FROMMER'S
DOLLARWISE GUIDE TO ENGLAND & SCOTLAND

by Darwin Porter

1985-86 Edition

Published by Frommer/Pasmantier Publishers
A Division of Simon & Schuster, Inc.
1230 Avenue of the Americas
New York, NY 10020

ISBN 0–671–52442–9

Manufactured in the United States of America

*Although every effort was made to ensure the accuracy
of price information appearing in this book,
it should be kept in mind that prices
can and do fluctuate in the course of time.*

CONTENTS

MAPS

To Stanley Haggart

Acknowledgment

I wish to acknowledge the field research of Mr. and Mrs. Peter J. E. Barnes of London, England, and the editorial assistance of Margaret Foresman, of Key West, Florida, and of Danforth Prince, of New York City.

A DISCLAIMER: Although every effort was made to ensure the accuracy of the prices and travel information appearing in this book, it should be kept in mind that prices do fluctuate in the course of time, and that information does change under the impact of the varied and volatile factors that affect the travel industry.

Readers should also note that the establishments described under Readers' Selections or Suggestions have not in many cases been inspected by the author and that the opinions expressed there are those of the individual reader(s) only. They do not in any way represent the opinions of the publisher or author of this guide.

Inflation Alert!!!

It is hardly a secret that a wave of inflation has battered the countries of northern Europe, and Britain has been hard hit. The author of this book has spent laborious hours researching to try and ensure the accuracy of prices appearing in this guide. As we go to press, I believe we have obtained the most reliable data possible. However, in a system that in 1982 alone saw one London hotelier raise his prices three times in one season, I cannot offer guarantees for the tariffs quoted. In the lifetime of this edition—particularly its second year (1986)—the wise traveler will add *at least* 20% to the prices quoted.

DOLLARWISE GUIDE TO ENGLAND AND SCOTLAND

The Reason Why

ENGLAND, AND SCOTLAND too, sent her children across the waves to settle North America, Australia, New Zealand, and a host of other lands. Today the offspring of those children are returning to visit their mother lands at a rate that is practically an invasion.

What's the big attraction?

England, as in Restoration days, has thrown out the Puritan and is experimenting in all sorts of imaginative, creative ways. Vigorous and exciting changes are taking place, and England today is, in a word, fun. The island may be small, but, like Mighty Mouse, it packs a powerful punch.

On the other hand, Scotland fulfills romantic myths—a land of shimmering lochs, pepper-pot towers and crow-stepped castles, clans with bagpipes, and balladeers. Scotland is very different from England. When English people go to Scotland, they are, in effect, "going abroad."

Connecting you with the life forces of both countries is one of the aims of this book.

I have set for myself the formidable task of seeking out the best of England and Scotland and condensing it between the covers of a guide. The best includes not only descriptions of hotels, restaurants, pubs, and nightspots, but descriptions of cities, towns, and sightseeing attractions. Part of the philosophy of this book is based on the fact that the best need not be the most expensive. Hence, my ultimate aim—beyond that of familiarizing you with the offerings of merrie old England and romantic Scotland—is to stretch your dollar power, to show you that you need not always pay scalper's prices for charm, top-grade comfort, and food.

In this guide, I'll devote a great deal of attention to the tourist meccas of London, Edinburgh, Stratford-upon-Avon, and Oxford. But these ancient cities and towns are not the full "reason why" of the book. Important as they are, they simply do not fully reflect the complexity and diversity of both countries. Unlike most nations of Europe, England and

Scotland defy a clear, logical, coherent plan of sightseeing. Both lands are a patchwork quilt of treasures, with many of the most scenic items tucked away in remote corners—an Elizabethan country estate in Devon, a half-timbered thatched cottage by the sea in Cornwall, a Regency manor in the Lake District, an old whitewashed coaching inn at Loch Ness.

Meeting the English and the Scots is perhaps the most important reason for making the trip. If possible, try to arrive with few preconceived ideas. For example, generalizing about the character of the English in a land filled with "soopah" swinging dukes, Cockney porters, Rudyard Kipling adventurers, and Miss Marple-type ladies is fraught with hazards. Suffice it to say, they'll surprise you—particularly if you think of the English as a cold, snobbish, withdrawn people. A few visits to the haunts of Soho, or to a local pub for a "lager and lime," or even a look at the racy London tabloids, will cure you of stereotypes.

A TRAVELER'S ADVISORY: During the past three years Great Britain has been able to hold **inflation** to a fairly manageable level, so I hope we have seen the last of the wild and sometimes unnecessary price increases. However, you should take the figures quoted in this guide only as an indication of the regular charges of a hotel or other establishment. Almost all hotels have special offers at various times of year, and some, such as the Priory in Bath, may offer as much as a 40% discount for a two-night stay. Management has improved, and staffs, especially in lovely little country places, have become more English and friendly.

The standard of **cooking,** the use of high-quality products, and the current wave of chefs born, bred, and trained in England and Scotland has led to the appearance, during the last few years, of a number of pleasant small hotels where the main attraction for guests is the cooking and the comfort. These hotels are generally in attractive buildings on the outskirts of interesting towns. "Very Professional Amateurs" is how one food writer described the chef-proprietors of these new-wave restaurants and inns, a number of which I have included in this edition. *A word of warning,* however: Do not be misled by prominently displayed plaques denoting awards for the culinary arts. If you wish to use such an award as a quick guide, ask if the chef who won it is still in charge of the kitchens. I have found on occasion that the hotel/restaurant claims the award, while the chef who actually earned it has already moved on! Also many of these places do not permit smoking in the dining room or anywhere near it, so check this out before you light up.

The historic buildings for which the country is famous are well worth a visit, although many top places, such as Woburn Abbey, find it uneconomical to remain open during the winter, except on weekends. Security staffing costs are astronomical, I am told. Also, many of the fine houses looked after by the National Trust close at the end of October and do not reopen until the following Easter. However, there are still many places to see for the winter visitor who seeks history and a taste of the real Britain.

Traveling in Britain is becoming easier, with many destinations now served by economical express buses, which are equipped with aircraft-type reclining seats, toilets, TV, and a hostess who serves light refreshments. Train service continues to improve, and although porters are often hard to find, the railways are becoming highly competitive with airlines for internal travel. Some services even have telephones now. Improved night sleeper accommodations enable you to enjoy dinner and a theater in London, catch the train, and be awakened for coffee and cookies some 500 miles away, before you arrive for breakfast in Scotland. Airlines offer all sorts of special tickets. Starting soon, there will be an air travel ticket similar to the BritRail Pass, good value but with certain restrictions.

Tourist information on Great Britain is now a little more difficult to get because of the closing of the British Tourist Authority's central London Information Bureau. Where a single visit would once give you answers to questions on England, Scotland, and Wales, you must now go to three different locations in London. Area Tourist Offices, however, work hard to assist the traveler.

If you are writing for information to one of the organizations or individuals mentioned in this book, it is important that you include an International Reply Coupon, obtainable from your local post office. It won't cover the full cost of reply postage, but it helps. Remember that yours is probably only one of many inquiries.

Many visitors wonder what **VAT (Value Added Tax)** is. This is a Common Market tax, set in 1979 at 15% for Britain, which is lower than in some other Common Market countries. Basically, the tax is added to your hotel or restaurant bill, unless otherwise stated. Restaurants must include the tax in menu prices displayed outside their premises. In most stores and shops, it is included in the price of the item you purchase. If in doubt, ask if VAT is included or must be added to the cost of accommodation, food, or goods. If you wish to export an item on which the tax is charged, you can avoid paying it, provided certain requirements are fulfilled, but you must arrange this at the time of purchase and complete the appropriate forms.

The most interesting tourist attraction I visited in updating this guide was the Jersey Museum in St. Hieler in the Channel Islands—small but filled with much of interest. My favorite hotel find was the Grosvenor Hotel, Chester, an outstanding example of comfort, friendliness, superb cuisine, and excellent location. In the entertainment field, an interesting new wrinkle is the trial by one London theater of being open Sunday and dark Monday. If this system continues to be successful, perhaps other theaters will follow suit.

Happy traveling!

DOLLARWISE—WHAT IT MEANS:
This is a guidebook giving specific, practical details (including prices) about the hotels, restaurants, pubs, sightseeing attractions, and nightlife of England and Scotland. First-class to rock-bottom-budget establishments have been documented and described, from the elegant May Fair Hotel in London to a bed-and-breakfast house in an old fishing village in Scotland. Each establishment has been judged by the strict yardstick of value.

The major focus of the book is on the average voyager who'd like to patronize the almost wholly undocumented establishments of England and Scotland—that is, the second-class hotels and some of the better, although less heralded, restaurants where you can often get a superb dinner.

The sights of England and Scotland have been set forth in what I believe is a human, personal, and practical style. In both England and Scotland, the bewildered visitor is faced with a staggering number of attractions from the most catholic collection of art and artifacts in the world (the British Museum), to George Washington's ancestral home, to Anne Hathaway's Cottage at Stratford-upon-Avon, to some of the Scottish castles where Mary Queen of Scots lived during her brief, tragic reign.

What the Dollarwise Guide attempts is to lead the reader through the maze of important sights, such as the Tower of London and Edinburgh Castle, then introduce him or her to a number of lesser known locales, such as the little hamlets, flint churches, and historic houses of East Anglia, perhaps the mellow old towns of the Scottish "Borders." The hours and prices of admission to these attractions have been detailed.

SOME DISCLAIMERS: No restaurant, inn, hotel, guest house, or shop paid to be mentioned in this book. What you read are personal recommendations—in many cases, proprietors never knew their establishments were being investigated.

A word of warning: Unfortunately, prices change, and they rarely go downward, at least not in Britain. The government does not control hotel prices, as is customary in Spain and Italy. Nearly all British hotels are fond of quoting a rate of "from so many pence up," and many establishments simply refuse to quote anything else. The hotelier, anxious about inflation or a sudden tax imposed by the government, doesn't want to commit himself or herself too far in advance to a specific price. However, the "from" rate often—but not always—means the average price you're likely to be charged.

Always, when checking into a hotel, inquire about the price—and agree on it. This policy can save much embarrassment and disappointment when it comes time to settle the tab. In no circumstances can you invariably demand to be charged the price quoted in this book, although every effort has been made to state the accurate tariff as much as it was foreseeable when this guide was published.

This guide is revised every other year, yet even in a book that appears fresh every year it may happen that that cozy little family dining room changes colors, blossoming out with cut-velvet walls and dining tabs that include the decorator's fee and the owner's new Bentley. It may be that some of the people, animals, and settings I've described are no longer there or have been changed beyond recognition.

AN INVITATION TO READERS: Like all the Dollarwise books, *Dollarwise Guide to England and Scotland* hopes to maintain a continuing dialogue between its author and its readers. All of us share a common aim—to travel as widely and as well as possible, at the best value for our money. And in achieving that goal, your comments and suggestions can be of tremendous help. Therefore, if you come across a particularly appealing hotel, restaurant, store, even sightseeing attraction, please don't keep it to yourself. I'll send free copies of the next edition of *this* book to readers whose suggestions are used. Unfortunately, I cannot send copies of other guides to other countries published in the series, but only the book in which your specific recommendation appears. The solicitation for letters applies not only to new establishments, but to hotels or restaurants already recommended in this guide. The fact that a listing appears in this edition doesn't give it squatter's rights in future publications. If its services have deteriorated, its chef grown stale, its prices risen unfairly, whatever, these failings should be known. Even if you enjoyed every place and found every description accurate—that, too, can cheer many a gray day. Send your comments to Darwin Porter, c/o Frommer/Pasmantier Publishers, 1230 Avenue of the Americas, New York, NY 10020.

The $25-a-Day Travel Club—How to Save Money on All Your Travels

In just a few paragraphs, you'll begin your exploration of England and Scotland. But before you do, you may want to learn how to save money on all your trips and travels; by joining the $25-a-Day Travel Club, now in its 22nd successful year of operation.

The Club was formed at the urging of readers of the $-a-Day Books and the Dollarwise Guides, many of whom felt that such an organization could bring financial benefits, continuing travel information, and a sense of community to economy-minded travelers in all parts of the world.

In keeping with the budget concept, the membership fee is low and is immediately exceeded by the value of your benefits. Upon receipt of U.S. $15 (U.S. residents), or $18 U.S., by check drawn on a U.S. bank or via international postal money order in U.S. funds (Canadian, Mexican, and other foreign residents) to cover one year's membership, we will send all new members the following items:

(1) *Any two* of the following books

Please designate in your letter which two you wish to receive:

Europe on $25 a Day
Australia on $25 a Day
England and Scotland on $25 a Day
Greece on $25 a Day
Hawaii on $35 a Day
India on $15 & $25 a Day
Ireland on $25 a Day
Israel on $30 & $35 a Day
Mexico on $20 a Day
New York on $35 a Day
New Zealand on $20 & $25 a Day
Scandinavia on $25 a Day
South America on $25 a Day
Spain and Morocco (plus the Canary Is.) on $25 a Day
Washington, D.C. on $35 a Day

Dollarwise Guide to Austria and Hungary
Dollarwise Guide to Canada
Dollarwise Guide to the Caribbean (including Bermuda and the Bahamas)
Dollarwise Guide to Egypt
Dollarwise Guide to England and Scotland
Dollarwise Guide to France
Dollarwise Guide to Germany
Dollarwise Guide to Italy

Dollarwise Guide to Portugal (plus Madeira and the Azores)
Dollarwise Guide to Switzerland and Liechtenstein
Dollarwise Guide to California and Las Vegas
Dollarwise Guide to Florida
Dollarwise Guide to New England
Dollarwise Guide to the Northwest
Dollarwise Guide to the Southeast and New Orleans
Dollarwise Guide to the Southwest
(Dollarwise Guides discuss accommodations and facilities in all price ranges, with emphasis on the medium-priced.)

Dollarwise Guide to Cruises
(This complete guide covers all the basics of cruising—ports of call, costs, fly-cruise package bargains, cabin selection booking, embarkation and debarkation and describes in detail over 60 or so ships cruising in Alaska, the Caribbean, Mexico, Hawaii, Panama, Canada, and the United States.)

How to Beat the High Cost of Travel
(This practical guide details how to save money on absolutely all travel items—accommodations, transportation, dining, sightseeing, shopping, taxes, and more. Includes special budget information for seniors, students, singles, and families.)

The New York Urban Athlete
(The ultimate guide to all the sports facilities in New York City for jocks and novices.)

Museums in New York
(A complete guide to all the museums, historic houses, gardens, zoos, and more in the five boroughs. Illustrated with over 200 photographs.)

The Fast 'n' Easy Phrase Book
(The four most useful languages—French, German, Spanish, and Italian—all in one convenient, easy-to-use phrase guide.)

Where to Stay USA
(By the Council on International Educational Exchange, this extraordinary guide is the first to list accommodations in all 50 states that cost anywhere from $3 to $25 per night.)

A Guide for the Disabled Traveler
(A guide to the best destinations for wheelchair travelers and other disabled vacationers in Europe, the United States, and Canada by an experienced wheelchair traveler. Includes detailed information about accommodations, restaurants, sights, transportation, and their accessibility.)

Marilyn Wood's Wonderful Weekends
(This very selective guide covers the best mini-vacation destinations within a 175-mile radius of New York City. It describes special country inns and other accommodations, restaurants, picnic spots, sights, and activities—all the information needed for a two- or three-day stay.)

Bed & Breakfast—North America
(This guide contains a directory of over 150 organizations that offer bed &

breakfast referrals and reservations throughout North America. The scenic attractions, businesses, and major schools and universities near the homes of each are also listed.)

(2) A one-year subscription to The Wonderful World of Budget Travel

This quarterly eight-page tabloid newspaper keeps you up to date on fast-breaking developments in low-cost travel in all parts of the world bringing you the latest money-saving information—the kind of information you'd have to pay $25 a year to obtain elsewhere. This consumer-conscious publication also features columns of special interest to readers: **The Traveler's Directory** (members all over the world who are willing to provide hospitality to other members as they pass through their home cities); **Share-a-Trip** (offers and requests from members for travel companions who can share costs and help avoid the burdensome single supplement); and **Readers Ask . . . Readers Reply** (travel questions from members to which other members reply with authentic firsthand information).

(3) A copy of Arthur Frommer's Guide to New York

This is a pocket-size guide to hotels, restaurants, nightspots, and sightseeing attractions in all price ranges throughout the New York area.

(4) Your personal membership card

Membership entitles you to purchase through the Club all Arthur Frommer publications for a third to a half off their regular retail prices during the term of your membership.

So why not join this hardy band of international budgeteers and participate in its exchange of travel information and hospitality? Simply send your name and address, together with your annual membership fee of $15 (U.S. residents) or $18 U.S. (Canadian, Mexican, and other foreign residents), by check drawn on a U.S. bank or via international postal money order in U.S. funds to: $25-A-Day Travel Club, Inc., Frommer/ Pasmantier Publishers, 1230 Avenue of the Americas, New York, NY 10020. And please remember to specify which *two* of the books in section (1) above you wish to receive in your initial package of members' benefits. Or, if you prefer, use the last page of this book, simply checking off the two books you select and enclosing $15 or $18 in U.S. currency.

GETTING THERE

PRESIDENT CARTER'S DEREGULATION of the airline industry made world headlines in 1979, and ever since then any vestiges of simplicity and uniformity in price structures for transatlantic flights have disappeared. Airlines now compete fiercely with one another, offering a confusing barrage of pricing systems and package deals, changing some of the public's preconceived ideas about the best available prices.

Travel agents laughingly refer to the masses of documentation they have received as "chaos." However, that can mean beneficial chaos to the alert traveler willing to study and consider all the choices available. The key to bargain air fares is to shop around.

1. Plane Economics

Latter-day pilgrims making the return trip to Britain will find the voyage a lot easier than their ancestors did, yet they will still have to overcome the hurdles of a complicated series of flight options. In what follows, I'll try to unravel the red tape of some attractive possibilities of air travel to Britain.

Of course, citing any actual fares in the fast-changing America-to-Britain routes would make this book obsolete before publication. All fares must be checked with the airline of your choice and/or your travel agent before departure.

Many **charter flights** exist to London with organizations that profit from group discounts. They are too numerous to describe here, and difficult to recommend because of the low capitalization of many of these companies and the changing legalities of the airline industry. Check with your travel agent for *legitimate* plans.

LEAST EXPENSIVE "REGULAR" FARES: Currently, your cheapest option with regular airlines falls into two categories: Super APEX and Standby.

Super APEX Fares

This is now the most heavily used fare to London from North America. On most airlines, APEX tickets are valid for a stay abroad of from seven days to six months, and must be purchased at least 21 days in advance. Travel dates in both directions must be reserved at the time of purchase, with a $50 penalty assessed for alterations or cancellations.

Standby Fares

Many airlines flying to London offer standby fares sold at the airport on the day of departure, and subject to availability. You'll have to risk waiting hours at the airport to find out whether you're confirmed, and you'll also risk being stranded at the airport for anywhere from one to several days on either leg of your trip if no seats become available. If you're emotionally prepared to hazard those risks, and if your travel plans are flexible enough, then a standby ticket might be for you.

Remember that high season, which, depending on the ticket, can stretch from April 1 until September 30, is *the most expensive time to travel*. It is also the most crowded. So if you are a budget-minded traveler (and if your schedule permits it), you should try to schedule your departure for the "shoulder" or low season.

CHOICE OF AIRLINE: This is a difficult question for some, as there are many airlines competing for your dollar on the heavily traveled routes between North America and Great Britain. These include British Airways, Trans World Airlines, Delta Airlines (which flies from Atlanta nonstop to London), and Northwest Orient Airlines (which has services from Minneapolis through Boston, flying to London's Gatwick Airport).

As part of my continuing policy to travel on many airlines and report on the services of dozens of national carriers, I recently chose Trans World Airlines for my flight from New York to London's Heathrow Airport. In a previous edition, I had reported on the services of British Airways, the premier airline of the United Kingdom.

TWA carries more people to Europe from North America than any other airline. Flights on TWA to London from each of the 61 American cities serviced by TWA are conveniently scheduled to interconnect with one of the three or more daily transatlantic flights leaving from the TWA terminal in New York's Kennedy Airport, or with one of the daily flights leaving from Boston, Chicago, Los Angeles, and (in summer only) Philadelphia.

The airline offers a wide selection of fares, and many of them feature discounts for midweek or midwinter travel in either direction.

The cheapest fare offered is the Super APEX, previously mentioned. Conditions require a purchase at least 21 days in advance and a stopover that must last at least seven days but not more than 180 days.

Another attractive alternative is called a point-to-point special economy fare. These cost more than the Super APEX, although no restrictions are made as to the stopover time or the number of days of advance booking. Other competing airlines have similar plans.

The Ambassador Class, which offers seats as wide as the first-class seating on many airlines (six across on a 747 or an L-1011), is ideal for business travelers or long-legged passengers who prefer wide, roomy comfort. Drinks are free, and the food served includes a choice of three entrees presented on fine china along with a selection of international wines.

Naturally, for those who can afford it, TWA, like all the major carriers flying across the North Atlantic, has a premier service in its first-class compartment. Here you get very special attention and lots of extras, but this is, obviously, the most expensive ticket you can purchase.

If you want everything done for you, once you land, you can ask about TWA's many tour options, as it is the largest tour operator in the world.

THE NO-FRILLS FLIGHT: People Express, the U.S. cut-rate airline, has inaugurated a no-frills flight from Newark, New Jersey, to London's Gatwick Airport. The service is designed to fill the void in cheap transatlantic service left by the bankruptcy of Sir Freddie Laker's Skytrain service. Obviously, any information reported here is likely to be vastly out of date by the time of your actual flight, so any prices and scheduling should be verified with a travel agent or with People Express (if you can ever get them on the phone!). Just to give you some idea, though, the current price is $159 one-way.

The no-frills is no joke. For example, on a flight I took on the airline to investigate it, I was charged for each piece of luggage checked in the baggage compartment, and I paid extra for my meal. The fare is collected by airline personnel once passengers are in flight. They take British or American currency, travelers checks, personal checks (with two forms of identification), or major credit cards.

Don't think, however, that you'll get away with showing up on a plane without funds and bluffing your way free to England. A People Express spokesperson said such passengers are arrested on felony charges at Gatwick.

Passengers should reserve space *way, way in advance* through a travel agent or with a phone number listed in your local area. If you try the latter route, good luck. I called 18 times over a period of three days in the New York area, and each time heard about five minutes of canned music before I was eventually cut off. Therefore, the travel agent route is more recommendable unless you have endless patience.

As we go to press, People Express is being challenged by a new airline, **Virgin Atlantic Airways.** Virgin Atlantic flies from Newark Airport in New Jersey to Gatwick Airport on the outskirts of London. The actual fare that Virgin Atlantic will charge at the time of your visit is not known. In fact, it isn't known if there will be a Virgin Atlantic at the time of your visit. However, it's an airline to investigate if you want to get your transatlantic fare bone-trimmed.

As of this writing, Virgin Atlantic charges $189 for a one-way fare from New Jersey to London. Even though that fare is slightly higher than that offered by People Express, the new airline is still competitive in that it offers free meals, free luggage (within certain guidelines), and free stereo headphones. At People Express, you are charged extra for those amenities.

In high season, if early bookings are any barometer, Virgin Atlantic is likely to be booked solidly, especially on weekends. But check with your travel agent or else call 212/242-1330 in the New York area. Regrettably, you are likely to get only a tape-recorded message (that is, if you get through at all). You might also try to make ticket purchases at the airline's offices at 166 West 32nd Street in New York City or else through Teletron or Ticketron.

2. By Ship

Traveling to England by ship is for those who crave a sea experience—either on a luxury liner, with resort-level facilities, or else on a more relaxed, time-consuming freighter.

Here is a description of the major service offered from the Atlantic seaboard to various ports in England (most often Southampton, where you'll pay a small debarkation fee):

Cunard Line, 555 Fifth Ave., New York, NY 10017 (tel. 212/880-7500), boasts the *Queen Elizabeth 2* as its flagship—self-styled, quite accurately, as "the most advanced ship of the age." It is the only ocean liner providing regular transatlantic service—23 sailings from April to November—between New York and Cherbourg, France, and Southampton, England. Designed for super cruises, the *Queen Elizabeth 2* is reaching a younger market, those leery of the traditional liner-type crossing. Hence, you'll find four swimming pools, a sauna, nightclubs, a theater with a balcony, an art gallery, cinemas, chic boutiques (including the world's first sea-going branch of Harrods), as well as four restaurants, a gymnasium, paddle tennis courts, and a children's playroom staffed with English nannies.

Recent additions to the tempting lifestyle available on the ship include access to an on-board branch of California's Golden Door Health Spa, a computer skills learning center, seminars by trained professionals on astrology, cooking, art, fitness, and medicine, and a Festival of Life series that introduces you to such personalities as Larry Hagman or Meryl Streep.

The vessel is a two-class ship, with both first and transatlantic classes. Each class has some public rooms for its exclusive use, although many of the public lounges, such as the on-board casino, are used in common.

The prices quoted are per person, based on double occupancy. (Tariffs were those charged at press time, and will invariably change by the time of your actual trip, but they'll give you a good idea of what to expect.) Fares are extremely complicated, based on the desirability of the cabin and the season of sailing. I'd suggest that you call your travel agent or a Cunard representative at their toll-free number (tel. 800/221-4770). In New York City, call 212/661-7777.

On the air/sea passage, you go over by ship, returning by British Airways to one of the almost 30 gateways in the continental U.S. (you can reverse the direction of your sailing if you want to), but conditions strictly state that the amount of time spent abroad cannot exceed 20 days for transatlantic-class passengers and 40 days for first-class passengers.

A series of complicated maneuvers are possible (including an air allowance if you return on British Airways from a point in Europe other than London), but in thrift season (approximately October and November eastbound, and November/December westbound) you'll usually pay a minimum fare of $1250 in transatlantic class and $2370 in first class. In intermediate season, you'll pay $1440 in transatlantic and $2590 in first class; and in high season (approximately July eastbound; July/August westbound), $1520 in transatlantic and $2735 in first class. Each passenger pays a $60 port tax for each direction of sailing regardless of the options he or she chooses.

Another ticket is known as one-way-free sailing. That means you pay for a one-way ticket by ship, but get your return by ship included "free." Of course, you have to adjust your sailing dates to those of Cunard's. Since the availability is limited for each sailing, the farther in advance you make your reservation, the more likely your chances are of being included.

If you depart in low season but return in high season, you'll have to pay the more expensive fare. Minimum per-person fares in thrift season are $1590 for transatlantic class and $2470 in first class; in intermediate season, $1745 in transatlantic and $2710 in first class; and in high season, $1835 in transatlantic and $2850 in first class.

First-class passengers can also arrange reduced return fares on a faster-than-sound British Airways jet, the SST.

Last, a very limited number of youth fares in transatlantic class are available at $525 per person, plus the $60 port tax. The person will share a "quad" with others of his or her own age.

3. Traveling Within Britain

BY TRAIN: There is something magical about traveling on a train in Britain. You sit in comfortable compartments, on upholstered seats, next to the reserved and well-dressed British; you're served your meal in the dining car like an aristocrat; and the entire experience can become a relaxing interlude.

You should, of course, be warned that *your Eurailpass is not valid on trains in Great Britain.* But the cost of rail travel in England, Scotland, Northern Ireland, and Wales can be quite low—particularly if you take advantage of certain cost-saving travel plans, some of which can only be purchased in North America, before leaving for Great Britain.

BritRail Pass

This pass gives unlimited rail travel in England, Scotland, and Wales, and is valid on all British Rail routes, on Lake Windermere steamers, and on Sealink ferry services to the Isle of Wight. It is not valid on ships between Great Britain and the continent, the Channel Islands, or Ireland. A seven-day **economy-class pass,** as of 1984, cost $115 for one person, rising to $155 in first class. A 14-day pass was $175 in economy, $230 in first class; a 20-day pass, $220 and $290; and a one-month ticket, $260 and $335.

Children up to 4 years of age travel free, and those from 5 to 15 go for half the adult price. Persons from 16 to 25 may travel at reduced rates in economy class, but they must pay the full adult fare if they choose to go first class. The youth rates in economy class are $95 for seven days, $150 for 14 days, $190 for 21 days, and $225 for a month. BritRail also offers a **Senior Citizen Pass** to persons 65 or older. This is a first-class pass, but passengers pay only the adult economy-class fare. Prices for BritRail passes are higher for Canadian travelers.

BritRail Passes cannot be obtained in Britain, but should be secured before leaving North America either through travel agents or by writing or visiting BritRail Travel International, 630 Third Ave., New York, NY 10017; 510 West Sixth St., Los Angeles, CA 90014; 333 North Michigan Ave., Chicago, IL 60601; or P.O. Box 58047, World Trade Center, Dallas, TX 75258. Canadians can write to BritRail Travel International, 55 Eglinton Ave., East Toronto M4P 1G8, ON; or 409 Granville St., Vancouver V6C 1T2, BC.

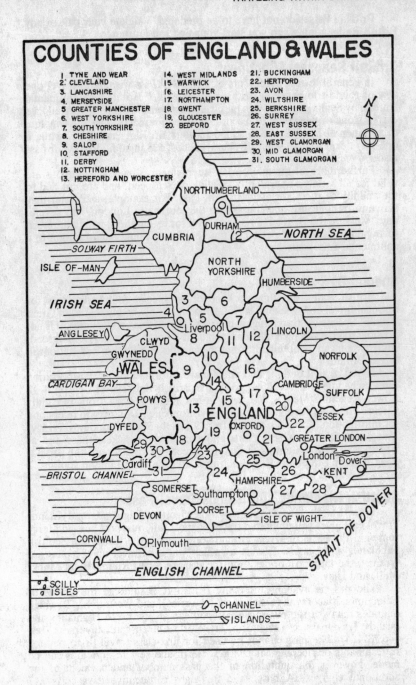

COUNTIES OF ENGLAND & WALES

1. TYNE AND WEAR
2. CLEVELAND
3. LANCASHIRE
4. MERSEYSIDE
5. GREATER MANCHESTER
6. WEST YORKSHIRE
7. SOUTH YORKSHIRE
8. CHESHIRE
9. SALOP
10. STAFFORD
11. DERBY
12. NOTTINGHAM
13. HEREFORD AND WORCESTER

14. WEST MIDLANDS
15. WARWICK
16. LEICESTER
17. NORTHAMPTON
18. GWENT
19. GLOUCESTER
20. BEDFORD

21. BUCKINGHAM
22. HERTFORD
23. AVON
24. WILTSHIRE
25. BERKSHIRE
26. SURREY
27. WEST SUSSEX
28. EAST SUSSEX
29. WEST GLAMORGAN
30. MID GLAMORGAN
31. SOUTH GLAMORGAN

BritRail Passes do not have to be predated. Validate your pass at any British Rail station when you start your first rail journey.

BritRail Seapass—Continent

In general terms, purchasers of a BritRail Pass wishing to travel one way or round trip between Britain and Ireland or Britain and continental Europe by Sealink services can purchase an extension of their BritRail Pass carrying one or two coupons, according to requirements. The one-way fare to continental Europe is $26 added to your BritRail Pass price, while a one-way ticket to take you to Ireland will cost $38 in addition to your pass price.

Furthermore, if the appropriate supplement is paid, the coupons are valid for all services operated by Sealink or Seaspeed, and are not tied to the validity of the associated BritRail Pass. For example, a traveler may arrive in Ireland, use one coupon for the journey to London, stay several days, validate the BritRail Pass and travel for its duration, and then return to London for another period of time before traveling from London to a continental European port.

Special Bargain Fares

British Rail from time to time offers special round-trip fares for optional travel and weekend travel, which may only be purchased in Great Britain. Because of the changing nature of these fares and facilities, it is not possible to give advance information about them to travelers from abroad. Information can be obtained from travel agents and British Rail stations in Great Britain.

If you're in London, and want more information on transportation rates, schedules, or facilities, go to the **British Rail Travel Centre,** 4–12 Lower Regent Street, S.W.1, only a few minutes' walk from Piccadilly Circus. This office deals with personal visitors only. Don't try to telephone for information. The office is open from 9 a.m. to 5 p.m. Monday to Friday. You can also make reservations and purchase rail tickets there and at British Rail Travel Centres at Oxford Street, Victoria Street, the Strand, King William Street, Heathrow Airport, and the main London stations.

Scottish Highlands and Islands Travel Pass

From March 1 to October 31, the Scottish Highlands and Islands Travel Pass gives you unlimited travel on most rail, bus, post bus, and ferry routes in the parts of Great Britain contained in the name, the Scottish Highlands and islands. Islands to which you can travel on the pass are Orkney, the larger Hebrides, and the inshore Skye, Rhum, Eigg, Muck, Mull, and Islay.

The pass is available at many British Rail stations, the offices of Caledonian Macbrayne (which runs the ferries), and Western SMT (which operates many of the bus services). You can also write to Highlands and Islands Travelpass, c/o Pickfords Travel, 25 Queensgate, Inverness (tel. 0463/32134). The pass cannot be used for first-class travel or to pay for refreshments or sleeping-car charges. Berth and seat reservations can be made, however, on quotation of the pass number and payment of the additional charges. A pass valid for eight consecutive days costs £47 ($70.50) in low season (March, April, and October), £55 ($82.50) in mid-season (May, June, and September), and £68 ($102) in high season (July and August). A 12-day pass is £56 ($84) in low season, £65 ($97.50) in mid-season, and £83 ($124.50) in high season.

•

BY AIR: British Airways offers a **Discover Britain Airpass,** valid for up to eight separate journeys over the airline network in England and Scotland, costing £160 ($240). The pass must be purchased before you start your trip, at the time you buy your ticket for your international flight. You can select the route you wish to take or purchase a voucher to be exchanged for tickets when you arrive in London. The pass is valid for one month from the date of your first air trip in the United Kingdom.

You can make reservations or travel on a standby basis, but you must not travel over the same route more than once. There are one or two other restrictions: for instance, you cannot fly on some peak-time shuttle services, and you must take your chances on standby on some other services, such as helicopter flights to the Isles of Scilly. You cannot get a refund after you begin your trip, and a $50 (U.S.) penalty is charged for cancellations before takeoff.

The airpass can mean substantial savings for you if you plan well and take advantage of the flights offered. If you're based in London, for example, you can make round trips to Jersey, Manchester, Newcastle, and Edinburgh for about £250 ($375) less than normal fares. From Glasgow, you can visit Stornaway, Inverness, and the Shetlands at a saving of £210 ($315). You don't have to keep making round trips, either, as the pass will also cover a flight such as London to Manchester to Belfast to Glasgow to Aberdeen to London to Jersey and back to London.

CAR RENTALS: Once you get over the initial awkwardness of driving on the left-hand side, you'll quickly discover that the best way to see the real Britain is to have a car while you're there. It gives you the freedom that nothing else can provide—to visit that out-of-the-way antique shop that doesn't know about tourist prices, or to escape the cities for a picnic lunch beside a quiet mill pond, or whatever. And for two or more persons, economy can be a major advantage in traveling by car.

All you need to do to rent a car from most companies in England or Scotland is to be between the ages of 21 and 72 and in possession of a valid driver's license. You should also possess a major credit card or be prepared to make a cash deposit at the time of pickup.

There are many car-rental services in England, including **Hertz** (with offices at both Gatwick and Heathrow, for example), **National, Kemwel,** and **Avis.** There are also dozens of British-owned car-rental firms, such as **Godfrey Davis Europcar,** most of them charging rates to match their American competitors.

However, some of these smaller firms can be tricky. For example, lured by its rates (lower than the more famous car-rental companies), I recently used a minor firm. The car was in a poor condition, and two breakdowns occurred. Because of the small operation of many of these firms, they are unable to afford service depots throughout Britain in case of breakdowns. On the one hand, you can save money temporarily, but then again, you might find yourself stranded on a Devon lane with no one to help but a kindly farmer. My phone call to London to the firm's head office brought the response from a recorded message that the company's offices were "closed until Monday morning." For me, it was a lonely, stranded Saturday afternoon. Fortunately, I was able to locate a mechanic in the neighboring village.

So when booking a car in the British Isles, you may want to consider one of the larger firms with branches placed at strategic locations throughout the country.

As part of my continuing policy over the years of sampling various firms and reporting on them in these pages, I recently used **Budget Rent-a-Car** in updating this guide. Budget maintains locations at both Gatwick and Heathrow Airports, as well as at seven inner London locations, including Earl's Court, Knightsbridge, Mayfair, Piccadilly, the Tower of London, and Victoria. All the vehicles are late-model, carefully inspected cars, each of which is given a thorough going over after each rental. Even the cheaper models have more options than you might expect, including radios.

Prices charged by all the major car-rental companies of England and Scotland are subject to change. However, I will cite a few just to give you an idea if you're preparing a budget. Rentals are usually priced by the day or by the week (which usually works out to be cheaper), with unlimited mileage included.

The cheapest car available is a two-door Ford Fiesta or similar vehicle with manual transmission. This will conveniently seat between three and four persons, although if you have lots of luggage you might want to graduate to a medium-size car. A slightly larger Ford Escort rents for £22 ($33) per day for between one and two days, for £17 ($25.50) per day for between three and six days, and for £104 ($156) per week. You will, of course, pay for your own gas (the English call it "petrol").

If you want to travel in slightly better circumstances, Budget maintains a fleet of cars that can seat up to five persons and their luggage comfortably. A medium-size Ford Sierra costs £25 ($37.50) per day for rentals of between one and two days, £21 ($31.50) per day for rentals of between three and six days, and £125 ($187.50) for a full week. The same car with automatic transmission costs around £8 ($12) more per day. More luxurious cars are also available, but these should be reserved well in advance. All car-rental companies in Britain are required to collect around 15% as tax.

If you should encounter difficulties on the road, Budget maintains a 24-hour-a-day number within Britain, which you can call for emergency assistance. You can get more information in North America by calling a toll-free number anytime between 7 a.m. and midnight (Central Standard Time) seven days a week. From points within the United States, call 800/527-0700 and ask for the international department. In Canada, call 800/268-8900 (in Toronto, 482-0222); in British Columbia, 112-800/268-8900; and in Québec, 800/268-8970.

Car Insurance

An examination of the fine print of any car-rental agreement can be intimidating, but the amount of public liability, personal liability, and property-damage insurance automatically written into most contracts is adequate for the average driver. Most car-rental firms in Britain have standard contracts; however, some of the smaller firms have widely different insurance arrangements, and if you're renting from one of these obscure firms, it pays to ask a lot of questions.

For example, in my Budget rental agreement, I noted that I would be responsible roughly for the first £300 (about $450) of any accidental damage to the car. However, for around £3 ($4.50) a day, I could—and did—purchase additional insurance to cover the deductible. The counter agent called this a "waiver" (that is, you waive responsibility for paying the deductible in case of an accident).

Also, if you're like me, you'll purchase additional personal accident insurance for around £1 ($1.50) per day, which will apply to both you and your passengers.

Driving Requirements

To drive a car in Britain, your passport and your own driver's license must be presented along with your deposit; no special British license is needed. The prudent driver will secure a copy of the *British Highway Code*, available from almost any stationer or news agent.

Although not mandatory, a membership in one of the two major auto clubs in England can be helpful: the **Automobile Association** and the **Royal Automobile Club.** The headquarters of the AA are at Fanum House, Basingstoke, Hampshire (tel. Basingstoke 20123); the RAC offices are in London at 49 Pall Mall, S.W.1 (tel. 01/839-7050). Membership in one of these clubs is usually handled by the agent from whom you rent your car. Upon joining, you'll be given a key to the many telephone boxes you see along the road, so that you can phone for help in an emergency.

BUSES IN ENGLAND: For the traveler who wants to see the country as even a train cannot reveal it, but who can't afford to rent a car, the old, reliable, and inexpensive (at least half the cost of railway fares) bus offers a fine form of transportation. While the trains do go everywhere, passing through towns and villages, they rarely bring you into contact with country life, and they almost never carry you across the high (main) streets of the villages, as the buses do. Moreover, distances between towns in England are usually short, so your chances of tiring are lessened. Every remote village is reachable by a bus.

The express motorcoach network covers the greater part of Britain. It links villages, towns, and cities with frequent schedules, convenient timetables, and efficient operation in all seasons. Most places off the main route can be easily reached by stopping and switching to a local bus. Fares are relatively cheap, making travel on the express motorcoach network economical.

The departure point from London for most of the bus lines is **Victoria Coach Station,** 164 Buckingham Palace Rd., S.W.1 (tel. 730-0202), which is a block up from Victoria Railroad Station. You'll be well advised to have reservations for the express buses; the locals can usually be boarded on the spot.

BritExpress Travel Card

This card gives you five or ten separate days of unlimited travel by express bus among 60 cities and towns in Britain. Stop over where you like. The card is only stamped for the days you use it, and you can spread your five or ten days over a whole month. Modern buses with panoramic windows cover the distance from London to Bristol in 2½ hours, to

Plymouth in 4 hours, and to Edinburgh in 9 hours. Travel cards can be bought in the U.S. and Canada, as well as in 17 other countries, or you can purchase them at the National Express Office, Victoria Coach Station, 164 Buckingham Palace Rd., London, S.W.1. The card has no validity until it is stamped at any National Express office in Britain, with the date on which you wish your month of travel to begin. The cost of five days' travel for adults is £25 ($37.50); for students 17 to 25 years of age, £20 ($30); and for children from 5 to 16, £15 ($22.50). For ten days' travel, adults pay £40 ($60); students, £30 ($45); and children, £20 ($30).

Green Line Buses

For trips to the immediate suburbs of London, and the towns nearby, you needn't go to Victoria Coach Station, however. Most of the spots are serviced by the Green Line coaches, which you can board throughout the city wherever you see green bus signs. To the south, these buses go as far as Crawley, Horsham, and Tunbridge Wells, all 30 to 40 miles from the center of London. To the north, they go as far as Stevenage, Luton, Hitchin, or Bishops Stortford—all around 20 to 25 miles from Piccadilly Circus. To the west, they reach Guildford, High Wycombe, Windsor, and Aylesbury, within 20 to 40 miles from London. And to the east, they go to Brentwood, Grays, or Gravesend, approximately 15 to 26 miles from the center of London.

A Golden Rover Ticket costs £2.95 ($4.43) per person, purchased as you board your first bus. Pick up a map of the system to plan your journey. **An Outback Ticket,** off-peak day return, will save up to 40% on two tickets.

Explorer gives an unlimited-mileage ticket that costs adults about £2.50 ($3.75) per day and £1.50 ($2.25) for children, and can be used on some 20 national carriers (especially those around London), except Green Line.

Heathrow/Gatwick Green Line link, so useful for interlining passengers, costs £4 ($6) for a single ticket during the day. Children under 5 years of age travel free. However, from midnight to 5 a.m., the cost goes up to £8 ($12). All tickets can be purchased from the London Transport Office at the Heathrow Airport underground station.

For more precise information on the Green Line routes, fares, and schedules, write to the **London Country Bus Services Ltd.,** Lesbourne Road, Reigate, Surrey RH2 7LE (tel. Reigate 42411).

Find a green-and-white sign mounted on a metal post, and stop the bus by signaling with your left hand.

Country Buses

The Country Bus Lines ring the heart of London. They never go into the center of London, although they hook up with the routes of the red buses and the Green Line coaches that do. You can get free maps of Country Buses from London Country Bus Services Ltd., Bell Street, Reigate, Surrey (see above). For more information about this form of touring, refer to "One-Day Trips from London," Chapter IV.

BIKES: This is the cheapest transportation apart from walking, and you can get a wealth of assistance from the *Cyclists' Touring Club,* Cotterell

House, 69 Meadrow, Godalming, Surrey (tel. 04868/7217). It costs £11 ($16.50) to join, with membership being good for one year. The club helps with information and provides maps, insurance, touring routes, and a list of low-cost accommodations, including farmhouses, inns, guest houses, and even private homes that cater especially to cyclists. You can rent bikes by the day or by the week from a number of businesses, such as **Savile's Stores,** 97 Battersea Rise, Battersea, S.W.11 (tel. 228-4279), which has been renting out bikes for some 75 years. Stan Savile's father started the company back in 1912!

The **London Bicycle Company** has two addresses: 41–42 Floral St., Covent Garden, W.C.2 (tel. 836-2969), and 55 Pimlico Rd., S.W.1 (tel. 730-6898). This company has Britain's largest fleet of rental bikes. A three-speed machine rents for £3 ($4.50) a day or £15 ($22.50) a week. A ten-speed touring bike costs £5 ($7.50) a day, £25 ($37.50) a week. They also have speed bikes, tandems, and a big selection of panniers. A deposit of £10 ($15) is required, but it is refunded if you return the bike in good condition. The company also provides maps and accessories. Write for a brochure and reservation form. If you wish, you can buy a genuine English racer here, and they'll show you how to take it home with you tax free.

CRUISES ON THE THAMES: This is a venture for those who have visited London before, and want to spend a day—or even a week—cruising the Thames. The idea is to show overseas visitors a side of England they might not otherwise see.

The craft used are traditional river day launches, designed especially for their elegance and grace. They are privately owned, and this is not an advertised hire service. The boats have awnings in case of rain.

Passengers are collected from their London hotel in the morning by car and driven to Runnymede where they embark. There they cruise downstream through Runnymede Fields past Magna Carta Island, where King John is reputed to have signed the famous document. Then they turn upstream and cruise through Windsor, under the shadow of the castle, Eton College, and Bray, to Maidenhead, so popular in Edwardian times with young sportsmen and their ladies.

Lunch is taken either as a picnic while moored in some quiet backwater or else in a riverside hotel or pub. At Maidenhead, Skindles Hotel grounds run down to the river, making it a popular stopping-off place.

Passengers then turn downstream again during the afternoon, disembarking at Windsor Town Quay within yards of the railway station. From there, the journey back to London is quick, cheap, and easy.

The cost for up to five people is £145 ($217.50) per day. A picnic lunch is provided at an extra cost of £10 ($15) per person with wine or beer.

Extended cruises can be arranged to suit the time available and the passengers' inclination. The journey from Oxford to Hampton Court takes three or four days, but shorter or longer cruises can be planned. They are carefully arranged so that not more than four or five hours a day are spent traveling. There is time for everyone to go ashore and explore riverside towns and villages, shop for antiques, walk in the fields, or talk to the locals in pubs.

Overnight accommodation must be arranged in advance, as many of the riverside hotels are small, although they do provide accommodations

with private facilities. All are personally selected and offer good food with a fine standard of accommodation. Baggage is transferred between hotels by taxi, as there is no room for cabin trunks in the dayboats.

Passengers are transferred from and to London at the start and finish of the cruise. They are expected to pay their own overnight expenses and all meals during the day.

These extended cruises cost £145 ($217.50) per day for up to six persons, excluding all meals and accommodations. For one-way trips, a charge is made for the unused return.

Advance booking is essential. Write to **Peter J. E. Barnes,** Willow Point, Friary Island, Wraysbury, near Staines, Middlesex TW19 5JR (tel. 078481/2259).

PLANNING YOUR ITINERARY: If you plan to drive yourself around the country, you can save time and fuel by having a route specially prepared to your requirements. Simply tell Peter and Caryl Barnes how many days you have, where you wish to start and finish, and what you are interested in. State what sort of accommodation you want (with or without private bath, for example), and any particular places you wish to visit. They will send back a driveable itinerary covering the days you have available.

There are two types, standard and budget. The budget gives you the basic road and route numbers and all information you need to make the tour, mentioning sights along the way, noting lunch stops (historic pubs, for example) and overnight accommodations in suitable places at economical prices. The standard itinerary gives all the same information but in greater detail with data on sights, opening hours, a suggestion for each day's lunchtime stop, and a wider choice of recommended overnight accommodations in hotels, countryside inns, and pubs, most of which will take advance reservations.

The minimum is for seven days and that will cost $35 (U.S.) for a standard itinerary, plus $5 for each additional day. A budget seven-day itinerary will cost $25, plus $3.75 per extra day. If you pay by personal check, add $5 to cover bank clearance charges.

Simply send your request and payment to **Peter and Caryl Barnes,** Willow Point, Friary Island, Wraysbury, near Staines, Middlesex TW19 5JR (tel. 078481/2259). Don't forget that mail can take as much as ten days each way across the Atlantic, even by air, and up to one month to go by surface.

If you're coming to London for the first time, you may want to have Peter Barnes take you on one of his orientation tours of London, lasting seven hours with a lunch stopover in a pub. He will show you all the major sights and, as a Londoner born and bred, quite a lot of other corners and buildings that visitors rarely see. It is a nonstop tour costing $140 for up to five people maximum in the car (the cost of lunch is not included).

For more information, write him at the address given above. He will also conduct his own personally escorted tours by private car or minibus into the countryside.

4. The ABCs of Britain

The aim of this "grab bag" section—dealing with the minutiae of your stay—is to make your adjustment to the British way of life easier. It is maddening to have your trip marred by an incident that could have been avoided had you been tipped off earlier. To prevent this from happening, I'll try to anticipate the addresses, data, and information that might come in handy on all manner of occasions.

ACCIDENT COMPENSATION: There is no automatic compensation. Some auto insurance companies operate a "knock for knock" cover. All other claims are settled by the courts. I would advise you to carry good personal accident and "third party" insurance. If you consider it necessary in the United States or Canada, the same rules apply in Britain.

AIRPORTS: London has two main airports, **Heathrow** and **Gatwick.** It takes 45 to 60 minutes by Underground train from Heathrow to Piccadilly Circus, costing £1.50 ($2.25). From Gatwick, the train takes one hour to London's Victoria Station, and costs £3.60 ($5.40). There are also three Airbus services from Heathrow to Victoria, Paddington, and Bloomsbury. Regular express services go for £2.50 ($3.75). Travel time depends on the traffic, ranging from about 45 minutes up to 1½ hours. Taxis from Heathrow charge by the meter—about £15 ($22.50) for up to four persons, plus a tip. Those from Gatwick have a set fee, which should be confirmed before departure. There is also a bus service between the two airports, leaving every hour for the 70-minute trip, costing £3.50 ($5.25). In addition, there's an expensive helicopter service that takes only 15 minutes between airports. For flight information, telephone Heathrow (tel. 01/759-4321) or Gatwick (tel. 0293/31299). Airline phone numbers are listed in the telephone directory.

AMERICAN EXPRESS: The main office is at 6 Haymarket, London, S.W.1 (tel. 930-4411). There are some ten other London locations.

BABYSITTERS: These are hard to find, and the safest way is to get your hotel to recommend someone—possibly a staff member. Expect to pay around £5 ($7.50) an hour and the cost of travel to and from your hotel by taxi. There are a number of organizations advertised in the Yellow Pages of the telephone directory that provide sitters using registered nurses and carefully checked mothers, as well as trained nannies. One such company is **Childminders,** 67A Marylebone High St., W.1 (tel. 935-9763). You pay a membership of around £14 ($21), then a charge of £1.50 ($2.25) an hour by day, £1.75 ($2.63) an hour at night, for a minimum of four hours plus transportation to and from your address. Another is **Babysitters Unlimited,** 313 Brompton Rd., S.W.3 (tel. 730-7777). There's also **Universal Aunts,** 36 Walpole St., S.W.3 (tel. 730-9834), which runs a comprehensive service, acting as substitute parents for children.

BANKS: Hours generally are 9:30 a.m. to 3:30 p.m. Monday to Friday, although some banks in the suburbs are open on Saturday from 9:30 a.m. to

12:30 p.m. There are also Bureaux de Change, which charge for cashing travelers checks or personal (United Kingdom) checks and for changing foreign currency into sterling. Bureaux are often open seven days a week, 12 hours a day. There are branches of the main banks at London's airports. You'll always get the best rates at banks.

BOAT TRIPS: Touring boats operate on the Thames between April and September, taking you various places within London and also to nearby towns along the Thames. Main embarkation points are Westminster Pier, Charing Cross Pier, and Tower Hill Pier—a system that enables you, for instance, to take a "water taxi" from the Tower of London to Westminster Abbey. Not only are the boats energy-saving, bringing you painlessly to your destination, but they permit you to sit back in comfort as you see London from the river.

Pleasure boats operate down the Thames from Westminster Pier to the Tower of London and Greenwich all year, departing every 20 minutes in summer, from 10 a.m. to 4 p.m., and every 30 minutes in winter. It takes 20 minutes to reach the Tower and 40 minutes to arrive at Greenwich. In the summer, services operate upriver to Kew, Richmond, and Hampton Court from Westminster Pier. There are departures every 30 minutes from 10:30 a.m. to 4 p.m. for the 1½-hour journey to Kew and three departures daily for the 2½-hour Richmond trip as well as to Hampton Court, a 3- to 5-hour trip each way. For information on these and other boat trips, call the London Tourist Board's **Riverboat Information Service** (tel. 730-4812).

BUS TERMINALS: Victoria Coach Station, 164 Buckingham Palace Rd., S.W.1 (tel. 750-0202), is the main bus terminal. Tube: Victoria. Other bus stations are at Kings Cross Coach Station and at Gloucester Road beside the Forum Hotel.

CIGARETTES: Most U.S. brands are available in major towns. Expect to pay more than £1.10 ($1.65) per pack. *Warning:* Smoking is banned at an increasing number of places. Make sure you enter a "smoker" on the train or Underground, and only smoke on the upper decks of buses or in the smoking area of single-deckers, in theaters, and at other public places. Some restaurants restrict smoking.

CLIMATE: British temperatures can range from 30° to 110° Fahrenheit. The British Isles, however, have a temperate climate with no real extremes, and even in summer evenings are cool. No Britisher will ever really advise you about the weather—it is far too uncertain. If you come here from a hot area, bring some warm clothes. If you're from cooler climes, you should be all right.

CLOTHING SIZES: Women will find the size of stockings the same in Britain as in America. Likewise, men will find suits and shirts the same size. However, there are some exceptions.

For Women

Dresses, Coats, and Skirts

American	7	8	9	10	11	12	13	14	15	16	17	18
British	9	10	11	12	13	14	15	16	17	18	19	20

Blouses and Sweaters

American	10	12	14	16	18	20
British	32	34	36	38	40	42

Shoes

American	4½	5	5½	6	6½	7	7½	8	8½	9	9½	10
British	3	3½	4	4½	5	5½	6	6½	7	7½	8	8½

For Men

Shoes

American	7	8	9	10	11	12	13
British	6	7	8	9	10	11	12

CRIME: Theft is not as bad, perhaps, as in the U.S. Mugging is limited in the main to the poor areas. As for murder and assault, reports say that most of these occur within families and related groups. The best advice is to use discretion and a little common sense.

CURRENCY: At the time of writing this book, the **pound** is worth $1.50. Each pound breaks down into 100 **pence**. There are now £1 coins as well as banknotes, plus coins of 20p, 10p, 2p, and 1p. The ½p coin has been officially killed, but they'll still be around for some time.

CUSTOMS: Visitors from overseas may bring in 400 cigarettes and one quart of liquor. If you come from the EEC area, you are allowed to bring in 300 cigarettes and one quart of liquor, provided you bought them and paid tax on them in that EEC country. If you have obtained your allowance on a ship or plane, then you may only import 200 cigarettes and one liter of liquor. There is no limit on money, film, or other items for your own use, except that all drugs other than medical supplies are illegal. Obviously, commercial goods such as video films and nonpersonal items will require payment of a bond and will take a number of hours to clear Customs. Do not try to import live birds or animals. You may be subject to heavy fines if you try to sneak one through, and the pet will be destroyed. When you return home, you may take $400 worth of merchandise duty free if you have been outside the U.S. for 48 hours or more. A flat 10% duty is charged on your next $1000 worth of purchases. Keep your receipts to prove the value of various items. On gifts, the duty-free limit is $50.

DENTIST: In London, telephone 584-1008 for the name of the dentist nearest to you. Expect to pay about £15 ($22.50) for treatment unless it is a genuine emergency. You can also get in touch with the **Royal Dental**

Hospital, 32 Leicester Square, W.C.2 (tel. 930-8831). Inquire about the likely cost when you telephone. The **Emergency Dental Service** (tel. 584-1008) offers private treatment 24 hours a day, and another private 24-hour, 365-day service is available by phoning 749-5704. Outside London, ask the nearest sympathetic local resident—perhaps your hotelier—for information.

DOCTORS: Hotels have their own lists of local practitioners for whom you'll have to pay. For information on free emergency treatment, see "Hospitals," below. Outside London, dial 100 and ask the operator for the local police, who will give you the name, address, and telephone number of a doctor in your area. Emergency treatment is free, but if you visit a doctor at his or her surgery (office) or if he or she makes a "house call" to your hotel, you will have to pay. It's wise to take out adequate medical/accident insurance coverage before you leave home.

DOCUMENTS FOR ENTRY: Every U.S. citizen must have a valid passport to enter the United Kingdom.

DRIVING REQUIREMENTS: A passport and a current driver's license are required. It is not necessary to obtain an International Driving License. Most car-rental companies include AA or RAC membership with their cars. If yours does not, get in touch with the **Automobile Association,** Fanum House, Basingstoke, Hampshire (tel. 0256/20123); or the **Royal Automobile Club,** 83 Pall Mall, London, S.W.1 (tel. 839-7050). Upon joining the AA or RAC, you will receive a key to the many telephone boxes you'll see along the road so that you can phone in an emergency.

DRUGSTORES: In Britain, they are called chemist shops. Every police station in the country has a list of emergency chemists. Dial "0" and ask the operator for the local police, who will give you information as to a druggist you can reach. The only 24-hour drugstore in London is **Bliss the Chemist,** 50–56 Willesden Lane, Kilburn, N.W.6 (tel. 624-8000). Emergency drugs are normally available at most hospitals, but you'll be examined to see that the medication you request is really necessary.

ELECTRICAL APPLIANCES: The current is 240 volts, AC (50Hz). Buy a transformer and an adapter before leaving home, as they are not readily available in Britain. A good adapter will convert your plug to almost any other sort of plug. If it is just a question of an electric razor, most hotel rooms have special sockets that can be changed from 240-v to 110-v at the flick of a switch. These are not suitable, however, for hair dryers and some other electrical appliances.

EMBASSY AND HIGH COMMISSION: The **U.S. Embassy** is at 24 Grosvenor Square, London, W.1 (tel. 499-9000), and the **Canadian High Commission** is at Canada House, Trafalgar Square, London, S.W.1 (tel. 629-9492).

EMERGENCY: In London, for police, fire, or ambulance, dial 999. Give your name and address, plus the telephone number and state the nature of the emergency. Misuse of the 999 service will result in a heavy fine. Cardiac arrest, yes. Sprained ankle, no. Accident injury, yes. Dented fender, no.

ETIQUETTE: How many chapters? Be normal, be quiet. The British do not like hearing other people's conversations. In pubs you are not expected to buy a round of drinks unless someone has bought you a drink. Don't talk politics or religion in pubs.

FILM: All types are available, especially in London. Processing takes about 24 hours although many places, particularly in London, will do it almost while you wait. There are few restrictions on the use of your camera, except where notices are posted, as in churches, theaters, and certain museums. If in doubt, ask.

FOOD AND CUISINE: A continental breakfast consists of rolls, croissants, or toast with jam or marmalade, coffee, or tea. An English breakfast can include porridge, kippers, smoked haddock, eggs, bacon, sausages, grilled tomatoes, mushrooms, toast and marmalade, and tea or coffee. Some London hoteliers have started listing a "London breakfast," which is more like many served in the U.S.; juice, eggs, bacon or ham, and toast are the major menu items. National dishes range from steak-and-kidney pie (with pastry crust) or pudding (encased in suet crust) and roast beef and Yorkshire pudding to the more imaginatively named starry-gazey pies, haggis and neaps, or collops and mash (these last two from Scotland). Desserts include apple pie and cheese as well as other fruit pies and cobblers, trifle, summer pudding, and a host of other sweets. Nowadays, hamburgers and pizzas are available in almost every British hamlet, but don't confuse them with real British cooking.

GAS: It's called "petrol." Prices are fairly stable at the moment at £1.84 ($2.76) per gallon, although most filling stations measure petrol in liters. Luckily, most pumps still show a comparative list of prices and measures. You'll probably have to serve yourself.

GLASSES: Lost or broken? Try Selfridges Optical in Selfridges Department Store, 400 Oxford St., W.1 (tel. 629-1234, extension 3889). If the prescription is simple, you can be fitted and back in vision within one or two hours. Cost including examination will be around £45 ($67.50). You will pay more for elaborate frames. It's always wise to take a copy of your glasses prescription with you when you travel.

HAIRDRESSING: Ask at your hotel. It may even have its own salon. You should tip the hairwasher 20p (30¢) and the stylist 50p (75¢) or more if you have a tint or permanent. Hairdressing services are available in most department stores. For men, barbershops are to be found at the main railway stations in London.

HITCHHIKING: It is not illegal and is normally safe and practical. However, it is illegal for pedestrians to be on motorways. The cleaner and tidier you look, the better your chances of getting a ride. Have a board with your destination written on it to hold up for drivers to see.

HOLIDAYS AND FESTIVALS: Christmas Day, Boxing Day (December 26), New Year's Day, Good Friday, Easter Monday, May Day, and spring and summer bank holidays are observed. Scotland also takes January 2 as a holiday but does not recognize the summer bank holiday, taking the first Monday in August instead of the last for a holiday. Scotland does not observe Easter Monday as a bank holiday.

HOSPITALS: The following offer emergency treatment in London 24 hours a day, and it's free under the National Health Service. If you have an existing condition, however, it may not be treated free, and if you are admitted to the hospital or referred to an Outpatient Clinic, you must also pay. Emergency care is available in London at the **Royal Free Hospital,** Pond Street, N.E.3 (tel. 794-0500); **Middlesex Hospital,** Mortimer Street, W.1 (tel. 636-8333); and **University College Hospital,** Gower Street, W.C.1 (tel. 387-9300). Only actual emergency treatment is free. Any referrals, the provision of medication, X rays, and all further treatment must be paid for. Many London hospitals have closed their outpatient departments.

INSOMNIACS: Late-night and all-night movies are shown in London at the **Gate Cinema,** 87 Notting Hill Gate, W.11 (tel. 727-5750); **Paris Pullman,** 65 Drayton Gardens, S.W.1 (tel. 373-5898); and the **Classic,** Leicester Square, W.C.2 (tel. 930-6915).

LAUNDRY AND DRY CLEANING: Most places take two days to complete the job and most hotels require the same length of time. London and most provincial towns have launderettes where you can wash and dry your own clothes, but there are no facilities for ironing. Many launderettes also have dry-cleaning machines. Otherwise, there are establishments that will do dry-cleaning for you with one-day service. The **Association of British Launderers and Cleaners,** 319 Pinner Rd., Harrow, Middlesex (tel. 01/863-7755) will give you a list if you can't find a facility close to you.

LIBRARIES: Every town has a public library, and as a visitor you can use the reference sections. The borrowing of volumes, however, is restricted to local citizens.

LIQUOR LAWS: No alcohol is served to anyone under the age of 18. Children under 16 aren't allowed in pubs, except in special rooms. Pub hours vary, but as a general guide, they are open from 11:30 a.m. to 2:30 p.m. and from 6 to 10:30 p.m. Monday to Saturday; from noon to 2:30 p.m. and from 7 to 10 p.m. on Sunday. Many general stores have "off license" hours when you can buy liquor for home consumption, hours generally being from 9 a.m. to 5 p.m., depending on the store. There are also "off license" shops, which are usually open from 11 a.m. to 3 p.m. and from 5 to 9 p.m. *Don't drink and drive:* Penalties are high and inconvenient, even if you are visiting from overseas.

LITERATURE: If you're really dedicated in your exploring, I suggest Churchill's *History of the English Speaking Peoples* (four volumes) and Trevelyan's *History of England.* These tomes will help you to understand a lot more about what you'll be seeing. Otherwise, just read this guidebook, and use a good map if you are touring. I recommend the Collins *Road Atlas of Britain,* which costs around $6 (U.S.) and makes a good souvenir.

LOST PROPERTY: Don't give up hope if you leave your prize possession on the tube, in a taxi, or elsewhere. Report the loss to the police first, and they will advise where to apply for its return. Taxi drivers are required to hand lost property to the nearest police station. London Transport's Lost Property Office will try to assist personal callers only at their offices at the Baker Street Underground station. Lost passports must be reported to the nearest police station and to your embassy. Loss of credit cards or travelers checks should be reported to the appropriate organization.

LUGGAGE STORAGE: You may want to leave your heavy gear in London while making excursions into the country. Very few B&B places and many of the larger hotels have no facilities for storing lots of luggage. There are **Left Luggage Offices** at the main rail terminals in London, or try **Michael Gibbons & Co., Ltd.,** 25 Great Windmill St., W.1 (tel. 437-2866), just off Shaftesbury Avenue. Storage charges are around 25p (38¢) per case per day. The office is open Monday to Friday from 8:45 a.m. to 5 p.m. You can have free access to your luggage during these hours.

MAIL DELIVERY: Any letter sent to **Poste Restante,** London, is available for collection at the Head Post Office, St. Martin-le-Grand, E.C.1, near St. Paul's Cathedral. Mail must be called for in person. Outside London, have mail addressed Poste Restante at any large town post office, or give your hotel address. When claiming your mail, always carry some sort of identification. Letters generally take seven to ten days to arrive from the U.S.

MEASURES: At present, Britain uses miles and inches to measure distances, although they may soon switch to the metric system.

1 inch = 2.54 centimeters (cm)
1 foot = 0.30 meters (m)
1 yard = 0.91 meters (m)   1 meter = 3.3 feet
1 mile = 1.61 kilometers (km)   1 kilometer = 0.62 miles
                                                     (roughly ⅔ mile)

Weights and measures are, for the most part, already metric.

1 ounce	= 28.35 grams (g)	1 gram	= 0.035 ounces
1 pound	= 0.45 kilograms (kg)	1 kilogram	= 2.2 pounds
1 imperial pint	= 1.2 U.S. liquid pints	= 0.56 liters	
1 imperial quart	= 1.2 U.S. liquid quarts	= 0.946 liters	
1 imperial gallon	= 1.2 U.S. liquid gallons	= 4.5 liters	
1 British ton	= 1 U.S. long ton	= 2240 pounds (In the U.S. the more commonly used short ton = 2000 lb.)	
1 metric ton	= 1000 kilograms	= 1.102 U.S. short tons.	

MEDICAL SERVICES: See "Doctors," "Dentists," "Hospitals."

NEWSPAPERS: *The Times* is the top, then the *Telegraph,* the *Daily Mail,* and the *Guardian,* but all papers carry the latest news. Others have some news but rely on gimmicks to sell. The *International Herald Tribune,* published in Paris, is available daily. *What's On* and similar publications appear weekly and are sold at all magazine stands in London.

OFFICE HOURS: Business hours are from 9 a.m. to 5 p.m. Monday to Friday. The lunch break lasts an hour, but most offices stay open all day.

PETS: See "Customs." It is illegal to bring in pets, except with veterinary documents. Most are subject to six months in quarantine. Hotels have their own rules, but usually dogs are not allowed in restaurants or public rooms, and often not in bedrooms.

POLITICS: There are two main parties, Conservative and Labour. The Conservatives believe in free enterprise and freedom of the individual to make his or her own decisions, with some government support. Labour believes in state ownership and control, with the state providing maximum support for the individual. The Liberals and the SDP have joined in an uneasy alliance to form the Social Democratic and Liberal Party, but have not yet made any noticeable impact.

POLICE: The best source of help and advice in emergencies is the police. Stop a "bobby" in the street, or dial 999 if the matter is serious. If the local force cannot help, they will know the address of the person who can. Losses, theft, and other criminal matters should be reported to the police immediately.

POST OFFICE: Post offices and sub-post offices are centrally located and open from 9 a.m. to 5 p.m. Monday to Friday, 9 a.m. to noon on Saturday. The Trafalgar Square Post Office in London is open from 8 a.m. to 8 p.m.

Monday to Friday, from 10 a.m. to 5 p.m. on Saturday. All post offices are closed on Sunday.

RADIO AND TELEVISION: There are 24-hour radio channels operating throughout the United Kingdom, with mostly pop music and chat shows during the night. TV starts around 6 a.m. with breakfast TV and educational programs. Lighter entertainment begins around 4 or 5 p.m., after the children's programs, and continues until around midnight. There are now four television channels—two commercial and two BBC without commercials.

RAILROAD INFORMATION: In London, personal callers are welcome at the **British Rail/Sealink** office, Lower Regent Street, S.W.1, and at the **British Rail Travel Centres** in the main London railway stations where they deal mainly with their own regions (there are five). For general information, phone 246-8030 or call the appropriate station. All numbers are listed in the telephone directory. Elsewhere, get in touch with the local station or a travel agent who holds a British Rail license.

RELIGIOUS SERVICES: Times of services are posted outside the various places of worship. Almost every creed is catered to in London and other large cities, but in the smaller towns and villages you are likely to find only Anglican (Episcopalian), Roman Catholic, Baptist, and Nonconformist forms of worship. The **Interdenominational American Church** is on Tottenham Court Road, London, W.1 (tel. 637-4858).

REST ROOMS: These are usually found at signs saying "Public Toilets." Expect to put from 2p (3¢) to 5p (8¢) in the slot to enter a stall if you're a woman. Men usually go free. Hotel facilities can be used, but they discourage nonresidents. Garages (filling stations) also have facilities for the use of customers only, and the key is often kept by the cash register. There's no need to tip except in hotels where there is an attendant.

SENIOR DISCOUNTS: These are only available to holders of a British Pension book.

SHOE REPAIRS: Many of the large department stores in Britain have "Shoe Bars" where repairs are done while you wait.

STORE HOURS: In general, stores are open from 9 a.m. to 5:30 p.m. Monday to Saturday. In country towns, there is usually an early-closing day when the shops shut down at 1 p.m. The day varies from town to town. Late shopping in London is on Thursday, when stores are open until 8 p.m. In the East End, around Aldgate and Whitechapel, many shops are open on Sunday from 9 a.m. until 2 p.m. There are a few all-night stores, mostly in the Bayswater section, and you'll find a 24-hour supermarket for food and household goods at 68 Westbourne Grove, W.2, near Paddington Station.

SUBWAY INFORMATION: Stations are identified by the distinctive sign and the words "London Underground." If you ask for the subway, you risk ending up in a tunnel for pedestrians running beneath a road. On the Underground, or tube, you pay a flat 40p (60¢) for any journey within the central area, 50p (75¢) to go farther afield. There are higher prices for the trip to Heathrow Airport, for example. Destinations are listed on ticket machines, or you can buy yours from the booking office if you don't have the correct change. Maps showing the Underground network are displayed in every station and on each platform. You can transfer as many times as you like so long as you stay in the Underground and don't leave the network on ground level.

TAXES: There is no local sales tax in cities and towns, but 15% Value Added Tax (VAT) is added to all hotel and restaurant bills. VAT is also included in the cost of many of the items you purchase to take home with you. When shopping, inquire as to the tax-free export scheme, which may save you the 15% tax.

TAXIS: You can pick up a cab in London either by heading for a cab rank or by hailing one in the street (it's available if the light on the roof is on). You can phone 286-6010, 286-6128, or 272-3030 for a radio cab. The minimum fare is 60p (90¢). Each passenger over 1 year old is charged extra, and there is a surcharge of 40p (60¢) on weekends and at night. *Be warned:* If you telephone for a cab, the meter starts when the cab driver receives the instruction from the dispatcher, so you could find 60p (90¢) or more on the clock already when you begin your ride. Cab-sharing is not often done.

TELEGRAMS: Inland telegrams have been replaced by telemessages at £3 ($4.50) for 50 words. If your message is telephoned before 8 p.m. Monday to Saturday, the message will be delivered by the first mail delivery the next morning (Monday morning if it is sent on Saturday) or you get your money back. Overseas cables can still be sent from any main post office or by telephone, costing £5 ($7.50) for 50 words sent to the U.S., including the address. You'll probably be advised at the post office that it would be less expensive to telephone home.

TELEPHONES: To make a call from a call box, you'll need 5p (8¢) and 10p (15¢) pieces. Phone numbers in Britain don't have any consistency or pattern, although it is gradually sorting itself out. One person may have a six-figure number, while the next-door neighbor's number has eight figures. In some cases, you have an exchange name; in others, sets of figures. You'll need all the figures, which can vary from ten down to six. Consult Directory Enquiries to aid you. Dial 192, give the operator the town to which you wish to call, and the name and address of the person you are calling. (Dial 142 for this information if the number you want is within the London postal code area.)

A guide to telephone costs: A call at noon from London to Reading, 40 miles away, lasting three minutes costs 84p ($1.26). A local call within the radius of one mile can cost 21p (32¢) for three minutes. These costs are roughly halved between 6 p.m. and 8 a.m. You will have to pay far more if you use a hotel operator at any time.

The **Westminster International Telephone Bureau**, 1 Broadway, London, S.W.1, is open daily from 9 a.m. to 5:30 p.m., including Sunday. Here you can call all countries not available through call boxes (i.e., outside Europe). A receptionist will help you and take your money when you've finished the call.

TELEX: These are mostly restricted to business premises and hotels. If your hotel has a Telex, they will send your message, and you can arrange in advance for receipt of replies.

TIME: England and Scotland are based on Greenwich Mean Time, five hours ahead of the U.S. East coast, with British Summer Time (GMT + 1 hour) during the summer, roughly from the end of March to the end of October.

TIPPING: Many establishments add a service charge. If the service has been good, it's usual to add an additional 5% to that. If no service is added to the bill, give 10% for poor service, 15% or more for good. If the service is bad, make it known and don't tip. Taxi drivers expect about 15% but never less than 15p (23¢) on a 60p (90¢) ride.

TRANSPORTATION IN GREATER LONDON: If you know the ropes, transportation within London and its immediate environs can be unusually easy and cheap, because London enjoys one of the best Underground and bus systems in the world.

The **Underground:** The electric subways are, to begin with, comfortable—the trains have cushioned seats, no less. You purchase your ticket in advance either at a ticket booth or from an automatic ticket machine. Fares vary according to the number of zones traveled within Greater London, from 30p (45¢) in one zone to £1.30 ($1.95) for five zones, but the flat fare in the central zone is 40p (60¢). Fares from Heathrow are higher, costing £1.50 ($2.25) to Piccadilly Circus.

Be sure to keep your ticket: it must be presented at the end of the line. If you owe extra, you'll be billed then by an attendant.

Each subway line has its own distinctive color, and all you need follow is the clearly painted arrows. On every stairway, at every corridor turning, on every platform, are additional diagrams in color, giving the routes of the various trains. More diagrams are inside the trains themselves.

The Piccadilly line serves Heathrow Airport, giving London Transport the world's first connection between an airport and a major underground transportation system. Built with special consideration for airline travelers, the Heathrow extension has trains with additional luggage space as well as moving walkways from the airport terminals to the Underground station. The link enables incoming passengers to dash from Heathrow to Piccadilly Circus in only 40 minutes.

The Piccadilly line has frequent service to accommodate the demand created by the Heathrow extension, but be warned: if you're out on the town and are dependent on the Underground, watch your time carefully—many of the subways stop running at midnight (11:30 p.m. on Sunday).

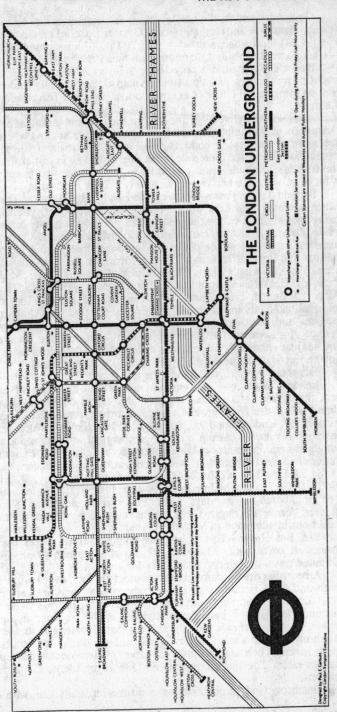

THE LONDON UNDERGROUND

On Sunday and public holidays there is a maximum fare to anywhere (except Heathrow and stations outside Greater London) on the network of 80p ($1.20) for a single journey and £1.20 ($1.80) for a round trip. These are not Rover tickets and therefore each ticket can be used only once.

Buses: The comparably priced bus system is almost as good. To find out about current routes, pick up a free bus map at the Piccadilly Underground Station Information Office or at any London Transport Travel Information Centre.

After you have lined up (queued) for the bus, and picked a seat either downstairs or on the upper deck (where you can smoke, and where you'll see more of the city), a conductor will come by to whom you tell your destination. He or she then collects the fare and gives you a ticket. As with the subways, the fare varies according to the distance you travel. If you want to be warned when to get off, simply ask the conductor.

Bargain Travel Passes—Underground and Buses: London Transport, which operates one of the world's biggest urban transport systems, offers many special facilities for the visitor, and produces a handy information guide, *London Transport's London,* which includes bus and Underground maps and a useful street plan. It is available free from Underground stations and London Transport Travel Information Centres. These centers are at Victoria, King's Cross, Oxford Circus, Piccadilly Circus, St. James's Park, and Heathrow Central Underground stations, as well as at Heathrow Airport Terminals 1 and 2 and Victoria British Rail station. They provide information on bus and Underground services and on a wide range of other facilities and places of interest. They sell special visitors' tickets, take bookings for London Transport's guided tours, and have free Underground and bus maps and other information leaflets. A 24-hour telephone information service is available (tel. 222-1234).

Of special value to visitors are the following:

London Explorer—These special visitors' bus and tube tickets give one, three, four, and seven days' unlimited travel on all red buses and almost all of the Underground, including travel from and to Heathrow Airport by Underground or Airbus. London Explorers are also the passport to valuable savings on a range of tourist attractions and can be bought at London Transport Travel Information Centres and Underground stations and from appointed travel agents worldwide. In London, they cost £3 ($4.50) for adults, £1.30 ($1.95) for children for one day; £8 ($12) for adults, £3 ($4.50) for children for three days; £10.50 ($15.75) for adults, £4 ($6) for children for four days; and £13 ($19.50) for adults, £5 ($7.50) for children for seven days. These tickets also carry discounts, such as reductions in admission to Madame Tussaud's.

Red Bus Rover—This is another unlimited-travel ticket useful to visitors. It costs adults £1.80 ($2.70) and children 60p (90¢), allowing unlimited travel on London's red buses for a day.

Airport Services—Many London visitors (in fact, most) will want to go to and from Heathrow by public transport, as taxis are very expensive. London Transport's express bus services provide links from Euston, Victoria, and Paddington stations, as well as from major hotel areas. All Airbus routes pick up and set down passengers at the three Heathrow air terminals. Airbus is particularly useful to visitors with heavy suitcases because the buses are large, modern double-deckers with luggage racks. The single fare is £2.50 ($3.75) for adults, £1 ($1.50) for children.

Heathrow Underground station is on the Piccadilly line, with direct services from King's Cross/St. Pancras and easy one-change journeys from Liverpool Street, Fenchurch Street, and Charing Cross.

These fares, although valid at the time of writing, will surely change during the lifetime of this edition, and are therefore presented only for general background information, so that you will know the range of travel options available to you.

USEFUL TELEPHONE NUMBERS: Alcoholics Anonymous, 01/834-8202. Gamblers Anonymous, 01/352-3060. **Rape Crisis Centre,** 01/340-6145. **Gay Switchboard,** 01/837-7324. **Consumer Association,** 01/839-1222. **Law Society,** 01/969-7473. **Help Advisory Centre,** 01/937-6445 (this is for when you don't know where to get the sort of help you need). **The Samaritans,** 01/283-3400 (for the suicidal or depressed). **Traveline** (travel information), 01/246-8021 in London, 031/246-8021 for Scotland. **Leisureline** (local events), 01/246-8041 in London, 031/246-8041 for Scotland May to September only. **Children's London,** 01/246-8007. **Weather,** 01/246-8091 for London; 0752/8091 foɪ Devon and Cornwall; 0224/8091 for Scotland's Highlands; 031/246-8091 for Edinburgh and Lothian.

Part One

ENGLAND

Chapter II

LONDON: HOTELS FOR EVERY BUDGET

LONDON IS A HYBRID, a gathering place for people from the far corners of a once-great Empire. Both the country gentry and the blue-collar worker from the provinces visit London somewhat in the mood of going abroad.

The true Londoner, usually from the East End, is called a Cockney, the name for a person born within the sound of the Bow Bells, the chimes of a church in Cheapside. But the city is also the home of the well-bred English lady who has had to sell her family estate of 400 years and take meager lodgings in Earl's Court; of the expatriate Hollywood actress living in elegance in a Georgian town house; of the islander from Jamaica who comes seeking a new life and ends up collecting fares on one of London's red double-decker buses; of the young playwright from Liverpool whose art reflects the outlook of the working class.

Cosmopolitan or not. Europe's largest city is still like a great wheel, with Piccadilly Circus at the hub and dozens of communities branching out from it. Since London is such a conglomeration of sections—each having its own life (hotels, restaurants, pubs)—the first-time visitor may be intimidated until he gets the hang of it. In this chapter, I'll concentrate on the so-called West End, although nobody has been able to come up with a satisfactory explanation as to what that entails. For the most part, a visitor will live and eat in the West End, except when he or she ventures into the old and historic part of London known as "The City," or goes on a tour to the Tower of London, or seeks lodgings in the remote villages such as Hampstead Heath.

The East End—the docks, the homes of the Cockney working class, the commercial and industrial districts—is rarely visited by tourists, except the more adventurous travelers bent on discovering the true London.

A LIVABLE METROPOLIS: The government has moved strongly against pollution. For example, residents can't burn anything but smokeless fuel. The legendary smog that once hung over the city is gone. When a trout was caught in the Thames, it made headlines in the world press. Nostalgia buffs miss the fogs, but eight million Londoners are getting 50% more winter sunshine than they used to.

In this day of energy crisis and inflation, London has many problems she's yet to tackle. But she has made inroads to create a better city in which to live.

She's wrinkled with age and was severely scarred by the war, but her presence is impressive. Tradition is maintained in the face of world change and upheaval. Mutton-chopped veterans of World War I still exist—hiding behind the Dickensian, dark-mahogany walls of their gentlemen's clubs, poring over the memoirs of long-forgotten generals.

But they are clichés. London today is filled with vital people, both young and old, pursuing their interests. Gambling clubs, discos, strip shows, and experimental theater make London an adventure all night long, as art galleries, museums, curiosity shops, and historic monuments fill the day.

THE HOTEL OUTLOOK: The hotel picture has changed drastically since the 19th century, when the Hotel Victoria had only four bathrooms for its 500 guests. London now offers accommodations to satisfy all purposes, tastes, and pocketbooks—ranging from the deluxe suites to army cots that rent to students in hostels.

One or two hotels sprout up every year, and others are on the drawing boards. For too long London hotels seemed lost in the days of Victoria (many still are). Now, increased pressure from overseas has brought about a discernible upgrading. Of course, in the name of progress, Edwardian architectural features have often given way to the worst and most impersonal of modern; and showers (even bedrooms) are placed in broom closets best left to serve their original functions. Nevertheless, a hotel revolution is in the air, as evidenced by low-budget town-house hotels now forced to install central heating.

Before launching into actual recommendations, I should issue a . .

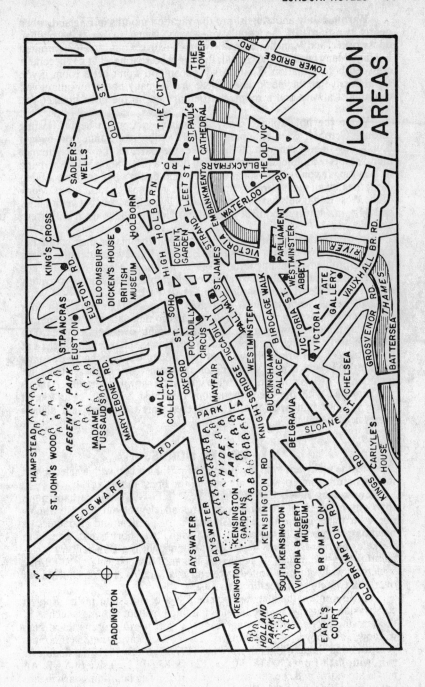

Warning: July and August are the vacation months in England, when nearly two-thirds of the population—every Jaguar maker, Liverpudlian dockworker, and Manchester textile worker—strikes out for a long-awaited holiday. Many head for the capital, further exacerbating what has become a crowded hotel situation. That doesn't mean you won't get a room if you should arrive at this peak time. There are so many hotels nowadays you can almost always find a room, but perhaps not in the price bracket you want.

When the holidays are over, the season in London begins, lasting through October. Even in September and October, as in June, low-budget hotels are tight—although nothing like they are in the peak summer months. It is recommended that you nail down a reservation before arriving in London. If you're a personal shopper who doesn't like to book a blind date, then by all means arrive early to begin your search for a room. Many of the West End hotels have vacancies, even in peak season, between 9 a.m. and 11 a.m., but by noon they are often packed solidly again with fresh arrivals.

In the sections to follow, I'll explore all the major districts of the English capital of interest to visitors. But first I'll devote attention to the pressing problem of finding a room—be it the Oliver Messel Suite at "The Dorch" or a beautifully decorated, comfortable guest house—privately owned—near Kensington Gardens and Hyde Park.

All hotels, motels, inns, and guest houses in Britain, with four bedrooms or more (including self-catering accommodations), are required to display notices showing minimum and maximum overnight charges. The notice must be displayed in a prominent position in the reception area or at the entrance. The prices shown *must* include any service charge and *may* include VAT, and it must be made clear whether or not these items are included. If VAT is not included, then it must be shown separately. If meals are provided with the accommodation, this must be made clear too. If prices are not standard for all rooms, then only the lowest and highest prices need be given.

1. Deluxe Hotels.

For the lucky few who can afford them, I'll lead off with a selection of luxury hotels, some of which are among the finest in the world.

Connaught Hotel, Carlos Place, W.1 (tel. 499-7070), perhaps more than any other hotel in London captures an elegant old English atmosphere. It ranks at the top with Claridge's for prestige and character. Its position is supreme, in the center of Mayfair, two short blocks from both Berkeley and Grosvenor Squares. The Connaught is a 19th-century architectural treasure house of a way of life fast disappearing. It's a brick structure, with a formal Rolls-Royce entrance, and its tall French windows overlook two curved, tree-lined streets.

As you enter, the staircase reminds you of an estate in the English countryside. Throughout the hotel you'll find excellent antiques, such as in the drawing room with its formal fireplace, soft lustrous draperies at high windows, and bowls of fresh flowers. The cost of staying here is the same year round: a single with bath from £65 ($97.50) to £78 ($117), a double or twin with bath from £100 ($150) to £125 ($187.50), inclusive of VAT. All meals are extra, and the service charge is 15%. The bedrooms vary in size but all are furnished with well-selected antiques and tasteful reproductions.

All of the rooms have well-equipped bathrooms and niceties galore. It is imperative to reserve well in advance.

The paneled bar-lounge is old-school-tie conservative; the fashionable (everybody from movie stars to bestselling novelists) dining room is also wood paneled, but it glitters with mirrors and crystal. The chef has perfected the English cuisine and a selection of French dishes. The bowing and attentive waiters, the fresh flowers, set the proper mood. Luncheon or dinner from the à la carte menu will cost about £45 ($67.50) per person. The food lives up to its reputation as superb. Reservations are essential for nonresidents of the hotel.

At four o'clock at the Connaught guests head for the circular sun room just off the entry lounge, where the English ritual of afternoon tea is practiced at its best, with all the proper accoutrements.

The Dorchester, Park Lane, W.1. (tel. 629-8888), faces Hyde Park on the fringe of Mayfair. Built and opened in 1931, it enjoys many of the benefits of early 20th-century design, with large rooms and bathrooms. Several British government ministers stayed here during World War II, joined by General Eisenhower and some of his aides after the United States entered the fracas. In 1976 the Dorchester was purchased by an Arab consortium for £9 million and since then, some £11 million has been spent on a renovation program. The hotel is presently owned by a publicity-shy Near Easterner, who lives in the hotel. A big refurbishing program of the public rooms on the first floor has been completed. Paris-based decorator Alberto Pinto was responsible for the bar, the Terrace Restaurant, and the promenade. The bar, decorated with mirrors and ceramics, is London's smart meeting place, particularly in the evening when guests relax to piano music. The new promenade, which extends from the lobby through the old lounge to the ballroom entrance, provides elegant and comfortable seating accommodation for afternoon tea or for cocktails before lunching or dining.

The Oliver Messel Suite is as popular as ever, and his penthouse and Pavilion Room for small parties have been refurbished exactly as he originally designed them. All the rooms and suites in the hotel are tastefully decorated in different colors and styles. Singles start at £90 ($135) and doubles at £110 ($165), including tax and service. The Dorchester offers numerous amenities, such as valet and maid service, hairdressing salons, a florist, in-house films, and radio and television in every room.

The Terrace Restaurant seats 85 at tables that are given an illusion of privacy, with alcoves, gilded palm fronds, rose-pink columns, pale jade and rose curtains, and dining chairs in green Regency chinoiserie. A pianist plays from 7 to 10 p.m., and from 10 p.m. until 1 a.m. you can dance to a three-piece trio.

The Terrace, with a view across Hyde Park and impeccable service, complements the superb cuisine presided over by Anton Mosimann, maître chef de cuisine at the Dorchester for nearly a decade. Mosimann began learning his trade at a small restaurant owned by his parents in a Swiss village near Bern and has gone on to win acclaim as one of the world's finest chefs, being now in charge of all food service at the Dorchester, with a staff of 75.

In addition to à la carte dishes, you can enjoy a three-course table d'hôte dinner at the Terrace Restaurant for £19 ($28.50) per person, or try Mosimann's menu surprise, six courses at £50 ($75) for two persons, including service and VAT. On the menu surprise, you may have such dishes as hot puff pastry filled with cheese, spinach, and leek, followed by a terrine of wild mushrooms with a light sauce and decorated with endive and carrots. After beef consommé garnished with vegetables, perhaps you'll have pike mousse with watercress sauce and bits of frog legs and then mignons of veal with orange sauce, celery mousse, and fresh vegetables. When I was last there, the main course was followed by warm goat cheese served with brown bread and grapes, then sherbet in puff pastry with strawberry sauce. Sounds heavy? It's not, really, as the portions are small so that the amount you eat does not make you feel stuffed.

Mosimann changes the menu as the seasons change, and on the à la carte offering you may find rosettes de boeuf aux echalotes (small beef filets in shallot sauce) or a variety of seafood with a light herb sauce. The master chef specializes in dishes that are original, light, simple, and attractive. The Grill Room serves only the best of English dishes.

Ritz Hotel, Piccadilly, W. 1 (tel. 493-8181), along with its namesake on the Place Vendôme in Paris, made the word "Ritzy" synonymous in the English vernacular with luxury. Of the Ritz in the "other city," a French writer once said, "It isn't a hotel, it isn't even a big hotel, it's a monument." Much the same can be said of the London Ritz. For the incurable romanticist, it remains the leading choice in the capital, seemingly cut off from busy Piccadilly, especially if you get a room overlooking Green Park. The Ritz world is one of sparkling crystal, gleaming gilt, rich Italian marble, all that epitomizes the elegantly frivolous comfort of Edwardian high life.

Through extensive renovation, Cunard Leisure has restored the lovely hotel to much of its original elegance, the way César Ritz wanted it back in 1906. The public places are spacious and dramatic. The Palm Court is like a stage setting: oval shaped with its centerpiece the extravagantly sculptured fountain in exhellon marble, adorned by the gilt figure *La Source*. The restaurant has a paneled wall lining of melting marbles and a hand-painted ceiling depicting skies with billowing clouds. The sumptuous chandeliers are linked to each other around the room by a chain of gilt bronze garlands, so that the dining area appears to be permanently *en fête*. Sunday-afternoon tea dances, dancing during dinner, and musical performances are some of the regular features, and the food and service are of the highest standard.

Staying here costs from £85 ($127.50) in a single, from £110 ($165) to £130 ($195) in a double or twin, VAT and service included. The 139 bedrooms and suites are traditionally decorated in soft pastel shades of champagne and pale blue. Some of the original Victorian brass beds, cara-marble fireplaces, and crystal lighting fixtures are found in the rooms, giving them the elegance of an English stately home.

The Ritz offers a unique atmosphere of warmth, friendliness, and timeless good taste.

The Savoy, The Strand, W.C.2 (tel. 836-4343), is a landmark. Lucius Beebe maintained that its position has "ranked with the great hotels of all time." He went on to say that it "is perfumed with an aura lingering from the rich and regal England of Edward VII." The London institution looks to Richard D'Oyly Carte, the Victorian impresario who managed the first Gilbert and Sullivan operas, as its founding father. Through it have walked many of the famous personages of yesterday and today, everybody from the Divine Sarah, to acting partners Dame Ellen Terry and Sir Henry Irving, to rock stars.

Its position is choice, right on the Strand overlooking the Thames and adjacent to the new Covent Garden Market redevelopment. The lounges of the Savoy are comfortable and restrained, with intimate nooks. Bedrooms are skillfully planned and furnished with color-coordinated accessories; the furnishings are a blend of antiques, an eclectic combination of such pieces as gilt mirrors, Queen Anne chairs, and Victorian sofas. Singles cost £90 ($135), £150 ($225) with a river view. Doubles and twins go from £115 ($172.50), to £150 ($225) with a view of the Thames. VAT and service charge are included. Every chambermaid, every waiter, is groomed for attentive service; the Savoy has long been a training ground for employees desiring to learn top-level hotel service. The Savoy Grill and the Savoy Restaurant are world famous.

London Hilton on Park Lane, Park Lane, W.1 (tel. 493-8000), is better than ever. It's been a legend ever since it was built in 1963, and in 1984 the 500-room deluxe hostelry was completely renovated and upgraded in a tasteful, conscientious program. From the beginning, this was a smoothly running Anglo-American alliance. A skyscraper, it offers bedrooms facing Hyde Park. The site, so to speak, was always prime, ideal for what is Hilton International's flagship hotel in the United Kingdom.

When it was built, one of the most persistent allegations was that from some of the high-altitude windows (30 stories), you could look down into Queen Elizabeth's boudoir. Not so! It would take a powerful spyglass to let you see the queen putting on her diamond tiara.

The Hilton rooms have such amenities as extra-long beds, TV, radios and intercom systems, air conditioning, message signal lights, showers in the baths, and circulating ice water. Year-round rates, with VAT included, range from £89 ($133.50) to £115 ($172.50) in a single and from £112 ($168) to £140 ($210) in a twin-bedded chamber. The hotel not only sets high-level comfort and standards, but does so in style. As important as its slick bathrooms and bedrooms with every convenience is the quick and efficient service tailored to the needs of today's travelers.

As part of the new, major renovation, floors 24 to 27 now have nine luxury suites, two executive suites, and six junior suites, along with 38 bedrooms and a private lounge. Separate check-in and -out facilities are offered on these floors.

The Hilton's latest restaurant is called the British Harvest, which serves only the best and freshest of local produce in season. Pickled pine, a high coffered ceiling, and arched windows combine with pink marble, cherry-colored upholstery, and planted troughs to achieve an airy, cheerful effect. Breakfast here includes oatcakes from Scotland, Welsh seaweed bread, black and white pudding, kippers, and deviled kidneys, along with eggs, bacon, sausage, and steak. Lunch and dinner feature seasonal "harvest" menus.

The front lobby of the Hilton is a modern interpretation of 18th-century Georgian traditions. Finishes are mainly of mahogany and marble, with accessories in crystal and brass. Nearby, the St. George's Bar has become a favorite London rendezvous. Earth colors—brown, beige, peach, ocher, rust, and tan—predominate, and the furnishings reflect a Hepplewhite and Chippendale influence. A dramatic marble and brass spiral staircase sweeps up to the first-floor level and the British Harvest Restaurant.

You can patronize the Lobby Lounge for breakfast, snacks, afternoon tea, and evening drinks. The atmosphere is elegant but relaxed. Beginning at tea time, guests are entertained by a pianist, harpist, or string quartet. Other hotel facilities include a library of video films, a host of concessionaires in the arcade (where you can arrange car rentals, book theater tickets, etc.), a sauna, and a Jacuzzi. There has also been a major upgrading of the fire detection and safety systems.

Management and staff are among the most professional and highly trained in London.

Churchill, Portman Square, W.1 (486-5800), is a 500-room luxury hotel in Mayfair. It's owned by an Arab conglomerate, and design and taste are combined here with the best of traditional London hotel keeping. Interior designer Ellen Lehman McCluskey dipped into England's great periods to give the hotel style and flair. At No. 10, a restaurant, the decor is Regency, the tented effect reminiscent of the field headquarters of the Iron Duke; all is glamorous, with much gilt and marble, columns and Egyptian-style paintings. You dine in a simpler fashion in the Greenery, with its skylit roof. Drinks are served in the swank Churchill Bar, where soft piano music plays in the background; afternoon tea is taken in the sunken lounge. The bedrooms tastefully blend traditional pieces with classic modern. Every room has individually controlled temperature, two phones (one in the bath), radio, TV, and bath. Singles rent for £85 ($127.50); doubles, £98 ($147). Service and VAT are extra.

Brown's, Dover street and Albemarle Street, W.1 (tel. 493-6020), is the London base of many of the gentry who desert their stuffy manors for "the season" in the capital, quietly booking into their "usual" room. They know that Brown's resists the brassy new and doesn't appeal to flashy tourists.

This traditional hotel was the creation of Lord Byron's manservant, James Brown, who wanted to go into business for himself. He accepted "fine gentlemen only." The location is appropriate—in Mayfair, just off Berkeley Square. The rates for a single room with private bath are £75 ($112.50) and from £96 ($144) for a twin-bedded room with a bath, VAT and service included.

The bedrooms vary considerably, and are a tangible record of the past history of England. Even the wash basins are semi-antiques. The rooms have restrained taste, with good soft beds and telephones. The lounges on the street floor are inviting and cozy. There's a paneled lounge for the drinking of "spirits," another for afternoon tea.

The dining room has a quiet dignity and unmatched service. Á la carte meals are served, plus a set luncheon menu at £20 ($30) and a set dinner at £23 ($34.50), including service and VAT.

HOTELS IN THREE PRICE RANGES

After this look at life at the top, I'll now discuss my remaining recommendations, the bulk of those in this guide. These establishments are divided into districts, such as Mayfair, Belgravia, Bloomsbury. All of the hotels have one thing in common: they are less expensive than the deluxe, but even they reveal wide price differences. Therefore, I've broken them down into categories, beginning with the upper bracket, with first-class amenities. The medium-priced range follows with a listing of the best of London's moderately priced hotels with or without private baths. In this category a full English breakfast is usually (but not always) included in the rates quoted. Finally, for those who want to keep travel costs bone-trimmed, I'll list budget-range choices wherever possible. Establishments in this category are most often converted town houses with only a handful of rooms with private baths, if any.

First-class hotels in London have generally abandoned the time-honored English tradition of serving you a full English breakfast (bacon and eggs) for the price of the room. The hotels in the medium-priced range are a toss-up—the majority still maintain this custom, although many establishments rely on skimpy continental fare instead of the works.

Most budget hotels in London, with many exceptions, still provide a full English breakfast for the price of the room. Because the policy of charging extra for breakfast is so erratic, always inquire before checking in.

Further, nearly all upper and middle-bracket hotels, and even some budget accommodations, charge a service fee ranging from 10% to 15%. Again, inquire about all such hidden extras *before* checking in so as to avoid a surprise when the bill's presented.

2. St. James's

This section, the beginning of Royal London, starts at Piccadilly Circus and moves southwest. It's frightfully convenient, as the English say, enclosing a number of important locations such as American Express on Haymarket, many of the leading stores (Burberry's of raincoat wear), and Buckingham Palace.

It basks in its associations with royalty—it was the "merrie monarch" himself, Charles II, the famous skirt chaser (Nell Gwynne the favorite), who founded St. James's Park. And it was in St. James's Palace that his father, Charles I, spent his last troubled night, awaiting his beheading the following morning. At one time the palace was a hunting lodge of Henry VIII and his wife of the moment, Anne Boleyn.

For the traditionalist in particular, living in the heart of aristocratic London has many advantages—none more important than its well-run and discriminating hotels themselves. Their number is limited, but their addresses are most fashionable, just as they were in the society heyday of the 18th century.

THE UPPER BRACKET: **Cavendish Hotel,** Jermyn Street, S.W.1 (tel. 930-2111), has an old name, but a new body with a lively spirit. It was built in 1966 on the site of the old Cavendish, the subject of numerous stories about the days of Edward VII, when it was thronged with theatrical and royal personages. The hotel grew to fame under its colorful proprietor Rosa Lewis, known as "The Duchess of Jermyn Street" in a biography written about her. In the St. James's district ("Royal London"), just off Piccadilly and a five-minute walk from Pall Mall, this former landmark has been transformed into an ultra-contemporary hotel. Its first two floors are devoted to shops, lounges, restaurants, and bars; the 250-bedroom tower is set back, rising above it.

The rooms are bright and airy, with wall-to-wall curtains, a sitting area, and TV. Double-thickness windows keep out traffic noises. All rooms have private baths. A single rents for £68 ($102), doubles from £85 ($127.50). A continental breakfast is included in the rates.

The second-floor lounge and drinking bar are approached by a curious "floating staircase." The Sub Rosa bar-lounge, named in honor of the former proprietor, captures some of the flavor of the Edwardian era with brass lamps and black tufted banquettes. The Cavendish Restaurant is suitable for an after-theater supper (special menu from 11:30 p.m. to 7

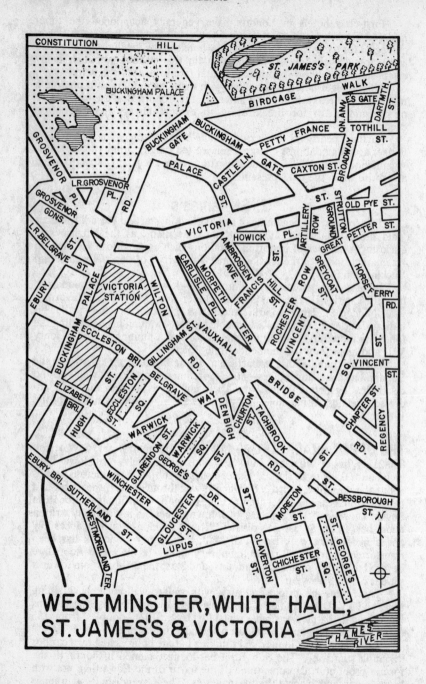

WESTMINSTER, WHITE HALL, ST. JAMES'S & VICTORIA

a.m.) and also offers an alternative menu in the style of *cuisine minceur* (cooking without fats) during the lunch and dinner service. Tube: Green Park.

The **Goring Hotel,** Beeston Place, Grosvenor Gardens, S.W.1 (tel. 834-8211), achieves the seemingly impossible: it provides the charm of traditional, dignified English living and at the same time offers all modern comforts. Hotelier Goring built the establishment in 1910 with "revolutionary ideas"—that is, that every room should have a private bath, foyer, and central heating. His grandson, George Goring, continues to provide top service.

The 100 rooms (here they are called apartments) rent for £65 ($97.50) in a single, £85 ($127.50) in a double or twin. Rates include color TV, service, and VAT. You can have a three-course table d'hôte luncheon for £15 ($22.50), and dinner from £18 ($27). Afternoon teas are served by waiters from a trolley in the large, paneled Garden Lounge, where you can sit and view the garden or take cocktails before meals in the new bar by the window. The recently refurbished dining room reflects the charm and elegance of an English country hotel. The Goring's situation is choice, close to Victoria Station, and a ten-minute walk from Buckingham Palace, Westminster Abbey, and the Houses of Parliament. Tube: Victoria Station.

Stafford Hotel, 16–18 St. James's Pl., S.W.1 (tel. 493-0111), dates from Edwardian days, romantically lying in a cul-de-sac off St. James's Street. The hotel can be entered via St. James's Place or else through the more colorful Blue Ball Yard (but only when the hotel's cocktail bar is open). The hotel has been completely brought up to date with all the modern amenities, and some of its rooms are the most tranquil in heartbeat London. The Stafford is often used by those who need a place near court, as well as the embassy and political life of London.

Its 60 bedrooms retain a home-like country-house atmosphere that many hotels seem to have forgotten. There is a small, comfortable restaurant and a bar (reputed to have exported the martini). The staff is attentive to your needs, and there is easy access to good shopping and to "theaterland." Rates are £92 ($138) in a single, rising to £112 ($168) in a double, plus VAT. Service is included, but breakfast is extra. Tube: Green Park.

Duke's Hotel, 35 St. James's Pl., S.W.1 (tel 491-4840), is a small, turn-of-the-century hotel in the St. James's district, only a five-minute walk from Piccadilly, a hundred feet or so from Green Park (which abuts Buckingham Palace) and near St. James's Palace. A bit of leftover Victorian architecture, it sits on a postage-stamp square lit by gas lamps and adorned with flowers. It's all pure Regency, and frequented mainly by gentry who avoid the large impersonal hotels and gravitate to an establishment where the staff knows their quirks ("Welcome back, Lady Cooper-Plympton, will you want your morning tea at the usual time?").

There is central heating throughout, every bedroom has its own private bath and direct-dial telephone, and each suite is named after a duke. A single rents for £78 ($117), a double or twin for £100 ($150), inclusive of service and VAT. Light refreshments are available in a charming little bar or in the sitting room at all times. Main meals are served in the St. James's Room restaurant from 12:30 to 2:30 p.m. and from 6:30

to 10:30 p.m. Room service functions 24 hours a day. Tube: Piccadilly Circus.

Royal Westminster Thistle Hotel, Buckingham Palace Road, S.W.1 (tel. 834-1821), has one of the most fashionable addresses in London, within minutes of Buckingham Palace (in fact, this hotel is passed during the Changing of the Guard). A shining concrete and glass structure, the Royal Westminster charges from £65 ($97.50) in a double or twin, £55 ($82.50) in a single. Rates are inclusive of service charge and VAT, although breakfast is extra. Each bedroom is spacious, with many fine touches; you get private baths, radio and TV, and there's a free ice machine on every floor. Thatcher's, the Royal Westminster's à la carte restaurant, is designed on a charming English rustic theme and offers an English and international menu appealing to business persons and visitors alike. The attractive cocktail bar, conveniently situated next to Thatcher's Restaurant, is ideal for a relaxing pre-lunch or dinner drink. Light refreshments and drinks are also served to residents in the comfortable, elegant lounge-bar, adjacent to the reception. The notable feature of the hotel is its collection of 18 "royal suites," each portraying a different theme—you go from Braganza and Botticelli to Victoria and Gladstone to Sayonara to Du Barry. Tube: Victoria Station.

THE MEDIUM-PRICED RANGE: **Hamilton House,** 62 Warwick Way, S.W.1 (tel. 821-7113), is composed of early Victorian houses, joined and recently modernized. James Burns, the owner, was born in Pimlico, a few yards from the hotel. Since buying the property with his Danish wife, who was a TWA stewardess, he has constantly improved the facilities. There are now 45 rooms of which 30 have private baths and toilets, renting for £36 ($54) per night, breakfast and tax included. All rooms have telephone, radio, and TV. There is a residents' bar on the premises, and a fine restaurant for 60 people. Open to the public, it serves traditional English dishes and American fast foods. American guests are particularly welcome. Tube: Victoria Station.

3. Piccadilly Circus

If you want to be in the middle of the West End, right at Piccadilly Circus and Leicester Square, then the following will appeal to you. Most of London's theaters, Soho, Regent Street, and many famous restaurants and pubs will be at your doorstep.

THE MEDIUM-PRICED RANGE: **Regent Palace Hotel,** Piccadilly Circus (tel. 734-7000), is one of the largest hotels in Europe. It's a mammoth establishment, some 1068 rooms, all with hot and cold running water (i.e., without private baths) and color TV. There is no more centrally located hotel in London—in fact, some of its rooms overlook the Eros statue on Piccadilly Circus. It charges £28 ($42) for a single, £42 ($63) for a double. Prices include a continental breakfast. Best of all, there is plenty of well-brewed coffee, an item that makes the Palace popular with North Americans. Facilities include a booking office for theaters and concerts, pressing, cleaning, and laundry service, shops for gifts, clothing, jewelry, and confectionery, and a hairdressing salon. Within the building is a Grill

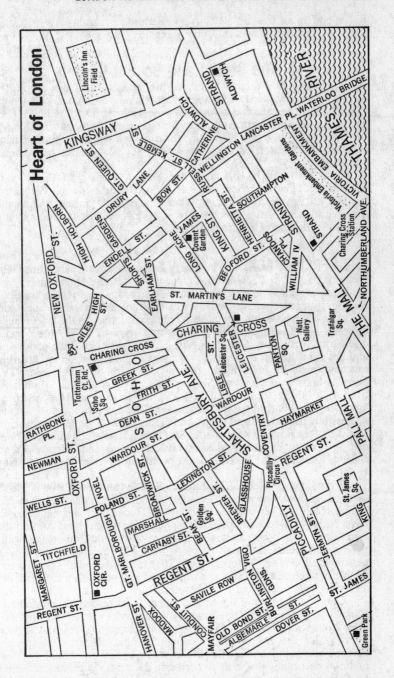

Heart of London

Room and an all-you-can-eat Carvery. A third restaurant, Garry's Coffee Shop, is open until 1:30 a.m. Tube: Piccadilly Circus.

4. The Strand and Covent Garden

Beginning at Trafalgar Square, the Strand runs east into Fleet Street. Londoners used to be able to walk along the Strand and see the Thames, but the river has receded. In the 17th century, the elegant and wealthy built their homes on the Strand, their gardens stretching to the Thames. But today it's changing to something less grand—flanked as it is with theaters, shops, hotels, and such landmarks as Somerset House.

Peaceful lanes jut off from the Strand, leading to the Victoria Embankment Gardens along the river. Opposite the gardens is Cleopatra's Needle, an Egyptian obelisk, London's oldest (and dullest) monument. You might want to stroll along the river if weather permits. You may also want to book a hotel along the Strand.

THE UPPER BRACKET: The **Drury Lane Hotel,** 10 Drury Lane, High Holborn, W.C.2 (tel. 836-6666), a Queens Moat House hotel, is a concrete and glass structure in the heart of theaterland. Once you're inside its confines, however, the atmosphere is relaxed and subdued, suggesting neither a chain hotel nor one of such severe modernity as the facade might indicate. Built with terraced gardens and its own plaza, the hotel is a self-contained entity. All of its 128 spacious bedrooms have good views and are furnished in a subtle, harmonious fashion, with many luxurious touches, such as individually controlled central heating, color TVs, even 24-hour room service. Singles range from £55 ($82.50), doubles from £72 ($108). Tariffs include VAT and service. All the bedrooms have fully tiled baths kept sparkling clean. The decor in the public rooms successfully uses green and beige, and plants evoke a garden atmosphere. Maudie's Restaurant is named after Sir Osbert Lancaster's famous arbiter-of-chic cartoon character Maudie Littlehampton, and offers a French cuisine. Maudie's Bar makes a good posttheater rendevous. Tube: High Holborn.

Strand Palace Hotel, The Strand, W.C.2 (tel. 836-8080), is ideally situated for those who want to be in the theater district, near points such as Trafalgar Square, yet within a block of the Thames Embankment. Rooms have baths, wall-to-wall draperies, innerspring mattresses, comfortable furnishings. Sun-bright colors contrast vividly with chalk-white walls. Behind the scenes is a staff of more than 400 standing by to provide personalized service. Rates are £42 ($63) in a single, £49 ($73.50) in a double or twin, and £58 ($87) in a triple. VAT and service are included, and all rooms have private baths or showers.

One of the assets of the Strand Palace is its restaurants, including a Carvery where every day but Sunday you can gorge yourself on England's finest roasts at £9.50 ($14.25) per person, including VAT and service. There's also the 369 Strand, a coffeeshop that attracts show people. Favored also is the intimate Mask Bar, with a collection of Saul Steinberg cartoons decorating the wall. To complete the dining possibilities, there is La Pizzerie where you can select from an à la carte menu. Tube: The Strand.

5. Westminster

This section has been the seat of British government since the days of Edward the Confessor. Dominated by the Houses of Parliament and Westminster Abbey, Parliament Square symbolizes the soul of England. Westminster is a big name to describe a large borough of London, including Whitehall, headquarters of many government offices. A good part of the sprawling area in and around Victoria Station with its many budget hotels is also a part of Westminster. Known as the gateway to the continent, Victoria Station is where you get boat trains to Dover and Folkestone for that trip across the Channel. The area also has other advantages: the Green Line Coach Station and the Victoria Coach Station are just five minutes from Victoria. From the bus stations, you can board many a Green Line coach for the suburbs. And an inexpensive bus tour of London departs from a point on Buckingham Palace Road, just behind Victoria Station. From Grosvenor Gardens, you can get a bus direct to Heathrow Airport, and from Victoria Station, trains to Gatwick Airport.

THE MEDIUM-PRICED RANGE: Dolphin Square, Dolphin Square, S.W.1 (tel. 834-3800), is what dollarwise is all about. One of the largest blocks of flats (apartments) in all of Europe, it offers one of the best values in the city. The location, if not prestigious, is interesting—set back from Thames-bordering Grosvenor Road, between Chelsea and the Tate Gallery. Its past closed-door policy has changed to admit transient guests, many of whom want to create an instant home in London. To do so, you can book, say, a one-room apartment with a double bed for £48 ($72) nightly. A two-room apartment with twin beds goes for £58 ($87). Three- and four-room apartments are available also. You get handsome reductions with minimum stays of one week, even better bargains if you stay a month. Besides the fully equipped and furnished apartments, all of which have color TV, guest rooms, including early-morning tea and biscuits, are also rented at £20 ($30) in a single, £32 ($48) in a double, plus VAT. Dolphin Square was created to provide luxury living and has a vast inner courtyard and lots of gardens and lawns. The reception lounge is impressive, and a restaurant overlooking the heated swimming pool serves meals from breakfast until after the theater is out. Luxurious sauna baths for both men and women are available. For those who want to go English all the way, eight squash courts beckon. It's best reached by taxi.

Stakis St. Ermins Hotel, Caxton Street, S.W.1 (tel. 222-7888), an elegant, turn-of-the-century, red-brick hotel, is ideally located in the heart of Westminster and only a few minutes' walk from Buckingham Palace, the Houses of Parliament, and Westminster Abbey. Its 244 bedrooms all have private bathrooms, radios, TV, and individually controlled central heating, with 24-hour room service. In addition, there are 15 banqueting rooms.

The hotel has two restaurants: the Caxton Grill offers an excellent-value à la carte menu, while the Carving Table has a set price for lunch and dinner, serving joints of roast beef, lamb, and pork. The lounge bar offers an alternative, serving light snacks 24 hours a day. The rates at the hotel are £51 ($76.50) in a single, rising to £62 ($93) in a twin-bedded room. These rates include a continental breakfast and VAT. The hotel is near New Scotland Yard, halfway between Victoria Station and Big Ben. Tube: St. James's Park.

6. Victoria

Directly south of Buckingham Palace is a section in Pimlico often referred to as "Victoria," with its namesake, sprawling, bustling Victoria Station, as its center. Known as the "the Gateway to the Continent," Victoria Station is where you get boat trains to Dover and Folkestone for that trip across the Channel to France.

The section also has many other advantages from the standpoint of location, as the British Airways Terminal, the Green Line Coach Station, and the Victoria Coach Station are all just five minutes from Victoria Station.

THE MEDIUM-PRICED RANGE: The **Airway Hotel**, 29 St. George's Dr., S.W.1 (tel. 834-0205), holds a warm, friendly welcome behind its elegant 19th-century facade, in a neighborhood that was once the London residence of English aristocracy. Its character has been preserved in the interest of historic and architectural integrity. The Airway is within walking distance of Buckingham Palace, Westminster Abbey, the Houses of Parliament, and Hyde Park, as well as being immediately accessible to Victoria Station and the Victoria Coach Terminal.

The hotel offers 33 comfortable rooms with personal service, immaculate cleanliness, and friendly management. It has recently been completely refurbished. Most of the bedrooms have private bath and toilet facilities, and color TV is available on request. Bathless singles rent for £16 ($24); with bath, £19 ($28.50). Doubles and twins without bath go for £23 ($34.50); with bath or shower, £28 ($42). For a bathless triple, you'll pay £28 ($42); triple with bath, £33 ($49.50). A large family room, bathless, costs £9.50 ($14.25) per person; with bath or shower, £10.50 ($15.75) per person. All prices include a full English breakfast, service and tax. Tube: Victoria Station.

7. Chelsea

This stylish district stretches along the Thames, south of Hyde Park, Brompton, and South Kensington. Beginning at Sloane Square, it runs westward toward the periphery of Earl's Court and Brompton. Its spinal cord: King's Road, center for boutique hopping. The little streets and squares on either side of King's Road have hundreds of tiny cottages used formerly by the toiling underprivileged of the 18th and 19th centuries (although Carlyle lived there—see "Homes of Famous Writers and Artists" in Chapter IV). Now, except for Belgravia and Mayfair, Chelsea couldn't be more chic. To become a part of the scene, you can, like Carlyle, "take up abode" in one of the following recommendations.

THE UPPER AND MEDIUM-PRICED RANGE: **Royal Court Hotel,** Sloane Square, S.W.1 (tel. 730-9191). In the heart of Chelsea, this fashionable hotel sits directly on Sloane Square, with an entrance marked by a trio of curved canopies festooned with hanging baskets and plants. The inside has attractively detailed walls and ceilings, crystal chandeliers, and comfortably elegant furniture. On the premises are a garden-style restau-

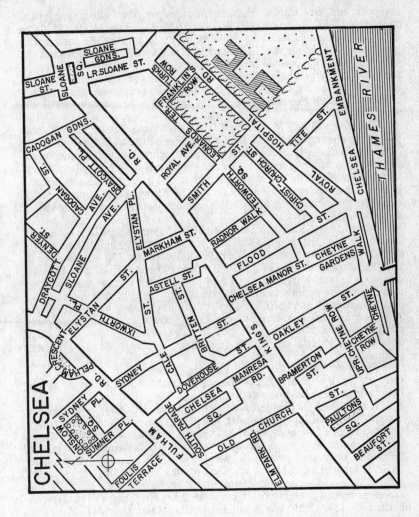

rant, the Old Poodle Dog, a darkly paneled tavern with accents of exposed brick, and reception rooms with chandeliers that originally hung in the Vatican. The well-furnished bedrooms are tastefully outfitted with contemporary colors such as lilac, biscuit, and fern green, and filled with French and Italian headboards. Singles cost from £55 ($82.50) nightly, with doubles going for £70 ($105). Breakfast is extra. The hotel has stood on this site for a century, but the present Royal Court was completely rebuilt into a four-star hotel.

   11 Cadogan Gardens, Sloane Square, S.W.3 (tel. 730-3426), is a Victorian house—or four—converted into comfortable single rooms, doubles, and suites. Quietly situated opposite private gardens, the hotel is traditionally furnished with antiques. Prices, on a "no extras" basis, comprise bed, full English breakfast, newspaper, shoe cleaning, service charge, and VAT. Rates are £60 ($90) to £70 ($105) in a single, £80 ($120) to £100 ($150) in a double. There is no license for liquor, but the porters will gladly send out for a bottle. Laundry and dry cleaning can be taken care of, with same-day service or 24-hour return. A chauffeur-driven Rolls-Royce is available to take you to the airport, theater, or on sightseeing and business trips. The porter can arrange for theater tickets and excursions for you. The managers—Mark Fresson, Alan Eyers, and Clare Armstrong—will look after you.

The **Fenja Hotel,** 69 Cadogan Gardens, Sloane Square, S.W.3 (tel. 589-1183), is an unusually interesting town house that has maintained much of its individualistic architecture. Some modern amenities have been slipped in, including a tiny elevator between a pair of marble pillars in the entry. A true English way of living is maintained here, and the atmosphere is quiet (no children), the clientele discriminating. Many embassy staff members stay here, along with owners of country manors who like to spend a season in London.

Mr. and Mrs. Kaulbeck charge £23 ($34.50) in a single in low season, November to April, and £35 ($52.50) in the same accommodation in high season; May to September/October. For a double, the low season price is £32 ($48), rising to £58 ($87) in high season. The rates include a London breakfast in bed. This consists of fruit juice; boiled eggs or ham, cheese, and tomato or cereal; toast with butter, jam, honey, and marmalade; and tea, coffee, or chocolate. (Note that the London breakfast differs slightly from what is referred to as a full English breakfast in some parts of the country, and which usually includes porridge, eggs of various kinds, fish, kidneys, and bacon, in addition to toast and other accompaniments.)

The rooms at the Fenja are cheerily furnished and each contains a radio or TV (if requested), a phone, and central heating. There are ample bathrooms and toilets on each floor.

Willett Hotel, 32 Sloane Gardens, S.W.1 (tel. 730-0634), opening onto the gardens, is a 19th-century town house with many architectural curiosities, including a Dutch-style roof and varying styles of bay windows. It's an intimate hotel with many luxurious and stylish features. Each of the pleasantly decorated bedrooms has a radio, TV, dressing table, and facilities for making coffee or tea. Best of all is the full English breakfast served in a club-style room with black leather chairs. Most of the accommodations contain private baths. Bathless twins cost £28 ($42); with bath, £36 ($54)—including a full English breakfast and VAT. An extra single bed in a family room costs an additional £10 ($15). Tube: Sloane Square.

8. Belgravia and Knightsbridge

Belgravia, south of Hyde Park, is the so-called aristocratic quarter of London, challenging Mayfair for grandness. It reigned in glory along with Queen Victoria, but today's aristocrats are likely to be the top echelon in foreign embassies, along with a rising new money class of actors and models.

Belgravia is near Buckingham Palace Gardens and Brompton Road. Its center is Belgrave Square, one of the more attractive plazas in London. A few town houses once occupied by eminent Edwardians have been discreetly turned into moderately priced hotels (others were built specifical-

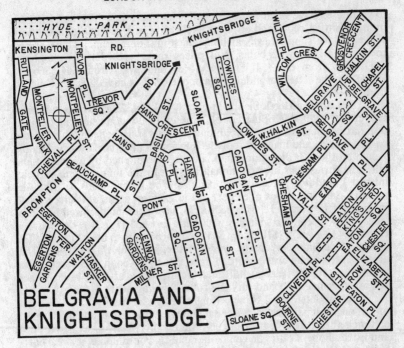

BELGRAVIA AND KNIGHTSBRIDGE

ly for that purpose). For those who prefer a residential address, Belgravia is choice real estate.

Adjoining Belgravia is Knightsbridge, another top residential and shopping district of London. Just south of Hyde Park, Knightsbridge is close in character to Belgravia, although much of this section to the west of Sloane Street is older—dating back in architecture and layout to the 18th century. Several of the major department stores, such as Harrods, are here (take the Piccadilly subway line to Knightsbridge). Since Knightsbridge is not principally a hotel district, my recommendations are limited.

THE UPPER AND MEDIUM-PRICED RANGE: The **Belgravia-Sheraton,** 20 Chesham Pl., S.W.1 (tel. 235-6040), reopened in the spring of 1984 after a major refurbishing program that converted it into one of the city's most intimate luxury hotels. It is in fashionable Belgravia, close to the embassies, Harrods, and Buckingham Palace (how elegant can your address be?). The rooms are luxuriously contemporary, and you get a phone in your tiled bath, 24-hour room service, and a helpful concierge. The staff offers a total of 90 bedrooms, including seven suites, each fully air-conditioned. For your amusement, there is color TV, plus a radio, along with free in-house movies. Personal services include a laundry and a valet. Singles range in price from £80 ($120) to £90 ($135), with twins costing from £90 ($135) to £100 ($150). On the premises is an elegant restaurant with a fine wine list, and the lobby lounge is the ideal venue for morning coffee and afternoon tea. Tube: Sloane Square.

Wilbraham Hotel, Wilbraham Place, off Sloane Street, S.W.1 (tel. 730-8296), is as dyed-in-the-wool British as you can get. On this quiet little street, just a few hundred yards from busy Sloane Square, three Victorian town houses have been joined together as one hotel. The hotel has an intimate sitting room and an attractively old-fashioned bar/lounge where you can have simple meals at both lunch and dinnertime. There are 57 rooms in all, plus 42 baths, and prices range according to plumbing. Singles go from £28 ($42) to £42 ($63) and twins from £44 ($66) to £50 ($75), the latter for a deluxe chamber. VAT is added. Tube: Knightsbridge.

The **Cadogan Hotel,** Sloane Street, S.W.1 (tel. 235-7141), is a colorful Edwardian hotel, one of the few older hotels in London whose modernization has not been destructive. Untouched is its fussy belle époque facade, corner towers, and mansard roof. Its interior architecture, designed by the Adam brothers, is also untouched, although brightened by red velvet and gilt. The furnishings are traditional, as seen in the lounge, with its gold, mirrored, and colored walls and ceilings. The lounge leads to the Lillie Langtry Bar, which was once part of the London home of "Jersey Lily," mistress of Edward VII. The bedrooms have been modernized and provide plenty of comfort. Singles with bath cost £55 ($82.50); doubles and twins, £64 ($96), £72 ($108), or £80 ($120), according to their location. The Oscar Wilde Suite, where he was arrested, goes for £100 ($150). (That arrest, incidentally, was recorded in a poem by John Betjeman.) The hotel's restaurant serves full and light meals at the usual times. All rates include VAT and service. Tube: Sloane Square.

Capital Hotel, Basil Street, Knightsbridge, S.W.3 (tel. 589-5171), is one of the most personalized hotels in the West End. Small and modern, it's a stone's throw from Harrods. The proud owner, David Levin, sat down and listed all the niceties he could offer guests. For example, it's one of the few hotels anywhere that will provide an emergency pack for the stranded traveler—robe, toothbrush, razor. From the modest lobby, an elevator will take guests to each floor, each corridor and staircase being treated as an art gallery, with original oil paintings. In all, 60 rooms are offered, the singles having more space than the doubles. The furniture is handmade, with color-coordinated fabrics. Singles rent for £60 ($90). Doubles go for £70 ($105) to £80 ($120). The Capital Restaurant is among the finest in London, offering such exquisitely prepared main dishes as filet de canard (duckling) aux choux rouges and carré d'agneau persillé. Fresh vegetables are used, and a sachertorte is often the featured dessert. Tube: Knightsbridge.

Basil Hotel, Basil Street, Knightsbridge, S.W.3 (tel. 581-3311), has long been a favorite little hotel of discerning British, who make an annual pilgrimage to London to shop at Harrods and perhaps attend the Chelsea Flower Show. This Edwardian charmer, totally unmarred by pseudo-modernization, is managed by Stephen Korany, who prefers guests who can appreciate his highly individualistic hotel. The open mahogany staircase seems ideal as a setting for the entrance line of a drawing room play: "You're just in time for tea, Braddie." There are several spacious and comfortable lounges, appropriately furnished with 18th- and 19th-century decorative accessories. Off the many rambling corridors are smaller sitting rooms.

The pleasantly furnished bedrooms are priced according to size and location. Single rooms range from £35 ($52.50) to £58 ($87), the latter with private baths. Doubles without bath go for £54 ($81), increasing £to 76 ($114) with bath. The dining room serves a three-course lunch for about £10.50 ($15.75). Dinner is à la carte. Candlelight and piano music recreate the atmosphere of a bygone era. The Upstairs Restaurant is suitable for lighter meals and snacks, and the Downstairs Wine Bar selection of wines and inexpensive food. Tube: Knightsbridge.

Ebury Court, 26 Ebury St., S.W.1 (tel. 730-8147), was created out of a group of small town houses. You notice the country-house flavor right away; it's brightly painted (turquoise and white), with railings to match and flower-filled window boxes. The little reception rooms are informal and decorated with flowery chintz and quite good antiques. Best of all, it has a cordial and informal staff. The hotel is close to the airline terminals. Terms quoted include an English breakfast and VAT. The rate in a single ranges from £27 ($40.50) to £29 ($43.50), from £40 ($60) in a bathless twin-bedded room or a double. Doubles with private bathrooms cost from £50 ($75). Each of the rooms has hot and cold running water, as well as a telephone and radio. An asset is the night porter, handy for late arrivals. In the small restaurant, you can order either a lunch or dinner.

The A1 bus, which goes to Heathrow every 20 minutes, leaves from Grosvenor Gardens, approximately 1½ minutes from the Ebury Court. Porters from the hotel will help visitors with their luggage on a trolley if required. Guests can apply for temporary membership in the hotel club, which allows them access to the bar. Tube: Victoria Station.

Knightsbridge Hotel, 10 Beaufort Gardens, S.W.3 (tel. 589-9271), sandwiched between the restaurants and fashionable boutiques of Beauchamp Place and Harrods, still retains the feeling of a traditional British hotel. On a tree-lined square that is peaceful and tranquil, and free from traffic, it has a subdued Victorian charm. The place is small—only 20 bedrooms—and personally run by the manager, Robert A. Novella. Units have phones, radios, and central heating, and there's a lounge with a color "telly" and a bar on the premises. Most expensive are rooms with private baths, costing £28 ($42) in a single, from £42 ($63) in a twin. The best for the budget are the bathless specials—from £20 ($30) in a single and from £27 ($40.50) in a twin. A family room with shower for three guests rents for about £46 ($69) per night. All tariffs include a continental breakfast, VAT, and service charge. Tube: Knightsbridge.

Claverley House Hotel, 13–14 Beaufort Gardens, Knightsbridge, S.W.3 (tel. 589-8541), offers fair value for the dollar, considering its chic location. Many guests are regulars, including two millionaires who drop in occasionally. The hotel has been extensively renovated and decorated. Fifteen of its 31 rooms have private baths, although none contains a toilet. The cost of a bathless single is £18 ($27), £24 ($36) with bath. Doubles range from £24 ($36) to £32 ($48), depending on the plumbing. All tariffs include VAT and an English breakfast. Tube: Knightsbridge.

28 Basil Street, which is, of course, at that address, S.W.1 (tel. 589-6286), has been converted by David and Margaret Levin, owners of the nearby Capital Hotel in Basil Street, into a 12-room inn with pleasant countrified bedrooms, with modern bathrooms. Downstairs is the Metro, a café/wine bar where breakfasts are served, with dishes of the day offered later. A machine dispenses better than average wine to be sold by the glass, keeping the drink fresh for quite a while. Peter Lowe, manager of 28 Basil Street, will rent you a room, either single or double occupancy, for £55 ($82.50) per night, which includes a continental breakfast. If you'd like an excellent gourmet meal, try the Capital Hotel's well-known restaurant, just down the street. Tube: Knightsbridge.

9. Kensington, South Kensington, and Earl's Court

Although the Royal Borough draws its greatest number of visitors from shoppers (Kensington High Street), it also attracts with a number of fine, medium-priced hotels, for the most part on Kensington Gardens. In Victoria's day, the rows of houses along Kensington Palace Gardens were inhabited by millionaires (although Thackeray also lived there). Today the houses are occupied largely by ambassadors.

South Kensington, south of Kensington Gardens and Hyde Park, is essentially a residential area, not as elegant as that bordering Belgravia and Knightsbridge. However, the section is rich in museums, and it has a number of colleges.

Staying in South Kensington has much to recommend it. Besides its proximity to the Kensington museums, such as the Victoria and Albert, the area encompasses Albert Hall, and is within walking distance of Kensington Gardens and Harrods department store. At the South Kensington station, you can catch trains for Kew Gardens and the Thames River town of Richmond.

For the most part, the hotels in this area recall yesterday more than today, although contemporary furnishings and modern amenities are grudgingly creeping in. It's an ideal spot for the traditionalist.

Earl's Court, below Kensington and bordering the western half of Chelsea, is one of the most popular middle-class hotel and rooming-house districts. A 15-minute subway ride from Earl's Court station will take you into the heart of Piccadilly, via either the District or Picadilly lines. The bus from Grosvenor Gardens to Heathrow Airport stops on Cromwell Road, outside the Penta Hotel.

THE UPPER BRACKET: The **John Howard Hotel,** 4 Queen's Gate, S.W.7 (tel. 581-3011), is just across the road from Royal Kensington Palace and Gardens, on a tree-lined street in the vicinity of Albert Hall. This Regency building has fine, high-ceilinged rooms that have been lavishly restored and decorated. In its category, the John Howard is one of the leading small hotels of London. The manager, H. Michael Krause, is a first-rate hotelier who has done much to turn this into one of those special hotels of character that more and more discriminating people seek out when they travel.

There are 50 spotlessly clean rooms and 12 apartments, all with room lighting bright enough to read by, a feature often lacking in hotel bedrooms. The units are individually designed and offer an atmosphere of quiet luxury, with personal service you don't find in larger hostelries. Facilities include free in-house movies, individual air conditioning, soundproof windows and double doors, color TV, four-channel radio, direct-dial telephone, mini-bar, and trouser press. All rooms have private bath and/or shower.

For a longer stay, you may prefer an apartment with video and hi-fi, where you can either use the fully equipped kitchen or the hotel's room service and restaurant facilities.

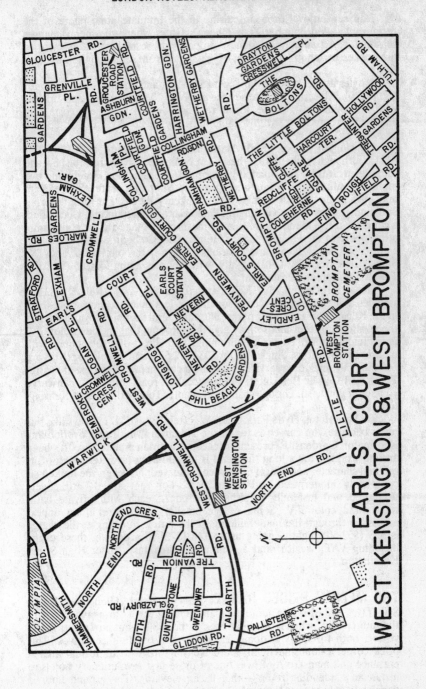

You can enjoy European cuisine in the intimate atmosphere of the restaurant called Number Four Queen's Gate, where the menu changes seasonally. An authentic Japanese teppan yaki restaurant offers meat or fish cooked on a hotplate in front of you. Snacks are served in the Captain's Bar.

Singles at the John Howard cost £50 ($75), and doubles or twins go for £80 ($120). All tariffs include service and VAT. The luxurious apartments, with reproduction antique furniture and kitchen facilities, cost from £350 ($525) per week, with a minimum stay of 22 days. Bus 9, 33, 49, or 52.

Kensington Palace Thistle Hotel, De Vere Gardens, W.8 (tel. 937-8121), although built in 1951 has been comprehensively refurbished and remodeled. It is ideally situated just opposite Kensington Gardens and two minutes' walk from Kensington High Street shopping center. The elegant and spacious foyer is decorated with a Regency theme. For formal wining and dining, there is the Kensington Piano Bar and Restaurant, which offers a comprehensive menu. More relaxed meals can be taken in the continental atmosphere of the Pavilion Coffee House. The 320 bedrooms have stylish, color-coordinated decor, and each has its own bathroom, radio, and TV. Singles rent from £52 ($78) nightly, with doubles going for £65 ($97.50). Tube: High Street Kensington.

Royal Kensington, 380 Kensington High St., W.14 (tel. 603-3333), supplies a near-luxurious accommodation at less-than-luxurious prices. It's in the Kensington area, near parks, museums, and shopping. You can enjoy the comforts of the handsomely styled bedrooms that include color TV, individually controlled air conditioning, and direct-dial telephones with bathroom extensions. Singles go for £35 ($52.50), and doubles or twins are £45 ($67.50), including service. VAT and a continental breakfast are extra. The Royal Carver Restaurant offers succulent roast joints you can carve yourself if you wish. Garage space is available. Tube: High Street Kensington.

De Vere Hotel, Hyde Park Gate, W.8 (tel. 584-0051). I always like this place because you can have tea in the Adam drawing room overlooking Kensington Gardens. Representing classic Victorian architecture, it's been around London for a long time and is an enduring favorite. Much of its original character and charm have been preserved; however, the building is completely modernized and up to date. For rent are 84 attractively decorated and tastefully furnished bedrooms, each with private bath, radio, and color TV. Some of the smaller rooms are in an annex, accessible through the main building of the hotel. In a single, the charge is £35 ($52.50) nightly, going up to £48 ($72) in a double, these tariffs including VAT, service, and a continental breakfast. Tube: High Street Kensington.

THE MEDIUM-PRICED RANGE: Bailey's Hotel, Gloucester Road, S.W.7 (tel. 373-8131), to quote the management, was a "firm favourite with the squirearchy" when it was built back in the 1880s—but now caters to the visitor, both foreign and domestic, along with budding executives. This brick corner establishment in South Kensington, with its formal arched entrance and mansard roof, was one of those first revolutionary hotels to install an "ascending room"—that is, an elevator. The ground floor is paneled in oak, mixing antiques with reproductions. All 154 bedrooms have a private bathroom/shower, color TV, radio, and direct-dial telephones. The hotel has finished an extensive upgrading program, and many amenities have been added, such as automatic elevators, a good coffeeshop, a hotel bar, and a restaurant specializing in Indian food. There's also a fully computerized reservation and billing system. Single rooms are £44 ($66), and twin rooms are £52 ($78) per night. All prices include VAT, a continental breakfast, and service. Tube: Gloucester Road.

Number Sixteen, 16 Sumner Pl., S.W.7 (tel. 589-5232), is considered a luxury "pension" in central London. Just off Old Brompton Road, it's a three-minute walk to the South Kensington Underground station. Michael Watson is the creator of this offbeat hotel, built in 1860, which is much patronized by people in the performing arts. The hotel, which now comprises 15, 16, and 17 Sumner Pl., is classically Victorian, with high-ceilinged period rooms converted to self-contained bed-sitting accommodations, with private shower/bathrooms (some of them have tubs as well). Rooms are decorated with antiques and Victorian pieces, along with pictures, Hans Holbein prints, and lithographs. Mr. Watson prefers guests who will stay more than a night or two. Singles range from £32 ($48) to £40 ($60), doubles and twins from £55 ($82.50) to £72 ($108). These rates include VAT and a continental breakfast. Tube: High Street Kensington.

Milestone Hotel, Kensington Court, W.8 (tel. 937-0991), is a great old building facing Kensington Gardens. There's an ornate roof with decorative gables and chimneys, plus large bay windows. The decor is modified neoclassic, the best example being the dining room with bright pastel colors. The bedrooms, each with radio and telephone, are spacious. A bathless single rents for £20 ($30); a single with bath is £22 ($33). Bathless doubles or twins range from £30 ($45). A twin with bath costs £40 ($60). Rates include a continental breakfast, VAT, and service. Tube: High Street Kensington.

The **Alexander,** 9 Sumner Pl., S.W.7 (tel. 581-1591), is between Brompton and Fulham Roads, on the borderline of Kensington and Chelsea. This small, attractive hotel looks like a private residence and has a pleasantly relaxed, almost private atmosphere. One of its most attractive features is a secluded little garden, well kept and entirely reserved for hotel guests. Behind a white-pillared 19th-century facade, the hotel is surprisingly modern. The dining room decor is natural pine, and the small television lounge looks like a living room and boasts a color TV. However, the bedrooms also have their own television sets. The licensed hotel has an attractively designed private bar in the lounge.

The units are fairly spacious, with nicely matched ivory and green color schemes, soft russet carpeting, and built-in cupboards and dressing tables. Each centrally heated unit has a private bath, telephone, radio, and dual-shaver razor points. The reception desk downstairs will not only organize theater tickets for you but also looks after car rentals and tour reservations.

The hotel is only 200 yards from the South Kensington Underground station, which is on a direct link to Heathrow Airport. It also has a 24-hour dry-cleaning and laundry service. In a single, tariffs are £36 ($54) nightly, rising to anywhere from £44 ($66) to £52 ($78) in a double or twin. There are some triple-bedded rooms at £58 ($87) and a studio suitable for four at

£88 ($132). Rates include service, VAT, and an English breakfast. Tube: South Kensington.

The **Regency Hotel,** 100–105 Queen's Gate, S.W.7 (tel. 370-4595), is a skillful conversion of six lively old houses to provide 200 simply furnished, comfortable rooms with bathroom or shower, color TV, radio, and telephone. There are elevators to all floors and 24-hour porterage. The high-ceilinged, warm red-walled dining room serves a set lunch or dinner, three courses for around £10 ($15). They also do a limited à la carte menu where a meal will cost around £15 ($22.50) per person. The bar is large and cheerfully decorated with green walls, dark wood, and button chairs, and serves coffee, tea, and sandwiches as well as drinks. The tariffs are a very good value at £38 ($57) single, £50 ($75) twin or double, £60 ($90) triple, including a continental breakfast, service, and VAT. South Kensington museums are close by. In addition, the Underground stations at South Kensington and Gloucester Road, with direct link to Heathrow Airport, are just a five-minute walk away.

Albany Hotel, Barkston Gardens, S.W.5 (tel. 370-6116), has combined five Victorian town houses on tree-shaded Barkston Gardens—secluded, yet only one minute from Earl's Court Road and conveniently near Underground and bus service to Heathrow Airport. Rebuilding and tasteful furnishing have transformed these former private residences into attractive public places in which to stay. Most of the 100 rooms contain private bath and toilet, and all have color TV, radio, and telephone. A single without bath rents for £16 ($24); a single with bath, £22 ($33); a bathless twin or double, £26 ($39); a double or twin with bath, £35 ($52.50). These tariffs include a continental breakfast, service, and VAT. Highly popular is an old-style pub, with a beamed ceiling, rough brick walls, and Windsor chairs. The dining room is stylish and airy. Tube: Earl's Court.

Burns Hotel, Barkston Gardens, S.W.5 (tel. 373-3151), stands near its sister, the already-recommended Albany. Small and intimate, it was once the home of Ellen Terry (1848–1928), who was especially acclaimed for her Shakespearean roles and was also known for her correspondence with G. B. Shaw. Most of the rooms overlook the trees of Barkston Gardens. Singles rent for £15 ($22.50) to £20 ($30) nightly, doubles or twins for £28 ($42) to £32 ($48), depending on the plumbing. The higher tariffs are for private baths. Tariffs include VAT, service, and a full English breakfast. Tube: Earl's Court.

The **Ambassadors Hotel,** 16 Collingham Rd., S.W.5 (tel. 373-1075), is a neat, bandbox-modern hotel, in Earl's Court opposite the Airbus stop. It's only a short block away from the heavy Cromwell Road traffic, where finding a quiet room is almost impossible. Its bedrooms are as compact and as utilitarian as some motels in America—built-in headboards, radios, direct-dial phones, dressing tables. Every room has a private bath. The rates in a single are £32 ($48), £38 ($57) in a double or twin, and £45 ($67.50) in a triple. All tariffs include a continental breakfast, service, and VAT. One of the reasons for staying here is the ease with which you can check in anytime day or night. On the premises is a coffeeshop/bar serving snacks, full meals, and refreshments at any time. Tube: Gloucester Road or Earl's Court.

Onslow Court Hotel, 109–113 Queen's Gate, S.W.7 (tel. 589-6300), is a long-established family hotel. The plain but comfortable rooms have color

TV, phone, and central heating, and there is an elevator to all floors. Units have private bathrooms as well. A single goes from £29 ($43.50) to £34 ($51), a double from £42 ($63) to £54 ($81). If you're traveling with children, an extra bed can be brought in at £10 ($15) per night. All rates include a continental breakfast, VAT, and service. The hotel is licensed, and a coffeeshop offers both snacks and full meals. Tube: South Kensington.

Eden Plaza, 68–69 Queensgate, S.W.7 (tel. 370-6111), completed in 1972, is an attractive, white-painted corner building, offering bedrooms furnished in modern style and tastefully decorated. An elevator carries guests to all floors, where bedrooms with double glazing await them. Other amenities include color TV sets, along with private baths and showers. The cost in a single is £30 ($45), rising to £43 ($64.50) to £46 ($69) in a twin or double. These tariffs include a full English breakfast and VAT. Both business people and vacationers meet in the cocktail lounge and bar, and later go to the restaurant, offering à la carte continental and English cuisine. Two-course meals cost from £7 ($10.50). On the ground level are such additional facilities as a sauna, massage room, and solarium. The location is near Hyde Park, close to the London Air Terminal, and convenient for shoppers heading for such emporiums as Harrods and Selfridges. Tube: Gloucester Road.

THE BUDGET RANGE: **Strathmore House,** 12 Strathmore Gardens, W.8 (tel. 229-3063). You'd never guess this is a hotel. There's no sign, only a street number, and its location near Embassy Row and Kensington Palace makes it appear like a private town house. It's a corner house, with a low wall and shrubbery. Mr. and Mrs. Haskell, the proprietors, charge from £11 ($16.50) to £14 ($21) per person per night inclusive, according to length of stay. Terms include a complete English breakfast, but don't expect private baths. The bed-sitting rooms, opening off the central hallway, are large and comfortable. There are some nice old pieces mixed in with the nondescript furniture, and the total effect is homey and immaculate. You get hot and cold running water in the rooms, as well as the free use of the corridor baths. Breakfast is brought to your room, and you have a gas ring and kettle so you can make your own tea or coffee. Tube: Notting Hill Gate.

Princes Lodge Hotel, Prince of Wales Terrace, W.8 (tel. 937-6306), is a family hotel in the literal meaning of the word. A number of rooms have been specially designed to accommodate families; there are also family suites, rooms for parents and children separated by a private bath. There are day and night "baby-watching" and "child-minding" services; the hotel has cribs and cots. Large families are never met with a sigh here, but are always given a welcoming smile. Singles range in price from £12 ($18) to £20 ($30), and doubles go from £22 ($33) to £26 ($39). A family room with bath costs £40 ($60). The difference in price depends on location, plumbing, and season, and all tariffs include a full English breakfast, service, and VAT. The Princes Lodge is opposite Kensington Palace Gardens. Tube: High Street Kensington.

Vicarage Private Hotel, 10 Vicarage Gate, W.8 (tel. 229-4030), is the domain of Ellen and Martin Diviney, who charge £9.50 ($14.25) per person double occupancy, and £11 ($16.50) in a single. Each guest in a triple room

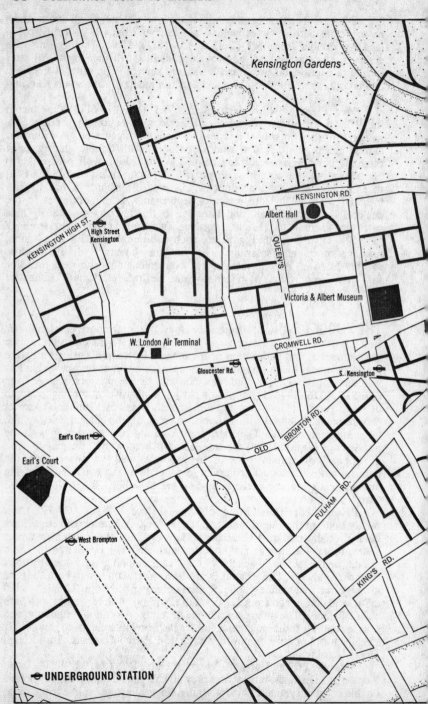

Kensington Gardens

KENSINGTON RD.

Albert Hall

KENSINGTON HIGH ST.

High Street Kensington

QUEEN'S

Victoria & Albert Museum

W. London Air Terminal

CROMWELL RD.

Gloucester Rd.

S. Kensington

BROMTON RD.

Earl's Court

OLD

Earl's Court

FULHAM RD.

West Brompton

KING'S RD.

⊖ UNDERGROUND STATION

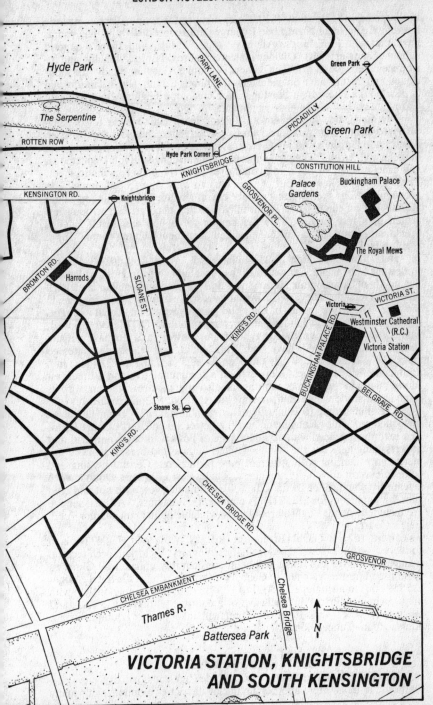

Hyde Park

The Serpentine

ROTTEN ROW

PARK LANE

Green Park

PICCADILLY

Green Park

Hyde Park Corner

KNIGHTSBRIDGE

CONSTITUTION HILL

GROSVENOR PL.

Palace Gardens

Buckingham Palace

KENSINGTON RD.

Knightsbridge

The Royal Mews

BROMPTON RD.

Harrods

SLOANE ST.

VICTORIA ST.

Victoria

Westminster Cathedral (R.C.)

BUCKINGHAM PALACE RD.

KING'S RD.

Victoria Station

BELGRAVE RD.

Sloane Sq.

KING'S RD.

CHELSEA BRIDGE RD.

GROSVENOR

CHELSEA EMBANKMENT

Thames R.

Chelsea Bridge

N

Battersea Park

VICTORIA STATION, KNIGHTSBRIDGE
AND SOUTH KENSINGTON

is charged £8 ($12), £6.80 ($10.20) in a room for four. All rates include breakfast, and as of November 1 charges are reduced slightly. The rooms have pleasant furnishings. All have water basins, and there's a good supply of showers. Mrs. Diviney makes each breakfast individually, and introduces her guests to each other. Vicarage Gate is handy for boutiques and restaurants on Kensington Church Street, and a laundromat is nearby. The nearest tube stops are Kensington High and Notting Hill Gate.

Mr. and Mrs. A. Demetriou, 9 Strathmore Gardens, W.8 (tel. 229-6709), operate this small, privately owned guest house very close to Kensington Gardens and Hyde Park. Reader Joseph A. Wilson, a sergeant in the army, wrote, "They are without a doubt the most helpful, courteous, and gracious pair of hosts you could ever have the good fortune to meet. These kind people went out of their way to make me feel at home. The accommodations were immaculately clean. To use a cliché, 'You could literally eat off the floor.'" Beautifully kept and decorated, the rooms are rented at a rate of £10 ($15) per person for a bed and a full English breakfast served in an often-sun-filled basement dining room. Tube: Notting Hill Gate.

Hotel One Two Eight, 128 Holland Rd., W.14 (tel. 602-3395), is a somewhat offbeat place at which to live, located as it is in Holland Park to the north of Kensington High Street and to the south of Holland Park Avenue. Here the converted town houses still retain spacious gardens in the rear. The white facade of the hotel greets you with its small wrought-iron balconies and abundant flowers in summer. Of the 36 colorful, well-equipped bedrooms, 13 have private showers and 16 have private showers and toilets. All have bed lights, radio, and telephone. Rates go from £19 ($28.50) to £24 ($36) in a single, £25 ($37.50) to £32 ($48) in a double. Besides two guest lounges with a communal TV, and a breakfast room, guests in the warmer months can also enjoy the rear garden, with its large lawn, stone walls, and towering trees. Tube: Shepherd's Bush.

Camellia Hotel, 16 Longridge Rd., S.W.5 (tel. 373-3848), lies in an unspoiled section of Kensington, on the better side of Earl's Court Road. The exterior is graced with an abundance of flowers in boxes and urns and baskets hanging from the windows. The lounge and breakfast room are made more inviting with Austrian pine furnishings. Central heating and color television add to the amenities. Singles cost £10 ($15). Doubles with private bath and toilet go for £20 ($30), although a few with hot and cold running water rent for £18 ($27). A continental breakfast, VAT, and service are included. A full English breakfast is available at an extra charge. Tube: Earl's Court.

Hotel 167, 167 Old Brompton Rd., S.W.5 (tel. 373-0672), is a converted corner town house, maintaining its Victorian architectural features, although the decor has been considerably updated by Christina Rasmus, a Finnish designer. In clean, comfortable rooms, the hotel charges £15 ($22.50) in a single, £22 ($33) to £25 ($37.50) in a double or twin with private shower. Prices are inclusive of a continental breakfast, VAT, and service. A short walk from the hotel will take you to boutique-strewn King's Road. Tube: Gloucester Road.

10. Bayswater

North of Bayswater Road, west of Hyde Park and north of Kensington Gardens, is Bayswater, another unofficial district of London, with many

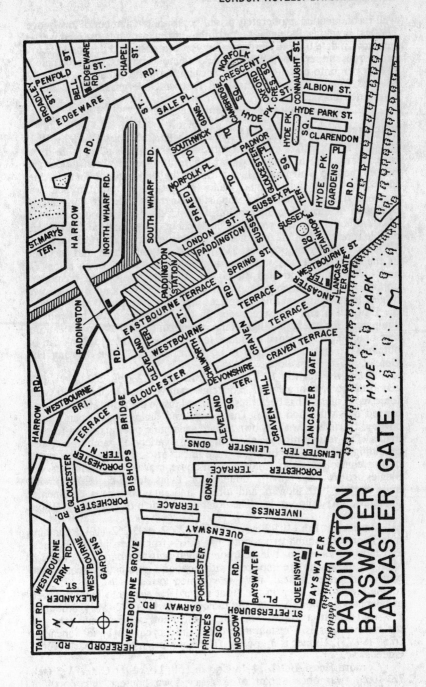

well-recommended, moderately priced hotels, plus a number of low-budget bed-and-breakfast lodgings. Many of these former town houses, converted into hotels, date back to the days when Bayswater spelled the good life to a prosperous, upper middle class. Some of the town houses, often lined up in rows, open onto pleasant squares. Serving Bayswater Road are buses 12, 88, and 289. Both the Central and District Underground lines run to Bayswater tube station.

THE MEDIUM-PRICED RANGE: Portobello, 22 Stanley Gardens, W.11 (tel. 727-2777), makes me green with envy, as it fulfills a secret desire to take over a couple of antiquated, threadbare, 19th-century town houses and restore them to their former luster. Under the leadership of Tim Herring, his wife, Cathy, and designer Julie Hodgess, a 30-room miracle was created. It has all that cool sophistication that goes with an eclectic collection of furnishings harmoniously blended. A single room costs £38 ($57), although you can request a single cabin (very small) at £42 ($63), a double room at £55 ($82.50), or a twin-bedded room at £68 ($102), all plus VAT. A continental breakfast is provided in your room and included in the cost. Each bedroom has a private bath, as well as color TV and individually controlled air conditioning. Natural wood pieces are upholstered in bright colors, an oval gilt mirror in the lounge hangs over a gleaming white marble fireplace, and the reception area echoes the Edwardian era. Shuttered doors in the bedrooms hide do-it-yourself equipment for preparing light fare and mixing drinks. At a beautiful restaurant, again designed by Julie Hodgess, good food and drink can be obtained at any hour. There is no room service. Tube: Notting Hill Gate.

Henry the Eighth, 19 Leinster Gardens, W.2 (tel. 262-0117), is a glamorous remake of an older, more conservative hotel. Its fine facade with Ionic-style columns has been preserved, and inside the restoration has been carried out with good taste. The lounge and dining room open onto a covered courtyard, with its own heated swimming pool and semi-tropical plants. The restaurant specializes in a large variety of hamburgers, also providing steaks. The bedrooms are most attractive; each has push-button control of radio, color TV, in-house movies, and maid service. Singles go for £32 ($48), doubles or twins for £45 ($67.50). All units contain bath/showers and toilets, and rates include a continental breakfast, VAT, and service. The hotel is just north of Hyde Park. Tube: Queensway.

Hospitality Inn, 104 Bayswater Rd., W.2 (tel. 262-4461), contains nine floors of ultramodern rooms. It's across from Kensington Gardens, and most of its studio-style bedrooms open onto the park. The hotel is ideal for those who are impatient with London's antiquated accommodations, and prefer a neat, new, streamlined look. All of the 175 bedrooms (air conditioning in the front rooms) have private baths, as well as telephones, color TV sets, and radios. A single is £42 ($63); a double, £54 ($81); and a triple, £62 ($93)—including service and tax. On the second floor is a restaurant where you can have a buffet lunch for £6.50 ($9.75). Dinner is à la carte. The hotel has a free car park. Tube: Queensway.

Cordova House Hotel, 14–16 Craven Hill, Lancaster Gate, W.2 (tel. 723-1065), was once a pair of Regency town houses lying north of Kensington Gardens. It's been converted into an informal establishment that is one of the best run hotels in the area. All the redecorated rooms contain private baths and toilets, and single rates are £26 ($39); doubles, £32 ($48)—including VAT and a continental breakfast. There is no service charge. The restaurant is new, and the hotel offers an intimate bar, a sauna, and a swimming pool. Tube: Paddington.

The **Royal Bayswater Hotel,** 122 Bayswater Rd., W.2 (tel. 229-8887), is a charming economy hotel overlooking Hyde Park. The friendly atmosphere, comfortable rooms, and reasonable prices attract the visitor who is looking for high standards at moderate prices. The 36 rooms are modern, tastefully furnished, with wall-to-wall carpets, private bath/showers, central heating, and radios. Wardrobe space is adequate, and there's a built-in "vanitory unit" with specially lit mirror. Tea- or coffee-making facilities are available in all rooms. The hotel charges no service tax as there is none, except for room cleaning. Singles with bath rent for £20 ($30), a double with bath going for £32 ($48). VAT is included. Tube: Queensway.

THE BUDGET RANGE: Garden Court Hotel, 30–31 Kensington Gardens Square, W.2 (tel. 229-2553), is run by Mr. and Mrs. Stefan Lis, who fled Poland during the war. The family found this old town house on a private garden square and began the long task of making it the home-like hotel it is today. For the occupants of a bathless double room, the B&B charge is £23 ($34.50), plus VAT. Most of the rooms are singles, renting for £15 ($22.50) to £18 ($27), the latter with private showers, but families may be interested in one of the four triple rooms ranging in price from £30 ($45) to £35 ($52.50), the latter with private bath. The ten double rooms with private bath cost from £26 ($39) nightly. Each room has a water basin, along with telephone, radio, and intercom. You'll enjoy meeting and talking with guests from many lands who frequent the Garden Court; there's a bar-television lounge on the ground floor, where you can lower the stock of beer on hand and hear candid opinions about world affairs. Tube: Queensway.

READERS' HOTEL SELECTION: "**Redland House Hotel,** 52 Kendal St., Hyde Park, W.2 (tel. 723-7118), is a double town house just off Edgware Road. The proprietors are Mr. and Mrs. H. Newlands, who charge £14 ($21) for singles, £12 ($18) per person for doubles or twins, plus VAT. This is just at the edge of the W.1 area. A two-minute walk from buses serving the Strand, this is a first-rate choice for budgeting time as well as money. Nearby are teashops and a variety of restaurants, plus laundromats. Further, one can walk to Oxford and Regent Streets and the parks. Redland House is attractive, clean, centrally heated, and most efficiently operated. No private baths are available, but there are ample facilities near all rooms. Reservations are desirable; in our experience inquiries were promptly answered. It is but a short walk to Selfridges and the Marble Arch tube stop, but the Newlandses point out that using buses saved money. They are Welsh, intelligent, and interesting people. The establishment is well ordered and quiet for sleeping" (Mr. and Mrs. Arthur Thurner, Chicago, Ill.).

11. Paddington and Little Venice

Another popular hotel area, particularly for budget travelers, is the Paddington section, around Paddington Station, just to the northwest of Kensington Gardens and Hyde Park. Here you'll be within walking distance of the great Marble Arch, the entrance to Hyde Park. The main

Paddington avenue, Sussex Gardens, has been known for years to pence-shy travelers who seek out its bed-and-breakfast houses. But as more and more town houses are being razed on Sussex Gardens to make way for expensive flats, Norfolk Square is gaining importance as the area in which to shop for budget hotels. Allowed to deteriorate after World War II, the square was formerly one of the most prestigious squares of London, especially in the reign of Victoria when the eminent built large, beautiful town houses ideal for big families, maids, and nannies.

On the periphery of Paddington is an unofficial district dubbed Little Venice, a seldom-visited hideaway off Edgware Road, north of Paddington Station. Little Venice gets its name because two branches of the Grand Union canal meet at Blomfield Road and Warwick Avenue. Bus 6 from the West End runs to Warwick Avenue, or else you can take the Bakerloo line to the Warwick Avenue station. From this district, you can book a ride on Jason's boat through Regent's Park, or board a boat in summer to the London Zoo.

THE MEDIUM-PRICED RANGE: Colonnade Hotel, 2 Warrington Crescent, W.9 (tel. 286-1052), is an imposing town house in a pleasant residential area, just a block from the Warwick Avenue tube station. Owned and managed for some 35 years by the Richards family, the hotel is run in a personal and friendly manner. The bedrooms are spacious (some with balconies), and are equipped with either private bath/shower or hot and cold water. The rates, including a full English breakfast, are: £25 ($37.50) in a single without bathroom, £35 ($52.50) in a bathless double. For a single with private bath, the charge is £32 ($48) to £36 ($54); for a double with private bath, £42 ($63) to £54 ($81). VAT is included. Mr. Richards emphasizes: "Every bedroom, bathroom, and corridor is centrally heated 24 hours a day of every day from the first chill wind of autumn until the last breath of retreating winter, even in summer if necessary." He's installed a water-softening plant as well. All rooms have TV, video, radio, phone, hair dryer, and electrically heated trouser press. Seven have four-poster beds. The hotel now has a restaurant and a garden bar.

READER'S HOTEL SELECTION: "We stayed at the **Dylan Hotel,** 14 Devonshire Terrace, Lancaster Gate, W.2 (tel. 723-3280). The rates with breakfast are from £22 ($33) to £30 ($45) in a double, the latter with private shower or bath, plus a toilet. Singles rent from £18 ($27). VAT is included. The rooms are large, cheery, and very clean, and the breakfast more than adequate. The hotel has been redecorated and recarpeted from top to bottom. Accommodations have radio intercoms, shaver points, and central heating. Guests gather in the lounge to watch color TV. The hotel is convenient to the Paddington Underground and Hyde Park" (Ann Calhoun, Los Angeles, Calif.).

12. St. Marylebone

Below Regent's Park, northwest of Piccadilly Circus, is the district of St. Marylebone (pronounced Mar-li-bone), a residential section that faces Mayfair to the south and extends north of Marble Arch. A number of simple but gracious town houses in this section are being converted into private hotels. Many visitors arriving in London in peak season without a

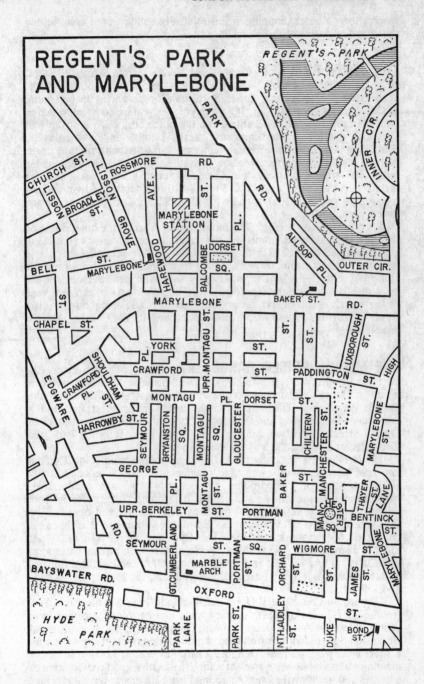

reservation go hotel shopping in this relatively undiscovered area, letting the crowds fight it out in Bloomsbury.

THE UPPER BRACKET: Cumberland Hotel, Marble Arch, W.1 (tel. 262-1234), will please those who want to be in the center—at Marble Arch, at the corner of Hyde Park, with its Speakers' Corner, and at the beginning of Oxford Street and Mayfair. It's a modern, well-equipped hotel, which in North America would be described as a top-notch business persons' place. You may get lost in the corridors, as the Cumberland is a colossus, containing 900 bedrooms. Those rooms are furnished with built-in units, bedside lights, telephones, radios, private baths with showers, color televisions, trouser pressers, mini-bars, and small sitting areas. The rates include service charge and VAT. From April to October, a twin-bedded room rents for £70 ($105), a single for £55 ($82.50). Off-season prices are lower.

A plus is the ownership: Trusthouse Forte. Also, in the hotel is one of the best bargain restaurants in the capital, the all-you-can-eat Carvery, costing from £12 ($18). And there's a quick-meal coffeeshop. The hotel's other restaurant, Wyvern, offers traditional recipes from the 18th and 19th centuries. Another offering is sole with prawn sauce, based on a dish devised by the head cook to Queen Victoria in the first year of her marriage to Albert. Yet another specialty is salamagundy, a salad from *The British Housewife,* a book published in 1749. Tube: Marble Arch.

THE MEDIUM-PRICED RANGE: Hart House, 51 Gloucester Pl., Portman Square, W.1 (tel. 935-2288), is a well-preserved building, part of a group of Georgian mansions occupied by the French nobility during the French Revolution. The hotel is in the heart of the West End and is convenient for shopping and theaters. It is within easy walking distance of Oxford Street, Selfridges, Marble Arch, Hyde Park, Regent's Park, the Zoo, Madame Tussaud's, and the Planetarium.

Hart House is centrally heated, and all rooms have color TV, hot and cold water, phone, radio, and razor points. This is a small family B&B consisting of 15 bedrooms, all spotlessly clean and comfortable. More than half the units have private bathrooms. Except for a short period, 1980 to 1982, the hotel has long been owned and operated by the Welsh family of Graham E. Bowden, whose son has been in charge of operations since 1983. The Bowdens charge £18 ($27) per night in a single, £29 ($43.50) in a double or twin with private bathroom, and £38 ($57) to £42 ($63) in a family room. All prices include a full English breakfast, but VAT is extra. Buses 1, 2, 2B, 13, 26, 30, 59, 74, 113, and 159.

Bryanston Court Hotel, Great Cumberland Place, Marble Arch, W.1 (tel. 262-3141), is three 19th-century town houses joined together by a central reception lounge, decorated with Delft Blue canvas. Just off restful Bryanston Square, with its well-tended gardens and trees, the hotel is only a short walk from Marble Arch and a rarity in central London in that it maintains a moderate price level. It is furnished with a good combination of antiques and traditional pieces. All rooms have bath or shower. Singles rent for £36 ($54), doubles or twins for £49 ($73.50), and triples for £60 ($90), these tariffs including a continental breakfast, service, and VAT. It's a good choice year round, as it's centrally heated, and each room has a radio and telephone. Tube: Marble Arch.

THE BUDGET RANGE: Merryfield House, 42 York St., off Baker Street, W.1 (tel. 935-8326), is a refreshingly pleasant remake of a 19th-century pub, the Lord Keith. Ale drinkers of old would look askance at the bright facade and the flower boxes filled with red geraniums. Owned by Mr. and Mrs. G. K. Tyler-Smith, the hotel is a haven for those who cling to the old English ways. Resisting continental breakfasts, the manager, Bridget, serves a "jolly good breakfast" right in your room. Radio and TV can be had on request. According to the season and location, doubles (no twins or singles) range in price from £25 ($37.50), and every room has its own private toilet and shower. The house is small enough so that a tiny staff can keep everything shiny, polished, scrubbed, and laundered. The location is also convenient for budget-conscious shoppers, as it lies near Selfridges and Marks and Spencers. York Street is just two blocks south of Marylebone Road. Tube: Baker Street.

13. Mayfair

Mayfair, bounded by Piccadilly, Hyde Park, and Oxford and Regent Streets, is an elegant section of London. Luxury hotels exist side by side with Georgian town houses and swank shops. Here are the parks, names, and streets that have snob appeal the world over, including Grosvenor Square (pronounced Grov-nor) and Berkeley Square (pronounced Barkley). If you can't afford Claridge's try:

THE UPPER BRACKET: May Fair Intercontinental Hotel, Berkeley Street, W.1 (tel. 629-7777), has been completely redecorated and refurnished. The circular cantilevered lobby staircase sets the pace. If you're not of international celebrity material, and can't afford one of the posh suites, then you may settle for one of the decorator bedrooms. Those I've inspected have been colorfully and tastefully conceived. All the bedrooms contain private baths, and rent for £60 ($90) in a single, £82 ($123) in a double, service included. All rooms have color TV. A new bedroom wing with a high standard of luxury has been refurbished also. Here, singles cost £80 ($120); doubles, £95 ($142.50).

You can dine in the Chateaubriand, with its excellent French cuisine. In addition, there's a coffeehouse, really a grill, open from 10 a.m. until midnight. The facilities seem endless: bars, a movie house that operates as a private club (but is available to all hotel residents), and a theater. Tube: Piccadilly Circus.

The **London Marriott Hotel** (formerly the Europa), Grosvenor Square, W.1 (tel. 493-1232), right by the American Embassy, has been revamped to become Marriott's flagship hotel in Europe. Its bedrooms, nearly 300 in all, have been furnished in the modern manner, in good taste, with an emphasis on simplicity. All rooms have private baths. Singles rent for £90 ($135), doubles or twins for £102 ($153), and triples for £112 ($168), all tariffs including VAT and service. All rooms have color TV, in-house films, radios, central heating, air conditioning, mini-bars, hair dryers, and complimentary shampoo packs. On the premises are the well-known

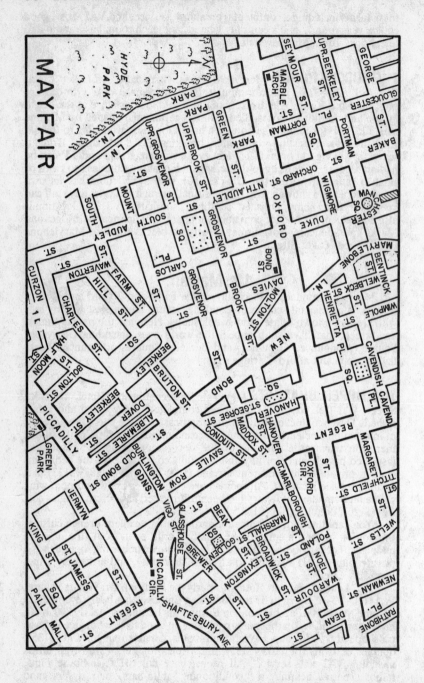

Diplomat Restaurant and the Diplomat Bar, as well as the Regent Lounge Coffee Shop. Tube: Bond Street.

Flemings Hotel, 7–12 Half Moon St., W.1 (tel. 499-2964), is a flat-fronted building in a terrace of old houses and offices with an uncluttered reception and a large lounge. It also has a pleasant bar where you can sit at a bamboo table in a wicker chair or perch on a stool by the bar. The airy, informal dining room, the Mermaiden Restaurant, has a pleasant, simple menu of light appetizers, soups, omelets, grilled fish, and steaks, backed up by an adequate wine list.

For the most part, the bedrooms have baths; some units are a little small where the plumbing had to be added. They include color TV, radio, phone, a refrigerator for water and ice cubes, 24-hour room service, and in-house movies. Rates are £40 ($60) in a single with bath, rising to £50 ($75) in a double or twin, also with bath. Even more expensive and larger "executive rooms" are available, and tariffs include a continental breakfast, service, and VAT. Tube: Green Park.

The **Londoner,** Welbeck Street, W.1 (tel. 935-4442), has retained its traditional facade, but completely modernized its interior. The contrast, the moment you walk in, is delightful. Tucked away in Mayfair off Wigmore Street (near Cavendish Square and Wigmore Hall), the hotel is an excellent remake of an older building.

Now all of its 142 comfortably furnished bedrooms contain private baths, phones, radios, TVs, and free in-house movies. There is also 24-hour room service. Singles rent for £42 ($63), with doubles or twins costing from £52 ($78), inclusive of VAT and a continental breakfast. Oliver's Restaurant is comfortably traditional and welcoming, serving British fare at breakfast, lunch, and dinner. The Chesterfield Bar offers a range of "spirits" and beer. Tube: Bond Street.

14. Bloomsbury

To the northeast of Piccadilly Circus, beyond Soho, is Bloomsbury, a world unto itself. It is, among other things, the academic heart of London, where you'll find London University, several other colleges, the British Museum, and many bookstores. Despite its student overtones, the section is fairly staid and quiet. Its reputation has been fanned by such writers as Virginia Woolf (it figures in her novel, *Jacob's Room*). She and her husband, Leonard, were once the unofficial leaders of a coterie of artists and writers known as the Bloomsbury Group, nicknamed Bloomsberries.

The exact heart of Bloomsbury is difficult to pinpoint. There are those who say it is Russell Square, with its university buildings, private homes, and hotels. Others feel it is the nearby British Museum. Still others are convinced it's the sprawling University of London, which also contains the Royal Academy of Dramatic Art on Gower Street. In any case there are at least four other old tree-filled squares—Bloomsbury, Bedford, Gordon, and Tavistock—each one an oasis of green in the midst of some of London's finest buildings. The unquestioned northern border is Euston Road, with its three railway stations—St. Pancras, King's Cross, and Euston—and its southern border is New Oxford Street.

THE UPPER BRACKET: **Hotel Russell,** Russell Square, W.C.1 (tel. 836-6470), is a late Victorian hotel facing the gardens of Russell Square and within easy reach of theaters and shopping. It is run by Trusthouses Forte

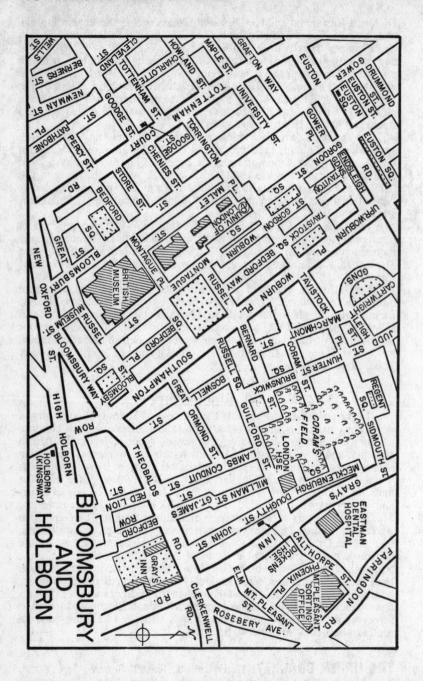

and offers 318 rooms, all with private baths or showers. Rates for a single are from £54 ($81) and from £68 ($102) for a twin. The public rooms have been refurbished and include an excellent Carvery restaurant and the Hansom Cab Grill Room, which offers a full range of dishes, plus quick grills and drinks at pub prices in an Edwardian atmosphere. The King's Bar has become one of London's most popular cocktail bars. Other facilities include a theater ticket agency, secretarial services, and a car-rental agency. Tube: Russell Square.

THE MEDIUM-PRICED RANGE: "Y" Hotel, 112 Great Russell St., W.C.1 (tel. 637-1333), is actually a modern hotel in the heart of London. Single rooms with shower rent for £24 ($36) a night, prices rising to £35 ($52.50) in a double or twin-bedded room with shower. It was built by the London Central Young Men's Christian Association for men and women of all ages. At the Oxford Street end of Tottenham Court Road, this new "Y" Hotel may not be like any you've ever seen before. Its facilities include squash courts, a gymnasium, a swimming pool, a shop, and an underground garage for car parking. Other facilities include a lounge and bar, plus a restaurant. Every bedroom has a private shower and bath, central heating, color TV, and radio. The furnishings are up to date and comfortable, and there's even wall-to-wall carpeting. Tube: Russell Square.

THE BUDGET RANGE: Lonsdale Hotel, 9–10 Bedford Pl., W.C.1 (tel. 636-1812), is a Georgian town house, within the shadow of the British Museum. It's elegantly positioned on one of the most attractive tree-lined streets in London, midway between Russell and Bloomsbury Squares. It is a particular favorite of professors and scientists from the continent who find it a convenient place to stay while researching at the museum. The B&B rate in a double or twin is £32 ($48), although singles pay £19 ($28.50), including VAT. There is no other charge. All rooms have razor outlets, and central heating assures cozy warmth. The hotel is privately owned and has a little garden in the rear. Tube: Russell Square.

READERS' HOTEL SELECTION: "Staunton Hotel (B&B), 13–15 Gower St., W.C.1 (tel. 580-2740), stands near the British Museum and many shops. It is also convenient to good city transportation. The rooms are very clean, and the breakfast is excellent. The rate is £10 ($15) per person (lower off-season). Mr. and Mrs. W. G. D. Morgan permitted us to leave luggage while on other tours, keeping the lodgings for us upon our return. Anxious to please, they are personable proprietors. Tube: Russell Square" (Mr. and Mrs. Samuel C. Levin, Chicago, Ill.).

15. Euston Station and King's Cross

Accommodations generally less expensive than those we have been considering so far can be found in these rather nondescript sections just a few blocks north of Bloomsbury. The hotels here are mainly around three large railway stations—Euston, St. Pancras, and King's Cross—and they are serviced by three tube stations: King's Cross, Euston, and Euston Square.

THE MEDIUM-PRICED RANGE: Kennedy Hotel, Euston, Cardington Street, N.W.1 (tel. 387-4400), opened in 1968 and is perhaps the most American-inspired hotel in London. Next to Euston Station, it is a gray

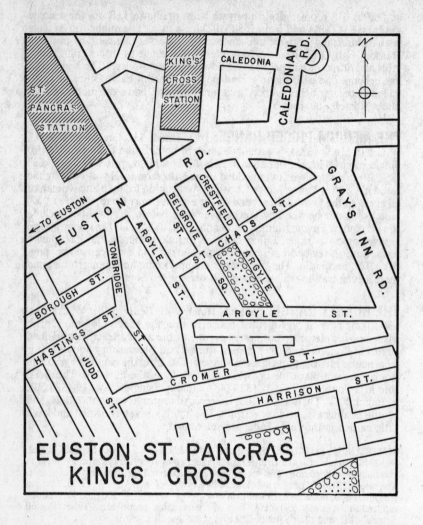

EUSTON ST. PANCRAS
KING'S CROSS

building with a drive-in entrance. Inside, everything is bright and you'll find top-grade accommodations with many touches of luxury. Yet the prices are moderate—£43 ($64.50) in a single with bath, £55 ($82.50) in a double with bath. A continental breakfast is included. The rooms are expertly designed, with innerspring mattresses, TV, and air conditioning throughout. Decorator fabrics and colors are used—even the lamps are stylish.

The hotel's novelty is its Planters Restaurant. A profusion of greenery, full air conditioning, and an intriguing decor make this an attractive place to enjoy anything from a cup of coffee to a three-course meal with wine.

London Ryan, Gwynne Place, King's Cross Road, W.C.1 (tel. 278-2480), is one of London's new efficiency hotels, where there are no hidden extras. Everything in the bedrooms is streamlined and self-contained, that is, complete private baths, direct-dial telephones, radios, color televisions, free in-house movies, and central heating. Even your continental breakfast is served in your chamber. From April to October, singles rent from £35 ($52.50), twins from £49.50 ($74.25), and triples from £59.50 ($89.25). These charges include a continental breakfast, service, and VAT. Facilities include a restaurant, a shop, Victorian Bar, and a private 50-car park. The location is convenient, near King's Cross railway and tube station, in back of Sadler's Wells, and within walking distance of the Dickens house.

16. On the Fringe

SOUTHEAST LONDON: Time was when no one would think of building a hotel in unchic Elephant and Castle, across the Thames in Southeast London. But this is a new day and a new London—and here it is . . .

The Budget Range
London Park Hotel, Brook Drive, S.E. 11 (tel. 735-9191), is an enormous warehouse across the Thames that has been completely overhauled and turned into a streamlined modern hotel. It now boasts 380 bedrooms, most with showers or tubs, plus a large restaurant, coffeeshop, and two bars. Rooms are very contemporary and contain built-in headboards with telephones and radios (some even have "baby-listening" devices). Bathless singles go for £16.50 ($24.75), increasing to £19 ($28.50) with private bath or shower. In a bathless twin-bedded or double-bedded room, the cost is £27 ($40.50) nightly, rising to £30 ($45) with private bath or shower. Prices include a continental breakfast and VAT. There are fast elevators, express laundry and dry-cleaning service, and a theater ticket bureau. Meal prices are low for London: a set lunch is £7 ($10.50); a set dinner, from £8.50 ($12.75). Numerous buses pass by the hotel, and there's a tube stop at Elephant and Castle.

HAMPSTEAD: The old village of Hampstead, sitting high on a hill, is the most desirable residential suburb of London. The village borders a wild heathland, which contains sprawling acres of wooded dells and fields of heather. Yet the Northern line of the Underground reaches the edges of the heath, making it possible for Londoners to enjoy isolated countryside while living only 20 minutes from city center. These advantages have caused many young artists to discover what Keats could have told them years ago—Hampstead is the place to live. The little Georgian houses have never received so much attention and love as they get now.

The Budget Range
Sandringham Hotel, 3 Holford Rd., N.W.3 (tel. 435-1569). You'd never guess this is a hotel, because it stands on a residential street in one of the best parts of London. After getting off at the Hampstead tube station, you walk up the hill past interesting shops, pubs, and charmingly converted houses. Shortly, at the Turpin Restaurant, you turn right into Hampstead Square, which leads into Holford Road. A high wall and trees screen the house from the street (if you have a car, you can park in the driveway). It is

a well-built, centrally heated house, and the comfortable rooms often house professional people who want to be near the center of London, yet retain the feel of rural life. The B&B charge is £16 ($24) in a single, increasing to £28 ($42) in a twin or double if bathless, but rising to £32 ($48) with private bath. The breakfast room overlooks a walled garden; from the upper rooms you have a panoramic view over the heath of the center of London. You'll find a home-like lounge furnished with color TV. Owners Mr. and Mrs. Dreyer and their two sons live on the premises.

SWISS COTTAGE: If you prefer life on a tree-lined residential street in north London, the following choice may appeal to you. It lies only ten minutes by underground from the heart of the West End.

Swiss Cottage Hotel, 4 Adamson Rd., N.W.3 (tel. 722-2281). This is rather an intriguing sort of place, an elegant family house furnished with paintings and antique furniture, Persian rugs, and chandeliers. The glass-fronted reception desk contains a fine collection of porcelain figures, and each bedroom has an old-fashioned bureau or writing desk. The lounge boasts a fine grand piano, a select place for afternoon tea. There is a pleasant quiet bar and a handsome dining room where à la carte meals are served.

Behind the hotel is a small formal town garden with trees, ferns, and geraniums, plus the Tea House area. This is the honeymoon suite, but you need not be on honeymoon to rent it. Bedrooms in the main hotel are very comfortable and, except for some singles, have modern showers or bathrooms. All have TV and telephone. The whole place is centrally heated. Singles go from £25 ($37.50) to £52 ($78) for sole occupancy of a large double with bathroom. Doubles are £42 ($63) to £60 ($90), and the Tea House rents for £80 ($120). All rates include a full breakfast and VAT. Tube: Swiss Cottage.

FULHAM: This is a pleasant part of West London. A tree-lined road stretches from St. Ethelred's Church (that's the bus stop you should ask for) to Bishop's Walk, a shady park running down to the river where in the afternoons a band often plays. And just around the corner is Fulham Palace, home of the bishop of London. In such a setting you're likely to discover London's most elegant B&B.

Off Fulham Palace Road, which runs from Hammersmith to Putney Bridge, at 10 Doneraile St., Fulham, S.W.6 (tel. 731-2192), Lady Hartley has two comfortable doubles available at £20 ($30) single occupancy, £32 ($48) double occupancy. In this elegant Edwardian house, renovated by Lady Hartley herself, you can come and go as you please.

The rooms are well furnished with comfortable beds. Guests share a bathroom but have their own tea- and coffee-making equipment. Knowing North American tastes, Lady Hartley willingly provides ice for your drinks.

Guests have the use of the front room to sit in, and this is where breakfast with hot croissants is served. Lady Hartley decided to take in guests purely because she and her two pug dogs enjoy meeting people. She does all she can to make you comfortable.

17. Airport Hotels

As one of the major gateways to Europe (not to mention England), London's two major airports are among the busiest in the world. Many readers have expressed a desire to be near their point of departure, spending the night in ease before "taking off." With that in mind, I'd suggest the following accommodations, beginning—

AT GATWICK: Gatwick Hilton International Hotel, Gatwick Airport, Crawley in Surrey (tel. 0293/518080), a deluxe, five-floor hotel of the Hilton chain, is the airport's most convenient resting place. A covered footbridge links the hotel and air terminal with a five-minute walk. You can also obtain porterage to the airport, and there are trolleys and electric cars if you can't cope with a walk.

A desk in the airport's arrival hall allows you to check your baggage and register, then catch the express city-link train into London to return later to your hotel room where your baggage awaits you.

The most dramatic part of the hotel is the first-floor lobby, where a glass-covered portico rises through four floors, containing a full-scale replica of the de Havilland Gypsy Moth airplane *Jason,* used by Amy Johnson on her solo flight from England to Australia in 1930. The reception is close by, an area of much greenery, trees, flowering shrubs, and trailing ivy and fig.

There is a well-equipped health club with a sauna, massage room, and a heated swimming pool (indoor), along with other temptations, available to guests. On the ground floor is a restaurant serving both English and continental dishes. Opening for breakfast at 7 a.m., it serves dinner until 11 p.m.

The Jockey Club bar, with its masculine, Edwardian decor, is mainly for drinking, although sandwiches are available. There is also a cozy lounge bar, where light refreshments are available 24 hours a day.

Rooms have the amenities expected of a Hilton: full air conditioning, double-glazed windows, phone, radio, and color TV with a full-length feature film shown daily in addition to normal stations (plus a mini-bar). Laundry and dry cleaning are returned within the day if collected at 9 a.m. The 333 bedrooms, each with private bath and shower, cost from £55 ($82.50) in a single and from £68 ($102) to £80 ($120) in a double.

The hotel staff provides many services for the business traveler who needs to contact his or her associates in a hurry. Up-to-date flight information is also flashed on the TV screen.

Gravetye Manor, near East Grinstead, West Sussex (tel. 0342/810567), is a 16th-century Elizabethan manor just 12 miles from Gatwick, part of an estate set in the hills, standing in its own 30 acres of woods, orchards, and a trout lake. It's approached by a mile-long winding driveway leading into an entrance courtyard. Later, you can discover the restored formal gardens, the lifetime creation of one of England's leading horticulturists, William Robinson.

The spacious drawing room has tasteful furnishings, oak-paneled walls, and many antiques. You can enjoy quiet conversation while you sip tea and munch on home-baked scones and cake. Guests and area residents gather in the pleasant sitting room, warmed by a large oak fireplace, for apéritifs before dinner. The 14 bedchambers are individual, each one named after trees on the estate: ash, bay, beech, whatever. My favorite is the Willow, an elegant, comfortable double with Tudor windows in both bedroom and bath from which you have a panorama of the gardens. Doubles or twin-bedded rooms range in price from £62 ($95) to £115 ($172.50) nightly.

One is the former master bedroom, with a massive carved four-poster, as well as wood-carved portraits of the original owners over the fireplace (Richard and Katherine Infield in 1598). The rates in a single with private bath are from £52 ($78). These prices are inclusive of a continental breakfast. Service is also included, but VAT is added to the entire account. Write well in advance for reservations in high season.

Dinner is to be savored, not rushed. Jacketed waiters are trained by the restaurant manager, Helmut Kircher. He supervises what some wine experts claim to be the best cellar in England, some 500 listings. The kitchen is the domain of a true Englishman, Allan Garth. He delights not only with his British dishes, but also he has been trained in imaginative French cuisine—a happy combination. You may find on the menu, depending on the season, saddle of rabbit with pistachio and chicken mousse, coquille St. Jacques au saffron, braised Scottish river salmon topped with pike mousse, and many tempting desserts, including muscat sabayon, almond pastry filled with hazelnut cream, plus mango, prune, or Armagnac homemade ice cream. Expect to spend £23 ($34.50) to £30 ($45) for a complete meal.

This is an excellent place to stay if you like horseback riding or golf, which can be arranged nearby, croquet, or clock golf on the lawn. Fly fishermen may try their luck on the three-acre lake filled with brown and rainbow trout.

Cisswood House Hotel, Lower Beeding, near Horsham in Sussex (tel. 040-376/216), was called "Harrods in the country" by the locals when it was built in the late 1920s for Sir Woodman Burbridge, owner of Harrods store, and his wife, Cicely. Its name, Cisswood, was derived from the couple's first names. Craftsmen from the Harrods workshops were employed to create the wood and plasterwork and give the house its character, even if it is mock country Tudor. It is surrounded by traditional gardens with shrubs and flowering creepers, herbaceous borders, and well-kept lawns, with dovecotes and trees.

Othmar and Elizabeth Illes have owned Cisswood since 1979 and have built a reputation for their high-quality cooking and the comfort of their rooms. Othmar, who was trained at a hotel school in his native Austria, is the chef as well as the proprietor. He uses fresh ingredients from the London markets and from local farms. The dining room is beamed, carpeted, and pleasant, and there is a cheerful bar. The bedrooms are furnished with flower prints and potted plants, with some good reproduction antiques and modern bathrooms. You'll pay £30 ($45) in a single, £46 ($69) in a double, including a continental breakfast, service, and VAT. No dinner is served on Sunday or Monday. Lunches are offered daily from Tuesday to Friday. Cisswood lies about 12 minutes from Gatwick Airport, and you can order a taxi for an early departure if necessary.

The **Copthorne Hotel,** Copthorne, near Crawley in Sussex (tel. 0342/714971), is a 16th-century farmhouse with various additions, set in a large garden with a peaceful lake. A garden room overlooks the central patio with its tinkling fountains and weeping willows. The bar and many of the bedrooms in the old part of the house have ancient beams. Floral bedspreads and chintz curtains add to the ambience. Bathrooms are modern, but most singles have showers only. The restaurant is dark, with a low beamed ceiling and wooden balustrades. Meals include mainly French dishes, such as onion soup and bouillabaisse. The vegetables are fresh, and you have a good choice of desserts from the trolley. A set dinner costs £7.50 ($11.25), with an à la carte meal going for about £15 ($22.50) for three courses. As befits an airport hotel, food is available from 6:30 a.m. to 10:45 p.m. A single bedroom with a shower rents for £39 ($58.50) to £51 ($76.50), while doubles go for £63 ($94.50) to £68 ($102). Breakfast is included in the tariffs. There are some ground-floor rooms suitable for the handicapped. Transportation to nearby Gatwick is available.

Russ Hill Hotel, Charlwood, near Horley, Sussex (tel. 0293/862171), is a pleasant country-house hotel set in wooded grounds with views over the Surrey hills. All the bedrooms have well-appointed bathrooms, radios, and phones. There is a comfortable lounge, and for the more energetic, an indoor swimming pool, a sauna, and a games room. You can enjoy a drink in the bar and good, simple meals in the restaurant. Singles cost from £31 ($46.50); doubles, from £45 ($67.50)—both with breakfast included.

READER'S HOTEL SELECTION: "**Trumble's Hotel and Restaurant** on Stanhill (the road to Newdigate), Charlwood, Surrey (tel. 0293/862212), is a wonderful place to stay overnight, or just to dine, if your plane comes in at Gatwick Airport. The hotel is only ten minutes by car from there, in lovely rolling country. Its rooms are large and beautiful, some furnished with fine antiques (two bedrooms have canopied four-poster beds). All bedrooms have private bathrooms, radio, and color TV. In a double room, the cost of B&B is £35 ($52.50) for two. There's nothing gloomy—everything's airy and cheerful and comfortable, and the 'full' heat is really that. Proprietors Sue and Peter Trumble will advise on touring and car rental, and often have maps you can borrow. Dinner here averages about £12 ($18) per person and is of gourmet quality. We had black currant pie that was the best pie we had ever tasted. House specialties are traditional roast beef for Sunday lunch, roast duckling with orange sauce and fresh wheels of orange, very tender steaks, and plenty of fresh English fish. Also try the homemade lemon meringue pie. Excellent wines and liqueurs are available. There's a small Victorian bar. Trumble's would be a splendid place to spend a week or two. With a car, you could travel to Canterbury, Oxford, the South Coast, or Winchester, to name a few good spots, and get back in time for a memorable dinner. Also you can drive to Gatwick Airport, leave your car, and take the short train ride to London for the day. Trains run every 15 minutes during the day, every hour at night. Charlwood village is full of historic houses, some more than 300 years old. The church has a wall pre-William the Conqueror and 1066. My husband and I thought this the nicest place and the best buy on our 1000-mile tour of England. It is advisable to reserve ahead by telephone" (Mrs. Janet Kay, Rochester, N.Y.).

AT HEATHROW: Sheraton Skyline Hotel, Bath Road, Hayes, Middlesex (tel. 759-2535), is a square, red brick building set back from the road just off the airport, with a large car park in front. The main feature of the hotel is a covered central patio with exotic plants blooming among tables around the heated swimming pool. Caribbean and tropical nights are held in the patio on some evenings, with entertainment by a steel band or Hawaiian guitarists and a supper served at a set price of £5 ($7.50). More intimate and less noisy is Diamond Lil's Klondyke Saloon, while the Edwardian Colony Bar is elegant and sedate. The light and airy coffeeshop is open from 6 a.m. to 2 a.m. If you prefer, you can dine in the Colony Room, selecting from a more expensive menu offering continental and some international dishes, a meal costing around £20 ($30) per person, without wine.

The bedrooms are modern, with double-glazed windows and air conditioning, as well as TV and in-house movies. A single rents for £64 ($96), a double for £72 ($108), with VAT added. This is probably the best hotel at Heathrow, having a little more atmosphere than the usual commercial operation. Frequent transportation to the terminal buildings and into central London is available.

Heathrow Penta Hotel, Bath Road, Hounslow, Middlesex (tel. 897-6363), is within the perimeter of the airport, many of the rooms having fantastic views of Concorde and jumbo-jet takeoffs, with double-glazed windows protecting your ears from the sound. The bedrooms have up-to-date amenities such as tea- and coffee-making equipment, mini-bars, TVs, and in-house movies. All units have bathrooms, and there is an indoor swimming pool and health center, plus a hairdresser and 24-hour laundry service. Singles are £58 ($87); twins, £64 ($96); and large doubles, £70 ($105)—including VAT and service. Besides the 24-hour coffeeshop, there is a restaurant, as well as a Flying Machine Bar decorated with flying prints and models.

In a lower price range, you might like to try the **Osterley Comfort Inn,** Great West Road, Isleworth, Middlesex (tel. 568-9981), a roadside inn about 15 minutes from Heathrow on the road that leads into London. Most of the bedrooms have private baths, while others contain showers. Singles run from £20 ($30) for a room with shower to £26 ($39) for an accommodation with bath. Doubles and twins are £33 ($49.50) to £40 ($60), and all tariffs include breakfast. There is a cheerful pub-style bar and a restaurant serving meals such as grills, steaks, and fish dishes.

Another convenient choice for a first or last night near the airport is the **Post House Hotel,** Sipson Road, West Drayton, Middlesex (tel. 759-2323). The multistory building rises above the M4 motorway. It is surrounded by a car park and a helipad from which busy aircraft make trips between the hotel and both Heathrow and London. Most people, however, make use of the frequent bus service to reach the terminal buildings.

Bedrooms have TV, radio, tea- and coffee-making facilities, mini-bar, and bathroom. Singles cost £40 ($60); doubles and twins, £47 ($70.50). The hotel has a cocktail bar and a grill room, but most people gravitate toward the Carvery in the evening, where a central table groans beneath joints of beef, pork, and lamb. You can start with melon, soup, or pâté, and then help yourself to as much as you like from the meat counter, with a selection of vegetables. Cold cuts and a variety of salads are also offered, and there's a dessert trolley. A meal will cost about £9 ($13.50).

Elstree Moat House, Barnet Bypass (A1), Borehamwood, Hertfordshire (tel. 953-1622), sits beside the A1 to the north, some 15 miles from Heathrow and London's West End. The original building dates from the 16th century, but much has been added and modernized to provide a very pleasant motel. Furnished with oak paneling and reproductions of antiques, all 60 bedrooms contain baths, color TVs, radios, telephones, and tea- and coffee-making facilities. Single occupancy costs £40 ($60). In a double or twin, the rate is £55 ($82.50). There are also rooms for three persons at £60 ($90). All tariffs include service, VAT, and a large English breakfast. The candlelit, oak-beamed dining room serves well-prepared meals and hot grills, and there are also two bars that provide snacks besides the usual range of drinks. Facilities include an Olympic-size swimming pool. Close by is St. Albans and the remains of the Roman city of Verulanium. Also nearby is Ayot St. Lawrence where Sir George Bernard Shaw lived.

18. Alternatives to Hotels

STAYING WITH A FAMILY: At least ten agencies in Britain can arrange stays with a private family, either in London or in the country. As much as is possible, interests are matched. This program is an intriguing way to involve yourself in the social life of a country, seeing it from the inside. Also it's a great bargain. Some agencies limit themselves to teenagers, others welcome older readers.

Try one of the following: **Host & Guest Service**, 529a King's Rd., S.W.6 (tel. 731-5340), will provide a place for you at a cost that begins at £40 ($60) weekly for B&B and £55 ($82.50) with evening meals, added. Write or call Mrs. Rutter.

Ball Tourist Services, 9 Norbury Ave., Thornton Heath (tel. 653-8467), specializes in arranging accommodation for any length of visit with selected host families in many places throughout the United Kingdom including the southwest suburbs of London (about 15 minutes by train to central London), Kingston-upon-Thames (west London near Hampton Court), Canterbury (southeast England), Eastbourne (south coast), the Isle of Wight (off the south coast), Cambridge (east England), and the Lake District (northwest England). Prices for lodging and an English breakfast, booking fee, and VAT range from £7.50 ($11.25) per person per night. Evening meals are also available for from £4 ($6) per person.

London Home to Home, 26 Ascott Ave., W. 5 (tel. 567-2998), is operated by Anita Harrison and Australian Rosemary Richardson. When their children were grown, the two women looked around for something to do. Since both of them had a never-ending stream of friends from overseas coming to stay, they hit on the idea of providing "home from home" accommodations on a wider basis. They have more than 100 homes on their books, mostly in the London suburbs, all of which offer comfortable beds, a full English breakfast, tea, coffee, access to the house and to the family living area at all times, use of the TV, the lounge, bathrooms, and laundry facilities. Mrs. Harrison and Mrs. Richardson try to match homes and guests, so you will be asked to list your interests briefly when you make a reservation.

The cost of this service is £10 ($15) per person per night. Family rooms are available accommodating two adults and one child over 2 years old and under 12, for a total of £27 ($40.50) per night. Breakfast is included in the price at all the homes, and an evening meal can be arranged for £5 ($7.50) extra. For an additional £15 ($22.50) the service will include a transfer from Heathrow to your accommodation (more from Gatwick). All arrivals are given a traveler's information package of maps, bus and tube timetables, and sightseeing brochures so that you can become familiar with the territory, with the help of your host family.

A small deposit is required when you reserve your rooms, and you pay the balance to your host on arrival. If you have to cancel, your deposit, minus a small administrative cost, will be refunded if at least four weeks' notice is given.

ACCOMMODATION SERVICE: The **London Tourist Board**, at 26 Grosvenor Gardens, Victoria, S.W.1 (tel. 730-3488), will make same-day bookings (in writing) in a wide range of accommodations, from guest houses to hotels, for a basic price of £6 ($9) per person, including bed, breakfast, and VAT. At this price, however, the accommodation would be shared in a guest house or a hostel. Singles are available, beginning at £8 ($12). The board performs this service for those who go in person to its information centers at Victoria Station and at Heathrow Underground station. You're charged a small booking fee regardless of the number of persons in your party, plus a refundable deposit. In addition, the centers supply information on accommodations at campsites and in dormitories, plus other types of accommodations below the minimum price of £6 ($9). However, staff members will not book such accommodations through their centers.

LIVING LIKE A LORD AND LADY: If you have always wanted to spend the night inside a castle, **Country Homes and Castles**, 118 Cromwell Rd., S.W.7 (tel. 491-4272), may be able to arrange just the suitable abode for you. More than 100 houses, ranging from cottages to historic manor houses to turreted fortresses, are available to paying guests through this program. Since the owners naturally vary in their interests, ages, and professional backgrounds, the agency makes every effort to match you with suitable hosts so that both will benefit from an enjoyable experience.

The organization will arrange a one- or two-night stay in a single house to fit in with your travel plans, or it will try to plan a complete tour with stops throughout the country, bearing in mind your personal interests. Prices for accommodations range from £105 ($157.50) to £200 ($300) per couple per night. The rate includes drinks, dinner with wine, accommodations with private bath, and breakfast. All payments are made in advance to the agent so that you can enjoy your guest-host relationship without embarrassment. Make arrangements through Sue Duncan, 6265 Courtside Dr. N.W., Norcross, GA 30092 (tel. 404/448-2185).

STAY ON A FARM: Country Farm Holidays, The Place, Ham Lane, Powick, Worcester (tel. 0905/830899). For two or three nights or longer in the country, all you have to do is get in touch with Country Farm Holidays which will fit you up with a lovely Elizabethan farm in Salop, amid paneled walls and old oak beams, or with a 15th-century moated farmhouse in Suffolk where you can enjoy the country life, dinner, bed, and breakfast for as little as £12.50 ($18.75) a night per person. They have a wide selection of attractive and often historic farms on their books, and will give you details of how to get there, what to see and do. Many of the places allow guests to help with the animals and the working of the farm. They also have a list of self-catering cottages and apartments available for rentals of seven nights or more, sleeping from two to ten persons in comfort. Prices vary, obviously, but in June four to five persons can have an accommodation for around £80 ($120) for seven nights, including VAT.

YOUR OWN COTTAGE: "England's most exclusive and individual self-catering holiday homes," they claim, and it could well be so. These cottages are the dream-child of Maj. G. M. S. Bowlby, who controls the operation. His idea originated at Vere Lodge, where he lives, tucked away in the Norfolk village of South Raynham, and at one time the cottages at Vere Lodge were the only ones owned and rented as self-catering properties by Major Bowlby. Since then, **English Country Cottages** has expanded beyond all expectations and now offers a choice of more than 900 properties, ranging from mini-apartments to converted boathouses, farmhouses, and stately homes in most parts of England and Wales, all of which are inspected by a senior member of the staff before acceptance.

Visitors therefore have a choice not only of a wide range of types of accommodation but also of a variety of locations. They can choose to take a holiday either in the upland moorland of Yorkshire; in the spacious, corn-growing country of East Anglia; in Dorset, where Thomas Hardy lived and wrote; or in the lush pastureland of Devon and Cornwall, with tall, bright-red cliffs, narrow lanes with high banks bright with wildflowers, and hundreds of pretty fishing villages. This part of England is the mecca of vacationers and provides everything you could possibly want—surfing, sailing, pony trekking, riding, old-world inns, high-class restaurants—all in a climate that is the kindest and softest England has to offer.

The cottages sleep from two to 14 persons. A brochure provides full details of all the properties available, with a color photo of each. Prices range from £81 ($121.50) per week to £132 ($198) in high season, from £291 ($436.50) to £690 ($1035) for the more expensive places. The interior appointments range from the simple to the luxurious. Prices, of course, depend not only on the quality of the decor but also on the location of the cottage or house and the amenities that accompany it, such as a heated swimming pool, a hard tennis court, or a barbecue patio.

The great advantage of this type of holiday is that you can do your own thing in your own way in your own time. You can get up when you like, eat what and when you like, and wear what you like. A self-catering vacation with English Country Cottages offers outstanding value for the money, complete freedom from all restrictions, and an opportunity of sampling English country life in its many and varied aspects.

A word of advice: Most cottages are in villages or on the grounds of mansions and farms. Many are quite difficult to find. Don't worry, however. When you make your reservation, the major will send you detailed instructions on how to get there. The head office is Claypit Lane, Fakenham, Norfolk NR21 8AS. The telephone numbers for reservations are: for East Anglia, 0328/51155; for the southwest, 0328/51411; for Wales, the North of England, the Cotswolds, the southeast, and other areas, 0328/51331. You can even "Dial-a-Brochure," 1328/4041.

YOUR OWN APARTMENT: The **South London Accommodation Agency,** 2 Mount Ephraim Rd., S.W.16 (tel. 769-2117), is an established business, serving visitors to London who are looking for nice and inexpensive self-catering accommodation. The agency will try to provide you with a fully equipped, private, clean, cozy, modern flatlet, flat, or house, depending on the number in your party and your needs. Mini-flatlet prices start at £80 ($120) per week for one or two persons. Family mini-flatlets cost from £110 ($165) per week for one to four persons. A whole London house will cost from £300 ($450) for from one to seven persons. Reduced rentals are granted for two, four, six, eight, and 26 weeks. For example, a mini-flatlet for two persons for four weeks costs from £45 ($67.50) per week. For the most part, accommodations are in quiet, pleasant suburbs only about five miles from the center of London, reached by excellent public transport service.

Upon arrival, you will be presented with a free Welcome Pack containing bus and train maps and advice on things to do, places to see, and how to get there. Advance reservations can be made. Discounts are available if you mention that you obtained the address from this guide. The bureau also offers a free pickup service from the local station to take you to the accommodation upon arrival.

The offices are open Monday through Friday from 9:30 a.m. to 4 p.m. and on Saturday from 9:30 a.m. to noon; closed Sunday and bank holidays.

A free airmail brochure by return mail is available upon request. If you do not have time to reserve in advance, simply telephone the agency when you arrive, and the staff will usually be able to help you.

Rentals are for a minimum of seven days, plus any number of additional days or weeks you require, and start on any day except Sunday or English public holidays, ending on any day, including Sunday. No lease is required, no extra fees, no fuss—in fact, it's as simple as booking into a hotel, but it costs only about half the price of comparable accommodations.

The **Regency Suites,** 130 Queen's Gate, S.W.7 (tel. 370-4242), are well-furnished apartments. Style varies from rather masculine brown leather buttoned chairs, indoor plants, and sober carpeting to warm apricot and white net curtains, flowery armchairs, and soft lights. The kitchens are fully equipped with modern electrical appliances and kitchen utensils, the glass is good, and all the china comes from Wedgwood. The penthouse suites even have a dishwasher to cope with your entertaining program, and all suites are serviced daily. There is 24-hour porterage as well. A wide range of provision shops are just around the corner so you should have to lack for nothing. Several of the larger apartments have their own terraces, equipped with garden furniture and electrically operated sunblinds. All have direct-dial telephone and a doorlock with a TV monitor. There is remote-control TV in all bedrooms and in the lounges. Bathrooms are well equipped, and all linen is provided. A studio flat with large reception and bedroom, bath, and kitchen costs from £300 ($450) per week; a double room, lounge, kitchen, and bath from £450 ($675). Three-room flats run from £525 ($787.50) per week; and the penthouses, each with enormous living rooms, three bedrooms with bath, kitchen, and entrance lobby, are from £1800 ($2700) per week. All rates include VAT and service, and rentals of 22 days or more are preferred. Tube: Gloucester Road.

Draycott House, 10 Draycott Ave., S.W.3 (tel. 584-4659), and its fellow block, 41 Draycott Pl., just across the street, offer what may seem the ultimate in the way of facilities. The old London houses are well converted to provide self-contained luxury apartments and studio flats, furnished in Edwardian style but with modern kitchens and bathrooms. All have private telephone lines and color TV. There are a resident porter and housekeeper, plus maid service five days a week. On your arrival the refrigerator will be stocked with basic provisions, and daily milk and newspapers will be delivered to you. Garage parking is also available. Rates compare £850 ($1275) favorably with London hotels. A two-bedroom apartment is about £700 ($1050) per week, and a three-bedroom apartment from £850 ($1275) to £1000 ($1500) per week. Studios and one-bedroom apartments range from £125 ($187.50) to £500 ($750) per week. No service charge or VAT is added. The rub is that minimum rental is for three weeks. Miss Linda Coulthard is the resident administrator, young and highly experienced in the travel, hotel, and catering industry. In addition to the more domestic details, they can provide Telex, secretarial and translation services, and rental of video equipment for the business person, and will recommend eating places.

Accommodations in South London can be arranged by John and Myra Slade, **Slade Holdings,** 49 Woodcrest Rd., Purley, Surrey (tel. 660-2967), for those who prefer to look after themselves in a clean, cozy flat (efficiency) or flat (apartment). All units are equipped for a minimum of two persons up to a maximum of seven. Prices start at £90 ($135) per unit for seven nights, with reductions for longer stays. The accommodations are at Streatham Hill, London, S.W.16, in quiet, pleasant suburbs about five miles from the center of London, reached by excellent public transportation in less than 30 minutes. There are no parking restrictions at the apartments for those who wish to rent a car and use this as a base to travel around Britain. Upon your arrival, you are presented with a free welcome pack containing bus and train maps and advice on things to do, places to see, and how to get there.

The office is open seven days a week, but it is advisable to reserve your apartment as much as two months in advance if possible, as this type of low-cost, good-quality accommodation is quite popular. Rentals may start on any day, minimum of seven days. No lease is required and there are no extra fees.

FOR GOLFERS ONLY: The Golfers Club was started in 1893. It has now opened its doors to overseas members, and an annual subscription (price listed on application) will give you access to more than 50 golf clubs in England and Scotland, as well as privileged greens fees of around half the normal rates. Membership also permits you to use the Sloane Club in London where accommodations are available at around £25 ($37.50) a night. The 400 or so United Kingdom members will arrange introductions for overseas visitors in the particular area they are visiting. Matches and friendly games are also arranged, and members will even help in lending clubs and equipment. Members are often able to obtain concessionary rates for car rentals, restaurants, and hotels. The club also makes up special golf packages for aficionados of the game. Write to Golfers Club, International House, Windmill Road, Sunbury-on-Thames, Middlesex (tel. 09327/85666).

LONDON: RESTAURANTS AND PUBS

WHEN ELIZABETH I was released from the Tower, with her stiff neck intact, she feasted on loin of pork and overcooked English peas. Up until the last few years, most of the English agreed with Queen Bess's idea of a feast, sometimes varying the peas with gray cabbage and boiled-to-death brussels sprouts. But the England of Elizabeth I is not the England of Elizabeth II, as your palate will quickly reveal to you if you sample some of the wares in the upcoming restaurants.

A new wave of skilled cooking, inspired by the continent and visitors' demands, has swept the country, but is most noticeable in London. Of course, the trend toward continental dishes is not without its pretensions. As novelist-historian-gourmet Raymond Postgate pointed out, boiled beef and carrots are still served, passed off as "la pièce de boeuf salée londonienne." A striking feature of the dining scene in London and the country is the emergence of the personality restaurant—that is, a dining spot based on the character, charm, and individual recipes of one exceptional chef.

Many Americans accustomed to spices and mixing and blending of foods find English cooking dull. Of course, the French show their disdain by calling anything plain, boiled, or cooked in the blandest way possible "à l'anglaise." However, simplicity doesn't mean bad food, and it's good to keep that in mind as you dine in London and elsewhere in England and Scotland.

All restaurants and cafés in Britain are required to display the prices of the food and drink they offer, in a place where the customer can see them before entering the eating area. If an establishment has an extensive à la carte menu, the prices of a representative selection of food and drink currently available must be displayed as well as the table d'hôte menu, if one is offered. Charges for service and any minimum charge or cover charge must also be made clear. The prices shown must be inclusive of VAT.

1. The Top Restaurants

Waltons, 121 Walton St., S.W.3 (tel. 584-0204), is a restaurant of considerable merit, beginning first with its creative chef, David Nicholls, an inventive Englishman, and his young, well-trained staff. The cuisine is international, with a strong emphasis on traditional English dishes, including such attractive delicacies as moneybag of salmon, noisette of veal with ribbons of vegetables, royale of lobster with a matching lobster butter sauce, and paupe of pink trout with vegetables. For dessert, try the strawberry soufflé glacé.

The setting helps: on a quiet street in Chelsea where dining is leisurely. The decor is in an intimate modern style, using Trianon gray with buttercup yellow and mauve tiles. The cutlery is Georg Jensen, the china Royal Copenhagen. Many guests arriving early make their menu selections in the bar on the second floor.

A three-course lunch, called "Simply Waltons," is served for £9 ($13.50). You can also order à la carte, a three- or four-course luncheon or dinner going for around £22 ($33). A Sunday luncheon is offered for £12.50 ($18.75), a Sunday dinner for £18.50 ($27.75), and a late-night supper (three courses) for £14.50 ($21.75), which might be ideal for an after-theater rendezvous. VAT is included, but service is extra.

The menu is backed by an extensive and comprehensive wine list, with a large range of mature château-bottled clarets, domaine-bottled red and white burgundies, and what is generally considered the best champagne list in London, plus a careful selection of the best from Alsace, the Loire, the Rhône, the Rhine, and the Mosel. There is a unique selection of rare single-vintage cognac, and the vintage port is decanted every morning to make certain that it arrives at the table in perfect condition that evening.

The restaurant is open daily, including Sunday, from 12:30 to 2:30 p.m. and from 7:30 to 11:30 p.m. The nearest tube stop is South Kensington, but it's more customary to arrive by taxi.

Savoy Restaurant, The Strand, W.C.2 (tel. 836-4343), in the Savoy Hotel, has a prime position: its tables open toward the river, and as you have breakfast or lunch, you can watch the boats passing by on the Thames. Lucius Beebe, in his history of the hotel, wrote: "Supper at the Savoy became legendary. It remains to this day a formidable tradition of London nightlife." At the apex of his fame, Auguste Escoffier was the director of the cuisine, earning for himself the title of "the king of chefs and the chef of kings." It is said that here Escoffier invented peach Melba, one of the world's most imitated desserts, and named it after the celebrated singer, Nellie Melba.

The river restaurant has an intimate dance floor, surrounded by tables, where a four-person band plays for dinner. (The great Russian dancer, Anna Pavlova, once appeared here.) Dinner starts at 7:30 p.m. and is served until midnight, until 11 p.m. on Sunday. Lunch is offered daily from 12:30 to 2:30 p.m. Music for dancing begins around 9 p.m. Monday through Saturday.

The à la carte menu is most ambitious. Nearly every dish is prepared to perfection, and only the most exacting gastromome will find fault.

Specialties include caneton (duckling) du Norfolk poêlé à l'orange and grilled chateaubriand with pommes soufflées for two persons. Crêpes suzette make a lavish dessert, although the peach Melba is more classic. Under "les savouries," perhaps you'll try "devil on horseback." On weekdays, a set dinner is offered for £15.50 ($23.25) per person, a set lunch costing £11.50 ($17.25) per person. Otherwise, expect to pay up to £50 ($75) for two persons for a complete à la carte meal, and make an evening of it.

The Thames Foyer makes an ideal meeting place where coffee, pre-lunch and dinner drinks, afternoon tea, and light refreshments are served. Tube: Temple.

Savoy Grill, The Strand, W.C.2 (tel. 836-4343), basks in its own glory. "Let's dine at the Grillroom" is an invitation often repeated since the days of Edward VII and Lillie Langtry. Unlike many other dining legends, the modestly named grill continues to maintain unimpeachable quality when dispensing the haute cuisine of France. It's been especially popular with a theatrical clientele since its patronage by Sarah Bernhardt, and to accommodate this group, it remains open until late, last orders being taken up to 11:30 p.m. Reservations are necessary, even after final curtain time at West End productions.

The chef's specialties include filet de boeuf en croûte François Villon (beef wrapped in puff pastry and garnished with artichokes, celery heart, and foie gras) and omelette Arnold Bennett. Excellent hors d'oeuvres include smoked trout and lobster mousse. For dessert, try a selection from the extensive and colorful sweet trolley. There's a distinguished collection of vintage wines, although you can order a large carafe of hock. Expect to pay around £25 ($37.50) per person, including tax and service, for a complete meal and a reasonable bottle of wine. Tube: Temple.

Carrier's, 2–4 Camden Passage, The Angel, N.1 (tel. 226-5353), is the special domain of Robert Carrier, one of the leading cookbook writers in the British Isles. His restaurant is in a tiny antique row district of Islington, where little shops and booths are crammed to the ceiling with antiques and bric-a-brac. Everybody makes the trip, and Mr. Carrier proves a point—if you serve exciting food, the world will find its way to your door.

To simplify matters, both the four-course lunch and dinner have set prices, the former costing from £25 ($37.50), the latter from £30 ($45). In addition, the chef does a three-course club luncheon menu at £20 ($30). He also does a three-course supper menu at £20 ($30) per head (available from 10:30 p.m.). All prices include VAT and service. Appetizers are likely to include the house specialty, brandade of smoked trout. You might follow with leek and pumpkin soup. For your main course, you can make selections from "the open fire" or else "the great dish of the day." All the main dishes are served with a choice of gratin Dauphinois or saffron rice, as well as a green salad with herb dressing. A dessert treat, when featured, is a cold chocolate soufflé. The wine list is modest, but sufficient. Carrier's is open Monday through Saturday from 12:30 to 2:30 p.m. and from 7:30 till 11:30 p.m. Tube: Angel.

2. The West End

I'll begin the pleasant task of exploring the cuisine in the major districts of the West End:

ST. JAMES'S: In the former playground of royalty is a well-recommended French restaurant.

The Upper Bracket
A l'Ecu de France, 111 Jermyn St., S.W.1 (tel. 930-2837), offers the quintessence of French cuisine. It's not cheap, but then you wouldn't expect it to be. A short block from Piccadilly, the restaurant attracts Londoners with bowlers and briefcases, as well as numerous well-heeled visiting French diners. The atmosphere is traditional, without ostentation. Pillars with mirrors reflect the dark walls in discreet lighting. There's a relaxing atmosphere with a touch of elegance. On the right of the menu, there is a prix-fixe luncheon choice for £12.75 ($19.13). A set dinner is offered for £16.50 ($24.75). Otherwise, expect to spend about £26 ($39) and up for an à la carte meal. Singled out for special praise are the coquilles St-Jacques (scallops baked in their shells), the crêpe de volaille (poultry) princess, and the boeuf en croûte (filet of beef cooked in pastry and served with truffle sauce). The veal served in a delicate wine sauce is outstanding. There is a good selection of desserts, including soufflé aux liqueurs and gâteau fromage. Sunday dinner hours are from 7 to 10:30 p.m. Weekday hours are from 12:30 to 3 p.m. and from 6:30 to 11:30 p.m. No lunch is served on Saturday or Sunday. Tube: Piccadilly Circus.

PICCADILLY CIRCUS: Garish, neon, crowded, but exciting Piccadilly Circus keeps time with the heartbeat of a mighty city. Here, from all sections of the city, come the aristocrat, the housewife, the revolutionary, the government official, the secretary, the pimp, the financier. They converge around the statue of Eros.

Much of your London activity will center here, so finding the right restaurant is important, as many establishments are unabashed tourist traps or sleazy joints. The following restaurants have been selected not only for the quality of their food but because they offer the best value for the money.

The Budget Range
Richoux of London, 172 Piccadilly, W.1 (tel. 493-2204), is a restaurant with a fresh clean decor, along with attractive serving girls in starched aprons and caps. Comfortable, well-arranged tables give a degree of privacy. It is open from 9 a.m. to 1 a.m., seven days a week.

Breakfast can be a simple juice and scrambled eggs or a big brunch-type meal. Throughout the day the waitresses serve omelets. House specialties are steak-and-kidney pie and a chicken-and-mushroom vol-au-vent. There's also a variety of well-stuffed sandwiches, everything from club to smoked salmon.

Afternoon tea sees hot scones brought out, along with strawberry jam and freshly whipped cream. Pastries from the trolley include a chocolate fudge cake. All prices include VAT, but service is extra. The smallest tab is likely to be £2.50 ($3.75), although, depending on what you order, you can spend from £8 ($12) for a big meal here. There are several Richoux of London restaurants. One is on South Audley Street. Tube: Piccadilly Circus.

The Granary, Albemarle Street, W.1 (tel. 493-2978), is open from 10 a.m. to mid-evening, serving throughout this time a good variety of hot dishes, all of which have a real home-cooked flavor. For prices £ranging from 2 ($3) to £4.20 ($6.30), you can order such dishes as stuffed avocado with spinach, prawns, and cheese. Salads are also available. Everything can be taken in foil containers to eat elsewhere. (Remember, no VAT is charged for food carried away.) A number of desserts and homemade cakes are offered, including crème brûlée and tipsy cake. A meal averages £5 ($7.50), including a glass of wine. Tube: Piccadilly Circus.

Hard Rock Café, 150 Old Park Lane, W.1 (tel. 629-0382), is a down-home southern-cum-midwestern funky American roadside diner with good food at reasonable prices, a loud jukebox, and service with a smile. Almost every night there is a line waiting to get in, as this is one of the most popular places in town with young people. It is also the favorite of visiting rock stars, film stars, and tennis players from America. They give generous portions of all their food items, and the price of a main dish comes with not only a salad but fries.

Naturally, you can get corn on the cob, and their specialties include a smokehouse steak, filet mignon, and a T-bone special. They also do char-broiled burgers and, in winter only, hot chili. Their dessert menu is equally tempting, including homemade apple pie, thick cold shakes, and "real American homemade country ice cream." There is also a good selection of beer. They are open seven days a week from noon to 1 a.m., charging from £6 ($9) and up for a meal. Naturally, if you order one of the beef specialties, you'll pay far more. Tube: Green Park or Hyde Park Corner.

LEICESTER SQUARE: Named for the Earl of Leicester, and once the site of the home of Sir Joshua Reynolds, Leicester Square has since become the movie center of London. The 19th-century square is a congested area of stores, theaters, movie houses, even churches. It also has some inexpensive restaurants and pubs (popular with West End actors) in its little offshoot lanes and alleyways.

The Medium-Priced Range

London Swiss Centre Restaurant, New Coventry Street, W.1 (tel. 734-1291), is a showcase restaurant complex where Switzerland wins friends and influences palates. Opened in 1968 and dedicated to bettering people-to-people relationships between England and Switzerland, this group of restaurants prepares Swiss cuisine with consummate skill.

It is managed by a Swiss, Mr. Baumann, who claims that the Rendez-Vous has the best coffee in town, a special blend from Switzerland. Suitable for lunch or afternoon tea, they serve 100% chopped beef steaks known as Toggenburgers, as well as steak tartare. You can also try one of their cakes, as they have their own bakery and pâtisserie. All the food is made and prepared right on the premises.

The Taverne offers both Swiss and Italian dishes, including the famed air-dried beef from the Grisons and the Engadine. They also serve the celebrated raclette Valaisanne and other regional dishes.

The Locanda is the newest restaurant, specializing in fondues, ranging from traditional to Chinese to chocolate. Last orders go in here at midnight. There is also a serve-yourself salad bar.

The Chesa is the most expensive dining room, offering such dishes as minced veal served with rösti potatoes. The cookery here is creative, the service excellent. The Imbiss is a self-service coffee bar.

In such a complex, meals are naturally wide-ranging in price, beginning at £2.50 ($3.75) for a quick lunch but going up to around £10 ($15) for an average meal. At the Chesa, however, you can spend far more, with meals beginning at £15 ($22.50). Tube: Leicester Square or Piccadilly Circus.

J. Sheekey Ltd., 29–31 St. Martin's Court, W.C.2 (tel. 240-2565), is an 1896 restaurant and an art nouveau oyster bar that over the years has been a gathering place for show people (autographed celebrity photos on the wall). Trying to get a table may make you feel like a salmon going upstream, but it's worth it. Sheekey serves a pre- and after-theater meal. For a beginning, I suggest the terrine de poisson. Naturally, the chef features jellied eels. Most fish dishes are either grilled or poached. A complete meal will cost from £18 ($27) to £25 ($37.50), more if you order lobster and wine, £7 ($10.50) per bottle. The restaurant is open Monday through Saturday from 12:30 to 3 p.m. and from 5:30 to 11:30 p.m. It faces the stage doors of the Albury and Wyndham's theaters. Tube: Leicester Square.

Manzi's, 1–2 Leicester St., off Leicester Square, W.C.2 (tel. 734-0224), is London's oldest seafood restaurant. Here you can get that jellied eel you've heard so much about, or else real Dover sole that overflows your platter. This lively Soho seafood restaurant doesn't waste much effort on decor, but the fish is fresh and it's proved so reliable that a loyal clientele has patronized Manzi's for years. Perhaps the waiters aren't English any more, but otherwise the recipes are much the same. You can begin with a prawn cocktail or perhaps half a dozen Whitstable oysters. Recently I sampled the legendary jellied eels, and I also enjoy the fresh sardines and crab salad. Other recommendable courses include the Dover sole and grilled turbot. You can dine well for about £18 ($27), including the house wine. If you don't prefer the ground-floor restaurant, then you can ask to go up to the Cabin Room on the next floor. Hours are from 12:30 to 2:40 p.m. and from 5:30 till 11:45 p.m. Tube: Leicester Square.

ON THE STRAND: In another major geographic and tourist center, the Strand, you can have a nostalgic taste of American cuisine.

The Medium-Priced Range

Joe Allen's, 13 Exeter St., W.C.2 (tel. 836-0651), has invaded London with his red-checked tablecloths and spinach salad, not to mention barbecued ribs and bowls of chili. Londoners, of course, by now are long familiar with American invasions, so Mr. Allen didn't create a revolution. The decor is actually an improvement on its New York namesake, the London restaurant appearing more openly inviting. I even enjoy the food better in the English eatery. The food is solid, reliable, uninspired, but on the other hand rarely disappointing. Try the familiar specialties: black bean soup, barbecued ribs, the regular spinach salad, a bowl of chili, calf liver and onions, steak, and the really tasty pecan pie. Expect to spend at least £7

($10.50) to £12 ($18). The items of the day are listed on a blackboard menu. Naturally, show business posters adorn the walls. Service is by friendly waiters and waitresses who just may be out-of-work actors and actresses. The guests are often people connected with the world of the theater and attracts after-theater crowds. Joe Allen's is open until 1 a.m. every day (till midnight on Sunday). The bar closes from 3 to 5:30 p.m. (from 2 to 7 p.m. on Sunday). Tube: The Strand.

The Budget Range

Lyons Corner House, 450 The Strand, W.C.2 (tel. 930-9381), is a whisper from the past. Once Lyons Corner Houses were much more prominent, having fed hungry Londoners for decades. This white-fronted place with gold trimmings offers a wide variety of fast food and traditional English dishes at reasonable prices. Meals are served by a new generation of waitresses known, as their predecessors were, as "Nippies," for the way they get around among the tables. Dressed in black frocks and natty white aprons, they serve hamburgers and brunches in the coffeeshop on the ground floor, along with soft drinks, tea, or coffee throughout the day.

The Garden Restaurant serves more substantial meals, including steak-and-kidney pie and fried fish and chips. In the evening they offer a set Dine and Wine menu when £7.50 ($11.25) will buy you a cocktail, dinner, and a quarter bottle of wine. The establishment is open from 10 a.m. to 8 p.m. daily. Alcoholic drinks can only be served during licensing hours. Tube: The Strand.

COVENT GARDEN: In 1970 London's flower, fruit, and veg market celebrated its 300th anniversary. But Auld Lang Syne should have been the theme song that day, as the historic, congested market was transferred in 1974 to a $7.2-million, 64-acre site at Nine Elms, in the suburb of Vauxhall, 2½ miles away, across the Thames.

Covent Garden dates from the time when the monks of Westminster Abbey dumped their surplus home-grown vegetables there. In 1670 Charles II granted the Earl of Bedford the right to "sell roots and herbs, whatsoever" in the district. The king's mistress, Nell Gwynne, once peddled oranges on Drury Lane (and later appeared on the stage of the **Drury Lane Theatre).**

Before that, in the 1630s, Inigo Jones designed the square. He hoped to complete a plaza in the Florentine style, but the work on it got bogged down. Even his self-tabbed handsomest barn in England, **St. Paul's Covent Garden,** burned down in the late 18th century and was subsequently rebuilt. The English actress, Dame Ellen Terry (noted in particular for her letters to G. B. Shaw), is buried there, incidentally. St. Paul's eastern face looks down on the market where Pygmalion's Professor Higgins met his "squashed cabbage leaf," Eliza Doolittle.

On the wall of St. Paul's Church is a carving commemorating the first performance in England of Punch's Puppet Show, witnessed in 1662 by Samuel Pepys. Nowadays there are often guitarists, flautists, and violinists busking and just playing in the area for their own pleasure, generally the center of an admiring crowd. Close to the **Punch and Judy pub** there are also conjurers, jugglers, and escape artists trying their latest illusions and tricks on the passersby. In the Punch and Judy, a good warm lunch of lamb provençale with rice, savory mince and mushroom pie, or steak casserole will cost under £2.50 ($3.75).

Also in the area is the **Royal Opera House** on Bow Street, housing the Royal Ballet and the Royal Opera Company. On nearby Russell Street, Samuel Johnson met his admirer, Boswell, and coffeehouses in the district were once patronized by Addison and Steele. Just as chicly dressed people once flocked to Les Halles in Paris to have onion soup, so London revelers used to drop in at Covent Garden's pubs to drink with Cockney barrow boys in the early dawn hours. The tradition will be sadly missed.

Covent Garden has now been turned into a commercial and entertainment district, complete with restaurants, hotels, and a convention center. Conservationists won a major battle in 1973, when the Department of Environment ruled that 250 buildings near the market site be preserved as historic, plus 80 already designated. What Londoners set out to achieve was something like the preserved character of Bourbon Street in New Orleans.

An old cabbage warehouse was reopened as the Jubilee Market. Monday is the antique market, and Saturday and Sunday are the days of a crafts market. Cockney costermongers (vegetable traders) have moved in in force, including Barry Teeden, the fastest apple polisher in the business, and Ginger Hurd, purveyor of jellied eels.

There are new exclusive clubs here, such as the **Zanzibar** and the **Rock Garden**. The **Blitz** offers snacks, and **Brahms and Liszt** offers drinks.

And the area has begun to attract art galleries, such as the Acme, the Hammond Lloyd, the Covent Garden, and the William Drummond. A new plant shop, the Neal Street, specializes in Chinese vases used as planters.

It's appropriate that art galleries should be returning to Covent Garden. In the 18th century it was a beehive of artists, including Lely and Kneller (famous portrait painters, the latter of whom is buried at St. Paul's Church, around the corner). Others who lived here were Thornhill, Richard Wilson, Fuseli, Daniel Mytens, the sculptor Roubiliac, Zoffany, and Flaxman. The American painter Benjamin West also lived here after he got out of jail for trying to study in London during the Revolution.

The Upper Bracket

Inigo Jones, 14 Barrick St. (tel. 836-6456), is one of the lights of Covent Garden, and although it has been around for some 17 years it's better than ever. It occupies a former stained-glass studio, but some of the carvings and stained glass have been removed, making the place more garden-like than ecclesiastical. The banquettes and chairs are now in a brick color, and the waiters are dressed in black trousers, white shirt, black tie, and white apron.

But what has made the restaurant such a renewed success is the cookery of the chef de cuisine, Paul Gayler, formerly of the Dorchester Hotel. I can't recommend any specialties, because he depends for his inspiration on the daily offerings of the market place. However, I will cite only some dishes enjoyed in the past to give you an idea: a minestrone of frog legs with fresh herbs, a salad of smoked rabbit with its own liver and kidney (served with a sweet orange vinaigrette), a light ragoût of salmon and mussels with cucumbers and a delicate dill sauce, a roast saddle of lamb with honey and sesame (served with a sherry vinegar sauce), or perhaps a saddle of hare with a walnut and celery cream sauce. The selection of sorbets is often flavored with bay leaf, thyme, cinnamon, and clove.

Hours are Monday to Friday from 12:30 to 2:30 p.m. and from 6 to 11:30 p.m. (on Saturday, from 6 to 11:30 p.m. only). It is best to telephone for a reservation. Count on spending around £26 ($39) to £29 ($43.50) per person with wine. Tube: Covent Garden.

Boulestin, 25 Southampton St., W.C.2 (tel. 836-7061). This famous old restaurant, founded by Marcel Boulestin, the first Fleet Street restaurant critic, more than half a century ago has had a facelift. It's reached by a side door that leads down into the basement beneath a bank. Kevin Kennedy, who is both the manager and the chef, is one of the new British-bred cuisine experts who has style, flair, and imagination in the kitchen. He has brought new life to the place.

The chandeliers are still there, and the menu still has many of the old Boulestin dishes, including crab with artichaut, coquilles St-Jacques, and magret de canard. You might also try the tulipe de sorbets maison. But Mr. Kennedy is also free to experiment—and he does so every week, much to the pleasure of his guests.

He offers a set lunch for £16.60 ($24.75), but, be warned, dinner could run as high as £30 ($45) per person, including some wine. The restaurant is open from 12:30 to 2:30 p.m. and from 7 to 11:15 p.m. It is closed for lunch on Saturday, all day Sunday, on bank holidays, and during most of the month of August. Tube: Covent Garden.

The Medium-Priced Range

Poons of Covent Garden, 41 King St., W.C.2 (tel. 240-1743), is one of the best Chinese restaurants in London. The place is run by Wai-Lim (Bill) and his wife, Cecilia Poon. Mr. Poon's great-great-grandfather cooked for the Chinese emperors, and succeeding generations of the family have all interested themselves in traditional Chinese cookery. The decor is reminiscent of *The World of Suzie Wong*. Tables surround an island see-through kitchen, which has been the subject of some controversy. I personally like it, as it's fascinating to stand and watch the chefs go through their intricate steps. The house specializes in wind-dried meat, including sausage, which is quite different in flavor from smoked. Two of the most recommendable courses include Poons special crispy duck and Poons special wind-dried meat with seasonal greens. For a beginning, you might select the sharkfin broth or the bird's-nest soup. Other preferred specialties include Poons special crispy chicken (one half) and sweet-and-sour pork based on an original recipe.

If you're a serious and dedicated gourmet of the Chinese cuisine, as are many people these days, you'll find Poons willing to provide you with some rare and delectable specialties, providing you give them 24 hours' notice. Ever had stewed duck's feet with fish lips? Cecilia Poon is usually on hand to explain the niceties of the menu and to discuss the ingredients of any particular dish. They also do a set lunch at £13 ($19.50) for two persons, £19 ($28.50) for three persons, or £25 ($37.50) for four diners. An à la carte dinner costs £15 ($22.50). The restaurant is open from noon to midnight daily except Sunday. Tube: Covent Garden.

Rules, 35 Maiden Lane, off the Strand, W.C.2 (tel. 836-5314), dates back to 1798 when it made its debut as an oyster bar. Over its long and legendary history, it has been the steady haunt of actors and actresses, newspaper columnists, and barristers. In the Gay '90s, the Prince of Wales (later Edward VII) was its most famous patron, accompanied, as always, by the Jersey Lillie. The prince dined on the second floor, now the Edward VII Room. Pictures of Lillie hang in the alcove where they used to sit. Another alcove honors Charles Dickens, who used to dine and do some of his writing at Rules. The restaurant is under the care of John Shrimpton.

You enter via the front bar, with its red plush settees. The walls are hung with cartoons George Whitelaw did in the '20s and '30s. Rules specializes in dishes such as jugged hare, grilled Dover sole, grouse, steak, and kidney pie, and Rules duckling, the latter served for two persons. In season, hare soup is a specialty. Apple and blackberry pie with fresh cream makes a good finish. Meals begin at £15 ($22.50) per person, plus the cost of your drink. Reservations are important, and a pretheater dinner is available between 6 and 7:30 p.m. Rules is open for lunch and dinner Monday to Friday, and dinner only on Saturday. The restaurant is closed on Sunday and bank holidays. Tube: Covent Garden.

Tuttons, 11–12 Russell St., W.C.2 (tel. 836-1167), sits on the side of Covent Garden's piazza with wide windows overlooking the square and the Opera House. The restaurant has stone floors and clean wooden tables. It has an adjoining bar which is open from 9 a.m. for breakfast, coffee, and fresh croissants. The restaurant itself opens for lunch at noon and remains open for tea and dinner, with the last orders going in at 11:30 p.m. The atmosphere is informal and businesslike, the service quick and cheery. In the summer, when there are lots of tables placed outside, you can also dine al fresco.

Appetizers include a homemade pâté, baked brie with almonds, and a smoked salmon mousse. Main courses are likely to feature steak-and-kidney pie, a game pie and salad, spiced chicken kebab, and salmon trout mayonnaise. Omelets are also served, as well as hamburgers. A dessert specialty is crème brûlée. Meals begin at £9 ($13.50), plus the cost of your drink.

Downstairs is another restaurant, serving the same menu in surroundings that are quieter and more comfortable. It's best to reserve a table for dinner, as it can fill up easily.

Tuttons is open seven days a week (noon on Sunday) until the last orders go in. Tube: Covent Garden.

The Budget Range

Penny's Place, 6 King St., W.C.2 (tel. 836-4553), is a wine and food bar in an old Victorian pub still with the mirrors and the antique mahogany woodwork. Snacks include various pâtés, crab, taramasalata, crab vol-au-vents, liver in orange and white wine sauce, garlic mushrooms, and cous-cous at £2 ($3) to £3 ($4.50). There is a wide selection of wines, a glass costing around 85p ($1.28). The place is open from 11 a.m. to 3 p.m. and from 5:30 to 11 p.m. Closed Sunday. There is live music on Friday and Saturday nights. Tube: Covent Garden.

Calabash Restaurant, 38 King St., W.C.2 (tel. 836-1976), is the only African restaurant in London, underneath the Africa Centre. A simply furnished place with a bar, it has an informal atmosphere. Dishes from all over Africa are offered, with fish and chicken a specialty. The menu changes weekly. For an appetizer, you may be given a choice of pepperpot soup with bread, delice de Calabash (avocado, coconut, and black-eyed beans), or mashy, an Egyptian stuffed green pepper. Main courses come in a wide variety, each tempting. Kuku wa kupake (chicken cooked in coconut cream) is a dish from Zanzibar. Nyama yo phika, from Malawi, is beef stew with sweet peppers and potatoes. I like egusi, a Nigerian beef stew with melon seeds, spinach, and dried shrimps, as well as gombiona (fish, spinach in palm oil, and rice). A good dessert is ananas flambé au rhum (pineapple fritter flambeed in rum). A complete meal will cost from £6 ($9) up. The restaurant is open Monday to Friday from noon to 3 p.m. and from 6:30 to 11 p.m., on Saturday from 6:30 to 11 p.m. Closed Sunday. Tube: Covent Garden.

READER'S RESTAURANT SELECTION: "Food for Thought, 31 Neal St., W.C.2 (tel. 836-0239), is a small place with inexpensive vegetarian food. Better go at odd hours—perhaps in the middle of the afternoon. Otherwise, it's likely to be crowded. Everybody ends up sitting with and often talking with everybody else. It's most congenial. The establishment is a basement café in the heart of the theater and movie district. From the Covent Garden tube station, walk along Neal Street toward Shaftesbury Avenue. The restaurant will be in the second block on the left. It's open Monday through Friday from noon to 8 p.m. The price of a meal for two is around £8 ($12)" (Vicki Banks, London, England).

HIGH HOLBORN: In "legal London," you can join barristers, solicitors, and law clerks at the following recommendation.

The Budget Range

My Old Dutch, 132 High Holborn, W.C.1 (tel. 242-5200), is a cheerful, friendly place, resembling a Dutch kitchen with scrubbed pine tables at which you can be served 101 different pancakes—all enormous—on huge Delft plates. Fillings and garnishes include cheese, meats, and vegetables, as well as sweet fillings such as Adam's Downfall—that is, figs and avocado. The cost of an average meal is around £5 ($7.50) at lunchtime, £6 ($9) in the evening. If you don't want a pancake, you can order a cold platter of meat and a salad. Fresh ground coffee and hot chocolate are available to wash it all down. My Old Dutch stays open from noon to midnight Sunday through Wednesday, and noon to 1 a.m. on Thursday, Friday, and Saturday. Tube: Holborn.

WESTMINSTER: Our dining expedition to Westminster begins in one of London's famous fish houses:

The Medium-Priced Range

Bumbles, 16 Buckingham Palace Rd., S.W.1 (tel. 828-2903), gives you a chance to dine just 300 yards from Buckingham Palace. John D. Forbes places emphasis on cooking originality, above-average but moderately priced food, and gracious service by young women once described as "very sweet." There is a full wine list, including English wines, from £5 ($7.50), including VAT. The staff will make menu suggestions. Serving hours are Monday to Friday from noon to 2:15 p.m. and from 6 p.m. to midnight (last orders at 10:30 p.m.). Saturday hours are from 6:30 p.m., with the last orders placed at 10:30 p.m. The restaurant is closed all day Sunday and on bank holidays.

Bumbles soup of the day is invariably good, and there's a large selection of main courses. On my most recent visit I enjoyed a leg of lamb stuffed with mushrooms, onions, and rosemary, then roasted and cut into steaks, caramelized with red-currant jelly and served with sauteed potatoes and cauliflower. Count on spending from £15 ($22.50) up. Tube: Victoria Station.

Pomegranates, 94 Grosvenor Rd., S.W.1 (tel. 828-6560). The owner of this basement restaurant, Patrick Gwynn-Jones, has traveled far and collected dishes from throughout the world. Asian and Indonesian delicacies vie for a place on the menu with European dishes, spiced pickled salmon with sweet mustard sauce, leg of lamb with herbs, veal kidneys deviled lightly. The decor is purely European—soft amber lights, mirrors, and well-laid tables. Bread is baked fresh twice a day, and vegetables are cooked when fresh, adding to the pleasure of a good meal. You should get away for about £20 ($30) a person, including wine, but if you start in on the more exotic dishes or the luscious desserts—grapefruit and gin sorbet, honey and brandy ice cream—it will probably cost more. The place is open for lunch from 12:30 to 2:15 p.m. Monday to Friday, and for dinner from 7:30 to 11:15 p.m. Monday to Saturday. There is a very good wine list and some reasonable house wines. A set lunch of three courses costs from £10 ($15), excluding wines. It's best reached by taxi.

The Budget Range

Slinky, 49–51 Whitehall, S.W.1 (tel. 930-9877). Walk down Whitehall from Trafalgar Square for a couple of hundred yards and, on the left, next to the Clarence pub, you will find a bright new place for the diet-conscious. Pat Gibbon is the lively manager of London's first quick-food restaurant for the dieter. It is open from 9 a.m. to 8 p.m. seven days a week, serving a wide selection of hot dishes and salads. These include filets of sole stuffed with artichoke hearts and mushrooms, boned breast of chicken baked in a spicy sauce, a hot dish of the day, and salads made from seasonal produce. Portions are carefully controlled for quantity, quality, and calorie content, and random samples are regularly checked. The place is pleasantly decorated, with potted plants and blue chairs and tables. You order and pay at one end of the cash "tills" as you enter, then select your table. Your food is served immediately. At the end, you receive a printout of the calories consumed. Meals begin at £5 ($7.50). Tube: Trafalgar Square.

BELGRAVIA: Belgravia after dark used to be a gastronomic wilderness. Happily, that situation has changed.

The Medium-Priced Range

Drones, 1 Pont St., S.W.1 (tel. 235-9638), was labeled by one newspaper columnist the "unofficial club for the bright people, at least half of whom seem to know each other." David Niven & Friends launched this two-floor restaurant, and its reputation for charm and chic has long ago spread. Reservations are imperative, preferably a day in advance. There's no elaborate menu, no fancy sauces, just simple but good food. At lunch have the Droneburger, a favorite. For dinner, the calf liver with bacon is delicious (have it cooked pink if you prefer). As an appetizer, the chef's pâté poivre vert is worthy. A main-dish specialty is the chili. My heartiest recommendation goes to the sole à la Drones with prawns and truffles. Hot apple pie and fresh pineapple vie for your attention in the dessert department. The menu is wisely limited, and it never changes, although plats du jour are featured. A meal, not including wine selection, costs from £12 ($18).

You sit on bentwood armchairs with green velvet cushions at white wrought-iron tables. The simple white walls are perfect foils for oil paintings and framed copies of children's comics and magazines. Try to get a table downstairs. If you're lingering in the bar while waiting for a table (a likely possibility), take a look at the collection of movie-star photos. But John Wayne as a baby is hardly recommended as an appetizer! Open seven days a week, Drones serves lunch from 12:30 to 3 p.m. and dinner from 7:30 p.m. to midnight. Tube: Sloane Square.

Papillon, at the Chelsea Holiday Inn, Sloane Street, S.W.1 (tel. 235-4377), is a restaurant built around the pool. In good weather the clear roof rolls back for al fresco eating. Around the pool are bamboo tables and chairs. A piano player entertains in the evening and on Sunday from noon to 4 p.m., when those who come to eat and drink may also use the pool free. A wide menu of appetizers is offered, then omelets, lasagne, or spaghetti. Steaks and grills are served with french fries, baked or croquette potatoes, or rice. A mixed grill Chelsea is a specialty.

If this is all too much for you, hamburgers are also served. Sandwiches, too, are filling, and you can have a very ample snack meal, a club sandwich, steak sandwich, or buck rarebit (cheese with fried egg on top). Ordering à la carte is likely to cost you from £8 ($12) to £18 ($27). In addition, there is a buffet from which you can choose as much as you like for £12.50 ($18.75), including a glass of wine. There is always a roast, plus two other hot dishes, cold meats, pies, and salads. The place is fully licensed and specializes in an impressive list of cocktails and apéritifs. All prices include VAT and service. Tube: Sloane Square.

KNIGHTSBRIDGE–BROMPTON ROAD: After splurging at the high-priced shops of Knightsbridge, these choices will make you feel better:

The Medium-Priced Range

Shezan, 16 Cheval Pl., off Montpelier Street, S.W.7 (tel. 589-7918), is generally considered the finest Pakistani restaurant in London, and I heartily concur. In a cul-de-sac behind Harrods, this brick-and-tile establishment in Kensington turns out exquisite dishes from its clay tandoor ovens. By all means, order murgh tikka lahori (marinated tandoori chicken), which is usually served slightly pink and is delicious. Another specialty is bhuna gosht (lamb cooked with tomatoes and spices). Tandoori charcoal barbecues and grills are always featured, as are kebabs. The tandoori breads are excellent, especially roti, a dark whole-wheat bread. Expect to spend from £18 ($27) for a complete meal. The restaurant is one of the most sophisticated in the city, and the service is flawless. Lunch is from noon to 3 p.m. and dinner from 7 p.m. to midnight. Closed Sunday and bank holidays. Tube: Knightsbridge.

In a small street, just off Knightsbridge, the **Upper Crust,** 9 William St., S.W.1 (tel. 235-8444), is a modest, simply decorated country sort of place with bare brick walls, wheel-back chairs, and warm lights. Pies, rather obviously, are the house specialty, and they are served filled with steak and giblets, savory chicken, curried fish, and a magnificent steak and pickled walnut. Main dishes are accompanied by fresh country bread and herb butter, plus a selection of fresh seasonal vegetables. Cold dishes with salads are also available. Puddings have a definitely old-world air, including traditional plum with custard or Yorkshire pudding with mincemeat. A three-course meal, including cover charge, a glass of wine, and coffee, is around £11.50 ($17.25). Before you begin your shopping or sightseeing trip, you can come here to feast on a full English breakfast of fresh orange juice, bacon, fried or scrambled eggs, toast, and coffee, all for £3.50 ($5.25), or a continental breakfast of croissants and tea or coffee, at £1.80 ($2.70). Devonshire cream teas with scones, jam, and cream cost £1.75 ($2.63). All food is homemade in the Upper Crust's bakery. The Franks family, who own and run the place, have a secret in that Mr. Franks also owns the superbly entitled butchershop, Wainwright and Daughter. Naturally, they select meat of prime quality for their restaurant showcase. Hours are 10 a.m. to 11:15 p.m., Monday to Saturday. On Sunday, hours are only from 6 to 11 p.m. Tube: Knightsbridge.

Paper Tiger, 10 and 12 Exhibition Rd., S.W.7 (tel. 584-3737). The dishes here are Szechuan rather than Peking cuisine, more spiced and beginning to be closer to Malaysian dishes than the blander Japanese ones. At Ricky Cheung's basement restaurant in South Kensington, you can order a Szechuan feast. Dishes include "bang-bang" sesame chicken salad, pickle soup, prawns, pork and peppers, chili chicken, and bamboo shoots. A less piquant Peking feast for the same price includes duck with trimmings, sweet-and-sour pork, chicken and almonds, fried dumplings, and hot-and-sour soup.

There is an extensive à la carte menu of reasonably priced dishes— spicey soups, entrees such as seaspice chicken shreds with peppers, chicken with yellow bean sauce and almonds, and lemon chicken. Vegetable dishes include stir-fried bean sprouts and Mother-Ma's hot pork mince and bean curd. Toffee apples and bananas are the featured desserts, followed by Chinese tea or coffee.

Lunchtimes they have platters—pork loin slices, meat and noodles, sweet-and-sour pork, beef slices and spring onions. In the off-season, they have a gourmet winter menu, including a sharp Chinese salad, a fish dish, spring rolls and wonton, three meat dishes (chicken, pork, and lamb), vegetables, rice, and a dessert. You should go there to sample the house specialty, aromatic crispy duck with pancakes, hoisin, and cucumber, or with green ginger and spring onions. A set lunch or dinner costs £10 ($15) for two persons. Ordering à la carte will run about £15 ($22.50) per person. Lunch is served Saturday and Sunday only from noon to 2:30 p.m.; dinner daily from 7 p.m. to 1 a.m. Tube: South Kensington.

The Budget Range

Harveys at the Top, the rooftop restaurant above Harvey Nichols store, S.W.1 (tel. 235-5000, ext. 149 for table reservations), is a light, airy place among the rooftops of Knightsbridge. In summer you can eat in the open air, but there is also a large restaurant inside. The day starts with an English breakfast at 9:30 a.m., costing £5.50 ($8.25), or just tea or coffee at about 75p ($1.13). The staff serves morning coffee, luncheon, and then afternoon tea until 5:30 p.m. when the store closes (6:30 p.m. on Wednesday).

There is a selection of appetizers, then you choose your main dish from the long buffet of hot dishes or from the salad table. The meal ends with dessert or cheese and coffee. The cost is around £10.50 ($15.75). They also do a real old cream tea for £3.50 ($5.25), with homemade scones, strawberry jam, and clotted Devon cream to revive the flagging shopper. Waitresses offer pleasant service in this nice atmosphere. It's rather Knightsbridge and British. Tube: Knightsbridge.

KENSINGTON: If Meg didn't ask you to stay to dinner at Kensington Palace, you'll be just as happy with:

The Medium-Priced Range

Flanagans, 11 Kensington High St., W.8 (tel. 937-2519), recaptures the splendor of turn-of-the century dining. One of London's bounciest restaurants, it offers bountiful food in a fun-loving atmosphere. It's a trip back through the years to a world of handlebar mustaches, cut-velvet walls, a honky-tonk piano player, gas lights, sawdust on the floor —and the inevitable sing-alongs. All the Florrie Forde favorites are aired here, everything from "Has Anybody Seen Kelly?" to "Flanagan" itself.

The pièce de résistance is Lobster Lillie Langtry, Edward VII's favorite. The shelled lobster is sauteed in chablis with tarragon and thyme and covered with a piquant cream sauce, then sprinkled with parmesan cheese and grilled. The Dover sole is so huge it extends over the edges of your plate; it is accompanied by a large helping of french fries. For an adventure in old English fare, order the homemade game pie, with mashed potatoes, and perhaps a side dish of pease pudding, for those who want to go Cockney all the way. A large dish of Irish stew, big enough for two, is a popular item, or you may prefer tripe or jellied eels. For an appetizer, there's an order of cockles, and for dessert, the original golden sponge pudding. A three-course meal, with a half liter of wine, costs less than £10 ($15). The original Flanagans is at 100 Baker St., W.1 (tel. 935-0287). Both are open from noon to 3 p.m. and from 6 p.m. to midnight, daily. Just mind your manners, and "Please Do Not Expectorate." It is advisable to make a reservation. Tube: High Street Kensington.

The Budget Range

Fu Tong, 29 Kensington High St., W.8 (tel. 937-1293). On recommendation I tried Mr. Shin Syn Chin's delightful Chinese restaurant and found it to be, in my opinion, one of the best in town. The comfortable booths offer a great degree of privacy. However, the bell button on your table will bring the waiter in a moment. Hot towels come between courses, and when you become a regular, you will be presented with your own chop-sticks engraved with your name. The cuisine is Cantonese/Peking style, and all the usual dishes are available. If you want Peking duck or another complicated dish, order it when you reserve your table or you'll have to wait when you arrive. The average meal begins at £8 ($12). It is open seven days a week from noon to 11:30 p.m. Tube: High Street Kensington.

SOUTH KENSINGTON: When you're exhausted from South Kensington's museums, try a feast at the following:

The Upper Bracket

Eleven Park Walk, 11 Park Walk, S.W.10 (tel. 352-3449), is a high-key, airy, two-level restaurant, with a winding staircase for "entrances." Coming down that staircase nightly is a bevy of chic Londoners, including many from the art, fashion, and photographic worlds. A smart establishment, modern and beautiful, it is a haven for the sophisticated and glamorous. In addition to being seen, you can also order some good food. Even the service is friendly.

The restaurant's owners, Signors Zanelleto, Movio, and Livesi, serve mainly Italian dishes, beginning with minestrone primavera, and a number of good pasta dishes, principally taglierini verdi. Fish specialties include calamari fritti and sea bass with herbs. Main meat courses include roast baby chicken, bollito misto with green sauce, quail cooked in white wine, saltimbocca, and calf liver veneziana. For dessert, try crêpes soaked in Tía Maria. A three-course meal, including half a liter of wine, goes for £20 ($30) per person and up. Hours are from 12:30 to 3 p.m. and 7 p.m. to midnight. Closed Sunday. It's best reached by taxi.

The Medium-Priced Range

Chanterelle, 119 Old Brompton Rd., S.W.7 (tel. 373-5522), used to be a part of the South Kensington Public Library. But times have changed. The smell is not of old books, but of highly original English and continental cookery in a restrained setting of wood paneling. Fergus Provan, the owner, organizes the kitchen, while Darryl Coutts, the manager, oversees the upstairs. A set lunch weekdays goes for £6.50 ($9.75), £9.50 ($14.25) on Sunday. In the evening a set meal is £10 ($15). The luncheon menu changes every second day, the dinner listing every three weeks. A typical main course might be braised oxtail with red wine. They also serve game when it is in season. Desserts are luscious in flavor and texture. Wines are limited but well selected, the house wine going for £5 ($7.50). VAT is included in all prices. Chanterelle is open for lunch daily from noon to 2:30 p.m., for dinner from 7 to 11:30 p.m. Tube: South Kensington or Gloucester Road.

The Budget Range

Chompers, 2 Exhibition Rd., S.W.7 (tel. 589-8947), is probably the oldest established bistro in town. It boasts an art nouveau decor, but doesn't get lost in its stage setting. Chompers serves good food prepared on the premises at moderate prices, a meal costing from £12 ($18). Helpings are generous. You can order barbecued spare ribs, onion soup, and pâté maison. The main-course specialties include chicken ratatouille, kidneys in sherry, and trout with capers. Chompers sells a lot of filet steak. The chef's specialties are filet with stilton and garlic butter. Chompers is open for dinner from 6 p.m. to 1 a.m. Monday to Saturday (on Sunday from 6 p.m. to midnight), and for lunch seven days a week from noon to 2:30 p.m. On Sunday it offers lunch. Reservations at this fully licensed restaurant are recommended between 8 and 10:30 p.m. Tube: South Kensington.

ST. MARYLEBONE: In Mar-li-bone you're in for a treat when you visit:

The Medium-Priced Range

The **Baker & Oven,** 10 Paddington St., W.1 (tel. 935-5072), may be in an out-of-the-way neighborhood, but it's a big success—a little corner bakery, with a sales shop converted into a tavern with a genuine pub atmosphere. The neighborhood people mingle with the fashionable West End visitors. Meals are served in the cellar kitchens, attractively done in a rustic style. The very English food often pleases the most critical; the portions are enormous, the tabs moderate. With a bit of luck, you'll be given a bare wooden table in one of the brick cove-ceilinged nooks, the former ovens.

The onion soup is a fine beginning, as is the country pâté. For the main course, there are several good choices, including roast Aylesbury duckling with stuffing and applesauce and jugged hare with red currant jelly. All entrees include vegetables. For dessert, you can order a thoroughly English hot fruit pie and cream. Meals begin at £8 ($12), plus the cost of your drink. The restaurant is open Monday to Friday from noon to 3 p.m. and from 6:30 to 11 p.m. On Saturday, it's open only in the evenings. Tube: Baker Street.

NOTTING HILL GATE: From a gourmet treat to fish 'n' chips, your choice in this area is wide ranging.

The Upper Bracket

Leiths, 92 Kensington Park Rd., W.11 (tel. 229-4481). Prudence Leith, a lovely young woman from South Africa, has brought her culinary talents to the most unlikely Notting Hill Gate district of London, a few blocks from the Portobello Road Market and near the Portobello Hotel. Pru, as she is called, discovered "how good food could really be" when she worked as an *au pair* girl in a French family. In time, she studied at the Cordon Bleu in Paris and also at the Cordon Bleu in London. Nowadays she relies on her managing director, French-born Jean-Baptiste Reynaud, who was a chef by trade until joining her as a manager in 1973, to produce the menus and to maintain the established high quality, ably supported by the chef, John Armstrong. Like the Four Seasons in New York, there are four seasonal menus. A fixed-price meal costs £25 ($37.50), including service and VAT. One recent spring menu included such dishes as trout stuffed with chicken and ham, tarragon chicken, stuffed quail in pastry, and poached salmon with a hollandaise sauce. I especially like the pink breast of duck with lime and orange sauce. There is an ambitious wine list. To end your meal, you can make a selection from the dessert trolley, perhaps a ginger syllabub. The restaurant is open daily from 7:30 p.m. to midnight. Tube: Notting Hill Gate.

The Medium-Priced Range

Hungry Viking, 44 Ossington St., W.2 (tel. 727-3311), is a modern restaurant on a street of mews houses. You descend past flower-draped boxes into a Scandinavian parlor, where waitresses in national costume will help you select from a gigantic smörgåsbord for a set price of £9.50 ($14.25). It's called the traditional Viking table, and includes the usual array of delicacies, such as prawns, herring, smoked fish, aspics, salads, cheeses, and meats, both hot and cold. The salads are especially good. The amount of food you can eat is your own capacity. The restaurant is closed on Monday but open otherwise Tuesday to Saturday from 6:30 to 11:30 p.m. (on Sunday, 7 to 11 p.m.). Tube: Queensway or Notting Hill Gate.

The Budget Range

Geale's, 2 Farmer St., W.8 (tel. 727-7969), is worth the investment in a subway ride to the western part of London if you're seeking some of the best fish and chips in the English capital—all at prices for around £2.50 ($3.75). The fish is bought fresh daily, and it's not greasy as it is in most establishments in London. Cod, haddock, and plaice are the featured mainstays of the menu. This corner restaurant, at the end of a mews street, is owned by Christopher A. Geale, who is proud, and rightly so, of his offerings. The place is run on very informal lines, and is open Tuesday to Saturday from noon to 3 p.m. and from 6 to 11 p.m. Tube: Notting Hill Gate.

MAYFAIR: Stick a few extra pounds in your pocket and join the swells for a memorable meal in Mayfair (less expensive Mayfair restaurants coming up too):

The Upper Bracket

Trader Vic's, at the London Hilton on Park Lane, W.1 (tel. 493-7586), is a dream fulfilled for its founder, who set for himself a high culinary level. The restaurant specializes in "fantasy dishes" that satisfy one's romantic concept of what South Sea islands food tastes like. Trader Vic once said that if travelers were to sample the truly native food, nine times out of ten they would reject it as unpalatable to the Western taste. His dishes, therefore, reflect the cuisine of the Pacific area, including China, but are original creations. The atmosphere matches the culinary offerings, relying on a forest of bamboo, coconuts, native drums, masks, spears, cork floats, nets, and exotic shells—a successful melange.

The menu is divided into parts, including "at the beginning" Trader Vic's tidbits: fried prawns, spare ribs, crab Rangoon, and sliced pork. One of the house specialties is paper-thin filets of beef flambé. From the "lakes, rivers, and sea" come such selections as filet of Dover sole Trader Vic. The curry dishes are by now world renowned, including such susu (cream) specialties as lobster curry. A personal favorite is the pressed duck, steamed with delicate spices, then boned and shaped into cakes with water-chestnut flour, fried, and served with a spicy plum sauce and sprinkled with crushed almonds. "At the end," you're faced with such a bewildering choice that you may remain the rest of the evening, or else settle for coconut honey ice cream. Expect to spend from £20 ($30) up for a meal here.

Lunch is served from noon to 3 p.m.; dinner, 6:30 to midnight (the restaurant is closed for lunch on Saturday). A postscript: Try one of the exotic drinks, but be forewarned—their potency is hard to determine, as the wallop is hidden by the beguiling fruit juices. Tube: Marble Arch.

Langan's Brasserie, Stratton Street, W.1 (tel. 493-6437), has maintained its popularity since its opening in late 1976. Owned by restaurateur Peter Langan and actor Michael Caine, along with the chef de cuisine, Richard Shepherd, the café is reminiscent of a Parisian bistro. The walls are covered with pictures, and the combination of overhead fans and potted palms creates a 1930s atmosphere. A complete meal, including wine, VAT, and service, comes to about £18 ($27). The long menu always has a good choice of English dishes, such as kipper pâté and roast joints and pies, along with the classic French dishes. Live music is played during the dinner hour. Lunch is served Monday to Friday from 12:30 to 3 p.m. and dinner is offered from 7 p.m. to midnight Monday through Friday. On Saturday, hours are from 8 p.m. to 1 a.m., and the restaurant is closed on Sunday. Upstairs is a more intimate dining room with silver service, although prices are the same as downstairs. The Venetian decor was the work of Patrick Proctor, the artist. Tube: Green Park.

Bentley's, 11–15 Swallow St., W.1 (tel. 734-4756), is one of the most prestigious fish restaurants in London; tradition permeates the place. There's a certain type of Mayfair gentleman, with bowler and cane, who heads for Bentley's at sunset. There, standing at the shellfish bar, he slowly and deliberately downs one oyster after another, a ritual unchanged in years. Then he fades away, seemingly having no life before or after swallowing those oysters until he shows up the following evening.

This club-like restaurant is on a tiny street connecting Regent Street with Piccadilly (a three-minute walk from Piccadilly Circus). On the ground floor, you'll find the Oyster Bar, usually crowded with people feasting on the riches from Bentley's oyster beds near Colchester, Essex. Upstairs is a dining room filled with devotees of good fish dishes. A half dozen oysters seems to be everybody's favorite appetizer, although you may prefer the iced lobster soup, another house specialty. Every day of the week there's a different specialty from the chef. On Monday it might be sole Véronique, poached in white wine and garnished with grapes. You'll find other exciting menu selections from the scampi, scallop, lobster, mussel, plaice, trout, turbot, and sole families. Especially delectable is the Scottish salmon, grilled or poached, or the lobster thermidor.

The owner, Peter Bentley, keeps his place open for lunch from noon to 2:45 p.m. and for dinner from 6 to 10:30 p.m. On Saturday, hours are from 6 to 10 p.m.; the restaurant is closed on Sunday. Count on spending from £15 ($22.50) or more for a superb seafood dinner. Tube: Piccadilly Circus.

The Medium-Priced Range

Gaylord, 16 Albemarle St., W.1 (tel. 629-9802), has established an enviable reputation among local connoisseurs of Indian cuisine in spite of its relative youth—it just opened in 1974. An elegant Oriental atmosphere pervades the restaurant, creating an air of festive expectancy. The ornate hanging lamps, the gold-studded door, and the unusual glass ceiling imported from India set off the rich color scheme of royal purple and gold. And the delicacies on which you dine do not disappoint you.

So many regional dishes are available that one hardly knows where to begin. The restaurant features three different types of regional cooking: tandoori centers on the tandoor, an oven of Indian clay that is used for cooking foods while retaining the flavor and natural moisture. A good example of this cooking style is tandoori fish.

Mughlai cooking dates from the Moghul period of Indian history in which exotic dishes were prepared with rich combinations of spices. If you like curried foods, you may wish to try the chicken noor jehani, a chicken, minced lamb, and egg dish cooked in a thick curry sauce.

Kashmiri specialties frequently include combinations of lamb and yogurt, as exemplified in the roghan josh, pieces of lamb cooked alternately between smoking butter and beaten yogurt to develop a unique flavor. Vegetarian entrees are also available. As a dessert treat, try an Indian delicacy from the trolley. Meals cost from £10 ($15) up. The Gaylord is open daily for lunch and dinner. Tube: Green Park.

Coconut Grove, 3–5 Barrett St., W.1 (tel. 486-5269), is a bright, shiny restaurant at the end of St. Christopher's Place, just off Oxford Street. Upstairs you'll find a decor of brown wood and pink napery, along with green frondy plants. There are more seats downstairs, and in summer, tables tumble onto the pavement to accommodate tired and thirsty shoppers. Find a table or seat at the bar and relax with a margarita, a Mississippi Mule, or perhaps a Singapore Sling. For a long, frosty glass, you'll pay £3 ($4.50).

Then choose a meal from a bewildering list of dishes with an international flavor. Guacamole, eggs Benedict, and chili vie with deep-fried potato skins with sour cream and chives or brie baked in almonds and served with hot garlic bread. The dozen or so salads include Waldorf and Caesar, and the chef's salad is called "indescribable." A 12-ounce T-bone is another popular item, served with fries and the vegetable of the day. You might also select lamb kebab with tomatoes and onions, perhaps a hamburger. Desserts are luscious, including hot pecan pie and deep apple pie. Expect to spend from £10 ($15). VAT is included, but not service. The Grove is open seven days a week from noon to 1 a.m. Tube: Bond Street.

The Budget Range

Cranks Health Food Restaurant, Marshall Street, W.1 (tel. 437-9431), around the corner from Carnaby Street, took its name from "cranks." But instead of the colloquial meaning of an eccentric, impractical person, the restaurant defines the word as those "who have the courage to pursue a line of thinking against the general stream of orthodox belief." Their "line," by the way, is excellent—the best of homemade soups, fresh fruit salads, homemade fruit pies, pastries, and cakes, and breads made from wholemeal, compost-grown, stone-ground English flour. Meals cost from £5 ($7.50). Cranks became famous when it operated on Carnaby Street, and first drew its young health-conscious clientele. The food-reform restaurant even tempts full-fledged carnivores by its fresh-tasting selections—such as the mix-it-yourself salad platter at lunch. If you've got a small waist, you can order a bowl of choice salads from the main buffet counter, although if you've already lost the battle of the bulge, you may prefer a large bowl. Cranks serves the best tiger's milk and dandelion coffee in town. It's open Tuesday to Saturday from 10 a.m. to 11 p.m.; it closes at 8:30 p.m. on Monday.

Cranks Health Food also has a restaurant at Peter Robinsons, on Oxford Circus. More recently a branch has been opened in Covent Garden Market that specializes in Cranks take-out food, a small food and juice bar, and downstairs a whole-grain shop. Tube: Piccadilly Circus.

The **Chicago Pizza Factory,** 17 Hanover Square, W.1 (tel. 629-2669), specializes in deep-dish pizza covered with cheese, tomato, and a choice of sausage, pepperoni, mushrooms, green peppers, onions, and anchovies. The regular-size pizza is enough for two or three diners, and the large one is suitable for four or five persons. The restaurant was introduced to London by a former advertising executive, Bob Payton, an ex-Chicagoan.

The atmosphere is pleasant and friendly, even though they are quite busy. It's one of the few places where a doggy bag is willingly provided. There are smoking and nonsmoking tables. The menu also includes stuffed mushrooms, garlic bread, salads, and homemade cheesecakes served with two forks. The cost begins at £7 ($10.50) for a meal.

The restaurant also has a large bar with a wide choice of cocktails, including a specialty known as St. Valentine's Day Massacre. A video over the bar shows continuous American baseball, football, and basketball games. The 275-seat restaurant is full of authentic Chicago memorabilia, and the waitresses wear *Chicago Sun-Times* newspaper-sellers' aprons. The factory is just off Oxford Street behind Woolworth's, opposite John Lewis and within easy reach of Regent Street as well. The factory is open Monday to Saturday from 11:45 a.m. to 11:30 p.m. Tube: Bond Street.

Justin de Blanc, 54 Duke St., W.1 (tel. 629-3174), stands just off Oxford Street by Selfridges. It serves breakfast, then runs into lunchtime when it is very popular with tired shoppers. Choose your meal from a variety of hot dishes: lamb and eggplant casserole, barbecued spare ribs, or roast beef and three vegetables. The dishes of the day are written over the bar, and it can be quite a problem to select among them. The array of salads includes rice and celery, cucumber and yogurt, orange and beetroot. Desserts are all homemade, including fruit pies, cheesecakes, and fruit salad. They bake their own bread, and the fresh granary rolls are tempting. Meals cost from £10 ($15). A glass of wine costs £1.50 ($2.25). It is open from 8:30 a.m. to 3:30 p.m., then from 4:30 to 9:30 p.m. on weekdays (on Saturday from 9 a.m. to 3:30 p.m. only). Closed on Sunday. Tube: Bond Street.

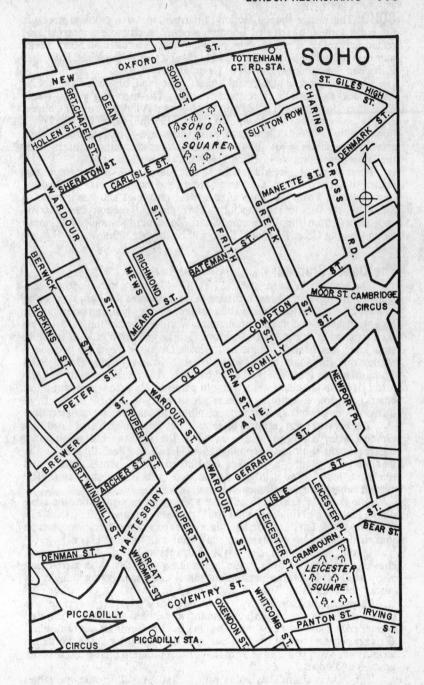

SOHO: This wedge-shaped section of narrow lanes and crooked streets is the main foreign quarter of London, where the city's best international restaurants reside. The life of the continent echoes throughout Soho. Large numbers of French people are found here, and so are Italians and all other European nationalities, as well as Orientals.

One writer wrote of Gerrard Street: "The smell of pickled ginger and roast duckling seeps from restaurant doors. The men scurry into stores from afternoon games of fan-tan and mah-jongg. A lilting twang of Chinese rock 'n' roll envelops the downtown street." Gerrard Street has succeeded in becoming London's Chinatown. Strip shows and honky-tonk clubs have given way to Chinese restaurants and bookstores keeping you informed of the latest developments in Hong Kong and the wisdom of Mao.

Soho starts at Piccadilly Circus, spreading out like a peacock and ending at Oxford Street. One side borders the theater center on Shaftesbury Avenue. From Piccadilly Circus, walk northeast and you'll come to Soho, to the left of Shaftesbury. This jumbled section can also be approached from the Tottenham Court Road tube station. Walk south along Charing Cross Road and Soho will be to your right.

The Upper Bracket

The Ivy, 1–5 West St., W.C.2 (tel. 836-4751). It's difficult to concentrate on the top-notch French cuisine here; diners are too busy star gazing in what is often a celebrity-filled dining spot. The Ivy is strong on tradition, an entrenched London restaurant since World War I. In the past it drew such regulars as Prime Ministers Lloyd George and Sir Winston Churchill, who knew his French viands and wines. Over the years, it became a rendezvous for show folk—Noël Coward, Gracie Fields, Dame Sybil Thorndike, Rex Harrison used to be habitués. The interior gleams with the luster of Paris—paneled walls with old paintings, bronze lamps, cut-plush chairs, art nouveau bronze figures set in window ledges. In the front drinking lounge you can wait for your table while making menu selections.

The Ivy had been getting a bit désuet, but with the arrival of Lord Lew Grade's wife, Kathleen, who now owns the Ivy, the old tradition of theatrical star-spotting is coming back. Her son, Paul Grade, is the manager. The paintings, paneling, and luxurious furnishings remain, and the menu tends to be a little old-fashioned in its length and detail. The cuisine is basic English/French.

Sole is available with 13 different sauces and garnishes, but the table d'hôte luncheon or dinner is what you'll probably go for at £12.50 ($18.75). If you don't see anything you like, then order one of the lunchtime plats du jour, including a gigot of lamb or roast beef with the trimmings.

In the evening you can try a chateaubriand steak for two, steak chasseur, or escalope of veal, among an array of dishes. À la carte meals begin at £15 ($22.50) per person, but this is quite amusing for a night out among the celebrities. Tube: Tottenham Court Road.

Terrazza, 19 Romilly St., W.1 (tel. 437-8991), at one time was considered the most voguish restaurant in London. But the West End theater crowd and "society" are, alas, fickle. Whether in or out of fashion, Terrazza remains one of the best places in the capital for authentic Italian food. If you visit, you'll have a choice of three different dining rooms, both upstairs and down.

The food is classic, beginning with cocktail Amalfi. House specialties include spaghetti with clams, fritto misto mare (scampi, octopus, and other sea products deep-fried), and rolled and stuffed breast of chicken. You can finish with a smooth zabaglione. A complete meal is likely to cost around £12 ($18), with a bottle of wine going from £5.50 ($8.25) up. Lunch is served from noon to 3 p.m., dinner from 6 p.m. to midnight. Tube: Tottenham Court Road.

Au Jardin des Gourmets, 5 Greek St., W.1 (tel. 437-1816), draws many a discriminating diner to some of the best French food in Soho. The restaurant has a Frenchman as its chef, and the traditional Gallic cuisine reflects the highest standards of his country. For appetizers, you can have such a treat as pâté maison. The soups are exceptionally good: vichyssoise and soupe à l'oignon gratinée. House specialties include carré d'agneau, red snapper with fennel sauce, roast duck with orange sauce, and a hot seafood dish in wine sauce. Vintage wines are available, but you can also order by the glass. The average price of a meal, including half a bottle of the house wine, is £20 ($30) per person. However, a set lunch or dinner is offered for just £10 ($15). The restaurant is open Monday to Friday from 12:30 to 2:15 p.m. and from 6:30 to 11:30 p.m. It is open on Saturday from 6:30 to 11 p.m. but closed on Sunday. Tube: Tottenham Court Road.

The Budget Range

Romano Santi, 50 Greek St., W.1 (tel. 437-5268), established in 1886, in the very heart of Soho, is one of the best values in this district, considering the grade of its cuisine. It's run by a friendly and polite international staff, under the direction of the Santi family. The management has made it a duty to keep this building, which was erected in 1735, in its original condition. The continental restaurant features an excellent three-course luncheon for £5 ($7.50) to £6.50 ($9.75). A typical meal might include an assortment of hors d'oeuvres, followed by chicken chasseur, with a green vegetable, and peach Melba for dessert. The helpings are generous, and there are several main dishes from which to choose. Expect to spend at least £10 ($15) to £18 ($27) for an à la carte dinner. Main courses include tournedos Romano Santi, veal piccatine al Marsala, chicken Kiev, and trout San Remo (with prawns and tomatoes). You'll find the lack of elbow room either a plus or a minus, depending on the person you're elbowing at the next table. Romano Santi is open from noon to 3 p.m. and from 6 to 11:45 p.m. It is also open Sunday and bank holidays. Tube: Tottenham Court Road.

The **Dumpling Inn,** 15a Gerrard St., W.1 (tel. 437-2567), in a small Chinese district of Soho, attracts a number of devoted regulars. Don't be fooled by the name or the Venetian murals—this is an elegant Chinese restaurant serving classical Mandarin dishes. The haute cuisine of China, Mandarin cooking dates back nearly 3000 years, and employs a number of unique cooking rituals, including the Mongolian hot pot. The fact that this restaurant serves somewhat small portions can be turned into an advantage because it gives you an opportunity to sample a variety of this delectable cuisine. You can savor the special tastes of Mandarin cooking in the sharkfin soup, the beef in oyster sauce, or the grilled pork or beef dumplings. Pancakes stuffed with discreetly flavored minced meat are a house specialty. Dinner reservations are recommended, and you should allow plenty of time for dining here since most dishes are prepared to your special order. The average meal will cost £10 ($15) per person, but just a large plate of grilled pork and dumplings will go for only £3 ($4.50). Tube: Leicester Square or Piccadilly Circus.

Chuen Cheng Ku, 17 Wardour St., W.1 (tel. 437-1398), is one of the finest eateries in Soho's "New China." A large restaurant, Chuen Cheng Ku is noted for its Singapore noodles. Specialties are paper-wrapped prawns, rice in lotus leaves, steamed spare ribs in black bean sauce, shredded pork with cashew nuts, all served in generous portions. Dim sum (dumplings) are served from 11 a.m. to 6 p.m. The Singapore noodles, reflecting one of the Chinese-Malaysian inspirations, are thin rice noodles, sometimes mixed with curry and pork or else shrimp with red and green peppers. A set dinner costs £8 ($12) per person. Featured à la carte dishes include fried oysters with ginger and scallions, sliced duck with chili and black bean sauce, and steamed pork with plum sauce. The average à la carte meal costs £10 ($15), plus 10%. The restaurant is open daily until midnight. Tube: Leicester Square or Piccadilly Circus.

HYDE PARK: If you crave greenery, this choice in the center of Hyde Park is welcome:

The Medium-Priced Range

The **Serpentine,** Hyde Park, W.2. (tel. 723-8784), is like a World's Fair exhibition center. It's in the center of Hyde Park, with an unobstructed view of the Serpentine Lake; the restaurant is a free-form glass structure built on different levels, with a separate area for drinks. The food is decidedly good, beginning with a selection of freshly prepared soups or a full range of fish and fruit appetizers. The menu features a full range of seafood and grilled meats. Main-course specialties include smoked and poached finnan haddock and roast lamb, pork, and beef carved at your table, and Yorkshire pudding. The average meal will cost about £15 ($22.50) to £18 ($27) per person. A set meal with a roast featured goes for £11.50 ($17.25), including a vegetable. For half a carafe of the house wine, expect to pay from £5.50 ($8.25). Meals are served daily from noon to 3 p.m. and from 6 to 11 p.m. It's best reached by taxi.

THE CITY: When the English talk about The City, they don't mean London. The City is the British version of Wall Street. Not only is it an important square mile of finance and business, but it contains many sights. Here are the buildings known the world over: the **Bank of England** on Threadneedle Street (entrance hall open to the public); the **Stock Exchange,** where you can watch transactions from a special gallery; **Lloyd's of London,** on Leadenhall, one of the world's great insurance centers. Lloyd's will insure anything from a stamp collection to a giraffe's neck.

Typical English food—shepherd's pie, mixed grills, roast beef—is dished up in dozens of the old pubs of The City. Here you can eat inexpensively along with the English, whether they be the man in the bowler worried about his country's inflation, or a Cockney secretary anxious to get back to the sound of the Bow Bells.

The Budget Range

The **George & Vulture,** 3 Castle Court, Cornhill, E.C.3 (tel. 626-9710), is for the Dickens enthusiast, ye olde Pickwickian hostelrie, etc. This chophouse, founded in 1660, claims that it is "probably" the world's oldest tavern, and refers to an inn on this spot back in 1175. The George &

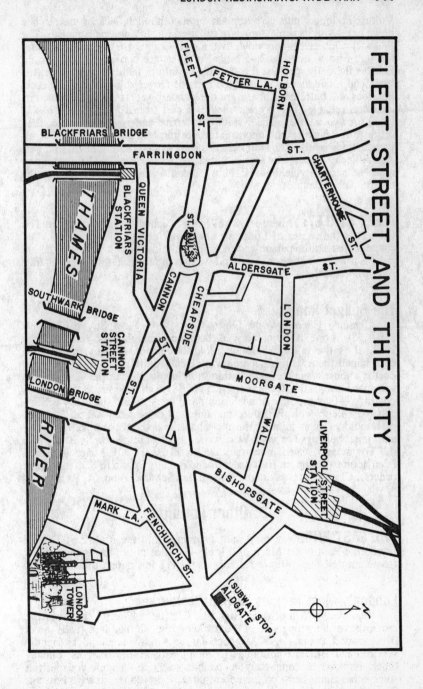

Vulture no longer puts up overnight guests (although Dickens used to bed down here), but its three floors are still used for serving English meals. The Pickwick Club meets here now, by the way. Come here for lunch, Monday through Friday, noon to 2:45 p.m. No tables are booked after 1:20 p.m. Besides the daily specials, the George & Vulture features a mixed grill, a "loin chop, chump chop," or fried filets of Dover sole with tartar sauce. Potatoes and buttered cabbage are the standard vegetables. The apple tart is always reliable. The average meal will cost from £9.50 ($14.25) to £12 ($18) for two courses. The system is to arrive and give your name, then retire to the Jamaica pub opposite for a drink. You are then fetched when your table is ready. The staff claims the wait is no more than 20 minutes. After lunch, explore the intricate nearby passageways, and discover the maze of shops, wine houses, pubs, and old buildings surrounding the tavern. Tube: Bank.

FLEET STREET: This street of ink, as it is called, is the gateway to The City. It is the center of London's newspaper and publishing world. The chances are that the person you're rubbing shoulders with in one of the old pubs is a writer or editor. Men and women of letters gather here, as they have for centuries.

The Budget Range

Cheshire Cheese, Wine Office Court, 145 Fleet St., E.C.4 (tel. 353-6170), is one of the greatest of the old city chophouses, running since 1667. It is the place where Dr. Johnson dined with his friends and entertained them with his acerbic wit. This is quite possible, as the good doctor's house was practically within shouting distance of the Cheese. The two specialties of the house cost £4.25 ($6.38) each. The first is "ye famous pudding"—(steak, kidney, mushroom, and game)—and the other is Scottish roast beef, with Yorkshire pudding and horseradish sauce. The hot plate holds a giant joint of the roast beef, and the waiters will give you additional helpings (on your Wedgwood plate) warning you "not to waste it." For dessert, "ye famous pancake" is £1.20 ($1.80). Lunch is served from noon to 2:30 p.m. (last orders), and dinners from 6 to 8:30 p.m. (last orders). Closed Saturday nights and all day Sunday. Tube: St. Paul's.

3. Other Locales

THE EAST END: You may want to plunge into the drab East End of London at least once. Much of it looks like slice-of-life background shots from countless films: But in restaurants it has a few potent drawing cards.

London's Most Famous Jewish Restaurant

Bloom's, 90 Whitechapel High St., E.1 (tel. 247-6835), is worth the crossover to the wrong side of the tracks. Although the place tends to get overcrowded, the manager, Mr. Nicholas, sees to it you get quick, friendly service, and Bloom's continues to tempt with kosher delights. Sunday lunch, however, is completely impossible, so try to schedule your visit at some other time. Feast on a chicken blintz, followed by cabbage borscht. The main dishes are reasonably priced, with specialties such as sauerbraten and salt beef (corned). For dessert, you can order apple strudel. An average meal will cost £9 ($13.50), with light snacks costing around £3.50 ($5.25). The restaurant is open 11 a.m. to 10 p.m., except on Friday when it closes at 3 p.m. (last orders at 2:30). It's closed all day Saturday and on all Jewish holidays. Tube: Aldgate East.

Chinese Food in Limehouse

Remember "Limehouse Blues"? The limekilns, from which the East End parish takes its name, were abolished before the war, but the legend lives on. On the North Bank of the Thames, the district is unattractive, with lots of ugly buildings—but therein lies its charm. Populated by broken-down or retired seamen by day, Limehouse at night is often filled with fashionable West Enders on a slumming spree. The big attractions are the Chinese restaurants known as "The Friends" (a few originals and a host of imitators).

New Friends Chinese Restaurant, 53 West India Dock Rd., E.14 (tel. 987-1139), is so popular, it's adopted a reservations-only policy during weekends. The pocketsize licensed restaurant near the Tower of London, open from noon to midnight, doesn't concern itself with decoration—just food and a reputation for some of the best quality Cantonese dishes in England. Although the menu is filled with surprises (many diners call in advance to order special dishes), you will fare handsomely just by sticking to the routine listings: items such as beef fried with green peppers, crunchy yet tender spare ribs, sweet-and-sour pork, and Kupar prawn. Meals cost from £12 ($18). If you want a truly special dinner, ask for Mr. Chung. West India Dock Road lies off Commercial Road and Burdett Road.

Young Friends, 11 Penny Fields, Poplar, E. 14 (tel. 987-4276), is just around the corner from New Friends. This is the domain of Raymond Low, and many West Enders cross the city to sample his gray mullet (on 24-hour notice). From the tiniest kitchen imaginable come excellent meals, served in a dining room that couldn't be more basic. Here are my suggestions for a memorable dinner: wonton soup, sharkfin soup, sweet-sour wonton, and stuffed chicken wings in oyster sauce. You can top your dinner with lichee nuts. A set meal goes for £8 ($12), and a complete à la carte repast costs from £10 ($15). Bring your own wine, as the restaurant is unlicensed. Penny Fields lies just off West India Dock Road. Lost? Call Raymond Low for directions.

READER'S RESTAURANT SELECTION: **"Slender's Health Food Restaurant,** 41 Cathedral Pl., E.C.4, is exactly in front of St. Paul's tube station. The menu at this fine eating place includes such items as tomato and watercress soup, lasagne verdi, and baked potato with butter. Herb teas and decaffeinated coffee are always served. They serve luscious desserts, such as apple-date pie, apricot meringues, and cheesecake, all at reasonable prices, from £5 ($7.50) for a full meal. The young people serving you are most pleasant, the food very well prepared and attractive. One may either eat in the restaurant or take food out. Beans, whole grains, and dried fruits are also sold. Hours are 8:30 a.m. to 6:15 p.m., Monday through Friday" (Jean See, Spokane, Wash.).

SOUTH OF THE THAMES: The **George Inn,** 77 Borough High St., S.E.1 (tel. 407-2056), across the bridge at Southwark, is a National Trust property, the only remaining London pub with an outside gallery. A touch of old England safely tucked away in an alley, the present building dates back some 300 years. Some claim that Shakespeare and his troupe performed in an old inn that stood on the same ground. Dickens not only frequented the George, but he also wrote about it in *Little Dorrit*. Recently the building next door was acquired by the owners and the pub has been enlarged to include a wine bar, where hot and cold snacks are offered for £1.25 ($1.88) to £2.50 ($3.75) from a serve-yourself buffet.

You enter the George through a gateway into the "old bar," noteworthy for its functioning beer engines, which are nearly as old as the building itself, and a bar area complete with a fire for nippy days and the Act of Parliament clock. This bar offers a variety of hot snacks, while the newer wine bar has a large cold buffet counter. The remaining bar on the first floor is for more serious drinkers. Two original staircases lead to each of the two restaurants, where a traditional three-course English luncheon costs £11.50 ($17.25). Lunch is served Monday through Friday from noon to 2 p.m., and dinner Monday through Saturday from 6 to 9 p.m.

South of the Border, 8–10 Joan St., S.E.1 (tel. 928-6374). The name reflects the attitude a lot of people have toward London "South of the River" as the locals say, and it is rare to find a fashionable place to eat after a visit to the Royal Festival Hall, National Theatre, and Young Vic Theatre. Joan Street is at the junction of the Cut and Blackfriars, within easy reach of all. Once a mattress factory, the ground floor and gallery can seat more than 80 people, and in summer there are also tables on the outdoor terrace. The decor is wood and brick walls with rugs, tapestries, and modern paintings.

The menu is changed frequently, and a vegetarian dish is included, as are a choice of various appetizers. There's always a homemade soup such as minestrone or white bean. Main dishes consist of a variety of chicken, lamb, beef, and fish dishes, such as chicken escalope, carbonnade of beef cooked in beer with potatoes and onions and served in its own pot, and fish pie stuffed with cod, shellfish, mullet, and crab. The price range is from £7 ($10.50) to £12 ($18). Desserts have such succulent names as Belvoir pudding steamed with fruits and custard. There is a good selection of wines and a choice from seven house wines. The menu is frequently changed so a return visit can be recommended. The restaurant is open Monday to Saturday from 6 to 11:30 p.m. and from Monday to Friday from noon to 2:30.

555, 555 Battersea Park Rd., S.W.11 (tel. 228-7011), is a most unprepossessing café (in looks only) in a dreary commercial sector of London, south of the Thames. But surprise! The food is winning, the ingredients fresh. A gemütlich feeling prevails at night, and soon you're joining in the fun. The posters on the walls are more permissive than ever. You can get a number of good Baltic dishes here. Vera, the owner, oversees everything. By all means, try the homemade sausage. The pâté is also delicious, a bit crude but good. The suckling pig is highly recommended, and seems to be a house specialty. Vegetables come with everything; red cabbage is often featured. An entire meal will run about £11 ($16.50) to £12 ($28). Meals are served to a cosmopolitan crowd against a background of taped music. Vera says it's all in great fun, and I agree. It is closed Sunday and Monday, but open otherwise for dinner only from 7:30 p.m. till midnight. Take a taxi: you'll never find the place if you don't.

HAMPSTEAD: Keats, Downshire Hill, Hampstead, N.W.3 (tel. 435-1499), is a "small, serious restaurant for committed gourmets," just around the corner from Keats's house. The well-prepared food is the best in Hampstead. Considering the size of the restaurant—it has a capacity of only about 50 diners—the French menu is exceedingly ambitious, containing some 40 delectable dishes that are varied every five weeks. Proprietor Aron Misan's special pride is his wine cellar, which houses at least 100 varieties, including a collection of classified clarets in great vintages. An average dinner at Keats comes to about £18 ($27), not including wine. Keats is open every evening except Sunday. Reservations are a must. Tube: Hampstead.

Le Cellier du Midi, Church Row, N.W.3 (tel. 435-9998), is a basement French bistro, off Hampstead Heath Street. It's decorated with odd Victorian knickknacks, with bunches of garlic and onions hanging from the roof beams. Rough wooden tables are covered with red cloths. It's run by Henri Saux, who offers classical French cooking with the day's specialties shown on the blackboard. For £15 ($22.50) you're given a four-course meal with a choice of some 16 appetizers, including pâté and mussels marinières, then 20 main dishes such as pot au feu or boeuf Alaric. A tempting array of at least 15 desserts is offered nightly. It is wise to reserve, particularly on weekends. Le Cellier is well recommended for the quality of its cuisine and its general ambience. Tube: Hampstead.

Pippin, 83–84 Hampstead High Street, N.W.3 (tel. 435-6434), offers a fine array of strictly vegetarian dishes to tempt even the most skeptical nonvegetarian. Clever adaptation of traditional dishes will surprise you. Try the English "Lancashire hotpot" made of soya mince and the Greek "moussaka" concocted of lentils and soya. You serve yourself from a selection of salads. Prices go from £3 ($4.50) to £7 ($10.50) for a meal. The freshly baked breads and cakes are prepared from Pippin's own organically grown wheat flour. The restaurant's Copella pure apple juice is the favorite beverage to accompany any dish. It's open daily from noon to midnight. Pippin offers morning coffee, lunch, afternoon tea, or dinner on its terrace restaurant. Tube: Hampstead.

NEAR OLYMPIA EXHIBITION HALL: Jonathan's Restaurant, 71 Blythe Rd., W.14 (tel. 602-2758), is in an almost suburban street, well away from the normal tourist haunts, behind Olympia Exhibition Hall. You enter the restaurant via a short flight of stairs down to a small bar, where you will be met by Joseph, who will pour your drinks or mix you one of his cocktails while you peruse the extensive French menu. The restaurant is Victorian and subtly romantic with lace curtains, soft lighting (but not so dark that you strain to see your dining partner), and candles and fresh flowers on the linen tablecloths.

A hot avocat Jonathan, filled with seafood in a béchamel sauce, might be your appetizer, or perhaps you'll prefer escargot (snails) à la bourguignonne or saumon fumé en mousse à la Brasil (a nest of tender palm hearts filled with smoked salmon mousse). A filet with stilton cheese and port wine is a special main dish, as is roast duckling coated with honey and served with apple sauce. Most items on the menu can be served plain grilled if preferred. There is also an interesting selection of desserts and English and French cheeses. An excellent wine list provides an ideal accompaniment to your meal, with a bottle of the house wine priced at £4.75 ($7.13). In addition to the à la carte menu, costing from £12 ($18), there are attractively priced set luncheon and dinner menus, from £6.50 ($9.75), consisting of three courses. VAT is included in all prices, but service is extra. The restaurant is open for lunch Monday through Friday from noon

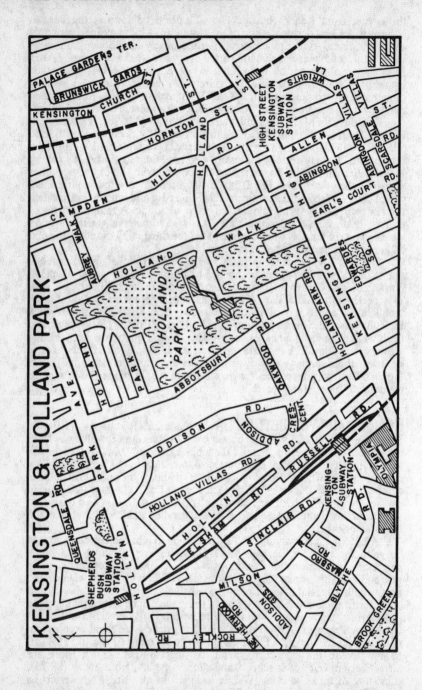

to 2:30 p.m. and for dinner Monday through Saturday from 7 to 11:30 p.m. It is recommended that you make a reservation to avoid disappointment. It's best to go by taxi.

ISLINGTON: Frederick's Restaurant, Camden Passage, N.1 (tel. 359-2888). Originally, in 1789, the building was a pub called the Gun. Then in 1834 it was rebuilt and renamed "The Duke of Sussex" in honor of George III's sixth son, Prince Augustus Frederick. So when the restaurant opened in 1970, what more natural than to name it after the prince? As well as tables inside, you can eat in the Garden Room, designed like a Victorian glasshouse with a domed ceiling. It is air-conditioned and heated, with glass doors leading to a terrace and the large garden. There is much open brickwork and plants to create a pleasant, relaxed place in which to enjoy the delicacies of the excellent French cuisine.

Jean-Louis Pollet, chef de cuisine, changes the menu every fortnight, but there are so many delightful alternatives to each course that you would be hard put to work through it in two weeks. There are several fish dishes, or, from the charcoal grill, a variety of steaks and cutlets served with garlic butter and béarnaise sauce. Desserts are all homemade, and there is a good cheese board. A three-course meal with coffee will cost around £19 ($28.50), including VAT.

There is a long and excellent wine list and a very palatable house wine is £5 ($7.50) a bottle. If you are in the area on Saturday, they do a set luncheon for £7.50 ($11.25). The set lunch on Saturday offers a choice of three appetizers, two main dishes with vegetable, and a choice of three desserts. VAT and service are included. This is the area for the antique hunter, so you may very well find yourself up there with time to enjoy a delicious meal. Tube: Angel.

4. A Dining Miscellany

For a memorable experience, take a taxi, tube, or bus to Aldgate East and spend a hectic hour or so at **Petticoat Lane.** That's the street market where, on Sunday, even if you don't want to buy the goods, you can see the full wit and expertise of the Cockney street vendors. Look for the one who sells tea services, buy a toffee apple or a hot dog, and then go around the corner to **Club Row,** a street market for animals and birds.

A short walk will bring you down to the Tower of London and, right beside it, just below Tower Bridge, **St. Katharine's Dock.** After you've had a look around, you may be interested in dining or just having a snack to tide you over. Some places you'll see are overpriced and have become careless about the quality of their cuisine, while others still provide good food and good value.

Tower Hotel, St. Katharine's Way, E.1 (tel. 481-2575). At the Carvery Restaurant at this modern hotel built overlooking the Thames, you can enjoy all you want of some of the most tempting roasts in the Commonwealth.

For example, you can select (rare, medium, or well done) from a standing rib of prime beef with Yorkshire pudding, horseradish sauce, and the juice; or from tender roast pork with crackling accompanied by a spiced bread dressing and apple sauce; or perhaps the roast spring Southdown lamb with mint sauce. Then you help yourself to the roast potatoes, the green peas, the baby carrots. Perhaps you'll prefer a selection of cold meats and salads from the buffet table. No one counts—even if you go back for seconds or thirds.

Before going to the carving table, you will be served either a shrimp cocktail, a bowl of soup, or a cold slice of melon. Afterward, you can end the meal with a selection from the dessert trolley (especially recommended is the fresh fruit salad, ladled out with thick country cream poured over). You also receive a large cup of American-style coffee. The cost is £10.50 ($15.75) for "the works," and the price is the same at both lunch and dinner. No telephone reservations are accepted. Buses 23, 42, and 78 run down here. Hours are from noon to 3 p.m. and from 5:30 to 10 p.m.

Before or after dinner you might want to visit the Thames Bar, which has a nautical theme and a full panoramic view of its namesake, along with Tower Bridge and the river traffic. There is a small balcony outside for drinks in summer.

Nearby is the **Dickens Inn by the Tower,** St. Katharine's Way, E.1 (tel. 488-2208), a very carefully reconstructed 19th-century warehouse. Incorporating the original redwood beams, stock bricks, and ironworks, it is a balconied pub/restaurant on three levels. Sitting on a wooden chair and an old table, you can enjoy such bar snacks as cockles, mussels, rollmops, and a ploughman's lunch. Prices begin at £2 ($3) for one of the snacks, around £4 ($6) for the hot dish of the day, accompanied by a vegetable.

A REAL BRITISH BREAKFAST: The fame of the British breakfast has spread around the world. For a breakfast at its best, try the **Fox and Anchor,** Charterhouse Street, E.C.1 (tel. 253-4838). Charterhouse Street leads into a lovely tree-lined square where most of the buildings that survived the bombs in 1941 date back to the 16th century. At the other end of the short, narrow street is the famous Smithfield meat market.

"Mine host," Peter Zeid, has been serving the traders from the market for the past 17 years with breakfast in his Victorian pub, starting at 6 a.m. and finishing at 11 a.m., when he reverts to being a publican and "pulling" ale.

The breakfasts are gargantuan, especially if you order "the full house," which will have at least eight different items on your plate, including sausage, bacon, mushrooms, kidney, eggs, and a fried slice of bread to mention just a few, along with unlimited tea or coffee, toast, and jam. For the lot, expect to pay £3 ($4.50). If you fancy a glass of ale to wash it down, you can order a glass for 50p (75¢) from 6 to 9 a.m.

Or perhaps you want a more substantial meal? Then toast and jam, a T-bone steak with mushrooms, chips, tomatoes, and salad will cost about £8 ($12). Add a Black Velvet (champagne and Guinness) at £2 ($3), and the day is yours.

EATING AFLOAT: An increasingly popular London activity is dinner aboard. On Wednesday, Saturday, and Sunday lunchtimes, **Catamaran Cruises** leave Westminster Pier, S.W.1 (tel. 839-2349). The cost is £13 ($19.50) per passenger. Evening floodlit supper cruises are also offered on Wednesday, Friday, and Sunday at 9 p.m. (you're back at 10:30 p.m.). Tours leave from Westminster Pier, and the cruise costs £4 ($6). If you purchase supper, the cost goes up to £10 ($15). The boat is licensed to serve drinks, and there is a commentary on the historic buildings as you ply between Albert Bridge and Tower Bridge.

A showboat dinner cruise leaves every Sunday from May to December at 7 p.m., departing from Westminster Pier. This showboat recaptures the atmosphere and gaiety of a Victorian music hall. A three-course English dinner, including wine, is served during the cruise for £23 ($34.50). You return at 10:30 p.m.

The Regents Canal, which winds and twists through London, is the home of **The Fair Lady,** departing from 250 Camden High St., N.W.1, two minutes from the Camden Town tube station. There are cruises most nights starting at 7:30 p.m. and costing £15 ($22.50) per person for a three-hour trip. Searchlights illuminate the banks and buildings, and there is live entertainment, a singer with a guitar. Dinner is a choice of three appetizers, then a selection of meat, poultry, or fish, dessert or cheese, and coffee. House wines go for £4.50 ($6.75) a bottle. The Sunday lunch is presented at 12:30 p.m. at a cost of about £10 ($15). Advance reservations are imperative (tel. 485-4433 or 485-6210).

Capital Cruises of DCW House, 45a Heathfield Rd., Wandsworth, S.W.18 (tel. 870-6158), runs luncheon, buffet/disco, and dinner/dance cruises on the Thames. The luncheon excursion costs £12.50 ($18.75) per person. You can intersperse disco dancing with buffet goodies for £7.95 ($11.93) per person, and the cost of a dinner cruise with dancing is £16.95 ($25.43). All prices include VAT.

LUNCHTIME THEATER: There is a drama on the menu these days in

many of the small theaters and pubs of London. The actors often include well-known names, and the plays the work of established writers, although this is an outlet for many a would-be Olivier, Ayckbourn, or Stoppard. With the play, which usually lasts about an hour, the audience can often enjoy a light, inexpensive meal, and prices are deliberately kept low so that the spectacle is available to all.

The **King's Head Theatre Club,** 115 Upper St., N.1 (tel. 226-1916), run by American-born Dan Crawford, charges £12.50 ($18.75) for a dinner and show. You pay a little extra for beer or wine. Your three-course dinner might consist of an appetizer, a choice of roast joint with vegetables, and a dessert. You can also order vegetarian meals. Dinner is served one hour before show time, at about 6:45 p.m. with most shows starting at 7:45 p.m. If you only want to attend the show, you can purchase a ticket for £5.50 ($8.25) for the evening performance, £2 ($3) for the lunchtime show.

After your visit to the Changing of the Guard ceremony, the **Institute of Contemporary Arts,** Nash House, The Mall, S.W.1 (tel. 930-3647), charges 60p (90¢) a day for membership, which gives you access to three galleries, the restaurant, the bar, and the bookshop. The building also houses two cinemas and a theater with a lively program concentrating on all aspects of contemporary art. Admission to the cinema, which shows contemporary and avant-garde productions, is £3 ($4.50). The ICA is by the Duke of York's Steps in the Mall.

ALMOST 24-HOUR EATERIES: Sometimes you'll want to dine at odd

hours, when most of the eating establishments in London are shut down. However, in a city as vast as London, some chef (not always a great one) is cooking. Here are some random selections:

Try **Canton Chinese Restaurant,** 11 New Port Pl., W.C.2 (tel. 437-6220), which is open 24 hours a day.

Or patronize **Rockafella's Café**, 3 New Burlington St., W.1 (tel. 734-3075), which serves American and continental dishes, and has a full take-away service. It is open from midday until 6:30 a.m., and a cabaret is also presented at night.

You might also visit the appropriately named **Up-All-Night Restaurant**, 325 Fulham Rd., S.W. 10 (tel. 352-1996).

Or **Great British Success**, a restaurant at 85 Gloucester Rd., S.W.7 (tel. 370-4404), with another branch at 22 Terminus Pl., S.W.1, close to Victoria Station.

At London's **Heathrow Airport**, all three terminals serve hot food 24 hours a day.

Most branches of **Kentucky Fried Chicken** are open 24 hours a day. The most central one is at 247 Old Brompton Rd., S.W. 5 (tel. 370-3951).

The **Wimpy Bar**, 27 London Rd., W.2 (tel. 723-4721), is also open 24 hours a day.

5. The Pubs of London

No activity is more typically British than to head for that venerated institution, the Public House, affectionately known as pub. Many are dreary Victorian monstrosities, patronized by the working men and women in the neighborhood. Others, particularly those in the West End, have glamour, basking in associations real (Charles Dickens, Samuel Johnson) or imagined (Sherlock Holmes). Pub crawling is a real part of your English experience.

Many North American visitors who don't usually go to bars at home become rabid enthusiasts of the English pub. And most single women feel comfortable in pubs.

Licensing hours are unpopular in England—generally from 11 a.m. to 3 p.m. and from 5:30 to 11 p.m. On Sunday the hours are usually from noon to 2 p.m. and from 7 to 10:30 p.m. Persons under 16 are generally not allowed in pubs, and those under 18 aren't served alcoholic beverages.

The most noticeable change in English pubs, especially those in the West End, is in the improved standard of food served. However, many pubs still rely on snacks, as typified by the little meat pies, drab dough wrapped around last week's pork roast. Others serve superb sandwiches (fresh salmon stuffed between healthy slices of brown bread), even hot dishes, such as shepherd's pie. Some London pubs are pursuing a fine cuisine in a separate dining room on their premises—the fare ranging from lobster soup to river trout grilled in butter to roast Aylesbury duckling in orange sauce.

My pub recommendations in all major tourist centers of the West End follow, the emphasis on those having historic interest (the Prospect of Whitby, Ye Olde Cock Tavern) or else those catering to special-interest groups, such as theater buffs and actors (Salisbury).

ST. JAMES'S: The **Red Lion**, 2 Duke of York St., St. James's Square, S.W.1 (tel. 930-2030), is only a short walk from Piccadilly Circus. Ian Nairn compared its spirit to that of Edouard Manet's painting *A Bar at the Folies-Bergère* (see the collection at the Courtauld Institute Galleries). Try to avoid peak hours, so that you'll be able to introduce yourself to the friendly owners, Roy and Corinne Hamlin, who pride themselves on the number of friends they have made. They offer pub luncheons at noon: steak pie with vegetables and a wide variety of sandwiches—all on healthy brown bread. Roasts are regularly featured, vegetables included. Good meals cost from £6 ($9) up. Everything is washed down with Ind Coope's fine ales in this little Victorian pub, with its posh turn-of-the-century decorations—patterned glass, deep-mahogany curlicues—that recapture the gin-palace atmosphere. It is open six days a week from 11 a.m. to 3 p.m. and from 5:30 to 11 p.m. (on Sunday from noon to 2 p.m.). Single women can be at ease here. Tube: Piccadilly Circus.

The **Captain's Cabin**, 4 Norris St., S.W.1 (tel. 930-4767), just off Haymarket, close to Piccadilly Circus, lies on a narrow street with a narrow pavement. On the first floor is a bar with pool tables and a darts alley. The room has one of those amazing 1930s art deco ceilings. On the ground floor is a Captain's Cabin logbook, dating back to 1930 and containing signatures of some former patrons, including Sir Winston Churchill (when he was prime minister) and Errol Flynn. The whole pub follows a nautical theme, with ship memorabilia throughout, and the upstairs bar is open until 1 a.m. You can order Director's Bitter, which is pure English beer, and have cold meats and salads, hot sausages, steak-and-kidney pie, or a ploughman's lunch, at prices ranging from £1.20 ($1.80) to £2.40 ($3.60). On a nostalgic note, the Dive Bar in the basement was famous in World War II as a rendezvous for airmen and servicemen on leave. Tube: Piccadilly Circus.

LEICESTER SQUARE: The **Salisbury**, 90 St. Martin's Lane, W.C.2 (tel. 836-5863), is one of the most famous Victorian pubs of London, attracting today a largely gay patronage. Its glittering cut-glass mirrors reflect the faces of English stage stars (and would-be stars) sitting around the curved buffet-style bar, having a cold joint snack. A plate of the roast leg of pork on the buffet, plus a salad, costs from £4 ($6). Fruit pies go for 75p ($1.13), and other dishes, priced from £2.50 ($3.75) to £5 ($7.50), include curry, vegetarian dishes, spaghetti, and quiche. The Salisbury is ably run by George Wynne. If you want a less prominent place to dine or to nibble oysters, choose the old-fashioned wall banquette with its copper-topped tables, and art nouveau decor. The light fixtures, veiled bronze girls in flowing togas holding up clusters of electric lights concealed in bronze roses, are appropriate. In the saloon, you'll see and hear the Olivier of yesterday and tomorrow. Tube: Leicester Square.

TRAFALGAR SQUARE: The **Sherlock Holmes**, 10 Northumberland St., W.C.2 (tel. 930-2644), is for fans of the legendary English detective and his creator, Arthur Conan Doyle. You can order your mug of beer and then look at the recreation upstairs of 221B Baker Street's living room, where get-togethers of "The Baker Street Irregulars" are held. Such "Holmesiana" are included as the cobra of the *Speckled Band* and the head of the *Hound of the Baskervilles*. The food served upstairs reflects both an English and continental influence. Main-dish specialties include Dover sole, trout, steaks, and veal escalope Cordon Bleu. A three-course meal with coffee comes to around £12.50 ($18.75). In the snackbar downstairs, you can have a salad and cold meat plate for about £2.50 ($3.75). Other dishes and the hot dish of the day go for £2 ($3). Tube: Trafalgar Square.

SOHO: **Maison Berlemont**, 49 Dean St., W.1 (tel. 437-2799), is popularly known as the French House. Run by Monsieur G. R. Berlemont, it once was the unofficial headquarters of the French resistance in exile in London during the war. Nostalgic Frenchmen still come here, talking about the old days and purchasing outstanding *vins* by the glass. The pub has a plain exterior, and the decor is not remarkable. However, the hospitality of the patron is laudable, as are his bar-room snacks, especially the pâté and the excellent quiche Lorraine. Count on spending from £3.50 ($5.25). A lot of authors, theater and film people are also attracted to "the French." Tube: Tottenham Court Road, Piccadilly Circus, or Leicester Square.

CHELSEA: **King's Head & Eight Bells,** 50 Cheyne Walk, S.W.2 (tel. 352-1820), is a historic Thames-side pub in a fashionable residential area of London, that has reopened after extensive redecoration and some reconstruction. It's popular with stage and TV personalities as well as writers. Many distinguished personalities once lived in this area. A short stroll in the neighborhood will take you to the former homes of such personages as Carlyle, Swinburne, and George Eliot. Press gangs used to roam these parts of Chelsea seeking lone travelers who were abducted for a life at sea. The snackbar has been upgraded to Cordon Bleu standards at pub prices. The landlord, Mary Timmons, supervises bars and food. The best English beers are served here, as well as a goodly selection of wines and liquors. In season some specialties include sea trout, turkey coronation, and stuffed lamb cutlets. All year you can order such delights as lasagne, shepherd's pie, or steak-and-kidney pie. One English critic wrote of the "elegant pud" (meaning desserts) served here. Among them are chocolate roulade and fresh fruit soufflés. You can dine here for £5.50 ($8.25). It's best reached by taxi.

BELGRAVIA: The **Grenadier,** Wilton Row, S.W.1 (tel. 235-3400), is an oldtime pub on a cobblestoned street, sheltered by higher buildings, and protected from the noise of traffic. The Grenadier is one of the special pubs of London—associated with the Iron Duke. But today the smell is not of the horses of Wellington's officers. The scarlet front door of the one-time officers' mess is guarded by a scarlet sentrybox and shaded by a vine. The bar is nearly always crowded with blue-bloods and their thin, pale girl-friends. Very English meals are served in front of fireplaces in two of the small rooms behind the front bar. Luncheons and dinners are offered daily, including Sunday, from noon to 3 p.m. and from 7 to 11 p.m. A soup of the day is invariably featured. Main courses include such dishes as baked Virginia ham, followed by desserts including apple pie and cream. Lunch snacks at the bar range in price from £1 ($1.50) to £1.40 ($2.10) a plate. In the evenings, only hot sausages are available in the bar, going for 30p (45¢). A three-course lunch or dinner in the small restaurant will average £8 ($12) to £12 ($18). Naturally, filet of beef Wellington is a specialty.

There is a gentle ghost, that of an officer who died after being flogged for cheating at cards. The decor is definitely Wellingtonian. At the entrance to Wilton Row (in the vicinity of Belgrave Square), a special guard ("good evening, guv'nor") is stationed to raise and lower a barrier for those arriving by "carriage." May British tradition never die. Pub enthusiasts are fanatic about the Grenadier. If anyone tries to tear it down, he may meet his Waterloo. Tube: Knightsbridge.

The **Antelope,** 22 Eaton Terrace, S.W.1 (tel. 730-7781), on the fringe of Belgravia, at the gateway to Chelsea, caters to a hotchpotch of clients, aptly described as "people of all classes, colours and creeds who repair for interesting discussion on a whole gamut of subjects, ranging from sport to medieval history, wicker-work, bed-bug traps, and for both mental and physical refreshment." 'Nuff said? You can wine and dine upstairs, or else have lunch in a ground-floor chamber offering a cold buffet. Meals cost from £5 ($7.50) to £9 ($13.50). For openers, try the soup of the day, followed by steak-and-kidney pie, and topped off by red-currant pie and cream. The trappings have long ago mellowed, as the history of the Antelope goes back to 1780. Tube: Sloane Square.

SHEPHERD MARKET (MAYFAIR): Shepherd's Tavern, 50 Hertford St., W.1 (tel. 499-3017), is a nugget, considered the pub of Mayfair. It attracts a congenial mixture of English, from those who read *The Times* every morning to a rather advanced set of young 'uns. There are many fine touches, including a collection of antique furniture. Attention is focused on the sedan chair that once belonged to the son of George III, the Duke of Cumberland (it's now fitted with a telephone for those very private "ring ups"). Many of the locals like to recall the tavern's associations with the pilots in the Battle of Britain. Bar snacks and hot dishes include shepherd's pie, curry, or fish pie with vegetable. Upstairs, the restaurant has reopened, serving chicken and steak-and-kidney pie, as well as shepherd's and fish pies, along with a coterie of curry dishes and roast joints daily. Meals begin at £10 ($15). The tavern is popular with local business folk, and it's a good place for the visitor wanting to study local Mayfair life. Tube: Green Park.

BLOOMSBURY: The Museum Tavern, 49 Great Russell St., W.C.1 (tel. 242-8987), opposite the British Museum, is a turn-of-the-century pub, with all the trappings: velvet, oak paneling, and cut glass. It's right in the center of the London University area, and popular with writers and publishers. At lunch you can order real, good-tasting, low-cost English food. Such standard English fare is featured as shepherd's pie or beef in beer with two vegetables. A fish pie with two vegetables is also tasty. A cold buffet is offered, including herring, Scottish eggs, and veal and ham pies, as well as salads and cheese. Count on spending from £4 ($6) for a meal. Tube: Russell Square.

THE CITY: Old King Lud, 78 Ludgate Circus, E.C.4 (tel. 236-6610), is a Victorian pub built in 1855 on the site of the Old Fleet Prison. The former dungeons are now the cellars of this old-world pub, which bills itself as the home of the original Welsh rarebit. However, it no longer serves that specialty for which it became famous. Rather, it offers a selection of pâtés that ranges from venison to duck with orange. Both hot and cold dishes are dispensed. Snacks start at £1 ($1.50) and plates at £2.50 ($3.75). Wine is £1 ($1.50) per glass. You can also order good Marlow Bitter here. The pub has recently been refurbished, and the 40-seat restaurant is open Monday to Friday, with waitress service. Tube: Blackfriars.

Ye Olde Watling, 29 Watling St., E.C.4 (tel. 248-6235), is associated with Sir Christopher Wren; it was built after the Great Fire of London in 1666. On the ground level is a mellow pub, with an intimate restaurant upstairs that serves lunch from noon to 2:15 p.m., Monday through Friday. Under oak beams and on trestle tables, you can have a good choice of English food, with such traditional dishes as steak, kidney, and mushroom pudding, the house specialty. Steak-and-oyster pie is also good. On the ground floor, buffet bar salads, along with hot dishes, are in the £1.60 ($2.40) to £2.50 ($3.75) range. Upstairs, a small steak with vegetables or salad, plus a dessert, will run you about £7 ($10.50). Tube: Mansion House.

FLEET STREET: Ye Olde Cock Tavern, 22 Fleet St., E.C.4 (tel. 353-9706), boasts a long line of ghostly literary comrades, such as Dickens, who have favored this ancient pub. After having a half pint on the ground floor, diners go upstairs to have lunch in a former horse stall, a meal here costing around £12 ($18). "Ye fare" is served from 12:30 to 3 p.m. Of course, the food is traditionally English, priced from 75p ($1.13) to a high of £2.50 ($3.75) for a steak-and-kidney pie. Tube: St. Paul's.

ALONG THE THAMES: The Prospect of Whitby, 47 Wapping Wall, E.1 (tel. 481-1095), is one of London's oldest riverside pubs, having been founded originally in the days of the Tudors. The Prospect has many associations—it was visited by Dickens, Turner, Whistler, in search of local "colour." Come here for a "tot," a "noggin," or whatever it is that you drink. The Pepys Room honors the diarist, who may—just may—have visited the Prospect back in its rowdier days, when the seamy side of London dock life held sway here. The pub is named after a ship, the *Prospect*, which sailed from its home port of Whitby and used to drop anchor outside the pub. Live music is heard every night from 8:30 to 11.

At the restaurant upstairs, you should reserve early and ask for the bow window table with fine views over the Thames. Here, a meal will cost you around £12 ($18). In the bar, you can have a giant hot sausage in french bread for £1 ($1.50), a variety of other snacks, or a hot plate of beef, Mexican style, costing £2.50 ($3.75). "Mine Host" is Brian Parkin.

Take the Metropolitan line to Wapping station. When you emerge onto Wapping High Street, turn right and head down the road along the river. Wapping Wall will be on your right, running parallel to the Thames. It's about a five-minute walk.

The City Barge, Strand-on-the-Green, Chiswick, W.4 (tel. 994-2148). Londoners head here for an outing and an evening pint of ale on a summer night. A little country pub, a nostalgic link with the past—it can be reached in 45 minutes from the center of London. Take the tube to Hammersmith, then change to bus 27 and get off at the beginning of Kew Bridge (during the day this can be combined with a visit to Kew Gardens). Then walk down a towpath (about a five-minute jaunt), past moored boats and a row of little Regency, Queen Anne, Georgian, and Dutch houses, till you reach the pub. Or you can go by boat from Westminster Pier to Kew Gardens, then visit the City Barge, and return to London by train. Regulars often bypass the little tables set outside (in summer) so as to have their pint while sitting on the embankment wall under a willow tree, and enjoying the boats chugging or gliding by.

The Anchor, 1 Bankside, Southward, S.E.1 (tel. 407-1577), is steeped in atmosphere, standing near what used to be the infamous debtors' prison, Clink (hence, the expression—"putting a man in the clink"). The original Anchor burned down in 1676 but was rebuilt and survived the bombs of World War II. Much of the present tavern, however, is aptly described by the management as "Elizabeth II." After getting off at the tube stop, you pass by Southwark Cathedral through a warehouse district that looks at night like Jack the Ripper country till you reach the riverside tavern. There's a viewing platform—especially popular during the day—right on the Thames. You'll find a number of bars named after the historical associations of the inn (Thrale Room, Dr. Johnson's Room, the Globe Bar, the Clink Bar, and the Boswell Bar). In addition, you can dine either upstairs or down in such "parlours" as the Boswell Grill or the Elizabethan Long Gallery Restaurant. The food is good, and meals begin at £7 ($10.50). The Anchor is open from noon to 2 p.m. for lunch and from 7 to 10 p.m. for dinner Monday through Saturday. On Sunday, lunch is from noon to 1 p.m.; dinner, 7 to 9 p.m. Tube: London Bridge.

Just up the road is the house on Bankside where Sir Christopher Wren stayed during the building of St. Paul's Cathedral. Catherine of Aragon also stayed there when she first landed in London prior to her marriage to Henry VIII. It is hoped that rebuilding will start soon on the nearby site of the old Globe Playhouse, to recreate the theater in its original 1599 form. One of the members of the cast of players first appearing at the Globe was one William Shakespeare, and later many of his plays, including *Hamlet,* had their first nights here—or rather their first afternoons, as daylight was essential in the open-air theaters of that day.

ELEPHANT & CASTLE: South of the Thames, the following pub is easily reached by underground train to Elephant & Castle. From the station where you get off, it's a five-minute walk.

The **Goose and Firkin,** 47–48 Borough Rd., S.E.1 (tel. 403-3590), is a pub that brews its own beer. The owner of this unique enterprise is David Bruce, who worked as a brewer for one of the big companies for many years until his chance came to buy the Goose and Firkin. He obtained his own license to brew, and set about producing his own beers. A large mirror proclaims "Bruce's Brewery, established 1979." He brews three special strengths, Borough Bitter, 60p (90¢) for a half pint, Dog Bolter, 65p (98¢) for a half, and, for special occasions, Earth Stopper, 90p ($1.35), all only served in halves. Be warned: This one is a real man's beer, and your 90p worth is the equivalent of three measures of whisky in strength.

Food is also available in this lovely old London pub. Each day there is a different hot dish costing from around £2.50 ($3.75). Or else you can order extra-large baps (bread buns) filled with your choice of meat and salad, costing from £1.10 ($2.15).

The whole operation is managed by Jean and Dave Torr, and the brewer is Nigel Gray. Most evenings, there is a pianist playing all the old numbers in a good old "knees-up" style. On weekends, groups of Morris dancers provide an unusual form of entertainment.

HAMPSTEAD: This residential suburb of London, beloved by Keats and Hogarth, is a favorite excursion spot for Londoners on the weekend. The Old Bull and Bush, made famous by Florrie Forde's legendary song, is long gone (the pub bearing that name today is modern). However, there is a pub up here with an authentic historical pedigree. To reach it, take the Northern line of the Underground to the Hampstead Heath station.

Jack Straw's Castle, North End Way, N.W.3 (tel. 435-8374). This weather-board pub is on the summit of the heath, about 443 feet above sea level. The nearby Whitestone Pond was used in the war as an emergency water tank, and previously Shelley used to sail paper boats on the pond.

The pub has been altered and added to, but Dickens knew it well. Jack Straw was one of the leaders of the peasants who revolted along with Wat Tyler in 1381 against what was, basically, a wage freeze. Prices were allowed to rise.

The pub was created in Jack's old home, now a bustling place with a large L-shaped bar and quick-snack counter where there are cold salads, meats, and pies, plus three hot dishes with vegetables served every day. Tabs start at around £2 ($3) a plate, and you can eat in the bar or on the large patio overlooking part of the heath.

The upstairs restaurant has a carvery, offering three courses for £8.25 ($12.38). The place is not often frequented by tourists. After leaving the Underground station, it's a five-minute walk up the hill, where you can enjoy the good fresh air. It's open seven days a week, keeping regular pub hours.

6. The Wine Bars

For years, the stark, atmospheric, and ancient wine cellars of the old City have been patronized by businessmen in bowlers, and were almost a well-kept secret, as you never ran into a tourist or a woman there. However, that has changed now. Wine bars are the fashion, and the pub no longer completely dominates the drinking scene in the English capital.

With the coming of newer and trendier wine bars, London's drinking habits have undergone significant change. Wine bars are not only places at which to drink, but also to meet friends and enjoy good food. A few of the older, more established ones still offer only wine, but in today's terms a wine bar is likely to mean anything, including a disco!

The English taste for wine has increased, hence the number of wine bars springing up in all parts of the city. Nearly all the establishments recommended below sell wine by the glass, although if you're traveling in a party you may want to order by the bottle and share as it's less expensive that way.

I'll lead off with the most interesting collection of wine bars that still lie in the City and are best visited weekdays for lunch. In the other sections of town you can go for both lunch and dinner.

THE CITY: Olde Wine Shades, 6 Martin Lane, off Cannon Street, E.C.4 (tel. 626-6876), is the oldest wine house in the City, dating from 1663. Today's joint hosts are Chris Mitchell and Vic Little. It was the only City tavern to survive the Great Fire of 1666, not to mention the blitz of 1940. Only 100 yards from the Monument, the Olde Wine Shades used to attract Charles Dickens who enjoyed its fine wines. In the smoking room the old oil paintings have appropriately darkened with age, and the 19th-century satirical political cartoons remain enigmatic to most of today's generation. Some of the fine wines of Europe are served here, and port and sherry are drawn directly from an array of casks behind the counter. The owners, El Vino, the City wine merchants, boast that they can satisfy anyone's taste in sherry. A candlewick bar and restaurant is found downstairs, but upstairs, along with your wine, you can order french bread with ham off the bone, Breton pâté, sandwiches, jacket potatoes filled with cheese, steak-and-kidney pie, venison pie with salad garnish, and a large beef salad. Meals range from £7.50 ($11.25). Jackets, collars, and ties are required for men. Jeans or cords are not permitted for women. Hours are from 11:30 a.m. to 3 p.m. and from 5 to 8 p.m. Closed Saturday, Sunday, and bank holidays. Tube: Monument.

Mother Bunch's Wine House, Arches F & G, Old Seacoal Lane, E.C.4 (tel. 236-5317), is a maze of vaults underneath the arches of Ludgate Circus. My favorite of all the wine houses, Mother Bunch's is one of the most atmospheric places for dining in the City, boasting a "well-stocked larder," with the best of hams and all manner of cheeses as well as game and other pies. Port wines of the most noted vintages are decanted daily "for gentlemen in the proper manner." In season, grouse, partridge, pheasant, and Scottish salmon are featured. Guests can dine in the mellow room downstairs or perhaps in the elegantly furnished upstairs room where many are seated around a large table and served family style. Sherry, port, and madeira "from the wood" are served, as well as table wines. The favorite dish is a plate of smoked ham off the bone, although game pie is also praised. Strawberries and raspberries in season make fine dessert. Meals go from £7.50 ($11.25) up. The wine house is open from 11:30 a.m. to 3 p.m. and from 5:30 to 8:30 p.m., Monday to Friday. Tube: Blackfriars.

Bow Wine Vaults, 10 Bow Churchyard, E.C.4 (tel. 248-1121), has existed long before the current wine bar fad. The atmosphere is staunchly masculine, and the vaults attract a loyal following of business and professional people who somehow manage to find their way back to their offices after a heavy eating and drinking session here. Sherries, port, and madeira are available by the glass, as are an assortment of table wines at prices ranging from £1 ($1.50) to £6.50 ($9.75), the latter price for a 1901 vintage Bual madeira. A cold buffet with a salad will run you £4 ($6), the minimum charge. The vaults are open from 11:30 a.m. to 3 p.m. and from 5 to 7 p.m., but closed weekends and bank holidays. Tube: Mansion House.

Jamaica Wine House, St. Michael's Alley, off Cornhill, E.C.3 (tel. 626-9496), lies in a tangle of City alleyways, and if you do manage to find it, you'll be at one of the first coffeehouses to be opened in England. In fact, the Jamaica Wine House is reputed to be the first coffeehouse in the Western world. Pepys used to visit it and mentioned the event in his Diary. The coffeehouse was destroyed in the Great Fire of 1666, rebuilt in 1674, and has remained, more or less, in its present form ever since. For years London merchants and daring sea captains came here to lace deals with rum and coffee. Nowadays, the two-level house dispenses beer, ale, lager, and fine wines, among them a variety of ports, to appreciative drinkers. The oak-paneled bar on the ground floor is more traditional, as the downstairs bar has been modernized. The Bank of England is only a stone's throw away. Tube: Bank.

NEAR LEICESTER SQUARE: Slatters, 3 Panton St., S.W.1 (tel. 839-4649), lies off Haymarket, a split-level wine bar convenient for theatergoers. It makes a good rendezvous for pre-theater and after-theater suppers. A stylish informality reigns. Classical music plays in the background and the paintings on the wall are for sale. Some are originals; others are lithographs—all with theatrical and dance themes, executed and signed by Tome Merrifield and priced from £30 ($45). The house wine is from France, and you can drink it at £1.10 ($1.65) a glass, along with food offered by owner Kenneth Slatter. The smoked trout is a favorite opener, followed by the underdone pink roast beef. Try also the mackerel pâté served with french bread or perhaps baked ham or chicken. The cheese board is first class. The average three-course meal here will cost from £8

($12), or try pink roast beef at £4 ($6) a plate. Closed on Sunday, Slatters is open for lunch or dinner until midnight. Happy hour is from 8 to 10 nightly. Tube: Leicester Square.

Cork and Bottle Wine Bar, 44–46 Cranbourn St., W.C.2 (tel. 734-7807), is in the theater district. Don and Jean Hewitson, the owners, devote a great deal of love and care to this establishment. Jean has revitalized the food, with a wide range of hot dishes, so that it is not a typical glass of wine and a slice of pâté type of bistro. Her most successful dish is her raised cheese-and-ham pie at £2 ($3). In just one week she sold 500 portions of this alone. She bagged, or else begged, the recipe for this from her favorite little bistro in the Rue Monge in Paris. It has a cream-cheesy filling, and the well-buttered pastry is crisp—not your typical quiche.

She also offers a mâchon Lyonnaise, a traditional worker's lunch in Lyon. The Hewitson's import their own saussiçon from a charcuterie in Lyon, serving it hot with warm potato salad, a mixed green salad, spicy Dijon mustard, and french bread for about £3 ($4.50). Don has expanded the wine list, and he doubts if anyone in the U.K. has a better selection of Beaujolais Cru and wines from Alsace. They also stock a good selection of California labels.

In fact, Don, a New Zealander, has been called the "kiwi guru of the modern wine bar movement." Their bar is open Monday to Saturday from 11 a.m. to 3 p.m. and from 5:30 to 11 p.m. Tube: Leicester Square.

MAYFAIR: Downs Wine Bar, 5 Down St., W.1 (tel. 491-3810), attracts "the beautiful people" of Mayfair, who live in and around that square mile at the Hyde Park end of Piccadilly, near the Athenaeum Hotel. In fair weather, there are sidewalk tables. Every evening you can descend a spiral staircase to a simple, admission-free disco. Nearly 100 wines are available, each bottled in its country of origin. The food specialty is ham cooked in marmalade. Hot and cold dishes have prices ranging from £2 ($3) to £6.50 ($9.75). The upstairs dining room is decorated in a modern style with chrome and cane chairs, along with banquettes. Hours are from 11:30 a.m. to 3 p.m. and from 5:30 to midnight daily, from noon to 3 p.m. and from 7 p.m. to 12:30 a.m. on Sunday. Tube: Green Park.

IN BLOOMSBURY: Entrecôte, 124 Southampton Row, W.C.1 (tel. 405-1466), invites you to go downstairs to its Edwardian precincts. Attractive women students are the waitresses, and they will serve you the house specialty, an entrecôte with french fries. Selections from the cheese board are first rate. Other daily specials are offered as well—perhaps homemade turtle soup, steak flambé, coq au vin, or beef bourguignonne. In fact, the food is generally French inspired, and the wine list includes some Haut Médoc selections. The price of a meal ranges from about £8 ($12) to £13 ($19.50). A three-piece band plays nightly from 8 to 9; otherwise, there is disco music. The restaurant is open Monday to Saturday from 11:30 a.m. to 3:30 p.m. and from 3:30 p.m. to 1 a.m. On Sunday its hours are from 5:30 p.m. to midnight. This has become a popular candlelit, romantic nightspot with many young people in the London University area. Tube: Russell Square.

IN BELGRAVIA: Motcomb's, 26 Motcomb St., S.W.1 (tel. 235-6382), opposite Sotheby's Belgravia, is one of the handsomest and most charming wine bars in London. A small, friendly place above the main restaurant, it is run by Betty, Don, and Jani Phillips. The bar is decorated with old paintings and mementos and has a club-like atmosphere. Only sandwiches are served in the evening. Otherwise, a complete range of hot and cold homemade food is served, with a buffet for each. Lunch averages £3.50 ($5.25), and you can feast on things like crab with mushrooms, shepherd's pie, and turkey with sage. Motcomb's is open from noon to 3:30 p.m. and from 7 to 11 p.m. in the restaurant and from 11:30 a.m. to 3 p.m. and 5:30 to 11 p.m. in the bar, Monday to Friday. Tube: Knightsbridge.

Bill Bentley's, 31 Beauchamp Pl., S.W.3 (tel. 589-5080), stands on this restaurant- and boutique-lined street near Harrods. A small Georgian house, it offers many ground-floor rooms and a little sun-filled patio in back. Cozy and atmospheric, it presents a varied list of reasonably priced wines, including a fine selection of bordeaux. If you're in the neighborhood for lunch, you can enjoy a pub-style lunch, such as ham and salad. Hot main dishes are likely to include skate in black butter with capers and grilled lemon sole. Meals cost from £12 ($18). It's open daily from 11:30 a.m. to 3 p.m. and from 5:30 to 11 p.m., on Saturday from 6:30 to 11 p.m. Closed Sunday and bank holidays. Tube: Knightsbridge.

CHELSEA: **Blushes**, 52 King's Rd., S.W.3 (tel. 589-6640), is the nearest you will get to a singles bar in London. This attractively decorated watering hole serves drinks and food all day from morning to midnight. Food is the main consideration here, wine a close second. You can select from dishes such as chicken in fennel, creamy chicken with tarragon, and taramasalata with pita bread. A well-filled plate will cost around £4.20 ($6.30). Blushes is open from 11 a.m. to midnight Monday to Saturday, from noon to 11:30 p.m. on Sunday, but it's closed Christmas Day. At night, there is a busy cocktail bar in the basement. Be prepared to be kept waiting before you get in. They call the dress "smart" around here. Tube: Sloane Square.

Charco's/Searcy's, 1 Bray Pl., S.W.3 (tel. 584-0765), has an entrance on two streets in Chelsea, lying right off King's Road. A very bright crowd patronizes this establishment, enjoying the reasonably priced wines and the home-cooked food, which makes a tempting sight when you enter and see the cold meats, salads, and cheeses spread out before you. On the blackboard are listed such foods as leek soup, seafood vol-au-vents, chicken casserole, and beef bourguignonne. Fresh fruit salad or rich homemade chocolate cake will make a good dessert. A two-course meal costs £4.50 ($6.75). In the evening, your table will be candlelit, and in summer you may dine at one of the sidewalk tables. The wine bar is open from 11 a.m. to 3 p.m. and from 5:30 to 11 p.m. daily (Sunday, noon to 2 p.m. and 7 to 10:30 p.m.). Tim Connolly is the manager. Tube: Sloane Square.

Chapter IV

LONDON: WHAT TO SEE AND DO

1. Seeing the Sights
2. Shopping for Value
3. London After Dark
4. Taking the Tours
5. One-Day Trips from London

DR. JOHNSON SAID: "When a man is tired of London, he is tired of life, for there is in London all that life can afford." And that holds true today.

Come along with me as we survey only a fraction of that life: ancient monuments, boutiques, debates in Parliament, art galleries, Soho, dives, museums, theaters, flea markets, and castles. Some of what we're about to see was known to Johnson and Boswell, even Shakespeare, but much of it is new.

1. Seeing the Sights

London is not a city to visit hurriedly. It is so vast, so stocked with treasures that the visitor does himself or herself a disservice if he or she plans to "do" London in two or three days. Not only will a person miss many of the highlights, he or she will also fail to grasp the spirit of London and to absorb fully its special flavor, which is unique among cities. Still, faced with an infinite number of important places to visit and a time clock running out, the tourist will have to concentrate on a manageable group. I'll survey a personal list of the indispensable sights for those with a minimum of time, then follow in this section with "The Best of the Rest," But first, a digression.

BARGAIN TIP: The **Department of the Environment**, 25 Savile Row, W.1 (tel. 734-6010), offers a **Season Ticket to History,** which allows the holder free and unlimited entry to all those places in England, Scotland, and Wales that are maintained by the British government. The cost of the ticket, payable only by international money order (sterling only) is £10 ($15) for adults, £5 ($7.50) for children under 16. Valid for one year, it can be purchased by mail only from Department of the Environment (St),

AMHB Store, Room 32, Building 1, Victoria Road, South Ruislip, Middlesex HA4 ONZ, or at any of the Ancient Monuments that have custodians. A list of sights to be seen, including the Tower of London, Hampton Court Palace, Stonehenge, and Edinburgh Castle, citing opening times and available facilities, is given free with each ticket order.

An **Open to View** ticket sells for $26 (U.S.) for adults, $13.50 for children, and includes free admission to more than 500 properties in Britain, including Edinburgh Castle, Churchill's Chartwell, Woburn Abbey, Hampton Court Palace, and Windsor Castle. It is good for one month after you first use it, and covers all properties in care of Britain's National Trust and those run by the Department of the Environment. It is estimated that anyone visiting as many as five of these sightseeing attractions will get back the initial outlay. In the U.S., inquire at **BritRail Travel International Inc.,** 630 Third Ave., New York, NY 10017; 333 North Michigan Ave., Chicago, IL 60601; 510 West 6th St., Los Angeles, CA 90014; or P.O. Box 58047, World Trade Center, Dallas, TX 75258.

THE TOWER OF LONDON: This ancient fortress on the north bank of the Thames continues to pack 'em in because of its macabre associations with all the legendary figures who were either imprisoned or executed here, or both. James Street once wrote, ". . . there are more spooks to the square foot than in any other building in the whole of haunted Britain. Headless bodies, bodiless heads, phantom soldiers, icy blasts, clanking chains—you name them, the Tower's got them."

Back in the days of the axman, London was "swinging" long before *Time* magazine discovered that fact. Ranking in interest are the colorful attending Yeoman Warders, the so-called Beefeaters, in Tudor dress, who look as if they are on the payroll for gin advertisements (but don't like to be reminded of it).

Many visitors consider a visit to the Tower to be the highlight of their sightseeing in London—so schedule plenty of time for it. You don't have to stay as long as Sir Walter Raleigh (released after some 13 years), but give it an afternoon. Take the tube to Tower Hill or bus 13 to Monument. The Tower is open March to October Monday to Saturday from 9:30 a.m. to 5 p.m., and from 2 to 5 p.m. on Sunday. Off-season hours are usually from 9:30 a.m. to 4 p.m. The Jewel House is closed in February. In summer, admission is £3 ($4.50) for adults, £1.50 ($2.25) for children under 16. Winter rates are £2 ($3) for adults, £1 ($1.50) for children. The Jewel House requires a separate admission of 80p ($1.20) for adults, 40p (60¢) for children. For further information about opening times and visiting privileges, telephone 709-0765, extension 303.

Don't expect to find only one tower. The fortress is actually a compound, in which the oldest and finest structure is the White Tower, begun by William the Conqueror. Here you can view the Armories, the present collection dating back to the reign of Henry VIII. A display of instruments of torture and execution will be spread before you, recalling some of the most ghastly moments in the history of the Tower. At the Bloody Tower, the Little Princes (Edward V and the Duke of York) were allegedly murdered by their uncle, Richard III.

The hospitality today far excels that of years ago, when many of the visitors left their cells only to walk to the headsman's block on Tower Hill. Through Traitors' Gate passed such ill-fated, but romantic, figures as Robert Devereux, a favorite of Elizabeth I, known as the second Earl of Essex. Elizabeth herself, then a princess, was once imprisoned briefly in Bell Tower. At Tower Green, Anne Boleyn and Katharine Howard, two wives of Henry VIII, lost their lives. The nine-day queen, Lady Jane Grey, and her husband, Dudley, also were executed, along with such figures as Sir Thomas More.

According to legend, the disappearance of the well-protected ravens at the Tower will presage the collapse of the British Empire (seen any around lately?).

To see the Jewel House, where the Crown Jewels are kept, go early in summer, as long lines usually form by late morning. Get a Beefeater to tell you how Colonel Blood almost made off with the crown and regalia in the late 17th century. Of the three English crowns, the Imperial State Crown is the most important—in fact, it's probably the most famous crown on earth. Made for Victoria for her coronation in 1838, it is today worn by Queen Elizabeth when she opens Parliament. Studded with some 3000 jewels (principally diamonds), it contains the Black Prince's Ruby, worn by Henry V at Agincourt, the battle in 1415 when the English defeated the French. In addition, feast your eyes on the 530-carat Star of Africa, a cut diamond on the Royal Sceptre with Cross. The Jewel House is closed for four to six weeks early in each year for the annual cleaning and overhaul.

The Tower of London has an evening ceremony called the **Ceremony of the Keys.** It begins with visitors who have tickets being admitted by a Beefeater around 9:35 p.m. It is, in fact, the changing of the guard and the ceremonial locking up of the Tower for yet another day in its 900 years. Nothing stops the ceremony. During World War II, a bomb fell within the castle walls during the ceremony, and nobody flinched—but the Tower was locked up two minutes late. Rumor has it that the guard that night was censured for tardiness, the pilot of the plane that dropped the bomb blamed as the culprit. The Beefeater will explain to guests the significance of the ceremony. For tickets, write to the Governor, Tower of London, London, E.C.3, England, requesting a specific date but also giving alternate dates you'd like to attend. One-week notice is preferred.

WESTMINSTER ABBEY: No less than such an illustrious figure as St. Peter is supposed to have left his calling card at the abbey. If it's true, I wouldn't be surprised—for nearly everybody else, at least nearly everybody in English history, has left his mark. But what is known for certain is that in 1065 the Saxon king, Edward the Confessor, rebuilt the old minster church on this spot, overlooking Parliament Square (tube to Westminster), and founded the Benedictine abbey.

The first English king crowned in the abbey was Harold in 1066, who was killed at the Battle of Hastings that same year. The man who defeated him, Edward's cousin, William the Conqueror, was also crowned in the abbey; the coronation tradition has continued to the present day, broken only twice (Edward V and Edward VIII). The essentially Early English Gothic structure existing today owes more to Henry III's plans than to any other sovereign, although many architects, including Wren, have contributed to the abbey.

Adults pay £1.40 ($2.10) and children pay 40p (60¢) to visit the Royal

Chapel, the Royal Tombs, the Coronation Chair, and the Henry VII Chapel. Hours are Monday to Friday from 9:20 a.m. to 4:45 p.m., and on Saturday from 9:20 a.m. to 2:45 p.m. and 3:45 to 5:45 p.m. On Wednesday, the abbey, including the Royal Chapels, are open with free admission from 6 to 8 p.m. This is the only time photography is allowed. On Sunday, the Royal Chapels are closed, but the rest of the church is open between services.

Built on the site of the ancient Lady Chapel, in the early 16th century, the Henry VII Chapel is one of the loveliest in Europe, with its fan vaulting, colorful Knights of Bath banners, and Torrigiani-designed tomb of the king himself over which is placed a 15th-century Vivarini painting of *Madonna and Bambino*. The chapel represents the flowering of the Perpendicular Gothic style. Also buried here are those feuding sisters, Elizabeth I and Mary Tudor ("Bloody Mary"). Elizabeth I was always vain and adored jewelry. The effigy that lies on top of her tomb has been fitted out with a new set of jewelry, a gilded collar and pendant, a modern copy derived from a painting now at Hatfield House. The originals were stolen by souvenir hunters in the early 18th century. Her orb and sceptre were added earlier. In one end of the chapel you can stand on Cromwell's memorial stone and view the R.A.F. chapel containing the Battle of Britain memorial stained-glass window, unveiled in 1947 to honor the R.A.F.

You can also visit the most hallowed spot in the abbey, the shrine of Edward the Confessor (canonized in the 12th century). In the saint's chapel is the Coronation Chair, made at the command of Edward I in 1300 to contain the Stone of Scone. Scottish kings were once crowned on this stone (in 1950 the Scots stole it back, but it was later returned to its position in the abbey). Nearby are the sword and shield of Edward III.

Another noted spot in the abbey is Poets' Corner, to the right of the entrance to the Royal Chapel, with its monuments to everybody from Chaucer on down—the Brontë sisters, Shakespeare, Tennyson, Dickens, Kipling, Thackeray, Samuel Johnson, "O Rare Ben Johnson" (his name misspelled), even the American Longfellow. The most stylized and controversial monument is Sir Jacob Epstein's sculptured bust of William Blake. The latest tablet commemorates Dylan Thomas.

Statesmen and men of science—such as Disraeli, Newton, Charles Darwin—are also either interred in the abbey or honored by monuments. Near the west door is the 1965 memorial to Sir Winston Churchill. In the vicinity of this memorial is the tomb of the Unknown Soldier, symbol of British dead in World War I. Surprisingly, some of the most totally obscure personages are buried in the abbey, including an abbey plumber.

Many visitors overlook such sights as the 13th-century Chapter House, where Parliament used to meet (special shoes must be worn to walk across the 700-year-old floor). The Chapter House in the Great Cloister is open from 9:30 a.m. till 6 p.m. (closed on Sunday) from March through September. It shuts down at 3:30 p.m. off-season.

Even more fascinating are the treasures in the museum in the Norman undercroft (crypt), part of the monastic buildings erected between 1066 and 1100. The collection includes effigies—figures in wax, such as that of Nelson, and woodcarvings of early English royalty. Along with the wax figures—the abbey's answer to Madame Tussaud—are ancient documents, seals, replicas of coronation regalia, old religious vestments (such as the cope worn at the coronation of Charles II), the sword of Henry V, and the famous Essex Ring that Elizabeth I is supposed to have given to her favorite earl. The museum, which charges 35p (53¢) for adults, 10p (15¢) for children, is open daily from 9:30 a.m. till 6 p.m., April 1 to September 30, 10:30 a.m. till 4 p.m. from October 1 to March 31. It is not open on Sunday during the winter.

For tours of the abbey with an expert guide, the cost is £3 ($4.50) per person. These tours operate Monday through Friday at 10:15 and 10:45 a.m., 2:15 and 2:45 p.m. On Saturday, the hours are 10:15 and 10:45 a.m. Inquire at the West Door for the meeting point.

For times of services and other information, telephone the Chapter Office, (tel. 222-5152).

Off the Cloisters, **College Garden** is the oldest garden in England, under cultivation for more than 900 years. Surrounded by high walls, flowering trees dot the lawns, and park benches provide comfort where you can hardly hear the roar of passing traffic. It is open on Thursday throughout the year, from 10 a.m. to 4 p.m. in winter, to 6 p.m. in summer. In August and September, band concerts are held at lunchtime from 12:30 to 2 p.m. Admission is free.

HOUSES OF PARLIAMENT:
These are the spiritual opposite of the Tower, the stronghold of Britain's democracy, the assemblies that effectively trimmed the sails of royal power. Strangely enough, both Houses (Commons and Lords) are in the formerly royal Palace of Westminster, the king's residence until Henry VIII moved to Whitehall.

Although I can't assure you of the oratory of a Charles James Fox or a William Pitt the Elder, the debates are often lively and controversial in the House of Commons (seats are at a premium during crises). The chances of getting into the House of Lords when it's in session are generally better than they are in the more popular House of Commons, where even the Queen isn't allowed. The old guard of the palace informs me that the peerage speak their minds more freely and are less likely to adhere to party line than their counterparts in the Commons.

The general public is admitted to the Strangers' Gallery in the House of Commons on "sitting days"—normally about 4:15 p.m. on Monday to Thursday and about 9:30 a.m. on Friday. You have to join a public queue outside the St. Stephen's entrance on the day in question. Often, there is considerable delay before the head of the public queue is admitted. You might speed matters up somewhat by applying at the American Embassy or the Canadian High Commission for a special pass, but this is too cumbersome for many people. Besides, the embassy has only four tickets for daily distribution, so probably you might as well stand in line. It is usually easier to get in after about 6 p.m.

The head of the queue is normally admitted to the Strangers' Gallery of the House of Lords after 2:40 p.m. from Monday to Wednesday (often at 3 p.m. on Thursday).

The present House of Commons was built in 1840, but the chamber was bombed and destroyed by the German air force in 1941. The 320-foot tower that houses Big Ben, however, remained standing and the celebrated clock continued to strike its chimes—the signature tune of Britain's wartime news broadcasts. "Big Ben," incidentally, was named after Sir Benjamin Hall, a cabinet minister distinguished only by his long-windedness.

At press time, the Houses of Parliament and Westminster Palace were both closed to the public (except for the Strangers' Galleries during sessions of the Lords and Commons). However, they might be open by the time of your visit. Check with the House of Commons by phoning 219-4272.

In the Palace of Westminster is a handsomely decorated Robing Room and the Royal Gallery with the sunburst theme on the ceiling, as well as the Princes' Chamber, with portraits of Henry VIII and his many wives. From the days of Edward the Confessor to the much-married Henry, the palace was a royal residence.

Westminster Hall, scene of the trials of Guy Fawkes and of Charles I, is the oldest surviving structure in the complex and the oldest public building in London. It was built by William Rufus in 1097. He intended it to be "but a bedroom" of the real palace he was going to erect, but he was prevented by death, three years later, from carrying out his plans. The hall is stupendously large. During a 15th-century flooding, rescuers actually rowed around it in boats.

THE BRITISH MUSEUM: Within its imposing citadel on Great Russell Street in Bloomsbury (tube to Holborn or Tottenham Court Road), the British Museum shelters one of the most catholic collections of art and artifacts in the world, containing countless treasures of ancient civilizations. To storm this bastion in a day is a formidable task, but there are riches to see even on a cursory first visit. Basically, the overall storehouse splits into the National Museum of Antiquities and Ethnography and the Department of Coins and Medals—each of which, in its own way, has much to offer. On occasion, special exhibits of the Department of Prints and Drawings are shown.

As you enter the front hall, you may want to head first to the Assyrian Transept on the ground floor, where you'll find the winged and human-headed bulls and lions that once guarded the gateways to the palaces of Assyrian kings, along with a rare Black Obelisk from about 860 B.C. From here you can go into the angular hall of Egyptian sculpture to see the Rosetta Stone, whose discovery led to the deciphering of the mysterious hieroglyphics, explained in a wall display behind the stone.

Also on the ground floor is the Duveen Gallery, housing the Elgin Marbles, consisting chiefly of sculpture from a frieze on the Parthenon showing a ceremonial procession that took place in Athens every four years. Of the 92 metopes from the Parthenon, 15 are housed today in the British Museum. The metopes depict the to-the-death struggle between the handsome Lapiths and the grotesque, drunken Centaurs. The head of the horse from the chariot of Selene, goddess of the moon, is one of the pediment sculptures.

The classical sculpture galleries hold *The Caryatid* from the Erechtheum, a temple started in 421 B.C. and dedicated to Athena and Poseidon. Also displayed here is a statue of Mausolus, Prince of Caria, who died in 353 B.C. His tomb at Halicarnassus was listed among the seven wonders of the world. Look also for the blue and white Portland Vase, considered the finest example of ancient cameo carving, having been made about A.D. 30.

The Department of Medieval and Later Antiquities has its galleries on the first floor, reached by the main staircase. Of its exhibitions, the Sutton Hoo funeral deposit, discovered at Ipswich, Suffolk, is, in the words of an expert, "the richest treasure ever dug from English soil"—containing gold jewelry, armor, weapons, bronze bowls and cauldrons, silverware, and the inevitable drinking horn of the Norse culture. No body was found, although the tomb is believed to be that of a king of East Anglia who died in the seventh century A.D. You'll also see the bulging-eyed Lewis Chessmen, Romanesque carvings by the Scandinavians of the 12th century, and the Ilbert collection of clocks and watches.

The featured attractions of the Upper Floor are the Egyptian Galleries, especially the mummies. The fourth Egyptian room is extraordinary, looking like the props for *Cleopatra,* with its cosmetics, domestic utensils, toys, tools, and other work. Some rare gems of Sumerian and Babylonian art—unearthed from the Royal Cemetery at Ur (southern Iraq)—lie in the room beyond: a bull-headed queen's harp (oldest ever discovered); a queen's sledge (oldest known example of a land vehicle); and a figure of a he-goat on its hind legs, crafted about 2500 B.C. In the Iranian room rests "The Treasure of Oxus," a hoard of riches, probably from the fifth century B.C., containing a unique collection of goldsmith work, such as a nude youth, signet rings, a fish-shaped vase, and votive plaques.

The museum is open weekdays from 10 a.m. till 5 p.m. (on Sunday from 2:30 to 6 p.m.). It is closed Good Friday, Christmas Eve, Christmas Day, Boxing Day, New Year's Day, and the first Monday in May. Admission to all parts of the museum is free.

Incidentally, the Ethnography Department is housed at 6 Burlington Gardens, W.1, where the galleries are open to the public during the same hours as above.

The British Library

In the east wing the galleries form part of the British Library (tel. 636-1544). In the Grenville Library you'll see the Benedictional (in Latin) of St. Ethelwold, Bishop of Winchester (A.D. 963–984), regarded as one of the most splendid medieval works of art in England. The library also contains the Manuscript Saloon, with its collection of autographs by such men as Cromwell, Disraeli, Sir Walter Raleigh, Newton, Pepys, Wren, Milton, Dr. Johnson, Pope, Fielding, and Swift.

There are also seven major exhibits (at least) of world interest: the Codex Sinaiticus (a Greek version of the Bible, written in the fourth century A.D.); the Lindisfarne Gospels (a masterpiece, viewed by experts as one of the important treasures from early Northumbria, written and illustrated about A.D. 698); Shakespeare's mortgage deed (with his signature, of course) to the Blackfriars Gate House: Capt. Robert Scott's journals telling of his attempt to reach the South Pole in the expedition of 1910-1912; a memorandum by Admiral Nelson explaining his plans for engaging the allied French and Spanish fleet, taken from the *Victory* logbook, and a letter to Lady Hamilton written two days before he died in the Battle of Trafalgar; and finally, documents relating to the Magna Carta, including the Articles of the Barons, demands accepted by King John at Runnymede in June 1215, along with John's seal of white wax and two of the four surviving exemplifications of Magna Carta issued over his seal.

In the King's Library rests a First Folio (1623) of the comedies, histories, and tragedies of Shakespeare. In addition, don't miss the Gutenberg Bible, the first substantial book ever printed with movable type (of the copies known, the British Library possesses one printed on paper, another on vellum—circa 1455). There is also a display of priceless Oriental manuscripts and books.

Like the museum, the British Library often changes part of its permanent gallery displays to set up special exhibitions in rotation, for example, to mark a centenary. The opening times of the British Library's exhibition galleries are the same as those of the museum. Admission is free.

The Museum of Mankind

The Museum of Mankind, the Ethnography Department of the British Museum, is housed at 6 Burlington Gardens, W.1 (tel. 437-2224), where the galleries are open to the public during the same hours as those of the Bloomsbury museum. It has the world's largest collections of art and material culture from tribal societies. A selection of treasures from five continents is displayed, and a number of exhibitions show the life, art, and technology of selected cultures. New exhibitions are mounted every year. Seek out, in particular, the pre-Columbian Mexican turquoise mosaics. Weekday hours are from 10 a.m. to 5 p.m.; on Sunday 2:30 to 6 p.m.; and there is no admission charged.

MADAME TUSSAUD'S: Strasbourg-born Marie Tussaud was to become world-famous as the madame of the macabre. She went to Paris at the age of six to join her uncle, Dr. Curtius. In 1770 he opened an exhibition of life-size wax figures. During the French Revolution, the head of almost every distinguished victim of the guillotine was molded by Madame Tussaud or her uncle.

After the death of Curtius, Madame Tussaud inherited the exhibition, and in 1802 she left France for England. For 33 years she toured the United Kingdom with her exhibition, and in 1835 she settled on Baker Street. The exhibition was such a success that it practically immortalized her in her day; she continued to make portraits until she was 81 (she died in 1850). The perennially popular waxworks (tel. 935-6861) are visited by some tourists even before they check out Westminster Abbey or the Tower of London.

Some of the works displayed came from molds cast by the incomparable Madame Tussaud herself. But to keep from becoming stilted the waxworks continue to make new figures, whoever is *au courant*. Of course, good old reliables, such as Sir Winston, can always be counted on to be there. Some of the figures—that of Voltaire, for example—were taken from life.

In the Chamber of Horrors, redesigned in 1980, you can have the vicarious thrill of meeting such types as Dr. Crippen, and walking through a Victorian London street where special effects include the shadow terror of Jack the Ripper. The instruments and victims of death penalties contrast with present-day criminals portrayed within the confines of prison.

An enlarged Grand Hall, as well as high-speed elevators and air conditioning, are welcome improvements. In "Heroes," with a sequence of sound, light, and projection, each hero is presented in turn, including David Bowie, Humphrey Bogart, and Elvis Presley. On the ground floor, you can relive the Battle of Trafalgar, complete with Nelson's recreated flagship. Madame Tussaud's costs £4 ($6) for adults, £2.20 ($3.30) for children under 16. You can visit both Madame Tussaud's and the neighboring **Planetarium** for £5 ($7.50), £3 ($4.50) for children under 16. Take the tube to Baker Street (entrance on Marylebone Road). Madame Tussaud's is open daily from 10 a.m. till 5:30 p.m., including Saturday and Sunday. It's closed only on Christmas Day.

TATE GALLERY: This building, beside the Thames on Millbank, houses the best grouping of British paintings from the 16th century on, as well as England's finest collection of modern art, from the French impressionists to the latest developments. The Tate is open from 10 a.m. to 6 p.m. weekdays (on Sunday from 2 to 6 p.m.). To reach it, take the tube to Pimlico or bus 88 or 77A. The number of paintings is staggering. If time permits, try to schedule at least two visits—the first to see the classic English works, the second to take in the modern collection (circa 1870 to the present). Since only a portion of the collections can be shown simultaneously, the works on display vary from time to time. However, the most time-pressed individual may not want to miss the following, which are almost invariably on view:

The first giant among English painters, William Hogarth (1697–1764), is well represented, particularly by his satirical *O the Roast Beef of Old England,* (known as *Calais Gate),* with its caricatured figures, such as the gluttonous monk. The ruby-eyed *Satan, Sin, and Death* remains one of his most imaginative works.

Two other famous British painters of the 18th century (exhibited in Galleries 4 and 5) are Sir Joshua Reynolds (1723–1792) and Thomas Gainsborough (1727–1788). Reynolds, the portrait painter, shines brightest when he's painting himself (three self-portraits hang side by side). Two other portraits, that of Francis and Suzanna Beckford, are typical of his early work. His rival, Gainsborough, is noted for his portraits too, and also landscapes ("my real love"). His landscapes with gypsies are subdued, mysterious; *Wooded Landscape with Peasant Resting* is more representative. One of Gainsborough's most celebrated portraits is *Edward Richard Gardiner,* a handsome boy in blue (the more famous *Blue Boy* is in California). Two extremely fine Gainsborough portraits have recently been acquired: *Giovanna Baccelli* (1782), who was well known both as a dancer and as the mistress of the third Earl of Dorset, and *Sir Benjamin Truman,* the notable brewer.

In the art of J. M. W. Turner (1775–1851), the Tate possesses its greatest collection of the works of a single artist. Most of the paintings and watercolors exhibited here were willed to the nation by Turner (collection divided among the Tate, the National Gallery, and the British Museum). Of his paintings of stormy seas, none is more horrifying than *Shipwreck* (1805). In the Petworth series, he broke from realism (see his *Interior at Petworth).* His delicate impressionism is best conveyed in his sunset and sunrise pictures, with their vivid reds and yellows. Turner's vortex paintings, inspired by theories of Goethe, are *Light and Color—the Morning After the Deluge,* and *Shade and Darkness—the Evening of the Deluge.*

In a nation of landscape painters, John Constable (1776–1837) stands out. Some of his finest works include *Flatford Mill,* a scene from his native East Anglia, and in a different mood, the stormy sketch for *Hadleigh Castle.*

American-born Sir Jacob Epstein became one of England's greatest sculptors, and some of his bronzes are owned and occasionally displayed by the Tate. Augustus John, who painted everybody from G. B. Shaw to Tallulah Bankhead, is also represented here with portraits and sketches.

The Tate owns some of the finest works of the Pre-Raphaelite period of the mid-19th century. One of the best of the English artists of the 20th century, Sir Stanley Spencer (1891–1959) is best represented by his two versions of *Resurrection* and three remarkable self-portraits.

The Tate has many major paintings from both the 19th and 20th centuries, including Wyndham Lewis's portraits of Edith Sitwell and of Ezra Pound, and Paul Nash's *Voyages of the Moon*. But the drawings of William Blake (1757–1827) attract the most attention. Blake, of course, was the incomparable mystical poet and illustrator of such works as *The Book of Job, The Divine Comedy,* and *Paradise Lost.*

In the modern collections, the Tate contains Matisse's *L'Escargot* and *The Inattentive Reader,* along with works by Dali, Chagall, Modigliani, Munch, Ben Nicholson (large collection of his works), and Dubuffet. The different periods of Picasso bloom in *Woman in a Chemise* (1905), *Three Dancers* (1925), *Nude Woman in a Red Armchair* (1932), *Goat's Skull, Bottle, and Candle* (1952), and *Reclining Nude* (1968).

Truly remarkable is the room devoted to several enormous, somber, but rich abstract canvases by Mark Rothko, the group of paintings by Giacometti and sculptures by Giacometti (1901–1966), and the paintings of two of England's best known modern artists, Francis Bacon (especially gruesome, *Three Studies for Figures at the Base of a Crucifixion)* and Graham Sutherland (see his portrait of W. Somerset Maugham).

Many world-famous pieces of sculpture are usually on display, including works by Rodin, Henry Moore, and Barbara Hepworth.

Downstairs is a coffeeshop offering tea, coffee, sandwiches, and cakes. There is also a restaurant.

Admission to the general gallery is free, but for special exhibitions, a charge of approximately £1.50 ($2.25) is made (half price for children).

For the **Tate Gallery Restaurant,** Millbank, S.W.1, telephone 834-6754 for reservations. The menus, at least the main dishes, are selected from a vast array of cosmopolitan dishes. It is essential to reserve, as this place is very popular with Tate visitors as well as local business people. It's still the choice for taking a maiden aunt out to lunch, as the service, by pleasant young women, is good and polite, the dishes well prepared.

NATIONAL GALLERY: On the north side of Trafalgar Square, in an impressive neoclassic building, the National Gallery houses one of the most comprehensive collections of European paintings, representing all the major schools from the 13th to the early 20th centuries. The largest part of the collection is devoted to the Italians, including the Sienese, Venetian, and Florentine masters.

Of the early Gothic works, the *Wilton Diptych* in Room 1 (French school, late 14th century) is the rarest treasure. It stands in a niche by itself, and depicts Richard II being introduced to the Madonna and Child by such good contacts as John the Baptist and the Saxon king, Edward the Confessor.

A Florentine gem, a Virgin and grape-eating Bambino, by Masaccio (one of the founders of modern painting) is in Room 3. In Room 4 are notable works by Piero della Francesca, particularly his linear *The Baptism.*

In a specially lighted hall, Room 7, is the famous cartoon (in the fine arts sense) of *The Virgin and Child with Saint John and Saint Anne* by Leonardo da Vinci. Matter and spirit meet in the haunting nether world of the *Virgin of the Rocks,* a Leonardo painting, now hung in Room 8. Also in Room 8 are two other giants of the Renaissance—Michelangelo (represented by an unfinished painting, *The Entombment),* and Raphael *(The Ansidei Madonna,* among others).

The Venetian masters of the 16th century, to whom color was

paramount, fill Room 9. The most notable works include a rare *Adoration of the Kings* by Giorgione; *Bacchus and Ariadne* by Titian; *The Beginning of the Milky Way* by Tintoretto (a lush galaxy, with light streaming from Juno's breasts); and *The Darius Family Kneeling Before Alexander the Great* by Veronese (one of the best paintings at the National). Surrounding are a number of satellite rooms, filled with works by major Italian masters of the 15th century—artists such as Andrea Mantegna of Padua *(Agony in the Garden);* his brother-in-law, Giovanni Bellini (his portrait of the Venetian doge, Leonardo Loredano, provided a change of pace from his many interpretations of Madonnas); finally, Botticelli, represented by *Mars and Venus, Adoration of the Magi,* and *Portrait of a Young Man* in Room 5.

The painters of northern Europe are well displayed. In Room 24, for example, is Jan van Eyck's portrait of G. Arnolfini and his bride, and Pieter Brueghel the Elder's Bosch-influenced *Adoration* (Room 25), with its unkingly kings and ghoul-like onlookers. In Room 28 the 17th-century pauper, Vermeer, is rich on canvas in a *Young Woman at a Virginal,* a favorite theme of his. Fellow Delft-ite Pieter de Hooch comes on sublimely in a *Patio in a House in Delft* (Room 28).

One of the big drawing cards of the National is its collection of Rembrandts in Rooms 15, 19, 26, and 27. Rembrandt, the son of a miller, became the greatest painter in the Netherlands in the 17th century. His *Self-Portrait at the Age of 34* shows him at the pinnacle of his life, his *Self-Portrait at the Age of 63* is more deeply moving and revealing. For another Rembrandt study in old age, see his *Portrait of Margaretha Trip* (Room 27). *The Woman Taken in Adultery* shows the artist's human sympathy. Rembrandt's portrait of his mistress, Hendrickje Stoffels, last displayed in public in the 1930s, has been bought and is now displayed by the National Gallery (Room 26). The picture is signed and dates from 1659. The purchase price has not been disclosed, but the market value is believed to be in the region of $2,000,000. Part of the prolific output of Peter Paul Rubens is to be seen in Room 20, notably his *Peace and War* and *The Rape of the Sabine Women.*

Five of the greatest of the home-grown artists—Constable, Turner, Reynolds, Gainsborough, and Hogarth—share their paintings with the Tate. But the National owns masterpieces by each of them. Constable's *Cornfield* is another scene of East Anglia, along with *Haywain,* perhaps his best known work, a harmony of light and atmosphere. Completely different from Constable is the work of Turner, including his dreamy *Fighting Téméraire* and *Rain, Steam, and Speed.* Room 34 is essentially a portrait gallery, hung with several works by Sir Joshua Reynolds, along with a Gainsborough masterpiece, *The Morning Walk,* an idealistic blending of portraiture with landscape. Finally, in a completely different brush stroke, Hogarth's *Marriage à la Mode* caricatures the marriages of convenience of the upper class of the 18th century.

The three giants of Spanish painting are represented in Room 41 by Velázquez's portrait of the sunken-faced Philip IV; El Greco's *Christ Driving the Traders from the Temple;* Goya's portrait of the Duke of Wellington (once stolen) and his mantilla-wearing *Dona Isabel de Porcel.*

Room 33 is devoted to 18th-century French painters such as Delacroix and Ingres; Room 44, 19th-century French impressionists such as Manet, Monet, Renoir, and Degas; and Room 45, 19th-century French post-impressionists such as Cézanne, Seurat, and Van Gogh.

The National Gallery (tube to Charing Cross) is open weekdays from 10 a.m. to 6 p.m., on Sunday from 2 to 6 p.m. It is closed on January 1,

Good Friday, Christmas Eve, Christmas Day, Boxing Day, and bank holidays. Admission is free.

KENSINGTON PALACE: Home of the State Apartments, some of which were used by Queen Victoria, this is another of the major attractions of the city, at the far western end of Kensington Gardens. The palace was acquired by asthma-suffering William III (William of Orange) in 1689, and was remodeled by Sir Christopher Wren. George II, who died in 1760, was the last king to use it as a royal residence.

The most interesting chamber to visit is Queen Victoria's bedroom. In this room, on the morning of June 20, 1837, she was aroused from her sleep with the news that she had ascended to the throne, following the death of her uncle, William IV. Thus the woman who was to become the symbol of the British Empire and the Empress of India began the longest reign in the history of England. In the anteroom are memorabilia from Victoria's childhood—a doll-house and a collection of her toys.

In Queen Mary's bedroom, you can see her mid-17th-century writing cabinet with its tortoise-shell surface. Incidentally, Mary II reigned with William III, and is not to be confused with the late Queen Mary (1867–1953), who also has many relics at Kensington. The late Queen Mary was born in Victoria's bedroom.

As you wander through the apartments, you can admire many fine paintings, most of which are from the Royal Collection. The State Apartments are open Monday through Saturday, 9 a.m. to 5 p.m.; on Sunday, 1 to 5 p.m. Adults pay an admission of 50p (75¢), and children pay 25p (38¢) January through March and October through December; £1 ($1.50) for adults and 50p (75¢) for children April through September. You enter from the Broad Walk, and you reach the building by taking the tube either to Queensway or Bayswater on the north side of the gardens, or High Street Kensington on the south side. You'll have to walk a bit from there, however. For more information, telephone 937-9561.

The palace gardens, originally the private park of royalty, are also open to the public for daily strolls around Round Pond, near the heart of Kensington Gardens. The gardens adjoin Hyde Park. Also in Kensington Gardens is the Albert Memorial to Queen Victoria's consort. Facing Albert Hall, it is a wart on the face of London, a statue that reflects all the opulent vulgarity of the Victorian era—it's fascinating, nonetheless.

ST. PAUL'S CATHEDRAL: During World War II, newsreel footage reaching America showed the dome of St. Paul's Cathedral lit by bombs exploding all around it. That it survived at all is miraculous, as it was hit badly twice in the early years of the Nazi bombardment of London. But St. Paul's is accustomed to calamity, having been burned down three times and destroyed once by invading Norsemen. It was in the Great Fire of 1666 that the old St. Paul's was razed, making way for a new Renaissance structure designed (after many mishaps and rejections) by Sir Christopher Wren.

The masterpiece of this great architect was erected between 1675 and 1710. Its classical dome dominates the City's square mile. Inside, the cathedral is laid out like a Latin cross, containing few art treasures (Grinling Gibbons's choir stalls are an exception) and many monuments, including one to the "Iron Duke" and a memorial chapel to American servicemen who lost their lives in the United Kingdom in World War II. Encircling the dome is the Whispering Gallery, where discretion in speech is advised. In the crypt lie not only Wren but the Duke of Wellington and Lord Nelson. A fascinating Diocesan Treasury was opened in 1981.

The cathedral (tube to St. Paul's) is open daily from 8 a.m. to 5 p.m. (until 6 p.m. from mid-April to September). The crypt and galleries, including the Whispering Gallery, are open only from 11 a.m. to 4:15 p.m. weekdays, to 3:15 p.m. in winter. Guided tours, lasting 1½ hours, and including the crypt and other parts of St. Paul's not normally open to the public, take place twice daily, at 11 a.m. and 2 p.m. when the cathedral is open (except Sunday), costing £2.50 ($3.75) for adults, £1.25 ($1.88) for children.

St. Paul's is an Anglican cathedral with daily services held at 8 a.m. and 5 p.m. in summer, at 4 p.m. in winter. On Sunday, services are at 10:30 and 11:30 a.m. and 3:15 p.m. In addition, you can climb to the very top of the dome for a spectacular 360-degree view of all of London, costing 70p ($1.05) per person.

VICTORIA AND ALBERT MUSEUM: When Queen Victoria asked that this museum be named after herself and her consort, she could not have selected a more fitting memorial. The Victoria and Albert is one of the finest museums in the world, devoted to fine and applied art of many nations and periods, including the Orient. In many respects, it's one of the most difficult for viewing, as many of the most important exhibits are so small they can easily be overlooked. To reach the museum on Cromwell Road, take the tube to the South Kensington stop. The museum is open weekdays, except Friday, from 10 a.m. to 5:50 p.m., on Sunday from 2:30 till 5:50 p.m.

I have space only to suggest some of its finest art. The early medieval art in Room 43 includes many treasures, such as the Eltenberg Reliquary (Rhenish, second half of the 12th century). In the shape of a domed, copper-gilt church, it is enriched with champlevé enamel and set with walrus-ivory carvings of Christ and the Apostles. Other exhibits in this same salon include the Early English Gloucester Candlestick, and the Byzantine Veroli Casket, with its ivory panels based on Greek plays. Devoted to Islamic art, Room 42 contains the Ardabil carpet from 16th-century Persia (320 knots per square inch).

In the Gothic art exhibition (Rooms 22 through 25), there are some fine pieces—such as the Syon Cope, made in the early 14th century, an example of the highly valued embroidery produced in England at that time; a stained-glass window from Winchester College (circa 1400); a Limoges enameled triptych for Louis XII. The Gothic tapestries, including the Devonshire ones depicting hunting scenes, are in Room 38.

Renaissance art in Italy, Rooms 11 through 20, include such works as a Donatello marble relief, *The Ascension;* a small terracotta statue of the Madonna and Child by Antonio Rossellino; a marble group, *Samson and a Philistine,* by Giovanni Bologna; a wax model of a slave by Michelangelo. The highlight of the 16th-century art from the continent is the marble group *Neptune with Triton,* by Bernini (Room 21).

In Room 48 are displayed the cartoons by Raphael, which are owned by the Queen. These cartoons—conceived as designs for tapestries for the Sistine Chapel—include scenes such as *The Sacrifice of Lystra* and *Paul Preaching at Athens.*

A most unusual, huge, and impressive exhibit is the Cast Room, with life-size plaster models of ancient and medieval statuary and architecture, made from molds formed over the originals.

Of the rooms devoted to English furniture and decorative art during the period from the 16th to the mid-18th century, the most outstanding exhibit is the Bed of Ware (Room 52), big enough for eight. In the galleries of portrait miniatures, two of the rarest ones are by Hans Holbein the Younger (one of Anne of Cleves, another of a Mrs. Pemberton). In the painting galleries are many works by Constable. His *Flatford Mill* represents a well-known scene from his native East Anglia. All paintings, prints, drawings, and photographs are in the new Henry Cole wing. The museum's phone number is 589-6371.

THE BEST OF THE REST: Now, for those with more time to get acquainted with London, we'll continue our exploration of this sight-filled city.

Royal London

From Trafalgar Square, you can stroll down the wide, tree-flanked avenue known as **The Mall.** It leads to **Buckingham Palace,** the heart of Royal London (English kings and queens have lived here since the days of Victoria). Three parks—St. James's, Green, and the Buckingham Palace Gardens (private)—converge at the center of this area, where you'll find a memorial honoring Victoria.

London's most popular daily pageant, particularly with North American tourists, is the **Changing of the Queen's Guard** in the forecourt of Buckingham Palace. The regiments of the Guard's Division, in their bearskins and red tunics, actually are five regiments in one, including the Scots, Irish, and Welsh. The guards march to the palace from either the Wellington or Chelsea barracks, arriving around 11:30 a.m. for the half-hour ceremony. To get the full effect, go somewhat earlier. There is usually no ceremony when the weather is what the English call "inclement." But remember that your idea of inclement may not be a weather-toughened Londoner's idea of inclement. When in doubt, phone 730-3488 for information; tube to St. James's Park or Green Park. These ceremonies are curtailed in winter, between October 1 and March 31. During those months, the official schedule is that the changing of the guard takes place on even calendar days in October, December, and February, and on odd calendar days in November, January, and March.

You can't visit the palace, of course, without an invitation, but you can inspect the **Queen's Gallery** (entrance on Buckingham Palace Road). It may be visited from 11 a.m. to 5 p.m. Tuesday through Saturday (from 2 to 5 p.m. on Sunday) for an admission of £1 ($1.50) for adults, 40p (60¢) for children. As is known, all the royal families of Europe have art collections —some including acquisitions from centuries ago. The English sovereign has one of the finest, and has consented to share it with the public. I can't predict what exhibition you're likely to see, as they are changed yearly at the gallery. You may find a selection of incomparable works by old masters, and sometimes furniture and objets d'art. The Queen's collection contains an unsurpassed range of royal portraits, from the well-known profile of Henry V, through the late Plantagenets, the companion portraits of Elizabeth I as a girl and her brother, Edward VI, and four fine Georgian pictures by Zoffany, to recent works including two portraits of Queen Alexandria from Sandringham and paintings of Queen Elizabeth II and other members of the royal family.

You can get a close look at Queen Elizabeth's coronation carriage at the **Royal Mews,** on Buckingham Palace Road. Her Majesty's State Coach, built in 1761 to the designs of Sir William Chambers, contains emblematic and other paintings on the panels. Its doors were executed by Cipriani. It is used by sovereigns when opening Parliament in person and on other state occasions. Queen Elizabeth used it upon her coronation in 1953 and in 1977 for her Silver Jubilee Procession. It is traditionally drawn by eight gray horses. Many other official carriages are housed here as well, including the Scottish and Irish state coaches. The Queen's horses are also housed here. The mews is open to the public on Wednesday and Thursday from 2 to 4 p.m. and charges an admission of 40p (60¢) for adults, 20p (30¢) for children. It is closed during Ascot week in June and at some other times as announced.

Official London

Whitehall, S.W.1, the seat of the British government, grew up on the grounds of Whitehall Palace, turned into a Royal residence by Henry VIII, who snatched it from its former occupant, Cardinal Wolsey. Beginning at Trafalgar Square, Whitehall extends southward to Parliament Square (Houses of Parliament and Westminster Abbey, described earlier). On this street you'll find the Home Office, the Old Admiralty Building, and the Ministry of Defence.

Visitors today can see **The Cabinet War Rooms,** the bomb-proof bunker, that suite of rooms, large and small, just as they were left by Winston Churchill in September 1945 at the end of World War II. Many objects were removed only for dusting, and the Imperial War Museum studied photographs to replace everything exactly as they were, including notepads, files, and typewriters—right down to pencils, pins, and clips.

You can see the Map Room with its huge wall maps, the Atlantic map a mass of pinholes. Each hole represents at least one convoy. Next door is Churchill's bedroom-cum-office, reinforced with stout wood beams. It has a very basic bed and a table with a microphone suspended above it for his broadcasts of those famous speeches that stirred the nation.

The Transatlantic Telephone Room, to give it its full title, is little more than a broom cupboard, but it had the Bell Telephone Company's special scrambler phone by the name of Sig-Saly. From here, Churchill and Roosevelt conferred. The scrambler equipment was actually too large to house in the bunker, so it was placed in the basement of Selfridges Department Store on Oxford Street. The actual telephone was still classified at the end of the war and was removed.

The entrance to the war rooms is by Clive Steps at the end of King Charles Street off Whitehall near Big Ben (tube: Westminster). It is open Tuesday to Saturday from 10 a.m. to 5:30 p.m., on Sunday from 2 to 5:30 p.m. It is closed on Monday and on certain state occasions when access would be impossible.

At the **Cenotaph** (honoring the dead in two World Wars), turn down unpretentious Downing Street to the modest little town house at **No. 10,** flanked by two bobbies. Walpole was the first prime minister to live here; Churchill the most famous.

Nearby is the **Horse Guards Building,** where the changing of the

Queen's Life Guard takes place daily at 11 a.m. and at 10 a.m. on Sunday. The ceremony lasts 20 minutes—a spectacle provided by the Life Guards and the Royal Horse Guards, combined to form the Household Cavalry. Mounted on their black horses, the guards in their white and red plumes, red and blue tunics, make for an exciting and dramatic show.

Across the street is Inigo Jones's **Banqueting House** (tel. 212-4785), site of the execution of Charles I. William and Mary accepted the crown of England here, but preferred to live at Kensington Palace. The Banqueting House was part of Whitehall Palace, which burned to the ground in 1698, although the ceremonial hall escaped razing. Its most notable feature today is an allegorical ceiling painted by Peter Paul Rubens. The Banqueting House may be visited weekdays from 10 a.m. to 5 p.m., except Monday; on Sunday, 2 to 5 p.m. Admission is 50p (75¢) for adults, 30p (45¢) for children.

Finally, you may want to stroll to Parliament Square for a view of **Big Ben,** the world's most famous timepiece.

Legal London

The smallest borough in London, bustling **Holborn** (pronounced Hoburn) is often referred to as Legal London, the home of the city's barristers, solicitors, and law clerks. It also embraces the university district of Bloomsbury. Holborn, which houses the ancient Inns of Court, was severely damaged in World War II bombing raids. The razed buildings were replaced with modern offices housing insurance brokers, realtors, whatever. But the borough still retains quadrangled pockets of its former days.

Turn south from busy Fleet Street down Middle Temple Lane, leading to the Embankment. You'll come to an area known as **The Temple,** named after the medieval order of the Knights Templar (originally formed by the Crusaders in Jerusalem in the 12th century). Here you'll find the Temple Church, one of four Norman "round churches" left in England. First completed in the 12th century, it has been restored. Look for the knightly effigies and the Norman door anytime from 10 a.m. to 5 p.m. (4 p.m. in winter). Readers Manly and Mary Johnson, from Tulsa, Oklahoma, were impressed with "a circle of grotesque carved portrait heads, which have to be seen to be believed—a goat in a mortar board, characters making faces, rolling their eyes, lolling tongues, and even a couple of them with little fierce creatures biting their ears. There's also a 'dungeon' one flight up—ask the caretaker to show you."

The **Middle Temple** contains a Tudor hall completed in 1570 with a double hammer-beam roof. It is believed Shakespeare's troupe played *Twelfth Night* here in 1602. A table on view is said to have come from timber from Sir Francis Drake's *The Golden Hind.* The hall may be visited from 10 a.m. to noon and from 3 to 4:30 p.m. weekdays.

While in this district, you may also want to explore the area north of Fleet Street and the Temple. **Staple Inn,** near the Chancery Lane tube stop, is the last of the old Tudor fronts to be found in London. The inn, lined with shops, was constructed and reconstructed many times, originally having come into existence between 1545 and 1589. Dr. Johnson moved here in 1759, the year *Rasselas* was published.

On Chancery Lane you can visit the **Public Record Office** (see "Other Museums," below), or else walk through a Tudor gateway into **Lincoln's Inn,** dating back to 1422. Another of the ancient Inns of Court, Lincoln's Inn forms an important link in the architectural maze of London. In the

17th century Inigo Jones erected a chapel here; Cromwell lived here at one time. To the east of Lincoln's Inn is the large square known as Lincoln's Inn Fields, with the Soane Museum (see "Other Museums"). Near the south of the fields on Kingsway is the **Old Curiosity Shop,** immortalized by Charles Dickens.

North of Lincoln's Inn in High Holborn stands the last of the four great Inns of Court—**Gray's,** restored after being heavily damaged by World War II bombings. Francis Bacon (not the modern artist) was the most eminent tenant to have resided here. Off Gray's Inn Road, it contains a rebuilt Tudor hall.

Other Museums

The present **Guildhall,** on King Street in Cheapside, The City, E.C.2 (tube to Bank; tel. 606-3030), was built in 1411. But the Civic Hall of the Corporation of London has had a rough time, notably in the Great Fire of 1666 and the 1940 blitz. The most famous tenants of the rebuilt Guildhall are *Gog* and *Magog,* two giants standing over nine feet high. The original effigies, burned in the London fire, were rebuilt only to be destroyed again in 1940. The present giants are third generation. Restoration has returned the Gothic grandeur to the hall—replete with a medieval porch entranceway; monuments to Wellington, Churchill, and Nelson; stained glass commemorating lord mayors and mayors; the standards of length; a 15th-century crypt; and colorful shields honoring fishmongers, haberdashers, merchant tailors, ironmongers, and skinners—some of the major Livery Companies. The Guildhall and Crypt may be visited Monday through Saturday from 10 a.m. to 5 p.m. (on Sunday, May to September only, from 10 a.m. to 5 p.m.).

The museum of the **Public Record Office,** on Chancery Lane, W.C.2 (tube to the Temple or Chancery Lane; tel. 405-0741), is one of the finest of the small museums of London, deserving far more attention than it gets. A mere recitation of some of its exhibits is all the selling it needs. You'll find two volumes of the *Domesday Book,* a general survey of England ordered by William the Conqueror in 1085. Here also are the navy log of the H.M.S. *Victory,* showing Nelson's dispatches relating to the Battle of Trafalgar; Elizabeth II's signed oath "to govern Great Britain"; exemplars of Magna Carta (Case VIII); John Bunyan's preaching license; one of the six authentic signatures known of Shakespeare, on his Last Will and Testament, dated March 25, 1616; a letter from George Washington (Case XII) to his "great and good friend," King George III; letters from Maria Theresa, Frederick the Great, Catherine the Great, Marie Antoinette, and Metternich; the first confession of Guy Fawkes about the gunpowder plot to blow up the king, signed November 9, 1605; scads of royal autographs—Richard II, Edward IV, Catherine Parr, Anne Boleyn. The museum is open Monday through Friday from 1 to 4 p.m.

Sir John Soane's Museum, 13 Lincoln's Inn Fields, W.C.2 (tel. 405-2107), is the former home of an architect who lived from 1753 to 1837. Sir John, who rebuilt the Bank of England (not the present structure, however), was a "spaceman" in a different era. With his multilevels, fool-the-eye mirrors, flying arches, and domes, Soane was a master of perspective, a genius of interior space (his art gallery, for example, is filled with three times the number of paintings a room of similar dimensions would be likely to hold). That he could do all this—and still not prove a demon to claustrophobia victims—was proof of his remarkable talent. Even if you don't like Soane (he was reportedly a cranky fellow), you may still want to visit this museum to see William Hogarth's satirical series, *The Rake's Progress*, containing his much reproduced *Orgy*, and the less successful satire on politics in the mid-18th century, *The Election*. Soane also filled his house with paintings (Watteau's *Les Noces*, Canaletto's large *Venetian Scene*) and classical sculpture. Finally, be sure to see the Egyptian sarcophagus found in a burial chamber in the Valley of the Kings. Soane turned his house over to his country for use as a museum. It is open Tuesday through Saturday from 10 a.m. till 5 p.m. Take the tube to Chancery Lane or Holborn.

The **Royal Academy of Arts,** Piccadilly, W.1 (tel. 734-9052), founded in 1768, is the oldest established society in Great Britain devoted solely to the fine arts. The academy is made up of a self-supporting, self-governing body of artists, who conduct art schools, hold exhibitions of the work of living artists, and organize loan exhibits of the arts of past and present periods. A summer exhibition is held annually, with contemporary paintings, drawings, engravings, sculpture, and architecture on display. This summer show has been held without a break for more than 200 years. The Royal Academy is known worldwide.

Situated in Burlington House, which was built in Piccadilly in the 1600s, the Royal Academy's first president was Sir Joshua Reynolds. Purchases and gifts have provided a rich collection of artworks, and the ongoing program of loan exhibitions provides opportunities to see fine art examples on an international scale. The Royal Academy Shop and a restaurant are open during exhibition hours, usually 10 a.m. to 6 p.m. daily, and the framing workshop can be visited from 10 a.m. to 5 p.m. Monday to Saturday. The upstairs gallery and business art galleries are open Tuesday to Friday from 10 a.m. to 6 p.m., on Saturday from 11 a.m. to 5 p.m., and on Monday by appointment. You can see works of Gainsborough, Constable, Reynolds, Wilkie, Etty, Angelica Kauffman, Landseer, and even Michelangelo here. Burlington House is opposite Fortnum and Mason. Tube: Piccadilly Circus.

Just across the Thames in Lambeth Road, S.E.1, is the **Imperial War Museum** (tube to Lambeth North or Elephant and Castle; tel. 735-8922). This large domed building, built around 1815, the former Bethlehem Royal Hospital for the Insane, or Bedlam, houses the museum's collections relating to the two World Wars and other military operations involving the British and the Commonwealth since 1914.

A wide range of weapons and equipment is on display: aircraft, armored vehicles, field guns, small arms, and models, decorations, uniforms, posters, photographs, and paintings. You can see a Mark V tank, a Battle of Britain Spitfire, a German one-man submarine, and the rifle carried by Lawrence of Arabia, as well as the German surrender document, Hitler's political testament, and a German V2 rocket. There is an exhibition on trench warfare in the First World War. Paintings on display include works by well-known war artists such as William Orpen, Paul Nash, Stanley Spencer, and Jacob Epstein. There is also a collection of propaganda posters from the First and Second World Wars, plus Field Marshal Montgomery's three campaign caravans. The museum is open Monday to Saturday from 10 a.m. to 5:50 p.m., on Sunday from 2 to 5:50 p.m. It is closed on Good Friday, Christmas Eve, Christmas Day, Boxing Day, New Year's Day, and the first Monday in May. Admission is free.

The **National Army Museum,** Royal Hospital Road, S.W.3 (tel. 730-0717), in Chelsea (tube: Sloane Square), traces the history of the

British, Indian, and Colonial forces from 1485. (The Imperial War Museum above concerns itself with World Wars I and II.)

The **National Army Museum** stands next door to Wren's Royal Hospital. The museum backers agreed to begin the collection at the year 1485, because that was the date of the formation of the Yeomen of the Guard. The saga of the forces of the East India Company is traced, beginning in 1602 and going up to Indian independence in 1947. The gory and the glory—it's all here, everything from Florence Nightingale's lamp to the French Eagle captured in a cavalry charge at Waterloo, even the staff cloak wrapped round the dying Wolfe at Québec. Naturally, there are the "cases of the heroes," mementos of such outstanding men as the Dukes of Marlborough and Wellington. But the field soldier isn't neglected either. Displays have been brought up to date with the opening of a permanent new gallery, Flanders to the Falklands. The museum is open weekdays from 10 a.m. to 5:30 p.m., on Sunday from 2 to 5:30 p.m. It is closed on New Year's Day, Good Friday, from December 24 to 26, and on the May bank holiday.

The **Wellington Museum,** at Apsley House, 149 Piccadilly, Hyde Park Corner, W.1 (tel. 499-5676), takes us into the former town house of the Iron Duke, the British general (1769–1852) who defeated Napoleon at the Battle of Waterloo. Wellington's London residence was opened as a public museum in 1952. Once Wellington had to retreat behind the walls of Apsley House—even securing it in fear of a possible attack from Englishmen, outraged by his autocratic opposition as prime minister to reform. In the vestibule you'll find a colossal statue in marble of Napoleon by Canova—ironic, to say the least. Completely idealized, it was presented to the duke by King George IV. In addition to three good paintings by Velázquez, the Wellington collection includes Correggio's *Agony in the Garden,* Jan Steen's *The Egg Dance,* and Pieter de Hooch's *A Musical Party.* You can see the gallery where Wellington used to invite his officers for the annual Waterloo banquet (the banquets were originally held in the dining room). The house also contains a large porcelain and china collection—plus many Wellington medals, of course. Also displayed is a magnificent Sèvres porcelain Egyptian service, made originally for Empress Josephine and given by Louis XVIII to Wellington. In addition, superb English silver and the extraordinary Portuguese centerpiece, a present from a grateful Portugal to its liberator, are exhibited. The residence was designed by Robert Adam and built in the late 18th century. The museum is open Tuesday, Wednesday, Thursday, and Saturday from 10 a.m. to 6 p.m., on Sunday from 2:30 to 6 p.m. Admission is 60p (90¢) for adults, 30p (45¢) for children. Tube: Hyde Park Corner.

The **Commonwealth Institute,** Kensington High Street, W.8 (tube to Kensington High Street or no. 9 bus from Piccadilly Circus; tel. 603-4535), is a center of information on the 40 or so countries of the modern Commonwealth. There are continuous exhibitions on each country, and you can capture some of the atmosphere and flavor of places as different as Sri Lanka and Papua, New Guinea, Malaysia, and Trinidad. Admission is free, and there is an attractive and inexpensive restaurant called Flags, plus a shop selling Commonwealth crafts, gifts and books. The institute also has a free library and art gallery. It plays host to many cultural events, including dance, drama, music, and exotic food-tastings and festivals. Many, perhaps most, of these events are free. It's open Monday through Saturday from 10 a.m. to 5:30 p.m. and on Sunday from 2 to 5.

In London's Barbican district, E.C.2, the **Museum of London** at 150 London Wall (tel. 600-3699) allows visitors to trace the history of London from prehistoric times to the present—through relics, costumes, household effects, maps, and models. Exhibits are arranged so that visitors can begin and end their chronological stroll through 250,000 years at the main entrance to the museum. The pièce de résistance is the Lord Mayor's coach, built in 1757 and weighing in at three tons. This gilt and red, horse-drawn vehicle is like a fairytale coach. Visitors can also see the Great Fire of London in living color and sound; a Roman dinner, including the kitchen and utensils; a cell in Newgate Prison made famous by Charles Dickens; and most amazing of all, a shop counter with pre-World War II prices on the items.

The museum overlooks London's Roman and medieval walls and, in all, has something from every era before and after—including little Victorian shops and recreations of what life was like in the London area in the Iron Age. Anglo-Saxons, Vikings, Normans—they're all there, arranged on two floors around a central garden. With quick labels for museum sprinters, more extensive ones for those who want to study, and still deeper details for scholars, this new museum, built at a cost of some $18 million, is an enriching experience for *everybody*.

A small coffeeshop helps sustain the visitor with various soft drinks, tea and coffee, plus sandwiches and other cold snacks. At least an hour should be allowed for a full (but still quick) visit to the museum, which will surely rank as one of the most worthwhile hours you'd spend in any museum in London. Free lectures on London's past are given during lunch hours. These aren't given daily, but it's worth inquiring at the entrance hall. You can reach the museum by going up to the elevated pedestrian precinct at the corner of the London Wall and Aldersgate, five minutes from St. Paul's. It is open Tuesday through Saturday from 10 a.m. to 6 p.m., on Sunday from 2 to 6 p.m.; admission is free. Closed Monday. Tube: St. Paul's, Barbican.

The **London Transport Museum**, Covent Garden, W.C.2 (tel. 379-6344), is in a splendidly restored Victorian building that formerly housed the flower market. Horse buses, motorbuses, trams, trolley buses, railway vehicles, models, maps, posters, photographs, and audio-visual displays illustrate the fascinating story of the evolution of London's transport systems and how this has affected the growth of London.

There are a number of unique working displays. You can "drive" a tube train, a tram, and a bus, and also operate full-size signaling equipment. The exhibits include a reconstruction of George Shillibeer's omnibus of 1829, a steam locomotive that ran on the world's first underground railway, and a coach from the first deep-level electric railway.

The museum is open every day of the year except Christmas and Boxing Day from 10 a.m. to 6 p.m. (last admission at 5:15 p.m.). Admission charges are £2 ($3) for adults, £1 ($1.50) for children. A family ticket for two adults and two children is £4.80 ($7.20).

The **R.A.F. Museum**, Grahame Park Way, Hendon, N.W.9 (tel. 205-2266), shelters what must be the largest and most comprehensive collection of airplanes and equipment from every stage of British aviation. The aircraft are housed in a gigantic hangar, and there is also a special section, the Battle of Britain Museum, with souvenirs, photographs, and exhibits explaining and portraying those days when "so much was owed by so many, to so few." The museums are open Monday to Saturday from 10 a.m. to 6 p.m., on Sunday from 2 to 6 p.m. Admission to the R.A.F. Museum and the Battle of Britain Museum next door is £1 ($1.50); children, 50p (75¢). Facilities include a cinema, a licensed restaurant, a shop, and free car parking. Tube: Colindale.

The **National Postal Museum,** King Edward Building, King Edward Street, E.C.1 (tel. 432-3851), contains the post office's collection of British postage stamps, a worldwide stamp collection from 1878, and a philatelic correspondence archives covering postage stamps of 200 countries from 1855 onward. The museum is open Monday to Thursday from 10 a.m. to 4:30 p.m. and on Friday from 10 a.m. to 4 p.m.

The **Science Museum,** Exhibition Road, S.W.7 (tel. 589-3456), traces the development of both science and industry, particularly their application to everyday life—meaning that there's a minimum of "pure science." Exhibits vary from models and facsimiles to the actual machines. You'll find Stephenson's original *Rocket,* the tiny locomotive that won a race against all competitors and thus became the world's prototype railroad engine. The earliest motor-propelled airplanes, a cavalcade of antique cars, and steam engines from their crudest to their most refined form may be seen here. Greatest fascination is with the working models of machinery (visitor-operable by push buttons). The most recent galleries are two of the Wellcome Museum of History of Medicine and "Telecommunications, a Technology for Change." Take the tube to South Kensington or bus 14. The museum is open weekdays from 10 a.m. to 6 p.m., on Sunday from 2:30 to 6 p.m.

The **London Toy & Model Museum** is housed in a restored Victorian home at 23 Craven Hill, W.2 (tel. 262-7905), off Bayswater Road. Allen Levy and David Pressland pooled their collections to open this museum of special treasures, mainly model trains and toys that predate World War I. Some of the trains are displayed in action. Many of the toys once sold for a penny in the heyday of the Industrial Revolution. One toy is a scale model of a Cadillac sports roadster from 1916. The collection also includes teddy bears and dolls in regional costume, along with a Victorian dollhouse. The museum is open Tuesday to Saturday from 10 a.m. to 7:30 p.m., and on Sunday from 11 a.m. to 7 p.m. Admission is £1.50 ($2.25) for adults and 50p (75¢) for children up to 14. Tube: Lancaster Gate.

A unique private museum in London, the home of **Dennis Severs,** 18 Folgate St., E.1 (tel. 247-4013), is a delight. Dennis is a young Californian who has lived in London since he was 16 years old and is utterly involved with England, the history and the culture of the place. He has restored a house on the edge of the City to the way it was in 1725 when it was occupied by the Huguenot family Jervis, who were silk weavers.

More Dennis's home and way of life than a museum, there is no electric lighting, and coal fires warm the house in which the absolute minimum of 20th-century paraphernalia is evident. Visit the house and enjoy an experience you will find nowhere else in Britain. Put yourself in Dennis's hands for three hours, and he, with the help of Dominic, his footman, and Whitechapel, the black cat who claims to have been born in the grounds of Buckingham Palace, will take you through two centuries of the life of the house. Rooms have different smells, background music is of the time, and social history is brought to life. This is not a theatrical performance but a sincere effort to involve the visitor in a feel of the life and times of the house.

You see the kitchen á la Beatrix Potter, with its blackened range holding simmering pots (they really do simmer). Gleaming copper and china glint on the candlelit Welsh dresser. You explore the Dickens Room with Bob Cratchit's high desk in the corner and learn the life of Dickens's time. The "withdrawing" room has high-back chairs and ornaments, all of which add to a fascinating picture of bygone times.

To visit and live this unique experience, you must use one of those new-fangled telephones and make a reservation, as there are only three tours a week with a maximum of eight people on each. The cost is £12.50 ($18.75) per person. This tour is especially suitable for social historians, sensitive people, and those who genuinely wish to go back into the past. The house is five minutes from Liverpool Street Underground at the back of Spitalfields Market.

You can step back into the days of Queen Victoria when you visit the **Linley Sambourne House,** 18 Stafford Terrace, W.8, which has remained unchanged for more than a century. The house, part of a group built between 1868 and 1874, is a five-story, Suffolk brick structure to which Linley Sambourne brought his bride in 1874. Sambourne was a draftsman who later became a cartoonist for *Punch,* attaining the position of chief political cartoonist which he held until his death in 1910. The Sambourne family owned and occupied the house until 1980, when it was purchased by the Greater London Council and leased to the Victorian Society, which had been born at 18 Stafford Terrace in 1958. From the moment you step into the entrance hall, you see a mixture of styles and clutter that typified Victorian decor, with a plush portière, plush fireplace valance, an orange tree in a blue and white bowl, and a large set of antlers vying for attention with several of Sambourne's framed *Punch* cartoons, plus other drawings and prints on the walls. An 1877 inventory of the house furnishings found in a cupboard shows that little has been changed. The drawing room alone contains an incredible number of items, making you wonder how the Victorians managed to navigate through it after a glass or two of sherry or port. The total number of objects, including furniture, ceramics, pictures, photos, books, clocks, and memorabilia of the family, is 640 in this room.

Sambourne's daughter Maud was the mother of the noted stage designer Oliver Messel. His son Roy never married. When Roy died in 1946, the house in which he had lived all his life was taken charge of by Maud and her daughter Anne, the mother of Lord Snowdon. Anne and her husband, the Earl of Rosse, made this their London home from the mid-1950s until 1978, preserving the house undisturbed except for a few minor alterations in a bedroom and changing the wallpaper. Admission to the house, which is open Wednesday from 10 a.m. to 4 p.m. and Sunday from 2 to 5 p.m. March 1 to October 31, is £1.50 ($2.25).

Another unique London museum is **Whitbread's Brewery,** Chiswell Street, E.C.1 (tel. 606-4455). Although beer is no longer brewed in Chiswell Street, the old brewery remains the headquarters of Whitbread's, which has opened the magnificent old building to the public. The most impressive of the rooms is the Porter Tun Room, completed in 1784 and renowned for its massive unsupported King Post timber roof, the second largest of its kind in Europe. Also on display in the brewery is the Speaker's Coach. A magnificent affair of gold and finery, it was built in 1698 and is still used, drawn by dray horses, to convey the Speaker of the House of Commons on state occasions. The stables can be visited by appointment.

The coffeeshop is open Monday to Saturday from 8:30 a.m. to 5 p.m. and provides light snacks from £2 ($3) to £5 ($7.50).

Across the road on the north side of Chiswell Street, in the vaults below the Georgian terraces, is a cellar wine bar, **Chiswell Vaults,** operated by Mr. Burford in the ancient vaults belonging to the brewery. The subterranean bars are bright with cream painted walls, candlelit tables, and flagstone floors, with wine-barrel tables and benches. Cold meats, salads, smoked mackerel, and quiches are served as well as hot dishes of the day. For £4 ($6), I got a large pile of cold roast beef and two salads. Those who wish to avoid the hassle of lining up at the buffet can proceed through the tunnel-like rooms with curved brick ceilings and sawdust-covered floors to the posh area where waitresses serve at elegant tables. Expect to pay around £8 ($12) here for two courses.

Other Galleries

National Portrait Gallery, St. Martin's Place, W.C.2 (entrance around the corner from the National Gallery on Trafalgar Square; tel. 930-1552), gives you a chance to outstare the stiff-necked greats and not-so-greats of English history. In a gallery of remarkable and unremarkable portraits, a few paintings tower over the rest, including Sir Joshua Reynolds's first portrait of Samuel Johnson ("a man of most dreadful appearance"). Among the best are Nicholas Hilliard's miniature of a most handsome Sir Walter Raleigh (Room 1); a full-length Elizabeth I (painted to commemorate her visit to Sir Henry Lee Ditchley in 1592), along with the Holbein cartoon of Henry VIII (sketched for a family portrait that hung, before it was burned, in the Privy Chamber in Whitehall Palace)—both in Room 1. In Room 1, also, is a portrait of William Shakespeare (with gold earring, no less). The artist is unknown, but the portrait bears the claim of being the most "authentic contemporary likeness" of its subject of any work yet known. The John Hayls portrait of Samuel Pepys adorns Room 4. Whistler could not only paint a portrait, he could also be the subject of one (Room 24). One of the most unusual portraits (Room 17) in the gallery—a group of the three Brontë sisters (Charlotte, Emily, Anne)—was painted by their brother, Branwell. An idealized portrait of Lord Byron by Thomas Phillips is pleased with itself in Room 13. For a finale, treat yourself to the likeness of the incomparable Aubrey Beardsley (Room 24). For sheer volume of portraiture, Queen Victoria reigns supreme. The admission-free gallery is open from 10 a.m. to 5 p.m. Monday to Friday, from 10 a.m. to 6 p.m. on Saturday, and from 2 to 6 p.m. on Sunday. Special exhibitions are held at the gallery from time to time.

The **Wallace Collection,** Manchester Square, W.1 (tel. 935-0687), off Wigmore Street, has an outstanding collection of works of art of all kinds bequeathed to the nation by Lady Wallace in 1897 and still displayed in the house of its founders. There are important pictures by artists of all European schools, including Titian, Rubens, Van Dyck, Rembrandt, Hals, Velázquez, Murillo, Reynolds, Gainsborough, and Delacroix. Representing the art of France in the 18th century are paintings by Watteau, Boucher, and Fragonard, and sculpture, furniture, goldsmiths' work, and Sèvres porcelain. Valuable collections also are found of majolica and European and Oriental arms and armor. Frans Hals's *Laughing Cavalier* is the most celebrated painting in the collection, but Pieter de Hooch's *A Boy Bringing Pomegranates* and Watteau's *The Music Party* are also well known. Other notable works include Canaletto's views of Venice (especially *Bacino di San Marco*), Rembrandt's *Titus,* and Gainsborough's *Mrs. Robinson (Perdita).* Worthy also is Boucher's portrait of the Marquise de Pompadour. The

Wallace Collection may be viewed daily from 10 a.m. to 5 p.m., on Sunday from 2 to 5 p.m. Closed Christmas Eve, Christmas Day, Boxing Day, New Year's Day, Good Friday, and the first Monday in May. Tube: Bond Street.

The **Courtauld Institute Galleries,** Woburn Square, W.C.1 (tel. 580-1015), is the home of the art collection of London University—noted chiefly for its superb impressionist and post-impressionist works. It has eight works by Cézanne alone, including his *A Man with a Pipe.* Other notable art includes Seurat's *La Poudreuse,* Van Gogh's self-portrait (with ear bandaged), a nude by Modigliani, Gauguin's *Day-Dreaming,* Monet's *Fall at Argenteuil,* Toulouse-Lautrec's delicious *Tête-à-Tête,* and Manet's *Bar at the Folies Bergère.* The galleries also feature classical works, including a *Virgin and Child* by Bernardino Luini, a Botticelli, a Giovanni Bellini, a Veronese, a triptych by the Master of Flémâlle, works by Pieter Brueghel, Matsys, Parmigianino, 32 oils by Rubens, oil sketches by Tiepolo, three landscapes by Kokoschka, and wonderful old master drawings (especially Michelangelo, Brueghel, and Rembrandt). The artworks may be viewed Monday to Saturday from 10 a.m. to 5 p.m. and on Sunday from 2 to 5 p.m. Tube: Euston Square, Goodge Street, or Russell Square.

The **Hayward Gallery,** South Bank, S.E.1 (tel. 629-9495), presents a changing program of major exhibitions organized by the Arts Council of Great Britain. The gallery forms part of the South Banks Arts Centre, which also includes the Royal Festival Hall, the Queen Elizabeth Hall, the Purcell Room, the National Film Theatre, and the National Theatre. Admission to the gallery varies according to exhibitions, with cheaper entry on Monday and in the evening from 6 to 8 p.m. on Tuesday and Wednesday. Hours are Monday to Wednesday from 10 a.m. to 8 p.m.; Thursday, Friday, and Saturday from 10 a.m. to 6 p.m.; and Sunday from noon to 6 p.m. The gallery is closed between exhibitions, so check the listings before crossing the Thames. Tube: Waterloo Station.

The **Serpentine Gallery,** Kensington Gardens, W.1 (tel. 402-6075). The Old Teahouse, near the Albert Memorial, was an inspired choice for the Arts Council's London platform for professional artists whose work has not been seen in commercial galleries. Its four large rooms, spacious and adaptable, are well suited to the experimental, and large-scale works are often shown here. The fact that the gallery is in popular parkland not only means that there are excellent adjacent outdoor facilities for sculpture and events, but that it draws a crowd who generally would not think of going to a Bond Street exhibition. Usually a minimum of four artists is shown at a time and given freedom to use the space as they wish. The exhibitions are principally for those interested in the most outstanding contemporary trends and tendencies, and are carefully watched by the more far-sighted commercial gallery owners. The gallery now has a winter program as well, and stages some international shows, exhibitions by more established artists, and occasional retrospectives devoted to just one artist. The gallery is open daily from 10 a.m. to 6 p.m., April through October, and from 10 a.m. to 15 minutes before dusk during November through March. Admission is free. Closed Good Friday, Christmas Eve, Christmas Day, Boxing Day, and New Year's Day. Tube: High Street Kensington.

Homes of Famous Writers

Dr. Johnson's House: The Queen Anne house of the famed lexicographer is at 17 Gough Square (tel. 353-3745). It'll cost you £1 ($1.50), and it's well worth it. Students and children pay only 50p (75¢). It was there that

Dr. Johnson and his copyists compiled his famous dictionary. The 17th-century building has been painstakingly restored (surely "Dear Tetty," if not Boswell, would approve). Although Johnson lived at Staple Inn in Holborn and at a number of other houses, the Gough Square house is the only one of his residences remaining in London. He occupied it from 1748 to 1759. It is open from 11 a.m. to 5:30 p.m., Monday through Saturday, May through September, closing half an hour earlier off-season. Take the tube to Blackfriars, then walk up New Bridge Street, turning left onto Fleet. Gough Square is a tiny, hidden square, north of the "street of ink."

Carlyle's House: 24 Cheyne Row (tel. 352-7087), in Chelsea (bus 11, 19, 22, or 39). For nearly half a century, from 1834 to 1881, the handsome author of *The French Revolution* and other works, along with his letter-writing wife, took up abode in this modest 1708 terraced house, about three-quarters of a block from the Thames, near the Chelsea Embankment. Still standing and furnished essentially as it was in Carlyle's day, the house was described by his wife as being "of most antique physiognomy, quite to our humour; all wainscotted, carved and queer-looking, roomy, substantial, commodious, with closets to satisfy any Bluebeard." Now who could improve on that? The second floor contains the drawing room of Mrs. Carlyle. But the most interesting chamber is the not-so-soundproof "soundproof" study in the skylit attic. Filled with Carlyle memorabilia—his books, a letter from Disraeli, a writing chair, even his death mask—this is the cell where the author labored over his *Frederick the Great* manuscript. The Cheyne (pronounced chainey) Row house may be visited weekdays, except Sunday, Monday, and Tuesday, from 11 a.m. to 5 p.m. Admission is £1 ($1.50) for adults, 50p (75¢) for children up to 16 years of age. Closed November through March.

Dickens's House: In Bloomsbury stands the house of the great English author Charles Dickens, accused in his time of "supping on the horrors" of Victoriana and read by Russians today to find out "what Britain is really like." Born in 1812 in what is now Portsmouth, Dickens is known to have lived at 48 Doughty St., W.C.1 (tube to Russell Square; tel. 405-2127) from 1837 to 1839. Unlike some of the London town houses of famous men (Wellington, Soane), the Bloomsbury house is simple, the embodiment of middle-class restraint.

The house contains an extensive library of Dickensiana, including manuscripts and letters second in importance only to the Forster Collection in the Victoria and Albert Museum. In his study are his desk and chair and from the study at Gad's Hill Place, Rochester, on which he wrote his last two letters before he died (also the table from his Swiss chalet on which he wrote the last unfinished fragment of *The Mystery of Edwin Drood*). Dickens's drawing room on the first floor has been reconstructed, as have the still room, wash house, and wine cellar in the basement. The house is open daily, except Sunday and bank holidays, from 10 a.m. to 5 p.m. Admission is £1 ($1.50) for adults, 75p ($1.13) for students, and 50p (75¢) for children.

Keats's House: The darling of romantics, John Keats lived for only two years at Wentworth Place, Keats Grove, Hampstead, N.W.3 (tel. 435-2062). Take the tube to Belsize Park or Hampstead or bus 24 from Trafalgar Square. But for the poet, that was something like two-fifths of his creative life, as he died in Rome of tuberculosis at the age of 25 (1821). In Hampstead, Keats wrote some of his most celebrated *Odes*—in praise of a Grecian Urn and to the Nightingale. In the garden stands an ancient mulberry tree that the poet must have known. His Regency house is well preserved, and contains the manuscripts of his last sonnet ("Bright star, would I were steadfast as thou art"), a final letter to the mother of Fanny Brawne (his correspondence to his Hampstead neighbor, who nursed him while he was ill, forms part of his legend), and a portrait of him on his death bed in a house on the Spanish Steps in Rome. Wentworth Place is open weekdays 10 a.m. to 1 p.m. and 2 to 6 p.m. On Sunday, Easter, and spring and summer bank holidays hours are from 2 to 5 p.m. Closed Christmas Day, Boxing Day, New Year's Day, Good Friday, Easter Eve, and May Day. Admission is free.

The Parks of London

London's parklands easily rate as the greatest, most wonderful system of "green lungs" of any large city on the globe. Not as rigidly artificial as the parks of Paris, those in London are maintained with a loving care and lavish artistry that puts their American equivalents to shame. Above all, they've been kept safe from land-hungry building firms and city councils, and still offer patches of real countryside right in the heart of the metropolis. Maybe there's something to be said for inviolate "royal" property, after all. Because that's what most of London's parks are.

Largest of them—and one of the biggest in the world—is **Hyde Park.** With the adjoining Kensington Gardens, it covers 636 acres of central London with velvety lawns interspersed with ponds, flowerbeds, and trees. At the northwestern tip, near Marble Arch, is Speakers Corner, where any orator can declaim on any subject under the sun. He or she had better be good at it, however, as the audience is great on heckling and usually more sardonic than impressed.

Hyde Park was once a favorite deer-hunting ground of Henry VIII. Running through the width is a 41-acre lake known as the Serpentine, where you can row, sail model boats, or swim—providing you're not expecting it to be like Florida water temperatures. Rotten Row, a 1½-mile sand track, is reserved for horseback riding and on Sunday attracts some skilled equestrians.

Kensington Gardens, blending with Hyde Park, border on the grounds of Kensington Palace. Kensington Gardens also contain the celebrated statue of Peter Pan, with the bronze rabbits that toddlers are always trying to kidnap. Unfortunately, it also harbors the ghastly Albert Memorial—but you don't have to look.

East of Hyde Park, across Piccadilly, stretch **Green Park** and **St. James's Park,** forming an almost unbroken chain of landscaped beauty. This is an ideal area for picnics, and you'll find it hard to believe that this was once a festering piece of swamp near the leper hospital. There is a romantic lake, stocked with a variety of ducks and some surprising pelicans, descendants of the pair that the Russian ambassador presented to Charles II back in 1662.

Regent's Park covers most of the district by that name, north of Baker Street and Marylebone Road. Designed by the 18th-century genius John Nash to surround a palace of the prince regent that never materialized, this is the most classically beautiful of London's parks. The core is a rose garden planted around a small lake alive with waterfowl and spanned by humped Japanese bridges. In early summer, the rose perfume in the air is as heady as wine.

Regent's Park also contains the Open-Air Theatre (see Section 3) and the London Zoo. Also—as at all the local parks—there are hundreds of deckchairs on the lawns in which to sunbathe. The deckchair attendants, who collect a small fee, are mostly college students on vacation.

Churches

St. Martin-in-the-Fields, overlooking Trafalgar Square, is the Royal Parish Church, dear to the hearts of many an English person, and especially the homeless. The present classically inspired church, with its famous steeple, dates back to 1726. James Gibbs, a pupil of Wren's, is listed as its architect. The origins of the church go back to the 11th century. Among the congregation in years past was George I, who was actually a churchwarden, unique for an English sovereign. From St. Martin's vantage position in the theater district, it has drawn many actors to its door—none more notable than Nell Gwynne, the mistress of Charles II. On her death in 1687, she was buried here. Throughout the war, many Londoners rode out an uneasy night in the crypt, while blitz bombs rained down overhead. One, in 1940, blasted out all the windows.

Along the Thames

There is a row of fascinating attractions lying on, across, and alongside the River Thames.

All of London's history and development is linked with this winding ribbon of water. The Thames connects the city with the sea, from which it drew its wealth and its power. For centuries, the river was London's highway and main street.

Some of the bridges that span the Thames are household words. London Bridge, which, contrary to the nursery rhyme, has never "fallen down," but has been dismantled and shipped to the United States, ran from the Monument (a tall pillar commemorating the Great Fire of 1666) to Southwark Cathedral, parts of which date back to 1207.

Its neighbor to the east is the still-standing Tower Bridge (tel. 407-0922), one of the city's most celebrated landmarks and possibly the most photographed and painted bridge on earth.

Tower Bridge was built during 1886 to 1894 with two towers 800 feet apart, joined by footbridges that provide glass-covered walkways for the public who can enter the north tower, take the elevator to the walkway, cross the river to the south tower, and return to street level. It's a photographer's dream, with interesting views of St. Paul's, the Tower of London, and in the distance, Big Ben and the Houses of Parliament. You can also visit the main engine room with its Victorian boiler and steam-pumping engines, which raise and lower the roadway across the river.

There are models showing how the 1000-ton arms of the bridge can be raised in 1½ minutes to allow ships passage upstream. These days the bridge is only opened once or twice a week, and you'll be lucky to catch the real thing. You'll know if it is going to open, however, as a bell sounds throughout the bridge and road traffic is stopped. Admission is £2 ($3.90) with reductions for children. It is open daily in summer from 10 a.m. to 6:30 p.m. (to 4:45 p.m. in winter).

The piece of river between the site of the old London Bridge and the Tower Bridge marks the city end of the immense row of docks stretching 26 miles to the coast. Although most of them are no longer in use, they have long been known as the Port of London.

But the Thames meant more to London than a port. It was also her chief commercial thoroughfare and a royal highway, the only regal one in the days of winding cobblestone streets. Every royal procession was undertaken by barge—gorgeously painted and gilded vessels, which you can still see at the National Maritime Museum in Greenwich. All important prisoners were delivered to the Tower by water—it eliminated the chance of an ambush by their friends in one of those narrow, crooked alleys surrounding the fortress.

When Henry VIII had his country residence at Hampton Court, there was a constant stream of messenger boats shuttling between his other riverside palaces all the way to Greenwich. His illustrious daughter, Queen Elizabeth I, revved up the practice to such a degree that a contemporary chronicler complained he couldn't spit in the Thames for fear of hitting a royal craft.

The royal boats and much of the commercial traffic disappeared when the streets were widened enough for horse coaches to maintain a decent pace. But a trip up or down the river today will give you an entirely different view of London from the one you get on dry land. You'll see exactly how the city grew along and around the Thames, and how many of her landmarks turn their faces toward the water. It's like Manhattan from a ferry.

There are pleasure launches sailing from Charing Cross and Westminster piers from April to September. You can take them upstream, past the Houses of Parliament, to Kew, Richmond, and Hampton Court. The downstream journey takes about 50 minutes and ends at Greenwich.

For inquiries, telephone 930-2074.

Ships on the River

For anyone with even the faintest nautical bent, there's a fascinating collection of craft permanently moored along the river. Each is totally different from the other, and you could spend an entire day inspecting the contrasting marine worlds they represent.

Just below Tower Bridge stands the relatively new development of **St. Katharine's Dock** (nearest Underground station is Tower Hill). This development was created out of the old London dock area where the "breakfast ships," carrying bacon and eggs from Holland, used to tie up. It is gradually becoming a vast open-air pleasure area—but with a difference.

In the East Basin of the dock (behind the Dickens Inn) lie many old and famous vessels. This is the **Historic Ship Collection** of the Maritime Trust (tel. 730-0096). For an admission charge of £1.70 ($2.55) for adults and 80p ($1.20), for children, you can go on board seven historic ships, from the royal research vessel *Discovery,* Captain Scott's ship, which was moved here from its former berth at Victoria Embankment, to the old *Nore* lightship. Also docked here are the Thames sailing barge *Cambria,* an East Coast herring drifter, a "dirty British coaster" of 1890 as described by John Masefield in his poem "Cargoes," and a steam tug. In contrast to these, you'll usually see elegant yachts from all over the world.

The Trust provides walk-around guide leaflets to help visitors interpret what they see, and souvenirs are sold aboard the *Cambria.* There are plenty of places for a snack lunch or a pint in a pub, and of course the Tower of London is just across the road. For information, call 481-0043.

A floating museum, **H.M.S.** *Belfast,* Symons Wharf, Vine Lane, S.E. 1 (tel. 407-6434), is an 11,500-ton cruiser, the last of the great British warships. She's moored on the opposite bank of the Thames, looking out onto the Tower of London. The first shots were fired from her guns during the sinking of the *Scharnhorst,* and she saw distinguished service during the D-Day bombardment of Normandy. She also was in action in Korea. Exhibitions show the history not only of the H.M.S. *Belfast* but of cruisers in general. The huge engine and boiler rooms can be seen, together with many other working and living spaces. The price of admission is £2 ($3) for adults, half price for children. The hours are 11 a.m. to 5:50 p.m. daily. In winter the ship closes at sunset. Nearest tube stations: Tower Hill, Monument, and London Bridge. Boats run from Tower Pier in summer and on weekends in winter.

The Dungeon

The **London Dungeon,** 34 Tooley St., S.E.1 (tel. 403-0606), simulates a ghoulish atmosphere designed deliberately to chill the blood while reproducing faithfully the conditions that existed in the Middle Ages. Set under the arches of London Bridge Station, the dungeon is a series of tableaux, more grizzly than Madame Tussaud's, depicting life in Old London. The rumble of trains overhead adds to the spine-chilling horror of the place. Bells toll and there is constant melancholy chanting in the background. Dripping water and live rats make for even more atmosphere.

The heads of executed criminals were stuck on spikes for onlookers to observe through glasses hired for the occasion. The murder of Thomas à Becket in Canterbury Cathedral is also depicted. Naturally, there's a burning at the stake, as well as a torture chamber with racking, branding, and fingernail extraction.

If you survive, there is a souvenir shop selling certificates to testify that you have been through the works. The dungeon is open from 10 a.m. to 5:45 p.m. April through September, to 4:30 p.m. October through March, seven days a week. Admission is £4 ($6) for adults, £2.50 ($3.75) for children under 14.

Cleopatra's Needle

Rising from the Victoria Embankment along the Thames is a tall white stone obelisk, popularly misnamed "Cleopatra's Needle." The pillar is, in fact, far older than Cleopatra and once stood in front of the temple of Heliopolis, erected sometime between 1600 and 1500 B.C. In 1878 it was presented to Britain by the khedive of Egypt and brought here in a ship specially fitted for the purpose.

On its reerection by the Thames, the Victorians couldn't resist adding some contemporary objects to the interior of the foundation stone. To wit: a Bible, a straight razor, several morning newspapers, a baby's feeding bottle, and a box of hairpins, presumably to impress whoever would excavate the site with the splendors of 19th-century civilization.

Highgate Cemetery

This cemetery is the ideal setting for a collection of Victorian sculpture. Described as everything from "walled romantic rubble" to "an anthology of horror," the 20-acre cemetery in North London's old Highgate section attracts tombstone fanciers. The unkempt look of overgrown weeds combined with the clutter of obelisks and crosses give the graveyard a rare, Gothic kind of beauty. Several of the tombstones are masterpieces in themselves, including the full-size concrete grand piano, its top opened as if ready for a concert, marked only with the name Thornton and a poetic phrase by Puccini. Another grave, that of a sporting goods manufacturer, is decorated with crossed tennis rackets, cricket bats, and balls. The most tender marker is a life-like statue of a small boy with a ball, placed over the grave of a five-year-old boy. Highgate's most famous grave is that of Karl Marx, the founder of modern Communism, who died in Hampstead in 1883. On his tomb is a huge bust of Marx, inscribed with his quotation, "Workers of all lands, unite." The grave is seldom without a wreath or bouquet of red flowers, usually placed there by an Eastern embassy or a local Communist group. The cemetery adjoins Waterlow Park, a 29-acre landmark of Highgate. In the nearby community are also several historic houses, including the Cromwell House, dating from 1638, and the home of Samuel Taylor Coleridge.

Free Sights—London in Action

Those who have grown museum-weary might like to see workaday London engaged in its task of, say, trying to start a revolution at Speakers Corner or sentencing a modern-day Jack the Ripper at Old Bailey. Here are a few of the action items available:

First, at the northwest extremity of Mayfair, head for **Marble Arch,** an enormous *faux pas* that the English didn't try to hide but turned into a monument. Originally it was built by John Nash as the entrance to Buckingham Palace, until it was discovered that it was too small for carriages to pass through. If you see a crowd of people nearby who look as if they are plotting revolution, you might be right. In this part of Hyde Park (tube to Marble Arch) is **Speakers Corner,** where you will see English free speech in action. Everybody from Communists to Orgone theorists mounts the soapbox to speak his or her mind. The speeches reach their most violent pitch on Sunday, the best day to visit Marble Arch.

If you are intrigued with the operation of the courts, you may want to include a visit to the **Central Criminal Court** while you are in the area of St. Paul's. On the corner of Old Bailey and Newgate Street, E.C.4, the court was built on the site of the infamous Old Newgate Prison. Affectionately called Old Bailey, it has witnessed some great—and some dubious—moments in the history of British justice. The public is permitted to enter from 10:20 a.m. to 1 p.m. and from 1:50 to 4 p.m. Monday through Friday. Entry is strictly on a first arrival basis. Guests queue up outside (where, incidentally, the final public execution took place in the 1860s). Courts 1 to 4, 17, and 18 are entered from Newgate Street, and the balance from "Old Bailey." No persons under 14 are admitted, and teenagers from 14 to 17 must be accompanied by a responsible adult. No cameras or tape recorders are allowed. If you prefer civil cases to criminal ones, you can visit the **Royal Courts of Justice** on The Strand, W.C.2; (tube to Temple; tel. 405-7641, extension 3439), which are open Monday through Friday from 10 a.m. to 4 p.m.

The **Stock Exchange** has replaced New York as the world's leading money mart. On the trading floor of this money center, one of the most modern in the world, you can catch a glimpse of brokers and jobbers. Guides explain what the action means, and later you are shown a film in an adjoining cinema, giving you an insight into the world of high finance. The Visitors' Gallery entrance is in Old Broad Street, and the nearest Underground station is Bank. Admission is free, and visiting hours are weekdays from 9:45 a.m. to 3:15 p.m. For more information, phone 588-2355.

London Zoo

One of the greatest zoos in the world, the London Zoo (tel. 722-3333) celebrated its 150th birthday in 1976. Among the thousands of animals, the most famous are the two giant pandas, Ching-Ching and Chia-Chia, a gift to Britain from the People's Republic of China. One of the most fascinating exhibits is the Snowdon Aviary. Many families budget almost an entire day to spend with the animals, watching the sea lions being fed or the elephants bathed on fine summer days. Also of interest is the Moonlight World, where animals of the night—the "nocturnal beasties"—wander in their special world, everything from Australian fruit bats to primitive echidnas.

The London Zoo occupies 36 acres of Regent's Park, and is open every day except Christmas from 9 a.m. in summer and from 10 a.m. in winter, till 6 p.m. or dusk, whichever is earlier. You can go by Underground to Baker Street or Camden Town and then take the no. 74 bus (Camden Town is nearer and an easy ten-minute walk). On the grounds are two fully licensed restaurants, one self-service, the other with waitresses. Admission is £3.50 ($5.25) for adults, £1.50 ($2.25) for children 5 to 16 (under 5, free).

The Jewish Museum

The major communal building for English Jewry is **Woburn House,** Upper Woburn Place, W.C.1, near Euston Station. In these precincts you'll also come upon the hard-to-find Jewish Museum (tel. 388-4525), tucked away on a lovely square. Walk along Euston Road, and turn right onto Upper Woburn Place. When you reach Tavistock Square, turn right again, and there's the entrance. After entering, you're invited to sign a guest book, then you're guided up to the museum, a large salon filled with antiques relating to the history of the Jews. You'll come across many artifacts used in Jewish rituals. All the exhibits, in fact, are of interest to those concerned with Anglo-Judaica. It is open Monday to Thursday from 12:30 to 4 p.m. and on Sunday from 10:30 a.m. to 12:45 p.m. It is closed on Friday, Saturday, bank holidays, and Jewish holidays. The Jewish Historical Society runs the **Mocatta Library** at the neighboring University College on Gower Street.

Wembley Stadium

To the soccer and rugby buff (football fan), this stadium is the ultimate. A guided tour of the hallowed ground gives you a chance to visit the players' changing rooms, then walk up the players' tunnel to the roar of the crowd. You can even relax in the Royal Box and Retiring Rooms. There is a multiscreen slide show depicting the activities at Wembley, including the first cup final and Henry Cooper's fight with Muhammed Ali. Tours leave at 10 and 11 a.m., noon, and 2, 3, and 4 p.m., taking one hour and ten minutes. Tours are conducted daily except Thursday and the day before, of, and after any event, as well as Christmas, Boxing Day, and New Year's Day. Admission is £2 ($3) for adults, £1.25 ($1.88) for children. For

tion boxes as well. There is a City branch at 27b Throgmorton St., E.C.2 (tel. 588-1306). Tube: Green Park.

Prestat, 40 Moulton St., W.1 (tel. 629-4838), is chocolate maker "to Her Majesty the Queen by appointment." Why not impress your friends by taking home a box of assorted Napoleon truffles, £6.50 ($9.75) a pound in a carton or £7 ($10.50) packed in a box? A box of truffles and an assortment of connoisseur chocolates also cost £7 ($10.50) a pound. Coffee or double mints and brandy cherries may tempt you. The boxes give Prestat products an extra touch of elegance.

CLOCKS: **Strike One (Islington) Limited,** 51 Camden Passage, N.1 (tel. 226-9709), sells clocks, watches, and barometers. It's in the heart of the Camden Passage Antiques Village in Islington (tube: Angel). Strike One clearly dates and prices each old clock, and every clock is guaranteed for a year against faulty workmanship. A wide selection of clocks is displayed, ranging from early English dial clocks to long-case clocks. Strike One specializes in Act of Parliament clocks. They issue a quarterly illustrated catalog, which is mailed internationally to all serious clock collectors. They also undertake to find any clock to a customer's requirement, if they do not have a suitable example in stock. The shop is owned by John Mighell, a former mining executive who loved clocks more than his job. He gave up his business more than a decade ago to found Strike One. The shop is open daily except Sunday from 9 a.m. to 5 p.m. (at other times by appointment).

CONTEMPORARY ART: **Christie's Contemporary Art,** 8 Dover St., W.1 (tel. 499-3701), offers original etchings, and lithographs, and screenprints by up-and-coming artists for around £30 ($45) to £100 ($150). You will certainly not end up with an absolute "pup," and your holiday purchase may turn out to be a first work of a second Picasso. The gallery also has the works of such masters as Henry Moore, David Hockney, Joan Miró, and John Piper. Each work is an authentic original, numbered and signed by the artist, then stamped with Christie's seal of authentication before delivery. You can send for a catalog or just go along. Tube: Green Park.

Auction sales are held by Christie's at 85 Old Brompton Rd., S.W.7 (tel. 581-2231), as advertised in the Monday editions of the *Daily Telegraph* and *Times.*

COVENT GARDEN ENTERPRISE: In the Central Market Building an impressive array of shops, pubs, and other attractions has opened. Judging from the already-existing enterprises in the area, the new Covent Garden will prove exciting for the visitor. After all, who would expect to find in central London a kite shop?

The **British Crafts Centre,** 43 Earlham St., Covent Garden, W.C.2 (tel. 836-6993), is a gallery and display center promoting the best of British crafts through exhibitions, information, and events. Many of the leading craftspeople in Britain exhibit their work through the center, much of which is for sale. A program of changing exhibitions attempts to cover all the craft disciplines and their various applications, with the emphasis on contemporary original and professional work. The exhibition program is comple- mented by a second display area with a range of work changed each month. The ceramics, glass, jewelry, leather, metal, silver, textiles, and wood shown in the center have an appeal for the serious collector of fine crafts through to the person wanting an individual gift for a friend. Information is available about craft organizations, galleries, and studios throughout Britain. The center is open Tuesday to Friday 10 a.m. to 5:30 p.m. (until 7 p.m. on Thursday), on Saturday from 11 a.m. to 5 p.m.

The following are places that have caught my interest.

The **Covent Garden General Store,** 111 Long Acre, W.C.2 (tel. 240-0331), offers a conglomeration of gifts and household items, ranging from pots, pans, glass and china, cups, mugs, money boxes, packing boxes, walking sticks, handbags, and shopping bags. It's ideal for browsing to find that odd souvenir which will have some use. Prices range from a few pence to several pounds, and they also sell herb teas, sea salt, spices, and country jam, as well as natural soaps.

At 21 Neal St., W.C.2 (tel. 836-5254), the **Natural Shoes Store** sells all manner of comfortable and quality footwear from Birkenstock to the best of the British classics. Also, at 40 Floral St., W.C.2 (tel. 379-7856), the **Plum Line** offers exclusive designer shoes for both men and women.

Neal Street East, 5 Neal St., W.C. 2 (tel. 240-0135), is a vast shop devoted to Oriental or Orient-inspired merchandise. Here you can find artificial flowers, pottery, baskets, glassware, chinoiserie, and toys. There is also an Oriental cooking section and book department, as well as a gallery for Oriental themes. The **Tea House,** 15a Neal St., and the **Kimono Shop,** 23 Neal St., are also part of the Neal Street East organization. The Tea House is a shop devoted to tea and "teaphernalia," which includes anything associated with tea, tea drinking, and tea time. Kimono deals in second- hand and antique kimonos, kasuri jackets and trousers, yukatas (casual kimonos), scarves, purses, and sandals—everything you need to dress the way the Japanese do.

Coppershop, 48 Neal St., W.C.2 (tel. 836-2984), is another one of the enthusiastic enterprises to blossom in the market, with the widest range of exclusively English-manufactured copper goods in Britain. For the kitchen, you'll find jelly molds depicting lions, unicorns, fruit, whatever—along with hard-wearing frying and omelet pans, plus more exotic sauté pans, pomme anna pans, and zabaglione pans. In addition to fish kettles, jardinières, and traditional coal scuttles, ideal as flowerpot holders, Coppershop has copper clocks, lamps, cocktail shakers, ice buckets, trays, watering cans, and much else besides. The shop is run by Sally and Michael Crosfield, and they will airmail your goods home at a low cost, because on exports they can deduct the VAT and put this against postage.

Naturally British, 12 New Row, W.C.2 (tel. 240-0551), specializes in items made in Britain, including handmade pottery from Devon and Cornwall, tweed and knitwear from Scotland, leather goods, wrought-iron work, and carved woodwork. A perfectly carved rocking horse will cost upward of £350 ($525), but a three-dimensional jigsaw-puzzle monkey, dog, or cat will go for only about £9 ($13.50).

The Glasshouse, 65 Long Acre, W.C.2 (tel. 836-9785), sells beautiful glass, and also invites visitors into the workshops to see the craftspeople producing their wares. At street level, passersby can see glassblowers at work. An intensive weekend course in the art of glassblowing is offered. The Glasshouse is open from 10 a.m. to 5:30 p.m. Monday to Friday, from 11 a.m. to 4 p.m. on Saturday.

Penhaligon's, 41 Wellington St., W.C.2 (tel. 836-2150), established in 1870 as a Victorian perfumery, holds a Royal Warrant to H.R.H. the Duke of Edinburgh. It offers a large selection of perfumes, aftershave, soap, and bath oils for men and women. Perfect gifts include antique silver perfume bottles.

Behind the Warehouse off Neal Street runs a narrow road leading to **Neal's Yard,** a mews of warehouses that seem to retain some of the old London atmosphere. The open warehouses display such goods as vegetables, health foods, fresh-baked breads, cakes, sandwiches, and in an immaculate dairy, the largest variety of flavored cream cheeses you are likely to encounter.

At the top of Burleigh Street, off the Strand, beside the old Flower Market, is the **Covent Garden Flea Market.** This is a real browser's paradise, with its good, bad, and indifferent clothing, fruit, and vegetables —you name it. The stalls are mainly under cover, and stallholders range from the aristocratic through punk.

There are many tiny shops, mostly of a specialized nature, where artists and craftspeople seem to have gathered to form a new community. In Bedfordbury, one of the tiny streets, Cherry Saltzer specializes in—not surprisingly—cats, in her shop called **Catz.** There are model cats, teapot cats, ashtray cats, cat calendars, cat badges, books, posters, and cat umbrellas. **Nubia,** 29 Bedfordbury, sells clothing and accessories from the '30s through the '60s. Elsewhere there are silversmiths, pewter, and copperware shops, and several small snackbars and restaurants. It's well worth making your own voyage of discovery and enjoy finding odd shops and souvenirs to take home.

DEPARTMENT STORES: Harrods, Brompton Road, at Knightsbridge, S.W.1 (tel. 730-1234), is the department store to end all department stores. As firmly entrenched in English life as Buckingham Palace and the Ascot Races, it is an elaborate emporium, at times as fascinating as a museum. In a magazine article about Harrods, a salesperson was quoted as saying: "It's more of a sort of way of life than a shop, really." Aside from the fashion department (including high-level tailoring and a "Way In" section for young people), you'll find such incongruous sections as a cathedral-ceilinged and arcaded meat market, even a funeral service. Harrods has everything: men's custom-tailored suits, tweed overcoats, cashmere or lambswool sweaters for both men and women, hand-stitched traveling bags, raincoats, mohair jackets, patterned ski sweaters, scarves of hand-woven Irish wool, pewter reproductions, a perfumery department, "lifetime" leather suitcases, pianos. Tube: Knightsbridge.

Much more economical, however, is **Selfridges,** on Oxford Street, W.1 (tel. 629-1234), one of the biggest department stores in Europe, with more than 550 divisions, selling everything from artificial flowers to groceries. The specialty shops are particularly enticing, with good buys in Irish linen, Wedgwood, leather goods, silver-plated goblets, cashmere and woolen scarves. There's also the Miss Selfridge Boutique, for the young or those who'd like to be. To help you travel light, the Export Bureau will air freight your purchases to anywhere in the world, completely tax free. On the ground floor, the London Tourist Board will help you find your way around London's sights with plenty of maps, tips, and friendly advice. Tube: Bond Street.

Liberty & Company Limited, Regent Street (tel. 734-1234), celebrated its centenary in 1975. In 100 years the store became known worldwide for its exquisite fabrics. One whole floor of the department store is devoted to fabrics of all kinds from all over the world, including Liberty printed cottons, silks, and pure wool. Liberty printed Tana lawn costs approximately £4.95 ($7.43) a meter, and Liberty printed silk around £9.95 ($14.93) a meter. Liberty printed silk squares in all sizes and colors, for both men and women, can be found in the country's largest scarf department. Twenty-seven-inch squares cost approximately £16.50 ($24.75).

Other exciting departments include treasures from the Orient, a wide range of modern furniture, an extensive furnishing fabric department, including Liberty's own fabrics, plus the best china and glass from all over the world. Tube: Oxford Circus.

Marks & Spencer has several branches in London, attracting the thrifty British, who get fine buys, especially in woolen goods. The main department store is at 458 Oxford St., W.1 (tel. 935-7954), three short blocks from Marble Arch. Cashmere sweaters for women are in the £35 ($52.50) to £40 ($60) range, women's suits from £45 ($67.50) to £75 ($112.50). Cashmere sweaters for men cost from £45 ($67.50) to £50 ($75), and men's suits go for around £60 ($90) to £110 ($165). Tube: Marble Arch.

In addition, you might visit **British Home Stores,** on Oxford Street, W.1 (tel. 629-2011), near the Oxford Circus tube station, between John Princes Street and Holles Street. Similar to Marks & Spencer, it is patronized almost exclusively by the English themselves, and is known for its buys in woolens. Look for bargains. British Home Stores also operates next to the Marks & Spencer building on Kensington High Street, just a few minutes from the tube station.

THE WORLD'S MOST ELEGANT GROCERY STORE: Fortnum and Mason Ltd., 181 Piccadilly, W.1 (tel. 734-8040), down the street from the Ritz, draws the carriage trade, the well-heeled dowager from Mayfair or Belgravia who comes seeking such tinned treasures as pâté de foie gras or a boar's head. She would never set foot in a regular grocery store, but Fortnum and Mason, with its swallow-tailed attendants, is no mere grocery store; it's a British tradition dating back to 1707. In fact, the establishment likes to think that Mr. Fortnum and Mr. Mason "created a union surpassed in its importance to the human race only by the meeting of Adam and Eve." At the Patio Restaurant on the mezzanine, which closes at 4:30 p.m., you can mingle at lunch with the caviar and champagne shoppers, choosing from a menu that ranges from soup and sandwiches to chicken pie and steak-and-kidney pie. American-style milkshakes, sundaes, and ice-cream sodas are also available here, as well as at the Fountain Restaurant in the basement. With entrances from both the store and Jermyn Street, the Fountain stays open from 9:30 a.m. until midnight and is a popular after-theater place for snacks or light meals. The elegant St. James's Restaurant on the fourth floor is open during regular store hours, 9:30 a.m. to 6 p.m., offering a more extensive and more expensive menu than the other two restaurants. Look for the ornate Fortnum and Mason clock outside on the front of the store. Tube: Piccadilly Circus.

IRISH WARES: The Irish Shop, 11 Duke St., W.1 (tel. 935-1366), and 80 Buckingham Gate, S.W.1 (tel. 222-7132), unites northern and southern Ireland by stocking so much stuff in such a small area. Directed by Charles

(heavy on clothes and sundries); **The Cut,** behind Waterloo Station (small but fairly bustling in the morning); and **Berwick Street,** in the heart of Soho, which is heavy on fresh fruits and busiest around noon" (G. Berkowitz, DeKalb, Ill.).

STYLISH CLOTHING: **Carnaby Street,** just off Regent, is a legend, and legends take time to build. Often, by the time they are entrenched, fickle fashion has moved on elsewhere. Alas, Carnaby no longer dominates the world of pace-setting fashion. But the street is still visited by the curious, and some of its shops display lots of claptrap and quick quid merchandise. For value, style, and imagination in design, the **Chelsea** (King's Road) and **Kensington** boutiques have left Carnaby behind.

WELSH HANDICRAFTS: The **Welsh Craft Centre,** 36 Parliament St., S.W.1 (tel. 839-5056), is a gallery of things Welsh, ranging from hand-woven rugs, tapestries, and tweeds to Welsh lovespoons, brass miners' lamps, horse brasses, pottery, and stoneware. You can learn about the people and the history of the goods before buying at very genuine prices. Tube: Westminster.

WOOLENS: See Harrods, where the standards are high. But for a specialty shop, **D. & L. Estridge,** 62 Regent St., W.1 (tel. 734-0195), next to the Café-Royal Grill Room, is a good choice (and it's not as expensive as one would judge from its location). Cashmere, camel's hair, shetlands, tartan kilts and skirts—Estridge is a virtual showcase of Scottish crafts. Good values are to be found in cashmere sweaters. Lambswool sweaters are also sold, as are shetland Fair Isle, authentic tartans, and cashmere and lambswool scarves. Tube: Piccadilly Circus.

READERS' SHOPPING SUGGESTIONS: "In London an outdoor (weather permitting) art show takes place on Saturday and Sunday on Piccadilly at Green Park (Underground shop is Hyde Park or Green Park). The show extends for almost half a mile, and you can pick up good-quality drawings, watercolors, oils, and crafts" (Ray R. Conley). . . . "In London combine a Sunday afternoon outing at the Hyde Park Speakers Corner with a stroll down Bayswater Road. Along the edge of the park, from Marble Arch for four blocks toward Lancaster Gate, stretches an outdoor art fair. Every possible type of art and craft is exhibited, from paintings on velvet to handmade pottery—and most at reasonable prices" (Phyllis and Steve Wilson, Chicago, Ill.). "My husband and I want to add a suggestion about shopping for gifts that we found helpful on our trip to England. We restricted our buying to museum and cathedral shops. This is a good idea for several reasons. We found many wonderful people in these shops and learned a good deal about local history, their family backgrounds, and their historic ties. The items bought were well priced and quite lovely, e.g., note paper in the Jewish Museum in London; placemats and trivets in Warwick Castle; paperweights in the Ashmolean Museum at Oxford; and a facsimile of Wordsworth's 'Tintern Abbey' at the abbey. Also we felt that in making such purchases we contributed to the preservation of these sights and made it possible for other visitors to follow" (Henry and Gertrude Langsam, Malverne, N.Y.).

3. London After Dark

London is crammed with nighttime entertainment. You'll have a wide choice of action—from the dives of Soho to elegant clubs. So much depends on your taste, pocketbook, and even the time of year. Nowhere else will you find such a panorama of legitimate theaters, operas, concerts, gambling clubs, discos, vaudeville at Victorian music halls, striptease joints, jazz clubs, folkmusic cafés, nightclubs, and ballrooms. For information about any of these events, ask a newsstand dealer for a copy of *What's on in London*, 50p (75¢).

THEATERS: The fame of the English theater has spread far and wide. In London, you'll have a chance to see it on its home ground. You may want to spend a classical evening with the National Theatre Company (formerly the Old Vic), or you may settle for a new play by Harold Pinter. You might even want to catch up on that Broadway musical you missed in New York, or be an advance talent scout for next year's big Stateside hit.

You can either purchase your ticket from the theater's box office (the most recommended method), or else from a ticket agent, such as the one at the reservations desk of American Express (agent's fee charges, however). In a few theaters, you can reserve your spot in the gallery, the cheapest seats of all, but in some cases the inexpensive seats are sold only on the day of performance. This means that you'll have to buy your ticket earlier in the day, and—as you don't get a reserved seat—return about an hour before the performance and queue up for the best gallery seats. Occasionally you can enjoy a preshow staged by strolling performers called "buskers," next year's Chaplin—or last year's (the theater has its peaks and valleys).

If you want to see two shows in one day, you'll find that Wednesday, Thursday, and Saturday are always crammed with matinee performances. Many West End theaters begin their evening performances at 7:30.

Students and senior citizens get a break at most theaters (subject to availability) by being granted a discount at the local box offices. Currently, such discount tickets sell at a price beginning at £3.50 ($5.25) each.

The **Leicester Square Ticket Booth,** Leicester Square, W.C.2, sells theater tickets on the day of performance for half price, plus a 75p ($1.13) service charge. Open from noon to 2 p.m. for matinee performances and from 2:30 to 6:30 p.m. for evening performances, they have a wide selection of seats available. Tickets for "hits" are obviously not available often. There is frequently a long line, but it moves quickly and it is well worth the effort if you want to take in a lot of theater while you are in London—and save money. The shows for which tickets are available are well displayed at the booth, so you can make up your mind on what to see as you wait in the queue.

Of London's many theaters, these are particularly outstanding:

The **National Theatre,** a concrete cubist fortress—a three-theater complex that stands as a $32-million landmark beside the Waterloo Bridge on the south bank of the Thames. It was first suggested in 1848, and it took Parliament 101 years to pass a bill vowing government support. Flaring out like a fan, the most thrilling theater in this complex is the **Olivier,** named after Lord Olivier, its first director when the company was born in 1962. (Olivier was succeeded in 1973 by Peter Hall, who created the Royal Shakespeare Company.) The Olivier Theater bears a resemblance in miniature to an ancient Greek theater. It's an open-stage, 1160-seat theater that is intended primarily for the classics. The **Cottesloe** is a simple box theater for 400 people, offering experimental plays. Finally, the 890-seat **Lyttelton** is a traditional proscenium-arch house that doesn't have one bad seat for any theater-goer. In the foyers there are two bookshops, eight bars, a restaurant, and five self-service buffets (some open all day except Sunday), and many outside terraces with river views. For everyone, with or without tickets for a play, there is live foyer music, free, before evening performances and Saturday matinees, and free exhibitions. The foyers are open 10 a.m. to 11 p.m. except Sunday. Also guided theater tours are available daily, including backstage areas, for about £1.75 ($2.63).

Tickets range from £4 ($6) to £12.50 ($18.75), but midweek matinees are cheaper. Group bookings can be arranged in advance. Credit cards are accepted. You can book through a travel agent or with the theater in advance, and some tickets are available on the day of performance at £5 ($7.50).

For general information, telephone 633-0880. For ticket information, call the box office at 928-2252.

The National Theatre Restaurant will serve you a good meal for around £10 ($15), but at one of the coffee bars a snack will run around £3.50 ($5.25). If the weather is good, you can just sit and look out over the river and the London skyline spread before you. Tube: Waterloo Station.

The Old Vic: a 165-year-old theater on Waterloo Road, S.E.1 (tel. 928-2651, or the box office at 928-7616), has reopened after a mammoth facelift and modernization. The facade and much of the interior have been restored in their original early 19th-century style, and most of the modernization is behind the scenes. The proscenium arch has been moved back, the stage trebled in size, and more seats and stage boxes added. It is air-conditioned and contains five bars. There are plans for short seasons of varied plays, and several subscription offers have been introduced with reductions of up to £3 ($4.50) a seat if you purchase six tickets for different shows at once. Otherwise, top prices vary, with the best stalls or dress circle going for about £11 ($16.50) a ticket. Tube: Waterloo.

The **Royal Shakespeare Company** has its famous theater in Stratford-upon-Avon and is also housed in the Barbican Theatre, Barbican Centre, E.C.2 (tube to Barbican or Moorgate; tel. 628-8795 in London, or Stratford 295-623). A program of new plays and Shakespearean and other classics is performed here. Plays run in repertoire and are presented two or three times a week each. The company also has two smaller theaters where new and experimental plays are performed as well as classics: **The Other Place,** in Stratford, and **The Pit,** also in the Barbican Centre.

Royal Court Theatre, Sloane Square, S.W.1 (tel. 730-1745; tube to Sloane Square). The English Stage Society has operated this theater for more than 25 years. The emphasis is on new playwrights (John Osborne got his start here with the 1956 production of *Look Back in Anger*). Also on the premises is the Theatre Upstairs, the studio theater also devoted to the work of new playwrights. Prices of tickets vary according to the play, those in the main theater averaging from £4 ($6) to £12 ($18). At the Theatre Upstairs, the tickets go for £1.50 ($2.25) to £3 ($4.50).

The **Young Vic,** The Cut, Waterloo, S.E.1 (tel. 928-6363), aims primarily at the 15 to 25 age group, with some productions specifically for younger audiences. The Young Vic's repertoire includes such authors as Shakespeare, Ben Jonson, O'Casey, and Pinter, as well as specially written new plays. Performances begin normally at 7:30 p.m. Seats cost an average of £3 ($4.50). Tube: Waterloo Station.

Sadler's Wells Theatre is on Rosebery Avenue, E.C.1 (tel. 278-8916). Apart from its resident companies, Sadler's Wells Royal Ballet and new Sadler's Wells Opera, it also plays host to other outstanding companies. Prices fluctuate from £2.50 ($3.75) to £12 ($18). Take the Underground to Angel Station (Northern line). The theater is a three-minute walk. Or you can go by bus direct from Piccadilly (no. 19 or 38), from Holborn (no. 19,

38, or 172), from the Angel (no. 30, 43, 73, 104, 214, 277, or 279), and from Waterloo (no. 171 or 188), and change at Holborn. The theater operates its own "Stagecoach" service before and after every evening performance, collecting patrons at mainline and Underground stations and setting them down on the return journey. Service A starts from Victoria via Waterloo and Holborn; Service B from Paddington via Marble Arch, Baker Street, Euston Road, and King's Cross. The fare is 60p (90¢) one way, £1 ($1.50) round trip.

Many theaters will accept bookings by telephone if you give your name and credit-card number when you call. Then all you have to do is go along before the performance to collect your tickets, which will be sold at the theater price. All theater booking agencies charge a fee. Once confirmed, the booking will be charged to your account even if you don't use the tickets. Only card holders can collect the tickets charged to their accounts.

THEATER CLUBS: Besides the productions in the regular theaters, several theater clubs have been established, originally to avoid the censorship of the Lord Chamberlain, although that is no longer necessary. These clubs are where the most experimental and avant-garde productions are staged. By stopping by at their box offices and paying a nominal fee, you can become a temporary member. The clubs include the **Mountview Arts Centre** and **Mountview Theatre School,** with two theaters, the Mountview Theatre and the Judi Dench Theatre, both at 104 Crouch Hill, N.8 (tel. 340-5885), and have been established for some 40 years. About 40 plays and musicals are presented annually, plus 30 films. Membership is free. Many courses are offered, mainly full time, although some evenings part-time courses are also given. Affiliated theaters include the New Arts Theatre Club in London, the Hampstead Theatre Club, and the Traverse Theatre Club, Edinburgh. Performances on weekday evenings begin at 7:30 p.m. Matinees are at 3:30 p.m. There is no charge for seats, although donations are invited for the students' scholarship fund. Take the subway on the Piccadilly line to Finsbury Park and then a W2 or W7 bus (terminus). The theater is on the main road.

The **Holland Park Open Air Theatre** is a charming open-air stage in Holland Park, W.8, close to the Commonwealth Institute. It really has the air of a court theater in some Renaissance palace yard. There is a weekly program in June, July, and August of opera and drama. Free band concerts are presented on Sunday at 3 p.m. Tickets are £2 ($3) Tuesday through Saturday. Shows begin at 7:30 nightly, at 2:30 p.m. for Saturday matinees. The Dutch Garden is floodlit until midnight, and the theater is closed on Monday. For program inquiries, telephone 633-1707. Tube: Kensington High Street.

PUB THEATER: In 1969 a "new" movement developed in London's theatrical world, which was delightful but certainly not new in terms of stage history. Live theater penetrated the pubs. Within a year the movement gathered such momentum that a string of pubs began to display regular playbills alongside their beer ads. Saloon regulars who normally wouldn't have dreamt of theater-going picked up their pint mugs and slipped into the auditorium—and frequently became devoted fans and critics.

There is no uniformity about either the material presented or the premises involved. The former ranges from wildly experimental efforts by unknown young playwrights to established classics, the latter from elaborately decorated and lit stages to pretty primitive backroom assemblies. But that's part of the movement's peculiar charm. You never know what you're going to get, the monetary risk is minimal, and you don't even have to buy a drink to see the show. Some pubs feature lunchtime performances only, while others put on another, often different, play at night as well. It's an experience you shouldn't miss, since you're not likely to find it anywhere else.

The line-up of public houses doubling as theaters changes frequently and abruptly and your best bet for finding them is to look in *What's On in London.*

MOVIES: The films shown in London are much like those you'd see in any large American city, but with a stronger international flavor. Screenings, however, are not continuous, and the last performances start around 8 p.m., so you'd better consult a newspaper for the exact showtimes. Prices vary according to seats—all of them considerably cheaper than at home. Don't forget that movie theaters are called cinemas.

London has a dozen or so real movie palaces in the old meaning of the term, gigantic citadels with plush loges, grand buffets, and triple curtains. But her prime piece is the kind of ultramodern movie mansion you might expect to find in Hollywood—but won't.

The **Cinecenta** is a streamlined, black-and-white block on Panston Street, off Leicester Square, S.W.1 (tel. 930-0631), housing four superb theaters under one roof. They share one sleekly plush lobby, but each runs a separate program, always including at least one European film. Tube: Leicester Square.

MUSIC HALLS: Players, Villiers Street (formerly the famous Gatti's "Under the Arches"), W.C.2 (tel. 839-1134). Nowadays, the Players is a Victorian music hall variety club. Top-notch entertainers often perform here. The presentation is professionally staged, with the appropriate settings and costumes. The master of ceremonies, the chairman, asks members to introduce their guests, who stand for a bow (and comments). Insults are exchanged in jest, especially if a guest is from one of the "colonies."

You can enjoy the entire show, having drinks only, although it's best to make an entire evening of it, order dinner, and stay for the dancing session after the show. To do that, you can have a generous dinner à la carte. Temporary membership is available for overseas members for £6 ($9) a week, £12 ($18) quarterly. It is essential that 48 hours elapse before a membership becomes valid. Incidentally, memberships must be paid in sterling. Application must be made in person. Dinner at £9 ($13.50) per head is served in the restaurant from 6:45 p.m. (reserve a table ahead). The show starts nightly at 8:30. Performances are given every night, except Sunday, but check in advance by calling the box office. Tube: Charing Cross Station. (Directly across the street from the Players, incidentally, is a house with a plaque commemorating the fact that Rudyard Kipling lived there between 1889 and 1891.)

Cockney Cabaret and Music Hall, 18 Charing Cross Rd., W.C.2 (tel. 408-1001), recaptures the atmosphere of a Victorian music hall. At the whisky and gin reception, you'll have the cockles of your heart warmed and learn about "mother's ruin" (large gins). The lively waiters and waitresses join the guests to sing along to the sounds of a honky-tonk piano. An East End meal, four courses of Cockney nosh, is served, along with unlimited beer and wine. Music to sing and dance marks the evening. The show is divided into two parts, featuring cabaret with both production numbers and solo performances. The hall is open daily in summer; however, in winter it is open only from Wednesday to Saturday. Admission is £20.95 ($31.43) per person Wednesday to Friday, rising to £22.90 ($34.35) on Saturday. The club is open from 8 p.m. Tube: Charing Cross.

Aba Daba, 328 Gray's Inn Rd., W.C.1 (tel. 722-5395), near King's Cross Underground station, is not a club, like the Players' Theatre, and its admission charges are £5 ($7.50) per person. Charges must be paid 24 hours in advance. In winter the club is especially popular, and reservations are suggested. The place is more like a pub than a supper club, although in addition to drinks from its well-stocked bar you can also order typically British meals. Decorated in red, Aba Daba seats more than 100 guests at tiny tables. On show nights about half a dozen performers entertain, exchanging banter with members of the audience. This music hall presents shows on Thursday, Friday, and Saturday nights.

The **Pindar of Wakefield,** 328 Gray's Inn Rd., W.C.1 (tel. 722-5395 for reservations), perpetuates the convivial world of the Victorian music hall. Aided by tankards of foaming ale and authentic Cockney entertainment, the boisterous days of communal friendliness live on. As your chairman, the "garrulous glossarist" puts it, the Pindar is for "booze, ballads, and bonhomie," not to forget "bangers & mash and faggots." The admission charge is £4 ($6), £3.50 ($5.25) if you buy a one-year membership for £2 ($3). In the pub you can order chicken, sausage, or scampi in the basket, at a cost ranging from £1.75 ($2.63) to £3.50 ($5.25). The show is billed as "a gargantuan garish gala gloriously gathered for your gracious gratifications." Usually six performers belt out tearjerkers, and you're given a song-sheet to help in the sing-alongs. Tube: King's Cross Station.

The **Rheingold Club,** Sedley Place at 361 Oxford St., W.1 (tel. 629-5343), has brought the old-world charm of an ancient Rhineland inn to the heart of Mayfair for a quarter of a century. Appropriately housed in a 100-year-old wine cellar, this nightspot provides a relaxed atmosphere where the strains of popular and Latin music are freely mingled with German drinking songs and Viennese waltzes. Wrought-iron lanterns cast a soft glow across Rhenish coats-of-arms, dark wooden beams, and historical copper etchings. Although celebrities frequently perform at the midnight cabaret, the patrons themselves are responsible for most of the entertainment. Respectable single women are welcome and safe here.

The temporary membership you purchase at the entrance costs £5 ($7.50) for men and £4 ($6) for women, and entitles you to one free admission. You can also buy a one-night membership for £2.50 ($3.75). The menu offers such wholesome German dishes as pickled knuckle of pork and sauerkraut served with pease pudding and boiled potatoes for £3.80 ($5.70). It also has a strong German draft beer at 60p (90¢) for a half pint, and excellent German and French wines, from £4.50 ($6.75) for a simple qualitatswein to £8.50 ($12.75) for an Auslese The Rheingold is open every night except Sunday and bank holidays from 7:30 p.m., closing at 1:30 a.m. on Monday and Tuesday, at 2 a.m. on Wednesday and Thursday, and remaining open until 2:30 a.m. on Friday and Saturday. Tube: Bond Street.

The luxury catamaran *Naticia* is a music hall showboat, leaving

Westminster Pier on Sunday, Monday, and Tuesday at 7 p.m. for a 3½-hour cruise on the River Thames, returning at 10:30 p.m. There is a bar for a drink while you watch the landmarks slip by. Dinner is a three-course meal with wine. At dinnertime a first-class, oldtime music hall program entertains you. Advance reservations are essential. Telephone **Catamaran Cruisers Ltd.,** Westminster Pier, S.W.1 (tel. 839-2349). The dinner and cruise costs £23 ($34.50).

NIGHTCLUBS: There are several kinds of nightclubs where you can eat or drink, be entertained, dance—even gamble. Most often these clubs are private—but don't turn away yet. To avoid the unpopular early closing hour of 11 p.m. for licensed public establishments, the private club has come into existence and may stay open till 3 and 4 a.m. In most cases, the clubs welcome overseas visitors showing passports, granting them a temporary membership. The cost of a temporary membership may even be deducted from the price of dinner; however, there is no hard-and-fast rule. Many clubs offer dinner, a show, and dancing. No visitor to London should be afraid to ask about membership in a private club. After all, most of the clubs are in business to make money, and welcome foreign patronage.

The Top Nightclubs

Eve, 189 Regent St., W.1 (tel. 734-0557), is London's longest estab-ished late-night club. Doyen of London's nightlife, owner Jimmy O'Brien launched it in 1953. Strip cabaret and erotic entertainment (at 1 a.m.) have replaced the floor shows previously presented. Dancing is to disco, alternating with live music of a high standard. Eve is open Monday to Friday from 10 p.m. to 3:30 a.m. Admittance is by membership only. There is an annual subscription of £5 ($7.50), but a special temporary membership for overseas visitors, valid for one night only, is granted for £1 ($1.50). Only one person in a party need be a member, and overseas visitors may be admitted on application without waiting the customary 48 hours. There is an entrance fee or cover charge of £5 ($7.50) for a member and each guest. An à la carte menu is available throughout the night. All prices include VAT. Charming girls, many of whom speak more than one language, are available as dining or dancing partners for unaccompanied men. Tube: Oxford Circus.

Royal Roof Restaurant, Royal Garden Hotel, Kensington High Street, W.8 (tel. 937-8000), lies on the top floor of the hotel, is elegant and refined, and overlooks Kensington Gardens and Hyde Park. From your table you will see the lights of Kensington and Knightsbridge, with a view of London's West End skyline. In a romantic candlelit aura, you can enjoy a three-course dinner for between £25 ($37.50) to £28 ($42), with a £3 ($4.50) entertainment charge. Prince Vince and Troubled Waters will serenade you at your table, and if you wish, you may dance the night away to the sounds of their music. The restaurant is open Monday to Saturday, 8 p.m. to 2 a.m. Reservations are necessary. Tube: High Street Kensington.

L'Hirondelle, Swallow Street, W.1 (tel. 734-6666), is a small but popular nightspot just off Regent Street. The spectacular hour-long stage shows put together by producer Ken Roland are performed in what appears to be an all-gold environment, complete with golden-colored wallpaper, accessories, and sparkling chandeliers to reflect the entire scene. The company of glamorous showgirls go skillfully through their routines in colorful—and often scanty—costumes with overwhelming headdresses. Singers and dancers add their talents to the hour of variety and music. Two bands assure you of constant music for dancing throughout the rest of the evening.

You'll pay a minimum charge of £7.50 ($11.25) if you don't dine here, but L'Hirondelle offers a very good three-course meal package for about £18 ($27), which allows you to choose from a number of items in each course. There's also a more expensive à la carte menu. Wines are expensive, ranging from £15 ($22.50) for the house wine. A service charge and VAT are added to the tab. The entire staff of L'Hirondelle is courteous and efficient, assuring you of an enjoyable evening of dining, dancing, and entertainment. The club is open from 8 p.m. to 3:45 a.m., and dancing is from 9 p.m. to two live bands. The floor shows are at 11 p.m. and at 1:30 a.m. It's closed Sunday. Tube: Piccadilly Circus.

Bouzouki and Plate Smashing

The **Elysée**, 13 Percy St., W.1 (tel. 636-4804), is for *Never on Sunday* devotees who like the reverberations of bouzouki and the smashing of plates. The domain of the Karegeorgis brothers—Michael, Ulysses, and the incomparable George—it offers hearty fun at moderate tabs. You can dance nightly, including Sunday (until 3 a.m.), to music by Greeks. At two different intervals (last one at 1 a.m.) a cabaret is provided, highlighted by brother George's altogether amusing act of balancing wine glasses (I'd hate to pay his breakage bill). You can book a table either on the ground floor or the second floor, but the Roof Garden is a magnet in summer. The food is good too, including the house specialty, the classic moussaka, and the kebabs from the charcoal grill. Expect to pay about £20 ($30) for a complete meal, including a bottle of wine. There's a £2 ($3) cover charge. Tube: Goodge Street.

A Theater Restaurant

A unique theater restaurant in a unique setting, that's **The Talk of London** (tel. 831-8863), in the New London Centre, an entertainment complex at Parker Street, off Drury Lane, W.C.2, the heart and soul of the city's theaterland. The restaurant is ingeniously designed so that every guest gets "the best seat in the house." By using a circular layout and varying floor levels, everyone has an uninterrupted view of the show.

The Talk of London offers a complete evening's entertainment from 8 p.m. to 1 a.m.: a four-course dinner of your choice, dancing to the Johnny Howard orchestra, Europe's top show band, Afrodisiac, and an international cabaret at 10:30 p.m. All this and coffee, service, and VAT are included in the price of £18.45 ($27.68) Monday to Friday and £20.45 ($30.68) on Saturday. Drinks are extra. Phone for reservations, which are essential. Tube: Covent Garden or Holborn.

From Madrigal to Modern

Tiddy Dols Eating House, 2 Hertford St. (entrance on Shepherd Market), Mayfair, W.1 (tel. 499-2357), set amid the lanes, curio shops, and taverns of Shepherd Market and occupying eight charming 1741 houses with twisting staircases, low ceilings, and secluded alcoves, has become one of London's top choices for dinner, entertainment, and dancing, costing about £20 ($30) to £40 ($60) per person, inclusive. A young, friendly English staff serves you with personal flair five nights a week from 6 p.m. to 2 a.m. (last orders at 1 a.m.). John Campbell, once an army officer, has turned his civilian expertise as an economist, market researcher, and management consultant to making a success of this establishment of which he is owner/director.

The cuisine is traditional English, featuring such dishes as beef Wellington, rack of lamb, roast pheasant, jugged hare, and the medieval Tiddy Dol gingerbread. There is also one of the best wine lists in the United Kingdom, featuring fine wines with low markups. Tiddy Dols is named after Tiddy Dol, the eccentric seller of gingerbread who attended the May Fair in the 18th century, singing "Tid-dy Ti, Tid-dy ti ti, Tid-dy Tid-y Dol" as he sold the produce of his special recipe, which the restaurant still makes. Tiddy Dol was immortalized by Hogarth in a 1747 picture of a London scene.

Two English musical acts alternate half hourly every night from 7 to 11 p.m. and include the Elizabethan Garlande, playing Tudor and Stuart songs for courtiers and commoners; Father Footsteps, offering Victorian music hall; the Food of Love, with great British composers from Henry VIII to Andrew Lloyd Webber; and Instant Sunshine, three urban English gentlemen who appear on Friday. Each evening, Lord Julian Shepherd, Mayfair's town crier, "paralyzes, pulverizes, and punishes" the latest news. Finally, there is dancing every night from 11 o'clock until the restaurant closes at 2 a.m. Tube: Green Park.

Mediaeval Feestes

Beefeater by the Tower of London, Ivory House, St. Katharine's Dock, E.C.3 (tel. 408-1001), is housed in the historic vaults alongside the Thames where ivory was stored in days of yore. During the Napoleonic wars, the vaults served as a prison for captured French soldiers.

In this historic setting, Merrie Olde England comes alive every night from 8 p.m. to midnight in the form of an enormous, rollicking, medieval feast. When you first arrive, you'll be led down into the vaults where you're greeted by no less a personage than Henry VIII, surrounded by serving wenches, jester, and madrigal singers. In no time at all you'll be caught up in the spirit of the celebration and forget that these are actors playing the parts of characters who lived 400 years ago.

Entertainment begins at the reception, where you sip honeyed wine to the tune of a few fa-la-lahs and hey-nonny-noes, and continues between courses ("removes") during the meal. Your party will be led in procession to the long trestle tables, where you'll dine in typical Tudor fashion, using no utensils except a knife. The leader of each procession becomes the "head boy" who is host for the table, filling all the plates and calling for more bread or wine as necessary. If you are lucky enough to be chosen, you'll be given a tall white hat to mark your distinguished position.

The dinner consists of a five-course sumptuous feast, topped off by all the wine and ale you can drink. During the meal, the entertainment, in the forms of magicians, acrobats, and musicians, continues. There's even a very believable duel between two knights. Be sure to hiss the villain! Dinner is followed by dancing. The cost for the entire evening of food, entertainment, and dancing is £21.95 ($32.93) weekdays, rising to £23.95 ($35.93) on Saturday. In season, the Beefeater is open nightly. Otherwise it is open only Wednesday through Saturday. Tube: Tower.

1502 A.D. Tudor Rooms, 80–81 St. Martin's Lane, W.C.2 (tel. 240-3978). If you want to eat, drink, and be merry, then this is the place to be. A sumptuous banquet with a choice of many main courses in the atmosphere of the Tudor period. There is continuous entertainment throughout the evening, with actors impersonating King Henry VIII, Anne Boleyn, Jane Seymour, the court jester, minstrels, and a dancing bear, while guests are served by so-called wenches. The feast is made up of pâté, served with toast, a glass of Olde English mead, a choice of soups, Henry's tidbits, a selection of baby chicken, fresh river trout, beef casserole, roast pork, or roast lamb, followed by a medley of sherbets and then cheese and apple.

There's a star cabaret with a Turkish belly dancer, jugglers, and comedians, followed by disco dancing from midnight until 2 a.m. The cost is £16.50 ($24.75) per person for the evening, plus your drinks. All rates include VAT.

Additionally, King Henry's luncheon is available Monday to Friday from noon to 3 p.m. At that time, for £8.50 ($16.58), including VAT, you can sample a choice of soups and main courses, followed by sherbet. From 3 to 5 p.m. the staff serves a traditional English tea with sandwiches and pastries in medieval surroundings. Tube: Trafalgar Square.

Eroticism in Soho

Once upon a time, Britain's film censors were kept busy snipping the bare patches out of those "daring" French movies, and London's stage regulations permitted braless belles only on condition that they didn't move a limb while thus exposed. All this might just as well have happened in the last century for all the relevance it has today. Sheer acreage of undress currently on view in London outshows anything in Paris, New York, San Francisco, or Hamburg. Only Tokyo might be on a par.

Some of this clothes-shedding mania is undoubtedly a reaction to the years of Mrs. Grundy's dictatorship, when even a semi-transparent nightgown had to be struck out of a play as "bordering on the indecent." But by now it has gone past the saturation point. London's entertainment world, in fact, is in danger of being smothered by a pink tidal wave of nudity, lapping every nook and cranny of the West End and sweeping before it every other brand of amusement.

Entire blocks of Soho now consist of little else but strip shows, sometimes two in one building. Along Frith Street, Greek Street, Old Compton Street, Brewer Street, Windmill Street, Dean and Wardour Streets, and the little courts and alleys in between, the disrobing establishments jostle cheek by jowl. Big ones and small ones, fancy and dingy, elaborate and primitive, they all sport outsize photos of the inside attractions, gloriously exotic names, and bellowing speakers to draw your attention in the right direction.

The basic commodity is the same, but the packaging varies considerably. Some of the large—and fairly expensive—places are regular theaters, putting on lavish productions, complete with musical scores, choreography, trained dancers, and intricate, if insufficient, costuming.

At the other extreme are dozens of cellar dens, holding a few rows of creaking chairs, a torn curtain, and a few boards knocked together as a stage. The women appearing there can neither dance nor strip gracefully, but they can take their clothes off. And they do. Regarding their acts, you'd better forget what you know about American burlesque. There's no trace of humor, no slapstick gags with girdles, no wisecracking with the boys in the front row, and no fans or fluttering pigeons. Here the stripping is total and basic, minus modesty gimmicks such as flickering strobe lights or climactic blackouts. The women go through a series of vaguely undulating movements and strip right down to their skins. And that's that.

The big, plush establishments, of course, have regular and highly paid casts, and among the most spectacular is—

The **Nell Gwynne,** 69–70 Dean St., W.1 (tel. 437-3278), entrance on Meard Street, is a showcase for some of the most interesting and novel striptease acts in London. The acts at the Nell Gwynne Club begin at 6 p.m. and run until 11 p.m. with shows at two-hour intervals. It is noted for the unique sensual routines and comedy striptease. Audience participation is also there, but the management likes to keep it subtle. The entrance fee of £5.50 ($8.25) includes VAT.

That admission fee also admits you to the **Comedy Store** on the same premises. Otherwise, you pay from £3.50 ($5.25) Wednesday through Friday and £4.50 ($6.75) on Saturday. There is dancing to disco music, with live shows by up-and-coming (and some arrived) comedians at 11 p.m. on Wednesday, Thursday, and Friday (also 8 p.m. on Friday and Saturday as well as midnight on Saturday). Drinks cost £2.50 ($3.75) for a double, and there are light snacks, pizzas, chicken in the basket, and scampi, with a meal priced at about £5.50 ($8.25) per person. Tube: Tottenham Court Road.

THE DISCOS: A firmly entrenched London institution, the disco is nevertheless as vulnerable as the Stone of Scone. Many of them open, enjoy a quick but fast-fading popularity, then close. Some possible favorites that may still be going strong upon your arrival are the following.

The **Marquee,** 90 Wardour St., W.1 (tel. 437-6603), is considered one of the best known centers for rock in Europe. Its reputation goes back to the '50s, but it remains forever young, in touch with the sounds of the future. Famous groups such as the Stones played at the Marquee long before their names spread beyond the shores of England. Fortunately, you don't have to be a member—you just pay at the door. If you have a Student Union Card from any country, it will cost you less to enter. The entrance fees vary, but usually fall in the £2 ($3) to £3 ($4.50) range, depending on who is appearing. There's a coffee and a Coke bar for light snacks; those 18 or older can order hard drinks. Many well-known musicians frequent the place regularly on their nights off. The quite small and very crowded club is one of the few that features live music. Hours are from 7 to 11 p.m. seven nights a week. Tube: Piccadilly Circus.

Studio Valbonne, 62 Kingly St., off Regent Street, W.1 (tel. 439-7242), offers disco music noisy and heavy on the beat. The decor is modern, with mirrors and futuristic furniture. Masses of flashing and changing colored lights make a feature of the glass dance floor. There's a 100-inch video screen, showing a multitude of pictures. A light machine flashes words and sentences on the walls. There is a large cocktail bar offering a variety of exotic drinks and a long wine bar. The disco music has been updated to meet the discerning taste of the international disco crowd. This is a disco theater with live acts, talented artists, and surprise cabaret distractions.

You can eat as much as you like at the sumptuous salad bar for £1.95 ($2.93), or if you're too hungry to be satisfied with salads, try the Gallery Grill Room, where you can order from the à la carte menu or enjoy a set-price dinner for less than £10 ($15) per person, including VAT.

Reservations are advisable for dining in the Gallery Grill Room. A special breakfast is served from 2 to 3 a.m., and snacks and steak sandwiches are available throughout the evening in either the disco or the restaurant.

Admission Monday to Wednesday is £4 ($6) for men, £3 ($4.50) for women. Otherwise, men and women pay £5 ($7.50). Your entrance fee is refunded if you order in the restaurant before 11 p.m. (inform reception when you enter). Tube: Oxford Circus.

Samantha's, 3 New Burlington St., W.1 (tel. 734-6249), just off Regent Street, has been one of London's most popular discos and nightspots since it opened about two decades ago. The central feature of the club is, of course, the disco, with its sound and light system controlled by a disc jockey who has taken up residence inside an E-type Jaguar. Flashing colored lights and curved mirrors create a surrealistic setting for the endless parade of youthful, energetic dancers. Besides the two bars that flank the disco, Samantha's offers several other facilities for those who require a momentary escape from the hectic vibrations of the main dance floor.

"Samantha's Playroom" is the favorite gathering spot for pinball or pool enthusiasts. A second area of bars and a smaller dance floor with quieter music are set apart from the disco so that even the highest decibels do not penetrate. Upstairs is one of Samantha's later creations, Sir Harry's Bar, where you can sip cocktails in a tropical atmosphere of cane furniture and animal skins. Admission to Samantha's is £3.50 ($5.25) per person, which gives you access to any part of the club. Drinks average about £1.50 ($2.25), but you'll pay more for the "super cocktails" in Sir Harry's.

Stringfellows, at the Hippodrome corner of Charing Cross Road and Leicester Square, W.C.2 (tel. 437-4311). Peter Stringfellow has created what he hopes is the greatest disco in the world, an enormous place where light and sound beam in on you from all directions. Revolving speakers even descend from the roof to deafen you in patches, and you can watch yourself on closed-circuit video as you disappear in the atmosphere created by the smoke machine. There are six bars, plus a fast-food counter. Lasers and a hydraulically controlled stage for visiting international performers are part of the attraction. Overseas visitors must produce passports for a temporary membership of £10 ($15). Admission charges range from £4 ($6) to £7.50 ($11.25). The club is open Tuesday to Saturday from 9 p.m. to 3 a.m. Tube: Leicester Square.

Le Beat Route, 17 Greek St., W.1 (tel. 734-1470), is a luxurious club with both live and disco music, open every day except Sunday. Top recording artists make personal appearances here. There's a superb sprung dance floor, as well as a pool room with its own bar. Admission ranges from £1 ($1.50) to £6 ($9). It opens at 9 p.m., closing at 3:30 a.m. Tube: Tottenham Court Road.

MUSIC IN PUBS AND CLUBS: Pubs offering music for the price of a drink include the **New Golden Lion,** 490 Fulham Rd., S.W.6 (tel. 385-3942; tube to Fulham Broadway). Unlike most London pubs, which close at 11 p.m., it is open till midnight.

Other places where you can enjoy the music at no extra charge are **Blakes Wine Bar,** 34 Wellington St., W.C.2 (tel. 836-5298; tube: Covent Garden); the **Rock Garden,** 6–7 The Piazza, King Street, W.C.2 (tel. 240-3961; tube: Covent Garden); **Bull and Gate,** 389 Kentish Town Rd., N.W.5 (tel. 485-5358; tube: Kentish Town); and the **Greyhound,** 175 Fulham Palace Rd., W.6 (tel. 385-0526; tube: Hammersmith).

Bananas, 201–203 Wardour St., W.1 (tel. 434-4285), is open to nonmembers from 8:30 p.m. to 3:30 a.m. Monday to Saturday, charging £4 ($6) for admission. It's free to women on Wednesday, and they can get in at reduced rates at other times. Friday night is Prohibition Night, when all drinks cost 2p (4¢), but admission that night costs members £8 ($12) and nonmembers £10 ($15). There's lots of room here, with a restaurant serving American dishes, and two bars. No sloppy dress, please.

Elle et Lui Club Français, 53 Berwick St., W.1 (tel. 437-6830), has music for all tastes. Admission is £3 ($4.50). You can wear casual dress to come here, so long as you're tidy.

ROCK: **Rockgarden Restaurant & Dancehall,** 6–7 The Piazza, Old Covent Garden, W.C.2 (tel. 836-1929). Virtually every current major rock band in Britain has played at the Rockgarden in their infancy. The restaurant is open Monday till Wednesday from 11 a.m. to 2 a.m., on Thursday, Friday, and Saturday from 11 a.m. till 4 in the morning of the next day, and on Sunday from noon till midnight. You can always order such dishes as spare ribs or hamburgers, a light meal costing from £6 ($9). Tube: Covent Garden.

JAZZ: **Ronnie Scott's,** 47 Frith St., W.1 (tel. 439-0747), has long been the citadel of modern jazz in Europe. Featured on almost every bill is an American band, often with a top-notch singer. The best English and American groups are booked. It's in the heart of Soho, a ten-minute walk from Piccadilly Circus via Shaftesbury Avenue, and worth an entire evening. You can not only saturate yourself in the best of jazz, but get reasonably priced drinks and dinners as well. There are three separate areas: the Main Room, the Upstairs Room, and the Downstairs Bar. You don't have to be a member, although you can join if you wish. The nightly entrance fee is £3 ($4.50) to £8 ($12), depending on who is appearing. If you have a student ID you are granted considerable reductions on entrance fees, providing you come before 9:30 p.m., Monday through Thursday, without making a reservation beforehand. Drinks cost around 85p ($1.28) for whisky. The Main Room is open Monday through Saturday from 8:30 p.m. to 3 a.m. You can either stand at the bar to watch the show or sit at a table, where you can order a three-course dinner for around £9 ($13.50). The Downstairs Bar is more intimate, a quiet rendezvous where you can meet and talk with the regulars, usually some of the world's most talented musicians. The Upstairs Room is a disco, with unusual sculptured foam seating, where you can either dance or drink. On most nights a live band is featured. Incidentally, if you bypass the other two floors, you can get in here at a reduced entrance fee of around £3 ($4.50). Tube: Tottenham Court Road.

The **100 Club,** 100 Oxford St., W.1 (tel. 636-0933), is a serious contender for the title of London's finest jazz center. The emphasis here is strictly on the music, which begins each evening at 7:30 p.m. and lasts until midnight. Admission is usually between £2.50 ($3.75) and £3.50 ($5.25). On Thursday nights, West Indian reggae is presented, but jazz—all kinds of jazz—is performed on the other six nights. The scheduled performers vary every night, so you'll have to phone ahead for that evening's program. However, you're sure to see the cream of jazz at the 100 Club, including such bands as Ken Colyer's All Star Jazzmen, Chris Barber's Band, and Mr.

Acker Bilk and his Paramount Jazz Band. The club's menu features Créole cooking. There's also a fully licensed bar, serving liquor, wine, and beer. Tube: Tottenham Court Road.

Kettner's, 29 Romilly St., W.1 (tel. 437-6437), is a well-known old rendezvous that is now part of the Pizza Express group, serving the wide variety of the pizzas that group concocts. The difference is that here you get your pizza served to the tune of some excellent jazz piano playing. There's a champagne bar, and if you're not in the mood for pizza, you can have a salmon sandwich while you listen to the music. Jazz is offered Friday and Saturday night and at lunchtime on Sunday.

Pizza on the Park, 11 Knightsbridge, S.W.1 (tel. 235-5550), is just another pizza parlor downstairs, but upstairs two superb grand pianos provide almost nonstop jazz piano music from 8:30 p.m. to 12:30 a.m. Entrance ranges between £3 ($4.50) and £5 ($7.50).

A much cheaper way to hear jazz is at one of the many pubs in the West End offering it on certain nights of the week. Some charge admission; others allow you to listen for the price of your drink.

The **Bull's Head,** Barnes Bridge, S.W.13 (tel. 876-5241), offers live jazz all week, with musical happenings that sometimes get very lively indeed. The modern jazz is said by many to be the best in town. Weekdays it attracts shoppers and fashion designers to its old English snackbar, which is a fine place to meet for lunch.

GAMBLING: London was a gambling metropolis long before anyone had ever heard of Monte Carlo and when Las Vegas was an anonymous sandpile in the desert. From the Regency period until halfway into the 19th century, Britain was more or less governed by gamblers. Lord Sandwich invented the snack named after him so he wouldn't have to leave the card table for a meal. Prime Minister Fox was so addicted that he frequently went to a cabinet meeting straight from the green baize table.

Queen Victoria's reign changed all that, as usual, by jumping to the other extreme. For more than a century games of chance were so rigorously outlawed that no barmaid dared to keep a dice cup on the counter.

The pendulum swung again in 1960 when the present queen gave her Royal Assent to the new "Betting and Gaming Act." According to this legislation, gambling was again permitted in "bona fide clubs" by members and their guests.

Since London's definition of a "club" is as loose as a rusty screw in a cardboard wall, this immediately gave rise to the current situation, which continues to startle, amaze, and bewilder foreign visitors. For the fact is that you come across gambling devices in the most unlikely spots, such as discos, social clubs, and cabaret restaurants. All of which may, by the haziest definition, qualify as "clubs."

The more legitimate gambling clubs offer very pleasant trimmings in the shape of bars and restaurants, but their central theme is unequivocally the flirtation with Lady Luck. There are at least 25 of them in the West End alone, with many scattered through the suburbs. And the contrasts between them are much sharper than you find in the Nevada casinos.

Owing to a new law, casinos are not allowed to advertise, and if they do, they are likely to lose their licenses. Their appearance in a travel guide that doesn't accept advertising is still considered "advertising"—hence, I cannot recommend specific clubs as in the past.

However, most hall porters can tell you where you can gamble in London. It is not illegal to gamble, just to advertise it. You'll be required to become a member of your chosen club, and must wait 24 hours before you can play the tables, then strictly for cash. Most common games are roulette, blackjack, punto banco, and baccarat. Most casinos, as mentioned, have restaurants where you can expect a good standard of cuisine at a reasonable price.

FOLK MUSIC: The 20th-century troubadour makes his way to a smoke-gets-in-your-eyes candlelit haven called the **Troubadour Coffee House,** 265 Old Brompton Rd., S.W.5 (tel. 370-1434). The Troubadour is open to nonmembers. At one time this club was young at heart, a pacesetter in a new kind of unpretentious, natural entertainment. It still offers many happy nights to an attractive, young crowd (if you can squeeze in).

You can dine upstairs, again if you can find a seat. From the ceiling hang musical instruments of every shape and size; the walls are covered with unusual trade signs of the Victorian era. Prices are quite reasonable, and the food consists of omelets, spaghetti bolognese, salads, and the like. The average dish goes for £1 ($1.50), the price going up to no more than £2 ($3). Tube: Earl's Court.

BALLROOMS: Although the straight dance hall is by now almost defunct in America, it continues to draw crowds in London. There are several reasons for this survival, all of them having to do with the boy-meets-girl syndrome. As places for casual encounters, the ballrooms are unbeatable. The music is not so loud that you can't hear each other's names, the illumination is bright enough to see whom you're meeting, and the floors are sufficiently large for actual dancing—as distinguished from the postage stamp that passes for a dance floor in the discos. The hunters of both sexes usually prowl in pairs but will split up as readily as amoebas as soon as opportunity beckons.

Café de Paris, Coventry Street, off Piccadilly Circus, W.1 (tel. 437-2036), is a legend. Once Robert Graves considered it a worthy subject for a book; the Duke of Windsor went there to see Noël Coward perform. Now part of the Mecca chain, it is elaborately decorated with chandeliers. Changing lights set the mood. A band alternates with disco for dancing seven nights a week. According to the day and time (it's cheaper before 9:30 p.m.), admission prices range from £2 ($3) to £3 ($4.50). On Tuesday, women are admitted free. A three-course meal with a glass of wine and coffee comes to about £9 ($13.50). They do tea dances, with an admission costing £1.35 ($2.03). Another £2.20 ($3.30) gets you a pot of tea, a sandwich, and a piece of cake. Tube: Piccadilly Circus.

The **Empire Ballroom,** Leicester Square, W.C.2 (tel. 437-1446), is another dance giant of the type now virtually extinct in the United States. Vast and plushly ornate, it operates on several levels centering around a magnificent dance floor. Liquid refreshment is dispensed from no fewer than five bars, and the sign above the entrance says "Disco Dancing" in 14 languages.

The Empire, the largest dance hall of its type in Europe and situated in the heart of London's most renowned entertainment area, was the scene of the World Disco Dancing Championship in 1984. Every night of the week, among the best in live bands, groups, and DJs are featured. A wine bar is also in operation in the evening. Dancing is Monday to Thursday from 8 p.m. to 2 a.m., on Friday and Saturday till 3 a.m. According to the day of the week and the time (early is cheaper, of course), admission prices range from £3 ($4.50) to £4.50 ($6.75). Both disco and live groups are regularly featured. Tube: Leicester Square.

A CULTURAL COMPLEX: In the old **Riverside Studios,** Crisp Road, Hammersmith, W.6, an enterprising young group has developed a complex of theaters and exhibition rooms where, under the directorship of David Gothard, unknown and not-so-unknown artists can demonstrate their skills. In the film theater, seasons of movies demonstrate the producer's art or that of the camera person; visiting orchestras and dance teams perform nightly; and in the restaurant, there is generally an exhibition of paintings or collages.

The restaurant is open from 11 a.m. to 11 p.m. Tuesday through Saturday, 12:30 to 11 p.m. on Sunday, and 11 a.m. to 6 p.m. on Monday, serving mostly homemade meals. A filling repast will cost about £4 ($6). The bar serves real ale among other beverages during licensing hours. Current programs are available throughout London, and the studios are well worth a visit, lying just a five-minute walk from Hammersmith Underground station. Telephone the box office at 748-3354. Tickets for concerts, films, and plays cost about £4 ($6), but are increased on occasions when well-known performers appear.

VAUDEVILLE: This lives on in London on a grand scale.

Palladium, Argyle Street, W.1 (tel. 437-7373). World-famed for the best of vaudeville, it is equivalent to the former Palace in New York. Performers from America, the continent, and England can be seen here in acts that sometimes border on the spectacular. Seats normally range from around £4.50 ($6.75) to £12 ($18) for orchestra stalls, but it depends on who's appearing. Prices can go much higher. Tube: Oxford Circus.

Victoria Palace, Victoria Street, S.W.11 (tel. 834-1317), near Victoria Station, presents mainly drama but with some comedy, variety, and light entertainment, all at popular prices. Tube: Victoria Station.

GAY NIGHTLIFE: The most reliable source of information on all gay clubs and activities is the **Gay Switchboard** (tel. 837-7324). The staff there runs a 24-hour service of information on places and activities catering openly to homosexual men and women. The *Gay News,* available from some street news stalls, also carries advertisements. However, here are some suggestions: most are membership clubs which, nevertheless, welcome overseas visitors.

The Heaven, The Arches, Villiers Street, Charing Cross, W.C.2 (tel. 839-3852), is considered to be the largest and most high-energy disco and nightclub in Europe, with fantastic lasers, lights, and sounds. There is no membership requirement and no dress code. The cover charge varies from £1.50 ($2.25) to £5 ($7.50). The club is open almost every night. Tube: Charing Cross.

The Copacabana, 180 Earls Court Rd., S.W.5 (tel. 373-3407), is a gay drinking place, with a £3 ($4.50) membership charge. There is free entrance to members until midnight; after that, a £1 ($1.50) fee. Others pay a £2 ($3) entrance fee at most times, more on weekends. Dress is optional, but no transvestites please. Drinks are half price until midnight, then you pay the whole whack. Tube: Earl's Court.

EAST END DRAG PUBS: In the East End is a series of pubs offering entertainment nightly. Drag acts (female impersonators) are the chief form of amusement. The English, especially the Cockneys of the East End, love to giggle and scream over the caricatures of men satirizing women. Many female impersonator acts find their way into the posh West End clubs, which many of our readers will find too expensive. However, talent without all the fancy trappings appears almost nightly in some of these Victorian pubs. You pay no admission, no cover, no minimum—one of the bargain entertainment values in London.

One of the best is the **Union Tavern,** 146 Camberwell New Road, S.E.5 (tel. 735-3605), capably managed by Chris Darnell. Some of London's top drag artists perform here at one of the two bars. You should arrive earlier to get a comfortable seat. The "ladies" tend to make for a hysterical night. Two of the favorites (by now all the habitués know their acts) are bejeweled, begowned, bewigged, even breasted—a couple of sex sirens who do mime recordings of stars. With luck, you'll hear their rendition of Shirley Temple in *Animal Crackers* or Carol Channing in *Gentlemen Prefer Blondes*. A half pint of lager costs only 45p (68¢). Drag shows with gay disco or live groups are presented from 8 p.m. on Wednesday, Friday, and Saturday. There are also performances at 12:30 p.m. on Sunday and again at 8 p.m. The other bar has disco nightly. Admission is free. The tavern closes nightly at 11 (at 10:30 on Sunday).

READER'S DRAG CLUB SUGGESTION: "I've often recommended two drag clubs to North American visitors. The **Black Cap,** 171 Camden High St., N.W.1 (tel. 485-1742), features a different drag act each night—some are hilarious, others grotesque, but it's excellent for a fun evening, seven nights a week, with no entry fee. The **Royal Vauxhall Tavern,** 372 Kennington Lane, S.E.11 (tel. 582-0833), lies on the south of the Thames, over the Vauxhall Bridge and near the Vauxhall tube station. It offers drag acts nightly—some of them original, some in pantomime to records. There's no cover charge—just the drinks you buy" (Howard Archer, London, England).

OPERA AND BALLET: London has treasures to offer the opera and ballet lover. The **Royal Opera House,** at Bow Street, is the center of the Royal Opera Company and the Royal Ballet. The Opera House advance box office, at 48 Floral St., is open from 10 a.m. to 7:30 p.m., Monday to Saturday (tel. 240-1066). A good seat can be had for £10 ($15), and sometimes one of the finest seats in the house will cost you no more than £16.50 ($24.75). Sixty-five rear amphitheater seats will be available for sale at 10 a.m. on the day of performance. Tube: Covent Garden.

English National Opera, London Coliseum, St. Martin's Lane, W.C.2 (tel. 836-3161 for reservations, or 240-5258 for credit-card booking and inquiries), is the state-supported opera company that performs in English and draws many enthusiastic audiences. Light operas are often included in the repertory, and tickets can cost as little as £3.50 ($5.25). These cheap seats are in the balcony and may be reserved in advance, although a limited number are available on the day of the performance only. The average visitor may find the upper circle seats preferable, with prices ranging for most performances from £7.50 ($11.25). Tube: Charing Cross or Leicester Square.

The **D'Oyly Carte Company** has no permanent home in London or elsewhere. Information can be obtained from the company's office address: Tabard House, 116 Southwark St., London SE1 OTA (tel. 928-7322).

At **Gilbert's House,** which is now run as a hotel and restaurant, Gilbert and Sullivan concerts are given every Sunday night during dinner. It is called Grim's Dyke Country Hotel, Old Redding, Harrow Weald, Middlesex (tel. 954-4227).

The **Barbican Centre,** The Barbican, E.C.2, is newly built and considered the largest art and exhibition center in Western Europe. It was created to make a perfect setting in which to enjoy good music and theater from comfortable, roomy seating.

The theater is now the home of the Royal Shakespeare Company, which of course performs a wide range of works other than plays of the Bard. The Concert Hall is the permanent home of the London Symphony Orchestra and host to visiting performers.

There are often lunchtime concerts where the admission is from £3 ($4.50) for the 45 minutes or so. Otherwise, seats are priced from £2.50 ($3.75) to £9.50 ($14.25) for evening performances. Matinees in the theater start at £2 ($3), going upward to £8 ($12).

There are a number of bars and a self-service café and wine bar open from 9 a.m. to 10:30 p.m. Monday to Saturday, and from noon to 10:30 p.m. on Sunday. Called the Waterside Café, it has views over the artificial lake. In good weather patrons can sit on the terrace in the open air.

The main restaurant, the Cut Above, also overlooks the lake, a more formal place with a pleasant Carvery open from noon to 3 p.m. and from 6 p.m. until the last orders are taken half an hour after the end of the performance. The cost of a meal where you carve as much as you want from the succulent joints of meats is £9.50 ($14.25). Table reservations can be made by telephoning 588-3008.

The following numbers will be useful—628-8795 for the box office for seats for concerts and theatrical performances; 928-9760 for 24-hour information on performances of concerts; and 628-2295 for information about theatrical performances. Tube: Barbican.

CONCERTS: In recent years, the musical focal point in London has shifted to a superbly specialized complex of buildings on the South Bank side of Waterloo Bridge. This Cultural Centre—including pleasure gardens and the National Film Theatre—houses three of the most stylish, comfortable, and acoustically perfect concert structures in the world: the **Royal Festival Hall,** the **Queen Elizabeth Hall,** and the **Purcell Room.** Here, more than 1200 performances a year are presented, and it's not all classical music: included are ballet, jazz, popular classics, pop, and folk. The Royal Festival Hall is open from 10 a.m. every day and offers an extensive range of things to see and do. There are free exhibitions in the foyers and free lunchtime music from 12:30 to 2 p.m., plus guided tours of the building, and book, record, and gift shops. The Festival Buffet has a wide selection of food at reasonable prices, and there are a number of bars throughout the foyers.

Tickets are available from the Royal Festival Hall box office (tel. 928-3191; for credit card bookings, phone 928-6544), or the usual booking agents. They usually range in price from £3 ($4.50) to £10 ($15). Tube: Waterloo Station.

Royal Albert Hall, Kensington Gore, S.W.7 (tel. 589-8212). Acoustic improvements and other alterations have made this one of the world's finest auditoriums. The BBC Promenade Concerts are held here for eight weeks in summer. Throughout the year there are performances by top orchestras and artists, brass bands, and all manner of events ranging from covered court lawn tennis to the annual Royal British Legion Festival of Remembrance. Ticket prices vary according to the type of event. Tube: South Kensington, High Street Kensington, or Knightsbridge.

Wigmore Hall, 36 Wigmore St., W.1 (tel. 935-2141). At this intimate auditorium, you'll hear excellent recitals and concerts. There are regular series, master concerts by chamber music groups and instrumentalists, song recital series, and concerts featuring special composers or themes throughout the year. In the summer, Wigmore Summer Nights and Sunday morning concerts are featured. Many good seats are in the £2.50 ($3.75) range. A free list of the month's concerts is available from the hall. Tube: Bond Street or Oxford Circus.

City of Westminster Arts Council, Marylebone Library, Marylebone Road, N.W.1 (tel. 828-8070, ext. 4052), sponsors concerts, recitals, and exhibitions throughout the year. These are held in small and often little-known halls around the city. For current information, refer to the address above. The average entrance charge is around £3 ($4.50), but some promotions, such as exhibitions, are free. In most cases, payment is at the door, and no advance reservations are necessary. A monthly diary of events lists a wide range of such promotions. Free copies can be picked up at any public library in Westminster. The events are mainly amateur, but a high level of accomplishment is achieved, and many programs are of artistic importance.

4. Taking the Tours

In addition to the sights you can see in London by foot, or by using the tubes, there are numerous attractions that can be reached via several inexpensive coach tours. As an added bonus, there are dozens of fascinating trips that can be made on the Thames.

EASIEST WAY TO SEE LONDON: For the first-timer, the quickest and most economical way to bring the big city into focus is to take a two-hour, 20-mile circular tour of the West End and The City, the **'Round London Sightseeing Tour,** which is offered by London Transport, the city's official bus company. The cost is £2.95 ($4.43) for adults, £1.50 ($2.25) for children under 16. Some journeys are by open-top buses. Tours pass virtually all the major places of interest in Central London. There is no guide. Passengers are given an illustrated diagram of the route, showing points of interest.

The one drawback is that seats cannot be reserved, but the buses run with great frequency every day (except Christmas). From March to October, tours are at least every hour from 10 a.m. to 8 p.m. (9 a.m. to 4 p.m. in the winter). The starting points for the tour are Piccadilly Circus, Marble Arch, and Victoria.

There is also a two-hour guided nonstop tour from Grosvenor Gardens, Victoria, and Piccadilly Circus, beginning at 9:30 and 11:30 a.m. and 2:30 p.m. Tickets, which may be purchased on board, cost £3.75 ($5.63) for adults, £2 ($3) for children. The guide tells you the history of the buildings you pass.

LONDON'S WEST END AND THE CITY: If you prefer a more detailed look at the city's sights, then **London Transport** offers two highly regarded conducted coach tours.

For a look at the West End, a three-hour tour is offered, passing Westminster Abbey (guided tour), Houses of Parliament, Horse Guards, Trafalgar Square, and Piccadilly Circus, including the changing of the guard. The tour starts at 10 a.m. every day except Sunday, and the fare is £6 ($9) for adults £4 ($6) for children under 14.

London Transport's other popular three-hour tour is of The City, and includes guided trips to the Tower of London and St. Paul's Cathedral. The fare for this is £8 ($12) for adults, £5 ($7.50) for children. The tour is operated Monday to Saturday at 2 p.m. In summer the tour also runs on Sunday.

These two tours are combined to form the London Day Tour, which costs £16.50 ($24.75) for adults, £10 ($15) for children under 14, including lunch. The tour leaves at 10 a.m,. The tours begin at Victoria Coach Station, at the corner of Buckingham Palace Road and Elizabeth Street. To reserve seats, go to the London Transport Travel Information Offices at: St. James's Park, Piccadilly Circus, King's Cross, Euston, Oxford Circus, or Victoria tube stations. Reservations cannot be made over the phone.

CULTURE BUS: Discover London's sights and many of the big stores by buying a ticket for the yellow double-decker bus tour by **Culture Bus Limited,** Falcon Estate, Central Way, Feltham, Middlesex (tel. 844-0880). The trip is an 18-mile, two-hour, 20-stop journey taking in Harrods, the Albert Hall, and Hyde Park to the west, Madam Tussaud's and the Planetarium to the north, and extending through the City to the Tower of London, Tower Bridge and H.M.S. *Belfast* in the east, after which the bus recrosses the river past St. Paul's and then back to see the National Theatre and Lambeth Palace before returning to the West End, past the Houses of Parliament and the Tate Gallery. You can travel as far as you like, get off and reboard the bus at any of the stops on the route, spend hours browsing in museums and art galleries, and rejoin a later bus—all for the price of a day's ticket.

You can buy a ticket from your hotel porter or from the driver of the Culture Bus, but remember that he does not carry change, so you must have the correct fare ready. Tickets bought after 3 p.m. can also be used the next day. The flat fare is £2.50 ($3.75) for adults, £1.50 ($2.25) for children. A family of two adults and two children under 16 can purchase a family ticket for £7 ($10.50). Buses start at 9 a.m. and run until 6:30 p.m. seven days a week. You get a map showing the route and the various stopping places together with a brief description of various sights.

HARRODS SIGHTSEEING BUS: A double-decker bus in the discreet green and gold livery of Harrods operates sightseeing tours around London's attractions, on an "upper-crust sightseeing" tour. The first departure from door no. 8 of Harrods in Brompton Road is at 9:15 a.m., and there are eight tours daily. Tea, coffee, and orange juice are served on board. The tour costs £10 ($15) for adults, £7.50 ($11.25) for children under

12. You can purchase tickets at the theater ticket desk on the store's fourth floor or at any Keith Prowse agency. You can obtain more information from Harrods (tel. 730-1234).

A CANAL BOAT IN LITTLE VENICE: When you get tired of fighting the London traffic, you might want to come here and take a peaceful trip (1½ hours) aboard the traditionally painted Narrow Boat *Jason* and her butty boat *Serpens*. Come for lunch along the most colorful part of the Regent's Canal in the heart of London. The boat is moored in Blomfield Road, just off Edgware Road in Maida Vale. Little Venice is the junction of two canals and was given its name by Lord Byron.

To inquire about bookings, including the Boatman's Basket Luncheon Trip, get in touch with **Jason's Trip,** Opp. No. 60 Blomfield Rd., Little Venice, W.9 (tel. 286-3428). Advance booking is essential during high season. If you come by tube, take the Bakerloo line to Warwick Avenue. Face the church, turn left, and walk up Clifton Villas to the end and turn right (about two minutes). If you arrive early, you can browse around the shop, which sells many brightly colored traditionally painted canal wares.

On the trip you'll pass through the long Maida Hill tunnel under Edgware Road, through Regent's Park, the Mosque, the Zoo, Lord Snowdon's Aviary, past the Pirate's Castle to Camden Lock and return to Little Venice. The season begins Good Friday and lasts through September. During April and May, the boats run at 12:30 and 2:30 p.m.In June, July, August, and September, there is an additional morning and afternoon trip. Always telephone first. Refreshments are served on all trips and prebooked lunches on the 12:30 and 2:30 p.m. cruises. The fare for a day is £2 ($3) for adults, £1 ($1.50) for children.

LONDON WALKS: J. W. Travel, 66 St. Michael's St., W.2 (tel. 262-9572). John Wittich, who owns J. W. Travel, started walking tours of London in 1960. He is a Freeman of the City of London and a member of two livery companies as well as having written six books on London walks. He is also director of the London History Fellowship. There is no better way to search out the unusual, the beautiful, and the historic, than to take a walking tour. The walks are conducted by guides who really know their business, and you don't need a reservation. Tours take place whatever the weather. The cost is £1 ($1.50) for adults, 50p (75¢) for students with ID cards, and free to children with adults. Some of the titles of the organized tours are "Steeple-chasing," "Dick Whittington," and "The Great Fire of London Walk."

Hunt for ghosts or walk in the steps of Jack the Ripper, the infamous East End murderer of prostitutes in the 1880s. Retrace the legal system through the Inns of Court. Visit peaceful Hampstead or elegant Mayfair. Investigate the London of Shakespeare, Dickens, and Sherlock Holmes, or taste the delights of an evening's drinking in four historic pubs. These and many other walks (Roman London; 1660s; Great Plague and Great Fire; Tudor and Stuart London) are included in the program of unusual and historical walks organized by **London Walks,** 139 Conway Rd., Southgate, London N14 7BH (tel. 882-2763). Walks take place on weekends all through the year and during the week April to October. The cost is £2 ($3) for adults; children under 16 go free. No reservation is required. Get in touch with the above address for details.

Another small and enthusiastic company, a husband-and-wife team, offering a vast variety of London walks, is **Discovering London.** It's operated by a Scot, Alex Cobban, a historian of some note whose guides are professionals. Mainly on Saturday and Sunday, but during the week as well, scheduled walks are planned, starting at easily found Underground stations, to Dickens's London, Roman London, Ghosts of the City, the Inns of Court-Lawyers' London, Jack the Ripper. Mr. Cobban's knowledge of Sherlock Holmes is immense. No advance booking is necessary, and the walks cost £1.50 ($2.25), children under 16 go free, and students with ID cards are charged £1.20 ($1.80). Each walk takes about 1½ to 2 hours, except for the pub tours, which usually are in the evening and allow time for drinking in interesting pubs. At these you pay for whatever you wish to drink, and enjoy the pleasure of jostling at the bar with the locals. Write, enclosing an international reply coupon, for a detailed schedule of the walks available during your stay in London. The address is Discovering London, 11 Pennyfields, Warley, Brentwood, Essex CM14 5JP, U.K. (tel. Brentwood 0277/213-704).

TOURS FOR CHILDREN: Junior Jaunts, 4A William St., S.W.1 (tel. 235-4750), is a responsible organization that will take children 5 to 15 years old off your hands for the entire day. The service provides tours for parties of no more than six children at a time to various points of interest in London. The small number in each group assures you that your child will be carefully supervised and that his or her interests will be taken into consideration. Tours range from a visit to the Regents Park Zoo to a trip to Buckingham Palace or the Tower of London to a museum tour that includes no less than six popular museums in London. Tours are flexible, and suggestions from the children are often incorporated into the activities. Tours cost about £20 ($30) per day, depending on what is done and transport costs. You pay on a cost-plus basis, and children are collected from their London hotel and returned to it. Tube: Knightsbridge.

5. One-Day Trips from London

It would be sad to leave England without ever having ventured into the countryside, at least for a day. The English are the greatest excursion travelers in the world, forever dipping into their own rural areas to discover ancient abbeys, 17th-century village lanes, shady woods for picnic lunches, and stately mansions. From London, it's possible to take advantage of countless tours—either by conducted coach, boat, or via a do-it-yourself method on bus or train. On many trips, you can combine two or more methods of transportation; for example, you can go to Windsor by boat and return by coach or train.

In this section, you'll find a sampling of what is available—but, first, some general tips.

DO-IT-YOURSELF: Many hidden sightseeing surprises are in store for the adventurous traveler who doesn't depend on guides and scheduled routes. And this is possible even if you don't rent a car. Several means of transportation are available: coach, train, or boat.

Highly recommended are the previously described Green Line Coaches, operated by London Country Bus Services. You can go to the

Green Line Enquiry Office at Victoria (Eccleston Bridge) and pick up Green Line timetables giving specific details on routes.

For longer tours, say, to Stratford-upon-Avon, you will find the trains much more convenient. Often you can take advantage of the many bargain tickets outlined in Chapter I. For further information about trains to a specific location, go to the British Rail offices at Lower Regent Street, off Piccadilly, S.W.1 (tube to Piccadilly Circus).

An **Explorer Bus Ticket** will let you visit Sevenoaks, Westerham, the stately homes of Knole and Chartwell or Windsor, then Aylesbury and Beaconsfield or Luton to see Luton Hoo, Dunstable, and Whipsnade Zoo, as well as Hatfield House—all in one day. Tickets are £2.50 ($3.76) for adults, £1.50 ($2.25) for children, or £5 ($7.50) for a family.

With a day return ticket, you can travel as far as Portsmouth to see the *Mary Rose* and the *Victory* for £5 ($7.50); to Coventry to see the modern cathedral, £4.50 ($6.75); to Bath or Bournemouth, £5.50 ($8.75). Brighton, Exeter, Norwich, and Stratford-upon-Avon are also within reach. For further information and tickets, phone 730-0202 from 8 a.m. to 10 p.m. or Victoria Coach Station at 730-3499 from 8 a.m. to 9 p.m. You must pick up your ticket at least 30 minutes before departure.

THE BRITAINSHRINKERS:

THE BRITAINSHRINKERS: This is a bonanza for travelers who want to make several quickie trips into the heart of England, without having to check out of their hotel room in London. Scheduled full-day tours are operated by Road 'n' Rail Tours Ltd. in cooperation with British Rail. You're whisked out of London by train to your destination, where you hop on a waiting bus to visit the various sights during the day. You have a light lunch in a local pub, and there is also free time to shop or explore. A guide accompanies the tour from London and back. Your return is in time for dinner or the theater. Included in the rates are entrance fees and VAT.

For more information, telephone 589-0156. It's possible to call this number, even on weekends, providing you do so before 4:30 p.m.

On one day trip, you can visit Warwick Castle, Stratford-upon-Avon, and Coventry Cathedral, at a cost of £27.50 ($41.25) for adults, £17.20 ($25.80) for children up to 16 years old, and a further reduction for Britrail Pass holders, making the cost £19.60 ($29.40) for adults, £13.30 ($19.95) for children. It's also possible to visit Scotland on an overnight trip, at a cost of £116.50 ($174.75) for adults, £77.40 ($116.10) for children, with substantial reductions for holders of Britrail Passes. One of the most heavily booked tours is to Bath and Stonehenge, taking in Salisbury Cathedral, costing £30 ($45) for adults, £18.70 ($28.05) for children under 16, again with additional reductions for Britrail Pass holders.

It's better to write **Britainshrinkers,** 22 Hans Pl., London, S.W.1, than to get in touch with British Rail.

London Transport Tours

The official bus company, **London Transport,** takes the lead in conducted coach tours to the places of interest in and around London. The coach tours are accompanied by an experienced guide, and they start from Victoria Coach Station. It is necessary to reserve seats; this is done at the London Transport Travel Information Centres at the St. James's Park, Piccadilly Circus, Oxford Circus, Victoria, King's Cross, and Euston Underground stations.

An outstanding coach tour is offered to **Windsor Castle** and **Hampton Court Palace,** a day's adventure that also includes Eton College, Runnymede, and the Kennedy Memorial. The tour departs daily at 10 a.m., getting back at 4:15 p.m. Adults pay £15 ($22.50); children under 14, £10 ($15). Rates include lunch and the admission charge to the State Apartments at Windsor. The tours are operated daily in summer and on Thursday and Sunday from October to March.

HAMPTON COURT: On the Thames, 13 miles west of London, this 16th-century palace of Cardinal Wolsey can teach us a lesson. Don't try to outdo your boss—particularly if he happens to be Henry VIII. The rich cardinal did just that. But the king had a lean and hungry eye. Wolsey, who eventually lost his fortune, power, and prestige, ended up giving his lavish palace to the Tudor monarch. In a stroke of oneupmanship, Henry took over, even outdoing the Wolsey embellishments. The Tudor additions included the Anne Boleyn gateway, with its 16th-century astronomical clock that even tells the high water mark at London Bridge. From Clock Court, you can see one of Henry's major contributions, the aptly named Great Hall, with its hammer-beam ceiling.

To judge from the movie *A Man for All Seasons,* Hampton Court had quite a retinue to feed. Cooking was done in the Great Kitchens. Henry cavorted through the various apartments with his wives of the moment—everybody from Anne Boleyn to Catherine Parr (the latter reversed things and lived to bury her erstwhile spouse). Charles I was imprisoned here at one time, and temporarily managed to escape his jailers.

Although the palace enjoyed prestige and pomp in Elizabethan days, it owes much of its present look to William and Mary of Orange—or rather to Sir Christopher Wren. You can parade through the apartments today, filled as they are with porcelain, furniture, paintings, and tapestries. The King's Dressing Room is graced with some of the best art. In Queen Mary's closet, you'll find Pieter Brueghel the Elder's macabre *Massacre of the Innocents.* Tintoretto and Titian deck the halls of the King's Drawing Room. Finally, be sure to inspect the Royal Chapel (Wolsey wouldn't recognize it). To confound yourself totally, you may want to get lost in the serpentine shrubbery Maze in the garden.

The State Apartments may be visited year round—April to September, weekdays from 9:30 a.m. to 6 p.m., on Sunday from 11 a.m. to 6 p.m.; October to March, weekdays from 9:30 a.m. to 5 p.m., on Sunday from 2 to 5 p.m. The admission is £2 ($3) for adults, £1 ($1.50) for children. The off-season admission is £1 ($1.50) for adults, 60p (90¢) for children. There is an extra charge for admission to any special exhibition held at the palace. Entrance to the maze is 10p (15¢).

Frequent trains run from Waterloo to Hampton Court Station. To come by boat, apply to the Westminster Passenger Service Association (Up River), Westminster Pier, S.W.1 (tel. 930-2062). Or take bus 201, 206, 216, or 264 weekdays; 267 on Saturday and Sunday only. Green Line Coaches 716, 716A, and 718 will deliver you to Hampton Court in about half an hour from London.

Where to Eat

After visiting the palace, lunch at **Bastians,** Hampton Court Road, in East Molesey, Surrey (tel. 977-6074), an attractive old building with a large stone-floored hall, roaring log fire, and comfortable chairs. Here you order an apéritif and select your meal. Then you go into the simple dining room or, in summer, into the tiny garden to eat al fresco.

The French menu includes such appetizers as moules marinières in season, an enormous platter, or trout mousse. Main dishes include filet steak, a whole small chicken, and lamb cutlets in a light mustard sauce. These courses are served with a delicious variety of sauces and well-cooked vegetables, depending on the season and availability. Desserts include crème brûlée, sorbets, and chocolate mousse, and there is a good cheese board. A carafe of house wine is always available. Expect to spend from £12 ($18), plus wine. Prices include VAT but not the 12½% service charge. The restaurant is open Monday to Friday from 12:30 to 2:30 p.m. for lunch, Monday to Saturday from 7 to 10:45 p.m. for dinner (until 11:15 p.m. Saturday evenings).

KEW GARDENS: Nine miles southwest of central London at Kew, near Richmond, are the **Royal Botanic Gardens,** (tel. 940-1171), among the best known in Europe, containing thousands of varieties of plants. But Kew is no mere pleasure garden—rather, it is a vast scientific undertaking that happens to be beautiful. A pagoda, erected in 1761–1762, represents the "flowering" of chinoiserie. One of the oddities of Kew is a Douglas fir flagstaff, more than 220 feet high. The Palm House, built in the heyday of Victoria by Decimus Burton, is replete with torrid temperatures and cannibalistic-looking vegetation—a sort of south of Pago Pago setting.

Much interest focuses on the red-brick **Kew Palace** (dubbed the Dutch House), a former residence of King George III and Queen Charlotte. It is reached by walking to the northern tip of the Broad Walk. Now a museum, it was built in 1631 and contains memorabilia of the reign of George III, along with a royal collection of furniture and paintings. It is open only April to September from 11 a.m. to 5:30 p.m. daily. Admission is 60p (90¢) for adults, 30p (45¢) for children. The gardens may be visited from 10 a.m. to 8 p.m. in summer, to 4 p.m. in winter. Admission is 15p (23¢). Closed Christmas Day and New Year's Day.

At the gardens, **Queen Charlotte's Cottage** has been restored to its original splendor. Built in 1772, it is half-timbered and thatched. George III is believed to have been the architect. The house has been restored in great detail, including the original Hogarth prints that hung on the downstairs walls. The cottage is open April to September on weekends and bank holidays. The least expensive and most convenient way to visit the gardens is to take the District line subway to Kew. The most romantic way to come in summer is via a steamer from Westminster Bridge to Kew Pier.

London's living steam museum, **Kew Bridge Engines,** Green Dragon Lane, Brentford, Middlesex (tel. 568-4757), houses a fine collection of steam and traction engines, a working forge, and two of the world's largest steam-operated beam engines, used for pumping London's water. One of these can produce 700 gallons per stroke. There are many models, and usually at least one steam engine will be in action during your visit. The museum is about a ten-minute walk from Kew Gardens. It's open Saturday, Sunday, and Monday holidays from 11 a.m. until the end of the afternoon. Admission is £1.20 ($1.80) for adults, 70p ($1.05) for children.

GREENWICH: Greenwich Mean Time, of course, is the basis of standard time throughout most of the world, the zero point used in the reckoning of terrestrial longitudes since 1884. But Greenwich is also home of the Royal Naval College, the National Maritime Museum, and the Old Royal Observatory. In drydock at Greenwich Pier is the clipper ship *Cutty Sark,* as well as Sir Francis Chichester's *Gypsy Moth IV.*

About four miles from The City, Greenwich is reached by a number of methods, and part of the fun of making the jaunt is getting there. Ideally, you'll arrive by boat, as Henry VIII preferred to do on one of his hunting expeditions. In summer, launches leave at regular intervals from either the Charing Cross or Westminster piers. Actually, Westminster is preferred, because the boats from Charing Cross are usually filled with tour-group passengers. You can take the tube to New Cross, then bus 171a or 177. Buses 70 and 188 run from the Surrey Docks tube station. The boats leave daily to Greenwich every 20 minutes from 10 a.m. to 7 p.m.

Unquestionably, the *Cutty Sark*—last of the great clippers—holds the most interest, having been seen by millions. At the spot where the vessel is now berthed stood the Ship Inn of the 19th century (Victorians came here for whitebait dinners, as they did to the Trafalgar Tavern). Ordered built by Capt. Jock Willis ("Old White Hat"), the clipper was launched in 1869 to sail the China tea trade route. It was named after the Witch Nannie in Robert Burns's *Tam o'Shanter* (note the figurehead). Yielding to the more efficient steamers, the *Cutty Sark* later was converted to a wool-clipper, plying the route between Australia and England. Before her retirement, she knew many owners, even different names, eventually coming to drydock at Cutty Sark Gardens, Greenwich Pier, S.E.10 (tel. 858-3445), in 1954. For £1 ($1.50) for adults, 50p (75¢) for children, the vessel may be boarded weekdays from 11 a.m. to 6 p.m., on Sunday from 2:30 to 6 p.m. It closes at 5 p.m. in winter.

A neighbor to the *Cutty Sark*—and also in drydock—is Sir Francis Chichester's *Gypsy Moth IV* (also tel. 858-3445), in which he circumnavigated the world in 1967. He single-handedly fought the elements in his vessel for 119 days. You can go aboard (same hours as *Cutty Sark).* It's usually closed on Friday.

The **Royal Naval College** (tel. 858-2154) grew up on the site of the Tudor palace in Greenwich in which Henry VIII and Elizabeth I were born. William and Mary commissioned Wren to design the present buildings in 1695 to house naval pensioners, and these became the Royal Naval College in 1873. The buildings are a baroque masterpiece, in which the Painted Hall (by Thornhill, 1708–1727) and the chapel are outstanding. It is normally open to visitors between 2:30 and 5 p.m. (latest time of admission, 4:45 p.m.) daily, except Thursday and certain public holidays. These days are published in daily papers.

The **National Maritime Museum,** built around Inigo Jones's 17th-century Palladian Queen's House, portrays Britain's maritime heritage. Actual craft, marine paintings, ship models, and scientific instruments are displayed, including the full-dress uniform coat that Lord Nelson wore at the Battle of Trafalgar. Other curiosities include the chronometer (or sea watch) used by Captain Cook when he made his Pacific explorations in the 1770s. At the **Old Royal Observatory,** see the Greenwich Meridian Line, the internationally accepted 0 degrees longitude, and an exhibit of mariner's instruments, from astrolabes to an atomic clock. The museum is open Tuesday through Friday from 9 a.m. to 6 p.m. (on Sunday from 2 to 5:30 p.m.) in summer, and Tuesday through Friday from 10 a.m. to 5 p.m. (on

Sunday from 2 to 5 p.m.) in winter. On Saturday all year, hours are from 10 a.m. to 5:30 p.m. It's closed Christmas Eve, Christmas Day, Boxing Day, New Year's Day, Good Friday, May bank holiday, and every Monday. Admission is free. Just off the Navigation Room, in the west wing, is a licensed restaurant. Before making the trip to the museum, telephone 01858/4422, extension 221, for information about opening hours.

Eating in Greenwich

Trafalgar Tavern, Park Row, S.E.10 (tel. 858-2437), overlooks the Thames at Greenwich and is surrounded by many attractions. Directly opposite the tavern is the Royal Naval College, and nearby are the *Cutty Sark,* the National Maritime Museum, Greenwich Royal Observatory, and the *Gypsy Moth IV.*

Traditional English dishes and seafood specialties are featured. Many of the fish have never seen the Thames, and, consequently, dishes such as whitebait do not appear on table d'hôte menus but only on the à la carte. To begin your meal, you can order deep-fried whitebait. You might follow with Dover sole or turkey breast Hamilton. Also good is steak, kidney, and oyster pie. A three-course meal costs from £18 ($27) per person, plus wine and service.

In its most recent redecoration, the tavern retained all the original artist's designs, and it has many antique and historical pieces of naval equipment. All its rooms are named after famous sea admirals. For example, there is the Nelson Room and the Hardy and the Hawke and Howe Bars.

Lunch is served from noon to 2 p.m., dinner from 7:30 to 10 p.m. Only dinner is served on Saturday, only lunch on Sunday. The restaurant is closed on Monday, but hot and cold bar snacks are available every day.

The **Cutty Sark Free House,** Ballast Quay, Lassell Street, S.E.10 (tel. 858-3146), has plenty of local color on its Thames-side perch. About a half mile from the railway station, this English riverside tavern will dispense drinks in an atmosphere in which you can eavesdrop on the conversation of oldtime salts (head to the second floor for the Captain's Bar). Bar meals, costing around £7.50 ($11.25), are served. Dinner, going for from £12 ($18), features traditional English fare.

RUNNYMEDE: Two miles outside Windsor is the meadow on the south side of the Thames, in Surrey, where King John put his seal on the Great Charter. John may have signed the document up the river on a little island, but that's being technical. Today, Runnymede is also the site of the John F. Kennedy Memorial, one acre of English ground given to the United States by the people of Britain.

In accommodations, the **Runnymede Hotel,** Egham (tel. 0784/36171), stands in ten acres of landscaped grounds on the Thames, bordering the Mede. The setting, near the spot where King John signed the Magna Carta, is just 17 miles from the heart of London (Waterloo can be reached by fast train in about half an hour). The water-view garden hotel is newly built, but not blatantly contemporary, providing a clean-cut freshness, open-view lounges, plus 90 well-equipped bedrooms, each with its own private bath or shower, renting for £42 ($63) nightly in a single, £54 ($81) in a double, a continental breakfast and VAT included.

English and continental cuisines are served in the River Room, which is built on two levels, giving every table a view of the garden and river. A set dinner costs £10 ($15), plus £1 ($1.50) if you chose your meat course from the trolley of roast joints. An à la carte meal will cost about £20 ($30). There's dancing on Friday and Saturday nights. At night the Anglers Bar is one of the most attractive along the Thames.

SYON PARK: Just nine miles from Piccadilly Circus, on 55 acres of the Duke of Northumberland's Thames-side estate, is one of the most beautiful spots in all of Great Britain. There's always something in bloom. Called "The Showplace of the Nation in a Great English Garden," Syon Park was opened to the public in 1968. A nation of green-thumbed gardeners is dazzled here, and the park is also educational, showing amateurs how to get the most out of their small gardens. The vast flower- and plant-studded acreage betrays the influence of "Capability" Brown, who laid out the grounds in the 18th century.

Particular highlights include a six-acre rose garden and the Great Conservatory, one of the earliest and most famous buildings of its type, housing everything from cacti to fuchsias. In it is also housed a walk-through aviary full of exotic and brilliantly colored birds. In the old dairy you will find an interesting aquarium.

Operated by the Gardening Center Limited, Syon was the site of the first botanical garden in England, created by the father of English botany, Dr. William Turner. Trees include a 200-year-old Chinese juniper, an Afghan ash, an Indian bean tree, and a "Liquidambar." The gardens are open all the year (except for Christmas and Boxing Day). The gates open at 10 a.m. and close at 6 p.m. April to September; from 10 a.m. to 5 p.m. or dusk October to March. Admission is 70p ($1.05) for adults, 40p (60¢) for children. On the grounds is **Syon House,** built in 1547, the original structure incorporated into the Duke of Northumberland's present home. The house was later remade to the specifications of the first Duke of Northumberland in 1766. The battlemented facade is that of the original Tudor mansion, but the interior is from the 18th century, the design of Robert Adam. Basil Taylor said of the interior feeling: "You're almost in the middle of a jewel box." In the Middle Ages, Syon was a monastery, later suppressed by Henry VIII. Katherine Howard, the king's fifth wife, was imprisoned in the house before her scheduled beheading in 1542. The house may be visited Sunday to Thursday from noon to 5 p.m. from Easter to the end of September. It is closed Friday and Saturday because the duke is in residence during the summer. Admission to the house costs 75 p ($1.13) for adults, 40p (60¢) for children. A combined ticket to visit both the house and park goes for £1.30 ($1.95) for adults, 65p (98¢) for children. There is a restaurant for light meals and snacks. For more information, telephone 560-0881.

A DAY AT THE RACES: Within easy reach of central London, there are horse-racing tracks at Kempton Park, Sandown Park, and the most famous of all, Epsom, where the Derby is the main feature of the summer meeting. Entrance to the courses for a day's racing can be as little as £1.50 ($2.25), but of course you pay more for a seat in a grandstand or on one of the most prestigious race days. Racing isn't conducted every weekend, so you should telephone **United Racecourses** at Epsom (tel. Epsom 26311) for information of the next meeting. You can drive yourself or, if you want to travel by rail, dial 928-5100 for details of train services.

Chapter V

WINDSOR, OXFORD, AND THE HOME COUNTIES

1. Windsor
2. Oxford
3. Hertfordshire
4. Buckinghamshire
5. Bedfordshire

WITHIN EASY REACH of London, the Thames Valley and the Chilterns are a history-rich part of England, and they lie so close to the capital they can be easily reached by automobile or Green Line coach. You can explore here during the day and return in time to see a show in the West End.

Here are some of the most-visited historic sites in England: the former homes of Disraeli and Elizabeth I, the estate of the Duke of Bedford, and of course, Windsor Castle, 22 miles from London, one of the most famous castles in Europe and the most popular day trip for those visitors venturing out of London for the first time.

Of course, your principal reason for coming to Oxfordshire, our second goal, is to explore the university city of Oxford, about an hour's drive from London. But Oxford is not the only attraction in the county, as you'll soon discover as you make your way through Henley-on-Thames. The shire is a land of great mansions, old churches of widely varying architectural styles, and rolling farmland.

In a sense, Oxfordshire is a kind of buffer zone between the easy living in the southern towns and the industrialized cities of the heartland. In the southeast are the chalky Chilterns, and in the west you'll be moving toward the wool towns of the Cotswolds. In fact, Burford, an unspoiled medieval town, lying west of Oxford, is one of the traditional gateways of the Cotswolds (dealt with in a later chapter). The Upper Thames winds its way across the southern parts of the county.

The "Home Counties" are characterized by their river valleys and gentle hills. The beech-clad Chiltern Hills are at their most beautiful in spring and fall. This 40-mile chalk ridge extends in an arc from the Thames Valley to the old Roman city of St. Albans in Hertfordshire. The whole region is popular for boating holidays, as it contains a 200-mile network of canals.

1. Windsor

If you hop aboard a 701 or 704 Green Line coach at Victoria Station, you'll be delivered in little more than an hour to Windsor, site of England's greatest castle and its most famous boys' school.

You can also take an express nonstop bus (no. 700). If you start your trip before 9 a.m., the fare each way is £1.70 ($2.55). After 9 a.m., you'll pay £2.10 ($3.15) each way. Children ride for half price.

Windsor was originally called "Windlesore" by the ancient Britons who derived the name from winding shore—so noticeable as you walk along the Thames here.

THE SIGHTS: Your bus will drop you near the Town Guildhall, to which Wren applied the finishing touches. It's only a short walk up Castle Hill to the following sights:

Windsor Castle

It was William the Conqueror who founded a castle on this spot, beginning a legend and a link with English sovereignty that has known many vicissitudes. King John cooled his heels at Windsor while waiting to put his signature on the Magna Carta at nearby Runnymede; Charles I was imprisoned here before losing his head; Queen Bess did some renovations; Victoria mourned her beloved Albert, who died at the castle in 1861; the royal family rode out much of World War II behind its sheltering walls. When Queen Elizabeth II and her entourage are at Windsor, the Royal Standard flies, which means the State Apartments are off limits then. Otherwise, they may be visited weekdays from 10:30 a.m. to 4:45 p.m. from March to October; 10:30 a.m. to 3:15 p.m. November to February; also on Sunday from 1:30 to 4:45 p.m. The price of admission is £1.20 ($1.80) for adults, 50p (75¢) for children. The apartments are closed for about six weeks at Easter and for around three weeks in June when the Queen and Philip come here for the Ascot races. The apartments themselves selves contain many works of art, porcelain, armor, furniture, three Verrio ceilings, and several Gibbons carvings from the 17th century. The world of Rubens adorns the King's Drawing Room and in his relatively small dressing room is a Dürer, along with Rembrandt's portrait of his mother, and Van Dyck's triple look at Charles I. Of the apartments, the grand reception room, with its Gobelin tapestries, is the most spectacular.

The guard is changed daily at 10:30 a.m., except on Sunday. The Windsor changing of the guard is a much more exciting and moving experience, in my opinion, than the London exercises. In Windsor, the guard marches through the town, stopping the traffic as it wheels into the castle to the tune of a full regimental band when the court is in residence. When the Queen is not there, a drum and pipe band is mustered.

Old Master Drawings

The royal family possesses a rare collection at Windsor of drawings by old masters—notably Leonardo da Vinci. One Leonardo sketch, for example, shows a cat in 20 different positions; another is a study of a horse; still a third is that of Saint Matthew, a warmup for the head used in *The Last Supper*. In addition, you'll find sketches by William Blake, Thomas Rowlandson, and 12 Holbeins (don't miss his sketch of Sir John Godsalve). The drawing exhibition may be visited at the same time as the State Apartments for an admission of 50p (75¢) for adults, 20p (30¢) for children. It remains open, unlike the State Apartments, when the Court is in residence.

Queen Mary's Dollhouse

Just about the greatest dollhouse in all the world is at Windsor. Presented to the late Queen Mary as a gift, and later used to raise money for charity, the dollhouse is a remarkable achievement and recreation of what a great royal mansion of the 1920s looked like—complete with a fleet of cars, including a Rolls-Royce. The house is perfect for Tom Thumb and family, and a retinue of servants. All is done with the most exacting detail—even the champagne bottles in the wine cellar contain vintage wine of that era. There's a toothbrush suitable for an ant. A minuscule electric iron really works. For late-night reading, you'll find volumes ranging from Hardy to Houseman. In addition, you'll see a collection of dolls presented to the monarchy from nearly every nation of the Commonwealth. The dollhouse may be viewed for an admission of 50p (75¢) for adults, 20p (30¢) for children, even when the State Apartments are closed.

St. George's Chapel

A gem of the Perpendicular style, this chapel shares the distinction with Westminster Abbey of being a pantheon of English monarchs (Victoria is a notable exception). The present St. George's was founded in the late 15th century by Edward IV on the site of the original Chapel of the Order of the Garter (Edward III, 1348). You enter the nave first with its fan vaulting (a remarkable achievement in English architecture). The nave contains the tomb of George V and Queen Mary, designed by Sir William Reid Dick. Off the nave in the Urswick Chapel, the Princess Charlotte memorial provides an ironic touch. If she had survived childbirth in 1817, she—and not her cousin, Victoria—would have ruled the British Empire. In the aisle are the tombs of George IV and Edward IV. The Edward IV "Quire," with its imaginatively carved 15th-century choir stalls (crowned by lacy canopies and colorful Knights of the Garter banners), evokes the pomp and pageantry of medieval days. In the center is a flat tomb, containing the vault of the beheaded Charles I, along with Henry VIII and one of his wives (no. 3, Jane Seymour). Finally, you may want to inspect the Prince Albert Memorial Chapel, reflecting the opulent taste of the era of Victoria. The chapel is closed during services, and it's advisable to telephone to check opening hours at other times (tel. Windsor 65538). The chapel is usually open from 10:45 a.m. to 3:45 or 4 p.m. Monday to Saturday, and from 2 to 3:45 or 4 p.m. on Sunday. The price of admission is £1.50 ($2.25) for adults, 75p ($1.13) for children.

Footnote: Queen Victoria died on January 22, 1901, and was buried beside her beloved Prince Albert in a mausoleum at **Frogmore** (a private estate), near Windsor (open only two days a year, in May). The Prince Consort died in December 1861.

Royal Mews Exhibition

After you've seen the changing of the guard, walk across the road and down St. Albans Street to the entrance of the Royal Mews exhibition in the red brick buildings of historic **Burford House,** built for Nell Gwynne in the 1670s. Her natural son by King Charles II was created Earl of Burford when he was six and later was made Duke of St. Albans, hence the name of the house and the street.

The exhibition displays large portraits of Queen Elizabeth II and the Duke of Edinburgh as well as other members of the royal family riding or driving with various celebrated horses sometimes stabled in the Royal Mews. There is also a room containing the state harness and a collection of driving and riding bits. Beyond the mews is the coach house with all sorts of coaches and carriages that are still used regularly.

The exhibition is open Monday to Saturday from 10:30 a.m. to 5 p.m., to 3 p.m. in winter. On Sunday in summer it is open from 10:30 a.m. to 4 or 5 p.m. Admission is 50p (75¢) for adults, 20p (30¢) for children.

Royalty and Railways

The **Station Master's House,** Thames Street (tel. 07535/57837), a part of Windsor Town Railway Station, has been taken over by the company that owns and operates Madame Tussaud's in London and is the scene of an exhibition of "Sixty Glorious Years" of Victorian history. At one of the station platforms, you will see life-size wax figures of guests arriving at Windsor for the jubilee celebration disembarking from the royal coaches. In one of the carriages, the Day Saloon, sits Queen Victoria and her family, with her faithful Indian servant, Hafiz Abdul Karim, the Munshi, waiting in the anteroom.

The platform is busy with royal servants, a flower seller, a newsboy, an Italian with a barrel organ, and others who have come to see the arrival of the train. Drawn up in the courtyard are the troops of the Coldstream Guards and the horse-drawn carriage that would take the party to the castle. With the sound of military bands in the background and the voices of officers commanding their troops, you really feel you are present in the courtyard for Her Majesty's arrival.

Afterward, at the end of the walkway through the Victorian Conservatory, you reach the 260-seat theater where a short audio-visual presentation with life-size animated models gives further glimpses of life during Victoria's reign. The entire visit takes about 45 minutes. The exhibition is open daily from 9:30 a.m. to 5:30 p.m. (closed Christmas Day). Admission is £1.85 ($2.78) for adults, £1 ($1.50) for children.

Sunday Entertainment

There are often polo matches in **Windsor Great Park**—and at Ham Common—and you may see Prince Charles playing and Prince Philip serving as umpire. The Queen often watches. For more information, telephone 07535/60633.

The Town Itself

Windsor is largely a Victorian town, with lots of brick buildings and a few remnants of Georgian architecture. In and around the castle are two cobblestoned streets—**Church** and **Market,** with their antique shops, silversmiths, and pubs. One shop on Church Street was supposedly occupied by Nell Gwynne who needed to be within call of Charles II's chambers. After lunch or tea, you may want to stroll along the three-mile, aptly named Long Walk.

STAYING OVER AT WINDSOR: If you don't have an engraved invitation to overnight at the castle, there's always room at one of the inns—except during Ascot Races and the Windsor Horse Show.

For those who decide to stay in Windsor and use it as a base for London sightseeing, trains run from Windsor Town Station and from Windsor and Eton Riverside Station to London. Trains leave London as late as 10:30 or 11 p.m., so it is quite easy to take in an early theater and dinner before returning to Windsor for overnight.

Alternatively, the **Royal Theatre** (tel. 07535/63444) has nightly performances. Run by John Counsell and his wife, Mary Kerridge, this is one of the best repertory companies around London. Tickets cost £2 ($3) to £8 ($12), depending on the day.

The Upper Bracket

Wrens Old House Hotel, Thames Street (tel. 07535/61354), was designed and lived in by Christopher Wren in 1676. Between Eton and Windsor, the former town house occupies a prime position on the Thames, its gardens overlooking the swans and boats. The owners, Wren House Ltd., have improved and completely redecorated the hotel, maintaining the beauty of the past, keeping the same architectural detail, furnishing it with a collection of antiques. The central hall is impressive, with a Queen Anne black marble refectory table. Wren's former study is inviting; it's in apricot and white paneling, with his Empire desk, along with a fireplace and shield-back Hepplewhite chairs. Another area is a small apple-green salon, with linenfold walls, Tudor oak and chintz-covered chairs. The bay-windowed main drawing room, decorated with mirrors, sconces, and a formal marble fireplace, opens into a garden and a riverside flagstone terrace for after-dinner coffee and drinks.

All of the 40 bedrooms have private baths and have been redecorated and brightened. Some have fine old furniture, and all are equipped with color TVs, direct-dial phones, and trouser presses. Some rooms overlook the river. Room 3, which was Sir Christopher Wren's bedroom, is said to be haunted. I couldn't find out whose ghost walks, but I was assured that it is not Sir Christopher's. Singles with bath range from £40 ($60) to £45 ($67.50) per night; doubles or twins with bath, from £54 ($81) to £62 ($93).

Chef Leon Carol, who has cooked for royalty and was congratulated by the Queen Mother on a fine meal, is in charge of the new kitchens. He comes from Provence in the south of France and has been cooking since he could walk. He holds the Maîtrise Escoffier Gold Medal. Every dish is cooked to order, with fresh ingredients used when possible. A table d'hôte dinner, including coffee and VAT, will cost you from £12 ($18), while an à la carte selection, also with coffee and VAT included, will cost two persons about £34 ($51). If you choose the latter approach, try the cocotte d'escargots bourguignons (snails in a fine burgundy sauce with walnuts), followed by julienne de caneton flambée au porto (breast of duck sauteed with orange segments) served with fresh french beans and lyonnaise potatoes.

Castle Hotel, High Street (tel. 07535/51011), a small link in the Trusthouse Forte circuit, sits in a prominent position facing the Guildhall, across from the castle. Formerly a Georgian posting house, it enjoyed many prestigious visitors, such as second-string royal cousins, in its heyday in the 18th century. Nowadays it's more likely to be patronized by parents visiting their sons at Eton. Its classic facade is a "parchment color." The interior may not contain the splendid furnishings of its former days, but the hotel is nevertheless comfortable and immaculate, with central heating throughout. A ballroom suite is its most attractive feature. Guests are housed in one of the well-furnished rooms in the main building or in a park wing that has been added. All units contain private bath, TV, and radio, as well as tea- and coffee-making facilities. A single rents for £42 ($63) in the park wing, for £48 ($72) in the main building. Doubles go for £50 ($75) in the wing, £58 ($87) to £68 ($102) in the original structure. Prices include VAT and service.

The Medium-Priced Range

Harte and Garter Hotel, High Street (tel. 07535/63426), stands right opposite the castle, beside the Castle Hotel. Recently revamped, it is decidedly the best location for lovers of castles. It's very accessible to the Windsor Town Railway Station. All rooms have color TV, phone, radio, and tea- and coffee-making facilities. A single without bath costs £26 ($39); with bath, £28 ($42). Twins or doubles with bath go for £46 ($69), including a continental breakfast and VAT. Grill room meals range in price from £5 ($7.50) to £11 ($16.50) and are likely to include rump steak or a mixed grill. Peas and jacket potatoes are always on the menu.

Royal Adelaide Hotel, Kings Road (tel. 07535/63916), is opposite the famous Long Walk leading to Windsor Castle, five minutes away. An old Victorian hotel, it offers single rooms from £16 ($24) without bath to £28 ($42) with bath, and doubles or twins from £24 ($36) without bath to £34 ($51) with bath, including breakfast. All units have radio, alarm, and tea-maker. There is good car parking at the rear for guests, and the hotel is warm and well furnished. The staff, used to a quick turnover of guests, may be a little offhand. A set lunch or dinner is available at £8 ($12) for a three-course meal.

On the Outskirts

On the river road, the A308, from Windsor to Maidenhead, the motorist comes across the **Oakley Court Hotel,** Windsor Road, Water Oakley, three miles from Windsor (tel. 0628/74141). This old house, once owned by the Avery family of weighing scales fame, has emerged from a semi-retirement and blossoms as a most attractive riverside hotel. The house with its turrets and chimneys contains the reception and the living rooms, and the restaurant. One new wing of bedrooms extends from the old house; another, built beside the river, is a 30-foot walk from the main building. This is, in my opinion, the best place to be, with lovely views of the river and the garden, but some may wish to be within closer walking distance of the main building.

Of the 75 rooms, those in the old house have high ceilings, interesting shapes, and one still contains the original paneling. The bookshelves are stocked with ancient tomes. In the two modern wings, the rooms are of generous size and have modern bathrooms en suite. All have color TV and radio with remote control and phone. There is full room service. Units go for £40 ($60) to £50 ($75) for two, including an English breakfast, VAT, and service.

The restaurant serves a set luncheon for £8.50 ($12.75), including such fare as roast stuffed breast of veal with spinach and ham, royal jugged hare, and lamb cutlets. The set dinner is more elaborate—perhaps a leg of lamb, filet of trout, or noisettes of lamb—all for £15 ($22.50). The à la carte menu is priced according to availability but includes a wide variety of hors d'oeuvres, soups, fish, and poultry. The chef's specialties include tournedos de boeuf Princesse and mignonettes de boeuf exotiques. A well-chosen meal will cost about £20 ($30) per person, including a bottle of wine for two diners.

The Oakley Court is three miles from Royal Windsor and about 20 minutes' drive from Heathrow. As well as being a delightful spot for a vacation stay, the hotel is close enough to London to attract those who have daytime business in the city. You can't miss the wide-open black iron gates with gold touches. The hotel sits grandly out of sight of the road on a tree-lined drive.

LUNCH AT WINDSOR: For lunch in Windsor, try the **William IV Hotel,** Thames Street, 100 yards from Eton Bridge (tel. 07535/51004). This lovely old place (circa 1500) with its armor, beams, and log fire, invites visitors in with its friendly and local atmosphere. Just outside is the Chapter garden where the Windsor martyrs were burned at the stake in 1544 for their religious beliefs. It was from this inn that they received their last cups of strong ale "in gratification of their last wish." The house built by Sir Christopher Wren for his own use is opposite the William IV, and the great architect of St. Paul's was reputedly a regular visitor to the old tap room, as were diarists Evelyn and Pepys. The present landlord is Ken Gardner, award-winning journalist and writer. Rub shoulders here with newspaper people and actors (nearby is the Theatre Royal), artists and rivermen, and drink traditional ale that is still pulled by old-fashioned beer engines.

The food is home-cooked, and the portions are guaranteed to satisfy gargantuan appetites. Scottish beef is served by two motherly locals, Lottie and Gert, who are quick and accurate. Try a steak or one of the house regional specials. A three-course luncheon costs £6 ($9), and might consist of soup, followed by a roast topside of beef with Yorkshire pudding, served with a selection of vegetables, and followed by a homemade apple pie with cream. Bar lunches are also available, costing from £1.50 ($2.25). You can sit at sidewalk tables in a pedestrian area by the Eton Bridge, gazing up at the castle while enjoying lunch. The William IV lies at the bottom of Windsor Hill on the approach road to the bridge, which is now open to pedestrians only.

The house also rents out three double bedrooms, one with shower, charging from £23 ($34.50) for two persons, these tariffs including a good English breakfast.

The **Court Jester,** Church Lane (tel. 07535/64257), is a pub with a restaurant serving traditional pub lunches and French cuisine in the evening. Publican John Chandler and Barbara will give you a warm welcome. The charges for food vary—between £3 ($4.50) and £6 ($9) for lunch, slightly more for a really excellent dinner. B&B terms are £12.50 ($18.75) in a single, £18 ($27) in a double. The tariffs include a full English breakfast and morning tea or coffee.

ETON: For our final sight, from Windsor Castle we must cross over a bridge spanning the Thames:

Eton College

Largest and best known of the public (private) schools of England, Eton College was founded by a teenage boy himself, Henry VI in 1440. Some of England's greatest men, notably the Duke of Wellington, have played on the fields of Eton. Twenty prime ministers were educated at Eton, as well as such literary figures as George Orwell and Aldous Huxley. Even the late Ian Fleming, creator of James Bond, attended. The traditions of the school have had plenty of time to become firmly entrenched (ask a young gentleman in his Victorian black tails to explain the difference between a "wet bob" and a "dry bob"). For 90p ($1.35) admission, the School Yard and Cloisters may be visited daily, 2 to 5 p.m., throughout the year, and also from 10:30 a.m. to 2 p.m. on school holidays, including most of July and all of August. If it's open, pay another 60p (90¢) to take a look at the Perpendicular chapel, with its 15th-century paintings and reconstructed fan vaulting.

Bernard Weintraub wrote, "Eton, the Gothic school on the Thames that has symbolized starched exclusiveness, is quietly lifting its cloak of privilege." In the future, along with the sons of diplomats and prime ministers, boys from poorer families will also be educated there, the tuition funded by scholarships. All of this represents the movement in England toward a classless society. One man put it this way, "The lifestyle of the young cuts across all classes—they're wearing the same clothes, listening to the same music, engaging in the same activities." However, the administration (at the moment) doesn't plan to go coed.

Lunch at Eton

Eton Wine Bar (tel. 07535/54921) is owned and run by William and Michael Gilbey of Gilbey's gin family, although no gin is served here. Just across the bridge from Windsor, it is a charming place set among the antique shops with pinewood tables and old church pews and chairs. There is a small garden out back. It is open seven days a week from 11:30 a.m. to 3 p.m. and from 6 to 10:30 p.m., but on Friday and Saturday they remain open until 11 p.m. Soups of the day are often imaginative and sophisticated (ever had watercress vichyssoise?). Another "starter" might be mussels marinated in a roquefort dressing. Main dishes include such treats as stuffed eggplant with a Provençal tomato sauce and rice. For a main dish and appetizer, expect to pay from £7.50 ($11.25). Each day two special dishes are featured, and desserts include pineapple and almond flan and damson crunch. Wine can be had by the glass or the bottle.

Antico, 42 High St. (tel. 07535/63977), is an old building with beams spreading through several rooms. On your way to the tiny bar you cannot help but pass the cold table, displaying a vast array of hors d'oeuvres, fresh fish, and cold meats. Grilled fresh sardines are also a feature. There is a wide choice of fish dishes, such as sole grilled, colbert, or with mushrooms, capers, and prawns. Beef filet is a favorite dish, as is a kidney brochette. Desserts from the trolley are offered. VAT and service are added to all bills. Meals range from £8.50 ($12.75) to £14 ($21). The restaurant is open for lunch daily except Saturday from noon to 2:30 p.m. Dinner is nightly from 7 to 11 p.m. Closed Sunday and holidays.

Eton Buttery, 73 High St. (tel. 07535/54479), is just on the Eton side of the bridge from Windsor, a new building among the boathouses of the college with magnificent views over the river and up toward the town and the castle. Open seven days a week from 9:30 a.m. to 10:30 p.m., it is decorated with plain red brick walls, brown carpets and tables, caneback chairs, and a mass of potted plants. This is an up-market self-service buffet owned by Mrs. Ron Stanton, owner of the House on the Bridge restaurant, opposite.

Food is well displayed along spotless counters. There are waitresses to clear away and to bring you wine and drinks; otherwise, you help yourself to the variety of quiches, cold sliced meats, and specialty salads and pâtés. There is also a hot dish of the day. Expect to spend £2 ($3) to £8 ($12). In the evening, a two-course meal of, say, steak (with salad) and a dessert costs £8.50 ($12.75).

SHOPPING IN WINDSOR: For those who have time to spare, Windsor

offers a great variety of attractive shops for browsing or more serious souvenir hunting.

Scots Corner, High Street (tel. 07535/51695), has Shetland sweaters for £8.95 ($13.43), 100% pure new wool tartan kilts at £18.95 ($28.43), matching tartan scarves at £2.95 ($4.43), men's hand-woven Harris tweed jackets for £54.50 ($81.75), and cashmeres from £39.50 ($59.25).

Woods of Windsor Ltd., at the Castle Perfumers, Queen Charlotte Street (tel. 07535/55777), established in 1770, right beside the Guildhall, is a heady experience where you can buy a scented leaf of paper to slip between your hankies for 50p (75¢) or an elegant potpourri for £12.50 ($18.75). In between are lavender and herb bags from £1.25 ($1.88) to £1.75 ($2.63), and oil to refresh potpourri for £1.75 also.

Opposite, the **Token House** has one of the best selections of china and porcelain of all well-known makes, and farther down the High Street, **Le Sac** has a wide selection of leather goods, handbags, wallets, scarves, and gloves.

A short walk down Peascod Street, opposite the Queen Victoria Statue, brings you to King Edward's Court. On the corner is **Hammick's Books,** 1 King Edward's Court (tel. 07535/56456). Charles Hammick, ex-army, now runs a string of bookshops where you can get the latest paperbacks and guidebooks, maps, and illustrated historical documentation on the town and the country.

At 34 King Edward's Court is **Le Pot,** a paradise of traditional cooking utensils, tableware, herbs, and spices. The large, once-bare shop is stuffed with cooking pots, garlic presses, earthenware casseroles, pepper mills, oven gloves, napkin rings, and egg cups. There is a large selection of kitchen knives, wooden spoons, and a gigantic stirring spoon. I counted 41 different herbs and spices, all small and easy to slip into a pocket, after being paid for, of course. Blue-and-white-striped butchers' aprons are also sold, and there is a mass of basketwork and an excellent selection of cookbooks. Souvenirs can be purchased from under £1 ($1.50), although prices go up to £10 ($15), even £20 ($30). This is the domain and brainchild of Graham Cooper and actor friend Anthony Davidson. They are helped by several young women who are always willing to discuss the merits of various pots and utensils. It's a lovely place in which to buy souvenirs at prices lower than in Central London.

AROUND WINDSOR SIGHTSEEING TOUR: A 35-minute tour of Windsor and the surrounding countryside is offered in an open-top, double-deck bus with commentary. The ten-mile drive starts from Windsor Castle and passes the Royal Mews, the Long Walk, the Royal Farms, Albert Bridge, Eton College, and the Theatre Royal. The departure point is Castle Hill, by the statue of Queen Victoria, starting at noon, with one or more tours an hour until 5 p.m. Adults pay £1.20 ($1.80); children, 80p ($1.20). Tickets and information are available from **Windsorian Coaches,** 17 Alma Rd. (tel. 07535/56841).

GUIDED TOURS: Every day except Sunday a guided tour of Windsor Castle and the town leaves from the **Tourist Information Centre,** (tel. 07535/52010) in the Central Station, the one opposite the castle. The walking tour includes a look at the Long Walk, then the Guildhall and Market Cross House, along with the changing of the guard when possible. In the castle precincts, you'll visit St. George's Chapel, the Cloisters, and the Albert Memorial Chapel, finishing in the State Apartments. Subject to demand, the tour leaves at 10:15 a.m., costing adults £3 ($4.50) and children £1.50 ($2.25) for two hours. There are further departures during the day if demand merits it. All tours are accompanied by a licensed guide and include inside visits where possible. The tour price does not include admission charges.

NEARBY SIGHTS: Two attractions of interest are in the surrounding area.

One of England's Great Gardens

The **Savill Garden,** Wick Lane, Englefield Green (tel. 07535/60222), is in Windsor Great Park and clearly signposted from Windsor, Egham, and Ascot. Started in 1932, the garden is now considered one of the finest of its type in the northern hemisphere. The display starts in spring with rhododendrons, camellias, and daffodils beneath the trees; then throughout the summer there are spectacular displays of flowers and shrubs all skillfully presented in a natural and wild state. It is open all year except at Christmas, from 10 a.m. to 6 or 7 p.m., and the admission is £1.30 ($1.95) for adults; accompanied children under 16 are admitted free. There is also a licensed, self-service restaurant on the premises.

Adjoining the Savill Garden are the **Valley Gardens,** full of shrubs and trees in a series of wooded natural valleys running down to Virginia water. It is open daily, free, throughout the year.

Windsor Safari Park and Seaworld

In the safari craze sweeping the world, even the Royal Borough of Windsor hasn't been spared. The Safari Park and Seaworld, Winkfield Road (tel. 07535/69841), is open just two miles from Windsor Castle on a site 23 miles from London. Take the M4 motorway and leave it at Junction 6. The park is on the B3022 road. There you can watch the performing dolphins and a killer whale, and drive through reserves of lions, tigers, baboons, giraffes, camels, and many other wild animals. It is open from 10 a.m. There are catering facilities, but you can picnic on acres of green. If you have a soft-top car or come on public transport from Windsor, take the safari bus through the reserves. Admission to Safari Park is £3.50 ($5.25) for adults, £3 ($4.50) for children. The dolphin and killer whale show, parrot show, and amusements are free.

THE WELLINGTON DUCAL ESTATE: If you'd like to make an interesting day trip in Berkshire, I'd suggest **Stratfield Saye** (tel. 0256/882882), between the A4 and the A30, just west of the city of Reading. It has been the home of the Duke of Wellington since 1817 when the 17th-century house was bought for the Iron Duke to celebrate his victory over Napoleon at the Battle of Waterloo. Many memories of the first duke remain in the house, including his billiard table, battle spoils, and pictures. Recently, the funeral carriage that since 1860 had rested in St. Paul's Cathedral crypt was added to the ducal collection.

In the gardens is the grave of Copenhagen, the charger ridden to battle at Waterloo by the first duke. The lovely plain stone face of the house looks over a country park, with its lake, woods, and meadows.

There is a fascinating National Dairy Museum, with relics of 150 years of dairying. Other attractions include a riding school, nature trails, boating, and sailing on the lake. On summer weekends a miniature railway goes through the parklands.

The house is open Easter to the end of September from 11:30 a.m. to 5 p.m. daily except Friday. Admission is £2.30 ($3.45) for adults, £1 ($1.50) for children. The country park is open March to October from 10 a.m. to 5 p.m. Adults are charged £1.40 ($2.10); children, 70p ($1.05). A combination ticket for house and estate costs £3.20 ($4.80) for adults, £1.50 ($2.25) for children.

MAPLEDURHAM HOUSE ON THE THAMES: The Elizabethan mansion home of the Blount family lies beside the Thames in the unspoiled village of Mapledurham and can be reached by car from the A4074 Oxford to Reading road. A much more romantic way of reaching the lovely old house is to take the boat that leaves the promenade next to Caversham Bridge at 2:15 p.m. on Saturday, Sunday, and bank holidays from Easter to the end of September.

The journey upstream takes about 40 minutes, and the boat leaves Mapledurham again at 5 p.m. for the journey back to Caversham. This gives you plenty of time to walk through the house and see the Elizabethan ceilings and the great oak staircase, as well as the portraits of the two beautiful sisters with whom the poet Alexander Pope, a frequent visitor here, fell in love. The family chapel, built in 1789, is a fine example of modern Gothic. Cream teas with homemade cakes are available at the house. On the grounds, the last working watermill on the Thames still produces flour.

The house is open from 2:30 to 5 p.m. Saturday, Sunday, and public holidays from Easter to the end of September; the mill, from noon on the same days in summer and on Sunday from 2 to 4 p.m. in winter. Entrance to the house and mill costs £2.10 ($3.15) for adults, £1.10 ($1.65) for children. To the mill only, the charge is 70p ($1.05) for adults, 40p (60¢) for children.

The boat ride from Caversham costs £1.50 ($2.25) for adults, 80p ($1.20) for children. Further details about the boat can be obtained from D.&T. Scenics Ltd., Mapledurham Village, Reading RG4 7TR.

INNS ALONG THE THAMES: For those who want to anchor into riverside villages with old inns along the Thames, I offer the following suggestions for the motorist.

Bray-on-Thames

Twenty-eight miles from London, you come upon this attractive Thameside village, with its beautiful old almshouses, timbered cottages, and small period houses. Windsor Castle is but just a short jaunt away. The town was once famous for its 16th-century "Vicar of Bray" who couldn't make up his mind about his religious or political affiliations.

In what was a traditional English riverside pub on an attractive stretch of the river, the Roux Brothers operate the **Waterside Inn,** Ferry Road, Bray (tel. 0628/20691), known for its impeccable cooking (and also for its astronomical prices). The restaurant has been given almost every superlative in the book. The Roux Brothers were brought up in the Saône et Loire region of France and first started serious cooking at the age of 14. Their father had a charcuterie (delicatessen), and the boys learned the basic skills from him and from their mother. Both went into private service in England and France, working in some of the best-known homes and at embassies. They then opened a London restaurant, Le Gavroche, and later came to the Waterside.

If you select from the à la carte menu, expect to pay around £90 ($135) for two persons, plus wine, if you have been extravagant in your choice of dishes. Actually, you can dine well for about £65 ($97.50) for two, including wine. At lunchtime, you can enjoy the set meal at £20 ($30). Chef Michel Roux has developed some interesting combinations, such as salmon and brill with ginger, a mousse using three different fish, and fileted young rabbit with marrons glacés. Recently, I feasted happily on the mousseline of volaille au roquefort, a cassoulette d'ecrivisses aux tagliatelles with sauce

Nantua, and Harlem sauce Drambuie. Roughly, in English that's a fine game pâté with roquefort cheese, baked crayfish with tagliatelli, and a tasty dessert. The Waterside is open from Tuesday dinner to Sunday lunchtime; closed in January and for the Christmas holiday. Hours for lunch are noon to 2 p.m.; dinner, 7:30 to 10 p.m. Reservations are essential.

If the Waterside is too rich for your pocketbook's blood, you should be well pleased with the following, more modestly priced recommendation.

The **Hinds Head Hotel**, Bray-on-Thames, Berkshire (tel. 0628/26151), lies on the bend of a very busy, narrow road, but there's ample parking in front of the restaurant. Although calling itself a hotel, the Hinds has no rooms to rent. There is a bar and you can take your pint in with you if you wish, as the wine list is expensive. A three-course lunch costs £8.50 ($12.75) and a four-course lunch is £16 ($24), plus VAT and service. A three-course dinner goes for £18 ($27); a four-course dinner, £21 ($31.50). There is a fish course before the roast beef, pork, or lamb, with all the trimmings. Be warned, the friendly waitresses bring around three sorts of potatoes and then about four different green vegetables. A bottle of the house wine is £8.50 ($12.75). Hours are from 12:30 to 2 p.m. and from 7:30 to 10 p.m. This is the sort of place to come to on a nice Sunday for a good old English "blow-out" lunch, £15 ($22.50). The portions are large, and the standard of cuisine pretty high on the plainer dishes.

Henley-on-Thames

At the eastern edge of Oxfordshire, only 35 miles from London, Henley-on-Thames is a small town and resort on the river. At the foothills of the Chilterns, it is the headquarters of the Royal Regatta held annually in July, the Number One event among European oarsmen. The regatta dates back to the first years of the reign of Victoria.

The Elizabethan buildings, the tearooms, and inns along the town's High Street live up to one's conception of what an English country town looks like—or should look like.

The life here is serene, and Henley-on-Thames makes for an excellent stopover en route to Oxford. Warning: During the Royal Regatta, rooms are virtually impossible to get at the fashionable inns of Henley, unless you've made reservations months in advance.

The **Red Lion**, Henley Bridge (tel. Henley-on-Thames 572161), is a former coaching inn, dating from the 16th century. A bedchamber used to be kept ready for the Duke of Marlborough, who would stop over on his way to his palace at Blenheim. The guest list reads like a hall of fame, including such notables as Johnson and Boswell, even George IV who, it is said, downed more than a dozen lamb chops one night. The red brick facade, with its climbing wisteria, remains untouched, but most of the interior has been renovated and modernized. Nowadays, wayfarers enjoy central heating and private baths in most of the rooms, some of which are named after famous personages who have stopped over. The decor in most of the bedrooms has been brightened with contemporary furnishings and color-coordinated pieces. A bathless single costs £24.50 ($36.75), rising to £40 ($60) with bath, and bathless doubles go for £40 ($60), increasing to £50 ($75) with bath, these tariffs including an English breakfast and VAT. Guests congregate in the low-beamed lounge. Opening onto views of the Thames, the Riverside Restaurant is cozy in green and gold. A three-course lunch goes for £6.50 ($9.75). On Saturday night, a pianist plays, and a four-course set meal is priced at £10 ($15). Otherwise, an à la carte dinner will average £12 ($18).

Streatley-on-Thames:

This Thameside village has some old buildings and a fine Priory church. And it has the **Swan Hotel,** Streatley-on-Thames, Berkshire (tel. 0491/873737), a pleasant riverside inn. The hotel Swan has now been much enlarged, but still it retains much of its old charm. It would take a lot to ruin the tranquility and eternity of the River Thames. Gardens slope down to the water, and your hire-cruiser will nestle happily alongside while you have dinner. The menu is unstartling, mainly grills, steaks, roast chicken, and desserts from the trolley. A set luncheon goes for £10 ($15), rising to £11.50 ($17.25) on Sunday. A set dinner costs £12.50 ($18.75).

If you're touring or spending a last night before going to Heathrow Airport, this is a pleasant place to stay. All rooms have private baths, and the prices include VAT and service. Singles rent for £35 ($52.50) and doubles from £45 ($67.50) to £55 ($82.50), which buys you a river room.

EN ROUTE TO OXFORD: Between Henley-on-Thames and Oxford (a 24-mile drive) lies the following recommendation.

The **Swan Inn,** Tetsworth, Oxfordshire (tel. Tetsworth 281), is an old inn that has been in business for at least 700 years. Over the centuries it has been added to, and examples of the various architectural styles can be seen around the house. Elizabeth I and then Queen Victoria stayed here. It is reputed to be haunted and could very well be, as it has had many occupants since the monks who ran the first hostelry left in the 14th century. Singles go for £18 ($27); doubles, from £30 ($45)—including a full breakfast and VAT. Lunch can be ordered for £7.50 ($11.25), and a set dinner begins at £8 ($12), depending on your choice from a selection of well-prepared roasts, grills, and salads. If you're ordering à la carte, expect to pay from £9 ($13.50). The Swan makes an ideal last-night stopover on the way back to Heathrow or for someone leaving the Cotswolds and Oxford and wanting to stop over before plunging into London.

2. Oxford

A walk down the long sweep of The High, one of the most striking streets in England; a mug of cider in one of the old student pubs; the sound of a May Day dawn when choristers sing in Latin from Magdalen Tower; the Great Tom bell from Tom Tower, whose 101 peals traditionally signal the closing of the college gates; towers and spires rising majestically; the barges on the upper reaches of the Thames; nude swimming at Parson's Pleasure; the roar of a cannon launching the bumping races; a tiny, dusty bookstall where you can pick up a valuable first edition. All that is Oxford—57 miles from London and home of one of the greatest universities in the world. An industrial city, the center of a large automobile business, as well as a university town, Oxford is better for sightseeing in summer. The students are wherever Oxford scholars go in the summer (allegedly they study more than they do at term time), and the many bed-and-breakfast houses—vacated by their gown-wearing boarders—will be happy to offer you an accommodation. But you'll be missing a great deal if you view Oxford without glimpsing its life blood.

However, at any time of the year you can enjoy a tour of the colleges,

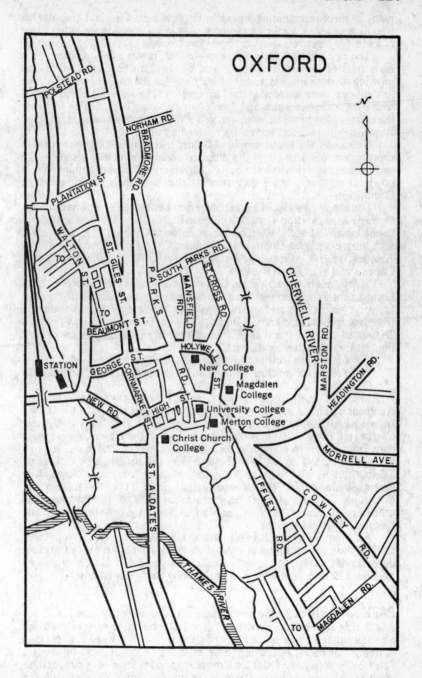

OXFORD

many of them representing a peak in England's architectural kingdom, as well as a valley of Victorian eyesores. Just don't mention the other place (Cambridge) and you shouldn't have any trouble.

The city predates the university—in fact, it was a Saxon town in the early part of the tenth century. And by the 12th century, Oxford was growing in reputation as a seat of learning—at the expense of Paris. The first colleges were founded in the 13th century. The story of Oxford is filled with conflicts too complex and detailed to elaborate here. Suffice it to say, the relationship between town and gown wasn't as peaceful as it is today. Riots often flared, and both sides were guilty of abuses.

Nowadays, the young people of Oxford take out their aggressiveness in sporting competitions, with the different colleges zealously competing in such games as cricket and soccer. However, all colleges unite into a powerful university when they face matches with their traditional rival, Cambridge.

Ultimately, the test of a great university lies in the persons it turns out. Oxford can name-drop a mouthful: Roger Bacon, Samuel Johnson, William Penn, John Wesley, Sir Walter Raleigh, Edward Gibbon, T. E. Lawrence, Sir Christopher Wren, John Donne, William Pitt, Matthew Arnold, Arnold Toynbee, Harold Macmillan, Graham Greene, A. E. Housman, Lewis Carroll, and even Dean Rusk.

Many Americans arriving in Oxford ask, "Where's the campus?" If an Oxonian shows amusement when answering, it's understandable. Oxford University is, in fact, made up of 28 colleges, including five just for women (scholars in skirts in years past staged, and won, the battle for equal rights). To tour all of these would be a formidable task. Besides, a few are of such interest they overshadow the rest.

For a bird's-eye view of the city and the colleges, climb Carfax Tower. This is the one with the clock and figures that strike the hours. Admission is 35p (53¢) for adults, 10p (15¢) for children.

In season (from Easter through October), the best way to get a running commentary on the important sightseeing attractions is to go to the **Oxford Information Centre,** St. Aldate's Street, opposite the Town Hall, near Carfax (tel. 0865/726871). Walking tours through the major colleges leave daily from Easter to mid-November at 10:45 a.m. and 2:15 p.m., last two hours, and cost £1.25 ($1.88). The tour does not include New College or Christ Church, which charge 50p (75¢). Minibus tours are offered daily except Sunday for £2 ($3) to see Oxford and £7 ($10.50) to tour the Cotswolds. You can also get reservations for the Oxford Playhouse and other entertainment facilities, as well as for Stratford-upon-Avon and London West End theaters.

At **Punt Station,** Cherwell Boathouse, Bardwell Road (tel. 0865/55978), you can rent a punt at a cost of £3 ($4.50) per hour, plus a £20 ($30) deposit which must be posted. Similar charges are made on rentals at Magdalen Bridge Boathouse and at the Folly Bridge Boathouse.

PARK AND RIDE: Traffic and parking are a disaster in Oxford, and not just during rush hours. However, there are three large car parks on the north, south, and west of the city's ring road, all well marked. Car parking is free at all times, but at any time from 9:30 a.m. on, and all day on Saturday, you pay 40p (60¢) for a round-trip bus ride into the city, getting off at St. Aldates or Queen Street to see the city center. On weekdays the fare is 50p (75¢) before 9:30 a.m. There is no service on Sunday, but then there's no need for it. The buses run every eight to ten minutes in each direction. The car parks are on the Woodstock road near the Peartree roundabout, on the Botley road toward Faringdon, and on the Abingdon road in the southeast.

WHAT TO SEE: Of the many well-known buildings in Oxford—Radcliffe Camera, whose dome competes in a city of spires; Sheldonian Theatre, an early work of Wren's; the Bodleian Library, one of the most important in the world—I have narrowed down the sights to a representative list of a few colleges.

A Word of Warning

The main business of a university, is, of course, to educate—and unfortunately this function at Oxford has been severely interfered with by the number of visitors who have been disturbing the academic work of the university. So, with deep regret, visiting is now restricted to certain hours and small groups of six or fewer. In addition, there are areas where visitors are not allowed at all, but your tourist office will be happy to advise you when and where you may "take in" the sights of this great institution.

Christ Church

Begun by Cardinal Wolsey as Cardinal College in 1525, Christ Church, known as The House, was founded by Henry VIII in 1546. Facing St. Aldate's Street, Christ Church has the largest quadrangle of any college in Oxford.

Tom Tower houses Great Tom, the 18,000-pound bell referred to earlier. It rings at 9:05 nightly, signaling the closing of the college gates. The 101 times it peals originally signified the number of students at the time of the founding of the college. The student body number changed, but Oxford traditions live on forever.

In the 16th-century Great Hall, with its hammer-beam ceiling, are some interesting portraits, including works by those old reliables, Gainsborough and Reynolds. Prime ministers are pictured, as Christ Church was the training ground for 13 prime ministers: men such as Gladstone and George Canning. There is a separate picture gallery.

The cathedral, dating from the 12th century, was built over a period of centuries. (Incidentally, it is not only the college chapel, but the cathedral of the diocese of Oxford.) The cathedral's most distinguishing features are its Norman pillars and the vaulting of the choir, dating from the 15th century. In the center of the Great Quadrangle is a statue of Mercury mounted in the center of a fish pond. The college and cathedral can be visited between 9:30 a.m. and noon and from 2 to 4:30 p.m. Entrance fee is 70p ($1.05).

Magdalen College

Pronounced "maud-len," this college was founded in 1458 by William of Waynflete, bishop of Winchester and later chancellor of England. Its alumni range all the way from Wolsey to Wilde. Opposite the botanic garden, the oldest in England, is the bell tower, where the choristers sing in Latin at dawn on May Day. The reflection of the 15th-century tower is cast in the waters of the Cherwell below. On a not-so-happy day, Charles I—his

days numbered—watched the oncoming Roundheads. But the most celebrated incident in Magdalen's history was when some brave Fellows defied
James II. Visit the 15th-century chapel, in spite of many of its latter-day
trappings. The hall and other places of special interest are open when
possible.

A favorite pastime is to take Addison's Walk through the water
meadows. The stroll is so named after a former alumnus, Joseph Addison,
the 18th-century writer and poet noted for his contributions to *The
Spectator* and *The Tatler*. The grounds of Magdalen are the most extensive
of any Oxford college, even containing a deer park. You can visit Magdalen
each day from 2 to 6:15 p.m.

Merton College

Founded in 1264, this college is among the trio of the most ancient at
the university. It stands near Corpus Christi College on Merton Street, the
sole survivor of Oxford's medieval cobbled streets. Merton College (tel.
0865/49651) is noted for its library, said to be the oldest in England, having
been built between 1371 and 1379. In keeping with tradition, some of its
most valuable books were chained. Now only one book is so secured, to
show what the custom was like. One of the treasures of the library is an
astrolabe (astronomical instrument used for measuring the altitude of the
sun and stars), thought to have belonged to Chaucer. You pay only 30p
(45¢) to visit the ancient library, as well as the Max Beerbohm Room (the
satirical English caricaturist who died in 1956). Both are open from 2 to 4
p.m. (4:30 p.m. March to October) on weekdays, and, in addition, the
college is open from 10 a.m. to noon on Saturday and Sunday only. You can
also visit the chapel, dating from the 13th century, at these times.

University College

On The High, University College is the oldest one found at Oxford,
tracing its history back to 1249 when money was donated by an ecclesiastic
called William of Durham. More fanciful is the old claim that the real
founder was Alfred the Great. Don't jump to any conclusions about the age
of the buildings when you see the present Gothic-esque look. The original
structures have all disappeared, and what remains today represents essentially the architecture of the 17th century, with subsequent additions in
Victoria's day, as well as in more recent times. For example, the Goodhart
Quadrangle was added as late as 1962. Its most famous alumnus, Shelley,
was "sent down" for his part in collaborating on a pamphlet on atheism.
However, all is forgiven today, as the romantic poet is honored by a
memorial erected in 1894. The hall and chapel of the University College can
be visited during vacations from 10 a.m. to noon and from 2 to 4 p.m.
(otherwise, from 2 to 4 p.m.).

New College

New College was founded in 1379 by William of Wykeham, bishop of
Winchester and later lord chancellor of England. The college at Winchester
supplied a constant stream of candidates. The first quadrangle, dating from
before the end of the 14th century, was the initial quadrangle to be built in
Oxford, forming the architectural design for the other colleges. In the
ante-chapel is Sir Jacob Epstein's remarkable modern sculpture of *Lazarus*,
and a fine El Greco painting of St. James. One of the treasures of the

college is a crosier (pastoral staff of a bishop) belonging to the founding father. In the garden you can see the remains of the old city wall and the mound. The college (entered at New College Lane) can be visited from 2 to 5 p.m. weekdays at term time (otherwise, from 11 a.m. to 6 p.m.). On weekends, it is open from noon to 6 p.m.

The **Oxford Union**, St. Michael Street (tel. 0865/56747), is the oldest debating club in the world. Many of Britain's leaders past and present gained invaluable experience in public speaking and in being heckled here. Although it is not normally open to the public, the union now offers a video presentation, "Inside Oxford," an intimate exposé of university life and customs. You are invited to the colorful ceremonies of the academic year and initiated into the mysteries of the university's system of teaching, take part in a summer ball at Oriel College, and go punting on the Cherwell. Lord Wilson, a former prime minister, talks about his Oxford student days, and Jeremy Thorpe describes the Oxford Union Society of which he was president. Entrance is £1 ($1.50). Refreshments are available throughout the day, and a licensed bar is open at lunchtime.

WHERE TO STAY: The accommodations in Oxford are limited, although the addition of motels on the outskirts has aided the plight of those who require modern amenities. Recently, some of the more stalwart candidates in the city center have been refurbished as well. In addition, motorists may want to consider two grand old country houses on the outskirts, which offer the best living in Oxford if you don't mind commuting.

When the tourist rush is on, why tire yourself further? The **Oxford Association of Hotels and Guest Houses** has provided an efficient accommodation secretary, Mr. J. O'Kane, who also operates the Earlmount Guest House at 322/4 Cowley Rd. (tel. 0865/240236). If Mr. O'Kane cannot accommodate you himself, he will spare no effort in helping you to find the kind of accommodation you require. Advance single or party bookings can also be made, long or short term. No fees are charged. B&B prices begin at £10 ($15) per person.

The **Oxford Information Centre** (tel. 0865/726871) operates a room-booking service for personal callers for a fee of £1 ($1.50) all year. If you'd like to seek out lodgings on your own, the staff at the center will provide a list of accommodations, or you may try one of the following recommendations:

The Upper Bracket

Randolph Hotel, Beaumont Street (tel. 0865/240236), is a recently refurbished Gothic-Victorian monument, dating back to 1864. For more than a century it has been Oxford's prestige hotel, centrally situated and commanding an impressive vantage point overlooking St. Giles, the Ashmolean Museum, and the Cornmarket. The lounges, although modernized, are still cavernous enough for dozens of separate conversational groupings; and the furnishings are bright and contemporary. Run as a member of Trusthouse Forte Ltd., the hotel contains 111 rooms, all with private bath, telephone, radio, and color TV. The price for a single is from £42 ($63), from £54 ($81) for a double. The Randolph Restaurant boasts a high standard of cuisine, and specializes in flambé dishes. The average price for a meal is £15 ($22.50), plus wine, and a wide selection of wines is available. The restaurant is open from 12:30 to 2:30 p.m. and from 7 to 9:45

p.m. Service charge and VAT are included in the tariffs. There is also a popular coffeeshop with an entrance off the street.

The Medium-Priced Range

The **TraveLodge,** Peartree Roundabout, Woodstock Road (tel. 0865/54301), is ideal for motorists who want to be within easy reach of the university and shopping districts of Oxford, yet set apart at the city edge for a quiet night's sleep. Easy to spot, near a large bus stop, the lodge invites with international flags fluttering in the breezes. Its lower-level bedrooms open onto private terraces. The furnishings are in the typical motel style, with compact, built-in necessities. Each of the rooms has a picture-window wall, a private bath with shower, a television and radio, individually controlled heating and tea-making facilities. Room rates in a single are £32 ($48), £44 ($66) for a double. A twin or double and a single combined costs £46 ($69); a double and two singles, £48 ($72). In the Autogrill (open at 7:30 a.m.), you can order an English breakfast. Otherwise, a continental breakfast is included in the room rates, as are service and VAT. On the grounds are a swimming pool, the fully licensed Blenheim Bar, a 24-hour cafeteria, and a garage. It's two miles from the city center.

The **Oxford Moat House,** Godstow Road, Wolvercote Roundabout (tel. 0865/59933), one of the Queens Moat Houses Group, incorporates the principles of advanced motel design, with an emphasis on spacious, glassed-in areas and streamlined bedrooms. Its position is ideal, hidden from the traffic at the northern edge of Oxford, two miles away, at the junction of the A40 and the A34. Although generally patronized by motorists, it can also be reached by bus. In a double or twin, with a full breakfast, you pay £48 ($72) for two, £34 ($51) in a single. On the second floor is a restaurant, and there are drinking bars as well, with traditional entertainment on most nights.

Eastgate Hotel, Merton Street, off The High (tel. 0865/248244), is a hotel of character, exquisitely placed opposite Merton College and on The High. It's smallish—in fact, it is a group of older buildings joined together and modernized. The bedrooms, all with baths, are clean-cut, borrowing their inspiration from the compact, serviceable designs of Scandinavia. Singles cost £44 ($66); doubles or twins, £52 ($78). All units have color TV sets, and tariffs quoted include a full English breakfast, VAT, and service. The lounge opening onto The High is pleasantly furnished; the dining room is airy and comfortable. A set Sunday lunch is offered for £7.50 ($11.25). Otherwise, a three-course à la carte meal averages about £12 ($18).

Royal Oxford Hotel, Park End Street (tel. 0865/248432), is an oldish establishment given a new lease on life by a drastic renovation of its interior. Near Oxford Station, about a ten-minute walk from the center of the city, it is a comfortable and convenient place at which to stay. Of its 25 bedrooms, 12 have private baths, and all have color TV, phone, and radio. A bathless single goes for £20.50 ($30.75); with bath, £30 ($45). A bathless twin or double rents for £32 ($48), increasing to £36 ($54) with bath. Triples are priced at £50 ($75). Prices include service and VAT. The bedrooms are well kept, with modern, compact furnishings, and all have television.

The Budget Range

The **Old Parsonage Hotel,** 3 Banbury Rd. (tel. 0865/54843), is so old it looks like an extension of one of the ancient colleges. Originally a

13th-century hospital named Bethleen, it was restored in the early 17th century. Today, it's slated for designation as an ancient monument. Near St. Giles Church, it is set back from the street behind a low stone wall and sheltered by surrounding trees and shrubbery. However, most of the rooms are in a modern wing that is more institutional in character. The owners charge from £18 ($27) per person nightly for bed and breakfast in a single, from £31 ($46.50) in a twin or double. Should you want a private shower, the price is increased to £35 ($52.50) for two persons. Twenty rooms have been added to the accommodations. Some of the large front rooms, with leaded-glass windows, are set aside for travelers. Many rooms are big enough to have a living-room area, armchairs, antique chests, and soft beds. You have breakfast in a pleasant Swedish-style dining room, overlooking the garden. A licensed restaurant and bar are on the premises.

Ascot Guest House, 283 Iffley Rd. (tel. 0865/240259), is ideally located in the quiet outskirts of Oxford, yet only minutes away by bus or car from the city center. The owner, Mrs. Elizabeth Neville, has performed the difficult task of combining friendliness, high standards, and reasonable prices in her recently refurbished home. All rooms have wall-to-wall carpeting, telephones, and hot and cold running water. The per-person charge of £8.50 ($12.75) per night includes breakfast and VAT. Parking facilities are plentiful here, and it's usually less expensive and more convenient to leave your car at the guest house and take the frequent buses into the city. When Mrs. Neville is unable to accommodate any more guests, she will cheerfully recommend other guest houses in the area.

Belmont Guest House, 182 Woodstock Rd. (tel. 0865/53698), is on a tree-lined avenue in the residential part of Oxford, about one mile from the city center. It's on the main road and close to Blenheim Palace, Stratford-upon-Avon, the Midlands, and the Lake District. All rooms have central heating and hot and cold running water. A few have private showers. Most rooms can be used as either doubles, twins, or family rooms. The charge is from £10 ($15) per person for B&B.

LIVING ON THE OUTSKIRTS: Weston Manor, Weston-on-the-Green

(tel. 0869/50621), is a moated stone manor house, only eight miles from Oxford (on the A43 Oxford–Northampton road)—ideal as a center for touring the district (Blenheim Palace is only five miles away). The manor, owned and run by the Price family, is rooted in the 11th century; portions of the present building date back to the 14th and 16th centuries, with later additions in Victoria's day. Although long owned by noblemen, the estate was an abbey until they were abolished by Henry VIII. Of course, there are ghosts, such as Mad Maude, the naughty nun who was burned at the stake for her "indecent and immoral" behavior. She returns to haunt the Oak Bedrooms. Prince Rupert, son of Charles II, hid from Cromwell's soldiers in one of the fireplaces, eventually escaping in drag as the "maiden of the milk bucket."

As you enter the driveway, you pass two elm trees, dating back to 1672, and proceed into a formal car-park area. The reception lounge is furnished with antiques, dominated by a Tudor fireplace and a long refectory table, the latter glowing from centuries of polishing. The various lounges have fine old pieces. Most of the bedrooms are spacious, furnished with antiques (often four-posters), old dressing tables, and chests. The cost of staying here is from £44 ($66) in a single, from £52 ($78) to £72 ($108) in a double. All these tariffs include a continental breakfast, VAT, and service. Breakfast is served in the yellow morning room, with your table set in front of the stone-mullioned and leaded windows. The view is of the formal garden, edged with animal and bird figures trimmed out of the old yew hedges.

In the Great Hall, one of the most beautiful dining rooms in England, you'll be served your lunch and dinner. It's like a chapel, with an open raftered and beamed ceiling, the lower portion solidly paneled with a rare example of linenfold. There's a minstrels' gallery and a large wrought-iron chandelier. The food is first rate. On any given dinner menu, you're likely to find roast Aylesbury duckling, spring chicken, sirloin steak, Scottish salmon, or rainbow trout. À la carte meals average £14 ($21), and the big Sunday lunch costs £13.50 ($20.25). In warm weather, you can enjoy the open-air swimming pool, surrounded by its gardens.

Studley Priory Hotel, Horton-cum-Studley (tel. Stanton St. John 203), may be remembered by those who saw *A Man for All Seasons*. The former Benedictine priory, now a hotel, was used for background shots for the private residence of Sir Thomas More. It is a stunning example of Elizabethan architecture, although it originally dates from the 12th century. Lived in for around 300 years by the Croke family, it is now managed by Jeremy Parke, who receives guests for £42 ($63) in a single, from £45 ($67.50) to £85 ($127.50) in a double. All of the rooms have private baths.

Only seven miles from Oxford, the manor is protected from noise by its gardens and lawns. Stone built, in the manorial style with large halls and long bedroom wings, Studley is gabled with mullioned windows. The rooms are large, the beds soft, and the furnishings tasteful. Even if you're not staying over, you may want to drop in for lunch or dinner, with a four-course meal averaging around £18 ($27). Getting here is a bit complicated—so be armed with a good map when you strike out from Oxford.

WHERE TO EAT: Restaurant Elizabeth, 84 St. Aldate's (tel. 0865/242230), is an intimate and special restaurant that (in spite of its name) owes the inspiration of its cuisine to the continent, notably Spain, France, and Greece. Under the watchful eye of Antonio Lopez, it attracts Oxonians who appreciate good food served in a friendly, inviting atmosphere. For appetizers, try either the ttoro (a Basque fish soup served with aïoli), or avgolemono (the Greek national soup—chicken bouillon laced with a beaten egg and lemon juice). Favorite main dishes that I highly recommend include delicate quenelles, trout stuffed with sea food mousse, charcoaled prawns with aïoli, and coq au vin. For dessert, the syllabub is a winner. Including wine and coffee, plus all the extras, the cost of a dinner is about £25 ($37.50) per person. Wine by the liter, both bourgogne and bordeaux, is available. The restaurant is open for dinner from 6:30 to 11 p.m. every day, except Monday. Sunday lunch is from 12:30 to 2:30 p.m. and dinner from 7 to 10:30 p.m.

La Sorbonne, 130A The High (tel. 0865/241320), in a 17th-century building, is tucked away on a narrow lane off The High. True to its name, it provides typically French meals from time-tested recipes. A good beginning is the chef's special, moules marinières, offered from October to March only. An alternative suggestion is escargots bourguignonnes or perhaps a fresh herb and vegetable soup. Mr. Chavagnon, the chef de cuisine and proprietor, offers not only the usual French dishes, but the following specialties as well: jugged hare, wild duck, and suprême de volaille estragon. A soufflé for two is a specialty. Mr. Chavagnon says: "We charge a lot for soufflés because they require a lot of care and attention. When we tried to charge less, everybody wanted one and we couldn't cope." Expect to pay, on an average, about £20 ($30) per head. The restaurant is open from noon to 2:30 p.m. and from 7 to 11 p.m. seven days a week.

The **Cherwell Boathouse Restaurant,** Bardwell Road (tel. 0865/52746), is owned by the people who rent out the punts, and it's run by a committee of cheerful enthusiasts who cater to impoverished undergraduates. The menu contains varied items (Patrick's pancake parcels, for example). Two fixed menus that are rarely repeated are offered at each meal, and the cooks are trying out new dishes all the time. Appetizers include soups or fish or meat pâtés, followed by casseroles, pies, and hot pots, then some exotic dessert—cikolatak pasta, rum soufflé, or fruit fool.

There is an extensive wine list, including brandy after dinner. The restaurant is open every evening from 8 to 10:30 p.m. and for Sunday lunch. For a regular dinner, the charge is £10 ($15), although Sunday lunch is only £9.50 ($14.25), including VAT. It's recommended that you make a reservation. Children, if they don't order a full meal, are granted half price. In summer the restaurant also does an all-day cold buffet in the Marquee for thirsty punters. This place surely must be one of the most English, most attractive, and least known of the eating establishments of Oxford. It also provides an opportunity to observe a most important aspect of Oxford undergraduate life.

Saraceno, Magdalen Street (tel. 0865/249171), is rather unobtrusive, hidden around the corner from the Randolph Hotel and opposite St. Mary Magdalen Church. It's in the basement so only the door and a small sign announce its presence. The kitchen is separated from the dining room by vast red glass panes, behind which a puppet show of figures dance and weave among the pots and pans.

Saraceno is, after all, an Italian restaurant, and all the usual pasta dishes are available with just the right sauces. After ordering one, you might settle later for scaloppine with sage and olives, baron of lamb with marsala, Dover sole Colbert, or rainbow trout with almonds. Appetizers include scrambled eggs with caviar, smoked mackerel, and prosciutto with melon. They have a very special dish of quail served in a rich wine sauce with plain cooked vegetables or salad. With ample portions of the Italian house wine, a meal will cost about £14 ($21) per person, including a creamy dessert from the trolley, perhaps a syllabub or Bavarian cream with liqueur.

Bevers Wholefood Restaurant, 36 St. Michael's St. (tel. 0865/724241), declares that everything is homemade with "free range" eggs, stone-ground flour, home-cured ham, honey from honey-fed bees, scrumpy cider from unsprayed apples, and meat from their own farm. It is a small street shop with lots of small tables and chairs, noisy with chatter and laughter. The clientele includes undergraduates and local business persons. A window door allows you to see the kitchen where the food is prepared. If you don't want to eat here, why not take away the ingredients for a tasty picnic?

THE SPECIAL PUBS OF OXFORD: The **Bear Inn,** Alfred Street, is an

Oxford tradition, a short block from The High overlooking the north side of Christ Church College. It's the village pub. Its swinging inn sign depicts the bear and ragged staff, old insignia of the Earls of Warwick, who were among the early patrons. Built in the 13th century, the inn has been known to many famous people who have lived and studied at Oxford. Over the years, it's been mentioned time and time again in English literature.

The Bear has served a useful purpose in breaking down social barriers, bringing a wide variety of people together in a relaxed and friendly way. You might talk with a rajah from India, a university don, a titled gentleman—and Dave and Des Beeson, who are the latest in a line of owners that goes back more than 700 years.

They may explain to you their astonishing hobby: collecting ties! Around the lounge bar you'll see thousands of snipped portions of neckties, which have been labeled with their owners' names. For those of you who want to leave a bit of yourself, a thin strip of the bottom of your tie will be cut off (with your permission, of course) with a huge pair of ceremonial scissors. Then you, as the donor, will be given a free drink on the house. After this initiation, you may want to join in some of the informal songfests of the undergraduates.

The shelves behind the bar are stacked and piled with delicious items to nibble on: cheese, crisp rolls, cold meats, flans. Homemade pie with french fries and beans cost £2 ($3); a ploughman's lunch, £1.50 ($2.25); and many salads are offered, from £1.80 ($2.70).

The **Trout Inn**, 195 Godstow Rd., near Wolvercote (tel. 0865/54485), lies on the outskirts of Oxford. Ask any former or present student of Oxford to name his most treasured pub, and his answer is likely to be the Trout. Hidden away from visitors and townspeople, the Trout is a private world where you can get ale and beer—and top-notch meals. Have your drink in one of the historic rooms, with their settles, brass, and old prints, or go out in sunny weather to sit on a stone wall, where you can feed crumbs to the swans that swim in the adjoining weir pool. Take an arched stone bridge, stone terraces, architecture that has wildly pitched roofs and gables, throw in the Thames River, and you have the Trout. If you don't have a car, take bus 520 or 521 to Wolvercote, then walk.

Daily specials are featured for lunch. The seafood platter's popular, as is a tempting seven-ounce entrecôte. For dessert, try the fruit tart with cream. The pub is open from noon to 2 p.m. and from 7 to 10 p.m. Salads are served during the summer and grills in winter. Expect to pay about £10 ($15) for a meal, unless you settle for just a plate of smoked trout or salmon with brown bread and butter. If so, you're likely to pay £4 ($6).

On your way there and back, look for the view of Oxford from the bridge. And go ahead and talk with the undergraduates, who usually like telling about their university. They may even ask you to have tea at one of their colleges, where the average visitor rarely penetrates.

EATING AND DRINKING NEAR OXFORD: White Hart, Fyfield, seven miles along the A420 Oxford/Swindon/West Country road (tel. Frilford Heath 390585), is high on the list of Oxford students who want to celebrate by taking their friends to a romantic inn—once the Fyfield Chantry—for a superb dinner. It's a public house, dating from the early 15th century, and owned since 1580 by St. John's College (although the present building is leased). In the 1960s the college renovated the inn, successfully restoring its old-world charm. It was once the home of a chantry priest and five almsmen until it was dissolved under Henry VIII. What was the lower chamber for the priest has now been transformed into a raftered dining room; and the ancient kitchen is the beamed lounge bar. The menu consists of house specialties, plus the dishes of the day. At lunchtime and in the evening, a wide range of bar snacks is offered, costing from £2 ($3) to £5 ($7.50), VAT included. An à la carte menu has dishes ranging in price from £7 ($10.50) to £12 ($18). The wines, an excellent selection, are extra. Specialties of the White Hart include traditional English food, with emphasis on game. The restaurant is open daily, and reservations are advised.

BLENHEIM PALACE: This extravagant baroque palace regards itself as England's answer to Versailles. Blenheim is the home of the 11th Duke of Marlborough, a descendant of the first Duke of Marlborough (John Churchill), an on-again, off-again favorite of Queen Anne's. In his day (1650–1722), the first duke became the supreme military figure in Europe. Fighting on the Danube near a village named Blenheim, Churchill defeated the forces of Louis XIV. The lavish palace of Blenheim was built for the duke as a gift from the queen. It was designed by Sir John Vanbrugh, who was also the architect of Castle Howard. Landscaping was carried out by Capability Brown.

The palace is loaded with riches: antiques, porcelain, oil paintings, tapestries, and chinoiserie. But more North Americans know Blenheim as the birthplace of Sir Winston Churchill. His birthroom forms part of the palace tour, as does the Churchill exhibition, four rooms of letters, books, photographs, and other Churchilliana. Today, the former prime minister lies buried in Bladon Churchyard, near the palace.

Blenheim Palace is open every day from mid-March to October, inclusive, from 11 a.m. to 6 p.m. The last admittance to the palace is at 5 p.m. On spring bank holidays, Sunday, and Monday, charity events take place in the park, when different prices and times apply. The admission fee is £2.70 ($4.05) for adults, £1.30 ($1.95) for children.

In the park is the Bleinheim Model Railway, second-largest in Britain, which you can usually ride on weekends in season. The palace is at Woodstock, eight miles north of Oxford on the A34 road to Stratford-upon-Avon. From Oxford, do-it-your-selfers take bus 44 from the Gloucester Green Bus Station, which makes the run to Woodstock. For information, telephone 0993/811325.

3. Hertfordshire

Like a giant jellyfish, the frontier of Greater London spills over into this county, once described by Charles Lamb as "hearty, homely, loving Hertfordshire." This fertile land lies northwest of London and supplies much of that city's food, although industry has crept in. Hertfordshire is sometimes called "the market basket of England."

Its most important tourist attraction, which is usually visited on a day trip from London, is:

HATFIELD HOUSE: One of the chief attractions of Hertfordshire, and one of the greatest of all English country houses, Hatfield House is just 21 miles north of London on the A1. To build what is now the E-shaped Hatfield House, the old Tudor palace at Hatfield was mostly demolished. The Banqueting Hall, however, remains.

Hatfield was much a part of the lives of both Henry VIII and his daughter Elizabeth I. In the old palace, built in the 15th century, Elizabeth romped and played as a child. Although Henry was married to her mother,

Anne Boleyn, at the time of Elizabeth's birth, the marriage was later nullified (Anne lost her head and Elizabeth her legitimacy). Henry also used to stash away his oldest daughter, Mary Tudor, at Hatfield. But when Mary became Queen of England, and set about earning the dubious distinction of "Bloody Mary," she found Elizabeth a problem. For a while she kept her in the Tower of London, but she eventually let her return to Hatfield (Elizabeth's loyalty to Catholicism was seriously doubted). In 1558, while at Hatfield, Elizabeth learned of her ascension to the throne of England.

The Jacobean house that exists today contains much antique furniture, tapestries, and paintings as well as three much-reproduced portraits, including the ermine and rainbow portraits of Elizabeth I. The Great Hall is suitably medieval, complete with a minstrel's gallery. One of the rarest exhibits is a pair of silk stockings, said to have been worn by Elizabeth herself, the first lady in England to don such apparel. The park and the gardens are also worth exploring. The Riding School and Palace Stables contain an interesting vehicle exhibition and the National (North) Collection of Model Soldiers.

Hatfield is usually open from March 25 through October 7 daily, except on Monday and Good Friday, from noon to 5 p.m. (on Sunday, from 2 to 5:30 p.m., and on bank holiday Mondays from 11 a.m. to 5 p.m.). Admission is £2.35 ($3.53). The house is across from the station in Hatfield. From London, take Green Line coach 724 or 732, or the fast trains from King's Cross. Luncheons and teas are available in the converted coach house in the Old Palace yard.

Elizabethan banquets are staged Tuesday, Thursday, Friday, and Saturday, with much gaiety and music. Guests are invited to drink in an anteroom, then join the long tables for a feast consisting of typical English food, ending with the classic syllabub. Wine is included in the cost of the meal, but you're expected to pay for your predinner drinks yourself. The best way to get there from London is to book a coach tour for an inclusive fee of £20 ($30) on Tuesday and Thursday, £22 ($33) on Friday, and £23 ($34.50) on Saturday. The Evan Evans agency has tours leaving from Russell Square or even from 41 Tottenham Court Rd. The coach returns to London after midnight. If you get there under your own steam, the cost is £18 ($27) on Tuesday and Thursday, £19.50 ($29.25) on Friday and Saturday. For reservations, telephone Hatfield 62055.

In Old Hatfield, a fine place for light lunches and good lager is Eight Bells, a pub on Park Street. For Dickens fans, it was the inn where Bill Sikes and his dog found temporary refuge after the brutal murder of Nancy. It's a rickety old corner inn with a central bar for drinks and dining nooks—in all, a forest of time-blackened beams, settles, and pewter tankards. A bowl of homemade soup costs 45p (68¢), and the cook's specialty is smoked mackerel filet at £1.75 ($2.63).

HERTFORD: This old Saxon city is the county town, containing many fine examples of domestic architecture, some of which date back to the 16th century. Hertford is reached via the A1 or A10 from London. Samuel Stone, founder of Hartford, Connecticut, was born here. The town's Norman castle has long been in ruins, although part of the still-standing keep dates from the 16th century.

For food and lodgings, try the **Salisbury Arms Hotel**, Fore Street (tel. 0992/53091), which has been called "always Hertford's principal inn." For

400 years it's been feeding and providing lodgings to wayfarers, or giving a hot grog to the coachman, a stable for his horses. Although the stables have long given way to a car park, a sense of history still prevails. In the cellar is medieval masonry predating the 16th-century structure around it. Cromwell is said to have lodged here, and both Royalists and Roundheads have mounted the Jacobean staircase. Bedrooms now spill over into a modern extension, a total of 22 functionally furnished rooms added to the 10 more antiquated original ones. Rates depend on the room occupied—single, double, or twin. Singles start at £19 ($28.50), going up to £21.50 ($32.25) for those requiring a private bath. Two persons pay from £28 ($42) to £34 ($51). Good, wholesome English "fayre" is provided. When most visitors stop by, a cut from the roast of the day goes for £7.50 ($11.25) with vegetables. The dining room is paneled and intimately partitioned. There is, as well, a well-stocked cellar. Dinners are from £5 ($7.50).

The **Marquee Restaurant,** 1 Bircherly Green (tel. 0992/5899), a recently opened establishment in historic Hertford, midway between London and Cambridge, has been called by Miss Barbara Cartland, the world's top-selling romantic novelist, "a perfect place to take someone you love." Norman Swallow, artist turned restaurateur, has created spectacular surroundings in which to serve excellent food, backed by a cellar of more than 300 wines. Exquisitely decorated with masses of fresh flowers, the restaurant has two dining rooms. The downstairs is opulent, with deep-pink and gray fabric walls, 18th-century chandeliers, and lamplit tables. Upstairs, there's a different mood, with sumptuous, glowing orange curtained walls and a center pleated ceiling, giving a rich, luxurious feel. The fabrics were created for Swallow by Michael Szell, designer and supplier to H.M. the Queen.

Specializing in classical English as well as international cuisine, the chef, Ernst Stark, formerly of Waltons in London, presents his dishes with care and originality. You might feast on brandade of pink river trout (choux swans filled with a delicate trout mousse) or a rack of Southdown lamb in pastry (the rack topped with a puree of mangetout and onion and wrapped in thin strudel pastry). For dessert, try burnt cream, made by the old Trinity College recipe, or moneybags of apple and pear, wafer-thin pancakes filled with fruit and flamed in Calvados. A typical meal for two, including wine, costs about £40 ($60). The Marquee is open for lunch and dinner every day except Good Friday and Christmas Day.

ST. ALBANS:
ST. ALBANS: This cathedral city, just 21 miles northeast of London, dates back 2000 years. It was named after a Roman soldier, the first Christian martyr in England. Don't ask a resident to show you to the **Cathedral of St. Albans.** Here it's still known as "The Abbey," even though Henry VIII dissolved it as such in 1539. Construction on the cathedral was launched in 1077, making it one of the early Norman churches of England. The bricks, especially visible in the tower, came from the old Roman city of Verulamium at the foot of the hill. The nave and west front date from 1235.

The new Chapter House, the first modern building beside a great medieval cathedral in the country, which also serves as a pilgrim/visitor center, was opened by the Queen in 1982.

The **Verulamium Museum** at St. Michael's stands on the site of the Roman city. Here you'll view some of the finest Roman mosaics in Britain. Part of the Roman town wall, a hypocaust, and a theater and its adjoining houses and shops are still visible. Visit in summer from 10 a.m. to 5:30 p.m.

weekdays (on Sunday from 2 to 5:30 p.m.), and in winter from 10 a.m. to 4 p.m. weekdays, 2 to 4 p.m. on Sunday, paying 60p (90¢) for adults, 40p (60¢) for children and students.

The **Clock Tower** at Market Place was built in 1402, standing 77 feet high, a total of five floors.

From St. Albans you can visit **Gorhambury House,** a classic-style mansion built in 1777, containing 16th-century enameled glass and historic portraits. It's open, May to September, only on Thursday (2 to 5 p.m.), charging adults £1.20 ($1.80) for admission; children pay 70p ($1.05). The location is 2½ miles north of St. Albans near the A5.

On the outskirts, the **Mosquito Aircraft Museum,** the oldest aircraft exhibit in Britain, lies on the grounds of Salisbury Hall, just off the main A6 London–St. Albans road near London Colney, about five miles south of St. Albans. The hall is no longer open to the public, but the museum can be visited from Easter Sunday to October 1 on Sunday from 2 to 6 p.m.; on Thursday from July to the end of September (also on bank holiday Mondays) from 11 a.m. to 6 p.m. Displayed is the prototype of the de Havilland "Mosquito" aircraft, which was designed and built at Salisbury Hall in World War II. There are also three Mosquitos that were used. Admission is 75p ($1.13) for adults, 50p (75¢) for children. For more information, telephone Bowmansgreen 22051, or write to Box 107, St. Albans.

Back in St. Albans, I offer the following recommendations for food and lodgings:

Food and Lodging

St. Michael's Manor Hotel, Fishpool Street (tel. 0727/64444), stands on five acres of landscaped gardens, with a private lake, about a ten-minute walk from the heart of St. Albans. At its core is an original manor house dating from the 16th century. To the original structure a William and Mary bow-fronted center section has been added, along with a Georgian-style extension.

The grounds of the hotel contain such trees as cedars of Lebanon, hornbeam, and Wellingtonia and all 22 attractively furnished bedrooms are named after the trees in the garden. The Lilac honeymoon suite, complete with a four-poster bed and lilac decor, is most impressive. All the bedrooms have baths en suite. A single costs £35 ($52.50), and doubles or twins, £50 ($75). Prices include a full English breakfast and VAT. Special bed-and-breakfast terms are offered on weekends. Direct-dial phones, color TV, and radios are in all rooms.

In the Georgian-style dining room, a well-prepared international menu is presented for both luncheon and dinner to residents and nonresidents. A lunchtime table d'hôte meal with coffee costs £10 ($15), and a "chef recommends" dinner goes for £12 ($18). The impressive à la carte offering is about £18 ($27), inclusive of VAT.

The **White Hart Hotel,** Holywell Hill (tel. 0727/53624), is a timbered inn of uncertain origin. It may have been a 13th-century coaching inn. At the White Hart, formerly called the Hartshorn, Hogarth painted the picture of himself that hangs in London's National Portrait Gallery. Of architectural interest is a lounge with a minstrels' gallery, oak timbering, and a collection of copper and antiques. The old-world dining room has Windsor chairs and paneled walls, and there are two lounge bars, all in the old English style.

The hotel was undergoing extensive alterations at press time, so no prices of rooms were available, but each will have a private bath or shower and toilet, and four will have four-poster beds. Kevin Taylor, the manager, will be pleased to quote rates if you telephone. He expects tariffs to include VAT, service, and a full English breakfast. In the dining room you can order from a table d'hôte menu and an à la carte selection. The White Hart stands opposite the cathedral, and a short walk through the abbey grounds leads to the ruins of Roman Verulamium.

For dining, **Zorbas Greek Restaurant**, 3 French Row (tel. 0727/60609), seems an incongruous choice in such an historic English town, but it is a good and fairly inexpensive eating place. Right in the old part of town, it is reached by going along a pedestrian mall. The Theocharides family welcome you if you've come to dine, although I've seen them politely turn away English ladies who drop in just for afternoon tea, which they don't serve, incidentally. The house specialty, served with rice, is a kebab. You might prefer to begin with a Greek salad or hummus (ground chick peas with garlic). Pita bread is also served, as is the classic Greek moussaka. Another house specialty is stuffed vine leaves. Meals begin at £8 ($12). The restaurant serves lunch until 3 p.m. and dinner from 6 to 11 p.m. It is closed on Sunday and holidays.

SHAW'S CORNER: Just southwest of Ayot St. Lawrence, three miles northwest of Welwyn, stands the home where George Bernard Shaw lived from 1906 to 1950. The house is practically as he left it at his death. In the hall, for example, his hats are still hanging, as if ready for him to don one. His personal mementos are in his study, drawing room, dining room, and writing hut, which can be visited in March and November on Saturday and Sunday, and from April 1 to October 31 on Wednesday through Sunday from 11 a.m. to 1 p.m. and from 2 to 6 p.m. (or sunset if it comes before 6). Admission is £1.20 ($1.80) for adults, half price for children. For information, telephone High Wycombe 28051.

4. Buckinghamshire

This is a leafy county, lying north of the Thames and somewhat to the west of London. Its identifying marks are the wide Vale of Aylesbury, with its sprawling fields and tiny villages, and the long chalk range of the Chilterns. Going south from the range, you'll find what is left of a once-great beech forest.

A good center for touring the Chilterns is—

AYLESBURY: Gourmets still speak of its succulent ducks, a prize-winning dish on any table, although ducks bearing that name are usually raised elsewhere these days. The county town, Aylesbury has a number of timbered inns, old houses, and a wide Market Square. Less than 40 miles from London, it remains cozily old world.

Six miles northwest of Aylesbury, **Waddeson Manor** contains an outstanding collection of decorative art of the 17th and 18th centuries and an exhibition of dresses of a lady in the 1860s. Among the paintings are portraits by Reynolds, Gainsborough, and Romney. The manor was built in the late 19th century for Baron Ferdinand de Rothschild and stands in 150 acres of grounds with rare trees, an aviary, and a herd of Sika deer. Visiting times are from the end of March until the end of October, Wednesday to Sunday from 2 to 6 p.m. It costs £2 ($3) to enter the house, grounds, and aviary. For information, apply to the administrator, Aylesbury (tel. 0296/651282).

The **Bell Inn,** Aston Clinton, Buckinghamshire (tel. 0296/630252), is a coaching inn and believed to have been built at the end of the 18th century. Under the guidance of the Harris family, the inn has won extraordinary acclaim for its cuisine. Advertised by a large bell instead of an inn sign, it stands unobtrusively by the road 40 miles from London and four miles from Aylesbury. It's a mossy brick structure, with crisp white windows and a Georgian portico. Inside, antiques are used liberally. The dining room in olive green is coolly elegant, with polished wood and sparkling glass and silver. You select your meal in a large stone-floored bar while having a drink. Lunch or dinner is a special event. The Bavarian chef, Jacques Dick, is a perfectionist. For a beginning, try his "smokies" or his pâté maison. Main dishes include poached salmon (in season only) and roast duck with apple sauce from the trolley, a specialty for two diners. I'd also recommend the tournedos Rossini, sea bass Provençal, and saddle of hare. The price of the average meal is about £24 ($36), including half a bottle of the house wine.

There are six bedrooms in the original inn, all with private baths, refrigerator, and mini-bar, and all tastefully decorated. Converted from a stable block are 15 more comfortable rooms, arranged around a courtyard across a narrow road from the inn. Such thoughtful touches have been added as bathrobes, bubble-bath powder, shampoo, whatever, all included in the luxuriously appointed baths. Room rates range from £40 ($60) in a single, from £53 ($79.50) to £74 ($111) for a double, including a full English breakfast, VAT, and service. A log fire in the lounge makes for a warm welcome to this old coaching inn.

Back in Aylesbury, you can find food and lodgings at the **Kings Head,** Market Square (tel. 0296/5158), a half-timbered hotel that was once a 15th-century coaching inn. It is one of the finest examples of Tudor architecture in Buckinghamshire. Its 15 bedrooms overlook a cobbled courtyard. Because of its heavy patronage by business people on weekdays, I've never been able to get a room unless reserved well in advance. Units cost from £22 ($33) in a single, and from £29 ($43.50) in a double. There are no private baths. Lunch is served from noon to 2 p.m. and dinner from 7 to 9 p.m. (from 7:30 to 10 p.m. on Saturday). Try to have a predinner drink in the cozy pub in back, with its collection of weapons. Bar lunches start at £2 ($3). A set dinner is offered for £8.50 ($12.75), although there is an à la carte menu as well, a complete meal costing from £11 ($16.50). The inn was much frequented by Cromwell, and his chair is still on view in the lounge bar. He slept in the Cromwell Room upstairs with its extra-large bed.

BUCKINGHAM: This old market town on the River Ouse was once the county town of Buckingham. It has a fine 13th-century Chantry Chapel and some 18th-century houses.

If you're motoring through, try to plan a luncheon or dinner stopover at **Old Market House,** Market Hill (tel. 0280/812385), housed in one of the town's most interesting buildings, a black-and-white timbered structure with leaded-glass windows. John Rawlings is the owner/chef. He offers a set Sunday lunch for £6.50 ($9.75). On other days, each lunchtime menu item is individually priced, with a main dish costing about £3 ($4.50). An à la carte evening meal can be expected to be around £9.50 ($14.25). Dinner is served every evening from 7 to 9:15 p.m. except Sunday and Monday.

Food and Lodging

White Hart, Market Square (tel. 0280/815151), is an oldish market-town hotel, with 18th-century origins, although the plaster facade and portico are Victorian additions. In recent years the hotel has been remodeled and equipped for modern comfort, its renovation bringing simplicity to the interior. All of the hotel's 20 bedrooms have private baths, television sets, and coffee-making facilities. Singles rent for £32 ($48) and doubles cost £40 ($60) with private bath. The hotel's dining room, called the Georgian Room, has its own small dance floor, and there is a lounge bar as well. They also have Hathaways Kitchen, serving steaks, trout, seafood pancakes, all with fresh salads and granary bread. Meals cost from £6.50 ($9.75) to £10 ($15).

JORDANS VILLAGE: Old Jordans, Jordans Lane, in Jordans Village (tel. Chalfont St. Giles 4586), is a farm dating back to the Middle Ages. But its recorded history starts in the early 17th century when one Thomas Russell, sitting tenant, bought the freehold, signing the deed with his thumbprint. The house was added to over the years, and in the mid-17th century William Penn, founder of Pennsylvania, and other well-known Dissenters stayed here and worshiped.

Now the property of the Quakers, the house is run as a conference center, but they have 30 simply furnished rooms available for overnight guests at £16 ($24) in a single, £24 ($36) in a double, including breakfast.

On the grounds is the Mayflower Barn, built almost indisputably from timbers from the ship *Mayflower* in which the first Pilgrims sailed to the New World. These days the beams ring to the strains of concert music and recitals performed by top-notch artists.

You can enjoy lunch at £3.50 ($5.25), served at 1 p.m., and supper for £5.50 ($11.25) at 7 p.m.; and reservations are a must.

It's a peaceful place, full of history, perhaps a little isolated from today's bustle but easily accessible to London and Oxford.

MILTON'S COTTAGE: The modern residential town of Gerrards Cross is often called the Beverly Hills of England, as it attracts the wealthy-chic who settle here in many beautiful homes. Surrounding this plush section are several tucked-away hamlets, including **Chalfont St. Giles,** where the poet Milton lived during the Great Plague in 1665. He completed *Paradise Lost* here. In this 16th-century cottage are two museum rooms containing 93 rare books, including first editions of *Paradise Lost* and *Paradise Regained* and other Miltoniana, with exhibits of interest to young and old. A beautiful cottage garden is a further attraction. The house is open daily, except Monday, from February 1 to October 31 (on spring and summer bank holiday Mondays from 10 a.m. to 1 p.m. and 2 to 6 p.m.; on Sunday from 2 to 6 p.m.). Charges are 70p ($1.05) for adults and 30p (45¢) for children. It is closed November, December, and January. For information, write to Milton's Cottage, Dean Way, Chalfont St. Giles, Bucks, HP8 4JH, U.K. (tel. Chalfont St. Giles 2313).

West of Gerrards Cross, the town of Beaconsfield, with its broad, tree-lined High Street, enjoys many associations with Disraeli. Visitors pass through here en route to—

HUGHENDEN MANOR: Outside High Wycombe, in Buckinghamshire, sits a country manor that gives us not only an insight into the age of Victoria, but acquaints us with a remarkable man. In Benjamin Disraeli we meet one of the most enigmatic figures of 19th-century England. At age 21, Dizzy published anonymously his five-volume novel *Vivian Grey*. But it wasn't his shining hour. He went on to other things, marrying an older widow for her money, although they developed, apparently, a most successful relationship. He entered politics and continued writing novels, his later ones meeting with more acclaim.

In 1848 Disraeli acquired Hughenden Manor, a country house that befitted his fast-rising political and social position. He served briefly as prime minister in 1868, but his political fame rests on his stewardship as prime minister during 1874–1880. He became Queen Victoria's friend, and in 1877 she paid him a rare honor by visiting him at Hughenden.

In 1876 Disraeli became the Earl of Beaconsfield: he had arrived. Only his wife was dead, and he was to die in 1881. Instead of being buried at Westminster Abbey, he preferred the simple little graveyard of Hughenden Church.

His library is preserved much as he left it. In fact, Hughenden contains an odd assortment of memorabilia, including a lock of Disraeli's hair. The letters from Victoria, the autographed books, and especially a portrait of Lord Byron, known to Disraeli's father.

If you're driving to Hughenden Manor on the way to Oxford, continue north of High Wycombe on the A4128 for about 1½ miles. If you're relying on public transportation from London, take coach 711 to High Wycombe, then board an Alder Valley bus (323, 324, 333, or 334). The manor house and garden are open daily except Monday and Tuesday from April to October, from 2 to 6 p.m. (from noon to 6 p.m. on Sunday and bank holidays). In March, they're open on Saturday and Sunday only from 2 to 5 p.m. (or sunset if earlier). Admission for adults is £1.70 ($2.55), half price for children. It is closed all December, January, and February, and on Good Friday. For more information, telephone 0494/28051.

WEST WYCOMBE: Snuggled in the Chiltern Hills 30 miles west of London, the village of West Wycombe still has an atmosphere of the early 18th century. The thatched roofs have been replaced with tiles, and some of the buildings have been removed or replaced, but the village is still two centuries removed from the present day.

In the mid-18th century, Sir Francis Dashwood began an ambitious building program at West Wycombe. His strong interest in architecture and design led Sir Francis to undertake a series of monuments and parks that are still among the finest in the country today. He also sponsored the building of a road using the chalk quarries on the hill to aid in the support of the poverty-stricken villagers. The resulting caves became the meeting place of "The Knights of St. Francis of Wycombe," later known as **The Hellfire Club.** The Knights consisted of a number of illustrious men drawn from the social circle surrounding the Prince of Wales. Its members "gourmandized," swilling claret and enjoying the company of women "of a cheerful, lively disposition . . . who considered themselves lawful wives of the brethren during their stay."

You can tour the caves, wandering through a quarter mile of winding passages, past colorful waxwork scenes brought to life by sound and light effects. The caves are open from 1 to 6 p.m. daily from March through September, and from 1 to 5 p.m. on weekends only during the rest of the year. Admission is £1.60 ($2.40) for adults, 85p ($1.28) for children.

Other sights at West Wycombe include the **Church of St. Lawrence,** perched atop West Wycombe Hill and topped by a huge golden ball. Parts of the church date from the 13th century; its richly decorated interior was copied from a third-century Syrian sun temple. The view from the hill is worth the trek up. Near the church stands the **Dashwood Mausoleum,** built in a style derived from Constantine's Arch in Rome.

A visit to **West Wycombe House,** home of the Dashwoods, is of both historical and architectural interest. Both George III and Ben Franklin stayed here, although not at the same time. The house is one of the best examples of Palladian-style architecture in England. The interior is lavishly decorated with paintings and antiques from the 18th century.

During your tour, you may also wander freely through the village, stopping for lunch at one of the public houses, or browsing through the gift shop. Four miles of nature trails also meander about the village, through forests and farmlands.

Although the Dashwood house is open only from June 1 to August 30, the rest of the village may, of course, be visited all year. The house is open Monday to Friday from 2:15 to 6 p.m. and charges an admission of £1.80 ($2.70) for adults and half price for children. If you just want to visit the grounds, the cost is reduced to £1 ($1.50).

The telephone number of the West Wycombe Park Office is 0494/24411.

5. Bedfordshire

This county contains the fertile, rich Vale of Bedford, crossed by the River Ouse. Most visitors from London head here on a day trip to visit historic Woburn Abbey (previewed below). Others know of its county town—

BEDFORD: On the Ouse, Bedford contains many riverside parks and gardens, but is better known for its associations with Bunyan. In Mill Street stands the 1850 **Bunyan Meeting House** (tel. 0234/58627), erected on the site of a barn where Bunyan used to preach. The bronze doors, considered to be artistically outstanding, illustrate ten scenes from *Pilgrim's Progress.* The Bunyan Meeting House contains the surviving relics of Bunyan and a famous collection of the *Pilgrim's Progress* in 400 foreign-language editions. Open Tuesday to Saturday April to October from 2 to 4 p.m., it charges 50p (75¢) for admission.

About 1½ miles south of Bedford lies Elstow, close to Bunyan's reputed birthplace. Here you can visit **Elstow Moot Hall,** a medieval market hall containing exhibits depicting the life and times of John Bunyan. It is open Tuesday through Saturday, from 10 a.m. to 1 p.m. and 2 to 5 p.m., on Sunday from 2 to 5:30 p.m. (to dusk in winter), charging 20p (30¢) for adults, 10p (15¢) for children. For more information, telephone 0234/66889.

The **Swiss Garden,** Old Warden, near Biggleswade, is an unusual romantic site dating from the early 19th century. It contains the original buildings and features, together with many interesting plants and trees, some of great rarity. A lakeside picnic area in adjoining woodlands is open at all times. Hours for the garden are from 2 to 6 p.m. (last admission at 5:15 p.m.) on Wednesday, Thursday, Saturday, Sunday, bank holiday Mondays, and Good Friday from the last Saturday in March to the last Saturday in October. The garden lies approximately 2½ miles west of Biggleswade adjoining the Biggleswade–Old Warden road about two miles west of the A1. For more information, telephone 0234/63222, ext. 30.

Stevington Windmill, dating from about 1770, is a particularly fine example of a post mill, fully restored in 1921. The Bedfordshire County Council acquired the mill in 1951, when further extensive restoration work was carried out. Stevington Mill was probably the last windmill in the country working with four common (i.e., cloth-covered) sails. Admission is 50p (75¢). Visitors to the mill may borrow the keys between the hours of 10 a.m. and 7 p.m. (dusk in winter) from the landlord of the Royal George, Silver Street, Stevington. The location is a half mile southeast of Stevington. For more information, telephone 0234/63222, ext. 30.

WOBURN ABBEY: Few tourists visiting Bedfordshire miss the Georgian

mansion of **Woburn Abbey,** the seat of the Dukes of Bedford for more than three centuries. The much-publicized 18th-century estate is about 42 miles from London outside Woburn. Its State Apartments are rich in furniture, porcelain, tapestries, silver, and a valuable art collection, including paintings by Van Dyck, Holbein, Rembrandt, Gainsborough, and Reynolds. A series of paintings by Canaletto, showing his continuing views of Venice, grace the walls of the dining room in the Private Apartments (Prince Philip said the duke's collection was superior to the Canalettos at Windsor—but Her Royal Highness quickly corrected him). Of all the paintings, one of the most notable from a historical point of view is the *Armada Portrait* of Elizabeth I. Her hand rests on the globe, as Philip's invincible armada perishes in the background.

Queen Victoria and Prince Albert visited Woburn Abbey in 1841. Victoria slept in an opulently decorated bedroom. Victoria's Dressing Room contains a fine collection of 17th-century paintings from the Netherlands. Among the oddities and treasures at Woburn Abbey are a Grotto of Shells, a Sèvres dinner service (gift of Louis XV), and a chamber devoted to memorabilia of "The Flying Duchess." Wife of the 11th Duke of Bedford, she was a remarkable woman, who disappeared on a solo flight in 1937 (the same year as Amelia Earhart). The duchess, however, was 72 years old at the time.

In the 1950s, the present Duke of Bedford opened Woburn Abbey to the public to pay off some $15 million in inheritance taxes. In 1974 he turned the estate over to his son and daughter-in-law, the Marquess and Marchioness of Tavistock, who reluctantly took on the business of running the 75-room mansion. And what a business it is, drawing hundreds of thousands of visitors a year and employing more than 300 persons to staff the shops and grounds.

Today, Woburn Abbey is surrounded by a 3000-acre park containing many rare and exotic animals (ten varieties of deer). Some people visit just to see the animals. While seated in one of 57 gondolas on the two-mile cable lift, you pass over lions, elephants, and giraffes. What would Humphry Repton, the designer of the estate's park in the 18th century, say?

Woburn Abbey is outside Woburn, near Dunstable. It is hard to reach by public transportation from London, so you may prefer to take one of the organized tours.

In February, March, and November the park is open daily from noon to 3:45 p.m. and the abbey from 1 to 4:45 p.m. From April 1 to October 31, the park hours are 10 a.m. to 4:45 p.m. weekdays, 10 a.m. to 5:45 p.m. on Sunday, while the abbey is open from 11 a.m. to 5:45 p.m. weekdays and 11 a.m. to 6:15 p.m. on Sunday. The last admission to the abbey is 45 minutes before closing time. The charge to enter the park is £2.20 ($3.30) for a car and passengers; for bus passengers, cyclists, and pedestrians, 40p (60¢) per person. Admission to the abbey is £2.40 ($3.60) for adults, £1.50 ($2.25) for children 5 to 15. To economize if it fits your needs, I suggest a family ticket, going for £6.50 ($9.75) for admitting two adults and two children, with similar reductions for more children.

The deer park admission charge does not apply to visitors purchasing the abbey entrance ticket as they enter the park. When not in use by the family, visitors may see the private apartments at an additional charge of 40p (60¢) for adults, 15p (23¢) for children. For more information, telephone 052525/666.

After visiting the abbey, a good spot for both food and lodgings is the **Bedford Arms,** George Street (tel. Woburn 441). This is a Georgian coaching inn with a checkered history that blends the old and new at the gates of the estate of the Duke of Bedford. Tastefully modernized, it still preserves a mellow charm. Its 75-seat Georgian dining room, Hollands, was designed by Henry Holland, architect of Woburn Abbey. Guests are housed in one of the pleasantly furnished bedrooms, all of which contain private baths or showers. Singles cost £40 ($60); doubles or twins, £45 ($67.50). Each unit contains coffee-making facilities, radio, phone, automatic alarm system, and color TV. A new block provides executive-style bedrooms furnished and decorated to extremely high standards. All these rooms have private baths, color TV, radio, and drinks facilities. This block brings the hotel's complement of bedrooms to 55. The Tavern adjoining the hotel's main restaurant has been restored, its old beams exposed as well as its inglenook fireplaces. By contrast, a cocktail bar has been designed as an ideal place for a predinner drink or cocktail. The bar, with its gray suede-covered walls and soft-pink draperies, creates an atmosphere of luxury.

Chapter VI

KENT, SURREY, AND THE SUSSEXES

LYING TO THE SOUTH and southeast of London are the shires (counties) of Kent, Surrey, and the Sussexes. Combined, they form a most fascinating part of England to explore, and are easy to reach, within commuting distance of the capital.

Of all the centers, **Canterbury** in Kent is of foremost interest, but the old Cinque ports of **Rye** and **Winchelsea** in East Sussex are equally exciting, as is **Brighton** in its own distinctive way. In and around these major meccas are dozens of castles and vast estates, monuments, homes of celebrated men, cathedrals, yachting harbors, and little villages of thatched cottages.

The range of accommodations varies from an old-world smugglers' inn at the ancient seaport of Rye to a 16th-century house in Canterbury featured in *David Copperfield*. Throughout the counties of the south coast, you'll discover some superb bargains, as the English themselves come to these coastal shires for the sun and are accustomed to paying reasonable rates.

In the fog-choked cities of northern England, the great dream for

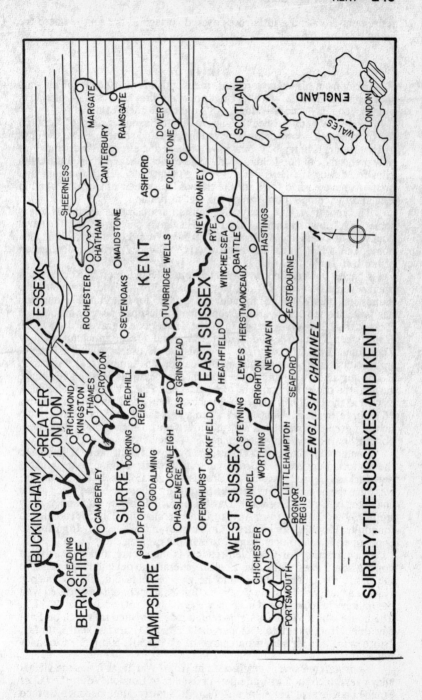

SURREY, THE SUSSEXES AND KENT

retirement is to find a little rose-covered cottage in the south, where the living's easier.

KENT

Fresh from his cherry orchard, the Kentish farmer heads for his snug spot by an inglenook, with its bright-burning fire, for his glass of cherry brandy. The day's work is done. All's right with the world.

We're in what was once the ancient Anglo-Saxon kingdom of Kent, on the fringes of London yet far removed in spirit and scenery. Since the days of the Tudors, cherry blossoms have pinkened the fertile landscape. Not only orchards, but hop fields abound. The conically shaped oasthouses with kilns for drying the hops dot the rolling countryside. Both the hops and orchards have earned for Kent the title of the garden of England. And in England the competition's rough for that distinction.

The country is also rich in Dickensian associations—in fact, Kent is sometimes known as Dickens Country. His family once lived near the naval dockyard at Chatham. At **Rochester,** 30 miles from London, you'll find his home, Gad's Hill, at the edge of town (in *Pickwick Papers* is a description of the Bull Inn).

Charles Dickens Centre, Eastgate House, High Street, in Rochester, is open seven days a week, from 10 a.m. to 12:30 p.m. and 2 to 5:30 p.m. Admission is £1.10 ($1.65) for adults, 55p (83¢) for children. The museum has tableaux depicting various scenes from Dickens's novels, including a Pickwickian Christmas scene, then the fever-ridden graveyard of *Bleak House,* scenes from *The Old Curiosity Shop* and *Great Expectations, Oliver Twist,* and *David Copperfield.* There is clever use of sound and light. Information is also available at the center on various other sights in Rochester associated with Dickens, including Eastgate House and, in the garden, the chalet transported from Gad's Hill Place, where Dickens died, as well as the Guildhall Museum, Rochester Cathedral, and the mysterious "6 Poor Travellers' House." Pick up a brochure that includes a map featuring the various places and the novels with which each is associated. For further information, telephone 0634/44176.

Canterbury, the road to Dover, the byways of Kent, were all known to the Victorian novelist. At Broadstairs, his favorite seaside resort, what is now **Dickens House Museum** (tel. Broadstairs 62853), on the main seafront, was once the home of Mary Pearson Strong, on whom he based much of the character of Betsey Trotwood, David Copperfield's aunt. It is open daily from 2:30 to 5:30 p.m. from April to October, charging 35p (53¢) admission for adults, 15p (23¢) for children. On Tuesday and Wednesday from July to September, it is also open from 7 to 9 in the evening.

An attraction for Canadian readers is the square, red brick, gabled home where James Wolfe, the English general who defeated the French in the battle for Québec, lived until he was 11 years old. Called Québec House, a National Trust property, it contains memorabilia associated with the military hero, who was born in Westerham (Kent) on January 2, 1727. The house which Wolfe's parents rented may be visited in March on Sunday only; from April to October daily except Thursday and Saturday, 2 to 6 p.m., for an admission charge of £1 ($1.50), 50p (75¢) for children.

Kent suffered severe destruction in World War II, as it was the virtual alley over which the Luftwaffe flew in its blitz of London. After the fall of France, a German invasion was feared. Shortly after becoming prime minister in 1940, Churchill sped to Dover, with his bowler, stogie, walking cane, and pin-striped suit. Once there, he inspected the coastal defense and gave encouragement to the men digging in to fight off the attack. But Hitler's "Sea Lion" (code name for the invasion) turned out to be a paper tiger.

In spite of much devastation, Kent is filled with interesting old towns and stately homes.

1. Kent's Country Houses and Castles

CHURCHILL'S HOME: For many years, Sir Winston lived at **Chartwell** (tel. 0732/866368), which lies 1½ miles south of Westerham in Kent. Churchill, a descendant of the first Duke of Marlborough, was born in grand style at Blenheim Palace on November 30, 1874. Chartwell doesn't pretend to be as grand a place as Blenheim, but it's been preserved as a memorial, administered by the National Trust. The rooms remain as Churchill left them, including maps, documents, photographs, pictures, and other personal mementos. In two rooms are displayed a selection of gifts that the prime minister received from people all over the world. There is also a selection of many of his well-known uniforms. Terraced gardens descend toward the lake with its celebrated black swans. In a garden studio are many of Churchill's paintings. Go if you want to see where a giant of a man lived and worked. The house is open from March until the end of November, weekdays except Monday and Friday from 2 to 6 p.m.; Saturday, Sunday and bank holiday Mondays from 11 a.m. to 6 p.m.; also open from 11 a.m. on Wednesday and Thursday in July and August. Admission to the house and garden is £2 ($3); to the garden only, £1 ($1.50). The restaurant offers light meals, salads, sandwiches, cakes, and a few hot dishes. It's open from 10:30 a.m. on the days the house is receiving visitors. An average snack costs £2 ($3).

SQUERRYES COURT: A William and Mary period manor house, Squerryes Court, Westerham (tel. 0959/62345), was built in 1681 and owned by the Warde family for 250 years. Besides a fine collection of paintings, tapestries, and furniture, in the Wolfe Room is a collection of pictures and relics of the family of General Wolfe. The general received his military commission in the grounds of the house at a spot marked by a cenotaph. See also the Museum of the Kent Sharpshooter Yeomanry Regiment. The house and grounds are open from March to October on Saturday, Sunday, and bank holidays (also Wednesday from May to September). Hours are 2 to 6 p.m., and admission charges are £1.20 ($1.80) for adults and 60p (90¢) for children.

KNOLE: Begun in the mid-15th century by Thomas Bourchier, archbishop of Canterbury, Knole (tel. 0732/450608) is one of the largest private houses in England, and is considered one of the finest examples of the purely British Tudor style of architecture.

Henry VIII confiscated it along with other church property in 1537, and it was later granted to Thomas Sackville, Earl of Dorset, by Queen Elizabeth I. Sackville, whose descendants reside in Knole to the present day (although the building was donated to the National Trust in 1946), extended the mansion by adding long gabled wings and the Great Hall.

It has been estimated that the completed house has a room for every day of the year, a courtyard for every day of the week, and a staircase for every week of the year. Virginia Woolf, often a guest of the Sackvilles, used Knole as the location for her novel *Orlando*. The manuscript is on display in the Great Hall. The elaborate paneling and friezework provide a background for the 17th- and 18th-century tapestries and rugs, the Jacobean furniture, and the collection of family portraits. The King's Room has heavy silver furniture and is dominated by a royal canopied bed made for King James II when he was Duke of York. It is covered in brocade woven from gold and silver threads.

Knole, in the village of Sevenoaks, about five miles north of Tunbridge and 25 miles from Central London, is open April to September, Wednesday to Saturday, bank holiday Mondays, and Good Friday from 11 a.m. to 5 p.m. (on Sunday from 2 to 5 p.m.). In October and November, it is open Wednesday to Saturday from 11 a.m. to 4 p.m. (on Sunday from 2 to 4 p.m.); last admissions one hour before closing time. It is closed from December to March. Admission is £2.50 ($3.75) for adults, £1.50 ($2.25) for children.

IGHTHAM MOTE: A perfect, medieval moated manor house, Ightham Mote, Ivy Hatch, Sevenoaks (tel. 0732/62235), is open only on Friday afternoon throughout the year and also on Sunday afternoon from April to September. If you're in the area visiting other stately homes and castles on the open days, you should see this ancient house. It was extensively remodeled in the early 16th century. The Tudor chapel with its painted ceiling, the timbered outer walls, and the ornate chimneys reflect that period.

A stone bridge crosses the moat and leads into the great central courtyard overlooked by the magnificent windows of the Great Hall. The rest of the house is grouped around the courtyard. From the Great Hall, a Jacobean staircase leads to the old chapel on the first floor, where you go through the solarium, with an oriel window, to the Tudor chapel.

Unlike many other ancient houses of England, Ightham Mote has passed from family to family, each leaving its mark on the place. The present owner is Charles Henry Robinson of Portland, Maine, who found the house for sale during a visit here in 1953 and promptly bought it. He has been responsible for a great deal of restoration and plans to leave it to the National Trust. The house is open from 2 to 5 p.m. on Friday and Sunday in summer, to 4 p.m. on Friday in winter. Admission is £1.10 ($1.65) for adults, 70p ($1.05) for children.

HEVER CASTLE: The castle was built at the end of the 13th century as a fortified farmhouse surrounded by a moat, and a dwelling house was added within the fortifications some 200 years later by the Bullen family. In 1506 the property was inherited by Sir Thomas Bullen, father of Anne Boleyn. It was here that Henry VIII courted Anne for six years before she became his second wife and later mother of Elizabeth, who became Queen of England. In 1530 Hever Castle was acquired by Henry VIII, who granted it to his fourth wife, Anne of Cleves, in 1540. This luckier Anne lived here for 17 years. In 1903 the castle was purchased by William Waldorf Astor, who spent three years restoring and redecorating it, as well as building the unique village of Tudor-style cottages connected to the castle, for use by his guests. Astor was responsible also for the construction of the spectacular Italian gardens and the 35-acre lake through which the River Eden flows.

The castle and gardens are normally open from April through September daily except Thursday from noon to 6 p.m. (last entry at 5 p.m.). Closed Good Friday. Admission is £2.70 ($4.05) for adults, £1.50 ($2.25) for children. For entrance to the gardens only, adults pay £1.25 ($1.88), and children, 75p ($1.13). Hot meals and light refreshments are available, and you are welcome to picnic in the grounds. You can park your car free.

For further information, call the Hever Castle Office, Edenbridge (tel. 0732/865224).

If you have a party, you can rent accommodations in rooms in the adjacent buildings for a minimum of eight persons, at £70 ($105) per night for a single, £82 ($123) in a double. You must reserve in advance.

HAXTED MILL: There seems to have been a watermill on the site of Haxted Mill, near Edenbridge (tel. 0732/862914), since 1361, but the present mill was built on the original foundations in 1680, the eastern half added in 1794. The three pairs of grinding stones that you see today have been grinding corn for more than 250 years, and the waterwheel that drives them is more than 140 years old. The old building is a museum in itself, but it contains a fascinating collection of mill machinery, early mill gas engines, and an old wooden drive shaft from Horsten Keynes mill. Woody Woodrow is the curator. After you've seen the mill pool and the waterwheels, you can go across the courtyard to a small tea room where light refreshment is served. The mill is open most afternoons from Easter to September. Drive west out of Edenbridge on an unnumbered road toward Haxted and Lingfield. Admission is 50p (75¢) for adults and 30p (45¢) for children.

CHILHAM CASTLE GARDENS: This former royal property six miles west of Canterbury was used as a hunting lodge until it was sold by King Henry VIII. It can be reached by the A28 Ashford–Canterbury road, the A252 Maidstone–Glastonbury road, or from the M2 Faversham turnoff. The gardens are open from mid-March to the end of October from 11 a.m. to 6 p.m. Admission is £1.50 ($2.25) for adults, 80p ($1.20) for children. This includes a pet park and falconry display. On Sunday jousting is staged, costing £2 ($3) for adults, £1 ($1.50) for children, and on a bank holiday Sunday and Monday there are medieval jousting tournaments costing £3 ($4.50) for adults, £1.50 ($2.25) for children. For further information, phone 0227/730319.

PENSHURST PLACE: This magnificent English Gothic-style mansion, one of the outstanding country houses in Britain (tel. 0892/870307), lies 33 miles from London and 3½ miles west of Tonbridge on the Tunbridge Wells road. Sir John de Pulteney, four times mayor of London, built the stone house whose Great Hall forms the heart of Penshurst, even after more than 600 years. The boy king, Edward VI, presented the house to Sir William Sidney, and it has remained in this family ever since, becoming, in 1554, the birthplace of the soldier-poet, Sir Philip Sidney. In the first half of the 17th century Penshurst was known as a center of literature, attracting such personages as Ben Jonson.

Visitors are shown through the premises, including the splendid State Dining Room and Queen Elizabeth's Room. In the Stable Wing is an interesting Toy Museum. The ten-acre walled garden is divided into hedged enclosures, a legacy from the Tudor era. The home park is grazed by rare sheep and the lake is the home of many wildfowl. The site is open daily except Monday from April 1 to October 8 and each bank holiday. The gardens and home park hours are from 12:30 to 6 p.m. and the house from 1 to 5:30 p.m. Admission is £2.35 ($3.53) for adults, £1 ($1.50) for children.

LEEDS CASTLE: This castle at Maidstone, dating from A.D. 857, was once described by Lord Conway as the loveliest castle in the world. Originally built of wood, it was rebuilt in 1119 in its present stone structure on two small islands in the middle of a lake, and it is an almost impregnable fortress. Henry VIII converted it to a royal palace.

The castle has strong links with America through the sixth Lord Fairfax who, as well as owning the castle, owned five million acres in Virginia and was a close friend and mentor of the young George Washington. The last owner, the Hon. Lady Baillie, who lovingly restored the castle with a superb collection of fine art, furniture, and tapestries, bequeathed it to the Leeds Castle Foundation.

Within the surrounding parkland, there is a wild wood garden and duckery where rare swans, geese, and ducks can be seen, and the aviaries contains a superb collection of birds, including parakeets and cockatoos. Dogs are not allowed here, but dog lovers will enjoy the Great Danes of the castle and the unique collection of dog collars dating from the Middle Ages. The Culpeper Garden is a delightful English country flower garden. Beyond are the castle greenhouses and the vineyard, recorded in the Domesday Book and now again producing Leeds Castle English white wine. A nine-hole and an 18-tee golf course are open to the public daily.

The castle is open from April 1 to October 31 daily except Monday in April, May, and October (not closed on bank holidays) from noon to 5 p.m.; from November 1 to March 31 on Saturday and Sunday from noon to 4 p.m. Admission is £3.25 ($4.88) for adults, £2.75 ($4.13) for students, and £2.25 ($3.38) for children up to 16.

From November 1 to the end of March, Sunday lunch is offered. A sherry reception is followed by a four-course lunch with wine and then a tour of the castle. The all-inclusive rate is £10.50 ($15.75) for adults, £8.50 ($12.75) for children. Advance reservations are essential.

Every Saturday from 7:15 p.m. to 1 a.m., a Kentish evening takes place in the Jacobean Tithe Barn, the Fairfax Hall where, after a sherry reception and an evening tour of the castle, a six-course meal is served with wine and musical entertainment, for £18.50 ($27.75) per person. Advance reservations are essential. Telephone 0622/65400.

The Three Chimneys, Biddenden (tel. 0580/291472), is a delightful timbered inn with a steep red-tile roof and low-ceilinged bars where an astonishing selection of draft bitters can be sampled as well as real ale and cider. Meals include fresh homemade soup or a delicate cucumber mousse, then roast pork with apple sauce or stuffed lamb with onion sauce. Desserts include date and walnut pudding and lemon meringue pie. Christopher and

Pippa Sayers, the hosts, take a keen interest in the well-being of their guests. Lunch, with a pint of beer, will cost around £6 ($9) per person. This is an ideal stop before a visit to Sissinghurst Castle gardens, 1½ miles up the road.

SISSINGHURST CASTLE GARDEN: V. Sackville-West and her husband, Harold Nicolson, created the celebrated Sissinghurst Castle Garden, Sissinghurst (tel. 0580/712850), now on view between the surviving parts of an Elizabethan mansion. The gardens are worth a visit at all seasons. There is a spring garden where bulb flowers flourish, a summer garden, and an autumn garden with flowering shrubs, as well as a large herb garden. The gardens are open from April to mid-October Tuesday to Friday from 1 to 6:30 p.m., on Saturday and Sunday from 10 a.m. to 6:30 p.m. Admission is £2 ($3) for adults, £1 ($1.50) for children. Light meals are available in the Oast House Restaurant.

FAN OF VICTORIA: Violet Bourne, 70 High St., Milton Regis, near Sittingbourne (tel. Sittingbourne 23762 in the evenings), owns the Elizabethan house in which she lives and has filled it with Victoriana. Each room has been furnished absolutely to period down to the last ornament and trinket—a tiny purse made of shells, polished and lacquered musical boxes, and chiming clocks. She is delighted to take visitors around, charging 75p ($1.13) to see her lovely collection. She prefers afternoon visitors, and receives guests from April to October only. Please telephone before arriving.

2. Canterbury

Under the arch of the ancient West Gate journeyed Chaucer's knight, solicitor, nun, squire, parson, merchant, miller, and cook—spinning racy tales. They were bound for the shrine of Thomas à Becket, archbishop of Canterbury, who was slain by four knights of Henry II on December 29, 1170. (The king later walked barefoot from Harbledown to the tomb of his former friend, where he allowed himself to be flogged in penance.) The shrine was finally torn down in 1538 by Henry VIII, as part of his campaign to destroy the monasteries and graven images. Canterbury, by then, had already been an attraction of long standing.

The medieval Kentish city, on the Stour River, is the mother city of England, its ecclesiastical capital. Mother city is an apt title, as Canterbury was known to have been inhabited centuries before the birth of Jesus Christ. Julius Caesar once went on a rampage near it. Although its most famous incident was the murder of Becket, the medieval city witnessed other major moments in English history—including Bloody Mary's ordering of nearly 40 victims to be burned at the stake. Richard the Lionhearted came back this way from crusading, and Charles II passed through on the way to claim his crown.

Canterbury was once completely walled, and many traces of its old fortifications remain. In the 16th century, weavers, mostly Huguenots from northern France and the Low Countries, fled to Canterbury to escape religious persecution. They started a weaving industry that flourished until the expanding silk trade with India ruined it.

The old city is much easier to reach today than it was in Chaucer's time. As it lies 56 miles from London, it is within a 1½-hour train ride from Victoria Station. The city center is closed to cars, but it's only a short walk from several car parks to the cathedral or walking-tour starting point.

From just below the Weavers House, boats leave for half-hour trips on the river with a commentary on the history of the buildings you pass. The charge is £1.50 ($2.25) per person. Umbrellas are provided to protect you against inclement weather.

Now, as in the Middle Ages, the goal of the pilgrim remains:

CANTERBURY CATHEDRAL: The foundation of this splendid cathedral (tel. 0227/61954) dates back to the coming of the first archbishop, Augustine, from Rome in A.D. 597, but the earliest part of the present building is the great Romanesque crypt built circa 1100. The monastic choir erected on top of this at the same time was destroyed by fire in 1174, only four years after the murder of Thomas à Becket on a dark December evening in the northwest transept, still one of the most famous places of pilgrimage in Europe. The destroyed choir was immediately replaced by a magnificent early Gothic one, and first used for worship in 1180. The cathedral was the first great church in the Gothic style to be erected in England and set a fashion for the whole country. Its architects were the Frenchman, William of Sens, and "English" William who took Sens's place after the Frenchman was crippled in an accident in 1178 that later proved fatal.

This part of the church is noteworthy for its medieval tombs of royal personages such as King Henry IV and Edward the Black Prince, as well as numerous archbishops. To the later middle ages belongs the great 14th-century nave and the famous central "Bell Harry Tower." The cathedral stands in spacious precincts amid the remains of the buildings of the monastery—cloisters, chapter house, and Norman water tower, which have survived intact from the Dissolution in the time of King Henry VIII to the present day.

Becket's shrine was destroyed by the Tudor king, but the site of that tomb is in Trinity Chapel, near the High Altar. The saint is said to have worked miracles, and the cathedral contains some rare stained glass depicting those feats. Perhaps the most miraculous thing is that the windows escaped Henry VIII's agents of destruction and Hitler's bombs as well (part of the cathedral was hit in World II). East of the Trinity Chapel is "Becket's Crown," in which is a chapel dedicated to "Martyrs and Saints of Our Own Time." St. Augustine's Chair, one of the symbols of the authority of the archbishop of Canterbury, stands behind the high altar.

ROMAN PAVEMENT: This site is off High Street down Butchery Lane. It contains some fine mosaic pavement remains and treasures from excavations in the city. The pavement is open daily from 10 a.m. to 1 p.m. and 2 to 5 p.m. (afternoon only, in winter). The entrance charge is 25p (38¢), or you can obtain a combined ticket to the Roman Pavement and the West Gate Towers Museum for 35p (53¢).

GUIDED TOURS: Guided tours of Canterbury are organized by the **Guild of Guides,** Virginia House, 12 St. Thomas Hill (tel. 0227/59779), costing £1

($1.50) per person. Tours of the cathedral are arranged by the Guides office at 11B The Precincts (tel. 0227/64212). They take place generally from April to October at 11:20 a.m. and 2:30 p.m. Monday to Friday, and at 11:20 a.m. on Saturday. No tours are conducted on Sunday. There is no charge to enter the cathedral, although tours cost 75p ($1.13) per person.

A SEARCH FOR ROOTS: Know Your Ancestors, Northgate (tel. 0227/ 68664), specializes in compiling family trees, establishing rights to coats-of-arms, and searching for ancestral British roots. The cost depends on the nature and complexity of the task, and the availability of records to be searched. A £50 ($75) retainer is required, but you will end up with your "roots" discovered and documented. If you have to return home before the task is completed, they will send the finished article to you.

WHERE TO STAY: Before you can begin any serious exploring, you'll need to find a hotel. You have several possibilities, both in the city and on the outskirts, ranging from craggy Elizabethan houses of historic interest to modern studio-type bedrooms with private baths. I'll proceed in descending order of cost.

The **County Hotel,** High Street (tel. 0227/66266), has been a hotel since the closing years of the reign of Victoria. But its recorded history goes back to the end of the 12th century, when Jacob the Jew built a private town house on the spot. Over the years it has undergone many changes and alterations, in both its structure and its name. It was first licensed in 1629. Today it offers 73 luxury bedrooms fully equipped with private bathrooms and showers, color TV, tea- and coffee-making facilities, radios, telephones, and a bowl of fruit. The intimate restaurant offers a full à la carte menu, or for a more informal meal the coffeeshop is open from 11 a.m. to 11 p.m. The rate for a single room is £40 ($60), and for a twin or double room, £55 ($82.50). All Prices include a full English breakfast, service, and VAT. The average cost of a three-course lunch in the restaurant is £6.50 ($9.75) and £10 ($15) for a three-course set dinner. The coffee-shop is open for quick grills and omelets.

Slatters, St. Margaret's Street (tel. 0227/63271), is a record of the city's changing past. Originally, its Jolly Miller Restaurant was built in the 17th century, and many of its old beams and stones are intact. But today the hotel has branched out, erecting a new structure on ground once occupied by buildings bombed in World War II. Slatters, as a result, has emerged as one of the most up-to-date establishments in the shire. The contemporary bedrooms, most with private baths, are motel-like in their efficiency. Most of the rooms convert into sitting areas during the day, with armchairs, a radio, and television. All rates include breakfast. A bathless single rents for £24 ($36), going up to £33 ($49.50) with bath. A bathless double is tabbed at £36 ($54), rising to £45 ($67.50) with bath, these tariffs including an English breakfast, service, and VAT. Parking is available even though you're in the heart of congested Canterbury, a five-minute stroll from the cathedral. The fully licensed Jolly Miller Restaurant serves lunch and dinner.

Chaucer, Ivy Lane (tel. 0227/64427), harmonizes modern features with its original Regency character. It's within strolling distance of the cathedral in the old part of the city. The bedrooms are well furnished, with good central heating, adequate storage space, and comfortable beds. The hotel has 51 bedrooms, 31 with private bathrooms. Facilities for making your own morning coffee or tea are available in the rooms, as well as color TV, radio, and telephone. A bathless single rents for £31 ($46.50) nightly, increasing to £38 ($57) with private bath. Bathless doubles go for £35 ($52.50), rising to £45 ($67.50) with bath. The Pilgrim's Bar is comfortable and tastefully decorated and offers a variety of bar snacks. The Dickensian restaurant is known for its local specialties, such as filet of beef and lamb. Service and VAT are included in the tariffs. A lunch costs £8 ($12) for three courses, a set dinner going for £11 ($16.50) for four courses.

The **Falstaff Hotel,** St. Dunstan's Street (tel. 0227/62138), is a restored coaching inn (you drive in where coaches from London to Dover used to unload their passengers). Just outside Westgate, near the River Stour, it is easy to spot, with its black-and-white timbered gables. Its street floor is devoted to pub-style lounges, the soul of Falstaff even after 500 years. On the floors above are a dining room, with its collection of antique clocks and framed Dutch tiles, and the well-kept bedrooms. Each of the rooms has hot and cold running water, and at least ten are fitted with private baths or showers. The rate in a single is £20 ($30). Twins range from £34 ($51) to £37 ($55.50), depending on the plumbing. Tariffs include an English breakfast. A three-course lunch or dinner costs from £8 ($12).

Cathedral Gate Hotel and Restaurant, 37 Burgate (tel. 0227/64381), is for modern-day pilgrims who want to rest their bones at an inn shouldering up to the cathedral's gateway. In 1620 this former hospice became one of the earliest of the fashionable coffee and tea houses of England. Its facade was added in the 19th century, however. The interior reveals many architectural features of the 17th century. Ms. Adsett is devoted to the hotel, and has done much to furnish it as authentically as possible. Two curved bay windows in the living room overlook the little square in front of the gateway. On chilly nights, log fires burn in an old fireplace, although the bedrooms are heated electrically. Each of the 33 bedrooms has hot and cold running water. Some contain private baths. Single rooms start at £12 ($18) for a top-floor unit (be warned, there's no elevator). A single with bath on the second floor costs £14 ($21). Doubles begin at £22 ($33), rising to £25 ($37.50) with bath, tariffs including VAT. The ground-floor restaurant serves morning coffee, luncheon, afternoon teas, and evening meals, and is licensed. A good meal in the restaurant will cost from £7 ($10.50).

The **House of Agnes Hotel,** 71 Saint Dunstan's St. (tel. 0227/65077), remains much as Dickens described it in *David Copperfield,* as the home of Agnes Wickfield, heroine of the novel. Built in the 16th century, the House of Agnes is an authentic, Tudor black-and-white timbered building—historic surroundings at budget prices. Mr. and Mrs. Roy Cook, who run it, quote B&B terms (depending on the room and the time of year) ranging from £12 ($18), inclusive. Some of the bedrooms are handsome and cozy; all ye olde chambers have hot and cold running water and free color TV. The hotel has a bar lounge, its own car park, and full central heating.

WHERE TO EAT: The **Castle Restaurant,** 71 Castle St. (tel. 0227/65658), is frequented by in-the-know "Canterburians" as the choicest dining spot in the medieval city (the building dates back to 1485)—choice not only because of its refined cuisine, but because of economy too. It is directed by Mr. and Mrs. Porter, who keep it unpretentious and unspoiled. For suggestions: The soups have rarely been found disappointing—a choice of two is offered daily. The specialties run to grills and fish dishes (prices include chips and garden peas), with such favorites as large Dover sole and rainbow trout. Two grilled lamb cutlets are another favorite. The desserts are especially good and widely varied, often featuring a gooseberry tart with fresh cream. Meals, not including your drink, begin at £7.50 ($11.25). The restaurant is open from 10 a.m. to 10 p.m. On Saturday, it's imperative to reserve before 4 p.m.

Adelaide Silver Grill, Adelaide Place (tel. 0227/65658), is part of the Castle Restaurant recommended above. It too is run by the Porters. Mr. Porter flits between one restaurant and the other via the "coalhole." The grill room has a slower turnover and higher prices. The food is good, and the place has a fine reputation among locals. Both restaurants are joined by a common kitchen, although much of the cooking in the Adelaide is on a grille in the dining room. The average price of a meal is £9 ($13.50), including drinks. For appetizers, try a selection of hors d'oeuvres from the trolley, which holds 18 different varieties. Grilled fish is a main-dish specialty, and a meat specialty is grilled Barnsley chop with mint sauce (a double loin lamb chop). Incidentally, steaks and chops are on display, and you can select your own if you wish. A choice from the sweets trolley will cost you an additional £1.50 ($2.25). With its reds and browns, the dining room is inclined to give one the feeling of a nightclubbish place. You need to reserve for Saturday luncheons.

The **Three Tuns,** Watling Street (tel. 0227/67371), has been an inn since 1600, but the house dates from the 13th century, standing on the corner of Watling Street, the Roman road to Dover, and Castle Street. The bars are open from 10 a.m. to 2:30 p.m. and 6 to 10:30 p.m. The pub serves breakfasts from 7:30 to 9 a.m. daily except Sunday, then coffee until lunch, which is available from noon to 2 p.m. Dinners, costing from £4 ($6) and served from 6 to 9 p.m., include beef-and-ale pie with two vegetables, moussaka with rice and vegetables, and chicken hotpot and curry. Light snacks and sandwiches are also served.

Waterfield's Restaurant, 5a Best Lane (tel. 0227/50276), is a pleasant 17th-century house with a light, bright dining room and attractive views across the river to the ancient houses beyond. Pine wood and white-painted brick walls make for a perfect setting for the expert cuisine of Michael Waterfield. There is a choice of different style and priced menus, ranging from saffron soup, kipper pâté, prawns in puff pastry, and terrine of eel to tournedos Rossini. All main courses are accompanied by fresh vegetables or potatoes and salad. Meals cost from £10 ($15) to £18 ($27), with 10% added to the bill for service. The restaurant is open from noon to 2:30 p.m. for lunch, from 7 to 10:30 p.m. for dinner, but closed all day Sunday and at lunchtime Monday.

Frogs, 26a/b Peter St. (tel 0227/68581), is a cheerful place where Mehrad Samimi, who hails from Iran, dispenses excellent food. At lunch, you might enjoy the stuffed crêpes, with a wide choice of filling, such as ham and cheese, asparagus and cheese, chicken livers, and caviar, followed by a sweet crêpe with banana and rum or Grand Marnier. Such meals cost from £3.50 ($5.25). The Brasserie caters to larger appetites with such courses as steak stuffed with stilton and cooked in red wine, served with petits pois and baked potato. Here, count on spending from £10 ($15) or more.

RIDE THE RAILS: In the area is the **Romney, Hythe & Dymchurch Light Railway Co.,** the world's smallest public railway. The engines are all steam driven, the carriages covered so there is no fear of getting wet. The line is 13½ miles long from Hythe (Kent) to New Romney and Dungeness, and the trains are one-third-size miniature versions of the kind of trains that ran on English or North American mainline railways in the 1920s. Fares depend on the distance traveled. Otherwise, you can purchase a runabout ticket valid for unlimited travel, costing about £18 ($27) per day. Children travel for one-third of the adult fare. It operates daily from Easter to the end of September. The railway is reached by road along the A259. The ride takes about half an hour. Naturally, the ticket includes freedom to travel for a whole day as services permit on the R.H.&D. Railway. Telephone 0679/62353 for train times. The terminal of the railway, Hythe, is near Folkestone, which can be reached by frequent trains from London.

By car, leave Canterbury on the Dover road, five miles out turn right and Elham's five miles farther. A right turn and another five miles will take you to Hythe.

3. Dover

Dover, one of the ancient Cinque ports, is famed for its white cliffs. In Victoria's day, it basked in popularity as a seaside resort. Today it is of importance mainly because it is a port for major cross-Channel car and passenger traffic between England and France (usually Calais). Sitting in the open jaws of the white cliffs, Dover was one of England's most vulnerable and easy-to-hit targets in World War II and suffered repeated bombings that destroyed much of its harbor.

Hovering nearly 400 feet above the port is **Dover Castle,** one of the oldest and best known in England. Its keep was built at the command of Becket's fair-weather friend, Henry II, in the 12th century. You can visit the keep year round, generally from 9:30 a.m. to 6:30 p.m. in summer (it closes earlier off-season), for an admission of £1.20 ($1.80) for adults, 60p (90¢) for children. Admission to the underground works is 60p (90¢) for adults, 30p (45¢) for children. Admission to the castle grounds is free. The ancient castle was called back to active duty as late as World War II. The "Pharos" on the grounds is a lighthouse built by the Romans in the first half of the first century. The Romans landed at nearby Deal in 55 B.C. and 54 B.C. The first landing was not successful. The second in 54 B.C. was more so, but after six months they departed, and did not return until nearly 100 years later, in A.D. 43, when they occupied the country and stayed 400 years.

This seaport handles more visitors from abroad than any other point of entry to Great Britain. At the **National Tourist Information Centre,** Townwall Street (tel. 0304/205108), I found a small band of dedicated workers tirelessly answering questions and booking accommodations. It is easy to be casual and offhand when dealing with the same old questions time and time again, but these people treat each inquiry as something of vital interest and importance and give endless helpful advice. I am sure they will solve any problem you may have.

WHERE TO STAY: The **White Cliffs Hotel,** Sea Front (tel. 0304/203633), is the traditional choice, with many of its bedrooms facing the Channel. Clinging tenaciously to the past, its facade is impressive, built like a string of attached town houses, with an unbroken seafront balcony and a glass-enclosed front veranda. The bedrooms are comfortable and tranquil. The rooms facing the sea carry the higher price tag, of course. A waterfront double with private bath rents for £38 ($57). A bathless double costs £33 ($49.50). A single without bath is £20 ($30), rising to £24 ($36) with bath or shower and a sea view. Tariffs include a full English breakfast and VAT. Meals and light snacks are available 24 hours a day, and there is a set lunch for £5.50 ($8.25), a set dinner for from £7 ($10.50). A covered garage is available. The hotel is close to the eastern and western docks and the hoverport for travel to and from France and Belgium.

The **Dover Stage Coachotel,** Sea Front (tel. 0304/201001), is for those who desire streamlined motel efficiency. Set back from the sea, it opens onto its own miniature plaza with flowers and fountain. Six floors of bedrooms attract cross-Channel overnighters. The entire waterfront facade zigzags, with angular bay-view units and individual balconies. The studio-style rooms have built-in furnishings, and hot and cold running water—but no private baths. The furnishings of this modern building have not stood up well to weathering, and the general impression now is of utilitarian austerity. Singles cost £23 ($34.50); doubles, £32 ($48); and the few doubles with showers, £36 ($54). Extra beds can be added, and there are some bunk rooms for families, costing £28 ($42). All prices include a full breakfast and VAT. No lunches are served here, but you can dine in the Burgundy Restaurant from 7 p.m., with last orders being taken at 8:45 p.m. Snacks are served in the Coach Bar at the same time. Coffee and sandwiches are available after the dinner hours.

The **Holiday Inn,** Townwall Street (tel. 0304/203270), stands in the center of town, just a few minutes away from the railway station, the seafront, and the international ferry and hoverport terminals. Small as Holiday Inns go in England, it offers 83 rooms, designed in the typical utilitarian chain motif, each with a private bath, color TV, radio, in-house movies, direct-dial phones, plus individually controlled air conditioning and heating. Singles rent for £38 ($57) nightly, the tariff increasing to anywhere from £48 ($72) to £50 ($75) in a double or twin. On the premises is an attractive heated indoor swimming pool, along with a fitness center. You can dine in a modern restaurant at the inn or order a snack in the coffeeshop, perhaps a drink in the Lord Warden bar.

Cliffe Court Hotel, Marine Parade (tel. 0304/211001), is a useful addition in a town lamentably short of good accommodations. It has a Regency facade with a wrought-iron balcony and steps up to the front door. It offers mostly large rooms, some with bath or shower and toilet, radio, color TV, and an alarm clock to wake you for an early start to France. Le Rendezvous Restaurant and bar behind the first-floor balcony serves good continental cuisine. Singles are £18 ($27); bathless doubles or twins, £29 ($43.50); doubles or twins with bath or shower, £32 ($48). Family rooms are £40 ($60) and £44 ($66) without bath, £48 ($72) with shower and toilet. All prices include breakfast, VAT, and service.

Tower Guest House, 98 Priory Hill (tel. 0304/208212), is an absolute gem, high above the town with fine views over the roofs out to sea and across to the castle atop the White Cliffs. Ron and Doreen Wraight inherited an old water tower at the bottom of their garden when they came to Tower House and promptly set about turning it into guest accommodations. Bedrooms in the round building are shaped like wedges or half moons, containing warm carpets, comfortable beds with downy duvets, and hot and cold running water. A bathroom, shower room, and two toilets are shared among the four double rooms, and there's a wedge-shaped breakfast room where Doreen serves ample breakfasts. Off the breakfast room is the immaculate kitchen where you can make tea or coffee anytime. Given warning, Doreen will prepare you an evening meal at £5.50 ($8.25). She prefers to serve steaks, rounding the meal off with Black Forest cake. The cost is £18 ($27) per night per couple. By use of bunk beds, family rooms can be provided, for which the Wraights charge £25 ($37.50) for three persons, £31 ($46.50) for four.

Priory Hill rises almost directly above Dover Priory Station, and for a quick descent to the town, there are steps leading down. It's better to drive up, however, in your own car or by taxi.

WHERE TO EAT: Britannia, Townwall Street (tel. 0304/203248), across from the Dover Stage Coachotel, near the seafront, brings imagination and flair to an otherwise dull restaurant town. In a modern pub setting, you can sample good English food: Canterbury lamb cutlets, grilled Dover sole. But the chef reaches out to France and Spain as well for inspiration. On my latest rounds, I spotted six Spanish specialties on the menu, including such treats as Valencian paella. The appetizers are tempting as well, including pâté maison and lobster soup with brandy. Among the desserts, I prefer the Tia Maria walnut parfait. Prices for the bar food downstairs start at £1.50 ($2.25) for soup and french bread, and go up to £2.50 ($3.75) for the hot dish of the day. The restaurant upstairs specializes mainly in grills. A complete meal chosen from the à la carte menu will cost about £10 ($15) per person. A set lunch is £6.50 ($9.75); a set dinner, £8.50 ($12.75).

For our next and final stopover in Kent, we go inland, 37 miles from London, to a once-fashionable resort.

4. Tunbridge Wells

Dudley, Lord North, courtier to James I, is credited with the discovery in 1606 of the mineral spring that started it all. His accidental find led to the creation of a fashionable resort that reached its peak in the mid-18th century under the foppish leadership of "Beau" Nash. Beau or Richard Nash (1674–1761) was a dandy in his day, the final arbiter of what to wear and what to say—even how to act (for example, he got men to take off their boots and put on stockings). But, of course, most of his time was devoted to Bath. Even so, Tunbridge Wells enjoyed a prime spa reputation from the days of Charles II through Victoria. Because so many monarchs visited it, Edward VII named it Royal Tunbridge Wells in 1919. Over the years the cure was considered the answer for everything from too many days of wine and roses to failing sexual prowess.

The most remarkable feature of Tunbridge Wells is its Pantiles, a colonaded walkway for shoppers, tea-drinkers, and diners, built near the wells. At the Assembly Hall, entertainment such as opera or vaudeville is presented.

Alas, there's nothing sadder in tourism than a resort that's seen its day. Still, it's worth a visit—just for a fleeting glimpse of the 18th century.

Canadians touring in the area may want to seek out the grave of the founder of their country's capital. Lt. Col. John By of the Royal Engineers (1779–1836) died at Shernfold Park in Frant East Sussex, near Tunbridge Wells, and is buried in the churchyard there. His principal claim to fame is that he built the Rideau Canal in Upper Canada and established what was later to be the capital of the Dominion of Canada—the city of Ottawa.

The Rideau Canal, some 124 miles long, links the city of Kingston on the St. Lawrence River with the city of Ottawa on the Ottawa River. Between 1826 and 1832 John By successfully constructed this canal through an unexplored wilderness for the British government. At the northern end of the canal he laid out "Bytown." Twenty years later this was renamed Ottawa, and it became the capital of a united Canada. His grave near Tunbridge Wells is marked with a plaque erected by the Historical Society of Ottawa in 1979.

FOOD AND LODGING: **Calverley Hotel,** Crescent Road (tel. 0892/26455), is an old stone hotel facing Calverley Park, gardens of special interest in themselves. The hotel's enormous lounge, furnished with comfortable chairs and decorated in relaxing colors, opens onto the terrace and gardens. The dining room also overlooks the gardens. The bedrooms, on the upper floors, are reached by elevator. Each room has central heating, telephone, radio, and many have private bath or shower. Guests frequently meet in the warm and friendly cocktail bar for drinks before dinner. Overnight rates at the Calverley range from £17 ($40.50) for a bathless single to £33 ($49.50) for a double with private bath. Breakfast is included, but you'll pay an additional £6 ($9) for the table d'hôte luncheon, and about £8.50 ($12.75) for dinner. VAT is added to all charges.

Wellington Hotel, Mount Ephraim (tel. 0892/42911), enjoys a regal position, overlooking the common. The Regency hotel suggest a Charles Addams drawing, with its mansard roof, rows of dormers, and original balconies. Catering mainly to business people and families, it is in an ideal position to be used as a base for visiting the southeast of England, being equidistant from London and the coast, centrally situated in the "Garden of England," with its beautiful old manor houses. For a luxury period double room with private bath, the charge is from £45 ($67.50) per night, including VAT and service. Less expensive doubles go for only £35 ($52.50). A four-course dinner will cost from £8 ($12).

READER'S HOTEL SELECTION: "The **Russell Hotel,** 80 London Rd. (tel. 0892/44833), charges £35 ($52.50) per night for two persons in a room with bath, including VAT but not service. It is clean, well furnished, and has a tiny bar and color TV. The dining room is run by a young French chef who does a superb job. The woman who owns the hotel is friendly, efficient, and helpful. This hotel was recommended to me by locals. It is an easy walk from the Pantiles" (Wanda S. Nadal, Fircrest, Wash.).

Instead of leaving London for Kent, you might head directly south of the capital to inviting Surrey.

SURREY

This tiny county has for some time been in danger of being gobbled up by the growing boundaries of London and turned into a sprawling suburb. Already some of the densely populated area in Surrey is now part of Greater London. But Surrey still retains much unspoiled countryside, largely because its many heaths and commons do not make good land for postwar suburbanite houses. Essentially, Surrey is a county of commuters (Alfred, Lord Tennyson was among the first), since a worker in the city can practically travel to the remotest corner of Surrey from London in anywhere from 45 minutes to an hour.

Long before William the Conqueror marched his pillaging Normans across its chalky North Downs, Surrey was important to the Saxons. In fact, early Saxon kings were once crowned at what is now **Kingston-on-Thames** (their Coronation Stone is still preserved near the Guildhall).

LIVING IN TUDOR SPLENDOR: The best of England—the best living accommodations, in particular—are to be found in the countryside. There you can sometimes live like a duke or duchess for the same amount you'd pay for only a fairly good room in London. Transportation facilities are often so good that you can enjoy the best of two worlds, darting into London for all its attractions, while enjoying the lower costs and better surroundings of rural England. For those who want to be in the vicinity of Heathrow Airport, yet within easy access of central London, I have the following recommendation in the upper bracket:

Great Fosters, Egham (tel. 0784/33822), is one of the most impressive old manor houses of England. It was built in 1550 and in its day belonged to Elizabeth I and was a hunting lodge in Windsor's Royal Forest. Although only 18 miles from London, it still preserves the link to its past. A red brick Tudor building, with stone-mullioned windows, many gables, and towering chimneys, it is placed in a private garden, where paths cut through formal grounds of clipped yew hedges, roses, and rhododendrons—and a swimming pool. The architectural features of the interior are in the grand style, as witness the main hall with its carved black oak Jacobean fireplace. In the 15th-century Tithe Barn, with its high vaulted and raftered oak beams, excellent English meals are served and an orchestra plays for dancing on Saturday night. Some of the master bedrooms are worthy of royalty. For example, the gilt-paneled Italian bedroom contains an overscale bed with hand-carved cherubs on the posts. Period-style rooms rent from £53 ($79.50), doubles and twins from £50 ($75), and singles from £30 ($45). These room rates include a full English breakfast, service, and VAT. Great Fosters is only a half mile from Runnymede and the Kennedy Memorial, and only seven miles in different directions from Windsor Castle and Hampton Court Palace.

5. Richmond

Want to spend an afternoon in a Thames river town? Richmond in Surrey is only a 30-minute ride from London, and can be easily reached by the Underground trains, or else Green Line coaches 716 or 716a from Hyde Park Corner. The old town, popular in Victorian times, has good public rail links with London, and it offers the escape many seek from the rush and bustle of the metropolis. If you're feeling lighthearted, take the boat trip down the Thames. Turner himself, art materials in hand, came here for inspiration.

Richmond is only one mile from Kew and its botanical gardens. You may prefer a combined excursion to Kew Gardens and Richmond on the same day. One of the attractions of the Thames town is the 2500-acre **Richmond Park,** first staked out by Charles I in 1637. It is filled with photogenic deer and waterfowl. Richmond has long enjoyed associations with royalty, as Henry VII's Richmond Palace stood there (an even earlier manor was razed). Queen Elizabeth I died in the old palace in 1603. Somebody's short-sightedness led to the palace's being carted away, and only a carriageway remains.

If you want to be like the English, you'll climb **Richmond Hill** for a view of the Thames considered by some to be one of the ten best views in the world. The scene reminded William Byrd of a similar view near his home on the James River in Virginia, inspiring him to name the city founded there in 1737 Richmond.

There are good shops and an excellent theater facing the green on which, in summertime, cricket matches are played. Boating happens on the river. Richmond Park has a public golf course, and you can rent a horse from the local stables. The Richmond Ice Skating Rink has been the nursery of many of England's skating champions. Wimbledon and the Tennis Championships are within easy reach, as is Hampton Court Palace.

At Petersham, the 13th-century St. Peter's Church is the burial place of Capt. George Vancouver. The Queen Mother's parents, Lord and Lady Glamis, were married there. It also has some very old wooden box pews. At St. Anne's Church at Kew Green, the painters Gainsborough and Zoffany were buried.

WHERE TO EAT: Londoners often go down to Richmond for the day, browse through its art galleries, and then dine out—which must account for the town's number of good restaurants. My recommendation follows:

Richmond Rendezvous, 1 Wakefield Rd. (tel. 940-5114), bills itself with some justification as "the leading Peking-style restaurant in the United Kingdom." You would never suspect it, however, to judge from the unprepossessing decor. The food is superb, especially if you stick to the chef's specialties and avoid the routine Chinese restaurant fare. Three dishes, designed to delight, include barbecued Peking duck, steamed and deep fried, or a variety of meats in a chafing dish. Also recommended are hot-and-sour Peking soup, scampi Peking style, sliced beef in oyster sauce, and diced chicken in yellow bean sauce. If there are six persons in your party, you can forgo the above and leave it to the chef, who will prepare you a Peking dinner at £12 ($18) per head.

WHERE TO STAY: The **Richmond Gate,** Richmond Hill (tel. 940-0061), and the **Petersham,** Richmond Hill (tel. 940-7471), are two privately owned hotels, 200 yards apart, that are operated and managed as one. From the top of Richmond Hill, both hotels enjoy a view of the Thames that has attracted famous artists for centuries, and both hotels have interesting historical features. The Richmond Gate comprises two adjoining Georgian buildings, one originally occupied by a member of the Penn family. The Petersham, built as a hotel in 1864, has a remarkable spiral stone staircase dominated by ceiling murals of well-known Renaissance painters. Bedrooms are a careful blend of old and new, all with private bathroom, color TV, radio, and telephone. Room service is offered until 10 p.m., and two restaurants are available. Nightingales restaurant at the Petersham enjoys a panoramic view of the river, and the à la carte menu offers a wide choice of international dishes. A three-course set menu is available at lunchtime for £9 ($13.50). Gates bar-restaurant at the Richmond Gate is an informal facility specializing in fresh seasonal produce. Snacks in the bar or an à la carte menu can be yours at lunchtime, and in the evenings a three-course menu is offered at £10.50 ($15.75). Single rooms cost £42 ($63). An extra bed in the room is £12 ($18). Specially reduced rates based on two- or three-night stays will be quoted. All tariffs include a full English breakfast and VAT.

6. Haslemere

A quiet, sleepy town, Haslemere attracts because early English musical instruments are made by hand there. Ever hear a harpsichord concert? An annual music festival (see below) is the town's main drawing card. Over the years, the Dolmetsch family has been responsible for the acclaim that has come to this otherwise unheralded little Surrey town, which lies in the midst of some of the shire's finest scenery. Haslemere is only an hour's train ride from Waterloo Station in London, about 42 miles away.

THE FESTIVAL: It isn't often that one can hear such exquisite music played so skillfully on the harpsichord, the recorder, the lute, or any of the instruments designed so painstakingly to interpret the music of earlier centuries. Throughout the year the Dolmetsch family makes and repairs these instruments, welcoming visitors to their place on the edge of Haslemere. They rehearse constantly, preparing for the concerts that are held in July and last nine days.

You can get specific information by writing to the **Haslemere Festival Office**, Jesses, Grayswood Road, Haslemere (or telephone 0428/2161 between 9 a.m. and 12:30 p.m. daily). During the festival, matinees begin at 3:15 p.m., evening performances at 7:30 p.m. For seats in the balcony, prices range from £2.50 ($3.75) to £3.50 ($5.25), with stall seats going from £1.50 ($2.25) to £3 ($4.50).

WHERE TO STAY: The **Georgian Hotel,** High Street (tel. 0428/51555), is in the middle of the town, within walking distance of the Dolmetsch Center. Antiques and period accessories are well placed throughout. The B&B rate per person ranges from £22 ($33) to £32 ($48) nightly, the latter for a single with private bath. (Of the hotel's 22 pleasingly furnished bedrooms, 15 have private baths.) The hotel, although Georgian, is actually named after the U.S. State of Georgia. James Edward Oglethorpe, a member of Parliament in the 18th century, who owned the hotel, founded the state of Georgia. The establishment is licensed, and before dinner you can have healthy-size drinks, which can be served to you from the magnificent new cocktail bar overlooking the split-level flower-surrounded patio. The garden is a favorite spot for afternoon tea.

A Hotel on the Outskirts

Lythe Hill Hotel, Petworth Road, near Haslemere (tel. 0428/51251), is a 14th-century farmhouse of historic interest set in 14 acres of beautiful parkland overlooking National Trust woodlands and just one hour from London, Heathrow, and Gatwick. Across the courtyard is the newer part of the hotel in converted 16th-century farm buildings that offer a luxurious accommodation, 28 rooms and suites, handsomely decorated public rooms, and a restaurant serving international and English dishes, both table d'hôte and à la carte. In the Italian garden, a dinner dance is staged on Saturday evenings.

The black-and-white timbered farmhouse has six period bedrooms with all modern comforts, and in the Tudor room stands a four-poster bed dated 1614. Downstairs in the oak-beamed and paneled dining room is the renowned **Auberge de France** restaurant, offering a fine French cuisine at candlelit, polished oak tables. Specialties include diplomat d'homard, pintadeau truffe au persil, turbot au champagne, and a cellar of fine wines. Dinner for two in the auberge costs around £35 ($52.50).

The table d'hôte menu in the main hotel restaurant is around £10 ($15) to £15 ($22.50); and a twin room with private bath for two, including a continental breakfast and VAT, plus the service charge, is £60 ($90).

Lythe Hill Hotel is really a French hamlet in Surrey, offering peace and comfort as well as a genuine French cuisine. The auberge is closed for lunch on Tuesday and all day on Monday.

GUILDFORD: The old and new meet in the county town on the Wey River, 40 minutes by train from Waterloo Station in London. Charles Dickens believed that its High Street, which slopes to the river, was one of the most beautiful in England. The Guildhall has an ornamental projecting clock which dates back to 1683.

Lying 2½ miles southwest of the city, **Loseley House** (tel. 0483/71881), a beautiful and historic Elizabethan mansion visited by Queen Elizabeth I, James I, and Queen Mary, has been featured on TV and in five films. Its works of art include paneling from Henry VIII's Nonsuch Palace, period furniture, a unique carved chalk chimneypiece, magnificent ceilings, and cushions made by the first Queen Elizabeth. The mansion is open from the end of May to the end of September on Wednesday, Thursday, Friday, and Saturday from 2 to 5 p.m., charging £1.20 ($1.80) for adults, 75p ($1.13) for children.

Sutton Place, Guildford, is on view by appointment only. For 17 years, J. Paul Getty, reputed to be the world's richest man, lived in isolated security here. In 1980 the house became the property of Stanley J. Seeger, who formed the Sutton Place Heritage Trust and set about spending millions of pounds on the house and gardens to restore them to their 16th-century spirit. Although it was built in the mid-1520s, the house today is of no particular period, but you'll find an interesting balance throughout.

The house has been given over to history and the arts. Concerts and special evenings when supper is served in the Long Gallery are held. A selection of artworks is displayed in the Small Gallery, changing from time to time. Visits to the house and garden are offered on Tuesday and Saturday, and you have your own special guide. Write or telephone in advance to the Booking Secretary, Sutton Place, Guildford, Surrey GU4 7QV (tel. 0483/504455 between 10 a.m. and 4 p.m.). The charge for admission is £2.50 ($3.75); half price for bona fide students. The tour lasts about 1½ hours.

Food and Lodging

Angel Hotel, High Street (tel. 0483/64555), is an old coaching inn in the middle of the steep main street of town. Its entrance and part of its courtyard are Tudor, and many other original features of this once-busy hostelry have been maintained. Inside, there is lavish paneling, plus a huge, open fireplace as well as exposed beams. Great oak timbers from old ships at Portsmouth were used to support the gallery.

Most of the two dozen bedrooms, including two family rooms, are simply furnished, although some are quite attractively decorated (these disappear first to those who reserve ahead). Each has a private bath, as well as a phone, radio, TV, and coffee maker. Rates begin at £45 ($67.50) in a single, going up to £60 ($90) in a double, including VAT and service. In addition to a well-decorated bar, the hotel has a quick-service coffeeshop as well as a unique 13th-century restaurant in the crypt, with medieval architecture making for cozy surroundings. The restaurant offers a wide range of dishes, including English roasts, at an average price of £15 ($22.50) per person.

DORKING: This country town lies on the Mole River, at the foot of the North Downs. Within easy reach are some of the most scenic spots in the shire, including Silent Pool, Box Hill, and Leith Hill. Three miles to the northwest stands **Polesden Lacey** (tel. Bookham 52048), a former Regency villa containing the Greville collection of antiques, paintings, and tapestries. In the early part of this century, it was enlarged to become a comfortable Edwardian country house when it was the home of a celebrated hostess, who frequently entertained royalty there. The 18th-century garden is filled with herbaceous borders, a rose garden, and beech walks, and in all the estate consists of 1000 acres. The house is open in March and November on Saturday and Sunday only from 2 to 5 p.m.; April to the end of October, daily, except Monday and Friday, from 2 to 6 p.m. (closed Good Friday and Tuesday after a bank holiday Monday, when it is open). The charge to visit both the house and garden is £2 ($3) for adults, half price for children. The garden is open daily all year from 11 a.m. to sunset. To visit just the garden, adults are charged £1 ($1.50) and children pay 50p (75¢). A licensed restaurant on the grounds is open from 11 a.m. on the days the house can be visited, plus a gift shop open 2 to 5:30 p.m.

Back in Dorking, you can find accommodations at the following:

Burford Bridge Hotel, Box Hill (tel. 0306/884561), offers stylish living in a rural town from which a train will zip you into London in less than half an hour. At the foot of the beauty spot of Box Hill, the hotel has a lot of historical associations. Lord Nelson was a frequent patron, and Keats completed *Endymion* here in 1817. Everyone from Wordsworth to Robert Louis Stevenson also frequented the place. You get the best of both the old and the new here, including a tithe barn (circa 1600) as well as 52 large, colorfully decorated bedrooms, renting for £42 ($63) in a single, from £48 ($72) to £60 ($90) in a double. Each room has its own bath or shower, plus a phone and color TV. The restaurant serves good English food, and a bar opens onto a flowered patio with a fountain. Light refreshments and afternoon teas are served in the comfortable lounge and pretty garden. In summer, you can enjoy the garden swimming pool and frequent barbecues.

White Horse Hotel, High Street (tel. 0306/881138). Just ten miles from Gatwick Airport, you can dine or lodge at a hotel that dates in part from 1500. Once the vicarage of Dorking, the White Horse by tradition was supposed to have been the "Marquis of Granby" in the *Pickwick Papers.* At least Dickens was known to have frequented the bar parlor.

An atmospheric place of creaking timbers and low beamed ceilings, the inn offers 70 bedrooms, including 18 family units, each with private baths or showers, plus phones, radios, TV sets, and coffee makers. A single with bath costs from £38 ($57), a double renting for £52 ($78), including VAT and service. Often called "the most interesting house in Dorking," the inn has a restaurant as well as a Pickwick bar offering à la carte meals for £10 ($15) to £13 ($19.50).

GODALMING: The **Inn on the Lake,** Godalming (tel. 04868/5575), is a haven of landscaped gardens with ducks drowsing on pools beside the lake and a pleasant old house, owned by Joy and Martin Cummings. Rooms are decorated with pretty country prints and simple furniture, each having TV, tea- and coffee-making equipment, and radio. The Cummingses charge £24 ($36) for a single, £31 ($46.50) for a double, including VAT and a large breakfast. Excellent snacks are served in a real old-world bar, where some of the timbers date from Tudor times. In summer, barbecues are held in the garden. For more substantial dinners, three fixed-price menus are offered at £9.50 ($14.25), £11.50 ($17.25), and £13.50 ($20.25) for five courses, with a varied selection of grills, English, and continental dishes.

The house was listed in the Domesday Book and has Tudor, Georgian, and Victorian associations. As you may know, Godalming was the starting point for the emigrés who eventually settled Allenton, Georgia, after landing in Savannah.

After visiting Surrey, you can head south toward the English Channel and the sprawling shires of Sussex.

THE SUSSEXES

If King Harold hadn't loved Sussex so much, the course of English history might have been changed forever. Had the brave Saxon waited longer in the north, he could have marshaled more adequate reinforcements before striking south to meet the Normans. But Duke William's soldiers were ravaging the countryside he knew so well, and Harold rushed down to counter them.

Harold's enthusiasm for Sussex is understandable. The landscape rises and falls like waves. The country is known for its Downlands and tree-thickened Weald, from which came the timbers to build England's mighty fleet in days gone by. The shires lie south of London and Surrey, bordering Kent in the east, Hampshire in the west, and opening directly onto the sometimes sunny, resort-dotted English Channel.

Like the other sections in the vulnerable south of England, the Sussexes witnessed some of the most dramatic moments in the country's history. Apart from the Norman landings at Hastings, the most life-changing transfusion of plasma occurred in the 19th century, as middle-class Victorians flocked to the seashore, pumping new spirit into Eastbourne, Worthing, Brighton, even old Hastings. The cult of the saltwater worshippers flourished, and has to this day. Although **Eastbourne** and **Worthing** are much frequented by the English, I'd place them several fathoms below **Brighton** and **Hastings,** which are much more suitable if you're seeking a holiday by the sea.

Far more than the resorts, the old towns and villages of the Sussexes are intriguing, particularly **Rye** and **Winchelsea,** the ancient towns of the Cinque Port Confederation. No Sussex village is lovelier than **Alfriston** (and the innkeepers know it too); **Arundel** is noted for its castle; the cathedral city of **Chichester** is a mecca for theater buffs. Traditionally, and for purposes of government, Sussex is divided into East Sussex and West Sussex. I've adhered to that convenient dichotomy.

I'll begin in East Sussex, where you'll find many of the inns and hotels within commuting distance of London.

7. Rye

"Nothing more recent than a Cavalier's Cloak, Hat and Ruffles should be seen in the streets of Rye," said Louis Jennings. He's so right. This ancient town, formerly an island, was chartered back in 1229. Rye, 65 miles below London, near the English Channel, and neighboring Winchelsea were once part of the ancient Cinque Ports Confederation. Rye flourished as a smuggling center, its denizens sneaking in contraband from the marshes to stash away in little nooks (even John Wesley's firm chastisements couldn't stop what was a strongly entrenched tradition).

But the sea receded from Rye, leaving it perched like a giant whale out of water. Its narrow, cobblestoned streets twist and turn like a labyrinth. It has long been considered a special place, having attracted any number of famous men, including Henry James, who once lived in the Lamb House on Mermaid Street.

Attacked several times by French fleets, Rye was practically razed in 1377. But it rebuilt sufficiently, decking itself out in the Elizabethan style so that Queen Elizabeth I, during her visit in 1573, bestowed upon the town the distinction of Royal Rye.

Today the city has any number of specific buildings and sites of architectural interest, notably the 13th-century **Ypres Tower** (sheltering the Rye Museum), and the 15th-century **St. Mary's Parish Church,** with its unusual clock.

The **Rye Museum** has collections of military gear, toys, Cinque Ports relics, Victoriana, and pottery, as well as displays showing the history of shipping and of inns of the area. It is open from Easter until mid-October from 10:30 a.m. to 1 p.m. and 2:15 to 5:30 p.m., opening at 11:30 a.m. on Sunday.

WHERE TO STAY: The **Mermaid Inn,** Mermaid Street (tel. 0797/223065), is one of the most famous of the old smugglers inns of England, known to that band of cutthroats, the real-life Hawkhurst Gang, as well as to Russell Thorndike's fictional character, Dr. Syn. One of the present rooms, in fact, is called Dr. Syn's Bedchamber, and is connected by a secret staircase—set in the thickness of the wall—to the bar. That room, with a private bath, rents for £24 ($36) per person nightly, as does the Elizabethan Chamber (with four-poster and private bath). Two other special rooms—the Fleur-de-Lys Chamber and the Tudor Rose Chamber—contain private baths and twin beds, and cost £22 ($33) per person. Terms include breakfast, and a 10% service charge is added. Other less expensive rooms are equipped with hot and cold running water, some with baths, attractive furnishings, and are available in single, double, or twin. The charge is from £18 ($27) per person, including breakfast. Some of the single rooms are so small, customers in the days of the plumed hat and sword must have had to leave their gear outside. The best rooms are in the main building overlooking the cobblestone street. The Mermaid has sheltered everybody from Queen Elizabeth I to George Arliss. When Elizabeth came to Rye in 1573, the inn had already been operating nearly 150 years. A covered carriageway leads to the car park. In the center of the hotel is a courtyard, where you'll see a pedestal fountain with water flowing down on the heads of water lilies. The Mermaid has also taken over the 16th-century Ship Inn at the foot of Mermaid Street which, with its 12 bedrooms and restaurant on the first floor, complements the Mermaid very well.

Monastery Hotel, 6 High St. (tel. 0797/223272), is an early 17th-century building that grew up over the ruins of a 13th-century friary of the Augustinian order. Its own monastic garden backs up against the walls of the old friary. Nowadays, the house offers eight modernized double- and twin-bedded rooms with hot and cold running water, private showers, central heating, and razor points, renting at £12 ($18) per person for B&B. One unit with a private bath costs slightly more. There is a comfortable lounge, with color television, and a restaurant installed in an attractive room overlooks the Old Friary Chapel. For nearly 50 years, the Monastery has been receiving guests, the welcome today provided by the resident manager, Colin G. Coombes.

WHERE TO EAT: The **Monastery Restaurant,** 6 High St. (tel. 0797/223272), is in the small High Street Monastery Hotel. Don Moore, restaurant owner, is the chef and produces dishes with undisguised enthusiasm. Leek and stilton soup with croutons or garlic bread, chicken breasts stuffed with avocado and prawns covered with watercress sauce, and lamb stuffed with rosemary and orange served with a garnish of onions, tomato, and mushrooms are specialties of the house. Desserts, including light flans and sorbets, are further examples of Don's expertise. A harpist plays at Sunday lunch and on Friday and Saturday night. Meals cost from £12 ($18) to £18 ($27). The house wine is £5.50 ($8.25). Sunday lunch, a gastronomical feast, is £8 ($12). Reservations are advised.

The **Flushing Inn,** Market Street (tel. 0797/223292), is in a 16th-century inn on a cobblestone street. It has preserved the best of the past, including a wall-size fresco in the restaurant dating from 1544 and depicting a menagerie of birds and heraldic beasts. A rear dining room overlooks a carefully tended flower garden. A special feature is the Sea Food Lounge Bar, where sandwiches and plates of seafood are available from £2.50 ($3.75) to £8 ($12). In the main restaurant, luncheons are offered for from £8 ($12); dinners run from £11.50 ($17.25). Besides these lunches and dinners, gastronomic evenings are held at regular intervals between October and April. For one of these specially prepared meals, including your apéritif, wine, and after-dinner brandy, you pay £22 ($33) per person. Fine Wine evenings cost £25 ($37.50) per person. The inn is closed Monday night, all day on Tuesday, and for three weeks after Christmas.

Another choice is offered at the **Bistro Down Under,** 1a High St. (tel. 0797/222829). You may not be immediately drawn here by the somewhat loud rock music and oilcloth or plastic-covered tables, but Nick Parking and Toni Fergusson-Lees make up for those minor characteristics with superb, fresh local fish, wild duck, rabbit, pigeon, and jugged hare. It's all there in pies, casseroles, and stews, accompanied by fresh vegetables properly cooked or a salad. A meal will cost £14 ($21).

The **Peacock Wine Bar,** Lion Street (tel. 0797/223161), is in a little cottage owned by Jane Edgar, who also does the cooking—pâtés, soups, steak-and-kidney pie, moussaka, chili, and turkey pie, priced from £1 ($1.50) to £2.50 ($3.75) per plate or bowl. Wine is £1 ($1.50) per glass. It's open in summer all week from noon to 2 p.m. and from 6:45 to 9:30 p.m., except for closing on Friday and Saturday evening. In winter, only lunches are served, from noon to 2 p.m. daily except Tuesday and Thursday. This is a busy place in summer, but if you're patient, you will get one of the small tables to use after collecting your food from the bar.

8. Winchelsea

The sister Cinque Federation port to Rye, Winchelsea has also witnessed the water's ebb. It traces its history back to Edward I, and has experienced many dramatic moments, such as sacking by the French. Today it is a dignified residential town (Ellen Terry's former cottage can be seen huddling up to Strandgate, on the road to Rye). In the words of one 19th-century writer, Winchelsea is "a sunny cream of centuries ago." Its finest sight is a badly damaged 14th-century church, containing a number of remarkable tombs.

WHERE TO STAY: The **New Inn** (tel. 0797/226252) is an old hostelry in the middle of this picture-postcard village, across the road from the 14th-century church. It has all the mellow associations of a country inn of England—pleasant, comfortable rooms, a tavern, good food, a garden in the rear, a fireplace, plenty of battered, but polished, brass and copper steins hanging from the ceiling, even a dart game going. Run by Richard and Eileen Joyce, the New Inn rents its well-furnished (many quite large) doubles for £28 ($42) per night (innerspring mattresses) including a big English breakfast and VAT. All the rooms have hot and cold water. Snacks and main meals are served in the inn's bars, with plenty of good food available for from around £2.50 ($3.75).

On the Outskirts

Justins Hotel, Bodiam, near Robertsbridge (tel. Staplecross 372), is a Tudor-style estate set in a well-tended two-acre garden, surrounded by tall trees and a view of the Sussex Downs. Only 12 miles from Rye and Winchelsea, it is close to Bodiam Castle, built in 1386 and considered one of the most magnificent castles of its kind in England.

Your resident owners are Joy and George Tipper, who have installed private baths in eight of their ten attractively furnished bedrooms, charging from £16.50 ($24.75) per person nightly for B&B, or £23 ($34.50) per person for half board. After enjoying a drink and friendly conversation in the cocktail bar, guests can order good cookery served in the oak-paneled dining room. Personal service is a hallmark of the establishment.

9. Hastings and St. Leonard's

The world has seen bigger battles, but few are as well remembered as the Battle of Hastings in 1066. When William, Duke of Normandy, landed on the Sussex coast and lured King Harold (already fighting Vikings in Yorkshire) southward to defeat, the destiny of the English-speaking people was changed forever. It was D-Day in reverse. The actual battle occurred at what is now Battle Abbey (nine miles away), but the Norman duke used Hastings as his base of operation.

Hastings suffered other invasions—it was razed by the French in the 14th century. But after that blow a Tudor town grew up in the eastern sector, and it makes for a good stroll today. The more recent invasion threat, that of Hitler's armies, never came to pass, although the dragons' dentures put up across the countryside stood waiting to bite into Nazi tanks.

Linked by a three-mile promenade along the sea, Hastings and St. Leonard's were given a considerable boost in the 19th century by that eminent tripper Queen Victoria, who visited several times. Both towns no longer enjoy such royal patronage; rather, they do a thriving business with Midlanders on vacation. Hastings and St. Leonard's have the usual shops and English sea-resort amusements. Only 63 miles from London, they are serviced by fast trains from Victoria Station.

The two chief attractions are:

HASTINGS CASTLE: In ruins now, the first of the Norman castles to be built in England sprouted up on a western hill overlooking Hastings, circa 1067. Precious little is left to remind us of the days when proud knights, imbued with a spirit of pomp and spectacle, wore bonnets and girdles. The fortress was ordered torn down by King John in 1216, and later served as a church and monastery until it felt Henry VIII's ire. Owned by the Pelham dynasty from the latter 16th century to modern times, the ruins have been turned over to Hastings. It is open from 10 a.m. to 5 p.m. daily from Easter to September, charging an admission of 60p (90¢) for adults, 35p (53¢) for children. From the mount, you'll have a good view of the coast and promenade.

THE HASTINGS EMBROIDERY: A commemorative work, the Hastings Embroidery was first exhibited in 1966. It is a remarkable achievement that traces 900 years of English history through needlework. Depicted are some of the nation's greatest moments (the Battle of Hastings, the coronation of William the Conqueror) and its legends (Robin Hood). In all, 27 panels, 243 feet in length, depicting 81 historic scenes, are exhibited at the Town Hall (tel. 0424/424182). The history of Britain comes alive—the murder of Thomas à Becket, King John signing the Magna Carta, the Black Plague, Chaucer's pilgrims going to Canterbury, the Battle of Agincourt with the victorious Henry V, the War of the Roses, the Little Princes in the Tower, Bloody Mary's reign, Drake's *Golden Hind,* the arrival of Philip's ill-fated Armada, Guy Fawkes's gunpowder plot, the sailing of the *Mayflower,* the disastrous plague of 1665 and the great London fire of the following year, Nelson at Trafalgar, the Battle of Waterloo, the Empress of India, Victoria, the Battle of Britain, and the D-Day landings at Normandy. Also exhibited is a scale model of the battlefield at Battle, depicting William's one-inch men doing in Harold's mini-soldiers. Admission is 75p ($1.13).

WHERE TO STAY: **Royal Victoria Hotel,** Marina (tel. 0424/433300), is peacock-proud of its seafront prominence. It owes its fame to Queen Victoria, who visited here several times. Most of its bedrooms face the sea, but others look onto St. Leonard's Gardens. Inside, the furnishings are fairly modern, although many of the grandest architectural features are still intact. It offers nearly 90 bedrooms, only 14 of which have private baths, although another 11 units contain private showers. Many of the rooms are quite large—good beds, sound comfort. The highest prices are charged from June 1 to September 30. Singles rent for £14.50 ($21.75) to £18 ($27), and doubles for £27.50 ($41.25) to £34 ($51), depending on the plumbing. These prices include breakfast, service charge, and VAT. Special rates for stays of more than three days are offered. Guests gather evenings in the Crown Bar, which has many fine old touches. Lunch is £6.50 ($9.75); dinner, £10 ($15). The chef's specialty is the local sole.

Beauport Park Hotel, Route A2100 (tel. 0424/51222), is one of the best places to stay in the Hastings–Battle district. It looks much older than it is. It was originally erected as the private estate of General Murray, once the governor of Quebec (he had previously served under General Wolfe). However, a fire in 1923 swept over it, and it was later reconstructed in the old style. Now run as a hotel accommodating 30 guests, it is surrounded by beautiful gardens (the Italian-style grounds in the rear contain statuary and vivid flowering shrubbery). The living room and drinking lounge are tastefully furnished, and the French windows in the dining room open onto the park-like rear. The B&B rate ranges from £26 ($39) to £34 ($51) per person daily. All units have private bathrooms with shower, direct-dial telephone, and TV.

The hotel offers an ambitious cuisine, well prepared and handsomely served. Some of the produce comes from the hotel's own gardens. A set lunch is featured for £7 ($10.50) at which a varied choice is available. The set dinner is £9 ($13.50), and again the choice is wide. The à la carte menu offers such tempting dishes as a half dozen escargots, real turtle soup, chateaubriand for two. A rich and creamy dessert is the zabaglione.

10. Battle

Nine miles from Hastings is the old market town, famed in history as the site of the Battle of Hastings in 1066. William the Conqueror founded **Battle Abbey** (some of the stone was shipped from Caen) to commemorate his victory over Harold, the last of the kings of the English. The town grew up around the abbey. Regrettably, stucco has been plastered over many of Battle's half-timbered buildings, a notable exception being the Pilgrim's Restaurant (see below). Even the church was torn down as part of the act approved by Henry VIII in 1537 to dissolve the monasteries.

But some buildings and ruins remain in what Tennyson called: "O Garden, blossoming out of English blood." The principal building is the Abbots' House, at present rented to a public (private) school for girls (not open to visitors). Of architectural interest is the Gatehouse, with its octagonal towers, standing at the top of the Market Square. All of the north precinct wall still stands, and one of the most interesting sights of the ruins is the ancient Dorter Range, where the monks once slept.

Harold was killed and dismembered by William, Duke of Normandy. Encircled by his house-carls, Harold battled bravely not only for his kingdom but his life. The abbey is open year round—from 9:30 a.m. to 5:30 p.m. (on Sunday from 2 to 5:30 p.m.) in summer; from 9:40 a.m. to 4 p.m. in winter (on Sunday from 2 to 4). Admission charges are £1.25 ($1.88) for adults in summer, 60p (90¢) for children. In winter, charges are lowered.

WHERE TO STAY: George Hotel, High Street (tel. 04246/4466), has been purchased by an ex-Californian, David M. Crum, who has brought modern standards to this old coaching inn, dating from 1699. All bedrooms now have private bathrooms and are beautifully decorated, featuring different Sanderson and Laura Ashley wallpaper prints and color schemes throughout. There is central heating in the entire hotel, open log fireplaces in the lounge and saloon bar, and the hotel has its own private car park. Prices, including a continental breakfast, are £18 ($27) in singles, £25 ($37.50) in a double or a twin, including free coffee- or tea-making facilities. Family rooms with a double bed and two single beds rent for £29 ($43.50). All prices include service and tax. Lunch is from £2.25 ($3.38), and dinner, featuring steak-and-kidney pie and local dishes, costs from £5.85 ($8.78). Special bargain terms are offered, for couples staying two nights or more, at a rate beginning at £18 ($27) per person, including dinner, bed, and a continental breakfast. There's no additional charge for couples in the four-poster or "honeymoon" bedrooms, but advance reservations are necessary.

WHERE TO DINE: The **Blacksmith's Restaurant,** 43 High St. (tel. 04246/3200), is in an oak-beamed building dating back to the 14th century, when it was the smithy for the village and the 11th-century manor house. Owned by Martin and Christine Howe, the restaurant they have created here since 1981 has become a much-talked-of place, mentioned frequently in write-ups by gourmets and other journalists. Martin was head chef at London's well-known Gay Huzzar for 14 years before finding this location in Battle when he felt the need of a place of his own. The result is a friendly, low-windowed restaurant with wheelback chairs, red and pink linen, and gleaming silver, decorated with antique blacksmith's tools and a large pair of bellows in one corner.

There is a small bar where Christine or one of the pleasant local women will take your order from the à la carte or supper menu while you sip an apéritif. The £9 ($13.50) supper menu had such a good choice when I visited that the other listing was not necessary. I sampled roast duck Blacksmith's style, crispy and coated with honey, served with cherry sauce accompanied by vegetables and finished off with a homemade dessert from the trolley. The meal was not only a delight, but reasonably priced for the generous portions served. Dinner is offered Tuesday to Saturday, and you must reserve a table. The restaurant is also open for lunch from Tuesday to Sunday, with Sunday lunch at £8 ($12), plus a 50p (75¢) cover charge. On weekdays, the set three-course lunch costs £4.50 ($6.75).

The **Gateway Restaurant,** 78 High St. (tel. 04246/2856), is owned and run by Ron and Penny Middleditch, experienced restaurateurs. Ron was also once a marathon runner. Their daughter Sue helps Penny serve in the restaurant.

The meals offered show their skills; everything that can be is homemade. The steak-and-kidney pie is superb, and there is always a joint roasted to perfection and served with fresh vegetables. Follow this with, perhaps, black currant pie or melt-in-the-mouth suet pudding (the old-fashioned kind) with syrup. Main dishes cost from £2 ($3) to £3.25 ($4.88). The accent is on English dishes, and the menu changes according to season. They are open at 10 a.m. for coffee, closing after the last tea is served around 5 p.m. In mild weather you can sit out on the smooth lawn, smell the roses, and enjoy the view of the abbey across the road. The restaurant is closed on Monday.

Pilgrim's Restaurant, Battle Village Green, High Street (tel. 04246/

2314), adjacent to Battle Abbey, is an early 14th-century, black-and-white timbered house—the preferred place for lunch or afternoon tea while in town. You'll not only receive good portions of homemade food, but you'll encounter an authentic atmosphere. Owned by Peter and Heather Randall-Nason, a husband-and-wife team who gave up the pressure of commercial life for the pleasure of restaurant life, the Pilgrim's is a treasure house of antiquity. You may have lunch in the two-story, high-pitched main room with its open brick hearth, exposed beams, and collection of antiques, or perhaps you'd prefer the smaller adjoining room where the tables are placed in front of an old open fireplace.

Peter and Heather both enjoy preparing and serving food. In fact, Peter's first job was working on Saturday at the age of 6 helping his grandfather, who was a master confectioner. All meals served at Pilgrim's are à la carte, but you can have just an appetizer for 75p ($1.13). A three-course meal with fresh roast beef costs around £5.50 ($8.25). Sandwiches are available all day except at lunchtime, for 75p ($1.13) up. Afternoon Sussex cream teas, £1.50 ($2.25), include enormous homemade scones produced by Peter. The restaurant is open from 10 a.m. to 5:30 p.m. seven days a week in high season, closing on Wednesday in spring and fall. In winter, it is closed on Tuesday, Wednesday, and Thursday.

11. Alfriston and Lewes

Nestled on the Cuckmere River, **Alfriston** is one of the most beautiful villages of England. Its High Street, with its old market cross, looks like one's fantasy of what an English village should be. Some of the old houses still have hidden chambers where smugglers stored their loot. Alfriston has several old inns, the best known of which is the Star, now a Trusthouses Forte hotel with its heraldic carvings outside.

During the day, Alfriston is likely to be overrun by coach tours (it's that lovely, and that popular). The village lies about 60 miles from London, northeast of Seaford on the English Channel, in the general vicinity of the resort of Eastbourne and the modern port of Newhaven.

Only about a dozen miles along the A27 toward Brighton lies **Lewes,** an ancient Sussex town, worth exploring. Centered in the South Downs, Lewes lies 51 miles from London. Since the home of the Glyndebourne Opera is only five miles to the east, the accommodations of Lewes are often frequented by cultured guests.

The county town has many historical associations, listing such residents as Thomas Paine who lived at Bull House, High Street, now a restaurant. The half-timbered **Anne of Cleves House,** so named because it formed part of that queen's divorce settlement from Henry VIII, is now a Museum of Local History and is cared for by the Sussex Archaeological Society. (Anne of Cleves never lived in the Anne of Cleves House, and there is no proof that she ever visited Lewes.) The museum has a furnished bedroom and kitchen and displays of furniture, local history, the Wealden iron industry, and other local crafts. It is found on Southover High Street and is open weekdays from mid-February to mid-November from 10 a.m. to 5 p.m.; on Sunday, April to October, from 2 to 5 p.m. Admission is 70p ($1.05) for adults, 35p (53¢) for children. Lewes, of course, grew up around its Norman castle. From the tower you can obtain a fine view of the countryside. To visit **Lewes Castle and Museum** (tel. Lewes 4379), a joint ticket costs adults 75p ($1.13); children, 40p (60¢). The castle and museum are open all year from 10 a.m. to 5:30 p.m., Monday through Saturday (also on Sunday, April to October, from 2 to 5:30 p.m.). Accommodations are difficult during the Glyndebourne Opera festival, but adequate at other times.

WHERE TO STAY IN ALFRISTON: If you're spending the night, try to get a room at one of the old inns.

The **Star Inn** (tel. 0323/870495) answers the craving of those who want all the charm of Tudor living without having to sacrifice 20th-century comfort. The present building dates from 1450, although it was originally founded in the 1200s, perhaps to house pilgrims en route to Chichester and the shrine of St. Richard. The timbered inn is a gem. In the center of the village, its carved front still unchanged, it boasts an overhanging second story of black and white timbers and bay windows. The lounges are on several levels, a veritable forest of old timbers, seasoned by the centuries. The furnishings and decorations blend well, with a Tudor refectory table, a bowl of English garden flowers, Windsor armchair, wrought-iron ceiling lights, old engravings, and several fireplaces.

Out back is a motel-type wing, with every studio-style room offering a private bath. Each is simply furnished in a tasteful style, well designed, with radio and telephone, heating, and built-in wardrobes. A single is £34 ($51) per night, a double or twin costing £48 ($72). These rates do not include breakfast, but if you plan to stay two or more nights, ask about the full-board prices.

WHERE TO STAY IN LEWES: White Hart Hotel, High Street (tel. Lewes 473794), was labeled by Thomas Paine as "the cradle of American Independence," owing to his founding of the volatile and aptly named Headstrong Club there in 1761. Originally it was the town house of the Pelhams, a kind of first family of Lewes. Later it became a coaching inn, although the facade today dates from the 19th century. In yet another century, the representative of the Soviet Union met here with the British foreign secretary as a prelude to the resumption of diplomatic relations between the two countries.

A single with bath costs from £32 ($48) to £35 ($53); a double or twin with bath, £43 ($64.50) to £50 ($75). A full English breakfast, service, and VAT are included in the rates. Most bedrooms have individual television color sets, and all have full central heating and are tastefully furnished. The wine cellars once whispered with the sighs of 16th-century Protestant martyrs (many were buried there).

The dining room, with its view of the Downs, is warmly decorated with paneling and a hand-carved formal fireplace. Here, while sitting on red banquettes, you can order some of the finest viands in Lewes. An excellent carvery meal costs from £6.50 ($9.75).

The **Shelleys Hotel** (tel. Lewes 2361) is a manor house dating back to 1526. In its day it was owned by the Earl of Dorset, before it was sold to the Shelley family, distant relatives of the poet. Radical changes were made to the architecture in the 18th century. Nowadays, the standards of the management are reflected in the fine antiques, the bowls of flowers, the paintings and prints, the well-kept garden, and most important, the staff. In the rear is a sun terrace and lawn for tea and drinks. Horse chestnuts and copper beech shade the grounds.

The central hall is characterized by Ionic columns, a Welsh cupboard, a domed ceiling, and the coat-of-arms of the Shelley family. The bay windows of the front drawing room open onto the rear gardens, and the drinking lounge is paneled. The bedrooms are personal, individually furnished, usually spacious and most comfortable. Singles with shower cost from £40 ($60); doubles with bath/shower, from £58 ($87). Service and VAT are included in all charges. Room 11 has a 16th-century frieze of Bacchanalian figures and a design of entwining grapes and flowers. You can, by the way, order meals at Shelleys. Lunch costs from £6 ($9); dinner is from £10 ($15).

12. Brighton

Back in 1753, when Dr. Russell propounded the seawater cure—even to the point of advocating the drinking of an "oceanic cocktail"—he launched a movement that was to change the life of the average English person, at least his or her vacation plans. Brighton was one of the first of the great seaside resorts of Europe.

The original swinger who was to shape so much of its destiny arrived in 1783, after just turning voting age; he was the then Prince of Wales, whose presence and patronage gave immediate status to the seaside town.

Fashionable dandies from London, such as Beau Brummell, began turning up. The construction business boomed, as Brighton blossomed with charming and attractive town houses, well-planned squares and crescents. From the Prince Regent's title came the voguish word "Regency," which was to characterize an era, but more specifically refers to the period between 1811 and 1820. Under Victoria, and in spite of her cutting off the patronage of her presence, Brighton continued to flourish.

Alas, in this century, as the English began to discover more glamorous spots on the continent, Brighton lost much of its old joie de vivre. It became more aptly tabbed as tatty, featuring the usual run of fun-fair-type English seaside amusements ("let's go down to Brighton, ducks"). Happily, that state of affairs is today changing rapidly, owing largely to the huge numbers of Londoners moving in (some of whom have taken to commuting, as Brighton lies only one hour—frequent train service—from Victoria Station). The invasion is making Brighton increasingly lighthearted and sophisticated.

The Lanes, a closely knit section of alleyways off North Street in Brighton (many of the present shops were formerly fisherman's cottages) were frequented in Victoria's day by style-setting curio and antique collectors. Many are still there, although sharing space with boutiques.

THE ROYAL PAVILION: Among the royal residences of Europe, the Pavilion at Brighton—a John Nash version of an Indian mogul's palace—is unique. Ornate and exotic, it has been subjected over the years to the most devastating wit of English satirists and pundits. But today we can examine it more objectively as one of the outstanding examples of the orientalizing tendencies of the romantic movement in England.

Originally the pavilion was built in 1787 by Henry Holland. But it no more resembled its present look than a caterpillar does a butterfly. By the time Nash had transformed it from a simple classical villa into an Oriental fantasy, the Prince Regent had become King George IV. He and one of his mistresses, Lady Conyngham, lived in the palace until 1827.

A decade passed before Victoria, then queen, arrived in Brighton. Although she was to bring Albert and the children on a number of occasions, the monarch and Brighton just didn't mix. The very air of the resort seemed too flippant for her—and the latter-day sea-bathing disciples of Dr. Russell trailed Victoria as if she were a stage actress. Further, the chinoiseries of the interior and the mogul domes and cupolas on the exterior didn't sit too well with her firm tastes—even though the pavilion would have been a fitting abode for a woman who was to bear the title Empress of India.

By 1845 Victoria and Brighton had had it. She began packing, and the royal furniture was carted off. Its tenants gone, the pavilion was in serious peril of being torn down. By a narrow vote, Brightonians agreed to purchase it. Gradually, it has been restored to its former splendor, enhanced in no small part by the return of much of its original furniture on loan by the present tenant at Buckingham Palace.

The caretakers put out the silverware, gold plate, and porcelain during the annual Regency Exhibition from June to September. But at any time you can walk through the world of crustacean ceilings, winged dragons, silk draperies, lacquered furniture, water-lily chandeliers, gilt dolphins, Chinese mythological figures, and serpents who hold everything up.

Of exceptional interest is the domed **Banqueting Hall,** with a chandelier of bronze dragons supporting lily-like glass globes. In the Great Kitchen, with its old revolving spits, is a collection of Wellington pots and pans, his *batterie de cuisine,* from his town house at Hyde Park Corner. In the State Apartments, particularly the domed Salon, dragons wink at you, serpents entwine, lacquered doors shine. The Music Room, with its scalloped ceiling, is a salon of water lilies, flying dragons, sunflowers, reptilian paintings, bamboo, silk, and satin. Currently this room is being painstakingly restored, and the fascinating work can be seen in progress. In the second-floor gallery, look for Nash's views of the pavilion in its elegant heyday. Finally, don't miss the sitting room of the king's "wife," Mrs. Fitzherbert, with some of her former furniture.

From June to early October the pavilion is open daily from 10 a.m. to 6 p.m. It closes at 5 p.m. off-season. The admission charges are: June to October (Regency Exhibition), adults £1.85 ($2.78); children 80p ($1.20). For the rest of the year, adults pay £1.50 ($2.25); children 65p (98¢). The Royal Pavilion is in central Brighton. Telephone 0273/603005 for information.

SEEING BRIGHTON: A walking tour is made every Wednesday at 7:30 p.m., June to September, costing 60p (90¢) per person, and plans at press time were for a more frequent bus tour to begin soon. Tours start from the **Tourist Information Centre,** Marlborough House, 54 Old Steine (tel. 0273/23755), by the Royal Albion Hotel and the bus terminal. You can also get help here if you have accommodations problems.

WHERE TO STAY: Hundreds of accommodations are to be found in all price ranges. Regrettably, many are establishments, to quote Norman Mailer, "where elderly retired India colonels brood through dinner. . . ." However, that situation is changing now, as the most celebrated relics of yesteryear are experiencing (or have experienced) extensive overhauling.

We'll survey the leading hotels, then proceed to a representative sampling of the accommodations awaiting those who must keep expenses trimmed.

The Upper Bracket

Grand Hotel, Kings's Road (tel. 0273/26301), unquestionably has grandeur. Built in 1864, it is listed as a building of architectural and historical importance by the Department of Environment. The interior is impressive, the outstanding features being the wrought-iron staircase and the dome. The Victorian era has been skillfully recreated on the ground floor, but the bedrooms, all with private bath, radio, and TV, are modern. There are 166 bedrooms, plus seven luxury suites for VIPs.

Singles range from £35 ($52.50). Doubles go from £62 ($93) facing the sea. Terms include an English breakfast and VAT. En pension terms are quoted as well. The Grand also offers a table d'hôte luncheon for £9 ($13.50) and a dinner for £10 ($15), both inclusive. There are special weekend rates available throughout the year, excluding public holidays.

The Medium-Priced Range

Royal Albion Hotel, Old Steine (tel. 0273/29202), stands right on the seafront, opposite the Palace Pier. As a hotel, it is one of the traditional choices of Brighton, with lots of Regency character and history, dating back to 1826. Inside, the hotel has been luxuriously decorated and furnished to a very high standard. All rooms have private bath/shower, color television, radio, telephone, and a tea- and coffee-making machine. The majority of the rooms have a superb sea view. Sir Harry's Bar, with a nautical theme, is named after the late Sir Harry Preston, who owned the hotel in the early 1900s. There is also a spacious lounge with magnificent views onto the seafront and a large Regency-style restaurant. The rates are £42 ($63) for a single, £54 ($81) for a twin or double room, £65 ($97.50) for a family room, all inclusive of VAT and service. Table d'hôte menus range from £9 ($13.50) per person.

Courtlands Hotel, The Drive, Hove (tel. 0273/731055), lies 400 yards from the sea, opening onto the wide thoroughfare known as "The Drive," about a mile from the center of Brighton. It is a comfortable Victorian building, recently modernized, with 65 rooms, of which 60 contain private baths or showers en suite and color TV. This includes units in the Courtlands complex—five particularly agreeable rooms in the cottage and coach house annex, which possess mini-bars and tea- and coffee-making facilities. Bedrooms are spacious and harmonious, with prices set according to plumbing. Per-person rates include a full English breakfast, service, and VAT. Bathless singles cost £24 ($36), rising to £40 ($60) with bath. Doubles with bath rent for £29 ($43.50) per person. This traditional hotel has more than adequate facilities, including the Golden Dolphin lounge bar and a dining room opening onto gardens. A good cuisine, both international and English, is assured. The hotel has a small children's playground, as well as a games room, and adequate parking is provided.

The Budget Range

Kennedy Palace Hotel, 11/12 Marine Parade (tel. 0273/604928), honors the assassinated American president, and is also a good place for B&B or full board. The proprietors, A. and Y. Stylianou, charge £13 ($19.50) per person without bath, £18 ($27) per person with bath. Their fully licensed restaurant and bar is open to nonresidents as well. Their house, a Regency treasure, with an authentic bow front and an encircling balcony, has tables out on the patio so that guests may enjoy the view of the sea. The service is personal, the welcome friendly at the family-run establishment.

The **Regency Hotel,** 28 Regency Square (tel. 0273/202690), is a charming Regency building with bow windows, carved doors, and a canopied balcony facing south across the square toward the pier and the sea. It was recently refurbished in a traditional style, yet incorporating modern comforts such as central heating and baths. Most units face the sea. For that romantic splurge night, you can reserve the Regency Suite, overlooking the water. This is an enormous room with a canopied bed, private sun balcony, and tented bathroom "just like something out of the Royal Pavilion." The rest of the hotel is comfortably furnished. The chandeliers are pure sparkling Waterford crystal. The hotel has a coal fire burning throughout the winter months in the original fireplace in the lounge. Overnight will cost from £17 ($25.50) per person, including a full English breakfast.

Ryford Private Hotel, 6 and 7 New Steine (tel. 0273/681576), on a Regency square adjacent to the Marine Parade, is within minutes of the seafront, the Palace Pier and the Aquarium. The comfortable lounge and some of the guest rooms offer views of the sea. All 25 rooms are carpeted and immaculate, complete with hot and cold running water. B&B rates per person per night are about £11.50 ($17.25). Dinner is also available in the spacious dining room where excellent cuisine is prepared and served under the personal supervision of the resident proprietors.

DINING OUT IN BRIGHTON: English's Oyster Bar and Seafoods Restaurant,

29/31 East St. (tel. 0273/27980), is my leading choice for superbly cooked fish, served in a well-preserved, 19th-century building conveniently opening onto "The Lanes." It combines a romantic setting with good food. For years, diners have been making such wise selections as a half dozen Colchester oysters or a hot lobster pâté. The chef is known for such specialties as Dover sole (plate-size) and fresh locally caught plaice. The pièce de résistance is the bouillabaisse. The chef also offers a set two-course table d'hôte menu, which is available for luncheon and dinner every day. You're given a selection of appetizers, plus a choice of five main courses. Expect to spend from £15 ($22.50) up if you order à la carte. The restaurant is open for lunch every day, including Sunday, from noon to 2:20 p.m., and for dinner from 6 to 10:20 p.m. every day except Sunday.

The **French Connection Restaurant,** 11 Little East St. (tel. 0273/24454), occupies a Georgian fisherman's cottage. Lionel Roberts and Bernard Brick run this elegant and comfortable little place, which is considered among the best restaurants in Brighton. All vegetables are purchased fresh daily, and the fish is caught locally. The restaurant is open Monday to Saturday for lunch and dinner, featuring an extensive table d'hôte menu for around £8 ($12), excluding wine, or a full à la carte menu from around £15 ($22.50) exclusive of wine. The restaurant is frequented by many show business and political personalities, and is very popular with American tourists and business people. All major credit cards are accepted. Reservations are suggested.

The **Swiss Restaurant** (also called the William Tell), 11–12 Queen's Rd. (tel. 0273/26865), is a miniature Alpine world, tucked away in a building a block north of the clock tower. In this pine-paneled room, run by Gordon Jones, you'll be served top-notch Swiss dishes, along with French fare. The national dish of Switzerland, fondue Neuchatelloise, is offered for two persons. For more elaborate dining, you can order the fondue bourguignonne for two persons. Other specialties include rösti, a Swiss potato dish. For dessert, try the pineapple with kirsch. A meal costs from £15 ($22.50). The place is open daily, except Sunday, from noon to 2 p.m. and from 6 to 10 p.m.

Henekeys, 4–6 Ship St. (tel. 0273/27492), is the leading pub (established in 1695), which makes it big on atmosphere. Even if it didn't serve good food and drinks (which it does), it'd make an interesting stopover, inviting with its old timbers, bricks, stones, and leaded-glass windows. In the center is a beer garden (open in summer only), and there's a lounge bar upstairs. Behind the Old Ship Hotel, it's especially popular at lunch. The fare is very English, and includes locally caught plaice, a grilled sirloin, and scampi. A completely satisfying meal can be ordered here for about £7.50 ($11.25). These main dishes, all served in the Steak Bar, come with pie or cheese. Henekeys keeps regular pub hours.

Tureen, 31 Upper North St. (tel. 0273/28939), is one of my favorite Brighton bistros, a rare one that makes available (see the blackboard for daily specials) some of the best of the English and continental dishes at low prices—including an always-good soup "from the tureen." The layered terrine of duck with Cumberland sauce makes an excellent appetizer, and might be followed by leek and chicken pancake; Elizabethan rabbit casserole with dried fruit, spices, and herbs; or loin steaks of pork grilled with apple sauce, cream, and Calvados. Dinners will run from £12 ($18). A three-course budget luncheon is offered on Saturday for £5.50 ($8.25) and on Sunday for £8 ($12). The Tureen is open for dinner Tuesday to Sunday in summer, Tuesday to Saturday in winter, from 6:30 p.m., with last orders being taken at 9:30 p.m.

Browns Restaurant and Coffee House, 3–4 Duke St. (tel. 0273/23501), is a charming, rather 1930s place with plain tables and hoop-backed chairs. Dishes have imaginative accompaniments. For example, spaghetti dishes are served with hot garlic bread and a salad; pies, including steak, mushroom, and Guinness, come with baked potatoes rather than the ubiquitous chips. American-style sandwiches are featured as well, along with spare ribs, chili, stuffed trout, and invariably a special of the day such as braised oxtail (game in season). Salads and grills make up the small but tasty menu. Followed by thick dark-chocolate cake and coffee, a meal will cost around £7 ($10.50) a person.

STAYING AT HOVE: The **Alexandra Hotel,** 42 Brunswick Terrace (tel. 0273/202722), was built in 1830 at the height of the Regency period. Ideally situated on the tranquil Hove seafront, it was at the heart of the Brunswick Estate, which was a small cluster of residences for "people of quality." Before being established as a hotel by a special Act of Parliament, the structure at this address was the home of the exiled Austrian diplomat, Prince Metternich. It was one of the first houses in England to have hot and cold running water.

The hotel has been fully modernized without detracting from its period atmosphere, with care taken to restore windows and exterior ironwork in the Regency style. Each of the 62 bedrooms has a private bath, color TV, tea- and coffee-making facilities, radio and alarm clock, phone, and central heating. Most rooms enjoy sea views, and special units are available for the handicapped. A single costs £30 ($45), a double going for £38 ($57), including service and VAT.

You can enjoy choice Sussex ale drawn from the wood in Alex's Bar, and have meals of English or continental cuisine in the 1830 Restaurant, with its Regency ambience. A table d'hôte luncheon costs around £8 ($12), with dinner from £10 ($15).

13. Arundel

This small and beautiful town in West Sussex, only 58 miles from London, four miles from the English Channel, nestles at the foot of one of England's most spectacular castles. The town was once an Arun River port, its denizens enjoying the prosperity of considerable trade and commerce. The harbor traffic is gone, replaced by coaches filled with visitors who come to visit Le Castle.

ARUNDEL CASTLE: The ancestral home of the Dukes of Norfolk, this baronial estate (tel. 0903/883136) is a much-restored mansion of considerable importance. Its legend is associated with some of the great families of England—the Fitzalans and the powerful Howards of Norfolk. Arundel Castle traces its history back to King Alfred; its keep goes back to around the Conquest.

Over the years, Arundel Castle suffered destruction, particularly during the Civil War when Cromwell's troops stormed its walls, perhaps in retaliation for the 14th Earl of Arundel's (Thomas Howard) sizable contribution to Charles I. In the early 18th century the castle virtually had to be rebuilt. In late Victorian times it was remodeled and extensively restored again. Today it is filled, as you'd expect, with a good collection of antiques, along with an assortment of paintings by old masters such as Van Dyck and Gainsborough.

The castle is open from April 1 until the last Friday in October, Sunday to Friday inclusive, from 1 to 5 p.m. It is open at noon during June, July, and August, and all bank holidays. The last admission time any day is 4 p.m. (the castle is not open on Saturday). Admission charges are £2.25 ($3.38) for adults, £1.50 ($2.25) for children 5 to 15 years of age. Surrounding the castle is an 1100-acre park (scenic highlight: Swanbourne Lake).

OTHER SIGHTS: Arundel Toy and Military Museum at "Doll's House," 23 High St. (tel. 0903/882908), displays a delightful and intriguing family collection spanning many generations of old toys and games, small militaria, dolls, dollhouses, tin toys, musical toys, Britain's animals and soldiers, arks, boats, rocking horses, and crested military models. Housed in a Georgian cottage in the heart of historic Arundel, it is open most days from Easter to October (in winter, weekends only), or it may be seen at any time by arrangement. Admission is 60p (90¢) for adults, 35p (53¢) for children.

The little **Museum of Curiosity,** 6 High St. (tel. 0903/882420), will delight children (and their parents) with its displays of small animals in storybook tableaux, including the life work of the Victorian naturalist and taxidermist Walter Potter. It is open from April to September 30, Monday to Friday from 10:30 a.m. to 5:30 p.m., on Saturday and Sunday from 11 a.m. to 5:30 p.m. It closes for lunch from 1 to 2:15 p.m. It is also open daily in October from 2:15 to 5 p.m. or dusk. Admission is 50p (75¢) for adults, 25p (38¢) for children.

WHERE TO STAY: **Norfolk Arms,** High Street (tel. 0903/882101), is a former Georgian coaching inn set in the center of the town, just a short walk from the castle. The lounges and dining room are in the typically English country-inn style—that is, unostentatious but unquestionably comfortable. The hotel has been restored with many modern amenities blending with the old architecture. The bedrooms are handsomely maintained and furnished, each with personal touches. Most rooms have private bathrooms, and all have color television. It is a medium-priced place. The B&B rate is £17 ($25.50) per person without bath, £19 ($28.50) per person with bath, VAT included. No service is charged.

In the restaurant you can order good English cooking with Host's Luncheon for £6 ($9). When available, fresh local produce is offered. You can also dine on a specialty menu for £10 ($15), which includes many traditional English dishes.

14. Chichester

According to one newspaper, Chichester might have been just a market town if the Chichester Festival Theatre had not been established in its midst. One of the oldest Roman cities in England, Chichester is in vogue, drawing a chic crowd from all over the world who come to see its theater's presentations.

Only a five-minute walk from the Chichester Cathedral and the old Market Cross, the 1400-seat theater, with its apron stage, stands on the edge of Oaklands Park. It opened in 1962 (first director: Lord Laurence Olivier), and its reputation has grown steadily, pumping new vigor and life into the former walled city. Of course, in some quarters there is still resentment, and occasionally you hear suggestions that the pounds could have been better spent on a municipal swimming pool. But others point to the success of the Chichester theater in having given fresh stimulus to the living theater in England.

THE FESTIVAL THEATRE: Booking generally opens in the middle of March, although the season might not start till the middle of May (it continues until late September). The price of seats ranges from £2 ($3) to £8 ($12) for the finest tickets in the house. A limited number of £2 ($3) seats go on sale at the box office on the day of each performance, and are sold on a first-come, first-served basis. Reservations made over the telephone will be held for a maximum of four days (call 0243/781312). It's better to mail inquiries and checks to the box office, **Chichester Festival Theatre,** Oaklands Park, Chichester. Matinee performances begin at 2:30 p.m., evening shows Monday to Thursday at 7 p.m. and Friday and Saturday at 7:30 p.m.

How to get there: If you would like to come down from London, 62 miles away, for a matinee, then catch the 11:28 train from Victoria Station, which will deliver you to Chichester by 1:05 p.m., in plenty of time. For an evening performance, board the 4:28 p.m. train from Victoria Station, arriving at 6:07 p.m. Regrettably, there is no direct late train back to London after the show. Visitors who must return can make a connection via Brighton, arriving at Victoria station shortly after midnight.

WHERE TO STAY: In Chichester, you have a choice of living either at one of the old inns inside the city, or at a motel on the outskirts.

The **Ship Hotel,** North Street (tel. 0243/782028), is one of the classic Georgian buildings of the city, only a few minutes walk from the cathedral, the Chichester Festival Theatre, and many fine antique shops.

The Ship was built as a private house in 1790 for Admiral Sir George Murray (one of Nelson's commanders) and still retains an air of elegance and comfort. A grand Adam staircase leads from the main entrance to the bedrooms (most with private bathrooms) which are all named after historic ships. Single room prices are around £19 ($28.50), and doubles go from £34 ($51). A full English breakfast is included. Good pub lunches are offered at around £3 ($4.50). The Victory Bar is one of Chichester's most popular meeting places. The welcoming restaurant offers excellent value for money with its à la carte and special four-course dinner menus each evening from £8.50 ($12.75).

Dolphin & Anchor, West Street (tel. 0243/785121), is two old inns   joined together and run as a Trusthouses Forte. The situation is prime, right at the historic 15th-century Market Cross and opposite the Chichester   Cathedral a ten-minute walk from the Festival Theatre. The tradition of good innkeeping is honored here, in a setting that blends 19th-century architectural features with 20th-century comforts, including an old coaching entrance, but a new wing of handsomely furnished bedrooms as well. The two-in-one inn has 54 bedrooms, all with baths, TV, radio, and telephone. A single with bath is £38 ($57), increasing to £48 ($72) in a twin with bath, these tariffs including service and VAT. There are lounges, bars, the Whig and Tory Restaurant, and the Roussillon Coffee Shop, which serves light meals and grills until 10 p.m.

Chichester Lodge Hotel, Westhampnett (tel. 0243/786351), is a boon to motorists because it's a mile from the city center on the main A27 with large car-parking facilities. A covered passageway connects it to the older White Swan Inn nearby. The attractively styled hotel offers 43 modern bedrooms tastefully furnished, containing private bathrooms, telephone, radio, tea-making facilities, and color TV. The rate is £52 ($78) for a double and £35 ($52.50) for a single, including VAT, service, and a full English breakfast. The hotel has an attractive cocktail bar and restaurant serving a set lunch for £8 ($12), a table d'hôte dinner for £10 ($15), including VAT and service. There is also an à la carte menu.

WHERE TO EAT: Unlike its limited number of accommodations, Chichester abounds with good restaurants. I find the following establishments superior, both for food and value.

Little London Restaurant, Little London, off East Street (tel. 0243/784899), nestles in a charming little building. The fully licensed restaurant serves a fine cuisine, each dish prepared individually. The service and reception are friendly as well. In an atmosphere of subdued taste, you can order from one of the small, but very select, menus, while seated on an upholstered chair at a pink-clothed table. At lunch, a three-course table d'hôte meal is served for £6.50 ($9.75), including, for example, pears with tarragon mayonnaise, roast rolled rib of beef, and profiteroles in chocolate sauce. In the evening, there is a small à la carte menu that varies during the year, serving such delicacies as caviar cream, nut cutlets, sweetbread pie, or guinea fowl in red wine and herbs. The vegetables of the day are included in the price of the main dishes. The desserts are homemade and mouthwatering. Expect to spend from £12 ($18) for an à la carte dinner. You must reserve. The restaurant is closed all day Sunday and Monday, but open otherwise from noon to 2 p.m. and 7 to 10 p.m. On Saturday nights, and also during the May to September Festival Theatre season, there are two sittings, at 7:30 and 9:45 p.m. The place is usually closed for one week in February.

Also on the premises is the fully licensed, self-service **Savourie,** offering a variety of soups, pâtés, and hot pies. Salads and jacket potatoes are also good. Such desserts as chocolate gâteau are offered. A two-course meal will cost you about £6 ($9). This place is well worth recommending for its good service and the high standard of its food. Wicker chairs are placed before clean white tables. As East Street is a pedestrian way, you must be prepared to walk to the restaurant, only a short distance.

The **Roussillon Coffee Shop,** Dolphin Anchor, West Street (tel. 0243/785121), serves snacks and light meals from 10 a.m. to 10 p.m. daily. Those on the sightseeing run might settle happily for a cheese and bacon burger, although fish dishes and sirloin steak (ten ounces uncooked weight, served with french fries) are also featured. A complete hot meal is likely to cost from £9 ($13.50). Children under 14 may choose from the main menu at half price.

The **Coffee House,** West Street (tel. 0243/784799), stands right beside the Dolphin & Anchor, opposite the cathedral. It has a good reputation for satisfying food at low prices. A small place, it provides plats du jour including a shrimp salad. Hot snacks such as Welsh rarebit with bacon are offered from 10 a.m. to closing. In the licensed restaurant you can have good-tasting omelets or a selection from the cold buffet. Complete meals run from £4.50 ($6.75) up.

THE LOCAL PUB: The **Royal Arms,** East Street, near the Market Cross, is a pub built in 1576 and known locally as the Punch House, as it became famous in the early 19th century for the making and sale of Chichester milk punch. Hosts Tim and Val Biggs offer a full range of hot and cold bar snacks lunchtime and evenings. Prices range from £1 ($1.50) to £3 ($4.50).

WEALD AND DOWNLAND OPEN AIR MUSEUM: In the beautiful Sussex countryside at Singleton, six miles north of Chichester on the A286 (London road), historic buildings that have been saved from destruction are being reconstructed on a 40-acre Downland site. The structures show the development of traditional building from medieval times to the 19th century in the Weald and Downland area of southeast England. The museum (tel. 0243/63348) is open daily April 1 to October 31 from 11 a.m. to 5 p.m. Admission is £1.75 ($2.63) for adults, £1 ($1.50) for children. The museum is continually developing. Exhibits include a 16th-century Market Hall from Titchfield in Hampshire, medieval houses, a blacksmith's forge, a carpenter's workshop, a 17th-century treadwheel, two 18th-century thatched barns and a granary, a charcoal burner's camp, a weather-boarded toll cottage, and a working watermill producing stone-ground flour.

FISHBOURNE: A worthwhile visit only two miles from Chichester is the **Roman Palace** (tel. 0243/785859), the largest Roman residence yet discovered in Britain. Built around A.D. 75 in Italianate style, it has many mosaic-floored rooms and even an underfloor heating system. The gardens have been restored to their original first-century plan. The story of the site is told both by an audio-visual program and by text in the museum. There is free parking and a cafeteria. The museum is open from March through November. Admission for adults is £1.20 ($1.80). Students pay 80p ($1.20), and children are charged 50p (75¢).

LIVING ON THE OUTSKIRTS: One of the most interesting ways to attend the theater in Chichester is from a base on the outskirts. That way, you get to enjoy the best of English village life, but can conveniently go into the city whenever you want. Some recommendations follow.

Old Bosham

One of the most charming little villages of West Sussex, Bosham was a Saxon hamlet (King Harold lived near here in a now disappeared palace). Its little church was depicted in the Bayeux Tapestry. Near the harbor, it is reached by a narrow lane. Its graveyard overlooks the boats (a daughter of King Canute is buried inside). The church is filled with ship models and relics, showing the villagers' link to the sea. Bosham is principally a sailing resort, linked by good bus service to Chichester.

The **Millstream Hotel,** Bosham (tel. Bosham 573234), is set on the road to the village of Bosham and its harbor, off the A27. Completely redecorated, the rooms have different colors, but all are outfitted with floral-patterned wallpaper. The decor is in keeping with the country cottage-type hotel. Beds are comfortable, and each of the 22 rooms has a private bath. The charge is £50 ($75) for a double, £30 ($45) in a single, with breakfast included in the rates. The cocktail bar at the entrance to the restaurant is tastefully furnished with white bamboo chairs and tables, plus green carpeting. At the adjoining restaurant, you can order such à la carte dishes as moules marinières and roast Sussex lamb with fresh herbs. A set luncheon is £8.50 ($12.75), and a set dinner costs £11.50 ($17.25).

Midhurst

The **Spread Eagle Hotel** at Midhurst (tel. Midhurst 2211) started life as a 15th-century coaching inn, and has been much lived in, altered, and loved ever since. The inn and the market town of Midhurst are so steeped in history that the room you sleep in, the pavement you walk have a thousand tales to tell. The rooms have beams, small mullioned windows, and unexpected corners, although most units have been modernized with bathrooms en suite, along with radio, color TV, and phone. The Queen's Suite with a four-poster bed goes for £100 ($150) a night. However, you can rent a double or twin room from £60 ($90) to £70 ($105) or a single from £40 ($60), including VAT, service, and a large English breakfast.

Dinner is served in the dining hall, lit by candles that flicker on the gleaming tables. In the winter, huge log fires blaze to greet travelers. The lounge with its timbered ceiling is where Queen Elizabeth I and her court might have sat to watch festivities in the Market Square outside. The eagle in the lounge is the actual one that decorated the back of Hermann Goering's chair in the Reichstag. It was acquired for its apt illustration of the hotel's name.

There are several bars where you can sit and watch the locals and sip a glass of sherry after a day of exploration. Midhurst lies only 12 miles from Chichester, only a bit farther from Arundel and Bosham; Brighton is just 36 miles down the road. It's also quite a good place for a first or last night for those boarding a flight at Gatwick Airport.

AT HOME WITH AN AMERICAN COUPLE: At Home Country Holidays, Lower House Farm, West Burton, Pulborough, West Sussex (tel. 079/881800). Bill and Gretchen Stevens, an American couple, live at Arundel Holt Court and offer two private bedrooms in their own house. The guest suite has a library lounge and tea- and coffee-making equipment. There is another bedroom under the roof, with a comfortable sitting area and drinks cupboard. Both have private bathrooms. The Stevenses will provide breakfast and evening meals either in your own suite or en famille in their own charming dining room. They are both good cooks and feature traditional American farmhouse, Italian, and Mexican dishes, with barbecues for hot summer evenings.

They will gladly give information on the various local sights and arrange for excursions to the coast, to Brighton, or Chichester for the theater, Goodwood for racing, or to Glyndebourne for the opera.

They are able to book you into some 50 private houses around England, Scotland, and Wales, apart from their own. The price for one night is £35 ($52.50) per person for a bed, private bath, use of a private sitting room, and breakfast. Lunch is served for £4 ($6), dinner for £10 ($15). However, if you order dinner with wine, expect to spend from £12 ($18). B&B for two persons is from £60 ($90); for four persons, from £100 ($150). Weekly rates are also available, and according to these terms you pay for six nights, getting the seventh one free.

Bill and Gretchen were traveling by ship from the United States to France. On board they met some English people and decided to stop over in England first. They've never left. Bill worked among the youth of Puerto Rico for many years.

You can write for a list of the other properties they represent in the area of England you intend to visit.

HAMPSHIRE AND DORSET

STONE FARMHOUSES—Burke's Landed Gentry—all this belongs to the countryside of the 17th century. Fireplaces where stacks of logs burn gaily. Wicker baskets of apples freshly brought in from the orchard (ever had homemade apple butter?). Chickens stuffed with dressing and roasted with strips of bacon on top to keep them tender and juicy. Milk that doesn't come from bottles. Old village houses, now run as hotels, possessing quality and charm. Beyond the pear trees, on the crest of a hill, the ruins of a Roman camp. A village pub, with two rows of kegs filled with varieties of cider, where the hunt gathers.

You're in Hampshire and Dorset, two shires guarded zealously by the English, who protect their special rural treasures. Everybody knows of Southampton and Bournemouth, but less known is the undulating countryside lying inland. Your car will take you through endless lanes, revealing tiny villages and thatched cottages untouched by the industrial invasion.

HAMPSHIRE

This is Jane Austen country—firmly middle class, largely agricultural, its inhabitants doggedly convinced that Hampshire is the greatest spot on

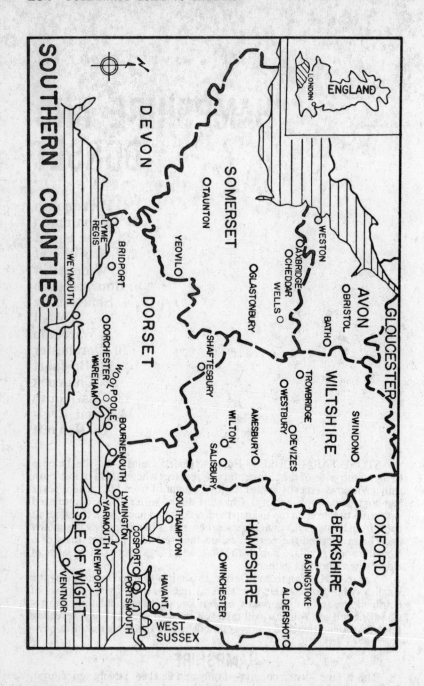

SOUTHERN COUNTIES

ENGLAND

DEVON

SOMERSET

○ TAUNTON

YEOVIL ○

WEYMOUTH

LYME REGIS

BRIDPORT

DORSET

DORCHESTER ○

WAREHAM

WOOL

POOLE

BOURNEMOUTH

LYMINGTON

YARMOUTH

NEWPORT

ISLE OF WIGHT

VENTNOR

COSPORT

PORTSMOUTH

WEST SUSSEX

HAVANT

SOUTHAMPTON

GLASTONBURY ○

WELLS ○

CHEDDAR ○

AXBRIDGE ○

WESTON ○

BRISTOL ○

BATH ○

AVON

GLOUCESTER

WILTSHIRE

TROWBRIDGE ○

WESTBURY ○

DEVIZES ○

SWINDON ○

WILTON ○

AMESBURY ○

SALISBURY ○

SHAFTESBURY ○

HAMPSHIRE

WINCHESTER ○

BASINGSTOKE ○

ALDERSHOT ○

BERKSHIRE

OXFORD

LONDON

earth. Austen wrote six novels of manners, including *Pride and Prejudice* and *Sense and Sensibility,* that earned her a room at the top among 19th-century writers. Her books provided a keen insight into the solid middle-class English who were to build such a powerful Empire. Although the details of the life she described have now largely faded ("At five o'clock the two ladies retired to dress, and at half-past six Elizabeth was summoned to dinner"), much of the mood and spirit of Hampshire depicted in her books remains.

Born in 1775, Jane Austen was the daughter of the Oxford-educated rector, the Reverend Mr. George Austen, a typical Hampshire country gentleman, who had much charm but little money. In keeping with a custom of the time, the Austens gave their second son, Edward, to a wealthy, childless family connection, Thomas Knight, whose heir the young man became. It was Edward who gave to his mother and sisters **Chawton Cottage,** near Alton (tel. 042/83263), where visitors can see the surroundings in which the novelist of manners spent the last 7½ years of her life, her period of greatest creation. In the unpretentious but pleasant cottage, you can see the desk on which Jane Austen penned new versions of three of her books and wrote three more, including *Emma* (her "handsome, clever, and rich" heroine, Emma Woodhouse). You can also see the rector's George III mahogany bookcase and a silhouette likeness of the Reverend Austen presenting his son to the Knights. It was in this cottage that Jane Austen died in 1817 of what would have been diagnosed by the middle of the 19th century as Addison's disease.

There is an attractive garden in which visitors are invited to have picnics, and an old bakehouse with Miss Austen's donkey cart. About a mile from the station, the home is open daily, including Sunday from 11 a.m. to 4:30 p.m. for 75p ($1.13) admission; children under 14, 25p (38¢). It is closed Monday and Tuesday from November 1 to March 31.

Hampshire embraces the **New Forest** (don't expect anything in England labeled "new" to be new), the **South Downs,** the **Isle of Wight** (Victoria's favorite retreat), the passenger port and gateway city of **Southampton,** and the naval city of **Portsmouth.**

Going west from Southampton, you'll come to the New Forest, more than 90,000 acres selfishly preserved by William the Conqueror as a private hunting ground (poachers met with the death penalty). William lost two of his sons in the New Forest—one killed by an animal, the other by an arrow. Today it is a vast and unspoiled woodland and heath, ideal for walking and exploring.

Although Hampshire is filled with many places of interest, for our purposes I've concentrated on two major areas that seem to hold the most appeal for visitors: Southampton for convenience and Winchester for history.

LUNCHEON STOPOVERS ON THE WAY: For those driving down to Winchester and the New Forest, there is a good lunch stop at **Selborne.** After taking the A31 from London to Chawton to see Jane Austen's home, take the signposted B3006 to Selborne, five miles away. In the 18th century, Gilbert White, the author of the *Natural History of Selborne* and a pioneering botanist, lived here.

At the **Queens Hotel** (tel. Selborne 272) you can order a pub lunch of homemade soup, Queensburger, and Welsh rarebit for £2 ($3), or else eat in the fantastically decorated dining room under a canopy of brass jugs, bits of farm equipment, corncobs, and "god-whattery" hanging from the old oak beams. David, son of the owner, Blake Paton, ladles out the special Peggy Paton's homemade soup (his mother's recipe), plus large portions of freshly roasted beef with all the trimmings, such as Yorkshire pudding, roast potatoes, and properly cooked cabbage (that is, al dente with a little butter and some pepper). On other days there is lamb with mint sauce and red currant jelly. Desserts are homemade, and the fruit pies and cream are especially good. The bill, including VAT, will come to around £5.50 ($8.25) per person. If you can drive after leaving the place, Winchester is not too far away if you retrace your steps on the A31. The hotel is open for lunches from 12:30 to 1:45 p.m. and for dinners from 7:30 to 8:45 p.m. Accommodation with a full English breakfast is available from £11 ($16.50) per night. Six of the nine bedrooms have private bath or shower and toilets.

Similarly at Hurstbourne Priors, between Andover and Whitchurch, on the B3400, stands the **Portsmouth Arms** (tel. 025682/2000), another country pub serving good food. The range of hot dishes isn't large, but there are usually two choices as appetizers—smoked mackerel, soup, pâté—followed by pork chops, ham steaks, or lamb, all served with freshly picked and freshly cooked vegetables in season. Cheese, homemade pie, or trifle finishes the meals which, with coffee, comes to £3 ($4.50) to £5 ($7.50) per person. The "Arms" is open for lunch from noon to 2:30 p.m. and for dinner from 7 to 10:30 p.m.

1. Portsmouth

Virginia, New Hampshire, even Ohio, may have their Portsmouths, but the daddy of them all is the old port and naval base on the Hampshire coast, 70 miles south of London. German bombers in World War II virtually leveled the city, hitting about nine-tenths of its buildings. But the seaport has recovered admirably.

Its maritime associations are known around the world. From Sally Port, the most interesting district in the Old Town, "Naval heroes innumerable have embarked to fight their country's battles." That was certainly true on June 6, 1944, when Allied troops set sail to invade occupied France.

Some 400 years earlier, an English navy ship didn't fare so well. The *Mary Rose,* flagship of the fleet of wooden men-o'-war of King Henry VIII, sank in the Solent in 1545 in full view of the king. In 1982 a descendant of that monarch, and heir to the throne, Charles, Prince of Wales, watched the *Mary Rose* break the water's surface after almost four centuries spent lying on the sea bottom, not exactly shipshape and Bristol fashion but surprisingly well preserved nonetheless. Now the remains are on view, although the hull must be kept permanently wet. The hull and the more than 10,000 items brought up by divers constitute one of the major archeological discoveries of England in many years. Among the artifacts on permanent exhibit are almost the complete equipment of the ship's barber, with surgeon's cabin saws, knives, ointments, and plaster all ready for use; long bows and arrows, some still in shooting order; carpenters' tools; leather jackets; and some fine lace and silk.

To see the *Mary Rose* exhibition, use the entrance to the Portsmouth Dockyard through the Victory Gate (as for H.M.S. *Victory*), and follow the signs. It is open Monday to Saturday from 10:30 a.m. to 5:30 p.m., on

Sunday from 1 p.m. to 5:30 p.m. Admission is £1 ($1.50) for adults, 40p (60¢) for children. The administrative offices of the Mary Rose Trust are at Old Bond Store, 48 Warblington St. (tel. 0705/750521).

On the 40th anniversary of the Normandy landings, the **D-Day Museum,** Clarence Esplanade, Southsea, was opened and dedicated to the Allied invasion of occupied France and to the forces that took part in it. The Overlord Embroidery was moved here from London to form the main attraction, showing the complete story of Operation Overlord, the men, and the machines that featured in the invasion operation. The appliquéed embroidery—probably the largest of its kind, 272 feet long and three feet high—was designed by Sandra Lawrence and took 20 women of the Royal School of Needlework five years to complete.

There is a special audio-visual program and displays, including reconstructions of various stages of the mission with models and maps. A hall is filled with tanks, Jeeps, field guns, and even a Duck, that incredibly useful vehicle equally at home on land or in the water. The museum next to Southsea Castle, is open seven days a week from 10:30 a.m. to 5 p.m. Admission is £1.25 ($1.88) for adults, 65p (98¢) for children.

Of major interest is Lord Nelson's flagship, H.M.S. *Victory,* a 104-gun, first-rate ship of the line, now at No. 2 Dry Dock in Portsmouth Naval Base, (tel. 0705/22351). Although she first saw action in 1778, her fame was earned on October 21, 1805, in the Battle of Trafalgar when the English scored a victory over the combined Spanish and French fleets. It was in this battle that Lord Nelson lost his life. The flagship, after being taken to Gibraltar for repairs, returned to Portsmouth with Nelson's body on board (he was later buried at St. Paul's in London). It is open March 1 to November 1, weekdays, 10:30 a.m. to 5:30 p.m.; on Sunday from 1 to 5 p.m. From November 1 to March 1, weekdays, 10:30 a.m. to 4:30 p.m. and on Sunday from 1 to 4:30 p.m. There is no admission charge.

The **Royal Naval Museum** (tel. 0705/822351, extension 23868) stands opposite H.M.S. *Victory* and close to the *Mary Rose* in the unique setting of the old naval dockyard. It is the only museum devoted exclusively to the overall history of the Royal Navy. Exhibitions include a special collection of Nelson memorabilia belonging to an American citizen, Mrs. Lily McCarthy, C.B.E. Also relics of Nelson and Lady Hamilton are shown, as well as displays on the pre-Nelsonian navy, the navy in the Napoleonic Wars, the Victorian navy, and the navy in the 20th century. There is also a large-scale panorama of the Battle of Trafalgar with full sound effects. The museum is open daily from 10:30 a.m. to 5 p.m. Monday to Saturday, 1 to 5 p.m. on Sunday (with some seasonal variations). Admission is 60p ($1.20). The museum complex includes a buffet and a well-stocked souvenir shop.

Portsmouth was the birthplace of Charles Dickens, and the small terrace house of 1805 in which the famous novelist made his appearance on February 7, 1812, and lived for a short time, has now been restored and furnished to illustrate the middle-class taste of the early 19th century. Called **Charles Dickens' Birthplace Museum,** it is at 393 Old Commercial Rd., Mile End (tel. 0705/827261). It is open daily from 10:30 a.m. to 5:30 p.m., except Christmas Day and Boxing Day. Admission is 50p (75¢) for adults, 20p (30¢) for students and children. Family tickets (four persons) are available for £1 ($1.50). Last tickets are sold at 5 p.m.

Jutting out into the harbor, **Portchester Castle** is the finest example of a complete Roman fortress in Europe. Within its walls, enclosing seven acres, stand a Norman castle and a Norman church. You can explore the

Roman stone walls and bastions. It was here that Henry V assembled his men for the assault on Agincourt in 1415.

WHERE TO STAY: Overnighting in Portsmouth? If so, try the following:

Keppel's Head Hotel, The Hard (tel. 0705/833231), is an impressive Victorian brick monument facing the train, bus, and ferry stations and overlooking the harbor. A prestigious hotel for generations, it has comfortable, well-furnished, and pleasantly decorated bedrooms, all with private baths or showers, color TVs, phones, and tea- and coffee-making facilities. Singles rent for £36 ($54) and doubles for £52 ($78) per night, including a full English breakfast and VAT. The hotel's restaurant, the Captain's Table, has English cuisine—thick slices of ribs of beef with Yorkshire pudding or roast loin of pork with apple sauce. This can be followed by cheesecake, cake, or a selection from the tempting cheeseboard.

WHERE TO EAT: The **Lone Yachtsman** at the Point (head up Broad Street; tel. 0705/24293) is a revamped pub that is the center of the local life of old Portsmouth. Decorated in a nautical theme, it commands a view of the harbor from its perch on the end of a promontory. You can drink in the Sir Alec Rose bar (popular with yachting people) or dine at the Lively Lady (hot luncheons every day from noon to 2:30 p.m.). Among the usual entrees are such tempting items as the soup of the day and steak, kidney, and mushroom pie. A tradition is the hot fruit pie, served with thick cream. A snack meal will cost around £1.50 ($2.25) to £4.50 ($6.75), with a set lunch going for £2.75 ($4.13).

The Hungry One, 15 Arundel Way, Arundel Street (tel. 0705/817114), is a clean and neat snackbar offering a wide choice of salads, plus an assortment of meats, chicken, plaice, and scampi, served with chips and salad. Meals cost from £7 ($10.50). This place is noted for its coffee served with fresh cream.

IN THE ENVIRONS: The **Old House,** The Square, Wickham, near Fareham (tel. 0329/833049), is a tiny village-square hotel built in 1702, in the time of Queen Anne. It is personally run by its owners, Mr. and Mrs. Skipwith. The hotel stands in a preserved Georgian square of Wickham, and is noted for its good restaurant, which is closed at lunchtime on Monday and Saturday (all day on Sunday).

The hotel's bedrooms, each with private bath, are not rented on Saturday and Sunday, and therefore it is open on weekdays only. Prices are from £35 ($52.50) in a single, from £52 ($78) in a double, these tariffs including a full English breakfast, service charge, and VAT.

The garden overlooks the Meon River, and the restaurant specializes in a French provincial cuisine, a complete meal costing from £18 ($27). The menu changes frequently, and care goes into the selection of the vegetables as well. On one occasion, local spring greens, with butter and black pepper, were excellent. Lunch is served from 12:30 to 2 p.m. and dinner from 7:30 to 9:30 p.m. Always reserve well in advance.

Off the Portsmouth–Southhampton road, follow the signs to **Hamble.** You will soon come to **Beth's Restaurant,** The Quay, in Hamble (tel. 0703/454314). Even in a village of ancient shops and houses, the Queen

Anne house stands out with its typical plain front, large windows, and welcoming front door. Inside, the bar with its roaring log fire and antique furniture is more a drawing room, and you might be excused for thinking you've come to the wrong place.

Never fear. Beth Cockburn has specially created the family home atmosphere, and you can relax in a deep armchair with an apértif while deciding on your meal. Upstairs, the restaurant has lovely views over the Hamble River, one of the best known yachting centers in the country.

The menu is changed frequently, along with the seasons and the availability of fresh produce. Mostly French dishes are offered, but there are some rather elaborate English ones as well. Appetizers include homemade pâté with a celery and orange salad, a hot fish pâté with a herb sauce, and gravad lax, home-cured salmon not often found outside Norway. Main dishes include guinea fowl baked with limes and cream cheese, fresh local fish, lamb kidneys with port Dijon mustard, and sirloin steak served with special butters—herb, garlic, or "alcoholic." Your meal is rounded off with a light homemade dessert or cheese. The average price is £12 ($18), including vegetables and VAT but not wine.

They also do a special two-course menu, with coffee, for £7.50 ($11.25). The restaurant is open for lunch from 12:30 to 2:30 p.m. and for dinner from 7 until the last orders are taken at 9:30 p.m. They are closed from Sunday night to Tuesday in January and February. They make sure that you're not hurried from your table and have time to enjoy a relaxing meal. Telephone to reserve a table, as they are very popular.

They also do breakfast from 9 a.m. if you happen to be touring in the area. In summer, they open the garden behind the house, weather permitting, and lunches and dinners are served there. The fare consists of various barbecues—steaks, hamburgers, chicken, local mackerel, and bass, all served with baked jacket potatoes and salads. Fresh lobster with lemon mayonnaise is a summer special.

Between Portsmouth and Southampton lies an increasingly popular attraction in this part of the country—

BROADLANDS: The home of Earl Mountbatten of Burma until his assassination in 1979, Broadlands, Romsey (tel. 0794/516878), lies on the A31, 72 miles southwest of London. Lord Mountbatten lent the house to Princess Elizabeth and Prince Philip (now H.M. the Queen and the Duke of Edinburgh) as a honeymoon haven in 1947, and in 1981 Prince Charles and Princess Diana spent the first nights of their honeymoon here. Broadlands is now owned by Lord Romsey, Lord Mountbatten's eldest grandson, who has created a fine exhibition and audio-visual show depicting the highlights of the brilliant career as a sailor and statesman of his grandfather, who has been called "the last war hero."

The house, originally linked to Romsey Abbey, was purchased by Lord Palmerston in 1736. It was later transformed into an elegant Palladian mansion by Capability Brown and Henry Holland. Brown landscaped the parkland and grounds, making the river (the Test) the main object of pleasure. Broadlands has long been a center of hospitality for royal and eminent persons. This tradition continues, but it remains very much a home for Lord and Lady Romsey. The house, the Mountbatten Exhibibition, and the riverside lawns are open April 1 to September 30 from 10 a.m. to 6 p.m. Closed Monday except in August, September, and on bank holidays. Admission is £3 ($4.50) for adults, £1.60 ($2.40) for children.

2. Southampton

To many North Americans, England's No. 1 passenger port, home base for the *Queen Elizabeth 2,* is the gateway to Britain. Southampton is a city of wide boulevards, parks, and shopping centers. It was rebuilt after German bomb damage, which destroyed hundreds of its old buildings.

In World War II, some 3½ million men embarked from here (in the First World War, more than twice that number passed through Southampton). Its supremacy as a port has long been recognized and dates from Saxon times when the Danish conqueror, Canute, was proclaimed king here in 1017.

Southampton was especially important to the Normans and kept them in touch with their homeland. It shares the dubious distinction of having imported the bubonic plague in the mid-14th century that wiped out a quarter of the English population. Near the docks is a memorial tower to the Pilgrims, who set out on their voyage to the New World from Southampton on August 15, 1620.

If you're waiting in Southampton between boats, you may want to use the time to explore some of the major sights of Hampshire that lie on the periphery of the port—the New Forest, Winchester, the Isle of Wight, and Bournemouth in neighboring Dorset.

WHERE TO STAY: The **Post House,** Herbert Walker Avenue (tel. 0703/28081), is a Trusthouses Forte oasis of style and taste, the pacesetter of modern hotels on the south coast. Ten floors tall, it was built near the New Docks to overlook the harbor, but is only five minutes away from the city center. You can unload your luggage under a sheltered drive, and walk straight into the reception area. The rooms, 132 in all (nine studio and eight syndicate accommodations), are handsome and spacious, decorated in strong bold colors, with fine built-in pieces, picture-window walls, private baths, telephones, radio, and television. Twin or double rooms cost £52 ($78) per person; a single, £42 ($63). Your breakfast is extra, but all rates include service and VAT. The facilities of the hotel are exceptional, especially the heated open-air swimming pool. The residents' lounge has a color television. The Harbour Bar adjacent to the restaurant has an intimate atmosphere. For dining in the Solent Room see my restaurant recommendations.

Dolphin Hotel, High Street (tel. 0703/26178), which dates back to the 13th century, was Jane Austen's choice, even Thackeray's when he was writing *Pendennis.* In time, Queen Victoria arrived in a horse-drawn carriage at this Georgian inn and coaching house. A classic brick building, with a pair of bow windows, it is in the center of the city, and is approached through an arched entrance, over which rests a coat-of-arms of William IV and Queen Adelaide. The 73 bedrooms vary widely in size, but are generally spacious and well furnished. All have baths. Singles cost £37 ($55.50); doubles and twins, £45 ($67.50). The lounge is dignified, nicely paneled, and tidily kept. The open staircase holds a rare collection of naval uniform prints. Meals at the Dolphin are quite good, with a table d'hôte dinner beginning at £10 ($15). Drinks are served in the Nelson Bar.

Polygon Hotel, Cumberland Place (tel. 0703/26401), 15 minutes to the Ocean Terminal, is the ideal hotel for transatlantic passengers just off the *Queen Elizabeth 2.* Set quietly back overlooking West Park and the Civic Centre, it is run as a member of Trusthouses Forte Hotels Ltd. It offers 119 well-furnished bedrooms, all with private baths, telephones, radios, and color TV sets. A single is £42 ($63), and a twin is £50 ($75). A bar and restaurant are on the premises; there is ample parking space, plus near-instant taxi service.

Southampton Moat House, 119 Highfield Lane, Portswood (tel. 0703/559555), stands in a quiet residential area on the outskirts of the city. This modern hotel, a member of Queens Moat Houses group, offers comfortable accommodations and friendly, efficient service. Its restaurant, the Mary Rose, serves both table d'hôte and à la carte menus, which are complemented by a comprehensive wine list. Lunch and dinner will cost from £6.50 ($9.75) for a three-course meal. Rooms are from £36 ($54) in a single and £46 ($69) in a double, including an English breakfast and VAT.

WHERE TO DINE: The **Solent Room,** Post House, Herbert Walker Avenue (tel. 0703/28081), is a distinguished restaurant in a colorful setting. On the ground floor of this ten-story modern hotel, top-notch meals are served against a background of bright-red floors and walls. The service is friendly and attentive and the cuisine is international. A four-course set lunch with three choices for each course costs £10 ($15), and a similar four-course dinner goes for £11.50 ($17.25). You can also order à la carte meals. All charges are inclusive of service and VAT. The headwaiter will present you with an excellent list of wines.

Cobbett's Restaurant, The Square, Botley (tel. 04892/2068), is run with flair by Mr. and Mrs. Charles Skipwith, who prepare French dishes with skill, using fresh ingredients whenever possible. Even the vegetables—too often neglected in restaurants in England—are well prepared, tender and crisp. Mr. Skipwith's wife, Lucie, comes from France, and she does the cooking, taking pride in selecting original and unusual dishes. To her, "deep freeze" are dirty words. Seating 40, the snug restaurant has a 16th-century beamed bar where pre- and postdinner drinks are served. The menus and prices change seasonally, so I can't recommend particular specialties. However, recent main courses included tournedos Curnonsky and a regional cassoulet. Fresh vegetables in season are always offered. The hors d'oeuvres are good, especially the salade des crudités. Although the list varies, depending on what's available at the market, a recent plate featured celery, tomatoes, fennel, watercress, chicory, cucumber, egg, artichoke hearts, and other vegetables. Expect to pay about £16 ($24) per head, including VAT. Lunch is served from noon to 2 p.m.; dinner, 7:30 to 10 p.m.

Mr. Skipwith takes special pride in his wine list, the main part of which is supplied by Yapp Brothers of Mere in Wiltshire, whose expertise is unsurpassed in the United Kingdom where Rhône and Loire wines are concerned. The restaurant's whole list changes two or three times a year. Closed at lunchtime Saturday, Sunday, and Monday, on Sunday evening, bank holidays, and for a two-week summer vacation. There's ample off-street parking here.

The Best Pub in Town

The **Red Lion**, High Street (tel. 0703/333595), is one of the few architectural jewels that survived World War II. The pub is rooted in the 12th century (a Norman cellar), but its high-ceilinged and raftered Henry V Court Room is in a later style. The room was the scene of the trial of the Earl of Cambridge and his accomplices, Thomas Grey and Lord Scrope, who were condemned to death for treason in plotting against the life of the king in 1415. The Court Room is adorned with coats-of-arms of the noblemen who served as peers of the trio. All this bloody history needn't deter you. The Red Lion is a friendly, fascinating place at which to stop in for a drink, a good old English pub lunch for around £4 ($6), and a chat.

SIDE TRIPS FROM SOUTHAMPTON: If postwar Southampton is too modern for your taste, and you want to capture the flavor of old England, then strike out for the **Fox and Hounds Inn,** Hungerford Bottom, Old Bursledon (tel. 042121/2784), between Southampton and Portsmouth—not far from the ferry to the Isle of Wight, and close to the Bursledon Railroad Station. It would take the writing ability of Dickens and the visual techniques of Hogarth to capture the spirited image of this inn, which dates back to 1338. You can have your wine-tasting experience in either the Hunter's Bar or the Farmer's Kitchen. Against a backdrop of horse brasses, a heavily beamed ceiling, and an open fireplace, the legendary mead—known to both the English and the Vikings—is dispensed. The Saxons considered it an elixir, and it is believed that the honey-based drink was the customary toast following a wedding—hence, the term honeymoon. Between lifting your maple and silver "mazer," you can sample Hampshire farm cheese served with good-tasting cottage bread. The Fox and Hounds, run by Terry and Lynne McEvoy, is also noted for its English wines, which can be ordered on draft. If you've tasted cowslip before, you surely haven't sampled damson dandelion! From your beer-barrel seat, you can also take your chance on some sloe gin. English wines cost 75p ($1.13) per glass; a small glass of real ale, 55p (83¢). At the rear of the inn is a timbered barn serving as both a museum of farming artifacts (old farm wagons, carts, and smithy tools) and a self-service dining room. Here you dine on benches at one of the longest, oldest tables in England. During winter, the table nearest the ten-foot-wide fireplace is favored. Summertime, tables are also available in the courtyard beside an ancient wine press, under a rose arbor. A large bowl of soup with crusty bread is £1 ($1.50), and salads and cold meats cost £2.50 ($3.75) to £3.50 ($5.25).

Directions: Go on road A27 from Southampton, toward Portsmouth. After passing Lowford, turn right onto Long Lane, pass the school on School Road, and you'll reach a road called Hungerford Bottom. The Fox and Hounds is on your right.

3. New Forest

The New Forest came into the limelight in the times of Henry VIII, who loved to hunt here, as venison abounded. Also with his enthusiasm for building up the British naval fleet, he saw his opportunity to supply oak and other hard timbers to the boatyards at Buckler's Hard on the Beaulieu River for the building of stout-hearted men-o'-war. Today you can visit the old shipyards, the museum with its fine models of men-o'-war, pictures of the old yard, and dioramas showing the building of these ships, their construction, and their launching. It took 2000 trees to build one man-o'-war.

Stretching for about 92,000 acres, New Forest is a large tract 14 miles wide and 20 miles long. William the Conqueror laid out the limits of this then-private hunting preserve. Those who hunted without a license faced the executioner if they were caught, and those who hunted but missed had their hands severed.

Nowadays, New Forest is one of those places traversed by a motorway by those motorists bound for the southwest. However, I'd suggest you stop a moment and relax.

This used to be a forest, but now the groves of oak trees are separated by wide tracts of common land that is grazed by ponies and cows, hummocked with heather and gorse, and frequented by rabbits. Away from the main arterial roads, where signs warn of wild ponies and deer, there is a private world of peace and quiet.

The **New Forest Butterfly Farm,** Longdown, Ashurst, near Southampton (tel. 042129/2166), is probably not everyone's cup of tea, but if you're interested in Orange-tips, Jezebels, or Delias, this is the place for you. This farm keeps not only endangered species of British butterflies but exotic numbers from Malaysia, Brazil, and Africa. They are bred in a paradise of lemon trees, bougainvillea, and passion flowers. Outside on the ponds, dragonflies and damselflies hover over the water and breed naturally among the reeds. More exotically, there are also locusts, mantids, and tarantulas carefully protected behind observation glass.

There are five acres of woodland, a tea shop, and a gift shop where you can buy mounted butterflies, jewelry, butterfly books, and caterpillars for home breeding. At the Old Spud Shed, a relic of some former garden, you can purchase tropical plants and good old-fashioned dandelions, thistles, and nettles to encourage butterflies in your own garden. The farm is open April 1 to October 31 daily from 10 a.m. to 5 p.m., charging adults an admission of £1.75 ($2.63), and children, £1 ($1.50).

FOOD AND LODGING: My recommendations for food and lodging follow, beginning with the finest establishment in the entire area.

New Milton

Chewton Glen Hotel, New Milton, Hampshire (tel. 04252/5341), is a gracious old country house on the fringe of the New Forest. It's within easy reach of Southampton and Bournemouth for those who want to escape from the bustle of the 20th century. Follow the signpost off the A35 New Milton–Christchurch road, through well-kept parkland to a private car park. The staff will arrange for you to be met if you intend to arrive by ship or train at Southampton.

Rooms are either in the old house or in the new wing. In your bedroom you'll find "a tot" of sherry along with a bowl of fresh flowers to greet you. In the old house, you take the magnificent staircase to one of the well-furnished chambers, decorated with chintz armchairs, good beds, and lovely views over the spacious grounds. In the new wing, you find yourself on the ground level with french doors opening onto your own private patio. Here the decor is in muted colors, the rooms named for the heroes of novels written by Captain Marryat (he was the author of *The Children of the New Forest*). There is full room service so you can retire fully from the world if that is your wish. In the old part, the rooms have eaves and dormer windows, and some have been combined to provide family accommodations.

Settle in and wander downstairs to explore the many lounges, arranged so that you can join the small crowd in the bar, or sit and talk in the big drawing room. Everywhere log fires burn and fresh flowers add fragrance. In the hall an information office provides details of local excursions, golf, sailing, and horse-riding. Guests can also swim in an open-air heated swimming pool. The garden sweeps down to a stream and then to rhododendron woods. In addition there are a tennis court, a billiard room, and a croquet and putting green.

In the dining room, the standard of cooking and the presentation of the food is high. Particular emphasis is placed on fresh ingredients. The chef de cuisine, Pierre Chevillard, favors nouvelle cuisine, complemented by excellent sauces and velvety-smooth desserts. Toni Ferrario is one of the most efficient restaurant managers in the country. Your dinner will be a treat. The set meal of three magnificent courses is changed daily. A set lunch is £10.50 ($15.75), going up to £15 ($22.50) on Sunday. A set dinner costs £20 ($30), rising to £21 ($31.50) on Saturday. The à la carte menu includes such delicacies as sweetbreads and Scottish salmon, and such daily specialties as lobster in season. An à la carte dinner will cost about £50 ($75) for two persons. But I find the set meal delicious and adequate for the best of trenchermen. A simpler but equally excellent luncheon is provided, and the kitchen will also prepare a succulent picnic for you to take on an excursion. The wine cellar contains a choice of well-chosen French and German wines—and some Italian ones too.

The price to stay here begins at £98 ($147) for two persons, including VAT, service, and a continental breakfast. The Marryat suite is priced at £155 ($232.50) for two, and the recently converted coach houses are delightful duplexes, with two bathrooms each, costing £140 ($210) for two.

The hotel is owned by Martin Skan and his family, and their influence and that of their general manager, David Brockett, can be seen in the many thoughtful touches, the friendly attitude of the efficient staff, and the spotless condition of the hotel and grounds.

Ashurst

Beaulieu Road Hotel, Ashurst (tel. Ashurst 2141), stands on the B3056 from Lyndhurst to Beaulieu. It was said to have been built by the grandfather of the present Lord Montagu close to the Beaulieu Road Railway Station to accommodate the overflow of guests arriving from London to shoot on the estate.

Nowadays the red brick building, surrounded by pine trees, has comfortable bedrooms, some with bath, which rent for £14 ($21) per person nightly, including a large English breakfast.

Dinners are mainly grills and roasts, particularly New Forest venison, a large meal costing around £8 ($12). They also have a snackbar at lunchtime with quiches, sandwiches, and several homemade hot dishes.

Every autumn, the highlight of the year is the Beaulieu Road New Forest Pony Sales in the stockyards of the local railway station, when ponies newly rounded up from the forest are sold. The hotel's drinking license is extended to cover the whole day.

Mrs. McGrath is the owner and manager of the hotel, and she'll see that you're well provided for. As an additional bonus, the hotel has a swimming pool and tennis court—and your horse can be stabled at low cost. The surrounding area is gentle walking country, as there are no startling or steep hills and dales to negotiate. It's also marvelous for horseback riding.

Lyndhurst

Lyndhurst Park Hotel, High Street (tel. 042128/2824), is a large old country house with trees and lawns, plus a swimming pool and golf practice net. Bedrooms are equipped with TV, in-house movies, radio, phone, and tea- or coffee-makers, costing from £20 ($30) per person with bath, including VAT and an English breakfast.

There are two bars with beams, high-backed settles, and harnesses decorating the brick walls and the high-ceilinged, woodpaneled dining room. A surprisingly wide selection of dishes is offered, both at lunch and dinner. Appetizers are likely to include scallops with lobster and cheese sauce or fried camembert cheese in breadcrumbs. Main dishes include grilled Lymington plaice (a local fish), pot-roasted local pheasant, and sirloin steaks. A three-course meal with coffee will cost about £11 ($16.50), except on Saturday night when they have dancing at dinnertime. Then the cost of the evening will be from £13 ($19.50). It's very pleasant and comfortable.

The **Crown Hotel,** High Street (tel. 042128/2722), stands on a spot where there has been a hostelry for centuries, on the main street of the village opposite the church with its tall spire. The present building is a mere 100 years old, and the bedrooms are snug with color TV, radio, phone, and a drink cabinet. Singles cost £34 ($51), and doubles, £45 ($67.50), including VAT and a full English breakfast.

Much local produce is used in the dining room, including venison Walter Tyrrell, commemorating the hunter who missed the deer and loosed the arrow that pierced the heart of William Rufus, king of England. This specialty is a rich concoction of meat, mushrooms, and onions cooked in red wine and cream with red currants and brandy. Steak Agamemnon is named for one of the wooden warships built at nearby Buckler's Hard.

A set lunch costs £8 ($12); a set dinner, £10 ($15). There are also à la carte selections. Sunday lunch is well patronized by the local people. They also do substantial bar snacks with at least one hot dish of the day with vegetables, plus afternoon teas for 75p ($1.13).

Brockenhurst

New Park Manor, Lyndhurst Road, Brockenhurst, New Forest (tel. 0590/23467), is a former royal hunting lodge dating from the days of William the Conqueror. It is the only hotel in the New Forest itself. In 1666 King Charles made New Park his favorite hunting lodge on his return from exile in France, and came here accompanied by Nell Gwynne.

Now a modern country hotel, the manor has some 20 bedrooms, which were opened to the public in 1970. The original rooms have been preserved, including such features as beams and open log fires. The owners have installed central heating throughout, and the bedrooms contain baths, color TV, and tea- and coffee-making facilities. The rate per person is £24 ($36) in a room on the second floor, £25 ($37.50) on the first floor. Included in the tariff is the use of a swimming pool, in a sheltered corner of the garden (heated in summer), and a hard tennis court. Riding from the hotel's stables is available at a reduced rate for guests.

The candlelit restaurant, with its log fire, specializes in flambé cookery. Backed up by a good wine list, the chef often uses fresh garden produce and the hotel's own bacon and pork from its pig farm. Saturday dinner-dances are increasingly popular. The hotel lies half a mile off the A337 Lyndhurst–Brockenhurst road past the 500-year-old thatched lodge to the manor.

Balmer Lawn Hotel, Brockenhurst (tel. 0590/23116), is a sophisticated place, with grounds blending with those of New Forest, a heated swimming pool, and pleasant comfortable lounges in which to relax. Lunch costs from £7.50 ($10.50); dinner, from £9.50 ($14.25). The menu offers many interesting selections. After a local fish or venison, you might try, for example, a date-and-ginger pie. Rooms, all with baths, go for £25 ($37.50) per person, including VAT and a full breakfast. Ideal for the visitor, the hotel lies on the A337, the Lyndhurst–Lymington road, about a mile outside of Brockenhurst. Opposite the hotel is the village cricket field, where on summer weekends guests can stroll out to watch the game played as it should be—by local enthusiasts.

Lymington

The **Angel Hotel,** 108 High St. (tel. 0590/72050), is a 13th-century inn right on the main street with a large car park behind it in the courtyard. The plain bedrooms have TV, radio, and tea- and coffee-making facilities, costing £18 ($27) per person in a double. They also rent out family rooms at reduced rates. A full English breakfast is served and included in the tariff. Meals of an informal nature are available at lunchtime and in the evening in the Tuck Inn. You can select from a traditional menu or just enjoy a light snack.

Marlo's Barge Restaurant, Bridge Yard (tel. 0590/72237). An old French river barge, *Maria II* has been converted into a restaurant open Wednesday to Sunday from 7 p.m. You're advised to reserve a table, as there's not much room. Appetizers range from the soup of the day to fresh trout. Main dishes include chicken with tarragon, noisettes of lamb, sweetbreads, fresh local fish such as plaice or monkfish, and especially crab, depending on availability. These platters go for about £6.50 ($9.75), including vegetables and a salad. It's a fun place with a cheerful atmosphere and good food, but it's not easy to find. Ask directions when you make your reservation.

The Old Bankhouse Bistro, 68 High St. (tel. 0590/78888), is a basement place with a wooden floor and an old brick wall behind the bar, which is long and narrow. It's very popular with the locals who like its friendly atmosphere and excellent value meals. It's open daily except Monday from noon to 3 p.m. and from 6 to 11 p.m. You lunch off chicken pâté or taramasalata, perhaps soup of the day. You can order basket meals such as scampi and chips, salads, and cold meats. A plate will cost from £1.20 ($1.80) to £2.50 ($3.75).

Fagin's Restaurant, 135 High St., is a real Dickensian-type, low-ceilinged restaurant, with oak beams, high-backed chairs, and dining alcoves with stools. Try the Fagin's cocktail of prawns, celery, apple, and walnuts in Marie-Rose sauce, or the homemade sardine and anchovy pâté with brown bread. I also enjoy the crudités (fresh raw vegetables) with a cheese dip. Perhaps you'll follow with a whole grilled local plaice, chicken casserole, or an entrecôte steak with mushrooms and brown sauce. Desserts from the trolley finish off the meal, and fresh vegetables cost extra. Expect to spend from £9 ($13.50).

The Buttery, 20 High St., is an ideal place for morning coffee or a quick snack lunch. Salads and omelets are good, costing from £2 ($3), and sandwiches start at 70p ($1.05). It's a busy, cheerful place with quick service. The cakes and pastries served are homemade, and the specialty is clotted-cream teas, served all day.

For those who just want "pub-grub," Mr. Keen at **King's Head,** at the bottom of High Street, offers a wide range of bar snacks from noon to 2 p.m. and also in the evening. Perhaps you'll sample his cannelloni with a meat and tomato sauce, or chicken in the basket with straw potatoes. Portions go for about £3 ($4.50). On Sunday, he does only a ploughman's lunch.

BEAULIEU ABBEY: This stately home is in the beautiful New Forest. The abbey and Palace House, as well as the National Motor Museum, are on the property of Lord Montagu of Beaulieu (tel. 0590/612345), five miles southeast of Lyndhurst and 14 miles south of Southampton. Originally a Cistercian abbey was founded on this spot in 1204, and the ruins can be explored. **Palace House** was the gatehouse of the abbey before it was converted into a private residence in 1538. The house is surrounded by gardens.

In the grounds, the **National Motor Museum,** one of the best and most comprehensive motor museums in the world, with more than 200 vehicles, is open to the public. It traces the story of motoring from 1895 to the present day. Famous autos include four land-speed record holders, among them Donald Campbell's *Bluebird*. The museum is based on the Montagu family's collection of vintage cars. All the facilities are open daily from 10 a.m. to 6 p.m., to 5 p.m. from November to March. Admission to the museum, house, abbey ruins, and garden is an inclusive £3 ($4.50) for adults, £1.50 ($2.25) for children.

Food and Lodging

Montagu Arms, in Beaulieu (tel. 0590/612324), was built with locally made bricks and tiles as well as timbers from the New Forest. This time-tested favorite combines the comfort of a country manor house with the cozy hospitality of a mellow wayside inn. The hotel staff keeps up an old English garden, which is well sheltered and filled with some rare plants. The main lounge overlooks this garden, and the dining room, serving good food and wine, is oak beamed and paneled. In one of the three bars, the counter was fashioned from an old wine press.

The bedrooms are immaculately kept and modernized, most of them containing private baths and wall-to-wall carpeting. Singles rent from £34 ($51) to £39 ($58.50), and twins and doubles range from £48 ($72) to £56 ($84), including VAT, service, and a full English breakfast. The rates vary according to season and location of room. You can have a set lunch in the dining room for £8.50 ($12.75), a set dinner for £12.50 ($18.75).

Buckler's Hard

The **Master Builders House Hotel,** Buckler's Hard (tel. 059063/253), is a lovely 18th-century main house that was once the home of master shipbuilder Henry Adams, who was responsible for many of the wooden walls that dominate the seaways of the world. Today there is a new wing that accommodates guests in pleasant double rooms with bath, color TV, and tea- and coffee-making facilities. The main house has only four rooms available to guests. Singles rent for £28 ($42), doubles and twins for £44 ($66), including VAT and a full English breakfast.

The space in the main building is devoted to the Yachtsman Buffet Bar, which provides good, ample snack meals, and to the restaurant with its wide windows overlooking the busy river. A set lunch is offered for £7.50 ($11.25), a set dinner for £10 ($15). Some evenings, there's live music with dancing, and then an 80p ($1.20) cover charge is levied.

This is an ideal center from which to explore the New Forest and the coastline. This historic 18th-century village on the banks of the Beaulieu River is where ships for Nelson's fleet were built, including the admiral's favorite, *Agamemnon,* as well as *Eurylus* and *Swiftsure.* The **Maritime Museum** reflects the ship-building history of the village. Its displays include shipbuilding at Buckler's Hard; Henry Adams, master shipbuilder; Nelson's favorite ship; Buckler's Hard and Trafalgar; and models of Sir Francis Chichester's yachts and items of his equipment. The cottage exhibits are a recreation of 18th-century life in Buckler's Hard. Here you can stroll through the New Inn of 1793 and a shipwright's cottage of the same period or look in on the family of a poor laborer at home. All these displays include village residents and visitors of the late 18th century.

The museum is open daily from 10 a.m. to 9 p.m. in summer, closing earlier the rest of the year. The walk back to Beaulieu, 2½ miles, along the riverbank is well marked through the woodlands. During the summer, you can cruise on the Beaulieu River in *Swiftsure,* an all-weather catamaran cruiser.

4. Isle of Wight

Four miles across the Solent from the South Coast towns of Southampton, Lymington, and Portsmouth, the Isle of Wight is known for its sandy beaches and its ports, favored by the yachting set. The island, which long attracted such literary figures as Alfred Tennyson and Charles Dickens, is compact in size, measuring 23 miles from east to west, 13 miles from north to south. You can take regular ferryboats over, although hydrofoils cross the Solent in just 20 minutes from Southampton.

Long a favorite of British royalty, the island has as its major attraction **Osborne House,** Queen Victoria's most cherished residence, lying a mile southeast of East Cowes. Prince Albert himself designed the Italian-inspired mansion, which stands in lush gardens, right outside the village of Padmore. The rooms have remained as Victoria knew them, right down to the French piano she used to play and with all the cozy clutter of her sitting room. Grief-stricken at the death of Albert in 1861, she asked that Osborne House remain as it was, and so it has been. Even the turquoise scent bottles he gave her, decorated with cupids and cherubs, are still in place. It was at her bedroom in Osborne House that the queen died on January 22, 1901. Times of admission are April 5 to June 26 from 11 a.m. to 5 p.m. (same hours from September 6 to October 9). From June 28 to September 4, hours are 10 a.m. to 5 p.m. The house is closed on Sunday. Price of admission is £1.80 ($2.70) for adults, 90p ($1.35) for children.

A completely different attraction, **Carisbrooke Castle** is where Charles I was imprisoned by the Roundheads in 1647. This fine medieval castle is in the center of the island, 1½ miles southwest of Newport. Everybody heads for the Well House, concealed inside a 16th-century stone building. Donkeys take turns treading a large wooden wheel connected to a rope that hauls up buckets of water. The castle is open from mid-March to mid-October, weekdays from 9:30 a.m. to 6:30 p.m. In winter it closes at 4 p.m. On Sunday in season its hours are from 9:30 a.m. to 6:30 p.m., but from 2 to 4 p.m. in the other months. Admission is £1.50 ($2.25) for adults, half price for children. Charges drop to 75p ($1.13) for adults (half price for children) in winter.

You have a choice of several bases on the Isle of Wight unless you're what the English call a "day-tripper."

Cowes is the premier port for yachting in Britain. Henry VIII ordered the castle built there, but it is now the headquarters of the Royal Yacht Squadron. The seafront, the Prince's Green, and the high cliff road are worth exploring. Hovercraft are built in the town, and it's also the home and birthplace of the well-known maritime photographer, Beken of Cowes. It's almost *de rigueur* to wear oilskins and wellies, leaving a wet trail behind you.

Along the southeast coast are the twin resorts of **Sandown,** with its new pier complex and theater, and **Shanklin,** at the southern end of Sandown Bay, which has held the British annual sunshine record more times than any other resort. Keats once lived in Shanklin's Old Village.

Farther along the coast, **Ventnor** is called the "Madeira of England," because it rises from the sea in a series of steep hills.

On the west coast, the sand cliffs of **Alum Bay** are a blend of many different colors, a total of 21 claimed. The Needles, three giant chalk rocks, and the Needles Lighthouse, are further features of interest at this end of the island. If you want to stay at the western end of Wight, refer to my recommendations under **Totland Bay, Ullcase,** and **Freshwater Bay.**

Newport is the capital, a bustling market town lying in the heart of the island.

Visitors who'd like to explore the Isle of Wight just for the day can take an **"Around the Island"** six-hour bus tour which leaves from the Cowes Coach Park, Ryde Esplanade, or Yarmouth Harbor at 11:40 a.m. daily from May to October. The price is around £3.50 ($5.25) for adults, £2.75 ($4.13) for children. For further information, telephone 0983/292082 in Cowes, 0983/62264 in Ryde, or 0983/752275 in Yarmouth/Freshwater.

The ferry from Southampton to the Isle of Wight costs about £3.50 ($5.25) for a round-trip ticket, or else you can take a ferry/hydrofoil combination, a round-trip ticket going for around £5 ($7.50) for the ferry, £5.50 ($8.25) for the hydrofoil. Children go for half price.

The Lymington/Yarmouth (Isle of Wight) ferry charges about £5 ($7.50) for a medium-size car and about £3 ($4.50) for each passenger on a day round-trip ticket. The more usual way of reaching the island is by ferry from Portsmouth Harbour or by hovercraft from Southsea, both of which take you to Ryde, a busy seaside town in summer, the railhead for the island's communications system. Arriving in Yarmouth, however, is something else. Here you will find a typical busy little harbor, providing a mooring for yachts and for one of the lifeboats in the Solent area.

You can purchase an **Island Freedom Ticket,** which includes the cost of the ferry from Portsmouth Harbour to Ryde and the "freedom" of Southern Vectis buses as well as the British Rail electric train from Ryde to Shanklin, so you can visit the entire island in a day. To help you pinpoint Alum Bay, Carisbrooke Castle, and Shanklin Chine (ravine), you are provided with a free map of the island and the transport service network. A full-day ticket costs £5.75 ($8.63) for adults, £2.88 ($4.32) for children. A half-day Freedom Ticket, valid from Portsmouth after noon, is £4.75 ($7.13) for adults, £2.38 ($3.57) for children.

A **Round the Island coach tour** operates daily from April to September (not on Saturday in July and August) from Ryde at 11:30 a.m., returning at 5 p.m. The route includes pretty countryside, the seaside towns of Sandown and Shanklin and its Chine, Alum Bay, and the colored cliffs, Yarmouth, and Carisbrooke. The cost, including the ferry from Portsmouth, is £6.30 ($9.45) for adults, £3.70 ($5.55) for children. You must arrive in the Coach Park at Ryde by 11:20 a.m. to take this tour.

VENTNOR: Madeira Hall, Trinity Road (tel. 0983/852624), is perhaps one of the nicest places to stay on the Isle of Wight. In an estate garden of lawns, tall trees, and flowering shrubs stands this stone manor house, with mullioned windows, gables, and bay windows. It has housed interesting people, such as Lord Macaulay, who wrote some of his well-known essays here. And there are associations with Charles Dickens and some of his characters. On the grounds is a heated swimming pool and an 18-hole putting course. All bedrooms are fitted with bed lights and wash basins. There are ample baths and toilets in the corridors. Three rooms have been equipped with private baths, one with a private shower. Half-board terms are from £17 ($25.50) per person in a double or twin without bath, rising to £21 ($31.50) per person with private bath, including service and VAT. Mr. and Mrs. Waring are the resident hosts.

SANDOWN: St. Catherine's Hotel, 1 Winchester Park Rd. (tel. 0983/ 402392), stands in its own garden a few minutes' walk from Sandown's sandy beach, new leisure center, and pier complex, with its sun lounges and theater. St. Catherine's was built in 1860 of creamy Purbeck stone and white trim, for the dean of Winchester College; a modern extension was added for streamlined and sunny bedrooms. Bright colors have been used generously in the interior—the living room has a cherry-red carpet and draperies to match at the wide bay windows. The walls are soft sage green, and the dining room is done in rose pink and olive. Bedrooms have bright bedspreads, white furniture, and built-in headboards. Most of the bedrooms face the sun and are centrally heated. Tucked away in your bedroom are tea- and coffee-making facilities. Many of the rooms contain private baths or showers en suite. Jim and Maureen Hitchcock welcome you, charging a peak rate of £23.50 ($35.25) per person for room with bath or shower, breakfast, and dinner, including VAT and service. Bathless rooms are cheaper, costing £17.50 ($26.25) per person, and including only breakfast.

FRESHWATER BAY: Farringford Hotel, Bedbury Lane, Freshwater (tel. 0983/752500), once the home of Lord Tennyson, has a pleasant, old-fashioned country ambience. A holiday, recreational estate, it has at its core a fine stone manor house and is surrounded by cottages on attractively landscaped grounds. It's adapted to the taste of the English who are accepted from April until the end of October. Depending on the season, the B&B rate ranges from £25 ($37.50) to £29 ($43.50) per person. Half board goes from £32 ($48) to £38 ($57) per person, including VAT and service. Dinner is four courses of well-cooked simple dishes, and lunch can be a snack in the bar lounge. There is a nine-hole golf course free to hotel guests, as well as tennis courts, a swimming pool, a croquet lawn, and a sports pavilion.

In addition, the hotel also rents out self-catering suites available in cottages on the grounds. Four guests can live comfortably for anywhere from £35 ($52.50) to £60 ($90) per day. They can take their meals at the hotel where a dinner costs from £10 ($15), and a Sunday lunch, £7.50 ($11.25). These units have color TV and a fully equipped kitchen, where guests can hire the services of a maid if they don't want to do cleaning.

CHALE: Clarendon Hotel, Newport Road (tel. 0983/730431), lies on the most southerly part of the island, where the vegetation is almost tropical. From here, you have views over the Channel to the mainland coast. The Clarendon is a cheerful, friendly place at which to spend the night. The rooms are simple and comfortable, with tea- and coffee-making equipment. Breakfasts are included in the rate of £13.50 ($20.25) per person without bath, £16 ($24) with bath. They also offer a half-board rate of £20 ($30) per person daily. The meals are ample, with many fresh ingredients. In the Wight Mouse Inn, the pub of this old hostelry, they serve a large selection of beers, including real ales and malt whiskies, in addition to the more usual drinks. "Mine host," John and his wife Jean keep a tight rein on the place, seeing that everything is spotless and shining bright.

5. Winchester

The most historical city in all of Hampshire, Winchester is big on legends—it's even associated with King Arthur and the Knights of the Round Table. In the Great Hall, all that remains of Winchester Castle, a round oak table, with space for King Arthur and his 24 knights, hangs on the wall. But all that spells undocumented romance. What is known, however, is that when the Saxons ruled the ancient kingdom of Wessex, Winchester was the capital.

The city is also linked with King Alfred, who is honored today by a statue, and is believed to have been crowned here. The Danish conqueror, Canute, came this way too, as did the king he ousted, Ethelred the Unready (Canute got his wife Emma in the bargain). The city is the seat of the well-known Winchester College, whose founding father was the bishop of Winchester, William of Wykeham. Established in 1382, it lays claim to being the oldest public (private) school in England.

Traditions are strong in Winchester. It is said (although I've never confirmed the assertion) that if you go to St. Cross Hospital, now an almshouse, dating from the 12th century, you'll get ye olde pilgrim's dole of ale and bread (and if there's no bread, you can eat cake!). Winchester, 65 miles from London, is essentially a market town, on the Downs on the Itchen River.

WINCHESTER CATHEDRAL: For centuries Winchester Cathedral has been one of the great mother churches of England. The present building, the longest cathedral in Britain, dates from 1079, and its Norman heritage is still in evidence. When a Saxon church stood on this spot, St. Swithun, bishop of Winchester and tutor to young King Alfred, suggested modestly that he be buried outside. When he was later buried inside, it rained for 40 days. The legend lives on: just ask a resident of Winchester what will happen if it rains on St. Swithun's Day, July 15.

Of the present building, the nave with its two aisles is most impressive, as are the chantries, the reredos (late 15th century), and the elaborately carved choir stalls. Of the chantries, that of William of Wykeham, founder of Winchester College, is perhaps the most visited (it's found in the south aisle of the nave). The cathedral also contains a number of other tombs, notably those of Jane Austen and Izaak Walton (exponent of the merits of the pastoral life—*The Compleat Angler*). The latter's tomb is to be found in the Prior Silkestede's Chapel in the South Transept. Jane Austen's grave is marked with a commemorative plaque. Winchester Cathedral contains in chests the bones of many of the Saxon kings and the remains of the Viking conqueror, Canute, and his wife, Emma, in the presbytery. The son of William the Conqueror, William Rufus (who reigned as William II), is also believed to have been buried at the cathedral.

The Crypt is flooded for a large part of the year, and at such times is is closed to the public. When it's not flooded, there are regular tours at 10:30 a.m. and 2:30 p.m. The Library, in which is displayed the Winchester Bible and other ancient manuscripts, is open for limited hours throughout the summer season (except Monday mornings and Sunday, and on Wednesday and Saturday for the rest of the year). In January the library is open on Saturday only. The Treasury is open during the summer season from 11 a.m. to 5 p.m. It is small and does not require a guide.

OTHER SIGHTS: The **Royal Hussars Museum**, Southgate Street (tel. 0962/61781, extension 239), traces the history of the famous regiment in tableaux and pictures. You go from the days when the original regiments, the 10th and 11th Royal Hussars, were engaged in the Penisular War and fought at Waterloo, to their mechanization in 1928 and their amalgamation in 1969. All sorts of questions are answered, including why the 11th is known as "Cherrypickers." (The answer to that one is they had an engagement with the French in a cherry orchard during the Peninsular War.) The word "Hussar," you'll learn, is a derivation from old Hungarian relating to the method of conscripting "one in twenty" from the men of each village. The museum is open Easter until the end of October, Tuesday to Friday, from 11 a.m. to 4 p.m. On Saturday and Sunday its hours are from 2 to 4 p.m. Admission is 30p (45¢) for adults and 15p (23¢) for children.

The **Royal Green Jackets Museum,** Peninsular Barracks, Romsey Road (tel. 0962/61781, extension 288). In the same military complex as the Royal Hussars Museum, this other exhibition hall has a collection of weaponry and uniforms illustrating the history of the Oxfordshire and Buckinghamshire Light Infantry. Along with that, you'll see other mementos of the King's Royal Rifle Corps and the Rifle Brigade, which together form the Royal Green Jackets. The museum is open in March from 10:30 a.m. to 12:30 p.m. and 2 to 4 p.m. Monday to Saturday. From April to September it is open Monday to Friday from 10:30 a.m. to 12:30 p.m. and 2 to 4:30 p.m. On Saturday hours are 2:30 to 4:30 p.m.

WHERE TO STAY: Accommodations are limited, but adequate. I'll survey the most expensive recommendations first.

The Upper Bracket
Wessex Hotel, Paternoster Row (tel. 0962/61611), has won over critics who protested such a modern structure adjacent to the grounds of Winchester Cathedral. Two stories high, built of natural brick, it turns most of its walls of windows toward a view of the Norman Tower. The lounges and reception areas are built on several open levels. The coffeeshop is modern and international in design, and the cocktail lounge and restaurant are traditional with leather furniture, mahogany and brass. The hotel has 93 bedrooms and one suite, with 17 deluxe rooms facing the cathedral. The rooms are warmed by soft materials and have such amenities as telephones and bedlamps. A single rents from £45 ($67.50); a double, from £55 ($82.50). The coffeeshop is open from 10 a.m. until 10 p.m. daily, and the main restaurant has large picture windows overlooking the cathedral and its grounds.

The Medium-Priced Range
Royal Hotel, St. Peter Street (tel. 0962/53468), is a fine old hotel, built at the end of the 17th century as a private house. For 50 years it was used by nuns from Brussels as a convent before being turned into a hotel. As a hotel, however, it soon became the center of the city's social life. It's only a few minutes' walk to the cathedral, yet still enjoys a secluded position. Best of all is the garden hidden behind high walls. If you like a hotel where old-fashioned values and comfort predominate, you'll appreciate the Royal. Bathless singles go for £28 ($42), bathless doubles for £44 ($66). With bath, a single is £32 ($48); a double, £50 ($75). These prices include a traditional English breakfast, VAT, and service. Meals are served in a small, formal dining room, with a view of the private garden. A set dinner costs £10 ($15).

The Budget Range
Southgate Hotel, Southgate Street (tel. 0962/51243), is a brick house in the center of Winchester. It opens onto a rear garden with flowerbeds and an old walnut tree. Christopher Wren designed and built Southgate in 1715, and many of the original architectural details remain (note the front entry with the glass lights over the doorway). All the bedrooms are equipped with

hot and cold running water. The B&B rate is £16 ($24) per person, including VAT, service, and a full English breakfast. A set luncheon goes for £6 ($9), a dinner for £7.50 ($11.25).

WHERE TO EAT: The Elizabethan, 18 Jewry St. (tel. 0962/53566). In an atmosphere of another century, under hand-hewn timbers, you dine by candlelight, on sparkling white linen. You have a choice of cozy nooks or a galleried main dining room. Well run under the personal supervision of the Pitkin family, the kitchen offers an excellent Anglo-French cuisine. The licensed restaurant serves table d'hôte lunches at around £6 ($9) and a full à la carte menu. The extensive choice of dishes provides for an interesting lunch or dinner at about £15 ($22.50) per person. Light refreshments are served at lunchtime in the fully licensed modern bar. The restaurant is open from noon to 2 p.m., and from 7 to 10 p.m. On Sunday, only lunch is served. Closed Monday.

The **Old Chesil Rectory Restaurant,** Chesil Street (tel. 0962/53177), is just a short walk from the cathedral. Once a rectory, the unusual timber-and-stucco building dates from the 15th century. Inside and out the Old Chesil exudes an air of merrie Old England, but the food served in the heavily beamed dining room is the finest quality northern Italian cuisine. The menu is a wonderful melange of creative and classical dishes, including pollo sorpresa (chicken surprise), rolled, stuffed chicken breasts flavored with garlic and herbs; garlic snails and mushrooms covered in puff pastry; roast pheasant; or scaloppa alla Boccaccio, a delightful combination of veal, lobster, and cheese cooked with Orvieto wine. Appetizers include a prawn and melon cocktail and seafood hors d'oeuvres. Menus change quite frequently, depending on what is in season. A set dinner costs £10 ($15). Light lunches average around £8 ($12). In the evening, expect to pay £18 ($27) for a three-course à la carte repast. The Old Chesil is open daily except Sunday evenings and Monday. Otherwise, it serves lunch from noon to 2:30 p.m. and dinner from 7 to 10:30 p.m.

Splinters, 9 Great Minster St. (tel. 0962/64004). Downstairs in the Edwardian bar, soup of the day with roll and butter, plus several hot dishes, such as quiche with salad, moussaka, or cottage pie, are offered. Upstairs, the elegant plushy restaurant serves à la carte meals, including coq au vin and other French stalwarts or grills. You can choose from ratatouille, goulash, crab with cheese sauce, and cheese and cucumber mousse. A complete meal will cost from £8 ($12). There is a very good selection of more expensive French and German wines available by the bottle. Mike Sherret and his wife, Fiona, are the owners. It is open for lunch from 11 a.m. to 3 p.m. and for dinner from 6 to 10 p.m. Monday to Saturday.

Mr. Pitkin's Wine Bar and Eating House, 4 Jewry St. (tel. 0962/69630), has a pleasant wine bar on the ground floor. Upstairs is a restaurant with a luncheon menu, served from noon to 2 p.m. daily including Sunday. For £7 ($10.50) you can have three courses, two courses for £6.20 ($9.30). Appetizers include the chef's soup of the day or farmhouse pâté. For a small extra charge you can even have a smoked Scottish salmon and prawn cocktail. For a main dish, you might choose lamb kidneys turbigo, sirloin steak au poivre, or roast duck with orange sauce. All are served with fresh vegetables or a side salad. You can conclude your meal with a choice of dessert and coffee. VAT is included in the price, but 10% is added for service.

A Favorite Pub

Instead of lunching at one of the above restaurants, you may want to drop in at the **Royal Oak Pub** (tel. 0962/61136), which is to be found in a passageway leading from the High Street and next door to the God Begot House. Graham and Sue Moore, the proprietors, serve lunches at the bar from noon to 2 p.m. daily, Monday through Saturday. Various hot and cold snacks, hot meals, and an extensive serve-yourself cold buffet are available. The pub also contains the oldest bar in England, which is worth a visit, as indeed is the pub itself—a busy, friendly hostelry with lots of atmosphere. For those with a liking for live traditional or New Orleans jazz, this can be enjoyed in the bar on Sunday, Monday, Wednesday, and Thursday from 8:30 to 10:30 p.m. at no extra charge apart from the cost of your drinks. In summer, bar snacks are available on jazz evenings.

On the Outskirts

Lainston House, Sparsholt (tel. 0962/63588), two miles northwest of Winchester, is an early 17th-century manor house which Robin and Marie-José Oldland have converted into a fine hotel. The Oldlands bring a wealth of knowledge about how to run a hotel to this enterprise, Robin having been managing director of the Dorchester Hotel in London until 1978 and Marie-José being born a Seiler, one of Switzerland's leading families of hoteliers.

Each of the 29 bedrooms has a bath, TV, direct-dial phone, and private safe, and is decorated with chintz fabrics and polished woods. You can look out over the Downs, into the delightful kitchen garden, or over the ruins of a Norman chapel. For a single, the cost ranges from £48 ($72) to £56 ($84), with doubles going for £62 ($93) to £85 ($127.50).

The entrance hall of Lainston House has a huge fireplace framed in Delft tiles, and the room beyond has been made into a wood-paneled bar, where locals as well as residents gather for drinks before going into the dining rooms, done in apple green. The chef, Friedrich Litty from Germany, uses a judicious blend of regional products and continental cookery, offering such delicacies as a cheese-filled pancake with apple sauce and sliced veal and morels in white wine sauce, served with rösti potatoes. I recommend that you try his native trout with fresh watercress sauce. For a satisfying lunch that won't stuff you, order the platter of six sample salads with a glass of wine.

DORSET

This is Thomas Hardy country. By now, you've probably seen *Far from the Madding Crowd* or *Tess,* and know Dorset is the Wessex of Hardy novels. Some of the towns and villages, although altered considerably, are still recognizable from his descriptions. However, he changed the names to protect the innocent. Bournemouth, for example, became Havenpool, Weymouth converted to Budmouth. "The last of the great Victorians," as he was called, died in 1928 at the age of 88. While his tomb rests in a position of honor in Westminster Abbey, his heart was cut out and buried in his beloved Dorsetshire.

One of England's smallest shires, Dorset stretches all the way from the old seaport of **Poole** in the east to **Lyme Regis** in the west (known to Jane Austen). Dorset is a southwestern county, bordering the English Channel. It's big on cows, and Dorset butter is served at many an afternoon tea. Mainly, it is a land of farms and pastures, with plenty of sandy heaths and chalky downs.

The most prominent tourist center of Dorset is the Victorian seaside resort of Bournemouth. If you don't anchor there, you might also try a number of Dorset's other seaports, villages, and country towns. For the most part, we'll hug closely to the impressive coastline.

Incidentally, Dorset, as the vacation-wise English might tell you if they wanted to divulge a secret, is a friend of the budget traveler's.

6. Bournemouth

The south coast resort at the doorstep of the New Forest didn't just happen: it was carefully planned and manicured, a true city in a garden. Flower-filled, park-dotted Bournemouth contains great globs of architecture inherited from those arbiters of taste, Victoria and her son Edward. Its most distinguished feature is its Chines (shrub-filled, narrow steep-sided ravines) along the zigzag coastline. The real walking English strike out at, say, Hengistbury Head, making their way past sandy beaches, both the Boscombe and Bournemouth Piers, to Alum Chine, a distance of six miles, and a traffic-free walk to remember.

It is estimated that of the nearly 12,000 acres which Bournemouth claims for its own, about one-sixth is turned over to green parks and flowerbeds, such as the Pavilion Rock Garden, through which amblers pass both day and night. The total effect, especially in spring is dramatic, and helps explain Bournemouth's long-established popularity with the garden-loving English. Bournemouth was discovered back in Victoria's day, when seabathing became a firmly entrenched institution, often practiced with great ritual. Many of the comparatively elegant villas that exist today (now largely bed-and-breakfast houses and hotels) were once private homes.

Bournemouth, which along with Poole and Christchurch, forms the largest urban area in the south of England, is not as sophisticated as Brighton. Increasingly, it is becoming a retirement place for widowed or single English ladies. But Bournemouth and its neighbors also have some 20,000 students attending the various schools or colleges, who explore, in their off-hours, places written about or painted by such poets and artists as Shelley, Beardsley, and Turner.

The resort's amusements are wide and varied. At the Pavilion Theatre, for example, you can see West End–type productions from London. The Bournemouth Symphony Orchestra is justly famous in Europe. And there's the usual run of golf courses, band concerts, variety shows, and dancing.

Bournemouth is about 104 miles from London, easily reached in about one hour and 40 minutes on an express train from Waterloo Station. It makes a good base for exploring a historically rich part of England. On its outskirts are the New Forest, Salisbury, and Winchester, and the Isle of Wight (15 miles away, the former seaside retreat of Victoria).

WHERE TO STAY: Bournemouth offers accommodation choices in all price ranges. I'll begin with—

The Upper Bracket

Royal Bath Hotel, Bath Road (tel. 0202/25555), was built in the Victorian era to stimulate a French château, with towers and bay windows looking out over the bay and Purbeck Hills. In its own three acres of cliff-top gardens is a heated swimming pool. The rate is £40 ($60) per person per day, inclusive of service and taxes. The table d'hôte lunch and dinner prices start at £10 ($15). The resident band plays for a dinner-dance Saturday evenings. For health enthusiasts, there is a sauna bath, as well as Swedish massages and special diets. Every bedroom, 135 in all, has a private bath and television (the large accommodations contain sitting areas as well).

The Medium-Priced Range

Norfolk Hotel, Richmond Hill (tel. 0202/21521), is one of the oldest prestige hotels of the resort, built a few blocks from the seafront and the shopping area in the center of town. Disregarding what lies on its periphery, it is like a country estate, with a formal entrance and a rear garden and fountain shaded by trees. The public rooms are geared to holiday guests, with two drinking bars. The bedrooms—more than half with private baths—are furnished with traditional, serviceable pieces, comfortable and satisfactory. The Norfolk charges its highest rates from April 1 to the end of October.

In a room without bath, the rate is £27 ($40.50) per person nightly, rising to £34 ($51) in a unit with bath, these tariffs including an English breakfast, dinner that evening, VAT, and service. The set dinner-dance on Saturday is included in the above rates. However, if you're a nonresident and wish to attend, expect to pay from £10.50 ($15.75) for dinner and nothing extra on Saturday when you can dance.

Langtry Manor Hotel, 26 Derby Rd., East Cliff (tel. 0202/23887), originally called the Red House, was built in 1877 for Lillie Langtry, the famous Jersey Lily, as a gift from Edward VII to his favorite mistress. The house contains all sorts of reminders of its illustrious inhabitants, including initials scratched on a windowpane and carvings on a beam of the entrance hall. On the half-landing is the peephole through which the prince could scrutinize the assembled company before coming down to dine, and one of the fireplaces bears his initials.

Mrs. Pamela Hamilton Howard, the present owner, has carefully furnished the hotel in the Edwardian style, and on Saturday she has six-course Edwardian dinner parties. There is no menu; the dishes are just produced for inspection. Other evenings dinner is a more usual four-course affair at £10 ($15).

Bedrooms range from ordinary twins with bathroom from £18 ($27) per person, including breakfast. The Lillie Langtry suite, Lillie's own room, with a four-poster bed draped in Nottingham lace and a double heart-shaped bathtub (not to mention the more modern refinements of color TV, refrigerated bar, and toilet), goes from £30 ($45), or you can rent the Edward VII suite, furnished as it was when His Royal Highness lived in this spacious room. The huge carved oak fireplace has hand-painted tiles showing scenes from Shakespeare. The four-poster bed can be made up as either twins or a large double bed, and you have a bathroom en suite, color TV, a refrigerated room bar, and a telephone. The cost is £40 ($60) per person nightly. All rates are subject to VAT.

Apartments by the Week

Miami Court, 27a Surrey Rd., Westbourne, Bournemouth (tel. 0202/764329), will intrigue travelers tired of hotels and guest houses. Here, at these holiday flats, guests can enjoy a private life, preparing their own kind of food. This, of course, is an increasingly popular way of traveling in Europe. The apartments or "flats" are ideally situated, allowing you to explore the coast, inland country villages, and stately homes.

The new block of eight apartments has its own garden; and, best of all, there is a woods in the rear with a stream, as well as a pathway leading to the seafront and Bournemouth Square.

Owners Howard Archer and Michael Marshall used to run the Camelot Hotel in London, where they made many friends among American travelers, and incidentally won an award as the best small hotel of the year. To the Miami Court in Bournemouth they bring the same personal flair that distinguished them in London.

At their new location, they provide one-, two-, and three-bedroom apartments that are completely furnished. The flats are centrally heated as well and contain TV sets and refrigerators. The highest tariffs are charged from June to September, £55 ($82.50) per person weekly. Between October and April, the rates are slashed in half. Then the flats rent for only £30 ($45) per person weekly.

Write to them for a reservation and the amount of deposit required.

WHERE TO DINE: Trattoria San Marco, 148 Holdenhurst Rd. (tel. 0202/21132), small with an intimate atmosphere, is run by Angie and Ettore Longi. He is an English-born Italian, and she is from Parma, where the best salami and parmesan cheese come from. The cost of the menu varies with the season and availability of certain produce. Specialties include minestrone, suckling pig, stracciatella, salami, prosciutto con melone, piccatini (veal pieces), saltimbocca, and pasta. Try quail eggs, followed by escalope of Sofia Loren, with a walnut meringue to finish. In other words, there's veal something for everybody at a cost of about £32 ($48) for two persons, including wine. They won't serve cheap wines—"it should be used for cooking." The restaurant is open daily, except Monday and bank holidays, from noon to 2:30 p.m. and from 6:30 p.m. to midnight.

Fisherman's Haunt Hotel, Salisbury Road, Route B3347, Winkton, near Christchurch (tel. Christchurch 484071), is an ancient inn (built in 1673) just two miles from the English Channel. Authentic regional British dishes are the fare in the dining room, which overlooks the River Avon. Open from 12:30 p.m., Fisherman's Haunt offers a set luncheon for £5.50 ($8.25). Weeknight dinners are served from 7 to 10 p.m., costing from £10 ($15). A special feature of the restaurant is the traditional family-style Sunday midday meal. If you decide to bed down here for the night, your breakfast on the following morning is the classic, full English one. Most rooms contain private bath facilities.

7. Shaftesbury

The origins of this typical Dorsetshire market town date back to the ninth century when King Alfred founded the abbey and made his daughter the first abbess. King Edward the Martyr was buried there, and King Canute died in the abbey but was buried in Winchester. Little now remains of the abbey, but the ruins are beautifully laid out. The museum adjoining St. Peter's Church at the top of Gold Hill give a good idea of what the ancient Saxon hilltop town was like.

Today, ancient cottages and hostelries cling to the steep cobbled streets, thatched roofs frown above tiny paned windows, and modern stores vie with the street market in the High Street and the cattle market off Christy's Lane.

The town, right on the A30 from London, is an excellent center from which to visit the Hardy Country (it appears as Chaston in *Jude the Obscure*)), Stourhead Gardens, and Longleat House.

FOOD AND LODGING: The **Royal Chase Hotel** (tel. 0747/3355) is a Georgian house with Victorian additions, and as such has had varied occupants. Once a button-making factory and then a monastery, it is now a delightfully informal Best Western hotel run by George and Rosemary Hunt with their assistant, Liz Thomas. Most rooms have baths and go for £24 ($36) per person per night, including a full breakfast, early-morning tea, newspaper, service, and VAT. A meal in the Country Kitchen Restaurant, with its gingham cloths and hoop-backed chairs, will cost around £10 ($15) and includes several local dishes—pork filet cooked in cider or bluevinney cheese and Dorset knobs. House wine is about £5 ($7.50) a bottle.

From November to March they also offer bargain rates, among which is the Real Ale Break at around £32 ($48) per person for two nights, including accommodation, a full English breakfast, five pints of traditional ale, plus a free bottle of Thomas Hardy's Ale, featured in the *Guinness Book of Records* as the strongest beer brewed in a bottle. Even for less fanatical drinkers, the bar, dominated by an open-kitchen range and decorated with Dorsetshire bygones, is an attraction. There are traditional bar games, shove ha'penny, and table skittles at which to pitch your skill. On weekends, the Cellar Bar also offers snacks and a wide selection of wines at lunchtime and in the evenings if you don't want a full meal in the restaurant.

A "Meet the British" plan is extended to visitors staying two nights or more, in which, wherever practicable, you are invited into the home of a local resident for a predinner drink or after-dinner coffee.

IN THE ENVIRONS: Milestones, at Compton Abbas, lies between the church and the village post office, 2½ miles south of Shaftesbury on the A350. Just the telephone exchange of this ideal English tea room is enough to make one curious about it (tel. Fontmell Magna 811360). Two delightful old ladies, Mrs. Smith, the owner, and her friend, preside over the spotless, beamy little place with views over the Dorset hills. Their farmhouse teas, with boiled eggs, fresh sandwiches, homemade scones, and cakes are accompanied by tea or coffee. Expect to pay £1.75 ($2.63) per person for a set tea. Homemade cakes go for about 60p (90¢); sandwiches, from 75p ($1.13). Just a pot of tea costs 40p (60¢) per person. Morning coffee is served from 10 a.m. to 1 p.m. and afternoon tea from 2:30 to 5:30 p.m.

Plumber Manor, Sturminster Newton (tel. 0258/72507), a Jacobean manor house, has been lived in by the Prideaux-Brune family since the early 17th century. The present inhabitants, Richard Prideaux-Brune and his wife, Alison, have opened the lovely old place to guests. Downstairs, a large hall from which the staircase rises is decorated with family portraits. A comfortable lounge is furnished with antiques. There's a bar to serve the restaurant, made up of three connecting dining rooms where guests can sample the excellent cooking of Brian Prideaux-Brune, Richard's brother.

Upstairs, a gallery leads to six of the bedrooms, all with private baths and views over the gardens and the countryside. Six more large units in a long, low stone barn across the stable block (large umbrellas are provided to make the crossing if necessary) are well designed, with wide window seats and views over the gardens, good modern bathrooms, and expensive furnishings. The bedrooms in the house go for £39 ($58.50) per night for two, £34 ($51) for single occupancy. The large doubles in the annex are £55 ($82.50) for two, £39 ($58.50) for single occupancy. All rates include a full English or a continental breakfast, VAT, and service.

Dinner is a delight, a three-course meal costing £15 ($22.50), including VAT. Try the English lamb or roast pheasant in port sauce. All main courses are served with fresh vegetables. The restaurant is closed to nonresidents on Monday and also on Sunday in winter. On those days, a set meal is served for residents.

Plumber Manor has a family atmosphere, with the Prideaux-Brunes treating their clientele as houseguests.

8. Wool

Set in the midst of pastoral scenery, known to readers of Hardy, the sleepy hamlet of Wool is one of the most charming in East Dorset. On the Frome River, it has thatched cottages on either side of the road. The stream that winds its way through the maze of streets and lanes lures waders.

The district was also known to T. E. Lawrence, Lawrence of Arabia, who died in a motorcycle crash in 1935. His former home, **Clouds Hill,** lies four miles to the northwest (one mile north of Bovington Camp). It is open Wednesday to Friday (also Sunday) from April until the end of September, from 2 to 5 p.m. (from October until the end of March, it is open only on Sunday, from 1 to 4 p.m.), charging an admission of £1.25 ($1.88).

WHERE TO STAY: Woolbridge Manor Hotel (tel. Bindon Abbey 462313) is a small manor house edging up to the village. It owes its present fame to its Thomas Hardy associations, having been a setting in *Tess of the D'Urbervilles.* The owners, Mr. and Mrs. Peter Maddocks, have furnished the place attractively. The manor, which dates from medieval times, is a good backdrop for all the copper, brass, and oak. The only meal served is a full English breakfast. B&B costs from £30 ($45) in a double, including VAT.

9. Wareham

This historic little town on the Frome River is about a mile west of Poole Harbor. Many find it a good center for touring the South Dorset coast and the Purbeck Hills. It contains remains of early Anglo-Saxon and Roman town walls, plus the Saxon church of St. Martin with its effigy of Lawrence of Arabia.

FOOD AND LODGING: The Old Granary, The Quay (tel. Wareham 2010), is a riverside country pub, where you dine either inside or on a terrace overlooking the boats and swans. The interior dining room has a charm of its own, with bentwood chairs, a wine rack, a natural wood sideboard, and white walls displaying a collection of locally painted watercolors. A gracious and informal atmosphere prevails. The secret behind the success of the Old Granary is its fine cuisine; the owners, Mr. and Mrs. Michael Hipwell, try hard to stick to natural country foods. Homemade soups and pâtés are featured. Main dishes include filet of pork in a barbecue sauce and Dorset lamb chops with cheese and onion. A hefty portion of homemade fruit pie with cream finishes off the meal nicely. A five-course table d'hôte menu costs £10 ($15), and you can also order à la carte. The restaurant is open every day. If you wish to overnight here, the charge per person is £14 ($21) without bath, £18 ($27) with bath, including a full English breakfast and taxes.

A COUNTRY MANOR: At Culeaze, near Wareham, **Col. and Mrs. Anthony Barne** (tel. Bere Regis 471209), welcome you to this manor house, standing in the center of the estate known as Culeaze. They offer two double rooms and two single rooms, with private baths, charging £30 ($45) per person per night, including everything except lunch. Drinks are served before dinner and wine is offered at dinner. As their pillared manor house lies off the beaten track, a car is essential. For their own reasons, they don't encourage first-time visitors to stay more than three days. During the day you can visit Salisbury Cathedral, Wilton House, Abbotsbury, and Portland Bill, along with Stonehenge. Here is a rare chance to experience a fast-fading English way of life.

10. Dorchester

Thomas Hardy, in his 1886 novel *The Mayor of Casterbridge,* gave Dorchester literary fame. But it was known to the Romans; in fact, its Maumbury Rings, south of the town, is considered the best Roman amphitheater in Britain, having once resounded with the shouts of 12,000 spectators screaming for gladiator blood. Dorchester, a country town, was the setting of another bloodletting, the "Bloody Assize" of 1685, when Judge Jeffreys condemned to death the supporters of the Duke of Monmouth's rebellion against James II.

But it is mostly through Hardy that the world knows Dorchester. Many of his major scenes of love and intrigue took place on the periphery of Dorchester. The land was best known to Hardy, since he was born in 1840 at **Higher Bockhampton,** three miles northeast of Dorchester.

His home, now a National Trust property, may be visited by the public March to October from 11 a.m. to 6 p.m. or dusk, whichever is earlier. But to go inside, you must make an appointment with the tenant. You may write in advance to **Hardy's Cottage,** Higher Bockhampton, Dorchester, Dorset, England, or telephone 0305/62366. You approach the cottage on foot, a ten-minute walk after parking your vehicle in the space provided in the wood. The admission is £1 ($1.50).

You may also want to browse around the **Dorset County Museum** on High West Street (next to St. Peter's Church), with its gallery devoted to memorabilia of Thomas Hardy. In addition, you'll find prehistoric and Roman relics, plus natural history exhibits and others pertaining to the geology of the region. The museum is open weekdays from 10 a.m. to 1 p.m. and from 2 to 5 p.m.; admission is 50p (75¢) for adults, 25p (38¢) for children 5 to 16 years of age (children under 5, free).

WHERE TO STAY: The **Kings Arms Hotel** (tel. 0305/65353) is a typical inn, with great bow windows above the porch and a swinging sign hanging over the road. An archway leads to the courtyard and parking area at the back of the hotel. Most of the rooms—decorated in country style with chintz fabrics—have bathrooms attached, and all contain radio, TV, and phone, along with tea- and coffee-making equipment. The residents' lounge above the door has one of the bay windows. You have a choice of two bars from which you can observe the locals while you sip ale and eat lunchtime bar snacks. An evening meal of hors d'oeuvres, Dorset lamb cutlets with red currant sauce, and a selection of vegetables, plus a choice of dessert, costs £9 ($13.50), including service and VAT.

An overnight stay will cost £18.50 ($27.75) in a bathless single, £25 ($37.50) with bath. Doubles and twins are £34 ($51) without bath, £39 ($58.50) with bath. A four-poster-bedded double room with bath is £42 ($63). A full English breakfast, service, and VAT are included in the tariffs.

The **Wessex Hotel,** High West Street (tel. 0305/62660), is an architecturally interesting Georgian structure built on medieval foundations. In the town center, the quiet hotel offers 20 bedrooms with full residential services. Room rates range from £15 ($22.50) for a single room to £25 ($37.50) for a double or twin. Prices include a full English breakfast, service, and VAT. The Wessex also offers a small cozy bar for guests as well as a public restaurant. Lunch or dinner of two courses costs from £4.50 ($6.75) to £8 ($12).

The **Antelope Hotel,** South Street, Cornhill (tel. 0305/63001), was known in medieval times. Subsequently, it has received a Victorian overlay. The high point (or low) in its history, was when Judge Jeffreys held his Bloody Assize here. Old and traditional, it's been the wayfarer's choice for generations. It charges from £32 ($48) nightly for a double with bath, including breakfast. It's £24 ($36) for singles with bath, these tariffs including an English breakfast, VAT, and service. A table d'hôte dinner costs from £8 ($12).

WHERE TO EAT: **Judge Jeffreys' Restaurant,** High West Street (tel. 0305/64369), opposite the County Museum, is an attractive stop on your cross-country jaunt. Dating back to the 14th century, it had the dubious distinction of lodging that "cantankerous alcoholic," Judge Jeffreys, during the Bloody Assize. The restaurant today offers different services in each room. In the Judge's Room, a traditional three-course lunch is served. In the Tudor Room, an à la carte steak and trout menu is offered, and a roast joint is prepared daily. Try also the scallops, plaice, haddock, eggs, even their hamburgers. A set luncheon or dinner costs from £7 ($10.50) to £9 ($13.50). In the bar and lounge, snacks and salads can be ordered. Evening meals are served from mid-June to mid-October on Wednesday, Friday, and Saturday, the final orders taken at 10 p.m. The proprietor, Brian Bean, takes pride in the old English atmosphere of massive oak beams, an oak spiral staircase, stone-mullioned windows, paneled rooms, Tudor fireplaces. Most important, the restaurant's haunted. During its restoration in 1928, parts of a human skeleton were discovered in a bricked-up part of the east wall.

INNS ON THE OUTSKIRTS: Brace of Pheasants, Plush (tel. Piddletrenthide 357). Joan Chandler has transformed this row of two adjoining thatched cottages and a village forge, dating from the 16th century, although rebuilt in the old style after a fire. Formerly the owner of a toy factory, she sought and found a new way of life in this tiny hamlet, 15 miles from the coast. The major activity takes place in the all-purpose living, dining, and drinking room—a cozy setting with inglenooks, antiques, comfortable armchairs, and old decorative objects. Mrs. Chandler is an informal hostess, well known in the area for her Cordon Bleu meals. She offers a four-course meal for a set price of £10 ($15), with such dishes as fruits de mer, good-tasting soups and pâtés, quenelles de brochet, and main courses such as wild duck with orange sauce, pheasant, venison (in season), and homemade cakes and desserts.

The main restaurant, where meals are served on Friday and Saturday evening only, is in a recently added Hunter's Lodge, which is a skittle alley/party room, where folk clubs meet on Sunday evening. This is a spectacular building, in keeping with the Brace. It has low, black beams, is open to the roof, and has a large inglenook built in the local pirbeck stone with Canadian-style log finish. A 12-foot-long bar has been installed, and old pews add to a unique atmosphere. The skittle alley can be covered over with carpet to match the room, so that the restaurant is attractive. Reservations for dining here are imperative. A table is yours for the evening, as Mrs. Chandler only has one sitting per evening. The Charcoal Grill serves lunch and dinner daily, specializing in charcoal-flavored steaks, lobster, and jumbo prawns. There is also a children's menu.

The upstairs of the Brace (which was formerly a restaurant) has been turned into accommodations, with two doubles and one single with bathrooms en suite, beautifully furnished and decorated with chintz and velvet. In summer you can also enjoy a lovely big garden. How to get there: Take the B3143 out of Dorchester to Piddletrenthide, turning off at the sign to Plush. The inn will be on your left.

Summer Lodge, Evershot (tel. 093583/424), is a country-house hotel 12 miles north of Dorchester, where its resident owners, Nigel and Margaret Corbett, provide care, courtesy, and comfort. Once the home to the heirs of the Earls of Ilchester, the country house, in the attractive village of

Evershot, stands on four acres of secluded gardens. Evershot appears as Evershed in *Tess of the D'Urbervilles,* and author Thomas Hardy designed a wing of the house.

In this relaxed, informal atmosphere, guests rent rooms with views either of the garden or over the village rooftops to the fields beyond. Although centrally heated, the hotel offers log fires in winter. Guests sit around the fire getting to know each other in a convivial atmosphere. All rooms have a private bathroom en suite. Rates range from £30 ($45) to £37.50 ($56.25) per person, including a full English breakfast, a five-course dinner with after-dinner coffee, and VAT.

Mrs. Corbett, who does the cooking, specializes in traditional English dishes the way they should be done, placing the emphasis on home-grown and local produce. In addition to the dining room with its French windows opening onto a terrace, the Corbetts have a bar and a TV room. They will direct you to places of local interest, including National Trust houses.

Yarlbury Cottage, Lower Bockhampton, near Dorchester (tel. 0305/62382), is a beetle-browed thatched cottage with leaded windows in a small country village in the heart of Hardy country and, in fact, within walking distance of Thomas Hardy's cottage. Mr. and Mrs. Phillips came here when he tired of a job that took him away from home a great deal, and they have turned three smallish rooms downstairs into a delightful restaurant, with low beams and soft lights. The restaurant has rapidly gained local repute for good home-cooking.

Appetizers include homemade soup or Dorset pâté, and main dishes feature grilled trout with shrimp butter and steak Bombay cooked in garlic butter. All main dishes are served with fresh vegetables. Desserts include homemade profiteroles with chocolate or brandy sauce or English cheeses such as cheddar and limeswold. A satisfying meal will cost around £13 ($19.50). There is a small bar overlooking the garden where guests can spill out onto the lawn to enjoy their pre-dinner drinks. Upstairs, the Phillipses have three double rooms for rent: a small one at £12.50 ($18.75), the others (with washbasins) cost £19.50 ($29.25) for two. A full English breakfast is included in the price.

Wise Man Inn, West Stafford, near Dorchester (tel. 0305/3694), is a tiny, 400-year-old village pub with wooden seats in front (where you sit with your feet in the road), a thatched roof, and leaded windows. On the front wall is an old poem attributed to Thomas Hardy extolling the virtues of ale. Inside, decorating the bars is a magnificent collection of mugs and Toby jugs along with antique pipes. Host Michael Fisher runs the bars, and his wife provides simple lunches and dinners for around £4 ($6). Lunch is served from noon to 2 p.m. and supper from 6 to 10 p.m.

READER'S HOTEL SELECTION AT FRAMPTON: "Our very favorite place on our entire trip was **The Court** (tel. Maiden Newton 20242) at Frampton, a tiny village in Dorset, near Dorchester in the Thomas Hardy country. The Court is a beautiful manor house, elegantly furnished, run by two lovely women. It's on a secluded lane and contains 60 acres of woods and fields, a pond, and a charming menagerie of ducks, chickens, a golden retriever, a Siamese cat, and peacocks. There are ample bathrooms and a shower room. Our breakfast, served in their first-floor dining room overlooking the garden and pond, included hot homemade rolls, fresh milk and homemade butter from their Jersey cows, and generous servings of sausage, bacon, and eggs, with, of course, marmalade and tea. We had electric kettles in our rooms, and Mrs. Goddard brought us a doily-lined tray with a bone china cup and saucer and teapot for our early-morning tea. There was also a small covered pitcher of cream, sugar, and tea bags. Dinner, bed, and breakfast (no children) in the best English manor tradition are £20 ($30) per person" (Alice L. Jones, Au Sable Forks, N.Y.).

11. Bridport

On Thomas Hardy's fictional Wessex terrain, Bridport was "Port Bredy." The town lies inland, although there is a harbor one mile away at the holiday resort of West Bay, near the end of Chesil Beach. Ropes and fishing nets are Bridport specialties. Many a man dangled from the end of a "Bridport dagger"—that is, a rope—especially when Hanging Judge Jeffreys was around.

An interesting excursion from Bridport is to visit **Parnham House** at Beaminster (tel. 0308/862204). One of the loveliest houses in Dorset, it stands in a wooded valley beside the River Brit. Since Tudor times it has been surrounded by sweeping lawns and magnificent trees, along with terraces and falling water. In 1976 John Makepeace, a contemporary designer and furniture maker, moved into Parnham House, and in the following year, started the renowned School of Craftsmen in Wood. In these beautiful surroundings he makes exquisite modern furniture and trains young artisans. The well-restored rooms of the great house are furnished with recently completed commissions from the Makepeace workshops, and each month a different exhibition of contemporary artists' and craftspersons' work is shown amid the ornate plastered ceilings, paneled walls, and stone fireplaces, lit through the stained glass of the mullioned windows.

Perhaps the most noted of Makepeace's pupils has been Lord Linley, son of Princess Margaret, who is now well on his way to making his name as a designer and craftsman. Lately, he has also been following in the footsteps of his father, Lord Snowdon, as a photographer.

Light lunches and teas with homemade cakes and local clotted cream are served in the 17th-century Oak Room. The house, gardens, and workshops are open from April to October on Wednesday, Sunday, and bank holidays from 10 a.m. to 5 p.m. Admission is £1.75 ($2.63) for adults, 75p ($1.13) for children. The house is on the A3066 between Beaminster and Bridport.

WHERE TO STAY AND EAT: The **Bull Hotel,** East Street (tel. 0308/22878), a 16th-century coaching inn, now houses modern wayfarers in its 22 bedrooms, all with hot and cold running water, many overlooking the old courtyard. Rates range from £14 ($21) to £18 ($27) in a single without bath, from £15.50 ($23.25) to £19 ($28.50) in a single with bath. In doubles and twin-bedded rooms, the tariffs are £24 ($36) without bath, £30 ($45) with bath, and all prices include an English breakfast and VAT. The atmosphere is old-worldish, complete with a minstrels' gallery and enough bars to satisfy anybody. The bedrooms are simply, but comfortably, furnished. In 1939 George VI stopped off at the Bull. The hotel remains open all year and is run under the close personal supervision of the Terleski family. Fresh local food and fish dishes are a specialty. A three-course luncheon is £7 ($10.50) to £9 ($13.50). The tab for an à la carte dinner will probably be from £7 ($10.50) to £15 ($22.50).

Eype's Mouth Hotel, Eype, 1½ miles west of Bridport and one mile south of the A35 Bridport–Lyme Regis road (tel. 0308/23300), is a gracious country house, right on the sea, a five-minute walk from the beach. Most of the public rooms and bedrooms open south toward the water. At times, Eype's Mouth seems like an English version of a villa on the Riviera, with a sea-view front terrace, where you can relax and have drinks or tea. The hotel is managed by Mr. and Mrs. Shute, who also provide meals for nonresidents. The rooms are centrally heated, containing hot and cold water basins. There are convenient corridor toilets and baths, plus nine private bathrooms. Generally a guest stays here on what is called inclusive terms, meaning bed, breakfast, and dinner. The rate is from £21 ($31.50) per person daily, going slightly higher in June, July, August, and September. For straight B&B, you pay from £15 ($22.50) to £18 ($27) per person nightly, the latter in a room with private bath. The rooms are plain, but comfortable. There is a lounge bar and cellar bar with live entertainment, along with a dinner-dance every Saturday night.

12. Chideock

Chideock is a charming village one mile west of Bridport. It's a hamlet of thatched houses, with a dairy farm found in the center. About a mile away from the coast, it's a gem of a place for overnight stopovers, or especially longer stays. The countryside, with its rolling hills, makes excursions a temptation.

WHERE TO STAY: Chideock House Hotel (tel. 029-789/242) is perhaps the prettiest thatched house in Chideock, a village of winners. Set near the road, with a protective stone wall, the house opens onto a rear garden of flowers, shrubs, and fruit trees. A driveway through the gardens leads to a large car park (wood-burning fires on cool days). You can stay here on a B&B basis at a cost beginning at £17 ($25.50) per person nightly. The hotel has been extended, and most of its bedrooms have baths en suite. The 15th-century restaurant is renowned for fine cuisine. In addition to the à la carte restaurant, a Copper Grill has opened, decorated with antique pieces of copper and featuring large steaks and fish dishes. Especially interesting is the Tudor part of the house, and the Adam fireplace in the lounge. The house quartered the Roundheads in 1645, and the ghosts of the village martyrs still haunt, as their trial was held at the hotel. Resident owners are Alf and Barbara Way and Kevin and Alison Davies.

The **Thatch Cottage** (tel. 029-789/473). You'd never suspect that under the thatch of this 17th-century cottage are the comforts of home. The owners, Pat and Ron Shayler, accept paying guests year round. While this is essentially a summer resort, there are those who welcome the idea of staying winter weekends, snugly sitting in front of the fireplace after enjoying good home-cooking. Fresh local produce is a specialty. Most of the year the charge is £10 ($15) per person for B&B. If you want to walk to the beach, you can ask your hostess to pack a picnic lunch. It's best to make Chideock your center for a week, exploring the many sights in the area on day trips. Weekly costs for B&B and dinner range from £83 ($124.50). Reservations are necessary from June to September.

13. Charmouth

On Lyme Bay, Charmouth is another winner. A village of Georgian houses and thatched cottages, Charmouth contains some of the most dramatic coastal scenery in West Dorset. The village lies to the west of Golden Cap, which is—according to the adventurers who measure such things—the highest cliff along the coast of southern England.

WHERE TO STAY: The **Queen's Armes Hotel** (tel. 0297/60339). Catherine of Aragon, the first of Henry VIII's six wives and the daughter of Ferdinand and Isabella of Spain, is believed to have stayed in this hotel near the sea. It also figured in the flight of King Charles II, who spent the night here, with the Roundheads in hot pursuit. Since the Queen's Armes is right on the road, you may not suspect its inner charm: a rear flower garden, oak beams, pewter, old doors with creaky hardware, a dining room with dark oak tables and Windsor chairs, the living room with its Regency armchairs and antiques. The hotel has 11 rooms, nine with either bath or shower and toilet. One room has a four-poster bed. All of the upstairs has been redecorated by the owners, Mr. and Mrs. Peter Miles, with new carpets and beds being added. You can stay here for £18 ($27) per person for B&B, £24 ($36) per person for half board. The cuisine is excellent, offering a variety of traditional, Cordon Bleu, and modern dishes, with a good choice of wines from the well-stocked cellar.

14. Lyme Regis

On Lyme Bay near the Devonshire border, the resort of Lyme Regis is one of the most attractive centers along the south coast. For those who shun such big, commercial holiday centers as Torquay or Bournemouth, Lyme Regis is ideal—the true English coastal town, with a highly praised mild climate. Sea gulls fly overhead; the streets are steep and winding; walks along Cobb Beach brisk and stimulating; the views, particularly of the craft in the harbor, photogenic. Following Lyme Regis's career as a major seaport (the Duke of Monmouth landed here to begin his unsuccessful attempt to become king), one finds it was a small spa for a while, catering to such visitors as Jane Austen.

The seaside town was the location of the film *The French Lieutenant's Woman,* and the actors stayed in the town's two main hotels.

The town also boasts the 1979–1980 world champion and best dressed town crier. Richard Fox is just maintaining a tradition that has been handed down for 1000 years in Lyme Regis when he announces the local news. He'll also take visitors on a two-hour tour of the resort on Tuesday and Thursday at 2:30 p.m. to see the Cobb, the harbor from which ships sailed to fight the Spanish Armada. The walk heads up old Broad Street. Mr. Fox can be reached at the Witchcraft Gallery, Broad Street (tel. 02974/3803).

The surrounding area is a fascinating place for fossilism. Mary Anning discovered in 1810 at the age of 11 one of the first articulated ichthyosaur skeletons. She went on to become one of the first professional fossilists in the country. Books telling of walks in the area and the regions where fossils can be seen are available at the local Information Bureau in the Guildhall on Bridge Street.

WHERE TO LODGE AND EAT: The **High Cliff Hotel,** Sidmouth Road (tel. 02974/2300), is an impressive Regency house, placed in the midst of surrounding gardens on the edge of a cliff, providing views of the coast. Formerly the home of Lord Lister, the doctor who pioneered antiseptic surgery, it now accepts paying guests. The present manager and director is Patricia Webb. High Cliff was opened by her parents in 1935, and has continued to be personally owned and managed by her family ever since, with the 50th anniversary of the family's ownership being proudly celebrated. Inside, the central formal hallway, lounges and dining room are tastefully decorated, with a sprinkling of good antiques. Bedrooms are appropriately home-like, with good beds, hot and cold running water, and comfortable furnishings. The charge is from £17.50 ($26.25) per person for B&B. A three-course dinner goes for £7.50 ($11.25).

The **Mariners Hotel,** Silver Street (tel. 02974/2753), has been a coaching inn since 1641, and now it's owned by Leo and Mary Featherstone. They are proud, and rightly so, of the view from their lounge of the Dorset coastline—all the way around to the lighthouse at Portland Bill. This view of approximately 25 miles is considered the best in Lyme Regis. Modern plumbing has been installed, including hot and cold running water in all 16 bedrooms (12 with private bath or shower). Of course, the 17th-century rooms retain their special charm, crooked and irregular. Full fire precautions have been implemented.

In the low-ceilinged dining room, you are served excellent food. For bed, breakfast, and a four-course evening meal, the daily rate ranges from £28 ($42) to £35 ($52.50) per person, including VAT.

The building was immortalized by Beatrix Potter in her painting of "Susan the Cat and Stumpy the Dog," in *The Tale of Little Pig Robinson,* published in 1902. The tulip tree in the garden is one of the five oldest in England, more than 300 years old.

Kersbrook, Pound Road (tel. 02974/2596), lives up to its boast of being the "dream house of the Dorset Riviera." Stone built in 1790, Kersbrook is crowned by a thatched roof and sits on a ledge above the village, which provides a panoramic view of the coast. The public rooms have been refurnished with antique furniture, recreating old-world charm yet with all modern facilities. Mr. and Mrs. Eric Hall Stephenson are the proprietors of Kersbrook, charging from £15 ($22.50) for B&B, £22 ($33) for half board. Many of the rooms have private baths and showers available at a small extra cost. There is a good choice of an evening meal, with an extensive dessert trolley, for those who choose B&B and dinner.

The **Cobb Arms,** down by the Cobb (tel. 02974/3242), is a blue-painted pub right on the harborside where you can order bar snacks such as braised beef with vegetables. Or you can dine in the restaurant on fresh Lyme Bay plaice with a salad and vegetable, or local Dover sole. Fresh local scallops are often sauteed in herb butter and served with a salad and brown bread and butter. Appetizers include soups, pâtés, and smoked fish. There are also mixed grills, rump or T-bone steaks, served with jacket potatoes and salads. Meals cost from £12 ($18) up.

As you eat, you can look out over the harbor in very much the same way as the French lieutenant's woman did. It was in this pub that the members of the cast and the stars were dressed and made up for their parts in the film.

Next to the inn is the Lifeboat Station, with its lifeboat ever ready to put to sea to rescue sailors in distress.

The **Royal Lion,** Broad Street (tel. 02974/2768), is an old coaching inn, once known as the White Lion. On the side of a hill, it climbs up from the sea, with country-style furnishings in the oak-beamed bar and lounge. The bedrooms are also country style, including one with a canopied bed used regularly by Edward VII when he was Prince of Wales (his mistress, Lillie Langtry, was born in Lyme Regis). A room and a large breakfast costs £20 ($30) per person, including VAT and an early-morning cup of tea brought up with the daily papers. The owner, B. A. Sienesi, also quotes a half-board rate of £28 ($42) per person for those staying three days or more. Ordered separately, a dinner will cost around £10 ($15), and you're given a choice of fresh local fish along with grilled meat dishes. There is a separate buffet bar.

The **Three Cups Hotel,** Broad Street (tel. 02974/2732). Although this hotel is up the hill from the seashore, most of its rooms have views overlooking the Cobb. A building more than 200 years old, it has handsome bow windows over the main entrance, which was featured in the film. Window boxes brighten the stone exterior, and inside the rooms are light and airy with comfortable beds. All units contain hot and cold running water, as well as tea- and coffee-making equipment. TV can be provided, and each room already has a phone and radio. Corridors are narrow and the floors may creak, but no expense is spared to offer a friendly welcome to the traveler. Rooms go for £17.50 ($26.25) per person, including VAT and a full breakfast. A set dinner costs from £9.50 ($14.25), or you can enjoy some enterprising snacks in the bar, including crab salad, and fresh soup and french bread.

15. Donyatt

After Lyme Regis, you may want to journey to Donyatt, a village near Ilminster. Just outside the village of Donyatt, between the A303 and the A30 London–West Country roads, stands the following recommendation:

Thatchers Pond, Donyatt, near Ilminster (tel. Ilminster 3210), is a 15th-century thatched limestone farmhouse where Michael and Pamela Smith, both experienced caterers, offer a vast cold table for lunch and dinner daily except Monday. The house is warm and welcoming, with old clocks, guns, and swords adorning the walls of the flagstoned hall and dining room. Meals are served from a vast table laden with fresh lobster, salmon, crab, and prawns, cold roast beef, ham, tongue, homemade pâté, quiches, and mousse. You're offered a choice of any two meats and then are allowed to help yourself from a selection of 25 different salads. The dessert trolley is laden with succulent sweets, and there is cheese if you prefer it. The bar offers beers and wines, and coffee is available, but no tea. The main course is large enough, but if you're a good trencher person an appetizer can be provided. Lunch from the buffet costs £8 ($12); dinner, £10 ($15). Thatchers is open from noon to 2 p.m. for lunch. There are two sittings for dinner, one at 7:30, another at 9 p.m. Closed on Sunday evening and Monday.

READER'S HOTEL SELECTION IN CHEDINGTON: "**Chedington Court** in the tiny village of Chedington, near Beaminster (tel. 093589/265), is situated so that you have panoramic vistas of the green, rolling hills of Dorset, Somerset, and Devon. The gardens of the court are splendid, replete with pond, running brook, lovely flowers, greenery, and even a croquet court and putting green. The rooms are large and uniquely furnished. One even has a magnificent old four-poster bed. The bathrooms are larger than most hotel rooms. The units have TV and various amenities such as tea sets and bottled water. Doubles cost from £23 ($34.50) to £28 ($42) per person, plus service.

"The furnishings of the manor house are interesting and comfortable. You can settle down and read in the cozy living room or relax on the patio. The court is operated by Philip and Hilary Chapman, who are attentive to their guests. Hilary does the cooking, and on our two nights there, we were served the best meals we had in England. Many of the vegetables are from the Chapmans' garden and are fresh and well prepared. Dinner includes a fish and a meat course, both excellent, and is topped off by fine desserts, the most scrumptious of which was a nectarine Pavlova. Fresh flowers from the garden grace the tables in the dining room" (Susanne Stanford, San Diego, Calif.).

Chapter VIII

DEVON

THE GREAT PATCHWORK QUILT area of the southwest of England, part of the "West Countree," abounds with cliffside farms, rolling hills, foreboding moors, semitropical plants, and fishing villages—all of which combine to provide some of the finest scenery in England. The British approach sunny Devon with the same kind of excitement one would normally reserve for hopping over to the continent. Especially along the coastline, the British Riviera, many of the names of the seaports, villages, and resorts have been synonymous with holidays in the sun: Torbay, Clovelly, Lynton-Lynmouth.

Many small towns and fishing villages do not allow cars to enter. These towns provide car parks on their outskirts, but this can involve a long walk to reach the center of the harbor. In high season, from mid-July to mid-September, the more popular villages get quite crowded, and one needs reservations in the limited number of hotels available.

It's easy to involve yourself in the West Country life, as lived by the British vacationers. Perhaps you'll go pony trekking across moor and woodland, past streams and sheep-dotted fields, stopping at local pubs to soak up atmosphere and ale. Chances are your oddly shaped bedroom will be in a barton (farm) mentioned in the Domesday Book or in a thatched cottage neither straight, level, nor true.

Fishermen can catch their lunch (salmon and trout in such rivers as the Dart), then take it back to the kitchen of their guest house to be grilled. Life is usually very informal. The hosts here, many of farming stock, don't like to "muck about" putting on airs for tourists. In the morning, your landlady might be out picking runner (string) beans for your dinner. Later, she'll bring up pails from the milk house, and you can watch her create her own version of clotted Devonshire cream—cooked on the back of the stove. For dessert that night, you'll get a country portion heaped on your freshly picked gooseberries.

When a Devonian invites you to walk down the primrose path, he or she means just that. The primrose is practically the shire flower of this most beautiful of counties. Devon is a land of jagged coasts—the red cliffs in the south facing the English Channel, the gray cliffs in the north opening onto the Bristol Channel.

Aside from the shores, a great many of the scenic highlights appear in the two national parks, **Dartmoor** in the south, **Exmoor** in the north. First, we'll explore:

SOUTH DEVON

It's the lazy life in South Devon, as you sit in the orchard, enjoying the view of the coast from which Raleigh and Drake set sail. Almost every little hamlet, on some level, is geared to accommodate tourists, who flock here in great numbers from early spring to late fall. There is much to see and explore (although a minimum of historical sights), but mainly the tranquil life prevails.

1. Exeter

The county town of Devonshire, on the banks of the Exe River, Exeter was a Roman city founded in the first century A.D. Two centuries later it was encircled by a mighty stone wall, traces of which remain today. Conquerors and would-be conquerors, especially the Vikings, stormed the fortress in the centuries to come. None was more notable than William the Conqueror. Irked at Exeter's refusal to capitulate (perhaps also at the sheltering of Gytha, mother of the slain Harold), the Norman duke brought Exeter to its knees on short notice.

Under the Tudors, the city grew and prospered. The cocky Sir Walter Raleigh and Sir Francis Drake cut striking figures strolling through Exeter's streets. In May 1942 the Germans bombed Exeter, destroying many of the city's architectural treasures. Exeter was rebuilt, but the new, impersonal-looking shops and offices couldn't replace the Georgian crescents and the black-and-white timbered buildings with their plastered walls. Thankfully, much was spared, including the major architectural treasure—

EXETER CATHEDRAL: Owing its present look to the Decorated style of the 13th and 14th centuries, the Exeter Cathedral of St. Peter actually goes back to Saxon times. Even Canute, the Viking conqueror, got in on the act of rebuilding around 1017. The cathedral of Bishop Warelwast came into being in the early 12th century, and the north and south towers serve as reminders of the Norman period. The remarkable feature of the present Gothic building is the nave, with its tierceron vaulting, stretching out for some 300 feet, broken only by an organ. The cathedral did suffer damage in the 1942 German bombings, losing its St. James's Chapel, which subsequently has been restored. But most of the treasures remained intact, including the rows of sculpture along the west front; the 14th-century Minstrels' Gallery, its angelic figures with Early English musical instruments in hand; and the carved oak 14th-century bishop's throne. The Dean

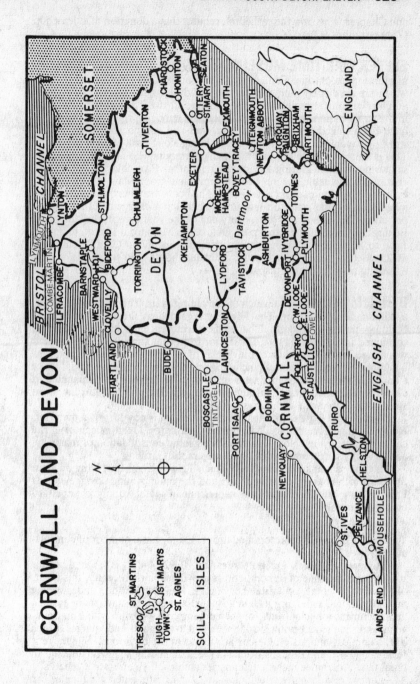

CORNWALL AND DEVON

and Chapter, who own the cathedral, request that a donation of at least 50p (75¢) per adult is made.

EXETER MARITIME MUSEUM: At The Quay (tel. 0392/58075), the maritime museum has a collection of more than 100 small craft, most of which are on display, and shelters the world's largest collection of English and foreign craft, ranging from the Congo to Corfu. The larger boats afloat in the canal basin can be boarded. There are canoes, proas, and boats that have been rowed across the Atlantic, and you can go aboard the oldest working steamboat or even picnic on a Hong Kong junk or an Arab dhow. This is an active museum, and the ISCA members who maintain the boats sail some of them during the summer months. Five colorful Portuguese chatas are available for rent at the museum from May to September, carrying a maximum of six passengers. The boats are rowed along the three miles of navigable water on the historic canal at a charge of £1.50 ($2.25) per hour. The museum is open every day of the year except Christmas and Boxing Day from 10 a.m. to 5 p.m. October to May; from 10 a.m. to 5 p.m. June to September. Adults pay an admission of £2.50 ($3.75); children, £1.25 ($1.88). *Note:* Occasionally, individual boats used for special events or sailing may not be on display.

OTHER MONUMENTS: Much of the old remains. The **Exeter Guildhall,** a colonnade building on The High, is regarded as the oldest municipal building in the kingdom. The earliest reference to the Guildhall is contained in a deed of 1160. The Tudor front that straddles the pavement was added in 1593. Inside is a fine display of silver in the gallery. It contains a number of paintings as well, including one of Henrietta Anne, daughter of Charles I (she was born in Exeter in 1644). The ancient hall is paneled in oak. The Guildhall is open throughout the year, Monday to Saturday, from 10 a.m. to 5:30 p.m., and admission is free.

   Rougemont Castle, with its Norman gateway, is now largely a memory. Rougemont was created for William the Conqueror. Over the centuries the castle fell into ruins. Now there has been some consolidation of masonry, and it is pleasant to stroll through Rougemont Gardens.

   If time remains, see also **St. Nicholas Priory,** The Mint, lying off Fore Street, a 15th-century craft building; and the underground passageways at **Princesshay,** off The High (the subterranean water supply channels of medieval times).

WHERE TO STAY: In accommodations, Exeter has a number of comfortable choices.

   Rougemont Hotel, Queen Street (tel. 0392/54982), is imbued with a stylish flair that none of its competitors provides. Fairly recently, this great, old-fashioned hotel, opposite the Central Railway Station, underwent a metamorphosis, emerging as a solid place at which to stay. Its neoclassic architecture is a background for the contemporary furnishings. The bone-white walls in the reception lounge are a foil to the golds and oranges. Much of the comfort and tasteful decor are found in the bedrooms. Singles rent from £32 ($48), and doubles from £42 ($63), including VAT and an English breakfast. Amenities include telephones, radios, TV, and private baths.

   Dinner is à la carte, beginning at £9 ($13.50). Guests gather in the Adam-style Cavendish Bar for drinks—sparkling with crystal and vibrant in gold and white. An excellent stock of wines comes from the cellar, which, incidentally, was once used as a debtor's prison.

Royal Clarence Hotel, Cathedral Yard (tel. 0392/58464), a Georgian-style building, miraculously escaped destruction during the war. A hotel full of history, it possesses modern amenities: all of the 63 bedrooms have private bathrooms, and many overlook the Cathedral Green. Comfortable lounges display a mixture of antiques, gilt mirrors, and modern pieces. The restyled restaurant is open to the public. A table d'hôte luncheon costs from £6.50 ($9.75), and a table d'hôte dinner from £9 ($13.50), but you can also order à la carte. A single room with bath rents from £36 ($54), a double with bath from £52 ($78). Prices include all taxes. The general manager is Arthur E. Barnes.

The **Devon Motel,** Exeter Bypass, Matford (tel. 0392/59268), lies on the outskirts of the city at the western sector of the bypass on the A38. Convenient to the airport and as a stopping-off point for those headed for the West Country, it is one of the Watney Lyons properties, built in a style familiar to most North Americans. You drive your car into your own open garage, and your bedroom and private bath are directly overhead. Singles pay £24 ($36) to £26 ($39); doubles, £30 ($45) to £36 ($54)—including a full English breakfast and VAT. Some cheaper singles are in the old part of the hotel and are without bath, but all doubles and units in the new wing have private baths. Inside, all is compact and built-in, with a picture window overlooking the meadows beyond. On the premises are a restaurant and drinking bars, serving a two-course lunch for £3.50 ($5.25) and a three-course meal for £7 ($10.50), coffee included. An à la carte dinner is around £12 ($18).

The **White Hart Hotel,** South Street (tel. 0392/79897), is one of the oldest inns in the city, with a statue of Suzanna greeting you as you enter the cobbled courtyard. The hotel is a mass of polished wood, slate floors, oak beams, and gleaming brass and copper. The comfortable sitting rooms are bright with chintz. Bedrooms skillfully combine old and new. Most have color TV and a bath or shower. All have phones. A single room with shower costs £32 ($48); a double room with bath, £44 ($66)—including breakfast and VAT. The dining room offers good English and continental dishes in a well-appointed and relaxed atmosphere. The hotel has an excellent wine cellar, which supplies the Ale & Port House (a bar with waiter service where you can feast on traditional English fare), plus the well-known Bottlescreu Bills wine bar, which offers beefsteak and oyster pie or, in summer, barbecue steak in the secluded wine garden. A substantial meal, including pâté and salad, is available for under £5 ($7.50).

WHERE TO EAT: The **Ship Inn,** Martin's Lane (tel. 0392/72040), a short walk from the cathedral, was often visited by Sir Francis Drake, Sir Walter Raleigh, and Sir John Hawkins. Of it Drake wrote: "Next to mine own shippe, I do most love that old 'Shippe' in Exon, a tavern in Fyssh Street, as the people call it, or as the clergie will have it, St. Martin's Lane." The pub still provides tankards of stout and lager and is still loved by both young and old. The reconstructed dining room on the second floor also retains the early English atmosphere: settles, red leather and oak chairs. The fare is hearty English, the service friendly. At either lunch or dinner, you can order such temptations as onion soup, grilled rainbow trout, or grilled rump steak. The price of the main courses includes vegetables, roll and butter. The portions, as in Elizabethan days, are large. A two-course meal ranges in price from £5 ($7.50) to £8.50 ($12.75). The restaurant is open from noon to 2 p.m. and from 6:30 to 10:30 p.m., Monday through Saturday. Closed Sunday, and all bank holidays. The bars are open from 10:30 a.m. to 2 p.m. and 5 to 10:30 p.m. weekdays.

Coolings Wine Bar, 11 Gandy St. (tel. 0392/34183). In one of the older and more interesting little streets of the city, this is a friendly place with beams above the checked cloths of the tables. Some of the dining space is in the cellars of the old building. All the food is prepared on the premises, and that includes a good selection of cold meats, pies, and quiches, as well as chicken Waldorf, sugar-baked ham, each served with a variety of salads, then two or three daily hot dishes, chalked up on the blackboard. Meals cost around £5 ($7.50). D. C. Belford is the proprietor. He keeps the place open daily except Sunday from noon to 2:15 p.m. and from 5:30 to 11:30 p.m.

The **Port Royal Inn,** The Quay (tel. 0392/72360), is a real ale house where Barry Weeks dispenses ale and nourishment. It's close to the maritime museum. On the city side of the river, turn left from the museum for about 200 yards. The good bar food includes platters of chicken-and-ham pie, seafood, roast chicken or lamb, plus sandwiches made with fresh granary bread. There are always two or three special hot dishes and various desserts. Meals begin at £2 ($3).

WHERE TO STAY AND EAT OUTSIDE EXETER: In the Exe Valley, four miles south of Tiverton and ten miles north of Exeter, lies **Bickleigh**, a hamlet with a river, an arched stone bridge, a mill pond, and thatch-roofed cottages—a cliché of English charm, one of the finest spots in all of Devon. In this village, I have a recommendation in the medium-priced range:

The **Fishermen's Cot Hotel** (tel. 08845/237) sits like a picture postcard across the way from Bickleigh Bridge. Even though it's thatched and blends beautifully into the local setting, it is newer than most of the houses here, and has all the heating and plumbing necessary. In a single, the rate ranges from £15 ($22.50) to £20 ($30), with doubles costing from £25 ($37.50) to £30 ($45). Tariffs depend on whether or not you have a private bath. VAT and a full English breakfast are included. Chances are you'll be served some of the best food in Devon. Ask if the cook will make you a chocolate mousse—light and airy, of country-fresh eggs. The Cot serves excellent trout dishes. Bar snacks are available at lunchtime, ranging from a soup with roll and butter up to a sirloin steak. A table d'hôte dinner costs from £8 ($12); a Sunday lunch, £5.50 ($8.25). Fishermen particularly like the place, because they can catch salmon and trout right in front of the hotel on the banks of the Exe. The hotel is fully licensed. There are dinner-dances on Saturday.

Trout, on the main Tiverton–Exeter road, A396, four miles south of Tiverton (tel. 08845/339), is a former 17th-century coaching inn, transformed skillfully into three pubs and a gourmet restaurant. Anthony Varney is in charge. The long, low thatched roof and white exterior with tiny leaded windows encloses the former stables, converted into a spacious and dramatic restaurant, with heavy dark beams and oak furniture. A collection of copper and glittering horse brasses, turkey-red table linens, and ladderback chairs provide a warm atmosphere for dining. Pre-dinner drinks are provided in one of the pubs, the most popular one containing an old open fireplace, made from the original bridge stone. A sign indicates that the inn was built in 1630 as a trout hatchery.

A buffet lunch and evening snacks are available in the bar seven days a week. A meal includes smoked trout, Austrian cheese, chicken or pâté, with a salad, and homemade desserts. The restaurant does only à la carte dinners. Appetizers might include pâté and a Cumberland sauce or whitebait, perhaps a homemade soup. Main-dish specialties are beef Stroganoff, beef créole, chicken in herbs, veal marsala, chicken mornay, and lamb cutlets. A hot cooked meal costs from £4 ($6) to £6 ($9).

An Old Manor at Ottery St. Mary

The sleepy little market town, where the incomparable Coleridge *(The Rime of the Ancient Mariner, Kubla Khan)* was born, lies in the Otter River Valley, only ten miles east of Exeter. See the almost perfectly preserved church from the 14th century. The old cloth town makes a good base for exploring the South Devon coastline, particularly if you center at the following medium-priced recommendation:

Salston Hotel (tel. Ottery St. Mary 2310), an old manor house, lies 1½ miles off the main A30 London road, and a mile from Ottery St. Mary. The hotel is officially listed as a building of historical and architectural interest. Even though it's lost most of its acreage and original furnishings, the exterior is intact—a rambling three-story brick hotel with dozens of chimneys and gables. The lounge is large, with two bay windows opening onto the gardens. A ballroom, built for the visit of Princess Alexandra of Teck (that name will send you rushing to your history books), has a Tudor fireplace. The Salston has just built a new 12-bedroom extension, with luxury rooms, each with shower, hairdryer, refrigerated mini-bar, and a double and single bed. Charges are £34 ($51) in a single with private bath in one of the new luxury rooms, or £29 ($43.50) in a single in one of the traditional rooms. B&B in a double luxury room is £50 ($75) for two persons, or £42 ($63) for two in one of the traditional rooms. Spa fans will find a health studio run in conjunction with the Salston, and two squash courts have been completed. There is a 20- by 48-foot swimming pool, plus an adjoining Norwegian pine cabin with sauna, solarium, and a massage and relaxing room, available at an extra charge. There is also a swimming instructor. Sometimes on Friday evening the years roll back to 1530. In front of the Henry VIII fireplace, a medieval banquet is spread, complete with costumed serving "wenches," minstrel singers, and a jester. Featured at a "six-remove" banquet are such items as game soup based on a 16th-century recipe, Tudor-style pâté, ribs of oxen, and lots of mead and ale. The latest innovation of the hotel is a French Cellar Restaurant in the original vaulted wine cellars, which is open Tuesday through Saturday until 10:30 p.m.

READER'S HOTEL SELECTION: "Louisiana-born James Henry and his English wife own one of the oldest (1487) continuously licensed pubs in England, the **Oxenham Arms,** South Zeal, Devon (tel. Sticklepath 244). The carefully preserved inn was originally built in the 12th century and used as a monastery. A cob-walled double room is £18 ($27) per person, tax included, with a choice of breakfast menus. Seventeen miles west of Exeter, the inn is just a short hike into the bracken- and gorse-covered hills of Dartmoor National Park" (A. Emerson Smith, Columbia, S.C.)

POWDERHAM CASTLE: The castle at Powderham (tel. 0626/890243) lies eight miles south of Exeter on the A379 Dawlish road. It was built in the late 14th century by Sir Philip Courtenay, sixth son of the second Earl of Devon, and his wife, Margaret, granddaughter of King Edward I. Sir Philip and Lady Margaret are interred in a magnificent tomb in the south transept of Exeter Cathedral. The castle suffered damage in the Civil War and was restored and altered in the 18th and 19th centuries, but its towers and battlements are still pure 14th century. The castle contains much fine furniture, including a clock that plays full tunes at 4 and 8 o'clock, at noon, and midnight, 17th-century tapestries, and a chair used by William III for his first Council of State at Newton Abbot. The staircase hall contains remarkable plasterwork set in bold relief against a brilliant turquoise background, more than 200 years old. The chapel dates from the 15th century, with hand-hewn roof timbers and carved pew ends. It contains a detailed pedigree of the Courtenay family, a document more than 12 feet high. The castle is open from June to September daily except Friday and Saturday, Easter Sunday and Monday, and on Sunday in May, from 2 to 6 p.m. Admission is £1.75 ($2.63) for adults, 90p ($1.35) for children. There is a tea room for light refreshments.

2. Dartmoor

Antiquity-rich Dartmoor lies in the southern part of the shire. The Tors (huge rock formations) of this granite mass sometimes soar to a height of 2000 feet. The national park is a patchwork quilt of mood changes: gorse and purple heather, Dartmoor ponies, a foreboding landscape for the experienced walker only, gorges with rushing water.

Some 13 miles west from Exeter, the peaceful little town of **Moreton Hampstead,** perched on the edge of Dartmoor, makes a good center. The heavily visited Dartmoor village of **Widecombe-in-the-Moor** is only seven miles from the town. Moreton Hampstead contains much that is old, including a market cross and several 17th-century colonnaded alms-houses.

Accommodation information and a booking service is operated by the **Dartmoor Tourist Association,** Pencroft, Widecombe Road, Postbridge (tel. 0252/3501). Local information centers will also provide a list of accommodations.

The **National Park Authority** operates a summer bus service throughout the moor. Services have such inviting names as the Pony Express and the Transmoor Link, and they are an ideal way to get onto the moor in order to hike some of the 500 miles of foot- and bridgepaths. The country is rough, and on the high moor you should always make sure you have good maps, a compass, and suitable clothing and shoes. Don't be put off, however. Unless you are a professional hiker, it is unlikely that you will go very far from the well-trodden paths.

For bus service information, apply at **Plymouth City Transport,** Bretonside Bus Station in Plymouth (tel. Plymouth 664014), or at the **Exeter Bus Station,** Western National, in Exeter (tel. 0392/56231). Apart from the regular service of buses linking the various villages and towns on the moor, the National Park Authority runs guided walks from selected starting points.

There are also **guided walking tours** of varying difficulty, ranging from one hour up to six hours for a trek of some 9 to 12 miles. All you have to do is turn up suitably clad at your selected starting point, and there you are. Details are available from the **Dartmoor National Park Information Centres** or from the **Dartmoor National Park Board,** Parke, Haytor Road, Bovey Tracey, Newton Abbot (tel. Bovey Tracey 832093). The charge for walks is 75p ($1.13) for 1½ hours, £1 ($1.50) for up to three hours, or £1.50 ($2.25) for six hours.

Throughout the area are stables where you can arrange for a day's trek on horseback across the moors. For horse-riding on Dartmoor, there are too many establishments to list. All are licensed, and you are accompanied by an experienced rider/guide. The moor can be dangerous, with sudden fogs descending without warning on treacherous marshlands. All horse-rental stables are listed in a useful free publication, the *Dartmoor Visitor,* obtainable from tourist and visitor centers or by mail. Send an International Reply Coupon to the Dartmoor National Park Board (address above). Prices are around £3.50 ($5.25) per hour, £7 ($10.50) for a half day, and £15 ($22.50) for a full day.

The **Wild Life Gallery and Bird Sanctuary,** Mearson Manor, Cross Street in Moretonhampstead (tel. 0647/40483). Terry and Betty Tilson-Chowne, who own the manor, decided that the house should be put to good use. They have opened the halls and rooms to house a great collection of contemporary paintings and sculpture. You can browse through these rooms until you find just the one you want. There are beautiful, delicate pastels and crayon drawings of wildlife on Dartmoor by Brian Carter, otters, a fox chasing a pheasant, whatever. Other rooms contain Eastern brassware and bronze work, among other items. The oldest part of the house is, in fact, a restaurant, with two magnificently preserved fireplaces. The menu is entirely homemade, including scones with fresh butter and Devonshire cream teas at £1.50 ($2.25). They do light lunchtime snacks as well. Before you leave, say hello to the talking crow and the other birds in the aviary.

The **Museum of Dartmoor Life** is at the rear of 3 West St., Okehampton (tel. Okehampton 3020). The market town of Okehampton owes its existence to the Norman castle built by Baldwin de Bryonis, sheriff of Devon, under orders from his uncle, William the Conqueror, in 1068, just two years after the conquest. The Courtenay family lived there for many generations until Henry VIII beheaded one of them and dismantled the castle in 1538. The museum is a group of authentic buildings around a courtyard. These include two 19th-century cottages, an agricultural mill, and a printer's workshop. They display farm machinery and some old vehicles, a Devon box wagon of 1875, a 1922 Bullnose Morris motorcar, a 1937 motorcycle. There is a reconstructed wheelwright's shop, a farm kitchen, a dairy, and much more. It is open from April to October daily except Sunday from 10:30 a.m. to 4:30 p.m. Admission is 40p (60¢) for adults and 20p (30¢) for children. The castle is open from mid-March to mid-October Monday to Saturday from 9:30 a.m. to 6:30 p.m., on Sunday from 2 to 6:30 p.m. In winter, it closes at 4 p.m. Admission is 40p (60¢) for adults, 20p (30¢) for children.

WHERE TO STAY AND EAT: Manor House Hotel (tel. 0647/40355), at the edge of Dartmoor, is a converted, gabled, Jacobean manor. It is in the midst of 200 acres of parkland, much of which has been cultivated for the pleasure of guests. This upper-bracket hotel is a favorite with fishermen (trout in the Bovey and Bowden Rivers, salmon in the Teign), and with golfers as well who are drawn to the 18-hole course, which hotel guests can use free of charge. Built for a distinguished family, the manor has lost its old grandeur, but added the new lure of modern amenities. The halls, reception lounge, drawing and dining rooms are for life on a large scale; the bedrooms are often outsize (some suitable for a diplomatic reception); the furnishings are comfortable, with good beds, and all the rooms have private baths. Expect to pay from £29 ($43.50) to £44 ($66) in a single with a shower for B&B, £40 ($60) to £54 ($81) in a twin or double with shower for B&B. Dinner and B&B in a room with bath costs £40 ($60) to £60 ($90) per person, and all prices include VAT and service. Bar snacks are available at lunchtime. A set dinner goes for £13.50 ($20.25).

Moorwood Cottage Restaurant, Lustleigh, near Newton Abbot (tel. Lustleigh 341). It's easy to drive past the small 17th-century cottage with beetling thatch and leaded windows on the A382 highway between Morgtonhamstead and Bovey Tracey. Take it easy and stop for lunch in this tiny dining room, furnished with antiques, a log fire burning on nippy days, and fresh flowers on the tables. Michael Harris is the inspired chef, and his wife, Claudia is the self-styled wine waitress, barmaid, and reception committee.

You're given a warm greeting, then asked to make your selection from six or so appetizers, likely to include a homemade soup, spinach-and bacon pâté, or a Moorwood cocktail of prawns, corn, apple, and fresh celery with dressing. The main courses include veal with spices, herbs, onions, and tomatoes; roast duckling in wine with pineapple and ginger; poached Devon salmon with sorrel mayonnaise; and filet of beef in cream, madeira, and green peppercorns. All dishes are accompanied by potatoes and fresh vegetables or a salad on the side.

The homemade desserts are luscious, particularly a chocolate and brandy mousse with Devonshire cream, or black currant sorbet with Kirsch and cream. Coffee ad infinitum is served in the lounge with liqueurs. A three-course meal will cost around £10 ($15), but you can dine majestically for £7.50 ($11.25). There's a good wine list, including some California and South African vintages, with a bottle costing as little as £6 ($9). Lunch is served from 12:30 to 1:45 p.m., dinner from 6:45 to 9 p.m.

Lydford House Hotel, Lydford, near Okehampton (tel. Lydford 347), is a family-run country house hotel, peacefully set in more than three acres of grounds, just on the edge of Dartmoor. It was built in 1880 by the well-known Dartmoor artist, William Widgery. Several of his paintings hang in the residents' lounge. The hotel is particularly known for its food and features home-cooking, using fresh and local produce whenever possible. Owners Ron and Ann Boulter have set the following rates: £13.50 ($20.25) per person nightly for room and English breakfast, £15 ($22.50) for a room with private bath. For room, breakfast, and table d'hôte dinner, the charge is £20 ($30), £22.50 ($33.75) with private bath. Weekly terms are available, and all prices include service and taxes. Lydford House has its own riding stables in the grounds. Superb riding on Dartmoor is available by the hour, or you can enjoy inclusive riding holidays. Beginners are welcome, and expert tuition is offered. The stables are under the personal supervision of Claire Boulter, BHSAI.

The **Castle Inn,** Lydford, near Okehampton (tel. Lydford 242), is a 16th-century inn next to Lydford Castle. The low inn, with its pink facade and row of rose trellises, is the hub of the village, along with the all-purpose grocery store and post office. The inn's owners, Mr. and Mrs. Reed, have maintained the character of the commodious rustic lounge, with its valuable collection of old furniture and accessories, including wing chairs, grandfather clocks, and antique prints. One room is called the "Snug," containing a group of high-backed oak settles arranged in a circle. Meals are served buffet style, from noon to 2 p.m., a great spread set out on a long table. The cost depends on your selection of a main course. The salads are on a help-yourself basis. Buffet salads at lunch cost about £3 ($4.50) with a main course. Snacks are available as well, and you can take your plate, along with a lager, and sneak off to an inviting nook. A three-course dinner will run about £8 ($12). For a bed and a large country-style breakfast, the charge is £13 ($19.50) in a single, £22 ($33) in a double. The bedrooms are not large but are well planned and attractively furnished, often with mahogany and marble Victorian pieces, each room with its own color scheme.

Holne Chase Hotel (tel. Poundsgate 471) is a white-gabled country house, within sight of trout- and salmon-fishing waters. You can catch your lunch and take it back to the kitchen to be cooked. Although the mood of the moor predominates, Holne Chase is surrounded by trees, lawns, and pastures, a perfect setting for walks along the Dart. It's off the main Ashburton–Princetown road, between Holne Bridge and New Bridge. Holne Chase is run by Mary and Kenneth Bromage, who returned to their native Devon to preserve the house "as a sanctuary of peace and hospitality." Every bedroom in the house is named after a tributary of the River Dart. The best way to stay here is to take the half-board rate, which ranges from £28 ($42) to £39 ($58.50) in a single, from £49 ($73.50) to £58 ($87) in a double or twin. The more expensive tariffs are for units with private baths.

The house is furnished in period style, with a fine English 18th-century oak dresser base serving as the bar. The cooking combines the best of English fare with specialty dishes that are made all the better whenever produce from the gardens is used or fresh fish from the Dart River and Torbay. Devon beef and lamb are also featured. The old cellars hold a good selection of wines.

Leusdon Lodge Guest House, Poundsgate (tel. Poundsgate 304), is a 150-year-old stone country house, with gables, chimneys, and beyond the garden, views of Dartmoor National Park. Its owners are Neelia and Denis Hutchins, who probably know more about this area than anyone else. Denis was once the chairman of the Dartmoor Tourist Association, and likes to help guide you to the best local sights, to a picnic beside a crystal-clear brook, or to tell the history of the moor and its mystical folklore. On cool nights he lights a log fire in the living room, joining guests in talks. There are seven rooms with soft beds and hot and cold water basins. Your breakfast will be abundant and varied. Dinners are English at their traditional best. The charge is £20 ($30) per person for half board, the only terms offered. However, you'll be charged an extra £2 ($3) per person for a room with private bath. Meals are served in the dining room with its hand-carved paneled walls and an ornate fireplace. Specialties include steak-and-kidney pudding, Dartmoor rabbit in cider, and beefsteak casserole with dumplings. In winter there is full central heating, even a festive Christmas house party, as well as medieval banquets.

Old Walls Farm, Ponsworthy, near Ashburton (tel. Poundsgate 222), is a substantial, stone-colored plastered country home set remotely on a working farm and reached by very narrow lanes. Here you are comfortable in the heart of the moors, and in the safe, knowing hands of owner Bill Fursdon, an expert on the area. He is a genial, handsome, white-haired gentleman with a gracious smile who is by avocation a naturalist. He'll take you on a short walk around his farm, showing you his collection of cows, mongrel dogs, ducks, a pet goat (its milk is served at breakfast, but it's strictly optional), and a beautiful little river, lying a short distance from the house. He'll make handmade maps, pinpointing the places of interest within driving distance.

His house is a living tribute to a fast-disappearing era. He is assisted by his wife, Elizabeth, who plays the organ on Sunday at the village church, and their son who lives in a separate home close by. Guests relax around a stone fireplace in the drawing room, or on a sunny day enjoy a crescent-shaped, all-glass sun room. From the latter, the view of the moorland is exceptional. The living room has an old grand piano, a Victorian card table, a soft arm sofa, and armchairs placed in a curving bay recess.

The B&B rate is about £12 ($18) per person. Breakfast is a special event in the dining room, and you can have as much food as you want, including mouslie, a concoction of oats, bran, wheat germ, raisins or dates, served with brown sugar, goat's milk, and a glob of clotted Devonshire cream.

Old Walls Farm is reached from the A38 dual carriageway, which runs between Exeter and Plymouth. Turn onto the B3357 (signposted Dartmoor) at Ashburton, then right at Poundsgate, going through the hamlet of Ponsworthy, passing the all-purpose post office and store.

A VISIT TO AN ABBEY: Sir Francis Drake's House, Buckland Abbey, Yelverton, (tel. 0752/668000), was originally a Cistercian monastery in 1278. It was dissolved in 1539 and became the country seat of Sir Richard Grenville and later Sir Francis Drake (two great sailors). It remained in the Drake family until 1946 when the abbey and grounds were handed over to the National Trust. The abbey is now a museum, housing portraits, mementos, including Drake's drum, banners, and a superb collection of model ships. (You probably won't get a chance to beat Drake's drum, but if you do, remember the words of Henry Newbold's poem: "Drake will quit the port of heaven and come to England's aid once more.") The abbey lies three miles west of Yelverton off the A386. It is open Monday to Saturday from 11 a.m. to 6 p.m. (on Sunday from 2 to 6 p.m.). In winter it is open only on Wednesday, Saturday, and Sunday from 2 to 5 p.m. Admission is £1.20 ($1.80) for adults, 60p (90¢) for children. Light snacks are available in the old kitchen from Easter to September.

3. Chagford

Six hundred feet above sea level, Chagford is an ancient Stannary Town. With the moors all around, it is a good base for your exploration of the region of North Dartmoor. It is approximately 20 miles from Exeter, Torquay, and Plymouth. Chagford overlooks the Teign River in its deep valley and is itself overlooked by the high granite tors. There's good fishing in the Teign (ask at your hotel). From Chagford, the most popular excursion is to **Postbridge,** six miles to the southwest, a village with a prehistoric clapper bridge.

Near Chagford stands **Castle Drogo,** in the hamlet of Drewsteignton (tel. 06473/3306). This massive granite castle was designed and built by Sir Edward Lutyens and the castle's owner, Julius Drewe, in the early 20th century. It stands high above the River Teign, with gorgeous views over the moors. The family can trace its origins back to the Norman Conquest. Drewe, who wanted to create a home worthy of his noble ancestors, found the bleak site high above the moors, and he and Lutyens created a splendid modern castle. The tour includes the elegant library, the drawing room, the dining room with fine paintings and mirrors, and a simple chapel, along with a vaulted-roof gunroom. There is a restaurant open daily from 11 a.m. to 6 p.m. The castle is open from April until the end of September from 11 a.m. to 6 p.m., charging an admission of £1.85 ($2.78) for adults, half price for children. If you wish to visit only the grounds, the fee is £1.25 ($1.88) for adults, half that for children.

WHERE TO STAY AND EAT: Gidleigh Park Hotel, Chagford (tel. 06473/2367), is set one mile from the edge of Dartmoor in beautiful countryside. A visit to this hotel is highly recommended, if you can find it. Its owners, Kay and Paul Henderson, have renovated and refurnished the house with flair and imagination.

In a park of 30 acres, the mansion is Tudor style, lying just two miles from Chagford. Large beech and oak trees abound. Inside, the oak-paneled public rooms and the open log fires invite a return to yesterday. The windows open onto views of the garden and the Teign Valley, with Dartmoor lying beyond.

Most of the bedrooms, 12 in all, are on the second floor and are approached by a grand staircase. All rooms contain private bath, color TV set, and phone. Half board ranges from £65 ($97.50) per person nightly, plus VAT.

Good-tasting meals are served in an oak-paneled dining room. The menu is changed daily, and only the best and freshest products are used. Cheeses are supplied by Patrick Rance, Streatley, Berkshire, and the wine cellar is one of the most extensive and reasonably priced in England. Kay Henderson trained at Cordon Bleu in London and Paris. She believes it is better to make up a meal from the freshest produce available each day from local farmers, fishermen, and the hotel's own garden, than to offer a large choice of indifferently prepared à la carte dishes. She was joined in 1980 by John Webbe, former sous-chef at the Dorchester.

How to get there: From Chagford Square turn right into Mill Street at Lloyds Bank. After 200 yards, fork right and down the hill to the crossroads. Cross straight over into Holy Street, following the lane passing Holy Street Manor on your right and shifting into low gear to negotiate two sharp bends on a steep hill. Over Leigh Bridge turn a sharp right into Gidleigh Park. A half-mile drive will bring you to the hotel.

The **Great Tree Hotel,** Sandypark, near Chagford (tel. 06473/2491), is a comfortable country house set in 18 acres of private gardens and woodland. Here in the early morning the only sounds you are likely to hear are the calls of birds, the noise of white water running through the wood, and the occasional moo of a cow. All bedrooms have bath and shower, color TV, radio, and tea- and coffee-making facilities. Many of them are on ground level, with lovely views over the gardens and Dartmoor. A single room with bath or shower costs £28.30 ($42.45) in low season, rising to £33 ($49.50) in summer. A double with bath goes for £27 ($40.50) per person in low season, £32 ($48) per person in high, while a deluxe double with bath and shower is priced at £30.90 ($46.35) per person in low season, rising to £35 ($52.50) per person in summer. All tariffs include a full English breakfast and VAT.

There's a cozy lounge with high beams. A roaring log fire burns on cold days. In the snug cocktail lounge, bar snacks are served at lunch, including homemade soup, toasted sandwiches, a ploughman's lunch, cold meats, salads, and fresh scampi. The standard of food is high, and there's a good à la carte menu as well as a set dinner. Much of the fruit and vegetables come from the hotel's own gardens, and they pride themselves on providing fresh fish and local meat. A set lunch costs about £8.50 ($12.75), and picnic lunches can be packed if you ask the evening before. Cream teas are served on the terrace in summer and by the fire in winter at a cost of £2.50 ($3.75).

Moor Park Hotel, Chagford (tel. 06473/2202), is another charming place in the heart of Dartmoor, where B&B costs £12.50 ($18.75) in a single without bath. Doubles without bath rent for £15 ($22.50) per person, going up to £18.50 ($27.75) with bath, all plus VAT. Bedrooms are simply furnished but comfortable, and the lounges are cozy with deep armchairs, wood fires, and highly polished furniture. Meals consist of simple dishes, such as leek-and-potatoe soup, smoked fish pâté, and roast joints, accompanied by fresh seasonal vegetables and followed by such desserts as grilled bananas with honey or trifle with clotted cream. Expect to spend from £8.50 ($12.75) for the set menu.

An à la carte bill of fare provides roast pork filet, Widecombe "fayre," Madagasker peppercorn steak, and rainbow trout Cleopatra. If you want to branch out and order an exotic dessert, I'd recommend the crêpes suzette or the peach and cherry flambé. An average meal without one of these exotic concoctions will cost from £11 ($16.50). The place has a friendly atmosphere, extending a hearty welcome to passersby. Mr. and Mrs. Edwards are the proprietors.

Teignworthy Hotel, Frenchbeer, near Chagford (tel. 06473/3355), is an attractive granite and slate country house where John and Gillian Newell and their family welcome you as guests. Teignworthy stands 1000 feet up on Dartmoor with a view of the South Teign River. The house has central heating, but log fires in the main living rooms add to the ambience. There are nine comfortable and individual double bedrooms, six in the main house and three in the hayloft. All bedrooms have baths, color TVs, and phones, and there is room to relax in privacy. They have a drawing room with an open log fire and a small bar for predinner drinks.

John does most of the cooking, aided by the Newells' daughters, Debbie and Rebecca, plus various local girls. His individual style is becoming very popular in the area, and dinner can include trout baked with fennel and lemon juice, calf kidneys with brandy and green peppercorns, or peppered sirloin steak. A complete dinner, including VAT, costs about £17 ($25.50). Wherever possible, local fresh produce is used. A liter of house wine is £6 ($9) and up. There is also a good, well-thought-out wine list.

Overnight stays, including an English breakfast and dinner, will cost £50 ($75) per person, including VAT.

4. Torbay

In April 1968, the towns of Torquay, Paignton, and Brixham combined to form the "County Borough of Torbay," as part of a plan to turn the area into one of the super three-in-one resorts of Europe. Vacationers from the factories of the Midlands find it easier to bask in the home-grown Devonshire sunshine than to make the pilgrimage to Rimini or the Costa del Sol.

Torquay, set against a backdrop of the red cliffs of Devon, contains 11 miles of coastline, with many sheltered pebbly coves and sandy beaches. With its parks and gardens (including numerous subtropical plants and palm trees), it isn't hard to envision it as a Mediterranean-type resort (and its retired residents are fond of making this comparison, especially in postcards sent back to their cousins in Manchester). At night, concerts, productions from the West End (the D'Oyly Carte Opera appears occasionally at the new Princess Theatre), vaudeville shows, and ballroom dancing keep the holiday-makers—and many honeymooners—regally entertained.

If you suddenly long for an old Devonshire village, you can always ride the short distance to **Cockington,** still in the same borough, which contains thatched cottages, an old mill, a forge, and a 12th-century church. Furthermore, if you want to visit one of the great homes of England, you can call on **Oldway,** in the heart of Paignton. Started by the founder of the Singer sewing-machine dynasty, Isaac Merritt Singer, and completed the year after he died (1875), the neoclassic mansion is surrounded by about 20 acres of grounds and Italian-style gardens. Inside, if you get the feeling you're at Versailles, you're almost right, as many of the rooms were copied. Open all year, Oldway may be visited weekdays from 9 a.m. to 1 p.m. and from 2 to 5:15 p.m. (on Saturday and Sunday from 2:30 to 5 p.m., May to September only). Admission is free. The gardens are always open.

WHERE TO STAY AND EAT: Rainbow House, Belgrave Road (tel. 0803/211161), is like a complete resort, having been enlarged and integrated with the adjoining San Remo Hotel. Facing south and open throughout the year, the hotel has been in the Marshall family for about two decades. Once a large and stately house, the hotel has expanded until now it has more than 100 bedrooms, each with bath en suite, plus a number of self-catering apartments. The peak B&B rate per person charged is £20 ($30) in low season, £25 ($37.50) in summer. Singles pay a £4 ($6) supplement.

Facilities include a heated pool and sun terraces, a Caribbean coffeeshop, an apéritif bar, plus a sauna and solarium. Public rooms are furnished in bright, modern colors. In the hotel's nightclub, you can dance to a first-class band and often enjoy cabaret entertainment. The hotel's à la carte specialty restaurant, the Pot of Gold, serves an international menu, or you can patronize the grill for late-night dining. In addition to that, the hotel also offers a main restaurant, serving some local specialties among its traditional repertoire. If you're not booked on half-board terms, expect to pay from £10 ($15) for dinner.

Palm Court Hotel, Sea Front (tel. 0803/24881), is a Victorian crescent built facing south onto the esplanade overlooking Torbay, and offers style and good living. Two lounges are wood-paneled with leaded-glass windows. In the dining room is a minstrels' gallery. There are two up-to-date bars and a coffeeshop, open all day. All rooms have been modernized and have color TV, tea- and coffee-making facilities, central heating, telephone, and radio. Of the bedrooms, 42 have private bathrooms. There is an elevator. From June through September, B&B rates are from £18 ($27) to £21 ($31.50), including service. With garden chairs and tables on the sun terrace outside the coffeeshop, the Palm Court becomes a social center. At night the colored floodlighting around the bay evokes a Riviera atmosphere outside the hotel.

Lanscombe House, Cockington Village (tel. 0803/607556), is a 250-year-old Georgian "Dower" house, with its own trout pond. It's the only hotel in this village, famous throughout England for its thatched cottages, old forge, riding stables, and country walks. The considerate hosts are Mr.

and Mrs. Malcolm Goldby, who do much to see that your stay is an enjoyable one. Set in a two-acre garden, the house resembles a church rectory, with large lounges and dining rooms opening onto views. The owners rent out about ten bedrooms at prices ranging from £11.50 ($17.25) to £15 ($22.50) per person, depending on the accommodation and time of year. However, it's best to take the half-board rate, costing from £18 ($27) to £23 ($34.50) per person nightly, including VAT and service. The dinner is home-cooked, typically English fare. The eggs served here, for example, are called "free range" in England, meaning the chickens are allowed to roam the estate. Everything is backed by a good wine cellar, and before dinner you can enjoy a drink in the wood-beamed and thatched bar.

Colindale, Rathmore Road (tel. 0803/23947), is a good choice. And it's about as central as you'd want, opening onto King's Garden, as well as lying within a five-minute walk of Corbyn Beach, and three minutes from the railway station. The B&B rate, set by Messrs. Spencer and Gold, is £10.50 ($15.75) per person in high season. But the best arrangement in one of their nine well-kept double rooms is to take the partial board weekly rate—£90 ($135) per person. Colindale is one of a row of attached brick-built Edwardian houses, with gables and chimneys. It's set back from the road, with a tiny parking court in front. Messrs. Spencer and Gold have a wine list far superior to most large hotels and an attractive cocktail bar.

A Gourmet Cooking School (off-season only)

South Devon Technical College, Newton Road (tel. 0803/35711), is a hotel cooking school that serves inexpensive—but gourmet-level—lunches during the school terms (closed July, August, and the first two weeks in September, as well as on weekends). You pay a set £6 ($9) including coffee—and are offered the results of the day's lesson. Supervised by expert teachers, the young chefs turn out excellent meals. Lunch is served at 12:30 p.m. (you must reserve no more than seven days in advance; telephone between 10:30 a.m. and 4:30 p.m.). You leave tips at your discretion. It's pointless to give menu suggestions, as the bill of fare changes daily. It's usually in French, beginning with hors d'oeuvres and following with soup, then fish, such as filet of sole, the main course, perhaps entrecôte tyrolienne, accompanied by vegetables, and finally, dessert. The modern-looking restaurant is licensed, and offers a selection of table wines, apéritifs, and liqueurs. The linen is starched stiff white, the silver sparkling, and the copper chafing dishes shining.

5. Totnes

One of the oldest towns in the West Country, the ancient borough of Totnes rests quietly in the past, seemingly content to let the Torbay area remain in the vanguard of the building boom. On the Dart River, 12 miles upstream from Dartmouth, Totnes is so totally removed in character from Torquay that the two towns could be in different countries. Totnes has several old historic buildings, notably the ruins of a Norman castle, an ancient guildhall, and the 15th-century church of St. Mary, made of red sandstone. In the Middle Ages, the old cloth town was encircled by walls, and the North Gate serves as a reminder of that period.

WHERE TO STAY: Royal Seven Stars Hotel (tel. 0803/862125) is a coaching inn, rebuilt in 1660 although tracing its origins back 500 years before that. Whitewashed and severe, it stands on a street not far from the Dart at the bottom of Fore Street. The interior courtyard, built for horses and carriages, has been enclosed in glass, with an oak staircase leading to the second-floor bedrooms, which have been upgraded with built-in furniture. In the courtyard are interesting antiques, such as a heraldic shield, hand-carved chests, and an inlaid grandfather's clock, forming the most inviting part of the inn. The rooms are in the old style—nothing fancy, but heartily recommendable for their comfortable beds, soft eiderdowns. There's hot and cold running water; half of the rooms have private baths. All rooms have color TV and tea- and coffee-making facilities. You pay £19 ($28.50) to £24 ($36) in a single room, from £29 ($43.50) to £35 ($52.50) for a double, inclusive of VAT and breakfast. A buffet bar is open for low-cost meals, or you can have a three-course lunch in the dining room for £6.75 ($10.13). A four- or five-course dinner costs £9.75 ($14.63), and there is a choice of à la carte dishes. Olde Tyme Music Hall, dinner, dance, and cabaret are offered in the Star-lite Room every Saturday night. Reservations are necessary.

Broombrough House Farm, on the outskirts of Totnes (tel. 0803/863134), is a gracious 100-year-old, many-gabled stone manor house set on a hill about a ten-minute walk from Totnes. Owner Joan Veale loves to show guests around the farm, which was designed by Sir George Gilbert Scott. Four spacious and well-furnished bedrooms are on the first floor (two shower rooms and one bathroom are shared). They are centrally heated, each containing twin beds, innerspring mattresses, and hot and cold running water. The daily charge is £9 ($13.50) to £10 ($15) for bed and a farm-style breakfast, plus another £7 ($10.50) for dinner. Guest lounges are spacious and comfortable. This place is highly recommended, especially to those who have never experienced life on a farm. The farm is situated first left on the B3210 after leaving Totnes.

WHERE TO EAT: The **Elbow Room,** 6 North St. (tel. 0803/863480), is a one-time cider press and adjoining cottage converted into an intimate rendezvous for diners. The original 300-year-old stone walls have been retained and decor matched to them to give a unique atmosphere. Mr. and Mrs. B. J. Sellick provide a standard of food and service that attracts gourmets. Mrs. Sellick combines technical skill with inspiration and a flair for the unusual in the selection, preparation, and presentation of her appetizers, main courses, and homemade desserts. Main courses are accompanied by, and inclusive of, fresh vegetables. The menu is restricted to a maximum of ten international dishes, ranging from truite farci de Georges Bernard (trout, boned and stuffed with salpicon of shellfish, wrapped in a pancake, and baked) to escalope de veau Maître Martino, an original of scalloped veal filled with cream cheese, chives, gherkins, mushrooms with cream and white wine. The price of a complete meal, with full silver service and including a half bottle of wine, is about £40 ($60) for two persons. Dinner is served daily except Sunday and Monday from 7:30 to 9:30 p.m. Simpler luncheon meals are offered daily from noon to 2 p.m. except Saturday, Sunday, and Monday, with a three-course menu that usually includes a roast joint costing around £6 ($9). Mr. Sellick presides over the restaurant with charm and unobtrusive expertise, and offers a wine list to match the food. The Elbow Room extends a warm welcome.

WHERE TO STAY AND EAT ON THE OUTSKIRTS: In and around this area is some of South Devon's finest scenery. The hamlets, such as **Dartington,** are especially pleasing. Here, a Yorkshireman and his American-born wife (one of the Whitneys) poured energy, courage, imagination, and money into the theory that such a village could be self-sufficient. They used historic **Dartington Hall,** built in the late 14th century and restored by them after 1925, as their center. In the surrounding acres of undulating hills and streams, several village industries were created—housing construction, advanced farming, cloth milling, and an experimental school. During the day, visitors are welcome to tour the extensive grounds and can make purchases of handmade crafts in the community store. My food and lodgings recommendations in the village follow.

The **Cott Inn** (tel. 0803/863777), on the Old Ashburton–Totnes turnpike, is the second-oldest inn in England, built in 1320. It is a low, rambling, two-story building of stone, cob, and plaster, with a thatched roof and walls three feet thick. The owner, Nigel Shortman, charges £15.50 ($23.25) per person, including VAT, for a full English or a continental breakfast and occupancy of one of their low-ceilinged old beamed rooms upstairs, where modern conveniences, including hot and cold running water, have been skillfully installed.

The inn is a gathering place for the people of Dartington, and here you'll feel the pulse of English country life. Even though it is a lowly pub, it is sophisticated—and you'll hear good talk here. In winter, log fires keep the lounge and bar snug. You'll surely be intrigued with the tavern, perhaps wanting to take a light meal there. Eating out in restaurants today is an expensive proposition, so Mr. Shortman offers his customers a superb hot and cold buffet where prices for the numerous dishes vary between £2.50 ($3.75) and £7 ($10.50). Even if you're not staying over, at least drop in at the pub.

Stoke Gabriel

About four miles southeast of Totnes sits the little village of Stoke Gabriel, one of the loveliest in Devon. Famous as a fishing hamlet, it lies on a creek of the Dart River. Dartmouth is only six miles south of the village (equidistant to Torquay). Desirable as a base is:

The **Gabriel Court Hotel** (tel. 080/428206), is a manor house that until recently had been owned by one family since 1485. What must the ghosts have thought when Michael and Eryl Beacom acquired it and guests started to fill up the rooms, chasing away the cobwebs of the past? The gleaming white house is surrounded by gardens, hedges, and magnolia trees. A heated swimming pool has been added. B&B rates are from £20 ($30) per person. You might get a room in the new wing, containing eight bedrooms, all with private baths. The majority of the other comfortable rooms also have private baths or shower and toilet facilities, and the remaining few feature hot and cold running water only. Gabriel Court enjoys a reputation for its well-cooked English food, enhanced all the more by fruit and vegetables from the garden, as well as trout and salmon from the Dart and poultry from nearby farms. The hotel has a bar offering moderately priced wines. It remains open all year.

6. Dartmouth

At the mouth of the Dart River, this ancient seaport is the home of the Royal Naval College. Traditionally linked to England's maritime greatness, Dartmouth sent out the young midshipmen who ensured that Britannia ruled the waves. You can take a river steamer up the Dart to Totnes (book at the kiosk at the harbor). The view along the way is of Devon's most beautiful river.

Dartmouth's 15th-century castle was built during the reign of Edward IV. The town's most noted architectural feature is the Butterwalk, lying below Tudor houses. The Flemish influence in some of the houses is pronounced.

WHERE TO STAY: The **Royal Castle Hotel,** The Quay (tel. 08043/2397), has been a coaching inn since 1639, having slept a host of visitors, including Sir Francis Drake, Queen Victoria, Charles II, and Edward VII (bedrooms named after them commemorate their visits). Horse-drawn carriages (as late as 1910) would dispatch their passengers in a carriageway, now enclosed to make the reception hall. Everywhere you look, you see reminders of the inn's rich past. The glassed-in courtyard, with its winding wooden staircase, has the original coaching horn and a set of 20 antique spring bells connected to the bedrooms. Many of the rooms opening off the covered courtyard and the rambling corridors have antiques, and the beds are soft.

A single without bath costs £22 ($33), rising to £29 ($43.50) with bath. A double without bath is £34 ($51), going up to £40 ($60) with bath. These tariffs include breakfast and VAT. The meals are excellent, in the best of the English tradition. A set lunch goes for £5.50 ($8.25), a set dinner for £7.50 ($11.25). A favorite place to settle in is the Galleon Bar, once two old kitchens, with double fireplaces and large hand-hewn beams said to have been rescued from Armada ships. There are two other pub-style bars, with settles, popular with the locals. Guests lounge on the second floor in a room with a bay window overlooking the harbor.

The **Victoria Hotel,** Duke Street (tel. 08043/2572), is an unheralded little hotel, just 150 yards from the harbor. However, it is a sophisticated oasis, showing excellent taste in both the hotel and restaurant. The Victoria is a favorite retreat of the officers of the Naval College (at times, you feel that Gilbert and Sullivan wrote their operettas there). For B&B guests pay £28 ($42) in a twin, £15 ($22.50) in a single. A favorite place for before-dinner drinks is one of the Victorian slipper chairs in front of the lounge fireplace. The bedrooms are immaculate, tidy, and personal, the beds fresh and restful, and some rooms have baths. Recommended on the à la carte menu are the chef's own pâté, T-bone steak, and locally caught fish. Try Ushers Best real ale or the local cider.

WHERE TO DINE: **Taylors,** The Quay (tel. 08043/2748). Almost out of place in a peaceful south-coast river town, Taylors's decor is straight out of Arabia, a huge black tent decorated with goatskins and brilliantly colored tassels. A camel comes at you through a mirage on one wall. Diana Taylor was an assistant master of horses for the film *Khartoum* and was in charge of the boats used in *A Man for All Seasons.* Her theatrical flair for the dramatic shows now that she has settled in rural England, and is reflected in the black chairs and tables as well as the dim lights.

Diana excels in buying fresh ingredients for the dishes, which feature plenty of fresh fish and seafood. One of the charming young women on the staff will lead you to the bar where an open fire burns, provide your apéritif, and help you to choose your meal. For an appetizer, you might select the homemade pâté, moules marinières, hot prawns in oil, garlic, and chili, or grilled sardines in garlic butter. Vegetarians are catered to with vegetable curry, risotto, and fresh vegetables simmered in cream with nuts and herbs. For main dishes, other diners might choose pork steak cooked in cream and wine with peppers and onions, chicken with honey and toasted almonds, chicken curry with poppodums and chutney, or a steak—rump, filet, or au poivre. Meals cost around £15 ($22.50) and up. Fresh vegetables are always featured, and rice or a salad accompanies all main dishes. There are lovely views from the bow window down the River Dart to the sea.

The restaurant is open daily from noon to 2 p.m. and from 7 to 10:30 p.m. It is closed for a month from mid-January to mid-February.

The **Cherub,** Higher Street (tel. 08043/2571), was built around 1380 and maintains much of its original decor, the uniqueness of the old timbered building an attraction to North Americans. The owners of this very attractive and friendly pub, Roy and Lois Thwaites, serve bar meals at lunch for £1 ($1.50) to £2.50 ($3.75) each. In the evenings they offer a popular, although intimate, candlelight restaurant, seating just 20 persons. The average meal there costs about £12 ($18) with drinks. Every item is home-cooked, and the chef specializes in local crab and seafood dishes such as Dover sole and turbot in a Devonshire cream sauce. You can even pick your own lobster from the live ones in the tank. It's open seven days a week.

Bay Tree Restaurant, Fairfax Place (tel. 08043-3167), is a typical English tea shop with cakes for sale in the windows. Inside it has wheelback chairs placed around dark mahogany tables. Cheerful local women hover about to serve. A Devon cream tea for two costs £1.50 ($2.25), and they have a mouthwatering selection of toasted scones and teacakes, along with sandwiches and toasted buns, all served from 3:15 to 5:30 p.m. Light meals include poached eggs, fried fish and chips, and beans on toast, served from noon to 2 p.m. and again from 6:30 p.m. when a dish will cost around £2.50 ($3.75). A set lunch is featured for £3.50 ($5.25), including such items as a homemade vegetable soup, roast chicken or beef, lamb curry, and steak-and-kidney pudding (the sort with the crust rather than the pie), followed by, say, lemon meringue or apple pie.

7. Plymouth

The historic seaport of Plymouth is more romantic in legend than in reality. But this was not always so. In World War II, the blitzed area of greater Plymouth lost at least 75,000 buildings. The heart of present-day Plymouth, including the municipal civic center on the Royal Parade, has been entirely rebuilt—the way that it was done the subject of much controversy.

For the old you must go to the Elizabethan section, known as the **Barbican,** and walk along the quay in the footsteps of Sir Francis Drake (once the mayor of Plymouth), and other Elizabethan seafarers, such as Sir John Hawkins, English naval commander and slave trader. It was from here in 1577 that Drake set sail on his round-the-world voyage. An even more famous sailing took place in 1620 when the Pilgrim Fathers left their final port in England for the New World. That fact is commemorated by a plaque at the harbor.

While playing bowls on Plymouth Hoe, Drake was told that the Spanish Armada had entered the Sound. In what must surely rank as one of the greatest displays of confidence of all time, he finished the game before taking off.

Apart from the Hoe, the most interesting part of the city is the area around the departure point of the Pilgrim Fathers in 1620, the already-mentioned Barbican. Here you'll find the Memorial Gateway to the Waterside whence, as tradition has it, they embarked on the *Mayflower.* Here too is the Blackfriars Refectory Room, dating from 1536, in Southside Street. The building is a national monument and one of Plymouth's oldest surviving buildings. It's now owned by Plymouth Gin Distillery, which welcomes visitors Monday to Friday to see the small exhibition of the history of the building. It was here that the Pilgrims finally met prior to setting sail for the New World.

The Barbican is a mass of narrow streets, old houses, and quayside shops selling antiques, brasswork, old prints, and books. Fishing boats still unload their catch at the wharves, and passenger-carrying ferry boats run short harbor cruises. A one-hour trip from Phoenix Wharf includes a visit to Drake's Island in the Sound, the dockyards, and naval vessels, plus a view of the Hoe from seaside. The cost is £1.20 ($1.80) per person. For other cruises, get in touch with **Millbrook Steamboat and Trading Co.,** Cremyll Quay (tel. 0752/822202).

The **Barbican Craft Centre,** White Lane, in the Barbican, has workshops and showrooms where you can watch and talk to the people engaged in crafts. You'll see such sights as a potter throwing a special design or a glass-blower fashioning a particular glass. Woodcarvers, leather workers, and weavers are also busy, and you can buy their products at reasonable prices, even commissioning your own design if you're lucky. Prices range from a few pounds for a hand-tooled belt to £20 ($30) for a hand-woven blanket rug.

WHERE TO STAY: Still a major base for the British navy, Plymouth makes for an interesting stopover. The pick of the lot in accommodations follows.

Duke of Cornwall, Millbay Road (tel. 0752/266256), is a Gothic-Victorian monument. Spared from World War II bombings, it looms like a château. Many of its bedrooms open onto balconies with views of the harbor. Considerable modernization has enlivened the interior. The bedrooms have been successfully upgraded, with compact, streamlined furnishings, most with bath or shower. A single with bath rents for £28 ($42) to £34 ($51) nightly, the cost rising to £40 ($60) to £46 ($69) in a double, these tariffs including an English breakfast and VAT. In the paneled Clan Bar, you can order good drinks in a setting of tartan floors and country-keg stools. The dining room is contemporary, with draped walls, a circular ceiling, and banquettes for cozy dining. A set lunch costs £6.50 ($9.75); a set dinner, £10 ($15). Latecomers are drawn into the Spider's Web in the cellar.

Holiday Inn, Armada Way (tel. 0752/662866), would probably have upset the departure plans of our forefathers. If they'd known how luxurious the new Holiday Inn would be, they might never have sailed. It's one of the most distinguished hotels in the West Country, set beside a park, overlooking the harbor and the Hoe. Rising like a midget skyscraper, it contains 222 good-size bedrooms with long double beds. Singles go from £39.60 ($59.40), and doubles from £49.50 ($74.25), plus VAT. The rooms are fashionable, with air conditioning, wide picture windows, TV, radios, telephones, and private baths. Babysitting is available. A covered swimming pool is on the grounds, and there's a sauna and sun terrace as well, with garden tables set up for poolside refreshments. On the top floor is the Penthouse, with superb views across Plymouth Sound, and on the ground floor there's a specialty fish and meat restaurant, Mongers.

Blackfriars Restaurant and Hotel, 58 Southside St. (tel. 0752/668827), owned and run by David King and family, lies at the top of a paved courtyard and built on the site of an old malthouse that probably belonged to the Blackfriars Monastery. This is the only hotel within the historic Barbican area of the city. You can almost believe yourself back two or three centuries as you arrive at this small hotel.

Family run, it offers a bed and a continental breakfast for £18 ($27) in a single, from £28 ($42) in a double. All the smallish Swedish pine-paneled units have showers and toilets en suite, as well as coffee- and tea-making facilities (TV is also available on request).

The restaurant is open from 10:30 a.m. to 3 p.m. and 6 to 10 p.m. Monday to Friday and from 10:30 a.m. to 5 p.m. on Saturday. It's run by Sally, daughter of David King. It serves mainly whole foods, using local produce. I recently enjoyed the lettuce soup. There's a wide range of salads, at least 20 in all, and you can take your choice of any four with a sunflower oil dressing. Also offered are savory flans, hot dishes such as beef stew with a jacket potato, the queen of bread puddings, junket, an Elizabethan sorbet, and a large selection of homemade cakes, cookies, baps, rolls, and sandwiches, which are available to take away if you don't want to eat in.

Mayflower Post House, The Hoe (tel. 0752/662828) was built in 1970 to celebrate the 350th anniversary of the Pilgrims' voyage. It's a white, nine-story building, standing high on a hill above Plymouth Hoe, commanding a view over the wide sweep of Plymouth Sound. The hotel has a resort character, with a heated outdoor swimming pool, three bars, a restaurant, and a buttery with a naval flag decor. Each of the 104 bedrooms is decorated as a bed-sitting room, with wall-wide windows, desks, armchairs, TV, telephone, and private bath, even facilities for making your own tea or coffee. Higher rates are in effect from May 25 till October, with singles costing approximately £48 ($72); doubles or twins, £62 ($93). Breakfast is extra, but VAT and service are included.

The **Anchorage,** Grand Parade, West Hoe (tel. 0752/668645), boasts a choice location, on the Grand Parade by the sea, overlooking Plymouth Sound. Owned by Mr. and Mrs. Willmott, the hotel is simply furnished in a modified modern style. Without flair or frills, it provides its own drama. The rooms have innerspring mattresses, hot and cold running water, and electric heaters. The rate for B&B is from £10 ($15) per night. An evening meal is available from £5 ($7.50).

The **Imperial Hotel,** 3 Windsor Villas, Lockyer Street (tel. Plymouth 27311), is for anyone who prefers a small, friendly place, rather than a commercial hotel. The proprietors are great characters who enjoy making guests feel at home. Mr. Brooks was a rubber planter in Malaya, but retired here and he and Mrs. Brooks bought this attractive Victorian house. The hotel is tastefully furnished, indicating the experienced travel background of its owners. The rate is £14 ($21) in a single, rising to £30 ($45) in a double, including breakfast, VAT, and service. Some ground-floor rooms are offered to those who have difficulty with stairs. The cocktail bar is well stocked, and a four-course evening meal with coffee is £6.30 ($9.45).

WHERE TO EAT: If you're pressed for time and are only passing through, try at least to visit the Barbican—perhaps for a meal. My dining choice is **Green Lanterns,** 31 New St. in the Barbican (tel. 0752/660852). A 16th-century eating house, on a Tudor street, the Green Lanterns lies 200 yards from the Mayflower Steps—about as close to the Pilgrim Fathers as you can get.

Even to this day, it's a good restaurant. At lunchtime, an extensive menu of reasonably priced dishes is served from £3.50 ($5.25), including such items as plaice fritters, Wiltshire porkies (balls of fresh pork sausage dipped in batter and deep fried with apple rings), and cottage pie. All main courses at both lunch and dinner are served with the fresh vegetables of the day.

Some unusual dishes are offered on the dinner menu, such as cidered sole, pigeon pupton (made from an old English recipe in which the pigeon is oven baked with mixed vegetables, hard-boiled egg, stock gravy, and a tasty sausage-and-liver forcemeat topping), venison cobbler, and walnut crumbed lamb (lamb cutlets coated with liver pâté and chopped walnuts, fried and served with a tomato sauce). Desserts include several tempting hot and cold dishes: cinnamon plum crumble, berry grunt, lemon syllabub, and orange delicious. They're rich but worth the calories. All the desserts are served with Devon clotted cream (if you wish). Expect to spend from £10 ($15) for dinner.

Family owned, the Green Lanterns is run by Sally M. Russell and Kenneth Pappin, who are fully aware that voyaging strangers like the Elizabethan atmosphere, traditional English fare, and personal service. The restaurant is near the municipally owned Elizabethan House. It's licensed until 11:30 p.m. and closed Sunday. Reservations for dinner are advisable.

Oysters Restaurant and Wine Bar, 48 Southside St. in the Barbican (tel. 0752/25656). A glass-fronted hallway leads to a rather pleasant wine bar, dimly lit yet welcoming with a crackling log fire and lights dancing off stone walls. Sit at the bar or in one of the snug alcoves to imbibe the house wine, tempered by a bar snack, such as soup, sandwiches, omelets, or the more enterprising chicken-and-mushroom pie, curry, mussels marinière, or half a dozen oysters. Prices range from £1 ($1.50) to £4 ($6) per portion. Try french bread toasted with a filling of onion, mushrooms, tomato, pepper, and mixed herbs.

Behind the bar, the Restaurant at the Back, managed by Philip Cook, is open at the same hours as the bar. The cook features many fish dishes, such as crab, whitebait, clams, herring, oysters, prawns, mullet, sole, and skate, along with some meat and poultry specialties. The steak and pot-roast pigeon is to be eaten in the fingers with a rich bilberry sauce. The average three-course meal costs £18 ($27).

The Barbican Wine Lodge, Quay Road in the Barbican (tel. 0752/660875), lies right on the quayside, across the water from the Customs House. The lodge is an old building with wooden floors softened by sawdust. Vintage wines are stacked in racks behind the bar under an oak-beamed ceiling. Parking is possible directly outside if you can find a space among the local cars, as this is a popular place, owned and run by Peter Stadnyk. It is open from 11 a.m. to 2:30 p.m. and from 6 to 10:30 p.m. Monday to Saturday (closed on Sunday).

This is an ideal place to stop during your exploration of Plymouth. There is a good ambience, plus a wide range of snacks to sate the appetite, including avocado vinaigrette, pâtés, hot soups, quiches, salads, and cold plates of meat—ham, beef, pork, or lamb, costing £1.50 ($2.25) to £3 ($4.50) per plate. Upstairs in the restaurant, you can order steaks and homemade dishes such as Barbican vol-au-vents and Dunster chicken, a meal costing around £10 ($15). You can listen to live music nightly—blues, folk, jazz, whatever.

The **Queen Anne House,** White Lane, in the Barbican (tel. 0752/ 262101), stands next to the previously recommended Barbican Craft Centre. It's a bow-fronted, white-painted tea shop where from 11 a.m. to 1 p.m. you can order fresh coffee, tea, savories, cakes, delicacies, and sandwiches which, as the menu says, titillate the tastebuds. White wood tables and chairs, along with white-paneled walls, make for a bright and cheerful place. It's ideal for a quick snack or a Devonshire cream tea, costing £1.25 ($1.88) per person. The tea shop is open from 8 a.m. to 6 p.m., serving a complete menu daily.

NORTH DEVON

"Lorna, Lorna . . . Lorna Doone, my lifelong darling," is the wailing cry you'll think of as you lie abed in your North Devon farmhouse. A wildness seems to enter the air at night on the edge of the moody Doone Valley. Much of the district is already known to those who have read Victorian novelist R. D. Blackmore's romance of the West Country, *Lorna Doone.*

The bay-studded coastline is mysterious. Pirates and smugglers used to find havens in crooked creeks and rocky coves. The ocean crashes against the rocks, and the meadows approach so close to the cliff's edge that you wonder why they don't go spilling into the sea, sheep and all. The heather-clad uplands of Exmoor, with its red deer, extend into North Devon from Somerset, a perfect setting for an English mystery thriller. Favorite bases are Clovelly and the twin resorts of Lynton and Lynmouth. Our first stopover is the best:

8. Clovelly

This most charming of all Devon villages is overpopular in summer. Still, it remains one of the main attractions of the West Country. Starting at a great height, the village cascades down the mountainside, with its narrow, cobblestoned High that makes travel by car impossible. (You park your car at the top and make the trip by foot.) Supplies are carried down by donkeys. Every yard of the way provides views of tiny cottages, with their terraces of flowers lining the main street. The village fleet is sheltered at the stone quay at the bottom.

To avoid the climb back up the slippery, cobblestoned incline, go to the rear of the Red Lion Inn and "queue up" for a Land Rover. In summer, the line is often long, but considering the alternative, it's worth the wait. Two Land Rovers make continuous round trips, costing 50p (75¢) per person.

WHERE TO STAY: A warning: It's hard to get a room in Clovelly. Advance reservations, with a deposit, are imperative during the peak summer months, although you can always telephone in advance and just possibly get a bed.

A tip: To avoid the flock of tourists, stay out of Clovelly from around 11 in the morning till teatime. After tea, settle in your room, and have dinner—perhaps spend the night in peace and contentment. The next morning after breakfast, you can walk around the village or go for a swim in the harbor, then visit the nearby villages during the middle of the day when the congestion sets in. Bideford, incidentally, is 11 miles away.

The **New Inn** (tel. Clovelly 303), about halfway down the High Street, is the village pub, a good meeting place at sundown. It offers the best lodgings in the village, in two buildings on opposite sides of the steep street (but only a 12-foot leap between their balconies). B&B ranges from £10 ($15) to £12 ($18) per person, inclusive. If you're only stopping over, then this little country inn is recommended for meals. A wide choice of moderately priced à la carte meals is offered in the oak-beamed dining room. The local fare, including genuine Devonshire cream, is featured whenever possible. Locally caught lobsters are prepared by a skilled chef exactly as you want them. The hotel is open most of the year. Motorists can park in the car park or in the garage at the top of the street. It is advisable to pack an overnight case, as the luggage has to be carried down (but is returned to the top by donkey).

Red Lion, The Pier (tel. Clovelly 237), may well have the best location in the village—at the bottom of the steep cobbled street, right on the stone seawall of the little harbor. Rising three stories, it is an unspoiled country inn, the life centering on an antique pub where the villagers gather to satisfy their thirsts over pints of ale. Most of the bedrooms look directly onto the sea. All have hot and cold running water and adequate furnishings. The cost is £11.50 ($17.25) per person nightly, including breakfast. Other meals are available in the sea-view dining room. The manager can arrange for boating in the bay, and suggests that the Red Lion is not suitable for children under 7 years of age.

On the Outskirts

Beaconside, Monkleigh, near Bideford (tel. 02372/77205), was built around 1860 and still retains its high ceilings and the large rooms typical of that era. Your hosts, John and Stella Pucker, and their four daughters, Linella, Elaine, Celestine, and Lucinda, have brought their own personal style and a dash of humor to the running of this place that they like to think of as typical of "visiting friends in the country." They offer only nine pleasantly furnished bedrooms, each with private bath or shower, plus color TV. The daily rate for B&B is £18 ($27) to £22 ($33) per person, depending on the season. Stella cooks good, traditional English dishes, served in the dining room, which the Puckers have expanded, also adding a bar.

9. Lynton-Lynmouth

The north coast of Devon is set off most dramatically in Lynton, a village some 500 feet high. It is a good center for exploring the Doone Valley and that part of Exmoor that spills into the shire from neighboring Somerset. The Valley of Rocks, west of Lynton, offers the most spectacular scenery.

The town is joined by a cliff railway to its sister, Lynmouth, about 500 feet lower. The rivers of East and West Lyn meet in Lynmouth, a resort popular with the English. For a panoramic view of the rugged coastline, you can walk on a path halfway between the two towns that runs along the cliff. From Lynton, or rather from Hollerday Hill, you can look out onto Lynmouth Bay, Countisbury Foreland, and Woody Bays in the west.

FOOD AND LODGING: The **Tors Hotel** (tel. 05985/3236), set high on a cliff, opens onto a view of the coastline and the bay of Lynmouth. It was built in the fashion of a Swiss château, with more than 40 gables, Tyrolean balconies jutting out to capture the sun (or the moon), black-and-white timbered wings, and some 30 chimneys. Surrounding the hotel are a terrace and a heated swimming pool. The interior has been modernized, and much attention has been paid to the comfortable bedrooms. All prices are per person. B&B goes for £18 ($27) per night up to £25 ($37.50), the cheapest rate being for a single without bath and without view. The top charge is for a grade-A room with a sea view and private bath, toilet, radio, and color TV. All tariffs include VAT and a full English breakfast. A set lunch costs £5.50 ($8.25); a set dinner, £9.50 ($14.25). Lunch on Sunday is priced at £6.50 ($9.75). The hotel is closed from November to March.

The **Rising Sun Hotel** (tel. 05985/3223) is perhaps one of the most colorful thatched inns in England—especially as it's right at the end of the quay at the mouth of the Lyn River. Not only is the harbor life spread before you, but you can bask in the wonder and warmth of an inn in business for more than 600 years. In bedroom after bedroom, with crazy levels and sloping ceilings, you'll have views of the water, the changing tides, and bobbing boats. The place is owned by hoteliers Mr. Wade and Mr. Jeune. The inn is closed in January; otherwise, they make sure that either one or the other of them is there to supervise things. They charge from £16 ($24) per person for an overnight stay, including an English breakfast, service, and VAT. Even if you're not staying over, you may want to sample the English cuisine: dinners from £10 ($15). It's a delight dining at the Rising Sun, as everything is 101% British in the dining room, with its deeply set window and fireplace. See the original 14th-century fireplace in the bar.

Rock House, Lynmouth (tel. 05985/3508), stands in the Manor Grounds between the Lyn River and the shore overlooking the Bristol Channel as well as Lynmouth Harbour. Run by Paddy and Paul Green, it is reached by a bridge and occupies one of the most dramatic positions in the village. The bedrooms, each with hot and cold running water, central heating, and much home-like comfort, rent for £12 ($18) per person nightly, including breakfast and VAT. Children sharing their parents' room get a reduction of 10%. Also, rates are reduced in the spring and autumn. Half board costs from £18 ($27) per person daily. Meals, served in a Regency dining room with its original ceiling moldings, are personally prepared by Mrs. Green. The fare is typically English, using fresh local produce and including homemade desserts served with clotted cream. From Easter to September, morning coffee, a buffet lunch, and cream teas with Mrs. Green's homemade scones are also available. Outside is a large sheltered garden with parking on the premises.

Ye Olde Cottage (Spinning Wheel Restaurant) (tel. 05985/3297) is a miniature, quayside inn, centered in this tiny resort with an unspoiled view of the harbor. Here you can get inexpensive teas and meals. For five generations the Wakeham family has been operating the inn. Chef Peter Wakeham and his wife, Heather, are always to be found at the place— either in the kitchen or in the dining room looking after their guests. Peter's mother and father are called in when things get hectic. It's a favored spot for a thoroughly English Devonshire cream tea with all the trimmings. At mealtime you can order a two-or three-course meal based on such traditional English "fayre" as roast beef or West Country chicken and homemade pies and tarts. From the à la carte menu you can select such delights as rainbow trout, Lyn salmon, and a full range of steaks. Expect to pay from £7 ($10.50) to £11 ($16.50) for an à la carte dinner. Peter has also introduced a line of dishes cooked in wine and cider, to his own recipes. The restaurant is open daily from 10:30 a.m. to 9:30 p.m. from March to November.

READERS' HOTEL SELECTION: "The Bonnicott Hotel, on Watersmeet Road (tel. 05985/3346), is the former vicarage of Lynmouth's Anglican church. Resting slightly back and above the sea, the Bonnicott has a beautiful dining room with large picture windows providing a wonderful view of the water. Ten cozy rooms have an equally good sea view, and the downstairs bar, with an open-hearth fire, is well stocked. The owners, Pam and George, are a husband and wife who personally execute every detail of the running of the hotel. George gives most attentive service to his guests at breakfast, dinner, and at night when he tends the bar until whatever time his guests choose to retire. Pam, who prepares all the food for breakfast and dinner, is truly a gourmet cook. Each of the five four-course dinners we were served during our stay was English cuisine at its finest, and much of it was local to Devon. From the thick clotted cream that graced the fresh homemade berry pies to the stuffed brook trout pulled from the neighboring streams, each course was different and delicious on each of our five nights there. The service did not stop with fine food and spirits, however. Pam and George were available for our every need, providing invaluable information about the best hikes, best local shopping, and best of all, local color and history, including, of course, the real-life locations of the scenes from the novel *Lorna Doone*. The cost is £11.50 ($17.25) per person for B&B, £18 ($27) per person for half board" (Tom and Laura Groce, Austin, Texas).

10. Combe Martin

Noted for its strawberry fields and mild climate, Combe Martin is surrounded by magnificent scenery: high, rugged cliffs, wild moors, and rocky shorelines. Among the rocks are some of Britain's favorite beaches, and local boatmen can take you to spots, impossible to reach on foot, where the scenery is breathtaking. The village is small, with the High Street as its shopping district. An old English church built in the Perpendicular style of architecture is the main historical structure in the town. Just six miles from Ilfracombe, Combe Martin is a good base for excursions into Exmoor.

WHERE TO STAY: Saffron House, King Street (tel. Combe Martin 3521), is an old farmhouse successfully adapted into a popular small hotel. Just a short walk from the village harbor, the house is set back from the road where it overlooks the village and surrounding countryside. The owners, Mr. and Mrs. Chantler, are sincerely interested in your comfort, and from the moment of your friendly reception, you know you're going to enjoy your stay. The guest rooms are clean and comfortable, with the benefit of full central heating. There are also two lounges, one with color TV, the other with a well-stocked bar. B&B rates are about £10 ($15) per person per night, including VAT. Guests have use of a heated swimming pool. The

Chantlers are only too happy to point out local areas of interest, and if they aren't too busy, they may just accompany you on a walk through the cliff paths.

The **Dragon House,** Bilbrook, near Minehead (tel. 0984/40215), is reached by driving from the A82 through a wide gateway into the inn's driveway and walking into the charming old house, with a comfortable lounge and cozy bar. Everything is spotlessly clean, with old furniture lovingly polished and gleaming in the firelight. The beamed bedrooms are individually furnished in country-cottage style, with good beds and some antiques. One has a half-tester bed. All the units have radios, and some also have TV. Most of the rooms have baths or showers and views over the moors or the garden. From the elegant hall, an ancient staircase leads to a gallery around the first floor off which many of the bedrooms open. Staircases lead to other units with dormer windows in the roof. B&B costs £23 ($34.50) in the first-floor rooms, £21.50 ($32.25) for the smaller ones on the second floor. There is a £6 ($9) supplement for single occupancy.

At lunchtime, excellent bar meals are served, costing about £3.50 ($5.25) to £6.50 ($9.75). For dinner in the antique-furnished dining room, a good selection is offered on the à la carte menu, including local trout with white wine sauce or honey-roast duck taken off the bone. Such a meal will cost around £15 ($15), unless you should demand a whole Dover sole. A set four-course dinner goes for £9.50 ($14.25).

Chapter IX

CORNWALL

THE ANCIENT DUCHY OF CORNWALL is the extreme southwestern part of England, often called "the toe." But Cornwall is one toe that's always wanted to dance away from the foot. Although a peninsula, it is a virtual island—if not geographically, then spiritually. Encircled by coastline, it abounds with rugged cliffs, hidden bays, fishing villages, sandy beaches, and sheltered coves where smuggling was once practiced with consummate skill. Many of the little seaports with their hillside-clinging cottages resemble towns along the Mediterranean, although Cornwall retains its own distinctive flavor.

The true Cornish people are generally darker and shorter than the English. Their Celtic origin still lives on in superstition, folklore, and fairy tales. King Arthur, of course, is the most vital legend of all. When Cornishmen speak of King Arthur and his Knights of the Round Table, they're not just handing out a line to tourists. To them, Arthur and his knights really existed, romping around Tintagel Castle, now in ruins—Norman ruins, that is—lying 300 feet above the sea, 19 miles from Bude.

The ancient land had its own language up until about 250 years ago, and some of the old words ("pol" for pool, "tre" for house) still survive. The Cornish dialect is more easily understood by the Welsh than by those who speak the Queen's English.

The Cornishmen, like the Welsh, are great miners (tin and copper), and they're fond of the tall tale. Sometimes it's difficult to tell when they're serious. One resident, for example, told me that he and his wife had been walking in the woods at twilight, but had lost their way. He claimed that the former owner of the estate (in Victoria's day) appeared suddenly in a dog-carriage and guided them back to where they'd taken the wrong turn. If this really had happened, I wouldn't be surprised—at least not in Cornwall.

The English come here for their holidays in the sun. But some of the places where everybody goes, I'd recommend that you avoid. For example, there's little point in going to Land's End, the westernmost tip of England, a narrowing hunk of bleakness and crude cottages set up to peddle ice cream and souvenirs.

In lieu of such a trip, I'd suggest berthing at one of the smaller fishing villages, such as East and West Looe, Polperro, Mousehole, or Portloe—where you'll experience the true charm of the duchy. Many of the villages, such as St. Ives, have now become artists' colonies. In some of the pubs and restaurants frequented by painters, a camaraderie prevails, especially in the nontourist months. Recently, for instance, at one of the artists' hangouts (bleached wooden tables, handmade stools), three young men who had finished dining brought out guitars and spontaneously launched into folk songs for the rest of the evening. Detecting the accent of some visiting Americans, they sang (with appallingly perfect accents) several country music favorites, although it was their repertoire from Ireland and Wales that cast the greater spell.

Except for St. Ives and Port Isaac, most of my recommendations lie on the southern coast, the so-called Cornish Riviera, which strikes many foreign visitors as being the most intriguing. However, the north coast has its own peculiar charm.

A SIDE TRIP TO LIZARD: The most southerly point of England is The Lizard, with jagged rocks reaching out into the sea where cormorants and gulls fish.

Right on the point, beneath the lighthouse, is the workshop of a man who must surely be one of the most perfect one-man cottage industries in the country. P. L. Casley runs **Lizard Point Serpentine Works,** (tel. The Lizard 290706) in one of the small shacks by the car park. There he turns, polishes, and fashions into pots, vases, ashtrays, and dishes, the serpentine stone found only in this part of the country. The veins in the stone can be green, gray, or sometimes red.

Ornamental barometers and clocks are not cheap, but these are absolutely genuine souvenirs made by a man who is entirely at peace with himself and the country he lives in. The family, his son, and his brother assist with the quarrying of the stone, which comes from under Coonhilly Down close by, the site of the country's largest radio receiving and space-tracking station. Mr. Casley's son, another blue-eyed Cornishman, is fast learning the trade so there is every hope that still in 50 years there will be someone whistling happily in the tiny workshop on the tip of The Lizard.

POLDARK MINING CO. LTD.: **Wendron Forge** (tel. 03265/3173), stands three miles north of Helston on the B3297 road. As you have driven around Cornwall, the old workings of the tin mines will have been evident everywhere. Here you have the chance of visiting a mine and walking through the old workings, which extend for several miles beneath the surface. They have discovered yet another cavern, and the tour of the mine will soon take longer than the present three-quarters of an hour. Above ground is a museum of mining artifacts, mining equipment, steam engines, drills, and a history of mining. There is a souvenir shop and another selling good-quality local products, a snackbar, and a children's play area if they don't want to see the exhibits. Entrance to all above ground is 1 halfpenny (that's right, ½p, less than 1¢ U.S.). Admission to the mine is £2 ($3) for adults, £1 ($1.50) for children. Hours are 10 a.m. to 10 p.m. in June, July, and August, to 6 p.m. the remainder of the year.

1. Looe

After your visit to Plymouth, about 15 miles away in Devon, you can either take the Tamar Suspension Bridge to Cornwall, or else cross by ferry from Plymouth. You'll soon arrive in the ancient twin towns of East and West Looe, connected by a seven-arched stone bridge that spans the river. In the jaws of shrub-dotted cliffs, the fishing villages present a stark contrast to Plymouth. Houses scale the hills, stacked one on top of the other in terrace fashion.

In both fishing villages you can find good accommodations and interesting people. Fishing and sailing are two of the major sports, and the sandy coves, as well as East Looe Beach, make choice spots for seabathing. Beyond the towns are cliff paths and downs worth a ramble. In these villages you'll find varied lifestyles: the traditional Cornish fishermen landing pilchard; the sophisticates enjoying the unspoiled atmosphere; summer visitors down for a week or so; and the artists and artisans who live and work here.

Looe is noted for its shark-angling, but you may prefer simply walking the narrow, crooked medieval streets of East Looe, with its old harbor and 17th-century guildhall.

WHERE TO STAY: Space and prices are at a premium in July and August. Some hotels are so heavily booked that they can demand Saturday-to-Saturday clients only. I have not recommended such establishments, as I feel that their managers aren't interested in patronage by international visitors.

Hannafore Point Hotel, West Looe (tel. 05036/3273), is a rambling, many-gabled structure commanding an advantageous view of the harbor, overlooking miles of Cornish coastline and one of the most beautiful bays in Cornwall. In addition to the older bay-windowed chambers, newer sections of the hotel have been built with walls of glass for viewing the harbor and St. George's Island. The entrance opens onto several levels of comfortable lounges and bars, with cantilevered stairs, balconies, and birch paneling. The modern bedrooms all include either private baths or showers, and most of the front rooms have their own balconies. B&B rates vary depending on the view, location of the room, and the time of year. From May to October, a single or double room rents for about £28 ($42) per person. The panoramic view adds to the pleasure of dining in the St. George's Restaurant, where fresh, first-class ingredients are used in the fine Cornish and French cuisine. There is also a heated outdoor swimming pool.

Hannafore Point is in the main center for shark and deep-sea fishing, and is ideal for exploring either Cornwall or parts of Devon.

The **Boscarn Hotel,** The Seafront. (tel. 05036/2923). This hotel has 22 bedrooms and sits right on the beach of East Looe, the safest bathing beach in Cornwall. Built more than half a century ago, it is a beautiful old building that provides modern facilities. There are two nicely decorated large bars, one available as a function room and providing entertainment and disco action (which may affect your sleep if your room is near). There is a cozy residents' bar as well. A large family room provides plenty of free games for children of all ages, and swings and slides are found in the garden overlooking the beach. An excellent English breakfast is served, as is lunch, although dinners aren't offered. Prices, inclusive of VAT, are £15 ($22.50) in a single, £22 ($33) to £29 ($43.50) in a double, breakfast included. Families are welcome. The Boscarn is a comfortable and well-recommended hotel for a relaxed holiday. Closed November to March.

Klymiarven Hotel, Barbican Hill, in East Looe (tel. 05036/2333), is a 180-year-old manor house, standing in its own wooded and terraced gardens above the harbor. It is owned and run by Daphne Henderson who, until a few years ago, ran a fashion shop in London. She and her husband traveled a lot and learned the pitfalls and likes of sojourners from all sorts of places. Daphne put experience to good use in this lovely old house, mainly Regency, with cellars that have Tudor associations. The main beams reputedly came from ships of the Spanish Armada sunk by Drake. These cellars are now a pleasant after-dinner meeting spot, with a fireplace to warm the cooler nights. On occasion, music is played for dancing. Daphne runs the whole place with special attention to the kitchen, which, in my opinion, produces some of the finest meals in the area. Dinners are five courses and cost nonresidents £10 ($15). For residents the price is covered in the inclusive per-person charge of £15 ($22.50) in low season, £26 ($39) high season for half board. The hotel is small, containing only eight bedrooms in the older part of the house, plus six modern accommodations, each with a private bath and a balcony. Guests gather in the hotel's attractively furnished lounge with french windows opening onto the garden. In addition, there is a sun lounge bar with a terrace.

The **Smugglers House,** Middle Market, near the old Guildhall (tel. 05036/2397), built in the 15th and 17th centuries, was once the headquarters of smugglers. The hotel is tucked away right in the center of the village, a few minutes' walk from the quay, the seafront, and the shops. The hotel has an original Cornish granite fireplace, and the beams in the restaurant and bar are believed to be from the ships of the Spanish Armada. There is a tunnel in the restaurant that was used by the ancient smugglers, now in process of being excavated. Rooms without bath rent for £12 ($18) per person nightly, increasing to £15 ($22.50) per person with private bath, plus VAT. The breakfasts are super, with bacon, eggs, sausage, and tomato, all the trimmings. Residents can enjoy a four-course dinner for £6 ($9). Your room will be immaculate, and the beds will be fresh and soft. There is also a Dungeon Restaurant (open to both residents and nonresidents), an authentic smugglers' haunt, known for its fresh English steaks and locally caught fresh fish.

The **Fisherman's Arms,** Higher Market Street (tel. 05036/2215), the main street in East Looe, is housed in a building dating from 1611. It is about 70 yards from the beach. Mr. and Mrs. Bissex provide an array of sandwiches and locally caught crabs and shellfish. The average price for a "cutting" is from £1.20 ($1.80) to £1.50 ($2.25). The decor is provided by antique guns, spears, brass, and copper.

If you wish, you can strike out from Looe on the cliff walk, a distance of 4½ miles, to Polperro. The less adventurous will drive.

WHERE TO STAY AND EAT OUTSIDE LOOE: The **Old Rectory Hotel,** St. Keyne, Liskeard (tel. 0579/42617), five miles from Looe, set in the countryside of southeast Cornwall, makes a good base for touring the area, which is known for its natural beauty, much of it under the care of the National Trust. Some of the Redgrave family's ten recently redecorated rooms have private baths/showers and toilets en suite. The cost of B&B and dinner starts at £25 ($37.50) per person. There is not a large à la carte menu, but the four-course table d'hôte dinner offers fish, meat, and vegetables bought daily from local suppliers. The approach to the hotel is by a winding drive, off the little-used B3254, to the rear of the house. The front overlooks gardens and farmlands. One of the stone outbuildings has been converted into a table-tennis room and another into a children's den. There are also swings for children in the garden.

2. Polperro

This ancient fishing village is reached by a steep descent from the top of a hill. Motorists in summer are forbidden to take their cars down unless they are booked in a hotel. Why? Because otherwise they'd create too much of a traffic bottleneck in July and August. At one time it was estimated that nearly every man, woman, and child in the village spent time salting down pilchards for the winter, or smuggling. Today, tourists have replaced the contraband.

You'd have to search every cove and bay in Cornwall to turn up with a village as handsome as Polperro, which looks almost as if it had been removed intact from the 17th century. The village is tucked in between some cliffs. Its houses—really no more than fishermen's cottages—are bathed in pastel-wash. A small river, actually a stream called the Pol, cuts its way through Polperro. The heart of the village is its much photographed, much painted fishing harbor, where the pilchard boats, loaded to the gunnels, used to dock.

There's a large car park, the price based according to the length of your stay. For those unable to walk, a horse-drawn bus carries visitors to the town center for 50p (75¢).

WHERE TO STAY: Noughts and Crosses Hotel (tel. 0503/72239). One side of this 16th-century pub-hotel faces a narrow street, and the other a five-foot-wide "river" that goes through the center of the village. Eddy T. Barlow, Noughts and Crosses' owner, charges £10 ($15) per person nightly for B&B. Children are not accepted, and booking in season must be for at least three nights. Its name came from the bookkeeping habits of a baker, its one-time owner. She made a small "o" whenever she sold a small loaf of bread and a large "O" when she sold a large loaf. When the loaves were paid for, she would cross them off with an "X." The hotel has windows opening by the Pol. You may remember the crooked stairway, the time-aged beams. The quite-good bedrooms are pleasingly furnished, with hot and cold running water and beds with inner-spring mattresses. Basket meals, snacks, and chilled beer are served in the two well-equipped bars. Steaks, scampi in a basket, and fried chicken are served with fried potatoes. There is a dining room upstairs in which residents of the hotel can eat their bar snacks. Expect to spend from £8 ($12) for a complete meal. No accommodations are offered from November through January.

WHERE TO EAT: The Kitchen, Fish na Bridge (tel. 0503/72780), is a pink cottage on the right, about halfway down to the harbor from the car park. This was once a wagon builder's shop but is now a restaurant, an extension of David and Judith Porter's house next door. David runs the 22-seat Kitchen, while Judith cooks in an area that is visible to diners. Since David retired from outside business at the age of 31, the Porters have built up a restaurant of repute, offering English cooking and using local produce from the sea and the land. Pink is the predominant color inside as well as outside, reflected in the tablecloths and napkins, but the furniture is a natural color beechwood.

The supper/dinner hours are from 7 to 9:30 p.m. daily except Monday in summer, only on Friday and Saturday in winter. The Kitchen is closed for a month after Christmas. The atmosphere is informal, and your meal will be served by a cheerful David. The place is popular, so it's best to reserve a table. In summer, dinner can be arranged as early as 5:30 p.m. if required. There are two menus, the tourist supper costing £6.50 ($9.75) and a house menu for £9 ($13.50). For the latter price, you can choose from a wide range of dishes, such as old English beef pie cooked in beer or tipsy Cornish rabbit braised in cider. If you fancy the more exotic fish dishes, lobster, or scallops, you must order in advance. A vegetarian meal is available for £6 ($9). The winter menus at £7.50 ($11.25) and £10 ($15) include such dishes as braised oxtail, rabbit stew with dumplings, venison pie, and pheasant braised with bacon and onions in wine.

The **Captain's Cabin,** Lansallos Street (tel. 0503/72292), owned by Mr. and Mrs. Victor S. Moore, is run by their son and daughter-in-law, Anthony and Petrina. They are pleased when Americans come by. While they don't have bedrooms for overnight guests, they can give you tips about where to find a room, but you're sure to want to dine with the Moores, among the antique furniture in their low-beamed dining room. The cuisine is comprehensive, and Anthony has a fine reputation for his fish dishes, from among which you may order crab mornay, trout à la Bretonne, or grilled sole. At lunchtime, you can order à la carte meals for £5 ($7.50) to £8 ($12), or special snacks such as a crabber's lunch, a plate of crab and salad, for £3.50 ($5.25). At dinner, if you order à la carte, you can feast lavishly for £12 ($18) to £15 ($22.50). However, if you don't feel like making decisions, there are three set dinners: one of three courses for £6.50 ($9.75) and two four-coursers, one for £10 ($15) and the other for £12 ($18).

The **Pengelly,** near the harbor, is where locals and visitors go for their evening pints of beer and social activity; it is a large L-shaped room with a fireplace that burns brightly at night. Why don't you sit in the window seat and listen to the talk of the villagers? That isn't really as rude as it sounds—since you probably won't be able to understand a word of their thick Cornish dialect. You may like the absence of quaint bits of decor in this honest pub, the center of life in Polperro.

WHERE TO STAY AND EAT ON THE OUTSKIRTS: If you find the busy activity of the two little harbors of Looe and Polperro too much for you, then you can live in far greater style at two of England's outstanding inns, just outside. **Pelynt,** about three miles north of Polperro, is a small, sleepy village; and **Lanreath,** lying off the road to West Looe, is another peaceful, pleasant community.

The **Jubilee Inn,** Pelynt (tel. 0503/20312), was restored as part of a scheme to honor Queen Victoria's Jubilee, by using only the best hand-made Victorian furnishings, even in the bedrooms. Today, the rate for a handsomely decorated room and big English breakfast is £11.50 ($17.25) per person without bath, £15 ($22.50) per person in a room with bath. These tariffs include breakfast, VAT, and service. The food is good, and the vegetables come fresh from the inn's own garden. Sunday lunch is served for £7.50 ($11.25). Otherwise, you have lunch in the bar, where hot and cold dishes are offered for £2 ($3) to £4 ($6). Dinner is à la carte and will cost between £10 ($15) and £18 ($27), depending on what you choose and how much. The inn is a comment on, rather than a monument to the past. The lounge has a hooded fireplace, with a raised hearth, Wind-sor armchairs, antique porcelain, and copper bowls filled with flowers cut from the garden behind the building. The dining room is elegantly Victorian, with mahogany chairs and tables. The only sound you hear is the rustling of the starched aprons of the maids. A fairly sophisticated crowd of people come here to eat and drink at the public bar. A circular, glass-enclosed staircase takes you to the bedrooms. Fitting onto the out-side, the winding stairway has been built to serve as a combined tower and hothouse. The stone steps are covered with carpeting, and vines and plants grow happily in the sunlight streaming in through the glass walls.

The **Punch Bowl Inn,** at Lanreath (tel. 0503/20218), has had a checkered past, serving in turn as a courthouse, coaching inn, and rendezvous for smugglers. Now its old fireplaces and high-backed settles, and its bedrooms with their four-posters, provide hospitality to travelers from abroad, as well as to the discriminating English. The B&B rate is £19 ($28.50) per person. Even if you're only stopping over, you may want to sample the fare or drinks in one of the kitchens (really bars, among the few "kitchens" licensed in Britain as "bars"). In the Stable Restaurant, with its Tudor beams and fireplace, you eat à la carte, choosing to have just a bowl of soup, or perhaps you'd like a steak. Prices go from £1 ($1.50) up to £8 ($12), which is what you'll pay for a big grill. There is a modern lounge, TV room, air-conditioned cocktail bar, and an additional bed-room wing. Many rooms have their own private bathrooms. Advance bookings of less than three nights are not accepted during the high season.

3. Fowey

Called the Dartmouth of Cornwall, Fowey is a town of historical interest (one of the most ancient seaports in the West Country). Once the Fowey Gallants sailed the seas and were considered invincible when raiding French coastal towns. However, occasional retaliation was inevitable. At the time of the Armada, Fowey sent more ships than London. With its narrow streets and whitewashed houses, it has remained unspoiled over the years, enjoying a sheltered position on a deep-water channel. Its creeks and estuary attract sailors and fishermen. If you climb to St. Catherine's Point, you'll be rewarded with a view of the harbor. Sandy beaches and coves are there to explore as well (there's also an 18-hole golf course within easy reach of Carlyon Bay).

WHERE TO STAY: Riverside, Passage Street (tel. 072-683/2275), is the all-purpose ferry-landing hotel of Fowey. Directly on the water, the hotel is at the little car-ferry station where regular crossings leave for Bodinnick. Paintings by Mrs. T. B. Featherstone, wife of the owner, decorate the walls of the hotel, and glass and china ornaments, as well as potted plants, make the place extremely warm and inviting. The 14 bedrooms are handsomely decorated in a bright, cozy, comfortable manner. Six have private bath or shower, and all have hot and cold running water. From the rooms there are views of the river, where a variety of scenery is created by the passing river craft and ferries. Rates are based on the time of the year and the view. Bed and a full English breakfast costs from £18 ($27) to £25 ($37.50) per person daily, depending on the plumbing and the view, VAT included. Half board ranges from £28 ($42) to £33 ($49.50) per person, the latter including private bath. The chef specializes in hot and cold salmon and lobster dishes; the produce bought locally is fresh. The hotel also offers an excellent wine list with a comprehensive choice of both English and continental wines. The menu is changed daily to ensure that variety is a key factor.

Marina Hotel, The Esplanade (tel. 072-683/3315), is a Georgian-style shuttered hotel with sweeping verandas stretching across its symmetrical facade. Originally built for a bishop of Truro, the house sits on top of a well-constructed retaining wall that rises steeply above the boats moored in the estuary of the Fowey (pronounced "Foy") River. The modernized interior still retains some of the best of the original architectural features, as well as a walled garden with views of the water. A well-managed restaurant is on the premises, and if in the unlikely event you arrive by boat, the hotel will provide you with a mooring. Some of the comfortable and big-windowed bedrooms have private balconies. Half-board rates range from £28 ($42) to £32 ($49.50) per person.

4. Truro

This ancient town on the Truro River is the only cathedral city in Cornwall. As such, it is the ecclesiastical center of Cornwall. The cathedral church of St. Mary was begun in 1880 in the Early English style (the spires are in the Norman Gothic design). The town is within 8 to 20 miles of the Cornish beaches. It can be used as a base to explore the countryside, which ranges from bleak Bodmin Moor to fertile farmland and the Winter Roseland of the Falmouth Estuary.

Trelissick Garden (tel. 0872/862090) lies on both sides of the B3289 south of Truro, overlooking King Harry Passage. The entrance is just off the King Harry Ferry up the hill and by the circular tower. In this beautiful wooded park with peaceful walks through the well-tended trees and shrubs, the rhododendrons are a brilliant splash of color in early summer. Upon arrival, you pick up a map and set out on a woodland walk that will take you through the plantations to the banks of Lamouth Creek and all along the edge of the River Fal and Channals Creek before you return to the center of the garden, about a one-hour stroll. Then you can visit the gardens where the vegetation is more controlled and see the special plant section where experiments on acclimatization are made.

The restaurant here is open from 12:15 to 2:15 p.m. for lunch, with afternoon teas served until 6 p.m. The emphasis is on wholesome, fresh food, such as homemade soup and Cornish ice creams and clotted cream. A lunch will cost around £4 ($6) on weekdays or £6.50 ($9.75) for a three-course meal on Sunday, which includes a roast and coffee. You can also have sherry Cornish cider or one of the various lagers, as well as a house wine or a light English Barningham Riesling.

The garden is open April to October from 11 a.m. to 6 p.m. on weekdays, from 1 to 6 p.m. (or to sunset if earlier) on Sunday.

WHERE TO STAY: Penscowl, 12 Ferris Town (tel. 0872/74946), is a centrally situated corner house close to the town center, train station, and County Record Office, which you may want to look into if you're trying to trace your Cornish family history. Mr. and Mrs. C. S. Brockbank rent rooms with color TV, tables and chairs, fridges, toasters, and kettles, as well as crockery and cutlery, in addition to the normal bedroom furniture. There are two kitchens for the use of guests. Linen is provided, and the rooms are cleaned daily except Sunday. Prices are from £8.50 ($12.75) per person per night for accommodation only. Weekly charges range from £36 ($54) to £48 ($72), also per person.

5. Portloe

If you really want to get away from it all and go to that hidden-away Cornish fishing village, then Portloe is for you. On the slope of a hill, opening onto Veryan Bay, it is reached by a road suitable for cars—but chances are you may get sidetracked and spend the rest of the afternoon on byways, opening and closing gates to keep the cattle from straying.

Portloe is an ideal stopover on the south Cornish coast if you're traveling in July and August, when the popular tourist centers, such as Looe and St. Ives, are overrun with sightseers.

WHERE TO STAY: The Lugger, Portloe (tel. Truro 322), is a prestigious inn, yet the narrow lane that leads the way to the establishment was obviously created by a goat. You'll find the inn fresh, sparkling clean—a good spot at the top of the harbor slip, with a bay and boats at hand. The whole picture—water dashing and pounding the nearby rocks, the sunsets, the beach, the stone walls, the crazy roofs of the houses of the fishermen—requires that you take dozens of rolls of film with you . . . or none at all. The 17th-century establishment is managed by the Powell family. They'll put you up for £28 ($42) to £33 ($49.50) per person per night for bed, an English breakfast, and a dinner. All rooms have private baths. The charge for an excellent bar lunch will average around £5 ($7.50). All prices are inclusive of tax. The inn, open late February to early November, is believed to have been a smugglers' hideaway, on the coast between St. Austell and St. Mawes. Guests at the Lugger can also dine at the Idle Rocks Hotel at St. Mawes, just eight miles away, on a reciprocal arrangement. Reduced greens fees are allowed at nearby Truro Golf Club.

6. St. Mawes

Overlooking the mouth of the Fal River, St. Mawes is often compared to a port on the Riviera. Because it's sheltered from northern winds, subtropical plants grow here. From the town quay, you can take a boat to Frenchman's Creek, Helford River, and other places. St. Mawes is noted for its sailing, boating, fishing, and yachting. Half a dozen sandy coves lie within 15 minutes by car from the port. The town, built on the Roseland Peninsula, makes for interesting walks, with its color-washed cottages and sheltered harbor. On Castle Point, Henry VIII ordered the construction of St. Mawes Castle. Falmouth, across the water, is only two miles away.

WHERE TO STAY: **Tresanton** (tel. 0326/270544), is a member of the Relais de Campagne. It is really three buildings, the oldest one dating from the 18th century. One is on the roadside, another halfway up, and the third—the main part of the hotel—on top of the hill and away from the traffic noise. In the middle is an attractive cocktail lounge, with a veranda overlooking the sea. The upper level also has spacious veranda terraces—so there are a lot of places to sit outside among the flowers, looking across the bay. This is one of the highest rated hotels in the area. To quote an AA inspector, it's "quite simply the most charming and delightful hotel I have ever stayed in. The owner, Mrs. Farquharson-Oliver, will probably hold court near the piano on the evening.

The bedrooms are fresh and bright, furnished for the most part in the French country-house manner. All have private baths and are stocked with sewing kits, tissues, books to read, whatever. All accommodations face the sea. A single with dinner and B&B rents for £55 ($82.50), a similar double going for £125 ($187.50). The lounge has an open fireplace and comfortable chairs. The dining room, also overlooking the sea, has attractive murals and a verdant decor that is designed to carry the eye from the house to the sun terraces, the subtropical gardens, and the sea beyond. The menu is limited but good, including such dishes as caneton (duckling) à l'orange and grilled Dover sole. Nonresidents can dine here, enjoying the table d'hôte meal for £18 ($27) or selecting from the à la carte menu, with dinner costing £25 ($37.50).

The **Idle Rocks** (tel. 0326/270771) proudly stands on a terrace above St. Mawes Harbor, commanding views of the open sea and the mouth of the River Fal. The building is a bit of old Cornwall, with its mansard roof and white stucco walls. Diners at the excellent restaurant can view the sea from any table as they enjoy a blend of English and continental cuisine. The cocktail bar opens onto the 145-foot promenade where you may sip an apéritif while you take in the warm and sparkling scene.

The hotel has a total of 22 guest rooms, 15 in the main building and the remaining units in the annex, 50 yards away. All have private baths, and both buildings offer the comfort of central heating. Daily rates per person range from £28 ($42) for a double or single in the annex to £33 ($49.50) for a double or single in the main building overlooking the sea. Rates include bed, full English breakfast, morning and afternoon teas, and the table d'hôte dinner, as well as tax. For an evening at Portloe, just eight miles away, on a reciprocal agreement. Golf is available at Truro Golf Club at reduced greens fees.

The **Rising Sun** (tel. 0326/270233) is a colorful inn on the seafront—made of a row of white fishermen's cottages, with a slate roof, and a flagstone terrace out front. Inside, every square inch oozes with tasteful charm. The locals gather in the pub, with its Windsor chairs grouped around the fireplace. The dining room has lush gold walls with paintings by Michael Oelman in the form of two poems, *Kubla Khan* and *Jacob's Ladder*. English gentility reigns here. The proprietor, Mrs. Campbell Marshall, sets the gracious pace, and is known for her cuisine. You can stay here for anywhere from £22 ($33) to £24 ($36) per person in rooms with bath, including an English breakfast and VAT. Table d'hôte meals cost around £8.50 ($12.75). The dining room has become very popular, with its changing menu of imaginative dishes using local produce whenever possible. Bar snacks are available at lunchtime, and dinner is from 7:30 to 8:45 p.m. Closed November and December.

Braganza, Grove Hill (opposite the Catholic church), St. Mawes (tel. 0326/270281), is a Regency house, furnished with antiques and furniture of the period. You will be warmly welcomed by Polish-born Mrs. Zofia Moseley, now a confirmed Cornishwoman, who loves meeting people and speaks several languages. The house offers five twin-bedded rooms, three of which have private baths. All are centrally heated. Visitors gather in the lounge to watch television. The staircase is a perfect Regency one. The charge is £10.50 ($15.75) per person per night for rooms with a private bathroom, £9.50 ($14.25) per night without bath. These tariffs include an English breakfast, which can be served in your room at no extra cost. The house has an extensive garden overlooking the harbor of St. Mawes where the racing of yachts takes place each Sunday and Thursday in season. Lord Byron, who stayed in Falmouth in 1809, may have visited this house, for he mentions its name in one of his poems. It's said that his limping step can be heard at Braganza.

7. Falmouth

A lot of cutthroat ship wreckers used to live in the area. In fact, when John Killigrew, a leading citizen, started to build a lighthouse on Lizard Head, they protested that the beacon in the night would deprive them of their livelihood and "take away God's Grace from us." Falmouth, 26 miles Penzance, is today a favorite base for the yachting set, who consider it one of the most beautiful harbors in Europe. On a small peninsula, Falmouth's old section overlooks the land-locked inner harbor. The newer part, center for most of the hotels, faces the bay and commands a panorama from St. Anthony's Lighthouse to Pendennis Castle. Warmed in winter by the Gulf Stream, Falmouth has become a year-round resort. Built on a promontory overlooking the estuary of the Fal, it was once occupied in part by the captains of old mail-carrying packet ships. Many find it a good center for touring the rugged Cornish coastline. It's possible, for example, to take a ferry from Falmouth to St. Mawes, a 20-minute ride.

WHERE TO STAY: Greenbank Hotel, Harbourside (tel. 0326/312440), hangs tenaciously to the old days of the Post Office Packet Services (1688–1850). Beside the shore road, this hotel overlooks the water with its own landing pier. Over the years it has been expanded, but it remains traditional in every sense. The spacious lounges have views of the harbor, and the rooms are comfortably furnished. In a single, the rate ranges from £32 ($48), increasing to from £65 ($97.50) in a double or twin. Even if you don't stay here, consider an old-fashioned English meal in the water-view dining room favored by local yachting people. Lunches cost from £6 ($9), and dinners from £11 ($16.50).

The **Tudor Court,** Melville Road (tel. 0326/312807), once part of the local manor house, is within 200 yards of the sea and offers a variety of rooms, some with private bath and a view of the bay. The hotel has a licensed bar and a comfortable lounge with color TV. All meals are prepared and cooked on the premises by the resident proprietress, Mrs. Edna Jefferys. Fresh local produce is used whenever possible. The court is open throughout the year, including Christmas. The top rate per person in high season for dinner and B&B is £18 ($27), £11.50 ($17.25) in low season for B&B only.

The **Old Post Office,** Mylor Bridge (tel. 0326/72713), has been converted by Peter and Joan Davis into a delightful private home where they offer B&B for between £10 ($15) and £12 ($18) per night. The Davises are interesting people who like to meet new friends from overseas and tell them of local attractions. You get sent off in the morning with a good, full English breakfast under your belt.

READER'S B&B SELECTION: "By far the best value we encountered in our month's vacation in England was the **Chelsea House Hotel,** 2 Emslie Rd. (tel. 0326/311138), where Rose and Allan Sutcliffe provide spacious, spotlessly clean rooms and excellent food. B&B costs £11 ($16.50) per person, and an evening meal, optional, goes for £4 ($6). We found that Falmouth is a good base for touring the surrounding area. I am sure that advance reservations will soon be necessary at this fine, small hotel as it is sure to become better known" (H. F. Dinner, Belleair, Fla.).

On the Outskirts

Budock Vean Hotel, Golf and Country Club, near Falmouth (tel. 0326/250288). Since this place lies a few miles from Falmouth, a cab will be sent to meet you at the railway station. Or else you can drive there yourself, among the pines and subtropical vegetation sloping sharply to the Helford River. You come to an old stone house with a stout front door and bright welcoming hall. There Peter, the porter, will grab your bags and hurry them to your room. Afternoon tea is laid out on the polished table for you to help yourself; tea comes in large pots to be drunk in the depths of a chintzy armchair in the drawing room. Some bedrooms are in the old house, others in the new wing, and all have bathroom and toilet. A few units have magnificent views over the gardens and down to the distant river, and others overlook the private golf course.

The chef, Howard Roberts, down from the north, is a man of great skill, and meals are a selection of international and English dishes. Portions are large. Included in the cost of your room is the free use of the indoor, heated swimming pool. The glass walls roll back in summer to join it to the garden, and in winter an enormous log fire burns on the open grate for additional heating. The main attraction for many is the 18-hole golf course with greens fees of £4 ($6) a day, £18.50 ($27.75) a week. But for those who just want to walk, the gardens slope down to a private cove where sailboats lie at anchor and gulls wheel raucously above the water.

Peter Whiteside, a Canadian, owns and runs the place with the help of his son, Justin. Their boast is that a Whiteside is always on duty, and they certainly have an excellent staff to back up their efforts. Dinner, bed, and a full breakfast in low season costs £32 ($48) per person, rising to £44 ($66) from mid-June until the end of September. VAT is included. A set lunch costs £8 ($12); a set dinner, £10.50 ($15.75). You can also order à la carte in the dining room.

A Gourmet Stopover

Riverside, Helford, near Helston (tel. 032-623/443), is run by George Perry Smith, proprietor/chef, who says that the war taught him simplicity and good housekeeping. He used that training to open and build up the highly successful Hole in the Wall restaurant in Bath before moving to Helford. Here he has repeated his success, offering a fixed-price menu in his small, French-provincial-style restaurant in two 18th-century cottages beside the Helford River in a magic and romantic part of Cornwall. There are 12 tables with a capacity of 40 diners. Furnishings are in keeping with the cottage style of the house. Heather Crosby and six young local women see that you are well looked after. A table is yours for the evening, so there's no rushing to clear up for the next serving. Reservations are essential, or your trip here could be wasted.

Try the rissoles à la Parisienne with consommé or the brandade of smoked mackerel in pastry, followed by salmon baked in pastry with currants and ginger. Perhaps you might prefer the bourride, a Provençal fish stew with aioli and rouille sauce. Main courses include chicken, Georgian style, with grapes and oranges, or shoulder of lamb Boulangere, cooked slowly with coriander, garlic, and potatoes. Some succulent desserts include walnut treacle tart, St. Emilion au chocolat, and iced lemon soufflé. The set price of £20 ($30) includes VAT and service. All dishes are made of fresh local produce.

The Riverside also has overnight accommodations. The six double rooms have private baths, some with TV and some with fine views. The cost is £50 ($75) to £55 ($82.50) per night for two persons, with a continental breakfast of fresh homemade croissants and homemade marmalade, VAT, and service all included. Although the place is open from March to October, dinner is provided to nonresidents only Tuesday to Saturday from 7:30 to 9:30 p.m. Residents may take all their meals here daily.

8. Penzance

This little Gilbert and Sullivan harbor town is the end of the line for the Cornish Riviera Express. A full 280 miles southwest from London, it is noted for its equable climate (it's one of the first towns in England to blossom out with spring flowers), and summer throngs descend for fishing, sailing, and swimming. Overlooking Mount's Bay, Penzance is graced in places with subtropical plants, as well as palm trees.

The harbor is used to activity of one sort or another. *The Pirates of Penzance* were not entirely fictional. The town was raided by Barbary pirates, destroyed in part by Cromwell's troops, sacked and burnt by the Spaniards, and bombed by the Germans. In spite of its turbulent past, it offers tranquil resort living today.

The most westerly town in England, Penzance makes a good base for exploring Land's End, The Lizard peninsula, St. Michael's Mount, the old fishing ports and artists' colonies of St. Ives, Newlyn, and Mousehole—even the Isles of Scilly.

THE SIGHTS: St. Michael's Mount is reached at low tide by a causeway three miles east of Penzance. Rising about 250 feet from the sea, St.

Michael's Mount is topped by a partially medieval, partially 17th-century castle. At high tide the mount becomes an island, reached only by motor launch from Marazion. A Benedictine monastery, the gift of Edward the Confessor, stood on this spot in the 11th century. The castle, with its collections of armor and antique furniture, is open, weather and tide permitting, April to October on Monday, Tuesday, Wednesday, and Friday from 10:30 a.m. to 4:45 p.m. (November to March, on Monday, Wednesday, and Friday when possible). It charges £2 ($3) for adults, £1 ($1.50) for children. In winter, you can only go over when the causeway is dry. If you mistime it, they won't send a boat over to pick you up and rescue you from the island. There is, however, a tea garden and a café on the island, both of which are open in summer so you probably won't starve to death. *Warning:* The steps up to the castle are steep and rough, so wear stout shoes.

From Penzance, take bus 20, 21, or 22, then get off at Marazion, the town opposite St. Michael's Mount. To avoid disappointment, it is a good idea to telephone the office of St. Michael's Mount (tel. 0736/710507) to learn the state of the tides, especially during the winter months when a regular ferry service does not operate.

Craggy **Land's End** is where England comes to an end. Here you'll find the last of everything. Land's End, lying nine miles west of Penzance, is reached by bus 1 or 1B.

The **Minack Theatre** in Porthcurno, nine miles from Penzance, is unique. It's carved out of the Cornish cliff-face with the Atlantic as its impressive backdrop. In tiered seating, similar to that of the theaters of Ancient Greece, 550 persons can watch the show and the rocky coast beyond the stage. The theater is generally open to visitors, who come sometimes just for sightseeing, although you may want to attend an evening performance. To reach Minack, leave Penzance on the A30 heading toward Land's End. After three miles, bear left onto the B3283 and follow the signposts to Porthcurno. Or you can take bus 4 or 4A from Penzance. For details, telephone St. Buryan 471 during the season, lasting from the end of June to mid-September. Seats cost around £1.50 ($2.25) at the box office.

WHERE TO STAY: Back in Penzance, it is time to find a room.

The **Abbey Hotel,** Abbey Street (tel. 0736/66906), is a well-preserved old place that is frequented by discerning guests. The bonus is its situation (on a narrow sidestreet, on several terraces, directly overlooking Penzance harbor). The owners, the Cox family, have brought their vitality, style, and charm into the hotel business. You can stay at the Abbey, having only your room and breakfast, or all of your meals in the restaurant downstairs, where dinners, for around £10 ($15), include what Mrs. Cox describes as grand nursery food—good, wholesome, and filling. She was the world-renowned model of the '60s, Jean Shrimpton. The B&B rate per person averages around £18 ($27), including VAT. Some of the larger and better appointed rooms may run higher. Behind the hotel is a tiny formal garden on two tiers, each with a view of the water. Here the herbs are grown that are used to spice the delicately flavored meats in the restaurant downstairs.

Richmond Lodge, 61 Morrab Rd. (tel. 0736/5560), is one of the friendliest guest houses in Cornwall, in a convenient position making it an ideal center from which to explore the whole of the Land's End peninsula. An informal atmosphere prevails. The owners, Jean and Pat Eady, possess a wealth of local knowledge and are always at hand to attend to your needs. Good home-style cooking is served in an attractively furnished Delft blue and white dining room. You have the opportunity to experience living in a delightful early (1890) Victorian town house on the B&B plan for £7 ($10.50) nightly. Dinner costs an additional £3.50 ($5.25) per night.

READER'S HOTEL SELECTION: "The **Georgian House,** Chapel Street (tel. 0736/5664), once the home of the mayors of Penzance, has been completely renovated into a cozy, intimate hotel. The proprietors, Derek and Brenda Gibbard, with their friendly manner made us feel right at home and attended to all our needs promptly and cheerfully. The relaxed atmosphere of the dining room with its sea motif goes well with the excellent Cornish menu. The hotel is centrally heated and carpeted throughout. Our room was newly furnished, well lighted, and had a full bath. The rate in a room without a private bath is £8.50 ($12.75) per person per night, rising to £10.50 ($15.75) per person with bath, including breakfast. The location is a plus in that it is directly across the street from the Admiral Benbow Restaurant, and only two blocks from the town center in one direction and the harbor and Promenade in the other" (Ben N. Cox, Wabash, Ind.).

WHERE TO EAT: **Harris's Restaurant,** 46 New St. (tel. 0736/4408), is owned and run by a husband-and-wife team, the Harrises. It's a pleasant, warm, and candlelit place with a relaxed atmosphere. Ron Harris cooks tempting dishes served upstairs for light lunches, costing about £1.80 ($2.70) to £4 ($6) per plate. Foods include sauteed kidneys with fresh vegetables and liver and bacon with tomatoes, plus homemade soup, fresh pâté, and smoked fish. Both lunch and dinner can be ordered à la carte in the restaurant, with pâtés, soups, avocados, and crab appetizers. Main dishes of steak, pheasant, lamb, sole, and venison can be followed by fresh-made desserts. Lunch in the restaurant will cost about £12 ($18) to £15 ($22.50) with wine. Dinner with wine will come to £15 ($22.50) to £18 ($27). Harris's is open Monday to Saturday from 7 to 10 p.m. (closed Monday in winter).

Le Tarot, 19 Quay St. (tel. 0736/3118), brings sophistication and intimate ambience with flair to the cuisine offered in Penzance. Classic French dishes and local specialties are prepared by expert chefs under the watchful eye of the proprietor, Keith Kennedy. When he left industry to become a restaurateur in Cornwall, he hired chef Martin Robbins, who came from Leiths in London. Each dish is cooked to order, so plan a leisurely meal on such dishes as bonne femme turbot Nelson, lobster Américaine, steak au poivre, to name but a few. All ingredients are the freshest possible. A three-course meal goes for £10 ($15), plus another £3 ($4.50) for the French house wine. A three-course traditional Sunday lunch is offered for £6.50 ($9.75). The restaurant is open seven nights a week from June to October. During the rest of the year, it closes on Tuesday and Sunday.

The **Admiral Benbow,** Chapel Street (tel. 0736/3448), is a restaurant-cum-museum dedicated to the sea that has to be experienced to be believed. What started out as a simple two-story timbered inn has grown into a showcase of nautical objects. Open every day of the week for morning coffee, lunch, and dinner, it serves meals on the lower floor with its nooks and crannies, benches and booths. On the upper level there's a lounge bar (you wait here for a table if Admiral Benbow can't take any more on board downstairs). If you prefer to eat in the bar, a hot and cold buffet luncheon is served, where for £3 ($4.50) you may choose from a wide selection of cold meats, pâtés, and quiches, all served with fresh salad. The inn is owned by Roland Morris, a professional diver who has been discovering treasures for years on old wrecks around Cornwall and the Isles of Scilly.

When you get a table, consult the "Tavern Vittals Chart and Grog Log," the latter studded with everything from fine French bottled clarets to Hungarian Bull's Blood. You'll find the Cornish crab soup as an appetizer. Among the principal à la carte selections are Cornish lobster, roasts, grills, curries, and desserts. For dessert try one of the old English standbys, such as home-cooked fruit tart, although an order of Cornish cream would make it sparkle. Expect to spend £8 ($12) to £11 ($16.50) for a three-course meal.

Attached to the inn is a nightclub, open from 9 p.m. till 1 a.m. It charges half-price admission to the patrons of the restaurant.

On the Outskirts

Lesceave Cliff Hotel, Praa Sands, near Penzance (tel. 073-676/2325), is reached down a tiny lane, well marked off the A394 from Helston to Penzance. You drive down between high banks with nary a view of anything until you suddenly emerge with the spread of Praa Sands lying below you. The hotel owns much of the land between it and the sea, and the uninterrupted views are magnificent. A typical seaside hotel with much white paint, chintz-covered chairs, and bright furnishings, its cheapest low-season rate is £22 ($33), rising to £30 ($45) in high season for a room with a bath and a sea view, including VAT, breakfast, and a five-course dinner. The whole of the Cornish peninsula is close at hand.

LAND'S END: Craggy Land's End, where England comes to a stop, is where you'll find the last of everything. It lies nine miles west of Penzance and is reached by bus 1 or 1B. America's coast is 3291 miles away to the west of the rugged rocks that tumble into the sea beneath Land's End.

Big business has taken over Britain's most southwesterly peninsula, where you are often blown almost horizontal by transatlantic winds, and you must pay £1.50 ($2.25) to drive to "The End." You can park outside and walk in free, however. Besides the view, there are two museums and a crafts center where young artists and artisans practice and demonstrate their crafts. You can purchase pots, jewelry, and souvenirs. The snackbar has simple fare if you're hungry.

Old Success Inn, Sennen Cove (tel. 073-687/232), is a popular spot, because from here you can walk the cliffs to Land's End. If you come by car, turn right just before you reach Land's End and follow the road to Sennen Cove. The Old Success lies at the bottom, facing the sea and wide sandy beaches. Surfing rollers come in from the Atlantic almost to the foot of the sea wall beneath the 17th-century fishermen's inn. Over the years it has been extended and modernized, now offering bright, clean rooms, many with private bath, all with radio, tea and coffee maker, electric heater, and wash basin. Gillian and Tony Webster, who have run the place for the past few years, charge £13 ($19.50) per person for B&B in low season, £18 ($27) per person in high.

Downstairs, there is a lounge with color TV and fantastic panoramic views over the Atlantic, a cozy lounge bar, and Charlie's Bar, where the locals and fishermen join the inn residents in the evening. The chef, Don

Woodward, provides hot and cold snacks at lunch and a set three-course evening meal for £8 ($12). Fresh local fish with fresh vegetables are featured. Try the grilled river trout or the fresh Cornish crab with salad. Bar snacks start at £1.50 ($2.25) for a crab sandwich. A few hot dishes are offered, but generally salads with seafood predominate.

For those who seek more energetic exercise than an evening walk along the sand or the cliffs, there is the Surf Bar by the beach, which is separated from the inn by a large car park. Disco music is played on summer evenings.

9. The Isles of Scilly

Perhaps the most interesting and scenic excursion from Penzance is a day trip to the Isles of Scilly, which lie off the Cornish coast about 27 miles west-southwest of Land's End. There are five inhabited and more than 100 uninhabited islands in the group, some consisting merely of a few square miles of land while others, such as the largest, St. Mary's, encompass some 30 square miles. Two of these islands attract tourists, St. Mary's and Tresco.

These islands were known to the early Greeks and the Romans, and in Celtic legend they were inhabited entirely by holy men. There are more ancient burial mounds in the islands than anywhere else in southern England, and artifacts found establish clearly that people lived more than 4000 years ago.

Today there is little left of this long history to show the visitor. Now these are islands of peace and beauty where early flowers are the main export and tourism the main industry.

St. Mary's is the capital, with about seven-eighths of the total population of all the islands, and it is here that the ship from the mainland docks at Hugh Town. However, for the day visitor, I recommend the helicopter flight from Penzance to **Tresco,** the neighboring island, where you can enjoy a day's walk through the 735 acres, mostly occupied by the celebrated **Abbey Gardens.** These gardens were started by Augustus Smith in the mid-1830s. When he began work, the area was a barren hillside, a fact visitors find hard to believe.

The gardens are a collector's dream, with more than 5000 species of plants from some 100 different countries. The old abbey, or priory, is a ruin said to have been founded by Benedictine monks in the 11th century, although some historians date it from A.D. 964. Of special interest in the gardens is **Valhalla,** a collection of nearly 60 figureheads from ships wrecked around the islands. There is a rather eerie atmosphere surrounding these gaily painted figures from the past, each one a ghost with a different story to tell.

After a visit to the gardens, walk through the fields, along paths, and across dunes thick with heather. Flowers, birds, shells, and fish are so abundant that Tresco is a naturalist's dream and a walker's paradise. Birds are so unafraid that they land within a foot or so of you and feed happily.

HOW TO GET THERE: The **Isles of Scilly Steamship Company Ltd.,** Quay Street, Penzance (tel. 0736/2009), has daily departures from March to October, except Sunday. The trip from Penzance to Hugh Town, St. Mary's, takes about three hours. Steamships leave Penzance at 9:30 a.m. and return from Scilly at 4:30 p.m. In winter, there is a restricted service. Rates start with a walk-on one-way fare of £8 ($12) for adults,

£4 ($6) for children. A same-day round trip costs £15 ($22.50) for adults, £7.50 ($11.25). A short-stay round-trip ticket, which you can use to go back and forth for four days, sells for £22.50 ($33.75) for adults, £11.25 ($16.88) for children. However, if you are staying at one of the better establishments in the islands, you should check with the management, as they can often arrange discounted tickets for the crossing. To visit the other islands, go first to St. Mary's and take the small inter-island boat. For information, phone Kathie Stedford at 0720/22886.

British Airways, at the Penzance Airport (tel. 0736/3871), operates a year-round **helicopter service** between Penzance and St. Mary's, as well as to Tresco from March to October. Flight time is 20 minutes. The standard fare from Penzance to either of the islands is £17 ($25.50) each way. There also is a round trip at £31 ($46.50) if you return the same day, and you should ask when you make your reservations whether there are any special offers. Flights start at 8 a.m. in high season, July to October, and at 8:50 a.m. the remainder of the year. They continue regularly throughout the day, with the last flight back to Penzance at 6 p.m. in high season, 4 p.m. otherwise. For people arriving in Penzance on the overnight train from London, there is a bus service between the railway station and the heliport. The cost is 50p (75¢), and travel time is about five minutes. Helicopter departures are timed to connect with the trains.

Brymon Airways, City Airport, Crownhill, Plymouth (tel. 0752/707023), operates airplane flights from Heathrow and Gatwick via Plymouth to St. Mary's. The charge is £68.50 ($102.75) per person one way from London to St. Mary's. Flying time is 2 hours and 10 minutes, with a short stop at Plymouth. The one-way fare from Plymouth to St. Mary's is £31.50 ($47.25). There are no flights on Sunday.

Whatever the transportation you take, there is a 50p (75¢) landing fee for Tresco.

British Rail runs express trains from Paddington Station, London, to Penzance. BritRail passes can be used. Otherwise, the second-class round-trip fare is £81 ($121.50), with a first-class round trip costing £120 ($180). Travel time is about five hours. There are special offers on the Night Riviera Express, with a first-class, one-way ticket, including a sleeper, going for £55 ($82.50). The round-trip fare on this train is £110 ($165). These prices, of course, compare favorably with the cost of driving some 350 miles, plus one night's accommodation.

For those who wish to travel to Penzance by road, there are good express **bus** services. The Rapide costs £13 ($19.50) per person one way, £19.75 ($29.63) round trip, for the journey from London, 7½ hours each way. The slower service takes 9 hours and costs £9 ($13.50) one way, £14.50 ($21.75) round trip. The buses are fitted with toilets, and the Rapide service has reclining seats, television, and a hostess who dispenses coffee, tea, and sandwiches. These buses are run by the **National Bus Co.,** Victoria Coach Station, 172 Buckingham Palace Rd., London, S.W.1 (tel. 01/730-0202).

WHERE TO STAY AT TRESCO: The top hostelry here is the **Island Hotel** (tel. 0720/22883), a modern establishment on the northeast side of the island with views that have been compared to those seen in the Greek islands. The building blends with the sea and the rocks, and long, low extensions have been added to an original cottage. Some rooms overlook the sea, some facing inland. Most have private bathrooms, toilets, drying racks, color TV, phones, and razor points. All are comfortably furnished with easy chairs and reasonable storage space. Managers John and Wendy Pyatt charge rates that vary considerably, according to location and time of year. The cheapest single without bath is £31.50 ($47.25) in low season, rising to £36.50 ($54.75) at peak time for dinner, bed, a full English breakfast, and VAT. Doubles and twins without bathrooms go for the same per-person rate. The top charge is £64 ($96) per person per night for half board in a suite. A room with land and sea views in the cottage wing, the original and best part of the hotel, costs £40 ($60) per person per night for half board. Understandably, one-night stays are not encouraged, a three-night minimum being preferred. The hotel is closed from October to March.

Don't forget: On Tresco, you walk or bicycle. There are no cars or buses on the island.

The only other hotel on Tresco is the **New Inn** (tel. 0720/22844), run by Bruce Hopkins. His pub, built of stone and standing on the island's road, has an outdoor area for those who wish to picnic and drink a glass of ale. Inside, the bar is the meeting place for locals and tourists alike. Chances are that lunchtime will see Roy Cooper, the island historian and postmaster, swapping gossip with gardener Peter Clough, who heads the Abbey Gardens staff.

Lunch snacks are available: homemade soup, hot smoked mackerel with lemon sauce, grilled whole sole, steaks, the hot dish of the day, lobster salad, and fruit pie. The price per selection is £1.50 ($2.25), going up to £7.50 ($11.25) for lobster or T-bone steak. You can have what the English call a good fill for around £6 ($9). Dinners are £10 ($15). All the day's specials are put on the bar blackboard. The pictures in the bar are worth a look. They show many of the ships that sank or foundered around the islands in the past, as well as some of the gigs used in pilotage, rescue, smuggling, and pillage.

The inn has 12 rooms, all twins and doubles with private bathrooms. Here too there is a wide range of prices. In high season—July, August, and early September—reservations are taken for three nights maximum, so as to give other people a chance to stay on the island for a short period. Other times of year the hotel offers a number of special packages, which include, for example, the cost of the flight from Penzance and a three-day stay at the New Inn for £65 ($97.50) per person. Prices range from £26 ($39) per person to £32 ($48) per person, all tariffs including a full English breakfast, a four-course dinner, and VAT. The inn has a heated outdoor swimming pool.

Tresco also has a number of **self-catering cottages** available. One sleeping four persons in two double rooms costs from £90 ($108) per week up to £300 ($450) per week in high season. A cottage accommodating ten persons in four double and two single rooms rents for £125 ($187.50) to £470 ($705) per week. An apartment in Tresco Abbey with one twin-bedded room goes for £90 ($108) to £225 ($337.50) per week. All properties are fully furnished and equipped with central heating, gas cookers, and color TV, but bed linen and food are not provided. Many cottages have a sea view and their own small, trim gardens. For further information on the cottages in the Abbey Gardens, write to Kenneth Christopher, the Tresco Estate, Isle of Scilly, Cornwall (tel. 0720/22849).

WHAT TO DO AND SEE IN TRESCO: The Tresco Estate has **boats** for rent through the office. An 18-foot Starfish with outboard, gunter rig, and foresail is £15 ($22.50) per day, and there are **boat trips** organized to various other islands and out to the noted Bishop Rock lighthouse, at prices ranging from £2.50 ($3.75) to £3.50 ($5.25) per person. Seafishing and private cruises with experienced boatmen can be arranged by the Estate office.

David Hunt leads **naturalist safaris** around the island and to other uninhabited islets for from £2.50 ($3.75) per person, according to the trip's length and the boating involved.

The **Abbey Gardens** and **Valhalla** are open daily from 10 a.m. to 4 p.m. Admission is £1.75 ($2.63) for adults, 75p ($1.13) for children. An adult ticket valid for one week costs £3.50 ($5.25) and allows you to make repeat visits.

No cars or motorbikes are allowed on the island, but **bicycles** can be rented for £2 ($3) per day. The hotels use a special wagon towed by a farm tractor to transport guests and luggage from the harbor.

WHERE TO STAY AT ST. MARY'S: Hotel Godolphin (tel. 0720/22316)

gives the impression, as you approach it, of being a substantial stone-built private house—which is what it was until the Mumford family, who own and operate it, decided to make it into a hotel. This they have done with skillful additions, creating a fine hostelry in the town. There are 32 bedrooms, most with bathrooms and all with central heating, tea- or coffee-making equipment, color TV, three-channel radio, and intercom. The best rooms overlook the garden. Rates vary according to location and season, going from £21 ($31.50) per person in low season in a room without bath to £25 ($37.50) in high season for the same accommodation. In low season, a room with bath and a garden view is £27 ($40.50) per person, the same facilities renting for £32 ($48) per person in high season. There are some ground-floor twins. The hotel offers reductions for stays of four nights or more. All rates include a full English breakfast, a four-course dinner, service, and VAT. B&B only can be arranged, but you are likely to want to have dinner here also.

Good bar snacks are available at lunchtime, including salads, hot dishes, and sandwiches, or else picnic lunches can be arranged. Dinners, priced at £10 ($15), offer a wide choice. There is always a roast joint or two, fish, and poultry.

Incidentally, the hotel's name comes from the name of the estate on which the building stands, originating in the reign of Queen Elizabeth I, who gave the island to Francis Godolphin in 1571.

Star Castle Hotel (tel. 0720/22317) is in a structure built as a castle in 1593 in the shape of an eight-pointed star. It was erected for the defense of the Isles of Scilly against attacks by Spain in retaliation for the 1588 defeat of the Armada by Sir Francis Drake and the English fleet out of Plymouth —plus an assist by Mother Nature. Because of the purpose of the original building, the hotel, owned and operated by Lesley and Don Reynolds, has magnificent views out to sea as well as over the town and the harbor. The great kitchen has a huge fireplace where a whole ox could be roasted. The oak-beamed dining room was the original officers' mess. An early Prince of Wales (later King Charles II) took shelter here in 1643 when he was being hunted by Cromwell and his parliamentary forces.

In 1933 another Prince of Wales was here to officiate at the opening of the castle as a hotel. This was the man who succeeded to the throne as King

Edward VIII but was never crowned, abdicating in order to marry Mrs. Wallis Simpson.

The hotel has 25 bedrooms, some in the Scandinavian-style garden annex, which is about 50 yards from the castle, surrounded by pine trees and overlooking part of the four acres of gardens. Most rooms have private bathrooms. In the castle, four of the six double or twin rooms have their own baths. The two double rooms in the castle without bathrooms have wash basins and are, I think, the most interesting, as they are in points of the star overlooking the sea and the town. They are much favored for their isolation on the ramparts, although the bathroom is a few yards away— across those ramparts. All rooms are well heated and have tea- and coffee-making facilities. Rent for a room with bath in the castle in low season is £20 ($30) per person; without bath, £18.50 ($27.75) per person. In high season, the rates in a bathless room are £20 ($30) per person, £24 ($36) per person with bath. All tariffs include a full English breakfast and dinner, but VAT and 10% service are added to your bill.

There is an open-air, heated swimming pool, and the garden has many sheltered places for you to relax. Lunch and dinner orders are taken in the Cellar Bar, where lunchtime snacks are available. A four-course dinner costs £7.50 ($11.25), plus VAT and service. Typical English food is served, and many of the vegetables come from the hotel's large gardens.

Carnwethers Country Guest House, Pelistry Bay (tel. 0720/22415), is a modern, two-story house with a one-story extension, standing on top of a hill looking down to fields, beach, and the sea. Pelistry Bay is a secluded part of St. Mary's island, the sandy beach well sheltered. For lovers of the countryside who don't want to travel to Tresco but wish for quiet, open space to walk in, this is the spot. I am told that once a guest was disturbed when a cow got into a nearby field and grazed on the lush grass in a noisy manner! If you really want seclusion, you can walk at low tide across to the nearby uninhabited island of Tolls. A heated, outdoor swimming pool can add to your pleasure at the guest house.

There are eight bedrooms—four doubles, three family units, and one single. All but two have private bathrooms, and all are spotless, warm, and comfortable. The place is owned and operated by Roy and Joyce Graham, with Joyce personally supervising the kitchen. For dinner, although the choice is limited, traditional English fare is offered in good quantity to satisfy appetites whetted by the sea air. Dinner, served at 6:30 p.m., is never precooked or reheated. Only fresh local produce and home-grown vegetables are used. Breakfast is a substantial meal, the marmalade being a particular pride of the house. Rates per person, including breakfast, dinner, and VAT, start at £19 ($28.50), rising to £24 ($36) from May to September. An extra £3 ($4.50) is charged for private facilities. The single-room supplement is £4 ($6). For B&B only, deduct £4 ($6) from the prices quoted.

WHAT TO DO AND SEE IN ST. MARY'S: Carnwethers Marine Study Centre, Pelistry Bay (tel. 0720/22415), is operated by genial, bearded Roy Graham, who also owns the guest house reviewed above. He was, for 20 years, a Royal Navy diving officer and has more than 15 years of experience in exploring the waters around the Isles of Scilly. He offers facilities for individuals and small groups who wish to study the local marine environment, whether their interest is conservation, archeology, biology, or underwater photography. He has his own darkroom, so if you plan to do underwater photography, let him know in advance if you want to get your pictures developed quickly.

Graham can direct you to the best wrecks to view, and arrange diving boats. He says there are more than 1500 ships to which names can be put that have been lost around the islands. He has an extensive library with many photos and video film on underwater matters. Tanks, weights, and regulators can all be arranged for, but you must provide your own wetsuit. The waters around the Scillies are ideal for underwater activities, the temperature ranging between 50° and 55° Fahrenheit, being coldest in March and warmest in September.

If Roy cannot help you personally, he knows who to put you in touch with to pursue your particular nautical interests.

As secretary to the Islands Tourist Committee, Graham organizes various lectures, given on Tuesday and Sunday in the church hall, some illustrated with slides. They cover general subjects, such as the history of the islands, the flora and fauna, and local legends.

To rent a boat for a trip or for fishing, get in touch with **St. Mary's Boatman's Association,** an organization that keeps an eye on all craft, making sure that they have certificates of seaworthiness from the Board of Trade (the government body that controls the regulations) and that they carry more than the statutory safety equipment. The address is St. Mary's Boatman's Association, St. Mary's, Isles of Scilly (tel. 0720/22469).

At the **Isles of Scilly Underwater Centre,** Warleggan, Church Street, High Town, St. Mary's (tel. 0720/22563), two dives will cost around £9 ($13.50) per day, and diving partners can be arranged.

There is a nine-hole **golf** course at Telegraph Tower (tel. 0720/22692). Daily greens fees are £5 ($7.50); club rental, £1.75 ($2.63); and club cart rental, 60p (90¢). Weekly membership is £15 ($22.50). There is a good clubhouse where you can get light lunches and dinners.

Isles of Scilly Wildlife Safaris, Porthcressa, St. Mary's (tel. 0720/22740), offer a weekly excursion program with a local naturalist, for birdwatching, boat trips, and wild flower study. If you write, include an International Reply Coupon.

The **Isles of Scilly Museum,** St. Mary's, is open daily in summer from 10 a.m. to noon, 1:30 to 4:30 p.m., and 7 to 9 p.m. In winter, it is open only on Wednesday, from 1:30 to 4:30 p.m. Admission is 25p (38¢). The museum shows the history of the islands from 1500 B.C., with artifacts from wrecked ships, drawings, and relics discovered in the Scillies. It is an interesting small museum, well looked after.

Cars are available to rent, but they're hardly necessary.

The **Island Bus service** has a basic charge of 30p (45¢) for adults, 10p (15¢) for children.

Bicycles can be rented for £1.50 ($2.25) for 24 hours, £7 ($10.50) for a week. Apply to D. Guy, Atlantic View, High Lanes, near Telegraph, St. Mary's (tel. 0720/22684).

St. Mary's **gig races** are rowing events held for men on Friday for 22 weeks of the year, with women's races taking place on alternate Wednesdays. The gigs were mostly built by one man in the 1800s and have survived until now. Rowed by six men, they recall the olden days when the gig was used to ferry a pilot out to sailing ships entering the English Channel so that he could guide them safely to Bristol or London. The pilotage charge was split between the pilot and the crew of the gig. The races have their origin in the competition between gigs to get to the ship first, to put a pilot aboard, and win the fee. Oars were limited by the Excise men to six per gig so that the crews, inclined to do a bit of smuggling on the side, could not outrun the revenue cutter. The races are the islands' most popular sport and are always well attended by fiercely partisan backers.

10. Newlyn and Mousehole

For even more interesting living than that described above, we turn to the outlying district of Penzance, heading south to Newlyn and Mousehole.

NEWLYN: From Penzance, a promenade leads to Newlyn, a mile away, another fishing village of charm on Mount's Bay. Stanhope Forbes, now dead, founded an art school in Newlyn. The village has an artists' colony, attracting both the serious painter and the amateur sketcher. From Penzance, Newlyn is reached by taking bus 1 or 1B. For a dining or overnighting recommendation, try the following.

The **Smugglers Hotel and Restaurant,** Fore Street (tel. 0736/4207), is the central mecca for those who create in clay and paint. An artist's dream-come-true, this little two-story inn lies right on the roadside, across from the Newlyn Harbor. You pay £15 ($22.50) in a single, £26 ($39) in a double for a good bed and a big Cornish breakfast. The rooms are bright and sparkling clean, with innerspring mattresses and water basins. With a bath en suite, a room costs an extra £5 ($7.50) per day. Good shore dinners are served till around 10 p.m. All meals are à la carte, averaging from £9 ($13.50) to £15 ($22.50) per person, depending on your selection. David and Debra Reeve are the hosts, and Pirate the parrot keeps the entertainment side going. Conversation in the lounge or in the dining room is often most rewarding. The bar is found in the granite-walled cellars, with tables and benches made from local driftwood. The original tunnel used by smugglers, although now blocked, can still be seen.

MOUSEHOLE: Still another Cornish fishing village, Mousehole lies three miles south of Penzance (take bus 9). The hordes of tourists who flock here haven't changed it drastically: the gulls still squawk, the cottages still huddle close to the harbor wall (although they look as if they were built more to be photographed than lived in), the fishermen still bring in the day's catch, the salts sit around with their pipes talking about the good old days, and the lanes are as narrow as ever. About the most exciting thing that's occurred around here was the arrival in the late 16th century of Spanish galleons, whose sailors sacked and burnt the village. In a sheltered cove, off Mount's Bay, Mousehole (pronounced mou-sel) has developed an artists' colony, which is home to both painters and potters. For rooms and meals, try the following recommendations in the village.

Old Coastguard Hotel, The Parade (tel. 0736/731222), is a 19th-century structure, on the edge of Mousehole, with a private, unspoiled view of the bay. Open all year, it's a center for artists and others who enjoy such an atmosphere. The old inn has stairways and halls leading directly to the oddly shaped bedrooms. For a bathless double, the owners, L. J. and K. J. Best, experienced hotel and pub operators, charge from £15 ($22.50) per person nightly. This rate includes a full breakfast with, if you wish, mackerel, fresh Newlyn sole or kippers, or perhaps sausage, egg, and bacon, served with fruit juice, tea, or coffee. Dinners, served from 7 to 9:30 p.m., are exceptional too. Every night you can select from the à la carte menu, which has a wide range of seafoods. They also have two special menus that offer a three-course meal for residents only. Also served between 6 and 9:30 p.m. is an extensive range of hot and cold bar meals. All prices are inclusive of service and VAT.

On the Outskirts

Lamorna Cove Hotel, at Lamorna Cove, near Penzance (tel. 073-673/411). This is one of the most perfect Cornish coves, seemingly inaccessible down a winding, narrow road, dropping always toward the sea until you suddenly emerge onto the sea wall of the tiny cove.

Above the cove, signposted off the approach lane, lies the Lamorna Cove Hotel. The present owners, Mr. and Mrs. Gordon Bolton, have carefully added to the old stone building, once a tiny chapel with a bell tower. They once even blasted several tons of rock from the cliff face to provide more room, a peaceful haven with views over the sea and the cove. The bar is in the chapel. A large dining room runs the length of the building, and there are several lounges full of comfortable chairs, with a roaring log fire in winter.

Accommodations are in the main hotel with bath or shower, some with balcony. There are also two cottages, one suitable for four, the other for five persons. A rocky garden clings to the cliffside and then surrounds a small swimming pool with a sun-trap terrace overlooking the sea. B&B ranges from £28 ($42) per person in low season to £34 ($51) per person in summer in double accommodation. There is also a suite available and a deluxe double room, costing from £38 ($57) to £43 ($64.50) per person per night. From October until the end of May, prices are substantially reduced.

If you do not have the time to stay at the hotel, their bar lunches can be well recommended. On Sunday, a traditional luncheon of sirloin of beef, filet of sole, or pork chops, buttered cabbage, rutabagas, roast potatoes (fresh vegetables in season), followed by pie with Cornish cream, brandy snaps, or cheese costs around £8 ($12). Dinners at £12 ($18) are quite a feast.

A DINING SELECTION: Between Sennen and St. Ives lies a worthy stop. The **Count House Restaurant,** Botallack, St. Just (tel. 0736/788588), is the most southwesterly place to dine on the English mainland to be recommended in this book. It is worth every mile you'll travel to taste the cookery of Ann Long, who with husband, Ian, runs this place. High on the cliffs among ancient tin mines, the building was the old mine workshop and settlement house where miners were paid for their labors. Rough stone walls and a high peaked roof shelter well-spaced assorted tables (there are only ten) set with bright white Wedgwood crockery. A roaring log fire in winter and a warm welcome anytime from Ian and daughter Suzanne help you enjoy your visit.

Dinner is served on Wednesday, Thursday, Friday, and Saturday from 7:30 p.m. It's likely to include pigeon with bacon in mustard sauce with mushrooms or fresh salmon with cream sauce. An average three-course meal will set you back between £11 ($16.50) and £15 ($22.50) per person.

The view of one of the best sunsets in England is free. Only lunch is served on Sunday, a set meal costing £5.50 ($8.25). Reservations are essential.

To find the Count House, take the B3306 out of St. Ives. When you reach the Queen's Arms, you will have just passed the track on the right that leads to the restaurant. That's how a local resident directed me.

11. St. Ives

This north coast fishing village, with its sandy beaches, is England's most famous art colony. Only 20 miles from Land's End, 10 from Penzance, it is a village of narrow streets and well-kept cottages. The artists settled in many years ago and have integrated with the fishermen and their families.

The art colony was established long enough ago to have developed several schools or "splits," and they almost never overlap—except in a pub where the artists hang out, or where classes are held. The old battle continues between the followers of the representational and the devotees of the abstract in art, with each group recruiting young artists all the time. In addition, there are the potters, weavers, and other craftspeople—all working, exhibiting, and selling in this area. There are several galleries to visit, with such names as the Sail Loft.

A word of warning: St. Ives becomes virtually impossible to visit in August, when you're likely to be trampled underfoot by busloads of tourists, mostly the English themselves. However, in spring and early fall, the pace is much more relaxed, and a visitor can have the true experience of the art colony.

Park and Ride: During the summer months, many of the streets in the center of town are closed to vehicles. You may want to leave your car in the Lelant Saltings Car Park, three miles from St. Ives on the A3074, and take the regular train service into town, an 11-minute journey. Departures are every half hour. It's free to all car passengers and drivers, and the car-park charge is about £1.75 ($2.63) a day. Otherwise, you can use the large Trenwith Car Park, close to the town center, for 35p (53¢) a day, and then walk down to the shops and harbor or take a bus, costing 20p (30¢) for adults and 10p (15¢) for children.

BARBARA HEPWORTH MUSEUM: At Trewyn Studio and Garden, on Barnoon Hill (tel. 0736/796226), the former home of Dame Barbara Hepworth contains a museum of sculpture by the artist from 1929 until her death in 1975 together with photographs, letters, and other papers documenting her life and background. The garden too contains sculpture and is well worth a visit. The museum is open year round from 10 a.m. to 5:30 p.m., Monday to Saturday. Closed on Sunday. Admission is 60p (90¢) for adults, 35p (53¢) for children and students. There is limited parking some 200 yards away, but visitors may like to leave their cars at Lelant Station some three miles away and use the park-and-ride service into St. Ives.

WHERE TO STAY: **Tregenna Castle Hotel** (tel. 0736/795254), standing on its own 100 acres, was once a castle. It was optimistically earmarked by Von Ribbentrop to be Hitler's British Berchtesgaden. Approached by a long driveway, it crowns a hill high above the fishing village of St. Ives. While the interior is spacious and a good background for gracious living, the grounds contain gardens and lawns, an open-air, heated swimming pool with a flagstone edging for sunbathers, three lawn tennis courts, three hard courts, a croquet lawn, a putting green, a squash court, a badminton court, and an 18-hole golf course. There are riding stables situated within the grounds and arrangements can be made for shark, mackerel, and fly fishing. The bedrooms usually are of good size, handsomely maintained with contemporary furniture, and more than 80% have private bathrooms. The rates vary according to the season and the location of the room. From June 16 to September 15, the B&B rate, inclusive of service charge and VAT, is from £20 ($30) in a bathless single, £35 ($52.50) in a single with bath. A bathless double costs from £33 ($49.50), from £48 ($72) with bath. A set buffet lunch goes for £8 ($12) and a set dinner for £12 ($18), inclusive of service and VAT. In addition, there is a well-stocked cellar, and an orchestra plays for dancing two nights a week in season.

Garrack Hotel, Higher Ayr (tel. 0736/796199), from its two-acre cliff knoll, commands a panoramic view of St. Ives and Portmeor Beach. The vine-covered little hotel, once a private home, is reached by heading up a narrow lane. It's one of the friendliest and most efficiently run small medium-priced hotels on the entire coast, with rooms furnished in a warm, homey manner. The atmosphere in the living room is inviting, with a log-burning fireplace, antiques, and comfortable chairs. The Garrack belongs to Mr. and Mrs. Kilby, who are proud of their meals (see my dining recommendations).

The Kilbys have added a pleasant wooden leisure building to the hotel with a swimming pool that has a Jacuzzi whirlpool and swim jet, a solarium, and a sauna, all with changing rooms and a small bar overlooking the lovely bay. There is even a small patio where you can sunbathe outside. Some new rooms with baths have been added, including a honeymoon suite. Unlike those in the main house, these are furnished in modern style and all have superb views across the bay. There is a mini-launderette. Rates range from £11 ($16.50) to £15 ($22.50) per person for B&B without bath, £18 ($27) to £22 ($33) per person with bath. The Garrack is open all year.

The **Trecarrell Hotel,** Carthew Terrace (tel. 0736/795707), is housed in a 140-year-old building in a quiet quarter of St. Ives. The restaurant, bar, and kitchen are under the close personal supervision of the proprietors, Don and Liz Fraser, who take pride in their table. The best local produce and meats are used, along with fish caught fresh from the Atlantic Ocean. They make many "Olde English" dishes and offer specialties, such as a citrus and ginger trifle made with fresh oranges, lemons, eggs, and Cornish cream. Continental dishes are also available. The hotel is centrally heated throughout and is small, with 16 guest rooms in all. But each room is individually decorated, and many have private bathrooms or showers.

Rates start with a low-season single with washbasin at £12 ($18) for B&B, £15 ($22.50) if you want a four-course dinner and a room with bath. A double in high season peaks at £25 ($37.50) for two in a room with bath, including dinner, bed, and breakfast. There are 16 different prices for the time of year and the type of room. Dinner for nonresidents is £8.50 ($12.75). The bar is well stocked with beers, liqueurs, and liquors, and a wide range of table wines is available. The Trecarrell is a friendly, spotlessly clean hotel, with excellent service and good food.

WHERE TO EAT: The **Chef's Kitchen,** Halsetown (tel. 0736/796218), stands on a point above St. Ives on a back road to Penzance. It's in an old granite post office, very unobtrusive among the cottages. It's on the left as you come up the main street from St. Ives. Since it's so easy to miss, go slowly. The old post office has been converted into a bar lounge, plus an adjoining cottage that is the restaurant, seating 32 guests. When you reserve a table (and reservations are imperative), you have it for the evening. Orders are taken between 7 and 10:30 p.m. Mr. and Mrs. Wright are joint owners, with Mr. Wright supervising the kitchen. As a chef and chef lecturer, he has had some 20 years of experience, mainly in Oslo and Geneva. Menus are changed every two weeks and range in price from £8.50 ($12.75) to £17 ($25.50) for a three-course dinner with four vegetables and a full seasonal side salad. VAT is included, and there is no service charge.

On my latest rounds, such outstanding dishes were offered as crab claws in almond with prawn sauce, seafood pancakes Cardinal, roast grouse à la anglaise, a ballontine of chicken with a truffle sauce, and salmis of pheasant forestière. A diner seeking a high-class cuisine will not be disappointed here.

The **Garrack Hotel,** Higher Ayr (tel. 0736/796199), the domain of Mr. and Mrs. Kilby, is outstanding, producing an excellent cuisine—using, when possible, fresh vegetables from their own garden. The hotel dining room, open to nonresidents, offers regular à la carte listings, plus cold buffet or snacks at the bar, and an £8.50 ($12.75) dinner from 7 to 8:30 p.m. The menu reflects some of the finest of English dishes, such as roast shoulder of lamb with mint sauce, fried filet of plaice, and a wide sampling of continental fare, such as filet of bass meunière and escalopes de veau Cordon Bleu. If you order before 10 a.m., they will provide a special meal from the shellfish menu—everything will have been brought in that morning by the fishermen, prepared, cooked, and served to you in the evening. Two trolleys are at your service, one with continental cheeses and two antique cheesebells covering half a stilton wheel or a farmhouse cheddar cheese and the other with a wide choice of desserts. (You can have Cornish cream with any dessert, if you wish.) A 10% service charge and VAT are added. The Kilbys' son Michael has joined his parents in the operation of the hotel and restaurant after completing a training period with Claridges in London.

The **Sloop** is right on The Quay, next to the art colony on the hill. The pub has old charm, tracing its history back to 1644, but it's the life here that's important. The Lounge Bar is for daintier types, the Cellar Bar for intimate rendezvousing. But in the Public Bar, you're likely to find artists and old sea dogs mixing congenially. The local fishermen come in for their evening game of darts and to talk to the owner-bartender. Apparently, the success of the pub depends a great deal on the gift of gab of the bartender. A recent visit was memorable. Six rugged Breton sailors made room at their long table for me. Their words were unfathomable, but not their friendliness. They were in port overnight and were sampling the English beer. The youngest, the cabin boy, was tagging along, trying to imitate his older companions. The walls of the interior are covered almost entirely by the works of a master who exchanged them for his nightly ration of good English ale. Bar snacks cost from 50p (75¢) to £2 ($3).

12. Port Isaac

The most unspoiled fishing village on the north Cornish coastline is Port Isaac, nine miles from Wadebridge. This Atlantic coastal resort retains its original character, in spite of the intrusions of large numbers of summer visitors. By all means wander through its winding, narrow lanes, gazing at the whitewashed fishermen's cottages with their rainbow trims.

WHERE TO DRINK AND SNACK: The **Golden Lion,** Fore Street (tel. 020-888/336), is perhaps the most handsomely positioned pub in the old fishing harbor. Owned by Mr. and Mrs. Spry, it offers good drinks, snacks, and crab sandwiches. Light meals cost from £5 ($7.50).

For meals, try the **Harbour Café,** Fore Street (tel. 020-888/237), in the center of the village. It has a special fame, featured several times on British television and once in scenes from the Sherlock Holmes thriller, *The Devil's Foot.* The unique café is designated as a building of architectural and historic interest, and is one of several buildings on this treacherous stretch of coast that used the timber of wrecked galleons in construction. The owners, Messrs. Wooding and Muller, offer complete meals as well as snacks. On the menu are such local dishes as crab and mackerel salads, plus a number of other specialties, with selected table wines. Meals begin at around £6.50 ($9.75). Perhaps you will arrive in the afternoon, when you can have a real Cornish cream tea, and if your appetite is still unsatisfied, you may care to try some homemade cake topped with a portion of clotted cream.

READERS' HOTEL SELECTIONS: "The **Tre-Pol-Pen Hotel** (tel. 020-888/232) is in the newer part of the village, just before the steep descent down into the cove and the old section. Charges are £12 ($18) per person during the main season for clean, bright rooms, a substantial breakfast (several choices), use of a lounge with color TV, and free baths. There is a large dining area where breakfast is served, and Cornish cream teas can be ordered during the afternoon. A meal at night costs from £6 ($9) per person. Some of the rooms have beautiful views of the coast. There is a car park, which is necessary, as to drive down into the village is difficult in winter and virtually impossible in summer. All rooms have hot and cold water and are centrally heated. Bookings are necessary in summer" (Mr. and Mrs. David Peters, Highgate, Australia). . . . "The **Hathaway Guest House** (tel. 020-888/416), is beautifully situated on the cliff on the western side of Port Isaac harbor. The house overlooks not only the village and harbor, but also the coastline and beyond. Resident proprietor Enid Andrews offers colorfully decorated rooms with breakfast year round, at £8 ($12) to £10 ($15) per person. Dinner is available for £5 ($7.50). It is less than a five-minute walk to the pub and shops, and a two-mile cliff walk begins at the door. There's a car park, and children are welcome" (A. Emerson Smith, Columbia, S.C.).

13. Tintagel

On a wild stretch of the Atlantic coast, Tintagel is forever linked with the legends of King Arthur, Lancelot, and Merlin. The Norman ruins, popularly known as "King Arthur's Castle," stand 300 feet above the sea on a rocky promontory. The colorful writing of Lord Tennyson in *Idylls of the King* greatly increased the interest in Tintagel, as did the writings of Geoffrey of Monmouth. The ruins, which date from Geoffrey's time, are what remains of a castle built on the foundations of a Celtic monastery from the sixth century.

In summer, many visitors make the ascent to Arthur's lair, 100 rock-cut steps. You can also visit Merlin's Cave and the "Old Post Office," a miniature 14th-century manor in the center of the village (open May to September, weekdays, 10 a.m. to 8 p.m., and on Sunday from 1 to 5 p.m.).

If you become excited by legends of Knights of the Round Table, you can go to **Camelford,** five miles inland from Tintagel. The market hall there dates from 1790, but more interestingly, the town claims to be Camelot.

The **Old Post Office** (tel. 0208/4281) at Tintagel is a National Trust property. It was once a 14th-century manor, but since the 19th century it has had connections with the post office. In the village center, it has a genuine Victorian post room that is open, April to October, daily from 11 a.m. to 6 p.m., or sunset if earlier. Admission is 80p ($1.20).

WHERE TO STAY: Bossiney House Hotel (tel. 0840/770240) stands in an inviting spot on the right as you approach Tintagel from Boscastle. Two brothers, John and Reg Wrightam, and their families operate the hotel, and everybody combines to make guests feel welcome. The hotel is comfortable, with a TV lounge and a well-stocked bar/lounge, which has a fine view of surrounding meadows marching right up to the tops of the cliffs, as well as of the wide expanse of lawn with a putting green. Rooms are comfortably furnished and have private baths and central heating. The large dining room—where a big English breakfast is served and you can enjoy other well-prepared meals brought to you by smiling Cornishwomen—is so situated as to give a view of the front, side, and back lawns. The price is £20.50 ($30.75) per person for a room with dinner, bed, breakfast, and morning tea served in your room before you go to the dining room for your morning meal. The Wrightams will direct you to interesting places you might otherwise miss seeing in the area. Ask about the nearby pottery. The hotel is closed from early October until spring. Look for the old phaeton and farm implements in the front garden.

Trebrea Lodge, Trenale, near Tintagel (tel. 0840/770410), may appear as a dignified stately home, but in truth it looks and feels inside like an old Cornish farmhouse, although it is centrally heated. It dates back to 1315, and was lived in by the same family for more than 600 years. The house, now owned by Ann and Guy Murray, looks straight out across fields to the sea, and each bedroom has a good view. Rooms are available in many sizes, and each has hot and cold water, color TV, radio, intercom (and even a baby-listening service). Most of the units have private bathrooms. Evenings are cozy in the drawing room around an open fire. You can have drinks in the, bar which is installed in an old fireplace. There is a Victorian smoking room as well. Dining is most informal, and all food is homemade by Mrs. Murray, who has mastered true English recipes. The cost is £16.50 ($24.75) per person for half board.

TALL TREES RIDING CENTRE: At Davidstow, near Camelford (tel. 0846/249), Mrs. Margaret Harrison, with her two daughters and various other assistants and working pupils, runs stables of 23 horses and majestic Bodmin Moor, through forests, and along bridle paths and country lanes. One week of riding, B&B, and dinner starts at £120 ($180) for adults, £60 ($90) for children. A day's riding and lunch costs £18 ($27), while by-the-hour riding is £5 ($7.50).

Chapter X

WILTSHIRE, SOMERSET, AND AVON

1. Salisbury
2. Castle Combe
3. Lacock
4. Wells
5. Bleadney
6. Glastonbury
7. The Caves of Mendip
8. Bath
9. Bristol

FOR OUR FINAL LOOK at the West Countree, we move now into Wiltshire, Somerset, and Avon, the most antiquity-rich shires of England. When we reach this area of woodland and pastoral scenes, London seems far removed—even divorced from the bucolic life here.

On cold, windswept nights in unrecorded times, the Druids used to steal across these plains, armed with twigs. Sheltered by boulders, they'd burn their sloe with rosemary to ward off the danger of witchcraft.

Most people seem to agree that the West Country, a loose geographical term, begins at Salisbury, with its Early English cathedral. Nearby is Stonehenge, England's oldest prehistoric monument. Both Stonehenge and Salisbury are in Wiltshire.

Somerset is even more varied—the diet richer not only in historical cities, but in wild scenic grandeur, especially in Exmoor, the home of the red deer. The legendary burial place of King Arthur at Glastonbury and the cathedral city of Wells also await you on your visit to Somerset. The old Roman city of Bath is the main target in the county of Avon.

WILTSHIRE

When you cross into Wiltshire, you'll be entering a county of chalky, grassy uplands and rolling plains. Most of the shire is agricultural, and a large part is devoted to pastureland. Wiltshire produces an abundance of England's dairy products, and is noted for its sheep raising. In this western shire, you'll traverse the Salisbury Plain, the Vale of Pewsey, and the Marlborough Downs (the last gobbling up the greater part of the land mass). Unquestionably, the crowning achievement of Wiltshire is:

1. Salisbury

Long before you've made the 83-mile trek from London, the spire of Salisbury Cathedral comes into view—just as John Constable painted it so many times. The 404-foot pinnacle of the Early English and Gothic cathedral is the tallest in England. But Salisbury is also a fine base for touring such sights as Stonehenge.

Salisbury, or New Sarum, lies in the valley of the Avon River. Filled with Tudor inns and tea rooms, it is known to readers of Thomas Hardy as Melchester and to the Victorian fans of Anthony Trollope as Barchester.

SALISBURY CATHEDRAL: You can search all of England, but you'll find no purer example of the Early English, or pointed, style than Salisbury Cathedral. Its graceful spire has already been mentioned, but the ecclesiastical building doesn't depend totally on the tower for its appeal.

Construction began as early as 1220, then took 38 years to complete, which was jet-age speed in those days (it was customary to drag out cathedral-building for three centuries at least). The spire began soaring at the end of the 13th century. Despite an ill-conceived attempt at revamping in the 18th century, the architectural harmony of the cathedral was retained.

The cathedral's octagonal Chapter House (note the fine sculpture) is especially attractive, dating from the 13th century. It also contains one of the four copies of Magna Carta, together with treasures from the diocese of Salisbury and manuscripts and artifacts belonging to the cathedral. There is a charge of 20p (30¢) per person to visit the Chapter House. The cloisters enhance the beauty of the cathedral. The Close, with at least 75 buildings in its compound (some from the early 18th century and others predating that), is exceptionally large, setting off the cathedral most fittingly. A donation of 50p (75¢) is asked of each visitor.

The cathedral has a good **Brass Rubbing Centre** where you can choose from a selection of exact replicas molded perfectly from the original brasses. The small charge made for each rubbing includes the cost of materials and a donation to the church from which it comes. The center is open at the cathedral early June to early September Monday to Saturday from 10 a.m. to 5 p.m., from 2 to 5 p.m. on Sunday.

One of the houses in the Close is **Mompesson House,** built by Charles Mompesson in 1701. The home of the Townsend family for more than a century, it is well known for its fine plasterwork ceilings and paneling. There is also a magnificent collection of 18th-century drinking glasses. It is open April to October daily except Thursday and Friday from 12:30 to 6 p.m. or dusk, charging an admission of £1.25 ($1.88).

Also in the Close is the **Regimental Museum** of the Duke of Edinburgh's Royal Regiment, the Berkshire and the Wiltshire. Admission is 75p ($1.13) for adults, 40p (60¢) for children.

TOURS: Wessexplore runs leisurely guided walks through the city and tours of the surrounding countryside, including Stonehenge and Avebury. Telephone Don Cross at 0722/26304 for further information. There are

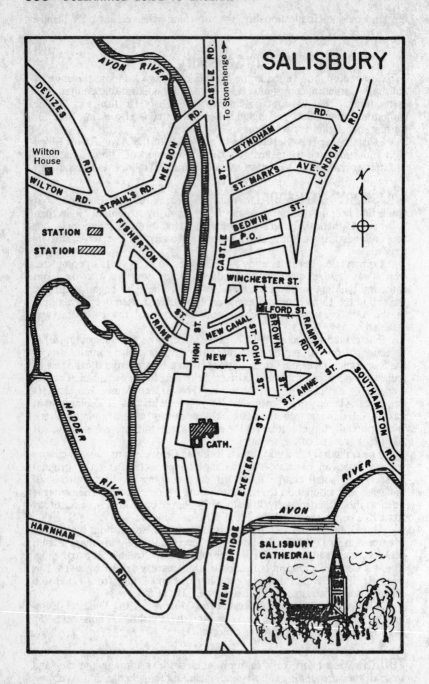

SALISBURY

To Stonehenge →

Wilton House

STATION ▨
STATION ▨▨

WILTON RD.
DEVIZES RD.
AVON RIVER
ST. PAUL'S RD.
NELSON RD.
CASTLE RD.
WYNDHAM ST.
RD.
LONDON RD.
ST. MARKS AVE.
BEDWIN ST.
P.O.
CASTLE ST.
FISHERTON
WINCHESTER ST.
MILFORD ST.
RAMPART RD.
BROWN ST.
CRANE ST.
HIGH ST.
NEW CANAL
NEW ST.
ST. JOHN ST.
ST. ANNE ST.
SOUTHAMPTON RD.
NADDER RIVER
CATH.
EXETER ST.
AVON RIVER
HARNHAM RD.
NEW BRIDGE

N

SALISBURY CATHEDRAL

regular guided walks of about 1½ hours' duration through the city, visiting St. Thomas's Church and the Cathedral Close. The starting point is the noticeboard on the side of the Guildhall facing Queen Street. Departures are daily at 2 and 8:30 p.m. in summer. The cost is 60p (90¢) for adults, 30p (45¢) for children. An entire family can go on the walk for £1.50 ($2.25).

WHERE TO STAY: The **Rose and Crown,** East Harnham (tel. 0722/27908), is an inn-collector's gem. An unspoiled, half-timbered, 13th-century hostelry, it lies at the edge of Salisbury. The Avon River winds its way within a few feet of the Rose and Crown, and beyond the water you can see the tall spire of the cathedral. The lawns and gardens between the inn and the river are shaded by old trees, and chairs are set out so you can enjoy the view and count the swans. The inn, part of the Queens Moat House Hotels chain, contains both a new and an old wing. The new wing is modern, but, to me, the old wing is more appealing, with its sloping ceilings, antique fireplaces, and furniture. A single rents for £44 ($66), a double with bath going for £55 ($82.50), including an English breakfast, service, and VAT. You can have lunch overlooking the river. The fare is English. A set luncheon goes for £6 ($9), and a dinner from £10 ($15). Across the courtyard (where there's free parking) are two taverns. You can easily walk over the arched stone bridge to the center of Salisbury from here in ten minutes or so.

White Hart, St. John Street (tel. 0722/27476), combines the best of the old and the new worlds. The White Hart has been a Salisbury landmark since Georgian times. Its classic facade is intact, with tall columns crowning a life-size effigy of a hart. The older accommodations are traditional, but a new part has been added with skill, making for a total of 72 bedrooms. It's in the rear, opening onto a large car park—like a motel. New-wing units are tastefully conceived and attractively decorated. The highest prices are charged from April 1 to October 31, when singles range from £38 ($57), doubles from £55 ($82.50). The higher prices are for rooms with private baths. The service charge and VAT are included. You can have your before-dinner drink in Wavell's Bar.

The **Kings Arms Hotel,** St. John Street (tel. 0722/27629), is a former coaching inn, in black-and-white Tudor style, with leaded-glass windows, an old pub sign out front, and a covered entranceway. It is unsophisticated without being self-consciously so. The Kings Arms charges from £21 ($31.50) in a single without bath to anywhere from £30 ($45) to £35 ($52.50) in a double or twin, the more expensive tariffs including a private bath or shower. A special feature of the Kings Arms is its attractively styled chamber with a four-poster bed. Rates include breakfast, service, and VAT. The rooms are good, with wash basins, radios, heating, and soft beds.

No one seems to know the age of the inn, although it's generally assumed it was built around the time of the completion of the cathedral. Conspirators helping Charles II flee to France were thought to have met here in the mid-17th century. The hotel contains fine old oak beams, the original ironwork, a priest's hiding hole, the Elizabethan fireplace. Have a pint of ale in the oak-beamed pub, sitting in a high-backed settle, warming yourself in front of the flames.

The **Grange Hotel,** St. Marks Avenue, off London Road Roundabout (tel. 0722/25321), stands in the highest part of Salisbury, on 1½ acres of pleasant gardens. Its architecture is an example of "Victorian Mock

Tudor." When constructed, the hotel incorporated the space and comforts required by wealthy Victorians. It is built of brick, with many bay windows, gables, carved fireplaces, and a dark oak central hall with an open winding staircase. The furnishings and decor are in keeping with the style of the building. Most of the bedrooms have private baths and are individually decorated, each bearing the name of a cathedral. Depending on the plumbing, rates in a single range from £15 ($22.50) to £18 ($27), in a double from £30 ($45) to £35 ($52.50). All these tariffs include an English breakfast, VAT, and service, and most rooms contain TV and telephones. Good food is served in the restaurant, a set dinner costing from £7 ($10.50). Lunchtime bar snacks include curries, pies, and quiches, costing about £2 ($3).

Grange Hotel owner Michael Robbins also owns the closest hostelry to Stonehenge, the **Bustarh Hotel** on the Amesbury–Shrewton A360 road. The Bustarh building is more than 250 years old. Michael charges £12 ($18) per person here.

READER'S HOTEL SELECTION AT AMESBURY: "The **Fair Lawn Hotel** (tel. 0980/22103) is ideally located for an in-depth visit to the archeological sites on Salisbury Plain. It is only two miles from Stonehenge and one mile from Woodhenge and Durrington Walls. The hotel, owned by Laurie Miles, is a Georgian building well into its third century. Bed and breakfast cost is £12 ($18) to £13 ($19.50) in a single, £19 ($28.50) to £21 ($31.50) in a double, and £21.50 ($32.25) to £23 ($34.50) in a twin or double with shower, all tariffs including VAT and a full English breakfast. The rooms are immaculate and sunny. The hotel also has a cocktail lounge and restaurant, serving a three-course dinner for £8 ($12) to £11 ($16.50), depending on the main course you choose. Gerald Hawkins, author of *Stonehenge Decoded*, stayed at the Fair Lawn when he visited the area. The Tourist Information Centre in Salisbury will gladly make your reservations to assure the availability of a room before you start for Amesbury" (Edward Pasahow, San Diego, Calif.).

WHERE TO EAT: **Provencal**, 14 Ox Row, Market Place (tel. 0722/28923), provides the most sophisticated setting of any dining place in Salisbury, and has the most ambitious French cuisine as well. This second-story restaurant overlooks the Market Place, has a sedate bistro setting, and a friendly staff to serve you. The menu is changed frequently, depending on the availability of produce and the season. Edward Moss, the owner, is in the kitchen. He offers a table d'hôte luncheon for around £8 ($12), a set dinner for £12 ($18). The restaurant is open from noon to 1:30 p.m. and from 6 to 10:30 p.m. (except for Saturday lunch and all day Sunday). The wine list contains a number of really good French-bottled wines, as well as an excellent carafe.

The **Haunch of Vension,** Minster Street (tel. 0722/22024), deserves its popularity. Owned and run by Anthony and Victoria Leroy, right in the heart of Salisbury, this creaky-timbered, 14th-century chophouse serves some excellent dishes, especially English roasts and grills. Stick to its specialties and you'll rarely go wrong. Diners with more adventurous palates will sample a bowl of game soup. The pièce de résistance of the inn is its roast haunch of vension, with chestnut purée and red currant jelly. All this good food and hospitality is offered in a treasured building, dating back to 1320. The centuries have given a gleam to the oak furnishings, and years of polishing have worn down the brass. Twisting steps lead to tiny, cozy rooms (there is one small room with space for about four to sit where you can saturate yourself in the best of England's yesterdays and todays). Two windows of the barroom overlook St. Thomas's cloisters (naturally, it's called the Cloisters Chamber). Dancing fires are kept burning in the old fireplace; heavy beams are overhead; antique chairs encircle the tables. A table d'hôte luncheon costs £5.50 ($8.25); a set dinner, £10 ($15). If you choose to have a plate of venison with vegetables, the price is £9 ($13.50). Hours are from noon to 2 p.m. and from 7 to 9:30 p.m. The restaurant is closed on Sunday.

The Local Pub

The **New Inn,** 43 New St. (tel. 0722/27679), isn't new at all. Backing up to the cathedral Close wall, it's definitely part of old England. The center of the inn is the serving bar, which is a common counter for three outer rooms—one is a tiny sitting area, another a tavern with high-backed settles and a fireplace, the third a lounge with a dart board. You'll find stacks of little pork pies, to be eaten cold and washed down with pints of ale. Prices range from 55p (83¢) to £2 ($3). A half pint of draft cider costs 75p ($1.13). The Historical Society, incidentally, once discovered several human bones in an oven behind an old doorway.

On the Outskirts

The **Silver Plough,** Pitton, near Salisbury (tel. 0722/72266), lies just off the A30 road from London to Salisbury. It's a pretty country pub with a skillfully added restaurant. The pub has a reputation for country wines and English cheeses. You can sup at least 17 varieties and eat home-baked cottage loaves with a wide selection of cheese for your lunch, in the beamed lounge bar, hung with tankards, coachhorns, and other country memorabilia. In addition to the cheese served for lunch, the restaurant is also open. The bar, incidentally, serves a full snack menu of homemade dishes, featuring steak-and-kidney pie, grilled steak, and various pastas.

There is also a dining room, where the chef does succulent grills and roasts for the set meals or else provides you with an à la carte dinner. He also prepares Scottish salmon, pheasant, and partridge dishes. The owners pride themselves on providing everything from a simple ploughman's lunch to a full meal, a set dinner costing from £15 ($22.50). On the table d'hôte are featured such tempting items as roast duckling with orange and brandy sauce, chicken cooked in red wine and mushrooms, trout poached in white wine with shrimp and mushrooms. The Silver Plough has known many famous visitors, but apart from displaying a signed letter from Queen Victoria, the management prefers to stick to its quiet country atmosphere and to concentrate on making its guests feel at home.

SIDE TRIPS FROM SALISBURY: Less than two miles north of Salisbury is **Old Sarum,** the remains of what is believed to have been an Iron Age fortification. The earthworks were known to the Romans as Sorbiodunum, and later to the Saxons. The Normans, in fact, built a cathedral and a castle in what was then a walled town of the Middle Ages. Parts of the old cathedral were disassembled to erect the cathedral at New Sarum.

Wilton House

In the small borough of Wilton, less than three miles to the west of Salisbury, is one of England's great country estates, Wilton House (tel.

0722/743115), the home of the Earl of Pembroke. The stately house dates from the 16th century, but has seen modifications over the years, as late as Victoria's day. It is noted for its 17th-century state rooms by Inigo Jones. Many famous personages have either lived at or visited Wilton. It is believed that Shakespeare's troupe entertained here. Plans for the D-Day landings at Normandy were laid out here by Eisenhower and his advisers, in the utmost secrecy, with only the silent Van Dycks in the Double Cube room as witnesses. The house is filled with beautifully maintained furnishings, especially a collection of Chippendale. Wilton House displays some of the finest paintings in England, including works by Rembrandt, Rubens, Reynolds, and the already-mentioned Van Dycks. An exhibition of 7000 model soldiers and the "Pembroke Palace" dollhouses are also to be seen.

The estate lies in the midst of 20 acres of grounds, with giant cedars of Lebanon, the oldest of which were planted in 1630. The Palladian Bridge was built in 1737. Wilton House may be visited from Tuesday through Saturday and bank holidays from 11 a.m. to 6 p.m. and Sunday from 1 to 6 p.m. April to mid-October. Admission is £2 ($3) for adults, £1.20 ($1.80) for children under 16. This is admission to the house and grounds. There is a small extra charge for the exhibitions. The fully licensed, self-service restaurant offers excellent values in home-cooking. It's open the same hours as the house. There is an adventure playground for children.

Stonehenge

Two miles west of Amesbury and about nine miles north of Salisbury is the renowned Stonehenge, believed to be anywhere from 3500 to 4000 years old. This huge oval of lintels and megalithic pillars is the most important prehistoric monument in Britain.

Some Americans have expressed their disappointment after seeing the concentric circles of stones. Admittedly, they are not the pyramids, and some imagination has to be brought to bear on them. Pyramids or not, they represent an amazing engineering feat. Many of the boulders, the bluestones in particular, were moved dozens of miles (perhaps from southern Wales) to this site by the ancients. If you're more fanciful, you can always credit Merlin with delivering them on clouds from Ireland.

The widely held view of the 18th- and 19th-century romantics that Stonehenge was the work of the Druids is without foundation. The boulders, many weighing several tons, are believed to have predated the arrival in Britain of the Celtic cult. Recent excavations continue to bring new evidence to bear on the origin and purpose of Stonehenge. Controversy surrounds the prehistoric site especially since the publication of *Stonehenge Decoded* by Gerald S. Hawkins and John B. White, which maintains that Stonehenge was an astronomical observatory. That is, a Neolithic "computing machine" capable of predicting eclipses.

Others who discount this theory adopt Henry James's approach to Stonehenge, which regards it as "lonely in history," its origins and purposes (burial ground? sun-worshipping site? human sacrificial temple?) the secret of the silent, mysterious Salisbury Plain.

If you don't have a car, getting to Stonehenge can be difficult unless you're athletic. First take the bus to Amesbury, then walk about 2½ miles to Stonehenge. The British do this all the time, and they don't complain. But if that is too strenuous, you'd better take one of the organized coach tours out of Salisbury.

On weekdays from 9:30 a.m. and on Sunday from 2 p.m., you can pay an admission of 60p (90¢) for adults, 30p (45¢) for children that permits you to go all the way up to the fence that now encloses the stones to protect them from vandals and souvenir hunters. The ticket booth usually closes at 5 p.m.

Longleat House

Between Bath and Salisbury, Longleat House (tel. Maiden Bradley 551), owned by the sixth Marquess of Bath, lies four miles southwest of Warminster, 4½ miles southeast of Frome on the A362. The first view of this magnificent Elizabethan house, built in the early Renaissance style, is romantic enough, but the wealth of paintings and furnishings within its lofty rooms is enough to dazzle.

A tour of the house, from the Elizabethan Great Hall, through Libraries, the State Rooms, and the Grand Staircase, is awe inspiring in its variety and splendor. The State Dining Room is full of silver and plate, and fine tapestries and paintings adorn the walls in rich profusion. The Library represents the finest private collection in the country. The Victorian kitchens are open during the summer months, offering a glimpse of life below the stairs in a well-ordered country home. Various exhibitions are mounted in the Stable Yard. Events are staged frequently in the grounds, and the Safari Park contains a vast array of animals in open parklands.

A maze, believed to be the largest in the world, has been added to the attractions by Lord Weymouth, son of the marquess. It has more than 1½ miles of paths among yew trees. The first part is comparatively easy, but the second part is very complicated, with bridges adding to the confusion. It knocks the Hampton Court maze into a cocked hat, as the British say.

Longleat House is open from 10 a.m. to 6 p.m. Easter to the end of September, to 4 p.m. the rest of the year. Safari Park is open mid-March to late October from 10 a.m. to 6 p.m., or sunset if earlier. Admission to the house is £1.80 ($2.70) for adults, 70p ($1.05) for children. The fee for Safari Park, including free boat cruises and a visit to Pets Corner, is £2.30 ($3.45) for adults, £1.60 ($2.40) for children. To make the trip by safari bus, with the boat cruises and Pets Corner visit free, adults pay £2.50 ($3.75); children, £1.80 ($2.70). A ride on the railway is 65p (98¢) for adults, 35p (53¢) for children. It costs 30p (45¢) to see the Victorian kitchens. A trek through the maze (allow 30 minutes to an hour) is 30p (45¢) for adults, 20p (30¢) for children. There are also fascinating exhibitions, a whole-food shop, souvenir shop, bookshop, and garden center.

The **Bath Arms,** Horningsham, Warminster (tel. 09853/308), is an old gray stone house that lies just beyond the main gatehouse of Longleat House. It is set among fine trees, among them more Glastonbury cockspur plants (the thorn tree that legend says was planted by Joseph of Arimathea), than you find at Glastonbury. The place has been an inn for well over 200 years, owned by the big house and leased to a succession of tenant landlords. Today, the Lovatt family, Joe and his wife, Beryl, assisted by son Paul, are the landlords who operate the inn in a personal way, providing a warm welcome to passersby and overnight guests. They have seven well-furnished bedrooms with baths and TV, which go for £26 ($39) single, £32 ($48) double, including a large English breakfast.

There is a cheerful bar that serves the local citizenry as well as guests, and a pleasant dining room where Beryl is rapidly acquiring a reputation for her country food, homemade meat and fish pies, and international dishes, interspersed with seasonal specialties. When I was there, the three-course Sunday lunch at £5.50 ($8.25) included roast venison from the estate. Regular meals begin at £12 ($18) per person. On a summer evening, you can sit until late in the garden and listen to the soft sounds of the countryside.

Stourhead

After Longleat, you can drive six miles down route 3092 to Stourton, a village just off the B3092, three miles northwest of Mere (A303). Stourhead, a Palladian house, was created in the 18th century by the banking family of Hoare. The magnificent gardens became known as *le jardin anglais* in that they blended art and nature. Set around an artificial lake, the grounds are decorated with temples, bridges, islands, and grottos, as well as statuary. The gardens are open all year, daily from 8 a.m. to 7 p.m. (or until dusk if earlier). The house is open April, September, and October on Monday, Wednesday, Saturday, and Sunday, from 2 to 6 p.m. In May, June, July, and August it can be visited daily, except Friday, from 2 to 6 p.m. Picnicking in the gardens is welcomed. Admission to the house is £1.80 ($2.70) for adults, £1 ($1.50) for children; to the gardens, £1.40 ($2.10) for adults, 80p ($1.20) for children. For more information, telephone Bourton 840348.

Avebury

One of the largest prehistoric sites in Europe, Avebury lies about six miles west of Marlborough, on the Kennet River. It is gaining in popularity with visitors now that the government has had to rope off the sarsen circle at Stonehenge (see above). Explorers are able to walk the 28-acre site at Avebury, winding in and out of the circle of more than 100 stones, some weighing up to 50 tons. They are made of sarsen, a sandstone found in Wiltshire. Inside this large circle are two smaller ones, each with about 30 stones standing upright. Native Neolithic tribes are believed to have built these circles. The village of Avebury, some of which is in the ownership of the National Trust, has been called the Ancient Capital of England.

Dating from before the Conquest, **Avebury Manor** (tel. 06723/203) was built on the site of a Benedictine cell. An early Elizabethan manor house, it stands beside the great stone circle of Avebury. The manor is carefully restored and is now the family home of D. and S. Nevill-Gliddon. Year round, it can be visited by appointment. Admission is £1.50 ($2.25) for adults, half price for children.

Inside, you'll find oak-paneled rooms and coved plasterwork ceilings. Throughout is much early oak and fine furniture in a period setting. Portraits date from 1532. The state rooms were visited by Queen Anne and by King Charles II. The Queen Anne bedroom, with its imposing state bed, is of particular note, as is the Cavalier bedroom, which is linked with tales of the supernatural, recounted by more than one visitor who stayed at the manor. The surrounding garden and parkland are equally intriguing. The topiary—old yew and box—pleasantly emphasizes the historic atmosphere. Outside attractions include the walled garden, herb border, wishing well, and a 16th-century dovecote. There's car parking within the manor grounds as well as a tea room and souvenir shop.

The manor lies one mile north of the London–Bath road, the A4, on the A361.

The **Alexander Keiller Museum** (tel. 06723/250) houses an important collection of archeological finds from the Avebury area and a display illustrating prehistoric monuments. From mid-March to mid-October it is open from 9:30 a.m. to 6:30 p.m. weekdays, from 2 to 6 p.m. on Sunday. Off-season hours are 9:30 a.m. to 4 p.m. weekdays, 2 to 4 p.m. on Sunday. Admission is 75p ($1.13) for adults, 35p (53¢) for children under 16.

The **Great Barn** (tel. 06723/333) is a center for the display and interpretation of Wiltshire during the past three centuries. It houses a museum dealing with local geology, farming, crafts, and domestic life. April to October it is open from 10 a.m. to 5:30 p.m. Monday to Saturday, from 10:30 a.m. to 5:30 p.m. on Sunday. Admission is 75p ($1.13) for adults, 40p (60¢) for children. Or you can purchase a ticket for your whole family at £1.50 ($2.25).

After sightseeing—and still in the same vicinity—you may be ready for a bite to eat. The **Red Lion** (tel. 06723/266) is a typical English country inn complete with thatched roof and Tudor half-timbering. It even has its own resident ghost, Florrie, supposed to have been killed by her husband when he returned from the wars and discovered she had been unfaithful. Parts of the building are from the 1600s, but there isn't any record as to just how long Florrie has been on hand. The Red Lion is a good choice for lunch or dinner. You can choose a bar meal, costing from £1.50 ($2.25) to £4 ($6), or eat in the dining room, the Barber Stone Grill, where a complete meal, including dessert, will be yours for £4 ($6) to £7.50 ($11.25). I recently enjoyed a rump steak, chips, peas, garnish, roll, butter, and a dessert for only £5 ($7.50). The inn is open for lunch daily from 11 a.m. to 2:30 p.m. and for dinner from 6 to 10:30 p.m.

2. Castle Combe

Once voted Britain's prettiest village, Castle Combe was used for location shots for *Dr. Doolittle*. About 9½ miles from Bath, this little Cotswold village is filled with shops selling souvenirs and antiques. The village cottages are often set beside a trout stream, and are made of stone with roofs laden with moss. The church is unremarkable except for its 15th-century tower. An old market cross and a triple-arched bridge are much photographed.

FOOD AND LODGING: The **Manor House Hotel,** Castle Combe (tel. 0249/782206), is a country estate whose original manor was a 14th-century baronial seat. Set in 26 acres of gardens and parkland, it is a family-run hotel. Mr. and Mrs. Oliver Clegg are the hosts. To the south, the lawns sweep down to the trout-stocked Bybrook River where fishing is permitted for a fee. Thirty-three rooms, 30 with bath, three with shower, are offered overlooking the garden. A double is £56 ($84) to £65 ($97.50) with private bathroom. A single costs £28 ($42) with private bath. The bedrooms are clean and well decorated, furnished mostly with sunny yellow carpeting and light wallpaper. Some contain antiques, and two have four-posters. The garden wing annex consists of a row of genuine Cotswold stone cottages at the entrance to the grounds. These were gutted and rebuilt to provide good-size rooms with baths.

From the à la carte menu, you can order such dishes as roasts from the trolley, £10 ($15). At Sunday lunch, a table d'hôte is featured for £8.50

($12.75). Although casual informality prevails during the day, men in the evening should wear a jacket and tie. Jeans and denims are not acceptable. The hotel has an outdoor swimming pool for summer use only, and an all-year tennis court.

The **White Hart Inn,** at Ford, near Chippenham (tel. 0249/782213) is run by Ken Gardner and his wife, Lily, who cater to the local population swelled during the summer months by passing tourists. The inn is a lovely old 16th-century building with gardens running down to the river. They have added a heated swimming pool to the amenities, but the bars remain low-ceilinged with blackened beams and open fires. Various local souls help in the bars and in the dining room, where residents can dine for £10 ($15) from a menu including braised venison (caught, matured, and marinated locally in port wine). If this is not enough, bar food offered can be anything from chicken casserole in cider to home-cooked ham.

Bedrooms, some with four-poster beds, contain private baths, renting from £30 ($45) a night, including an enormous breakfast with lots of real coffee. The honeymoon suite, which includes a dressing room, is £35 ($52.50) a night. Ken, who claims that his American-bred boxer dog is better looking than he is, reckons he must have a sense of the ludicrous. Otherwise, how would he, an award-winning newspaperman who has traveled the world, exist in a place like this? He enjoys the constantly changing stream of folk who while away the hours in the bar and has a marvelous store of tall stories with which to regale them when conversation falters.

The Local Pub

No accommodation but plenty of local color is offered at the **White Hart,** (tel. 0249/782295), on the main road through the village. It's a pub painted white and built of Cotswold stone with a stone tile roof. Dating from either the 13th or 14th century, it has low ceilings (in the cellars are Norman arches). The main bar is divided into two friendly parts, with a cold buffet counter for meals. The garden is also open to visitors, and the parlor bar admits children. This is the first venture of Dennis and Cath Wheeler (she calls it "my husband's indulgence"). Den, as he is known, works in London, commuting daily, and Cath is helped by her attractive daughters. Den's specialty is a landlord's pâté, and he claims the ingredients aren't poached. Home-cooked ham or beef, with coleslaw, bread, and butter, is offered at £3 ($4.50). In winter, hot soups, chili, and toasted sandwiches are available. Traditional bitter beer from wooden barrels is popular with the locals. They have a black cat, Pussy Galore, who drinks milk with her paw from a wine glass, and a King Charles spaniel known as Jack the Ripper. This is one of the few traditional English pubs in the Cotswolds recommended for evening visits.

3. Lacock

This is a National Trust village, with a 13th-century abbey in ruins and adjoining 16th-century houses and gardens. Within an easy drive of Bath, it contains a delightful 14th-century inn, **Sign of the Angel,** Church Street (tel. Lacock 230), ideal for a meal. Mr. and Mrs. Levis run this small inn, offering gourmet meals in an atmosphere that makes one feel he or she has stepped back into Shakespeare's time, maybe even earlier. Before an open fire on nippy days, food is served under a heavily beamed ceiling. Roasts are often featured on the menu. A set luncheon or dinner runs around £15 ($22.50) per person, and a reservation is essential. Lunch is served from 1 to 1:30 p.m. and dinner from 7:30 to 8 p.m. (one sitting only). The Sign of the Angel is closed for luncheon on Saturday and for dinner on Sunday (also it shuts down for Christmas holidays).

In addition, you'll find six "quaint" rooms, some with patchwork quilts and all with private bathrooms. Bed and full English breakfast ranges from £38 ($57) to £45 ($67.50) in a double room, including VAT and service. In all, it's an overnight stop that can be one of lasting memories (no guests under 12 are permitted, however).

SOMERSET

When writing about Somerset, it's difficult to avoid sounding like the editor of *The Countryside Companion,* waxing poetic over hills and valleys, dale and field. The shire embraces some of nature's most masterly scenic touches in England. Mendip's limestone hills undulate across the countryside (ever had a pot-holing holiday?). The irresistible Quantocks are the pride of the west, especially lovely in spring and fall. Here too is the heather-clad **Exmoor National Park,** a wooded area abounding in red deer and wild ponies, much of its moorland 1200 feet above sea level. Somerset opens onto the Bristol Channel, with Minehead the chief resort, catering primarily to the English.

Somerset is rich in legend and history, and is particularly fanciful about its associations with King Arthur and Queen Guinevere, along with Camelot and Alfred the Great. Its villages are noted for the tall towers of their parish churches.

A Norman castle was erected in the village of Dunster, three miles southeast of Minehead, but unfortunately no trace of that building remains, the oldest surviving feature being the 13th-century gateway to the lower ward. The present **Dunster Castle,** built on the site (tel. Dunster 314), and Dunster village lie just off the A39. The National Trust owns the property and 30 acres of surrounding parkland. Terraced walks and gardens command good views of Exmoor, the Quantock Hills, and the Bristol Channel. Outstanding among the contents of the castle are the 17th-century panels of embossed, painted, and gilded leather depicting the story of Antony and Cleopatra, and a remarkable 16th-century portrait of Sir John Luttrell shown wading naked through the sea with a female figure of peace and a wrecked ship in the background. The 17th-century plasterwork ceilings of the dining room, servery, and staircase, and the finely carved stair balustrade of cavorting huntsmen, hounds, and stags, are particularly noteworthy. The castle may be visited from April until the end of September daily except Thursday and Friday from 11 a.m. to 5 p.m. (last entrance at 4:30 p.m.). In October it is open from noon to 4 p.m. (last entrance at 3:30 p.m.). Visitors are advised to check times before arrival. Admission is £2 ($3) for adults, £1 ($1.50) for children.

A quiet, unspoiled life characterizes Somerset. You're likely to end up in an ivy-covered old inn, talking with the regulars, and being served broiled salmon that night by the fireside. Or you may stop at a large estate that stands in a woodland setting, surrounded by bridle paths and sheep walks (Somerset was once a great wool center). Maybe you'll settle down in a 16th-century thatched stone farmhouse, set in the midst of orchards in a vale. Somerset is reputed (and I heartily concur) to have the best cider anywhere. When you lounge under a shady Somerset apple tree, downing a tankard of refreshingly chilled golden cider, all the types you've drunk in the past taste like apple juice.

My notes on Somerset, accumulated over many a year, would easily fill a book. But because space is limited I've confined myself in the main to the shire's two most interesting towns—Wells and **Glastonbury.**

4. Wells

To the south of the Mendip Hills, the cathedral town of Wells is a medieval gem. It lies only 21 miles from Bath, 123 from London. Wells was a vital link in the Saxon kingdom of Wessex—that is, important in England long before the arrival of William the Conqueror. Once the seat of a bishopric, it was eventually toppled from its ecclesiastical hegemony by the rival city of Bath. But the subsequent loss of prestige has paid off handsomely in Wells today. After experiencing the pinnacle of prestige, it fell into a slumber—hence, much of its old look remains. Wells was named after wells in the town, which were often visited by pilgrims to Glastonbury in the hope that their gout could be eased by its supposedly curative waters. The crowning achievement of the town is:

WELLS CATHEDRAL: Dating from the 12th century, Wells Cathedral is a well-preserved example of the Early English style of architecture. The medieval sculpture (six tiers of hundreds of statues now in process of conservation) of its west front is without peer in England. The western facade was completed in and around the mid-13th century. The landmark central tower was erected in the 14th century, with its attractive fan vaulting attached later. The inverted arches were added to correct the sinking of the top-heavy structure.

Much of the stained glass dates from the 14th century. The star-vaulted Lady Chapel, also from the 14th century, is in the Decorated style. To the north is the vaulted Chapter House, built in the latter 13th century. Look also for a medieval astronomical clock (knights in armor jousting). There is no mandatory charge to enter the cathedral. However, visitors are asked to make voluntary donations of at least 50p (75¢) for adults, 20p (30¢) for students and children. For information, telephone the cathedral offices (tel. 0749/74483).

After a visit to the cathedral, walk along its cloisters to the moated Bishop's Palace. The swans in the moat ring a bell when summoned to eat at 11 a.m. and 4 p.m. Its former Great Hall, built in the 13th century, is in ruins. Finally, the small lane known as the Vicars' Close is one of the most beautifully preserved streets in Europe.

FOOD AND LODGING: The **Star Hotel** (tel. 0749/73055) had its origins somewhere in the 16th century, but is best associated with the great coaching era. The cobbled carriageway is still a feature and leads to the dining room—once the stables. The hotel has been modernized, yet retains its old charm and unhurried pace. Copper and brass are used extensively for decoration, and several original stone walls and timbers have been exposed. The hotel front was restored in the Georgian period. A single ranges from

£16 ($24) if bathless to £19 ($28.50) with bath, a double without bath costing £28 ($42) going up to £34 ($51) with bath, including VAT and an English breakfast. Tariffs are reduced in the off-season, so inquire when reserving a room. Five rooms have four-poster beds. Under the resident proprietor, Mark Nandi, the inn is fast gaining a reputation for good food. A set menu at lunchtime goes for £6 ($8), increasing to £11 ($16.50) for an à la carte dinner.

The **Crown Hotel,** Market Place (tel. 0749/73457), was built in the 15th century as a coaching inn. In Elizabethan times, it witnessed a number of additions. You'll find open beams in at least one of the bedrooms. A bathless single rents for £25 ($37.50); with bath, £16.50 ($24.75). Doubles without bath cost £40 ($60); with bath, £42 ($63). However, a few with four-poster beds cost from £40 ($60); per night. These terms include a full English breakfast and VAT. Tea- or coffee-making facilities and color TV are in all the rooms. Lunch or dinner in the restaurant begins at £10 ($15), à la carte. They also have the Pen Coffee Shop, serving light snacks. The Crown is just two minutes from Wells Cathedral.

The **Red Lion,** Market Place (tel. 0749/72616), is an attractive old inn. Here a single with bath starts at £18 ($27). A double rents for £30 ($45), increasing to £41 ($61.50). The dining room serves a good meal for £10 ($15), with such English specialties as homebaked ham and steak-and-kidney pie. There is a pretty courtyard with tables and chairs for a pleasant drink in the evening.

The **Ancient Gate House,** across from the cathedral (tel. 0749/72029), is ideal all year for good English or Italian meals or slumber, Tudor style. Part of the Great West Gate, called Browne's Gate, it overlooks the stunning west front of the cathedral. In fact, it is part of the ecclesiastical precincts. Three of its rather worn-looking bedrooms have intricately carved four-poster beds. One, for example, was carved by a craftsman who specialized in Tudor roses and monstrous dream-haunting figures, which appear on the headboard. The oak-beamed rooms have lovely furniture. Modern facilities, such as electric heaters, water basins, and TV have been installed without wrecking the spirit of the building.

The hosts, Mr. and Mrs. Rossi, charge from £18 ($27) per person for B&B. The price for bed, breakfast, and evening dinner is from £22 ($33).

If you can't stay here, at least stop in for lunch, noon to 2 p.m. For a luncheon of three courses you'll pay £6.50 ($9.75). It is a mystic and moving experience to sit on the lawn, 60 feet of frontage on the cathedral green, and take afternoon tea in the shade of the limes.

The **City Arms,** 69 High St. (tel. 0749/73916), is the former city jail, but now it's been converted into a local pub and restaurant. It has a high beamed ceiling, and around the dining tables are dark-oak Windsor chairs. On the ground floor is a pub, with an open-air courtyard and umbrella-crowned tables, a popular gathering place for the youth of Wells, who order hot and cold bar snacks, averaging £2 ($3) per order and including quiches, pies, salads, sandwiches, and chili. The restaurant upstairs is a carvery, where for £6.50 ($9.75) you can feast from a joint. Even if you're not hungry, drop in for a pint and soak up the atmosphere.

5. Bleadney

The unspoiled character of the West Country has been preserved in the quiet rural village of Bleadney, just four miles west of Wells on the B3139.

Overlooking the moors toward the Cheddar Valley and Mendip Hills, the village is a convenient center for the exploration of the beauty and history of Somerset with its medieval castles and cathedrals as well as its serene countryside and miles of coastline.

WHERE TO STAY: **Threeways Country Hotel and Restaurant** (tel. 0749/78870) stands on five acres of garden and paddock through which flows the Axe River. Guests can waken to a refreshing view of the moors and valleys surrounding the village. The inn provides clean, comfortable double- or twin-bedded rooms with hot and cold running water and central heating. Rooms are also available with private baths and toilets, and color TV. A double costs £9.50 ($14.25) without bath, £13.50 ($20.25) with bathroom facilities, in low season; £12.50 ($18.75) to £16.50 ($24.75) in summer. Prices include a continental breakfast. In summer the restaurant at Threeways is open six days a week, serving dinners from £5 ($7.50), the higher prices being charged for trout or one of the inn's succulent filet steaks. Meals are available in winter for residents if they are arranged in advance.

6. Glastonbury

The goal of the medieval pilgrim, **Glastonbury Abbey,** once one of the wealthiest and most prestigious monasteries in England, is no more than a ruined sanctuary today. But it provides Glastonbury's claim to historical greatness, an assertion augmented by legendary links to such figures as Joseph of Arimathea, King Arthur, Queen Guinevere, and St. Patrick.

It is said that Joseph of Arimathea journeyed to what was then the Isle of Avalon, with the Holy Grail in his possession. According to tradition, he buried the chalice at the foot of the conically shaped Glastonbury Tor, and a stream of blood burst forth. (You can scale this more than 500-foot-high hill today, on which rests a 15th-century tower.)

At one point, the saint is said to have leaned against his staff, which immediately was transformed into a fully blossoming tree. A cutting alleged to have survived from the Holy Thorn can be seen on the abbey grounds today. It blooms at Christmastime. Some historians have traced this particular story back to Tudor times.

Joseph, so it goes, erected a church of wattle in Glastonbury. The town, in fact, may have had the oldest church in England, as excavations have shown.

The most famous link—popularized for Arthurian fans in the Victorian era by Tennyson—concerns the burial of King Arthur and Queen Guinevere on the abbey grounds. In 1191, the monks dug up the skeletons of two bodies on the south side of the Lady Chapel, said to be those of the king and queen. In 1278, in the presence of Edward I, the bodies were removed and transferred to a black marble tomb in the choir. Both the burial spot and the shrine are marked today.

A large Benedictine Abbey of St. Mary grew out of the early wattle church. St. Dunstan, who was born nearby, was the abbot in the tenth century, later becoming archbishop of Canterbury. Edmund, Edgar, and Edmund "Ironside," three early English kings, were buried at the abbey.

In 1184 a fire destroyed most of the abbey and its vast treasures. It was eventually rebuilt after much difficulty, only to be dissolved by Henry VIII.

Its last abbot, Richard Whiting, was hanged by the neck at Glastonbury Tor. Like the Roman forum, the abbey for years later was used as a stone quarry.

The modern-day pilgrim to Glastonbury can visit the ruins of the Lady Chapel, linked by an Early English "Galilee" to the nave of the abbey. The best preserved building on the grounds is a 14th-century octagonal Abbot's Kitchen, where oxen were once roasted whole to feed the wealthier of the pilgrims (that is, the biggest donors). You can visit the ruins and museum from 9:30 a.m. till dusk for 60p (90¢) for adults, 30p (45¢) for children under 16.

Glastonbury may be one of the oldest inhabited sites in Britain. Excavations have revealed Iron Age lakeside villages on its periphery. Some of the discoveries dug up may be viewed in a little museum in the High Street.

After the destruction of its once-great abbey, the town lost prestige. It is a market town today. The ancient gatehouse entry to the abbey, by the way, is a museum, its principal exhibit a scale model of the abbey and its community buildings as they stood in 1539, at the time of the dissolution.

SOMERSET RURAL LIFE MUSEUM: Abbey Farm, Chilkwell Street (tel. 0458/32903). The main part of the exhibition is Abbey Barn, the home barn of the abbey, built in 1370. The magnificent timbered roof, the stone tiles, and the sculptures outside, including the head of Edward III, make it special. There are also a Victorian farmhouse and various other exhibits illustrating farming in Somerset during the "horse age" and domestic and social life in Victorian times. In summer they have demonstrations of butter making, weaving, basketwork—anything that has reference to the rural life of the country, now rapidly disappearing with the invention of the engine, the freezer, and the instant meal. The museum is open daily from 10 a.m. to around sunset (on Saturday and Sunday from around 2 p.m. to sunset). Admission is 60p (90¢) for adults, half price for children. There is a snackbar for light meals and soft drinks.

WHERE TO STAY: If you're one of the lucky few who can stay over in this town rich in history, you can lodge where the wealthy pilgrim of yore did.

The **George & Pilgrims Inn,** High Street (tel. 0458/31146), is one of the few pre-Reformation hostelries still left in England. Once it offered hospitality to Glastonbury pilgrims; now it accepts modern travelers. In the center of town, the inn has a facade that looks like a medieval castle, with stone-mullioned windows with leaded glass. Some of the bedrooms are former monk's cells; others have four-posters, carved monuments of oak. You may be given the Henry VIII Room, where the king watched the burning of the abbey in 1539. Major and Mrs. Richardson charge £25 ($37.50) for a single room, £19 ($28.50) per person in a double, VAT and an English breakfast included. A well-worn spiral staircase was in use by the monks for centuries, and if your dressing robe looks anything like a monk's robe, you may stir up the ghosts of the past as you walk along the corridors. You could be drawn to the old kitchen, which is now the Pilgrim's Bar with its old oak beams. Even if you don't stay over, you may want to stop in for lunch or dinner in the Regency Restaurant to enjoy the excellent à la carte or table d'hôte menus, both of which feature traditional local dishes, or homemade fare in the snackbar. A set luncheon goes for £6 ($9), a dinner for £12.50 ($18.75).

LIVING IN THE ENVIRONS: Hayvatt Manor Guest House, Hayvatt (tel. 0458/32330), is an attractive stone house, set back from the road, with true English gardens, even a hothouse where grapes are grown for making wine. The manor house is three miles from Glastonbury via Shepton Mallet Road. The owners, Mr. and Mrs. E. N. Collins, quickly become Norman and Molly, they are so down-to-earth and hospitable. They have three doubles and one single room, for which they charge £10 ($15) per person for B&B, plus £7.50 ($11.25) for an evening dinner of three courses and coffee. They grow their own vegetables and fruits for their meals. Families may want to inquire about one of their attached apartments, where you can cook meals for yourself. These go for a weekly rate of £70 ($105), and for that you get a sitting room, two bedrooms, and bath, plus a folding bed and cot. Besides making his own wine, Norman has many hobbies, including playing a Hammond organ in the living room and doing special woodwork on boats. The Collinses are justly proud of their house, which has been designated by the government as worth preserving.

7. The Caves of Mendip

The Caves of Mendip are two exciting natural sightseeing attractions in Somerset—the great caves of Cheddar and Wookey Hole, both easily reached by heading west out of Wells. After leaving Wells, you'll first come to **Wookey Hole** (tel. 0749/72243), less than two miles away, the source of the Axe River. In the first chamber of the caves, you can see, as legend has it, the Witch of Wookey turned to stone. These caves are believed to have been inhabited by prehistoric people at least 60,000 years ago. Even in those days there was a housing problem, with hyenas moving in and upsetting real-estate values. A museum nearby exhibits prehistoric relics.

In 1973 Madame Tussaud's bought the ravine and joined the cele- brated caves and an old paper mill into one remarkable sequence. You can now see paper made by hand as it has been since the 17th century, and Lady Bangor's Fairground Collection, as well as heads of the funny, the famous, and the unspeakable, modeled in wax by Madame Tussaud's and brought to Wookey Hole for safekeeping. There is also a museum covering the history of the caves from prehistoric times to modern cave-diving expeditions, as well as a Penny Arcade, a collection of vintage penny slot machines in full working order. The caves are open every day except Christmas from 9:30 a.m. till 5:30 p.m. (last admission) March to October, from 10:30 a.m. till 4:30 p.m. November to February, charging £3 ($4.50) for adults, £2 ($3) for children. Allow at least two hours for a tour.

At **Cheddar,** eight miles from Wells, you'll find an attractive village, giving its name to cheddar cheese. The village is at the foot of Cheddar Gorge, a two-mile-long pass through 450-foot-high limestone cliffs. The top of the cliffs can be reached by various footpaths or by way of Jacob's Ladder, a series of 322 steps. The views are well worth the effort, with panoramic sights of the Mendip Hills and Somerset moors. The main attractions of the gorge, however, are the famous Cheddar caves, compris- ing **Gough's Cave** and **Cox's Cave,** both with impressive formations. There is also a museum containing artifacts of prehistoric man found in the caves, dating back to more than 10,000 B.C. Gough's Cave and

Cox's Cave are open all year, from 10 a.m. to 6 p.m. Easter to October, 11 a.m. to 5 p.m. in winter. Admission to Gough's Cave is £1.30 ($1.95); to Cox's Cave, 70p ($1.05); Jacob's Ladder, 30p (45¢); and to the museum, 25p (38¢). For further information, phone the manager (tel. 0934/742243).

WHERE TO STAY: In and around this area, you'll find some interesting accommodations, as typified by the **George Hotel** (tel. Wedmore 712124), which lies three miles south of the Cheddar Gorge in the modest village of Wedmore. Here, King Alfred made peace with the Danes, and their ruler Guthrum in A.D. 878, forcing him to be baptized. Faced with such antiquity, nothing but an old-world coaching inn will do. The George, part of which dates back to the 1350s, has for centuries been giving strangers a refreshing pint of ale and a restful night's sleep in one of the 12 upstairs bedrooms. The B&B rate is £13 ($19.50) per person nightly. Bar lunches are available for £2 ($3), dinner from £7.50 ($11.25).

Behind the cellar bar are barrels of ales and beer, and rows of mugs hang from an overhead, time-blackened beam. Everywhere there is a sense of living in the past. It was in 1926 that the custom of holding "court leet of Wedmore" (a special type of manorial court) was abandoned, but the inn still functions as the center of village life. Today it is owned and run by Mr. and Mrs. K. James.

THE CHEESE TOUR: Chewton Cheese Dairy, Priory Farm, Chewton Mendip (tel. 076-121/666), is one of the six remaining dairies in England still making cheddar in the traditional way. Visitors are welcome to watch the cheesemaking process, which takes place every morning, usually from 9 a.m. to 12:30 p.m. After the tour, you may wish to purchase a "truckle" (or wheel) of mature cheddar to send home. A six-pound wheel costs about £17 ($25.50), including shipping. The knowledge that Prince Charles is also a customer adds even more flavor to one of England's unique products.

AN INN NEAR MINEHEAD: The Ship Inn, Porlock Weir, near Minehead (tel. Porlock 862753). As you drive along the A39 road from Bridgewater, through the Quantock Hills and toward North Devon and Exmoor, signs on your right will lead you down from Porlock to Porlock Weir, a tiny little port on the Bristol Channel backed by the Exmoor foothills. The Ship Inn is very old—almost 1000 years of history may have swept past it. Typical of many hard-working seaside harbors, timbers dragged from the sea have been used in the construction of the inn. Ceilings are low and windows are small.

All rooms but one have private bathrooms. Overnight, including a large English breakfast, will cost you around £18 ($27). Dinner is priced from £9 ($13.50) per person, and lunches are somewhat cheaper, about £6 ($8) for three courses.

AVON

Avon is the name that has been given to the area around the old port of Bristol—an area that used to be in Somerset.

8. Bath

Victoria didn't start everything. In 1702 Queen Anne made the 115-mile trek from London to the mineral springs of Bath, thereby launching a fad that was to make the city the most celebrated spa in England. Of course, Victoria-come-lately eventually hiked up too, to sample a medicinal cocktail (which you can still do today), but Bath by then had passed its zenith.

The most famous personage connected with Bath's scaling the pinnacle of fashion was the 18th-century dandy, Beau Nash. He was the final arbiter of taste and manners (one example: he made dueling déclassé). The master of ceremonies of Bath, he cut a striking figure as he made his way across the city, with all the plumage of a bird of paradise. While dispensing (at a price) trinkets to the courtiers and aspirant gentlemen of his day, Beau was carted around in a liveried carriage.

The gambler was given the proper setting for his considerable social talents by the 18th-century architects John Wood the Elder and his son. These architects designed a city of stone from the nearby hills, a feat so substantial and lasting that Bath today is the most harmoniously laid out city in England.

Their work done, the Georgian city on a bend of the Avon River was to attract a following among leading political and literary figures—Dickens, Thackeray, Nelson, Pitt. Canadians may already know that General Wolfe lived on Trim Street, and Australians may want to visit the house at 19 Bennett St. where their founding father, Admiral Philip, lived. Even Henry Fielding came this way, observing in *Tom Jones* that the ladies of Bath "endeavour to appear as ugly as possible in the morning, in order to set off that beauty which they intend to show you in the evening."

Bath has had two lives. Long before its Queen Anne, Georgian, and Victorian popularity, it was known to the Romans as Aquae Sulis. The foreign legions founded their baths here (which may be visited today), so they might ease rheumatism in the curative mineral springs.

Remarkable restoration and careful planning have ensured that Bath retains its handsome look today. The city suffered devastating destruction from the infamous Baedeker air raids of 1942, when Luftwaffe pilots seemed more bent on bombing historical buildings, such as the Assembly Rooms, than in hitting any military target.

The major sights today are the rebuilt Assembly Rooms, the abbey, and the Pump Room and Roman baths. But if you're intrigued by architecture and city planning, you may want to visit some of the buildings, crescents, and squares. The North Parade, where Goldsmith lived, and the South Parade, where Fanny Burney (English novelist and diarist) once resided, represent harmony, the work of John Wood the Elder. The younger Wood, on the other hand, designed the Royal Crescent, an elegant half-moon row of town houses copied by Astor architects for their colonnade in New York City in the 1830s. Queen Square is one of the most beautiful (Jane Austen and Wordsworth used to live here—but hardly together), showing off quite well the work of Wood the Elder. And don't miss his Circus, built in 1754, as well as the shop-flanked Pulteney Bridge, designed by Robert Adam and compared aptly to the Ponte Vecchio of Florence.

BATH ABBEY: Built on the site of a much larger Norman cathedral, the present-day abbey is a fine example of the late Perpendicular style. When

Queen Elizabeth I came to Bath in 1574, she ordered that a national fund be set up to restore the abbey. The west front is the sculptural embodiment of a Jacob's Ladder dream of a 15th-century bishop. When you go inside and see its many windows, you'll understand why the abbey is called the "Lantern of the West." Note the superb fan vaulting, achieving at times a scalloped effect. Beau Nash was buried in the nave and is honored by a simple monument totally out of keeping with his flamboyant character.

PUMP ROOM AND ROMAN BATHS: Founded in A.D. 75 by the Romans, the baths were dedicated to the goddess Sul Minerva. In their day they were an engineering feat, and even today are considered among the finest Roman remains in the country. They are still fed by the only hot spring water in Britain. After centuries of decay, the baths were rediscovered in Victoria's reign. Further major excavations are now taking place (under cover) to locate the temple of Sul Minerva and these excavations are open to the public. The museum connected to the baths contains many interesting objects from Victorian and recent digs (look for the head of Minerva). Coffee, with music, can be enjoyed in the 18th-century Pump Room, or you can have a drink at the licensed restaurant on the terrace. The Pump Room, Roman baths, excavations, and museum are open daily in summer from 9 a.m. to 6 p.m. In winter, weekday hours are from 9 a.m. to 5 p.m., on Sunday from 11 a.m. to 5 p.m. Admission is £1.40 ($2.10) for adults, 85p ($1.28) for children. A joint ticket covering the Pump Room, Roman baths, and the abbey is £2.20 ($3.30) for adults, £1.10 ($1.65) for children. For more information, telephone 0225/61111.

THE ASSEMBLY ROOMS: Lying right off the Circus, the Assembly Rooms were originally designed by John Wood the Younger in 1769. Partly destroyed by 1942 air raids, the rooms have been restored to the height of their 18th-century elegance, when the fashionable dandies and their ladies paraded about. Today they house a Costume Museum (tel. 0225/61111, extension 425), founded on the collection of Mrs. Doris Langley Moore, and greatly enlarged and enriched by donations from many sources. The display of clothes covers more than 300 years of fashion history—Madame Recamier's lounging ladies, Jane Austen's upper-middle-class look, styles right out of Watteau paintings, the Alice B. Toklas post-World War I garb, up to Dior haute couture and a '60s mini by Mary Quant.

Men's apparel isn't neglected in the exhibition, and there are embroidered silk suits of the 18th century, tailored coats worn by Victorian gentlemen, and outfits brought up to the present day by some of the world's leading fashion designers. There are also several dresses belonging to the British royal family, children's clothes, underwear, jewelry, and dolls. Head first for the Card Room, known to Dickens readers from the descriptions in *Pickwick Papers*. The museum is open weekdays in summer from 9:30 a.m. to 6 p.m., on Sunday from 10 a.m. to 6 p.m. Winter hours are 10 a.m. to 5 p.m. weekdays, 11 a.m. to 5 p.m. on Sunday. Admission is £2 ($3) for adults, 70p ($1.05) for children.

BATH FESTIVAL: This annual festival of the performing arts lasts 17 days and takes place at the end of May and beginning of June. Essentially it's a festival of music under the artistic direction of William Mann. Concerts are held in the Assembly Rooms, the Guildhall, the abbey, Wells Cathedral, and many other historic houses and churches in the area. The varied program includes concerts by the major British choirs and chamber orchestras, an international line-up of soloists and chamber groups, library events, exhibitions, lectures, garden and church tours. All information can be obtained from the Bath Festival Office, 1 Pierrepont Pl., Bath, BA1 1JY (tel. 0225/62231).

THE THEATRE ROYAL: The Theatre Royal, Sawclose, has been restored and refurbished with plush red velvet seats, red carpets, and a painted proscenium arch and ceiling. It is a tiny theater with a small pit and then grand circles rising to the upper circle. Beneath the theater, reached from the back of the stalls or by a side door, are the theater vaults. There you will find a pleasant bar in one of the curved vaults with stone walls. In the next vault is the Brasserie, where lunch and pre-performance meals are served. French onion soup, eggs Benedict, and seafood salad lead the appetizers with game pie and roast ham with mustard and peach sauce among the main dishes. Desserts are all homemade. Meals cost from £8 ($12).

The theater advertises a surprisingly sophisticated list of forthcoming events with a repertoire that includes, among other offerings, West End shows. The box office (tel. 0225/62065) is open from 10 a.m. to 7 p.m. Monday to Saturday.

A GEORGIAN HOUSE: No. 1 Royal Crescent (tel. 0225/28126) was given to the Bath Preservation Trust by Bernard Cayzer in 1968. By 1970 it had been carefully restored and the main rooms redecorated and furnished to create an authentic 18th-century interior. Thus visitors may see for themselves what the inside of a house in Bath looked like in its heyday. It is open March through October, Tuesday to Saturday from 11 a.m. to 5 p.m., 2 to 5 p.m. on Sunday; closed Monday. Admission is 75p ($1.13) for adults, 50p (75¢) for children.

THE AMERICAN MUSEUM IN BATH: Some 2½ miles outside Bath, you get a glimpse of life as lived by a diversified segment of American settlers until Lincoln's day. It was the first American museum established outside the United States. In a Greek Revival house, designed by a Georgian architect, Claverton Manor, the museum (tel. 0225/60503) sits proudly in its own extensive grounds high above the Avon valley. Among the authentic exhibits—shipped over from the States—are a New Mexico room, a Conestoga wagon, an early American beehive oven (ever had gingerbread baked from the recipe of George Washington's mother?), the dining room of a New York town house of the early 19th century, and (on the grounds) a copy of Washington's flower garden at Mount Vernon. You can visit the museum from the end of March to the end of October, daily except Monday from 2 to 5 p.m. There is now an American arboretum in the grounds for which an extra charge is made. Admission to the house and gardens is £2 ($3) for adults, £1.80 ($2.70) for children. The charge to visit the grounds only is 50p (75¢).

READER'S SIGHTSEEING TIP: "The mayor's **Corps of Honorary Guides** conducts free walking tours of the City of Bath every day during the summer (end of May to end of September), bank holidays and every Sunday and Wednesday from October to May. Guides are also available for private parties at other times if required. These guides, all local people are unpaid and act in a purely honorary capacity: they do not accept gratuities. A tour lasts approximately 1¾ hours and visitors see the main points of historical and architectural interest within the city. For further information, write to Mr. J. Clifton, Assistant Director, Department of Leisure and Tourist Services, Pump Room, Bath, BA1 1LZ, Avon" (R. Alter, Lexington, Ky.).

WHERE TO STAY: In accommodations, Bath offers a wide choice—some in architectural landmarks.

Lansdown Grove Hotel, Lansdown Road (tel. 0225/315891), is a well-run hotel outside the center of the city, set on the northern slopes with magnificent views, 600 feet above sea level. Its drawing room is informal, with flowering chintz draperies, a large gilt and marble console, and comfortable armchairs. A modernization program has produced not only carpeting and fresh paint, but full central heating throughout and private bathrooms and showers and color TV in all the cheerful, comfortable bedrooms. Single rooms with bath cost from £33 ($49.50); doubles with bath, from £48 ($72). All rates include VAT and a full English breakfast. It's a pleasure to eat in the sunny dining room, with its bay window that opens onto the garden. Before-dinner drinks are available in the cocktail bar, which is decorated with delightful murals of Edwardian fairground scenes, while a bar annex is adorned with illustrations of oldtime music halls, bringing a uniquely charming atmosphere. Bathonians as well as visitors to the hotel patronize this place. There is an area for parking your car, as well as a covered garage.

Royal York Hotel, George Street (tel. 0225/61541), was a coaching inn in Georgian days, and now provides moderate comfort at a location within easy walking distance of the abbey. Every room is centrally heated, and there are elevators to all floors. Each unit contains a radio, telephone, and razor outlet—and is furnished with tasteful, traditional pieces, appropriate to the genteel character of the hotel. Most rooms have private baths. The rate in a single ranges from £26 ($39) to £35 ($52.50), the latter with private bath. Twins range from £42 ($63) to £54 ($81). Tariffs include VAT, service, and a full English breakfast. Try to get an accommodation in the rear, as these rooms are much quieter. The hotel has its own continental-style café-bar and a traditionally English tavern.

The **Priory Hotel,** Weston Road (tel. 0225/331922), was converted from one of Bath's lovely Georgian houses in 1969. The original house dates from 1835 and is built of Bath stone in Gothic style. The gateway from Weston road leads to a large gravel courtyard with many shrubs, trees, and bushes. In front of the house are two acres of garden, manicured lawns and flowerbeds, a discreetly placed swimming pool, and a croquet lawn. The atmosphere exudes peace and tranquility.

John Donnithorne, the owner, is a hotelier of considerable experience, having managed some of Europe's well-known hotels during the past 35 years. In London he was the general manager of Browns Hotel in its heyday. The Priory reflects this experience. There are 15 rooms, each individually decorated and furnished with antiques, direct-dial phone, color TV, and easy chairs to complement the comfortable beds, one a genuine antique four-poster with a specially made modern mattress and a cunningly adapted commode from which to climb into bed. My personal favorite is the Turret Room, a duplex within a circular turret. Private bathrooms are attractive, carpeted, and well appointed.

The restaurant spreads between two rooms, one a small dining room in the old house, the other adjoining it in an extension overlooking a courtyard with an ornamental pond and fountain. The kitchen is in the hands of Michael Collom. The menu is varied and reflects seasonal availability. Partridge, hare, and venison are served in different recipes in season, as is the best end of lamb roasted with herb-flavored breadcrumbs. The average meal price is £18.50 ($27.75) for a three-course repast. A cold buffet luncheon is set out on a large circular table in the dining room for guests to select from. There is also a Sunday lunch served with traditional roast meats.

Prices for one night in a single room start at £40 ($60) with private shower, £42 ($63) with private bath. Twin and double rooms with private bath are from £72 ($108) per night, and luxury rooms with four-poster beds are £82 ($123). All tariffs include a continental breakfast.

Pratt's Hotel, South Parade (tel. 0225/60441), is convenient for sightseeing, on a wide street with a large car park close by. Several elegant terraced town houses were skillfully joined into a comfortable place with warm, cheerful lounges, a bar, and a high-ceilinged dining room. Bedrooms all have private baths, color TV with in-house movies, radio, telephone, and tea- or coffee-making equipment. A single goes for £26 ($39); a twin or double, £38 ($57). All rates include a full English breakfast and VAT. If you stay two nights, you can have dinner from the table d'hôte menu in addition to B&B and VAT for £25.50 ($38.25) per night per person; £31.50 ($47.25) per night in a single. Children under 15 sharing a room with two adults stay free overnight.

Fernley Hotel, 1 North Parade (tel. 0225/60603), is one of three houses on the parade—nos. 1, 2, and 3—that were built by John Wood the Elder in 1743 close to the Roman baths and the abbey. Now it is a hotel with a varied selection of rooms, some with private baths added. Bathless singles are £21 ($31.50); with bath, £30 ($45). Doubles or twins with bath or shower and toilet go for £40 ($60); without bath, £32 ($48). All rates include a full English breakfast and VAT. Downstairs, the coffeeshop, the Danish Terrace, offers a light meal for around £3 ($4.50). The hotel has a grill room and a pub, the Entertainer, where bar snacks are served as well as real ale. On some evenings live jazz is presented.

Number Nine, 9 Miles Buildings, George Street (tel. 0225/25462), is one of the most delightful small hotels of Bath, personally cared for by the owners, Sue and Paul Hayward. The hotel dates from the 18th century, having been built according to the plans of the celebrated architect, John Wood the Elder. The Haywards have taken care to retain its Georgian overtones, selecting furniture appropriate to the era.

In the center of Bath, near the Royal Crescent, the Assembly Rooms, and the Circus, the little hotel lies on one of the city's walkways, cut off from the roar of traffic. Parking space is available nearby.

Rooms are attractively furnished and individually decorated, often with half-tester beds. A bathless double costs £35 ($52.50), the cost rising to £45 ($67.50) and up in a double or twin with a bathroom en suite. A single with bath begins at £30 ($45). The hotel, incidentally, does not cater to children.

The bay windowed public rooms look out onto an old world garden. The hotel also offers international meals, with a good selection of wines. Guests who cannot be accommodated in the main building are housed in a mews cottage nearby. Ask about the membership arrangement with the Bath House, where you can enjoy steam baths, saunas, and a jacuzzi.

Christopher Hotel, High Street (tel. 0225/60029), is an attractive, well-run hotel, with an 18th-century facade, one of Bath's oldest coaching inns. Opposite a side of the abbey and overlooking the Grand Parade, it is only a one-minute walk from the Roman baths. The residents' lounge combines traditional and modern elements. The bedrooms are pleasantly furnished and well kept; a double with bath costs £40 ($60) nightly. The rates include an English breakfast. You can order good food in the restaurant, which has both a table d'hôte and an à la carte menu. The hotel has two bars but no elevator. A multistory car park is nearby.

Living on the Outskirts

Homewood Park, Hinton Charterhouse (tel. Limpley Stoke 2643), is set in ten acres of garden, just five miles south of Bath on the A36 Bath–Warminster road. Stephen and Penny Ross, who ran the successful Popjoys restaurant in Bath, have converted the property and now offer ten bedrooms with private baths. This small, family-run hotel was built in the 18th century, then subsequently enlarged in the 19th century. Overlooking the Limpley Stoke Valley, it is a large Victorian house, its grounds adjoining the 13th-century ruin of Hinton Priory.

The B&B rate is from £28 ($42) per person nightly. Of course, most visitors come here for the cuisine, served in a dining room facing south, overlooking the gardens. The French and English cooking is prepared with skill and flair, and you should expect to spend from £20 ($30) for a meal. The service is friendly and efficient.

On the grounds is a tennis court, and riding can be arranged with the stables next door.

WHERE TO DINE: Bath is increasingly gaining a reputation as a gourmet citadel. **Popjoy's,** Beau Nash House, Sawclose (tel. 0225/60494), is housed in a 1720 Regency building that was once the home of the notorious Beau Nash, the "King of Bath." The restaurant is named after Julianna Popjoy, Nash's last mistress. Her ghost is said to haunt the drawing room. When Nash died in 1761, Julianna vowed never again to sleep in a bed, and spent the rest of her life gathering herbs and living in a hollow tree in Wiltshire.

In 1981 Popjoy's was bought by Alison Golden, who promptly closed it and set about restoring it exactly as it had been in 1720, even down to scraping the centuries of paint from the walls to discover the original colors. Now the discreet town house has a neat sign beneath the bell, and you will not be admitted without a reservation. The hall and stairs are yellow and gray, the drawing room stone colored, with comfortable armchairs and sofas where you can sip your coffee and liqueurs. The dining room is done in Russian red.

Everything is freshly prepared in Alison's basement kitchen. The cost of a meal depends on your choice of main dish, all of which are priced from £10 ($15) to £12 ($18), including lamb kidneys braised with red wine, roast quail, Marseillaise fish pot, and grilled beef filet. Meat comes from Devon, fish from Cornwall, and fresh vegetables from the local farmers. The menu is changed every ten weeks, and ever since the place reopened in 1983, there has hardly been an empty seat. The house wine is specially bottled in France and imported for the restaurant. The atmosphere is informal and relaxed, with quiet music, mostly Mozart, played discreetly.

Alison owned and ran a restaurant in Devon for many years and trained in Switzerland. Her husband, Gregory, assists, but, as he says, this is Alison's place. They are open daily except Sunday, serving only dinner, from 6 p.m. Now that the theater is open just next door, you can take pre-theater meals here or enjoy an unhurried dinner after the performance.

The Hole in the Wall, 16 George St. (tel. 0225/25242). You enter what looks like the living room of a Georgian town house, where a hostess greets you, takes your name and order for a drink, and presents you with the impressive menu. She'll even help you plan your meal if you prefer. All the selections are especially prepared for you. When your table is ready, you descend into a colorful, old-world dining room, with an attractive decor that includes a great "dungeon" fireplace. The benches, tables, and chairs are antiques.

A huge table of hors d'oeuvres is on display and available only in summer. An à la carte menu is offered, or you can order a set meal at £14.50 ($21.75) for two courses, £17 ($25.50) for three. You get a choice of soup of the day, boudins blancs with apple sauce and celeriac purée, or a mixed selection of terrines, then grilled chicken with lime, a veal chop with spinach and cream cheese, goose, or fish, all served with a green salad and potatoes. The vegetables are fresh. For dessert, if you wait 20 minutes, you can have the prune, armagnac, and almond tart.

Tim and Sue Cumming have carefully converted the upper floors of the Georgian house to provide eight bedrooms with good baths, color TV, and phone. A continental breakfast is included in the room rates of £40 ($60) to £55 ($82.50) per night for doubles, from £28 ($42) for single occupancy. The restaurant is closed on Sunday, but residents may have a table d'hôte meal for either lunch or dinner by prior arrangement.

Beaujolais, 5 Chapel Row (tel. 0225/23417), is run by French proprietors, Jean-Pierre Auge and Philippe Wall, on true bistro lines. You enter through the undistinguished front door and find a seat in one of the three rooms of brightly clad tables. Then you're greeted by a member of the friendly and knowledgeable staff. Call in advance for a reservation, as this cheerful place has become very popular. You'll definitely need to give notice if you want one of the more private tables for four with settles. Fresh materials are used in the dishes served. Specialties include sea bass, half a roast pheasant, or venison. A new menu is offered every day, and it attaches importance to fish. Among the most popular appetizers are crêpe au camembert, fish soup, and piperade, to be followed by poulet en croûte Napoléon, coquilles St-Jacques à la Provencale, and entrecôte steak moscovite. Meals cost £12 ($18) and up. The Beaujolais is open from 12:30 to 2:30 p.m. for lunch on Saturday only, and from 7:30 to 11:30 p.m. for dinner Monday to Saturday. Faint music plays in the background, and the atmosphere is informal, the value excellent.

Binks Restaurant, Abbey Churchyard (tel. 0225/66563), stands across the pavement from the Roman baths and the abbey. Inside, in the two double-fronted shops that Nicky Binks pulled together, the bakers start early in the morning, preparing rolls and croissants for breakfast, together with the renowned Bath buns made from a recipe handed down from Dr. Oliver to his coachman. Bread, cakes, chocolates, and ice cream are sold at the counter just inside. On the same floor is the coffeeshop, which starts serving with breakfast and goes on until late at night. They admit to serving "disgustingly good" cream teas. Downstairs is a light and cheerful restaurant with music on Tuesday, Thursday, and Saturday. An area is set aside for intimate meals and secluded chats. There is a salad bar where, from 11 a.m., you can help yourself to a choice of three or four joints and ten different salads.

Lunch includes rough country pâté served with crusty bread and butter, followed by Binks's traditional English pie. Dinners include braised haunch of venison with bacon, celery, and walnuts, or English lamb cutlets, served Binks style with Worcestershire sauce and fresh lime juice. Desserts are all made from original 19th-century English recipes and include "You Just Can't Leave Me Alone," a lemony confection with raspberry jam, and Taunton rolypoly tipsy trifle. All the dairy products come from their own farms, and the milk is really fresh. A team of enthusiastic young people serve at the counter and wait tables. You can eat for as little as £3 ($4.50) for a club sandwich or cold savory pie with pickles and salad. Or you can "push the boat out," as the English say, with a three-course meal of chicken liver pâté with peppercorns and rump steak with champagne and oyster sauce, followed by negrita (dark chocolate brandy and orange mousse) for £8.50 ($12.75).

Clarets Wine Bar, Kingsmead Square (tel. 0225/66688), is a cellar with whitewashed walls beneath one of Bath's Georgian houses. Simple slate floors and mahogany tables and benches and a plain decor show that Lisa Tearle is an experienced restaurateur who offers simple surroundings and high-quality food. Casseroles include beef and orange, chicken in red wine, and country-style lamb. Interesting salads and pâtés are on the menu, or you might like deep-fried camembert, carbonnade of beef with noodles, beef and mushroom pie, or stuffed aubergine (eggplant) with rice. Meals cost from £8 ($12). In summer they go really "bistro" and have tables outside for al fresco eating. It is open from 10 a.m. to 2:30 p.m. and from 6:30 to 11 p.m. Monday to Saturday, on Sunday from 7 to 10:30 p.m. only.

Sally Lunns House, North Parade Passage (tel. 0225/61634), is a tiny gabled stone coffeeshop, with a Georgian bay window, original early Tudor fireplaces, and "bow and arrow" cupboards. The house is a landmark in Bath, built in 1482 and considered the oldest structure in the city. Sally Lunn was known by legend to all Bathonians for her buns baked in the cellars here in 1680. The same tradition of good cakes is carried on today (also salads and light meals are served all day). Take your coffee, tea, or hot chocolate at a natural-wood tavern table, or while seated in a settle. A Sally Lunn bun costs 65p (98¢), and cakes run to 85p ($1.28) a slice. Sandwiches, salads, meats, and hot dishes are all available, a plate costing from around £1.50 ($2.25). From the various dishes, it is possible to have a three-course meal for around £4 ($6). Sally Lunn's is licensed, with wines available at 85p ($1.28) a glass. At press time, the place was not open in the evening, but the owner, Norma Tugday, says that she may resume serving dinner before long. The house is easy to spot—near the abbey, off Church Street.

9. Bristol

Bristol, the largest city in the West Country, is a good center for touring western Britain. Its location is 10 miles west of Bath, just across the Bristol Channel from Wales, 20 miles from the Cotswolds, and 30 miles from Stonehenge. This historic inland port is linked to the sea by seven miles of the navigable Avon River. Bristol has long been rich in seafaring traditions and has many links with the early colonization of America. In fact, some claim that the new continent was named after a Bristol town clerk, Richard Ameryke. In 1497 John Cabot sailed from Bristol, which led to the discovery of the northern half of the New World.

In Bristol, the world's first iron steamship and luxury liner is being restored to her 1840 glory. She's the 3000-ton S.S. *Great Britain,* and was created by Isambard Brunel, a Victorian engineer. Visitors can go aboard this "floating palace" between 10 a.m. and 5 p.m. for an admission of £1 ($1.50), (half price for children), (tel. 0272/20608).

At the age of 25 in 1831, Brunel began a Bristol landmark, a suspension bridge over the 250-foot-deep Avon Gorge at Clifton.

The best way to discover the sights of Bristol, both obvious and hidden, is to take one of the guided walking tours operated by the city, costing 50p (75¢) for adults, children free. Lasting an hour and a half, these walks leave from the Exchange on Corn Street at 11 a.m. and from Neptune's statue in the city center at 2:30 in the afternoon. On Sunday, guided tours cover the suburb of Clifton, where the visitor finds the biggest concentration of Georgian buildings, particularly the Royal York Crescent, overlooking Avon Gorge. Visitors are often astonished to find that Bristol has more Georgian buildings than its neighbor, Bath.

The city's floating harbor was formed by damming up the Avon River in 1809. **Bristol Packet Tour Boats,** Wapping Wharf (tel. 0272/28157), operates one-hour tours from the harbor daily at noon and at 2, 3, and 4 p.m. from Easter to November. The trip takes you past S.S. *Great Britain*. Tours cost £2 ($3) for adults, half price for children. You embark from the S.S. *Great Britain* car park.

Bristol Cathedral was begun in the 14th century on the site of a Norman abbey. The central tower was added in 1466. The Chapter House and Gatehouse are good examples of late Norman architecture, and the choir is magnificent.

Another church, **St. Mary Redcliffe,** was called "the fairest, goodliest, and most famous parish church in England" by such an authority as Elizabeth I. Built in the 14th century, it has been carefully restored.

Cobbled King Street is known for its Theatre Royal, the smallest English playhouse and the oldest in continuous operation. Many old taverns line this quayside area, principally the 17th-century **Llandoger Trow,** once the haunt of pirates. A few blocks up King Street from the Lightship, Llandoger Trow is reputed to have figured in *Treasure Island* by Robert Louis Stevenson. Guests drop in for a drink at the Smuggler's Bar or the Old Vic Bar, later perhaps enjoying a plaice or a steak dinner in an atmosphere of time-worn beams and old fireplaces.

This is also the home of the **Bristol Old Vic,** the city's repertory company. For information about tickets or its current presentation, telephone the box office at 0272/27466.

FOOD AND LODGING: Holiday Inn, Lower Castle Street (tel. 0272/ 294281), is a modern city-center hotel, ideal for the business traveler, but also suitable to the tourist who makes it to this part of the West Country. The heated swimming pool is impressive, and the foyer is spacious. Public areas are well groomed, comfortable, and stylish, in the tradition of this popular chain. You have a choice of two bars, and the Restaurant Panache serves an à la carte menu as well as snacks. Bedrooms are uniformly furnished, bright, and cheerful, with double beds (doubles have two) and good tiled bathrooms. Singles cost £45 ($67.50) nightly, and the double tariff ranges from £48 ($72) to £58 ($87).

Instead of finding lodgings in Bristol, many visitors prefer to seek out the accommodations in the leafy Georgian suburb of Clifton, near the famous suspension bridge.

There you'll find **Oakfield,** Oakfield Road, off Whiteladies Road (tel. 0272/735556), an impressive guest house that would be called a town house in New York, with an Italian facade. It's on a quiet street, and everything is kept spic and span under the watchful eye of Mrs. D. L. Hurley. Every pleasantly furnished bedroom has hot and cold running water and central heating. The charge is £11.50 ($17.25) daily in a single, from £19 ($28.50) in a double, these tariffs including breakfast. For another £5 ($7.50) you can enjoy a good, home-cooked dinner.

Alandale Hotel, Tyndall's Park Road, Clifton (tel. 0272/35407), is an elegant early Victorian house that retains a wealth of its original features, including a marble fireplace and ornate plasterwork. The hotel is under the supervision of Mr. Johnson, who still observes the old traditions of personal service. For example, afternoon tea is served, as are sandwiches, drinks, and snacks in the lounge (up until midnight). A continental breakfast is available in your room until 10 a.m., unless you'd prefer a full English breakfast in the dining room. Terms are from £12 ($18) per person nightly in a twin-bedded unit, plus VAT.

Among the restaurants, the most creative cookery is found at **Michael's** 129 Hotwell Rd. (tel. 0272/276190), run by Michael McGowan. His charming and well-patronized restaurant is near Clifton, on a highway leading toward the Avon Gorge. In his pleasant bar, decorated like an Edwardian parlor, an open fire burns. The dining room is also bright and inviting. Michael's menu is imaginative, and he likes to change it, depending on the availability of seasonal produce. Service is informal and enthusiastic. Sunday lunch is offered in winter only for £6.50 ($9.75) and up. Dinner is served Monday to Friday until midnight (on Saturday till 1 a.m.). Expect to pay about £13 ($19.50) per person, including the wine of the house. Always call for a table. There's no smoking in the dining room. If you want a cigarette, stick to the bar.

Behind a Georgian facade lies **Parks Brasserie,** 51 Park St. (tel. 0272/28016), a favorite for university students but also of an older clientele. Here you can sample steak-and-kidney pie, Breton crêpes, burgers, and good salads. A main meal with wine costs about £10 ($15) per person.

On the Outskirts

Hunstrete House, Chelwood, near Bristol (tel. 07618/578), is operated by Thea and John Dupays, who ran a rather exclusive school in Bath before they found this interesting 18th-century house set in 90 acres of private parkland. The village of Hunstrete was first recorded in A.D. 936 when King Athelstan passed through on his way to the abbey in Glastonbury. The fine Georgian house has 20 bedrooms with private baths. Six units are in the Courtyard House, attached to the main structure and overlooking a paved courtyard with its Italian fountain and flower-filled tubs. Swallow Cottage, which also adjoins the main house, has its own private sitting room, double bedroom, and bath. Units in the main house are individually decorated and furnished in attractive colors, comfortable, and spotless. They vary in size as reflected by the rates. A small double is £54 ($81); a normal-size double, £64 ($96); a four-poster room, £81 ($121.50); and the cottage, £95 ($142.50). A single person will pay from £42 ($63) to £48 ($72), depending on the room. Tariffs include a continental breakfast, VAT, and service.

Part of the pleasure of staying at Hunstrete is the food. Chef Alain Dubois, a native of Normandy who trained extensively throughout France, heads the kitchen. French provincial cuisine is the main feature of the restaurant, although these days it could also be considered to be English country cooking. Try the terrine of venison with Cumberland sauce. The main course sets the price of a meal, which will range from £15 ($22.50) to £19 ($28.50). Try roast pheasant with fresh chanterelles and madeira sauce. Chef Dubois will also provide plainer dishes if you wish. All vegetables are fresh and lightly cooked. Among the desserts, you might enjoy scotch mist (iced meringue and cream with malt whisky and honey).

At Thornbury

Thornbury Castle Hotel (tel. 0454/412647), in the southern outskirts of Thornbury village near Bristol, is the achievement of Kenneth Bell, who was made a Member of the British Empire several years ago by Queen Elizabeth II, the award being given for his services to the culinary arts. With typical British restraint, this man so honored does not blazon his accomplishments with much show: as you drive through the fine gates of the hotel drive, the only sign is a brass plaque about five by eight inches saying simply, "Thornbury Castle. K. Bell, Restaurateur."

In 1966 Bell acquired the castle and set about to convert it. He planted vineyards from which sufficient white wine is produced to serve in the restaurant. Today you can also stay here overnight and dine in the splendor of a genuine English castle with a history dating back to William Rufus, who ascended the English throne in 1087 upon the death of William the Conqueror. Henry VIII owned Thornbury Castle for 33 years, staying here for several days with Ann Boleyn. Mary Tudor lived at Thornbury for some years before she became queen.

The main apartments on the first floor of the south wing have been converted to provide ten large bedrooms with private baths. Each is individually decorated and furnished with good furniture, including comfortable sofas. Many have fine oriels overlooking the walled garden. The four-poster room reflects the curve of the tower, and the ceiling is beamed, the timbers radiating from a central boss like the spokes of a wheel. Baths are well equipped and have such accessories as hair dryers, sewing kits, bath foam, and large towels. All bedrooms have the added modern touch of color TV, phone, and central heating. Room rates are £42 ($63) for a small single, £61 ($91.50) for a smallish double, £83 ($124.50) for a large double, and £110 ($165) for the four-poster room. Prices include a continental breakfast, VAT, and service.

The large dining room and the tower dining room are decorated in a baronial style with paneled walls and large open fires. The menu is the same in both rooms, but on Tuesday, Thursday, and Friday a pianist plays during dinner in the large room, and there is a cover charge of £1.50 ($2.25). Lunch is served from 12:30 to 2 p.m. and dinner from 7 to 9:30 p.m. The restaurant is open seven days a week, except for two weeks during the Christmas season. A table d'hôte luncheon is offered at £18 ($27). An à la carte dinner will cost around £20 ($30), without wine. Main dishes include rack of lamb, roast pheasant in season, fresh salmon, and barbary duck, all cooked with appetizing sauces and served with a choice of fresh vegetables. All prices include VAT and service.

Chapter XI

THE COTSWOLDS

1. Burford
2. Clanfield
3. Minster Lovell
4. Bibury
5. Cirencester
6. Painswick
7. Cheltenham
8. Royal Sudeley Castle
9. Malmesbury
10. Tetbury
11. Wotton-under-Edge
12. Shipton-under-Wychwood
13. Chipping Norton
14. Bourton-on-the-Water
15. Lower Swell
16. Upper and Lower Slaughter
17. Stow-on-the-Wold
18. Moreton-in-Marsh
19. Broadway
20. Chipping Campden

THE COTSWOLDS, the once-great wool center of the 13th century, lie mainly in the county of Gloucestershire, although parts dip into Oxfordshire, Warwickshire, and Worcestershire. If possible, try to explore the area by car. That way, you can spend hours surveying the land of winding goat paths, rolling hills, and sleepy hamlets, with names such as Stow-on-the-Wold, Wotton-under-Edge, Moreton-in-Marsh, Old Sodbury, Chipping Campden, Shipton-under-Wychwood, Upper and Lower Swell, and Upper and Lower Slaughter, often called "The Slaughters." These most beautiful of English villages keep popping up on book jackets and calendars.

Cotswold lambs used to produce so much wool they made their owners very rich—wealth they invested in some of the finest domestic architecture in Europe, made out of the honeybrown Cotswold stone. The wool-rich gentry didn't neglect their church contributions either. Often the simplest of villages will have a church that in style and architectural detail seems to rank far beyond the means of the hamlet.

Picture yourself as part of the life of these hills:

"Come on in through the kitchen" is all you need hear to know that you've found a home-like place where naturalness and friendliness prevail. Many readers will want to seek out comfortable (although decidedly unchic) accommodations in little stone inns that survive among the well-known and sophisticated hotels that advertise heavily. Perhaps you'll be served tea in front of a two-way fireplace, its walls made of natural Cotswold stone. Taking your long pieces of thick toasted bread, saturated with fresh butter, you'll find the flavor so good you won't resist putting on more chunky cherry jam.

Or maybe you'll go down a narrow lane to a stately Elizabethan stone manor, with thick walls and a moss-covered slate roof. Perhaps you'll arrive at haying time and watch the men at work in the fields beyond, as well as the cows and goats milked to produce the rich "double cheese" you'll be served later. Your dinner that night? Naturally, a roast leg of Cotswold lamb.

Or you may want to settle down in and around Cheltenham, where the view from your bedroom window of the Severn Valley to the Malvern Hills to the Welsh mountains is so spectacular that old King George III came for a look. The open stretches of common, woodlands, fields, and country lanes provide the right setting for picnics. Life inside your guest house may be devoted to comfort and good eating—baskets of fresh eggs, Guernsey milk, cream, poultry, and a variety of vegetables from the garden.

If your tastes are slightly more expensive, you may seek out a classical Cotswold manor (and there are dozens of them), with creamy field stone, high-pitched roofs, large and small gables, towering chimneys, stone-mullioned windows, a drawing room with antique furnishings, a great lounge hall, and ancient staircase, flagstone floors. Such Cotswold estates represent England at its best, with clipped hedges, rose gardens, terraces, stone steps, sweeping lawns, old trees, and spring flowers. Here you can revel in a fast-disappearing English country life.

The adventure begins in:

1. Burford

In Oxfordshire, Burford is the gateway to the Cotswolds. This unspoiled medieval town, built of Cotswold stone, is 19 miles to the west of Oxford, 31 miles from Stratford-upon-Avon, 14 miles from Blenheim Palace, and 75 miles from London. Its fame rests largely on its early Norman church (c. 1116) and its High Street, lined with coaching inns. Oliver Cromwell passed this way, as did Charles II and Nell Gwynne. Burford was one of the last of the great wool centers, the industry surviving into Victoria's reign. You may want to photograph the bridge across the Windrush River, where Queen Elizabeth I once stood. Burford is definitely equipped for tourists, as the antique shops along The High will testify.

WHERE TO STAY: Whether you're staying over or simply stopping off for lunch, there's a choice of some romantic old inns.

The **Bay Tree Hotel**, Sheep Street (tel. 0993/823137), would astonish the former owner of this 400-year-old, stone-gabled home. Surely Sir Lawrence Tanfield would never have predicted that this stately old house would become a quiet and peaceful setting for retreat-seekers. In his time, he was the unpopular Lord Chief Baron of the Exchequer to Elizabeth I—and was not noted for his hospitality. But time has erased the bad memory, and the splendor of this Cotswold manor house remains. The owners, Mrs. J. S. King and Mr. and Mrs. Peter King, charge between £20 ($30) and £25 ($37.50) per person for B&B, with a reduction in winter for stays of three days or more.

This is one of the showplaces of England. The house has oak-paneled rooms with huge stone fireplaces, where logs burn in chilly weather. There is a high-beamed hall with a minstrel's gallery. Room after room is furnished tastefully with antiques. The 20th-century comforts, such as central heating and a large number of bathrooms, have been discreetly installed. And the beds are a far cry from the old rope-bottom contraptions of the days of Queen Elizabeth I. You will sleep peacefully on soft mattresses. Try to get one of the rooms overlooking the terraced gardens at the rear of the house. As the season changes, new flowers come into bloom against the old stone walls. Flagstone walks, tidy lawns, and comfortable garden furniture will lure you into a lazy afternoon. A servant will bring you a tray at teatime.

You dine at night by candlelight: the meals are first class, some of the finest you'll be served in Cotswolds. A recent lunch consisted of a smoked salmon omelet, served with string beans and potatoes, and a spicy hot mince pie with brandy butter for dessert. Dinner is £7.50 ($11.25), and the big Sunday lunch costs the same. Have after-dinner coffee on the terrace and experience twilight. Slowly the soft shadows grow darker and longer: this is the moment of enchantment in England. You may even hear a meadow lark.

The **Lamb Inn,** Sheep Street (tel. 0993/823155), is a thoroughbred Cotswold house, built solidly in 1430 of thick stones, with mullioned and leaded windows, many chimneys and gables, and a slate roof mossy with age. On a quiet street, it opens onto a stone-paved rear garden, with a rose-lined walk and a shaded lawn. The inn is under the management of a family partnership of Richard and Caroline de Wolf and Ken and Bunty Scott-Lee. They charge £20 ($30) per person for B&B without bath, £23.50 ($35.25) with bath. Half-board rates are from £23 ($34.50) per person in a bathless room to £28 ($42) with bath. The bedrooms are a mixture of today's comforts, such as soft beds and plentiful hot water, and yesterday's antiques. The public living rooms contain heavy oak beams, stone floors, window seats. Oriental rugs, and fine antiques (Chippendale, Tudor, Adam, Georgian, Jacobean). In the drinking lounge, a special beer, made in an adjoining brewery, is served. In addition, a four o'clock tea is offered in front of the fireplaces, or else, weather permitting, out on the flagstoned courtyard.

Light lunches and snacks are served in the bars and lounges, or in the garden in summer, costing about £3.50 ($5.25) per person for an average meal. Dinner as well as a traditional Sunday lunch are served in the beamed dining room with a garden view. A three-course dinner costs from £10 ($15); a Sunday lunch, also three courses, goes for £8.50 ($12.75) per person. If you're dining here in the right season, you can feast on treats of the rivers or forest, such as salmon, venison, and trout.

2. Clanfield

Clanfield lies at the foot of the Cotswolds, near the upper reaches of the Thames. In the heart of "hunting country," it is convenient to

Cheltenham and the Newbury race courses. Golf and fishing are available nearby. Clanfield lies 20 miles from Oxford, eight miles from our last stopover in Burford, and 16 miles from Swindon, and also makes a center for visits to Blenheim Palace, Stratford-upon-Avon, Henley-on-Thames, and the Cotswold Wild Life Park, only a ten-minute drive from the following recommendation.

WHERE TO STAY: The **Plough Hotel and Restaurant**, Clanfield (tel. 0367/81222), is a perfect example of a mid-16th-century Elizabethan manor house. Throughout the summer, climbing roses cover the honey-colored Cotswold stone walls. Its attractive gardens just opposite the village green offer a peaceful spot for meditation. Under protection as a landmark building, the Plough maintains an air of authenticity inside as well, with cloistered halls, massive fireplaces, and fine antiques and tapestries.

The restaurant has become internationally recognized, having won various awards for its cuisine every year since 1970. Dinners are served in the Knights' and Tapestry Rooms with their authentic period furnishings. During the summer months, luncheon is frequently served in the small walled garden. Drinks are available in the beamed lounge with its magnificent Elizabethan fireplace. The Plough is open seven days a week, offering a set lunch of three courses and coffee for £10 ($15) between noon and 2 p.m. and an à la carte dinner from 7:30 to 9:30 p.m. You may select snails, melon, salad, or homemade soup as an appetizer. Main dishes include beef Wellington, sole William, rack of lamb, and steak, kidney, and oyster pie; there is a wide range of desserts. An average three-course meal will cost £15 ($22.50) to £18 ($27), with a bottle of the house wine going for £5.50 ($8.25).

The owners, Jeffrey and Lorraine King, have several small but attractively furnished rooms for rent. B&B costs £25 ($37.50) to £32 ($48) in a single, £38 ($57) to £42 ($63) in a double, VAT included in the prices.

3. Minster Lovell

From Oxford along the A40, you pass through Witney. Soon after, you turn right at the Minster Lovell signpost, about half a mile off the highway between Witney and Burford. The village's main attraction is **Minster Lovell Hall,** the remains of a moated house where an early Lovell supposedly hid out and starved to death after a battle in the area.

By the Windrush River, Minster Lovell is mainly built of Cotswold stone, with thatch or stone-slate roofs. It's rather a pity there is a forest of TV aerials, but the place is still attractive to photographers.

The **Old Swan Hotel,** Minster Lovell (tel. 0993/75614), has been an inn for some 600 years. It offers a unique blend of Cotswold stone and half-timbering. The Swan and the manor house (now in ruins) were once the two most important buildings in the village. The manor house was the home of the Lovell family, close friends of Richard III, whom they entertained there while his servants slept at the Swan. Polished flagstone floors and traditional log fires are evidence of those times. Today, the Old Swan offers 20th-century comfort in historic surroundings. All ten bedrooms have private baths, phones, and color TVs, and are individually furnished. There's even an impressive four-poster suite. A twin- or double-bedded room costs from £46 ($69), and a single, £32 ($48). The price includes VAT and a full English breakfast.

The beamed candlelit restaurant is a romantic setting in which to enjoy fine food, some of which is grown in the gardens of the hotel. Luncheon is from £8 ($12), dinner from about £14 ($21), and a light snack is available in the bar during the week.

4. Bibury

On the road from Burford to Cirencester, Bibury is one of the loveliest spots in the Cotswolds. In fact, the utopian romancer of Victoria's day, poet William Morris, called it England's most beautiful village. On the banks of the tiny Coln River, Bibury is noted for **Arlington Row,** a gabled group of 15th-century cottages, its biggest and most-photographed drawing card. The row is protected by the National Trust.

Arlington Mill, which houses the **Cotswold Country Museum,** dates from the 11th century and was in use as a mill until 1914. Mill machinery, agricultural implements, cobbler's and blacksmith's equipment, printing and weaving devices, and Victorian costumes and wedding finery are on display. There are William Morris and John Keble rooms, and you can see arts and crafts exhibits, including furniture. There is also pottery for sale. The museum is open from 10:30 a.m. to 7 p.m. (or dusk, if earlier) from March to October daily; from November to February on weekends. Admission is 80p ($1.20) for adults, 30p (45¢) for children.

WHERE TO STAY: Bibury is a good base for touring the old wool towns of the North Cotswolds. For those who prefer a secluded roadside oasis, I have the following recommendations:

Bibury Court Hotel (tel. 0285/74337) is a Jacobean manor house built by Sir Thomas Sackville in 1633 (parts of it date from Tudor times). Its eight acres of grounds are approached through a large gateway, the lawn extending to the encircling Coln River. The house was privately owned until it was turned into a hotel in 1968. The structure is built of Cotswold stone, with many gables, huge chimneys, leaded-glass stone-mullioned windows, and a formal graveled entryway. Inside there are many country manor furnishings, and antiques, as well as an open stone log-burning fireplace. In a double, the inclusive B&B rate is £35 ($52.50), dropping to £22 ($33) in a single. Many of the rooms have four-poster beds, original oak paneling, and antiques. Meals are an event in the stately dining room, where lunches and dinners start at £8.50 ($12.75). After tea and biscuits in the drawing room, walk across the lawn along the river where you find a doorway leading to a little church. On your return, head for one of the coaching houses that has been converted into a drinking lounge, a restful place for a glass of stout.

The **Swan Hotel** (tel. 0285/74204) is a scene-stealer. Before you cross over the arched stone bridge spanning the Coln, pause and look at the vine-covered facade. Yes, it's the same view that has appeared on many a calendar. The former coaching inn will bed you down for the night in one of its handsomely appointed chambers, all with bath or shower, charging £22.50 ($33.75) per person nightly. A traditional English breakfast and VAT are included. All of the rooms have been modernized, and there are many comforts. The special feature of the Swan is the small stretch of trout stream reserved for guests. If you're just passing through for the day, you may want to stop over and order the £9.50 ($14.25) lunch or the £12.50 ($18.75) dinner.

When you see the gardens at the Swan, your exploring days may be over.

5. Cirencester

Don't worry about how to pronounce the name of the town. Even the English are in disagreement. Just say "siren-sess-ter" and you won't go too far wrong. Cirencester is often considered the unofficial capital of the Cotswolds, probably a throwback to its reputation in the Middle Ages when it flourished as the center of the great wool industry.

But even in Roman Britain, five roads converged on Cirencester, which was called Corinium in those days. In size, it ranked second only to London. Today, it is chiefly a market town, a good base for touring, as it lies 34 miles from Bath, 16 from the former Regency spa at Cheltenham, 17 from Gloucester, 36 from Oxford, and 38 from Stratford-upon-Avon. The trip from London is 89 miles. In the heart of the town itself are two important sights:

Corinium Museum, Park Street (tel. 0285/5611), houses one of the finest collections of archeological remains from the Roman occupation, all found locally in and around Cirencester. Mosaic pavements found here on Dyer Street in 1849 and other mosaics are the most important exhibits. Provincial Roman sculpture, such as figures of Minerva and Mercury, pottery, and bits and pieces salvaged from long-decayed buildings provide a link with the remote civilization that once flourished here. The museum has been completely modernized to include full-scale reconstructions and special exhibitions on local history and conservation. It is open from 10 a.m. to 6 p.m. weekdays, 2 to 6 p.m. on Sunday throughout the year, closing at 5 p.m. in winter. It is closed Monday from October to April. Admission is 50p (75¢) for adults, 30p (45¢) for children.

Cirencester Parish Church, dating back to Norman times and Henry I, is the Church of John the Baptist, overlooking the Market Square. (Actually, a church may have stood on this spot in Saxon times.) In size, the Cirencester church appears to be a cathedral—not a mere parish church. The present building represents a variety of styles, largely Perpendicular, as in the early 15th-century tower. Among the treasures inside are a 15th-century pulpit and a silver-gilt cup given to Queen Anne Boleyn two years before her execution.

WHERE TO STAY AND EAT: Stratton House Hotel, Gloucester Road (tel. 0285/61761), on the outskirts of town, has a delightful country-house atmosphere in a building that is part Jacobean and part Georgian. This mellow old house, which stands in its own beautiful grounds with a walled garden and herbaceous borders, is inviting and extremely comfortable. The bedrooms are large and most have bathrooms en suite. In the dining and drawing rooms, some fine antique furniture and oil paintings may be seen. The half-board rates range from £32 ($48) to £35 ($52.50) per person. These tariffs include an English breakfast and a well-served dinner with a wide choice of British dishes. There is a timbered-beam bar, and in winter log fires blaze in this bar and in the main hall.

If you don't want to stay at a hotel, you might try **La Ronde Guest**

House/Restaurant, 52–54 Ashcroft Rd. (tel. 0285/4611), run by Mr. and Mrs. N. E. Shales, who charge approximately £14 ($21) per person for B&B. They have family rooms, as well as doubles and twins. In the town center, within walking distance of Cirencester Park, the Abbey Grounds, and the museum and parish church, the small hotel is licensed and is a good center for exploring all the Cotswolds. The dining room offers a varied menu and an extensive wine list. Dinner is from £10 ($15). VAT is included in all prices. The hotel offers central heating, hot and cold running water in all the rooms, and has a color TV lounge as well.

6. Painswick

The sleepy little town of Painswick, four miles northeast of Stroud, is considered a model village. All of its houses, while erected at different periods, blend harmoniously, as the villagers used only Cotswold stone as their building material. The one distinctive feature on the Painswick skyline is the spire of its 15th-century parish church. The church is linked with the legend of 99 yew trees, as well as its annual Clipping Feast (not the yew trees—rather, the congregation joins hands and circles around the church as if it were a Maypole, singing hymns as they do). Ancient tombstones dot the churchyard. Finally, you may want to visit **Court House,** a private Cotswold manor (see the court room of Charles I), open to the public for 30p (45¢) on Thursday only, June to mid-September, from 2 to 5 p.m. It is also open by special appointment (tel. 0452/813689).

WHERE TO STAY: The **Painswick Hotel,** Kemps Lane (tel. 0452/812160), stands at the rear of the church. Completely refurnished, this beautiful Georgian house was once a royal vicarage and is encircled by terraces of formal gardens. The hotel reception area was once the private chapel. For the upcoming season, I think this hotel offers exceptional value. Many readers have reported it to be the highlight of their Cotswold tour. In rooms, cuisine, and service, it merits consideration enough to rate a major detour from wherever else you were going. There are rooms both with and without private bathrooms, and the rates for bed and an English breakfast start at £22 ($33) per person, including VAT. The hotel has high standards of cuisine and service. It is managed by resident proprietors, who give particular attention to their North American guests.

WHERE TO DINE: The **Country Elephant** (tel. 0452/813564) is an excellent restaurant serving fine, English country-style cuisine. Owned and operated by Michael and Jane Medforth, the restaurant has a distinct personal touch. Mrs. Medforth does the cooking, keeping the menu limited so that only the freshest ingredients are used. In the simple dining room done in modern style, you can enjoy steak-and-mushroom pie with bacon and red wine, pork chops stuffed with apricots, almonds, and raisins and baked in cider with herbs, or a fresh grilled trout with cream and chives. Appetizers may include a homemade cream of watercress soup or an individual prawn and cheese quiche. The menu changes twice a week and sometimes even more often depending on what is available at the local markets. A meal will cost about £13 ($19.50) per person, plus 10% for service. Although they offer the finest California wines in their cellar, an inexpensive French wine will cost from £6 ($9) a bottle. The restaurant is open Tuesday through Saturday from 7 to 11 p.m., and also for Sunday lunch from 12:30 to 2:30 p.m.

ON THE OUTSKIRTS: Edge Farm Cottage, Edge, near Stroud in Gloucestershire (tel. 0452/812476), is a carter's dwelling dating from 1800, nestled in what has been called "a secret part of the Cotswolds." Aside from the charm of the house, what makes Edge Farm Cottage special is its owner, Barbara Blatchley, who, along with her doctor husband, welcomes guests. They've modernized their spacious house and have centrally heated it. They rent two guest bedrooms, each with twin beds, basin, and shower. Parties of two, three, or four persons are preferred.

The cost is £30 ($45) per person per day, including not only the bed and a full breakfast, but a good dinner with wine. Mrs. Blatchley offers personalized home-cooking, well-prepared British food, including roasts, game such as pheasant and venison, and salmon when in season. Guests eat together in a dining room with an old bread oven, enjoying the conversation.

As a qualified guide for the Heart of England Tourist Board, Mrs. Blatchley will also offer her services with a car, charging about £65 ($97.50) for a full day's tour.

7. Cheltenham

In a sheltered area between the Cotswolds and the Severn Vale, a mineral spring was discovered by chance. Legend has it that the Cheltenham villagers noticed pigeons drinking from a spring, and observed how healthy they were. The pigeon has therefore been incorporated into the town's crest.

Always seeking a new spa, George III arrived in 1788 and launched the town. The Duke of Wellington also came to ease his liver disorder. Even Lord Byron came this way too, proposing marriage to Miss Millbanke.

Some 100 miles from London, Cheltenham is one of England's most fashionable spas. Its architecture is mainly Regency, with lots of ironwork, balconies, and verandas. Attractive parks and open spaces of greenery make the town especially inviting.

The main street, the Promenade, has been called "the most beautiful thoroughfare in Britain." Rather similar are such thoroughfares as Lansdowne Place and Montpelier Parade. The design for the dome of the Rotunda was based on the Pantheon in Rome. Montpelier Walk, with its shops separated by caryatids, is one of the most interesting shopping centers in England.

You can take guided tours of Cheltenham on foot by checking in at the Tourist Information Centre on the Promenade. However, an advance notice of at least two days is required.

WHERE TO STAY: Queens Hotel, Promenade (tel. 0242/514724), can be safely considered the best hotel at the spa. At the head of the Regency Promenade, this upper-bracket hotel looks down on the gardens. Architecturally, it is imposing, built in 1838 in the style of the Roman temple of Jupiter. This distinguished hotel has a Regency decor and an unusually fine staircase. There are 77 bedrooms, all with private baths, radios, and color televisions. Accommodations at the back are quieter. Everything is well furnished, although decidedly old-fashioned. A single rents for £46 ($69),

KENILWORTH

WARWICK

WARWICK

A46

A41

STRATFORD-UPON-AVON

WORCESTER

WORCESTEP

A34

OEVESHAM

CHIPPING CAMPDEN

A 38

BROADWAY

MORETON-
IN-MARSH

Royal Sudeley Castle □ WINCHCOMB

STOW-ON-THE-WOLD

LOWER SWELL

UPPER AND LOWER SLAUGHTER

CHIPPING
NORTON

CHELTENHAM

BOURTON-ON-THE-WATER

GLOUCESTER

SHIPTON-UNDER-WYCHWOOD

PAINSWICK

GLOUCESTER

OXFORD

A 40

BURFORD

A16

A4I7

CLANFIELD

BIBURY

N

GLOUCESTER, WORCESTER
AND WARWICK

NAILSWORTH

CIRENCESTER

WOTTON-
UNDER-EDGE

TETBURY
MALMESBURY

ENGLAND

LONDON

and a double for £60 ($90), including service and VAT. The restaurant serves a luncheon from £10 ($15). The budget-conscious can enjoy a Queen's Table buffet lunch from £6 ($9). A complete set dinner is £18 ($27).

The **Hotel De la Bere and Country Club,** Southam, near Cheltenham (tel. 0242/37771). The year A.D. 1500 is a long time ago. This beautiful house was built at the turn of that century and was owned by the De la Bere family for three centuries. It was not converted into a hotel until 1972, and every effort has been made to ensure that the original charm of the building still remains. The dining room, the Elizabethan Room, and the Royalist Room are all paneled in oak, and there is also a Great Hall, complete with its minstrel's gallery. The menu is impressive, and there are some interesting first courses. A more informal atmosphere is offered in the French Bistro Restaurant, which is quite popular. Dinner à la carte costs £13 ($19.50), with a fixed-price menu available for lunch at £7.50 ($11.25) and for dinner at £11 ($16.50).

The bedrooms, six of which boast double four-poster beds, all have private bath, color TV, and tea- and coffee-making facilities. They have all been tastefully decorated and furnished to preserve their individual charm and character. Traditional architecture and 500 years of history are tactfully combined with the luxuries of modern-day living to provide the hotel guest with the ultimate in service and comfort. Single bedrooms cost from £32 ($48) to £40 ($60), and double or twin-bedded rooms range from £54 ($81) to £60 ($90) per night. Reductions are offered for children sharing their parents' room. All tariffs include a continental breakfast, service, and VAT.

In addition to normal hotel facilities, all guests are offered honorary membership in the hotel's own Sports and Country Club, providing an excellent range of sporting facilities and dancing in the nightclub.

Malvern View Hotel, Cleeve Hill (tel. 0242/672017), thinks of itself justifiably as a restaurant *avec chambres*. It offers only seven double bedrooms, with central heating, color TV, and private baths or showers (one chamber has a four-poster bed). These rent for £20 ($30) per person, with an extra £14 ($21) charged for dinner. The hotel's reputation for food is the finest for 20 miles around. Commanding views over Severn Vale to the Malvern Hills and the Welsh mountains beyond, the hotel is five miles north of Cheltenham, on the A46 to Broadway. It's a long, low, stone structure, with white shutters and a surrounding garden. The country-style dining room is furnished with antiques, including wheelback chairs. The silverware is real silver and the glassware cut glass. The menu is wide, including various good French dishes. On my most recent rounds, I ordered ratatouille. This appetizer was followed by a large quail stuffed with pâté in brandy. No lunch is served, and the restaurant is closed Sunday to nonresidents. Otherwise, dinner is offered from 7:30 to 9:30 p.m. If you're driving out from Cheltenham, you should telephone first.

On the Outskirts

The **Mill Inn,** Withington, near Cheltenham (tel. 024289/204), has a long history of hospitality, lying as it does opposite the Mill House, which was a working grist mill until early in this century, powered by water from the River Coln. It was here that farmers refreshed themselves while waiting for their grain to be processed. In fact, around 1870 the miller, Thomas Field, ran both the mill and the inn, enriching himself doubly. The Mill Inn has changed little over the centuries, except that today, in addition to providing snack meals and drinks, it also offers B&B accommodation. Its bedrooms are comfortable and attractive, all with central heating. If you appreciate the simple delights of a country inn, you'll like this one, with its log fires in winter and a delightful riverside garden in which you can have lunch in summer. The proprietor, Michael Stourton, charges £15 ($22.50) per person per night for a bed and a full English breakfast, VAT included.

Withington, at the head of the Coln Valley in lovely country, is an ideal center for touring the Cotswolds. It lies 11 miles north of Cirencester on the old Roman road, Whiteway.

WHERE TO EAT: Le Beaujolais, 15 Rotunda Terrace, Montpelier Street (tel. 0242/25230). Kevin Jenkins did much of his training at the Waterside Inn, Bray-on-Thames, with the Roux brothers and has now opened a good little restaurant with French flavor in the heart of Cheltenham. The kitchen is on the ground floor, and the restaurant beneath it in the basement. There is a log fire and a relaxed atmosphere, in which you can discuss the menu with Kevin's French wife. You can choose from such viands as chicken mousseline with cream and wine sauce, duck breast with garlic sauce, kidney dijonnais, turbot, mussels, snails, hot duck pâté, and skate in black butter, with perhaps a pear Charlotte or apple flan for dessert. Properly cooked vegetables accompany the main courses. A bottle of wine is £5.50 ($8.25); a set lunch, £6.50 ($9.75). For an à la carte dinner, expect to pay from £13 ($19.50) to £18 ($27) per person.

Montpelier Wine Bar and Bistro, Bayshill Lodge, Montpelier Street (tel. 0242/527774), is an imposing Regency building converted from an old established shop to a cellar bistro and first-floor wine bar. Very busy at lunchtime, but worth the effort to get in, it offers a choice of some 15 wines by the glass at around 75p to 85p ($1.28). Then you can select a hot meal from the blackboard menu. A soup is always featured among the various appetizers, then cold meats, homemade quiche, prawns, smoked fish, lasagne, interesting salads, and a good selection of desserts. Pay around £5 ($7.50) for a satisfying meal either in the cellar or, in good weather, on the terrace. It is open from Monday to Saturday, noon to 2:30 p.m. and 6 to 10:30 p.m.

That Sandwich Place, Regent Street (tel. 0242/529575), is a good luncheon choice, located in back of Cavendish House, a department store. Mr. Whittaker is the owner, and he is assisted by several very helpful local women who know how to make at least 200 different kinds of sandwiches, costing from 35p (53¢) to £1.50 ($2.25), plus an additional 30p (45¢) if you request salad garnishes such as lettuce and tomato. The repertoire uses such ingredients as peanut butter, cheese, prawns, pâté, beef, even bananas. Milkshakes, tea, and coffee are sold as well. You have a choice of eating on the premises or else ordering from the take-away service.

Forrest Wine Bar, Imperial Lane (tel. 0242/38001), is an extraordinarily economical place to eat. It's a small wine bar in an old bakery with tables given some intimacy by stall seats that divide the room. Presiding is Mrs. Henry Forrest-Hamdon (a true Cheltenham name if ever there was one). She provides a super menu with a daily homemade soup. There is a selection of homemade pâtés served with French bread and Middle Eastern dips with pita bread. Also available is a different hot dish daily, including homemade quiche, pizza, or pancakes with a cheese and spinach filling. You could have such dishes as spicy Mexican tacos with salad, lasagne with salad, chili con carne, or spaghetti Bolognese. Also, continental dishes are prepared, including roast lamb flavored with rosemary and coriander or beef roulade with red cabbage Alsacienne and sauté potatoes. Upward of 20 different wines are available by the glass, so you can conduct your own tasting if you don't have to drive farther. Prices range from about £7 ($10.50) for a meal. The house is open daily except Sunday from 10:30 a.m. to 2:30 p.m. and 7 to 10:30 p.m. (to 11 p.m. on Friday and Saturday).

8. Royal Sudeley Castle

In 1962 Elizabeth Chipps of Lexington, Kentucky, met and married Mark Dent-Brocklehurst, the wedding taking place in the 16th-century chapel of Royal Sudeley Castle. In 1970 her husband died, and Elizabeth inherited the 15th-century castle in the Cotswold village of Winchcombe, six miles northeast of Cheltenham. The history of the castle dates back to Saxon times, when the village was the capital of the Mercian kings.

Elizabeth Dent-Brocklehurst, now Lady Ashcombe, first opened the castle to visitors shortly after her husband's death, to enable people to share the treasures of royal relics, stained glass, tapestries, and paneling. The gardens are formal and surrounded by rolling farm and parkland. The herb garden dates from the time when Catherine Parr, sixth wife of Henry VIII, lived and died at Sudeley. There are several permanent exhibitions, some magnificent pictures and furniture, and peacocks that strut on the grounds.

There is now a permanent exhibition of toys and dolls, with more than 9000 items, the best known of which is the rocking horse said to have belonged to King Charles I in the early 1600s. The collection belongs to Mrs. Kay Desmonde, who has at last found a place where the public can see what is said to be the largest assembly of toys in Europe. No extra admission is charged to the exhibition, which lies to the right of the keep as you enter the castle.

The castle also has a restaurant good enough to participate in the "Taste of Britain" scheme, offering particularly good local recipes of an international standard. Lunch can be a ploughman's variety or else a hot dish of the day or cold local ham.

The castle is open daily from noon to 5 p.m. Easter to October 31. The grounds are open from 11 a.m. Admission prices are £2.80 ($4.20) for adults, £1.60 ($2.40) for children. For more information, telephone 0242/602308.

If you feel like a meal after visiting the castle, wander down to the village and to **Isbourne House,** Castle Street in Winchcombe (tel. 0242/602281). This is a lovely period Cotswold stone house surrounded by a well-kept garden, stone walls, and wrought-iron gates. Here Ted Saunders and his friend and colleague, Dick, provide elegant dinners for £15 ($22.50) per person for three or four courses, including half a bottle of excellent wine. Ted is a great equestrian and can advise on horseback-riding facilities in the area. Dick keeps his own mount and also owns several dogs, which live at Isbourne.

In the house—part Elizabethan, part Georgian—you can have B&B for £28 ($42) to £31 ($46.50) per night for two, depending on whether you have the room with bath and toilet or with just a shower.

Dinner is likely to include an appetizer such as chicken liver pâté, then veal escalope in ginger wine or pigeon breasts with juniper berry sauce, followed by a dessert, perhaps a strawberry and pernod mousse. Meals for nonresidents are provided by arrangement only. If you ring Ted in good time, he will be prepared to discuss the menu with you, advising on local products and what's in season.

9. Malmesbury

At the southern tip of the Cotswolds, the old hill town of Malmesbury is encircled by the Avon River. In the center of England's "Middle West," it makes a good base for touring the Cotswolds. Cirencester is just 12 miles away; Bibury, 19 miles; and Cheltenham, 28 miles. Malmesbury is a market town, with a fine market cross. Its historical fame is reflected by the Norman abbey built there on the site of King Athelstan's grave.

Malmesbury is considered the oldest "borough" in England, as it was granted its charter by Alfred the Great in 880. In 1980 it celebrated its 1300th anniversary. Some 400 years ago the Washington family lived there, leaving their star-and-stripe coat-of-arms on the church wall. In addition, Nancy Hanks, Abraham Lincoln's mother, came from Malmesbury. The town still has members of the family, noted for their lean features and tallness. The Penns of Pennsylvania also originally came from Malmesbury.

WHERE TO STAY: The **Old Bell,** Abbey Row (tel. Malmesbury 2344), is an unusual place—once a monastic retreat—to use as a touring center. It sits in the heart of the town, adjoining the Norman abbey. Its facade is wisteria-covered stone, with six gables and two towering chimneys; an iron picket fence guards the flowers and shrubbery. The inn opens onto a formal garden, with graveled monks' walks leading to the rear back wall, with its little stone gazebo bordering the Avon below. Architecturally, much remains of the original building, including a 13th-century window. There are 19 centrally heated bedrooms, 12 of them with private baths (otherwise, hot and cold running water). Singles range from £24 ($36) to £38 ($57), and doubles range from £40 ($60) to £52 ($78), including VAT. Open year round, the inn is often used by sportsmen, especially during Saturday hunts. Guests congregate in the dining room and the informal lounges and bars. The dining room is more modern (Regency), serving lunch for £8.50 ($12.75); dinner, £12 ($18).

WHERE TO DINE: **Apostle Spoon,** 6 Market Cross (tel. Malmesbury 3129), is run by Mr. and Mrs. Smalley, who serve tasty food. The restaurant stands facing the octagonal market cross, adjoining the abbey. A two-course meal is featured for anywhere from £8 ($12) to £16 ($24). Included in this à la carte meal are such main dishes as sirloin on the bone, kidneys in wine, pepper steak, salmon steak, chicken Wellington, and grilled ham. The restaurant is open daily.

10. Tetbury

Tetbury, in South Gloucestershire, is a sleepy Cotswold town, with old stone houses, some fine medium-priced inns, and an antique market hall. It is here that Prince Charles and Princess Diana live at Highgrove. Although the house is not open to the public, and you cannot see it from the road, you may catch a glimpse of the princess shopping in the village.

WHERE TO STAY AND EAT: The **Close,** Long Street (tel. 0666/52272), dates from 1695 and takes its name from a Cistercian monastery to which it was linked. It was once the home of a wealthy Cotswold wool merchant. Architecturally, it is built of warm honey-brown Cotswold stone, with gables and stone-mullioned windows. The ecclesiastical-type windows in the rear overlook a garden with a reflection pool, a haven for doves. Inside, you'll find a Georgian room with a domed ceiling (once it was an open courtyard), where predinner drinks are served and you can peruse the menu. Dining is in one of two rooms. Owners Jean-Marie and Sue Lauzier have spared none of their attractive antiques and silver, proudly sharing their treasures with guests. Candlelight on winter evenings, floral arrangements, sparkling silver and glass are just the background for the fine food.

The cooking is superb, and an à la carte menu offers specialty dishes. At lunch or dinner, appetizers might include homemade soup. Main dishes feature chicken cooked in champagne and encased in light pastry; steaks, beef, and fish; even an exotic guinea fowl for two persons. Desserts from the trolley are always tempting. A dinner à la carte costs from £16 ($24) per person. Fixed menus are also offered for lunch from £7.50 ($11.25) to £10 ($15), and for dinner at £12 ($18).

Most of the 12 bedrooms (all contain private baths) are spacious and handsomely furnished with antiques. A single room ranges in price from £28 ($42) to £40 ($60), and a double from £26 ($39) to £38 ($57) per person. A child sharing a room with parents is granted a reduction. A continental breakfast, service, and VAT are included.

11. Wotton-under-Edge

At the western edge of the Cotswolds, in Gloucestershire, Wotton-under-Edge is in the rural triangle of Bath (23 miles), Bristol (20 miles), and Gloucester (20 miles). Many of its old buildings indicate its former prosperity as a wool town. One of its obscure claims to fame is that it was the home of Sir Isaac Pitman, who invented shorthand. Its grammar school is one of the oldest in England, founded in 1834 and once attended by Dr. Edward Jenner, discoverer of the smallpox vaccine.

WHERE TO STAY AND EAT: The **Swan Hotel,** Market Street (tel. 0453/842329), lures with its Georgian facade, painted a distinctive blue. It offers comfortable rooms with and without private bath, but it is the fine French cuisine that attracts locals and visitors alike. Premeal drinks are taken in the Lounge Bar with an open fireplace. Meals are served in the restaurant, with its heavy beams, Windsor chairs, polished tables, and fireplace. In the Cotswold Restaurant, you can order à la carte. A three-course meal costs from £15 ($22.50). Specialties include beef Stroganoff and steak Diane maison. The Grill Restaurant is open for light meals starting from £5 ($7.50). A three-course meal starts at £7.50 ($11.25). On Saturday night, there's a dinner-dance with the resident band. Bathless singles cost £28 ($42), £35 ($52.50) with bath. A double room without bath is £36 ($54), with bath, £44 ($66). Tariffs are inclusive of VAT and breakfast.

12. Shipton-under-Wychwood

Taking the A361 road, en route from Burford to Chipping Norton, you arrive after a turn off at the little village of Shipton-under-Wychwood in Oxfordshire. It's about four miles north of Burford; but don't blink—or you'll pass it right by. The monks of Bruern Abbey used to run a hospice in the village and that hospice is now an inn.

WHERE TO STAY AND EAT: **The Shaven Crown,** High Street (tel. 0993/830330), was originally a hospice operated by monks as part of Bruern Abbey. In the 13th century it served as a center for dispensing aid to the poor. Built of rugged Cotswold stone during the reign of Queen Elizabeth I, it is on the main village road, and opens onto a triangular village green in the shadow of a church. Most of the rooms overlook a cobblestoned courtyard and garden, and have attractive antiques. Hot and cold running water have been installed in every bedroom, and there are adequate hallway baths and toilets, and two of the bedrooms have private baths. The charge is £45 ($67.50) nightly for B&B in a double room with private bath, although this is lowered to £38 ($57) in a bathless double. Tariffs include a full English breakfast. Singles are charged £18 ($27) nightly on the B&B arrangement.

The **Lamb Inn,** High Street (tel. 0993/830465), is a small stone Cotswold inn and perfect if you're seeking a simple village stopover serving a superior cuisine. It's owned by Hugh and Lynne Wainwright, who give a cordial welcome. Twins and doubles with bath cost £32 ($48) per night, including a full English breakfast, service, and VAT. A single costs £22 ($33). Each room in the inn is country style.

A three-course dinner goes for around £10 ($15). Main dishes are based on the season and the day's buying, but are likely to include roast pheasant, grilled trout with almonds, and duck cooked in various ways, a specialty. Another house specialty is filet Wychwood, filet steak in a cream sauce. At Sunday lunch the traditional roast beef or lamb is offered, with all the trimmings, £8.50 ($12.75). At lunch a hot and cold selection of snacks is available in the bar, with the list shown on the blackboard. Irish stew is popular, or you can have salads with duck, beef, ham, or salmon. Expect to spend about £4.50 ($6.75). The restaurant is closed on Sunday evening.

On the Outskirts

The **Wychwood Arms Hotel,** Ascott-under-Wychwood (tel. 0993/830271). Until recently the Wychwood Arms was a local pub, a Cotswold-stone building among many. Now, Peter and Eunice Bailey use the upper floor to provide five comfortable double bedrooms, all with private bath and color TV. The rate for a room and a full English breakfast, including VAT and service, is £25 ($37.50) in a double, £18 ($27) in a single. The furnishings are those of a country pub, and the pictures and prints that adorn the walls follow a sport theme. There is central heating throughout, and the atmosphere is friendly.

Midday meals are served in the bar, when you can enjoy hot dishes and salads. Try the scampi, brown bread, and chips, or a prawn salad. À la carte dinners in the bar dining area cost around £10 ($15) for a meal that might consist of soup, steak, vegetables, and dessert. The location is good, only 18 miles from Oxford, 26 miles from Stratford-upon-Avon.

13. Chipping Norton

Just inside the Oxfordshire border is Chipping Norton, another gateway town to the Cotswolds. Since the days of Henry IV it has been an important market town, and its main street is a curiosity as it's built on a slope, making one side higher than the other.

Chipping Norton has long been noted for its tweed mills; also seek out its Guildhall, its church, and its handsome almshouses. If you're touring, you can search for the nearby prehistoric Rollright Stones, more than 75 stones forming a circle 100 feet in diameter—the "Stonehenge of the Cotswolds." Chipping Norton lies 11 miles from Burford, 20 miles from Oxford, and 21 miles from Stratford-upon-Avon.

WHERE TO STAY AND EAT: The **Crown and Cushion Hotel,** The High (tel. Chipping Norton 2533), dates back to 1497 and was originally a coaching inn. Half of the bedrooms are equipped with private shower baths, radios, phones, and television sets, and all are centrally heated. Rates are £15.50 ($23.25) per person in a room without bath, rising to £21.50 ($32.25) per person with bath, these tariffs including breakfast and VAT. The bar can provide hot and cold snacks morning and evening. The restaurant is à la carte. There's a color TV lounge, plus a residents' reading room. This is an ideal center for touring the Cotswolds, and it's close to Oxford, Stratford-upon-Avon, Cheltenham, and Silverstone. Resident proprietors are Jim and Margaret Fraser, who come from Limerick in Ireland, and visitors find it amusing when they discover this couple running an "Old English coaching inn." The Frasers are helpful in finding accommodations elsewhere in the Cotswolds when their hotel is full.

An Old Mill on the Outskirts

The **Mill Hotel and Restaurant,** Kingham (tel. 060-871/8188). In A.D. 1086 reference was made in the Domesday Book to a mill worth 44 pence in lease value situated at "Corsingham of the King." This same mill on the Cornwell Brook at Kingham in Oxfordshire turns leisurely today as the centerpiece in one of rural England's finest regional hotels, where the nostalgia of days gone by merges delightfully with today. The Mill Hotel envelops all that was charming of the original mill and bakehouse, and it has been possible to infuse modern amenities without detracting from the old-world charm and original purpose of the buildings. There are comfortable lounges with log fires and an abundance of old stone floors and oak beams. In the Lounge Bar, the original ovens of the old bakehouse line the wall.

All 20 bedrooms have private bath or shower, color TV, radio, and phone. The B&B rate is £18 ($27) in a single, £34 ($51) in a double. À la carte and table d'hôte dishes are served, complemented by a good range of moderately priced wines. The hotel stands in ten acres of grounds bounded by a trout stream. Guests are warmly welcomed by John and Valerie Barnett, the resident owners.

14. Bourton-on-the-Water

In this most scenic Cotswold village, you can be like Gulliver, voyaging first to Brobdingnag, then to Lilliput. Brobdingnag is Bourton-on-the-Water, lying 85 miles from London, on the banks of the tiny Windrush River.

To see Lilliput, you have to visit the Old New Inn. In the garden is a near-perfect and most realistic model village. It is open daily from 8:30 a.m. till dusk, and costs 50p (75¢) for adults, 30p (45¢) for children.

If you're coming to the Cotswolds by train from London, you'll find the nearest rail station is in Moreton-on-Marsh, eight miles away. Buses make connections with the trains, however.

READERS' SIGHTSEEING SUGGESTION: "Tourists should visit **Birdland** (tel. 0451/20689) nearby. It consists of a beautifully designed garden of 4½ acres, a veritable paradise for some 600 birds of 158 different species. The macaws (each named) are particularly interesting and colorful—they love entertaining visitors with their antics and chatter. There is an exquisite group of flamingoes and a large collection of penguins with an eye-level pool so that they can be seen feeding, which is a rare sight. Also there are hummingbirds and others in a tropical house. Admission is £1.50 ($2.25) for adults, 90p ($1.35) for children" (D. and R. Hosie, Balwyn, Victoria, Australia).

WHERE TO STAY AND EAT: Bourton-on-the-Water offers a handful of quite-good accommodations, all of them inexpensive in spite of its reputation as a tourist attraction.

The **Old New Inn** (tel. 0451/20467) can lay claim to being the leading hostelry in the village. Right in the center, overlooking the river, it's a good example of Queen Anne design. But it is mostly visited because of the miniature model village in its garden (referred to earlier). Hungry or tired travelers are drawn to the old-fashioned comforts and cuisine of this most English inn. The B&B rate is £16 ($24) per person nightly, including service charge and VAT. The rooms are comfortable, with homey furnishings, soft beds, and hot and cold running water. Packed lunches at £2.50 ($3.75) will be provided for your excursion jaunts. You may want to spend evenings in the pub lounge, playing darts or chatting with the villagers. Nonresidents may also want to stop in for a meal, with lunches at £4 ($6), and dinners from £10 ($15).

The **Old Manse Hotel** (tel. 0451/20642) is reminiscent of the setting of Nathaniel Hawthorne's *Mosses from an Old Manse*. A gem architecturally, the hotel is by the slow-moving river that wanders through the village green. Built of ivy-covered Cotswold stone, with chimneys, dormers, and small-paned windows, it has been modernized inside, and all rooms have radio, color TV, and central heating. The proprietors, Mary and Derek Hall, charge from £42 ($63) for two persons in a twin with private bath, a continental breakfast included. Rates are lowered off-season. The inn's best feature is the stone fireplace in the dining room, as well as the wood-paneled bar. Dining is a treat here. A three-course lunch or dinner costs about £8 ($12), but you can order from an à la carte menu as well. The manse is closed during the first week in January.

Chester House Hotel & Motel (tel. 0451/20286) is a weathered, 300-year-old Cotswold stone house, built on the banks of the Windrush River. Owned and managed by Mr. Davies, the hotel is an ideal center for touring. A double room without bath rents for £28 ($42), increasing to £33 ($49.50) with bath and TV.

15. Lower Swell

Near Stow-on-the-Wold, Lower Swell is a twin. Both it and Upper Swell, its sister, are small villages of the Cotswolds. The hamlets are not to be confused with Upper and Lower Slaughter.

WHERE TO STAY AND EAT: You may want to anchor in for the night or stop for a meal at the following recommendation:

Old Farmhouse Hotel (tel. 0451/30232) is a small, intimate 16th-century hotel in the heart of the Cotswolds, one mile west of Stow-on-the-Wold. The hotel has been completely refurbished and the original fireplaces restored, once again blazing with log fires. The relaxed, friendly atmosphere, together with excellent food and wine, has made this a popular stop for visitors, so reserving a room before arrival is strongly recommended. All bedrooms have color TV and tea- and coffee-making facilities. Most units now have private baths. Prices for a twin- or double-bedded room range from £28 ($42) in low season to £42 ($63) in high season for the four-poster bed. Light lunches are served Monday to Saturday from 12:15 to 2 p.m. and may be taken in the delightful garden, weather permitting. On Sunday, a traditional English lunch with roast beef is a popular feature, costing £7.50 ($11.25). Dinner is served daily from 7:30 p.m., with last orders taken at 9 p.m. The food is likely to be a tasty and filling repast, whether you choose the table d'hôte at £8 ($12) or select from the à la carte menu. The hotel is closed for the month of January.

16. Upper and Lower Slaughter

Midway between Bourton-on-the-Water and Stow-on-the-Wold are the twin villages of Upper and Lower Slaughter. Don't be put off by the name because these are two of the prettiest villages in the Cotswolds. Actually the name "Slaughter" was a corruption of "de Sclotre," the original Norman landowner. The houses are constructed of honey-colored Cotswold stone, and a stream meanders right through the street, providing a home for the ducks that wander freely about, begging scraps from kindly visitors. In Upper Slaughter you can visit a fine example of a 17th-century Cotswold manor house.

WHERE TO STAY AND EAT: **Lords of the Manor Hotel,** in Upper Slaughter (tel. 0451/20243), is a rambling 17th-century house standing on several acres of rolling fields and gardens that include a stream flowing through the grounds in which guests fish for brown trout. Completely modernized in its amenities, the hotel has still been successful in maintaining the quiet country-house atmosphere of 300 years ago.

The 15 guest rooms are equipped with private bath, and many rooms have pleasant views of the Cotswold hills. The walls in the lounge bar are hung with family portraits of the original Lords of the Manor. Another bar overlooks the garden, and chintz and antiques are everywhere.

The country atmosphere is carried into the dining room as well, with its antiques and mullioned windows. All the well-prepared dishes are fresh and home-cooked. You'll pay an average of about £12 ($18) for a meal that may consist of leek and potato soup or broiled scallops wrapped in bacon for an appetizer, grilled rainbow trout with almonds, or chicken Kiev for the main course, and a selection of rich homemade desserts from the trolley. Room rates, which include breakfast, VAT, and service charge, range from £49 ($73.50) to £65 ($97.50) for a double room, depending on facilities. Singles go from £35 ($52.50) a night.

17. Stow-on-the-Wold

This is an unspoiled Cotswold market town, in spite of the busloads of tourists who stop off en route to Broadway and Chipping Campden, about ten miles away. The town is the highest in the Cotswolds, built on a wold about 800 feet above sea level. In its open market square, you can still see the stocks where offenders in days gone by were jeered at and punished by the townspeople with a rotten egg in the face. The final battle between the Roundheads and the Royalists took place in Stow-on-the-Wold. The town, which is really like a village, is used by many not only for exploring the Cotswold wool towns but Stratford-upon-Avon, 21 miles away. The nearest rail station is at Moreton-in-Marsh, four miles away.

WHERE TO STAY AND EAT: A wealth of old inns is to be found here.

Stow Lodge Hotel (tel. 0451/30485) dominates the Market Place, but is set back far enough to maintain its aloofness. Its gardens, honeysuckle growing over the stone walls, diamond-shaped windows, gables, and many chimneys, capture the best of country living, while letting you anchor right into the heart of town. Mr. and Mrs. Jux, the owners, who are partners with their daughter and son-in-law, Mr. and Mrs. Hartley, offer 22 ample, well-furnished bedrooms, all with private baths, radio, TV, B&B, central heating, and tea- and coffee-making facilities. The B&B rate ranges from £25 ($37.50). Arrange to have your afternoon tea out back by the flower garden. The owners discovered an old (approximately 1770) open stone fireplace in their lounge, so they now offer log fires as an added attraction.

Unicorn Hotel (tel. 0451/30257) was a posting house and staging inn, putting up wayfarers on the old Fosse Way. Nowadays run as a hotel, it is built of the local stone—low and sprawling with miniature dormers. While there is a nicely furnished residents' lounge, even two pubs, the emphasis is placed on the dining room and the bedrooms overhead. They offer 20 rooms, all with private bath or shower and toilet, color TV, radio, telephone, trouser presser, and tea- and coffee-making facilities. The rooms have been recently redecorated, making them warmer and more comfortable. Singles rent for £34 ($51), and doubles for £45 ($67.50), including VAT and a full English breakfast. A number of them have been set aside for nonsmokers. The rooms are pleasant, excellent for sleeping, especially the chambers away from the road. The dining room provides table d'hôte and à la carte menus specializing in old English cooking with dishes of local origin. A set lunch goes for £8 ($12), and a set dinner for £11 ($16.50). There is an excellent choice of table wines. This heart of England hotel offers walks and historic places of interest within easy reach.

The **Kings Arms Hotel** (tel. 0451/30364) is a 500-year-old posting house, opening onto the Market Square. The much-traveled Charles I slept here, on May 8, 1645. You can too, surrounded by some fine old antiques. A single without bath is yours for £15 ($22.50), a single with bath costing £18 ($27). A double- or twin-bedded room is £25 ($37.50) without bath, £29 ($43.50) with such facilities. All tariffs include VAT, service, and a full English breakfast. The lucky ones get the King Charles room itself, with its carved bed and open fireplace. The other bedrooms are all comfortably furnished with all modern comforts—innerspring mattress, bedside lamp, TV, and wash basin. In the dining room, dinner averages from £10 ($15) to £12 ($18), depending on the main course. Hot and cold snacks are served in the lounge-bar at lunchtime, from 75p ($1.13) to £6 ($9), which buys a complete meal. The family-run hotel gives you personal service at all times and is fully centrally heated.

The **Talbot Hotel,** The Square (tel. 0451/30631), is an old house on the main square overlooking the church, the village stocks, and the bustling life of the small country town. The hotel has a lot of very comfortable bedrooms, mostly with bath or shower, in the main building and in the annex across the road. A single in the annex rents for £18 ($27), a single with bath in the main hotel for £24 ($36). Twins and doubles cost £28 ($42) to £34 ($51), according to their location. Ask for the bedroom with the half-tester bed. However, it is perhaps more for the excellence of the bar snacks that I include the Talbot here.

The lounges and bars are warm and cheerful, with open log fires burning, fresh flowers, and cozy chairs. Snack lunches are served daily and include such things as prawns in cheese sauce, jacket potatoes filled with cheese and onions, Welsh rarebit, cottage pie, and chicken and ham vol-au-vent. These hot or cold snacks cost from £1.50 ($2.25) to £4 ($6).

For those who stay at the hotel or passersby who require a more substantial and leisurely meal, the dining room specializes in many traditional dishes made from fresh local ingredients and accompanied by fresh vegetables. A set lunch goes for £8 ($12), and a set dinner for £9.50 ($14.25). If you order à la carte, you'll pay about £14 ($21) for a complete meal.

Food at an Old Inn

On the B4450 across country from Chipping Norton to Stow-on-the-Wold, right on the village green at Bledington, lies the **King's Head,** Bledington, Oxfordshire (tel. 060-871/365). This lovely 16th-century inn has been catering to travelers for more years than it's possible to remember. Nowadays, Graham and Rita Smith provide real ale to be quaffed in the beer garden or in the low-ceilinged bars. The Smiths' daughter Sarah, a Cordon Bleu–trained cook, assures that visitors will get good meals at the inn at reasonable prices, whether they select bar snacks, lunches, or complete dinners. Accommodations comprise three comfortable double bedrooms, decorated and furnished to a high standard to complement the old beams and unique characteristics. Each room is carpeted and has color TV. The price is £22 ($33) per room, including a full English breakfast.

18. Moreton-in-Marsh

As it's connected by rail to Paddington Station in London (83 miles away), Moreton-in-Marsh is an important center for train passengers headed for the Cotswolds. It is very near many of the villages of interest—Bourton-on-the-Water, 8 miles; Stow-on-the-Wold, 4 miles; Broadway, 8 miles; Chipping Campden, 7 miles; Stratford-upon-Avon, 17 miles away.

Each of the Cotswold towns has its distinctive characteristics. In Moreton-in-Marsh, look for the 17th-century Market Hall and its old Curfew Tower, and then walk down its High, where Roman legions trudged centuries ago (the town once lay on the ancient Fosse Way). Incidentally, if you base here, don't take the name Moreton-in-Marsh too literally. Marsh derives from an old word meaning border.

WHERE TO STAY: For accommodations, seek out the following:

Manor House Hotel (tel. 0608/50501) is a 300-year-old stone manor, complete with its own ghost, a priest's hiding hole, a secret passage, and a Moot Room used centuries ago by local merchants to settle arguments over wool exchanges. Placed prominently on the main village street, it is formal, yet gracious, and its rear portions reveal varying architectural periods of design. Here, the vine-covered walls protect the garden, a tranquil retreat. Inside are many living rooms, one especially inti-drinks and the exchange of "bump-in-the-night" stories. Servants are instructed to keep the log fires burning—"never spare the wood-pile."

You can't miss on most of the bedrooms, as they are tastefully furnished, often with antiques or fine reproductions. Many have fine old desks set in front of window ledges, with a view of the garden and ornamental pond. All contain color TV sets. A single without bath costs £20.50 ($30.75), increasing to £32 ($48) with bath. In a bathless double, the tariff is £39 ($58.50), going up to £54 ($81) with bath, including breakfast, VAT, and service. In addition, Apple House, between the garden and the hotel orchard, contains three double bedrooms, each with shower, toilet, and basin en suite. Centrally heated, it has proven very popular with visitors. The cost is £35 ($52.50) per room, with breakfast, service, and VAT included.

A favorite nook is the bar-lounge, with its garden view through leaded Gothic windows. Evening meals in the two-level dining room are candlelit. A table d'hôte lunch goes for £7 ($10.50), and dinner for £12 ($18).

The **Redesdale Arms** (tel. 0608/50308) is an old coaching inn, on the main village street, its original Cotswold stone features intact. Guests gravitate to the bar-lounge, where drinks are served in front of a six-foot-high stone fireplace. In warmer months, the rear paved terrace is the focal point, with tables set out for refreshments. The bedrooms are simply furnished, with soft beds, dressing tables with three-way mirrors, and hot and cold running water. A single without bath costs £17 ($25.50); a double or twin without bath goes for £32 ($48), and a double or twin with bath, £36 ($54). All prices include breakfast and VAT. The inn is also well known for its meals. A three-course dinner goes for £9 ($13.50), although a full à la carte menu is available as well. Bar snacks are available at lunchtime, and on Sunday you can enjoy the classic English roast luncheon for £6.50 ($9.75).

White Hart Royal Hotel, High Street (tel. 0608/50731), is one of the Trusthouses Forte hotels. It's also another one of the hostelries graced by Charles I (in 1644), who did a lot of sleeping around. The inn provides the amenities of today without compromising the personality of yester-year. There are two dozen well-furnished bedrooms, with hot and cold running water (some with private bath), innerspring mattresses, and a few antiques intermixed with basic 20th-century pieces. Singles start at £38 ($57), rising to £42 ($63). Twins and doubles go for £50 ($75) to £55 ($82.50). All rates include service and VAT. The old hallway is ro-mantic, as is the bar lounge, built of irregular Cotswold stone. You can have drinks in front of the ten-foot open fireplace. Over the bar and on the walls is a good collection of swords, pewter, and copper warming pans.

19. Broadway

This is the best known Cotswold village. Its wide and beautiful High Street is flanked with honey-colored stone buildings with mullioned windows remarkable for the harmony of their style and design. Overlooking the Vale of Evesham, Broadway is virtually mobbed with tourists in summer, a major stopover for bus tours. That it retains its charm in spite of the invasion is a credit to its character.

Broadway lies near Evesham at the southern tip of Worcestershire, more than just a sauce familiar to steak lovers. Many of the prime attractions of the Cotswolds as well as Shakespeare Country lie within easy reach of Broadway. Stratford-upon-Avon is only 15 miles away. The nearest rail stations are at Evesham and Moreton-in-Marsh.

WHERE TO STAY: For lodgings, Broadway has the dubious distinction of sheltering the most expensive inn in the Cotswolds. Even the guest houses can command a good price—and get it.

The **Dormy House Hotel,** Willersey Hill, near Broadway (tel. 0386/852711), is a manor farmhouse, standing high on a hill above the village of Broadway, with views in all directions. Its spectacular position has made it a favorite place for those who desire either a meal, afternoon tea, or lodgings. Halfway between Broadway and Chipping Campden, it was created from a sheep farm. The owners have transformed it, remaking an old adjoining timbered barn into studio-style rooms, with open-beamed ceilings, window seats, a few antiques, good soft beds, and full central heating. Some rooms in the old farmhouse include the penthouse suite at £80 ($120) for two and the four-poster rooms at £70 ($105) for two. Other singles and doubles or twins include a wing of studio rooms. However, they're over the conference center so they're a bit noisy if there's a function going on. The studio rooms rent for £33 ($49.50) or £44 ($66) single, £60 ($90) double. The cottage suite is £102 ($153) for two, £125 ($187.50) for four (making it good value, but it only has one bath), and the Emily Suite rooms (ground floor, overlooking the courtyard garden) are £76 ($114). All rooms and suites have color TV, radio clock alarm, and well-fitted baths, although some in the main house are somewhat small. Rates include a full English breakfast and VAT.

Tavern meals from £5 ($7.50) in the bar include at lunchtime the chef's special or a cold buffet and salad. A table d'hôte lunch is £9 ($13.50); dinner, £12 ($18). At dinnertime, Roger Child, formerly a chef with the Roux brothers and at Chewton Glen, gives his skills free rein, and the à la carte menu includes interesting pâtés of quail and sweetbreads among the appetizers. Main dishes, beautifully presented, include a magret of duck with champagne and pink peppercorns and prime scotch beef with truffles and madeira sauce. Such a meal will cost you around £18 ($27) for three courses. Whole-meal bread is made for the hotel by a little old woman in the village who has to resist taking further orders to fulfill her contract with the hotel.

Ingrid Sørrensen, wife of the owner, is responsible for much of the delightful decor, the use of fresh flowers, and the fascinating decorations made with dried flowers. As you arrive at the front door, you can smell the woodsmoke from numerous open fires. This place has a friendly atmosphere.

The **Broadway Hotel,** The Green (tel. 0386/852401), is right on the village green, perhaps one of the most colorful houses in Broadway. It is a converted 15th-century house, formerly used by the abbots of Pershore, combining the half-timbered look of the Vale of Evesham with the stone of the Cotswolds. While keeping its old-world charm, the hotel has been modernized and converted to provide comforts. It recently was refurbished, with more private baths being added. There is hot and cold running water in the bedrooms, as well as central heating and bedside telephones. A single costs £26 ($39) with bath; and doubles go for £48 ($72) with bath. All these tariffs include a full English breakfast, service, and VAT. A few of the rooms contain four-poster beds. The cooking is fine, the service personal, the dining room attractive, the bedrooms pleasantly furnished. The comfortable cocktail bar is well stocked.

On the Outskirts

The **Old Rectory,** Willersey, near Broadway (tel. 0386/853729), is a 19th-century stone house lying on a quiet street near the duckpond and green, just two minutes' walk from the main A46 road. The building has a home-like atmosphere and much charm. Mrs. Helen Jones charges from £13.50 ($20.25) to £16.50 ($24.75) for her doubles. All bedrooms have tea- and coffee-making facilities, comfortable chairs and beds, and color TV. A full English breakfast is included in the rates.

WHERE TO DINE: Hunter's Lodge Restaurant (tel. 0386/853247) is set back quietly from the long High Street, surrounded by its own lawns, flower beds, shady trees, and flowering shrubs. The stone gables are partially covered with ivy, and the windows are deep-set with mullions and leaded panes. There is a formal entrance, with a circular drive and a small foyer furnished with antiques. The Swiss chef/proprietor is Kurt Friedli. His wife, Dottie, greets you, discusses the menu, and makes sure you have everything you want in the way of food and service. That might include rabbit casserole, wild duck with orange and fresh cream, two quails on a skewer grilled with bacon and apples and finished with apple brandy, game pie, or pork steak in cider cream with rosemary and roquefort. In summer you can eat in the garden. Dottie says she doesn't try to make "every chair pay the maximum." If somebody wants only one course, that's all right with her. Three courses at dinnertime will cost around £38 ($57) for two. Lunch is lighter and simpler—perhaps chicken liver pâté followed by sea bream with herb butter and vegetables, topped off by a homemade dessert, a meal costing about £11 ($16.50). Lunches are served from 12:30 to 2 p.m., and dinners from 7:30 to 10 p.m. The Lodge is closed on Sunday nights and all day Monday.

20. Chipping Campden

The English themselves, regardless of how often they visit the Cotswolds, are attracted in great numbers to this town. It's neither too large nor too small. Off the main road, it's easily accessible to major points of interest, and double-decker buses frequently run through here on their way to Oxford (36 miles away) or Stratford-upon-Avon (12 miles away).

Chipping Campden is the winner of the "Best Kept Village Award" in the Bledisloe Cup competition. Rich merchants built homes of Cotswold stone along its model High Street. They have been so well preserved that Chipping Campden to this day remains a gem of the Middle Ages. Its church dates from the 15th century, and its old Market Hall is the loveliest of the Cotswolds. Look also for its almshouses.

WHERE TO STAY: Here are several good choices, all in the medium-priced range:

The **Noel Arms,** High Street (tel. 0386/840317), may make you a snob. You just may assume a title for the night, dreaming that this is your personal manor house, with its staff of servants. Dating back to the 14th century, the Noel Arms is a famous establishment. It charges £25 ($37.50) for a bathless single, £28 ($42) for a single with bath. Bathless doubles go for £32 ($48), and doubles with bath for £41 ($61.50), plus VAT, for a bed and a full English breakfast. You can drive your car under the covered archway and into the old posting yard, where parking is private.

Mr. and Mrs. R. P. Sargent, the owners, have had much experience in running hotels, and they offer a warm welcome to their visitors from overseas. Their food always draws praise. Lunch averages £6 ($9), and a dinner costs as little as £10 ($15), if you order from the la carte menus. The food is traditional English: poached salmon, roast sirloin of beef with Yorkshire pudding, roast leg of lamb with onion sauce, steak hollandaise, apple and loganberry pie.

There's a private sitting room for residents, but you may prefer the lounge, with its 12-foot-wide fireplace. The adjoining room is the public tavern—public in the sense that it's frequented by the locals. It's almost too quaint: old worn curved settles where you can drink beer from mugs of pewter, and soak up an atmosphere enhanced by racks of copper, brass pans, medallions, and oak chairs worn from centuries of use.

The **Cotswold House Hotel** (tel. 0386/840330) is a stately, formal Regency house, dating from 1800. Right in the heart of the village, opposite the old wool market, it is run by two gentlemen partners, Graeme Black and Geoffrey Douglass. They have teamed up to bring a high taste level to this handsome old house, and are rightfully proud of the winding Regency staircase in the reception hall. All of the bedrooms have been renovated and two medieval cottages in the garden have been turned into very comfortable bedrooms with bathrooms. Each bedroom has its own personality, enhanced in some cases by antiques. A bathless single goes for £20 ($30), and a double for £33 ($49.50). A double with private bath rents for £42 ($63).

Taking your meals in the elegant Adam dining room is one of the pleasures of stopping over. The food is prepared with imagination and skill, a set dinner going for £10 ($15). A typical meal might include cream of celery soup, baked rainbow trout with almonds or roast leg of pork with apple sauce, along with fresh vegetables, followed by a wide selection of desserts. Set lunches are served in the dining room on Sunday. They begin with the largest table of hors d'oeuvres outside Claridge's. Otherwise bar lunches, snacks, salads, sandwiches, and soups fill the public need, judging by their popularity. Both guests and nonresidents are welcomed in this elegant background of fluted columns, an ornate ceiling, and three arched windows opening onto the garden in the rear. The front drawing room is home-like and informal, with a fine collection of framed needlework. Fires burn during the winter months, and the drinking lounge is a cozy spot on a cold day. The friendly management will do much to try to provide tickets for the Shakespeare performances and will offer after-theater suppers if you arrange them in advance.

Kings Arm Hotel, Chipping Campden (tel. 0386/840256), stands right by the Market Square. It is partly Georgian, partly much older, a pretty house with a large garden in which you can wander and whence come the fresh vegetables for your well-prepared dinner. Bathless singles rent for £17.50 ($26.25); bathless doubles, £35 ($52.50); doubles with bath, £45 ($67.50). Tariffs include breakfast, service, and VAT. All the accommodations are well furnished and spotlessly clean. Sunday lunch in the traditional English style is served for about £9.50 ($14.25). A table d'hôte dinner is a good meal with interesting dishes, costing about £12 ($18).

TIME OUT FOR TEA: **Bantam Tea Rooms,** High Street (tel. 0386/840386). Real old-fashioned English afternoon teas are served in this lovely bay-windowed 17th-century stone house. You can almost feel the warmth from the much-used oven when you enter to be greeted by Joan Hood and her staff of cheerful local women. In the winter, a log fire roars out its welcome from the original open fireplace. Tea can be just a pot of tea and a teacake for £1.50 ($2.25), or you can indulge in homemade scones, crumpets, sandwiches, and homemade pastries and cakes. Tea is served from 2 to 5:15 p.m. Tuesday through Sunday. It is almost an anticlimax to say that they also serve lunches Tuesday through Saturday with a selection of locally produced ham and salad, game pie, pâtés, omelets, and salads for around £3 ($4.50). This is the brainchild of Mrs. Hood, a cookery writer, and her husband, and you can rely on them to see that everything is in "apple pie order."

Chapter XII

STRATFORD AND THE HEART OF ENGLAND

1. Stratford-upon-Avon
2. Warwick
3. Kenilworth Castle
4. Coventry
5. Hereford and Worcester
6. Salop (Shropshire)
7. Staffordshire

SO CLOSE TO LONDON, so rich in fascination, the Shakespeare Country in the heart of England is that district most visited by North Americans (other than London, of course). Many who don't recognize the county name, Warwickshire, know its foremost tourist town, Stratford-upon-Avon, the birthplace of England's greatest writer.

The county and its neighboring shires form a land of industrial cities, green fields, and sleepy market towns—dotted with buildings, some of which have changed little since Shakespeare's time. Here are many of the places that have magic for overseas visitors, not only Stratford-upon-Avon, but also Warwick and Kenilworth Castles, as well as Coventry Cathedral.

Those who have time to penetrate deeper into the chapter will find elegant spa towns, such as Great Malvern, historic cathedral cities such as Hereford and Worcester, and industrial archeology at Stoke-on-Trent (the famous potteries). Scenery in Salop ranges from untamed borderlands to gentle plains that give way in the north to wooded areas and meres.

AN ENGLISH JOURNEY: Short stay holidays arranged through **Caroline Clist** at Shelsley Beauchamp, Worcestershire WR6 6RL (tel. 08865/252), were started several years ago, and Caroline is now able to offer visitors the opportunity of staying in private manor houses throughout the heart of England. Your hosts and hostesses live in a variety of period houses, all of architectural interest. All bedrooms have baths en suite and are furnished to a high standard. Dinner, prepared by your hostess, will provide a time to talk and get to know the owners of these lovely houses. This is a way to meet the English in their own homes.

Optional day tours with a driver/guide are available to take you to the hidden corners of this part of England. If you have particular interests you wish to pursue or particular places you would like to visit, let Caroline know, and she'll arrange it.

Dinner, drinks, and B&B cost £105 ($162.50) per night per couple. A day tour with driver/guide is priced at £65 ($97.50) per couple. Reduced rates are granted for children 8 to 16. Lunches taken in historic pubs and entrance fees to museums and other attractions are not included in the price of the trip. You can arrange to be picked up at railway stations, from Central London, or at Heathrow or Gatwick Airports.

1. Stratford-upon-Avon

This town has a phenomenal tourist trade. Actor David Garrick really got it launched in 1769 when he organized the first of the Bard's birthday celebrations. It is no secret by now, of course, that William Shakespeare was born in Stratford-upon-Avon on April 23, 1564.

Surprisingly little is known about his early life, as the frankest of his biographers concede. Perhaps because documentation is so lacking about the writer, much useless conjecture has arisen (did Elizabeth I really write the plays?). But the view that Francis Bacon wrote all of Shakespeare's work would certainly stir up *The Tempest,* if suggested to the innkeepers of Stratford-upon-Avon. Admittedly, however, some of the stories and legends connected with Shakespeare's days in Stratford are largely fanciful, invented belatedly to amuse and entertain the vast number of literary fans making the pilgrimage.

Today's magnet, in addition to Shakespeare's birthplace, is the Royal Shakespeare Theatre, where Britain's foremost actors perform during a long season that lasts from Easter until January. Stratford-upon-Avon is also a good center for trips to Warwick Castle, Kenilworth Castle, Sulgrave Manor (ancestral home of George Washington), Compton Wynyates, and Coventry Cathedral. The market town lies 92 miles from London, 40 from Oxford, and 8 from Warwick.

THE SIGHTS: Besides the attractions on the periphery of Stratford, there are many Elizabethan and Jacobean buildings in this colorful town—many of them administered by the Shakespeare Birthplace Trust. One ticket—costing £3.50 ($5.25) for adults, £1.50 ($2.25) for children—will permit you to visit the five most important sights. You should pick up the ticket if you're planning to do much sightseeing (obtainable at your first stopover at any one of the Trust properties). The houses are open from 9 a.m. to 6 p.m. weekdays (on Sunday from 2 to 6 p.m.), from April through October; Shakespeare's birthplace and Anne Hathaway's Cottage open at 10 a.m. on Sunday during the summer. Off-season, the houses are open from 9 a.m. to 4 p.m. On winter Sundays, only Shakespeare's birthplace and Anne Hathaway's Cottage are open, from 1:30 to 4:30 p.m.

Shakespeare's Birthplace

On Henley Street, the son of a glover and whittawer, the Bard was born on St. George's day (April 23) in 1564, and died 52 years later on the same day. Filled with Shakespeare memorabilia, including a portrait, and furnishings of the writer's time, the Trust property is a half-timbered structure, dating from the early years of the 16th century. The house was bought by public donors in 1847 and preserved as a national shrine. You can visit the oak-beamed living room, the bedroom where Shakespeare was born, a fully equipped kitchen of the period (look for the "baby-minder"), and a Shakespeare Museum, illustrating his life and times. Later, you can walk through the garden out back. It is estimated that some 660,000 visitors pass through the house annually. If visited separately, admission is £1.55 ($2.33) for adults, 75p ($1.13) for children. Next door to the birthplace is the modern Shakespeare Centre, built to commemorate the 400th anniversary of the Bard's birth. It serves both as the administrative headquarters of the Birthplace Trust and as a library and study center. An extension to the original center, opened in 1981, includes a Visitors' Centre providing reception facilities for all those coming to the Birthplace.

Anne Hathaway's Cottage

One mile from Stratford in the hamlet of Shottery is the thatched, wattle-and-daub cottage where Anne Hathaway lived before her marriage to the poet. In sheer charm, it is the most interesting and most photographed, it would seem, of the Trust properties. The Hathaways were yeoman farmers, and—aside from its historical interest—the cottage provides a rare insight into the life of a family of Shakespeare's day. If the poet came a-courtin', he must have been treated as a mere teenager, as he married Miss Hathaway when he was only 18 years old and she much older. Much of the original furnishings, including the courting settle, and utensils are preserved inside the house, which was occupied by descendants of Shakespeare's wife until 1892. After a visit through the house, you'll surely want to linger in the garden and orchard. You can either walk across the meadow to Shottery from Evesham Place in Stratford (pathway marked), or else take a bus from Bridge Street. The admission is £1 ($1.50) for adults, 50p (75¢) for children.

New Place

This site is on Chapel Street, where Shakespeare retired in 1610, a prosperous man to judge from the standards of his day. He died there six years later, at the age of 52. Regrettably, only the site of his former home remains today, as the house was torn down. You enter the gardens through Nash's House (Thomas Nash married Elizabeth Hall, a granddaughter of the poet). Nash's House has 16th-century period rooms and an exhibition illustrating the archeology and history of Stratford. The heavily visited Knott Garden adjoins the site, and represents the style of a fashionable Elizabethan garden. New Place itself has its own Great Garden, which once belonged to Shakespeare. Here, the Bard planted a mulberry tree, so popular with latter-day visitors to Stratford that the cantankerous owner of the garden chopped it down. The mulberry tree that grows there today is said to have been planted from a cutting of the original tree. The admission is £1 ($1.50) for adults, 35p (53¢) for children.

Mary Arden's House

A timbered Tudor farm, this is the house where Shakespeare's mother, the daughter of a yeoman farmer, lived. The farmstead lies in the Village of Wilmcote, three miles from Stratford-upon-Avon. Look for the stone dovecote out back, and the farming museum in the barns. The admission is 95p ($1.43) for adults, 35p (53¢) for children.

By now, you will have seen the Trust properties, except for Hall's Croft (see "Where to Eat," farther on). Other interesting sights not administered by the Trust foundation include the following:

Harvard House

Not just of interest to Harvard men, Harvard House on High Street is a fine example of an Elizabethan town house. Rebuilt in 1596, it was once the home of Katherine Rogers, mother of John Harvard, founder of Harvard University. In 1909 the house was purchased by a Chicago millionaire, Edward Morris, who presented it as a gift to the American university. Its present furnishings are not original, although they are of the period when the Rogers family lived in the house. But the floors, made of the local flagstone, are authentic. Look for the Bible Chair, used for hiding the Bible during the days of Tudor persecution. Harvard House, charging admission of £1 ($1.50) for adults, half price for children, is open April through September from 9 a.m. to 1 p.m. and from 2 to 6 p.m. weekdays, from 2 to 6 p.m. on Sunday; restricted hours in winter. Finally, you may want to visit the:

Holy Trinity Church

In an attractive setting near the Avon, the parish church of Stratford-upon-Avon is distinguished mainly because Shakespeare was buried in the chancel ("and curst be he who moves my bones"). The Parish Register records his birth and death (copies of the original, of course). No charge is made for entry into the church, described as "one of the most beautiful parish churches in the world," but visitors wishing to view Shakespeare's tomb are asked to donate a small sum, at present 35p (53¢), toward the restoration fund.

AN ELIZABETHAN PAGEANT: The **Heritage Theatre,** Waterside (tel. 0789/69190), presents a full-time show, an Elizabethan pageant that recreates the time of Shakespeare. The theater stands near the Royal Shakespeare Theatre. Its presentation tells the story of the great pageant that Lord Leicester scheduled for Queen Elizabeth in the summer of 1575. After a Royal Progress across the country, it culminated in several days of dances, songs, plays, and pomp at Kenilworth Castle. As a young man, Shakespeare is believed to have witnessed and been influenced by this pageant. The Heritage uses music, an eight-track sound tape, lights, costumes, and scenery, and dialogue is spoken by members of the Royal Shakespeare Company. Shows are on the hour and half hour daily from 9:30 a.m. to 8:30 p.m., April to September; 9:30 a.m. to 5 p.m., October to March. Admission is £1.90 ($2.85) for adults, £1.40 ($2.10) for students and children over 6 (no charge for children under 6). A special family ticket costs £6.50 ($9.75).

TOURS: **Guide Friday,** 13 Waterside (tel. 0789/294466), has a central location near the theater and opposite the canal basin. They have opened a large information office, which will give out free town maps and brochures, as well as information on the area. Hotel and guest-house reservations will be made from 9 a.m. to 9 p.m. at a cost of £1 ($1.50) per reservation. Tickets for tours and the theater can also be purchased here.

Tour prices include the Shakespeare Lecture Tour at £4 ($6), Warwick and Kenilworth Castles at £5 ($7.50), the Cotswolds and villages at £5.50 ($8.25), and a visit to Blenheim Palace, birthplace of Sir Winston Churchill, £6 ($9). The Quick Town Tour includes Mary Arden's House and Anne Hathaway's Cottage at £2.50 ($3.75), and the Cotswold pub tour goes for £4.50 ($6.75). On the latter, you pay for your own drinks.

The Shakespeare Connection is a service operated by British Rail and Guide Friday Ltd., a combined road/rail ticket from London Euston Station to Stratford-upon-Avon. The cost is about £12 ($18) per person, second class, for the round trip, which drops you right outside Shakespeare's Birthplace. It's now possible to be standing by the Bard's bed in Stratford in about two hours from the time you leave London. You can leave Euston at 8:35 a.m. and arrive in Stratford at 10:45 a.m., returning to Euston at 5:30 p.m., or if you wish, go to the theater or take Guide Friday's Cotswolds Country Inns Tour, catching the train back to London at 11:40 p.m., arriving in the capital in the early hours. Ask for a Shakespeare Connection ticket at London's Euston Station or any British Rail London Travel Centre. British Rail pass holders using the service simply pay the coach fare from Coventry Station to Stratford-upon-Avon.

CAUGHT WITHOUT A ROOM?: During the long theater season, the hotels in Stratford-upon-Avon are jam-packed, and you may run into difficulty if you arrive without a reservation. However, if you should visit from April to October during regular office hours (9 a.m. to 5:30 p.m. weekdays, 2 to 5 p.m. on Sunday) you can go to the **Information Centre** at the Judith Shakespeare House, 1 High St. (tel. 0789/293127).

Here a staff person, who has had much experience with travelers on all budgets, will get on the telephone and try to book a room for you in the price range you are seeking.

It is also possible to reserve accommodations if you write well enough in advance. By writing to the Information Centre, you'll be spared having to get in touch with several hotels on your own and running the risk of getting turned down. If you do write, specify the price range and the number of beds required. The centre often gets vague letters, and the staff doesn't know whether to book you into a private suite at the Shakespeare Hotel, or else lend you a cot to put in front of the Royal Shakespeare Theatre. Don't be surprised. Stratford-upon-Avon visitors are a varied group. Recently a young man not only slept in front of the theater, but was seen frying an egg there over an open fire the next morning.

WHERE TO STAY: For my hotel recommendations, I'll lead off with the most expensive in:

The Upper Bracket

Alveston Manor Hotel, Clopton Bridge (tel. 0789/4581), is a black-and-white timbered manor, conveniently placed for attending the theater, just a two-minute walk from the Avon. It has more chimneys and gables than one can count—a hodgepodge of styles, everything from an Elizabethan gazebo to Queen Anne windows. Tracing the building's ancestry involves one in early English history, as its origins predate the arrival of William the Conqueror. A Ping-Pong game of ownership has been played with Alveston, which was mentioned in the Domesday Book.

Rooms in the Manor House are for those who enjoy an atmosphere of old slanted floors, overhead beams, and antique furnishings. However, in the modern block, attached by a covered walk through the rear garden, rooms have well-designed built-in pieces, baths with showers, heated towel racks, phones, radios, bedside lamps, dressing tables, and a color-coordinated decor. In a single room, the rate is £40 ($60), increasing to £52 ($78) in a double or twin. Breakfast is extra, but service charge and VAT are included. In the newer block, a number of large rooms are rented to three or four persons. It's almost impossible to get a room in the old house.

The lounges are in the manor; and guests gather in the Cedar Room for relaxation, enjoying the view of the centuries-old tree at the top of the garden—said to have been the background for the first presentation of *A Midsummer Night's Dream.* In the main living room, with its well-preserved linenfold paneling, logs burn in the Tudor fireplace. The bar-lounge is another cozy spot, with its stone fireplace, Tudor bench, and Windsor armchairs. Good food is served in the softly lit Tudor Restaurant, with its oak beams and leaded-glass windows.

Stratford-upon-Avon Moat House, Bridgefoot (tel. 0789/67511), a member of the Queens Moat Houses hotel group, was formerly the Hilton International. On five landscaped acres of lawns and gardens, laid out in a semi-Tudor style, this complex of red brick and stone stands right on the Avon, within walking distance of the theater. In fact, not since the construction of the theater back in the 1930s has a building sparked such controversy, and attracted so many defenders and detractors. It's only four stories high—the top floor semi-disguised by a mansard roof—and it's spread out, much like a hospital. Each of its 253 rooms contains individually controlled heating and air conditioning, plus views of the river, the theater, and the surrounding countryside. Each has a private bath and shower, with direct-dial telephones, taped music, color TV. High-season rates apply from April 1 to October 1; singles range from £42 ($63); doubles, from £52 ($78). Tax is included in the tariffs. The hotel has an Actors Bar, an unusual octagonal-shaped cocktail lounge, with windows overlooking the gardens and the Avon. A live group plays for dancing here from 10 p.m. to 2 a.m. It is joined to the main building by an enclosed walkway. Guests can reach the theater via a ten-minute boat ride on a barge docked in front on the canal. The Tavern restaurant is a coffeeshop open for lunch and dinner, serving a buffet of cold meats, salads, and desserts, plus at least two hot dishes. A carvery lunch will cost £10 ($15). The Warwick Grill, the prestige restaurant of the hotel, offers a wide range of international and English cuisine. A specialty is roast rib of Scottish beef. Dinners ordered à la carte average £18 ($27).

Welcombe Hotel, Warwick Road (tel. 0789/295252), is one of England's great Jacobean country houses, placed about a ten-minute ride from the heart of Stratford-upon-Avon. The home once belonged to Sir Archibald Flower, the philanthropic brewer who helped create the Shakespeare Memorial Theatre. Converted into a hotel, it is surrounded by 120 acres of grounds. It is now the property of Sea Containers Ltd., which also owns the Cipriani in Venice and the Orient Express.

It is reached by a formal entrance on Warwick Road, a winding driveway leading to the main hall. There's even an 18-hole, 6300-yard course on the estate. Guests gather on fair days for afternoon tea or drinks on the rear terrace, with its Italian-style garden and steps leading down to flower beds. The public rooms are heroic in size, with high mullioned windows providing views of the park. Although the antiques have been removed, the furnishings are suitable. The bedrooms—some big enough for tennis matches—have pleasant pieces. A single room with bath rents for £45 ($67.50). A double with bath costs £65 ($97.50) to £78 ($117), all prices including a full breakfast, service charge, and VAT. You can order either table d'hôte meals or from the à la carte menu. Lunch costs about £11 ($16.50); dinner, from £15 ($22.50). Greens fees on the golf course for residents are £6 ($9).

The **Shakespeare Hotel,** Chapel Street (tel. 0789/294771), a 16th-century building, now redecorated and run as a Trusthouses Forte Hotel, lies within a few minutes of the theater, the poet's grammar school, and New Place, where the Bard died. It's easy to spot, with its nine gables, black-and-white timbering, leaded diamond windows, bays, and hanging baskets of red geraniums. In 1769 David Garrick, the famous actor, named most of the lounges and bedrooms after plays or characters of Shakespeare. You may be assigned the Ophelia Bedroom or the Romeo and Juliet Bedroom. There's even a private Hamlet suite. Room rates are higher between April 1 and November 1, with a single going for £45 ($67.50). Double rooms rent for an inclusive £62 ($93). All meals are extra. The rooms are centrally heated and contain private baths, radios, and TVs.

Meals are served in the David Garrick dining room, where the old beams have been preserved. While there is an extensive à la carte menu and a fine wine list, the bargain is the table d'hôte dinner starting at £13.50 ($20.25). The table d'hôte luncheon begins at £9.50 ($14.25). The Froth and Elbow and the cocktail bar, both with open fireplaces lure one to the Shakespeare.

The Medium-Priced Range

The **Falcon,** Chapel Street (tel. 0789/5777), is a blending of the very old and the very new. At the rear of a black-and-white timbered inn, licensed a quarter of a century after Shakespeare's death, is a contemporary bedroom extension, joined by a glass-covered passageway. In the heart of Stratford, the Falcon faces the Guild Chapel and the New Place Gardens. The bedrooms in the mellowed part have oak beams, diamond leaded-glass windows, antique furnishings, and good reproductions. One arrives at the rear portion to unload luggage, just as horse-drawn coaches once dispatched their passengers. All bedrooms have private bathroom, radio, television, telephone, electric trouser press, and tea- and coffee-making equipment. Rates include accommodation, full English breakfast, space for your car, VAT, and service charge. A single with bath is £44 ($66); a double or twin with bath, £52 ($78).

The social lounges are tasteful and comfortable—some of the finest in the Midlands. In the intimate Merlin Lounge is an open copper-hooded fireplace where coal and log fires are kept burning under beams salvaged from old ships (the walls are a good example of wattle and daub, typical of Shakespeare's day). The Oak Lounge Bar is a forest of weathered beams, and on either side of the stone fireplace is the paneling removed from the poet's last home, New Place. A set luncheon costs £6.50 ($9.75), a set dinner going for £10 ($15), both tariffs including three courses, service, and VAT.

Haytor Hotel, Avenue Road (tel. 0789/297799), is a private hotel where friendly service is rendered by the resident proprietors, the Branston family, and their staff. Most rooms contain private baths, and all are individually furnished and fully carpeted. There are three four-poster bedrooms, including the Green Onyx, which has an antique four-poster. Charges are from £20 ($30) for a single and from £33 ($49.50) for a double room. These rates include a full English breakfast and VAT. Meals are served in a charming dining room, decorated with a number of old maps. A pleasant lounge bar can be enjoyed by guests, or they can relax in the comfortable sitting room or the gardens, free from traffic noise. The hotel is only 900 yards from the Royal Shakespeare Theatre, and the Branstons will purchase tickets on behalf of guests and give assistance regarding travel in the United Kingdom.

Grosvenor House Hotel, Warwick Road (tel. 0789/69213), is a pair of Georgian residences joined to form a hotel of 57 bedrooms, 53 of which have private baths or showers. It is a member of the Best Western hotel group and is run by the Adcock family and friendly staff. Lawns and gardens to the rear of the hotel lend attraction. All bedrooms have color TV, radios, and phones. Singles rent from £18.50 ($27.75) and doubles from £30 ($45), including service, VAT, and a full English breakfast. The hotel is centrally heated, and there is a large free car park for guests. The informal bar (open until midnight) and terrace offer pleasant relaxation before or after you lunch or dine in the large restaurant whose floor-to-ceiling windows look onto the gardens. Perhaps the happiest feature of the Grosvenor is its convenience to the heart of Stratford, lying as it does just a short stroll from the intersection of Bridge Street and Waterside so that you're right at riverside Bancroft Gardens and the Royal Shakespeare Theatre before you know it.

Stratford House, Sheep Street (tel. 0789/68288), is a pleasant Georgian house 100 yards from the Avon River and the Royal Shakespeare Theatre. A small hotel of only ten bedrooms (seven of which have private baths or showers), the agreeable B&B establishment is run by Peter and Pamela Wade, who extend a fond welcome for their North American clients. The house is furnished tastefully and with style, somewhat like a private home, with books and pictures along with a scattering of antiques. Everything is spotlessly maintained. On the side is a small walled courtyard, with flowering plants. A double with private bath rents for £23.50 ($35.25) per person, only £21.50 ($32.25) if bathless. Families can rent a room for four with private bath at a cost of £18 ($27) per person. Children under 9 are granted reduced prices. Singles, however, are charged from £35 ($52.50) with bath. No service charge is included. Rates quoted include a full English breakfast, VAT, and early-morning tea. Color TV, incidentally, is provided in every bedroom.

Peter Wade will drive guests around Stratford and the Cotswolds in his private car to suit the arrangements of the visitor. He will also organize a private car tour for you, arranging for you to stay in first-class small hotels in the Lake District, the Central Scottish Highlands, and York. The private cars in which these tours are taken are driven, Peter says, "by friendly natives such as myself." He will provide full details upon request.

The Budget Range

Stratheden Hotel, Chapel Street (tel. 0789/297119), is a small, tuck-away hotel, in a weathered building dating back to 1673, with a tiny rear garden and top-floor rooms with slanted, beamed ceilings. Owned by Mr. and Mrs. Wells (she's from Northern Ireland, he's a native of Warwickshire), the house has improved in both decor and comfort, with fresh paint, new curtains, and good beds. Most rooms have private showers and toilets, with B&B costing from £10 ($15) to £16 ($24).

The entry hallway has a glass cupboard, holding family heirlooms and collector tidbits. The house is sprinkled with old pieces. The dining room, with a bay window, has an overscale sideboard that once belonged to the "insanely vain" Marie Corelli, the eccentric novelist, poet, and mystic who wrote a series of seven books, beginning with *A Romance of Two Worlds* and ending with *Spirit and Power and Universal Love.* Queen Victoria was one of her avid readers. The Victorian novelist (1855–1924) was noted for her passion for pastoral paintings and objets d'art. You can see an example of her taste in bedchamber furniture: a massive mahogany tester bed in one of the rooms.

WHERE TO EAT: The **Box Tree Restaurant,** the Royal Shakespeare Theatre, Waterside (tel. 0789/293226), has dibs on the best position in town, in the theater, with walls of glass providing an unobstructed view of the Avon and its swans. The meals and service are worthy of its unique position. The restaurant is open on matinee days from 12:30 to 2 p.m., and in the evenings from 6 to 11 p.m. A three-course pre-theater dinner begins at £13.50 ($20.25), going up to £18 ($27). Lunches start at £8.50 ($12.75). After each evening's performance, you can dine by flickering candlelight. Such items are featured as duckling à l'orange, grilled sirloin steak, coq au vin, escalope of veal. Be sure to book your table in advance, especially on the days of performances (there's a special phone for reservations in the theater lobby).

In the **River Terrace Restaurant** (tel. 0789/293226), an assortment of snack meals, homemade pizzas, quiches, pâtés, pies, soups, and hamburgers, all with salads, is offered. With dessert to finish off your meal, expect to pay around £3 ($4.50) to £6 ($9).

Hills, 3 Greenhill St. (tel. 0789/293563), is a bistro-like restaurant, providing an authentic French cuisine. It is owned by Shaun Hills who, after his French training, worked in Montmartre and then went to the Capital Hotel, Knightsbridge, and its noted restaurant. Here at Hills, he has stuck to the same French dishes that were popular under previous ownership, when the restaurant was known as Marianne, but he insists on using English for his menus. The small two-story dining room has an open wooden staircase leading to additional tables on the mezzanine. The best value here is the table d'hôte dinner, which includes an appetizer, main course, and cheese or dessert. On the à la carte menu, appetizers are likely to include gratinée lyonnaise, a tasty onion soup, or perhaps escargots in sauce à la bourgignonne. The menu selections vary according to the season since Shaun makes every effort to obtain only fresh ingredients for his dishes. When you visit, you may find such items listed as scampi à l'estragon, a savory shrimp dish in a delicate tarragon sauce, or caneton au cassis, duckling served with a fragrant cassis glaze. Meals are à la carte, averaging about £14 ($21) per person. For dessert, you might like to sample one of the pastries prepared by the chef. Hills is open Monday through Saturday for dinner, and also offers lunch from 12:30 to 2 p.m.

Christophi's, 21–23 Sheep Street (tel. 0789/293546), is a bit of old Athens set down in the middle of Shakespeare's hometown. Owned by Nicos Christophi, the restaurant is laid out in Greek fashion, with an indoor courtyard. You may dine on both Greek and Cypriot dishes while live Greek music plays in the background. A number of items of standard British fare are included on the menu for the less adventurous. To begin your meal you might try the dolmadakia, a meat and rice ball wrapped in vine leaves, or the popular avgolemono, a chicken soup heavily laced with lemon juice. The entree portion of the menu includes moussaka, a casserole of chopped beef, eggplant, and potatoes, crowned with a wonderful cheese-flavored cream sauce. Christophi's features the meze, a typical Greek "taverna" dinner, consisting of a variety of individual dishes, including various hors d'oeuvres and a main course "to satisfy the most adventurous palate." Meals begin at £12 ($18). The restaurant is open for dinner from 5:30 p.m. to midnight. Closed Sunday.

Da Giovanni, 8 Ely St. (tel. 0789/297999), is an intimate spot, favored by actors at the theater. The yellow brick cottage is graced with an Italianate facade that shelters the entrance to a sophisticated cocktail lounge with antiques. Da Giovanni is in the trattoria style, its cuisine beginning fittingly enough with minestrone. The classic Italian menu includes such pasta dishes as lasagne and cannelloni, and such main dishes as escalope Pietmontese and spezzato di pollo alla casalinga (casserole of chicken cooked in wine with tomatoes and mushrooms). A good Italian dessert is the zabaglione, although at least two persons must order it. A selection of excellent continental ices is also featured, everything from Italian cassata to mela Stregata. Expect to pay from £12 ($18) for a complete dinner. A 10% service charge is added. It's closed on Sunday, but open other days from 12:30 to 2 p.m. and from 6 to 11:30 p.m.

Cobweb Restaurant and Cake Confectionery, 12 Sheep St. (tel. 0789/292554), is a black-and-white timbered building, with a high gabled wing, dating from about 1520. It's steeped in associations with the days of Shakespeare. On the ground floor is a bar selling coffee and snacks from the extensive range of sweets and savories displayed. Drinks may be served with the food during licensing hours, 10:30 a.m. to 2:30 p.m. and 5:30 p.m. to midnight. The bar window onto the street doubles as a shop during the daytime and is known as one of the finest in England for its cakes, pastries, cream cakes, meringues, apple strudel, and cheesecake. The floor above is a maze of three oak- and elm-beamed rooms with low ceilings, filled with antique Windsor chairs, settles, and oak tables. The restaurant provides morning coffee, a set two-course luncheon of steak-and-kidney pie or roast chicken for about £4 ($6), plus an à la carte menu that includes many light meals. Tea is served from 2 to 6 p.m., with a pot of beverage costing 75p

($1.13), and scones, jam, cream, and cake going for £2.25 ($3.38). There are also sandwiches, tea cakes, and other goodies to please your palate. On Sunday, teas are served from 3 to 6 p.m. The Cobweb's new venture, candlelight dinners à la carte at around £8 ($12), is an inviting prospect Monday through Saturday from 6 to 11 p.m.

The **Black Swan,** Waterside Street (tel. 0789/297312), is affectionately known as the Dirty Duck. By whatever bird it's called, it's been popular since the 18th century as a hangout for Stratford players. The autographed photographs of its patrons, such as Lord Laurence Olivier, line the wall. The front lounge and bar crackles with intense conversation. In the spring and fall an open fire burns moodily.

In the Dirty Duck Grill Room meals are served from noon to 2:30 p.m. and from 6 p.m. to midnight. An à la carte menu is offered. Typical English grills are featured from £6 ($9). In fair weather, you can drink while sitting in the front garden, and watching the swans on the Avon glide by.

The **Garrick Inn,** High Street (tel. 0789/292186), is a black-and-white timbered Elizabethan pub named after one of England's greatest actors, David Garrick. It has its own kind of unpretentious charm. The front bar is decked out with tapestry-covered settles, an old oak refectory table, and an open fireplace where the locals gravitate. The back bar has a circular fireplace with a copper hood, plus a buffet bar serving "ploughman's lunches." Hot meals cost from £4.50 ($6.75).

The **Hall's Croft Festival Club,** in the Old Town (tel. 0789/292107), makes an ideal headquarters during your stay in Stratford-upon-Avon. This skillfully preserved, timbered Elizabethan building can become your private club, where you can congregate with fellow Shakespeare enthusiasts, and dine inexpensively. Hall's Croft was the original town house of Susanna, daughter of William Shakespeare, and her husband Dr. John Hall. Parts of the authentically furnished house may be visited on your £3.50 ($5.25) ticket that admits you to five Shakespeare Trust Properties. The house lies about two blocks from the Royal Shakespeare Theatre, and a block from the Avon.

The cost of membership is £3 ($4.50) weekly. As a member, you'll be entitled to use the facilities of the club, including the comfortable rooms for lounging, lunching, or reading, as well as the garden. Lectures and poetry readings are held, books and pamphlets sold—and you can even get your mail here.

Eating at the club is inexpensive, and the food is quite good. A three-course meal of, say, roast beef will cost around £4 ($6). If the weather is good, you can eat in the garden. The club is open Monday to Saturday all year from 10:30 a.m. to 6 p.m. or later in summer, to 4 p.m. in winter.

ATTENDING THE THEATER: The **Royal Shakespeare Theatre** (tel. 0789/295623) on the banks of the Avon is the number one theater for Shakespearean productions. The season runs for nine months from March to January, with a winter festival of music and ballet in February. The present theater was opened in 1932, after the old Shakespeare Memorial Theatre, erected in Victoria's day, burned down in 1926. The theater employs the finest actors and actresses on the British stage. In an average season, five Shakespearean plays rotate in repertory.

Usually, you'll need reservations: there are three successive booking periods, each one opening about two months in advance. You can best pick these up from a North American or an English travel agent. If you wait until your arrival in Stratford, it may be too late to get a good seat. Stall (orchestra) seats range in price from £6.50 ($9.75) to £12.50 ($18.75), and if you're not subject to nose bleed, you may want to anchor in the high-altitude balcony in a seat that goes for £3 ($4.50).

Tip: Don't despair completely if you should arrive in Stratford without a ticket. The theater box office always holds back a block of £4.50 ($6.75) stall seats that go on sale the day of each performance at 10:30 a.m. An alternative course is to buy standing room at the same time for £2 ($3).

In the Victorian wing of the old Memorial Theatre—spared by the fire—is a Picture Gallery and Museum, filled with portraits of the Bard, oils of performances from his various classics showing 18th- and 19th-century costume designs, portraits of actors in memorable characterizations of Shakespearean roles, such as Lord Laurence Olivier as Macbeth and Dame Edith Evans as Volumnia. The gallery is open April to October weekdays from 10 a.m. to 1 p.m. and 2 to 6 p.m.; matinee days, 10 a.m. to 6 p.m.; Sunday, 2 to 6 p.m. December to March, open Sunday only. Admission is 50p (75¢) for adults, 35p (53¢) for children.

BOOK BROWSING: Although it seems ironic to call this shop at 21 Chapel St. the **Chaucer Head Bookshop** (tel. 0789/293136), it is still an interesting place to visit, offering both new and secondhand editions. A friend of Shakespeare's, Julius Shaw, who was one of the executors of his will, lived at this address from 1597 to 1629. It is owned and run by Dorothy Withey, who has opened a second-floor art gallery exhibiting current books on Shakespeare and the Elizabethan period, a room for displaying the work of living artists, and for prints and engravings as well.

STAYING AT WILMCOTE: **Swan House Hotel,** The Green (tel. 0789/ 67030), lies in the heart of the tiny hamlet of Wilmcote, where Shake-speare's mother, Mary Arden, lived. Really an upgraded village pub-hotel, the white-painted Swan is tranquil, restful, and gracious, offering not only attractive and fresh bedrooms at low prices, but good meals as well. It's owned by Harold and Pauline Poole, who have made the inn home-like. It has eight bedrooms, all with TV and tea- and coffee-making facilities. A bathless single rents for £20 ($30) per night, a bathless double for £32 ($48), and a double with bath costs £35 ($52.50). All tariffs are inclusive of service and VAT.

Mary Arden's Tavern Bar provides hot and cold bar snacks and real English ale at lunchtime and in the evening from Monday to Saturday. The beamed dining room at the rear is a good setting for an excellent English cuisine with some French overtones, all the food being cooked by Harry Poole, who is a chef de cuisine. You might start with an apple filled with a creamy mixture of stilton cheese. The restaurant is open to nonresidents also, and affords a wide choice of à la carte and table d'hôte menus. Drinks are offered in the little bar, with its log-burning fireplace, a bay window with a view of the Mary Arden cottage, which you can visit, and tiny rear courtyard and old well.

Loxley Farm, Loxley, near Warwick (tel. 0789/840265), is a storybook cottage with small-paned dormers peeping out of the crooked, thatched roof and creeper vines climbing on the black-and-white beamed walls. The garden is full of apple trees, roses, and sweet-scented flowers, through which a stone path leads across the grass to the front door and into the flagstone hall with old rugs and a roaring fire. Blackie, the cat, helps the owners, friendly and hospitable Roderick and Anne Horton, welcome you, and Flossy, the gray pony with a touch of Arab blood, whinnies a greeting from the paddock when you arrive here to have B&B in a dream house.

The Hortons have two double rooms and one family room, which they rent for £8.50 ($12.75) per person per day, including a farmhouse breakfast. Roderick leaves for work each day in the farm chemicals industry, but Anne is on hand to prepare a packed lunch if required and to have an evening meal ready for you, if you have given her advance notice that you'd like to eat in. The cost of the meal is £6 ($9). Incidentally, the dining room table is made from a panel that was once part of the wall of the Royal Mint in London.

To reach Loxley Farm, take the B4086 out of Stratford-upon-Avon toward Wellesbourne, cross the river bridge, and then take the first turning right to Loxley. Or take the small road signposted to Loxley from the A422 Stratford-upon-Avon to Banbury road.

SIGHTS AND LODGING AT ALCESTER: Ragley Hall (tel. 0789/762090)
is a magnificent Palladian country house built in 1680, the home of the Marquis of Hertford and his family. Among the contents of the house are fine paintings, china, and a valuable library. Perhaps the most spectacular attraction, however, is the lavishly painted south staircase hall. The present marquis commissioned the modern trompe l'oeil work on the subject, *The Temptation,* but this religious theme stops with the lavishly evil Devil offering a gold circlet to Christ in the central ceiling medallion. The walls of the halls are decorated with a striking garden vista, with temples and trees, plus a far view over the countryside. Exotic birds and other creatures crouch above doorways while flamingos spar on a balcony. Up the stairs and toward the ceiling are painted balconies on which the Marquis of Hartford, his family, and friends lean and talk, feed the birds, and look back at the interested observer. Depicted far above are the servants' quarters with Ragley's cook and butler peering down at the scene below. This is a fascinating work of art that blends with the ease of trompe l'oeil into the old house. Ragley Hall, its garden, and the park are open from the beginning of April to the beginning of October. Hours for the park are from 11:30 a.m. to 6 p.m. on Tuesday, Wednesday, Thursday, Saturday, and Sunday (also Monday and Friday in July and August). The house and garden are open from 1:30 to 5:30 p.m. Admission is £2 ($3) for adults, £1 ($1.50) for children. A visit only to the park costs £1 ($1.50) for adults, 50p (75¢) for children.

If you'd like accommodations nearby, seek out **Billesley Manor Hotel** at Billesley near Alcester (tel. 0789/763737), three miles west of Stratford-upon-Avon. A fine manor house built of Cotswold stone in the 16th century, the hotel lies in 11 acres of parkland, with tennis courts, indoor swimming in a heated pool, and other leisure activities. The reception area and lounge have polished wood floors spread with Chinese and Persian rugs, and there is some interesting Louis XIV furniture. There are 28 luxurious bedrooms and suites, all with private baths. Sixteen of the units are in a new extension. All have color TVs, radios, phones, and trouser presses. The older rooms are large, some paneled and with four-poster beds. Others, on the upper floor, are modern, with light-wood furniture and chintz fabrics. The Shakespeare Room has a priest's hideaway and an enormous bathroom with gold-plated fittings. Room rates are £40 ($60) for a single with bath or shower, £54 ($81) for a double or twin, and £56 ($84) for a room with a four-poster double bed. All charges include a full English breakfast, newspaper, VAT, and service.

The paneled and richly carpeted dining room offers the diner the chance of enjoying the efforts of young Ian Whittock, the chef. Traditional English country dishes and French nouvelle cuisine are his specialties. Dinners are £17 ($25.50). Try the rich game pâté, then breast of local pheasant in cream sauce with chestnuts and wild rice. As with all good chefs, Ian only uses first-class fresh produce and prepares each dish individually so some waiting between courses is necessary.

Most travelers approach our next stopover, Warwick, via route A46 from Stratford-upon-Avon, eight miles away. The town is 92 miles from London, and is on the Avon.

2. Warwick

Visitors seem to rush through Warwick to see Warwick Castle; then they're off on their next adventure, traditionally to the ruins of Kenilworth Castle. But the historic center of medieval Warwick deserves to be treated with greater respect. It has far more to offer than a castle.

In 1694 a fire swept through Warwick, destroying large segments of the town, but it still retains a number of Elizabethan and medieval buildings— along with some fine Georgian structures. (Very few traces remain, however, of the town walls, except the East and West Gates.) Warwick looks to Ethelfleda, daughter of Alfred the Great, as its founder. But most of its history is associated with the Earls of Warwick, a title created by the son of William the Conqueror in 1088. The story of those earls—the Beaumonts, the Beauchamps (such figures as "Kingmaker" Richard Neville)—makes for an exciting episode in English history, but is too detailed to document here.

WARWICK CASTLE: Perched on a rocky cliff above the Avon, this magnificent 14th-century fortress encloses a stately mansion in the grandest late 17th-century style.

The importance of the site has been recognized from earliest times. The first defense works of significance at Warwick were built by Ethelfleda, daughter of Alfred the Great, in A.D. 915. Her fortifications were further developed by the construction of a motte and bailey castle on the orders of William the Conqueror in 1068, two years after the Norman Conquest. There are now no remains of the Norman castle, as this was sacked by Simon de Montfort in the Barons' War of 1264.

The Beauchamp family, the most illustrious medieval Earls of Warwick, are responsible for most of the castle as it is seen today, and much of the external structure remains unchanged from the mid-14th century. When the castle was granted to Sir Fulke Greville by James I in 1604, he spent £20,000 (an enormous sum in those days) converting the existing castle buildings into a luxurious mansion. The Grevilles have held the Earl of Warwick title since 1759, when it passed from the Rich family.

The State Rooms and Great Hall house fine collections of paintings, furniture, arms, and armor. The armory, dungeon, torture chamber, ghost tower, clock tower, and Guy's tower give vivid insights into the castle's turbulent past and its important part in the history of England. The private apartments of Lord Brooke and his family, who in recent years sold the castle to Madame Tussaud's company, of waxworks fame, are open to visitors to display a carefully constructed Royal Weekend House Party of 1898. The major rooms contain wax models of the time: young Winston Churchill, the Duchess of Devonshire, Winston's widowed mother, Jennie, and Clara Butt, the celebrated singer, along with the Earl and Countess of Warwick and their family. In the Kenilworth bedroom, the Prince of Wales, later to become King Edward VII, reads a letter, and in the red bedroom, the Duchess of Marlborough prepares for her bath. Among the most lifelike of the figures is a little uniformed man, bending over a bathtub into which the water is running, to test the temperature. Surrounded by gardens, lawns, and woodland, where peacocks roam freely, and skirted by the Avon, Warwick Castle was described by Sir Walter Scott in 1828 as "that fairest monument of ancient and chivalrous spendor which yet remains uninjured by time."

The castle is open daily, except Christmas Day, March 1 to October 31 from 10 a.m. to 5:30 p.m., November 1 to February 28 from 10 a.m. to 4:30 p.m. Admission is £3.20 ($4.80) for adults, £2.15 ($3.23) for children.

OTHER SIGHTS: Other nearby sights worth exploring include the following:

St. Mary's Church

Destroyed, in part, by the fire of 1694, this church with its rebuilt battlemented tower and nave is considered among the finest examples of the work of the late 17th and early 18th centuries. The Beauchamp Chapel, spared from the flames, encases the Purbeck marble tomb of Richard Beauchamp, a well-known Earl of Warwick who died in 1439 and is commemorated by a gilded bronze effigy. The most powerful man in the kingdom, not excepting Henry V, Beauchamp has a tomb considered one of the finest remaining examples of Perpendicular-Gothic as practiced in England in the mid-15th century. The tomb of Robert Dudley, Earl of Leicester, a favorite of Elizabeth I, is against the north wall. The Perpendicular-Gothic choir dates from the 14th century, as do the Norman crypt and the Chapter House. For more information, get in touch with the Rectory, Warwick (tel. Warwick 491132).

Lord Leycester Hospital

At the West Gate, this group of half-timbered almshouses was also spared from the Great Fire. The buildings were erected in about 1400, and the hospital was founded in 1571 by Robert Dudley, the Earl of Leicester, as a home for old soldiers. It is still in use by ex-servicemen today. On top of the West Gate is the attractive little chapel of St. James, dating from the 12th century, although much restored. The hospital may be visited weekdays from 10 a.m. to 5:30 p.m. (closed Sunday) for £1 ($1.50) for adults, 35p (53¢) for children. Off-season, it closes at 4 p.m. Last admission is 15 minutes before closing.

Warwickshire Museum

At the Market Place, this museum was established in 1836 to house a collection of geological remains, fossils, and a fine grouping of British amphibians from the Triassic period. There are also displays illustrating the history, archeology, and natural history of the country, including the Sheldon tapestry map. It is open weekdays from 10 a.m. to 5:30 p.m., and on Sunday in summer from 2:30 to 5 p.m.

St. John's House

At Coten End, not far from the castle gates, there is a display of domestic life and costumes, and the house in which these exhibitions are displayed is a fund of beauty itself, dating from the early 17th century. A Victorian school-room, recently opened, is furnished with original 19th-century school furniture and equipment. During term time, Warwickshire children, dressed in replica costumes, can be seen enjoying Victorian-style lessons. Groups of children also use the Victorian parlor and the kitchen. An important collection of musical instruments is on view, including a Tabel harpsichord and three Stanesby recorders dating from the 18th century and a 16th-century lute by Hans Frei. On the first floor is a military exhibition, tracing the history of the Royal Warwickshire Regiment from 1674 to the present day. The house is open Tuesday to Saturday from 10 a.m. to 12:30 p.m. and 1:30 to 5:30 p.m., and also on Sunday May to September from 2:30 to 5 p.m. Admission is free.

Warwick Doll Museum

Housed in one of the most charming Elizabethan buildings in Warwick, Oken's House, the Warwick Doll Museum keeps alive the memory of childhood. It contains an extensive collection of dolls—be they wood, wax, or porcelain. Of particular interest is a swivel-necked, double-headed doll that moves from tears to smiles. The house is on Castle Street, near St. Mary's Church. It was the birthplace of Thomas Oken, a bailiff in Warwick in Tudor days, whose reputation rests largely on his philanthropic work. The dolls, however, are from the collection of Joy Robinson. The house is open weekdays from 10 a.m. to 6 p.m. (on Sunday from 2:30 to 5 p.m.), for 60p (90¢) for adults, 30p (45¢) for children.

WHERE TO STAY: Many prefer to seek lodgings in Warwick, then commute to Stratford-upon-Avon. If you're one of them, here are my hotel recommendations:

Tudor House Inn & Restaurant, West Street (tel. Warwick 495447), was built in 1472. It's at the edge of town, on the main road from Stratford-upon-Avon leading to Warwick Castle. It is a stunning black-and-white timbered inn, one of the few buildings to escape the fire that destroyed the High Street in 1694. Off the central hall are two large rooms, each of which could be the setting for an Elizabethan play. In the corner of the lounge is an open turning staircase, waiting for the entrance of a minstrel player. The minstrels' gallery is dominated by a large inglenook. A regular meal in the restaurant and steak bar costs about £10 ($15). The inn has nine bedrooms, all with wash basins, although some have baths en suite. The cost ranges from £18 ($27) to £34 ($51) per room nightly. Two of the rooms have doors only four feet high! There's the usual resident ghost—an old man who gets up early in the morning, leaving the front door open and heading toward Stratford-upon-Avon, without paying his bill. In addition, the old priest's hiding hole has become the Priest Hole Bar.

Lord Leycester Hotel, Jury Street (tel. Warwick 491481), is a remake of what was once the country house of the Earl of Leicester. Extensively renovated, it now accommodates guests comfortably in its 47 bedrooms, all of which have private baths. Its position is most central, within walking distance of the castle and other historic buildings of Warwick. A single goes for £30 ($45). In a double or twin, the price is £44 ($66). Prices include a full English breakfast and VAT. A nicety is the inclusion of early-morning tea and a newspaper. The bedrooms are furnished with moderately modern pieces, neat and attractive. Lord Leicester's former stables have been transformed into the Tavern, where imbibers sit on cobblers' stools at trestle tables. In the dining room a small à la carte menu is offered, or you can have snacks in the Tavern bar.

3. Kenilworth Castle

In magnificent ruins, this castle—the subject of Sir Walter Scott's romance *Kenilworth*—once had walls that enclosed an area of seven acres. It lies five miles north of Warwick, 13 from Stratford-upon-Avon. In 1957 Lord Kenilworth presented the decaying castle to England, and limited restoration has since been carried out.

The castle dates back to the days of Henry I, having been built by one of his lieutenants, Geoffrey de Clinton. Of the original castle, only Caesar's Tower, with its 16-foot-thick walls, remains. Edward II was forced to abdicate at Kenilworth in 1327, before being carried off to Berkeley Castle in Gloucestershire, where he was undoubtedly murdered. Elizabeth I in 1563 gave the castle to her favorite, Robert Dudley, Earl of Leicester. The earl built the Gatehouse, which was visited on several occasions by the queen. After the Civil War, the Roundheads were responsible for breaching the outer walls and towers, and blowing up the north wall of the keep. This was the only damage caused following the Earl of Monmouth's plea that it be "Slighted with as little spoil to the dwellinghouse as might be."

From March 15 to October 15, the castle is open Monday to Saturday from 9:30 a.m. to 6:30 p.m. Otherwise, hours are from 9:30 a.m. to 4 p.m. In summer, the Sunday visiting hours are 2 to 6:30 p.m. (from 2 to 4 p.m. off-season). The castle is closed on December 25 and 26, and on January 1. Admission charges are 60p (90¢) for adults, 35p (53¢) for children under 16.

FOOD AND LODGING: The **Clarendon House Hotel,** High Street (tel. 0962/54694), is a family-run hotel and restaurant in the old part of Kenilworth. The oak tree around which the original ale house was built in 1538 is still supporting the roof of the building today. The present owners, the Lea family, welcome guests to spend the night in any of the 14 bedrooms, all of which are tastefully decorated. Prices range from £25 ($37.50) to £26.50 ($39.75) for a single, from £36 ($54) for a double with private shower, toilet, and perhaps even a four-poster bed. Tariffs include a full English breakfast and VAT.

Before the evening meal, guests gather in the timbered lounge. The hotel's restaurant is housed in what was once the inn stable. The oddly timbered room is decorated with antique maps and armor, constant reminders that a Cromwellian garrison once stayed at the inn during a seige of Kenilworth Castle.

Game is a specialty at the Clarendon House, and in season you may dine on such specialties as pigeon Normandy, casseroled in cider with onions, venison casserole, and mallard (wild duck cooked in red wine). A complete dinner, inclusive of VAT, is available for around £10 ($15) per head. You can dine Sunday to Thursday from 7 to 9 p.m. (until 9:30 p.m. on Friday and Saturday). The Leas also have an interesting collection of small antiques and old maps for sale.

Restaurant Bosquet, Warwick Road (tel. Kenilworth 52463), is a tiny terraced town-house restaurant owned and operated by Bernard Lignier, a Frenchman who does the cooking, and his English wife, Jane. The à la carte menu is changed with the seasons but consists mainly of French dishes, such as magret of duck, sweetbreads, loin of lamb with tarragon, fish according to the market, and game according to the season. When I visited here recently, there was a choice of duck mousse, a fish soup, and a feuilleté of leeks with chive butter sauce for appetizers, then halibut with crayfish sauce, calf liver with green mustard sauce, or filet of beef in a red wine sauce, followed by a choice of dessert or cheese. There is a good selection of reasonably priced regional French wines, a good bottle costing about £6 ($9). A meal of three courses goes for about £15 ($22.50) per person. The set menu, at £11 ($16.50), is changed regularly and also includes seasonal produce. The restaurant is open for dinner daily except Sunday, and you can have lunch here by prior arrangement. It is essential to make reservations, as the place is quite small. Bosquet is something of a culinary oasis in Kenilworth.

4. Coventry

Although the Midlands city of Coventry, home of motorcar and cycle manufacturing, is principally industrial, you'll want to pay it a visit to see Sir Basil Spence's controversial **Coventry Cathedral,** consecrated in 1962. The city was partially destroyed during the blitz in the early '40s, but the rebuilding was miraculous. No city more than Coventry seems to symbolize England's power to bounce back from adversity.

Coventry has long been noted in legend as the ancient market town through which Lady Godiva made her famous ride, giving birth to a new name in English: Peeping Tom. The Lady Godiva story is clouded in such obscurity that the truth has probably been lost forever. It has been suggested that the good lady never appeared in the nude, but was the victim of scandalmongers, who, in their attempt to tarnish her image, unknowingly immortalized her.

The cathedral grew up on the same site as the 14th-century Perpendicular building. Many Coventry residents have maintained that the foreign visitor is more likely to admire the structure than the Britisher, who perhaps is more attached to traditional cathedral design.

Outside is Sir Jacob Epstein's bronze masterpiece, St. Michael slaying the Devil. Inside, the outstanding feature is the 70-foot-high altar tapestry by Graham Sutherland, said to be the largest in the world. The floor-to-ceiling abstract stained-glass windows are the work of the Royal College of Art. The West Window is most interesting, with its engraved glass, rows of stylized saints and monarchs with jazzy angels flying around between them.

Coventry is 19 miles from Stratford-upon-Avon, and only 11 from Warwick and 6 from Kenilworth.

St. Mary's Guildhall, Bayley Lane (tel. 0203/25555). Up a flight of steps leading from a small yard off Bayley Lane is one of the most attractive medieval guildhalls in England, dating from 1342. It was originally built as a meeting place for the guilds of St. Mary, St. John the Baptist, and St. Catherine. It is now used for the solemn election of the lord mayors of the city and for banquets and civic ceremonies. Above the north window is an arras (tapestry), added in the 15th century, and a beautiful oak ceiling with its original 14th-century carved angels, which was rebuilt in the 1950s. There is a minstrel's gallery and a treasury, and off the Armoury, Caesar's Tower where Mary Queen of Scots was imprisoned in 1569. By appointment only, you can also see a magnificent collection of 42 original watercolors by H. E. Cox, depicting Coventry before the bombings of 1939. City pensioners conduct guided tours.

Ford's Hospital, Greyfriars lane, is a house built in the very early 16th century to house the poor of the city. Today it is a wealth of old beams and mullioned windows restored during 1953. It is now the home once more of elderly Coventry residents. There is a beautiful inner courtyard surrounded by timbered walls hung with geraniums, ferns, and ivy. It is open from 10 a.m. to 5 p.m. throughout the year, and is well worth a visit.

At the Coventry Information Centre, 36 Broadgate (tel. 0203/20084 or 0203/51717), you can obtain free a useful brochure on the city, listing the main sights and where to eat cheaply or magnificently. It also guides you to shopping bargains, including those of the indoor retail market off Market Way and the craft shops on Spon Street.

The Museum of British Road Transport, on Cook Street, is some five minutes' walk from Coventry Cathedral in the city center. It houses the largest municipally owned collection in the United Kingdom, possibly in the world. The oldest car is an original Daimler, dating from 1897 (the first English Daimler was built in Coventry only one year before). The museum also displays some of the most antique vehicles still running—six of them are regular participants in the annual London–Brighton run (only vehicles manufactured before 1905 are eligible). Curiosities include a 1910 Humber taxi whose mileage is listed at more than one million. Exhibits are diversified, as the museum has the ambitious task of covering the total history of transport in the Midlands, internationally recognized as the home of the British transport industry. Indeed, Coventry has been the home of some 116 individual motor vehicle manufacturers, many of which are represented in the collections. Among the military vehicles is the staff car in which Montgomery rode into Berlin after the defeat of the Nazis. The museum is open daily throughout the summer (Easter through September) and on Friday, Saturday, and Sunday from October through March, although prebooked parties can gain entry outside the public hours in winter. Admission is 30p (45¢) for adults, 15p (23¢) for children. For further information, phone the manager, Museum of British Road Transport, Cook Street, Coventry (tel. 0203/25555, extension 2315).

FOOD AND LODGING: De Vere Hotel, Cathedral Square (tel. 0203/51851), is strikingly modern, designed to relate architecturally to the adjoining cathedral. Just off the Coventry inner ring road, it stands in the center of the city. For such a provincial hotel, it has an international first-class standard of comfort and service. Attracting a large business clientele, the hotel sounds an elegant tone in its public rooms, including the Terrace Room, a coffeeshop-restaurant where, in summer, glass doors slide back to give access to the terrace forming one side of Cathedral Square. In addition, the Taverna, the hotel's biggest bar, is decorated in an Italianate style, and the Three Spires Restaurant specializes in classical British and continental cookery, with prime Scottish beef a specialty. Bedrooms are spacious and equipped with rosewood furnishings, and each unit was designed as a twin-bedded studio with private baths and double-glazed windows to keep out traffic noises. Twins range in price from £54 ($81) to £60 ($90), and singles pay from £42 ($63) to £54 ($81), the latter in the "executive" class. These rates include VAT.

Leofric, Broadgate (tel. 0203/21371), named for Lady Godiva's husband, is the major hotel in the city, attracting, I suspect, far more business people than tourists. However, if you're overnighting in Coventry, it's the best choice, lying only two or three minutes from the cathedral, overlooking the famous statue of Lady Godiva. Each of the 90 bedrooms has a private bath, TV, phone, and central heating. The regular rate in a single is £45 ($67.50), increasing to £60 ($90) in a double or twin. Tariffs include VAT. The Leofric's Carving Room is perhaps the best value in Coventry and serves traditional English food. A three-course meal is offered for £10 ($15). The coffeeshop, Peep-in Tom's, is named after the legendary figure who took a look at Lady Godiva. For a predinner drink, I'd recommend one of the specials in Ray's Bar.

The **Post House**, Rye Hill, Allesley, near Coventry (tel. 0203/402151), is a motor hotel, built in rural surroundings three miles to the west of the center of Coventry, overlooking the main A45 road. There are nine floors and 200 bedrooms, each with wide-view window, private bath, radio, telephone, color TV, and central heating, as well as tea- and coffee-making facilities. You pay £45 ($67.50) in a single, £60 ($90) in a double, including service and VAT. Meals are rapid in the coffeeshop, more leisurely in the restaurant.

A TOUR OF A GLASS WORKS: Royal Brierley Crystal, North Street,
Brierley Hill, West Midlands (tel. 0384/70161), can be visited if you phone ahead to arrange for the 1½-hour tour, which is fascinating. You are shown the process of mixing the ingredients, including white sand, red lead, and arsenic, which are melted in the giant furnace in the center of the great hall before being taken to the smaller furnaces around the walls. From those, it is collected, blown, cut, and decorated. Every hand-blown item is unique, but the artisans are so skilled that items of a set are almost identical, and very few end in the Seconds Shop, where, to the layman's eye, they look perfect anyway.

Tours take place at 11 a.m. Monday to Friday and at 1 p.m. Monday to Thursday, for a charge of 20p (30¢). You can visit the Seconds Shop any day except Sunday from 9 a.m. to 4 p.m. to buy goods at advantageous prices. Items include export rejects and discontinued lines, as well as slightly imperfect glasses and vases. Anything can be packed and sent overseas for you. A tea shop is open for lunch or tea.

To get to the glassworks, turn off the M5 at Exit 4 on to the A491 Bromsgrove–Wolverhampton road, and turn right to Brierley Hill.

5. Hereford and Worcester

The Wye Valley contains some of the most beautiful river scenery in Europe. The river cuts through agricultural country, and there is no population explosion in the sleepy villages. Wool used to be its staple business, although fruit growing and dairy farming are important today.

The old country of Herefordshire has now combined with Worcestershire to form "Hereford and Worcester"-shire. Worcestershire's name, of course, has become famous around the world because of its sauce familiar to gourmets. It is one of the most charming of Midland counties, covering a portion of the rich valleys of the Severn and Avon.

Herefordshire's Black Mountains border the Welsh Brecon Beacons National Park, and between the two cathedral cities of Hereford and Worcester the ridge of the Malverns rises from the Severn Plain.

The heart of England is the best point to travel to by train from Paddington Station in London if you wish to use your BritRail Pass. The train takes you through many of the previously mentioned towns and villages, and you can stop and visit Windsor, Henley-on-Thames, and Oxford, not to mention the numerous Cotswold villages such as Chipping Campden. It must be one of the best train rides in the country, and you can also take a side trip by bus from Evesham to Stratford-upon-Avon. Or take the bus back from Stratford to Oxford via Woodstock, then the train back into London.

HEREFORD: One of the most colorful old towns of England, the ancient Saxon city of Hereford, on the Wye River, was the birthplace of both David Garrick and Nell Gwynne. Dating from 1079, the red sandstone **Hereford Cathedral** (tel. Hereford 59880) contains all styles of architecture, from Norman to Perpendicular. One of its most interesting features is a library of chained books—more than 1600 copies—as well as one of the oldest maps in existence, the Mappa Mundi of 1290. There is also a newly established Treasury in the crypt.

Hereford is surrounded by both orchards and rich pasturelands. Hence it has some of the finest cider in the world, best sampled in one of the city's mellow pubs. Hereford cattle sold here are some of the finest in the world too.

The Old House, High Town, is preserved as a Jacobean period museum, with the appropriate furnishings. The completely restored half-timbered structure was built in 1621. Furnished in 17th-century style on three floors, the house includes a kitchen, hall, and bedrooms with four-poster beds. It was originally part of Butcher's Row. The house is open from 10 a.m. to 1 p.m. on Monday, from 10 a.m. to 1 p.m. and 2 to 5 p.m. Tuesday to Friday, and to 5:30 p.m. on Saturday in summer (10 a.m. to 1 p.m. on Saturday in winter). Admission is 30p (45¢) for adults, 15p (23¢) for children.

Museum of Cider, The Cider Mills, 21 Ryelands (tel. 0432/54207), displays everything connected with the making of cider, the real wine of England, starting with the growing of the fruit. There is a reconstruction of a 16th-century farm cider house, cider mills, presses, barrels and barrel-making tools, jugs, and bottles. The shop sells cider by the bottle. They also offer a rare old cider brandy. A tea shop serves light refreshment during the day. Admission is 80p ($1.20) for adults, 40p (60¢) for children. The museum is open daily June through September. It is closed on Tuesday in April, May, and October, and shut completely from November to March. Take the A438 Hereford–Brecon road and turn off on Grimmer Road.

Food and Lodging

Green Dragon, Broad Street (tel. 0432/272506), hides behind an 18th-century Georgian facade, although the former coaching inn is considerably older. Convenient to the cathedral, the inn has a large, pillared main hall. It's warm and inviting, made especially so by the traditional old features that remain, including some early 17th-century paneling of Herefordshire oak. Next to the restaurant is a paneled cocktail bar, and there's also the Offa Bar on the ground floor.

Many of the bedrooms are spacious, and all are pleasantly decorated— 93 units in all, mainly with private baths and all with color TV and in-house movies. Depending on the plumbing, singles begin at £44 ($66), and doubles go from £58 ($87). The paneled restaurant is a room of character. Good food, including both English and continental dishes, are featured by the chef. Expect to pay about £4.50 ($6.75) for a buffet lunch, from £12 ($18) for an à la carte dinner.

Style House, in nearby Withington (tel. 0432/850772), is a spacious stone Georgian house dating from 1781, in a walled garden in the little village of Withington, four miles from Hereford. The house is tastefully decorated, carpeted, and centrally heated. Mrs. Vera Allen rents rooms on a B&B basis for £10 ($15) per person, with an evening dinner offered for £4.50 ($6.75). VAT and service are included in the prices. There's a small guests' kitchen where you can make yourself refreshments if you wish.

WEOBLEY: This small medieval village of old timbered houses lies west of the A49 Hereford–Ludlow road, only a few miles east of the border of Wales.

Red Lion Hotel (tel. Weobley 220) is a charming village inn, more than 500 years old, which has been carefully restored to offer seven rooms, all with private bath or shower, color TV, warm furnishings, and comfortable beds.

Michael and Rosemary Stacey run the place most efficiently, and everything is kept spotlessly clean. Rooms go for £26 ($39) in a single, from £33 ($49.50) in a double, including service and **VAT.** Breakfast, featuring cooked dishes, is also included. Lunch is served daily from 12:30 to 2 p.m., dinner from 7 to 10 p.m. (till 9 p.m. on Sunday). Aside from the bar occupied in the evenings by locals, there is a cozy lounge with a roaring fire and soft armchairs where your orders for dinner are taken. Bar food and such à la carte specialties as local salmon and trout, Herefordshire beef, a rack of Welsh lamb, sauteed suprême of duckling Grand Marnier, crab and fresh coconut cocktail, and Dover sole. Expect to spend from £12 ($18) for an evening meal. The service is good and friendly, and passersby are welcomed.

WORCESTER: This historic cathedral city, known for its gloves and porcelain, stands 27 miles from Birmingham and 26 miles from Stratford-upon-Avon.

Worcester Cathedral, set high on the bank of the River Severn, celebrated its 900th anniversary in 1984. The original crypt, refurbished to mark the ninth centenary, is still in daily use, and the Quire, rebuilt in 1224, has contained the tomb of King John since 1216. The Chapter House, with its single central supporting column, is one of the oldest and finest in England. The cathedral, which has a long tradition of good choral music, is in open daily from 9 a.m. to 6 p.m. (7:45 a.m. to 7:30 p.m. in summer).

DOLLARWISE GUIDE TO ENGLAND

A visit to the **Royal Worcester Porcelain Factory** (tel. 0905/23221) is worthwhile. A tour costs £1.40 ($2.10) for adults, 50p (75¢) for children, allowing you to see the craftspeople at work. Unfortunately it's necessary to book ahead if you wish to take a tour, but everyone can enjoy browsing in the shop at the factory. There you can buy examples of their craft. Many pieces are "seconds," all marked as such and sold at moderate prices. Most of the time you won't be able to tell why! There is a magnificent museum as well.

The city is rich in other sights as well, including the **Commandery** (tel. 0905/355071), a fine 15th-century timber-framed structure that was originally founded about 1085 as a hospital. Purchased by the City of Worcester in 1973, it contains a great hall with a hammer-beam ceiling and oriel window. It features displays on the city's history from Roman times. It's open Tuesday to Saturday from 10:30 a.m. to 5 p.m. (Sunday in summer only, 2:30 to 5 p.m.) Admission is free.

If time remains, see **King Charles' House,** where Charles II stayed before the Battle of Worcestershire in 1651; **Queen Elizabeth's House,** and the **Queen Anne Guildhall,** built in 1723 (outside, the Royalists honored Charles I and II with statues); and **St. Helen's,** the nation's oldest church, which may date back to 680.

On Sunday in summer, guided walking tours, lasting two hours, leave at 11 a.m. and again at 2:30 p.m. Check with the Tourist Information Office, the Guildhall (tel. 0905/23471), for when and where regarding departure of the tours. A two-hour walk costs 50p (75¢).

Food and Lodging

Giffard Hotel, High Street (tel. 0905/27155), is a modern hotel in the center of the city, built in a new shopping district, which contains a multistory car park. In the lounge, guests can gaze through picture windows that frame a view of the cathedral. Often used as a conference center, the hotel has more than 100 well-furnished bedrooms, each with private bath, radio, TV, phone, and coffee-making equipment. The cost is from £38 ($57) in a single, from £46 ($69) in a double, including both service and VAT. The pleasantly efficient staff will make your stay comfortable. Adjoining the Royal Worcester Room, the elegantly furnished restaurant, is a cocktail bar. A second bar, finished in marble and deep mahogany, is named the Royalist, its theme based on the Royalist connections in Worcester. The hotel is easily accessible from the M5 Motorway (Exit 7).

For meals, I'd suggest the **King Charles II,** 29 New St. (tel. 0905/22449), a mellow old half-timbered building where Charles II was believed to have hidden out following the Battle of Worcester. The paneled dining room is elegantly decorated with two open fireplaces. The specialties—continental with mainly Italian dishes—are enjoyable prepared from good ingredients. Expect to pay about £15 ($22.50) per person for dinner on the à la carte menu. The restaurant, however, serves a set lunch for £8.50 ($12.75). It is closed on Sunday, Monday, all bank holidays, and for the first three weeks in August.

Bottle's Wine Bar & Bistro, 5 Friar St. (tel. 0905/21958), is a favored rendezvous right in the historic center. The decor is handsomely subdued, with black painted wickerwork tables, and the selection of cold foods is very good. I prefer the clove-studded freshly baked ham, along with a nice crisp salad, costing £3 ($4.50) per platter. In addition, the good-tasting soups are also homemade, going for 60p (90¢) a bowl. The roast joints, seafood dishes and at least one hot specialty every day are also recommended. You might end your meal with cheesecake or gâteau, or even with brie or stilton cheese. The wine bar is open from noon to 2:30 p.m. (last orders are taken at 2 p.m.) and from 6:30 to 10:30 p.m. (until 11 p.m. on Friday and Saturday; last orders a half hour before closing). It's open Sunday from 7 to 10:30 p.m.

Food and Lodging at Abberley

The **Elms Hotel**, Abberley (tel. 029-921/666), is 12 miles northwest of Worcester on the border of the old county of Herefordshire, home of the widely known Hereford cattle breed. Queen Anne was on the throne when this magnificent country house was built in 1710. Twelve acres of rolling parkland surround formal gardens, and there are tennis courts, a putting green, and a croquet lawn for the use of the guests. This is a warm country house where open log fires burn all year in the comfortably furnished lounges to welcome visitors.

Bedrooms are mostly large, some with four-poster beds. All have radios, phones, and color TVs. Much antique and good English furniture is used. Bathrooms are supplied with such accessories as hair dryers. Rates for single rooms with bath start at £39 ($58.50); doubles and twins, from £62 ($93). A unit with a four-poster bed and bath is £65 ($97.50). All tariffs include a full English breakfast, VAT, and service. An extra bed placed in a room costs £18 ($27).

The Regency dining room with a recent addition in the same style is open daily for lunch and dinner. It's an elegant and restful place to enjoy the "nouvellish" cuisine of Nigel Lamber, who trained in London, Scotland, and France before settling at the Elms. Using only the finest and freshest ingredients and the lightly flavored sauces of nouvelle cuisine, Nigel admits that larger portions are served here than are usual in such restaurants, in order to satisfy the hearty country appetites of the local clientele. You can enjoy the view of the raised gardens, floodlit at night, through the arched windows while you wait for your freshly prepared meal to be served.

Luncheon, at £10 ($15), might include chilled carrot and lime soup, then lamb liver with avocado served with a Dubonnet and orange sauce. To finish, there are homemade desserts. Dinner, at £18 ($27), is likely to feature a light spinach soufflé served with anchovy butter sauce, followed by grilled lamb cutlets topped with a stilton mousse. There is a good wine list.

Museums on the Outskirts

Avoncroft Museum of Buildings, Stoke Heath, Bromsgrove, (tel. Bromsgrove 31886), is 11 miles from Worcester and 21 miles from Stratford-upon-Avon. It is open daily from March 1 to November 30 from 10:30 a.m. to 5:30 p.m. Admission is £1.20 ($1.80) for adults, 65 p (98¢) for children. You can hire a guide for £4 ($6) per party. The museum's cafeteria is open from 11 a.m. for coffee, lunch, and afternoon tea. Snacks are available from 60p (90¢), and tea or coffee costs 35p (53¢). The museum is an open-air site where a variety of historic buildings have been saved from destruction and reconstructed. There is a windmill in working order; a timber-framed merchant's house from the 15th century; an Elizabethan house; a cockfight theater, a stable, a wagon shed, and an ice house (all from the 18th century); chain- and nail-making workshops; and a blacksmith's forge. This gives one a fascinating insight into the construction of those buildings as done by English forefathers. The 14th-century Geusten Hall roof from Worcester has been reconstructed at ground level so that you can see how the joints were made by the skill of artisans of the past. These are just a few of the exhibits on display at this ten-acre site. Free car parking is available, and there is also a picnic area.

Sir Edward Elgar's Birthplace at Upper Broadheath is a brick cottage surrounded by stables and a coach house built by his father and uncle in the early 19th century. Nowadays the house contains a museum of photographs and drawings, original musical scores, and mementos of his youth. Musicians and conductors come from afar to check his music and their interpretations of it. To reach the house, drive out of Worcester on the A44 toward Leominster. After two miles, turn off to the right at the sign. The house is in the village, 2½ miles along a side road. There is a small admission charge, and it is open daily from 1:30 to 4:30 p.m.

The **Jinney Ring Craft Centre**, Hanbury, Worcestershire (tel. 052-784/272), is in the same area as the Avoncroft Museum, five miles away in the village of Hanbury on the B4091 from Stoke Prior to Vernon Arms. Two old farm buildings have been carefully restored and converted by ex-farmers Richard and Jenny Greatwood into artists' studios and craft workshops on 20 acres of land. The eight small studios house a jeweler, blacksmith, wood turner, stained glass designer, weaver, and toy maker, all of whom will demonstrate their craft. Many of the items they show can be purchased in the center's shop. It is open Easter to Christmas, Wednesday to Saturday from 10:30 a.m. to 5 p.m. and on Sunday from 2:30 to 5:30 p.m. They also do tasty lunchtime snacks served from noon to 2:30 p.m. By the way, the Jinney Ring was one of the first implements in the mechanization of farming. A series of complicated cogs and drives linked the cider press or the chaff-cutter with the patient horse, which plodded ever onward around the ring to drive the grinding wheels.

Also in the area, **Hanbury Hall** is a Wren-style red brick building erected in the early 18th century. It is remarkable for its painted ceilings and magnificent staircase by Thornhill. It is open April to October, Saturday and Sunday and on Easter Monday and Tuesday from 2 to 5 p.m. From May until the end of September, it is open Wednesday to Sunday and bank holidays from 2 to 6 p.m. Admission is £1.75 ($2.63) for adults, 65p (98¢) for children. Teas are served in the hall.

GREAT MALVERN: A holiday spa and splendid walking center, Great Malvern is the best spot for your headquarters if you want to tour the beautiful, historic Malverns, once part of the ancient kingdom of Mercia. Great Malvern became important in the 19th century as a spa town, and much of the Victorian splendor remains. The Malvern Hills stretch for nine miles, with six townships lying along their line.

A Farm Cottage Holiday

Whitewells Farm Cottages, Ridgeway Cross, near Malvern (tel. 088684/607), are just one example of the country cottages offered in the heart of England. Peter and Lynne Bennett have turned their farm buildings into unique holiday accommodations. The old hop kiln has a circular kitchen and bedroom; saddlestones and haywain have bedrooms on the ground floor, a lounge and kitchen in the old hayloft. The cottages have antique oak beams and country-style furnishings. An old stone barn has been turned into a cottage named Cider Press, which sleeps from two to four persons. In addition an old pigs' cot alongside the pony stables now provides a laundry room, with an automatic washing machine and dryer for the use of guests. The old pony stables act as the reception. Milk, bread, and newspapers are delivered here, and you'll find a telephone, a library of books, and local information. All cottages are well furnished with refrigerator, cooker, central heating, color TV, and electric blankets, plus little extras such as hair dryers, toasters, and irons. They will willingly tell you where to buy provisions and will make you welcome to their part of the country. Prices range from £120 ($180) per week for two, £175 ($262.50) for four to £200 ($300) for six persons. During the early spring, winter, and autumn, shorter rentals are possible.

Where to Dine

Restaurant Croque-en-Bouche, 221 Wells Road, Malvern Wells (tel. 06745/65612), is reached by driving two miles south of Malvern on the A449. It's opposite the filling station. The restaurant, run by Robin and Marion Jones, is in what was the bakery and grocer's shop in a five-story Victorian building. There is still an old oven in the basement where wine is now stored. How anyone as young (and attractive) as Marion can have gained the culinary experience that she displays is a wonder to me.

Dinner, at £16.50 ($24.75), including VAT and service, is a set five-course meal with a limited choice at each stage. Menus are likely to include skate with black butter or a crab pancake followed by lamb roast with sweetbreads and rosemary. As there are only Robin and Marion to look after you, you must reserve a table. Coffee is served, and since pipes and cigars are not permitted in the dining room, smokers adjourn to the bar at this stage. The restaurant is open from Wednesday to Saturday for dinner and on Sunday for lunch.

LEDBURY: **Hope End Country House Hotel,** Hope End, Ledbury (tel. 0531/3613), is owned and operated by John and Patricia Hegarty, who come from local families. John's ancestor helped build the canal and bring the railway to Ledbury, and Patricia's family has lived here for more than 500 years. Tired of work as a solicitor and a schoolteacher, the Hegartys settled at Hope End, where Elizabeth Barrett Browning lived during her first 23 years. The house is furnished with antiques, and paintings and other art adorn the walls of the drawing room. Bedrooms are centrally heated, and all have adjoining bathrooms. There are such pleasant touches as books to read while you relax in the easy chair in your room, Malvern water from their own well to drink, and a choice of bath oils. The charge for B&B, dinner, VAT, and service is £36 ($54) per person per night, £42 ($63) per person in one of the larger rooms or in the suite across the courtyard under the minaret.

Patricia is rapidly gaining a reputation for her cooking. She specializes in providing whole and fresh foods and bakes her own brown bread. Fresh fruit and vegetables come from the large walled garden. Fresh eggs, local beef and lamb, fish, and game, and a wide selection of English cheeses make meals a pleasure. Five-course dinners include such appetizers as haddock hotpots with cider, wild duck, or lamb served with fresh vegetables in season.

Perhaps the most pleasing aspect here is the peace and quiet, with no radio or TV in the bedrooms. The surrounding orchards and fields line some of the most pleasant country lanes in England, and you can walk for miles without seeing another person.

EVESHAM: A delightful market town on the Avon River, Evesham is known for its riverside parks. It contains several interesting buildings, including a 16th-century bell tower. It is a center of a famous fruit- and vegetable-growing region, and in springtime the Vale of Evesham is a mass of blossoms. Six miles southeast of Broadway and 14 miles northeast of Stratford-upon-Avon, it makes a good center for touring both the Cotswolds and the Shakespeare Country.

The **Evesham Hotel,** Cooper's Lane, off Waterside (tel. 0386/49111), lies down a small lane just where the A44 runs beside the River Avon to Evesham. It is owned and run by the Jenkinson family. John is general manager, and there is always a Jenkinson on duty. A dwelling has stood on the site since the 16th century, and the mulberry trees and cedars of Lebanon date back almost that far. The pleasant lounges and the restaurant look out over the gardens to the trees. There is a modern bar where the usual drinks are served, plus an amazing selection of malt whiskies and brandies.

In the Cedar Restaurant, dinner is a well-prepared à la carte event. You choose your meal from such dishes as medallions of beef with green pepper sauce or breast of chicken stuffed with brie and deep fried. All are served with a selection of fresh vegetables and followed by homemade desserts. The meal price for three courses is around £12 ($18). At lunchtime, a buffet offers homemade soup, selections from a serve-yourself buffet, and coffee, all costing around £5 ($7.50).

The simply furnished bedrooms are warm and comfortable, with color TVs, radios, phones, tea- and coffee-making equipment, and private bathrooms. A recently opened wing has 16 modern, well-equipped units with views over the garden. It's attached to the main house by a fully enclosed and heated corridor. The cost for B&B is £36 ($54) in a single, £51 ($76.50) in a double, and £73 ($109.50) in a family suite. All tariffs include VAT and a full English breakfast, or a continental breakfast served in your room if you prefer.

Salford Hall, Abbots Salford, near Evesham (tel. 0386/870561). Part of the original building dates back to the 15th century but, as with so many country houses of those times, it has been added to in the 17th century and later restored to provide ten bedrooms, six with baths. The Abbots Bar (this was once a nunnery) is oak paneled, and the lounge is full of comfortable chairs. The restaurant provides a lunchtime carvery on Sunday. A single room with bath is £19.50 ($29.25) a night, a double or twin renting from £32 ($48) to £36 ($54) a night, including a full breakfast. All rooms have tea and coffeemakers. VAT is included.

6. Salop (Shropshire)

Immortalized by A. E. Housman's "A Shropshire Lad," this hilly county borders Wales, which accounts for its turbulent history. The bloody battles are over today, and the towns of Salop, with their black-and-white timbered houses, are peaceful and quiet. Salop makes a good base for touring in the Welsh mountains.

SHREWSBURY: Lying within a horseshoe bend of the Severn River, Shrewsbury is the capital of Salop. The river almost encloses the town. Known for its cakes and ale, Shrewsbury contains one of the best known schools in England. It was also the birthplace of Charles Darwin.

Considered the finest Tudor town in England, Shrewsbury is noted for its black-and-white buildings of timber and plaster, including Abbot's House from 1450 and the tall gabled Ireland's Mansion from 1575 standing on High Street. It also has a number of Georgian and Regency mansions, some old bridges, and handsome churches, including the Abbey Church of Saint Peter and St. Mary's Church.

Shrewsbury Castle is 900 years old and was saved from destruction in 1790 when an engineer, Thomas Telford, had it restored as a private house. Built of red sandstone on a hill dominating the town, it is now a visitor center with permanent displays of the history of Shrewsbury. Called the **Information Centre**, it stands in the Square (tel. 0743/52019).

Rowley's House Museum, on Barker Street, is housed in a fine timber-framed house and an adjoining brick mansion. This musuem includes displays on art, local history, Roman and prehistoric archeology, geology, costumes, and natural history. The great treasures include the fine Hadrianic forum inscription and silver mirror, both from the nearby Roman city of Viroconium (Wroxeter). The museum is open six days a week (seven days a week in August) from 10 a.m. to 5 p.m. Admission is 25p (38¢), free in winter.

Clive House Museum, on College Hill (tel. 0743/54811), has displays of local ceramics, industrial archeology, art, costumes, and a Georgian room, besides being the regimental museum of the Queen's Dragoon Guards. Hours are from 10 a.m. to 1 p.m. and 2 to 5 p.m., except Monday when hours are from noon to 1 p.m. and 2 to 5 p.m. Admission is free.

At **Coleham Pumping Station,** Longden Coleham, you can see displayed compound rotative pumping engines from 1900. Open Tuesday to Saturday from 10 a.m. to 1 p.m. and 2 to 5 p.m.

Food and Lodging

Prince Rupert Hotel, Butcher Row (tel. 0743/52461), is a hotel of character—part of it dating from the 15th century—right on a quiet side street in the center of town. Its front has four peaked gables and, in summer, a wealth of flower boxes full of petunias and geraniums. The facade is characterized by peaked gables on the Old Church Street entrance. Even though the interior has been modernized, it still has exposed beams and uneven floors. A favorite gathering spot is the lounge, which is tapestried. There are three restaurants in all, including the Cavalier, which has an international reputation for fine cuisine. The rooms are bright and fresh, with compact, well-maintained baths found in 47 of the 60 units. Singles range in price from £30 ($45) to £35 ($52.50); doubles or twins go from £38 ($57) to £54 ($81). The hotel is privately owned by Mr. and Mrs. L. Morris-Jones, who work hard to make their guests comfortable. Those guests, incidentally, have included Margaret Thatcher and her husband, Denis, and George C. Scott, who stayed here for seven weeks when he made a new film based on Dickens's *A Christmas Carol*.

Lion Hotel, Wyle Cop (tel. 0743/53107), is a simple red brick structure, once a well-known posting inn, standing on the outskirts of town on the Telford road. In part the hotel dates from the 15th century, and oak beams and paneling from that period remain. Many famous people have stayed here, including Dickens, Jenny Lind, and De Quincey, who described the hotel's Adam-style ballroom in his *Confessions of an Opium Eater*. Bedrooms are simply furnished, and many are quite small. Depending on the plumbing, singles range from £40 ($60), and doubles cost from £60 ($90), including both VAT and service. Forty-four of the 64 bedrooms contain private baths. The Dickens Suite boasts a "half-tester" bed in which the Victorian novelist is reputed to have slept. The restaurant with its Victorian decor is named after him, and it serves both table d'hôte and à la carte meals. The hotel has two bars, the Tudor one featuring a buffet at lunchtime.

OSWESTRY: Near the Welsh border, this interesting old market town has some Yale monuments in its St. Oswald's Church and a 17th-century Griddle Gate nearby. At Old Owestry, an Iron Age hill fort with multiple ramparts can be seen.

LUDLOW: Looking down on the Teme River, this is a mellow old town with a historic Norman castle. Many Georgian and Jacobean timbered buildings stand on its quiet lanes and courts. The most colorful street is known as "Broad," rising from the old Ludford Bridge to Broadgate, the one remaining gateway from walls erected in the Middle Ages. See, in particular, the Church of St. Laurence, Butter Cross, and Reader's House.

Food and Lodging

The **Feathers,** Bullring (tel. 0584/5261), is one of England's most famous Elizabethan inns. Built in 1603 as a private residence, it is characterized by its half-timbered front and richly decorated interior. Bedrooms are bright and cheerful, and all of them contain private baths en suite, as well as phones, radios, television sets, and tea- and coffee-making facilities. Colors are in perfect harmony, with Welsh tapestry bedspreads. Singles go from £38 ($57), and doubles cost from £28 ($42) to £31 ($46.50) per person, including an English breakfast. If possible, ask for one of the units with a four-poster bed. The Richard III restaurant, with its original fireplace, is in the old-world style, serving good food and drink. Set meals go for £10.50 ($15.75), but there will be an à la carte menu as well. There are also two fully licensed bars, and polished brass and copper set the right decorative tone. In the James I lounge, you can enjoy a carved mantelpiece and an elaborately ornamented plaster ceiling.

For lunch, I'd suggest the **Bull Hotel,** Corve Street (tel. 0584/2962). Close to the castle, it's an old coaching inn which you enter under a typical arch into the courtyard. The oldest parts of the building are early Tudor. There is a large bar with roaring open fire where bar snacks are served at prices ranging from 75p ($1.13) to £2.50 ($3.75) for salads. Hot dishes cost from £2 ($3) to £3.50 ($5.25). In summer, you can take your drink and food into the courtyard, but it's better to be inside close to the fire in winter. The Bull isn't really a hotel at all but an inn opposite the Feathers Hotel.

IRONBRIDGE: Ironbridge Gorge is the location of an intriguing complex of museums, said to be the birthplace of the Industrial Revolution.

The **Ironbridge Gorge museum,** Ironbridge, Telford (tel. 095245/3522), is open daily from 10 a.m. to 6 p.m. April to October, to 5 p.m. November to March, and closed Christmas Day. This museum includes the Blists Hill Open Air Museum, the Severn Warehouse Visitor Centre, the Coalbrookdale Furnace Museum of Iron, and Coalport China Works Museum, as well as many other smaller sites, including the Coach House Gallery (industrial art housed in stables), Bedlam Furance downstream from the Iron Bridge, and the Maws Tile Works across the river from Coalport. The museum charges adults £3 ($4.50); children £2 ($3).

The Iron Bridge was the first in the world made of that metal, which was cast at Coalbrookdale in 1779 and gave its name to the area. Abraham Darby I, ironmaster, first smelted iron using coke as a fuel at the Old Furnace in Coalbrookdale, thus paving the way for the first iron rails, iron bridge, iron boat, iron aqueduct, and iron-framed building. The Ironbridge Gorge Musuem spreads over some six square miles of the Severn Gorge, encompassing a unique series of industrial monuments.

7. Staffordshire

Stoke-on-Trent is the name of the five towns known as the Potteries, the "Five Towns" of Arnold Bennett's novels. The Potteries are known throughout the world for the excellence of their fine porcelain and china.

The so-called "Black Country" of steelworks and coal mines has almost disappeared, although you can visit a coal mine and descend in the "cage" to the worked-out seams.

Within easy reach of the industrial town of Dovedale is a valley with some of England's most beautiful scenery, forming part of the Peak District National Park.

STOKE-ON-TRENT: Because of the worldwide interest in the making of pottery, this town has found itself something of a tourist attraction. It's the home of the pottery made famous by Josiah Wedgwood, along with other well-known names such as Coalport, Minton, and Spode.

The **Wedgwood Visitor Centre,** at Barlaston (tel. 078-139/4141), at present charges 50p (75¢) admission and is open from 9 a.m. to 5 p.m. Monday to Friday except over Christmas. In the demonstration hall you can watch the clay built up on the potter's wheel, see how the raised motifs so well known on Wedgwood Jasper are made and added to the pieces, as well as witness how plates are turned and fired, then painted.

The artisans working at the benches are highly skilled, and the work they produce is of the highest quality. They are happy to answer your questions about their special occupation.

There's a continuous film show in the large cinema, and the beginning of the movie is announced on the public address system. In the shop you can see samples of all the sorts of items made at the factory, and purchase souvenirs. Prices are the same as elsewhere, but they do sometimes have items of discontinued lines and some "seconds" available at reduced prices.

The fascinating museum has exhibits of more than 200 years of craftsmanship, showcases of old bills, working details, experimental pots and goblets, and drawings of machines invented by Josiah Wedgwood two centuries ago.

When you need a rest, there's a lounge with a snack cafeteria where for under £1 ($1.50) you can get a bowl of soup, a sandwich, or some steak-and-kidney pie with a glass of wine. Here you can write your postcards home and have them franked with a special stamp to say they were mailed at the Wedgwood Centre.

Afterward, a visit to the past is in order. The **Gladstone Pottery Museum,** Uttoxeter Road at Longton (tel. 0782/319232), is an old building with a paneled hallway leading to rooms piled with ancient machines and equipment used in the pottery trade. Tiles and saggars (something to do with the piling of plates in kilns) are stacked everywhere. There's a marvelous exhibit of washstand bowls and jugs, plus toilets of all shapes and sizes, including the original flush toilet made for Queen Elizabeth I in 1596. Called the Harington Water Closet, it is still in working order. It was in Stoke that the tiles used in the Capital in Washington were made, and they have examples displayed on the floor. Outside is a replica of a typical potter's home, plus a working pottery with its old Victorian bottle ovens, the last few in the area where there used to be several thousand. The area around the museum is known as Potters' Acre because of the number of shops specializing in rejects and discontinued lines. Here you may be able to replace that broken cup. Admission to the museum is £1 ($1.50). It is open from Monday to Saturday from 10:30 a.m. to 5:30 p.m. (closed Monday in winter). It is also open on Sunday all year from 2 to 6 p.m.

The **Stoke-on-Trent City Museum,** on Broad Street in Hanley (tel. 0782/29611), has departments of fine art, decorative arts, natural history, archeology, and social history. In addition, it houses one of the largest and finest collections of ceramics in the world. It's open Monday to Saturday from 10:30 a.m. to 5 p.m., to 8 p.m. on Wednesday. Admission is free.

Afterward, sustenance is required, and where better than at **Heath's Wine Bar,** Albion Street at Hanley (tel. 0782/272472), almost opposite the museum? The long bar groans beneath great dishes of pâté, cold meats, pies (veal, ham and egg, steak and kidney, grosvenor), chili, salads (several varieties), dressed crab, and hot soup. Mounds of french bread are stacked up, and jacket potatoes are a favorite item. For dessert, try the cheesecake or a fruit salad. Everything is fresh, and there is much that's homemade. Order and collect your meal and repair to one of the low coffee tables surrounded by sofas or the wheelbacked chair-surrounded tables. The music is soft, and the atmosphere is warm and red. A two-course meal will cost around £3 ($4.50) to £4.50 ($6.75).

The **Minton Museum,** London Road (tel. 0782/47771), is the starting point for a 1½-hour conducted tour through the major departments of the renowned pottery. A telephone call or a letter in advance is advised if you would like to join the £1 ($1.50) tour, which includes a visit to the department where Minton's celebrated raised gold designs are produced. Visitors will also have the opportunity of seeing free-hand painting of the highest order. Details are available of a new service offered by Minton enabling customers to commission a special hand-painted, personalized plate featuring an illustration of their own choice. The cost is around £130 ($195), and delivery takes three to four months. Ask the museum curator or factory guides.

The **Chatterley Whitfield Mining Museum,** at Tunstall, Stoke-on-Trent (tel. 0782/813337), is the only place in England where you can visit a coal mine, going down to the coal face. Before you start the underground tour, you will be shown a surface exhibition gallery including audio effects and striking visuals, painting a historical picture of the coal-mining industry. After seeing the exhibition, you are "kitted out" with lamp and helmet, and you can get overalls to cover your clothes. Stout shoes are also recommended. This mine was the first to produce one million tons of coal in a year. Coal was mined for 140 years, but the mine has been closed now for five years. The 700-foot shaft is 80 years old, and it takes 1½ minutes to descend to the face. Each party is accompanied by a retired miner. Mine was Joe, who was born in Poland, but settled in England in the '40s. He explains the techniques of mining, feeding you much information, including how the steam-winding engines work. The tour takes about an hour and costs £2.50 ($3.75). Other exhibits include a steam-winding engine and steam railway locomotives and wagons.

Alton Towers, North Staffordshire (tel. 0528/702449), lies on the B5032 four miles east of Cheadle and 15 miles east of Stoke-on-Trent. It must be the nearest thing to Disneyland this side of the Atlantic. The house, once the home of the Earls of Shrewsbury, now shelters the Planetarium, gift shop, and banqueting hall. In the park are roller coasters (the Dark Ride, Round the World, Thunderbirds, and Space 1999) and all sorts of miniature railways and cable cars, a log flume, and nature trails. There are rowboats and Indian canoes on the lake, plus a haunted house and exhibitions of natural history, dolls through the ages, and carriages. Cafés and restaurants of all sorts provide fast-food service, take-away orders, and regular table service, as at the Swiss Cottage and the Ingestre Restaurant. The place is well managed and in a lovely setting—just the thing to amuse young members of your party. The attractions are open from mid-March to the end of October daily. The grounds open at 9 a.m. and the rides are operated from 10 a.m. until 5, 6, or 7 p.m. Admission is £3.95 ($5.93), with a reduction for children. All rides and shows are free after you enter.

Food and Lodging

For those who wish to visit the Potteries and stay overnight in this industrial part of the country, I offer the following suggestions.

The **Crown Hotel,** High Street at Stone (tel. 0782/813535), is a solid 18th-century coaching inn, built on the site of a far more ancient staging post, one of the most important in the country in the reign of Charles II. Today the coach yard is roofed in to provide for the lofty paneled dining room. The sleek "carriages" of today's travelers are housed in a large yard behind the hotel.

Some of the accommodations are in the main hotel, reached by a fine galleried oak staircase; others are in a new extension at the back of the building. All units have bath (shower only in the newer part), color TV, and coffee- and tea-making facilities. Prices run from £38 ($57) per person in a double with bath. Singles run from £26 ($39) with bath. All prices include VAT, service, and an enormous breakfast.

Dinner in the magnificent paneled dining hall includes main-course specials at £4 ($6), salmon steaks at £6 ($9), and steaks from £7.50 ($11.25). Portions are huge, and you may not even want to think of an appetizer. I just managed to finish my main course and had to skip dessert on my latest rounds. If you want dessert, you face a choice from the groaning trolley. At lunch, a buffet provides substantial meals, including cold meats, quiche, and chicken-and-ham pie, along with an assortment of salads.

Haydon House Hotel, 5–9 Haydon St. at Basford (tel. 0782/629311), is a turn-of-the-century privately owned town house in the heart of the world-renowned Potteries. It offers single rooms for £26.50 ($39.75) without bath, £36 ($54) with. Doubles cost from £28 ($42) per person with bath or shower. All units have color TVs, radios, and phones, and prices include a large breakfast and a morning newspaper. If you make a reservation in advance, you may be able to get the antique four-poster bedroom with its original bathroom.

The Townhouse bar and dining room are Victorian in style and comfort, with antique clocks, lending a club atmosphere to the hotel. Haydon House is noted for good food prepared by an award-winning chef. A three-course luncheon chosen from the ample list of dishes will cost from £9 ($13.50) up. The table d'hôte dinner at £10 ($15) has a choice of five appetizers and five main dishes, plus dessert or cheese, then coffee. The à la carte menu is more extensive, including specially prepared steak dishes. Alternatively, Mrs. Beeton's Carvery will serve you a more casual meal until 10 p.m. English teas are served from 3 to 5 p.m. in the Garden Room.

NEWCASTLE-UNDER-LYME: This manufacturing and market town, 152 miles from London, has a history dating back 800 years. It is within easy reach of the Staffordshire Potteries, and might be your base for exploring them.

Grove Court Hotel, 100 Lancaster Rd. (tel. 0782/614406), is a large Victorian house with a rose garden, run by the James family, based on high standards of courtesy, cleanliness, and cuisine. All rooms have been fitted with showers and toilet facilities, and three motel-style chalets contain twin beds, showers, toilets, and TVs. There is a comfortable lounge and a small bar in the office. The hostess is a superb cook, who does outside catering in whatever spare time she can come up with. The charge is £20 ($30) for a room, including a full English breakfast and VAT.

STAFFORD: The county town was the birthplace of Izaak Walton, the British writer and celebrated fisherman. Its main industry is boot making, and it contains many historic buildings, notably St. Chad's, the town's oldest church; St. Mary's, with its unusual octagonal tower; and the William Salt Library, with its interesting collection of folklore.

Food and Lodging

Tillington Hall Hotel, Eccleshall Road (tel. 0785/535321), which has been extensively remodeled and renovated, stands in its own grounds just a mile from the center of the county town, yet less than half a mile from the M6 Motorway (junction 14). The attractive paneled reception lounge, where you are likely to stand next to Midlands business people checking in, leads to a modern bar and a lounge with an open fire on nippy nights. Eighty bedrooms, each furnished in a contemporary idiom, come equipped with private bath, radio, phone, color TV set, and coffee-making equipment. The cost is £38 ($57) to £44 ($66) nightly in a single, £48 ($72) to £52 ($78) in a double, including a full English breakfast, VAT, and service. Good food is served in the Izaak Walton Restaurant, where a set lunch costs £8 ($12); a set dinner, £9.50 ($14.25).

LICHFIELD: Fans of Samuel Johnson pay a pilgrimage here to this historic city where he was born in 1709, son of an unsuccessful bookseller and parchment maker. The city is noted for its cathedral, whose three spires are known as "Ladies of the Vale." The tallest spire rises more than 250 feet, and the west front of the cathedral was built from about 1280. You can walk around the beautiful Close and see a bit of the Vicars Close, with its half-timbered houses, along with the 17th-century Bishops Palace.

Dr. Johnson's Birthplace on Breadmarket Street contains mementos and pictures of the author and his contemporaries. It is open from 10 a.m. to 5 p.m., closing at 4 p.m. off-season and Sunday afternoons in the summer. The admission charged is 50p (75¢) for adults, half price for children.

Across the street from Dr. Johnson's Birthplace stands the **Lichfield Heritage Exhibition and Treasury,** in the Market Square. The exhibition portrays in exciting form the history of Lichfield through its men and women of arts and science and historic events. There is an audio-visual presentation of the Siege of Lichfield during the Civil War. The treasury displays examples of the silversmiths' art over the centuries, showing civic, church, and regimental plate. It is open daily from 10 a.m. to 5 p.m. Adults pay 70p ($1.05); children 30p (45/).

You can also visit the **Guildhall** behind the Heritage Exhibition. Over the city dungeons dating from the Middle Ages, the Guildhall was rebuilt in 1846. Prisoners were jailed here before they were burned at the stake in Market Square.

Incidentally, market days are Friday and Saturday in Lichfield.

TUTBURY: Once a stronghold of the Anglo-Saxon kings of Mercia, and mentioned in the Domesday Book, Tutbury is a small town on the Dove River, lying four miles north of Burton-upon-Trent. It has a fine Norman church and the ruins of Tutbury Castle.

Ye Olde Dog and Partridge, High Street (tel. 0283/813030), has been a colorful village inn for so long there is no clear record of its beginnings. Charming in appearance, it has an ornate black-and-white timbered facade, bay windows, and leaded glass, surviving elements from the 15th century. A popular coaching house in the 18th and 19th centuries, it offers a more modernized hospitality today. New luxury bathrooms have been installed for each bedroom, and singles rent for £30 ($45) a night, doubles going for £37 ($55.50), including a full English breakfast.

Inside, the inn still has a wealth of old timbering and fireplaces, maintaining a traditional character. On a more incongruous note, it has a French restaurant that is open from Monday evening through Saturday evening (Saturday lunches excepted). The à la carte menu, costing about £11 ($16.50) for a meal, is changed weekly. In addition, the inn also has a wine bar and carvery open seven days a week.

CAMBRIDGE AND EAST ANGLIA

"WE ARE FARMERS—great animal lovers," say two sisters who run a small farm in Essex. They delight in receiving paying guests at their old farm, feeding them fresh vegetables and home-grown fruit. They are not atypical of the East Anglians. The four counties of East Anglia—Essex, Suffolk, Norfolk, and Cambridgeshire—are essentially low-lying areas, where the bucolic life still reigns supreme.

East Anglia was an ancient Anglo-Saxon kingdom, under heavy domination of the Danes for many a year. Beginning in the 12th century, it was the center of a great cloth industry that brought it prosperity, as the spires of some of its churches testify to this day. Essentially, it is a land of heathland, fens, marshes, and broads in Norfolk.

Cambridge is the most visited city in East Anglia, but don't neglect to pass through Suffolk and Essex, Constable country, containing some of the

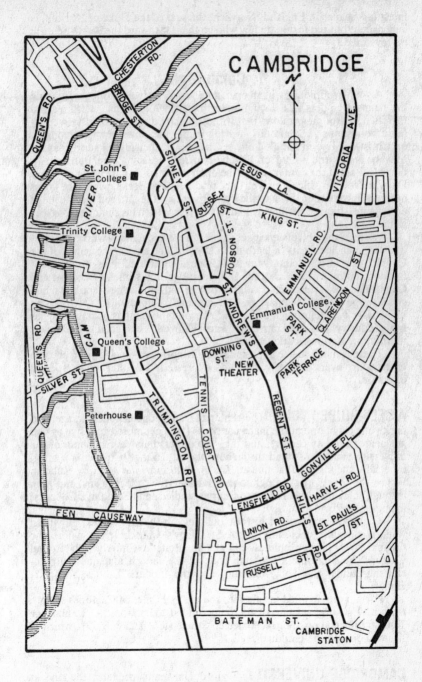

CAMBRIDGE

finest landscapes in England. Norwich, the seat of the Duke of Norfolk, is less visited, but the fortunate few who go that far toward the North Sea will be rewarded.

1. Cambridge

A young couple lying in an open green space between colleges, reading the Romantic poets . . . rowing under the Bridge of Sighs . . . spires and turrets . . . drooping willows that witness much punting . . . dusty second-hand bookshops . . . daffodils swaying in the meadows . . . carol singing on Christmas Eve in King's College Chapel . . . dancing till sunrise at the May balls . . . the sound of Elizabethan madrigals . . . the purchase of horse brasses at the corner stall in the open market . . . narrow lanes where Darwin, Newton, and Cromwell once trod . . . The Backs, where the lawns of the colleges sweep down to the Cam River . . . the tattered black robe of an upperclassman, rebelliously hanging by a thread to his shoulder as it flies in the wind.

We're in the university city of Cambridge, which, along with Oxford, is one of the ancient seats of learning in Britain. The city on the banks of the Cam River is also the county town of Cambridgeshire, 55 miles northeast of London, 80 miles from Oxford. In many ways, the stories of Oxford and Cambridge are similar—particularly the age-old conflict between town and gown (impoverished scholars vs. rent-gouging landlords). But Oxford is an industrial city, sheltering a thriving life beyond the campus. Cambridge has some industry, but if the university were removed, I suspect it would revert to an unpretentious market town.

There is much to see and explore in Cambridge—so give yourself time to wander, even aimlessly. For those pressed, I'll offer more specific direction.

A SELF-GUIDED TOUR: The center of Cambridge is pedestrianized, so park your car at one of the many car parks (they get more expensive as you get nearer the city center), and take the opportunity to visit some of the university buildings spread throughout the city. King's College is a must, especially the chapel that houses *The Adoration of the Magi* by Rubens. Follow the courtyards through to the "Backs" (the college lawns) and walk through to Trinity (where Prince Charles studied) and St. John's Colleges, including the Bridge of Sighs.

There are many other historic buildings in the city center, all within walking distance, including Great St. Mary's Church (from where the original Westminster chimes come), St. Benet's Church, the Round Church, the Fitzwilliam Museum (one of the largest and finest provincial museums), the Folk Museum, and the modern Kettles Yard Art Gallery.

For a more detailed insight into the life and times of Cambridge, both town and gown, join one of the daily guided tours from the **Cambridge Tourist Information Centre,** Wheeler Street (tel. 0223/358977), which is situated behind the Guildhall.

CAMBRIDGE UNIVERSITY: Oxford University predates the one at Cambridge. But in the early 13th century scholars began coming up to

Cambridge, as opposed to being "sent down." The choice of the market town as a seat of learning just happened—perhaps coming about as a result of a core of important masters, dissatisfied with Oxford, electing to live near the fens. Eventually, Cambridge won partial recognition from Henry III, rising and slumping with the approval or disdain of subsequent English monarchs. Cambridge consists of 29 colleges for both men and women. If you have time for only one sight, then make it:

King's College Chapel

The teenaged Henry VI founded the college on King's Parade in 1441. But most of its buildings today are from the 19th century. It is the Perpendicular Chapel that is not only the crowning glory, but one of the architectural gems in England inherited from the Middle Ages. The chapel, owing to the chaotic vicissitudes of English kings, wasn't completed until the early years of the 16th century. Its most characteristic features are its magnificent fan vaulting—all of stone—and its Great Windows, most of which were fashioned by Flemish artisans between 1515 and 1531 (the west window, however, dates from the late Victorian period). The stained glass, in hues of blues, reds, and ambers, reflects biblical stories. The long range of the windows, reading from the first on the north side at the west end right around the chapel back to the first on the south side, tell the story of the Birth of the Virgin, the Annunciation, the Birth of Christ, the Life, Ministry, and Death of Christ, the Resurrection, the Ascension, the Acts of the Apostles, and the Assumption. The upper range contains Old Testament parallels to these New Testament stories. The rood screen is from the early 16th century. Henry James called King's College Chapel "the most beautiful in England." It is open during vacation time on weekdays from 9 a.m. to 5 p.m., and on Sunday from 10:30 a.m. to 5 p.m. During term time the public is welcome to choral services, which are at 5:30 p.m. on weekdays (service said on Monday), and at 10:30 a.m. and 3:30 p.m. on Sunday. In "term" the chapel is open to visitors from 9 a.m. to 3:45 p.m. on weekdays, from 2 to 3 p.m. and from 4:30 to 5:45 p.m. on Sunday. Closed December 26 to January 1. It may be closed at other times for recording sessions.

Peterhouse

This college on Trumpington Street is visited largely because it is the oldest Cambridge college, having been founded as early as 1284. The founding father was Hugh de Balsham, the bishop of Ely. Of the original buildings, only the Hall remains, but this was restored in the 19th century and now contains stained-glass windows by William Morris. Old Court was constructed in the 15th century, but refaced in 1754, and the chapel dates from 1632. Ask permission to enter at the porter's desk.

Trinity College

On Trinity Street, Trinity College—the largest at Cambridge (not to be confused with Trinity Hall)—was founded in 1546 by Henry VIII from a number of smaller colleges that had existed on the site. The courtyard is the most spacious one in Cambridge, built when Thomas Nevile was master. Sir

Christopher Wren designed the Library. For admission to the college, apply at the porter's lodge, or telephone 0223/358201 for information.

Emmanuel College

On St. Andrew's Street, Emmanuel (tel. 0223/65411) was founded in 1584 by Sir Walter Mildmay, a chancellor of the exchequer to Elizabeth I. It is of interest at least to Harvard men, as John Harvard, founder of that university, studied here. With its attractive gardens, it makes for a good stroll. You might even visit the chapel designed by Sir Christopher Wren and consecrated in 1677. Both the chapel and college are open daily from 9:30 a.m. to 12:15 p.m. and 2 to 6 p.m.

Queens' College

On Queens' Lane, Queens' College (tel. 0223/65511) is considered by some as the loveliest in the architectural galaxy. Dating back to 1448, it was founded, then "refounded" by two English queens—one the wife of Henry VI, the other the wife of Edward IV. Its second cloisters are the most interesting—flanked with the half-timbered President's Lodge, dating from the first half of the 16th century. Normally, the college is open to visitors between 1:45 and 4:30 p.m. Entry and exit is by the Old Porters' Lodge in Queens' Lane only. The college is closed between mid-May and mid-June. An admission fee of 35p (53¢) is charged, and in return a short printed guide is issued.

St. John's College

On St. John's Street, the college was founded in 1511 by Lady Margaret Beaufort, mother of Henry VII. A few years earlier she had founded Christ's College. Before her intervention, an old monk-run hospital had stood on the site of St. John's. The impressive gateway bears the Tudor coat-of-arms, and the dining room, one of the largest in Cambridge, is handsome, dating from the early 16th century. But its best known feature is the Bridge of Sighs, crossing the Cam, built as late as the 19th century and named after the bridge in Venice. It connects the more dated part of the college with New Court—a Gothic revival—on the opposite bank. Wordsworth was an alumnus. The college may be visited any time before dusk, except during the summer examination period, May to early June.

Other College Sights

The above are only a representative selection of some of the more interesting colleges. **Magdalen College** on Magdalene Street was founded in 1542; **Pembroke College** on Trumpington Street was founded in 1347; **Christ's College** on St. Andrew's Street was founded in 1505; and **Corpus Christi College** on Trumpington Street dates from 1352. Only someone planning to stop in Cambridge for a long time will get around to them.

A Word of Warning: Unfortunately, because of the disturbances caused by the influx of tourists to the university, Cambridge has regretfully had to limit visitors, and even exclude them from various parts of the university altogether, and, in some cases, even charge a small fee for entrance. Small groups of up to six persons are generally admitted with no problem, and you can inquire from the local tourist office about visiting hours here.

OTHER SIGHTS: However, colleges aren't the only thing to see in Cambridge, as you'll assuredly agree if you explore the following attractions.

The Fitzwilliam Museum

On Trumpington Street, near Peterhouse, this museum was the gift of the Viscount Fitzwilliam, who in 1816 gave Cambridge University his paintings and rare books—along with £100,000 to build the house in which to display them. He thereby knowingly or unknowingly immortalized himself. Other gifts have since been bequeathed to the museum, and now it is one of the finest in England. It is noted for its porcelain, old prints, archeological relics, and oils (works by Titian and Rembrandt).

The museum is open weekdays from 10 a.m. to 5 p.m., on Sunday from 2:15 till 5 p.m. Closed Monday, Good Friday, December 24 to 31, and New Year's Day.

Great St. Mary's

Great St. Mary's, opposite King's College Chapel on King's Parade, is the university church (tel. 0223/350914). It is built on the site of an 11th-century church, but the present building dates largely from 1478. It was closely associated with events of the Reformation. The cloth that covered the hearse of King Henry VII is on display in the church. A fine view of Cambridge may be obtained from the top of the tower.

BOAT RENTALS: Scudamore's, at Granta Place adjacent to the Anchor Pub, has been in business since 1910. Costs are by the hour: £3.30 ($4.95) for a punt, £2.65 ($3.98) for a rowboat, or £2.45 ($3.68) for a canoe. A deposit of £16.50 ($24.75) is required, and it is refundable if you don't wreck the boat. Upriver you can go all the way to Grantchester, about a distance of two miles, made so famous by Rupert Brooke. Downstream, you pass along the Backs behind the colleges of the university.

READER'S BOATING SUGGESTION: "In summer, some enterprising undergraduates offer a delightful luncheon and boat tour of the campus, called the **Picnic Punt,** with embarkation point at the foot of the bridge over the Cam on Silver Street. My wife and I enjoyed a lunch served on the punt as we were slowly poled up and down the Cam along grassy banks lined with a lot of holiday trippers and students enjoying the sun. Our waiter and punt propeller gave a running commentary on the history of the college buildings and bridges we passed. We ate a lamb curry on rice, a side plate of celery and carrots, and strawberries in Devonshire cream. Lunch is served at your departure, on plywood planks attached to the gunwales, after you are comfortably seated on pillows in the punt. The price is £6 ($9) per person for all—punt ride, lunch, and tour comments. Wine is not provided, but the helpful woman making the reservations steered us to a good wineseller who supplied us with a splendid Vouvray. The trip lasts about 50 minutes and is a wonderful experience" (Gordon Beck, Olympia, Wash.).

PERSONALIZED TOURS: The person to know if you're in the Cambridge area is Mrs. Isobel Bryant, who runs **Heritage Tours** from her

200-year-old cottage, Manor Cottage, Swaffham Prior (tel. 0638/741440). A highly qualified expert on the region, she will arrange tours starting from your hotel or Cambridge railway station, to, say, the charming town of Lavenham with its thatched and timbered houses, to the fine medieval churches of the Suffolk villages, to Ely Cathedral, and to one of the grand mansions nearby with their many treasures. The charge of £40 ($60) for the day covers up to three passengers and all travel expenses, plus the services of the driver/guide. Lunch in a village pub and admission fees add £4 ($7.50) per person.

Mrs. Bryant can also arrange accommodation with local families in their lovely country houses. The charges range from £20 ($30) to £40 ($60) for two persons per night in double rooms with private baths, these tariffs including a full English breakfast. Often dinner can be arranged at around £7 ($10.50) per person, including wine. Rooms without private baths rent from £7 ($10.50) per person.

There are also walking tours around the colleges of Cambridge at £1.50 ($2.25) per person (minimum charge of £10, or $15), lasting approximately two hours. If you can make up a party of 15 or more persons, there is a fascinating tour of Newmarket, headquarters of the horseracing industry. That tour includes getting to watch training gallops, a visit to the Racing Museum or a stud stable, seeing the bloodstock-sales center, and being shown the celebrated Jockey Club. A whole day costs £12 ($18) per person; half a day, £7 ($10.50). If you want lunch at a private manor house with Cordon Bleu cooking, the cost will be £7 ($10.50), including wine. All prices include VAT.

WHERE TO STAY: Accommodations are limited in scope and facilities, although generally adequate for the purpose. Much of the overload in summer is siphoned off by little guest houses, filled at term time with scholars, but otherwise freed when most visitors arrive in July and August. I'll begin with a general survey of the best hotels in:

The Medium-Priced Range

University Arms Hotel, Regent Street (tel. 0223/351241), is a successful blending of the old and new. It originated late in Victoria's day as an inn operated by Marcus Dennis Bradford, grandfather of the present owner, William Bradford. One portion is traditionally designed, although a new wing was added in 1965, offering 58 modern bedrooms, all with private bath and tasteful decorations. Sliding glass doors open onto private balconies, with views of the cricket grounds of Parker's Place, known for its associations with cricketer Sir Jack Hobbs. The rooms opening onto Regent Street have soundproofed double-glass windows.

Each bedroom has its own telephone, central heating, private bath, electric razor outlets, radio, and color TV. The single rate is £32.50 ($48.75), and a twin-bedded room is £48 ($72). These rates include service, VAT, and a full English breakfast. Meals are served in the wood-paneled dining room, opening onto open parkland. The charge for a table d'hôte luncheon is from £6.50 ($8.75), rising to £8.50 ($12.75) for a set dinner. The older octagonal lounge, with its stained-glass dome, is still the best place to gather at teatime. Tip: The hall porter can arrange for a guide to show you the nearby colleges.

The **Royal Cambridge Hotel,** Trumpington Street (tel. 0223/351631), may be the answer to England's hotel problem. The facade of a row of town houses has been preserved, but the inside has been gutted and redesigned in a tasteful modern way. The 86 rooms are compact and handsomely appointed. The bedrooms use many of the built-in techniques of motel design. Rates depend on the season, plumbing, and floor. Singles range from £19 ($28.50) to £31 ($46.50); twins, £32 ($48) to £44 ($66). All prices include service and VAT. Each room is centrally heated, and has both radio and telephone. A lot of extras are found here, including a hairdressing salon. Meals are carvery or à la carte.

Cunard Cambridgeshire Hotel, Bar Hill (tel. 0954/80555), is four miles from Cambridge city center. It's a modern, four-star hotel with heated swimming pool, a sauna, three squash courts, two outside tennis courts, and an 18-hole championship golf course. The 100 bedrooms are spacious and furnished in a functional way, including private bathroom/shower, color TV, radio, early-morning call system, and tea- and coffee-making facilities. Singles are £45 ($67.50); doubles, £60 ($90). The main dining room, with a hammer-beamed ceiling, is overlooked by the lounge/cocktail bar in the Minstrels' Gallery. The food is traditionally English, including roast beef and Yorkshire pudding, steak-and-kidney pie, and grilled Dover sole. Bar lunches are also offered daily.

Blue Boar Hotel, Trinity Street (tel. 0223/63121), has an innkeeping fame that stretches back at least to the late 17th century. The most central of all my recommendations, it is run by Trusthouses Forte, attracting international visitors as well as parents of Cambridge students. Since its early days, it has been considerably modernized, with hot and cold running water added to every room (11 with private baths), as well as central heating and well-maintained furnishings. A pleasant brick building, directly opposite the Trinity Great Gate, it still keeps its original Blue Boar inn sign hanging over the arched doorway. Room prices are £32 ($48) for a single, from £48 ($72) to £60 ($90) in a double, including VAT and service. Being a small inn, the hotel offers a limited lounge area. The Athene Bar draws an interesting crowd of people. It couldn't be handier for visiting the colleges, and there's a public car park a few blocks away.

Gonville Hotel, Gonville Place (tel. 0223/66611), stands on its own grounds, opposite Parkers Place, only a five-minute walk from the center of the city. It's not unlike a country house—ivy covered, with shade trees and a formal car entry. In 1973 it was gutted and rebuilt as a commercial hotel, intending to attract business people as well as tourists in summer. Singles go for £34 ($51); doubles, £48 ($72). Prices include VAT, service charge, and an English breakfast. Special three-bedded family rooms rent for £60 ($90). Central heating is provided throughout, plus air conditioning in the restaurant, where you can get a set lunch for £6.50 ($9.75) or dinner for about £10 ($15). You can also order à la carte. The quality of comforts is good, the furnishings stylish.

WHERE TO EAT: The **Pentagon,** 6 St. Edwards Passage (tel. 0223/355246), is in the center of Cambridge, overlooking medieval cottages and the historic churchyard. Cold buffet meals and four hot specialties are served daily, the price per dish being about £4.50 ($6.75). There is a fine wine list, and fully licensed bar. Connected to and run by the Arts Theatre, the restaurant has a strong artistic atmosphere and is patronized by many stars of the English stage. It's open for lunch Monday to Saturday from noon to 2 p.m. and for supper from 6 to 10:30 p.m.

The **Arts Roof Garden Buffet**, perched above the theater, is popular in summer as it offers alfresco meals, self-service lunch, afternoon tea and supper, with a view of the Cambridge spires. You select from an array of hot and cold dishes, with meals averaging around £5 ($7.50). Wines are available by the glass, and there's a fully licensed bar. Local artists, incidentally, exhibit their work upstairs. It's open Monday to Saturday from 9:30 a.m. to 8 p.m.

Strudel's Restaurant, University Pitt Club Building, Jesus Lane (tel. 0223/311678), occupies part of a building originally constructed as an elegant Turkish bath. Since 1866 it has been used by the exclusive University Pitt Club, a young gentlemen's dining club founded in memory of William Pitt. Part of the building, including the original club dining room, with its high ceiling, huge central glass dome, and oak paneling, is now Strudel's Restaurant. Tables are draped in white, with fresh flowers and candles. In colder weather, a large, glowing fire makes a warm, inviting atmosphere.

The restaurant is run by Christopher Ryan and his partner, Alan Boorman. Mr. Ryan, who likes everything fresh insofar as possible, does most of the cooking, shopping in the market daily for fresh vegetables. Although the à la carte menu is fairly expensive, the restaurant also serves a three-course lunch for £8.50 ($12.75) and a three-course dinner for £11.50 ($17.25). The restaurant specializes in continental dishes, often using old family recipes, many of which date back more than 100 years. When available, fish and game, such as Sussex pheasant, are featured. The restaurant is closed Sunday but otherwise serves lunch daily from noon to 2:30 p.m. and dinner from 6 to 11 p.m. Reservations are necessary.

In the heart of the city center, between the Guildhall and Christs College, is the renowned Petty Cury, where, at no. 25, you will find the **Eros Restaurant,** (tel. 0223/63420), fully licensed and offering an interesting menu. Specialties include roast duckling with stuffing and orange sauce, roast lamb peperoni with cream cheese, kebab indienne with ginger and curry, marinated lamb and rice, all served with vegetables and a salad. There are many good appetizers, and crème caramel, cheesecake, and sorbets finish off the menu. The Greek coffee is thick and sweet. A three-course Greek meal costs about £9 ($13.50), and the Cypriot, Italian, and English dinners go for about the same price. Hours are from noon to 3 p.m. and from 5:30 to 11 p.m. Monday to Friday, from noon to 11:30 p.m. on Saturday and Sunday. It's popular with undergraduates who know they are getting good value for their money and who enjoy listening to the Greek music.

Shades Wine Bar & Restaurant, opposite King's College on Kings Parade (tel. 0223/359506), gives you a choice of having either a full meal in the restaurant or bar snacks from the wine bar buffet, which consists of pâtés, salads, cold meats, smoked fish, cheeses, and seasonal specialties, to be accompanied by excellent wines sold by the glass or bottle. It is open seven days a week from 11:30 a.m. to 2:30 p.m. and 6 to 11 p.m. Monday to Saturday, from noon to 2 p.m. and 7 to 10:30 p.m. on Sunday.

The restaurant is open from 6:30 to 10 p.m. Tuesday to Saturday. Appetizers include prawns in the shell with garlic mayonnaise, escargots, soup, and smoked oysters. For a main course, you might choose filet steak Madagascar, salmon steak tsar, or scampi marinière au riz. There is also a good selection of desserts and cheeses. The menu is good and imaginative, and portions are ample. A meal costs around £12 ($18), including wine.

The **Anchor Pub,** Silver Street (tel. 0223/353554), right beside the Silver Street Bridge, has a bar and terrace right on the waterside, where you can get snacks—a ploughman's lunch, french bread and pâté, ham salad, and various cold meats in sandwiches.

Upstairs is a restaurant where you can enjoy a prawn cocktail, soups, lamb cutlets with mint sauce, peas, jacket potato, plus vanilla meringue surprise, or grilled rump steak with potatoes, followed by dessert. A beefburger is another popular item. A three-course meal will cost about £7.50 ($11.25) per person. Below the pub is the Rock Revival snackbar where you can buy the makings of a picnic lunch to be taken on a boat on the River Cam or enjoy your morning coffee. The pub is by Scudamore's where you rent boats.

THE ARTS THEATRE: The outstanding attraction in Cambridge is the Arts Theatre, with its entrance on Peas Hill, squeezed among lodging houses and shops. It provides Cambridge and the surrounding area with its most important theatrical events. Almost all the leading stars of the British stage have performed here at one time or another. Call 0223/352000 to find out what's playing. The cheapest seats cost £4.50 ($6.75); the most expensive ones range from £5 ($7.50) to £6.50 ($9.75).

Nearby, on Market Passage, you'll find the principal **movie house,** the **Arts Cinema,** which usually has separate showings daily. Seats for the evening performances are "bookable" by telephoning 0223/352001.

2. Ely

The top attraction in the fen country, outside of Cambridge, is Ely Cathedral. The small city of Ely lies 70 miles from London, only 16 miles north of Cambridge. Ely used to be known as the Isle of Ely, until the surrounding marshes and meres were drained. The last stronghold of Saxon England, Ely was defended by Hereward the Wake, until his capitulation to the Normans in 1071.

ELY CATHEDRAL: The near-legendary founder of the cathedral was Etheldreda, the wife of a Northumbrian king, who established a monastery on the spot in 673. The present structure dates from 1083. Seen for miles around, the landmark octagonal lantern tower is the crowning glory of the cathedral. It was erected in 1322, following the collapse of the old tower, and represents a remarkable engineering achievement.

You enter the cathedral through the Galilee West Door, a good example of the Early English style of architecture. The already-mentioned lantern tower and the Octagon are the most notable features inside, but visit the Lady Chapel. Although it's lost much of its decoration over the centuries, it still is a handsome example of the Perpendicular style, having been completed in the mid-14th century.

The city, really a market town, is interesting—at least momentarily so—as it seems to be living in the past. If you choose to lodge or dine at Ely, here are my recommendations.

WHERE TO STAY AND EAT: The **Lamb Hotel,** Lynn Road (tel. 0353/3574), right in the center of the town, with ample car parking space available and in the shadow of the cathedral, is a Queens Moat House Hotel offering bedrooms with private baths and showers, TVs, and tea- and coffee-making facilities. The B&B rate in a double or twin is £45 ($67.50). A single costs £32 ($48). Tariffs are inclusive of an English breakfast and VAT. A table d'hôte lunch or dinner costs £10 ($15).

The Old Fire Engine House, St. Mary's Street (tel. 0353/2582), opposite St. Mary's Church, is one of the finer restaurants in East Anglia, worth a detour. It enjoys an interesting setting in a walled garden, in a complex of buildings with an art gallery. The restaurant was converted from a fire station. It is open for lunch from 12:30 to 2 p.m. and for dinner from 7:30 till 9 p.m. (closed Sunday). Reservations are required.

All the good English cooking is the result of the staff, a harmonious combination of unusual people who really care about food preparation. Materials are all fresh. Soups are served in huge bowls, and accompanying them is a coarse-grained crusty bread. Main dishes include duck with orange sauce, jugged hare, steak-and-kidney pie, baked stuffed pike, casserole of rabbit, and pigeon with bacon and black olives. Desserts include fruit pie and cream, although I'd recommend the syllabub. In summer, you can dine outside in the garden, even order a cream tea. The young and attractive Ann Ford owns the place, and not only does some of the cooking and serves but still has time to talk to customers. It's open weekdays from 11:30 a.m. to 5:30 p.m. and 7:30 to 10 p.m., on Sunday from 12:30 to 5:30 p.m. Do try for a table if you're just passing, but this place is quite popular with locals and people coming out from Cambridge, especially on weekends, so it's better to make a reservation.

A TOUR TO GRIME'S GRAVES: On the B1108, off the main A1065 from Swaffham to Mildenhall road east of Ely, you can visit Grime's Graves. This is well worth the short detour, as it is the largest group of Neolithic flint mines in the country. This is fir-wooded country with little population, and it's easy to imagine oneself transported back to ancient times.

The mines are well signposted, and you soon find yourself at a small parking lot presided over by a bearded enthusiast and his aging Labrador. Because the mines have no head machinery and are spread around a common area, they are all securely enclosed. But, on your arrival, the custodian will open up one or several of the shafts, allowing you to enter ancient Britain.

Climb down the ladder of the pit and imagine what must have been going on even before the time of the Anglo-Saxons. Take a flashlight so you can see into the dark corners. Restoration has been carried out during the intervening years, and it is now possible to see where work took place and, if you're lucky, you may find a worked flint of your own to present to the custodian. He has a vast knowledge of the working methods and the implements used in those far-off days.

The location is close to the air force bases so well known to countless American air crews during World War II.

The place is open for most of the year from 9:30 a.m. to 4 p.m. (longer in summer), charging adults an admission of 60p (90¢); children, 30p (45¢).

AN AIRCRAFT MUSEUM: Part of the **Imperial War Museum** (tel. 0223/833963), on the A505 Newmarket–Royston Road, is housed appropri-

ately at Duxford Airfield, the former Battle of Britain station. In hangars that date from World War I, you'll find a huge collection of historic civil and military aircraft, including the B17 Flying Fortress, the Super Sabre and Concorde 01, Britain's preproduction specimen of the controversial jet. Other exhibits include midget submarines, British and German tanks, and a variety of field artillery pieces. Duxford was also a U.S. Eighth Air Force fighter station in World War II. There are now more than 80 aircraft on display, including the only B-29 Superfortress in Europe, plus a BE2c and an RE8 from World War I, a B-52, and several Spitfires. Other exhibits include a giant 140-ton coastal artillery gun from Gibraltar and a special historical display on the U.S. Eighth Air Force in World War II.

The museum is open daily mid-March to early November except Good Friday and May Day, from 11 a.m. to 5:30 p.m., charging an admission of £1.50 ($2.25) for adults and 75p ($1.13) for children. Parking is free.

ESSEX

Even though it borders London, and is heavily industrialized in places, Essex still contains unspoiled rural areas and villages. Most tourists pass through it on the way to Cambridge. What they find, after leaving Greater London, is a land of rolling fields. In the east are many seaside towns and villages, as Essex opens onto the North Sea.

The major city is **Colchester,** in the east, known for its oysters and roses. Fifty miles from London, it was the first Roman city in Britain, the oldest recorded town in the kingdom. It's a rather dull-appearing city today, although parts of its Roman fortifications remain. A Norman castle has been turned into a museum, containing a fine collection of Roman Britain. Among the former residents of Colchester were King Cole, immortalized in the nursery rhyme, and Cunobelinus, the warrior king, known to Shakespearean scholars as Cymbeline.

However, Colchester is not the pathway of most visitors—so I have concentrated instead on three tiny villages in the western part of Essex: **Saffron Walden, Thaxted,** and **Finchingfield,** all three representative of the best of the shire. You can explore all of them quite easily on your way to Cambridge or on your return trip to London. Roughly, they lie from 25 to 30 miles south of Cambridge.

A BASE OUTSIDE LONDON: Moat House, London Road, Brentwood (tel. 0277/225252), stands on the London side of Brentwood, about three-quarters of a mile from the center of town and only 22 miles from London's West End. A remarkably well-preserved and modernized country mansion, this early 16th-century hotel claims associations with Henry VIII and Catherine of Aragon.

It's a handsome black-and-white timbered structure with a great hall for dining and a minstrels' gallery. Nowadays modern extensions give you a wide choice of accommodations, although traditionalists will gravitate to one of the original Tudor bedrooms, which have maintained their character, complete with four-poster beds. Depending on the plumbing, singles rent for £32 ($48) to £45 ($67.50), going up to £48 ($72) to £58 ($87) in a double, including VAT, service, and a full English breakfast.

The restoration of the public rooms has been skillful, and you're invited to enter a world of heavy old beams, oak paneling, inglenooks, and ceilings of carved plasterwork. In the dining room, meals are à la carte, lunch costing from £12 ($18); dinner, from £18 ($27).

3. Thaxted

Some 43 miles north of London, the Saxon town of Thaxted sits on the crest of a hill. It contains the most beautiful small church in England, whose graceful spire can be seen for miles around. Its bells are heard throughout the day, ringing out special chimes to parishioners who attend their church seriously. Dating back to 1340, the church is a nearly perfect example of religious architecture.

Thaxted is well known to newspaper and magazine readers because of the late iconoclastic Conrad Noel, the Red Vicar, whose son-in-law, the Rev. Jack Putterill, carries on in the traditions of the elder.

The Rev. Putterill has brought back to the church a sense of drama, which he feels has been gradually eliminated elsewhere. The parishioners often enter the church in a processional, carrying a banner or a long branch of leaves. Gay and colorful flags hang from the heights of the church; flowers are everywhere; the rare and ancient chairs are meant to be used. There are candles in great brass stands, and incense billows up as the purple-robed vicar and his assistants proceed with the ceremony. The choir kneels and sings at the rear of the church, near the bell tower. On a banner you'll see Picasso's dove of peace.

During the summer, folk dancing is performed by the townspeople, both in and out of church. The London Philharmonic Orchestra comes down to play. The vicar has encouraged the church to use music, and you can hear both the old and the experimental. The denizens of Thaxted are divided about the activities of the church, but one thing they like: their town is alive and flourishing because of it.

Thaxted also has a number of well-preserved Elizabethan houses and a wooded-pillared Jacobean guildhall.

WHERE TO STAY AND EAT: The **Swan Hotel,** Watling Street (tel. 0371/830321), is a 14th-century coaching inn, right in the middle of everything. From several of the bedroom windows you can see the church—even have a box seat if a processional should pass by. For many centuries the townspeople have patronized the Swan for drinks and gossip. It is owned by Charles Byrne, who respects the heritage of the inn. His B&B rate in bathless singles is £13.50 ($20.25), rising to £18.50 ($27.75) with bath. Doubles or twins cost £22 ($33) without bath, £25 ($37.50) with. All tariffs include VAT, service, and a full English breakfast. The hotel has been completely restored and decorated as the old inn it once was. A set lunch costs £5 ($7.50) and a set dinner is £6.50 ($9.75), or if you prefer, you can order à la carte. Bar snacks are also available for £1 ($1.50) for soup and french bread up to £5.50 ($8.25) for a steak. You can also have salads, cold meats, or a hot dish of the day.

4. Saffron Walden

In the northern corner of Essex, a short drive from Thaxted, is the ancient market town of Walden, renamed Saffron Walden because of the fields of autumn crocus that used to grow around it. Although it lies only 44 miles from London, it still hasn't succumbed to heavy tourist traffic. Residents of Cambridge, 15 miles to the north, escape to this old borough for their weekends.

One mile west of Saffron Walden (on the B1383) is **Audley End House** (tel. 0799/23207), considered one of the finest mansions in all of East Anglia. This Jacobean estate was begun in 1603, built on the foundation of a monastery. It is open from April 1 to September 30 except Monday bank holidays and on Good Friday, from 1 to 5:30 p.m., for an admission of £2 ($3) for adults, £1 ($1.50) for children. The grounds close at 6:30 p.m. James I is reported to have said, "Audley End is too large for a king, though it might do for a lord treasurer." At the north end of the hall is a screen dating from the early 17th century and considered one of the most ornamental in England.

Many of the houses in Saffron Walden are distinctive in England, in that the 16th- and 17th-century builders faced their houses with parget—a kind of plasterwork (sometimes made with cow dung) used for ornamental facades.

WHERE TO STAY: The **Saffron Hotel,** 10–18 High St. (tel. 0799/22676), stands in the center of the Cromwellian market town. Dating from the 16th century, the Saffron combines modern comforts with old-world charm, as reflected by its individually designed and decorated rooms. The hotel was completely refurbished in 1981 by its new owners. All rooms have color TV, telephone, central heating, and most have private baths. Most units overlook the High Street or the inner courtyard with its patio garden and small carp pool. Stories abound locally about the Saffron Hotel ghost, which several of the staff claim to have seen in recent years. B&B rates are £15 ($22.50) in a bathless single, £22 ($33) with shower. For a bathless double the rent is £24 ($36), £36 ($54) with a private bath. Children are welcomed at reduced prices. The hotel's restaurant is renowned locally and is in a Regency style. Dining is by candlelight overlooking the flood-lit patio garden. A three-course menu with several choices on each course ranges from £6.50 ($9.75) to £10 ($15). The cuisine at the Saffron is among the best in the area, combining traditional dishes with more ambitious specialties.

5. Finchingfield

This little village, only a short drive east of Thaxted, puts in a serious claim for being the model village of England. Even though you may have another personal favorite, you still must admit it's a dream village, surrounded by the quiet life of the countryside. If you're staying in either Saffron Walden or Thaxted, you might want to motor over here. It makes for an interesting jaunt.

FOOD AND LODGING: The **Fox Inn** (tel. 0371/810151), two hours from London airport, stands near the edge of the pond on the village green. It's an attractive old pub, with authentic pargeting (raised plaster) design on the facade. Roy Garner, owner of the Fox, offers bar snacks at 75p ($1.13) for cheese on toast to £5.50 ($8.25) for steak and salad. Sunday lunch is à la carte, but you can have a plate of roast beef and three vegetables for £3.50 ($5.25).

Near to the Fox, Joe King runs the little eight-room **Old Manse** (tel. 0371/810306), all accommodations with central heating, wall-to-wall carpeting, hot and cold running water, and shaving points. Most rooms overlook the village pond. There is a lounge with color TV, plus a large garden as well. Terms, including a full English breakfast consisting of farm produce, are £13 ($19.50) in a single, £24 ($36) in a double, including VAT and service.

6. Dedham

Remember Constable's *Vale of Dedham?* In this little Essex village on the Stour River, you're in the heart of Constable country. Flatford Mill is only a mile farther down the river. The village, with its Tudor, Georgian, and Regency house, is set in the midst of the water meadows of the Stour. Constable immortalized its church and tower. Dedham is right on the Essex-Suffolk border, and makes a good center for exploring both North Essex and the Suffolk border country.

In the village is **Castle House** (tel. 0206/322127), home of Sir Alfred Munnings, the president of the Royal Academy (1944–1949) and painter extraordinaire of racehorses and animals. The house and studio contain sketches and other works, and are open from the second Sunday in May to the second Sunday in October on Sunday and Wednesday, plus spring and August bank holiday Mondays, as well as Thursday and Saturday in August. Hours are 2 to 5 p.m. Admission is £1 ($1.50) for adults, 25p (38¢) for children.

WHERE TO STAY AND EAT: **Maison Talbooth** (tel. 0206/322367), is small and exclusive, each of its ten bedrooms really a spacious suite. This Victorian country house has been given a facelift, and each accommodation has been distinctively furnished by one of England's best known decorators. High-fashion colors abound; antiques are mixed discreetly with reproductions—and the original architectural beauty has been preserved. The super-luxury suite, with a sunken bath, goes for £85 ($127.50) nightly for two persons and has a draped bed. Other suites, each with its own theme, start as low as £55 ($82.50) for two. One person pays from £45 ($67.50) to £60 ($90). When you arrive, you're welcomed by your hostess who takes you to your suite, where fresh flowers, fruit, and a private bar are standard. A continental or cooked breakfast is brought in the morning. In an informal, yet stylish, drawing room, guests mingle with the hostess, making you feel as if you're a guest in her country home.

Maison Talbooth's restaurant nearby, **Le Talbooth** (tel. 0206/323150 for reservations), has an international reputation for its cooking and its wine list. It is in a 16th-century timbered weaver's house set in beautiful gardens on the banks of the River Stour in Constable country. The owner, Gerald Milsom, has brought a high standard of international cooking, backed by good wines. Dinner is served from 7:30 to 9 p.m. You can dine here for about £17 ($25.50) per person.

Dedham Vale, Gun Hill (tel. 0206/322273), is a handsome, Virginia-creeper-covered 19th-century residence, with tall windows overlooking spacious lawns, flowerbeds, and trees, plus a view of the Stour River. The hotel has recently been taken over by Mr. Gerald Milsom of Maison Talbooth and extensively upgraded. Delightful bedroom suites cost from £55 ($82.50) to £65 ($97.50), each including a private bath, phone, TV, a continental breakfast, and VAT. The magnificent glass-domed, plant-filled restaurant specializes in barbecue meats. The hotel is within easy reach of the ports of Harwich and Felixstowe for journeys to the continent.

SUFFOLK

The easternmost county of England—a link in the four-county chain of East Anglia—Suffolk is a refuge for artists, just as it was in the day of its famous native sons, Constable and Gainsborough. Through them many of the Suffolk landscapes have ended up in museums on canvas.

A fast train can make it from London to East Suffolk in approximately an hour and a half. Still, its fishing villages, dozens of flint churches, historic homes, and national monuments remain relatively unvisited by overseas visitors.

The major towns of Suffolk are **Bury St. Edmunds,** the capital of West Suffolk, and **Ipswich** in the east, a port city on the Orwell River. But to capture the true charm of Suffolk, you must explore its little market towns and villages. Beginning at the Essex border, we'll strike out toward the North Sea, highlighting the most scenic villages as we move easterly across the shire.

7. Newmarket

This old Suffolk town, 62 miles from London, has been famous as a racing center since the time of King James I. Visitors can see Nell Gwynne's House, but mainly they come to visit Britain's first and only **National Horseracing Museum,** 99 High St. (tel. 0638/66733).

The museum is housed in the old subscription rooms, early 19th-century rooms used for placing and settlement of bets. Visitors will be able to see the history of horseracing over a 300-year period. There are fine paintings of famous horses, pictures loaned by Queen Elizabeth II, and copies of old Parliamentary Acts governing races. There is also a replica of a weighing-in room, plus explanations of the signs used by the ticktack men who keep the on-course bookies informed of changes in the price of bets.

There is also a 53-minute audio-visual presentation showing races and racehorses, running continuously. At a shop at the entrance you can buy from an interesting collection of small souvenirs, along with books, tankards, a Derby chart showing the male descent line of every winner of the celebrated race since 1780, and silk scarves with equine motifs. Richard Kilburn is the curator of the museum, which is open daily except Monday from 10 a.m. to 5 p.m., 2 to 5 p.m. on Sunday. It is closed in December, January, and February, but those with a special interest in seeing it can telephone.

The **National Stud** (tel. 0638/3464) is *the* place for those who wish to see some of the world's finest horseflesh. You must write in advance, and visits can only be arranged on weekdays in August and September. Admission is £2 ($3) per car. Michael Bramwell is director of the National Stud, and he has plenty of staff members available to answer your questions. You may be lucky enough to see a parade of stallions and certainly some of the foals whose sires are valued at in excess of £1 million sterling.

WHERE TO STAY AND EAT: The **White Hart Hotel,** High Street (tel. 0368/663051), opposite the Horseracing Museum, offers bar snacks, a hot dish of the day, salads, cold meats, homemade soup and crusty bread, and cheese and apple pie. Two dishes cost about £3 ($4.50). In the hotel restaurant, you can order a three-course luncheon for around £7 ($10.50).

For accommodation, try the **Rutland Arms Hotel,** High Street (tel. 0638/664251), an imposing Georgian coaching inn dating in part from the reign of Charles II. The hotel is at the clock end of the High Street. There are 50 rooms, large and comfortably furnished, most with private bathroom. Prices start at £17 ($25.50) for a bathless single, going up to £40 ($60) for a twin or double with bath. An English breakfast, service, and VAT are included. A good three-course lunch, costing £5.25 ($7.86), is served between 12:30 and 2 p.m. Sunday lunch, at £6.50 ($9.75), and a set dinner, for £6 ($9), are also served.

The **Golden Lion Hotel,** High Street (tel. 0638/663916), is an old pub dating back to the reign of James I. The host, Ron Turner, offers morning coffee, bar snacks, and B&B. The bedrooms are warm, clean, and basic, and the charge is £13 ($19.50) for a single, £21 ($31.50) for a double. Evening meals are available by arrangement only.

There is an interesting history of Newmarket and the inn written on the wall, telling, among other things, how Newmarket developed as a place of escape from the plague when London was stricken. It also tells you that a minute's walk away from the inn lived the Marquess of Queensbury, noted for his rules governing the sport of boxing. He was popularly known as "Old Hugh."

8. Clare

Lying 58 miles from London, but only 26 east from Cambridge, the small town of Clare holds to the old ways of East Anglia. Many of its houses are bathed in Suffolk pink, the facades of a few demonstrating the 16th- and 17th-century plasterwork technique of pargeting, discussed previously. The Stour River, which has its source a few miles away, flows by, marking the boundary of Suffolk and Essex. The little rail station has fallen to the economy axe. The nearest station is now at Sudbury, where Gainsborough was born. The journey by road from London takes about two hours, unless you succumb to the scenery and the countryside along the way. For accommodations in Clare, I have the following recommendations in the budget range.

FOOD AND LODGING: The **Bell Hotel** (tel. 0842-277741) is considered one of the oldest inns in England. Once known as the Green Dragon, it served the soldiers of Richard de Clare, one of William the Conqueror's barons. Later it became a posting house, but in time the old stable gave way to a car park. Its owner, Hugh Jones, is responsible for its recent facelift. He maintains a friendly give-and-take with guests. B&B rates range from £32 ($48) for a single, £40 ($60) for a double, plus service and tax. The rooms have a fresh, pleasant style to them, and the beds are soft. The beamed dining room, with its high-back chairs and large brick fireplace, is ideal for winter dining. Lunch costs £8 ($12); dinner, around £10 ($15).

READERS' SIGHTSEEING TIP: "You might mention the **Ancient House Museum** (tel. 0842/2599), directly across from the churchyard. The house is a splendid example of pargeting and has many notable architectural features and numerous fascinating exhibits. One comes away from the Ancient House with a deeper understanding and appreciation of the rural life of Suffolk. The museum is open from Easter to the end of October Monday to Saturday from 10 a.m. to 5 p.m., 2 to 5 p.m. on Sunday. It

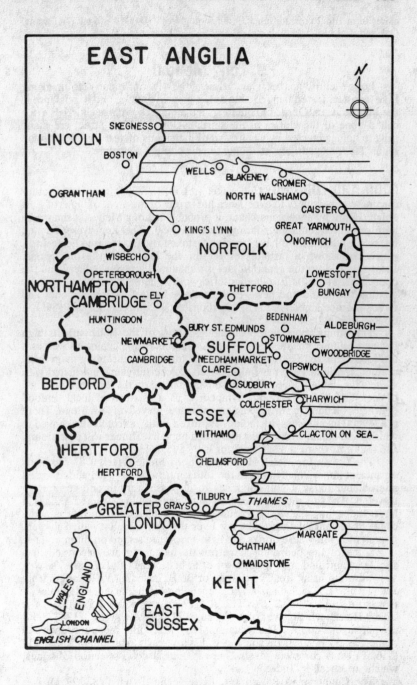

EAST ANGLIA

N

LINCOLN

SKEGNESS

BOSTON

WELLS   BLAKENEY   CROMER

GRANTHAM   NORTH WALSHAM

CAISTER

KING'S LYNN   GREAT YARMOUTH

NORWICH

NORFOLK

WISBECH

PETERBOROUGH   THETFORD   LOWESTOFT

NORTHAMPTON   BUNGAY

CAMBRIDGE ELY

HUNTINGDON   BEDENHAM

BURY ST. EDMUNDS   ALDEBURGH

NEWMARKET   STOWMARKET

CAMBRIDGE   **SUFFOLK**   WOODBRIDGE

NEEDHAM MARKET

CLARE   IPSWICH

BEDFORD   SUDBURY

COLCHESTER   HARWICH

ESSEX

HERTFORD   WITHAM

CLACTON ON SEA

CHELMSFORD

HERTFORD

TILBURY   *THAMES*

GREATER   GRAYS

LONDON

MARGATE

CHATHAM

MAIDSTONE

KENT

WALES   ENGLAND

LONDON

EAST

SUSSEX

ENGLISH CHANNEL

closes from 1 to 2 p.m. for lunch. Admission is free" (David and Jackie Allswang, Oakland, Calif.).

9. Long Melford

Long Melford has been famous since the days of the early clothmakers. Like its sister, Lavenham (coming up), it grew in prestige and importance in the Middle Ages. Of the old buildings remaining, the village church is often called "one of the glories of the shire." Along its High Street are many private homes erected by wealthy wool merchants of yore. While London seems far removed here, it is only 61 miles to the south.

FOOD AND LODGING: Bull Hotel (tel. 0787/78794) provides another fortunate opportunity to experience life in one of the great old inns of East Anglia. Built by a wool merchant, it probably is Long Melford's finest and best preserved building, dating back to 1450. The improvements and interior modernization have been undertaken by Trusthouses Forte Ltd., which has shown a tasteful respect for the beauty of the old beams. Incorporated into the general hotel is a medieval weavers' gallery and the open hearth with its Elizabethan brickwork. The bedrooms are a goodly mixture of the old and new—each centrally heated, with telephones and radios—a nice ambience. A single room with bath rents for £44 ($66), a double with bath for £64 ($96).

The dining room is the outstanding part of the Bull, with its high beamed ceilings, trestle tables, settles, and handmade chairs, as well as a ten-foot fireplace. There is a good menu for dinner, including many local seafood specialties such as half a dozen Colchester clams marinated with white wine, lemon juice, and olive oil and served on the half shell on a bed of ice. The "Mersea Island Symphony" is a mixture of local seafood delicacies blended in whisky and cream sauce, served on lava bread. There are several meat dishes, including "Drunken Bull," a scotch filet cooked in whisky and cream with onions and green peppers. Dinner will cost around £16 ($24), or there is a set meal for £10.75 ($16.13).

The **Crown Inn Hotel,** Hall Street, Long Melford (tel. 0787/77666), is an ancient inn originally built in the 16th century. It has been added to and altered, but today it still continues to dispense warmth and comfort to travelers. The tiny reception leads to snug bars with low-beamed ceilings, a large Tudor fireplace with a roaring log fire, much antique furniture, and a candlelit restaurant that looks out over the 15th-century walled garden, floodlit at night, where drinks and light snacks are served on summer days.

Some of the bedrooms have private baths and are decorated in a simple, countrified style with flower-print bedspreads and curtains, as well as plain wood furniture. The charge for B&B, including VAT, ranges from £20 ($30) to £24 ($36) in a single, depending on the facilities. Doubles or twins run from £18 ($27) to £19.50 ($29.25) per person. Rooms in the Coach House, which have color TV, cost £24 ($36) in a single, £19 ($28.50) per person in a double. The restaurant has a fixed-price menu for lunch and dinner, £6.50 ($9.75), or you can order à la carte, spending around £11 ($16.50) for a complete meal. There is quite a good selection of wines, which are stored in Tudor cellars.

The **Countryman Restaurant,** Long Melford (tel. 0787/79951), is a pretty little 15th-century country tea shop with blue awnings, on the main street. Inside, there are small tables and wheelback chairs. A set lunch, at £6 ($9), is likely to include minestrone, then rib of beef served with a selection of vegetables, followed by a dessert from the trolley and coffee. VAT is included. Afternoon teas, costing £1.50 ($2.25), offer fresh scones, jam, and cream. Dinners are chosen from several set menus at prices ranging from £7.50 ($11.25) to the most expensive at £13.50 ($20.25). A specialty is filet steak cooked in butter, with red wine and pimento sauce.

10. Lavenham

Once a great wool center, Lavenham is considered a model village of East Anglia. It is filled with a number of half-timbered Tudor houses, washed in the characteristic Suffolk pink. Be sure to visit its church, with its landmark tower, built in the Perpendicular style. Lavenham lies only seven miles from Sudbury, 11 from Bury St. Edmunds. For accommodations or meals, there is the following medium-priced recommendation.

WHERE TO STAY AND EAT: Swan Hotel, High Street (tel. 0787/247477), is linked to the Middle Ages—a lavishly timbered inn, probably one of the oldest and best preserved buildings in this relatively unmarred village. Its success has necessitated incorporating an adjoining ancient Wool Hall, which provides a high-ceilinged and timbered guest house and additional raftered, second-story bedrooms, opening onto a tiny cloistered garden. The Garden Bar opens onto yet another garden, with old stone walls and flowerbeds. Londoners often visit on September-to-March weekends for dinner and chamber music concerts. All the accommodations contain private baths. A single rents for £42 ($63), and doubles from £62 ($93). The bedrooms vary greatly in size, according to the eccentricities of the architecture. Most have beamed ceilings and a mixture of traditional pieces that blend well with the old. There are nearly enough lounges for guests to try a different one every night of the week.

Meals in the raftered, two-story-high dining room have their own drama, as you sit on leather and oak chairs with brass studding. Even if you're not spending the night, you can sample the three-course luncheon priced at £11 ($16.50). Evening table d'hôte dinners go for £13 ($19.50). From the à la carte menu, you can order such specialties as Norfolk duckling in a sauce with almonds and raisins or boned English saddle of lamb with artichokes. Expect to spend from £25 ($37.50). In World War II, Allied pilots (who made the Swan their second home) carved their signatures in the bar, a longish room with a timbered ceiling and a fine weapon collection—with placards advertising everything from the Huntingdon Steeplechase to a wine and cheese party for the Young Conservatives.

11. Woodbridge

A yachting center, 12 miles from the North Sea, Woodbridge is a market town on a branch of the Deben River. Its best known resident was Edward FitzGerald, the Victorian poet and translator of the *Rubáiyát* of Omar Khayyám (some critics consider the Englishman's version better than the original). The poet died in 1883 and was buried four miles away at Boulge.

Woodbridge is a good base for exploring the East Suffolk coastline and excursions to Constable's Flatford Mill, coming up. But first, a look at my medium-priced accommodations and dining recommendation, which is some 1½ miles from the Woodbridge rail station.

WHERE TO STAY AND EAT: Seckford Hall, A12 Road near Woodbridge (tel. 03943/5678), captures the spirit of the days of Henry VIII and his strong-willed daughter Elizabeth (the latter may have held court here). The estate is built of brick, now ivy covered, and adorned with crow stepped gables, mullioned windows, and ornate chimneys—pure Tudor. The hall was built in 1530 by Sir Thomas Seckford, a member of one of Suffolk's first families. You enter through a heavy studded Tudor door into a flagstone hallway with antiques. The butler will show you to your bedroom. Owners Mr. and Mrs. M. S. Bunn have seen to it that your stay is like a house party. All bedrooms have private baths en suite. A single room rents for £38 ($59) nightly, a double or twin for £48 ($72), and a four-poster unit for £50 ($75). Charges include a full English breakfast, service charge, and tax. One room is high-ceilinged with a monumental 1587 four-poster bed. In summer, reservations are helpful for those desiring bed, breakfast, and evening dinner. (Nonguests can stop by for dinner, which is à la carte. Best to phone first.)

If you arrive before sundown, you may want to stroll through a portion of the 34-acre gardens. As you proceed to the side and rear, you'll come upon a rose garden, herbaceous borders, and greenhouses. At the bottom of the garden is an ornamental lake, complete with weeping willows and paddling ducks. At four o'clock, you can have a complete tea in the Great Hall. Sip your brew slowly, savoring the atmosphere of heavy beams and a simple stone fireplace. Your chair may be Queen Anne, your table Elizabethan. Dinner will be announced by the butler. Good English meals are served in a setting of linenfold paneling and Chippendale and Hepplewhite chairs. After-dinner coffee and brandy are featured in the Tudor Bar.

The **Lane O'Gorman Wine Bar,** 17 Thoro'fare, upstairs (tel. 03940/2557). The homemade food (cooked in the bar) is offered from a seasonal menu that changes weekly and might include garlic mushrooms, stuffed pepper, game pie, and an inventive display of help-yourself salads, plus desserts such as chocolate roulade or apple and apricot Brown Betty. Vegetarians can almost always be satisfied. Meals cost from £6 ($9) up. Of course, customers are not obliged to eat, as this is not a restaurant. You are welcome to sit with a glass or bottle of wine, a beer, or just a cup of coffee. The wine bar is open from noon to 2:30 p.m. and from 7 to 11 p.m. It's closed Sunday and Monday but open on bank holiday Monday evenings.

12. Aldeburgh

Pressed against the North Sea, Aldeburgh is a favorite retreat of the in-the-know traveler, even attracting some Dutch tourists who make the sea crossing via Harwich, the British entry port for those coming from the Hook of Holland. The late composer Benjamin Britten (*Peter Grimes, The Rape of Lucretia*), used to live in the area. But the festival he started at Aldeburgh in 1948 is held at Snape in June, a short drive to the north.

Less than 100 miles from London, the resort was founded in Roman times, but legionnaires have been replaced by fishermen, boatmen, and fanciers of wildfowl. A bird sanctuary, Havergate Island, lies about ten miles offshore. Some take time out from their sporting activities (a golf course stretches 3½ miles) to visit the 16th-century **Moot Hall.**

WHERE TO STAY AND EAT: In August, the time of the regatta, accommodations tend to be fully booked. I'll survey the pick of the lot:

Brudenell Hotel, The Parade (tel. 072-885/2071), is Aldeburgh's prestige hotel, right on the waterfront. Built at the beginning of the 20th century, it was remodeled and decorated by its owner, Trusthouses Forte Ltd. An attractive and comfortable accommodation awaits the visitor exploring the East Anglian seacoast. The interior is most successful and pleasant, and from many of the bedrooms there's a view of the churning sea. All of the rooms contain private baths. Singles range in price from £32 ($48) to £33 ($49.50), and twins or doubles from £42 ($63) to £44 ($66), VAT and service included. During the months of October to May, many bargain-break offers are available, with golfing breaks and jazz weekends as specialties. Every room has TV, telephone, radio, tea and coffee makers, and central heating, as well as good, soft beds. The dining room with an all-glass wall overlooking the coast is an ideal spot for a three-course luncheon costing £6.50 ($9.75). A set dinner costs £10 ($15). There are à la carte selections also, a dinner averaging around £11 ($16.50) to £14 ($21). Excellent bar snacks featuring local fish are available.

Uplands Hotel, Victoria Road (tel. 072-885/2420), is as untouristy a retreat as you are likely to find. It's more like a private home run by Ron and Iris Porter, who take in paying guests. The inn dates from the 18th century. At one time it was the childhood home of Elizabeth Garrett Anderson, the first woman doctor in England. Uplands provides personally decorated bedrooms and excellently planned and well-prepared meals. Once inside the living room, you sense the informality and charm. They have furnished it with some good antiques, a few comfortable upholstered chairs, paintings, and books. The prices range from £18 ($27) to £20 ($30) for an overnight stopover. There are seven twin-bedded chalets in the garden, with private baths and TV. In the hotel are 12 individually designed units. The chef, who has won many cooking awards, offers an à la carte dinner for about £10 ($15). A typical meal might include escalope de veau "Uplands" or roast Aylesbury duck. You can have coffee in front of the fireplace, or in fair weather, in the garden.

The Local Pub

Ye Olde Crosse Keys, Crabbe Street, is a genuine 15th-century pub, with the real atmostphere of a Suffolk seaside local. In the summertime, everyone takes his or her real English ale or lager out and sits on the seawall, sipping, talking, and thinking. The pub is rustic—favored by local artists, who in the cooler months sit beside an old brick fireplace and eat plates of oysters or smoked salmon. Sandwiches, and very good ones, are available at from 75p ($1.13) up. Ye Olde Crosse Keys is easy to spot, a short walk from Ye Olde Curiosity Shoppe.

13. East Bergholt

The English landscape painter, John Constable (1776–1837), was born at East Bergholt. Near the village is **Flatford Mill** (tel. 0206/298283), subject of one of his most renowned canvases. The mill, in a scenic setting, was given to the National Trust in 1943, and since has been leased to the Fields Studies Council for use as a residential college. Weekly courses are arranged on all aspects of the countryside and the environment. None of the buildings contains relics of Constable, nor are they open to the general public, but students of all ages and capabilities are welcome to courses. The fee for one week is inclusive of accommodation, meals, and tuition. Details may be obtained from the warden, Flatford Mill Field Centre, East Bergholt, Colchester, Essex CO7 6UL.

THE LOCAL PUB: Red Lion Inn, Gaston Street (tel. 0206/298332), traces its ancestry back to around 1500. Numerous authors have written of the Red Lion, citing it as one of the unmarred inns of East Anglia.

The friendly, family-run pub has a good enclosed children's garden. There is a wide range of bar meals, costing from £1 ($1.50) to £4 ($6), including the best ploughman's lunch in the area. Steaks are offered in the evening. A short stroll from Flatford Mill and the heart of Constable land, the inn is opposite a historic church with a bell cage on the ground, where the bells are hand-rung. The Red Lion is reached by turning off the A12 Colchester–Ipswich road.

NORFOLK

Bounded by the North Sea, Norfolk is the biggest of the East Anglian counties. It's a low-lying area, with fens, heaths, and salt marshes. An occasional dike or windmill makes you think you've been delivered to the Netherlands. One of the features of Norfolk is its network of Broads, miles and miles of lagoons—shallow in parts—connected by streams.

Summer sports people flock to Norfolk to hire boats for sailing or fishing. From Norwich itself, **Wroxham,** the so-called capital of the Broads, is easily reached, only eight miles to the northeast. Motorboats regularly leave from this resort, taking parties on short trips. Some of the best scenery of the Broads is to be found on the periphery of Wroxham.

THE NORFOLK BROADS BY BOAT: From Wroxham on Tuesday and Friday at 11 a.m., you can embark on a day's cruise wandering past the boatyards and sailing clubs of Salhouse Broad, through Horning village, and along the River Bure, on tours operated by **Broads Tours** (tel. 06053/2207). The cruisers have all-round vision, comfortable seats, and sunroofs. The skipper tells of places of interest, and light refreshments are available on board. After a short stop for lunch ashore at Ranworth, you return to the boat for the trip back to Wroxham. If you only have time for half a day on the Broads, you can take an afternoon cruise that leaves daily at 2:30. There are also one- and two-hour trips, which allow you to see at least a little of the beautiful waterways. It is advisable to make a reservation for the day trip by phoning in advance.

An all-day cruise costs £5 ($7.50) for adults, £3 ($4.50) for children. The longer afternoon trip costs £3 ($4.50) for adults, £2 ($3) for children; the two-hour cruise, £2.75 ($4.13); and the one-hour trip, £1.60 ($2.40). Cruises run from April to October, with extra tours during peak season.

EN ROUTE TO NORWICH: If you're searching for a place to dine near the Suffolk–Norfolk border, before driving on to Norwich, you'll find none better than the recommendation below.

The Fox and Goose, Fressingfield, near Diss, Norfolk (tel. Fressingfield 247), is a charming old building with a wide gravel courtyard and a pond with ducks. It was the old guildhall, and is the only remaining inn I could find in England still owned by the church and originally provided by the church for the refreshment of parishioners instead of their eating in the nave after services. The place is a delight. It's open daily from noon to 1:30 p.m. and 7 to 9 p.m., except Tuesday and from December 21 to December 28.

The Clarke family runs it, and its members have been here for longer than a decade, serving lunches and dinners to locals (London is only 80 miles of fast road away so some come from there) and passersby.

If you can plan ahead, telephone and reserve a table. The Clarkes will send you the menu and you can select your meal in advance. The kitchen staff prefers one party to order the same entree if possible, as this place is very much a family concern. The selection is made from a wide variety of fresh fish and local meat dishes. Featured are smoked eel, mackerel, salmon and trout, sole normande, coquille St. Jacques, king prawns, lobster, and crab, followed by beef or pork en croûte, five sorts of steak, tournedos provençale, three duck dishes, venison in season or game, all served with a variety of vegetables. Desserts include fresh fruit dishes and sorbets and ices laced with liqueurs.

Mr. Clarke used to be a wholesale butcher, and the quality of the meat reflects his interest. Adrian, his young son, hated school but had a knack for cooking. He presides in the kitchen. The kitchen staff bakes its own whole-meal crusty bread to serve with masses of yellow butter.

The dining room seats only 26 "at a pinch," and punctuality is essential. But once you're there, the table is yours to enjoy your meal in comfort. Start in the bar with an apéritif. The wine list is long and excellent, although you can order a bottle of the house wine for £5.50 ($8.25). Service is unobtrusive in the simple dining room, with its low ceiling and wooden tables and chairs. A meal, not including wine, will cost from £12 ($18) to £18 ($27).

14. Norwich

Norwich is the most important shopping center in East Anglia and is well provided with hotels and entertainment. In addition to its cathedral, it has more than 30 medieval parish churches built of flint.

There are many interesting hotels in the narrow streets and alleyways, and a big open-air market, busy every weekday, where fruit, flowers, vegetables, and other goods are sold from stalls with colored canvas roofs.

The Assembly House (see below) is a Georgian building restored to provide a splendid arts and social center. The **Maddermarket Theatre,** the home of the Norwich Players, is an 18th-century chapel converted by Nugent Monck in 1921 to an Elizabethan-style theater. On the outskirts of the city, the buildings of the University of East Anglia are strikingly modern in design and include the Sainsbury Center (1978).

There is a **Tourist Information Centre** at Augustine Steward House in Tombland, near the cathedral.

THE CASTLE: In the center of Norwich, on an artificial mound, sits the castle, formerly the county gaol (jail). Its huge 12th-century Norman keep and the later prison buildings are used as a civic museum and headquarters of the county-wide Norfolk Museums Service (tel. Norwich 611277). The museum houses an impressive collection of pictures by artists of the Norwich School, of whom the most distinguished were John Crome, born 1768, and John Sell Cotman, born 1782. The Castle Museum also contains a fine collection of Lowestoft porcelain and Norwich silver. These are shown in the rotunda. There are two sets of dioramas, one showing Norfolk wildlife in its natural setting, the other illustrating scenes of Norfolk life from the Old Stone Age to the early days of Norwich Castle. You can also visit a geology gallery and a permanent exhibition in the keep, "Norfolk in Europe."

The Castle Museum is open weekdays from 10 a.m. to 5 p.m. (on Sunday from 2 to 5 p.m.). Charges from the spring bank holiday until September are 70p ($1.05) for adults, 10p (15¢) for children, and 35p (53¢) for students. The rest of the year, adults pay 35p (53¢); children, 10p (15¢); and students, 20p (30¢). There's a coffee bar, plus the licensed Buttery, which is open from 10:30 a.m. to 2:30 p.m.

THE CATHEDRAL: Principally of Norman design, the cathedral dates back to 1096. It is noted primarily for its long nave, with its lofty columns. Its spire, built in the late Perpendicular style, rises 315 feet, and shares distinction with the keep of the castle as the significant landmarks on the Norwich skyline. On the vaulted ceiling are more than 300 bosses (knob-like ornamental projections) depicting biblical scenes. The impressive choir stalls with the handsome misereres date from the 15th century. Edith Cavell—"Patriotism is not enough"—the English nurse executed by the Germans in World War I, was buried on the cathedral's Life's Green. The quadrangular Cloisters go back to the 13th century, and are among the most spacious in England.

The cathedral Visitors' Centre includes a refreshment area and an exhibition and film room with tape/slide shows about the cathedral. Admission is free.

A short walk from the cathedral will take you to **Tombland,** one of the most interesting old squares in Norwich.

SAINSBURY CENTRE FOR VISUAL ARTS: In 1973 Sir Robert and Lady Sainsbury gave their private art collection to the University of East Anglia, and their son David gave an endowment to provide a building to house the collection. The center, designed by Foster Associates, was opened in 1978, and since then the building has won many national and international awards. A feature of the structure is its flexibility, allowing solid and glass areas to be interchanged, and the superb quality of light, which allows optimum viewing of works of art. The Sainsbury Collection is one of the foremost in the country, including modern, ancient, classical, and ethnographic art. Other displays at the center include the Anderson collection of art nouveau and the university aggregation of 20th-century nonfigurative art. There is also a regular program of special exhibitions.

The center (tel. 0603/56161) is open from noon to 5 p.m. from Tuesday to Sunday. Admission to the permanent collections is 50p (75¢) for adults, 25p (38¢) for students; to both galleries, 75p ($1.13) for adults, 40p (60¢) for students.

The restaurant offers a self-service buffet from 10:30 a.m. to 2:30 p.m. Monday to Friday. Meal service is available from 12:30 to 2 p.m., also Monday to Friday. In the coffee bar, snacks are served from noon to 4:30 p.m. Tuesday to Sunday. A set lunch is offered for £4 ($6).

The university offers many of its modern student accommodations for holiday rentals during recess. The flats at Mary Chapman Court have fully equipped kitchens and are suitable for five persons. They cost £125 ($187.50). Large bed-sitting rooms in Orwell and Wolfson Closes rent for £9 ($13.50) per person for B&B, and there is also a kitchen shared by each eight units. No deposit is required, but payment should be made on arrival. For information, write to the Registry, University of East Anglia, Norwich NR4 7TJ (tel. 0603/56161).

THE MUSTARD SHOP: This fascinating attraction is at 3 Bridewell Alley (tel. 0603/27889). Early in the 19th century Jeremiah Colman went into partnership with his nephew, James, and started the firm of J. & J. Colman, a name that became synonymous with mustard over the years. To mark the 150th anniversary of the business (1973), the Mustard Shop was opened in an 18th-century building up a pretty little alleyway in Norwich's old center. It is now the town's major tourist attraction after the cathedral. Here, you can learn the history of mustard and buy useful and unusual souvenirs at the same time. More than a dozen different flavors of mustard made by Colman are on sale, including horseradish, chive, and tarragon. Various mustard pots, mustard spoons, and mustard paddles are sold here. They will pack and mail to anywhere in the world.

WHERE TO STAY: The **Post House,** Ipswich Road (tel. 0603/56431), is two miles from the center of the city on the A140 Ipswich road and one mile from the A11 London road. Free parking space is provided for 200 cars. Run as a Trusthouses Forte hotel, it charges £44 ($66) in a single, £58 ($87) in a double, VAT and service charge included. Each of the 120 bedrooms has a private bath, telephone, TV, radio, central heating, tea- and coffee-making equipment, and a small refrigerated bar. The rooms have combined sitting areas, with sofas and armchairs. The coffeeshop, which stays open till 10:30 p.m., reflects Norfolk's ties with agriculture (sturdy farming tools decorating the walls); the main restaurant specializes in traditional English fare, such as game in season, smoked fish, and potted meats. The modern Punch Bar is decorated with early *Punch* cartoons and drawings.

The **Maids Head Hotel,** Tombland (tel. 0603/28821), claims to be the oldest continuously operated hotel in the United Kingdom, in business since 1272. Situated in the oldest part of the city and next to Norwich Cathedral, it has two parts to its architectural personality, one being the Elizabethan black-and-white Georgian section with a prim white entry and small-paned windows. The 82 bedrooms have private baths or showers, with fresh fruit, newspapers, and the traditional services such as shoe cleaning, breakfast served in bed, and afternoon cream teas. The four-poster-bedded Queen Elizabeth I room (where the Tudor monarch allegedly once slept) is much sought after, renting for £55 ($82.50). Bathless singles are £30 ($45); singles with shower, £34 ($51); and singles with bath, £37 ($55.50). A double with bath and shower costs £47 ($70.50). A full English breakfast is included in all the tariffs. Meals are served in the Courtyard

Carvery at lunchtime, with an extensive buttery service all day. The Georgian paneled Minstrel Room offers dinner each night. Lunches cost from £6.50 ($9.75); dinners, from £8.50 ($12.75).

Santa Lucia Hotel, 38–40 Yarmouth Rd. (tel. 0603/33207), is one of the best for value of the hotels outside Norwich, only 1½ miles from the center. The combined hotel and guest house offers not only inexpensive rooms, but an attractive setting and a friendly atmosphere.

You pay £9 ($13.50) nightly for B&B. The food is quite good too, costing £3.50 ($5.25) for a dinner. Each of the rooms has running water and a radio. There are sun terraces for relaxing, modern bathrooms, and plenty of parking space. Three buses pass by the door heading for the center of the city.

WHERE TO EAT: The **Assembly House,** Theatre Street (tel. 0603/26402), is a good example of Georgian architecture. You enter the building through a large front courtyard, which leads to the central hall with its columns, fine paneling, and crystal chandelier. The restaurant is administered by H. J. Sexton Norwich Arts Trust.

On your left is a high-ceilinged room, with paneling, fine paintings, and a long chilled-buffet table—ready for self-service. After making your selection, take your plate to any one of the many tables. Often you'll share—perhaps with an artist or a woman who owns an estate in the country. You'll find an unusually varied selection of hors d'oeuvres and desserts. Hot entrees are prepared with fresh ingredients. The prices, like the food, are simple. For example, a home-cured ham and salad meal goes for £2.75 ($4.13), an omelet for £2 ($3). The restaurant is open from 10 a.m. to 2 p.m. and from 3 to 7:30 p.m.

After dining, you may want to stroll through the rest of the building. Art exhibits are usually held regularly in the Ivory and Hobart Rooms, open from 10 a.m. to 5:30 p.m. Concerts are sponsored in the Music Room, with its chandeliers and sconces. There's even a small movie house.

The **Quarter-Deck** at the Hotel Nelson, Prince of Wales Road (tel. 0603/28612), brings back memories of Norwich's most famous son, Horatio, Admiral Lord Nelson, after whom the hotel is named. The nautical name of the buttery also stems, of course, from the heroic naval exploits of Nelson, even up to his death at the Battle of Trafalgar. At the Quarter-Deck (or should I say "on" it?), you get fast, cheerful service and a choice of dishes such as Cromer fish pie or beef-and-beer casserole with mushrooms and noodles. Hot fruit pie is the best dessert. Lunch is served from noon to 2 p.m., costing £3 ($4.50) for a selection from meats, pies, fish, and pâté, including serve-yourself salads. For the same price you can have the admiral's hot dish of the day. The restaurant is open from 10:30 a.m. for coffee and drinks, from noon to 2 p.m. for lunch, and from 5:30 to 10:30 p.m. for informal dinners. The hotel is near the railway station and Foundry Bridge.

The **Britons Arms Coffee House,** 9 Elm Hill (tel. 0603/23367), over-looks the most beautiful cobbled street in Norwich, in the heart of the old city. Over the years, it's had several names, and traces its history back to the days of Edward III. It was already more than 100 years old when Columbus discovered America. Now it's one of the least expensive eating places in Norwich—certainly the most intimate and informal. The coffee-house has several rooms, including a back one with an inglenook. You'll find old beamed ceilings, Tudor benches, and pink-washed walls. This is one of the few places in the city with a garden for outdoor dining in summer.

It's open every day except Sunday, serving mostly lunches and coffee. Lunch begins at 12:15 p.m. (the staff is strict about that), ending at 2:30 p.m. Generally, you can have tea from 3:30 until 5 p.m.

The procedure here is to go to the little counter, where you purchase your lunch and bring it to the table of your choice. Everything I've tried has been tasty, and the items are homemade. In summertime the food is cold; in winter, hot. You'll find an assortment of soups, quiches, flans, fruit pies, and cheeses, a meal costing around £4 ($6). It's a good place to stop after your inspection of the cathedral, only a block away.

15. Shipdam

As you negotiate a sharp bend around the churchyard in Shipdam village, near Thetford, you come to an open gateway leading to the wide graveled front yard of **Shipdam Place,** Church Close (tel. 0362/820303). Ring the bell, and you will be welcomed into an old country house that was once the rectory. It dates back to the 17th century, with an elegant Regency block that was added in 1800. There are two lounges with comfortable chairs and a drinks trolley. You are trusted to help yourself and enter your drinks in the book for payment at departure. Behind the house, a peaceful garden is at the disposal of guests. You can take coffee on the terrace on a warm summer evening.

Upstairs, the five bedrooms come in varying shapes and sizes. Some have sloping ceilings. All are decorated in pretty country prints, and fresh fruit and flowers are placed in your room on arrival. Rates vary from £44 ($66) in a single and £49 ($73.50) in a double for the front units to £29 ($43.50) or £41 ($61.50) in a single and £35 ($52.50) to £45 ($67.50) for the others. All tariffs include VAT and a delightfully relaxed breakfast when you can have almost anything you want.

It is mainly for the cuisine that Melanie and Justin de Blank, the hosts, are nationally known. Justin has various restaurants in London, and Melanie is in charge of the kitchen at Shipdam. The set five-course dinner costs £18 ($27), including VAT. You may expect such original appetizers as Colchester clam and mussel salad. The main dish can be filet of beef with vintners butter sauce or medallions of English lamb with mint béarnaise sauce, all served with appropriate vegetables. A 10% service charge is added to all bills.

16. Tottenhill

This village can be a center for exploring some stately homes and gardens, the seaside resorts and fens and broads of East Anglia. Within a day's drive are the historic old port of King's Lynn, the country home of Queen Elizabeth (Sandringham), the lavender fields of Heacham, the tulip fields of Spalding, as well as the large man-made forest at Thetford and the neolithic flint mines at Grime's Graves. The following private hotel is recommended as a stopover.

Oakwood House, on Route A10 near Tottenhill, just four miles south of King's Lynn (tel. King's Lynn 810256), is a country house of Tudor origin with all the amenities of a modern hotel. The house was enlarged some 200 years ago and refaced with a typical Georgian exterior. Within a short drive of the Norfolk coast, Oakwood House offers visitors a peaceful alternative to the bustling seaside resorts and market towns.

Nestled in its own two acres of gardens, the hotel and its annex have 12 guest rooms with color TV, tea- and coffee-making facilities, hot and cold running water, individually controlled heating, and pleasant views over the Norfolk countryside and the gardens. Four rooms are equipped with private showers and toilets en suite. The comfortably furnished guest lounge contains a color TV, and the spacious dining room adjoins the well-stocked period bar.

The menu is carefully chosen to make the best use of local and homegrown produce whenever possible, and all cooking is under the personal supervision of Marjorie Rhodes, who, with her husband Geoff, sees that the needs of their guests are attended to. Rates per person for B&B begin at £14 ($21). The four-course dinner will cost you an additional £8 ($12). VAT is included in the price, and no service charge is made. Ample parking facilities are maintained within the grounds.

17. North Norfolk

This part is already well known by members of the American Eighth Air Force, for many Liberators and Flying Fortresses took off and landed from this corner of the country. Their captains and crews sampled most of the local hostelries at one time or another. Now it is just feathered birds that fly overhead, and the countryside is quiet and peaceful.

THE SIGHTS: This area is of considerable scenic interest, having some very good value in its offering of accommodations and food. Norfolk especially provides an alternative to the vastly overcrowded West Country in summer, and it's extremely convenient for a weekend out of London, as it lies only a three-hour drive away.

Sandringham

Some 110 miles northeast of London, Sandringham has been the country home of four generations of British monarchs, ever since the Prince of Wales (later King Edward VII) purchased it in 1861. The son of Queen Victoria, along with his Danish wife, Princess Alexandra, rebuilt the house, standing on 7000 acres of grounds, and in time it became a fashionable rendezvous of British society.

The red brick Victorian Tudor mansion consists of more than 200 rooms, and in recent times some of these rooms have been opened to the public, including two drawing rooms and a dining room. Sandringham joins Windsor Castle and the Palace of Holyroodhouse in Edinburgh as the only British royal residences that can be examined by the public. Guests can also visit a lofty saloon with a minstrels' gallery.

A group of former coach houses has been converted into a museum of big-game trophies, plus a collection of cars, including the first vehicle purchased by a royal, a 1900 Daimler Tonneau that belonged to Edward VII. The house and grounds are open, except when the Queen or members of the royal family are there, from Easter to the last week in September daily except Friday and Saturday. Hours are from 11 a.m. (noon on

Sunday) to 4:45 p.m. for the house, 10:30 a.m. (11:30 a.m. on Sunday) to 5 p.m. for the grounds. Admission to the house and grounds is £1.75 ($2.63) for adults, £1.50 ($2.25) for children. To visit the grounds only, adults pay £1 ($1.50); 90p children, ($1.35). The house is closed from the third week in July to the end of the first week in August, and the grounds and house are both closed for all but the first and last three or four days of that period. The 70-acre gardens, incidentally, are richly planted with azaleas, rhododendrons, hydrangeas, and camellias.

Sandringham lies 50 miles from Cambridge and 10 miles from King's Lynn. There is bus service between King's Lynn and Sandringham.

Blickling Hall

A long drive, bordered by massive yew hedges towering above and framing your first view of this lovely old house, leads you to Blickling Hall, near Aylsham (tel. 0263/733471). A great Jacobean house built in the early 17th century, it is perhaps one of the finest examples of such architecture in the country. The Long Gallery has an elaborate 17th-century ceiling, and the Peter the Great Room, decorated later, has a fine tapestry on the wall. The house is set in ornamental parkland with a formal garden and an orangery. Meals and snacks are available. It is open from April until the end of October, except Monday, from 2 to 6 p.m. The house is also open from 11 a.m. daily, except Monday and Thursday, from May to September. Admission is £1.70 ($2.55) for adults, 85p ($1.28) for children.

Norfolk Lavender Ltd.

At Caley Mill at Heacham (tel. 0485/70384), you can see how lavender is grown, the flowers harvested, and the essence distilled before appearing prettily packaged as perfume, aftershave, and old-fashioned lavender bags to slip between your hankies. The grounds are open from 10 a.m. to 6 p.m. May to September, from 9 a.m. to dusk in winter. Admission to the grounds, which include gardens of lavender, herbs, and roses, is free. The best time to see the lavender is mid-July to mid-August, and there are several tours of the distillery every day except Sunday. Admission is 50p (75¢) for adults, free to children. You will be able to discuss the merits of the various varieties and their suitability for your own particular garden. The Miller's Cottage Tearoom serves cream teas with homemade cakes, scones, and buns, as well as light lunches.

Alby Crafts Ltd.

This brainchild of Valerie Alston, on Cromer Road, Erpingham (tel. 0263/761590), is open from Easter to Christmas, daily, except Monday, from 10 a.m. to 5 p.m. The craft center is housed in an old Norfolk stone farmhouse and its outbuildings. Mrs. Alston scours the country to find genuine articles of country craft, including leatherwork, woodcarving, and ceramics. A rocking chair model, perfect in every detail, yet only four inches high, costs £18 ($27). A woodcarving of a Bedfordshire farmer and his pig goes for £58 ($87). Bronze and wrought-iron work can be made to order, a piece costing from £3 ($4.50) to £500 ($750). There are sometimes demonstrations and specialist exhibitions, and several of the workshops are made available to local craftspeople. The delight of this place is that the articles come from all over the country and are entirely genuine craftware. Homemade dishes and cakes are served throughout the day in the tea room.

Sutton Windmill

At Sutton (1½ miles southeast of Stalham off the A149) is the tallest mill in the country. But its main claim to fame, in a country where many windmills still work, is the exceptional quality and interest of the working machinery. Chris Nunn, the young man who owns the mill, decided it was time he put something back into the country instead of taking it out. So he left the construction business and now devotes his days to restoring the mill. When money runs short, he works on the North Sea oil rigs for a time. He hopes shortly to be grinding corn again, but the lower floors—there are nine in all—house a collection of tools and bygones reflecting the mill's 100 years of history. The mill is open April 1 to May 14 from 1:30 to 6 p.m., May 15 to September 30 from 9:30 a.m. to 6 p.m. Admission is 65p (98¢) for adults, 40p (60¢) for children. There is a telescope on the top floor, and the view over the countryside is magnificent. Crafts, pottery, books, and gifts are on sale. Telephone Stalham 81195 for more information.

The Thursford Collection

Just off the A148, which runs from Kings Lynn to Cromer, at Laurel Farm, Thursford Green, Thursford, near Fakenham (tel. Thursford 238), George Cushing has been collecting and restoring steam engines and organs for more years than you'd care to remember. His collection is now a trust, and the old painted giants are on display, a paradise of traction engines with impeccable pedigrees such as Burrells, Garretts, and Ruston Proctors. There are some static engines, the sort that run merry-go-rounds at funfairs, but the most flamboyant exhibits are the showman's organs, the Wurlitzers and concert organs with their brilliant decoration, moving figures, and mass of windpipes. The organs play at 3 p.m. There is a children's play area, and a Savages Venetian Gondola switchback ride with Gavoili organ, which operates daily. It was built at nearby Kings Lynn, and Disneyland has been after it for years. On many days during the summer, the two-foot gauge steam railway, the Cackler, will take you around the wooded grounds of the museum. There is a refreshment café and a souvenir shop to buy photographs, books, and records of the steam-organ music. The collection is open daily from 2 to 5:30 p.m. from Easter until the end of October. It is open on Sunday in November and March; closed in January and February. Admission is £1.75 ($2.63) for adults, £1 ($1.50) for children.

The North Norfolk Railway

This steam railway plies from Sheringham to Weybourne. The station at Sheringham is open daily from 10 a.m. from Easter to October. There are two museums of railway paraphernalia, steam locomotives, and historic rolling stock. Admission to the museums is 40p (60¢) for adults, 20p (30¢) for children. The round trip to Weybourne by steam train takes about 45 minutes through most attractive countryside. Days and times of departures vary so you should write or phone the Cromer Tourist North Lodge Park,

Cromer, Norfolk (tel. 0263/512497). The round-trip journey will cost £1.40 ($2.10) for adults; children, 70p ($1.05).

FOOD AND LODGING: The Maltings, Weybourne, near Holt (tel. 0263/70275). Almost on the edge of the sea but protected from its worst ravages, the Maltings is a delightfully friendly country "pub" in the best tradition. It is under the watchful eye of Ross Mears. Bedrooms are simple and comfortable with color TV and radio. They go from £22 ($33) to £26 ($39) in a single, and from £19.50 ($29.25) to £21 ($31.50) per person in a double, depending on whether or not you have a private bath. Rates include a large English breakfast, VAT, and service.

The original building dates back to the 16th century, and the flint walls and stout plain exterior bear witness to those times. The elegant restaurant has a sophisticated à la carte menu, including most of those haute cuisine dishes that you crave—coquilles St. Jacques frites, veal escalope with rosemary, beef filet with parsley butter—along with a Taste of England menu when a succulent set lunch will cost £8.50 ($12.75); a set dinner, £12 ($18). There are some interesting variations such as jugged hare cooked in red wine.

If you feel unable to sustain a whole meal, drift down the yard to the Inn and the Buttery where, in another solid old stone building, you can sup off a variety of salads complemented by fresh-caught seafoods, home-cooked meats, and, the main attraction, hot baked jacket potatoes, with a wide variety of fillings. John Boyle rules over the kitchens, but he has a superb team of chefs with him.

The **Blakeney Hotel,** The Quay, Blakeney, near Holt (tel. 0263/740797). As its address indicates, the hotel is right on the quay overlooking the harbor and across the flats from Blakeney Point where migrating birds rest on their way south. The village and neighboring Cley built many of the Elizabethan sailing ships, and the hotel bars are named for two of them, *Jacob* and *Revenge*. Rooms are cozy, have tea- and coffee-making facilities, as well as telephones and radios. Most have baths and color TVs.

Expect to pay from £21 ($31.50) to £34 ($51) in a single, £20 ($30) to £32 ($48) per person in a double including VAT. The cheaper rooms are without bath, the more expensive with private bath and color TV.

There is an indoor swimming pool, and the lounge has panoramic windows with superb views over the flats to the sea. Bar snacks at lunchtime start with soup and bread, salads, hot dishes, and sandwiches. The top price is £3 ($4.50), for steak-and-kidney pie with two vegetables. A set dinner costs £10 ($15) for three courses and coffee.

The **Buckinghamshire Arms Hotel,** Blickling, near Aylsham (tel. Aylsham 2133), is a pleasant 17th-century village inn with roaring fires in the bars. Offered are comfortable rooms—some with four-poster beds, others with half-tester beds (the canopy reaches over the sleeper's head only). Some come with just ordinary divans, although all have TV and coffee- and tea-making trays. The charge for two persons in one of the inn's four-poster beds is £35 ($52.50), including VAT and a full English breakfast. Dinner is £13.50 ($20.25). The soup comes from an aromatic stockpot, and Norfolk duckling and chicken are served with fresh vegetables. During the winter they hold special feasts once or twice a month with lobster, venison, and pheasant among the main dishes. Nigel Elliott leases the inn from the National Trust, which owns the nearby Blickling Hall. Real ale, featured in the bar, is often so strong that it only comes in "nips."

This is my idea of a real English inn, with log fires, country location, old oak trees all around, and the big house of the lord of the manor nearby.

The **Old Rectory,** Great Snoring, Fakenham (tel. Walsingham 597). The history of this old house is shrouded in mystery, but in 1500 it was believed to be hexagonal with stone-mullioned windows and heraldic shields of the then owners, the Shelton family, carved on the oaken front door. The Victorians did their bit to restore the house, but it still remains a solid part of medieval village life.

Rosamond Scoles and her family have six comfortable and elegantly furnished rooms for guests. Overnight is £22 ($33) to £28 ($42) in a single, from £42 ($63) in a double, the latter with bath, including a leisurely and substantial breakfast. There is a large lounge for guests, where an open woodstove burns, and the light flickers on antique woodwork.

Dinner is three courses, cheese, and coffee for £10 ($15) per person. Picnic hampers are provided for luncheon alfresco if you wish. The Old Rectory is licensed, so you can enjoy a sherry before dinner or a nightcap by the fire before retiring to your bed. It's an entirely elegant, relaxed experience, an insight into comfortable country life.

Gasche's Swiss Restaurant, Weybourne (tel. Weybourne 220), has been going on for about 40 years. These days it is run by Edgar Steiner, nephew of the original Herr Gasche. Nigel Massingham, the chef, trained here and has picked up those Swiss touches in the preparation of the dishes. The beamed dining room of the flint and thatch cottage is warmed by a log fire. You will be greeted as warmly by the staff as you partake of the set lunch, costing £5.50 ($8.25) for three courses. You have a choice of seven appetizers, a homemade soup, and eight main courses including wiener-schnitzel. Dinner, from £12 ($18), is chosen from a similarly large menu, including roast Norfolk duckling. There is an à la carte menu where a meal will cost around £18 ($27), but I think you will find enough choices on the set menus to satisfy all tastes. The restaurant is open daily except Monday throughout the year (except for dinner on Sunday).

Chapter XIV

EAST MIDLANDS

1. Northamptonshire
2. Leicestershire
3. Derbyshire
4. Nottinghamshire
5. Lincolnshire

THE EAST MIDLANDS contains several widely varied counties, both in character and scenery. This part of central England, for instance, offers miles of dreary industrial sections and their offspring row-type Victorian houses, yet the district is intermixed with some of Britain's noblest scenery, such as the Peak District National Park, centered in Derbyshire. Byron said that scenes there rivaled those of Switzerland and Greece. There are, in short, many pleasant surprises in store for you, from the tulip land of Lincoln to the 18th-century spa of Buxton in Derbyshire, from George Washington's ancestral home at Sulgrave Manor in North-amptonshire to what remains of Sherwood Forest.

1. Northamptonshire

This sprawling county in the middle of England is rather undistin-guished in scenery, although its meadows are pleasant in summer. The county town is—

NORTHAMPTON: This has long been an important shoe-making center, and the **Central Museum** on Guildhall Road commemorates that fact. In its collection it traces footwear through the ages, some of which dates back to Roman times. It can be visited from Monday to Saturday from 10 a.m. to 6 p.m. Admission is free. Most visitors pass through here en route to Sulgrave Manor, previewed below.

Food and Lodging

Saxon Inn, Silver Street (tel. 0604/22441), is a concrete-and-glass structure, attracting mainly the business client, drawn to its good location just off the Inner Ring Road (West). A first-class motor hotel, it checks you in and out smoothly and efficiently. The atmosphere isn't stiff at all—in fact it's rather informal, and the public lounges are attractively decorated. Portraits of sporting personalities decorate the Sportsman Bar, and light meals are served in the Little Mermaid coffeeshop. Or you can dine in a coaching-house atmosphere in the Saddle Room, with its large stone fireplace and heavy beams. The menu is international, and guests dine by candlelight, enjoying soft music from a piano player. A resident band entertains on Saturday nights. Rooms are well furnished and comfortable, each with private bath, shower, and toilet en suite, along with color TV, radio, phone, and wall-to-wall carpeting. Singles range in price from £40 ($60), and doubles cost from £52 ($78), including VAT, service, and a full English breakfast.

Westone Moat House, Ashley Way, Weston Favell (tel. 0604/406262), is a big 19th-century mansion that has seen much modernization. My favorite spot here is the cocktail lounge, which has a calm elegance, its windows opening onto the terrace and grounds. All of the 63 bedrooms have private baths, color TVs, radios, phones, and tea- and coffee-making equipment. B&B in a single starts at £36 ($54), at £41 ($61.50) in a double. Traditional English dishes are among the offerings in the restaurant which has good food, fine service, and a bright, cheery decor.

SULGRAVE MANOR: On your way from Oxford to Stratford-upon-Avon, you can visit Sulgrave Manor, the ancestral home of George Washington. First, you'll come to **Banbury,** a market town famed in the nursery rhyme, immortalizing the lady upon the white horse. The old Banbury Cross was destroyed by the Roundheads, but was replaced in Victoria's day. Eight miles northeast of Banbury will take you to Sulgrave Manor, a small Tudor manorial house, built in about the mid-16th century. Follow the A422 east from Banbury toward Brackley. Go left on the B4525 toward Northampton until you pick up the signs to Sulgrave.

As part of Henry VIII's plan to dissolve monasteries, he sold the priory-owned manor in 1539 to Lawrence Washington, who had been mayor of Northampton. George Washington was a direct descendant of Lawrence (seven generations removed). The Washington family occupied Sulgrave for more than a century. In 1656 Col. John Washington left for the New World.

In 1914 the manor was purchased by a group of English people in honor of the friendship between Britain and America. Over the years, major restoration has taken place (a whole new wing had to be added), with an eye toward returning it as much as possible to its original state. The Colonial Dames have been largely responsible for raising the money. From both sides of the Atlantic the appropriate furnishings were donated, including a number of portraits—even a Gilbert Stuart original of the first president. On the main doorway is the Washington family coat-of-arms—two bars and a trio of mullets—which is believed to have been the inspiration for the "Stars and Stripes."

The manor is open daily except Wednesday from April 1 to September 30, 10:30 a.m. to 1 p.m. and 2 to 5:30 p.m. From October to March the hours are from 10:30 a.m. to 1 p.m. and 2 to 4 p.m. It's closed in January. Admission is 80p ($1.20) for adults, 40p (60¢) for children. For more information, telephone 029-576/205.

Food and Lodging

Across from Sulgrave Manor is the **Thatched House Hotel** (tel. 029-576/232), a long, low group of thatched 17th-century cottages, with a front garden full of flowers. It's a good place to stop for afternoon tea, served at a table in either the beamed living or dining room, furnished with antiques. You'll get a pot of tea with homemade scones, jam, thick cream, and cakes for £1.50 ($2.25). In season, a tea with strawberries and thick cream may be served for an additional cost.

The owners, Eileen and Ron Walpole, assisted by Mark Harrison, offer single rooms at £23 ($34.50) and twin- or double-bedded rooms at £34 ($51), including VAT, service, and a full English breakfast. A set lunch costs £5.50 ($8.25) to £10 ($15), and a set dinner goes for £8.50 ($12.75) to £12 ($18). The difference in meal prices is according to your selection of a main course. On Tuesday, Wednesday, and Thursday, a four-course dinner with some six selections per course is offered for £7 ($10.50).

THE SPENCER HOME: Althorp, Northampton (tel. East Haddon 209), is the home of Earl and Countess Spencer, parents of the former Lady Diana Spencer, now the Princess of Wales. The house lies six miles northwest of Northampton and one mile from the village of Harlestone. Built in 1508 by Sir John Spencer, the house has undergone many alterations over the years.

It now contains a fabulous collection of pictures by Van Dyck, Reynolds, Gainsborough, and Rubens, as well as fine and rare French and English furniture, along with Sèvres, Bow, and Chelsea porcelain. The collection is quite as magnificent as that in better known stately homes. The present countess helps in the gift shop, and Lord Spencer's favorite sideline is the excellent cellar and wine store. There is a tea room for light refreshment.

The house is open all year daily from 2:30 to 5:30 p.m. (closed on Monday in August and on Friday during the other months). Admission is £2.50 ($3.75) for adults, £1.50 ($2.25) for children.

STOKE BRUERNE: The **Waterways Museum** (tel. 0604/862229) is on the Grand Union Canal at Stoke Bruerne near Towcester, just south of the Blisworth Tunnel (take the A508 from the M1 junction 15 and then the A5). The three-story grain warehouse has been lovingly restored and adapted to give an insight into the working lives of canal boatmen and their families—a dying breed. On display is a full-size replica of a "butty" boat cabin complete with cooking range, brassware, lace curtains, traditional ware, tools, and teapots. There is also an early semi-diesel Bolinger boat engine, a boat-weighing machine once used to determine canal toll charges. You can buy posters, books, illustrations of canal life, hand-painted miniatures of traditional canalware, models, and badges in a shop at the museum. It is open daily from 10 a.m. to 6 p.m. Closed on Monday from October to Easter and open till 4 p.m. Tuesday to Sunday. Admission is 60p (90¢) for adults, 30p (45¢) for children.

The **Boat Inn** (tel. 0604/862428) started as a row of humble cottages in the 17th century and has gradually progressed without losing its original character. It's still a limestone building with a thatched roof overlooking Grand Union Canal and the Stoke Bruerne Waterways Museum. The public house is the oldest part. It has stone floors and open fires. Bar food is served here. The restaurant offers a full range of dishes, including guinea fowl and grouse in season. A three-course meal, finished off with a choice from the dessert trolley or the cheeseboard, then coffee and mints, will cost around £10 ($15), including the VAT but with service added. The "Great

British Sunday Lunch," roast beef with Yorkshire pudding of course, costs £5.50 ($8.25) for adults, £3.50 ($5.25) for children. The Woodward family has owned and run the Boat Inn since 1877.

OUNDLE: A good stopover after Cambridge, if you're driving north, is Oundle in Northamptonshire, 80 miles from London. It's a pleasant old stone town with a fine church dating back to the 14th century. Its Latham almshouses date from 1611. Those motorists moving between East Anglia and northeastern England will find a warm welcome at—

The **Talbot Hotel,** Oundle, Northamptonshire (tel. 0832/3621), an ancient inn last reconstructed in 1626. An arch from the street leads to the yard and a pleasant garden in the rear. At this busy country-town pub, with its many beams and old pictures, the oak staircase is reputed to have come from Fotheringhay Castle where Mary Queen of Scots was imprisoned and then executed in 1587. Most of the bedrooms have private bath, color TV, and radio. B&B in singles goes for £28 ($42) to £38 ($57), and in doubles or twins for £48 ($72). The hotel is warm and well furnished. Meals are quickly and efficiently provided from a wide menu of grills and roasts. Lunches cost £8 ($12), and dinners, £10 ($15), from the table d'hôte menu. An à la carte meal will average about £15 ($22.50). This is a typical country-town inn, catering to local business people, but welcoming strangers too, in their long tradition as a coaching inn.

AT WEEDON: The **Crossroads Hotel,** High Street, Weedon (tel. Weedon 40354), is a true crossroads hotel, off the M1, the A5, and A45. The owners, Richard and Wendy Amos, have created a little nook where imagination and good taste reign. The clock tower of the hotel, standing in the garden, is a sign of hospitality. Inside there is a fascinating collection of old clocks throughout the dining room and lounges. The antique collection in the dining room is enhanced with stuffed fish, horse prints, birds in cages, a Victorian carved sideboard, old bicycles hanging from the ceiling, and etched mirrors. There's a large brick oven, and best of all, excellent meals are offered. The house specialty is "Wendy's famous steak, kidney, and mushroom pie," served with vegetables for £6 ($9). In new Garden House accommodations, 18 luxury rooms are offered, all with private bath, color TV, trouser press, hair dryer, and tea- and coffee-making equipment. All are attractively furnished. The cost of singles at the hotel is from £27 ($40.50) to £32.50 ($48.75), depending on where the rooms and the plumbing are located . Doubles range from £34 ($51) to £41.50 ($62.25). All tariffs include VAT and a full English breakfast. The Parlour, another recent addition, serves breakfast, morning coffee, and afternoon tea. The Crossroads is an affiliate of Best Western.

2. Leicestershire

Virtually ignored by most North American tourists, this eastern Midland county was the home of King Lear and is rich in historical associations.

LEICESTER: Although the county town is a busy industrial center, it was once a Roman settlement and has a forum and other sites that remind one of those days.

It also has a Norman castle-hall, a period museum, a 15th-century Guildhall (Shakespeare is said to have played here), and many interesting gardens. On its abbey park and grounds are the remains of Leicester Abbey, Cardinal Wolsey's grave, a boating lake, paddling pool, riverside walks, a miniature railway, ornamental gardens, and an aviary.

You can ask at the Information Bureau on Bishop Street (tel. 0533/20644) for details of guided walks around the city or inquire of the **City Transport** on Rutland Street (tel. 0533/24326) about double-decker bus tours.

Food and Lodging

Grand Hotel, Granby Street (tel. 0533/555599), is aptly named indeed. Built in the days when no expense was spared, the interior decoration is truly magnificent, oak and mahogany paneling abound, and the friendly welcome matches the setting, with the emphasis placed on making your stay as comfortable as possible and offering you good value for money. In the Grand Carving Room, you can choose from succulent joints of meat generously carved by the chef to satisfy the heartiest appetite. The completely refurbished bedrooms have a bright, cheery decor, and all have private bathrooms and color TV. Singles cost from £35 ($52.50); twins, from £44 ($66).

Holiday Inn, St. Nicholas Circle (tel. 0533/531161), is smart and stylish, much warmer on its interior than its rather plain facade would suggest. Its enclosed swimming pool is a special feature, and plants and flowers throughout the hotel soften the modernity. Bedrooms, for the most part, are well furnished, with good, large beds, carpeting, private baths, radios, color TV sets, in-house movies, direct-dial phones, and individually controlled air conditioning. Rates range from £29 ($43.50) on weekends to £40 ($60) midweek in a single, from £35 ($52.50) to £44 ($66) in a double. I'd suggest a meal in the Hayloft Restaurant, with its collection of rustically decorated small lofts. The menu is wide ranging, and the dishes are well prepared and presented. Lunch is priced from £8.50 ($12.75) to £10 ($15), and an à la carte dinner goes for about £14 ($21). A Saturday night dinner-dance costs £11.50 ($17.25).

TOURING THE COUNTRY: As long as people continue to read Sir Walter Scott's *Ivanhoe,* they will remember **Ashby-de-la-Zouch,** a town that retains a pleasant country atmosphere. Mary Queen of Scots was imprisoned in an ancient castle here.

If you're in the area, you might want to dine at the **Fallen Knight Restaurant,** 16 Kilwardby St. (tel. 0530/42230), a small place that takes its name from a resident suit of armor. A rustic decor is created by the plain wooden tables and ladderback chairs. The menu is like a "taste of England," with some good, country-style cookery and some imaginative dishes. Joints are carved from the trolley, and an extensive à la carte menu is available; a three-course meal costs from £12 ($18) to £16 ($24). Garry Brook and his wife Susan, who manage the place, rent rooms, all without bath, for £16 ($24) per night in a single, £26 ($39) in a double, all prices including a full English breakfast and VAT. Units contain color TV, a tea or coffee maker, central heating, and shaver points.

On the northern border of Leicestershire overlooking the Vale of Belvoir (pronounced "beaver"), **Belvoir Castle** has been the seat of the

Dukes of Rutland since the time of Henry VIII. Rebuilt by Wyatt in 1816, the castle contains paintings by Holbein, Reynolds, and Gainsborough, as well as tapestries in its magnificent state rooms. Seven miles west-southwest of Grantham, between the A607 to Melton Mowbray and the A52 to Nottingham, the castle was the location of the movie *Little Lord Fauntleroy,* and in summer it is the site of medieval jousting tournaments. From March 22 to October 1 it is open on Tuesday, Wednesday, Thursday, and Saturday from noon to 6 p.m. On Sunday its hours are from noon to 7 p.m. After October 1 it is open until the end of that month only from 2 to 6 p.m. Admission is £2 ($3) for adults, £1.10 ($1.65) for children. Further details are available from Jimmy Durrands, Estate Office, Belvoir Castle, Grantham, Lincolnshire (tel. Grantham 870262).

Other interesting towns to visit in Leicestershire include **Melton Mowbray,** a fox-hunting center and market town, which claims to be the original home of stilton cheese and is renowned for its pork pies.

For a sample of this town's gastronomy, I'd recommend **Dickinson & Morris Ltd.,** 10 Nottingham St., in Melton Mowbray (tel. 0664/62341), a 17th-century structure. By tradition, the first Melton pork pie was baked here, and you can sample it today, based on an old recipe, costing from £1.50 ($2.25). The Melton Hunt cake (rich fruit) is made in the bakery shop to the rear, going for 60p (90¢) a serving.

3. Derbyshire

The most magnificent scenery in the Midlands is found within the borders of this county, lying between Nottinghamshire and Staffordshire. Derbyshire has been less defaced by industry than its neighbors. The north of the county, containing the **Peak District National Park,** is by far the most exciting for touring, as it contains waterfalls, hills, moors, green valleys, and dales. In the south the land is more level, and the look becomes, in places, one of pastoral meadows.

Some tourists avoid this part of the country, because it is ringed by the industrial sprawl of Manchester, Leeds, Sheffield, and Derby. To do so, however, would be a pity, and this part of England contains the rugged peaks and leafy dales that merit a substantial detour, especially Dovedale, Chee Dale, and Millers Dale.

Chatsworth House, home of the Dukes of Devonshire, and **Haddon Hall,** home of the Duke of Rutland, are worth a visit. Melbourne Hall, Kedlestone, and Hardwick Hall are also open to view.

OTHER PLACES TO SEE: In addition to majestic scenery, you may want to seek out the following specific sights.

Tramway Museum, Crich, near Matlock (tel. Ambergate 2565). One young 65-year-old whom I know spends as much of his free time as his wife will allow in the paradise of trams—electric, steam, and horse-drawn. Your admission ticket is £1.60 ($2.40) for adults, 80p ($1.20) for children. This ticket allows visitors to have unlimited rides on trams that make a two-mile round trip to Glory Mine with scenic views over the Derwent Valley, then back through Wakebridge where a stop is made to visit the Peak District Mines Historical Society display of lead mining. It also includes admission to the tramway depot 5 and exhibition. It is open every Saturday and Sunday from April to October, and daily, except Friday, from Easter to September. Hours are from 10:30 a.m. until about 5 p.m.

Peak District Mining Museum, The Pavilion, Matlock Bath (tel. 0629/3834), is open year round, daily (except for Christmas Day) from 11 a.m. to 4 p.m. Admission is 70p ($1.05) for adults, 50p (75¢) for children. The main exhibit of this display of 2000 years of Derbyshire lead mining is a giant water-pressure engine, used to pump water from the mines and itself rescued from 360 feet underground by members of the society before being brought to the museum. The most popular feature is the children's climbing shaft, a twisting tunnel through which they can crawl.

The museum's **Temple Mine,** about five minutes away, is an old fluorite and lead mine that has been restored by volunteers of the Peak District Mines Historical Society so that visitors can experience conditions underground. The mine is electrically lit throughout, but safety helmets must be worn. Like the museum, the mine is open daily except for Christmas Day. Hours are 11 a.m. to 5 p.m. in summer and 2 to 4 p.m. in winter. Admission is 60p (90¢) for adults, 40p (60¢) for children.

Gulliver's Kingdom and Royal Cave, Temple Walk, Matlock Bath (tel. 0629/55970), is just off the A6 main road beside the Pavilion. Before going underground, you are given a brief audio-visual explanation of man's activities under the earth. Then you descend into the cavern, with its series of sound-and-light shows depicting the life of the earliest cavemen through hardships and disasters, as well as the life of the first Romans in Britain and on to the present day. There's a mineral museum, and after the tour the Gallery Cafeteria will revitalize or sustain you. The cave is open daily from Easter until the end of September from 11 a.m. to 4:30 p.m. (sometimes closed on Friday). Admission is £1.90 ($2.85) for everyone.

In Castleton, not so far away, is the **Blue John Cavern,** open all year from 9:30 a.m. to 6 p.m. or dusk. Admission is £1.40 ($2.10) for adults, 70p ($1.05) for children. Drive on the A625 through Winnats Pass from Matlock. These caves, discovered and recorded some 2000 years ago, are dramatic, with fine stalagmites and stalactites.

Magpie Mine, at Sheldon, near Bakewell, has been the site of much desperate toil, murders, vendettas, and enormous financial losses. The underground workings are dangerous and not accessible, but the extensive surface remains are open at all times. Care must be exercised on this site because of the numerous shafts. A guide is only available to organized parties, arranged by telephoning 0629/3834 well in advance. This is a specialist tour, but it is representative of conditions that existed in the 18th- and 19th-century English countryside. The cost of a guided tour is £10 ($15).

The **Red House Stables,** Old Road, Darley Dale, near Matlock (tel. 0629/733583). Caroline Dale's father collected coaches and carriages as a hobby, restored them, and used them for his own pleasure, driving through the Peakland countryside. Today, the carriages and horses are available for the pleasure of anyone who wants to learn to drive a four-in-hand (as Prince Philip does), a pair, or a tandem. An introductory course of three days costs £90 ($135), but if you already have some experience in driving, an intermediate course is available for £120 ($180). A special unaccompanied child's course of English riding and some driving costs £135 ($202.50), plus VAT, for seven days, including full board. No previous experience is necessary, and the course caters to the 8- to 16-year old age group, learners and more advanced pupils alike.

If you would rather someone else drove so that you could enjoy the scenery, Mrs. Dale operates special drives through Chatworth Park with halts at local inns for refreshment in traditional style. A stagecoach—yes, a real one—or a four-in-hand that seats 14 people costs £180 ($270). For a party of four, a landau and pair is more suitable at £70 ($105). These prices include the use of the coach and the services of the coachman, but your meal and drinks are at your expense.

Red House Stables is getting firmly established as a working Horse and Carriage Museum and is open to the public throughout the year. Mrs. Dale also has riding horses at livery. An hour will cost £5.50 ($8.25); a day's trek, £25 ($37.50) (bring your own picnic basket and bad-weather clothing).

The **Clock Warehouse,** London Road, Shardlow (tel. Darby 792844), was built in 1780 on the Trent and Mersey Canal at the junction with the navigable River Trent. It became part of the inland port where merchandise was stored on arrival by narrow boat and river barge. Nowadays the old building houses the Canal Story exhibition, which fills its three floors. There are life-size models of boats and barges, historic photographs, artifacts, and a diorama showing the history of the canal system and the flourishing trade carried on along the waterways. The Canal Shop will sell books, souvenirs, and mementos. Look out for the authentic canal boat painted buckets, jugs, and boxes. The Cider Warehouse Restaurant is a simple beamed room decorated with dozens of authentic "lace-plates" peculiar to the canals. It serves snacks and refreshments throughout the day, and an extensive à la carte menu is available. You may be lucky enough to be able to take a short trip on the canal in an authentic narrow boat. Admission is 80p ($1.20) for adults, 40p (60¢) for children. The warehouse is open during most of the year, but telephone to make sure.

BUXTON: One of the loveliest towns in Britain, Buxton was built in the 18th century to rival the spa at Bath. Although it eventually fell into a decline, it is now being considerably revived. The 18th-century opera house, for years the local movie palace, is being restored, and will be the centerpiece for a festival featuring Britain's National Theatre. Buxton is 20 miles southeast of Manchester and 163 miles northwest of London.

Of its old buildings, the finest is the Crescent, built by the fifth Duke of Devonshire between 1780 and 1784. The Pump Room, opened in 1894, now houses the **Tourist Information Centre,** in which you may drink the water from Buxton's natural springs.

Poole's Cavern, Buxton Country Park, Green Lane, in Buxton (tel. Buxton 6978), is a cave that was inhabited by Stone Age man, but now the only inhabitants are its visitors who marvel at the natural vaulted roof bedecked with stalactites. Explorers walk through the spacious galleries, viewing the incredible horizontal cave, electrically lighted. It is open from Easter until the first week in November from 10 a.m. to 5 p.m., charging a small admission fee.

Some 20 minutes away in Grin Low Woods is **Solomon's Temple,** a folly built in 1895 on a tumulus that dates from the Neolithic Age. Climb a small spiral staircase inside the temple for impressive views over Buxton and the surrounding country.

ASHBOURNE: This old market town has a 13th-century church, a 16th-century grammar school, and ancient almshouses.

For accommodations, I recommend—

The **Green Man & Blacks Head Royal Hotel,** St. John Street (tel. 0335/43861), in the town center, has many historical connections going back to 1710. In 1777 Dr. Samuel Johnson and his biographer, James Boswell, stayed at the inn, and Boswell writes, "I took my post-chaise from the Green Man, a very good inn." In the Tap Room you can still see the chairs of Boswell and Johnson. Even Princess Victoria and her widowed mother, the Duchess of Kent, halted here and gave the inn the right to add "Royal" to its name. This red brick posting inn has retained its traditional character, although modern amenities have been added. You can get a bathless double for £25 ($37.50); with bath, £32 ($48). Bathless singles are £18.50 ($27.75); with bath, £21 ($31.50). There are 17 rooms, each well decorated, and all tariffs include breakfast, early-morning coffee, and VAT. Service is extra. At lunch, you can enjoy the bar buffet, costing from £5 ($7.50) for three courses. Evening dinners are offered in the Shrovetide Restaurants, selections made from an à la carte menu.

On the Outskirts

Pervil of the Peak, Thorpe, near Ashbourne (tel. 033-529/333), is a low, rambling hotel that may have been the Thorpe rectory. Offering 29 handsomely furnished bedrooms, it stands at the foot of Thorpe Cloud, a 900-foot peak guarding the gateway to Dovedale, an area preserved by the National Trust that incorporates 5000 acres of the Peak District. A Trusthouses Forte hotel, it charges from £40 ($60) daily in a single with bath, including breakfast, service, and VAT. Doubles go for £55 ($82.50) with bath, including VAT and service. All units have private plumbing.

The interior is paneled in natural pine, combined with local stone walls, and large picture windows open onto the big country garden, where a hard tennis court is situated. The attractively decorated hotel restaurant offers à la carte meals.

DOVEDALE: Overhung by limestone crags, this beautiful wooded valley forms part of the Peak District National Park, with its views of Thorpe Cloud, a conical hill 900 feet high. It's best explored on foot. Fishermen know of its River Dove trout stream, because of its associations with such anglers as Izaak Walton and Charles Cotton. One is honored by the hotel named after him (previewed below).

The **Izaak Walton Hotel,** Dovedale (tel. 033-529/261). Even the telephone exchange—Thorpe Cloud—has a romantic ring about it. This is a very comfortable hotel in what was originally a 17th-century farmhouse. Most of the rooms have private bathrooms, and the views over the dales and peaks of Derbyshire are unsurpassed. This is ideal rambling country, with Dovedale spreading before you.

A single room with bath will cost £32 ($48) to £35 ($52.50); a double with bath, £45 ($67.50) to £48 ($72). These tariffs include service, an English breakfast, and VAT. A table d'hôte luncheon costs £5.50 ($8.25) to £8.50 ($12.75). A set dinner at £11.50 ($17.25) offers an excellent variety of appetizers, three entrees, and a cold buffet, followed by dessert and coffee.

This is the country for the fisherman, as the name implies, but if that is not your scene, it is an excellent center for touring, with Haddon Hall, Chatsworth House, and Hardwick Hall, to name but a few, lying within easy reach.

FOOD AND LODGING ELSEWHERE IN DERBYSHIRE: The **Howard Hotel,** Friar Gate, Derby (tel. Derby 43455), is a small elegant city house run by Geoffrey Price as a pleasant hotel, ideally situated for visitors to the peaks and dales or those just passing along the M1 from London to Scotland. Bedrooms are warm and comfortable, with color TV, radio, and wash basin, and go for £14 ($21) in a single, £18.50 ($27.75) to £19.50 ($29.25) in a double or twin. Room rates include a full English breakfast, and there is a pleasant dining room where a set meal costs from £7 ($10.50). In the cellars, reputedly part of the old Derby jail, lurks or burgeons the Judge Jeffreys, with music and dancing nightly until 2 a.m. Meals in the basket are served until 11 p.m.

Peacock Hotel, Rowsley, near Matlock (tel. 0629/733518), is a charming old house with a creeper covering the front door, where fishermen gather with tales of catches in the nearby Wye and Derwent Rivers. Just up the valley is Chatsworth House and down the road is Bakewell, where the tarts (a sort of macaroon with jam) come from. Accommodations reflect the informal country atmosphere, with patterned curtains, deep beds, and well-appointed baths. The lounge and dining room gleam with well-polished woods. The reception area is informal, decorated with trophies from bygone battles. A single room will cost £23 ($34.50) to £35 ($52.50), £36 ($54) to £46 ($69) in a double. Lunch is £7.50 ($11.25); dinner, £13.50 ($20.25). Meals are served beneath low beams in the dining room by friendly local waitresses. Details of nearby walks and other attractions are available, and the hotel has fishing rights on local waters.

Rutland Arms, The Square, Bakewell (tel. 062-981/2812), is a lovely old hotel on the edge of town, offering comfort and good food. There are a comfortable lounge and bar, plus a dining room that has an excellent local reputation. Dinner includes such delicacies as chicken suprême, wienerschnitzel, fresh seafood from the East Coast, and Scottish roast beef. A special three-course luncheon is offered for £5.50 ($8.25), £6.50 ($9.75) on Sunday. Rooms are well equipped and have private bathrooms. To keep costs down, there is no porterage or room service. Overnight will cost £28 ($42) in a single, £38 ($57) in a double, including VAT and service. Families can avail themselves of a three- or four-bed unit for £45 ($67.50).

Cavendish Hotel, Baslow, Bakewell (tel. 024-688/2311), built as the celebrated Peacock Inn in the 1780s, was restored in 1975 and extended in 1984. It has 23 well-equipped bedrooms, a commendable dining room, and drawing rooms with roaring log fires. The hotel is personally managed by its owner, Eric March, and run by his professional and friendly staff. The Cavendish is set on the Duke of Devonshire's Chatsworth Estate, which serves as a magnificent view from every room of the hotel and whose exclusive fishing is available for hotel guests. You look out upon the cavern-filled Derbyshire Peak District from your room, which has such amenities as TV, clock-radio, private bar, bathroom, and shower. Twins or doubles rent for £50 ($75); there are no singles. Lunch or dinner in the dining room costs from £10 ($15).

In the new wing of the hotel, for which the builders found secondhand stone to match exactly that in the original old fishing inn, the Mitford Rooms were named to honor the Duchess of Devonshire, each unit named after members of her Mitford family: Deborah, Diana, Jessica, Lucy, Nancy, Pamela, Sydney, Unity, Valkyrie, and Vivian. The duchess did the original Cavendish in 1975 and its sister hotel, the Devonshire Arms, at Bolton Abbey in 1981, borrowing furnishings from Chatsworth and also having much of the furniture made by hand in the Chatsworth workshop.

4. Nottinghamshire

"Notts," as it is called, was the county of Robin Hood and Lord Byron. It is also Lawrence country, as the English novelist, author of *Sons and Lovers* and *Lady Chatterley's Lover,* was also from here, born at Eastwood. Although Sherwood Forest isn't the green wood paradise it used to be, it did provide in its time excellent cover for its world-famous bandit and his band, including Friar Tuck and Little John.

Sherwood Forest is probably the most famous woodland in the world, yet very little of it was forest, even in the days of Robin Hood and his men. The area consists of woodland glades, fields, and agricultural land, along with villages and hamlets. The **Sherwood Forest Visitor Centre,** Sherwood Forest National Park at Edwinstowe, near Mansfield (tel. 0623/823202), has been opened in the area just by the Major Oak, known popularly as Robin Hood's tree. It's the center of many marked walks and footpaths through the woodland. There's an exhibition with life-size models of Robin Hood and the other well-known outlaws, as well as a shop with books, gifts, and souvenirs. Robin Hood's Larder offers light snacks and meals, with an emphasis on traditional English country recipes. It is open daily except Monday from 11 a.m. However, it is closed on Friday in winter. There is no admission charge to the center, which is on the B6034 north of Edwinstowe village, seven miles north of Mansfield.

Nottinghamshire is so rarely visited by foreign tourists that its beautiful landscapes could almost be called "undiscovered," although British trippers know of its hidden villages and numerous parks.

NOTTINGHAM: The county town is a busy industrial city, 121 miles north of London. On the north bank of the Trent, Nottingham is one of the most pleasant cities in the Midlands.

Overlooking the city, **Nottingham Castle** was built by the Duke of Newcastle on the site of a Norman fortress in 1679. After restoration in 1878, it was opened as a provincial museum (tel. 0602/411881), surrounded by a charmingly laid-out garden. See, in particular, the collection of medieval Nottingham alabaster carvings. The works of Nottingham-born artists are displayed in the first-floor gallery. The castle is open all year, except Christmas Day, from April to September, daily from 10 a.m. to 5:45 p.m. Otherwise, its hours are daily from 10 a.m. to 4:45 p.m. from October to March.

For 50p (75¢) you'll be taken on a conducted tour at the castle of **Mortimer's Hole** and underground passages. King Edward III is said to have led a band of noblemen through these secret passages, surprising Roger Mortimer and the queen, killing Mortimer, and putting his lady in prison. A statue of Robin Hood stands at the base of the castle.

More recently opened, the **Brewhouse Yard Museum** consists of five 17th-century cottages at the foot of Castle Rock, presenting a panorama of Nottingham life in a series of furnished rooms. Some of them, open from cellar to garret, have much local history material on open display, and visitors are encouraged to handle these exhibits. The most interesting features are in a series of cellars cut into the rock of the castle instead of below the houses. This is not a typical folk museum, but attempts to be as lively as possible, involving both visitors and the Nottingham community in expanding displays and altering exhibitions on a bimonthly basis. Open all year, the admission-free museum (tel. 0602/411881, extension 48) may be visited from 10 a.m. to 5 p.m. (except during the lunch hour from noon to 1 p.m.), but you must make reservations. It is closed Christmas.

An elegant row of Georgian terraced houses, the **Museum of Costume and Textiles** at Castle Gate, presents costumes from the 18th century to about 1960 in period settings, textiles, embroideries, and lace (one of the city's industries). You'll see everything from the 1632 Eyre map tapestries of Nottinghamshire to "fallals and frippery." The admission-free museum is open daily from 10 a.m. to 5 p.m.

On the outskirts of Nottingham, at Linby, **Newstead Abbey** (tel. 06234/2822) was once Lord Byron's home. It lies 11 miles north of Nottingham on the A60 (the Mansfield road). Some of the original Augustinian priory, bought by Sir John Byron in 1540, still survives. In the 19th century the mansion was given a neo-Gothic restoration. The poet's bedroom is somewhat as he left it. Mementos, including first editions and manuscripts, are displayed inside, and, later, you can explore a parkland of some 300 acres, with waterfalls, rose gardens, a Monk's Stew Pond, and a Japanese water garden.

The gardens are open all year from 10 a.m. to dusk. Adults are charged 60p (90¢) for admission; children pay 20p (30¢). The abbey is open from Easter to September 30, daily from 2 to 6 p.m. adults pay an admission of 50p (75¢); children, 10p (15¢). There is a tea room open during the summer.

Also on the outskirts of Nottingham, **Wollaton Hall** is a well-preserved Elizabethan mansion, housing a natural history museum, with lots of insects, invertebrates, British mammals and birds, reptiles, amphibians, and fish. The mansion is open April to September daily from 10 a.m. to 7 p.m., on Sunday from 2 to 5 p.m. From October to March daily, hours are 10 a.m. to dusk, from 1:30 to 4:30 p.m. on Sunday; closed Christmas Day. Admission is free except on Sunday and bank holidays. The hall is surrounded by a deer park and gardens.

Food and Lodging

Albany Hotel, St. James's Street (tel. 0602/40131), a Trusthouses Forte hotel, is a large tower block of 160 bedrooms in the heart of the city. Flanked by multistory car parks, it offers good rooms, each with private bath, double-glazed windows, air conditioning, and central heating, as well as a color TV, radio, direct-dial phone, and coffee-making facilities. Singles rent for £50 ($75) nightly and doubles go for £68 ($102).

In the hotel's Carvery, guests can carve as much as they wish from prime hot and cold joints, or else patronize the more elegant Four Seasons, which, in honor of its namesake, changes its menu and floral decorations quarterly. Along with seasonal specialties, continental dishes are featured. The Forum, the lounge and cocktail bar, is a sleek rendezvous.

Savoy Hotel, Mansfield Road (tel. 0602/602621), stands on the A60 Nottingham–Mansfield road, a little less than a mile from the city center. A bustling, modern hotel, it is immaculately maintained and efficiently run, and there's plenty of room to park your car. Attracting business people (and likely to be heavily booked on weekdays), it offers well-furnished, streamlined rooms for £28 ($42) daily in a single, £36 ($54) in a double, including private baths (some have showers), color TVs, radios, and phones. Have a predinner drink in Fagin's Bar, its decor inspired by the Dickensian atmosphere of the 19th century, before dining in one of two steak bars or the Colonial Restaurant. A five-course meal in the Colonial

Restaurant goes for about £7.50 ($11.25); however, an average meal in the Steak Bar ranges from £4 ($6) to £8 ($12).

Strathdon Hotel, 44 Derby Rd. (tel. 0602/418501), a favorite of traveling business people, lies about five miles from the M1, in the center of the city. Of the 67 bedrooms (the majority of which are singles), 23 come with private and pleasant tiled bath, the rest with shower, although all have color TV, phone, radio, and coffee-making facilities. Singles cost from £36 ($54) to £40 ($60); doubles or twins, from £42 ($63) to £46 ($69). The rate depends on the day of the week, weekends being cheaper. Some rooms have showers only. Drinks are ordered in the dark-paneled Mariners Tavern, decorated with fishing nets, ropes, ships' wheels, and portholes. In the hotel's restaurant, a good table d'hôte evening meal goes from £10 ($15), a set luncheon for £7.50 ($11.25), or you can order à la carte. The cookery is acceptable, and some international dishes are featured along with traditional English fare.

The **Castle Inn** (tel. 0602/413311), directly opposite the castle, is where Robert and Christina Latora provide excellent lunchtime snacks seven days a week. Quiches, ham, pâtés, and pork or chicken salad are featured, along with such hot dishes as chili con carne with french bread and a side salad. Fresh soup with french bread is a daily special, as are sandwiches. It is hard to believe, but the old building has only recently been converted into an attractive and olde-worlde-style pub. There is a circular staircase descending to a basement where the young can enjoy themselves while their elders relax upstairs after a visit to the castle.

Farmhouse Dining on the Outskirts

Grange Farm, Toton (tel. Long Eaton 69426), is an old English farmhouse, built in 1691, serving traditional English fare. This busy Nottinghamshire restaurant serves lunch Monday to Saturday from noon to 2 p.m., a set meal costing £6.50 ($9.75), inclusive of VAT, service charge, and coffee. The chefs prepare an excellent choice of interesting appetizers and many homemade English dishes—for example, steak-and-kidney pudding, venison pie, braised steak in burgundy sauce, followed by a large variety of desserts and cheeses. Dinner is served in two sittings, 7 and 8:30 p.m., a set meal costing £10 ($15), inclusive. Dinner is similar to lunch with an addition of an extra course. For example, you may also enjoy battered mushrooms in sweet-and-sour sauce or fried whitebait. It is advisable to telephone for a reservation to avoid disappointment. Saturday nights, the restaurant has a dinner-dance, which is popular. There is a fine collection of porcelain and ivories in the lounges which should be seen. Grange Farm has excellent car parking facilities and is six miles from Nottingham.

About a half-hour's drive from Lord Byron's Newstead Abbey leads to—

SOUTHWELL: This ancient market town is a good center for exploring the Robin Hood country. Byron once belonged to a local amateur dramatic society here. An unexpected gem is the old twin-spired cathedral, **Southwell Minster,** which many consider the most beautiful church in England. James I found that it held up with "any other kirk in Christendom." Look for the well-proportioned Georgian houses across from the cathedral.

Saracen's Head, Market Place (tel. Southwell 812701), is a historic coaching inn, where both Charles I and James I dined. In fact, Charles I was made a prisoner here before the Scots handed him over to the Parliamentarians. After he was beheaded, the name of the inn was changed from King's Arms to Saracen's Head. Commanding the junction of the main ancient thoroughfares of the town, the old hostelry also frequently entertained Byron. Today, your hosts are Joanna and René Koomen, who are proud of its old atmosphere, such as cozy bars with exposed beams and fine old paneling. The redecorated and refurbished bedrooms are up-to-date, however, each containing a private bath, TV, radio, and phone. Doubles cost from £47 ($70.50), and singles begin at £39 ($58.50). This includes a full English breakfast and VAT. From the well-stocked cellar emerges a good selection of wines to complement a meal, with both an à la carte and a table d'hôte menu.

East of Southwell, near the Lincolnshire border, is—

NEWARK-ON-TRENT: Here is an ancient riverside market town, on the Roman Fosse Way, lying about 15 miles across flatlands from Nottingham. King John died at **Newark Castle** in 1216. Constructed between the 12th and 15th centuries, the castle—now in ruins—survived three sieges by Cromwell's troops before falling into ruin in 1646. From its parapet, you can look down on the Trent River and across to Nottingham. The delicately detailed parish church here is said to be the finest in the country. The town contains many ancient inns, reflecting its long history.

Linked to the castle by a riverside walk, the **Millgate Museum of Folk Art** (tel. Newark-on-Trent 79403) was a 19th-century oil-seed mill, then a warehouse. Today it houses a fascinating collection of local products, domestic items in room settings, and dress, toy, and art shops. You'll see demonstrations of local crafts, such as matting, blacksmithing, and wood turning. Alongside are craft workshops where a host of young and enthusiastic artisans show and sell their wares. You can be sure of getting a unique and genuine article to take home.

THE DUKERIES: In the Dukeries, portions of Sherwood Forest, legendarily associated with Robin Hood, are still preserved. These are vast country estates on the edge of industrial towns. Most of the estates have disappeared, but the part at **Clumber**—covering some 4000 acres—is administered by the National Trust, which has preserved its 18th-century beauty, as exemplified by Lime Tree Avenue. Rolling heaths and a peaceful lake add to the charm. You can visit Clumber Chapel, built in 1886-1889 as a chapel for the seventh Duke of Newcastle. It is open April 1 to September 30 Monday to Friday from 2 to 7 p.m. On weekends its hours are noon to 6:30 p.m. Off-season hours are daily from noon to 3:30 p.m. There is no admission charge, but car entry charge to the park is £1.20 ($1.80). The location is at Clumber Park, five miles southeast of Worksop.

A few miles south of Clumber stands the greatest Victorian house in the Midlands, **Thoresby Hall,** a fine mansion in the heart of Sherwood Forest. Built by Salvin in 1864, this is the only palatial home in the Dukeries still occupied by the original owners' descendants. The hall is open to the public on Sunday and bank holidays during June, July, and August. For further information, telephone the estate office, Thoresby Park (tel. 0623/822301). It lies four miles north of Ollerton, just west of the Bawtry road, the A614.

EASTWOOD: Because of the increased interest in D. H. Lawrence these days, many literary fans like to make a pilgrimage to Eastwood, his hometown. The English novelist was born there on September 11, 1885. Mrs. Brown, a member of the D. H. Lawrence Society, conducts parties of visitors around the "Lawrence country." Hopefully, at the end, you'll make a donation to the society. If you're interested in taking a tour, write her in advance—Mrs. Moina Brown, D. H. Lawrence Society, 136 Moorgreen, Newthorpe, Notts. NG16 2FE (tel. Langley Mill 68139).

Lawrence's **Birthplace/Museum** is at 8A Victoria St. Admission is 25p (38¢).

SCROOBY: This is a tiny village of some 260 inhabitants where in 1566 William Brewster, a leader of the Pilgrim Fathers, was born. His father was bailiff of the manor and master of the postes, so it may have been in the Manor House that the infant Brewster first saw the light of day. The original house dated from the 12th century, and the present manor farm, built on the site in the 18th century, has little except historical association to attract.

Brewster Cottage, with its pinfold where stray animals were impounded, lies beside the village church of St. Wilfred. But it's uncertain whether the Pilgrim father ever lived there.

The village also contains Monks Mill on the River Ryton, now almost a backwater but once a navigable stream down which Brewster and his companions may have escaped to travel to Leyden in Holland and on to their eventual freedom.

In the 18th century the turnpike ran through the village, and there are many stories of highwaymen, robberies, and murders. The body of one John Spencer hung for more than 60 years as a reminder of the penalties of wrongdoing. He'd attempted to dispose of the bodies of the keeper of the Scrooby toll-bar and his mother in the river.

READER'S SEARCH FOR PILGRIM ROOTS: "Since so many North Americans are descended from the Pilgrims, I feel certain that there are many who, like me, might be eager to see the area from which their ancestors came. The Separatist movement started in a section north of Nottingham and south of York. The towns from which its members came are all in a small area, and include **Blyth, Scrooby, Austerfield, Bawtry,** and **Babworth.** Both the Scrooby and Babworth churches welcome North American visitors. William Brewster, the Pilgrim Father, lived in Scrooby, and his farmhouse is still standing, identified by a plaque. William Bradford's birthplace was a manor house in Austerfield, well maintained, which can be visited by arrangement with the occupant. We did not see Babworth, but of the other towns, Blyth was the most delightful, a village of 900 with a beautiful green surrounded by lovely old houses. The parish church was developed from the 11th-century Norman nave of a Benedictine priory church, and on the green is a 12th-century stone building, once the Hospital of St. John.

"Blyth can also boast of a fine, small hotel with an excellent dining room, the **Fourways Hotel** (tel. Blyth 235). Rates for a large room and breakfast are about £30 ($45) for two persons.

"This Blyth, by the way, is not to be confused with the Blyth on the northeastern coast of England" (Miriam C. Timbrell, Hackettstown, N.J.).

5. Lincolnshire

This large East Midlands county is bordered on one side by the North Sea. Its most interesting section is Holland, in the southeast, a land known for its fields of tulips, its marshes and fens, and windmills reminiscent of The

Netherlands. Although much of the shire is interesting to explore, time is too important for most visitors to linger long. Foreign tourists, particularly North Americans, generally cross the tulip fields, scheduling stopovers in the busy port of Boston before making the swing north to the cathedral city of Lincoln, lying inland.

BOSTON: This old seaport in the riding of Holland has a namesake that has gone on to greater glory, and perhaps for this reason it is visited by New Englanders. At Scotia Creek, on a riverbank near Boston, is a memorial to the early Pilgrims who made an unsuccessful attempt in 1607 to reach the promised land. They were imprisoned in the Guildhall in cells that can be visited today. A company left again in 1620—and fared better, as anybody who has ever been to Massachusetts will testify. Part of the ritual here is climbing the **Boston Stump,** a church lantern tower with a view for miles around of the all-encircling fens. In the 1930s the people of Boston, U.S.A., paid for the restoration of the tower, known officially as St. Botolph's Tower. Actually, it's not recommended that you climb the tower, as the stairs aren't in good shape. The tower, as it stands, was finished in 1460. The city fathers were going to add a spire, making it the tallest in England. But because of the wind and the weight, they feared the tower would collapse. Therefore, the tower became known as "the Boston Stump." An elderly gentleman at the tower assured me it was the tallest in England—that is, 272½ feet tall. Boston is 116 miles north from London, and 34 miles southeast of Lincoln.

The center of Boston is closed to cars, and you will have to walk to visit the church and the Guildhall.

Food and Lodging

White Hart Hotel, High Street (tel. 0205/64877), is a gleaming white hotel, built against the high wall of a canal embankment. Singles rent for from £22 ($33) to £28 ($42), and doubles or twins from £35 ($52.50) to £42 ($63), the difference depending on the plumbing. These tariffs include a full breakfast, service, and VAT. Rooms are pleasantly furnished, with central or electrical heating and a radio, and are kept immaculate. A bonus is the free car park at the rear of the hotel (you drive through an old coaching alleyway).

The White Hart contains half a dozen bars, each one decorated differently, serving draft sherries and beer, as well as spirits and food. Of the two restaurants, one features duck and steak dishes; the other, fish and chicken specialties. A meal costs around £10 ($15) to £15 ($22.50), and hours are from noon to 2:30 p.m. and 6 to 11 p.m.

LINCOLN: One of the most ancient cities of England, and only 135 miles north of London, Lincoln was known to the Romans as Lindum. Some of the architectural glory of the Roman Empire still stands to charm the present-day visitor. The renowned Newport Arch (the North Gate) is the last remaining arch left in Britain that still spans a principal highway. For a look at the Roman relics excavated in and around Lincoln, head for the **City and County Museum,** Broadgate (tel. 0522/30401), open daily from 10 a.m. to 5:30 p.m. (2:30 to 5 p.m. on Sunday).

Two years after the Battle of Hastings, William the Conqueror built a castle on the site of a Roman fortress. Used for administrative purposes, parts of the castle still remain, including the walls, the 12th-century keep, and fragments of the gateway tower. In addition, you can visit the High Bridge over the Witham River, with its half-timbered houses (you can have a meal in one of them). This is one of the few medieval bridges left in England that has buildings nestling on it.

Lincoln Cathedral

Towering over the ancient city, the Minster forms a grand sight, with its three towers. The central one is 271 feet tall, making it the second tallest in England, ranking under the Boston Stump, mentioned earlier. However, the central tower at Lincoln was once the tallest spire in the world (525 feet) until it blew down in 1549. There are regular summer trips up the tower on weekdays, for which a small fee is charged. The Norman cathedral was consecrated in 1092, but only the west front remains. The cathedral represents the Gothic style, particularly the Early English and Decorated periods. The nave, in its present form, was built in the early 13th century. In the Early English Great Transept, you can see a rose medallion window, known as the Dean's Eye. The rose window at the opposite end of the transept—in the Decorated style—is known as the Bishop's Eye. The Angel Choir, in the eastern end, consecrated on October 6, 1280, is named after the sculptured angels displayed in it. The exquisite carving in the choir dates from the 14th century. The black font of Tournai marble is from the 11th century. One of the most interesting features of the cathedral is the roof bosses, which date from the 12th and 13th centuries. While most of them are 70 feet in the air and not visible to the viewer below, those in the Cloister are of oak, and some are only 12 feet from the ground.

In the Seamen's Chapel is a window commemorating Lincolnshire-born Capt. John Smith, one of the pioneers of early settlement in America and the first governor of Virginia.

The Library, in the Cloister, was built in 1674 by Sir Christopher Wren. It contains many fine books and manuscripts, some of which are on view in the adjoining Medieval Library (1422), together with one of the four remaining original copies of the Magna Carta of 1215, the Cathedral Charter of 1072, and the Foresters' Charter of 1225. The Library is open Monday through Saturday, from 10:30 a.m. to 4:30 p.m., Easter through September, and in winter by appointment (tel. 0522/21089).

In the Treasury (open weekdays 2:30 to 4:30 p.m., Easter through September), there is fine gold and silver plate from churches in the diocese.

Required donation to the cathedral is 50p (75¢) for adults, 20p (30¢) for children, or £1 ($1.50) for a family.

Where to Stay

Eastgate Post House, Eastgate (tel. 0522/20341), should put to shame those critics who resist contemporary architecture, especially in old English cathedral cities. A hotel attached to a Victorian mansion (now the Eastgate Bar), the Trusthouse occupies a historic site: in fact, when workmen were digging its foundations in the mid-'60s, they discovered the remnants of the north tower of the East Gate of Roman Lincoln. The hotel is well sited, overlooking Lincoln Cathedral. A well-preserved part of the Roman city wall is included in the rear garden. All 71 bedrooms have private baths, showers, color TVs, radios, private bars, and tea- and coffee-making facilities. Rates are £39 ($58.50) in a single, £48 ($72) in a double- or twin-bedded room, including service and VAT.

Breakfast, lunch, and dinner are served in the Palatinate Restaurant, which also overlooks the cathedral and is known for its good service and cuisine. The cost of a table d'hôte lunch is £8 ($12), with a fixed-price dinner going for £10 ($15). Both are inclusive of coffee, service, and VAT, and offer a choice within each course. Alternatively, you may wish to choose from the extensive à la carte menu. The coffeeshop serves grills and snacks. There are two bars in the hotel, one of which, the Eastgate, is open late for residents. There is free car parking space for up to 120 vehicles at the front and rear of the hotel.

The **White Hart,** Bailgate (tel. 0522/26222), is a red brick Georgian inn, with its corner clock and miniature figure of a white hart, right in the shadow of the cathedral, within the range of its chimes. On Lincoln's historic mile, the inn is unpretentious, and skillfully operated by a well-trained staff. Oldtimers respect the ambience, as reflected in the large living room opening onto a hothouse and patio garden. High mahogany cabinets hold a collection of old silver and porcelain; overstuffed chairs are set around tables for after-dinner coffee; and there are antiques in the reception lounges and corridors, including the more intimate upstairs residents' lounge. The bedrooms have nice old furnishings, with such pieces as a pedestal swivel mirror or a mahogany table. Each has a telephone and radio, and many have private baths.

Depending on the facilities, singles range in price from £42 ($63), and doubles go from £54 ($81). In the olive and red dining room, you'll be served some of the finest English fare in Lincoln. Very good sandwiches are served with coffee or tea in the lounge throughout the day, and you can also enjoy the same in a patio and garden bar known as the Orangery, a bright and cheerful place to meet friends and enjoy a selection from the buffet of hot and cold dishes and from the self-service salad bar. Prices are around £3.50 ($5.25) for a plate and coffee.

Grand Hotel, St. Mary Street (tel. 0522/24211), is an extensively remodeled hotel, top-heavy with contemporary amenities and a cooperative staff. You'll pay around £40 ($60) for a double with a private bath. Singles go for £30 ($45) with bath. The Grand's program of redecorating has given it a pleasant, spacious look. The West Bar and the lounges are streamlined, but the Tudor Bar pays homage to the past. The bedrooms are compact, with many built-in features and coordinated colors. The Grand is easy to spot, as it lies opposite the bus depot. It's a long walk to the cathedral, however, but you can hop a bus. Its food is a top-notch bargain, both in price and taste. From 7 to 8:30 p.m., a table d'hôte dinner is offered for £7.50 ($11.25). Meals are inclusive, priced according to the entree. The food is not only good and typically English, but the portions are ample. You can also lunch at the Grand from noon to 2 p.m. A buttery is open from 11 a.m. to 10 p.m.

The **Duke William Hotel,** 44 Bailgate (tel. 0522/30257), is in the heart of historic Lincoln near the Roman arch, within walking distance of the cathedral. Although the structure has seen many architectural changes since its establishment in 1791, care has been taken to preserve the atmosphere of an 18th-century inn. Many of the rooms still have their original heavy timbers. All of them contain TV sets. A single rents for £15 ($22.50) to £21 ($31.50); doubles, £25 ($37.50) to £32 ($48).

The hotel has both an inexpensive and good restaurant and a cozy bar.

An unpretentious but tasty luncheon is served from noon to 2:30 p.m. Monday to Saturday. Only cold snacks are served on Sunday, from noon to 1:45 p.m. Dinners are more elaborate, served Monday to Saturday from 7:30 to 9:30 p.m. A three-course meal of pâté with toast, pork marsala with fresh vegetables, and a dessert costs about £10 ($15).

The **D'Isney Place Hotel,** Eastgate (tel. 0522/38881), is a small, family-owned hostelry close to the cathedral, the Minster Yard, the castle, and the Bailgate shops. It was built in 1735 and later extended. The cathedral close's wall and towers, built in 1285, form the southern boundary of the house gardens. Each room is uniquely decorated, with a large bath, radio, phone, color TV, and tea- and coffee-making facilities. The proprietors, David and Judy Payne, charge £29 ($43.50) for a single, £40 ($60) for a double, with either a full English or a continental breakfast served in your room. There is car parking space in the hotel grounds.

Where to Eat

Harveys Cathedral Restaurant, 1 Exchequergate, Castle Square (tel. 0522/21886), lies in the heart of the old town, a short walk from the cathedral and the castle. My favored dining spot in the city, it is run by Adrianne and Bob Harvey, whose children may occasionally be glimpsed helping in the background. It is housed in a stately Georgian building which, until recently, was reputed to be haunted, but the cozy Victorian decor has routed any dismal spirits. The motto of the Harveys is "Simple lunches—superb dinners," and they live up to this with a lunch menu offering traditional English dishes such as farmhouse chicken pie and beef in Guinness, followed by Victorian sherry trifle. Start with Bob's homemade pâté or warming soup, always freshly made. Lunch will cost around £6.50 ($9.75).

In the evenings the restaurant is candlelit and bubbles with a romantic atmosphere (reservations are essential on weekends). The Harveys offer a table d'hôte gourmet menu at £15 ($22.50), fully inclusive. This consists of a special soup or fruit dish, followed by the appetizer course, with a choice of fish, savory dishes, or pâté. Then there is a selection of seven main dishes, including French and "Taste of England" specialties. A massive choice of cheeses follows, with a finale of diet-beating homemade desserts and ice creams, plus the bottomless coffee cup and mints. Almost everything the Harveys serve is homemade, and all ingredients are fresh.

Finally, if you're in Lincoln over a weekend, take in a traditional Sunday lunch here. You won't taste better roast beef anywhere, but remember to reserve your table. The restaurant is open for lunch daily except Monday in winter, from noon to 1:45 p.m. Dinners are from 7:30 to 9:30 p.m. Tuesday through Saturday.

Green Dragon, Broadgate (tel. 0522/24950), near the river, about a block from The High, is one of Lincoln's most attractive buildings, sheltering both pubs and a dining room. Actually, it's comprised of a row of 16th-century houses, black-and-white timbered, joined together and heavily reconstructed to create an inviting ambience.

A set lunch is featured for £5.50 ($8.25). If you're ordering à la carte, you'll find a wide menu selection, with a meal costing from £8 ($12).

STAMFORD: This charming stone-built market town, lying 89 miles from London, is visited chiefly for the following attraction:

Burghley House (tel. 0780/52451) is the home of the sixth Marquis of Exeter. The house, on the outskirts of Stamford, was built in 1564 on the remains of a monastery founded in 1158. Ten years later, and again in 1589, additions were made. At this magnificent Elizabethan house you will see a collection of paintings which includes a Rubens, Chippendale furniture, and Adam fireplaces. It is said that nobody has slept in the Queen Elizabeth I bedroom since the monarch was last here. From the window you can see a lime tree she planted in the 16th century. The present growth sprang from the roots of the original tree. The kitchen found in the oldest part of the house is huge. A whole ox could be roasted on the spit. The house is open from 11 a.m. to 5 p.m., on Sunday from 2 to 5 p.m. Admission is £1.50 ($2.25) for adults, 70p ($1.05) for children.

Lady Anne's Hotel, 37–38 High St., St. Martins (tel. 0780/53175), is named after Lady Anne Cecil, a young and favorite sister of the ninth Earl of Exeter. She lived in the original building for many years, but it has seen many changes before emerging as a pleasant country hotel. Bedrooms come in a wide range: some have very small showers while others are light and airy with baths and toilets en suite. Prices range from £14 ($21) per person in a double without bath to £18.50 ($27.75) per person in a double with complete bath. Single occupancy starts at £16 ($24). These rates are inclusive of tea or coffee, a morning paper, and a large English breakfast. Outside is a good car park, and inside there's a welcoming log fire in the bar. Bedrooms have individual TV sets, although there's a large one in the chintz-decorated lounge. The hotel has 30 bedrooms.

The cottage-y dining room has a pleasant but simple menu of grills and fish dishes, including trout cooked in white wine and butter, scampi provençale, ham with pineapple, and duckling in orange sauce. You can also order a large grilled steak. In season, venison pie and pheasant are specialties. Desserts are luscious and homemade. Anne Hastings supervises the kitchen and makes the desserts herself. Expect to spend from £8.50 ($12.75) for a meal. It's also possible to order snack meals. Anne's husband, Geoffrey, cooks flambé meals in the restaurant. Together, they offer barbecues in the garden during the summer. In winter, dinner-dances are held on Saturday night.

WANSFORD-IN-ENGLAND: Instead of staying at Lady Anne's Hotel in Stamford, an ideal alternative lies just off the A1 road to the north in a pleasant village of stone houses with a wide, typical English main street.

It's the **Haycock Hotel**, at Wansford, near Peterborough (tel. 0780/782223). A stone in the garden dates the present building from 1632, although an inn has existed on this site for many years. The inn is built around a courtyard with stone archways and mullioned windows. It is said that Mary Queen of Scots, on her way to imprisonment in 1586 at Fotheringhay, visited the inn. In later years Queen Victoria stopped by when she was still a princess. Many stories of bygone times exist, and you need to visit the place to discover more of its history.

Many of the bedrooms have four-posters, some have private baths, and all contain phones and color TVs. Your overnight charge includes early-morning tea and a newspaper, then a full English breakfast. Singles range from £13 ($19.50) to £34 ($51), the cheapest rate being for a no-bath, weekend stay; the top price is charged for a midweek occupancy with bath. The same rules apply for twins and doubles, which start at £40

($60) and rise to £55 ($82.50), which provides you with a four-poster bed.

Downstairs the busy bar caters to locals and guests alike. If you don't want to order a full meal in the dining room, you can eat heartily from a wide range of bar snacks. Meals are à la carte, averaging about £11 ($16.50), and you might choose to start with pâté or a prawn, pineapple, and cucumber cocktail, followed by roast beef and Yorkshire pudding. For dessert, you can make a selection from the trolley. However, I prefer Melton Mowbray stilton cheese, as this is the homeland of that famous English cheese.

Chapter XV

CHESHIRE, LIVERPOOL, AND THE LAKES

ONE OF ENGLAND'S most popular summer retreats in Victoria's day was the Lake District in the northwest. It enjoyed vogue during the flowering of the Lake Poets, including Wordsworth, who was ecstatically moved by the rugged beauty of this area. In its time the district has lured such writers as S. T. Coleridge, Charles Lamb, Shelley, Keats, Alfred Lord Tennyson, Matthew Arnold, and Charlotte Brontë.

The Lake District is a miniature Switzerland condensed into about 32 miles, principally in Cumbria, although it begins in the northern part of Lancashire.

As an added bonus, I've included Liverpool, plus Cheshire, a county that lies south of Lancashire. I suggest that you make a pilgrimage to the ancient city of Chester, with its medieval walls, near the border of Wales.

The northwest of England is one of the special parts of the country, yet it is rarely visited by the agenda-loaded foreigner, who considers it too far removed. In many ways, however, its remoteness is part of its charm. Have you ever seen one of those English-made films depicting the life of the Lake District? A soft mist hovers over the hills and dells, sheep graze silently on the slope of the pasture—and a foggy enchantment fills the air.

But first—

CHESHIRE

This county is low lying and largely agricultural. The name it gave to a cheese—and a cat—(Cheshire) has spread across the world. This north-western county borders Wales, which accounts for its turbulent history. The towns and villages of Cheshire are peaceful and quiet—forming a good base for touring North Wales, the most beautiful part of that little country. For our headquarters in Cheshire, we'll locate at:

1. Chester

Chester is ancient, having been founded by a Roman legion on the Dee River in the first century A.D. It reached its pinnacle as a bustling port in the 13th and 14th centuries, declining thereafter following the gradual silting up of the river. The upstart Liverpudlians captured the sea-trafficking business. The other walled medieval cities of England were either torn down or badly fragmented, but Chester still retains two miles of fortified city walls intact.

The main entrance into Chester is Eastgate, itself dating back to only the 18th century. Within the walls are half-timbered houses and shops. Of course, not all of them came from the days of the Tudors. Chester is freakish architecturally in that some of its builders kept to the black-and-white timbered facades—even when erecting buildings during the Georgian and Victorian periods, with their radically different tastes.

The Rows are double-decker layers of shops—one tier on the street level, the other stacked on top and connected by a footway. The upper tier is like a continuous galleried balcony. Shopping upstairs is much more adventurous than down on the street. Rain is never a problem. Thriving establishments operate in this traffic-free paradise: tobacco shops, restaurants, department stores, china shops, jewelers, even antique dealers. For the most representative look, take an arcaded walk on Watergate Street.

At noon and at 3 p.m. daily at the City Cross, the world's champion town crier issues his news (local stuff on sales, exhibitions, and attractions in the city) at the top of his not-inconsiderable voice, to the accompaniment of a hand bell—at the junction of Watergate(!), Northgate, and Bridge Streets. Eastgate Street is now a pedestrian way, and musicians often play for their—and your—pleasure beside St. Peter's Church and the Town Cross.

You can go by boat bus to the Chester **Zoo.** An all-in ticket covers the cost of the ride to the zoo, one way by horse-drawn boat, one way by bus from the Town Hall Bus Exchange, and admission to the zoo. Boats leave Tower Wharf at noon every Sunday and Tuesday during summer, returning at 2:30 p.m. The voyage along the canal takes about 1½ hours. The zoo is one of the largest and most attractive in the country, and the canal enables you to see many of the exhibits by water. The cost of the ticket is £4 ($6) for adults, £2.75 ($4.13) for children. It's an ideal way to entertain youngsters.

After exploring The Rows, focus your attention on:

CHESTER CATHEDRAL: The present building founded in 1092 as a Benedictine abbey was created as a cathedral church in 1541. Considerable architectural restorations were carried out in the 19th century, but older parts have been preserved. Notable features include the fine range of monastic buildings, particularly the cloisters and refectory, the chapter house, and the superb medieval wood carving in the quire (especially the misericords). Also worth attention are the long south transept with its various chapels, the consistory court, and the medieval roof bosses in the Lady Chapel. A free-standing bell tower, the first to be built in England since the Reformation, was completed in 1975 and may be seen southeast of the main building. For more information, telephone 0244/24756.

CHESTER'S PAST: The **British Heritage Exhibition,** Vicars Lane (tel. 0244/42222), in a severe brick building opposite the Roman amphitheater, only minutes from the city center, shows a 20-minute audio-visual account of 2000 years of Chester's history. The drama ranges from the Roman occupation of the city to life in medieval times and up to the heyday of Victorian Chester. Afterward, you can wander through the exhibits, the reconstructed Victorian Chester street, the Map and Print Room with its fine drawings and large-scale architectural models of houses and shops. There is also a brass-rubbing center where materials and instructions are provided, and you can go away with a rubbing for as little as 60p (90¢). It is open from April to September weekdays from 9 a.m. to 5 p.m., on Sunday from 2 to 5 p.m. Admission is 90p ($1.35) for adults, 45p (68¢) for children. This is undoubtedly one of the most exciting living exhibitions in Chester and in the country.

WHERE TO STAY: The **Chester Grosvenor Hotel,** Eastgate Street (tel. 0244/24024), in a fine, half-timbered building in the heart of Chester, has a well-deserved high reputation. I always tend to gravitate toward "the Grosvenor," as the locals call it, where I can not only enjoy the attention and care the hotel offers but also see and sometimes talk with residents— wealthy landowners, industrialists, and lords and ladies of the manors who visit for morning coffee or spend a night or two of pampered relaxation from the hunting field and do a little shopping in the next-door Rows. The high, marble-floored foyer of the hotel, with its 200-year-old chandelier, carved wooden staircase, and antiques, sets the tone. The general manager and director, Richard Edwards, has placed his stamp firmly on the hotel. An expert, he has a happy and friendly staff to back him up.

The bedrooms are large and elegantly furnished. All have radios, color TVs, direct-dial phones, refrigerated bars, and in-house video. Private baths are well equipped with various accessories, such as hair dryers, bath salts, and emergency packs. Rates start at £40 ($60) for a single, rising to £56 ($84) in doubles and twins, and £65 ($97.50) in triples. VAT is included in the tariffs.

The hotel has two bars: the Arkle Bar, named after one of the world's most celebrated racehorses and furnished accordingly, and the Grosvenor Bar in the cellars, where at lunchtime you can get a light meal. If you are in town for lunch at the hotel, a buffet meal will cost £7.50 ($11.25). If you prefer, you can choose from the à la carte menu with a three-course meal costing around £13 ($19.50). Dinnertime is when the chef, Gilbert Schneider, excels. A set four-course repast goes for £11 ($16.50), or you can choose from the à la carte selection, with a three-course dinner, including coffee, tabbed at £15 ($22.50) to £18 ($27).

Blossoms Hotel, St. John Street (tel. 0244/23186), has been in business since the mid-17th century, although the present structure was rebuilt late in Victoria's day. Each of the 70 traditionally furnished bedrooms is equipped with central heating, and all have private baths. Each room has a telephone and radio, as well as color TV and coffee maker. The price for B&B in a single is from £35 ($52.50); in a twin or double, from £48 ($72). The old open staircase in the reception room sets the tone of the hotel. Dinner is served in the Egerton Room from 7 to 9:30 p.m., both a carving table selection at £6.95 ($10.43) and à la carte. The Snooty Fox coffeeshop, open from noon to 2:30 p.m., offers a limited menu served on Sunday from noon to 2 p.m. They have crusty "French logs" filled with cheese and onion, ham and salad, or beef and salad, baked potatoes with a number of toppings, and the chef's daily hot specialties, which might include the traditional English pork pie. Meals start at £4 ($6).

Rowton Hall, Whitchurch Road (tel. 0244/335262), is a stately home, two miles from the city center, which offers overnight accommodation for motorists. The gracious house, built in 1797, with a later wing added, is nearly covered with green ivy, and stands on its own eight-acre garden, with a formal driveway entrance. The Hall, owned by Stuart and Diana Begbie, has comfortable traditional and contemporary furnishings. All bedrooms have baths, a single renting for £30 ($45) and a double for £44 ($66). All prices include a full English breakfast and VAT. A set lunch costs from £6.50 ($9.75). Dinner ordered from the à la carte menu will probably come to £12 ($18) and up. The good English meals are served in the oak-paneled dining room with its Tudor fireplace. In winter, dinner-dances are sometimes held on Saturday. The hotel stands on the site of the battle of Rowton Moor, which was fought in 1643 between the Roundheads and the Cavaliers.

Ye Olde Kings Head, 48/50 Lower Bridge Street (tel. 0244/324855), is a 17th-century museum piece of black-and-white architecture. From 1598 to 1707, it was occupied by the well-known Randle Holme family of Chester, noted heraldic painters and genealogists (some of their manuscripts have made it to the British Museum). Since 1717 the Kings Head has been a licensed inn. The host rents out a dozen handsome bedrooms at £20 ($30) for a single room, £28 ($42) for a double. A full English breakfast is included. The bedchambers are linked with the past; many of the walls and ceilings are sloped and highly pitched, with exposed beams.

The residents' lounge, with its massive beams overhead, boasts a Tudor fireplace, and authentic furnishings, including an elaborate grandfather clock, an octagonal card table, high-backed Jacobean oak chairs, and soft upholstered pieces. The main lounge has a number of wall settles, barrel tables, wood paneling, and a Tudor fireplace. The 17th-century dining room is also a showcase of timberwork, with old furnishings, such as a Welsh cupboard and pewter and copper pieces. Hotel owners Marie and Robert Musker have a popular eating place too, in the Kings Kitchen, downstairs in the main bar. Here you can get bar snacks daily all year, and the salad bar in summer is excellent.

The **Belgrave Hotel,** City Road (tel. 0244/312138). Derek and Alma Wood have concentrated on friendly service in their Victorian-era hotel, within a stone's throw of the railway station and within easy walking distance of the city center. They charge around £14 ($21) a night for B&B.

WHERE TO EAT: The Courtyard, 13 St. Werburgh St. (tel. 0244/318973), was originally a stable courtyard, opposite the south transept of the

cathedral. Today, it's been turned into one of the finest dining spots in Chester. The narrow entrance, with its black-and-white decorative motif, sets the stage for a two-in-one restaurant. Opening into the inner courtyard is the ingeniously designed split-level bistro, which offers a luncheon buffet from noon to 2:30 p.m.

A smörgåsbord lunch is individually priced with hot dishes, cold meats, and salads. Prices range from £3 ($4.50). From 6 to 10 p.m. the restaurant offers a bistro dinner where you can serve yourself for an inclusive price of £10 ($15). It's good value. A more elaborate à la carte menu costing from £12 ($18) is available from 7 to 10 p.m., including items such as veal in orange and rum sauce. A specialty appetizer is Raymond's homemade pâté, or you might try mushrooms Armenienne cooked in red wine, bacon, and garlic. The chef's desserts include walnut fudge.

The Courtyard cellar is open nightly for dancing Monday to Friday. The restaurant is open Monday to Saturday and is closed on bank holidays.

The Witches Kitchen, Frodsham Street (tel. 0244/311836), is in the center of town, just a short walk from the station. It seats 100 and has old-world charm and good service. The ground-floor restaurant is 15 yards from the city walls and Chester Cathedral. It is open every day for luncheon (11:30 a.m. till 5:30 p.m.), afternoon tea (3 to 5 p.m.), and dinner (7 to 10:30 p.m.). Quick-lunch main-course dishes begin at £2 ($3). An à la carte menu with a wide variety of traditional dishes is served throughout the day—for example, roast beef and Yorkshire pudding and other roasts, beginning at £3.50 ($5.25). Included in the price is a selection of fresh vegetables in season. Desserts are excellent as well. On Sunday you can enjoy the traditional roast beef lunch, and on Saturday night a carvery with succulent roasts. A children's menu is always available, and the restaurant has a fully licensed cocktail bar.

Jean's Kitchen, 1 Newtown Close, St. Anne Street (tel. 0244/381313), owned by Ken Waterhouse, offers a table d'hôte luncheon that continues up to 7 p.m. at a cost of around £4.50 ($9.75). Dinner from the à la carte menu will cost about £12 ($18) per person. Specialties include mushrooms cooked in wine, seafood salad with rice, thin steak smothered in a cheese and tomato sauce, or boeuf bourguignon, followed by the richest desserts in Chester. Wine is French, a small bottle costing from £3 ($4.50).

The Royal Oak, Foregate Street (tel. 0244/314336), is a 17th-century building with a nice old paneled dining room where a set three-course lunch with two or three choices for each course will cost £4.50 ($6.75). Or else a meal chosen from the à la carte menu will go for £7.50 ($11.25). Choose from spicy tomato soup with cream, then chicken schnitzel with sweet corn relish, a jacket potato and vegetables, or lamb cutlets with peas and fried potatoes, grilled plaice with chips, followed by a large slice of Black Forest cake. Steaks, grilled to your specification and served with jacket or fried potatoes, peas, and tomato, are also served. You can have snacks in the Long Bar if you don't have time to stop for a meal.

Some Local Pubs

The **Bear & Billet Hotel,** 94 Lower Bridge St. (tel. 0244/321272), formerly the town house of the Earls of Shrewsbury, was built in 1644 and many of the original beams are still in place. It has been recently renovated and has three floors where food and drinks are served. All the food is good English "fayre." Prices range from 50p (75¢) to £7 ($10.50).

An alternative for drinking is the **Boot Inn,** Eastgate Street, established in 1643, making it even older than the Bear & Billet. It's the smallest and most unspoiled pub in Chester. Only oldtimers and those on the "in" know about it. It's reached by entering a passageway along the upper Rows of Eastgate Street. The publican has a multitude of mementos cluttering the walls—horse brasses, steins, curios from everywhere, even brass crocodiles and castanets.

AN EXCURSION TO CONWY CASTLE (WALES): The most popular

excursion from Chester is to the castle and walled town of Conwy in Wales, a distance of some 48 miles. The town contains many interesting old buildings, including the National Trust property of Aberconwy, Plas Mawr, and what is said to be the smallest house in Britain.

However, the major interest, of course, centers on **Conwy Castle,** built between 1283 and 1289 and considered a perfect specimen of medieval fortifications in Britain. Following the contours of a narrow strip of rock, the eight towers of the castle dominate the estuary of the River Conwy. The castle stands at the harbor where the river finds its way to the sea. From these old walls you can see the small fishing fleet at anchor in the sheltered harbor. Fishermen bring in their catch of mussels and Conwy dabs here.

The castle (tel. Conwy 2358) is open daily from 9:30 a.m. to 6:30 p.m. from mid-March to mid-October. Otherwise, it is open weekdays from 9:30 a.m. to 4 p.m. and on Sunday from 2 to 4 p.m. The summer admission charge is 60p (90¢) for adults, 30p (45¢) for children. In winter, charges are cut in half.

The town wall, which protected the borough laid out by Edward I below the castle, is still nearly intact. It is flanked by 21 towers and pierced by three twin-towered gateways.

2. Nantwich

The old market town on the Weaver River lies only 15 miles southeast of the county town of Chester, and can easily be tied in with a visit to that city. The town is particularly outstanding because of its black-and-white timbered houses. The most spectacular one, Churche's Mansion, is one of my dining recommendations.

WHERE TO STAY: Crown Hotel and Restaurant, High Street (tel.

0270/625283), is a black-and-white timbered structure, with leaded windows and an archway for carriages. The hotel was rebuilt in 1583 after a fire. Most attractive, the Crown offers guest rooms where you can immerse yourself in the charm of old England for £15 ($22.50) in a bathless single, £22 ($33) in a single with bath. In a twin or double without bath, the rate is £30 ($45), going up to £34 ($51) with bath, these tariffs including a full English breakfast, service, and VAT. The plank floors are so slanted you have to be careful not to lose your balance. The tavern and lounge blend antiquity with charm. The unique Georgian Assembly Room attached to the Crown has been restored, redecorated, and refurnished in the style of the period, and is now used as a dining and ballroom. You can have a set dinner for £10 ($15) or order from the à la carte menu. There is a bistro open seven days a week, where you can have steaks, hamburgers, and other quick hot and cold dishes. A two-course meal will cost about £10.50 ($15.75).

WHERE TO EAT: **Churche's Mansion Restaurant,** Hospital Street, is the most enchanting old restaurant in Cheshire, lying in Nantwich at the junction of Newcastle Road and the Chester bypass. Many years ago, Dr. and Mrs. E. C. Myott learned that this historic home of a wealthy Elizabethan merchant had been advertised for sale in America, and asked the town council to step in and save it. Alas, no English housewife wanted such a gloomy and dark home, so the Myotts attended the sale and outbid the American syndicate that wanted to transport it to the United States. Dr. Myott said that "our friends thought we were mad." They sought out the mysteries of the house; a window in the side wall, inlaid initials, a Tudor well in the garden, a long-ago love knot with a central heart (a token of Richard Churche's affection for his young wife). Today the house is widely known and recommended for its quality meals. A table d'hôte luncheon is offered for £7 ($10.50), and a set dinner for £14 ($21). You need to reserve a table, especially for dinner (tel. 0270/65933). No dinner is served on Sunday. Guests dine at candlelit tables. The mansion is "open to view" throughout the day for 50p (75¢) from April to October, and refreshments are available. It's open all year.

3. Liverpool

Liverpool, with its famous waterfront on the Mersey River, is a great shipping port and industrial center that gave the world everybody from Fannie Hill to the Beatles. King John launched it on its road to glory when he granted it a charter in 1207, and it quickly became a port for shipping men and materials to Ireland. At the time Victoria came to the throne, Liverpool had become Britain's biggest port.

Liverpudlians, as they are called, are rightly proud of their city, with its new hotels, two cathedrals, shopping and entertainment complexes (as exemplified by St. John's Centre, a modern pedestrian precinct), and the parks and open spaces (2400 acres in and around the city, including Sefton Park with its Palm House). Liverpool's main shopping street, Church, is traffic free for most of the day.

The **Metropolitan Cathedral of Christ the King** was built in a record-breaking short time—only five years—yet it has taken 120 years to reach fruition. It is called the Metropolitan Cathedral because Liverpool, in Catholic terms, is the mother city, the "metropolis" of the north of England. Yet it has had its own Catholic cathedral since only 1967. The cathedral's most striking feature is its Lantern Tower, containing more than 25,000 separate pieces of stained glass in a continuous progression of every color in the spectrum. Beneath the central tower lies the white marble high altar. This has been called a Space Age cathedral.

Among Liverpool's historic buildings, **St. George's Hall,** designed by a 24-year-old architect who never saw it realized, was completed in 1854. It has been called "England's finest public building." It contains law courts, and in the rear are pleasantly laid-out gardens.

Many visitors head for Liverpool these days just to see one attraction, the great new Anglican edifice, the **Cathedral Church of Christ,** completed 74 years after it was begun in 1904. On a rocky eminence overlooking the

Mersey River, the cathedral might possibly be the last Gothic-style one to be built on earth. Dedicated to Queen Elizabeth in 1978, it is the largest church in the country (the fifth largest in the world). England's poet laureate, Sir John Betjeman, hailed it as "one of the great buildings of the world." Its vaulting under the tower is 175 feet high, the highest in the world, and its length of 619 feet is second only to that of St. Peter's in Rome. The architect who won a competition in 1901 for the building's design was Giles Gilbert Scott. He later went on to rebuild the House of Commons, gutted by bombs after World War II. He personally laid the last stone on the highest tower pinnacle. The organ of the world's largest Anglican cathedral contains nearly 10,000 pipes, the biggest found in any church. The tower houses the highest (219 feet) and the heaviest (31 tons) ringing peals of bells in the world, and the Gothic arches are the highest ever built.

Want to visit the early Liverpool beginnings of the Beatles? The unofficial gathering spot for pilgrims come to worship is the **Cavern Mecca,** 18 Mathew St., a Beatles museum run by Mr. and Mrs. Jim Hughes. The Mecca displays a large collection of memorabilia on the Beatles and has a full-size replica of the Cavern, where many Liverpudlians first heard the Beatles. The museum is open Tuesday through Saturday from 10 a.m. to 5:30 p.m., charging an admission of 50p (75¢).

Beatle City Ltd., Seel Street (tel. 051/709-0017), is a permanent exhibition of Beatlemania, where a maelstrom of lights and sounds recreates the '60s and the story of the Beatles. Reconstructions of settings include the Cavern Club and a collection of original instruments, clothing, and photographs. A small souvenir shop sells Beatle records, books, and souvenirs, and a café offers light refreshments. It is open from 10:30 a.m. to 8:30 p.m. except over Christmas. Admission is £2 ($3) for adults, £1 ($1.50) for children.

Further information about Liverpool and souvenirs of the city are available from the Tourist Information Centre, opposite Lime Street Railway Station.

WHERE TO STAY: The **Brittania Adelphi Hotel,** Ranelagh Place (tel. 051/709-7200), is "the grand hotel" of Liverpool, known for its good rooms and fine cuisine. Past the elegant entrance, you enter a world of marble corridors, molded ceilings, and dark polished wood. However, these traditional features are complemented by a range of modern amenities, including a swimming pool. The hotel has undergone a complete refurbishing, with an increased bedroom capacity to 300 rooms, all with full facilities, including private baths, color TVs, and phones, and all well furnished and attractively maintained. Singles cost from £32 ($48) to £35 ($52.50), and doubles, from £40 ($60) to £50 ($75).

The new Radleys Restaurant is open seven days a week, until 10 p.m., for breakfast, lunch, and dinner. For dinner, expect to pay from £7.50 ($11.25) to £22 ($33) for two persons. In the basement of the hotel is Steiners Hairdressing Salon for both men and women. When current refurbishing is done, there will be two restaurants, a pub, a nightclub/disco, and a health club.

Holiday Inn, Paradise Street (tel. 051/709-0181), is large and modern, just what you'd expect. In the center of the city, it is one of the most comfortable hotels in Liverpool, if you like its particular brand of plush modernity. Close to the shopping and commercial area, the hotel offers 273 bedrooms, each with private tiled bath, color TV (showing free in-house movies), radio, and direct-dial phone, plus individually controlled heating and air conditioning. Each of the roomy bedrooms has two double beds. Rates are £50 ($75) in a single, from £65 ($97.50) in a double, including a full English breakfast. There's a spacious lounge bar that is most inviting, and in addition, guests can enjoy a heated indoor pool, complete with its own mini-gymnasium and sauna. Guests gravitate to either the Spyglass or the Warehouse for a drink before dinner in the well-appointed Chez Jacques.

St. George's Hotel, Lime Street (tel. 051/709-7090), a Trusthouses Forte hotel, was opened in the early 1970s in a modern shopping district, known as the St. John's Precinct development scheme, directly opposite Lime Street Station. In the heart of Liverpool, it is well run and of an international high standard, with color-coordinated bedrooms, 155 in all, each with a private bath, color TV, razor socket, phone, and coffee maker. Singles range in price from £48 ($72), and doubles go from £64 ($96). The large restaurant on the second floor has a modern look and an impressive menu of international dishes. There's also a coffeeshop for quick snacks or grills, where a three-course meal costs less than £6 ($9), although if you order steaks and a shrimp cocktail, your bill will be closer to £11 ($16.50). It's open Monday to Saturday from 10 a.m. to 10 p.m.

WHERE TO EAT: In food, **Jenny's Seafood Restaurant,** the Old Ropery, Fenwick Street (tel. 051/236-0322), is consistently good. In the vicinity of the harbor, it has a basement room that is both pleasantly decorated and softly illuminated. All this forms a backdrop for the good-tasting fresh seafood that is brought in daily. Everything we've sampled has been of fine quality and well prepared. The service, on my latest rounds, was excellent. Expect to pay about £15 ($22.50) to £18 ($27) per person. The restaurant is closed for lunch on Saturday and all day on Sunday, but is open otherwise until 2:30 p.m. for lunch, serving dinner from 6 to 9:30 p.m.

In a much more elegant, luxurious bracket, the **Oriel,** Oriel Building, Water Street (tel. 051/236-4664), presents a large menu of superb dishes, mainly fish, but with some excellent game and meat dishes as well. The special dishes of the place are lobster, turbot, scampi, and sole. You can choose from about ten different sorts of sole. The vegetables are always the freshest possible. Good ingredients are competently cooked, and the service is attentive. The backdrop consists of silver silk-textured wallpaper and a water garden lit at night. A set luncheon costs £7.50 ($11.25) for three courses and coffee, but in the evening you can expect to pay from £18 ($27) per person for an à la carte meal, unless you have caviar or lobster. The Oriel doesn't serve lunch on Saturday, and is closed all day on Sunday. Otherwise, it is open for lunch until 2 p.m., serving dinner until 10 p.m.

CUMBRIA

Driving in the wilds of this northwestern shire is fine for a start, but the best activity is walking, which is an art—practiced here by both young and old with a crooked stick. Don't go out without a warning, however. There is a great deal of rain and heavy mist. Sunny days are few. When the mist starts to fall, try to be near an old inn or pub, where you can drop in for a visit and warm yourself beside an open fireplace. You'll be carried back to the good old days, as many places in Cumbria have valiantly resisted change. If you strike up a conversation with a local, just make sure you know something about hounds.

The far northwestern part of the shire, bordering Scotland, used to be called Cumberland. Now part of Cumbria, it is generally divided geographically into a trio of segments: the Pennines dominating the eastern sector (loftiest point at Cross Fell, nearly 3000 feet high); the Valley of Eden; and the lakes and secluded valleys of the west—by far the most interesting. The area, so beautifully described by the Romantic Lake Poets, enjoys many literary associations. Wordsworth ("when all at once I saw . . . a host of golden daffodils") was a native son, having been born at Cockermouth.

The largest town is Carlisle in the north—not a very interesting tourist center, but possible as a base for explorations to **Hadrian's Wall.** The wall stretches from Wallsend in the east to Bowness on the Solway, a distance of about 75 miles. It was built in the second century A.D. by the Romans.

4. Kendal

A simple market town, Kendal contains the ruins of a castle where Catherine Parr, the last wife of Henry VIII, was born. With its 13th-century parish church, Kendal makes for a good stopover en route to the lakeside resort of Windermere, about nine miles away. Kendal is 270 miles from London.

The town was also associated with George Romney, the 18th-century portrait painter (Lady Hamilton his favorite subject) who used to travel all over the Lake District trying to get someone to sit for him. He held his first exhibition in Kendal, married and had children there. He deserted them in 1762, not returning until the end of his life. He died in Kendal in 1802.

WHERE TO STAY: Woolpack Hotel, Stricklandgate (tel. Kendal 23852), offers every modern convenience in this sprawling, motel-like establishment. Many of the 58 rooms are equipped with private bath, and some are suites which are ideal for families of three or more. Children under 12 are accommodated at no charge when sharing their parents' rooms. All the rooms are decorated in bright colors to add to the already cheerful atmosphere. Convenient parking is provided just outside. Singles range upward from £38 ($57), while doubles begin at £52 ($78). VAT, service, and a full English breakfast are included in the tab.

5. Windermere

The grandest of the lakes is Windermere, the largest one in England, whose shores wash up against the adjoining towns of **Bowness** and **Windermere.** Both of these lakeside resorts lie on the eastern shore of Windermere. A ferry service connects Hawkshead and Bowness. Windermere, the resort, is the end of the railway line. From either town, you can climb up Orrest Head in less than an hour for a panoramic view of England's lakeland. From that vantage point, you can even see Scafell Pike, rising to a height of 3210 feet—the peak pinnacle in all of England.

Windermere Steamboat Museum, Rayrigg Road, Windermere (tel. 09662/5565), is one of the most delightful working museums it has been my lot to visit for many years. It was founded and developed by George Pattinson, who discovered the fascination of steam many years ago and now has probably the best and most comprehensive collection of steamboats in the country. The wet boatsheds house some dozen boats, including the Veteran *Dolly,* probably the oldest mechanically powered boat in the world, dating from around 1850. It was raised from the lake bed in the early 1960s and run for several years with the original boiler and steambox.

Also displayed is the *Espérance,* an iron steam yacht registered with Lloyds in 1869, as well as many elegant Victorian steam launches and ferry boats. Attached to the boathouses is the speedboat *Jane,* dating from 1938, the first glider-plane to take off from the water in 1943, and the hydroplane racer *Cookie*—all jostling Beatrix Potter's rowing boat and other Lakeland craft for position. A new wet-dock extension has been completed (plus a new shop area), giving added space for a number of other boats. Boats that have been added to the collection include the hydroplane *White Lady,* the steam launch *Kittiwake,* the motorboat *Lady Hamilton,* and the fast speedboat *Miss Windermere IV.*

Ken Crowther is curator. He retired there in recent times, and is totally absorbed in the craft and concept of the museum.

There's a small shop selling books, postcards, and souvenirs of the historic craft. The museum is open from Easter to October, charging an admission of £1.50 ($2.25) for adults and £1 ($1.50) for children. The *Osprey* is regularly in steam, and visitors can make a 40-minute trip on the lake.

It's also possible to make trips on Ullswater and on Coniston, and there is regular steamer service around Windermere, the largest of the lakes, which serves the outlying villages as well as operating for visitors in summer.

WHERE TO STAY AND DINE: Miller Howe Hotel, Rayrigg Road (tel. 09662/2536), serves theatrically presented meals with dramatic flourish. This inn bears the unique imprint of its creator, former actor John Tovey. At the beginning of the 1970s he selected a country estate overlooking Lake Windermere, with views of the Langdale Peaks, and converted it to provide stylish accommodations and an exquisite cuisine.

His large, graciously furnished rooms have names—no number—and he treats each guest as if he or she were invited to a house party. Each accommodation is provided with binoculars to help absorb the view better, and even copies of *Punch* from the 1890s. Antiques are used lavishly throughout the house. Rates per person, including a full English breakfast, dinner, and VAT, range from £50 ($75) to £80 ($120), depending on the plumbing and the view. The hotel is closed from mid-December to mid-March. The public rooms, such as the lounge and library, are lushly decorated, evoking London sophistication.

Dinner at Miller Howe is worth the drive up from London. It's a joyful and satisfying experience. While Tovey is famed as a pastry chef, he is equally known for his original appetizers and main dishes. Even if you can't stay the night, at least consider a meal here. The set meal of five courses will cost £17.50 ($26.25) per person, including coffee and VAT. Regional dishes using local produce are a special feature. You might try Lake District lamb, fresh salmon, game pies (in season), Lancashire cheese, and Cumbria sausage. The lettuce and fennel soup with bacon is superb. Coats and ties are worn in the dining room. Dinners are served at 8:30 p.m. only, at 7:30 and 9:30 on Saturday. You're allowed half an hour for menu selections and apéritifs.

THE LAKE DISTRICT

NORTHUMBERLAND

CARLISLE

DURHAM

MARYPORT

WORKINGTON

KESWICK

PENRITH

CUMBRIA

GRASMERE

GOSFORTH

HAWKSHEAD

CONISTON

KENDAL
WINDERMERE

RAVENGLASS

NORTH
YORKSHIRE

GRANGE
OVER
SANDS

N

BARROW

LANCASTER

HEYSHAM

W.
YORK-
SHIRE

LANCASHIRE

BLACKPOOL

BURNLEY

PRESTON

BLACKBURN

WALES

ENGLAND

LONDON

GREATER
MANCHESTER

MERSEYSIDE

Overnight guests can request a picnic lunch, packed with goodies, including homemade rolls and quiches.

Langdale Chase Hotel, on the A591 between Windermere and Ambleside (tel. 0966/33220), is a great old lakeside house—built for grandeur—comparable to a villa on Lake Como, Italy. The story goes back to 1930 when the dynamic Ms. Dalzell and her mother took over the country estate, with its handsomely landscaped gardens, and decided to accept paying guests while retaining an uncommercial house-party atmosphere. Waterskiing, rowing, lake bathing, tennis, croquet on the grounds, and fishing attract the sports-minded. The rate for B&B ranges from £30 ($45) to £34 ($51) in a single, depending on the plumbing. In a double or twin, the rent is £55 ($82.50) to £65 ($97.50). The bedrooms are skillfully furnished, with excellent pieces.

The interior of the Victorian stone château, with its many gables, balconies, large mullioned windows, and terraces, is a treasure house of antiques. The main lounge hall looks like a setting for one of those English drawing-room comedies. The house was built in part with bits and pieces salvaged from the destruction of a nearby abbey and castle—hence, the ecclesiastical paneling. On the walls are distinctive paintings, mostly Italian primitives, although one is alleged to be a Van Dyck.

The dining room ranks among the finest in the Lake District—with guests selecting tables that are good vantage points for lake viewing. The cuisine is highly personal, mostly a liberated English fare, supported by a fine wine list. Open to nonresidents, the dining room charges from £9 ($13.50) for a set lunch, from £15 ($22.50) for a set six-course dinner. Next to the dining room is a cocktail bar, opening onto the terrace through two French windows. In this room are some old prints of the Lake District that have been collected over the years.

LAKE DISTRICT TOURS: **Mountain Goat Tours,** Victoria Street, Windermere (tel. 09662/5161), is one of the most enterprising ideas I have come across. Begun in 1972 by Chris Taylor, who had a strong desire to start his own business after spending some years in Australia, it has become firmly established in the Lake District as the fell-walking tours. For the less energetic, Mountain Goat has minibus tours that take you to many of the otherwise inaccessible beauty spots of the area.

For a full day's tour to the homes of the poet Wordsworth, the cost is £10 ($15) per person and includes the entrance fees. You retrace the poet's life and places he lived. This is called the In the Steps of Wordsworth Tour.

Another possibility for the more energetic is the tour up Hardknott and Wrynose Passes to Eskdale, following the old Roman route to Hardknott Roman Fort, where a pub lunch can be had in Eskdale. You can take a ride on the miniature Ravenglass-Eskdale railway before having tea at Ravenglass and returning over the fells to Duddon Bridge, Coniston, and Windermere. The cost is £9.50 ($14.25) per person.

Other tours visit Hawkshead and the home of Beatrix Potter for £5 ($7.50) for a half day, increasing to £9 ($13.50) for a full-day tour of Grasmere, Keswick, and Buttermere.

Mountain Goat Tours will also arrange two- or three-night stopovers in the Lakes, including a special discount rail ticket from London or wherever. Including travel to the lakes, the cost of two nights in a guest house, a full-day tour by minibus, a boat trip on Windermere, and taxis to and from

Windermere coach or bus station is £58 ($87) per person. An experienced guide can be hired for this tour. For a hotel with a bath or shower, the cost rises to £73 ($109.50) per person. Both tariffs are for half board.

There are also week-long walking tours available, if you are properly clad and reasonably fit, from £132 ($198). Required equipment can be hired locally. However, if you arrive without a suitable kit for this tour they will not take you out, for it is an area that calls for proper equipment. I suggest you inquire about what you will need for these specialized tours directly from Mountain Goat.

6. Ambleside

A good and idyllic retreat, Ambleside is one of the major centers attracting pony-trekkers, fell-hikers, and rock-scalers. The charms are essentially there year round, even in late autumn when it's fashionable to sport a mackintosh. Ambleside is superbly perched, at the top of Lake Windermere. Traditions are entrenched, especially at the Rushbearing Festival, an annual event.

WHERE TO STAY AND DINE: Rothay Manor, Rothay Bridge (tel. 0966/33605), at the edge of Ambleside, is like a French country inn, where the sparkling star is the cuisine, combined with a dedicated chef in the kitchen, well-selected French wines, and 16 comfortable, centrally heated bedrooms and two suites with bath, shower, phone and color TV. All this is possible because of a very special person, Mrs. Bronwen M. G. Nixon, who has installed herself in this gracious Regency house, bringing her energy, imagination, and taste to bear on its operation. She charges from £32 ($48) to £38 ($57) per person for B&B. The rooms are individually decorated, with a free use of vibrant colors. Most of them have shuttered French doors opening onto a sun balcony, with a mountain view. Throughout the estate you'll find an eclectic combination of antiques (some Georgian blended harmoniously with Victorian), flowers, and "get-lost" armchairs.

The manor is also a restaurant open to nonresidents. Mrs. Nixon's spacious dining room is decked with antique tables and chairs. Her appointments are flawless, and incorporate fine crystal, silver, and china. At night candles burn in silver holders. Lunches six days a week feature soup, cold meats, a variety of salads, desserts, cheeses, and coffee, and a traditional hot lunch on Sunday.

Dinners, from 8 till 9 p.m., are more ambitious, costing £16.50 ($24.75). Here is a typical selection: homemade chicken liver pâté laced with brandy, celery and almond soup, filet Talleyrand (beef filet rolled in a mirepoix of vegetables, baked in a flaky pastry case and served with a rich Espagnole sauce), an exciting selection of homemade desserts, fresh fruit, and a cheese trolley. Afterward good coffee awaits you in the lounges. All prices include VAT.

In the kitchen Mrs. Nixon directs everything herself with a wise and loving eye, and has trained a friendly young staff to produce the meals. I've saved the best news for last: that is, Mrs. Nixon herself, a forthright conversationalist and (that rarity) a sensitive listener—a winning combination.

Kirkstone Foot, Kirkstone Pass Road (tel. Ambleside 32232), is an architecturally simple 17th-century manor house whose lodging facilities have been increased with the construction of several slate-roofed and self-catering apartments in the surrounding park-like grounds. The original building is encircled by a well-tended lawn, while the interior is cozily furnished with overstuffed chairs and English-style paneling. The in-house restaurant offers home-cooked English meals under the direction of the co-owner, Jane Bateman, who personally runs this fine establishment along with her husband Simon. Fresh produce is used whenever possible. The comfortable accommodations, either in the main house or in one of the outlying units, are tastefully decorated in a family style of coziness. For a room with private bath, a full English breakfast, and a five-course dinner, expect to pay from £32 ($48) per person daily. If you're staying in one of their flats, you can drop in for dinner for another £12.50 ($18.75) per person.

Riverside Hotel & Lodge, near Rothay Bridge, Under Loughrigg (tel. 0966/32395), consists of two small country hotels beautifully situated in a lovely and peaceful riverside setting. They're secluded on a quiet lane away from traffic noise and yet only a few minutes' walk to the center of Ambleside. The hotel and lodge are jointly owned and run by Alan and Gillian Rhone, who can accommodate up to 30 guests and who provide good meals in an atmosphere as friendly and relaxing as it is professional. All bedrooms have color TV and tea- and coffee-making facilities. Rooms go for approximately £28 ($42) per person, inclusive of a private bath, a full English breakfast, and dinner. Breakfast is served at 9 a.m. and dinner around 7 p.m.

READERS' GUEST HOUSE SELECTION: "We were treated to the finest hospitality we've found throughout our entire six-month visit to Europe, when we discovered a truly fantastic place to stay with John and Sue Horne at **Horseshoe Guest House,** Rothay Road (tel. 0966/32000). An architect from London by profession, John has left the big city life behind and is creating an enviable lifestyle for Sue and himself in the Lake Country. For £19 ($28.50) per night for a double, you can stay in a large and immaculate room, bath down the hall, in a residence that has undergone complete restoration by the Hornes. Five new bedrooms, all with private shower, toilet, and balcony, have been added, and another £4 ($6) is charged for these units. John, an avid outdoorsman and member of the local Mountain Rescue Squad, has a complete knowledge of the surrounding area and he will gladly direct you to places of interest. Sue was up bright and early in the morning to fix us a fine breakfast of eggs, bacon, and sausage, all included in the room cost" (Phil Pritulsky and Pauline Dainty, Norfolk, Va.).

7. Rydal

Between Ambleside and Wordsworth's former retreat at Grasmere is Rydal, a small village on one of the smallest lakes, Rydal Water. Wordsworth lived at Rydal Mount, overlooking the lake, from 1813 until his death in 1850. The house is now a museum. The village is noted for its sheepdog trials at the end of summer.

WHERE TO STAY: **Rydal Lodge** (tel. 0966/33208), beside the roadway between Ambleside and Grasmere, is a good center for walking and touring the whole of the Lake District. The Rothay River runs beside the pleasant and secluded gardens; and Rydal Water, a beautiful lake, is at the end of the garden. Mr. and Mrs. Warren provide meals of high quality, and the menus are well planned. Strawberries and other fruit from the garden are provided in season, and the lodge has a license to serve wine with main meals. The bedrooms are equipped with hot and cold running water, shaving points, electric blankets, heaters, and innerspring mattresses, and there are two bathrooms and a shower room. There is also a private car park. Terms are from £14 ($21) for B&B, with dinner costing from £10 ($15), including VAT and service. Rydal Lodge is of historical interest. Matthew Arnold stayed here, and it is connected with Harriet Martineau. The older part of the house was an inn in 1655.

8. Grasmere

On a lake that bears its name, Grasmere was the home of Wordsworth from 1799 to 1808. The nature poet lived with his sister, Dorothy (the English writer and diarist) at **Dove Cottage,** which is now a museum administered by Dove Cottage Trust. Wordsworth, who followed Southey as poet laureate, died in the spring of 1850, and was buried in the graveyard of the village church at Grasmere. The other tenant of Dove Cottage was Thomas De Quincey *(Confessions of an English Opium Eater).* For a combined ticket costing £2.50 ($3.75) for adults, half price for children, you can visit both Dove Cottage and the **Wordsworth Museum.** This houses a collection of Wordsworth's manuscripts and memorabilia, as well as a collection of portraits of the Wordsworth circle, including Lamb, Coleridge, Keats, and Hazlitt, from the National Portrait Gallery. The trust property is open on summer weekdays from 9:30 a.m. to 5:30 p.m., on Sunday from 11 a.m. to 5:30 p.m. Off-season hours are from 10 a.m. to 4:30 p.m. weekdays, 11 a.m. to 4:30 p.m. on Sunday. It is closed from November 1 to March 1 except during the Christmas and New Year period. Telephone 09665/544 for further information.

A SHOPPING RECOMMENDATION: It isn't often that you get the opportunity to watch the material that you will later purchase being made. But at **Chris Reekie's,** in the Old Coach House at Grasmere (tel. 09665/221), you can see Mr. Reekie, one of his sons, or perhaps young apprentices, working at the traditional fly-shuttle loom that Mr. Reekie brought from his own apprenticeship employers in Selkirk. For about the last 30 years he has been weaving tartans and fine woolens for direct sale, thus keeping the prices down. His charges are below those in Scotland. Apart from a vast range of ready-made cloths and clothing, he will make to measure a garment within 14 days. If that is too long to wait, he will send articles anywhere in the world, so you can buy for relatives and friends.

FOOD AND LODGING: In this hiking and rock-scaling center, you'll find the following recommendations, beginning first with the most expensive, then descending in price level.

Michael's Nook, outside Grasmere (turn off the A591 at the Swan Hotel; tel. 09665/496), is a country-house hotel, once a private residence, standing in its own secluded garden of three acres. A Lakeland home of stone, it contains much fine mahogany woodwork and paneling, exemplified by its elegant staircase. Throughout the house, owned by Reg Gifford, are many fine antiques, which are only enhanced by the mellow glow of log fires or the discreetly placed vases of flowers.

The handsomely decorated bedrooms, ten in all, are individually furnished with grace and care. All are equipped with phones, private baths or showers, and TV. The minimum booking is usually three nights, but shorter visits will be accommodated where possible. The tariffs range from £45 ($67.50) to £65 ($97.50) per person per night and include a five-course dinner, bed, early-morning tea, an English or a continental breakfast, and VAT. After only a few hours here, guests become acquainted with Mr. Gifford's cats, Great Dane, and parrot. The feeling is very much that of living in a private home.

A limited number of guests can be accommodated in the dining room, and advance reservations are essential. Great care and an attention to detail go into the excellent English cooking, and the best of fresh ingredients are used whenever available. An attractive young staff serves the fine food, which costs from £17.50 ($26.25) for lunch, £23 ($34.50) for dinner, VAT included. The menus change, but you might have an appetizer of fresh scallop mousse in a light crayfish sauce, followed by roast local guinea fowl with black currants, Cumberland ham with a seed mustard sauce, or roast loin of Lakeland lamb with three purees.

The **Wordsworth Hotel** at Grasmere (tel. 09665/592) stands in the heart of the village and is owned by Reg Gifford of Michael's Nook Country House Hotel. An old stone Lakeland house (once the 19th-century Rothay Hotel), the Wordsworth has been gutted and rebuilt to provide large bedrooms with views of the fells and river, as well as modern baths, TVs, phones, and comfortable chairs. The rate of approximately £39 ($58.50) per person includes a full breakfast and VAT. There is a four-poster bedroom at £45 ($67.50) per person, with beams and dormer windows. The original master bedroom has a gorgeous Victorian bathroom, with a brass towel rail and polished pipes and taps.

There are several lounges, with sink-in armchairs grouped around log fires. A buffet lunch is served in the cocktail lounge, including the chef's hot dish of the day—perhaps ragoût, lasagne, or curry. The most expensive item is only £4.50 ($6.75).

A set dinner at £15 ($22.50) is likely to include a light fruit or vegetable appetizer, then soup, a choice of two meat dishes, then dessert or cheese, along with coffee and mints. The à la carte menu is more ambitious, and a three-course meal of, say, smoked haddock and cheese soufflé, clear beef broth with quail eggs, breast of chicken stuffed with walnuts, and rich chocolate fudge cake will cost around £16 ($24). Each dish is carefully explained on the menu so you know what you're getting.

After all this food, the hotel has a heated swimming pool, quite large, and there's also a sauna and a solarium.

White Moss House, Rydal Water (tel. 09665/295), is an old Lakeland cottage off the main A591 between Grasmere and Rydal Water. It overlooks the lake and the fells, where you're welcomed as a house guest to be pampered with morning tea in bed, your bedcovers turned down at night, and your culinary preferences remembered and adhered to.

The rooms are comfortably furnished and well heated in nippy weather. In all there are only five accommodations, so advance booking is essential. These units have baths en suite and go for £37 ($55.50) per person nightly including an elegant, if large, breakfast and a dinner to satisfy a gourmet.

There's also Brockstone, their cottage annex, a five-minute drive along the road, where two, three, or four guests can be accommodated in utter peace.

Dinner is a leisurely affair beginning at 8 p.m. You're served five courses—perhaps a celery and almond soup, then a fish soufflé, followed by a roast of lamb with an orange and red currant sauce, or quail with a chicken and brown rice stuffing, accompanied by a selection of intriguing vegetable dishes, cheesey potatoes, eggplant with lime, and cauliflower with herb cheese. For dessert, I hope Mrs. Beeton's chocolate pudding is featured, or the homemade brown bread ice cream, followed by English cheese and homemade "oat biscuits," coffee, and mints. If you're not a resident, dinner will cost from £14 ($21) without wines, but you must reserve a table early for, as you can imagine, residents very rarely pass up a chance to eat in. There isn't much space in the dining room.

Mr. and Mrs. J. A. Butterworth, their daughter Susan, and her husband Peter Dixon, work happily together in running the house. Mrs. Butterworth has been in charge of the kitchen for some years, and Peter helps her accomplish the fine cookery that has made her renowned throughout the country. You may be lucky enough to catch one of her rare appearances on TV, discussing and promoting English country cuisine. Susan works with her father at the front of the house, welcoming guests, serving diners, and helping with wine selections. All of the above rates include VAT, but service is left to the discretion of the guest. They don't take dogs, and they make no reductions for children.

Red Lion Hotel (tel. 09665/456) is a 200-year-old coaching inn in the heart of the village, owned by the Fawthrops, Mr. John and Mr. Stewart. It's only a short stroll to the waterside cottage once occupied by Wordsworth, and it's assumed that the poet often stopped in for a meal, a drink, or to warm himself by the fire. A rambling informal structure, it is imbued with a sophisticated rustic decor. In the spacious residents' lounge, the rugged stone fireplace is two-sided. Two of the three bars are paneled in mahogany, with refectory tables and chairs. In the dining room, you will be served some of the finest fare in the district: a set meal costing from £10 ($15), or you can order à la carte. A twin ranges from £36 ($54) without bath, from £52 ($78) with bath, and a single room is priced from £24 ($36) to £27 ($40.50) without bath to £25 ($37.50) to £29 ($43.50) with bath. Breakfast is included in the room rates, as are VAT and service. There is an elevator serving all 36 bedrooms, 21 of which contain private baths. As a family-run hotel, the Grasmere Red Lion maintains a personal atmosphere.

Swan Hotel (tel. 09665/551) has been renovated so that only the shell of the old building remains. However, there have been inns on this site for 300 years. Wordsworth mentioned it in *The Waggoner*. In fact, in one of the lounges is the poet's tapestry chair. The 31 rooms contain built-in furniture and good beds. Singles without bath rent for £40 ($60), going up to £46 ($69) with bath. Bathless doubles cost £52 ($78), rising to £64 ($96) with bath, these tariffs including service and VAT. The restaurant provides both table d'hôte and à la carte meals.

9. Hawkshead and Coniston

Discover for yourself the village of Hawkshead, with its 15th-century grammar school where Wordsworth went to school for eight years (he carved his name on a desk that still remains). Near Hawkshead, in the vicinity of Esthwaite Water, is the 17th-century **Hill Top Farm,** former home of Beatrix Potter, the author of the Peter Rabbit books, who died during World War II.

At **Coniston,** four miles away from Hawkshead, you can visit the village associated with John Ruskin. Coniston is a good base for rock climbing. The Coniston "Old Man" towers in the background at

2633 feet, giving mountain climbers one of the finest views of the Lake District.

Ruskin moved to his home, **Brantwood** (tel. 09664/396), on the east side of Coniston Water in 1872 and lived there until his death in 1900. The house today is open for visitors to view much Ruskiniana, including some 175 pictures by him. Also displayed are his coach and boat, the *Jumping Jenny*.

An exhibition illustrating the work of W. J. Linton is laid out in his old printing room. Linton was born in England in 1812 and died at New Haven, Connecticut, in 1897. Well known as a wood engraver and for his private press, he lived at Brantwood, where he set up his printing business in 1853. He published *The English Republic,* a newspaper and review, before emigrating to America in 1866, where he set up his printing press in 1870. The house is owned and managed by the Education Trust, a self-supporting registered charity. It is open daily from Easter to the end of October from 11 a.m. to 5:30 p.m., closed on Saturday. The admission is £1.50 ($2.25) for adults, 75p ($1.13) for children. Part of the 250-acre estate is also open as a nature trail, costing 50p (75¢) for adults, 30p (45¢) for children. A special £3 ($4.50) family day ticket (mother and/or father and children up to the age of 16) covers the house and nature trail. There is a gift and Ruskin book shop, and tea and coffee are available.

Literary fans may want to pay a pilgrimage to the graveyard of the village church, where Ruskin was buried; his family turned down a chance to have him interred at Westminster Abbey.

ACCOMMODATIONS: **Ivy House Hotel,** Main Street (tel. Hawkshead 204), is a friendly Georgian house that warms the austere Lake District. It's an ideal headquarters from which to branch out for visits on Lake Windermere. If you stay anywhere from one to three days, the B&B rate is £12 ($18) per person daily. Cheaper terms are quoted for longer stays. Dinner, bed, and breakfast cost £15 ($22.50). The hospitable proprietors, Mr. and Mrs. Williams, are used to welcoming overseas visitors, and Mrs. Williams tries to take a personal interest in all her lodgers. But because of her charming house and lovely situation, she is heavily booked—so it's imperative that you reserve well in advance. Some other points worth noting: All the rooms are centrally heated and have hot and cold running water. A modern, motel-type annex, with unrestricted electric heating, handles overflow guests. The house is open March to the end of October only. Log fires blaze in the lounge in early and late seasons.

10. Keswick

Lying 22 miles north of Windermere, Keswick opens onto Derwentwater, one of the loveliest lakes in the district. Robert Southey, poet laureate, lived for four decades at Greta Hall, and was buried at Crosthwaite Church. Coleridge lived here too, depending on Southey for financial aid. Sir Hugh Walpole, the novelist, in a different era also resided near Keswick.

Keswick is the natural geographical starting point for car tours and walks of exploration in the northern Lake District, including the John Peel country to the north of Skiddaw (quiet and little known), Borrowdale, Buttermere, and Crummock Water, as well as Bassenthwaite, Thirlmere, and Ullswater.

WHERE TO STAY: Royal Oak Hotel (tel. 0596/72965) dates back to the days of Queen Elizabeth I, although the present building more accurately reflects the architecture of the 18th century. As a posting house, it was a favored lakeland retreat of Sir Walter Scott, who is said to have written a section of *Bridal of Triermain* here. The famous hunter, John Peel, and authors Alfred Lord Tennyson and Robert Louis Stevenson also patronized the inn. Now redecorated and modernized under Trusthouses Forte auspices, the hotel is a cheerful and atmospheric place at which to stay. Rates are £25 ($37.50) for a bathless single, £36 ($54) for a single with bath. A bathless double or twin-bedded room costs £40 ($60), £50 ($75) with bath. Breakfast is extra, but service and VAT are included.

Borrowdale Hotel, near Keswick (tel. 059-684/224), is a typical Lakeland stone building, circa 1866, with log fires welcoming you when the weather is not kind. Its rooms are comfortable, many opening onto lovely views. All have private baths or showers and toilets, color TVs, radios, intercoms, baby-listening units, and hair dryers. Some traditional four-poster beds are available. The hotel has central heating throughout. The tariff for dinner, room, and breakfast, inclusive of VAT, depending on time of year and grade of room, starts at £28 ($42), rising to £35 ($52.50).

The main attraction of Borrowdale is its restaurant. A traditional English lunch on Sunday costs from £7.50 ($11.25). During the rest of the week, bar lunches with an imaginative choice of 25 main courses, costs in the £2 ($3) to £5 ($7.50) range. The seven-course dinner, consisting of appetizer, main, and dessert courses, each having a choice of at least six different dishes, starts at £12 ($18). Cuisine from all parts of the globe is offered, and the menu is changed daily. If you wish to have the daily roast, the chef will carve it at your table from a silver carving trolley. The hotel is owned and managed by Gunter and Jean Fidrmuc who, together with an efficient, friendly staff, assure you of a warm welcome.

Skiddaw Hotel (tel. 0596/72071) has a bone-white, clean-cut facade, and is built right onto the sidewalk in the heart of Keswick. The owners, Mr. and Mrs. Kitchin, have used natural elements in the interiors with walls of simple pine or rugged fieldstone. The meals are totally English, well prepared. The bedrooms are compact and eye-catching, renting at prices that vary according to the season and the view. The B&B rate ranges from £15.50 ($23.25) to £18 ($27) in a single, £29 ($43.50) to £33 ($49.50), for a double with bath, including VAT. Every room has hot and cold running water; the beds are bouncy soft, and the linen as clean as the lake air. Guests gather in the stone-walled lounge, or else in the pine-paneled cocktail bar.

A set four-course dinner goes for £6 ($9), the price going up to £8.50 ($12.75) for a six-course meal. A three-course Sunday lunch (always a roast) is £5.50 ($8.25). Lunch on other days is à la carte, but there is always a chef's special such as Lancashire hotpot, lamb cutlets, or pork chops, each platter costing from £2.50 ($3.75), including a vegetable.

The George Hotel, St. John Street (tel. 0596/72076), is a wayside tavern that has bedded down many a traveler who pulled in on a horse-drawn coach. Once associated with Coleridge, it brings a comfort and pleasure to the modern pilgrim. Guests still gather for a warming hot punch in the bar where Wordsworth and Southey met for quiet talks in high-backed settles in front of the fireplace. Modern amenities have been sneaked in, including central heating, electric razor outlets, and hot and cold running water. Six have private baths. Singles rent for £15 ($22.50), the cost going up to £28 ($42) in a double, including VAT and a full English breakfast. There is no service charge. Throughout the inn, modern furniture is blended harmoniously with well-chosen antiques.

READER'S HOTEL SELECTION: "We would like to recommend the **Grange Hotel** (tel. 0596/72500), the nicest, most elegant place we stayed in our two-week trip. The owners have completely remodeled and redecorated the interior to reflect its 1850 manor-house exterior. The furnishings are elegant (many are antiques), and the rooms are spacious. Ten of the bedrooms have baths en suite, and two share a bath. There is a reading room, a separate coffee lounge, and a cocktail bar. The units have built-in hair dryers and tea- or coffee-making facilities. One night at the Grange costs £14 ($21) in a single, £28 ($42) in a twin-bedded room, for B&B. We enjoyed a five-course dinner also, which was well prepared and beautifully served, costing £8.50 ($12.75). There is a choice from six main dishes, including venison, sole, and chicken" (Betty Brown, Orono, Maine).

WHERE TO DINE: The **Bay Tree Restaurant and Guest House,** 1 Wordsworth St. (tel. 0596/73313), is an old house on the main Penrith road, lying outside Keswick and overlooking the river and parkland. It has white walls with brown canopies over the windows, plus a glass door through which lights twinkle invitingly. The owner is Mrs. Joyce Shepherd, who is assisted by her sons. Her B&B rate is £10.50 ($15.75) per person nightly, rising to £13.50 ($20.25) per person for half board.

A few tables in the tiny dining room are open to nonresidents who should reserve a table for dinner between 6:30 and 7 p.m. The cost of a meal is £8.50 ($12.75), and dishes are likely to include ham steaks with a green salad and sauteed potatoes, or else lamb cutlets with a red currant and orange sauce. Appetizers always include a soup or pâté, and for dessert, such delights as black cherries in brandy with fresh cream. Coffee is served in the lounge. All prices include VAT and service.

Paprika Continental Restaurant, 70 Main St. (tel. 0596/72033), has a varied menu, with shrimp, accompanied by several sauces, rolls, and salad, being the specialty of the house. Also featured are smoked chicken, paprika chicken, and casserole of beef, pork, or local venison. Local fish dishes are also served, and regional specialties such as Cumberland sausage may tempt you. A typical à la carte dinner might include an appetizer of pâté, jumbo shrimp, tossed salad, rolls, cherry pie, and a beverage, costing about £9 ($13.50) per person. For lunch, Paprika serves delightful dishes to satisfy either large or small appetites. Weight-watchers and vegetarians will also find many satisfying foods. Especially popular are the savory cheese and prawn platters and homemade soup and a roll. Sherry, lager, and wines such as Hungarian Tokay, as well as that macho-sounding Hungarian drink, Bull's Blood, are sold at reasonable prices. Also, you get the chance of trying some good English wines here. The proprietor, Miss Judith Szucs, requests that no tips be left—"please just come back, and tell your friends," she says.

The restaurant is open daily including Sunday. Summer hours are 10 a.m. to 10 p.m. In winter it opens at 11 a.m. and closes at 9 p.m.

11. Bassenthwaite

With its fine stretch of water in the shadow of the 3053-foot Skiddaw, Bassenthwaite makes a good center for exploring the western Lakeland. In the village I have a choice recommendation.

The **Pheasant Inn,** Bassenthwaite Lake, near Cockermouth (tel. Bassenthwaite Lake 234), is a 16th-century inn with a neat exterior set against a wooded mountain backdrop. Inside, the bar is smoke-mellowed. Old hunting prints dot the walls, and real ale is on tap. The beamed dining room is bright and cheerful, with spotless white tablecloths and a menu of good-quality roasts, fish, and poultry with fresh vegetables. There are three pleasant lounges with an open log fire, and fresh flowers abound. The bedrooms are spotless and bright with chintz. Eleven have a bath or shower room attached, and there are electric blankets on the beds. There are also three bedrooms in the annex, which is a bungalow on the grounds. A single without bath is £23 ($34.50), going up to £25 ($37.50) with bath. A double without bath costs £40 ($60), rising to £50 ($75) with bath, including VAT, service, and an English breakfast.

12. Ullswater

A seven-mile sheet of water, stretching from Pooley Bridge to Patterdale, Ullswater is the second-largest lake in the district. Incidentally, it was on the shores of Ullswater that Wordsworth saw his "host of golden daffodils." The market town of Penrith lies seven miles to the east, and while housed in the area it is easy to explore several places of archeological interest, such as Hadrian's Wall, east of Carlisle, or Long Meg stone circle near Penrith.

WHERE TO STAY AND EAT: Sharrow Bay Country House Hotel, Howtown, Lake Ullswater, near Penrith (tel. 08536/301-483). Francis Coulson rules in the kitchen, Brian Sack in the dining room. Mr. Coulson bought this unusual Victorian house in 1949, and up to then it'd been a private house, similar to those one might find on Lake Maggiore, with a low angled roof and wide eaves. Sleeping on the floor during restoration work, he had the place rebuilt, turning it into one of England's finest country dining places, and offering accommodations as well, with daily terms in the range of £42 ($63) to £70 ($105) per person for room, dinner, breakfast, service, and VAT.

The atmosphere is relaxed, the lounges comfortable and handsomely decorated. From the picture window in the drawing room, a view opens across the lake to the Martindale Fells.

The six-course, £21 ($31.50) set menu contains a formidable list of choices. I recently counted 28 appetizers, including the chef's specialty, mousseline of fresh salmon with hollandaise sauce. The carefully chosen main courses seemed designed to make the best of home-grown food items, including roast Lancashire guinea fowl, a roast stuffed shoulder of young English lamb, or even a Cumberland ham from a cold table selection. The dessert selections are among the best you'll find in northwest England, including a fresh strawberry hazelnut brandy cream roulade. A feature as well is the Sharrow homemade cream ices, including prune and armagnac.

Brian Sack is a delightful host, and his staff is friendly and efficient, which makes Mr. Coulson's food all the more delectable.

If you're motoring through the area, and not stopping over for the night, I suggest you call in advance and make a reservation for the £17 ($25.50) set luncheon.

The hotel offers 29 antique-filled bedrooms, 17 of them in the lodge annex and cottages. In the main hotel, seven rooms have private baths, and 13 of the bedrooms in the cottages have private baths as well. Some rooms open onto views of the lakes, others onto fells and trees. Each of the individually decorated bedrooms has been given a name rather than a number, a nice touch.

You should write or telephone in advance, either for a meal or room. Closed December, January, and February.

Country Living

Farlam Hall Hotel (tel. 06976/234) is in Brampton, near Carlisle, making it a good base for visiting the Roman Wall, the Lake District, and the Yorkshire Dales. Farlam Hall is listed as a building of architectural and historic interest. It was just a farmhouse when it was erected in the 17th century, but in 1826 it changed hands and became a noted Border manor house. It stands today in four acres of grounds, with some fine old trees, a stream, and a small lake. John Wesley is said to have preached in the house, and George Stephenson, inventor of the steam railroad engine, stayed here.

The hotel is run by Alan and Barry Quinion and their families, who have set high standards of service and cuisine. Barry, an advanced Cordon Bleu chef, is in charge of the kitchens, offering interesting soups such as cream of stilton and celery, as well as roast Lancashire duckling with honey, almond, and raisin sauce and poached filets of turbot with shrimp sauce. A choice of at least six fresh vegetables accompanies the main courses. All ingredients are freshly brought in from the nearby coast or the local farms. Dinnertime is graced by the Quinion women, who serve the tables in full evening dress. Lunch is served on Sunday only, at £15 ($22.50), with dinners offered nightly, also at £15. Dinner in the formal dining room, with white linen cloths and napkins and silver table service, is at 8 p.m. Men are expected to wear jackets and ties, and for women, it is an occasion to dress up a bit and to enjoy the elegant surroundings, the careful attention, and the excellent food.

Accommodations consist of 11 bedrooms, all doubles and twins, with private baths or showers. Furnishings are antique, and everything is comfortable and warm. There are lovely views of the gardens and the lake. Helen Quinion is in charge of housekeeping. She sees to it that a mass of useful little things can be found in your room, such as magazines, hand cream, and shampoo. An overnight stay, including an English breakfast and VAT, costs £34 ($51) per person, with dinner and B&B priced at £40 ($60) per person, an excellent bargain. Service is left to the discretion of the guest.

The hotel is only four miles from the Roman Wall and 11 miles from the M6 motorway and Carlisle.

Chapter XVI

YORKSHIRE AND NORTHUMBRIA

1. York
2. North Yorkshire
3. West Yorkshire
4. Durham
5. Tyne and Wear
6. Northumberland

FOR THE CONNOISSEUR, the northeast of England is rich in attractions. **Yorkshire,** known to readers of *Wuthering Heights* and the works of James Herriot, embraces both the moors of North Yorkshire and the Dales. With the radical changing of the old county boundaries, the shires are now divided into North Yorkshire (the most interesting from the tourist point of view), West Yorkshire, South Yorkshire, and Humberside.

Away from the cities and towns that still carry the taint of the Industrial Revolution, the beauty of Yorkshire is wild and remote. It's characterized by limestone crags, caverns along the Pennines, many peaks, mountainous uplands, rolling hills, the chalkland wolds, heather blooming on the moorlands, broad vales, lazy rivers, and tumbling streams. Yorkshire lures not only with inland scenery but with some 100 miles of shoreline, with rocky headlands, cliffs, sandy bays, rock-strewn pools, sheltered coves, fishing villages, bird sanctuaries, former smugglers' dens, and yachting havens.

Across this vast region came the Romans, the Anglo-Saxons, the Vikings, the monks of the Middle Ages, kings of England, lords of the manor, craftsmen, hill farmers, and wool makers—each leaving his mark. You can still see Roman roads and pavements, great abbeys and castles, stately homes, open-air museums, and craft centers, along with parish churches, old villages, and cathedrals. In fact, Yorkshire's battle-scarred castles, Gothic abbeys, and great county manor houses from all periods are unrivaled anywhere in Britain.

Northumbria is made up of the counties of Northumberland, Cleveland, and Durham. Tyne and Wear is one of the more recently created counties, with Newcastle upon Tyne as its center.

The Saxons who came to northern England centuries ago carved out this kingdom, which at the time stretched from the Firth of Forth in

Scotland to the banks of the Humber in Yorkshire. Vast tracts of that ancient kingdom remain natural and unspoiled. Again, this slice of England has more than its share of industrial towns, but you don't go here to see them. Set out to explore the wild hills and open spaces, crossing the dales of the eastern Pennines.

The whole area evokes ancient battles and bloody border raids. Roman relics, Border castles, Saxon churches, and monastic ruins abound in Northumbria, none more notable than Hadrian's Wall, one of the wonders of the Western world. The finest stretch of the wall lies within the Northumberland National Park between the stony North Tyne River and the county boundary at Gilsland.

Let's begin our travels through this area of northeast England in its major historical and ecclesiastical center—

1. York

Few cities in England are as rich in history as York. It is still encircled by its 13th- and 14th-century city walls—about 2½ miles long—with four gates. One of these, Micklegate, once grimly greeted visitors coming up from the south with the heads of traitors. To this day, you can walk on the footpath of the walls of the Middle Ages.

The crowning achievement of York is its Minster or cathedral, which makes the city an ecclesiastical center topped only by Canterbury. In spite of this, York is one of the most overlooked cities on the cathedral circuit. Perhaps foreign visitors are intimidated by the feeling that the great city of northeastern England is too far north. Actually, it lies about 195 miles north of London on the Ouse River, and can easily be tied in with a motor trip to Edinburgh. Or after visiting Cambridge, a motorist can make a swing through a too-often-neglected cathedral circuit: Ely, Lincoln, then York.

There was a Roman York (Hadrian came this way), then a Saxon York, a Danish York, a Norman York (William the Conqueror slept here), a medieval York, a Georgian York, a Victorian York (the center of a flourishing rail business), and certainly a 20th-century York. A surprising amount of 18th-century York remains, including Richard Boyle's restored Assembly Rooms.

THE SIGHTS: The best way to see York is to go to the **Tourist Information Centre,** DeGrey Rooms, Exhibition Square (tel. 0904/21756) at 10:15 a.m. and 2:15 p.m. daily from Good Friday to the end of October, where you'll be met by a volunteer guide who will take you on an 1½-hour walking tour of the city, revealing its history and lore through numerous intriguing stories. There is no charge. Additional tours are made at 7:15 p.m. daily during June, July, and August.

At some point in your exploration, you may want to visit **The Shambles,** once the meat-butchering center of York, dating back before the Norman Conquest. But this messy business has given way, and the ancient street survives. It is filled with jewelry stores, cafés, and buildings that huddle so closely together you can practically stand in the middle of the pavement, arms outstretched, and touch the houses on both sides of the street.

Recently, special interest has been focused on discoveries of the Viking era, from 867 to 1066, when the city was known as Jorvik, the Viking capital and a major Scandinavian trade center. During excavations under York's

Coppergate prior to development, a wealth of artifacts was unearthed in the late 1970s and early 1980s, including entire houses and workshops of the Viking Age. Now, in the **Jorvik Viking Centre,** this whole street has been reconstructed in intricate detail, the sights, sounds, even smells of Viking Age York, in Coppergate, the very spot where it was first revealed. Visitors journey back in time to the Viking Age, then pass a mock-up of the excavation site itself, and finally enter an exhibition containing the best of the thousands of small objects rescued from Coppergate. For further information, inquire at the Jorvik Viking Centre, Coppergate, York, YO1 INT (tel. 0904/543211).

Incidentally, the suffix "gate" used for streets and sites in York is from the Scandinavian word for "street," a holdover from the era when Vikings held sway here.

York Minster

One of the great cathedrals of the world, York Minster traces its origins back to the early seventh century. The present building, however, dates mainly from the 13th century. Like the minster at Lincoln, York Cathedral is characterized by three towers, all built in the 15th century. The central tower is lantern shaped, in the Perpendicular style.

Perhaps the distinguishing characteristic of the cathedral is its medley of stained glass from the Middle Ages—in glorious Angelico blues, ruby reds, forest greens, and ambers. See in particular the large east window, the work of a 15th-century Coventry glass painter. In the north transept is an architectural gem of the mid-13th century, the "Five Sisters," with its lancets. The choir screen, from the late 15th century, has an impressive line-up—everybody from William the Conqueror to the overthrown Henry VI.

The undercroft is open Monday to Saturday from 10 a.m. to dusk (on Sunday from 1 to 4 p.m.), charging adults 50p (75¢) for admission; children pay 25p (38¢). The central tower is open Monday to Saturday, April to September, from 10:30 a.m. to 7 p.m. (October to March, 10:30 a.m. to 3:30 p.m.), costing adults 90p ($1.35), and children, 60p (90¢). The chapter house is open Monday to Saturday, May to October, from 10 a.m., costing adults 30p (45¢); children, 15p (23¢). The crypt is shown during conducted tours only. At an Information Desk in the south aisle of the Minster parties can be put in touch with a guide, if one is available, for a conducted tour. No charge is made, and the guides do not accept gratuities. Gifts toward the maintenance of the Minster are, however, always welcome. For information, telephone 0904/24426.

While this guide was being prepared York Minster was struck by a thunderbolt and severely damaged by fire. Although restoration is planned, the Minster may well be closed to the public for a long time, so make sure to check so that you won't be disappointed.

York Castle Museum

On the site of York's Castle, the York Castle Museum (tel. 0904/53611) is one of the finest folk museums in the country. Its unique feature is a recreation of a Victorian cobbled street, "Kirkgate," named for the museum's founder, Dr. John Kirk. He acquired his large collection while visiting his patients in rural Yorkshire at the beginning of this century.

The period rooms range from a neoclassical Georgian dining room through an overstuffed and heavily adorned Victorian parlor, to the 1953 sitting room with a brand-new television set purchased to watch the coronation of Elizabeth II. In the Debtors' Prison, former prison cells display craft workshops. There is also a superb collection of arms and armor, and the Costume Gallery, where displays are changed regularly to reflect the variety of the collection. Half Moon Court is an Edwardian street, with a gypsy caravan and a pub (sorry, the bar's closed!). During the summer, you can visit a watermill on the bank of the River Foss.

The museum is open April to September from 9:30 a.m. to 6:30 p.m. (from 10 a.m. on Sunday). October to March, hours are 9:30 a.m. to 5 p.m. (from 10 a.m. on Sunday). Last admission is one hour before closing, and it is recommended that you allow at least two hours for a visit to this museum. Admission is £1.50 ($2.25) for adults, 80p ($1.20) for children.

National Railway Museum

The first national museum to be built away from London, the National Railway Museum (tel. 0904/21261) has attracted millions of visitors. Adapted from an original steam locomotive depot, the museum gives visitors a chance to look under and inside steam locomotives or see how Queen Victoria traveled in luxury. In addition, there's a full-size collection of railway memorabilia, including an early 19th-century clock and penny machines for purchasing tickets to the railway platform. On display are more than 20 full-size locomotives. One, the *Agenoria*, dates from 1829 and is a contemporary of Stephenson's well-known *Rocket*. It's almost identical to the first American locomotive, the *Stourbridge Lion*, sent to the United States from England in 1828. Items on exhibition change from time to time, but there is always a fine selection of the beautifully colored British steam locomotives on display. Of several royal coaches, the most interesting is the century-old Royal Saloon, in which Queen Victoria rode until her death. It's like a small hotel, with polished wood, silk, brocade, and silver accessories.

The museum, on Leeman Road, can be visited weekdays from 10 a.m. to 6 p.m. and on Sunday from 2:30 to 6 p.m. It is closed on New Year's Day, Good Friday, May Day bank holiday, Christmas Eve, Christmas Day, and Boxing Day. Admission is free.

The Treasurer's House

In the Minster Yard, the Treasurer's House (tel. 0904/24247) stands on a site that dates from Roman times. However, the main part of the house was rebuilt in 1620 on the site of the official residence of the treasurer of York Minster, and was lived in as a private home until 1930. In the 20 rooms you will see fine furniture, glass, and china of the 17th and 18th centuries. An audio-visual program describes the work of the medieval treasurers and some of the personalities with which this York house is associated. The house has an attractive small garden. It is open from April until the end of October from 10:30 a.m. to 6 p.m., except on Good Friday. Admission is £1.30 ($1.95) for adults, 70p ($1.05) for children. On some evenings in summer, the house is open from 8 to 10 p.m., when you can enjoy coffee by candlelight in the main hall, then music in the drawing room.

Theatre Royal

Finally, Theatre Royal, St. Leonard's Place (tel. 0904/23568), is an old traditional theater building with modern additions to house the box office, bars, and restaurant. It is worth inquiring about the current production as the Royal Shakespeare Company includes York in its tours, the Arts Council presents dance, drama, and opera, and visiting celebrities appear in classics. There is also an excellent resident repertory company.

Seats go from £2 ($3) in the gallery to £5.50 ($8.25) in the dress circle, with most stall seats costing £4.50 ($6.75). The Theatre Royal Restaurant (tel. 0904/32596) provides a good meal for around £4 ($6). A buffet lunch will average £3 ($4.50). You don't have to buy a seat to eat here, and it's quite a relaxing experience to sit inside with your drink and a snack, looking out on the world passing by.

Brass Rubbing

In College Street, formerly Vicarage Lane, is the Treasurer's House, which stands on the site of a Roman villa. Nearby is St. Williams's College and the **York Brass Rubbing Centre,** which is open from 10 a.m. to 5 p.m. daily (on Sunday from 12:30 to 5 p.m.). The lovely old building was once the home of William Fitzherbert, great-grandson of William the Conqueror. Now a hive of activity, it offers rubbings ranging in price from 75p ($1.13) for a small dog to £7.50 ($11.25) for an elaborate medieval lady. Or you can purchase ready-made rubbings.

Afterward you can go to **The Restaurant,** across the courtyard, for coffee and homemade cakes and scones, served from 10 a.m. to noon. Lunch is from noon to 2 p.m., and teas follow from 2 to 4 p.m. At lunch, costing from £4 ($6), you can order such dishes as homemade soups, herb-flavored quiches, steak, kidney, and mushroom pie, chicken paprika, and wine by the glass. Among the more delectable desserts are lemon or chocolate mousse, honey pie, or a butterscotch tart.

An Unguided Walk-About

Starting from York Minster, walk down past Young's Hotel, reputedly the birthplace of Guy Fawkes. Turn right into Stonegate, a pedestrian area with lovely old shops, a 12th-century house on the right, and some old coffeehouses. Continue across Davygate into St. Helen's Square to see the Guildhall and Mansion House (not open to the public), then go left into Coney Street, taking a right into Lower Ousegate.

At the beginning of Ouse Bridge, take the steps down to Kings Staithe with a pub on the left for refreshment before continuing on into South Esplanade and St. George's Gardens beside the river.

At the bridge, join the road again, turning left and in front of you stand the Castle Museum, the Crown Courts, and Clifford's Tower. Walk up Tower Street and Clifford Street to Nessgate. Turn right into High Ousegate and continue across Parliament Street to the beginning of the Shambles on the left.

Walk up the Shambles past the attractive shops and ancient buildings to Kings Square, then bear right into Goodramgate. Walk down Goodramgate and, at the end, cross Deangate into College Street with St. William's College on the right. At the end a narrow road leads to the Treasurer's House.

You're now behind the east end of the Minster. Walk around to the west end and then up Bootham Bar, through the city gate and turn left into Exhibition Square. The Art Gallery is on the right, the Tourist Information Centre to the left, and beside it, York's Theatre Royal. Continue down St. Leonard's Street to the crossroads, turning right into Museum Street. Cross the river and go right to join part of the old Roman wall.

A Horse-Drawn Carriage Tour

While in York, what about a 15-minute trip in a horse-drawn Danish carriage around the city? One or two horses pull up to five persons, and an umbrella protects you in case it rains. The cost is £1 ($1.50) for adults and 50p (75¢) for children. Call Mr. B. W. Calam (tel. 0904/769490) for more information, or just turn up at the cathedral's west doors where he is likely to be found. He's also available for private rentals, including day country trips for four to six persons. You can stop at country pubs for drinks and farmhouses for tea. He also takes visitors on evening trips, with lantern lights, the price depending on the time.

WHERE TO STAY: My recommendations for rooms and meals follow.

The Upper Bracket

The **Viking Hotel,** North Street (tel. 0904/59822), is a nine-floor, 187-bedroom, ultramodern hotel within the ancient city walls, overlooking the River Ouse, with all the attractions of York only a few minutes' walk away. The bedrooms, many with views toward the Minster, have private baths, color TVs, trouser presses, phones, and tea- and coffee-making facilities. You'll be charged from £48 ($72) for a single, from £70 ($105) in a double- or twin-bedded room, all tariffs including a full English breakfast, VAT, and service. You can enjoy meals in the leisurely atmosphere of one of three riverside restaurants, the Regatta, the Carving Room, or Plumes Coffee Shop. The three dining areas have adjacent bars.

The **Judges Lodging,** 9 Lendal (tel. 0904/23587). The earliest historical fact about this charming house is that it was the home of a certain Dr. Wintringham in 1710. At the beginning of the 19th century it is listed as having been a judges' lodging, used when they traveled north from the London Inns of Justice. In 1979 it was bought by Gerald C. Mason, M.B.E., Her Majesty's consul in Biarritz, and his delightful Hungarian countess wife. Mme la Comtesse was brought up in Paris and has had a very wide experience of hotels. Her touch is evident throughout the elegant building. Drive around the sweeping drive, then up the broad stone steps to the stout front door. You will be greeted by the butler who will register your name and then lead you up a magnificent circular wooden staircase, the only one of its type in the United Kingdom, to one of the bedrooms. All have four-poster beds. If you want to spoil yourself, you can book the large Prince Albert suite, a twin-bedded room with three large windows overlooking the Minster. Prince Albert actually slept in the room once. Hand-embroidered sheets and French embroidered linen in the bathrooms are an additional elegant touch. Each room has a different decor and is named accordingly. One is known as the Queen Mother Room, and in fact it is with her blessing that the coffee cups you will use at dinner come from Clarence House. Singles cost from £40 ($60) to £55 ($82.50), depending on the type, while doubles and twins go for £65 ($97.50) to £80 ($120). The royal room is £90 ($135), rented as a single or a double. Rates include VAT and a full English breakfast.

There are two dining rooms, where candles flicker and the carefully trained French staff will attend to your every need. Dinner will cost around £15 ($22.50), with coffee and petits fours included, and the experience is worth it. All meat, fish, and vegetables are brought in fresh, and the countess does much of the selecting and cooking. The menu is a mouth-watering selection. Down in the old cellars where they found all sorts of bits of Roman pottery, antique pieces of glass, and other relics of the house's varied past, there is the Cocktail Bar, open to the public. Bar snacks at lunchtime include quiche Lorraine and smoked salmon with brown bread. You may be lucky enough to see one of the three ghosts—the countess has—perhaps that of Elizabeth Deltrey, who was shut in to stop her from eloping with her lover.

Royal York Hotel (tel. 0904/53681), outside the city, was built when it was fashionable to stop for the night at a railway station hotel. Owned by Sea Container and formerly called the Royal Station Hotel, it is a mammoth building, not unlike a palace. Most of its 129 bedrooms have private baths. Singles without baths rent for £28 ($42), going up to £48 ($72) with bath and garden view. Twins and doubles without bath go for £46 ($69), peaking at £66 ($99) with a complete bath and a view of the garden and the Minster, including a full breakfast, service, and VAT. The rooms are generally spacious, well furnished, and comfortable. There's an elaborate garden with a central fountain, and surrounding woods. York Minster is only a five-minute walk from the hotel. The public rooms were designed for Victorian grandeur, with high ceilings and miles of carpeting. In the lofty dining room, you can order an à la carte dinner from £10 ($15), including VAT and service. With a separate entrance at the side of the hotel, Bess's Coffee Shop offers steaks, omelets, curries, hamburgers, and salads.

The annex of the Royal York is the **Friars Garden Hotel** (tel. 0904/53681), which offers 22 comfortably furnished bedrooms, all with private baths and tea- and coffee-making facilities. It caters primarily to groups and tours, with £28 ($42) charged in a single, £40 ($60) in a twin or double, the prices including VAT, service, and a full English breakfast. Meals must be taken in the main hotel unless you are part of a large group to whom breakfast is served at Friars Garden.

The Medium-Priced Range

The **Post House,** Tadcaster Road (tel. 0904/67921), is a Trusthouses Forte enterprise, built on the grounds of a former manor house. Only a mile and a half south of the center of York, it is on the A1036, the main approach to York from the A1 and the south. Although contemporary in design, with picture windows in each bedroom, there are many traditional touches as well. The entrance hall and living room, for example, have authentic York flagstones and a montage of old prints and local family crests. A single in summer rents for £30 ($45), a double for £45 ($67.50). Service and tax are included, but breakfast is extra. Each room has a single color theme, with such amenities as air conditioning, color TV, radio, and tea- and coffee-making facilities. The Cedar Restaurant has wide-view windows overlooking a magnificent cedar of Lebanon planted many years ago. An international cuisine is offered. Light meals and snacks, as well as breakfasts, are served in the coffeeshop. Predinner drinks are to be had in the bar, where the wall cabinets are filled with heavy leather-bound books, such as one finds in a country house.

Mount Royale Hotel, The Mount (tel. 0904/56261), is excellent for the money, and the food is good too. Run by Richard and Christine Oxtoby, the Mount Royale is only minutes from the city center. Built in 1833, it is carefully furnished with some beautiful antiques blended with modern pieces. They have taken over the house next door, increasing their bedroom capacity to 20 units, each with bath, costing from £35 ($52.50) to £40 ($60) in a single, £40 ($60) to £56 ($84) in a double or twin, including VAT and a large breakfast. The hotel has a swimming pool. The menu consists of roast joints with interesting accompaniments—grilled York ham with eggs and spinach, fresh halibut with mushroom sauce, roast duckling with black cherry and brandy sauce, duckling with green pepper and corn sauce. The extensive set menu, costing £11.50 ($17.25), carries supplements for such items as fresh out-of-season asparagus or strawberries. The dining room opens onto an attractive garden.

Justifiably popular with locals, the restaurant requires advance reservations. As one local habitué told me, "I suppose that now my son is a week old, it's too late to book for his 21st birthday!" It's still worth the effort trying to get in, however.

Dean Court Hotel, Duncombe Place (tel. 0904/25082), is an ancient building lying right beneath the towers of the Minster. All rooms have bathroom or shower, telephone, radio, and color TV. Ian Washington, the owner, has done a lot recently to bring facilities up to the standards expected these days. B&B is £36 ($54) per person nightly. Lunch will cost £8 ($12), and dinner runs £12 ($18) for a meal from a well-chosen table d'hôte. VAT and service are included in all prices. There is a coffee lounge where snacks are served from 10 a.m. to 8 p.m.

The Budget Range

Lady Anne Middleton's Hotel, Skeldergate House, Skeldergate (tel. 0904/32257), is a delightful 17th-century house, originally built as a hotel for the widows of York's freemen. On the river right opposite the Castle Museum, it is run by Andrew Clark and his wife Kathe, who have lovingly restored the building and created a very comfortable overnight hostelry. There's good car parking, and close by is the world's largest O-gauge railway exhibition. And in the nearby Quaker burial ground lie John Woolman and Linley Murray, two well-loved American Quakers.

If you approach by car you should head toward Harrogate, then turn right to the back of Cromwell House and the car park. Rooms in the new building are cheerful and warmly decorated. Ten bedrooms have private facilities, although there are adequate public baths and toilets. The hotel consists of three separate buildings with extensions added. The overnight cost is £14 ($21) per person, including an English breakfast, but not VAT.

The restaurant is converted from an old sawmill. The dining room offers à la carte dinners such as ham with apricots, roast chicken, and lamb cutlets. The restaurant has a good local reputation, even though the menu is limited. Meals average around £10 ($15).

Beechwood Close Hotel, 19 Shipton Rd. (tel. 0904/58378). On the A19, north of the city, Beechwood is a large house surrounded by trees, a garden with a putting green, and free parking space. Mr. and Mrs. Bulmer have converted it into a hotel, with all modern comforts, such as hot and cold running water in the rooms (most with showers) and central heating. The charge for a bed and a good Yorkshire breakfast is £15.50 ($23.25) to £16.50 ($24.75), per person, including VAT. With its friendly atmosphere, Beechwood attracts many North Americans. It's a 15-minute walk to the Minster, either by road or along the river. However, a bus stop is close by.

Galtres Lodge, Low Petergate (tel. 0904/22478), is a Georgian brick building, owned by Mr. and Mrs. Adams, who have completely redecorated it, and in so doing found three priest holes, one Adam fireplace, and two Georgian fireplaces, which have greatly added to the charm of the hotel. The tariff is from £15 ($22.50) to £18 ($27) per person for B&B, including VAT. Some of the rooms open onto a view of the rose window of the cathedral, and a few contain private showers and four-poster beds. The price of your accommodation, according to manager Tonk Stroughair, depends on how many floors up you have to climb and whether your room has a shower. Lunch is offered à la carte from noon to 2 p.m. The location of the Galtres is faultless, lying only a hop from the Minster, and in the vicinity of the railway station. Historical note: There is a plaque attached to the wall outside the hotel, showing that the street was once the "via principalis" of the old Roman fortress of Eboracum.

Bootham Bar Hotel, 4 High Petergate (tel. 0904/58516), is a charming place, a scrupulously clean 18th-century house with bedroom views over various city sights. Right by the Minster, it is well situated for walking in the evening. Mr. and Mrs. M. Warren offer ten bedrooms at a rate of £10 ($15) per person nightly, including an English breakfast. A deposit will secure a room. All the accommodations, incidentally, are heated and contain wash basins and radios. There is a small lounge with TV. Mrs. Warren's tiny staff is pleasant and helpful.

Granby Lodge Hotel, Scarcroft Road (tel. 0904/53291), is a family-run hotel lying about a ten-minute walk from the historical "downtown" of York. Centrally heated, the hotel, run by the Jacksons, offers 57 pleasantly furnished bedrooms which contain hot and cold running water, shaver points, radios, TVs, and tea- or coffee-making facilities. Some of the units are equipped with private baths or showers. The cost is £15 ($22.50) per person nightly, including VAT, although you'll pay £18.50 ($27.75) per person with bath. The licensed restaurant, seating 200 diners, offers good English food, a reasonably priced dinner served between 6 and 7 p.m. A full English breakfast is included in the tariff quoted. The cozy cocktail bar provides an attractive old-world atmosphere, and private parking is available.

WHERE TO EAT: **Bettys Restaurant,** St. Helen's Square (tel. 0904/22323), is a good all-around eating house in York, regardless of the price range in which you travel. You can call in for a quick coffee and pastry or a full cooked English breakfast, for a Yorkshire cheese lunch or a Welsh rarebit, for a genteel afternoon tea with scones, or for a cooked "fish and chips" high tea. Bettys Tea Rooms are among the best known in England, and there's invariably a queue waiting for service, but the line moves fast and while you wait you can call in at the retail food counter where you may find exotic chocolates and cream cakes, Yorkshire specialties such as curd tart and Brontë fruit cake, or Bettys own roasted coffees and blends of tea. Meals cost from £6 ($9) up. Bettys is open from 9 a.m. to 5:30 p.m. except Sunday, when it is closed.

Kooks Bistro, 108 Fishergate (tel. 0904/37553), is an informal, relaxed eating place run by the owners, Stephanie Cooke and Richard P. Thiel, whose idea is "If *you* don't enjoy it, we don't." Pleasantly decorated in fresh greens and browns with plants and flowers, it features a varied and unusual menu of English, American, Mexican, French, and vegetarian dishes. All main courses are served with a choice of baked potato, french fries, hash browns, or a side salad included in the price. Special features include help-yourself french bread and unlimited coffee. Meals cost from £10 (15). The service is friendly and the atmosphere relaxed, with interesting background music and handmade jigsaws, games, and puzzles on every table. Kooks is fully licensed and open daily except Monday from noon to 3 p.m. and from 7 p.m. to midnight. It is within walking distance of the city center, and there is also plenty of easy parking.

Lew's Place, Kings Staithe (tel 0904/28167), is an old wharfside gathering place, run with charm by Trevor and Andrea Dawson, who admit, "We try to cater for most tastes." Even some of their rival restaurant and café owners drop in whenever they're free, it's that relaxed and friendly. The food is good too, certainly hardy. The menu changes daily. Main-course lunch prices average £4 ($6), increasing to £5 ($7.50) in the evening. The fare is likely to include a homemade moussaka, a savory seafood crêpe, a lamb steak (marinated in red wine, herbs, and garlic), even chili con carne. Usually a homemade soup is offered for a beginning course. Meals are served Monday to Saturday from 11:30 a.m. to 2 p.m. and 6:30 to 10 p.m. The place is smartly painted black and white, and it's cheerful inside with checked cloths on small tables jostling for room. It's a good atmosphere, and the service is efficient and friendly from the "wenches" in Lew's Place T-shirts.

Le Girondin, 30–32 High Petergate (tel. 0904/55344), is owned and operated by Pierre Dufau, who does most of the cooking along with his two assistants. His is probably the closest catering establishment to the Minster. The place opens at 9:30 a.m. for coffee, expanding to lunches from noon to 2:30 p.m. From 6 to 8:30 p.m., they do set dinners. However, they are open in the afternoon for snacks.

A set lunch or dinner includes a choice from four appetizers and about six main dishes. The menu features such exotic delicacies as snails and frogs' legs, mingled with the usual steaks and grills. A set lunch goes for £4.50 ($9.75), and a table d'hôte dinner is priced at £5.50 ($8.25).

Pierre's cousin owns a vineyard in his native Bordeaux region, and he imports his own label wine from his kinsman. A glass will cost £1 ($1.50).

Restaurant Bari, 15 The Shambles (tel. 0904/33807), stands in one of York's oldest and most colorful streets, originally the street of the butchers and mentioned in the Domesday Book. In a continental atmosphere, you can enjoy a quick single course or a full leisurely meal. Ten different pizzas are offered. Lasagne and cannelloni are superb. Lunch can cost as little as £4 ($6), and dinner from about £6 ($9). A main-dish specialty is escalope Sophia Loren (veal cooked with brandy and cheese with a rich tomato sauce). The restaurant is open seven days a week from 11:30 a.m. to 2:30 p.m. and 6 to 11 p.m.

Thomas's Wine Bar and Bistro, Museum Street (tel. 0904/54494). On a site where in the 1870s Eldrige's Royal Hotel was offering "a high standard of comfort and service to the nobility and country gentry," Thomas's now offers very good, economical meals or just a snack to sustain anyone who wants to stop. Downstairs, the wine bar has bare wooden floors and country-style wooden furniture; wine and sherry are dispensed from casks behind the bar. Pâtés, cheeses, pies, and salads are available at lunchtime. The bar is open seven days a week from noon to 2:30 p.m. and from 7 to 10:30 p.m.

The cheapest way to dine here is to order the set meal at £4 ($6), including VAT. For this you are likely to get a main course such as poached salmon or steak-and-kidney pie. Bistro dinners are likely to cost from £9 ($13.50). For this you might be served an appetizer such as deep-fried mushrooms or stuffed peppers, followed by pork Stroganoff with onions or beef with stilton sauce. Duck with orange sauce is another specialty, as are kidneys turbigo. The very pleasant atmosphere is created by Pam and Ian Postlethwaite, who run the place.

Plunkets, 9 High Petergate (tel. 0904/37722), is a bright, cheerful, busy place right beneath the shadow of the Minster yet seeming to fit in with its ancient surroundings. Hamburgers are served with french fries, salad with choice of dressing, and the relish tray. All the usual ones are there from plain quarter-pounder to Plunket Burger, a half-pounder with cheese or chili topping. A large club sandwich a good buy, or a rump steak may please you. There are milkshakes, ice creams, cheesecake, chocolate fudge cake, and banana splits.Meals cost from £12 ($18). At peak hours—lunch and suppertime—you must eat, but at other times just a coffee or milkshake is all you need have. There are several smaller rooms upstairs where you cannot hear the musak and can be a little more intimate if you wish to. The place is open from 11 a.m. to 11 p.m. daily, although in winter they close from 3 to 5 p.m.

The **Kings Arms,** Kingsnaith, is a historical public house in a prime position on the banks of the River Ouse. The house is one of charm, character, and intimacy, and is also bright and cheerful. Your hosts are John and Tina Winterbottom, who sell a full range of Samuel Smith's draft and bottled beers traditionally brewed in Tadcaster, which is only ten miles from York. Light meals cost from £3.50 ($5.25).

Jeeves, 39 Tanner Row (tel. 0904/59622), is a family-run restaurant with lace tablecloths and winking candlelight. It is open only in the evening from 7 to 10 p.m. (closed Sunday, and also on Monday in winter). The kitchen does an à la carte dinner, a full three-course meal costing about £10 ($15). Appetizers include homemade soup, fresh pâté, taramasalata, and mango stuffed with local crabmeat and dressing. Main dishes are likely to be chicken breast stuffed with mushrooms and served with mushroom and asparagus sauce, filet steaks, fresh salmon poached in wine, and other fish dishes in season, all served with a selection of fresh vegetables cooked in herbs. The meal is rounded off with a selection of homemade desserts, or for a special treat, ripe stilton cheese with a glass of rare vintage port. There are more than 200 wines in the cellar from which you can choose. VAT is included in the dinner price, but service is added. It is advisable to make reservations to dine here.

Taylors in Stonegate, 46 Stonegate, (tel. 0904/22865). Downstairs, the bow-windowed shop is filled with bags and jars of coffee. The old-fashioned till bears the prices of the various teas for sale. They boast 36 varieties of teas and coffee. When you see the shop, you'll know that is no idle boast. Teas come all the way from China and India, including exotic Moroccan mint and passion fruit. Upstairs, the coffeeshop dispenses these same beverages at 65p (98¢) for a pot of tea for one, 90p ($1.35) for a pot of coffee for one. They advertise a late breakfast for £2.50 ($5.25). You can also order Welsh rarebit, Yorkshire ham, and omelets with various fillings, costing around £2.60 ($3.90). Spiced Yorkshire teacakes and cinnamon toast are also on the menu. Service is from 9 a.m. to 5:30 p.m.

LODGINGS IN THE ENVIRONS: Just about 30 miles southeast of York lies a small market town, **Beverley**, in North Humberside. There are several medieval buildings in the town, and many travelers prefer to stay here instead of in York proper.

The **Beverley Arms Hotel**, North Bar Within, Beverley, North Humberside (tel. 0482/869241), is, in part, more than 300 years old. A wing has been added to provide bedrooms with bath, radio, phone, TV, and tea- and coffee-making equipment. A double room costs £52 ($78) a night, including VAT. The restaurant features many seafood and fish dishes, using produce caught daily in the North Sea and landed at Hull. There is also a coffeeshop, constructed in the old kitchens, with a stone-flagged floor and high-backed chairs where snacks and light meals are served from 10 a.m. to 7 p.m. The North Bar serves traditional ales, and good food.

Kings Head Hotel, Market Place, Beverley, North Humberside (tel. 0482/868103), is a Georgian inn where a double room will cost you £32 ($48); a single, £20 ($30)—including a full Yorkshire breakfast, service, and VAT. This is a typical small-town place where standards have to be kept up, otherwise you lose your regular customers. Lunch Monday to Saturday, costing £5 ($7.50), includes a choice of three appetizers, then from two roasts, steak-and-kidney pie, or several other hot dishes, plus dessert. A set lunch on Sunday goes for £6 ($9). An à la carte dinner, for around £10 ($15), is offered.

A CHANCE TO STAY WITH BRITISH ARISTOCRACY: Gunnerside Lodge is the family seat of the Earl and Countess Peel, a rambling house in Swaledale where Lord Peel (that is how you address him) owns and farms some 35,000 acres deep in the heart of the Herriot country and bordering on the Brontë country near the ancient city of York. The earl and countess have opened their home to small parties of six or more, who want to stay for at least three nights and learn something of this part of the country and the English way of life as lived here.

There are eight large double bedrooms with downy beds, modern literature, *The Sporting Life* and *Horse and Hound* on the bureau, and gorgeous views for miles over the dale. Four bathrooms are down the hall. Downstairs, the marble-floored main hall leads to the large drawing room, with the biggest set of antlers you'll ever see over the fireplace where a log fire often flickers. Beyond, the billiard room winds to the Orangery, with more views over the countryside.

Lady Peel supervises the kitchen, so if you have a particular dislike or dietary problem, it can be coped with. Breakfast in the paneled dining room is a leisurely, help-yourself-from-the-sideboard affair. Dinner is a candlelight occasion, with the earl and countess. The conversation flows— the conservation of land and wildlife, world affairs, or the latest debate attended by Lord Peel in the House of Lords.

During your days there's a trip to York, accompanied by the earl or the countess, including visits to the sights, lunch, and a drive through the Dales.

The cost of £400 ($600) for two people, inclusive of all food and drink for three days, as well as tobacco and other incidentals, is somewhat of a bargain if you figure that the same amount of time in a deluxe London hotel will set you back far more.

You must make up your own group, but that should be the least of your problems. Incidentally, for those history buffs, the earl is descended from Sir Robert Peel (his great-great-grandfather), once prime minister of England and the founder of the First Force to Protect Life and Property, the Peelers or Peelersmen, soon to become the policemen, bobbies, and rozzers.

For those worried about meeting the English aristocracy, chances are that within 24 hours you'll be on a first-name basis, inviting them to visit you.

For reservations and inquiries, write to the Secretary, the Gunnerside Estate Office, 8 Main St., Kirkby Lonsdale, Carnforth, Lancashire LA6 2AF (tel. 0468/71114), although Gunnerside Lodge is in Yorkshire.

A SIDE TRIP FROM YORK: The most interesting day trip from York is to:

Castle Howard

In its dramatic setting of lakes, fountains, and extensive gardens, Castle Howard (tel. Coneysthorpe 333), the 18th-century palace designed by Sir John Vanbrugh, is undoubtedly the finest private residence in Yorkshire. Principal location for the TV series "Brideshead Revisited," this was the first major achievement of the architect who later created the lavish Blenheim Palace near Oxford. The Yorkshire palace was begun in 1699 for the third Earl of Carlisle, Charles Howard, whose descendants still call the place home. The striking facade is topped by a painted and gilded dome, reaching more than 80 feet into the air. The interior boasts a 192-foot "Long Gallery," as well as a chapel with a magnificent stained-glass window by the 19th-century artist Sir Edward Burne-Jones. Besides the collections of antique furniture, tapestries, porcelains, and sculpture, the castle contains a number of important paintings, including a portrait of Henry VIII by Holbein, and works by Rubens, Reynolds, and Gainsborough.

The seemingly endless grounds around the palace also offer the visitor some memorable sights, including the domed Temple of the Four Winds, by Vanbrugh, and the richly designed family mausoleum by Hawksmoor. There are two rose gardens, one with old-fashioned roses, the other featuring modern creations. The stable court houses the Costume Galleries, the largest private collection of 18th- to 20th-century costumes in Britain. The authentically dressed mannequins are exhibited in period settings. Castle Howard, just 15 miles northeast of York, is open to the public daily from March 25 through October 31. The grounds are open from 10:30 a.m., the cafeteria from 11 a.m., and the house and Costume Galleries from 11:30 a.m. It all closes at 5 p.m., with last admission to the house and galleries at 4:45 p.m. Admission is £2.50 ($3.75) for adults, £1.50 ($2.25) for children. You can enjoy sandwiches, hot dishes, and good wines in the self-service cafeteria.

2. North Yorkshire

Yorkshire, known to readers of *Wuthering Heights* around the world, is now divided into three counties—West Yorkshire, South Yorkshire, and

North Yorkshire. For those seeking legendary untamed scenery, I'd recommend a tour of North Yorkshire, which also takes in the historic cathedral city of York.

North Yorkshire contains England's most varied landscape. Its history has been turbulent, often bloody, and many relics of its rich past are still standing, including ruined abbeys. Yorkshire is little known to the average North American visitor, but many an English traveler is familiar with its haunting moors, serene valleys, and windswept dales.

The hospitality of the people of Yorkshire is world renowned, and if a pudding which originated there doesn't accompany a slab of roast beef, the plate looks naked to the British. The people of Yorkshire, who speak an original twang often imitated in English cinema, are, in general, hardworking and industrious, perhaps a little contemptuous of the easy living of the south. But they are decidedly open and friendly to strangers, providing you speak to them first.

HARROGATE: If you head west from York for 20 miles, you reach Harrogate, North Yorkshire's second-largest town after York itself. In the 19th century Harrogate was a fashionable spa. Most of its town center is surrounded by a 200-acre lawn called "The Stray." Boutiques and antique shops—which Queen Mary used to frequent—make Harrogate a shopping center of excellence, particularly along Montpellier Parade. Harrogate is called England's floral resort, deserving such a reputation because of its gardens, including Harlow Car Gardens and Valley Gardens. The former spa has an abundance of guest houses and hotels, including the expensive Swan where Agatha Christie hid out during her mysterious disappearance —still unexplained—in the 1920s.

Food and Lodging

The Old Swan, Swan Road (tel. 0423/504051). This is the spot where the late mystery writer, Agatha Christie, suddenly surfaced after a mysterious 11-day disappearance that was the subject of the film *Agatha,* starring Dustin Hoffman. One of the most famous hotels in northern England, the Old Swan offers comfort, good food, fine wines, and impeccable service. It has been modernized, yet retains the atmosphere of a country home. There are 140 bedrooms and nine suites, all with private baths/showers, color TVs, and tea- and coffee-making equipment. The tariff for a twin-bedded room is £69 ($103.50), £49 ($73.50) in a single, both rates including VAT and a full English breakfast. Of the two restaurants, the Colours offers à la carte menus and the Wedgwood Carvery has a variety of roasts, fresh vegetables, salads, and other accompaniments.

Yorke Arms Hotel, Ramsgill, near Harrogate (tel. 0423/75243), is surrounded by moody moorland scenery, and is an ideal center for excursions. It's a widely spread manor house, with many well-preserved architectural features, plus a selection of antiques. The dining hall, for example, with its black oak sideboard, holds a collection of pewter, and you dine on Windsor armchairs in front of a time-blackened fireplace. The lounge has tufted velvet sofas drawn up around a stone fireplace. The exterior is stately, built of stone, with creeping ivy covering part of its gables and mullioned windows. The rooms are comfortably furnished and well maintained, and some contain private baths. The cost of half board here is about £35 ($52.50) per person nightly.

In this attractively furnished town house, built back in Victoria's day, **Number Six,** 6 Ripon Rd. (tel. 0423/502908), is one of the finest dining rooms at the spa, and I recommend that you skp a meal at your hotel to patronize this fine and well-run establishment with its outstanding wine list. The Di Silvestro brothers have hired a well-trained staff to serve their beautifully prepared dishes, which are likely to include such delicacies as quenelles of sole, quails en cocotte with raisins, fresh lobster thermidor, roast duckling with orange sauce, or roast mallard.

As you enter the restaurant you can head for the intimate bar to enjoy an apértif and, while sipping it, make menu selections from an imaginative choice of dishes, mostly continental in flavor and presentation. Ingredients are well chosen, and the wine list is above average. Expect to pay at least £15 ($22.50) per person, plus the cost of your wine. Only dinner is served, except Monday, and hours are from 7 to 10 p.m., when reservations are essential.

MOORS AND DALES:
The rural landscape is pierced with ruins of once-great abbeys and castles. North Yorkshire is a land of green hills, valleys, and purple moors. Both the Yorkshire Dales and the Moors are wide open spaces, two of Britain's finest national parks, with a combined area of some 1200 square miles. However, the term "national" can be misleading, as the land is managed by foresters, farmers, and private landowners. In fact, more than 90% of the land is in private ownership. The Dales rise toward Cumbria and Lancashire to the east, and the Moors stretch to the eastern coastline.

Of course, York, the major center, has already been previewed. But those with the time may want to explore deeper into the rural roots of England. From Harrogate, our last stopover, you can enjoy the wildest scenery of the region by heading out on day trips, anchoring at one of the inns coming up if you don't want to return to the old spa.

After leaving Harrogate, you can discover white limestone crags, drystone walls, fast-rushing rivers, and isolated sheep farms or clusters of sandstone cottages.

Malhamdale receives more visitors annually than any dale in Yorkshire. Of the priories and castles to visit, two of the most interesting are the 12th-century ruins of **Bolton Priory,** and the 14th-century pile, **Castle Bolton,** to the north in Wensleydale.

Richmond, the most frequently used town name in the world, stands here at the head of the Dales as the mother of them all. Here the Norman towers of Richmond Castle, the country's best known fortress, dominate the cobbled market town. The Georgian Theatre here, which was constructed in 1788, has a resident amateur company of the highest quality.

In contrast, the Moors, on the other side of the Vale of York, have a wild beauty all their own, quite different from that of the Dales. They are bounded by the Cleveland and Hambleton Hills. The white horse of Kilburn can be seen hewn out of the landscape.

Both **Pickering** and **Northallerton,** two market towns, serve as gateways to the Moors. Across the Moors are seen primordial burial grounds and stone crosses. The best known trek in moorland is the 40-mile hike over bog, heather, and stream from Mount Grace Priory inland to Ravenscar on the seacoast. It's known as **Lyke Wake Walk.**

Coxwold is on the southern border of the park, one of the most attractive villages in the Moors.

Along North Yorkshire's 45 miles of coastline are such traditional seaside resorts as **Filey, Whitby,** and **Scarborough,** the latter claiming to be the oldest seaside spa in Britain, standing on the site of a Roman signaling station. It was founded in 1622, following the discovery of mineral springs with medicinal properties. In the 19th century, its Grand Hotel, a Victorian structure, was acclaimed "as the best in Europe." The Norman castle on big cliffs overlooks the twin bays.

In and Around Helmsley

This attractive town, where a market is held every Friday, is a good center for exploring the surrounding area. Called the key to Ryedale, it is the mother town of the district, standing at the junction of the roads from York, Pickering, Malton, Stokesley, and Thirsk. On the southern edge of the North Yorkshire Moors National Park, Helmsley is well known as a center for walking and "potholing." It is in a section that contains many places and things of interest: remains of Bronze and Iron Age existence on the moors, prehistoric highways, Roman roads, and of course, the ruins of medieval castles and abbeys. Beyond the main square of the town are the ruins of its castle, built between 1186 and 1227, and its impressive keep.

A good reason for selecting Helmsley as a stopover is because it is near York and well located, but with hotel rates far below those of the larger city.

Three miles to the north of Helmsley are the ruins of **Rievaulx** (pronounced "reevo") **Abbey,** named for Rye Vallis, valley of the River Rye. The first Cistercian house in northern England, the abbey was founded in 1131 by monks who came over from Clairveaux in France. At its peak it had 140 monks and 500 lay brothers. Its size, architecture, and setting make even the abbey ruins among the most impressive in the country. The land was given by Walter l'Espec, a Norman knight who later entered the community as a novice, and died and was buried here. Admission to the abbey ruins is 80p ($1.20).

Rievaulx Terrace, now a property of the National Trust, is a land-scaped, grassy terrace about half a mile long, which was laid out in the mid-18th century by Thomas Duncombe of Duncombe Park. After a woodland walk, you emerge onto a wide lawn near a circular "temple," known as the Tuscan Temple. The walk along the terrace gives frequent views of the abbey ruins in the valley below. On a windy North Yorkshire spring day, I find this walk a real constitutional.

At the opposite end from the Tuscan Temple is the Ionic Temple, whose interior is beautifully decorated and furnished, with a classically painted ceiling and furniture of gilded wood with rose velvet upholstery. In the basement are two rooms that were originally used by servants to prepare food for guests above. The Ionic Temple was planned by Thomas Duncombe III as a banqueting house and a place of rest and refreshment after the long carriage ride from Duncombe Park.

Admission is £1 ($1.50) for adults, 50p (75¢) for children.

The **Black Swan** (tel. 0439/70466) has stood since the 16th century overlooking the marketplace. Part Tudor, part Georgian, part modern, this Trusthouses Forte hotel offers 38 well-furnished bedrooms, each with private bath, radio, TV, phone, and coffee-making facilities. These rent from £45 ($67.50) in a single, from £65 ($97.50) in a double, including service and VAT. A new wing of bedrooms has been added at the rear. Public rooms are full of character, with open fires, paneling, and time-aged beams. In the traditionally furnished restaurant, you can enjoy unusual Yorkshire dishes, such as Wensley fowl stuffed with dale cheese or jugged venison, a dinner costing from £12 ($18) per head. The hotel also has three bars.

Crown Hotel, Market Square (tel. 0439/70297), is of undetermined age, but at least from 1550. It's built of stone, standing at the edge of the village square, and the walls are covered by creepers, giving it charm. The owners, Mr. and Mrs. Mander, have spared no effort to make every room not only attractive, but comfortable. Nine of their bedrooms now have showers, all have hot and cold running water, and wherever possible, in the restoration old beams have been left exposed. The dining room is well furnished; there are two bars, one public and one better furnished for residents. In addition, there are two living rooms. B&B is priced according to the plumbing you get, £15.70 ($23.55) to £17.40 ($26.10) per person, including VAT. For dinner, bed, and breakfast, the cost is £20 ($30) to £21.50 ($32.25). Set lunches are from £6 ($9), dinners run from £10 ($15), and the food is typically English.

Near Skipton

The **Buck Inn,** Malham, near Skipton (tel. Airton 317), is a Victorian stone inn where Dale explorers can find excellent ale, a comfortable and cozy room, and a good breakfast and dinner. There are two bars, one especially for hikers, the other for residents. The inn offers ten centrally heated bedrooms, each with a wash basin, only one with a private bath, which costs £3 ($4.50) extra per night. The charge is £18 ($27) per person for B&B, £24 ($36) per person for half board, including VAT, between July 1 and mid-October, and after that, tariffs are reduced. You can order bar lunches noon and evenings if you don't want a full meal.

IN AND AROUND RIPON: Ripon has an ancient tradition of a watchman blowing a curfew horn in the center of town every night at 9 o'clock, a custom dating back to 886. This cathedral city, 27 miles north of Leeds by road, was once a Saxon village where a Celtic monastery was founded in 651.

Beneath the central tower of **Ripon Cathedral,** site of a Norman archbishop's church dating from 1154, is the original crypt built by St. Wilfrid more than 1300 years ago, one of the oldest buildings in England. The original plaster is still on the walls. The crypt contains silver chalices and patens dating from 1500 to the present.

Archbishop Roger built the nave of the Norman cathedral, the north transept, and part of the choir stalls. The twin towers of the west front are Early English, from about 1216, and the library (once the Lady Loft) is from sometime in the 14th century. The canons stalls were hand-carved, completed in 1495. Two sides of the tower date from the original construction in 1220, but in 1450 an earthquake caused the other two sides to collapse. They were reconstructed, and the central tower and south transept were added at the beginning of the 16th century. The completion of all the work was never carried out, as King Henry VIII took away all the cathedral endowments. Until 1664 the towers had tall spires, but they were removed to prevent fires caused by lightning.

Today the cathedral is a lively Christian Centre, with a study center and a choir school. It is the mother church of the Diocese of Ripon, which spreads over most of the Yorkshire Dales to the fifth-largest city in England, Leeds. For further information, telephone Ripon 4108.

Three miles west of Ripon lie the ruins of **Fountains Abbey,** which I consider the most magnificent abbey ruins in England. Founded in 1132, this former abbey was Cistercian in origin. It is set in 100 acres of meadow and woodland, with ornamental gardens, Fountains Hall, and a deer herd.

Newby Hall, on the northeast bank of the Ure River between Ripon (4 miles) and Boroughbridge (3½ miles), is a celebrated Adam house set in 25 acres of grounds filled with sunken gardens, magnolias, azaleas, and countless other flowering shrubs, along with many rare and unusual species. The house, built for Sir Edward Blackett circa 1695, is in the style of Sir Christopher Wren. In the mid-18th century Robert Adam redesigned the structure, extending it to display the antique sculpture, tapestries, and furniture of its owner, William Weddell, a connoisseur and art collector. Today it belongs to Robert Compton. Displayed are Gobelin tapestries, one of only five sets completed, with medallions by Boucher, appointed first painter to Louis XV.

On the grounds is a miniature railway, the Newby 10¼-inch gauge, providing rides for both children and adults.

In April, May, and September, the house is open from 1 to 5:30 p.m. Wednesday, Thursday, Saturday, and Sunday; from June to August, daily except Monday. The gardens are open April 1 to September 30 daily except Monday from 11 a.m. to 5:30 p.m. To visit the hall, park, and gardens costs £2.50 ($3.75) for adults, £1.25 ($1.88) for children. For more information, phone Boroughbridge 2583.

The **Unicorn Hotel,** Market Square (tel. Ripon 2202), is a coaching inn and posting house. It has welcomed travelers for some 400 years with true Yorkshire warmth and hospitality, and the same is true today. It's directly on the Market Square opposite the obelisk where the 1000-year-old tradition of setting the watch by blowing the horn takes place each evening. The facade of the inn is in Victorian style, with square bay windows and an elaborate front entrance. All of the 28 bedrooms have private facilities, central heating, tea- and coffee-making equipment, and phones. Singles rent from £24 ($36), and doubles or twins from £38 ($57), these tariffs including VAT and a full English breakfast. The cuisine in the Pykestolle Restaurant is Cordon Bleu, and in addition, bar lunches are served in the Tom Crudds bar, a typically English pub with locally brewed real ale.

The **Nordale,** 1 North Parade (tel. Ripon 3557), is a bargain at the daily per-person rate of £9.25 ($13.88), which includes not only a complete full-course breakfast but VAT. Some units have showers, and you will have hot and cold running water in your room. However, adequate baths are in the halls. Consider having a Yorkshire dinner as well, and this costs £16 ($24) per person, including your room and breakfast. The owners are John and Barbara Richmond. She will pack a picnic lunch for you if you are making a day trip. All their bedrooms are attractively furnished, with twins and doubles, according to your wish. Children can stay at reduced rates. The Nordale, which has a residential license, is a good center for exploring the Yorkshire Dales.

Black-a-Moor Inn, Risplith, near Ripon (tel. Sawley 214), is a 17th-century stone country inn well known for its hospitality and convivial atmosphere. It's on the Ripon–Pately Bridge road, the B6265, five miles from Ripon, well suited for visits to Fountains Abbey, the Brimham Rocks, and the Yorkshire Dales. The owners, Patricia and Byron Brader, have decorated the three bedrooms with taste, installing central heating as well as hot and cold running water. They charge £20 ($30) in a single room and £25 ($37.50) in a double for B&B, including VAT. A traditional English breakfast is served. A popular and varied menu is available at lunchtime and in the evening, including homemade steak-and-kidney pies, venison, and turkey Cordon Bleu. The Braders' son Martin presides over the bar.

READERS' RESTAURANT SUGGESTION: "The **New Hornblower Restaurant,** Duck Hill (tel. Ripon 4841), is a charming little eating place just off the central square in Ripon, where we had an excellent dinner. Everything is homemade, prepared and served by the husband-and-wife owners. We had beef-and-onion soup, chicken divan with three vegetables, potatoes, chocolate mousse, and coffee for about £10 ($15). Coffee refills are unlimited (unusual in the United Kingdom)" (Conrad and Virginia Bayley, Glendale, Ariz.).

At Thirsk

This pleasant old market town, lying in the Vale of Mowbray north of York, has a fine parish church. But what makes it such a popular stopover for visitors is the fame brought to the village by James Herriot, author of *All Creatures Great and Small* and other books about his experiences as a veterinarian serving this area of Yorkshire. Mr. Herriot still practices in Thirsk, and visitors can photograph his office, perhaps getting a picture of his partner standing in the door.

If you'd like to stay over, **Brook House,** Ingramgat (tel. Thirsk 22240), is a large Victorian house set in 1½ acres of land, some of which is bright with flower beds. It overlooks the open countryside, but a three-minute walk brings you to the Market Square. Mrs. Margaret McLauchlan charges from £11 ($16.50) per person for B&B, although she makes reductions for children. She is charming and kind, and has even been known to do a batch of washing for guests at no extra cost (however, I can't promise that). She serves a good Yorkshire breakfast, hearty and filling, plus an English tea in the afternoon. There is a spacious and comfortable living room with color TV, and the bedrooms are large and airy, opening onto views. The experience of knowing John and Margaret McLauchlan and enjoying their hospitality will remain long in your memory. They are personal friends of James Herriot.

Church Farm, at Sowerby, near Thirsk (tel. Thirsk 23655), offers rural peace. It's reached by a footpath from the town center, about a five-minute walk from Thirsk Market Square. It is both a Cordon Bleu restaurant and a farm offering accommodations. The owners, Olga and Roy Sheppard, were born in Yorkshire and are most helpful to guests touring in the area. Their home is some three centuries old, but it has been brought up to date and handsomely furnished, often with family heirlooms. Outside stand large lime trees, which were planted to honor Queen Victoria's Jubilee. Bedrooms are pleasantly furnished and have a personalized touch. My favorites are the two double rooms and a family room, all with bath en suite, installed in a former hayloft. The en suite accommodations are rented for £16 ($24) per person, or if you take one of the other double rooms, the charge is lowered to £12 ($18) per person.

The six-stall horse barn has been converted into the Sheppard's Table. It is possible to enjoy a quiet drink and a candlelit dinner on the very spot where James Herriot used to minister to the horses. The walls are of rough brick, and dark wood and farm equipment make for a rustic atmosphere. The cuisine is excellent because all the ingredients that go into making it are bought fresh daily. The cookery is both imaginative and served with flair. A traditional Sunday lunch is featured for £6.50 ($9.75), and a dinner from £10 ($15) to £15 ($22.50). There's also a full à la carte menu if you prefer. Lunch is served from noon to 2 p.m. and dinner from 7 p.m. The stable is closed Sunday evening and Monday. Reservations are advised.

The **Cleveland Tontine Inn** and **McCoy's Restaurant,** Staddle Bridge, Northallerton (tel. 060-982/207), could well be called a restaurant *avec chambres.* It is a solid coaching inn built at the midway point of all northern cities and equidistant from York, Leeds, Newcastle, and Sunderland, close to the Yorkshire Moors and the Dales, and near the main road to Scotland, just outside Northallerton. The veterinarian serving this area is James Herriot of Thirsk, so you know this is true Herriot country.

The place is run almost entirely by Eugene, Tom, and Peter McCoy, with staunch assistance from Alison. Eugene manages the front, and Tom and Peter do most of the cooking. They are a friendly and unconventional lot, given to a startling line in dress—jeans, T-shirts, and plimsolls (British shoes with rubber soles, mudguards, and canvas tops)—but they are masters in the art of hospitality which, as they say, even surpasses their food. Don't expect preferential treatment or discreet deference from Eugene as he discusses and translates the handwritten menu for you. Just sit back and enjoy the atmosphere of potted palms and art nouveau.

Then pay full attention to dinner, which can start with scallops in butter with a mouthwatering sauce of chablis, cream, basil, and tarragon; rock lobster poached in a cabbage leaf with a little caviar butter; or a roquefort quiche. Freshen your palate with a fresh fruit or champagne sorbet before sampling the filet of beef marinated in burgundy with shallots, juniper berries, and parsley, garnished with sauteed cucumber. Or you might prefer the partridge with port sauce and a fresh pear. There are some intriguing desserts, including a mixture of almond cream, Cointreau-soaked sponge cake, and fresh raspberries. Your meal will cost about £22 ($33), plus a bottle of wine. If you don't want such a rich spread, visit the cellar bistro where they serve homemade lasagne, hamburgers, steak, salad, mussels, spinach crêpes, and tandoori chicken.

The eight bedrooms rent for £34 ($51) single, £44 ($66) double, including VAT and a breakfast that includes exotic fruit, such as mangoes, pineapple, and papaya, plus home-laid "free range" eggs, homemade bread, honey, and jams.

3. West Yorkshire

HAWORTH: In West Yorkshire, this ancient stone village lying on the high moors of the Pennines—45 miles west of York via Leeds and 21 miles west of Leeds itself—is world famous as the home of the Brontë family. The three sister—Charlotte, Emily, and Anne—distinguished themselves as English novelists. They lived a life of imagination at a lonely parsonage at Haworth.

Anne wrote two novels, *The Tenant of Wildfell Hall* and *Agnes Grey,* and Charlotte's masterpiece was *Jane Eyre,* which depicted her experiences as a governess, and enjoyed popular success in its day.

But, of course, it was Emily's fierce and tragic *Wuthering Heights* that made her surpass her sisters, as she created a novel of such passion, intensity, and primitive power, with its scenes of unforgettable, haunting melancholy, that the book has survived to this day, appreciated by later generations far more than those she'd written it for. Haworth is the most visited literary shrine in England, after Stratford-upon-Avon.

From Haworth, you can walk to Withens, the "Wuthering Heights" of the immortal novel. In Haworth, Charlotte and Emily are buried in the family vault under the church of St. Michael's.

The parsonage where they lived has been preserved as the **Brontë Parsonage Museum** (tel. 0535/42323). Emily and Charlotte died there. It is open daily all year (except for three weeks in December) from 11 a.m. Closing time is 5:30 p.m. from April to September, 4:30 p.m. October to March. Admission is 50p (75¢) for adults, 25p (38¢) for children.

On the Haworth Moor stands a Brontë landmark, **Ponden Hall,** Stanbury, near Keighley (tel. 0535/44154), a distance of some three miles from Haworth. It lies half a mile from the main road on the wide rough track that is the Pennine Way. An Elizabethan farmhouse built in 1560 and extended in 1801, this reputedly is the model for Thrushcross Grange, Catherine's home after her marriage to Edgar Linton.

Today the hall provides a farmhouse accommodation, a hand-loom weaving studio, a residential weaving course, a bunkhouse accommodation, as well as camping.

The village of Haworth has frequent bus and train service to Keighley, Bradford, and Leeds in West Yorkshire.

Food and Lodging

The **Tourist Information Centre,** at 2–4 West Lane in Haworth (tel. 0535/42329), offers an accommodation-booking service, and the office is open daily from 10 a.m. to 5:30 p.m. Easter until the end of October, from 10:30 a.m. to 4:30 p.m. November to March. Otherwise, you might stay at one of my recommendations below.

A reminder: You must not expect such amenities as private baths, air conditioning, and the like in the lower priced places recommended. Just as in the United States, you get what you pay for.

The **Old White Lion Hotel** (tel. 0535/42313) stands at the top of a cobbled street. It was built around 1700 with a solid stone roof almost next door to the church where the Reverend Mr. Brontë preached and to the parsonage where the family lived. Phyllis and Don Wolstenholme welcome Brontë buffs and others in their warm, cheerful, and comfortable inn. They charge them £13 ($19.50) per person in a double, £16 ($24) in a single. For an additional £2 ($3) per person, you'll be given a room with a bath or shower. VAT is included, but service is extra. Dinners, except Sunday, are à la carte, and good local meats and fresh vegetables are used at a cost of £6.50 ($9.75) per person. A set Sunday lunch costs £6 ($9), usually featuring a roast. Bar snacks include the usual favorites—ploughman's lunch, hot pies, fish, and sandwiches.

The **Black Bull,** Main Street (tel. 0535/42249), owned by Ron and Kath Bennett, stands close to the parish church where Patrick Brontë was incumbent for 41 years and is closely associated with the son, Branwell Brontë. Although renovated and improved since Branwell's day, it is still interesting to spend time within the walls that drew him so strongly and even to sit in the chair that he occupied on his many visits to the place, still on the premises. Today the Black Bull is as comfortable an inn as you will find.

Conversion of the restaurant, which seats 40, has made use of a thick stone wall in forming a central arch. This is the room where Branwell's chair sits, and here is the original bell pull and bell that he used to ring for his many drinks. Luncheon and bar snacks are served from noon until 2:30 p.m. A three-course lunch with roast beef and Yorkshire pudding costs around £6.50 ($9.75). Snacks and assorted sandwiches are served in the lounge area. Chicken, scampi, and haddock with chips and peas or homemade steak pie are offered for around £3.50 ($5.25). Dinner is served from 7 until 10:30 p.m. The cuisine is excellent, and the à la carte menu, with a good supporting wine list, gives an ample choice. Morning coffee and high tea are served on Sunday. The Bennetts charge £25 ($37.50) for a double room, including a good breakfast.

Keepers Restaurant, The Fold, Haworth, near Keighley (tel. 0535/42919). Four cottages make up this delightful place presided over by Mrs. Starr, while her daughter, a qualified chef, does all the cooking. Although the present structure is not all that old (just a couple of hundred years), the original cottages date from the 15th century, and the decor reflects the period. More than 300 watercolor paintings decorate the walls, and a variety of simple dishes are served, such as roast beef and Yorkshire pudding, but they also do korma or hot Bengal curry with sambals (side dishes of relish). The dessert specialty of the house is a chocolate brandy cake made with fresh cream. A meal will cost around £5 ($7.50) to £7 ($10.50).

In the evenings, they like to have warning of your arrival for dinner (from 8 p.m.). A homemade soup followed by sirloin steak, beef Stroganoff, or chicken cooked with a sauce of cream, asparagus, and sherry, dessert, and coffee costs around £10 ($15) to £12 ($18). They bake all their own cakes and pastries, and are open from 11:30 a.m. to 7 p.m. daily in summer, noon to 6 p.m. in winter, when they also close on Friday. They also have a couple of rooms available in their cottage next door and charge £9 ($13.50) per person for B&B (you have to come along to the restaurant). The units are spotlessly clean and comfortable.

HAREWOOD HOUSE AND BIRD GARDEN: In West Yorkshire, at Junction A61/659, midway between Leeds and Harrogate and five miles from the A1 at Wetherby, stands Harewood House, home of the Earl and Countess of Harewood. It's one of the "magnificent seven" homes of England, which includes Blenheim Palace and Beaulieu Abbey. The 18th-century house was designed by Robert Adam and John Carr and has always been owned by the Lascelles family. It contains superb plasterwork, beautiful Chippendale furniture, and collections of Sèvres and Chinese porcelain, and of English and Italian paintings.

Harewood Bird Garden borders the lake and blends successfully with the fine landscape, created by Capability Brown. It houses some 180 exotic species from all over the world, including penguins, macaws, snowy owls, and flamingos, and has an undercover area housing tropical birds and small mammals. The extensive grounds offer terrace and lakeside walks, shops, a cafeteria, a picnic area, occasional exhibitions, a Courtyard Restaurant, and an Adventure Playground for the children.

Harewood is open daily from April 1 to October 31 and on Sunday, Tuesday, Wednesday, and Thursday in February, March, and November. Gates open at 10 a.m. (house at 11 a.m.). The bird garden and playground only are also open from December 26 to the first Sunday in January. Special events are often held on weekends. Admission rates vary during the year, but a summer Freedom Ticket, admitting the bearer to all facilities, is approximately £2.75 ($4.13) for adults, with reductions for children under 16. Call Harewood 886225 for recorded information, available 24 hours.

Incidentally, Harewood is on a regular bus route (Leeds/Harrogate/ Ripon), but the stop is about one mile from the house. Summer excursions run on varying days from those cities served by the regular buses and from York and Bradford, among other places. Ask at local tourist information centers and at your hotel for details.

4. Durham

This densely populated county of northeast England is too often pictured as a dismal, forbidding place, with coalfields, ironworks, mining towns, and shipyards. Yet it contains valleys of quiet charm and a region of wild moors in the west. Therefore if you have the time, it would be interesting to explore the Durham Dales, especially Teesdale with its waterfalls and rare wildflowers, and Weardale with its brown sandstone villages.

DURHAM: The county town is built around a standstone peninsula. It possesses a Norman **cathedral** which ranks as one of the most important in England. Adjoining the cathedral is **Durham Castle** (tel. Durham 65481), a Norman foundation of the prince bishops that has been used by Durham University since 1832. Except on the occasion of university or other functions, the castle is open to visitors from 10 a.m. to noon and 2 to 4:30 p.m., daily during the first three weeks in April and during all of July, August, and September; 2 to 4 p.m. on Monday, Wednesday, and Saturday the rest of the year. Admission is 90p ($1.35) for adults, 45p (68¢) for children.

Food and Lodging

The **Royal County Hotel,** Old Elvet (tel. Durham 66821), is a Georgian hotel tracing its origins back to Cromwellian times. In its well conceived modernization program, this antique riverside coaching inn blends yester-year with contemporary design, and does so effectively. The owner has decorated the public rooms with mementoes depicting the checkered history of the place. There are 126 bedrooms in the hotel, all with private baths, and you're given a choice of accommodations in the older building, with its traditional furnishings, or in the new block of rooms overlooking the river. Most units are fully equipped with TV set, radio, phone, and coffee-making facilities. Food is served in the Light Infantryman Restaurant, and the coffeeshop provides light snacks. Rates range from £40 ($60) in a single, from £54 ($81) in a double, including an English breakfast. In the foyer is an aviary, and there is an attractive cocktail bar with polished brasswork lining the walls, depicting historical data on the city.

BARNARD CASTLE: Near the River Tees in the town of Barnard Castle stands the **Bowes Museum** (tel. 0833/37139), at the eastern end. It was built in 1869 by John Bowes and his wife, the Countess of Montalbo, to house and display their art collection. Here you'll find masterpieces by Goya and El Greco, plus other paintings, fine tapestries, and ceramics. There are also collections of French and English furniture, superb costumes, musical instruments, a children's gallery, and many other exhibits of interest. The noted silver swan is switched on to perform its mechanical marvels at 1 p.m. daily. A tea room and ample parking are found on the premises. It is open all year, weekdays from 10 a.m. to 5 p.m., on Sunday from 2 to 5 p.m., charging £1 ($1.50) for adults, 25p (38¢) for children. It closes at 4 p.m. from November to February.

Where to Stay and Eat

Blagraves House Restaurant, The Bank (tel. 0833/37668), occupies a 15th-century house with a dining room which has been richly, warmly decorated by Mr. and Mrs. Davidson. They invite you to come by and "taste our food," which I've found to be excellently prepared and very wholesome. Fresh local produce and friendly service characterize the establishment. A fixed-price meal is offered for £15 ($22.50). Main dishes are likely to include rounds of filet of beef with a roquefort herb butter, duckling with peach and lemon sauce, or chicken breasts stuffed with asparagus in a white wine and cheese sauce. My favorite beginning, if featured, is a "very fine fish soup," made with lobster, crab, prawns, plaice, cream, and brandy. Only dinner is served, and it's offered nightly from 7 to 9, except Sunday. Call for a reservation.

The **Rose and Crown Hotel,** Romaldkirk, Teesdale (tel. 0833/50213), lies in a dale that often escapes the notice of the traveler in the north, at Romaldkirk, an attractive village set around a fine green with a water pump and punitive stocks (not in use today!). Higher up the dale, the River Tees goes over a sheer drop of 69 feet, and downstream is Barnard Castle and the Bowes Museum. In the main building are ten bedrooms, one with a four-poster bed. All have color TVs, radios, and phones, and across the courtyard in a modern extension, units have the same amenities, plus tea- and coffee-making facilities. An overnight stay costs from £22 ($33) to £28 ($42) per person, which includes a four-course dinner and a full English breakfast. There is a comfortable lounge, and the two bars have roaring log fires and are bright with the light glinting on the brassware. David and Jill Jackson are the resident owners.

BLANCHLAND: Near Consett, the village of Blanchland dates from the mid-12th century. It's a cobbled square with houses and little village shops. The post office still shows the arms of Queen Victoria over the mailbox.

The **Lord Crewe Arms Hotel** (tel. Blanchland 251) was the priory of the now-destroyed Abbey of Blanchland, and the bars are to be found in the crypt of the old building. You can walk through one of the enormous chimneys with a priest's hole above your head. It is easy to imagine the ghost of Dorothy Foster stalking the narrow passages.

Many of the rooms have baths, costing from £25 ($37.50) in a single and from £38 ($57) in a double, including a traditional cooked breakfast, VAT, and service. Additional bedrooms are now offered in the annex opposite the old building, all with direct-dial phones and tea- and coffee-making equipment. Rooms are decorated with fresh flowers, and a glass of sherry will be waiting to greet you. The owner, Ermes Oretti, is personally in charge. A four-course dinner at £8.50 ($12.75) is likely to include the house pâté with rough brown bread and salmon mayonnaise, seafood vol-au-vent, or fresh leek and potato soup, grilled lemon sole, roast duckling, rack of lamb, or grouse in season (a supplement is charged for a whole bird), followed by sorbets, fresh salad, baked apple pie with ice cream, coffee, and mints. There are also bar snacks for those who want to stop for a short while en route to Hadrian's Wall or Scotland.

5. Tyne and Wear

In the newly created county of Tyne and Wear, industrial Newcastle upon Tyne is the dominant focus, yet outside the city there is much natural beauty. Cattle graze on many a grassed-over mining shaft. There is such scenic beauty as moors and hills of purple-blue. The rugged coastline is beautiful. Americans like to pass through because of their interest in the ancestral home of George Washington (see below), and Newcastle itself also merits a stopover, particularly for motorists heading to Scotland.

The National Trust administers two sites in the region surrounding Newcastle:

Gibside Chapel, built in the classical style of James Paine in 1760, is an outstanding example of Georgian church architecture. A stately oak-lined avenue leads to the door of the chapel, which is the mausoleum of the Bowes family. The interior is decorated in delicate plasterwork and is furnished with paneled pews of cherrywood and a rare mahogany three-tiered pulpit. Hours are from 2 to 6 p.m. every day except Tuesday from April 1 to September 30. The entrance fee is 50p (75¢) per person. The location is six miles southwest of Gateshead and 20 miles northwest of Durham between Rowlands Gill and Burnopfield.

Washington Old Hall (tel. 0632/466879) is the ancestral home of the first president of the United States, and the place from which the family took its name. President Carter visited the manor house in 1977. The interior of the house, which dates back to 1183, is furnished with period antiques and a collection of Delftware. Relics of the Washingtons are also on display. The hall is open from March to October daily, except Wednesday, from 1 to 6 p.m. or sunset. From November to February, it is open on Saturday and Sunday, and by appointment, from 2 to 5 p.m. Admission is 80p ($1.20) for adults, 40p (60¢) for children. The location is in Washington on the east side of the A182, five miles west of Sunderland (two miles from the A1). South of Tyne Tunnel, follow signs for Washington New Town District 4 and then Washington Village.

At Stanley, just a few miles south of Newcastle upon Tyne is **Beamish,** the North of England Open Air Museum. Here the way of life of the people of this area around the turn of the century is being recreated. You can visit an old railway station and ride behind a steam locomotive, see bread being baked in a coal-fired oven in a row of furnished pit cottages, and go down a "drift" mine to witness how coal was worked around the turn of the century. You can also visit Home Farm to see animals and exhibitions and Beamish Hall in its beautiful parkland for a drink in the Victorian bar (summer only). For further information, telephone 0207/31811. The museum is open daily from 10 a.m. to 5:45 p.m. in summer, to 4 p.m. in summer. Admission is £2 ($3) for adults, £1 ($1.50) for children. Average visiting time is about three hours.

NEWCASTLE UPON TYNE: An industrial city, Newcastle is graced with some fine streets and parks, as well as many old buildings. After crossing its best known landmark, the Tyne Bridge, you enter a steep city that sweeps down to the Tyne, usually on narrow lanes called "chares." Once wealthy merchants built their town houses right on the quayside, and some of them remain.

For years Newcastle has been known as a shipbuilding and coal-exporting center, and gave rise to the expression of suggesting the absurdity of shipping coals to Newcastle.

Dominating the skyline, the **Cathedral of Newcastle** rises to a beautiful Scottish crown spire. It is England's most northerly cathedral, lying on a downward sweep between the Central Station and the quay. Its provost says that "the cathedral is one of the gems among the glorious churches of Northumberland." The cathedral's date of construction is unknown, and its recorded history predates 1122. The church was rebuilt in the 14th century, and John Knox preached from its pulpit.

The keep of the so-called New Castle, built by Henry II in 1170, contains the **Keep Museum,** on St. Nicholas Street, with a collection of medieval relics. It's open April to September on Monday from 2 to 5 p.m., Tuesday to Saturday from 10 a.m. to 5 p.m. From October to March, its Monday hours are from 2 to 4 p.m., Tuesday to Saturday from 10 a.m. to 4 p.m.

Food and Lodging

Royal Station Hotel, Neville Street (tel. Newcastle 320781), was built back in the days when the big, grand hotels were connected to the railway station by a covered way. This well-kept hotel has two restaurants, the main one called the Victoria, where an extensive à la carte menu is served. Otherwise, you can dine more inexpensively at their Oscars Viking Restaurant, which is on the lines of a coffeeshop/grill room with an interesting self-service cold table also available. Of the three bars, the Lord Mountbatten is the most recent. It has two sides, a nautical theme being used in one and an empire theme in the other.

Most of the bedrooms have been kept up to date, although some still have their heavy Victorian-style furniture. Bathless singles rent for £23 ($34.50), the rate increasing to £37 ($55.50) with bath. Twins and doubles with bath cost £48 ($72). Reductions are given on Friday, Saturday, and Sunday. The tariffs quoted include a full English breakfast, service, and VAT.

6. Northumberland

Unfortunately, most motorists zip through this far-northern county of England on their way to Scotland, missing the beauty and historic interest of the Border section. Because it is so close to Scotland, Northumberland was the scene of many a bloody skirmish. The county now displays a number of fortified castles that saw action in those battles. Inland are the valleys of the Cheviot Hills, lying mostly within the Northumberland National Park and the remainder of the Border Forest Park, Europe's largest man-made forest.

Northumberland's coast is one of Britain's best kept secrets. Here are islands, castles, tiny fishing villages, miles of sands, as well as golf and fishing among the dunes, and birdwatching in the Farne Islands—in all, an area of outstanding natural beauty.

Wallington, at Cambo, 12 miles west of Morpeth (take the A696 north from Newcastle), dates from 1688, but the present building reflects the great changes brought about in the 1740s when Daniel Garrett completely refashioned the exterior of the house. The interior is decorated with rococo plasterwork and furnished with fine porcelains, furniture, and paintings. Visitors may also visit the museum and enjoy an extensive display of dollhouses. The Coach House contains an exhibit of ornate carriages. The main building itself is surrounded by 100 acres of woodlands and lakes, including a beautifully terraced walled garden and a conservatory. The grounds are open all year; the house, April 1 to September 1 from 1 to 6 p.m. daily, October 1 to October 31 from 2 to 5 p.m. Wednesday, Saturday, and Sunday. Last admission is half an hour before closing time. Admission to the house and grounds is £2.20 ($3.30); to the grounds only, £1 ($1.50). Children pay half price. For more information, telephone 067-074/283.

Seaton Delaval Hall, the enormous country house near Whitley Bay (tel. Seaton Delaval 481493), represents the architecture of Sir John Vanbrugh at its most forbidding. It looks like the stage settings for 14 Roman tragedies piled one on top of another. Walk over and look through a window, and you can almost imagine knights and wenches feasting at long tables and drinking mead. The house is open to view from May to September on Wednesday and Sunday from 2 to 6 p.m., charging adults an admission of £1 ($1.50); children, 50p (75¢).

The **Farne Islands** are a group of small islands off the Northumbria coast, which provide a summer home for at least 20 species of sea birds as well as for one of the largest British colonies of gray seals. St. Cuthbert died here in 687, and a chapel built in the 14th century is thought to be on the site of his original cell. Only Inner Farne and Staple Island are open to the public. Visiting season extends from April through September, but access is more controlled during the breeding season. From mid-May to mid-July, you can visit Staple Island from 10:30 a.m. to 1:30 p.m. each day, and Inner Farne from 2 to 5 p.m. daily. From April 1 to mid-May and from mid-July until the end of September hours for both Staple Island and Inner Farne are from 10 a.m. to 6 p.m. Tickets are obtained on the island. During the peak season, adults pay £2 ($3) and children are charged £1 ($1.50). During the rest of the season, the admission is £1.50 ($2.25) for adults and 75p ($1.13) for children.

The best way to get to this most famous bird and animal sanctuary in the British Isles is to telephone or write Billy Shiel, the Farne Islands boatman at 4 Southfield Ave., Seahouses, Northumberland (tel. 0665/720308). He has been taking people in his licensed boat for the past 40 years, so he knows the tides and the best places to film seals, puffins, and guillemots. He runs 2½-hour trips in his 60-passenger craft at a cost of £3 ($4.50) per person.

Incidentally, these are the islands where Grace Darling and her father made their famous rescue of men from a foundered ship.

HOLY ISLAND: The site of the Lindisfarne religious community during the Dark Ages, Holy Island is only accessible for ten hours of the day, high tides covering the causeway at other times. For crossing times, check with local information centers.

Landisfarne Castle, on Holy Island, was built about 1550 as a fort to protect the harbor. In 1903 it was converted by Sir Edward Lutyens into a comfortable home for Edward Hudson, the founder of *Country Life.* It is open from April to the end of September every day except Friday (open Good Friday) from 11 a.m. to 5 p.m. In October it's open on Saturday and

Sunday from 11 a.m. to 5 p.m. Admission is £2 ($3) in June, July, and August; £1.40 ($2.10) the other months.

At Lindisfarne, you can stay at the **Lindisfarne Private Hotel** (tel. Holy Island 89273). This is a fine, substantial frame building with a trio of tall chimneys. It's run by members of the Massey family, who conduct it more like a private home than a hotel. Centrally heated bedrooms contain hot and cold running water (a few with private baths) and are decorated with personality, providing a home-like atmosphere. The charge ranges from £18 ($27) to £20 ($30) per person daily for bed, breakfast, and evening dinner. Boating excursions can be arranged to the Farnes.

BAMBURGH CASTLE: Guarding the British shore along the North Sea, the castle (tel. Bamburgh 208) stands on a site that has been occupied since the first century B.C. The Craggy Citadel where it stands was a royal center by A.D. 547. The Norman keep has stood for eight centuries, the remainder of the castle having been restored toward the end of the 19th century. This was the first castle to succumb to artillery fire, the guns of Edward IV. You can visit the grounds and public rooms from April to early October: 1 to 5 p.m. in April, May, June, and September; 1 to 6 p.m. in July and August; and 1 to 4:30 p.m. in October. Admission is £1.50 ($2.25) for adults, 75p ($1.13) for children. There is a restaurant and tea room in the clock tower. The castle is the home of Lord and Lady Armstrong and their family.

HADRIAN'S WALL: This wall, which extends across the north of England for 73 miles, from the North Sea to the Irish Sea, is particularly interesting for a stretch of 3½ miles west of Housesteads. Only the lower courses of the wall are preserved intact; the rest were reconstructed in the 19th century with the original stones. From several vantage points along the wall, you have incomparable views north to the Cheviot Hills along the Scottish border, and south to the Durham moors.

The wall was built following a visit of the Emperor Hadrian in A.D. 122. He wanted to see the far frontier of the Roman Empire, and he also sought to build a dramatic line between the so-called civilized world and the barbarians. Legionnaires were ordered to build a wall across the width of the island of Britain, stretching for 73½ miles, going over hills and plains, beginning at the North Sea and ending at the Irish Sea.

The wall is a premier Roman attraction in Europe, ranking among many people with Rome's Colosseum. The western end can be reached from Carlisle, with a good museum of Roman artifacts, and the eastern end from Newcastle upon Tyne (some remains are seen on the city outskirts and a good museum at the university). South Shields, Chester, Corbridge, and Vindolanda are all good forts to visit in the area.

At Housesteads you can visit a **Roman fort** (tel. Bardon Mill 363), built about A.D. 130 to house an infantry of 1000 men. Called Vercovicium in Latin, the fort held a full-scale military encampment, the remains of which can be seen today. The fort is open March 15 to October 15 from 9:30 a.m. to 6:30 p.m. on weekdays, 2 to 6:30 p.m. on Sunday; from 9:30 a.m. on Sunday April to September. From October 16 to March 14, hours are 9:30 a.m. to 4 p.m. weekdays, 2 to 4 p.m. on Sunday. Closed Christmas Eve, Christmas Day, Boxing Day, and New Year's Day. Admission in summer is £1 ($1.50) for adults, 70p ($1.05) for children.

Just west of Housesteads is **Vindolanda,** another fort south of the wall at Chesterholm. The building is very well preserved, and there is also an excavated civilian settlement outside the fort with an interesting museum of artifacts of everyday Roman life. Admission is £1.25 ($1.88) for adults, 60p (90¢) for children.

Not far from Vindolanda is the **Roman Army Museum,** Carvoran, on Hadrian's Wall near Greenhead, which traces the growth and influence of Rome from her early beginnings to the development and expansion of the empire, with special emphasis on the role of the Roman army and the garrisons of Hadrian's Wall. A barracks room shows basic Roman army living conditions. Realistic life-size figures make this a striking visual museum experience. Admission is 80p ($1.20) for adults, 45p (68¢) for children. For information, phone Gilsland 485.

Within easy walking distance of the Roman Army Museum lies one of the most imposing and high-standing sections of Hadrian's Wall, **Walltown Crags,** where the height of the wall and magnificent views to north and south are impressive.

HALTWHISTLE: About 20 miles east of Carlisle lies the town of Haltwhistle. There the **Grey Bull Hotel** (tel. Haltwhistle 20298) would be a good base of operations for seeing the best section of Hadrian's Wall and its Roman garrisons. These include Housesteads, Vindolanda (the largest site in Europe), the Chesters, and the Carvoran Roman Army Museum, all within 15 minutes' drive from the hotel. The Grey Bull has been modernized and reequipped. There are five bedrooms, each with its own wash basin with hot and cold running water. The inclusive price is £11 ($16.50) per person, including an English breakfast, service, and VAT. Packed lunches are available on request. The bar at the hotel is a lively gathering place for the local people.

HAYDON BRIDGE: Between Haltwhistle and Hexham, the **Anchor Hotel** (tel. 043-484/227), is in little Haydon Bridge, ideally situated for visitors to the wall and its surroundings. This riverside village pub was once an important coaching inn on the route from Newcastle to Carlisle. There is a friendly atmosphere in the cozy bar much used by locals. In the country dining room, wholesome evening meals are served.

Singles cost from £14 ($21) without bath to £18 ($27) with shower and toilet; doubles, £23 ($34.50) to £26 ($39) with shower and toilet. Some family rooms rent for £26 ($39) to £29 ($43.50) for a room for two adults and two children. All tariffs include a full English breakfast and VAT. If you stay two nights, the special rate for B&B and a choice of three courses from the à la carte dinner menu is £18 ($27) in a single with shower and toilet, £31 ($46.50) for two in a double with the same facilities. John and Vivienne Dees have owned and run the hotel since 1975 and have modernized the bedrooms by providing extra baths and tea- and coffee-making equipment. They will assist with information about the wall and the best places to walk. The hotel has a large car park.

HEXHAM: Above the Tyne River, this historic old market town is characterized by its narrow streets, old Market Square, a fine abbey church, and its Moot Hall. It makes a good base for exploring Hadrian's Wall and the Roman supply base of Corstopitum at Corbridge-on-Tyne, the ancient capital of Northumberland. The Tourist Office has masses of information on the wall for walkers, drivers, campers, and picnickers.

The **Abbey Church of St. Wilfred** is full of ancient relics. The Saxon font, the misericord carvings on the choir stalls, Acca's Cross, and St. Wilfred's chair are well worth seeing.

For accommodations, try the **Beaumont Hotel,** Beaumont Street (tel. 0434/602331), a family-run place across from the village park. It offers excellent facilities, including handsomely furnished and pleasantly decorated bedrooms, which are in the modern style, the effect enlivened by bright colors. Nearly all 20 bedrooms have private baths or shower units tucked in. A bathless single room costs £18 ($27), rising to £23 ($34.50) with bath. Doubles or twins with baths or showers rent from £28 ($42). Tariffs include VAT and service. Guests have a choice of two bars. Lunch is from £6.50 ($9.75), and dinner is à la carte.

The **Hadrian Hotel,** Wall, near Hexham (tel. Humshaugh 232), is the ideal place to stay when visiting Hadrian's Wall. It's an ivy-covered building erected of stones taken from the wall. The lounge has a collection of antiques, swords, guns, and curios, excellent for after-dinner coffee in front of the blazing fire. The dining room with three window walls has red tablecloths with white lace overcloths. You can look across the meadow toward the wall. There are eight bedrooms, all with hot and cold running water, innerspring mattresses, and electric blankets. The daily tariff in a single room is £18 ($27), from £34 ($51) in a double. Lunches are table d'hôte, costing from £5.50 ($8.25), and dinners begin at £10 ($15).

As a luncheon stopover, I'd suggest the **Country Kitchen,** 23 Market Pl. (tel. 0434/603835), where you can order a good-tasting homemade soup, followed by, perhaps, sugar-baked ham with a salad or vegetables, or smoked haddock flan. Desserts include the likes of baked banana sponge pudding. Expect to pay from £2.50 ($3.75) to £4 ($6), plus the cost of your drink. The kitchen is open daily except Sunday and Monday from 10:30 to 11:30 a.m. for coffee, then from noon to 2:15 p.m. for lunch.

Next door is an intriguing shop, selling all sorts of local crafts, exotic food, and souvenirs.

If you're spending the night in town, try dinner at the **Abbey Flags,** 19 Market Pl. (tel. 0434/603252). As the name suggests, it stands in the forecourt of the abbey, and it's open for dinner from 7 to 10 p.m. from Monday to Saturday.

Chilled honeydew melon or fresh pineapple or mushroom salad, along with fried sprats or homemade chicken liver pâté, jostle various cold and hot soups as appetizers. Main dishes include fish, pork with ginger sauce, turkey-and-walnut pie, or liver of lamb with Dubonnet. The whole meal, including dessert, coffee and VAT, is likely to cost from £10.50 ($15.75) per person. Abbey Flags is open daily except Tuesday and Sunday, with a tourist menu offered from 6 to 8 p.m. every day but Saturday. For £5.50 ($8.25), you can dine well. A glass of house wine is included. Close the door as you go out, or the rubber plant at the bottom of the stairs complains.

On the Outskirts

The **George Hotel,** Chollerford, Humshaugh, near Hexham (tel. 043-481/611), stands on the banks of the Tyne, an ingratiating, creeper-covered country hotel with well-tended gardens leading down to the riverbank. It's a convenient base for visiting the whole of the wall. The age of the hotel is unknown, and its drawing room maintains a country-house style, with ornate white woodwork including an original mantelpiece. Brightly colored chintz armchairs are drawn up for after-dinner coffee. Out the bay window you can see the river at the bottom of the garden. The bedrooms are small and nicely equipped, and come with private baths or showers and TV sets. Many of the units have been recently modernized, refurnished, and decorated. Singles rent for £28 ($42) to £32 ($48), and twins or doubles, from £40 ($60) to £48 ($72). All units have TV, some color and some black and and white. You can swim in the heated pool or sweat in the sauna. A large cooked breakfast, VAT, and service are included in the room rates.

Adjoining the restaurant is a cocktail bar and lounge, and locals gather in the Fisherman's Bar, which has the atmosphere of a country inn. Sandwiches are freshly made here. A set luncheon goes for £8 ($12), and a dinner runs from £10 ($15) to £12 ($18), depending on your choice of a main dish. Dinner is also offered à la carte. There's a very good wine list. In the lounge, except for Sunday, a salad bar dispenses pie, sausage, scotch eggs, along with mixed green and vegetable salads. For about £3 ($4.50) your plate will be heavily laden. A live band plays for dancing on Saturday night, when a £1 ($1.50) cover charge is levied.

LONGHORSLEY: Linden Hall Hotel, Longhorsley, near Morpeth (tel. 0670/56611), is a 19th-century mansion with large high rooms and tall windows. It's an elegant stopping place on your way to Alnwick and Holy Island on the coastal route to Edinburgh. There are several lounges where you can relax, plus a library to browse in, along with a tasteful cocktail bar with discreet lights and a cool, gracious dining room. The sweeping staircase leads to rooms with modern beds, except in the honeymoon suites, which are furnished with four-posters. All units have baths, color TV, radios, phones, and baby-listening service, with some antique furniture used to advantage. Fresh fruit greets you when you check into your room! Ten ground-floor rooms grouped around a sunny cobbled courtyard are especially suitable for physically handicapped guests. A single is £42 ($63), a double or twin costing £50 ($75). All rates include a full English breakfast, VAT, and service.

The chef offers a wide menu with some original appetizers such as pheasant and pear salad and chicken and artichoke salad. There is a bewildering array of fish dishes, including halibut with Dijon mustard and turbot Noilly Prat. You may prefer roast duckling, a julienne of filet of beef cooked with green and pink peppercorns, or veal kidneys and sweetbreads. Vegetables fresh from the field in summer accompany main dishes. A meal will cost around £13 ($19.50) to £17 ($25.50), including a dessert. There is a good selection of wines.

On the estate in the restored granary is the Linden Pub, a casual, cheerful place with a log fire and a good collection of those large enameled signs that used to advertise tobacco, Camp coffee, and cocoa. As well as serving North Country ales, the pub provides good bar food. They often have barbecues in the courtyard in summer, when guests can indulge in such pursuits as quoits, boule, and garden draughts.

ALNMOUTH: A seaside resort on the Aln estuary, Alnmouth attracts sporting people who fish for salmon and trout in the Coquet River or play on its good golf course.

The **Schooner Hotel**, Northumberland Street (tel. Alnwick 830216), is a well-preserved Georgian coaching inn, only a few minutes' walk to the water. The hotel is adjacent to the nine-hole Village Golf Course, the second oldest in the country, and also lies near an 18-hole course. The hotel has a squash court. A single room with breakfast is £15 ($22.50), £13.50 ($20.25) per person in a double, including VAT. Guests count on the good meals prepared and served at low prices. Set luncheons are £3 ($4.50) to £7 ($10.50); set dinners, £10 ($15). There are 24 bedrooms, a grill room, dining room, the Sea Hunter bar, the Chase Bar, and the Long Bar, as well as a resident's lounge with color TV.

On the seafront about 14 miles from Alnmouth, the **Dunes Hotel,** Seahouses (tel. 0665/720378), is a 30-bedroom establishment, from which you can view the Farne Islands with their bird and seal sanctuaries, Bamburgh Castle, and the sand dunes and Seahouses Harbour. Rooms are well kept and pleasantly furnished, and five doubles contain private baths. In a double or twin with bath, the B&B rate is £39 ($58.50), dropping to £34 ($51) without bath. Singles go for £19 ($28.50) without bath, £23 ($34.50) with, and all these tariffs include breakfast and VAT. There are three large lounges and a sun parlor overlooking the front lawn, plus a bright, sunny smoking room opening onto a flower garden. In the paneled restaurant, a good and varied cuisine is served, a set dinner costing from £10 ($15) to £14 ($21). The Dunes Hotel is an excellent center for exploring the Farne Islands, Holy Island, the Roman Wall, and the Border Country. The hotel lies just half a mile from Seahouses. It's closed from October to May.

ALNWICK: Set in the peaceful countryside of Northumberland, this ancient market town has had a colorful history. A good center for touring an area of scenic beauty, Alnwick is visited chiefly today by travelers wanting to see—

Alnwick Castle

In the town of Alnwick, 30 miles north of Newcastle, Alnwick Castle (tel. 0665/602722), the largest castle in England after Windsor, is the seat of the Duke of Northumberland. This border fortress dates from the 11th century, when the earliest parts of the present castle were constructed by Yvo de Vescy, the first Norman Baron of Alnwick. A major restoration was undertaken by the fourth duke in the mid-19th century, and Alnwick remains relatively unchanged to this day. The rugged medieval outer walls do not prepare the first-time visitor for the richness of the interior, decorated mainly in the style of the Italian Renaissance.

Most of the castle is open to the public during visiting hours. You can tour the principal apartments, including the armory, guard chamber, and library, where you can view portraits and landscapes painted by such masters as Titian, Canaletto, and Van Dyck. You may also visit the dungeons and the interesting Museum of Early British and Roman Relics. From the terraces within the castle's outer walls, you can look across the broad landscape stretching over the River Aln.

Alnwick is open to the public daily, except Saturday, from 1 to 5 p.m. May to September. Admission is £1.50 ($2.25) for adults and 75p ($1.13) for children. For an additional 20p (30¢) you can also visit the Regimental Museum of the Royal Northumberland Fusiliers, within the castle grounds.

Cragside, designed in the late 19th century by architect Richard

Norman Shaw for the first Lord Armstrong, is a grand estate stretching across 900 acres on the southern edge of the Alnwick Moor. Here groves of magnificent trees and fields of rhododendrons frequently give way to peaceful ponds and lakes. The Victorian house is open only for part of the season, but the grounds alone are worth the visit. At Rothbury, the house is just 13 miles southwest of Alnwick. The park is open April to the end of September from 10:30 a.m. to 6 p.m.; in October, daily from 10:30 a.m. to 5 p.m.; November to the end of March, on Saturday and Sunday from 10:30 a.m. to 4 p.m. Admission to the park only is 90p ($1.35). The house is open from April to the end of September daily except Monday (open bank holidays) from 1 to 6 p.m.; in October, on Wednesday, Saturday, and Sunday from 2 to 5 p.m. Admission is £2 ($3) for adults, £1 ($1.50) for children, including the park. For more information, telephone Rothbury 20333.

Dunstanburgh Castle, on the coast nine miles northeast of Alnwick, was begun in 1316 by Thomas, Earl of Lancaster, and enlarged in the 14th century by John of Gaunt. The dramatic ruins of the gatehouse, towers, and curtain wall stand on a promontory high above the sea. You can reach the castle on foot only, either by walking from Craster in the south or across the Dunstanburgh Golf Course from Embleton and Dunstan Steads in the north. The castle is open March 15 to October 15 weekdays from 9:30 a.m. to 6:30 p.m., on Sunday from 2 to 6:30 p.m. (from 9:30 a.m. on Sunday, April to September); and October 16 to March 14 weekdays from 9:30 a.m. to 4 p.m., Sunday from 2 to 4 p.m. Closed Christmas Eve, Christmas Day, Boxing Day, and New Year's Day. Admission is 40p (60¢) for adults.

Food and Lodging

White Swan, Bondgate Within (tel. Alnwick 602109), has a history going back to medieval days when it entertained highwaymen and passengers on the Edinburgh–to–London stagecoaches. A neoclassic-style coaching inn, just inside an ancient town gate, the Hotspur, it has also become the permanent home of the music room of the S.S. *Olympic*, sister ship of the *Titanic*. This beautiful paneled room was removed from the ship and completely reconstructed at the hotel. The hotel has 40 bedrooms, with bath and shower, and some of these are in a modern block and others in the older, more traditional part of the inn. Singles begin at £35 ($52.50) and doubles peak at £54 ($81), including a full breakfast, service, and VAT.

The **Warenford Lodge and Stable Restaurant,** Warenford, near Alnwick (tel. 066-83/453), is an old stone pub run by Ray and Marion Matthewman, who provide lunches and dinners daily in summer. From November to Easter, no meals are served on Monday. Appetizers include homemade soup and ramekins of smoked haddock and cream, and main dishes feature whole baked sole au gratin and jugged duck in red wine. Meals cost from £5 ($7.50). There are pleasant open fireplaces and a friendly atmosphere.

CORNHILL-ON-TWEED: This border village, on the River Tweed, faces Coldstream on the Scottish shore.

Tillmouth Park Hotel (tel. 0890/2255), built in 1882, is an imposing Victorian mansion, occupying a secluded position in its own parkland gardens overlooking the River Till at the heart of a 1000-acre estate. It stands about nine miles from Berwick, three miles from Cornhill-on-

Tweed, and four miles from Coldstream. Monumental and impressive, it rises four stories high, with many wings, gables, and chimneys, including a porch emblazoned with heraldic devices.

In spite of its size, there are only 14 bedrooms, each one exceptionally comfortable, seven containing private baths. Ask for the Sir Walter Scott room, with its stunning four-poster and private bath. Often Edwardian furnishings grace the private chambers, renting for £32 ($48) for one person, £28 ($42) per person for a couple. B&B costs £22.50 ($33.75) to £28 ($42) in a single, from £16.50 ($24.75) to £28 ($42) per person in a double, the latter price for the honeymoon bungalow called the Garden Suite. Christine and Tony Brooks-Sykes, resident managers, preside with skill over this establishment where modernity, as reflected by a cocktail bar, has been blended with tradition, as represented by a galleried lounge with a massive stone fireplace. Spacious lawns adjoin the hotel.

JERSEY, CHANNEL ISLANDS

ALTHOUGH THEY BELONG TO the Crown of England, the Channel Islands are really Norman: In A.D. 933 they became part of the estates of William, first Duke of Normandy, and their association with England began 133 years later, when Duke William II, better known as William the Conqueror, invaded the land of the Saxons and claimed the English crown. To this day the islanders drink the toast, "The Queen, our Duke."

These islands, off the northwest coast of France, are **Jersey, Guernsey, Alderney, Brechou, Great Sark, Little Sark, Herm, Jethou,** and **Lihou.** The entire population today is around 150,000.

In October 1941 German troops moved in, adding the Channel Islands to Hitler's Atlantic Wall, a line of fortifications from Normandy to the Spanish border. The islands became the only British territory to be occupied by invaders since 1066. Bunkers and other parts of the massive Third Reich construction program have been turned into museums of the occupation and can be visited today.

Jersey, the largest of the islands, has been inhabited by humankind for some 70,000 years. It lies about 85 miles from the south coast of England, 30 miles from France. English is spoken. The islands are self-governing, independent of each other and of Great Britain. Taxes are low, and there is no VAT. Drinks are served in larger measure here, and most prices in the shops are 15% to 20% lower than in England, although I advise you to shop wisely, even here.

The countryside is somewhat reminiscent of the Cotswolds or Cornwall —but only somewhat. Marvelous pink-granite buildings and very narrow lanes make the islandscape unique. Only 45 square miles in size and surrounded by the sea, Jersey is worth a visit, even briefly, just to sample the seafood. The islands are a paradise of lobster, crab, sole, and other fruits of the sea.

You can rent a car, a motorcycle, a bicycle (even a tandem), to get around, although taxis and buses are readily available. As in other parts of the British Isles, you drive on the left, but here the maximum speed limit is 40 miles per hour.

Additional information can be obtained from the **States of Jersey Tourist Information Office,** Weighbridge, St. Helier, Jersey, Channel Islands (tel. 0534/78000).

1. Getting There

You can fly to Jersey from London—Gatwick by British Caledonian, Heathrow by British Airways—and Southampton by Air UK. There is a wide difference in fares, and some tickets are only available for advance purchase. The cheapest price I found from London is £82 ($123) for a round trip, which takes 55 minutes each way. Air UK offers a day's round trip from Southampton for £55 ($82.50), which includes round-trip rail tickets from London to the airport. There is also an advance-purchase fare for a longer stay, £54 ($81); £63 ($94.50) if you want to include railway tickets from Waterloo.

Sealink operates a ferry service from Portsmouth and Weymouth, with a round-trip fare of £52 ($78), although in the middle of the week you can make the round trip for £46 ($69). The voyage takes from seven to nine hours. There is good train service from London to both Weymouth and Portsmouth. You can also make the round trip by bus from the Victoria Coach Station in London for £54.50 ($81.75). Berths on night sailings cost £7.50 ($11.25) per person per voyage.

Various companies offer holidays to Jersey. Some are day trips, while others include several nights' accommodation. Viscount Holidays runs a limited number of day jaunts from Southend, allowing 14 hours on Jersey. The round trip costs £51 ($76.50) to £54 ($81) in high season. The address is **Viscount Holidays,** Southend Airport, Southend on Sea, Essex 552 64L (tel. 0702/354435, extension 235).

2. Getting Around

There is a reasonably priced **bus** service operating on the island's narrow roads using specially built vehicles, with reduced service on Sunday and in winter. Smoking in the vehicles is prohibited by law. The main bus station is at the Weighbridge on St. Helier's seafront. If you want to explore the entire island by bus, you can buy a five-day unlimited bus pass for £9 ($13.50) for adults, £5 ($7.50) for children.

Taxis are more expensive but provide a useful method of transport if you want to pay an evening visit to one of the old inns in the north of the island or to Caesar's Palace at Grève de Lecq for the cabaret.

Blue Coach Tours, 70–72 Colomberie, St. Helier (tel. 0534/22584), operates sightseeing excursions, one a full day's coastal tour including visits to two of the sights for £5 ($7.50), not including admission charges. Lunch at the Château Plaisir is also extra at £2.50 ($3.75). There are also several morning and afternoon tours to the Jersey pottery, Jersey Zoo, and Mont Orgeuil, among other attractions, plus evening excursions to the Old World Inns or the various cabaret shows. All these tours cost around £3 ($4.50) per person. Admission fees are extra.

Self-drive cars can be rented from **Avis,** Airport Road, St. Brelade (tel. 0534/41131) or from **Falles Hire Cars,** Airport Road, St. Brelade (tel.

0534/43222). Charges vary from £8 ($12) per day or £46 ($69) per week for a small car in low season, including basic insurance, to £11 ($16.50) daily or £64 ($96) in high season. Collision damage waiver is around £2 ($3) per day extra. If you want to enjoy a convertible, you must pay about £15 ($25.50) per day or £102 ($153) per week.

The roads are narrow and often lined with high banks and hedges, with passing places well marked. Driving manners are usually excellent, but don't forget—drive on the left, and the speed limit is a maximum 40 miles per hour.

Hireride, 1 New St. John's Rd., St. Helier (tel. 0534/31995), has two-seater Yamaha **mopeds** for rent, for £30 ($45) per week, which includes a full tank of fuel and helmets. For the intrepid traveler, Unisex cycles with 20-inch wheels and three speeds rent for £2 ($3) per day or £8 ($12) per week. A deposit of £4 ($6) is required.

Jersey is an ideal place for walkers, with well-marked paths along the south and west coasts, mainly for level walking beside the sea. The routes along the north coast are more rugged, along cliff paths and across headlands. Maps and other information are available from the Tourist Information office at Weighbridge, St. Helier (tel. 0534/71179).

3. Where to Stay

Hotel de l'Horizon, St. Brelade's Bay (tel. 0534/43101), is a plain white building facing south, overlooking the beautiful, wide horseshoe of yellow sand that is St. Brelade's Bay. There is a heated indoor swimming pool area with doors opening along one side onto the sandy bay or the beach outside the hotel from which you can bathe in the sea when the weather is good. The 18-hole golf course of La Moye is close by. As many rooms of the hotel as possible face the sea, with balconies for sunbathing, evening drinks, and breakfast. You'll find a light, cool decor, large bathrooms, and color TVs—accommodations fit for the Queen of England, who stayed here on an official visit. Units go for from £33 ($51) to £44 ($66) per person in high season, including service and breakfast. Out of season, you can enjoy a stay here for as little as £28 ($42) per night. Little sitting rooms in some of the units can convert into sleeping quarters so that families can be accommodated.

The sea-facing restaurant does table d'hôte luncheons for £8 ($12), £10 ($15) on Sunday when roast beef dominates the sideboard. The dinner menu at £12 ($18) includes a wide enough choice to satisfy most palates, but the à la carte provides such delicacies as fresh fish dishes, Jersey lobster, Dover sole, and scallops. There is music for dancing most nights.

The Star Grill, a more intimate room with a low ceiling, plush pastel colors, and candlelight, has a superb menu offering such French delicacies as stuffed oysters or frog's legs, French onion soup, and green turtle soup, then lobster cooked in Pernod, salmon à la Hongroise, and mignons de filet de porc au roquefort. A celebration meal here will cost around £23 ($34.50) per person, including a modest bottle of wine.

Longueville Manor Hotel, St. Saviour (tel. 0534/25501), is a 12th-century manor house that has undergone some modernization but remains a lovely old creeper-clad Norman structure where you will be warmly welcomed to spend a night or two. It offers large, comfortable bedrooms with fresh flowers complementing the floral wallpaper and elegant furnishings. All units have the names of roses: Elizabeth of Glamis, Fragrant

Cloud, and the like. The bathrooms are supplied with robes and large bath towels. This is a place which you are invited to consider your home. Rooms go for from £33 ($49.50) to £39 ($58.50) per person for those sharing a double, depending on the time of the year. A small bed-sitting room or the four-poster room costs from £38 ($57) to £43 ($64.50). All rates include full breakfast and service, but you must expect a 10% service charge to be added to your restaurant and bar charges.

The dining room is wood-paneled with original beams. A large sideboard groans with a display of breads, and you can experience a memorable meal chosen from the menu for around £20 ($30). Specialties include rosette of monkfish with coriander and tarragon, and noisettes of lamb with braised turnips and pink peppercorns. You may prefer the set menu, however, for £12.50 ($18.75), plus service. Some 15 acres of gardens supply herbs and vegetables to the kitchens.

Besides the heated swimming pool and the beach facilities, the hotel has its own stables where you can go horseback riding for around £5 ($7.50) an hour. The joint owners of the hotel, the Lewis family and Simon Dufty and his wife, take great care to make you feel welcome at their house.

The **Moorings Hotel,** Gorey Pier (tel. 0534/53633), is on a half-moon road that bends around the tiny harbor on the way toward the castle of Mont Orgeuil. The serried buildings on the left overlook Gorey Pier and the small harbor beyond, across the rest of the wide bay. The Moorings opens directly onto the narrow road amid a seaside-town atmosphere, with sightseers mingling with local fishermen. Inside, there is a cheerful lounge and a bar, with a fire blazing beneath a large copper dome. Upstairs, the 16 bedrooms are bright and warm, with chintz fabric, large comfortable beds, well-fitted bath, color TV, and radio. The star rooms are those in the front overlooking the bay, the harbor, and the sea. Overnight stays cost from £18.50 ($27.75) per person in a room at the back, £20.50 ($30.75) with a sea view, all including breakfast. For half board—and the restaurant is good—add £5 ($7.50) per person per day for a three-course set meal.

The **Little Grove Hotel,** Rue de Haut, St. Lawrence (tel. 0534/25321), is another converted granite farmhouse set in acres of gardens. If you reserve your accommodations in advance, you will be given a little map showing how to reach the hotel either from the airport or from St. Helier. If you simply arrive, it is best to drive toward St. Helier, then turn inland at Bel Royal on the A11 and turn right just after you pass the Britannia Inn.

Inside the hotel, a lovely sitting room is warmed by two open fires, and light dances off the granite walls and polished furniture. There are reproduction oil paintings and gilt mirrors. A small bar leads off the sitting room, and in fact one of the fireplaces serves both rooms. Bedrooms are well appointed, some with sea views, and most with bath, TV, and telephone. Of the 14 units, three have four-poster beds. Rates run from £25 ($37.50) per person in low season to £30 ($45) in high season, including breakfast. Lunch is available at £5.50 ($8.25), including service. In the evening, you have a choice of appetizers, perhaps the house's special lobster mousse or shellfish bisque. For your main course, you might select grilled sole, plaice, or filet steak. A meal will cost around £12 ($18).

There is a heated swimming pool and a barbecue where summer evening parties are held. The gardens overlook St. Helier and beyond, out to sea. The Lapidus family, which owns and runs this personal operation, is highly experienced and professional.

St. Martin's House, St. Martin (tel. 0534/53271), is a good guest house, a beautiful Jersey granite structure set in wide gardens, perhaps one of the oldest houses on the island, dating from before 1490. Modernization allows for central heating, bathrooms, TVs, and a large swimming pool, but the antiquity of the building is reflected in the old ship's timber running down the length of the bar ceiling, plus the bread oven in the corner. The fireplace in the beamed dining room dates from 1760. Mary Lawrence, who runs St. Martin's, has lived on the island for years. She has a sitting room and a library of around 3000 books that are available to guests.

All bedrooms have hot and cold running water, razor points, and tea- and coffee-making equipment. Some have bathrooms en suite. Prices range from £10 ($15) per person in low season to £14 ($21) in high season. Add £4 ($6) per day for half board. For a room with bath, you'll have £2 ($3) tacked onto your bill. If you want to stay around the house or the pool all day, you can count on a salad or something simple for lunch. Evening meals are more elaborate.

Keep your eyes open for the "marriage stones," dates and initials carved in the stone and woodwork of the house to commemorate family marriages.

4. Where to Eat

The **Lobster Pot,** l'Etacq, St. Ouen (tel. 0534/82888), probably the island's best known restaurant, which has unfortunately resorted to plastic beams and decoration in a 17th-century farmhouse. The slightly fake atmosphere does not, however, detract from the excellence of the food, which, as the name implies, revolves around shellfish, and lobsters in particular. At the far end of Five Mile Road along St. Ouen's Bay, the place has been a restaurant for some 40 years, when Mancunian restaurateur Frank Grenelli first transformed West End Farm into a tea room and restaurant.

Now owned by Peter and Rosemary Gatehouse, the Lobster Pot opens from 12:30 to 3 p.m. for lunch, from 7:30 p.m. to 12:45 a.m. for dinner. The nine different lobster dishes start at £13 ($19.50), the price being governed by the size of the lobster. Other specialties include clams in garlic butter, moules à la crème, and poached king prawns. The gigantic assiette de fruits de mer—every kind of seafood you can think of, either grilled plain or with garlic butter—costs from £11 ($16.50). There are always fresh vegetables grown on the inn's own land, including characteristic kidney-shaped early Jersey potatoes. For those who prefer, there are steaks and game in season.

The Gatehouses have also renovated a wing of the building as the Coach House, a bar open from 10:30 a.m. to 11 p.m., where scrumptious buffet food is provided daily except on Sunday evening. Simple meals begin here at £6 ($9).

The **Old Court House Inn,** St. Aubin (tel. 0534/41156), is in a building whose front part overlooks the busy yacht harbor at St. Aubin. Once a wealthy merchant's house, the structure was built with huge cellars where cargoes were stacked and provisions for sailing ships stored. The 27-foot-deep well in the aptly named Well Bar must be kept pure for the use of ships' masters to draw from. The Westward Bar is built from timbers rescued from the gig of a schooner that foundered off Hurd's Deep, and the Mizzen Mast Bar is constructed like the stern of an old galleon. Relax in one of these drinking spots, choosing your meal before moving through into the old courthouse at the back where the judges sat to divide up the privateers' loot.

The restaurant is two stone-walled rooms with beams and low lights, small dark wood tables, and wheelback chairs. Being so close to the harbor and the sea, the kitchen inevitably emphasizes seafood. After an appetizer, settle down to deviled crab, a fisherman's platter, bouillabaisse, or a fresh lobster served with salad or vegetables of the day. A large meal will cost around £10 ($15), unless you settle for the fisherman's platter or lobster. Wine is served from stone jugs placed on the table.

The Sharps—Jonty and his sisters, Vicky and Caroline—who run the place make sure that there is always one of them available to oversee the inn, and they manage, with shifts of staff, to keep the place open from noon to 1 a.m. every day of the week during summer.

Upstairs, there are nine bedrooms and a penthouse suite. The rooms rent for £18 ($27) per person with bath, £15.50 ($23.25) without bath. The penthouse costs £28 ($42) per person for two in double rooms with bath, a lounge with TV, and a sea view. All rates include a full breakfast served in your room or in the lounge.

The **Moorings Hotel,** Gorey Pier (tel. 0534/53633), recommended earlier for overnight stays, has a long dining room managed by Pedro Martinez, who offers mixed hors d'oeuvres, whitebait and egg Florentine, homemade soups such as vichyssoise, various fish dishes, and grills, all served with fresh vegetables and salads. Desserts include crêpes suzette, rum omelets, and cassata siciliana. A meal costs around £11 ($16.50). The specialty list, based on the season and availability of produce, includes lobsters, skate with black butter, grilled turbot, oysters, and a dozen stuffed clams.

This is a warm, pub-style dining room with lots of stained wood and plain tables, wheelback chairs, and candles. The place has an informal air.

Apple Cottage, Rozel (tel. 0534/61002), is a little, low cottage in a flower-filled garden in a delightful village on the northeast corner of the island. Pat and Setti Pozzi specialize in seafood and scrumptious Jersey cream teas. In the beamed dining room with a stone fireplace are high-backed wooden seats between the tables. Brasswork decorates the chimneypiece. Main dishes include lobster mayonnaise with salad, hot or cold king prawns with garlic butter, and filet steak Apple Cottage, with cream and mushroom sauce. Desserts feature the highly recommended homemade apple pie. A meal will cost from £7 ($10.50) to £9 ($13.50). Also for a midday meal, a ploughman's lunch, sandwiches, and pasties are available. In the afternoon you can pig out on a renowned strawberry cream tea. The cottage is closed all day Monday and Saturday and on Sunday evening. Otherwise, lunch is from noon and dinner from 7 p.m. During the summer, it is usually open every day. Settimo comes from Stresa in the north of Italy.

The **Royal Yacht Hotel,** Weighbridge, St. Helier (tel. 0534/20511), is a typical Victorian seaside hotel with several bars and restaurants of which I've singled out the Victoriana Carvery for special mention. A large room on the first floor, it has carriage lamps and masses of pictures of sailing boats and yachts. Here a counter is laden with a dozen or so salads and a bewildering array of cooked fish—salmon, mackerel, mussels, prawns, fresh crab, and smoked trout—along with cold meats. The hot table has succulent joints of beef, lamb, and pork with appropriate sauces and garnishes. A choice of two of these meats with vegetables and garnishes costs £3 ($4.50), and a selection of three kinds of fish with mixed salad is £4 ($6). An unlimited choice—as much as you like of whatever you want—is

£7 ($10.50). The Carvery is open from noon to 2:30 p.m., including Sunday.

Le Pommier Coffee Shop, in the Pomme d'Or Hotel, The Esplanade, St. Helier (tel. 0534/78644), is open daily from 7 a.m. to 11 p.m. in summer, 10 a.m. to 9 p.m. in winter. It offers a good selection of light dishes, quiche, pizzas, sandwiches, fresh crab, and smoked salmon. Deep-fried chicken in breadcrumbs is featured, and you can also order an all-American charcoal-broiled beefburger. Steaks are the most expensive item on the menu. Meals begin at £6 ($9).

No. 10 Wine Bar, 10 Bond St., St. Helier (tel. 0534/73878), offers tasty bar snacks to accompany your wine in the semi-basement. On the ground floor, Joseph and his staff of young women fuss over your choice of dishes and wait quickly and quietly on the tables. The appetizers include oysters, hors d'oeuvres maison, moules marinières, and frog's legs. There are always fresh fish dishes and grills, including lemon sole meunière, crab salad, lobster, and specialties cooked at the table, such as steak au poivre, steak Diane, lamb kidneys, and veal escalopes. For dessert you might like fruit salad, cheesecake, or lemon sorbet. Complete your meal with an Italian coffee, or try the Jamaican coffee made with Tia Maria. Count on spending from £12 ($18). The wine bar is open from noon to 3 p.m. and 7 p.m. to 1 a.m., with last orders being taken at 10 p.m. Closed Sunday. In the early evening, drinks are accompanied by free munchies.

5. Some Favorite Pubs

Old Smugglers Inn, Ouaisne Bay, has foundations dating from the 13th century, and fishermen's cottages stood on this site until the early 1900s. They were enlarged and made into a small hotel. After World War II and the German occupation, the building underwent further alteration and became the Old Smugglers, an inn with a reputation for good food and fine ales. Beside the road just off the quay, it has granite walls five feet thick and low, beamed ceilings—a snug and friendly place to quaff ale with the locals after a walk along the bay past the martello tower.

At lunchtime, tables are set in the oldest part of the bar over the old well, where you can partake of hot pies—Smugglers beefsteak, steak and kidney, and chicken and mushroom—all served with crusty french bread, for £2 ($3). Brittany pâté and fresh homemade soup are also on the menu. Try the jacket potatoes topped with Jersey butter and cheese, along with charcoal-grilled steaks to order. Wine is around £2.75 ($4.13) for the house choice. Food is also served in the evening Monday to Saturday from 6 to 8:30 p.m., when the menu is much the same.

Les Fontaines Tavern, St. John, started life in the 14th century as an isolated farmhouse on the wild north coast of the island, and you can still see the smoking chains and the oven in the old fireplace in the bar. In winter, a bright fire burns, and the inglenook is popular in the public bar. The doorway into the pub is low as are the iron-bound beams, presenting a problem to drinkers and an incentive to sit at one of the tables set out on the stone floor, when they come here to enjoy bar snacks from noon to 2 p.m. On the menu, you'll find soup of the day with french bread and specials which include rabbit pie or, when the tide is right, crab sandwiches. Simple meals begin at £4.50 ($6.75). The publican has a mass of baseball caps from all over the world displayed behind the bar. This is a lovely place to relax before setting out on a walk along the cliffs—or afterward. You'll have a chance to meet the local farming folk, who speak a patois you may be at a loss to understand.

6. What to See

Elizabeth Castle, St. Aubin's Bay (tel. 0534/23971), was built on the historic Île de St. Helier in the late 16th century by Paul Ivey at the order of Queen Elizabeth I, to protect the island against invasion. It was further extended in 1626–1636 and 1646–1647. In 1668 the Outer Ward with the green and a fortified windmill were added. In the 1940s the Germans built a large bomb-proof shelter and a bunker armed with a French 110-mm gun captured from the Maginot Line, placed at the beginning of the Grand Battery.

Today, exhibits in the Militia Museum here show the progress of the fortress since Elizabethan days, and the Courthouse Bunker houses an exhibition of German militaria. Beside the castle is the Hermitage, where a man reputed to be St. Helier slept in a natural cavity in the rock during 15 years of prayer and fasting until he was beheaded in 555 by pirates.

The castle is reached by a causeway that runs for 1100 yards from West Park across the shingle ridge. This bridge is dry only about five hours at a time, and at spring tides it is often covered by 15 feet of water. Local boatmen are usually available to take you across at high water or to rescue tardy visitors. The castle is open daily March to October from 9:30 a.m. to 5:30 p.m. Admission is 60p ($1.05) for adults, 30p (45¢) for children. Refreshments are available.

The **Jersey Museum,** 9 Pier Rd., St. Helier (tel. 0534/75940), is housed in a Georgian merchant's house built of Jersey granite and displays exhibits depicting the island's social, political, and natural history. There is a courtyard with old weighing stones, an Edwardian telephone kiosk, and many nautical items. On the four floors above you will see reproduced rooms that have been, it would seem, lifted out of a house and transplanted intact: a bedroom, drawing room, and kitchen from the 1800s. There's a Victorian apothecary's shop that was taken complete with all the different jars from the St. Helier Pharmacy. Much of the Newgate Prison of St. Helier has been brought in and set up here.

The museum holds a fascinating marine biology room and a natural history room to acquaint you with the flora and fauna of Jersey. Perhaps you'll be interested in the art gallery or displays of old Jersey silver, medals, and coins. One room is devoted to the island's maritime history. The T. B. Davis Room recounts the story of *Westward,* a renowned racing schooner designed by Herreshoff of Rhode Island. The history of St. Helier, the island's capital, can be traced in one room. The pleasure is that you feel you're a part of all you see. The museum is open mid-January to the end of December Monday to Saturday from 10 a.m. to 5 p.m. Admission is 80p ($1.20) for adults, 40p (60¢) for children.

Fort Regent, St. Helier (tel. 0534/73000), is a modern entertainment and sports center that also houses the **Jersey Aquarium,** the **Museum of World Shells,** and the **States of Jersey Postal Museum.** There are also daily audio-visual presentations of the *Jersey Experience,* a journey through Jersey's history during the Napoleonic wars and the German occupation in World War II. The colorful Battle of Flowers exhibit serves as light relief. The fort is open daily from 10 a.m. to 10 p.m. in summer, to 6 p.m. in winter. Admission is £2.25 ($3.38) for adults and £1.50 ($2.25) for children from mid-May to the end of September, which allows entry to all exhibitions and museums plus free access to swimming pools, mini-golf, and other sports activities. The fee is reduced in winter to £1.50 ($2.25) for adults, 85p ($1.28) for children.

La Hougue Bie Museum, La Hougue Bie (tel. 0534/53823), lies in a green and pleasant park dominated by a fine cruciform Neolithic tomb built about 3000 B.C., with two medieval chapels on the massive mound. Other tombs (known as dolmens) exist, notably near St. Ouen and at Rozel, but this one at La Houge Bie is the finest to survive. Also in the park is the **German Occupation Museum** and the **Agricultural Museum** with a fine collection of mainly 19th-century farm implements, including the distinctive milk cans of Jersey, a hay cart showing its intriguing way of harnessing the horse, butter churns, hay forks, and wheat shovels. There is also the **Archaeological and Geology Museum.** Visitors may come here from March to early November daily except Monday from 10 a.m. to 5 p.m. Admission is 80p ($1.20) for adults, 40p (60¢) for children. You'll find refreshments and good parking available.

Mont Orgeuil Castle, Gorey, St. Martin (tel. 0534/53292), is a medieval concentric castle, which, until the construction of Elizabeth Castle in the 16th century, was the main fortress, built in the 13th century to protect the island from French raiders. There are tableaux and a small museum room illustrating the more important events in the castle's history, along with archeological finds from the Neolithic site on which the castle stands. It is open March to October daily from 9:30 a.m. to 5:30 p.m. Admission is 70p ($1.05) for adults, 30p (45¢) for children.

Reminders of the German occupation of the Channel Islands in the 1940s are everywhere in the Jersey countryside. At Noirmont Point at the southwest end of St. Brelade's Bay is **Noirmont Command Bunker,** built between March 1943 and April 1944 to command the naval coastal artillery battery that was placed on the headland in 1941. The building extends deep into the rock on two levels. It is open on selected dates during the summer. Admission and a guided tour are free. Telephone 0534/54383 for further information.

At Meadowbank, St. Lawrence, is the **German Military Underground Hospital,** started in 1942 but never completed. Visit the massive tunnel excavations, some still in an unfinished state, the operating theater, doctors' quarters, and a typical ward. Although all are empty now, it is easy to imagine the silent corridors filled with the bustle of a military hospital sheltering troops. It is open mid-March to early November daily from 9:30 a.m. to 5:30 p.m. (last admission at 5 p.m.). In winter it is open only on Thursday and Sunday from 2:30 to 5 p.m. Admission is £1 ($1.50) for adults, 50p (75¢) for children.

The most comprehensive collection of Nazi German memorabilia is at **St. Peter's Bunker,** St. Peter's Village (tel. 0534/81048 in summer, 0534/33825 in winter). The bunker was built in 1942 by the Germans, using slave labor, as a strong point guarding an important crossroads on the way to the airport. The six rooms contain a fascinating collection of proclamations and death warning notices, newspapers printed for German troops on the island, medical equipment, gas masks, the much-publicized "Enigma" decoding machine, and a butterfly bomb like the many thousands dropped on Britain during the war.

One room is reconstructed to show the bunk beds and personal possessions of the off-duty German soldiers, their weapons against the wall. Elsewhere are uniforms, caps, hats, helmets, and a vast display of weaponry and motorcycles, used largely for travel around the island. The bunker is open March to November daily from 10 a.m., with the last entrance at 4:45 p.m. Admission is 60p (90¢) for adults, 30p (45¢) for children.

Close by is the **Jersey Motor Museum,** St. Peter's Village (tel. 0534/82966), dedicated to preserving historic motor vehicles of all types, particularly with relation to Jersey's evolution. You'll also see American, British, and German military vehicles, plus bicycles and motorbikes. It is open March to November daily from 10 a.m., with the last visitor being admitted at 4:45 p.m. The charge is 60p (90¢) for adults, 30p (45¢) for children.

The **Jersey Wildlife Preservation Trust,** Les Augres Manor, Trinity, which celebrated its silver jubilee in 1984, is the outgrowth of the passionate enterprise of Gerald Durrell, author of many books about birds and animals and their care and preservation. The first of Durrell's specimens arrived at Les Augres in 1959 and were encouraged to breed and flourish in the rapidly expanding zoo, whose main aim is to protect endangered species throughout the world and help them replenish their population. The trust chose the dodo bird as its symbol, a large, harmless, flightless erstwhile inhabitant of Mauritius that was regarded as food and as a curiosity by mankind until it became extinct. This creature illustrates the shortsightedness and thoughtlessness which the trust seeks to change. A life-size stone dodo greets you as you enter the zoo.

The 32 acres ring to the cries, grunts, and whistles of the many beasts and birds that live happily in carefully designed houses and enclosures. The gorilla population is a particular achievement. Homes of endangered species are marked with the distinctive dodo sign to indicate their special importance. The trust has expanded and now boasts a sister organization, the Wildlife Preservation Trust International, in Philadelphia, Pennsylvania. Students come from all over the world, some 30% from the United States, to work and study at the Jersey zoo. The Wildlife Trust has more than 4000 members in the U.S., who are offered charter zoo trips along with special gifts when they visit here.

If you decide to join the trust at the zoo, Dodo Club membership for overseas visitors is £3 ($4.50). Admission to the zoo is £1.80 ($2.70). Le Café Dodo provides simple snacks. Bus 3A or 3B carries some of the 250,000 annual visitors from St. Helier to the zoo.

Elsewhere in the island is **St. Saviour's Church,** northeast of St. Heiler, where William Corbett le Breton, dean of Jersey, was rector. In the graveyard is his tomb, and in front of it, in the southeast corner of the churchyard, is the grave of Lillie Langtry, the Jersey Lily, his notorious daughter, born in 1853, who was widely known for her long love affair with Queen Victoria's son who became King Edward VII. She was brought here for burial after her death in Monaco in 1929.

St. Matthew's Church, Millbrook, St. Helier, on the road toward the airport, is known as the Glass Church. In 1934, a wealthy Millbrook inhabitant commissioned René Lalique of Paris to collaborate with the architect A. B. Grayson, and the church is decorated throughout with Lalique glass. The Great Cross behind the altar and the group of angels in the Lady Chapel are particularly fine examples. It is open weekdays from 9 a.m. to 6 p.m., on Saturday to 1 p.m.; closed Sunday except for services.

St. Luke's Churchyard on the A3 just outside St. Helier flies the American flag in honor of a number of American servicemen who died in World War II and are buried here.

The **Jersey Pottery,** Gorey Village, Grouville (tel. 1534/51119), is a modern studio behind the village, with pretty courtyards and a mass of climbing plants. This is a working pottery, and the people you see casting, throwing, and decorating are making the goods that will be on sale next month. There are all sorts of displays. The kilns are on show, and you can watch the process of making a vase from the moment the clay is first weighed before being placed on the wheel, right through to when the finished article emerges, glazed and decorated, from the kilns. In the "seconds" shop and large display hall, you can see all sorts of items on sale—cruets, napkin rings, egg timers, china table mats, flower holders, money boxes, and attractive pots.

The pottery and its restaurant are open Monday to Friday all year from 9:30 a.m. to 5 p.m.; closed Saturday and Sunday. In the light, airy restaurant, you can be served at a table by a waiter or serve yourself at the high counters where you perch on a bar stool to enjoy a meal alone or in a rush. In summer, you can eat in one of the two courtyards among the trees and plants. Take bus 1 or 2 from St. Helier.

The States of Jersey Postal Museum is in Fort Regent, but the main source of information is the sales and service counter at the **Main Post Office,** Broad Street, St. Helier (tel. 0534/26262). There you can get an enrollment form for opening a standing order account, through which you will receive the *Jersey Stamp Bulletin,* which will keep you up to date on new issues such as the one marking the anniversary of the Jersey Wildlife Preservation Trust.

There are two **golf courses** on Jersey, one by Gorey Common, the other at La Moye, St. Brelade. Aficionados of the sport may like to visit the Atlantic Hotel, La Moye, for lunch if they play that course.

Part Two

Scotland

Chapter XVIII

SOUTHERN SCOTLAND

1. The Border Country
2. Ayr, Prestwick, and District
3. Dumfries and Galloway

IN SCOTLAND, a land of bagpipes and clans, you'll find some of the most dramatic scenery in Europe. Stretching before you will be the Lowlands, but in the far distance, the fabled Highlands loom.

If you traverse all the country, you'll discover lochs and glens, heather-covered moors, twirling kilts and tam-o'-shanters, pastel-bathed houses and gray stone cottages, mountains, rivers, and sea monsters, as well as the sound of Gaelic, Shetland ponies, and misty blue hills, to name only some of Scotland's attractions.

Many visitors think of this country as Edinburgh and search no further. But if you travel northward, you'll find the real Scotland, along with overwhelming hospitality and a sense of exploration.

Scotland has its own legal system and issues its own currency, although English and Scottish banknotes have equal value and are readily accepted in both countries. The Church of Scotland is separate from that of England. The language of the Scot is said to be nearer to the original English than that spoken elsewhere these days, although many English-speaking people find it difficult to understand the speech of a true—and in modern times—gentle Highlander.

You will hardly be aware of crossing out of England into Scotland, either by road or rail, for the two countries have been joined constitutionally since 1707. But it has not always been that way, and indeed, although the border is just a line on the map, Scotland is still very much its own country.

For many centuries, from prehistoric times, a number of tribes effectively held sections of what is today Scotland, mainly the Picts and the Celts. The Romans, who initiated a takeover try in the first century of the Christian era, called the country Caledonia but were unsuccessful in crushing the tribes and occupied only the southern part of the country until their pullout in the fourth century. In the sixth century a tribe of Gaels sailed across from Ireland, the Scoti by name. They settled in, and it is from them that the country got the name it has today.

In A.D. 563 an Irish monk, St. Columba, landed on the island of Iona, a small rock of land to the west of Mull, built an abbey, and proceeded to preach Christianity to the heathen tribes.

Under various kings, Scotland gradually became more stable, and by the time William the Conqueror headed north from England in the 11th century, all the land was ruled by one sovereign, Malcolm III. From then on, battles great and small were waged between England and Scotland, and when they were not fighting the English, the Scots were fighting among themselves.

The first Irish invaders had started new families which, when they split from the original homesteads and resettled, had formed clans. "Clans" is a Gaelic word meaning "family" or "children of." The clan designation allowed them to trace their origins even when they moved to distant places. There was a strong hierarchy within each clan, with a chief at its head, followed by lesser chieftains, gentlemen, and then plain clansmen. The various families warred among themselves for territory, rights, and honor. The fighting among the clans abated in 1609 when, on the island of that name, the statutes of Iona were signed by most of the clan chiefs. However, sporadic fighting continued for years. The last real clan battle took place in 1688 at Keppoch near Glenroy, with the Macdonalds fighting the Macintoshes.

Today the clans—the ancient families—and those who enjoy common ancestry are distinguished mainly by the clan tartan, a word first recorded in 1471 to describe the previously named "chequered garment" or "mantle," now describing the particular plaid used for wearing apparel of the specific clan. Incidentally, it is not proper to use the word "tartan" in referring to a plaid carpet, nor is it allowed in Scotland to use an actual clan tartan pattern for carpeting or other decorative materials, except for use as clothing.

The kilt has an ancient history as a style of dress. It was recorded in Bronze Age frescoes in Crete and worn by Greek and Roman soldiers.

Highland gatherings or games have their origins in the fairs organized by the tribes or clans for the exchange of goods. At these gatherings, trials of strength were often held among the men, the strongest being selected for the chief's army. Many of these tests of brawn have continued until now at the gatherings, the most celebrated of which is at Braemar, held in early September of each year and patronized by the royal family.

GARB O' THE GODS: Few people realize that anywhere from seven to ten yards of tartan wool goes into the average kilt, and even fewer non-Scots know what is actually worn beneath the voluminous folds strapped onto the muscular thighs of a parading Scotsman.

For a Highlander purist, the answer to that last matter is "nothing." That answer is true for any defender of the ancient tradition that only a Stewart can wear a Stewart tartan, that only a MacPherson can wear a MacPherson tartan, and that only a Scotsman looks good in a kilt. Of course, any true Scot would wager his claymore (sword) that only a foreigner would stoop to wearing "unmentionables" (that's underpants to us) beneath his kilt.

Alas, commercialism has reared its ugly head with the introduction of undergarments to match the material making up the swirling folds of the kilts of bagpipe players. Nevertheless, salesmen in shops specializing in Highland garb tell the story of a colonel, the 11th Earl of Airlie, who had heard that the soldiers of his elite Highland Light Infantry were mollycoddling themselves with undershorts. The next day, his eyebrows bristling, he ordered the entire regiment to undress under his watchful eye. To his horror, he saw that half a dozen of his soldiers had disgraced the regiment by putting on "what only an Englishman would wear." He publicly ordered the offending garments removed. When he gave the order next day to "drop your kilts," not a soldier in the regiment had on "trews" (close-cut tartan shorts).

It was no doubt a long time before a similar level of indiscretion may have manifested itself among the Highland Light Infantry, if indeed it ever has. Even with the general decline of standards today, the mark of a man in the Highlands is still whether he can abide drafts up against his thighs and the feel of rough cloth against tender flesh.

If you're not fortunate enough to be of Highland extraction, or if you are distantly Scottish but can't discover possible clan connections, there is still hope. Long ago, Queen Victoria authorized two "Lowland" designs as suitable garb for Sassenachs (Saxons—Englishmen and, more remotely, Americans). If, during your jaunts in the Highlands, you decide to wear a kilt and a true Scot sees you in a Sassenach tartan, he or she will probably assume that you are also wearing "unmentionables."

GETTING THERE: From Newcastle upon Tyne, the A68 heading northwest takes you to where Scotland meets England, an area long known as "Carter Bar." At this point, all of Scotland lies before you, and an unforgettable land it is.

I recommend to visitors that they approach the Border Country after a stopover in the York area of England. That way, you can start exploring Scotland in the east with Edinburgh as your goal, then go up through Royal Deeside and on to Inverness, follow the Whisky Trail, and visit Glasgow, emerging at Gretna Green, near Carlisle in England's Lake District.

The Border Country is a fit introduction to Scotland, as it contains many reminders of the country's historic and literary past. A highlight of the tour is a visit to Abbotsford, the house Sir Walter Scott built on the banks of the salmon river, the Tweed.

However, if you're approaching Scotland from the west of England, you'll travel through Dumfries and Ayrshire—the Land of Burns, where the celebrated national poet was born, lived his short life, and died at the age of 37. This southwestern corner of Scotland, bounded by an indented coastline of charm and blessed with a gentle climate, attracts many artists who prefer the quiet, secluded life that prevails here. Distances aren't long, but many motorists take two or three or more days to cover some 100 miles, their progress slowed by the many places of interest to see along the way.

A large portion of the southwestern Lowlands comprises the shire of Dumfries and Galloway, the latter name being the ancient title of the area.

At Ayr, Troon, and Prestwick (with its international airport) you'll find sandy beaches and golf courses. There's also good fishing in southern Scotland, and pony-trekking over the low hills is a popular pursuit.

1. The Border Country

Castles in romantic ruins and Gothic skeletons of abbeys stand as reminders—in this ballad-rich land of plunder and destruction—of interminable battles that raged between England and the proud Scots. For a long time the so-called Border Country was a no-man's-land.

This is also the land of Sir Walter Scott, that master of romantic

SCOTLAND

THURSO
WICK
LYBSTER
LOCHINVER
Dunrobin Castle
LAIRG
Inverewe ULLAPOOL GOLSPIE
GAIRLOCH
DORNOCH
ACHNASHEEN
Hugh Miller's Cottage
Dunvegan Castle DINGWALL CROMARTY ELGIN CULLEN BANFF
NAIRN
PORTREE INVERNESS Cowdor Castle HUNTLY PETERHEAD
KYLE OF LOCHALSH HIGHLAND REGION Leith Hall Haddo House
Eilean Donan Castle Druminnor Castle INVERURIE Pitmedden
GRAMPIAN REGION Castle Fraser
FORT AUGUSTUS Kildrummy Castle Garden Drum Castle
Craigievar Castle ABERDEEN
Balmoral Castle Crathes Castle Provost Ross's House
Baemar Castle BANCHORY Provost Skene's House
BRAEMAR KINCARDINE Muchalls Castle
STONEHAVEN
Blair Castle Edzell Castle & Gardens Dunnottar Castle
BALACHULISH PITLOCHRY KIRRIEMUR BRECHIN
Barrie's Birthplace FORFAR
Angus Folk Museum
MULL TAYSIDE REGION Glamis Castle ARBROATH
Scone Palace DUNDEE Kellie Castle
OBAN CRIEFF PERTH Branklyn Garden
Drummond Castle Gardens GLENEAGLES Hill of Torvit
Inverary Castle Doune Castle FALKLAND ST ANDREWS
CENTRAL REGION Falkland Palace Kellie Castle
Menrtie KINROSS
LOCHGILPHEAD DUNBLANE Castle FIFE REGION
Benmore STIRLING DUNFERMLINE Luffness Castle
Stirling Castle NORTH BERWICK
JURA Rossdhu Culross Palace KIRKCALDY Dirleton Castle & Garden
DUNOON Loch Lomond The Town House Preston Mill
Park Hopetoun House Hamilton House HADDINGTON
STRATHCLYDE REGION The Binns Lamb's House Winton House
Achamore LINLITHGOW Suntrap Inveresk Lodge
ISLE OF LARGS Linlithgow Palace LOTHIAN REGION
GIGHA Weavers Cottage Malleny Garden Mellerstain
LANARK Dalkeith Park LAUDER Floors Castle
Brodick Castle Bachelor's Club PEEBLES KELSO
Traquair House Kailzie Gardens MELROSE Priorwood Gardens
Dawyck House Gardens Abbotsford House
Burns Cottage INNERLEITHEN
GLASGOW Abbotsford House Bowhill JEDBURGH
Culzean Castle MOFFAT House
Souter Johnnies Cottage BORDERS REGION
GIRVAN DUMFRIES AND GALLOWAY REGION
Drumlanrig Castle Rammerscales
LOCKERBIE
Waxwelton House DUMFRIES
CASTLE DOUGLAS
Castle Kennedy Gardens Arbigland Gardens
STRANRAER KIRCUDBRIGHT Threave Gardens
Logan Botanic
Garden PORT LOGAN

GLASGOW
Botanic Gardens
Linn Park
Rouken Glen Park
Victoria Park
Ross Hall Park
Pollok House
Bellahouston Park
Provand's Lordship
Greenbank
Provan Hall

EDINBURGH
Lauriston Castle
Palace of Holyrood House
Edinburgh Castle
Gladstone's Land
Royal Botanic Garden
The Georgian House

This map is taken from *Historic Houses, Castles & Gardens* with permission of ABC Historic Publications, a Division of ABC Travel Guides Ltd., Oldhill London Road, Dunstable LU6 3EB

adventure i
for such wc
   Southe
King David
Melrose, Je
   "The
Ridings" ga

JEDBURG

This royal b
founded by
abbeys in S
to Septemb
October to
Thursday a
   On Qu
08356/6333
November
Earl of Botl
killed her. 1
(her watch,
death mask
and 1 to 5:3

Kelso is also the home of the Duke of Roxburgh
Castle, built in 1721 by William Adam. Part of this
to the public, which is allowed to tour through
French antiques, Chinese porcelain, and
Gainsborough, Reynolds, and Landi. A
Courtyard Restaurant. Floors is open
from early May to late September (o
house is open at 1:30 p.m., the last
grounds and gardens may be visi
Centre is open daily from 10:

Food and Lodging

Ednam House H
Georgian house in
beside the river
atmosphere,
in 1761, the
Roxburgh
archite
is m

Food and

Mrs. A. Richardson, 124 Bongate (tel. 08356/62480), is more a private home than a guest house—in fact, it's an apartment in a block of four buildings. The Richardsons have two bedrooms, one with twin beds, the other with a double and single, which is classified as a family room. The per-person cost for an adult is £8 ($12) to £9 ($13.50) nightly. Mrs. Richardson gives you a hot beverage and cookies before you go to bed, and in the morning, a big breakfast. She'll also cook an evening meal, if asked beforehand, which she serves at 6:30 ("so I can go for a walk afterward").

The Carters' Restaurant (tel. 08356/63414), is a pub with downstairs dining room built of old abbey stones. The building has had a colorful history—a local grammar school from 1779, before finding its present role. This is the favorite gathering place of the people of Jedburgh who know that its owner, Michael Wares, serves good food and drink. Soups, bar snacks, and coffee are served daily in the lounge bar. The restaurant offers either British or continental dishes daily from £6.50 ($9.75). Lunches are served Monday to Saturday from noon to 2 p.m. Dinners are more elaborate, presented Monday to Thursday from 6 to 9 p.m. (till 10 on Friday and Saturday). Fish is fresh from Eyemouth, accompanied, if you wish, by a tomato and cole slaw salad.

If you follow the A698 northeast of Jedburgh, the road will lead to:

KELSO: Another typical historic border town, Kelso lies at the point where the Teviot meets the Tweed. **Kelso Abbey,** now in ruins, was the earliest and the largest of the border abbeys. In the town's marketplace, the "Old Pretender," James Stewart, was proclaimed king, designated James VIII.

e, who lives at **Floors**
Border house is on view
t, admiring the tapestries,
paintings by such artists as
ternoon tea is served in the
daily except Friday and Saturday
pen Friday in July and August). The
guests shown through at 4:45 p.m. The
ted from 12:30 to 5:30 p.m. The Garden
0 a.m. to 4:30 p.m.

otel (tel. 0573/24168) is a delightful conversion of a
o a 34-room hotel often referred to as "that lovely place
." The hotel, lying on the fringe of Kelso, has a good
nd the bedrooms are well kept, some with river views. Built
hotel was purchased by the Brooks family from the Duke of
e in 1928, and it is one of the finest examples of Georgian
cture in the Border Country. Still family owned, the hotel at present
anaged by R. Alastair Brooks, grandson of the original purchaser.

A few of the bedrooms are spacious and airy, although late arrivals
might be given the more cramped quarters. At least half the accommodations come equipped with private baths, and you pay more for these, of
course. Singles range in price from £18 ($27) to £20 ($30), and doubles from
£35 ($52.50) to £39 ($58.50). Rates include a full Scottish breakfast,
although service is extra. For those wanting to chance it with the highly
unreliable Scottish sun, there is a terrace.

From Kelso, it is only a short drive on the A699 to—

DRYBURGH: Scott himself is buried at **Dryburgh Abbey.** These Gothic
ruins are surrounded by gnarled yew trees and cedars of Lebanon, said to
have been planted there by knights returning from the Holy Land during
the years of the Crusades. Near Dryburgh is "Scott's View," over the
Tweed to his beloved Eildon Hills, considered one of the most beautiful
views in the region.
The adjoining town is—

ST. BOSWELLS: This old village, 40 miles from Edinburgh, stands on the
Selkirk–Kelso road, near Dryburgh Abbey. It lies four miles from Melrose
and 14 miles from Kelso. Because of the following hotel, many motorists
prefer to make St. Boswells their headquarters for touring "the Borders."
Dryburgh Abbey Hotel (tel. 0835/22261) actually stands beside the
ruins from which it takes its name. On the outskirts of St. Boswells, the red
sandstone hotel is surrounded by lovely grounds, made all the more so by
the gently flowing River Tweed. Built in the Scottish baronial manor, the
abbey hotel has all the amenities associated with the traditional country
house hotel, including large, extensive grounds. Modern conveniences have
been slipped in, however. About 30 rooms are offered, with singles renting
from 26 ($39) without bath, £30 ($45) with. Doubles range from £44 ($66)
to £64 ($96), and all these tariffs include a full English breakfast. You have
a choice of several lounges and a handsome dining room, plus a cocktail

bar. The hotel is open all year. Good Scottish fare is served, and that means fresh local salmon or perhaps roast gigot of "Borders" lamb, with its traditional accompaniment, red currant jelly. Soups are good too, especially the homemade ham and lentil broth. A three-course à la carte lunch costs about £10 ($15) and up, while dinner starts at around £12 ($18).

Four miles from Dryburgh Abbey is—

MELROSE: Lying 37 miles from Edinburgh, Melrose enjoys many associations with Scott. This border town, as mentioned, is also famous for its ruined **Melrose Abbey,** in the Valley of the Tweed. You can visit the ruins of the beautiful Cistercian abbey, founded in 1136, in which the heart of Robert I (the Bruce) is said to have been buried. Look for the beautiful carvings and tombs of other well-known Scotsmen buried in the chancel. In Scott's *The Lay of the Last Minstrel,* the abbey's east window received rhapsodic treatment, and in *The Abbot* and *The Monastery,* Melrose appears as "Kennaquhair." It is open Monday to Saturday April to September from 9:30 a.m. to 7 p.m., on Sunday from 2 to 7 p.m. October to March, hours are 9:30 a.m. to 4 p.m., 2 to 4 p.m. on Sunday. Admission is 90p ($1.35) for adults, 45p (68¢) for children.

The leading hotel in Melrose is **George & Abbotsford,** High Street (tel. 089-682/2308), a 19th-century coaching inn built overlooking the ruins of Melrose Abbey. The hotel is unpretentious, with well-equipped bedrooms, about half of which contain private baths. Singles range in price from £17 ($25.50) to £19 ($28.50) for B&B, and doubles rent from £30 ($45) to £34 ($51), the more expensive rooms with bath or shower. In the garden you can admire the roses—and think about the brave heart of the Scottish hero, Robert Bruce. Later on, you can fortify yourself for another day's exploration in one of the two lounges or bar, meeting a congenial blend of visitors and locals. A set lunch costs about £10 ($15); a dinner, £11 ($16.50).

At sunset you can stroll along the banks of the River Tweed, perhaps walk along a public footpath on a hill overlooking the town.

The next morning, you can drive three miles to—

ABBOTSFORD: This was the home of Sir Walter Scott that he built and lived in from 1812 until he died. It contains many relics collected by the author. Especially interesting is his study, with his writing desk and chair. In 1935 two secret drawers were found in the desk. One of them contained 57 letters, part of the correspondence between Sir Walter and his wife-to-be. The Scott home is open from March 22 to October 31, weekdays from 10 a.m. to 5 p.m., on Sunday from 2 to 5 p.m., charging £1.50 ($2.25) for adults, 75p ($1.13) for children.

After leaving Scott's house, you can continue along the Tweed to—

TRAQUAIR HOUSE: At Innerleithen, a few miles east of Peebles, Traquair is considered the oldest inhabited and most romantic house in Scotland. Dating back to the tenth century, it is rich in associations with Mary Queen of Scots and the Jacobite risings. Its treasures include glass, embroideries, silver, manuscripts, and paintings. Of particular interest is a brewhouse equipped as it was two centuries ago. The great house is still lived in by the Stuarts of Traquair.

The house and grounds are open from Easter Saturday until about the last week in October, daily from 1:30 to 5:30 p.m. In July and August, hours are from 10:30 a.m. to 5:30 p.m. (last admittance is at 5 p.m.). Rates are £2 ($3) for adults, £1 ($1.50) for children.

There are five craft workshops in the grounds as well as a tea room, home bakehouse, playground, woodland and River Tweed walks, and a maze. Tennis and croquet can be played by arrangement, and trout fishing is available on a private stretch of the Tweed. To make inquiries, telephone Innerleithen 830323.

Innerleithen is a modest little mill town, but the unmarred beauty of the River Tweed valley as seen from the town's surrounding hillsides remains constant. The famous Ballantyne cashmeres are manufactured here, and annual games and a Cleikum ceremony take place here in July. Scott's novel, *St. Ronan's Well,* is identified with the town.

From Innerleithen, it's only a six-mile ride to—

PEEBLES: This royal burgh and county town, 23 miles from Edinburgh, is a market center in the Valley of the Tweed. Scottish kings used to come here when they went to hunt in Ettrick Forest. The town is noted for its large woolen mills, although the **Scottish Museum of Wool Textiles,** where you can see how tartans and fine woolens are dyed and spun, and where you can buy lengths of cloth and garments to take home, lies nine miles east in the town of Walkerburn.

Peebles is also known as a "writer's town." John Buchan Tweedsmuir, the Scottish author and statesman who died in 1940 and is remembered chiefly for writing the Stevensonian adventure story *Prester John* in 1910, lived here. He was also the author of *The Thirty-Nine Steps* (1915), the first of a highly successful series of secret-service thrillers. In 1935 he was appointed governor-general of Canada. Robert Louis Stevenson once lived at Peebles, and drew upon the surrounding countryside in *Kidnapped,* which was published first in 1886.

On the north bank of the Tweed stands **Neidpath Castle,** its peel (tower) dating from the 13th century. Cromwell besieged and took it in 1650.

Food and Lodging

If you'd like to spend the night instead of heading on to Edinburgh, a good bet is the **Tontine Hotel,** High Street (tel. 0721/20892), which has a Scottish lion on a fountain in its forecourt. The hotel was built in 1808 by subscription—hence its name. It has been recently redecorated and re-styled, and in the comfortable main lounge is a fine display of silver belonging to the hotel. An extension has been added, housing a block of modern, studio-style rooms, all equipped with private baths, color TVs, and tea- and coffee-making facilities. Singles rent for £38 ($57), doubles for £56 ($84), including VAT and service. The staff is efficient and friendly. The restaurant, the Adam Room, has good views overlooking Glensax Hills. One bar is known as the Tweeddale Shoot Bar, named after the long-established Shooting Club of Peebles. The second bar, the Beltane, is decorated in pine and named after a local festival. It has one of the finest displays of working-horse harnesses in the country. Bar snacks are available at lunch, and there's always a chef's hot specialty, costing from £2 ($3).

The **Cringletie House Hotel,** at Eddleston, near Peebles (tel. Eddleston 233), is an imposing country hotel, with towers and turrets, standing on 28 acres of private grounds. It's like a small French château, built of red sandstone and lying slightly more than two miles from the center of Peebles, set back from the A703. Your hosts, Mr. and Mrs. Maguire, receive you as if you were a private guest in their baronial mansion.

Most of the bedrooms, 16 in all, are spacious, and all of them are comfortably appointed. Nine have private baths. Double- and twin-bedded rooms go from £22.50 ($33.75) per person with private bath. Top-floor bedrooms without private baths cost £19.50 ($29.25) per person. The public rooms are rich in character and style, as befits a Victorian mansion. There is an elevator as well. The bar is well stocked, and guests gather there before dinner, exchanging introductions.

Mrs. Maguire is in charge of the hotel's restaurant. In elegant surroundings, you are given a limited but extremely well-selected choice of dishes. The food is made even more enjoyable by the attentive service. In season the vegetables come fresh from Mrs. Maguire's garden. She has her own style of cooking, and her special dishes include a delectable smoked haddock mousse. A Sunday luncheon costs £8.50 ($12.75), and a four-course dinner is from 7:30 to 8:30, going for £12 ($18). Lunch is à la carte on weekdays. You must be punctual, because of the short hours of serving (the food is freshly cooked), and you'll need a reservation of course, particularly if you aren't a guest of the hotel. The restaurant and hotel are closed from mid-November to mid-March.

MELLERSTAIN: Seat of the Lord Binning, Mellerstain lies in "the Borders," although it is most often visited on a day trip from Edinburgh, 37 miles away. One of Scotland's famous Adam mansions, it lies near Gordon, nine miles northeast of Melrose and seven miles northwest of Kelso (tel. Gordon 225). It's open from May to September daily, except Saturday, from 1:30 to 5:30 p.m.

Mellerstain enjoys associations with Lady Grisel Baillie, the Scottish heroine, and Lord Binning is her descendant. William Adam built two wings of the house in 1725, although the main building was designed by his more famous son Robert some 40 years later.

You're shown through the interior, with its decorations and ceilings by Robert Adam, and are allowed to view the impressive library as well as paintings by old masters and antique furniture. Later, from the garden terrace, you can look south to the lake, with the Cheviot Hills in the distance, a panoramic view. Afternoon tea is served, and tweeds and souvenir gifts are on sale.

2. Ayr, Prestwick, and District

As Sir Walter Scott dominates the Borders, so does Robert Burns the country around Ayr and Prestwick. There are, in addition, a string of famous seaside resorts stretching from Girvan to Largs. Some of the greatest golf courses in Britain, including Turnberry, are found here, and Prestwick, of course, is one of the major airports of Europe.

AYR: Ayr is the most popular resort on Scotland's west coast. A busy market town, it offers 2½ miles of sands and makes for a good center for touring the Burns Country. This royal burgh is also noted for its manufacture of fabrics and carpets, so you may want to allow time to browse through its shops. With its steamer cruises, fishing, golf, and racing, it faces the Isle of Arran and the Firth of Clyde.

Ayr is full of Burns associations. The 13th-century **Auld Brig o' Ayr,** the poet's "poor narrow footpath of a street,/Where two wheelbarrows tremble when they meet," was renovated in 1910. A Burns museum is housed in the thatched **Tam o'Shanter Inn** in Ayr High Street, an alehouse in Rabbie's day.

The **Auld Kirk** of Ayr dates from 1654 when it replaced the 12th-century Church of St. John. Burns was baptized in the kirk.

Ayr is also the birthplace of the famous road builder **John L. MacAdam,** whose name was immortalized in road surfacing.

In Tarbolton village, 7½ miles northeast of Ayr, is the **Bachelors' Club,** a 17th-century house where in 1780 Burns and his friends founded a literary and debating society, now a property of the National Trust for Scotland. In 1779 Burns attended dancing lessons there, against the wishes of his father. There also, in 1781, he was initiated as a Freemason in the Lodge St. David. Eleven months later he became a member of Lodge St. James, which continues today in the village. Samuel Hay, 7 Croft St. (tel. 029-254/424), says the Bachelors' Club is open for visitors any time of day from April until October, and he will arrange to show it at other times if you telephone. Admission is 50p (75¢) for adults, 25p (38¢) for children. Tarbolton is six miles from Prestwick Airport.

For centuries, Ayr has been associated with horse racing, and it now has the top racecourse in Scotland. One of the main streets of the town is named Racecourse Road for a stretch near the town center.

Where to Stay

Pickwick Hotel, 19 Racecourse Rd. (tel. 0292/60111). It may seem ironic to have a hotel commemorating a character in a Charles Dickens novel in a town noted for its memories of Rabbie Burns. But this early Victorian hotel, set on its own grounds, does just that. The Pickwick is really a large-size house, renting out 15 well-furnished private bedrooms that contain either a private shower or else a complete bath. The B&B rate is £25 ($37.50) to £31 ($46.50) in a single and £38 ($57) to £48 ($72) in a double, including a full Scottish breakfast, VAT, and service. Each room bears a Dickensian title. All rooms have private bathroom facilities, color TV, radio, drinks dispenser, trouser press, and tea- and coffee-making equipment. In the paneled Pickwick Club you can soak up much Dickensian atmosphere. The food itself is simple but well prepared, a bar lunch costing around £6 ($9); a dinner, from £11 ($16.50). The hotel is personally supervised by Sheila and Edward Lynas, the proprietors, who endeavor to make everyone who stays at the Pickwick feel welcome.

Caledonian Hotel, Dalblair Road (tel. 0292/69331), occupies a convenient central location, offering comfortable although certainly not luxurious bedrooms, all 122 of which contain functional, compact private baths or showers plus TV. Singles rent for £34 ($51), doubles for £50 ($75), breakfast included. Flight crews from various international carriers stay here, a fact acknowledged by the Flight Deck Bar. The food is good, particularly in the hotel's theme restaurant, Chaplin's. There is also a sauna, souvenir shop, and a disco which is open five nights a week. A dinner-dance is held every Saturday night.

Marine Court, Fairfield Road (tel. 0292/67461), has long been a favorite with travelers. A substantial building in a cul-de-sac, it offers good, solid comfort, and many of its rooms open onto a sweeping view of the Firth of Clyde. The hotel also lies about 200 yards from the beach, and it makes for a charming oasis, especially as you wander through its garden. The bedrooms are well furnished and immaculately maintained, and all of them come equipped with private bath, color TV, tea- and coffee-making facilities, and in-house movies. Singles peak at £28.50 ($42.75), and doubles are rented for a top £45 ($67.50), including a full breakfast, service, and VAT. The food is well prepared and handsomely served. A normal set dinner goes for £10 ($15). On Saturday a band plays for a dinner-dance at a special price. The hotel has a heated swimming pool, a sauna, Jacuzzi, solarium, gymnasium, and leisure lounge.

The Local Pub

By all means, pay your respects to Burns by going to **Rabbie's Bar,** Burns Statue Square (tel. 0292/62112), right in the heart of town. A colorfully decorated pub, this place is of course dedicated to the memory of the poet. On the walls you'll find a selection of some of his most famous lines. In addition to the good drink which Burns enjoyed, you can also order snacks. Guests sit near a thatched bar counter. One reader reports that disco music wasn't what she expected to hear in a bar honoring Burns.

ALLOWAY: Some three miles from the center of Ayr is where Robert Burns, Scotland's national poet, was born on January 25, 1759, in the gardener's cottage—the "auld clay biggin"—his father, William Burns, built in 1757. More than 100,000 people visit the **Burns Cottage** annually, and it still retains some of its original furniture, including the bed in which the poet was born. Chairs displayed here were said to have been used by Tam o'Shanter and Souter Johnnie. Beside the cottage in which the poet lived is a museum, open all year from 9 a.m. to 7 p.m. during summer (shorter hours in the off-season). Admission to the cottage and the Burns Monument is 70p ($1.05) for adults, 35p (53¢) for children.

The Auld Brig over the Ayr, mentioned in *Tam o'Shanter,* still spans the river, and Alloway Auld Kirk, also mentioned in the poem, stands roofless and "haunted" not far away. The poet's father is buried in the graveyard of the kirk.

The **Land o' Burns Centre** near the monument is a good place to stop. You can watch the multiscreen presentation of highlights of Burns' life, his friends, and his poetry. Information is available from the friendly personnel, and a well-stocked gift shop is there. The Russians are particularly fond of Burns and his poetry, and many come annually to visit the cottage and pore over his original manuscripts.

Where to Stay

The **Burns Monument Hotel** (tel. Alloway 42466) is a 185-year-old inn that looks out onto the Doon River and the bridge, "Brig o'Doon," immortalized in *Tam o'Shanter*. The inn is an attractive, historical place, with riverside gardens and a whitewashed bar. The rooms are pleasantly and attractively decorated, bright and cheerful, some opening onto river views. All bedrooms have private baths. B&B averages around £18 ($27) in a single and from £32 ($48) in a double.

The **Balgarth Hotel** (tel. Alloway 42441), two miles south of Ayr on the A719 coastal road to the fishing village of Dunure, is within easy reach for touring the Burns Country and southwest Scotland. The hotel stands within its own pleasant grounds, complete with beer garden overlooking the Clyde and Carrick Hills, and offers special rates to golf enthusiasts with access to Royal Troon, Turnberry, and other scenic courses on the Ayrshire coast. The 15 rooms are bright and well furnished, with TV, telephone, and private bath. The tariff per person for B&B is £20 ($30), including VAT. Dinner is from £7 ($10.50). The Balgarth is open all year.

CULZEAN CASTLE: One of Robert Adam's most notable creations, although built around an ancient tower of the Kennedys, Culzean (pronounced Cullane), 12 miles south-southwest of Ayr, dates mainly from 1777 and is considered one of the finest Adam houses in Scotland. The castle, with a view of Ailsa Craig to the south and overlooking the Firth of Clyde, is well worth a visit and is of special interest to Americans because of General Eisenhower's connection with it and its National Guest Flat. In 1946 the guest flat was given to the general for his lifetime in gratitude for his services as Supreme Commander of Allied Forces in World War II. Culzean stands near the golf courses of Turnberry and Troon, a fact that particularly pleased the golf-loving Eisenhower.

An exhibition of Eisenhower memorabilia includes sound and audiovisual spectacles, and is seen by more than 100,000 people a year. The exhibition is sponsored by the Scottish Heritage U.S.A., Inc., and Mobil Oil. To illustrate his career, there is a capsule history of World War II demonstrated with wall maps. Mementos of Eisenhower include his North African campaign desk and a replica of the Steuben glass bowl given him by his cabinet when he retired from the presidency.

The castle is open April 1 through September daily from 10 a.m. to 6 p.m. (last admission at 5:30 p.m.), October 1 through October 31 daily from 10 a.m. to 4 p.m. Admission to the castle is £1.75 ($2.63) for adults, £1 ($1.50) for children.

In the castle grounds is **Culzean Country Park,** which in 1969 became the first such park in Scotland. It has an exhibition center in farm buildings by Adam. The 565-acre grounds include a walled garden, an aviary, a swan pond, a camellia house, an orangery, a deer park, miles of woodland paths, and beaches. Cars can drive through the Culzean Country Park at a cost of £1.60 ($2.40). For information, telephone Kirkoswald 269.

After leaving Culzean Castle, you might want to take a short drive to **Kirkoswald** near Maybole. This is the thatched cottage which was the home of the village cobbler, John Davidson (Souter Johnnie), at the end of the 18th century. Davidson and his friend Douglas Graham of Shanter Farm were immortalized by Burns in his poem *Tam o'Shanter.* The cottage contains Burnsiana and contemporary cobblers' workshop and tools. In the churchyard are the graves of Tam o'Shanter and Souter Johnnie, two of his best known characters. The cottage is open April 1 to September 30, daily except Friday, noon to 5 p.m. (other times by appointment). Admission is 70p ($1.05) for adults, 45p (68¢) for children. Telephone Kirkoswald 603 for more information.

GIRVAN: About eight miles south of Culzean Castle on the A77, Girvan is the leading coastal resort of southwest Scotland, with sandy beaches and good fishing. A whisky distillery offers guided tours (and samples) for visitors.

In summer entertainment is offered at the **Beach Pavilion,** featuring music, dancing, children's shows, variety shows, and concerts.

Ailsa Craig, a 1110-foot-high rounded rock ten miles offshore, is a nesting ground and sanctuary for seabirds and formerly provided granite for stones used in the Scottish game of curling. You can sail out to the rock for a modest charge.

Three miles northeast of Girvan is the 16th-century **Kilochan Castle,** stronghold of the Cathcarts of Carleton in the valley of the Water of Girvan.

Six miles north of Girvan are the scant remains of **Turnberry Castle,** where many historians believe Robert the Bruce was born in 1274.

The **Westcliffe Hotel,** Louisa Drive (tel. Girvan 2128), is on the seafront and overlooks the Promenade, putting greens, and a children's boating lake. This is a family hotel, and the resident proprietors, Mr. and Mrs. Robert Jardine, have carried out extensive alterations, adding six ground-floor bedrooms, all with private bathrooms, at the back. Some bedrooms in the original building have showers. All bedrooms have hot and cold water and electric shaving points, and are carpeted. Rooms without bath rent for £12 ($18) per person for B&B. With bath, the rent is £14 ($21). The Westcliffe is licensed, with a lounge bar and a small service bar at the end of the dining room that looks out over the seafront and Ailsa Craig. Mrs. Jardine personally supervises preparation of the food, which is very good. Dinner costs from £5.50 ($8.25). There are tea- and coffee-making facilities and color TVs in all bedrooms.

PRESTWICK: Prestwick is the oldest recorded baronial burgh in Scotland. But most visitors today aren't concerned with that ancient fact—rather, they fly in, landing at Prestwick's International Airport, which is in itself a popular sightseeing attraction, as spectators gather to watch planes take off and land from all over the world.

Behind St. Ninian's Episcopal Church is **Bruce's Well,** the water from which is reputed to have cured Robert the Bruce of leprosy. The **Mercat Cross** still stands outside what used to be the Registry Office and marks the center of the oldest part of Prestwick, whose existence goes back to at least 983. Prestwick is a popular holiday town, and is considered one of Scotland's most attractive resorts, with its splendid sands and golf courses. Prestwick opens onto views of Ayr Bay and the Isle of Arran.

Where to Stay

Adamton House Hotel, Monktown, near Prestwick (tel. 0292/70678), is an 18th-century, 30-bedroom hotel with views of the Isle of Arran and Ailsa Craig. As it lies only a few miles from Prestwick Airport, it provides an excellent opportunity to get over jet-lag. All rooms have bath or shower, tea-making equipment, and TV and radio. The beautiful curved wooden staircase leads down to a quiet, comfortable lounge, the restaurant, and the cocktail bar. In the Secret Room beneath the house, on weekends the hotel stages a historical banquet with candlelight and medieval entertainment. Including food and wine, the banquet costs £12 ($18) per person and lasts three hours. Singles with bath are £30 ($45), and doubles and twins with bath cost from £45 ($67.50), including a full Scottish breakfast, VAT, and service.

Towans Hotel, Prestwick Airport (tel. 0292/79691). The original building faces a side lawn and then looks out over the Firth of Clyde to the Isle of Arran. Much of the accommodation is in a new hotel/motel block that blends successfully with the old. The Martin family, conscious of the needs of international travelers passing through Prestwick Airport, are geared to catering for early and late arrivals. Rooms have private baths, and tea and coffee makers. Breakfast is served from 4 a.m., and the dining room has a good local reputation for well-cooked meals. A bed will cost you from £18 ($27). All meals are extra, but you can make as much tea and coffee as you want in your room.

The **Parkstone,** Esplanade (tel. 0292/77286), is more suited for a beach holiday center, as it opens onto the sea. Catering to families, it is handsomely perched, receiving guests all year in one of its bedrooms, many of which contain a private bath or shower. The single tariff is £17.60 ($26.40), rising to £30 ($45) in a double, including a full breakfast, VAT, and service. Rooms are comfortably and pleasantly furnished, and all have color TV. A two-course luncheon goes for £4.25 ($6.38), a set dinner for £8.50 ($12.75), and high tea from £4 ($6).

TROON: This holiday resort looks out across the Firth of Clyde to the Isle of Arran. It offers several golf links, including the "Old Troon" course. Bathers in summer find plenty of room on its two miles of sandy beaches, stretching from both sides of its harbor. The broad sands and shallow waters make it a safe haven also. From here you can take steamer trips to Arran and the Kyles of Bute.

Troon is mostly a 20th-century town, its earlier history having gone unrecorded. It takes its name from the curiously shaped promontory that juts out into the Clyde estuary on which the old town and the harbor stand. The promontory was called "Trwyn," the Cymric word for nose, and later this became the Trone and then Troon.

Fullarton Estate, on the edge of Troon beyond the municipal golf course, is the ancestral seat of the Dukes of Portland.

A massive statue of **Britannia** stands on the seafront as a memorial to the dead of the two World Wars. On her breastplate is the lion of Scotland emerging from the sea.

Where to Stay

Marine Hotel, Crosbie Road (tel. Troon 314444), is a large deluxe hotel that is enveloped by about 20 miles of seaside golf courses. One of the principal hotels along the Clyde coast, it offers a wide range of accommodations—70 rooms in all, each with bath, and each differing in style, space, and furnishings. The single rate is £39 ($58.50), rising to £59 ($88.50) in a double, including VAT, service, and a full breakfast. Not only are the views from the windows spectacular, but the hotel is most agreeable and makes a good base for touring the Burns Country. The helpful staff gives personal attention—if you come back a second time they'll know your name. The noise from Prestwick—three miles away—is kept out by double-glazed windows.

The hotel's restaurants offer excellent fare, although I prefer L'Auberge de Provence, where the French cookery is superb, as is the selection of fine burgundies. The auberge is decorated in a rustic style, serving dinner only, from 7 to 10.30 p.m. daily except Sunday, charging about £18 ($27) per person. The lounges are spacious, and there are two stylish bars.

Sun Court, Crosbie Road (tel. Troon 312727), was once the home of an industrialist, and it offers all the grand style of the Edwardian era. Like the Marine, it looks out onto golf courses and the sea. Its most delightful feature is a conservatory filled with flowers. The hotel also contains a Real Tennis Court, one of the few in Britain. A sandy beach along the Firth of Clyde is about a 100-yard walk away.

Open all year, the Sun Court offers 20 handsome bedrooms, 17 of which contain private baths. The single tariff ranges from £30 ($45) to £34 ($51), the double rate going from £48 ($72) to £52 ($78). There is as well a beautiful walled garden. The lounges are stylish and decorated in a conservative fashion. Try to get one of the more old-fashioned bedrooms, although you may be assigned a more modernized one. From a well-stocked cellar emerges a fine collection of wine, and the food at Sun Court is well prepared and served.

KILMARNOCK: This inland town is the site of the largest whisky-bottling concern in the world. Johnnie Walker, a grocer in King Street, started to blend whisky in Kilmarnock in 1820, and the product is known all over the world today.

The town also has Burns associations. The first edition of his poems was printed here in 1786. Burns published the poems to raise money to emigrate to Jamaica, but they were so successful he decided to remain in Scotland. In Kay Park, the **Burns Monument** is a red sandstone temple surmounted by a tower, which contains a good museum of Burnsiana.

Dundonald Castle, 4½ miles southwest of Kilmarnock, is a notable landmark high on an isolated hill. It was built by Robert II, the first Stuart king, who died there in 1390, as did Robert III in 1406. East along the River Irvine are the three lace-making towns of Galston, Newmilns, and Darvel where Dutch and Huguenot immigrants settled in the 17th century.

3. Dumfries and Galloway

Southwestern Scotland is often overlooked by motorists rushing north. But this country of Burns is filled with many rewarding targets—a land of unspoiled countryside, fishing harbors, artists' colonies of color-washed houses, and romantically ruined abbeys and castles dating from the days of the border wars.

It's a fine touring country, and the hotels are generally small, of the Scottish provincial variety, but that usually means a friendly reception from a smiling staff and good traditional Scottish cookery, using the local produce.

I've documented the most important centers below, but have included some offbeat places for those seeking a more esoteric trip.

LOCKERBIE: A border market town, Lockerbie lies in the beautiful valley of Annandale, offering much fishing and golf. It's a good center for exploring some sightseeing attractions in its environs.

Lockerbie was the scene in 1593 of a battle that ended one of the last great Border family feuds. The Johnstones routed the Maxwells, killing Lord Maxwell and 700 of his men. Many of the victims had their ears cut off with a cleaver, a method of mutilation that became known throughout the Border Country as the "Lockerbie Nick."

Of interest are the remains of **Lockmaben Castle,** 3½ miles west of Lockerbie, said to have been the boyhood home (some historians say the birthplace) of Robert the Bruce. This castle, on the south shore of Castle Loch, was captured and recaptured 12 times and also withstood six attacks and sieges. James IV was a frequent visitor, and Mary Queen of Scots was here in 1565. The ruin of the early 14th-century castle is on the site of a castle of the de Brus family, ancestors of Robert the Bruce. However, the charming little hamlet of Lochmaben, with its five lochs, is reason enough to visit, regardless of who was or was not born there.

Rammerscales lies five miles west of Lockerbie and 2½ miles south of Lochmaben on the B7020. It can easily be visited on your tour of Lochmaben and its lakes. Rammerscales is a Georgian manor house, dating from 1760. Set on high ground, it offers beautiful views of the Valley of Annandale. You can visit a walled garden of the period. It is open during the summer on Tuesday, Wednesday, and Thursday, and also on alternate Sundays from 2 to 5 p.m. Exact dates can be obtained from local information centers, hotels in the region, and the press. Admission is £1 ($1.50) for adults, 50p (75¢) for children. For more information, telephone 038-781/361 in office hours.

If you're heading north to Lockerbie on the A74, I'd suggest a stopover in the village of Ecclefechan. There you can visit **Carlyle's Birthplace,** five miles southeast of Lockerbie on the Lockerbie–Carlisle road. Even though the historian, critic, and essayist Thomas Carlyle isn't much read these days, the "arched house" in which he was born in 1795 is interesting in itself, containing mementoes and manuscripts of the author. It's open from Easter until the end of October, daily except Sunday, from 10 a.m. to 6 p.m., charging an admission of 50p (75¢) for adults, 25p (38¢) for children. For more information, telephone Ecclefechan 666.

In Lockerbie, you'll find the best accommodations at the **Dryfesdale House Hotel** (tel. Lockerbie 2427). The house was built in 1831 and was originally a Church of Scotland manse. This quiet hotel offers traditional comfort with log fires and tranquil surroundings. There is a choice of 15 bedrooms, seven of which have private bathrooms. Several of the bedrooms are quite spacious, and you can stay either in the main building or in an annex. Singles range from £18 ($27) to £24 ($36), and doubles run from £28 ($42) to £40 ($60). The hotel, known for its good food and wines, is fully licensed with two old-world bars. The sun lounge and elegant dining room open onto good views. The owners are always available to help.

MOFFAT: An Annandale town, Moffat thrives as a center of a sheep-farming area, symbolized by a statue of a ram in the wide High Street, and has been a holiday resort since the mid-17th century, because of the curative properties of its water. It was here that Robert Burns composed the drinking song "O Willie Brew'd a Peck o'Maut." Today people visit this border town on the banks of the Annan River for its good fishing and golf.

North of Moffat is spectacular hill scenery. Five miles northwest is a huge, sheer-sided 500-foot-deep hollow in the hills called the **Devil's Beef Tub,** where Border cattle thieves, called reivers, hid cattle lifted in their raids.

Northeast along Moffat Water, past White Coomb, which stand 2696 feet high, is the **Grey Mare's Tail,** a 200-foot hanging waterfall formed by the Tail Burn dropping from Loch Skene. It is under the National Trust for Scotland.

Food and Lodgings

Annandale Hotel, High Street (tel. 0683/20013), has been a coaching inn since the 18th century, housing travelers who crossed through the Border Country en route to Glasgow. However, the inn has been modernized and the amenities provided around here have improved considerably since the old days. Still, only five of the nearly 30 bedrooms contain private baths, and none of these has a shower. But the rates in the bathless rooms, to compensate, are low—from £14 ($21) in a single, from £28 ($42) in a double. In the more expensive chambers, expect to pay £18 ($27) in a single, from £31 ($46.50) in a double. The rooms, including the public ones, are kept immaculately. The proprietors have built up a good reputation for their cuisine, which includes both British and German specialties. The last dinner is served t 8:30 p.m., and the cost is from £8 ($12). Although it's in the center of town, Annandale provides ample car parking on its own grounds.

Beechwood Country House Hotel & Restaurant, off Harthope Place (tel. 0683/20210), has built its reputation more as a restaurant than a hotel. However, it does offer eight rooms, six of which contain private baths. The bedrooms are adequate for a short stay, costing from £16 ($24) in a single to £28 ($42) in a double, although the best doubles go for £32 ($48), including breakfast. All bedrooms are equipped with tea- and coffee-making facilities and radios, and most have telephones.

The owners, Mr. and Mrs. McIlwrick, serve some of the finest food in the area and offer a wide choice from an extensive wine list. A bar lunch costs about £3.95 ($5.93). When weather permits, you can take your coffee or afternoon tea in the garden. Dinner is served between 7:30 and 9:30 p.m., when reserving a table is essential. Mrs. McIlwrick sparkles as the chef. A set meal will run about £12 ($18). The dinner offers four courses, and the dishes are nearly always imaginative, certainly well prepared, and everything is made more enjoyable by the enthusiasm of the staff of local country girls. The freshly caught sea trout is a favorite, but if you arrive at the right season you are likely to find venison, even guinea-fowl, on the menu. The produce is fresh. For breakfast, you may enjoy oatcakes. The house is closed in January.

Mercury Motor Inn (tel. 0683/20464) makes a good place to stop off for the night as you're traveling through the Border Country. At the southern end of town, each of its compact, functional bedrooms contains a private bath, toilet, and coffee-making equipment. Some rooms open onto a public park with a boating pond. Bunk beds for children can also be rented, and there is ample car parking. The staff is helpful and friendly, and you'll be charged from £27 ($40.50) in a single, from £49 ($73.50) in a double, including VAT. The charming licensed bar is bedecked in an 1890s mauve, and the grill room provides goods and reasonably priced meals—including such treats as grilled Scottish trout—untl about 10 p.m. In the restaurant, a table d'hôte menu is offered for about £9.50 ($14.25), or you can select from the à la carte dishes. Dinner is served from 6:45 to 9 p.m.

The **Balmoral Hotel,** High Street (tel. 0683/20288), is an attractively furnished and decorated hotel that was once Ye Olde Spur Inn and Coaching House. The present lounge bar was originally the room where Robert Burns met his crony, Clark, the Moffat schoolmaster. Robin and

Denise Stewart, the resident proprietors, will give you a warm welcome and direct you to where to go for fishing, riding, walking, golfing, or just enjoying the views. They charge £18 ($27) in a single room for B&B, from £28 ($42) to £30 ($45) in a double.

READER'S SHOPPING RECOMMENDATION: "We visited the Moffat weavers at **Ladyknowe Mill**, High Street (tel. 0683/20134), a perfect place to purchase the least expensive tweeds, tartans, kilts, and knitwear that can be found in Britain. Wool kilts can be found for as little as £16 ($24). At the mill you can also watch the kiltmakers busy at work" (Anita T. Taylor, Hartsdale, N.Y.).

A Castle Hotel at Beattock

On the outskirts of Moffat, near the village of Beattock, the most luxurious accommodations in the area are found at **Auchen Castle Hotel** (tel. Beattock 407), a Victorian mock-castle, really a charming country house, built on the site of Auchen Castle. It's one of the most tranquil oases in the Scottish Lowlands, with terraced gardens, a trout-filled loch, and vistas from its windows. Beginning with your arrival at the reception desk, you are treated with graciousness and courtesy, and much effort is extended to make your stay a pleasant one.

The bedrooms, although lacking in fanciful decor, are often spacious and invariably comfortable, and each has a private bath or shower. Rates are £26 ($39) in a single, from £42 ($63) in a double, including a continental breakfast, service, and VAT. Rooms are spacious and well appointed in the annex, a double costing only £30 ($45).

The lofty dining room is exceptional for the area, its windows looking out over flowering ornamental grounds in late spring. Simple dishes are appetizingly good because of the excellent materials used. Roast Scottish beef is superb. The well-appointed tables and efficient staff complement the atmosphere of the peaceful country house. Lunch is from noon to 2 p.m. and dinner from 7 to 9 p.m. Bar lunches only are offered, and a table d'hôte dinner goes for £12.50 ($18.75). Closed in December and January.

DUMFRIES: A county town and royal burgh, this Scottish Lowland center enjoys associations with Robert Burns and James Barrie. In a sense it rivals Ayr as a mecca for admirers of Burns. He lived in Dumfries from 1791 until his death in 1796, and it was here that he wrote some of his most famous songs, including "Auld Lang Syne" and "Ye Banks and Braes of Bonnie Doon."

In **St. Michael's Churchyard**, a burial place for at least 900 years, stands the **Burns Mausoleum.** The poet was buried there along with his wife Jean Armour, as well as five of their children. Burns died in 1796, although his remains weren't removed to the tomb until 1815. In the 18th-century church of St. Michael's you can still see the pew used by the Burns family.

The poet died at what is now called the **Robert Burns House,** a simple, unpretentious stone structure, which can be visited by the public; it contains personal relics and mementoes relating to Burns. His death may have been hastened by icy dips in well water that the doctor prescribed. The house is on Burns Street (formerly Mill Vennel). The **Town Museum,** the **Globe Inn,** and the **Hole in the Wa' Tavern** all contain Burns relics, and a statue of him stands in the High Street. You can stroll along **Burns' Walk** on the banks of the River Nith.

St. Michael's is the original parish church of Dumfries and its founding is of great antiquity. The site was probably sacred before the advent of Christianity. It appears that a Christian church has stood there for more than 1300 years. The earliest written records date from the reign of William the Lion (1165-1214). The church and the churchyard are interesting to visit because of all their connections with Scottish history, continuing through World War II.

From St. Michael's, it's a short walk to the Whitesands, where four bridges span the Nith. The earliest of these was built by Devorgilla Balliol, widow of John Balliol, father of a Scottish king. The bridge originally had nine arches but now has six and is still in constant use as a footbridge.

The **Tourist Information Office** is near the bridge. The wide esplanade was once the scene of horse and hiring fairs and now is a fine place to park your car and explore the town. Tour buses park here.

The **Mid Steeple** was built in 1707 as municipal buildings, courthouse, and prison. The old Scots "ell" measure of 37 inches is carved on the front of the building. A table of distances on the building includes the mileage to Huntingdon, England, which in the 18th century was the destination for Scottish cattle drovers driving their beasts south for the markets of London.

At the **Academy,** Barrie was a pupil, and he later wrote that he got the idea for *Peter Pan* from his games in the nearby garden.

Where to Stay

Cairndale Hotel, English Street (tel. 0387/54111), is most reliable, a fine and substantial choice. Its bedrooms have been attractively decorated, with special care paid to modern amenities (at least the ones I inspected). Most of the color-coordinated chambers contain private baths, although there are a few bathless bargains offered. Depending on the plumbing, singles range from £19.50 ($29.25) to £28 ($42), and doubles go from £35 ($52.50) to £45 ($67.50), including VAT and service. You have a choice of a trio of bars, and guests quickly decide which one they'll make their local. The public lounges are handsomely decorated, and you can select your own favorite nook, perhaps a comfortable chair upholstered in velvet. Dinner, served until 9 p.m., is generally quite good, including such dishes as Galloway beef and grilled scampi. A three-course table d'hôte lunch goes for £6.50 ($9.75), a four-course dinner costing £10 ($15).

Station Hotel, 49 Lovers Walk (tel. 0387/54316), has been improved in recent years and now offers one of the best of the moderately priced accommodations in Dumfries. Rooms come in a variety of styles with differences in plumbing. The atmosphere is modest, although pleasant, and the hosts are most agreeable. Nearly 15 of their rooms contain private baths, and all units have color TV and tea- and coffee-making facilities. Singles cost £28 ($42) and doubles and twins run £35 ($52.50), including VAT, service, and a full Scottish breakfast. Bar lunches start at 80p ($1.20), going up to £5 ($7.50). You can enjoy a well-prepared and politely served dinner for £9 ($13.50) to £11 ($16.50). There's live music on Saturday night.

Newall House, 22 Newall Terrace (tel. 0387/52676), is owned by Charlie and Sheila Cowie. Together they run a friendly place, and do so cheerfully and well. Their rooms are clean and comfortable and include tea- and coffee-making facilities. They charge £10 ($15) for a single and £8.50 ($12.75) per person for double occupancy. The tariffs include a well-cooked breakfast. Mrs. Cowie will also prepare an appetizing dinner, if given fair warning, for just £5 ($7.50).

Fulwood Private Hotel, Lovers Walk (tel. 0387/52262), is run by congenial, friendly hosts, Mr. and Mrs. J. B. Rowland, who believe in giving wayfarers pleasure, cleanliness, and comfort in their tiny home, containing only five bedrooms (the bath must be shared). They have a wealth of information about touring in the area, and on one occasion Mr. Rowland drove a reader from San Jose, California, to some scenic spots. Their rate is £9 ($13.50) per person, including breakfast, VAT, and service.

The Waverley Hotel, St. Mary's Street, top of English Street (tel. 0387/54848), is another good bargain, close to the station, about a five-minute walk to the center of town. It's small, but fully licensed, and there is central heating. The owners, D. Solley and sons, offer 15 bedrooms, with hot and cold running water, shaving points, electric blankets, and floor lamps. Some family rooms are available, and there is a reduction for children sharing their parents' room. Singles cost from £15 ($22.50), and doubles are rented from £25 ($37.50), including VAT and a full breakfast. Drinks can be enjoyed in the Windmill Cellar Bar. In the evenings a "high tea" menu is available, giving you a choice of steaks, salads, fish, and bacon and eggs, a meal starting at £4 ($6). Everything tastes homemade in the attractively decorated, although petite. dining room.

Where to Eat

Bruno's, 5 Balmoral Rd. (tel. 0387/55757). It may seem ironic to recommend an Italian restaurant in the seat of Rabbie Burns, but Bruno's serves some of the best food in town. It is most unassuming, and that is part of its charm. Its minestrone is first rate, and its pastas such as lasagne are homemade. The chef doesn't serve the most imaginative Italian dishes ever sampled—in fact the repertoire is most familiar, such as saltimbocca alla Romana and pollo alla diavolo, but it's done with flair. The veal is particularly tender, and the tomato sauce well spiced and blended. Steak au poivre is also excellent. The waiters are friendly and skillful and offer good advice. Bruno's serves only dinner, from 6:30 to 10 p.m. nightly except Tuesday, and it will cost you about £14 ($21) per person, but it's worth it. There is also a special menu for £9 ($13.50).

If you're looking for a place to have lunch or tea, go to **Barbour's Department Store**, Buccleuch Street, where you can get tasty dishes in the dining room on the second floor for prices ranging from £2.50 ($3.75) for various salads to £4 ($6) for a full lunch. The dining room is licensed, and there's an elevator to take you up. Naturally, it's open only during store hours.

Several carry-out delicatessens are along the street across from the Tourist Information Office. The **Merry Chef**, for one, has a variety of goodies if you're in a hurry.

The Local Pub

The **Globe Tavern** was a favorite haunt of Burns. It was one of the "howffs" (taverns) where he imbibed. The location is on a little side street, so ask at your hotel for directions before heading out for your nightly game of "skittles."

Excursions from Dumfries

Based in Dumfries, you can set out on treks in all directions to some of the most intriguing sightseeing goals in the Scottish Lowlands.

South on the 710 leads to the village of **New Abbey,** dominated by the red sandstone ruins of the Cistercian abbey founded in 1273 by Devorgilla, mother of John Baliol, the "vassal king." When her husband, John Baliol the Elder, died, she became one of the richest women in Europe. Most of Galloway, with estates and castles in England and land in Normandy, belonged to her. Devorgilla founded Balliol College, Oxford, in her husband's memory. She kept his embalmed heart in a silver and ivory casket by her side for 21 years until her death in 1289 at the age of 80, when she and the casket were buried beside Baliol in the front of the abbey altar. So the abbey gained the name of "Dulce Cor," Latin for "sweet heart," which has since become a part of the English language.

Built into a wall of a cottage in the village is a rough piece of sculpture showing three women rowing a boat—an allusion to the bringing of sandstone across the Nith to build the abbey.

Directly south from New Abbey on the 710 to Southerness leads to the **Arbigland Gardens and Cottage** at Kirkbean, 15 miles soutwest of Dumfries. This is where John Paul Jones, one of the founders of the American navy, was born. You can visit the woodland with its water gardens arranged around a secluded bay, walking in the pathways where the great admiral once worked as a boy. The gardens are open, May to September on Tuesday, Thursday, and Sunday from 2 to 6 p.m., charging adults 60p (90¢); children, 30p (45¢).

Or, alternatively, you can head south from Dumfries on the B725 to **Caerlaverock Castle,** near the mouth of the River Nith, two miles south from Glencaple. Once the seat of the Maxwell family, this impressive ruined fortress dates back to the 1270s. In 1300 Edward I laid siege to it. In 1640 it yielded to Covenanters after a 13-week siege. The castle is triangular with round towers. The interior was reconstructed in the 17th century as a Renaissance mansion, with fine carving. Near the castle is the Caerlaverock National Nature Reserve, between the River Nith and Lochar Water. It is a noted winter haunt of wildfowl, including barnacle geese.

After leaving the castle, continue east along the B725 to the village of **Ruthwell,** about ten miles southeast of Dumfries. There at the early 19th-century Ruthwell Church you'll see one of the most outstanding crosses of the Dark Ages. Standing 18 feet high, the cross is believed to date from the eighth century. Engraved with carvings, it bears the earliest known specimen of written English (a Christian poem in Runic characters).

North from Dumfries on the A76 takes you to **Lincluden College,** two miles away. This is the richly decorated remains of a 15-century collegiate church.

Four miles away, still following the A76, is **Ellisland Farm,** where Robert Burns made his last attempt at farming, renting the spread from 1788 to 1791. The present occupants of the house will show you through the Burns Room. It was at this farm that Burns wrote *Tam o'Shanter.*

Continuing north, still on the A76, you reach **Thornhill,** a country resort—familiar to Burns—overlooking the River Nith. From here, it's possible to branch out for excursions in many directions.

The main target is **Drumlanrig Castle,** the seat of the Duke of Buccleuch and Queensberry, built between 1679 and 1689. It lies three miles north of Thornhill, off the A76. This exquisite pink castle contains some celebrated paintings, including a Rembrandt and a Holbein. In addition, it is further enriched by Louis XIV antiques, silver, porcelain, and relics related to Bonnie Prince Charlie. The castle stands in a parkland ringed by wild hills, and there's even an Adventure Woodland Playground.

The castle is normally open on Easter weekend and then daily except Friday from May 1 to the last Monday of August. Hours are from 2 to 6 p.m. on Sunday, from 12:30 to 5 p.m. weekdays in May and June; 11 a.m. to 5 p.m. weekdays in July and August. Last entry is 45 minutes before closing time. Admission is £1.50 ($2.25) for adults, 75p ($1.13) for children. For information, telephone 0848/30248.

Of almost equal interest, **Maxwelton House** (tel. Moniaive 384) lies three miles south of Moniaive and 13 miles north of Dumfries on the B729. It was the stronghold of the Earls of Glencairn in the 14th and 15th centuries. But it is more remembered today as the birthplace (1682) of Annie Laurie of the Scottish ballad. From Maxwelton you can see that the braes are just as bonnie as ever. The braes, of course, refer to the neighboring hills. The house, garden, chapel, gift shop, and an agricultural museum can be visited from May to September on Wednesday and Thursday from 2 to 5 p.m. Admission is £1.20 ($1.80) for adults, 20p (30¢) for children up to 12.

Back on the A76, you can branch northwest on the B797, heading in the direction of Mennock Pass. There, at **Wanlockhead,** you'll be in the highest village in Scotland. Once this village was a gold-mining center and known as "God's Treasure House." Gold was mined here for the Scottish crown jewels.

CASTLE DOUGLAS: A cattle and sheep market town, Castle Douglas makes a good touring center for Galloway. It lies about eight miles southwest of Dumfries, at the northern tip of Caringwark Loch. On one of the islets in the loch is an ancient lake dwelling known as a "crannog."

The favorite excursion is the **Threave Castle,** 1½ miles west on an islet in the River Dee west of town, the ruined 14th-century stronghold of the Black Douglases. The four-story tower was built between 1639 and 1690 by Archibald the Grim, Lord of Galloway. In 1455 Threave Castle was the last Douglas stronghold to surrender to James II, who employed "Mons Meg" (the famous cannon now in Edinburgh Castle) in its subjection. Over the doorway projects the "gallows knob" from which the Douglases hanged their enemies. The castle was captured by the Covenanters in 1640 and dismantled. Owned by the National Trust, the site must be reached by a *lengthy* walk through farmlands and then by small boat across the Dee. A ferry charge of 35p (53¢) is the only alternative to that very long walk. The castle is open April to September, Monday to Saturday from 9:30 a.m. to 7 p.m., from 2 to 7 p.m. on Sunday.

Threave Gardens (tel. 0556/2575) lie one mile west of the castle. The gardens are built around Threave House, a Scottish baronial mansion 1½ miles west of Castle Douglas, off the A75. They are under the protection of the National Trust of Scotland, which uses them as a school for gardening and a wildfowl refuge. In spring, more than 300 varieties of daffodils burst into bloom. There is also a walled garden. The gardens are open daily from 9 a.m. to dusk, charging admission of £1.50 ($2.25) for adults, 75p ($1.13) for children.

Food and Lodging

Back in Castle Douglas, I'd recommend the following selections for food and lodging.

Douglas Arms, King Street (tel. Castle Douglas 2231), was once an old coaching inn, but it has been turned into a modernized hotel, right in the center of this hamlet, situated at a busy crossroads. Therefore, it's not the most tranquil choice, but it is still inviting—made all the more so by the gracious hospitality extended by the owners, Mr. and Mrs. Wylie. Behind a rather stark, two-story facade, the public rooms are bright and cheerful, giving you a toasty feeling on a cold night. Bedrooms have color-coordinated schemes, and such new gadgets as razor sockets. At least 11 out of the 27 rooms contain private baths. Single rates go from £20 ($30) to £22.50 ($33.75), the higher tariff for a room with bath. Doubles cost from £35 ($52.50) to £38 ($57), all tariffs including VAT and service. Dinner is served until 9 p.m., and, of course, trout and salmon are featured along with good beef and lamb, of which the hamlet has plenty. A set dinner goes for £12 ($18).

King's Arms, St. Andrew's Street (tel. Castle Douglas 2097), is a good place at which to stop over, enjoying either a room or a meal or drink in the trio of tartan-clad bars, featuring the malt whisky collection of Mr. Iain MacDonald. The restaurant serves good, simple meals, using the freshest of fish and tender beef, a set meal costing from £10.50 ($15.75). It is attractively decorated, and the staff is most helpful. Bedrooms are comfortable, although modest, and four chambers contain private baths and toilets and two are equipped with showers and toilets. For these, the rate is £20 ($30) per person daily. However, in a bathless room, the tariff is £15 ($22.50) per person, including a full breakfast, VAT, and service. There is an attractive, sheltered, and secluded sun garden at the rear of the hotel which is a favorite rendezvous for coffee, tea, or a sundowner. Everything is maintained immaculately, and parking is provided. The hotel is under the personal management of the proprietors, Iain and Betty MacDonald.

An excellent hotel choice lies south of Castle Douglas, near Dalbeattie, in the hamlet of—

ROCKCLIFFE: An attractive seaside village, Rockcliffe has a bird sanctuary on its offshore Rough Island. From its sand and rock beach, you can look out to the Lake District mountains on the distant horizon.

Baron's Craig Hotel (tel. 055-663/225) is a stately country home, built of granite, and set back from the shoreline of Solway Firth. Because of its position sheltered from the cold north wind, its gardens bloom profusely in season. Lawns and grounds—nearly 12 acres—are well manicured. The public rooms are spacious and airy, brightly decorated and most welcoming. In the modern bar you can select at leisure your favorite whisky. The owners have paid special attention to the bedrooms, decorating them in warm, pleasing colors to suggest in summer a holiday atmosphere. From April to October, it rents singles (bathless) for £26 ($39), going up to £40 ($60) with bath. A bathless double costs £50 ($75), rising to £65 ($97.50) with bath, including breakfast. At least 21 of the rooms contain private baths, which are spotlessly clean.

Even if you're not staying here, you might want to drive down to enjoy the hotel's fine cookery. The dining room overlooks the water, and table appointments have flair and style. At lunch the menu is considerably shortened, but still quite good, a bar lunch costing from £4 ($6). In the evening, however, a table d'hôte is offered at £15 ($22.50) between the hours of 7 and 9 p.m. The menu is based on good local ingredients, and all dishes are acceptably prepared. The service is exceptional.

KIRKCUDBRIGHT: Stewartry's most ancient burgh, Kirkcudbright (pronounced Kir-coo-bree) lies at the head of Kirkcudbright Bay on the Dee Estuary. This intriguing old town contains color-washed houses inhabited, in part, by artists. In fact, Kirkcudbright has been called the "St. Ives [Cornwall] of Scotland."

In the old town graveyard are memorials to Covenanters and to Billy Marshall, the tinker king who died in 1792 at the age of 120, reportedly having fathered four children after the age of 100.

Maclellan's Castle, built in 1582 for the town's provost, Sir Thomas Maclellan, easily dominates the center of town. Kirkcudbright is an attractive town which is the center of a lively group of weavers, potters, and painters who work in the 18th-century streets and lanes.

The **Tolbooth,** a large building, dates back to the 16th and 17th centuries, and in front of it is a **Mercat Cross** of 1610. The Tolbooth is a memorial to John Paul Jones (1747-1792), the gardener's son from Kirkbean who became a slave trader, a privateer, and in due course one of the founders of the American navy. For a time, before his emigration, he was imprisoned for murder in the Tolbooth.

Art exhibitions are regularly sponsored at **Broughton House** (tel. 0556/2391), a 17th-century mansion that once belonged to E. A. Hornel, the artist. The house contains a large reference library with a valuable Burns collection, along with pictures by Hornel and other artists, plus antiques and other works of art. You can stroll through its beautiful garden. Broughton is open April to October seven days a week from 11 a.m. to 1 p.m. and 2 to 5 p.m., and November to March on Tuesday and Thursday from 2 to 5 p.m. Admission is 50p (75¢) for adults, 30p (45¢) for children.

In addition, the **Stewartry Museum** contains a fascinating collection of antiquities, depicting the history and culture of Galloway and its many and varied associations with John Paul Jones. It is open daily, except Sunday, from 10 a.m. to 5 p.m., charging adults 60p (90¢), and children, 30p (45¢). It's open from Easter to October.

North of town is the ruined **Tongland Abbey,** one of whose abbots, John Damian, once tried to fly from the battlements of Stirling Castle wearing wings of bird feathers, in the presence of James IV. He landed in a manure pile.

Dundrennan Abbey, seven miles southeast of Kirkcudbright, the ruins of a rich Cistercian house founded in 1142, includes much late Norman and Transitional work. Dundrennan is a daughter abbey of Rievaulx Abbey in Yorkshire and the mother abbey of Glenluce and Sweetheart Abbeys. The small village is partly built of stones "quarried" from the abbey. Mary Queen of Scots, after escaping from Loch Leven and being defeated at the Battle of Langside, spent her last night in Scotland at the abbey in May 1568. She went to England to seek help from Elizabeth who imprisoned her instead. The transept and choir, a unique example of the Early Pointed style, remain.

In accommodations, I'd suggest the **Selkirk Arms,** Old High Street (tel. 0557/20402), where Robert Burns stayed when he composed the celebrated Selkirk Grace. (The grace was actually given on St. Mary's isle, the seat of the Douglases, Earls of Selkirk, and, in part, it went as follows: "But we ha'e meat, and we can eat, And sae the Lord be thankit.") The hotel, a two-story 18th-century building, has 27 bedrooms, and the furnishings are in keeping with the character of the house. It has a homey atmosphere and a friendly staff, making it a pleasure to stay in such charming surroundings. The neighborhood evokes memories of John Paul Jones, and there are little art galleries displaying the works of local painters. In all, you'll enjoy a restful, tranquil atmosphere. You have a choice of rooms in the main building or in the annex, all with color TV and tea- and coffee-making facilities. Depending on the plumbing, singles range from £16 ($24) to £18 ($27), and doubles from £30 ($45) to £38 ($57), including breakfast. Dinner costs from £10 ($15) to £12 ($18) for three courses. The hotel is open all year. It has both a TV lounge and a cocktail bar, and there is ample parking. Live music is presented on Tuesday night.

GATEHOUSE-OF-FLEET: This sleepy former cotton town, on the Water of Fleet, was the **Kippletringan** in Sir Walter Scott's *Guy Mannering,* and Burns composed "Scots Wha Hae wi' Wallace Bled" on the moors nearby and wrote it down in the Murray Arms Hotel there.

The town's name probably dates from 1642 when the English government opened the first military road through Galloway to assist the passage of troops to Ireland. In 1661 Richard Murray of Cally was authorized by Parliament to widen the bridge and to erect beside it an inn that was to serve as a tollhouse, with the innkeeper responsible for the maintenance of a 12-mile stretch of road. This is believed to have been the original house on the "gait," or road, which later became known as the "gait house of Fleet," and by 1790 it was being written in its present form and spelling. This ancient "gait house" is now part of the Murray Arms Hotel, used as a coffeeroom, and is probably the oldest building still in existence in the town.

West of Gatehouse, on the road to Creetown, is the well-preserved 15th-century tower of the McCullochs, with its sinister "murder hole" over the entrance passage. Through this trapdoor, boiling pitch was poured onto attackers. **Cardoness Castle** was originally the seat of the McCulloch family, one of whom, Sir Godfrey McCulloch, was the last person in Scotland to be executed, at Edinburgh in 1697, by the "Maiden," the Scots version of the guillotine.

For accommodations, I recommend the following:

Cally Palace Hotel (tel. Gatehouse 341) is a large 18th-century mansion standing in 100 acres of beautiful gardens and wooded parkland. Especially popular with more mature readers, it is an oasis of peace and quiet—most comfortable, more suited for someone who wishes to spend a few days in Galloway than the fleeting overnight motorist. The public lounges are overscale with some fine period pieces, and a sun patio looks out onto a swimming pool. Amenities include a bar, table tennis, and pool, in addition to a hard tennis court, putting, croquet, a sauna, game fishing, loch boating, and dancing at certain times of the year. All of its 60 rooms contain private baths or showers, costing from £35 ($52.50) in a single, from £60 ($90) to £70 ($105) in a double, all prices including dinner and B&B. Some of the bedrooms have balconies opening onto the grounds. Rooms come in widely varying styles and sizes, but all have color TV and tea- and coffee-making facilities. A dinner-dance is held on Saturday night.

Murray Arms (tel. Gatehouse 207) is a long, low, white-painted building that was once a posting inn in the 18th century, its coffeehouse dating back even earlier, to 1642. Burns wrote his stirring song "Scots Wha'

Ha'e" while staying at the inn, the occasion still commemorated to this day by the Burns room with its Leitch pictures. The inn has been considerably updated and modernized by the laird of the Cally Estate, and that is as it should be, since it was James Murray of Cally who made the Murray Arms into a coaching inn so long ago. Now it's back in the same family after a long departure.

Standing by an old clock tower, the inn has long been known for its food and hospitality. In addition to three bars, the house has a sun lounge opening onto a roof terrace. The rooms are modestly furnished, and singles range from £18 ($27) to £25 ($37.50); doubles, from £32 ($48) to £48 ($72). Nearly half of the rooms contain private baths.

You can stop in for a complete dinner in its attractively decorated restaurant opening onto the garden. Between 12:30 and 2 p.m. typical bar lunches are offered. But at dinner, from 7:30 to 9 p.m., you can order a table d'hôte meal for £10 ($15). Specialties include Galloway beef and fresh Solway Firth salmon.

CREETOWN: "The Ferry Toon," as Creetown is called, lies west of Gate-house-of-Fleet, on the road to Newton Stewart. There are two ruined 16th-century castles about midway along the road, **Carsluith** and **Barholm.** Up the Kirkdale Burn from Barholm are the 4000-year-old standing stones and chambered tombs of Cairn Holy.

NEWTON STEWART: Sometimes called "the gateway to Galloway" and the "heart of Galloway," this small town on the River Cree was made a burgh or barony in 1677 after a son of the second Earl of Galloway built some houses beside the ford across the river and gave the hamlet its present name. When the estate was later purchased by William Douglas, he changed the name to Newton Douglas, but it didn't stick. The town has a livestock market and woolen mills. Cree Bridge, built of granite in 1813 to replace one swept away by a flood, links the town with **Minnigaff** where there is an old church with carved stones and some memorials.

Newton Stewart is associated with Scott, Stevenson, and Burns. Today it is chiefly a center for touring, especially north for nine miles to the beauty spot of **Loch Troolin** in the Glen Trool Forest Park, 200 square miles of magnificently preserved splendor. On the way to Loch Trool you go through the village of Glentrool, where you'll find the first car park for those wanting to take the Stroan Bridge walk, a distance of 3½ miles. The hearty Scots, of course, walk the entire loch, all 4½ miles of it.

Food and Lodging

Newton Stewart has a wide range of accommodations, making it one of the best bases for touring Galloway.

Bruce, Queen Street (tel. 0671/2294), is an exemplary up-to-date hotel. Although not lavish in appointments, it is completely modern and efficiently run, maintaining a high standard of comfort, but keeping its prices reasonable—from £23 ($34.50) in a single, from £36 ($54) in a double. The decor is bright, and the bedrooms well designed. All of the 20 bedrooms contain private baths. Guests enjoy a pleasant bar and congenial company, composed mainly of locals who frequent the Bruce. The restaurant, also in the modern style, offers a cold table at lunch from 12:30 to 2 p.m., costing

£4.50 ($6.75). Dinners, when the menu are more varied, are quite interesting, and everything tastes as if it were home cooked from fresh produce. A table d'hôte, served from 7:30 to 9 p.m., goes for £10 ($15).

Kirroughtree (tel. 0671/2141) is an impressive manor house, once the seat of the Herons of Galloway, built in 1719 and full of traditional character. The hotel has been completely refurbished and is now a luxurious Country House Hotel. All 24 bedrooms are attractively furnished and have colored bathroom suites, color TVs, and phones. There are two elegant dining rooms with period furnishings. The head chef, who came here from a similar position held for six years at Inverlochy Castle, has received the highest rating of any chef in Scotland for his cuisine. The hotel is fully licensed and has a cozy cocktail bar. Rates range from £48 ($72) per person per day for dinner and B&B, £160 ($240) for four days, these prices including VAT and free golf at several courses. The hotel is ideal for those who want complete peace and quiet, as it is surrounded by some eight acres of gardens with views of the Galloway countryside and Solway Firth. It also offers pony trekking and many pleasant walks. You can get a permit for salmon and trout fishing from the hotel.

WIGTOWN:
This former county town of the district is still a center for fishing and wildfowling although its harbor is silted up. Two market crosses, an 18th-century one topped by a sundial and another that was erected in 1816, stand in the town's central square. In 1685 two women, Margaret Maclauchlan and Margaret Wilson, Covenanters who were accused of attending meetings of their sect, were tied to stakes at the mouth of the River Bladnoch and drowned by the rising tide after refusing to give up their beliefs. An obelisk marks the traditional site of their martyrdom. A monument to all Covenanters stands on Windy Hill back of the town.

Three miles northwest of Wigtown, near Torhouskie Farm, are the Bronze Age **Stones of Torhouse,** 19 standing stones in a circle with three in the center.

The remains of **Baldoon Castle** are one mile from Wigtown. This was the setting for Sir Walter Scott's *The Bride of Lammermoor.* It was the home of David Dunbar and his wife, supposed to be the principal characters of the *Bride.* The castle was captured by Wallace in 1297.

WHITHORN:
Ten miles south of Wigtown, you come upon Whithorn, a modern town with a museum containing ancient crosses and tombstones, including the fifth-century **Latinus Stone,** the earliest Christian memorial in Scotland. St. Ninian, the son of a local chieftain, founded a monastery here in A.D. 397 and built his "Candida Casa" or "White House," probably the first Christian church in Scotland. In the 12th century Fergus, Lord of Galloway, built a priory. The church and monastery were destroyed in the 16th century. Excavations in the ruins have revealed fragments of wall covered in pale plaster believed to be from Ninian's Candida Casa. The ruins are entered through the Pend, a 17th-century arch on which are carved the Royal Arms of Scotland.

A moorland walk to the west coast 2½ miles away leads to **St. Ninian's Cave** in Port Castle Bay, used by the missionary as a retreat.

The **Isle of Whithorn,** three miles southeast of the town, is where St. Ninian landed about A.D. 395 on his return from studying in Rome, to bring Christianity to Scotland. The ruins of a plain 13th-century chapel are here but no signs of an earlier church. On the point of the promontory are the remains of an Iron Age fort and a late 17th-century tower.

Chapel Finian, near the shore road on the way from Whithorn to Glenluce, is a small chapel or oratory probably dating from the 10th or 11th century, in an enclosure about 50 feet wide.

An excellent place to stay just outside Whithorn is the **Castlewigg Hotel** (tel. 09885/213), a small licensed country hotel under the personal supervision of its owners, Stephen Summerson-Wright and Ronda Mussen. Castlewigg is two miles north of Whithorn on the A746, with views to the north toward Newton Stewart and to the east to Fleet Bay. More than 200 years old, the hotel building was the dower house of Castle Wigg, which lies in ruins, not open to the public, a mile or so off the road. The hotel has two singles, two doubles, and one family room, which rent for £11.50 ($17.25) per person for B&B. Guests may enjoy the residents' lounge with color TV, the spacious, colorful dining room, and the lounge bar. Dinner costs around £8 ($12). From the à la carte menu you can order such delicacies as prawn cocktail, venison in red wine and port, and rainbow trout. The hotel specializes in hunting and fishing holidays. The Castlewigg sits in seven acres of grounds, about 150 yards from the main road, so there's ample parking. It's open all year.

PORT WILLIAM: On Luce Bay, this little holiday resort is a center for tennis, golf, and swimming.

By taking the 714 west, you'll reach **Drumtrodden Stones,** a cluster of ring and cup markings from the Bronze Age on a rock face. Just 400 yards to the south is an alignment of three adjacent surviving stones. It's hardly Stonehenge, but interesting nevertheless.

While still on an antiquity search, you can drive directly south of Port William a short distance to **Barsalloch Fort,** the remains of a fort dating from the Iron Age.

In the pleasant village, you can stay at the **Monreith Arms Hotel** (tel. Port William 232), a big stone building at the roundabout where you will find immaculate bedrooms, innerspring mattresses, and comfortable public rooms, as well as a good garage accommodation for your car. Mr. and Mrs. A. R. Jardine, in their fully licensed hostelry, offer B&B for £13.50 ($20.25) per night per person. Dinner costs from £8.50 ($12.75). All prices include VAT and service charge. The hotel is open all year.

GLENLUCE: Lying on the Water of Luce near its estuary in Luce Bay, Glenluce is another attractive village. **Glenluce Abbey,** one mile northwest, is a ruined Cistercian house founded about 1190, which has intact a 15th-century vaulted chapter house of architectural interest. The Border "wizard," Michael Scott, is said to have lured the plague to the abbey in the 13th century and shut it in a vault. **Castle of Park,** a 16th-century mansion, overlooks the village from the brow of a hill across the river.

A convenient and pleasant place to stay in Glenluce is the **Judge's Keep,** in the center of town (tel. 05813/203), where Mrs. William Atkinson receives guests in her fully licensed hotel for £12.50 ($18.75) in summer, £11.50 ($17.25) in winter, per person for B&B. Dinner, prepared under Mrs. Atkinson's close supervision in the immaculate kitchen on the ground floor, costs from £8 ($12), and it's well worth it. There is a TV lounge for guests, as well as public and lounge bars and ample parking.

Snacks are served in the bar for those who don't want a large meal, and Bill Atkinson will keep your glass, as one patron said, "topped up with your choice of tipple." The hotel is open all year.

PORTPATRICK: Until 1849 steamers sailed the 21 miles from Donaghdee in Northern Ireland to Portpatrick, which became a "Gretna Green" for the Irish. Couples would land on Saturday, have the banns called on Sunday, and marry on Monday. When the harbor became silted up, Portpatrick was replaced by Stranraer as a port.

Commanding a clifftop to the south are the ruins of **Dunskey Castle,** a grim keep built in 1510 by John Adair.

Ten miles south of Portpatrick is the quiet little hamlet of **Port Logan.** In the vicinity is **Logan House,** the seat of the McDouall family, which could trace their ancestry so far back that it was claimed they were as "old as the sun itself." This family laid out the world-famous gardens at Logan, which are visited by people from all over the world. **Logan Botanic Garden,** an annex of the Royal Botanic Garden, Edinburgh, contains a wide range of plants from the temperate regions of the world. Cordylines, palms, tree ferns, and tender rhododendrons grow well in the mild climate of southwest Scotland. The garden is open April 1 to September 30 from 10 a.m. to 5 p.m. Admission is 50p (75¢). The site is 14 miles south of Stranraer off the B7065 road. Restaurant facilities are available.

Nearby is **Ardwell House,** with gardens that are at their best in April and May.

The ancient church site of **Kirkmadrine** lies in the parish of Stoneykirk, south of Portpatrick. The site now has a modern church, but there is an ancient graveyard and early inscribed stones and crosses, including three of the earliest Christain monuments in Britain, showing the chi-rho symbol and inscriptions dating from the fifth or early sixth century. There was an early Christian monastery and in the Middle Ages a parish church.

Instead of going to the larger town, Stranraer, you might stay at the **Knockinaam Lodge** (tel. 077/681471), a Victorian house with view looking out over the sea to Northern Ireland. People come to Knockinaam for the peace and relaxation, as the lodge stands in 30 secluded acres of private grounds right on the sea. It's run in the best country-house tradition by the resident owners Simon and Caroline Pilkington. In the heat of World War II, Churchill, who met Eisenhower here, enjoyed a long hot bath (in a tub that remains) while smoking a cigar. The hotel contains only ten rooms, most of which have private bath or shower. The rate is from £45 ($67.50) per person for dinner, bed, and a full Scottish breakfast, VAT included. The lodge serves the best food in the area. All ingredients used in the kitchen are fresh, and dishes on both the à la carte and table d'hôte menus are cooked to order. Service is polite and efficient, and the views open onto the water. Lunch from 12:30 to 2 p.m. is offered for £10 ($15); dinner is from 7:15 to 9 p.m., when a set meal costs £18 ($27), including VAT. The lodge is closed from mid-January until the end of February.

STRANRAER: The largest town in Wigtownshire, Stranraer is the terminal of the 35-mile ferry crossing from Larne, Northern Ireland. An early chapel, built by a member of the Adair family near the 16th-century **Castle of St. John** in the heart of town, gave the settlement its original name of Chapel, later changed to Chapel of Stranrawer and then shortened to

Stranraer. The name is supposed to have referred to the row or "raw" of original houses on the "strand" or burn, now largely buried beneath the town's streets. The Castle of St. John became the town jail and in the late 17th century held Covenanters during Graham of Claverhouse's campaigns of religious persecution.

To the east are **Castle Kennedy Gardens** and *Lochinch Castle* (tel. 0775/2024), a late-19th-century Scots baronial mansion. In the grounds of Lochinch Castle are the White and Black Lochs and the ruins of Castle Kennedy, which was built during the reign of James IV but burned down in 1716. The gardens, restored in the middle of the 19th century, contain the finest pinetum in Scotland. Go in the right season, and you can wander among rhododendrons, azaleas, and magnolias. The castle is not open to the public, but the gardens are, daily from 10 a.m. to dusk April to September. They are closed Easter, May Day, and on August bank holidays. Admission is £1.50 ($2.25) for adults, 75p ($1.13) for children.

Food and Lodging

North West Castle, Royal Crescent (tel. 0776/4413), overlooks Loch Ryan and the departure quay for Northern Ireland. The oldest part of the house was built in 1820 by Capt. Sir John Ross, R. N., the Arctic explorer. Of course, to honor the brave man, your bedroom window should face northwest, an allusion to his search for the "North West Passage." The hotel owners will give you a brochure that relates the exploits and disappointments of the explorer. The original building has been altered and extended to meet the hotel's increasing popularity. At last count, a total of 83 rooms are offered, all with private bath. Singles go from £25 ($37.50) and doubles from £43 ($64.50) for the well-appointed suites. Many of the best rooms are in the two more modern wings.

The lounges are cozy and pleasantly furnished, and the dining room is impressive, serving mainly continental fare with Scottish overtones. Fresh local ingredients are used. The bars downstairs are well stocked—I prefer the Explorers' Lounge with its views of the harbor. Further amenities include a garden, a sauna, and a solarium, plus a curling rink, game room, buttery, indoor swimming pool, and dancing to a live band on Saturday night.

George Hotel, George Street (tel. 0776/24878), stands right in the heart of town. I first stayed there many, many years ago, and on my most recent visit I found it considerably improved, a lot of money spent, in fact, to provide the latest up-to-date comforts for its guests, many of whom are embarking for Northern Ireland in the morning. Less than half the bedrooms contain private baths. Singles cost from £18 ($27) to £21 ($31.50) nightly, and doubles go for £30 ($45) to £35 ($52.50), including VAT, service, and a full breakfast. You can rent a family room—two doubles and a single—for £42 ($63). Most of the rooms contain such amenities as razor sockets and radio. Color-coordinated schemes are used in the bedrooms, and the baths are spotlessly clean. A friendly, cooperative staff is expert at giving touring advice. The hotel's restaurant is also good, making use of local produce, the cooking and service quite acceptable. The lighting is subdued and the ingredients fresh, the emphasis placed on "Taste of Scotland" dishes, costing £10 ($15) for four courses and coffee.

Chapter XIX

EDINBURGH AND CENTRAL SCOTLAND

**1. Edinburgh
2. Day Trips from Edinburgh
3. The Kingdom of Fife
4. Glasgow and the Clyde
5. The Trossachs and Loch Lomond**

SCOTLAND HAS OFTEN been compared to a sandwich in that the central belt is considered the meatier part. Within a relatively small compass of land, you can visit not only the capital at Edinburgh but enjoy such beauty as the Trossachs (the Scottish lake district), the silver waters of Loch Lomond, or take in the cragginess of Stirling Castle. Central Scotland should be treated as far more than just a gateway to the Highlands.

Edinburgh, often called the fairest city in Europe, is our first stopover. While based there you can take many day trips, such as to the seaside and golfing resort of North Berwick. The Scots suggest you take a "look aboot ye."

From Edinburgh, on the opposite shore of the Firth of Forth, reached by bridge, the Kingdom of Fife is rich in treasures, such as Falkland Palace, the hunting retreat of the Stuart kings, and the unspoiled fishing villages along the coast, collectively known as "East Neuk."

To the west of Edinburgh, a distance of some 40 miles, the industrial city of Glasgow is a target for some, although, to me at least, it has none of the charm of the capital. However, from Glasgow you can set out on a tour in many directions, including the glens and hills associated with the outlaw Rob Roy. Also on Glasgow's doorstep is the scenic estuary of the Firth of Clyde. You can cruise down the Clyde on a paddle-steamer.

But, assuming you're still back in the Lowlands, you can begin your descent upon—

1. Edinburgh

Scotland's capital city is Edinburgh, off the beaten path for those doing the mad whirlwind tour of Europe, as it lies 373 miles north of London. The city is associated with John Knox, Mary Queen of Scots, Robert

Louis Stevenson, Sir Arthur Conan Doyle (creator of Sherlock Holmes), David Hume, Alexander Graham Bell, Sir Walter Scott, and Bonnie Prince Charlie—to name-drop only a bit.

From the elegant Georgian crescents of the New Town, to the dark medieval "wynds" of the Old Town, down the wide, magnificent Princes Street (Stevenson's "liveliest and brightest thoroughfare"), Edinburgh lives up to its reputation as one of the fairest cities in Europe. Of course it's not as sophisticated as Paris, nor as fast-paced as London. And it's banal to call it the Athens of the North, although the Greek Revival movement of the 19th century made many of the buildings look like pagan temples.

What Edinburgh has to offer is unique. It's Scottish (scotch is a drink—so play it safe and refer to the hearty, ruddy-faced people as Scots)—and that means it's different from English. It wasn't sameness that made these two countries fight many a bloody border skirmish.

Most travelers know that since World War II Edinburgh has been the scene of an ever-growing International Festival, with its action-packed list of cultural events. But that shouldn't be your only reason for visiting the ancient seat of Scottish royalty. Its treasures are available all year. In fact, the pace the rest of the time—when the festival-hoppers have gone south—is more relaxed. The prices are lowered, and the people themselves, under less pressure as hosts, return to their traditional hospitable nature.

GETTING THERE: Edinburgh is two hours by bus or rail from the major international airport of Scotland, Prestwick, and it lies in the center of most of the rail and bus lines leading from Scotland to England. Edinburgh's own recently improved airport, connected by frequent 30-minute bus rides to midtown, receives flights only from within the British Isles, Dublin, and Amsterdam. Fares to London, 75 minutes away by air, begin at around £88 ($132) round trip.

BritRail passes are valid on all lines of the British rail system, which includes the corridor between London and Edinburgh. (See the "Travel by Rail" section in Chapter I.)

Regardless of the kind of ticket you hold, Edinburgh is well connected by rail and bus to all other points in Britain. Standard second-class round-trip rail fare from London is $121, but substantial amounts of money can be saved by booking a special InterCity Saver ticket in advance. The round-trip fare from London to Edinburgh is a surprisingly low £37 ($55.50), with special conditions attached; for more information, again refer to the "Travel by Rail" section of Chapter I.

GETTING AROUND: Edinburgh doesn't benefit from a modern underground (subway to Americans) system, so you'll find buses will probably be your chief method of transport in the Scottish capital. The fare you pay is determined by the distance you ride. The minimum fare is 15p (23¢) for three stops or less, and the maximum fare is 45p (68¢) for 20 or more stops. Children up to 10 years of age pay 15p regardless of the number of stops, and children under 5 travel free.

The Edinburgh city fathers (or mothers as the case may be) have devised several types of term bus passes for extended tourist visits to their city. The Edinburgh Freedom Ticket allows one day of unlimited travel on city buses at £1.25 ($1.88) for adults and 65p (98¢) for children. Another form of extended ticket is a TouristCard, allowing unlimited travel on all city buses for a time period of between two and 13 days, plus special discounts at certain restaurants and for tours of selected historical sites. A two-day TouristCard costs £7.40 ($11.10) for adults and £4.75 ($7.13) for children. A 13-day TouristCard goes for £18.40 ($27.60) for adults and £10.25 ($15.38) for children.

Finally, for daily commuters or for diehard Scottish enthusiasts, a RidaCard season ticket allows unlimited travel for adults on all buses at £8.25 ($12.38) for adults for two weeks and £14 ($21) for four weeks. Travel must begin on a Sunday. Prices for children are £4.15 ($6.23) for two weeks and £7 ($10.50) for four weeks.

These tickets and further information may be obtained at the **Waverley Bridge Transport Office,** Waverley Bridge in Edinburgh (tel. 226-4696) or the **Lothian Region Transport Office,** 14 Queen St., Edinburgh EHZ 1JL (tel. 554-4494).

As a last resort, try hailing a cab or waiting at a taxi stand. The rates are set at 70p ($1.05) for the first 1140 yards and 10p (15¢) for each additional 350 yards, not including tip.

WHERE TO STAY: Searching for a suitable hotel isn't too difficult in Edinburgh, as the city offers a full range of accommodations at different price levels throughout the year. However, during the three-week period of the festival, the establishments fill up with international visitors, so it's prudent to reserve in advance. To take care of emergency lodging 360 days a year, the **Edinburgh Tourist Information & Accommodation Service,** Waverley Market Complex, Princes Street (tel. 226-6591), compiles a well-investigated and lengthy list of small hotels and guest houses. The emphasis is on well-managed, clean, comfortable, and hospitable guest houses, usually catering to anywhere from 2 to 12 visitors, some for as little as £6.50 ($9.75) per person. The bureau's hours during the peak season, May 1 to September 30, are from 8:30 a.m. to 8 p.m. Monday through Saturday, and from 11 a.m. to 8 p.m. on Sunday (open til 9 p.m. during July and August). A 60p (90¢) booking fee is charged. There's also an information and accommodation desk at Edinburgh Airport, with a telephone link to the center. It's open according to the frequency of incoming flights.

You can write in advance, enclosing your requirements and the fee, but you should allow about four weeks' notice, expecially during the summer and particularly during the festival weeks.

Assuming you arrive in Edinburgh when the hotels aren't fully booked or that you will reserve a room in advance, I've prepared a representative sampling of the leading candidates, from the upper bracket to the budget range.

The Upper Bracket

The Caledonian, Princes Street and Lothian Road (tel. 225-2433), is the king of the hotels in Edinburgh, standing opposite its queen, the North British, at the other end of Princes Gardens. A British Transport hotel, it is the first choice for those who demand the best against an elegant background where service is keyed to personal tastes. It occupies the entire end

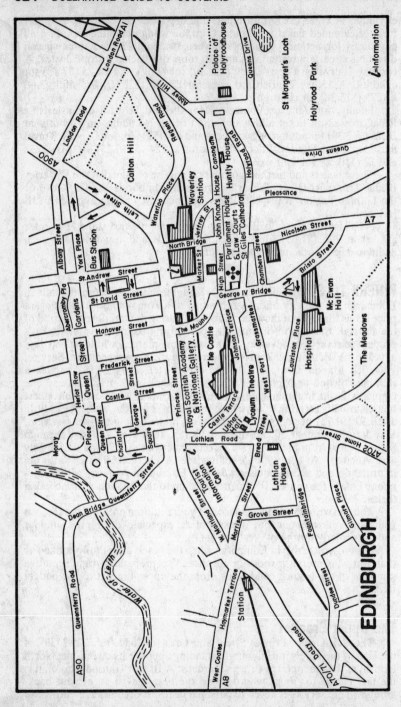

EDINBURGH

i=Information

of a block, with views of the castle and the park-like grounds. The interior is prestigious, drawing on some of the classic decorative and architectural features of both France and Scotland. The entrance hall achieves dignity with oyster-white paneled walls and desks, brass chandeliers, and a vibrant ceiling mural; and the main lounge is graced with neoclassic columns, a grand staircase, and chandelier.

The rates at the hotel are from £50 ($75) to £62 ($93) in a single, £75 ($112.50) to £85 ($127.50) in a twin or double. A full breakfast is included. The bedrooms are freshly decorated and pleasantly furnished.

For drinks, try the cave-like American Bar, with a curvy ceiling of cedar and walls of marble, spiked with flame-red accents. The Caledonia's Pompadour Restaurant, with its bona fide French cuisine, is such a highlight of the Edinburgh scene that I've featured it separately in the dining section, coming up. The most recent addition is the Gazebo Restaurant, where you can have breakfast, lunch, or dinner. A buffet lunch is available for £10 ($15), or you can order à la carte, choosing steak, chicken, burgers, and other main dishes, paying from £5 ($7.50) to £10 ($15). All prices quoted are inclusive of service and VAT.

The Roxburghe Hotel, Charlotte Square (tel. 225-3921), is an Adam building of dove-gray stone, trimmed in white, with a stately town house opening directly onto a tree-filled square. While only four floors high (including a row of dormered mansard windows), it is nevertheless the first choice for a number of discriminating people who prefer a dignified place at which to stay. Within five minutes of the British Airways Terminal, the hotel is central, a short walk from Princes Street. The atmosphere is genteel and traditional, as reflected in the drawing room, with its ornate ceiling and woodwork, and tall arched windows opening toward the park. The furnishings are mostly antique, with groups of Chippendale chairs.

Most of the 72 bedrooms, reached by elevator, have private baths or showers. All have color TVs, clock-radio alarms, phones, trouser presses, and tea and coffee makers, plus the usual amenities such as sewing kits, shower caps, and foam bath, as well as a basket of fruit. The units are handsomely traditional, a favorite scheme being Wedgwood blue-and-white Adam-style paneling. There are a few bathless singles for £40 ($60); with shower or bath, it's £50 ($75). The bathless doubles go for £60 ($90), the price rising to £65 ($97.50) with bath, service and VAT included. A smart place to congregate for drinks is the Consort Bar, with its festive decor of chinoiserie and bistro tables. A modern dining room serves not only good meals, but gives diners a view of the square.

The George Hotel, George Street (tel. 225-1251), is concentrated quality. A great deal is compressed into a comparatively small space. A member of the Grand Metropolitan Hotels Group, the George is only two short blocks from Princes Street, in the midst of a number of boutiques, bus, rail, and air terminals. Between April 1 and October 1 the highest rates are in effect: £50 ($75) in a single with bath, £65 ($97.50) in a twin- or double-bedded room, also with bath. In low season the same accommodations cost £35 ($52.50) single, £50 ($75) double. All prices include VAT. All of the bedrooms have been refurnished and redecorated, but the public rooms have retained the style, elegance, and old-fashioned comfort of a country house. The Carvers Table offers a selection of prime Scottish beef, roast lamb, or roast pork, including vegetables, an appetizer, a dessert, and coffee, all for £10 ($15). Le Chambertin, the hotel's new and exclusive French restaurant, is open Monday to Saturday, inclusive (refer to my dining recommendations).

King James Thistle Hotel, St. James Centre (tel. 556-0111 or 800/228-9290 toll free), at the end of Princes Street, is a large modern hotel with comfortable bedrooms, each equipped with bath, color TV, in-house movies, radio, phone, trouser press, hair dryer, tea- and coffee-making facilities, and double-glazed windows. Singles rent for £45 ($67.50), and doubles for £65 ($97.50), VAT and service included. This hotel is directly connected to Edinburgh's largest shopping mall and is also the site of *Jamie's,* Scotland's longest running show.

Carlton Hotel, North Bridge (tel. 556-7277), is in a unique position, just off the Royal Mile at the entrance to the North Bridge, with views of Princes Gardens. It's pure Victorian, with brick towers and turrets, reached by an unimpressive entrance from North Bridge. Even the public lounges give no clue to the quite up-to-date bedrooms that evoke Scandinavia in their design. Each pleasant bedroom has its own bath and costs £42 ($63) single, £62 ($93) for a double or twin, including a full breakfast, service, and tax. In the Carving Room, you can carve as much as you want, either at lunch or dinner, for £12 ($18). The hotel is 100 yards from Waverley Station (you can enter via a station-level doorway in Jeffrey Street).

The Medium-Priced Range

The Old Waverley Hotel, 43 Princes St. (tel. 556-4648), can be an ideal stopover for those desiring a central, clean, and comfortable establishment. The Old Waverley's world is that of the turn of the century, although a great deal of modernization has made it serviceable and fairly streamlined inside, with friendly personnel providing efficient service. All of the bedrooms have private baths. The B&B rate in a single is £40 ($60). In a double, the B&B charge is £55 ($82.50), including VAT and service. The lounges on the second floor have been given that contemporary look. The Waverley is a pleasant place to unwind after a day of sightseeing across loch and dale. Some of the rooms look onto Princes Street and at night the floodlit castle. The Waverley has a good restaurant serving à la carte meals.

The Mount Royal Hotel, Princes Street (tel. 225-7161), is right in the middle of the famed thoroughfare, complete with exclusive shops. A modern world emerges as you climb the spiral staircase or take an elevator to the second floor, with its reception rooms and lounges, and ceiling-to-floor windows opening onto views of the Old Town. In reality, Mount Royal is a remake of an old hotel, providing streamlined bedrooms with a view. The emphasis is utilitarian—not on frills, although the comfort is genuine. In summer, singles with bath go for £32 ($48), twins with bath rent for £46 ($69), and triples cost £51 ($76.50). Prices include a continental breakfast, service, and VAT. The main dining room serves reasonably priced lunches and dinners.

The lounge on the second floor, with floor-to-ceiling windows offering views over the Scott Memorial and Princes Street, provides a wide variety of sandwiches and snacks throughout the day and night.

Crest Hotel, Queensferry Road (tel. 332-2442), stands on the road leading to the airport and the Forth Road Bridge. A modern building, it is easily accessible in a city where you may find parking difficult. It offers lovely views over the Firth of Forth to the floodlit cathedral. Well-furnished bedrooms come with color TV, radio, phone, bath, and plenty of hanging space to catch up on your laundry. The standard rate is £44 ($66) in a single, from £54 ($81) in a double, including service, VAT, and a full Scottish breakfast.

The Rendezvous Écossais Restaurant offers the chef's table at lunch, a full menu in the evening. You can also obtain sandwiches and hot drinks from the porter throughout the night if you don't want to travel the five minutes or so downtown to Princes Street by bus or taxi. A three-course lunch costs from £7.50 ($11.25), and dinner is from £10 ($15). An à la carte meal will run about £13 ($19.50) to £18 ($27) per person, but the set meals are very good value and totally adequate, with such typically English fare as roast joints and fish or meat pies.

Howard Hotel, Great King street (tel. 557-3500). Three Georgian terrace houses have been combined to create a comfortable resting place. Singles renting for £35 ($52.50) contain showers, and doubles or twins have complete baths, costing from £48 ($72), including a full breakfast, VAT, and service. The decor is a combination of both traditional and modern. Units have tea- or coffee-making equipment, color TV, radio, and direct-dial phone.

After relaxing in the pleasant lounge, you might want to patronize an elegant restaurant in the basement, known as No. 36. Decorated in browns and cream, it has linen tablecloths and shining glassware. A three-course luncheon goes for £6.50 ($9.75). Specialties include such dishes as Highland game casserole and lamb sweetbreads in garlic butter with herbs and bacon. At dinner, two courses from a wide selection of dishes will cost from £11.50 ($17.25), and you are likely to be served grilled salmon filet or venison escalope with orange.

Across the passage in the basement is the Claret Jug, with paneled walls and touches of red, along with dark wood wheelback chairs. At lunchtime a popular cold buffet is served in the bar, with ample portions of cold poultry and meat. You can help yourself, too, to a selection of salads. The cost is from £3 ($4.50), and they have a good selection of wines by the glass, in addition to the usual pub ales. At the back is a car park, a blessing in busy Edinburgh.

The Budget Range

Belmont Hotel, 10 Carlton Terrace (tel. 556-6146), is right in the midst of a row of classic town houses, dating from the 18th and 19th centuries. A 15-minute walk from the center of Edinburgh, with views of the parks and rooftops from most of the windows, it is really two houses joined together by Mr. and Mrs. Stanley, who accept paying guests year round, charging them £28 ($42) in a double, £18 ($27) in a single in high season. The price includes breakfast. Your bed will be soft, the sheets freshly laundered, the furnishings comfortable. The dining room is as old-fashioned as the rest of the place, in typical Georgian style. The hotel was awarded a commendation prize by the Edinburgh New Town Conservation Committee for the extensive renovations to the dining room, restoring it to its natural Georgian splendor. The Belmont is ideal for those who want a simple, uncluttered life in a home-like atmosphere. It is open only from March to October.

Georgian Hotel, 5–6 Dean Terrace (tel. 332-4520), is a small, family-run hotel in central Edinburgh, and from it you can walk alongside the Water of Leith to historic Dean Village or to the Botanical Gardens. This Georgian house, under the personal supervision of Alistair Martin and

Betty Ross, has many fine Adam architectural features and tall, wide windows. The owners have a variety of nicely decorated bedrooms, renting from £15 ($22.50) in a single without bath, rising to £22 ($33) with bath. Doubles cost £24 ($36) without bath, £34 ($51) with bath. All these tariffs include breakfast, VAT, and service. Many of the units have their own shower and toilet en suite, and all have TV, radio, intercom, and a babylistening sereivce. Guests can enjoy drinks and the company in the hotel's bar, where home-cooked lunches are served every day at reasonable prices.

Teviotdale Guest House, 53 Grange Loan (tel. 667-4376), is a gem of a place to stay, where Mrs. Esther Riley welcomes visitors as if they were her house guests. It's in a peaceful area of the city, about a 15-minute walk from the University of Edinburgh and a 10-minute bus ride to Princes Street (the bus stop is only two blocks away). For B&B, Mrs. Riley charges £8.50 ($12.75) per person, and her breakfasts are special, all cooked by the landlady and including her own home-baked brown bread and scones. All seven of the bedrooms are equipped for modest self-catering, but Mrs. Riley will prepare dinner for you if you let her know in advance. The Teviotdale's halls and staircases have been made light and airy, and the decor is properly Edwardian. Mr. Riley is joined by her husband, Bob (who sings Gilbert and Sullivan), and her honey-colored chow, Chung, in making guests feel at home.

Hotels on the Outskirts

These hotels in the environs might be useful if Edinburgh gets heavily booked—at festival time and during the summer. Both are in the medium-priced range.

The Royal Scot Hotel, 111 Glasgow Rd. (tel. 334-9191), is close to EDI airport to the west of the city. It's a modern hotel with its own helicopter pad and good parking, yet it lies within easy reach of the city center. Facilities include the Sakura leisure complex, which comprises an indoor heated swimming pool, sauna, sunbeds, Jacuzzi, gymnasium, children's play area, cocktail bar, salad bar, and coffee lounge. Use of all these attractions is free to hotel guests, with the exception of the sunbeds. The hotel charges £45 ($67.50) in a single, £58 ($87) in a twin or double, including a full Scottish breakfast, service, and VAT. All rooms are equipped with private baths and showers, color TVs, radios, direct-dial phones, and tea- and coffee-making facilities, with central heating.

You can dine in the new carvery-style restaurant, which offers a set three-course dinner menu for £8.50 ($12.75) per person, or in the international à la carte restaurant.

Kings Manor Hotel, 100 Milton Rd. East (tel. 669-0444), is owned and run by the Solley family. The hotel lies within a ten-minute walk of the beach on the Firth of Forth, but still is within easy reach of the city center. It's a pleasant old building, comfortably modernized to provide most rooms with private baths. There is a bar and a lounge with a roaring fire. Rooms have color TV, radio, and phone. Singles rent for £22 ($33) to £26 ($39) without bath, £30 ($45) with bath. Bathless doubles are priced from £30 ($45) to £38 ($57), including VAT and service. A set luncheon is provided for £6 ($9), a table d'hôte dinner costing from £9 ($13.50), giving you a choice of 15 main dishes. However, if you want a filet steak, you'll pay slightly more.

Castle Hotels
To fulfill your fantasy, you might want to spend your first night in Scotland in a real castle surrounded by gardens and spacious grounds. If so, I have the following recommendations:

Dalhousie Castle, Bonnyrigg (tel. 0875/20153), dates back to the 12th century. It lies off the A7 Carlisle–Edinburgh road, just outside the village of Bonnyrigg, only eight miles from Edinburgh. It is now run by Neville Petts, who welcomes guests to this historic old castle. A turreted and fortified house, with ramparted terraces and battlements, it offers such delights as a dungeon restaurant where meals are served, including many local Scottish dishes. The rooms are large and all have private baths, color TVs, phones, radios, and plenty of space in which to sit and relax. Two of the suites have four-poster beds. The cost per night ranges from £55 ($82.50) in a single to £73 ($109.50) in a double- or twin-bedded room, while a triple rents for £97 ($145.50). For true palatial living, you might want to take one of the two-room suites with double or twin beds, costing £120 ($180). A full Scottish breakfast is included in the tariffs.

Borthwick Castle, North Middleton (tel. 0875/20514), lies 12 miles south of Edinburgh on the A7. This 15th-century structure recently celebrated its 550th anniversary and was the last refuge of Mary Queen of Scots and the Earl of Bothwell in 1567. Her apartments, the small chapel where she prayed, and the bedchamber once occupied by Bothwell are available to guests. Both bedchambers have four-poster beds. All the bedrooms have shower and toilet en suite and are centrally heated. Guests dine in the magnificent stone-vaulted Great Hall by roaring log fire and candlelight. On special evenings, pipers, dancers, and traditional entertainment are enjoyed. Borthwick Castle has become internationally famous for the excellence of its cuisine and personal service, its authentic medieval ambience, and the recreation of a gracious lifestyle that is unrepeatable. Miss Helen Bailey, the chatelaine of the castle, and the members of her household provide warm hospitality to all who enter this stately home. Room rates are £70 ($105) for a twin or double, including a full Scottish breakfast and VAT. There are no single rooms. A five-course menu is available for £20 ($30).

Melville Castle Hotel, Lasswade, Midlothian (tel. 031/663-6633), lies five miles from Edinburgh city center on the main A7 approaching Dalkeith, on the banks of the North Esk in acres of unspoiled forest. From medieval times, a castle has stood on the site of the present building. In the 16th century this was a hunting seat of Mary Queen of Scots. The twin-towered structure has fine interior architecture, with a spacious pillared entrance hall and an elegant "hanging" staircase, one of the few such in Britain. The hotel, owned by H. L. Weibye and managed by his daughter, has the intimate atmosphere of a country inn, with a cocktail bar and restaurant in what were once the castle's wine cellars and a dining alcove under an arch to the ancient structure. In the library are books from the 17th and 18th centuries, some handwritten by the first Viscount Melville.

You can rent a bedroom in this castle hotel for £20 ($30) to £26 ($39) in a single, £32 ($48) to £40 ($60) in a double. Miss Weibye and her staff of young people will make every effort to see that you enjoy your stay.

WHERE TO DINE: The Scots are hearty eaters—and you'll like the sizes of their portions as well as the quality of their fare, with choices from river, sea, and loch. You can dine on a cock-a-leekie soup, fresh Tay salmon, haggis, neeps, tatties, and whisky, Aberdeen Angus filet steak, potted hough, poacher's soup, and good old stovies and rumbledethumps. If none of the above tempts you, you'll find that French cuisine has made an inroad at many of the first-class hotels.

The Upper Bracket

Prestonfield House, Priestfield Road (tel. 667-8055), offers gourmet meals in the setting of a Jacobean country estate, in the midst of a 17-acre garden. King James II often visited before students burned down the house. Rebuilt, it was later to host Benjamin Franklin, then American ambassador, as well as Boswell and Johnson. The architect was William Bruce, who designed the Palace of Holyroodhouse. No matter which room you enter, you'll find fine furnishings and paintings, including two Ramsays over the dining room fireplace. Have a predinner toast in the Old Bar (drinks served from a Sheraton bookcase), while perusing the menu. If you arrive early enough, you can stroll through the gardens and pay your respects to the peacocks. The manager will guide you to one of the early-19th-century candlelit dining rooms, with their exquisite table settings.

All meals are à la carte, and the cuisine is essentially French. With so many fine dishes to recommend, I hesitate to point out a small group. Nevertheless, specialties include smoked haddock mousse and pâté maison. The Scottish national soup, cock-a-leekie, is also featured. Another local treat is trout fried in oatmeal. Main coures are likely to include escalope of pork. You can have after-dinner coffee in the second floor Mortlake Tapestry Room, with its ornate ceiling, Persian carpets, and antiques, or in the Leather Room, with its panels from Còrdoba. Expect to spend from £18 ($27) for dinner. Meals are served between 12:30 and 3 p.m. and between 7 and 10:30 p.m., including Sunday. It's essential to call ahead for a reservation.

Five bedrooms are available for those who book well in advance. The rooms are large and well furnished, with pieces from the 18th and 19th centuries. The rate for B&B, including VAT and service, is £45 ($67.50) for a single, £60 ($90) for a double. Two rooms have shower units, and the others have baths within easy reach. The breakfast is most generous, complete with Scottish oatmeal.

Pompadour Restaurant, Caledonian Hotel, Princes Street (tel. 225-2433), serves the haute French cuisine. At least 60 classic Gallic specialties are offered, augmented by an extensive wine list. The setting is convincing, in a drawing-room atmosphere of pale blue and white, with ornate bas-relief plaster paneling, fruitwood provincial armchairs, cerise draperies, and half-moon windows overlooking Princes Street. For your à la carte opening you might prefer escargots or smoked trout. Main dishes include chicken maréchal and sole Caledonian. Various specialty dishes are also offered, including filet d'angus chemise au poivre. Desserts range from ices to crêpes suzettes.

In addition to the French dishes, there's always a Taste of Scotland selection. Try, for example, scallops in wild Highland garlic butter or, for the more sophisticated, chicken suprême filled with scampi and creamed leeks. An average à la carte meal costs from £18 ($27) per person. The restaurant is open for dinner in summer from 7:30 to 10:30 p.m. (in winter from 7 to 10:30 p.m.). Closed Sunday.

Le Chambertin, George Hotel, 21 George St. (tel. 225-1251), provides a top-level French cuisine in intimate surroundings, between 12:30 and 2:30 p.m. Monday through Friday. A meal, inclusive of unlimited wines, is available for £11.50 ($17.25), £13.50 ($20.25), or £14.50 ($21.75).

In the evening, guests can select from a wide choice of wines, including some special bottles from the Chambertin district of France. The à la carte menu is well balanced and features many traditional French dishes and also, subject to availability, lobster, mussels, oysters, and many other dishes.

The Medium-Priced and Budget Range

The Consort, Roxburghe Hotel, Charlotte Square (tel. 225-3921), provides intimate dining in a plush atmosphere at one of Edinburgh's leading hotels. It and its adjoining cocktail bar attract sophisticated residents, and artists during the festival weeks. Through its separate entrance on George Street, you descend a stairway into an almost theatrical setting. Lunch is served between 12:15 and 2:30 p.m., dinner from 6:30 to 10 p.m. (Sunday till 9:30 p.m.). For appetizers, you might prefer either smoked Scottish salmon or escargots bourguignons. Many attractively prepared main dishes are offered, including the mixed grill and steak Diane. A set lunch goes for £7.50 ($11.25), a fixed-price dinner for £10 ($15), plus coffee.

Henderson's Salad Table, 94 Hanover St. (tel. 225-2131), is a Shangri-la for healthfood lovers as well as those who want an array of rich, nutritious salads—some of the most imaginative and original I've known. It's self-service, and you can pick and choose. The ingredients are combined ingeniously—eggs, carrots, grapes, nuts, yogurts, cheese, potatoes, cabbage, watercress, you name it. A variety of cosmopolitan international dishes is served on request, including stuffed eggplant or chop suey. You can have a number of hot plates, such as stuffed peppers with rice and pimiento. The soups are fabulous. Desserts are homemade, so rich and pure you'll strain trying to choose between them. Settle for a fresh fruit salad or a gâteau with double whipped cream and chocolate sauce. Average price of a meal starts at £8.50 ($12.75).

Henderson's is open regularly from 8 a.m. to 11 p.m. Monday through Saturday (on Sunday from noon to 9 p.m., closed on Sunday from October to June). The scene takes place in a semi-basement, and the furnishings are appropriate: pine-wood tables (often shared) and crude box-stools. The Vegetarian Society raises a provocative question: "Have you ever thought that killing for food is not necessary?" At Henderson's it certainly isn't. The Sherry Bar serves Spanish tapas (hors d'oeuvres). The wine cellar provides a choice of 50 wines, some 20 of which may be had by the glass. Live classical music is played most evenings. The bar may be reached by the same entrance as the Salad Table. Exhibitions of batik, sculpture, and ceramics by up-and-coming local artists add to the evening's entertainment.

Denzler's, 80 Queen St. (tel. 226-5467), offers a large à la carte menu with an appetizing choice of Swiss, Italian, French, and Scottish dishes, skillfully prepared using the highest quality ingredients. Portions are generous, and service is efficient although informal, the waiters contributing to the relaxed, friendly atmosphere. Air-dried Swiss ham with melon is an enticing appetizer. For a main course, choose from cuts of prime steak, fresh seafood, game in season, or else the pièce de résistance, fondue bourguignonne. For dessert, I endorse the apfelstrudel. Meals begin at £5 ($7.50). Open daily except Sunday, the restaurant serves lunch from noon to 2 p.m. and dinner from 6:30 to 10 p.m. You have a choice of the Garden Room, Cellar Restaurant, or the Thistle No-Smoking Restaurant for dining, or you can simply have drinks in the Cellar Bar.

Madogs, 38a George St. (tel. 225-3408), evokes a touch of American sophistication and flair in the Scottish capital. With its menu and movie posters (heavy on Bogart), it suggests someplace in California. Although English beer is very good, it's more chic here to order an American variety, such as Budweiser. The New England clam chowder is often very good, and better than you're likely to get at many places in New England these days. The kosher pastrami is popular; however, most guests prefer the hamburger with french fries and a salad. Chili con carne is another favorite. Eggs Benedict (the menu writer has to translate this for local diners) is also offered. At dinner the menu has a continental range—teriyaki steak, Long Island duck, even Bahamian grouper. Meals begin at £12 ($18). The split-level restaurant is graced with hanging baskets and potted palms, and the slim-hipped waitresses are attired in jeans. Lunch is until 3 p.m., and dinner is from 6 to 11:30. Closed Sunday.

Cosmo, 58a North Castle St. (tel. 226-6743), is one of the most heavily patronized Italian restaurants in the Scottish capital. Courtesy, efficiency, and good cookery are featured here. Cosmo Tamburro is your host. In season you can ask for mussels as an appetizer. Soups and pastas are always reliable. However, remember that the cost of your pasta is doubled if you order it as a main course. On the other hand, the portions are also doubled. I've found the veal dishes the best cooked and a good value, although you may be attracted to the seafood. The cassata Siciliana is well made and not unbearably sweet. Expect to pay from £15 ($22.50) for a complete meal. Closed Sunday and Monday, the restaurant serves otherwise until 2:15 p.m. for lunch and until 10:30 p.m. for dinner.

The **Luckpenny,** 88–90 Hanover St. (tel. 225-2227), caters to a leisurely clientele of visitors, shoppers, and students. The comfortable semi-basement restaurant is bright with polish, freshly decorated, and abounds in flowers and plants. There's a long salad bar where you can choose from some 20 different mixtures to go with baked potatoes, quiche, pizza, smoked mackerel, pâté, and cold meats. There is also a hot menu that changes daily, including such dishes as lasagne, seafood pie, Irish stew, and broccoli au gratin. Fresh cream trifle, chocolate mousse, cheesecake, cakes, and pies, all homemade, adorn the dessert counter. A meal will cost about £4 ($6), including a glass of wine, fruit juice, or beer. An added attraction is the totally separate no-smoking area with its own entrance. The restaurant is open daily from 10 a.m. to 8 p.m. but closed on Sunday during the winter.

The Witchery by the Castle, 352 Castle Hill, Royal Mile (tel. 225-5613), lies in a tiny court where James Boswell and Samuel Johnson are reputed to have met in 1770. Within 50 yards of the castle entrance, the dimly lit cellar restaurant is just the sort of place where the 17th-century witches of the city met with the devil and practiced their craft.

Present-day witches are asked to park their broomsticks at the door before lunching on hot-pot, scampi, finnan haddie, or broomstick pie. Duck with orange and venison in red wine and port sauce are available throughout the day. In the evening a soup is ladled from a bubbling cauldron, and later you might prefer White Witches (peaches stuffed with cottage cheese, walnuts, and raisins), or else Black Cat's Dream (seafood cocktail). The curried chicken is tasty, as is the chili con carne. Expect to spend from £6 ($9) for lunch, from £6 ($9) to £10 ($15) for an evening meal. The place is good fun, and the food is good too. Opposite the Camera Obscura, it's convenient for the hungry sightseer who can visit any time from 10 a.m. to 11 p.m.

Cousteau's Bar and Seafood Restaurant, 109 Hanover St. (tel. 226-3355), is reached down wide stone steps decorated by a mammoth pair of flippers and a diver's mask. Polished tables and green plants make for a simple but inviting decor. Obviously the emphasis is placed on the freshness and quality of the fish. Oysters are often available, and a savory opener would be the mussels marinière au gratin or perhaps crab en chemise. For a main course, I'd suggest the seafood platter. You might also order turbot, grilled or poached salmon, or trout. Most seasonal fish are available, and the prices vary with weather conditions. Expect to pay from £10.50 ($15.75) per person for a meal. There are simple desserts and a good wine list, which is perhaps a little expensive.

Restaurants on the Outskirts

At least once you should get out into the countryside surrounding Edinburgh. One way to do this is to take bus 41 for about five miles from the West End to the little Scottish village of Cramond. Few visible traces remain today of its Roman occupation.

Quietly nestling on a sloping street is the **Cramond Inn,** on Cramond Glebe Road, which has been serving food and drinks to wayfarers for 300 years (it was known to Robert Louis Stevenson). Picture upholstered booths, opera-red carpeting, some beerbarrel upholstered chairs, a collection of local watercolors, a low ceiling, large foot-square old beams, dark oak and creamy-colored walls, recessed windows, a small stone fireplace—and you'll begin to get the feel of the inn.

The restaurant can serve 60 diners, but you'd better call in advance (tel. 336-2035), as it's most popular. The prices are quite reasonable, considering the quality of food—some of the finest of Scottish dishes. The steak-and-kidney pie is delicious, but I'm drawn to the haggis, the famed dish of Scotland, made with an assortment of chopped meats, oatmeal, and spices. For an appetizer, the Scottish game soup is a favorite. A specialty of the house is roast duck. Desserts are extremely tasty. The inn serves lunch from noon to 2:30 p.m., dinner till 10:30 p.m. Most meals begin at £8 ($12), ranging upward. Bar lunches are served in the tastefully appointed lounge bar Monday to Saturday from noon to 2 p.m. and on Sunday from 12:30 to 2:30 p.m. The dining room is closed on Sunday.

THE TOP SIGHTS: Before leaving the Scottish capital, you'll want to take a look at both the Old Town and the New Town. Both have their different attractions—the Old Town's largely medieval; the New Town, Georgian. We'll begin our exploration on the Royal Mile of the Old Town, a collective term for Canongate, Lawnmarket, and The High. At one end on Castle Rock sits—

Edinburgh Castle

It is believed that the ancient city grew up on the seat of the dead volcano, Castle Rock. History is vague on possible settlements, although it is known that in the 11th century Malcolm III (Canmore), and his Saxon queen, Margaret, occupied a castle on this spot. The good Margaret was later venerated as a saint. St. Margaret's Chapel was built in the Norman style, the present oblong structure dating principally from the 12th century. The five-ton **Mons Meg,** a 15th-century cannon that formerly sat outside the tiny chapel, is now to be found in the French Prisons.

Inside the castle you can visit the **State Apartments**—particularly Queen Mary's Bedroom—where Mary Queen of Scots gave birth to James VI of Scotland (later James I of England). The Great Hall with its hammer-beam ceiling was built by James IV. It displays armaments and armor, although Scottish Parliaments used to convene in this hall.

The highlight, however, is the Crown Chamber, which houses the Honours of Scotland, used at the coronation of James VI, along with the sceptre and the sword of state of Scotland. The French Prisons can also be viewed. Turned into a prison in the 18th century, these great storerooms housed hundreds of Napoleonic soldiers during the early 19th century. Many of them made wall carvings that you can see today.

The castle may be visited April 1 to September 30 weekdays from 9:30 a.m. to 6 p.m., on Sunday from 11 a.m. to 6 p.m. From October 1 to March 31, hours are from 9:30 a.m. to 5:05 p.m. weekdays, 12:30 to 4:20 p.m. on Sunday. The price of admission ranges from £1.50 ($2.25) to £2 ($3) for adults, from 75p ($1.13) to £1 ($1.50) for children under 16.

The **Camera Obscura,** Castlehill (tel. 226-3709), is right beside the castle at the head of the Royal Mile. It's at the top of the Outlook Tower and offers a magnificent view of the surrounding city. Trained guides point out the landmarks and talk about Edinburgh's fascinating history. In addition, there are several entertaining exhibitions, all with an optical theme, and a well-stocked shop selling books, crafts, and records. Open from 9:30 a.m. seven days a week. Admission is £1.20 ($1.80) for adults, 60p (90¢) for children.

The **Scottish United Services Museum** (tel. 226-6907), at the castle, is the national museum for the armed forces of Scotland. Its collections are unique and comprehensive in their field, and its library, open for research by prior appointment, is a major source of reference on Scottish military subjects. The museum occupies display galleries on the east and west sides of Crown Square and has opened new galleries in the North Hospital Block. Entry to the museum's public galleries is included in the admission charge to the castle, its hours being the same as those of the castle.

Along the Royal Mile

Ideally, if you have the time, you should walk the full length of the Royal Mile—all the way to the Palace of Holyroodhouse at the opposite end. Along the way you'll see some of the most interesting old structures in Edinburgh, with their turrets, gables, and towering chimneys. Of all the buildings that may intrigue you, the most visited are John Knox's House and **St. Giles' Cathedral.**

Although it still bears the name "cathedral," which it once was, St. Giles' is now properly titled the High Kirk of Edinburgh (tel. 225-4363). Founded in 1120, the interior dates mainly from the 15th century. It contains the Thistle Chapel, designed by Sir Robert Lorimer and housing beautiful stalls and notable heraldic stained-glass windows. The chapel is open from 10 a.m. to 5 p.m. and may be visited for 40p (60¢). John Knox, the leader of the Reformation in Scotland, was minister of St. Giles' from 1560 to 1572.

Lady Stair's House lies in a close of the same name off Lawnmarket. It was built in 1622 by a prominent merchant burgess. It takes its name from a former owner, Elizabeth, the Dowager-Countess of Stair. Today it is a treasurehouse of portraits, relics, and manuscripts relating to three of Scotland's greatest men of letters: Robert Burns, Sir Walter Scott, and Robert Louis Stevenson. The house is open Monday to Saturday from 10 a.m. to 5 p.m., to 6 p.m. from June to September. During the festival it's open from 2 to 5 p.m. on Sunday.

The **Museum of Childhood,** 38 High St. (tel. 225-2424), stands just opposite John Knox's House on the Royal Mile. It was the first museum in the world to be devoted solely to the history of childhood. Three floors contain nearly every facet of the world of children, ranging from antique toys and games to exhibits on health, education, costumes, juvenile "arsenals," and many other items representing the childhood experience of members of different nationalities and periods. Because of the youthful clientele it naturally attracts, visitors are warned that it has been described as "the noisiest museum in the world." It is open weekdays from 10 a.m. to 6 p.m. June to September, to 5 p.m. the rest of the year, and from 2 to 5 p.m. on Sunday during the Edinburgh Festival. Admission is 60p (90¢) for adults, 50p (75¢) for children. (The museum was closed for alterations in 1984 but at press time was to reopen in time for the 1985 festival.)

Across the street at 45 High St. is **John Knox's House** (tel. 556-6961), whose history goes back to the late 15th century. Even if you're not interested in the reformer who founded the Scottish Presbyterian church, you may want to visit his house, as it is characteristic of the "lands" that used to flank the Royal Mile. All of them are gone now, except Knox's house, with its timbered gallery. Inside, you'll see the tempera ceiling in the Oak Room, along with exhibitions of Knox memorabilia. The house may be visited Monday to Saturday from 10 a.m. to 5 p.m., to 6 p.m. from June to October. During the festival it's open on Sunday from 2 to 5 p.m. Admission is 60p (90¢) for adults, 40p (60¢) for children.

After leaving John Knox's House, continue along Canongate in the direction of the Palace of Holyroodhouse. At 163 Canongate stands one of the handsomest buildings along the Royal Mile. The **Canongate Tolbooth** was constructed in 1591 and was once the courthouse, prison, and center of municipal affairs for the burgh of Canongate. It contains the **Scottish Stone and Brass Rubbing Centre,** which is open Monday to Saturday from 10 a.m. to 5 p.m., to 6 p.m. from June to September. Telephone 225-1131 for information. You can visit the center's collection of replicas molded from ancient Pictish stones, rare Scottish brasses, and medieval church brasses. No experience is needed to make a rubbing. The center will show you how and supply materials. These rubbings make beautiful wall hangings and gifts. You can also purchase ready-made rubbings on the spot.

Across the street is **Huntly House,** an example of a restored 16th-century mansion. It is now Edinburgh's principal museum of local history. You can stroll through period rooms and reconstructions Monday to Saturday from 10 a.m. to 5 p.m., until 6 p.m. from June to September. During the festival it is also open on Sunday from 2 to 5 p m

The Palace of Holyroodhouse

At the eastern end of the Royal Mile, the palace was built adjacent to an Augustinian abbey, established by David I in the 12th century. The nave, now in ruins, remains today. James IV founded the palace nearby in the early part of the 16th century, but of his palace only the north tower is left. Much of what you see today was ordered built by Charles II.

In the old wing occurred the most epic moments in the history of Holyroodhouse, when Mary Queen of Scots was in residence. Mary, who had been Queen of France and widowed while still a teenager, decided to return to her native Scotland. She eventually entered into an unsuccessful marriage with Lord Darnley but spent more time and settled affairs of state with her secretary, David Rizzio. Darnley plotted to kill the Italian, and he and his accomplices marched into Mary's supper room, grabbed Rizzio over her protests, then carried him to the Audience Chamber, where he was murdered with 56 stab wounds. A plaque marks the spot of his death on March 9, 1566.

Darnley himself was to live less than a year after, dying mysteriously in a gunpowder explosion. Mary, of course, was eventually executed on the order of her cousin, Elizabeth I. One of the most curious exhibits in Holyroodhouse is a piece of needlework by Mary, depicting a cat-and-mouse scene (Elizabeth's the cat).

The State Apartments also contain some fine 17th-century Flemish tapestries, especially a whole series devoted to Diana, as well as some Gobelins. In the Great Gallery are 89 portraits, depicting Scottish kings, including Macbeth, painted by a Dutchman, de Wet. (They either all looked surprisingly similar in the face, or else De Wet used the same model for the lot of them.)

The palace suffered long periods of neglect, although it basked in glory at the ball in the mid-18th century thrown by Bonnie Prince Charlie. The present Queen and Prince Philip live at Holyroodhouse whenever they visit Edinburgh. When they're not in residence, you can visit the palace weekdays from 9:30 a.m. to 5:15 p.m. (on Sunday from 11 a.m. to 4:30 p.m.). In the off-season, the palace is closed at 3:45 p.m. and on Sunday. Adults pay £1.50 ($2.25) to enter, but when the State Apartments are closed, the cost is 70p ($1.05) for the Historical Rooms tour. Children and students are admitted at half the adult rate. Light refreshments are available only in the summer months.

The New Town

At some point, the Old Town became too small. The burghers decided to build a whole new town across the valley, the marsh being drained and eventually turned into public gardens. Princes Street is the most striking boulevard. Architecturally, the most interesting district of the New Town is the north side of Charlotte Square, designed by Robert Adam. It was the young architect James Craig who shaped much of the Georgian style of the New Town, with its crescents and squares.

At No. 7 Charlotte Square, a part of the northern facade, is the restored building known simply as the **Georgian House** (tel. 225-2160). It is a prime example of Scottish architecture and interior design in the zenith of the New Town. Originally the home of John Lamont, 18th chief of the Clan Lamont, the house has recently been refurbished and reopened to the public by the National Trust for Scotland. The furniture in this Robert Adam house is mainly Hepplewhite, Chippendale, and Sheraton, all dating from the 18th-century. In a ground-floor bedroom is a sturdy old four-poster with an original 18th-century canopy. The dining room table is set for a dinner on fine Wedgwood china, and the kitchen is stocked with gleaming copper pots and pans. The house is open April to October from 10 a.m. to 5 p.m. (on Sunday from 2 to 5 p.m.). In winter its hours are from 10 a.m. to 4:30 p.m. on Saturday (on Sunday from 2 to 4:30 p.m.). Admission is £1.05 ($1.58) for adults, 50p (75¢) for children.

As an Old Town complement to the New Town Georgian House, the National Trust for Scotland has opened in a 1620 tenement in the Royal Mile, Gladstone's Land, Lawnmarket (tel. 226-5856), an upstairs apartment of four rooms furnished as it might have been in the 17th century. On the ground floor reconstructed shop booths display replicas of goods of the period. It is open April through October, Monday through Saturday from 10 a.m. to 5 p.m. (on Sunday from 2 to 5 p.m.). Admission is 80p ($1.20) for adults, 40p (60¢) for children.

The Gothic-inspired **Scott Memorial** lies in the **East Princes Street Gardens.** It is the most famous landmark of Edinburgh, completed in the mid-19th century. Sir Walter Scott's heroes are honored by small figures in the monument. You can climb the tower weekdays from May to October from 9 a.m. to 6 p.m. for 40p (60¢). Off-season, you must scale the monument before 3 p.m. Closed Sunday. At **West Princes Street Gardens** is the first ever **Floral Clock,** which was constructed in 1904.

ART TREASURES:
For the art lover, Edinburgh has a number of masterpieces, and many visitors come here just to look at the galleries. Of course, the principal museum is the **National Gallery of Scotland,** on The Mound (tel. 556-8921), in the center of Princes Street Gardens. Although the gallery is small as national galleries go, the collection came about with great care and was expanded considerably by bequests and loans. A few paintings are of exceptional merit. I'll highlight a representative sampling.

Italian paintings include Verrocchio's *Madonna and Child,* Andrea del Sarto's *Portrait of a Man,* and Domenichino's *Adoration of the Shepherds.* However, perhaps the most acclaimed among them is Tiepolo's *Finding of Moses.*

The Spanish masters are less well represented but shine forth in El Greco's *Saviour,* Velázquez's *Old Woman Cooking Eggs,* an early work by that great master, and *Immaculate Conception* by Zurbarán, his friend and contemporary.

The Flemish School emerges notably in Rubens's *Feast of Herod* and the Dutch in Rembrandt's *Woman in Bed,* superb landscapes by Cuyp, Ruisdael, and Hobbema, and in one of the gallery's most recent acquisitions, *Interior of St. Bavo's Church, Haarlem,* by Pieter Saenredam, his largest and arguably finest painting, bought in 1982. Hans Holbein the Younger's *Allegory of the Old and New Testaments* has added a new dimension to the representation of early northern painting in the gallery.

Among the paintings on loan to the gallery since World War II, from the Duke of Sutherland, are two Raphaels: *The Holy Family with a Palm Tree* and *The Bridgewater Madonna.* Titian gives us his favorite subject, Venus, this time rising from the sea, but he's even more masterly in his Diana canvases. A rare feature of the gallery: the *Seven Sacraments* paintings by Poussin, the 17th-century French painter, are also on loan.

The most valuable gift to the gallery since its founding, the Maitland Collection, includes Cézanne's *Mont St. Victoire,* as well as works by Degas, Van Gogh, Renoir, Gauguin, and Seurat, among others. Gauguin's *Vision of the Sermon,* a key work in the development of modern painting, is one of the gallery's masterpieces and a recent acquisition is an early Monet, *Shipping Scene—Night Effects.* Cézanne's *Big Trees* is one of the most notable acquisitions in recent years.

The great English painters are represented by excellent examples—Gainsborough's *The Hon. Mrs. Graham,* Constable's *Dedham Vale,* along with works by Turner, Reynolds, and Hogarth. Naturally, the work of Scottish painters decks the walls, none finer than Henry Raeburn, at his best in the whimsical *The Rev. Robert Walker Skating on Duddingston Loch.*

The gallery is open from 10 a.m. to 5 p.m. weekdays (2 to 5 p.m. on Sunday). During the festival, hours are from 10 a.m. to 6 p.m. weekdays and from 11 a.m. to 6 p.m. on Sunday. Admission is free.

Britain's only museum exclusively devoted to 20th-century art is the **Scottish National Gallery of Modern Art,** Belford Road (tel. 556-8921). In 1984 it moved from its temporary home in the Royal Botanic Garden into a former school building completed in 1828, which has been converted into an art gallery. It is set in 12 acres of grounds just 15 minutes' walk from the West End of Princes Street. The collection is truly international in scope and quality despite its modest size. Major sculptures sited outside the building include pieces by Henry Moore, Hepworth, and Epstein. Inside, the collection ranges from a fauve Derain and cubist Braque and Picasso to recent works by Richard Long and Chia. There is naturally a strong representation of English and Scottish art. Highlights of the collection include works by Matisse, Miró, Magritte, Léger, Jawlensky, Kirchner, Kokoschka, Dix, Ernst, Ben Nicholson, Nevelson, Pollock, Beuys, Balthus, Hanson, De Andrea, Lichtenstein, Kitaj, and Hockney.

It's worth starting at the Eye-Opener, which introduces the collection and the building through a tape-slide program. Prints and drawings can be studied in the Print Room. The licensed café sells coffee and nonalcoholic drinks as well as light refreshments and salads. Hours are from 10 a.m. to 5 p.m. on weekdays, from 2 to 5 p.m. on Sunday. These hours are extended during the Edinburgh Festival. The only bus that actually passes the gallery is the infrequent no. 13. However, nos. 18, 20, and 41 pass along Queensferry Road, leaving only a five-minute walk up Queensferry Terrace and Belford Road to the gallery.

Lauriston Castle

This fine country mansion standing in extensive grounds overlooking the Firth of Forth lies on the outskirts of Edinburgh, about 3¼ miles northwest of Princes Street. If you're going by car, take the Queensferry Road, the A90, as if you were heading for the Forth Road Bridge, but turn off to the right at the Quality Street junction (look for directional signs pointing to Lauriston Castle). Then proceed down Cramond Road South until you come to the entrance to the castle, on the right. If you're using public transport, take the Lothian Region bus no. 41 from the Mound, Hanover Street, or George Street.

The house is associated with John Law (1671–1729), the founder of the first bank in France. The house's collections are strong in English Georgian and French Louis styles of furniture. A visit here gives you a good picture of the leisure lifestyle of the upper classes before World War I. Look for the Derbyshire Blue John ornaments and the Crossley wool "mosaics."

The grounds are open from 9 a.m. to dusk, and each visitor to the castle is given a guided tour of about 40 minutes' duration, from April to

October daily except Friday at 11 a.m. and at 1, 2, and 5 p.m. (the last tour begins at 4:20 p.m.). From November to March, tours are only given on Saturday and Sunday at 1:20 and 3:20 p.m. Admission is £1 ($1.50) for adults, 50p (75¢) for children. For more information, phone 031/336-2060.

THE FESTIVAL: The highlight of Edinburgh's year—and the time of the greatest tourist invasion—is when the world-famous Edinburgh International Festival takes place. The annual festival is usually staged around mid-August to early September. Artists in all fields—music, drama, opera, ballet, painting—contribute their talents, and "Auld Reekie" takes on a cosmopolitan air.

One of the best attended spectacles is the military tattoo on the floodlit Esplanade in front of Edinburgh Castle. This is a chance for the spectator to witness some Highland dancing of the Scots and to watch a parade of Scottish regiments. In addition to operatic and dance presentations, choral and orchestral concerts, soloists, chamber concerts, and recitals (expect at least half a dozen every evening), there are a large number of dramatic shows and, to top it off, a widely attended film festival.

During these busy days, it's smart to make your headquarters at the **Festival Club,** a rendezvous for people participating in and witnessing the events. The club's headquarters are in the Edinburgh University Staff Club, 9–15 Chambers St. The licensed club operates a reasonably priced restaurant, cafeteria, snackbar, and lounges. The daily membership costs £1 ($1.50); a seven-day membership, £4 ($6); and for the season, £9 ($13.50).

For festival tickets, write to Festival Box Office, 21 Market St., Edinburgh EH1 1BW (tel. 226-4001). For accommodations, write to Tourist Accommodation Service, 9 Cockburn St., Edinburgh EH1 1BR.

THE SCOTTISH EXPERIENCE: This popular tourist center in Edinburgh's West End, 2 Rutland Pl. (tel. 228-2828), is the ideal introduction to a holiday in Edinburgh and/or Scotland. A 40- by 30-foot relief model of the country, the only one of its kind in Europe, displays more than 600 points of interest throughout Scotland. Castles, stately homes, wildlife parks, ski resorts—all light up at the touch of a button. Headphones provide guided tours around different areas of the country as seen on the map, ideal for helping you plan your trip. *The Making of Edinburgh* is a highly acclaimed 35-minute audio-visual presentation that traces the city's history from its volcanic origins right up to the present day. Gordon Jackson introduces the places and people who have helped shape Edinburgh through the years. Burke and Hare, John Knox, Mary Queen of Scots, Bonnie Prince Charlie, and the castle are all featured in this colorful insight into the history of Scotland's capital city.

An excellent restaurant caters to individuals and parties, and the Scottish Experience shop has gifts for all ages at reasonable prices. Summer hours are 9 a.m. to 6 p.m. daily from April to October. November to March it's open from 9 a.m. to 5 p.m. Monday to Saturday. The model of Scotland and *The Making of Edinburgh* are the only things to be seen on Saturday.

TOURS: If you want a quick introduction to the principal attractions in and around the capital, then consider one or more of the inexpensive tours offered by the **Lothian Region Transport,** 14 Queen St. (tel. 556-5656). You won't find a cheaper way to hit the highlights, and later you can go back on your own if you want a deeper experience. The luxury coaches leave from Waverley Bridge, near the Scott Monument. The tours start in April and run through late October. A winter program is also offered. A half-day coach tour (which takes about 3½ hours) leaves daily at 9:30 a.m. and 1:30 p.m. (Sunday at 1:30 p.m. only), costing £6 ($9) and visiting the castle, the Palace of Holyroodhouse, and St. Giles' Cathedral. Operating throughout the day are half a dozen shorter tours that show you some of the environs—such as the Sea City and the Hills. These tours are priced from £1.75 ($2.63). Also available is a wide selection of journeys that operate away from Edinburgh. These are on a special program called the "Waverley Series," composed of full-day and half-day excursions to destinations throughout Scotland and northern England.

SHOPPING: There are big and beautiful stores along Princes Street, facing the gardens and the castle, but there is just as much opportunity for seeking out souvenirs along the Royal Mile.

There you'll find the **Scottish Craft Centre,** Acheson House, Canongate, an exhibition of Scottish crafts—and everything is for sale. It is open Monday to Saturday from 10 a.m. to 5 p.m. At your leisure you can browse among all sorts of typically Scottish products, knitwear, pottery, glass, and jewelry. Everything is reasonably priced.

John Morrison, 461 Lawnmarket (tel. 225-8149), is a marvelous place at which to shop for a tartan. A woman's authentic hand-tailored kilt will cost around £70 ($105), but a semi-kilt or kilt skirt can be purchased for as little as £29 ($43.50). They will also provide evening sashes and stoles to match your skirt at £12 ($18) and £15 ($22.50).

For men, the tradition is far more complicated—kilts go for £85 ($127.50) to £165 ($247.50) for a heavy hand-woven worsted in your favorite tartan. To go with it, there are doublets and jackets, barathea at £75 ($112.50) and velvet at £98 ($147). That's followed up with accessories, a jabot and cuffs, £9 ($13.50) for the set, along with kilt hose at £7.25 ($10.88), a tie at £3.50 ($5.25), and plain green undertrews at £2.25 ($3.38) to answer the eternal question.

A belt with a sterling silver buckle is £21.50 ($32.25), and sporrans range from £15 ($22.50) for plain pig grain hide to £55 ($82.50) for a white sealskin evening model with silver mounts and skean dhus to tuck into your hose. Orders can be mailed throughout the world if you can't take personal delivery of your Highland dress.

The **Scottish Design Centre,** 72 St. Vincent St., G.2 (tel. 221-6121), is a good place to shop for items that are inexpensive, easy to pack, and distinctively Scottish, or just to look at exhibits of merchandise of Scottish design, as well as goods manufactured in other parts of Great Britain. You'll find toys, jewelry, cookware, and even furniture if you're in the market for large, handsome items.

NIGHTLIFE: The **Dalhousie Banquet** takes place every evening except Sunday in the summer season and most evenings during the winter at Dalhousie Courte, Cockpen, Bonnyrigg, a few miles south of Edinburgh. A four-course Jacobean banquet, with mead and wine, is served by the "gracious ladies of the courte" in medieval costume while the minstrels play. Afterward, you are regaled by their singing of traditional Scots songs and entertainment. There is also much merriment throughout the evening, good family fare. Advance reservations are essential. Telephone 663-5155. A free bus runs from central Edinburgh at 6:45 p.m. and will bring you back at the end of a happy evening in the past.

2. Day Trips from Edinburgh

Within easy reach of Edinburgh lie some of the most interesting castles and mansions in Scotland, the most important of which follow.

STIRLING: Almost equidistant from Glasgow and Edinburgh, Stirling is dominated by its impressive castle, perched on a 250-foot basalt rock. From Edinburgh, a bus takes about an hour and a half, traveling a distance of 37 miles.

This ancient town and its surrounding countryside was the scene of several battles, notably the Battle of Bannockburn in 1314 in which the Scots under Robert I routed the English forces of Edward II. Situated on the right bank of the Forth, Stirling Castle was certainly in existence in the early 12th century. At one time the castle was considered "the key to the Highlands," and is today the headquarters of the Argyle and Sutherland Highlanders, one of Britain's most celebrated regiments.

The castle and visitors' audio-visual center is open May 1 to October 31 from 9:30 a.m. to 6 p.m. (11 a.m. to 6 p.m. on Sunday); November 1 to April 30, hours are 9:30 a.m. to 5:05 p.m. weekdays (12:30 to 4:20 p.m. on Sunday). Admission is £1.50 ($2.25) for adults, 75p ($1.13) for children.

Other places of interest to visit in Stirling include the 15th-century **Church of the Holy Rood,** in which Mary Queen of Scots was crowned in 1543 at the age of nine months; the **Auld Brig** over the Forth, dating from the 14th century; and the **palace** built by James V in the 16th century.

Just outside the town is the **Robert the Bruce Memorial and Museum.** Admission is 35p (53¢) for a continual audio-visual presentation of stories of Bruce's times and history.

Food and Lodging

Portcullis Hotel, Castle Wynd (tel. 0786/2290), is my favorite place to stay in the area. It's a tall, 14th-century, rugged stone building hugging the walls of the castle. You enter through a lower courtyard of shrubbery and trees, protected by a high old stone wall. The inviting bar, which is colorful, is on the ground floor. Ron and Maggie Hill, who bought the hotel after his 34 years of service in the Royal Navy, serve candlelit and firelit dinners in the vaulted hall, which was formerly the second-floor lounge. This is the room where James VI of Scotland and I of England was educated before the union of the crowns in 1603. The atmosphere is pleasing, and the chef's cooking is superb. Maggie says they had a Texan diner who said the steak was the best he ever tasted, and he tried it more than once. The service is excellent and friendly. A three-course dinner costs about £15 ($22.50). You can have a pub lunch downstairs for £3 ($4.50) to £5 ($7.50). There's a good stock of whisky in the pub—80 different blends. For their customers from the States, they also have Jack Daniel's, and they're trying to find a supplier of Old Granddad, to keep Americans happy.

The bedrooms at the Portcullis are personal, each furnished informally and comfortably, renting at £16 ($24), including VAT, service, and a full breakfast. If you're lucky, Maggie says, you might even see the ghost.

If you're a Scottish history buff, you might try to find a room at the tiny

Heritage Hotel, containing only four bedrooms, all of which have private baths and showers. It's at 16 Allan Park (tel. 0786/3660). You're welcomed by the owner, Monsieur Marquetty, a Frenchman who married a Scottish lassie and settled in this unlikely spot. Their hotel is really like a private residence, and they have outfitted it as such, discreetly using antiques, paintings, and personal objects to make it warm and home-like. Their single rate is £16 ($24) per night, and two persons are charged from £30 ($45).

Monsieur Marquetty also offers a good cuisine in his adjoining restaurant, which features a set lunch at £6 ($9), served between noon and 3 p.m., and a table d'hôte dinner, four courses, for £11 ($16.50), offered between 6:30 and 11 p.m., the latter a surprisingly late hour for provincial Stirling.

DOUNE CASTLE: At Doune, on the banks of the Teith River, four miles west of Dunblane, stands this 14th-century castle, once a royal palace. Now owned by the Earl of Moray, it was restored in 1883, making it one of the best preserved of the medieval castles of Scotland. It is open daily April through October, charging adults 90p ($1.35) for admission; children pay 50p (75¢). It's closed on Thursday in April and October.

After visiting the castle, guests can drive 1½ miles to the **Doune Motor Museum,** which charges £1.50 ($2.25) for adults, 75p ($1.15) for children. The motor museum contains about 40 vintage and postvintage motor cars, including the second-oldest Rolls-Royce in the world. It is open daily from April 1 to October 31. In April and May the last admissions are at 4:30 p.m. June to August the hours are from 10 a.m. to 6 p.m., and in September and October the last admissions are again at 4:30 p.m. For more information, telephone 0786/841203.

South of Doune is the highly popular **Blair Drummond Safari Park** (tel. 0786/841456). It's open April until the end of September from 10 a.m., with last admission at 4:30 p.m. Apart from the zebras, you are likely to meet the typical safari-park cast of lions, tigers, giraffes, elephants, and Highland cattle, and there's even a Pets' Corner. Meals are offered in the Ranch Kitchen, and free picnic areas are provided. Cars are admitted for about £5 ($7.50), the one admission price allowing you to enjoy attractions such as the jungle cruise (a safari boat trip), the aquatic mammal show, the safari zoo, the wild animal reserves, giant astroslide, and adventure playground. Safari buses are available for those who don't have their own transportation. Take exit 10 off the M9 onto the A84 near Stirling.

Food and Lodging

The Woodside (tel. 07861/841237) is a pleasant stone structure standing on the A84 main Stirling–Oban road. In the heart of Perthshire, it was originally a coaching inn and dates back to the 18th century. It contains 14 well-furnished bedrooms, mostly with private baths. Singles rent for £20 ($30) and doubles go for £34 ($51), including a full breakfast. You can stay three nights for the price of two. The lounge is brightened by red plush seating and is brimful with antiques. The lounge bar has an open fire and offers a selection of more than 100 malt whiskies. You can enjoy a selection of traditional salad dishes on the bar luncheon menu with soused herring and homemade pâté salads. Grilled Aberdeen Angus steaks are also served. The dining room overlooks the garden, and you sit in high-backed carved Edwardian chairs, enjoying such specialties as venison, salmon, and fresh lobster in season. Dinner is likely to run about £10 ($15).

LINLITHGOW: In this royal burgh, a county town in West Lothian, 18 miles west of Edinburgh, Mary Queen of Scots was born. The roofless **Palace of Linlithgow,** site of her birth in 1542, can still be viewed here today, although it is but a shell of its former self. Once a favorite residence of Scottish kings, the palace was built square-shaped. In the center are the remains of a royal fountain erected by James V. The queen's suite was in the north quarter, but this was rebuilt for the homecoming of James VI in 1617. The Great Hall is on the first floor. Gen. Henry Hawley's dragoons burned the palace in 1746, destroying one of the gems in the Scottish architectural crown. It is open daily from 10 a.m. to 5 p.m. (on Sunday from 2 to 5 p.m.).

South of the palace stands the medieval kirk of **St. Michael the Archangel.**

From Linlithgow, it is but a 3½-mile drive east on the Queensferry road (A904) to the **House of the Binns** (tel. 050-683/255), the historic home of the Dalyells. The mansion, with its fine Jacobean plaster ceilings, portraits, and panoramic vistas, receives visitors Easter Week and then from May 1 to September 30—daily, except Friday, from 2 to 5:30 p.m. The parkland is open from 10 a.m. to 7 p.m. Admission is £1 ($1.50) for adults, 55p (83¢) for children.

For dining, **Champany,** on the A904, three miles northeast of Linlithgow (tel. 050-683/532), was once a farmhouse built of stone, but it has been handsomely converted into one of the finest places for dining in the area. The dining room is circular, with a steep hexagonal ceiling. Victorian mahogany furniture adds a sedate touch. They specialize in grills, and you'll find some of the best steaks in Scotland here. The owner has a butchery, and you can choose your own cut and watch it being grilled. On a recent visit I had rib loin, accompanied by chili sauce with tomatoes, a fresh, crisp salad, and to follow, pineapple shortcake made with fresh fruit. A set lunch costs £8.50 ($12.75). Dinner is à la carte, costing around £19 ($28.50) per person for a complete meal. The restaurant is open daily except Sunday from 12:30 to 2:15 p.m. and 7 to 10 p.m. Apart from the restaurant, there is the charming Country Life Bar, specializing in real ales.

HOPETOUN HOUSE: This is Scotland's greatest Adam mansion, that fine example of 18th-century architecture. It is the seat of the Marquess of Linlithgow, whose ancestors were once the governor-general of Australia and the viceroy of India. Set in the midst of beautifully landscaped grounds, laid out along the lines of Versailles, the mansion lies near the Forth Road Bridge at South Queensferry, off the A904. On a tour you're shown through splendid reception rooms filled with 18th-century tapestries, unique Cullen furniture, paintings, statuary, and other works of art. From a rooftop viewing platform, you look out over a panoramic view of the Firth of Forth. Even more enjoyable, perhaps, is to take the Nature Trail, explore the Deer Parks, investigate the Stables' Museum, or stroll through the formal gardens, all on the grounds. In the Ballroom Suite is a licensed restaurant that serves coffee, lunch, afternoon tea, and high tea. Hopetoun is open Easter weekend, then daily May to the end of September from 11 a.m. to 5:30 p.m. Admission to the house and grounds is £1.90 ($2.85) for adults and 90p ($1.35) for children under 16. For more information, telephone 031/331-2451.

NORTH BERWICK: This royal burgh, created in the 14th century, was once an important Scottish port. In East Lothian, 24 miles east from Edinburgh, it is today a holiday resort popular with the Scots and an increasing horde of foreigners. Visitors are drawn to its golf courses, beach sands, and colorful harbor life on the Firth of Forth. You can climb the rocky shoreline or enjoy the heated outdoor swimming pool in July and August.

At the tourist office (tel. 0620/2197), you can pick up information on how to take boat trips to the offshore islands, including **Bass Rock,** a breeding ground inhabited by about 10,000 gannets and one or two crusty lighthouse keepers. The volcanic island is one mile in circumference. It's possible to see the rock from the harbor. The viewing is even better at Berwick Law, a volcanic lookout point surmounted by the jawbones of a whale.

Some three miles east of the resort stand the dramatic ruins of the 14th-century diked and rose-colored **Tantallon Castle,** rising magnificently on cliffs. This was the ancient stronghold of the Douglases.

The favorite choice for accommodations in North Berwick is the **Marine Hotel,** Cromwell Road (tel. 0620/2406), one of those grand seaside resort establishments, standing in its own garden looking across the West Link golf course to the Firth of Forth. After a slumber, it has now blossomed out into a summer holiday hotel of the finest standing, ideal for families. In its modernization, all 85 of its bedrooms now contain private baths, and all have color TVs and tea- and coffee-making facilities. An airiness and freshness prevail. Rates vary according to the length of your stay. However, expect to pay from £36 ($54) in a single, £58 ($87) in a double, these terms including VAT and service. Tennis courts and a putting green are on the hotel's grounds. A resident orchestra plays for dancing on Saturday evening. The public rooms are spacious and nicely furnished. The hotel also has a heated outdoor pool in use from May to September, as well as squash courts and a sauna.

If you're seeking something less expensive, **Blenheim House** (tel. 0620/2385) is, I understand from readers' reports, a good bet, although I've never stayed there. It's tiny, offering only two singles (and these go fast), eight doubles, and a couple of family rooms. Rates are £14.50 ($21.75) in a single, from £29 ($43.50) in a double. The food—again, according to reports—is also good. Service is until 9 p.m. The hotel is very popular in summer, so reservations will be essential. In addition, Mr. and Mrs. Wight rent a garden apartment, consisting of two double bedrooms and one single room, at a rate of £160 ($240) per week.

DIRLETON: Another popular excursion from North Berwick is to the rose-tinted **Dirleton Castle,** with its surrounding garden and dovecote at Dirleton on the Edinburgh–North Berwick road, the A198. This 13th-century castle was the stronghold of the Anglo-Norman de Vaux family. It is well preserved and is open to visitors April to September from 9:30 a.m. to 7 p.m. (Sunday from 2 to 7 p.m.). October to March it closes at 4 p.m. daily. Admission is 70p ($1.05) for adults, 35p (53¢) for children. Dirleton vies for the title of "the prettiest village in Scotland."

For dining at Dirleton, the **Open Arms** (tel. Dirleton 241) will receive you in keeping with the promise of its name. This old stone hostelry has been transformed into a handsome restaurant, serving the finest food in the area. It lies off the A198, 2½ miles southwest of North Berwick. Overlooking the castle ruins, the hotel is owned by Arthur Neil, who has built up an enormous local reputation for serving Scottish dishes. Try, for example, cranachan (served with shortbread, this is a concoction of oatmeal, heavy cream, and brambles). Cold Scottish salmon is served encased in pastry, and is one of the inn's specialties. Another specialty is a stew made of fresh mussels and onions. On one recent occasion, the luncheon menu featured a first for me—smoked mackerel with gooseberry cream sauce. Before having, say, a venison casserole in red wine sauce, you might begin with a real "Taste of Scotland" specialty, lentil broth with oatmeal, about which, the Scots say, you can "stand up your spoon in it." The people who serve are quiet, informed, and skillful. A table d'hôte luncheon is offered for £8.50 ($12.75), although you can order à la carte as well, paying from £12 ($18). Hours are from 12:30 to 2:15 p.m. In the evening, between 7 and 10, a three-course set dinner is offered for £13 ($19.50), plus service.

The Open Arms will also receive you as an overnight guest. However, it's small, only eight bedrooms, each with private bath, and, joy of joys, room service available at no extra cost. A room rented for single occupancy costs £30 ($45), £42.50 ($63.75) for two persons, including a full breakfast, service, and VAT. Log fires crackle and blaze, and it must surely be a golfer's paradise, as it's surrounded by eight courses.

DUNBAR: In East Lothian, southeast of North Berwick, Dunbar, another royal burgh, is a popular seaside resort at the foot of the Lammermuir Hills. On a rock above the harbor are the remains of **Dunbar Castle,** built on the site of an earlier castle that dated from 856. Mary Queen of Scots fled there with Darnley in 1566, immediately after the murder of her secretary, Rizzio. Today the kittiwakes live where once the "Black Angus of Dunbar," the Countess of March, held off the English. The Battle of Dunbar was fought in 1650 between Cromwell's army and the Scots led by David Leslie. The Scots, fighting valiantly, lost and nearly 3000 were killed in one day.

Roxburghe Hotel, Queen's Road (tel. Dunbar 62755), is a rather old-fashioned hotel of much comfort, owned by E. H. Marcel and his sons. A large, 40-bedroom establishment, it stands in a sheltered position on the seafront, adjoining the Dunbar golf course. Bedrooms are often roomy and most comfortable, a large proportion containing private baths. B&B, depending on the plumbing, ranges from £15 ($22.50) to £26 ($39) per person, including a full breakfast. The public rooms are furnished in a homey fashion, often with open fires. The cocktail bar is modernized, and in the sea-view dining room the good food, using fresh produce, is supervised by Mr. Marcel, a well-known chef de cuisine.

The **Battleblent Hotel** (tel. Dunbar 62234) lies just outside Dunbar on the road to Edinburgh, 26 miles away. Jim and Faye Ferguson own the castle-like home set on a hill surrounded by three acres of their own land overlooking Balhaven Bay on the Firth of Forth. The bedrooms are large, high-ceilinged, and comfortable, all with divan beds, baths/showers, toilets, color TVs, and facilities for making tea and coffee. Assisted by their sons, Martin and Kevin, the Fergusons have a disco and lounge bar downstairs, and a small, charming, bright dining room on the first floor.

The bar and disco are popular with the people of Dunbar, so you can get acquainted with the local affairs of the day. Get Mr. Ferguson to show you his collection of international coins in the downstairs lounge bar. The tariff is £16.50 ($24.75) for bed and a continental breakfast, or £19.50 ($29.25) for bed and a big Scottish breakfast.

DALKEITH: This small burgh in Midlothian, seven miles southeast of Edinburgh, is the site of **Dalkeith Palace,** rebuilt and redesigned by Sir John Vanbrugh, circa 1700. Such monarchs as George IV, Victoria, and Edward VII have stayed here during visits to Edinburgh.

Visitors flock here for **Dalkeith Park,** to explore the woodland and riverside walks in and around the extensive grounds of the palace. Luring guests are natural trails and an adventure woodland play area, a tunnel walk, and an Adam bridge. The park is open daily from 11 a.m. to 6 p.m., April 2 to October 31. During November the park is open only on Saturday and Sunday from 11 a.m. to dusk. To reach the park, go seven miles south of Edinburgh on the A68. The price of admission is 60p (90¢).

On the same tour, it's easy to explore—

3. The Kingdom of Fife

North of Forth from Edinburgh, the county of Fife still likes to call itself a "kingdom." Its name, even today, suggests the romantic episodes and pageantry during the reign of the early Stuart kings. Fourteen of Scotland's 66 royal burghs lay within this shire. Many of the former royal palaces and castles, either restored or in colorful ruins, can be visited today, and I've previewed the most important ones, coming up.

As Edinburgh is so near, the temptation is to set up headquarters in one of the city's many elegant hotels or B&B houses and explore Fife from that base. However, serious golfers may want to stay at one of my recommended hotels in St. Andrews.

DUNFERMLINE: This ancient town was once the capital of Scotland. It is easily reached by ferry or by the railway crossing the Forth Bridge. Dunfermline lies five miles northwest of the Forth Bridge, a distance of 14 miles northwest of Edinburgh.

Dunfermline Abbey (tel. Dunfermline 422858) stands on a site occupied by a Christian house of worship for some time. Culdee Church dated back to the fifth and sixth centuries and was rebuilt in 1072. Traces of both buildings are visible beneath gratings in the floor of the old nave. In 1150 the existing church was replaced by a large abbey, the nave of which remains, an example of Norman architecture. Later, St. Margaret's shrine, the northwest baptismal porch, the spire on the northwest tower, and the flying buttresses were added. When Dunfermline was the capital of Scotland, 22 royal persons were interred within the abbey. Except for the sepulchers of Queen Margaret and King Robert the Bruce, no visible memorial or burial places are known. The tomb of Robert the Bruce lies beneath the pulpit. The abbey church is open daily from 9:30 a.m. to 5 p.m. April to September (from 2 to 5 p.m. on Sunday). From October to March it closes at 4 p.m.

The **Royal Palace** witnessed the birth of Kings Charles I and James I. Only the southwest wall remains of this once-gargantuan edifice. The last king to reside here was Charles II in 1651.

Andrew Carnegie, the American industrialist and philanthropist, was born here in 1835. The **Andrew Carnegie Birthplace** (tel. 0383/723638), a former weaver's cottage, lies at the junction of Priory Lane and Moodie Street and may be visited weekdays, May to August, from 11 a.m. to 1 p.m. and 2 to 5 p.m. From September, it's open from 11 a.m. to 1 p.m. and 2 to 4 p.m.; on Sunday from 2 to 5 p.m. all year.

After he retired from steelmaking and finance, Carnegie gave away $400 million for charitable purposes, mainly in Britain and America. Dunfermline received the first free library of many thousands, public baths, and **Pittencrieff Park,** rich in history and natural charm. Run by the trust that still provides extra benefits for his native town, the birthplace museum gives a glimpse of his humble origins and his benefactions.

From Dunfermline, you can take an excursion six miles west to—

Culross

This old royal burgh has been renovated by the National Trust for Scotland, and is one of the most beautiful in the country. As you walk its cobbled streets, admiring its whitewashed houses, you'll feel you're taking a stroll back into the 17th century. Many of the cottages have crow-stepped gables and red pantiled roofs.

Set in tranquil walled gardens, **Culross Palace** was built in the village between 1597 and 1611, containing a series of paintings on its wooden walls and ceilings. It has been restored and may be visited, April to September, daily from 9:30 a.m. to 7 p.m. (on Sunday from 2 to 7 p.m.). From October to March it's open daily from 9:30 a.m. to 4 p.m. (on Sunday from 2 to 4 p.m.). Admission is 40p (60¢) for adults, 20p (30¢) for children.

For food and lodging, try the **Red Lion Inn** (tel. 0383/880225), on the north side of the River Forth midway between Forth Road Bridge and the Kincardine Bridge. A local family runs this recently renovated, cozy place, charging £15 ($22.50) per person for B&B. There is a pub and a lounge where you can enjoy the above-average cooking and choose from the wide range of whiskies, including Royal Culross. The inn is on the main street, and there is ample parking in the rear. You'll like the old-world atmosphere.

FALKLAND: Now owned by Queen Elizabeth, Falkland was once the hunting retreat of the Stuart kings. This royal burgh of cobbled streets and crooked houses lies at the northern base of the hill of East Lomond, 21 miles north of Edinburgh.

Since the 12th century it has been connected with Scottish kings. Originally a castle stood on the site of today's palace, but it was replaced in the 16th century. Falkland then became a favorite seat of the Scottish court. A grief-stricken James V died here. Mary Queen of Scots used to come to Falkland for "hunting and hawking." It was also here that James Stewart, Earl of Murray, came with his men and tried to seize his cousin, James VI, son of Mary Queen of Scots. Bullet marks may be seen on the front of the towers of the gatehouse (1592). Cromwell's forces occupied Falkland in 1654.

The royal chapel and apartments are open from April 1 to September 30 weekdays from 10 a.m. to 6 p.m. (on Sunday from 2 to 6 p.m.). From October 1 to October 31, it's open only on Saturday and Sunday. The gardens, incidentally, have been laid out to the original royal plans. At

Falkland is the oldest royal tennis court in the United Kingdom. For a ticket to both the palace and gardens, adults pay £1.25 ($1.88); children, 60p (90¢).

Food and Lodging

Covenanter Hotel (tel. 03375/224) has been a popular inn since the early 18th century. With modest modernization, it offers a good standard of accommodation. It's built ruggedly of local stone, with high chimneys, wooden shutters, and a Georgian entry. The location is on a tiny plaza, opposite the church and castle. You enter a gleaming white entry hall with a circular staircase leading to the lounges and bedrooms. The dining room is strictly "old style" and for predinner drinks there is an intimate pub, the Covenanter Cocktail Bar. B&B costs £12 ($18) to £19 ($28.50) per person, including service and VAT. Pub luncheons go for £5 ($7.50), and a set evening meal is £8 ($12).

Kind Kyttock's Kitchen, Cross Wynd, stands right near the palace and welcomes you most of the year with a stone fireplace where logs burn brightly. The "kitchen" is also an art gallery, displaying local crafts and paintings. A specialty is oatcakes with cheese. The bread is always homemade, very fresh tasting, as you'll discover if you order an open sandwich. Locally grown potatoes in their jackets are served with a variety of fillings. For a tea, I'd suggest the homemade pancake with fruit and fresh cream. Even better, however, are the homemade tarts with fresh cream. Salads are good tasting, and you might try a cup of Scottish broth, served with a slice of home-baked whole-meal bread. The Kitchen now serves wine at £1 ($1.50) a glass or by the carafe at £4 ($6). Light meals cost from £5 ($7.50). The women who run the place serve from 10:30 a.m. to 5:30 p.m. Off-season, it is open only on weekends.

Back at Dunfermline you can connect with the coastal road, heading east to:

Largo

Alexander Selkirk, the original Robinson Crusoe, was born here in 1676. This Scottish sailor, son of a shoemaker and tanner, was once charged with "indecent behavior in church," but he never had to pay the penalty, whatever it was, as he was away at sea. He disappeared in the South Seas, but was discovered in 1709. He returned to Largo in 1712. A statue in the village honors this hometown boy, who was clearly the inspiration for the Daniel Defoe classic. A house Selkirk purchased for his father is still standing.

THE EAST NEUK: Within a half hour's drive of St. Andrews are some of the most beautiful and unspoiled fishing villages of eastern Scotland:

Pittenweem

If you're here in the morning, try to get caught up in the action at the fish auction held under a large shed (except Sunday). The actual time depends on the tides. Afterward you can go for a walk through the village, taking in the sturdy stone homes, some of which have been preserved by the National Trust for Scotland.

Anstruther

This is an important fishing port and a summer resort, with the **Scottish Fisheries Museum** (tel. 0333/310628) down by the harbor. Tracing the history of the fishing industry in Scotland, it charges 90p ($1.35) admission for adults, 45p (68¢) for children. The museum is open April 1 to October 31, Monday to Saturday from 10 a.m. to 6 p.m. (on Sunday from 2 to 5 p.m.). From November 1 to March 31, it may be visited every day except Tuesday, from 2 to 5 p.m. The museum also has a tea room and a marine aquarium. It has restored two large fishing boats in Anstruther Harbor. One, the 70-foot *Fifie,* is a sailing vessel. From the museum, you can walk to the tiny hamlet of Cellardyke which is really Old Anstruther, with many charming stone houses.

The **Craw's Nest Hotel,** Bankwell Road (tel. 0333/310691), was origi-nally an old Scottish manse before its conversion to a popular hotel, with beautiful views over the Firth of Forth and May Island. To the original building, many extensions were added under the direction of the owners, Mr. and Mrs. Edward Clarke, and their son-in-law, Ian Birrel. The black-and-white building is step-gabled, standing behind a high stone wall. Bedrooms are handsomely equipped and well appointed, costing from £24 ($36) per person nightly for B&B. Each of the units contains a private bath. Public areas are simply decorated and cozy, including a lounge bar as well as a bustling public bar. The food is good, and the wine is priced reasonably in the hotel's dining room.

Smuggler's Inn, High Street (tel. 0333/310506), stands in the heart of town, a warmly inviting inn that evokes memories of smuggling days around here. The original inn that stood on this spot dates back to 1300. In Queen Anne's day it was a well-known tavern. The ceilings are low, the floors uneven, and of course, the stairways are winding. Overlooking the harbor, rooms are rented for £17 ($25.50) per person if bathless, rising to £20 ($30) with bath. All rates include VAT, service, and a full breakfast. There is no table d'hôte lunch, but bar snacks are available. Bar suppers, served between 7 and 10:30 p.m., cost from £3 ($4.50). Dinner, served between 7 and 9:30 p.m., is à la carte, prices for a meal ranging between £10 ($15) and £15 ($22.50). If featured, ask for the local Pittenweem prawn. Otherwise, you are likely to have a choice of fried fish, lobsters, chicken, and local Scottish steak. All food is fresh except, as the owner, Mr. McSharry, said, the tomato soup. "We just can't catch the flavor like Heinz."

READER'S RESTAURANT SELECTION: "I recommend highly the **Cellar,** just back of the Fisheries Museum (tel. 0333/310378). The place is attractive, and the food is outstanding. Meals cost from £10 ($15)" (David L. Chalmers, Chevy Chase, Md.).

Elie

With its step-gabled houses and little harbor, this is my favorite village along the coast. Nearby is a good golf course, and there are rock-ribbed sands for bathing.

If you're passing this way, I'd suggest you drop in at the **Ship Inn** on the Toft, there to enjoy a pint of lager. In summer you can sit out in fair weather, overlooking the water. In colder months, a fireplace burns brightly. The pub has a nautical atmosphere, and doesn't do much in the way of food, but the friendly owner who runs it will prepare soup and a sandwich if you're hungry. Snacks cost from £3 ($4.50).

A paradise for golfers, the **Golf Hotel**, Elie (tel. Elie 330209), stands right on the Elie championship golf course, and there are 25 other courses within 25 miles, including St. Andrews and Carnoustie. It is a turreted gray stone building in the seaside village, where nongolfers can swim from the safe, sandy beaches and explore the countryside. It offers good comfortable bedrooms with radios and phones, many with private bathrooms. In the large lounge and cheerful bar, you can discuss your putting. The dining room offers good, wholesome food, with several "Taste of Scotland" dishes on the menu. Rates are from £15 ($22.50) per person without bath to £18 ($27) in a room with bath. Breakfast, service, and VAT are included in the price. There are reductions for stays of four nights or more. A set dinner is £7 ($10.50) to £9 ($13.50). Bar lunches are around £2 ($3), and afternoon teas go for £1.50 ($2.25). On Saturday during the season there is usually live music for dancing.

Mrs. Barbara Walker, Dalmore, The Toft (tel. Elie 330583), is the village librarian. She wisely began to accept guests so she could afford to keep her bayfront home. Since then she's won all sorts of new friends, especially among Americans, and she feels she's expanded her own horizons. "We feel less isolated—now we are a part of the world," Mrs. Walker told me. Her Tudoresque, tall and stylish 19th-century villa is on a grassy terrace, just 20 steps up from the harbor. It's still a private-seeming home, with many antiques in the sitting-breakfast room, the entry, and bedrooms. She personalizes the breakfasts, and charges £8 ($12) per person nightly. She also serves a beverage and cookies around 9 p.m. If you ask, she'll serve an evening meal for £4 ($6). If possible, it's wise to phone for a reservation and to get directions to the house.

Crail

Considered the pearl of the East Neuk of Fife, Crail is an artists' colony, and many painters have found cottages around this little harbor. Natural bathing facilities are found at Roome Bay, and there are many beaches nearby. The Balcomie Golf Course, in good condition, is one of the oldest in the world.

Croma Hotel (tel. Crail 239) is near the harbor with 14 bedrooms. It's the "home base" of famed all-American ballplayer Jack Healy and his attractive wife Rosemarie, originally from Ireland. Brooklyn-born Jack is a strapping, handsome former Pan Am executive. From Samoa he brought handicrafts and trinkets, and has hung them against the wall-size geographic maps from Pan Am. This, the Chart Room, is fully licensed, and it's Jack's domain. Rosemarie has decorated the dining room in green and white and used Windsor chairs set in front of the bay window. Many of the artists who live in this little fishing village come here for drinks and evening meals. Mr. and Mrs. Healy have hired an excellent local chef, who wisely uses farm-fresh vegetables, as well as local lobster, crab, and beef. The Healys charge £13 ($19.50) per person for B&B. They serve a table d'hôte lunch for £5 ($7.50), and an evening meal for £8.50 ($12.75).

ST. ANDREWS: On a bay of the North Sea, St. Andrews is sometimes known as the "Oxford of Scotland." Founded in 1411, the **University of St. Andrews** is the oldest in Scotland and the third oldest in Britain. At term time you can see the students in their characteristic red gowns.

The university's most interesting buildings include the tower and church of St. Salvator's College and the courtyard of St. Mary's College, dating from 1538. An ancient thorn tree, said to have been planted by Mary Queen of Scots, stands near the college's chapel. The church of St. Leonard's College is also from medieval days. The Scottish Parliament in 1645 met in the old University Library, now the Psychology Department. A new library building was opened in 1976 and contains nearly half a million books, with many rare and ancient volumes. Guided tours of the university are run twice daily during the summer months, usually in July and August.

The historic sea town in northeast Fife is also known as the home of golf in Britain. The world's leading golf club, the **Royal & Ancient** (tel. 0334/72112), was founded here in 1754. All of St. Andrew's four golf courses—the Old, the New, the Jubilee, and the Eden—are open to the public. Of course, the hallowed turf of the Old Course is the sentimental favorite. The clubhouse is not open to nonmembers, but in common with the rest of Scotland there's no problem in playing a round on the courses. It is advisable to reserve with the starter, however, or you may not get on, especially with the Old Course. If will cost around £6 ($9) for greens fees, and a caddy will charge another £5 ($7.50) or so. Of course he'll expect a tip, and deserves one if he knows the hazards and spots well. But do negotiate first, as they have a bit of a reputation—be warned. Club hire from the Pro Shop is £4 ($7.80) for an up-to-date set.

The old gray royal burgh of St. Andrew is filled with many monastic ruins and ancient houses; regrettably, they represent but a few mere skeletons of medieval St. Andrews.

The earliest part of **St. Andrews Cathedral and Priory** is the church and tower of St. Rule, although in 1160 a much larger cathedral was started and eventually consecrated in 1318. Built in both the Romanesque and Gothic styles, it was the largest church in Scotland, establishing St. Andrews as the ecclesiastical capital of the country. Today the ruins can only suggest the former beauty and importance of the cathedral. The east and west gables and a part of the south wall remain, and standing still is "the Pends," part of the old main gateway of the priory.

Within the restored refectory undercroft is a collection of early Christian and medieval monuments, as well as artifacts discovered on the cathedral site. It is open April to September daily from 9:30 a.m. to 7 p.m., on Sunday from 2 to 7 p.m. From October to March, hours are from 9:30 a.m. to 4 p.m. weekdays, from 2 to 4 p.m. on Sunday. Admission is 60p (90¢) for adults, 30p (45¢) for children.

The **Holy Trinity Church** ("the Town Kirk") is a beautifully restored medieval church, founded in 1410. John Knox preached his first sermon here. The stained glass, sacramental plate, Archbishop Sharp's tomb, and the Boyd memorial pulpit are of special interest. The original tower houses a 23-bell carillon. The 12th-century St. Regulus Tower stands in the grounds of a ruined cathedral, the largest church in Scotland before the Reformation (founded 1160, consecrated 1318). There is access to the tower of the church, which is 108 feet high.

You also can visit the ruined 13th-century castle, fortress, and residence of the bishops of St. Andrews. Notable features are a "bottle dungeon" and secret passage, a mine and countermine of 1546.

Food and Lodging

In hotels, many dedicated golfers prefer the **Old Course Golf and Country Club Hotel** (tel. 0334/74371), as it stands right in the middle of this legendary fairway—hence, the protective covering over the hotel's entrance. Fortified by finnan haddie and porridge, a real old-fashioned Scottish breakfast, you can face that diabolical stretch of greenery where nearly all of the world's golfing greats have played and the Scots have been whacking away since early in the 15th century.

The hotel is not ancient—far from it; it's bandbox modern, its balconies affording top preview seats at all tournaments. When Frank Sheridan bought it, he spent £7 million on creating saunas, Jacuzzi, massage salons, a Turkish bath, beauty therapy salons, a pool, changing and locker rooms, a pro shop, a gift shop, an indoor driving range, and completely refurbishing the whole of the existing building to create what is now one of the finest hotels in Scotland. The bedrooms are well equipped and always spotlessly maintained, renting for £60 ($90) in a single, £90 ($135) in a double. All 100 units contain private baths.

In the two restaurants, one a carvery and the other specializing in French and international cuisine, you can dine for about £15 ($22.50). Dinner is served from 7:30 to 11 p.m.

Try to pay a predinner visit to the Jigger Inn adjoining the hotel. In a former stationmaster's house, this pub evokes days of yore in sharp contrast to the modernity of the hotel.

Some golfers prefer the cozier retreat of **Rufflets Hotel,** on the B939, about a mile and a half from St. Andrews (tel. 0334/72594). Of the 21 bedrooms, all are equipped with private baths or showers, phones, radios, color TVs, tea- and coffee-making facilities, and alarm clocks, and all are well furnished in a warm, home-like way. Set in a garden of about ten acres, this is a substantial country house. The furnishings throughout are tasteful, as is the decor. The most modern bedrooms are in the new wing, although traditionalists request space in the handsome main building, and those in the know reserve well in advance, as Rufflets is very popular with the British. Singles rent from £29 ($43.50) and doubles cost from £48 ($72). The hotel is closed from mid-January to mid-February.

Even if you aren't staying here, you may want to call and reserve a table at the Rufflets Hotel Restaurant, a trio of dining rooms overlooking a well-laid-out garden. Excellent, fresh ingredients are used in the continental and British dishes, and everything I've sampled here has been accurately cooked. The service, too, is polite and friendly. A table d'hote dinner costs from £11 ($16.50), although there is also an à la carte menu. Lunch is served from 12:30 to 2 p.m. and dinner from 7 to 9 p.m. Like the hotel, the restaurant shuts down from mid-January to mid-February.

If you're seeking less formality, a favorite eating spot for years has been the **Grange Inn,** at Grange, about a mile and a half from St. Andrews on the A959 (tel. 0334/72670). In this country cottage, with its charming garden, an old-fashioned hospitality prevails. In such a homey atmosphere, tempting dishes are served, some of them continental in flavor, but all of them well cooked and pleasantly served. The fresh produce tastes home-grown. The proprietors are justly proud of the reputation they have acquired for food. Lunch is served from 12:30 to 2 p.m. and dinner from 7 to 10 p.m. Be sure to reserve, and expect to pay from £10 ($15) to £15 ($22.50) per person for a meal. The inn also has several bathless rooms to rent, going for £18 ($27) in a single, £15 ($22.50) per person in a double, tariffs including VAT, service, and a full Scottish breakfast.

Argyle House Hotel, 127 North St. (tel. 0334/73387), is a substantial renovated hotel in the center of town. While it has the rates of a simpler guest house, it offers many of the amenities of a larger hotel. There are three lounges—one for watching color TV, another where you can have a predinner drink, and the third for games such as chess, "snakes and ladders," backgammon, and bridge. Owners Tom and Joan Dowie and their courteous staff can make this an excellent stay. Their rooms have hot and cold water, good firm beds, and if you waken early you'll find each room has an electric kettle for making your own coffee. The rate per person, including VAT, for B&B is £10 ($15) to £11 ($16.50). Evening meals are offered for £5.50 ($8.25).

Number Ten, 10 Hope St. (tel. 0334/74601), is run by Ken and Maureen Featherstone, who have set reasonable rates per person for B&B—£9.75 ($14.63). With an evening meal, which I strongly recommend, it's £14.25 ($21.38) per person. They invite parents to bring their children along, as they charge half price for them, providing they share their parents' room and are under 12. Prices include VAT, and there is no service charge. Every room has hot and cold water, and some have private showers. You are invited to watch the color TV set in the lounge. There are ample shower or bath facilities. The hotel, which is of great architectural interest, is only 400 yards from the first tee on the Old Course.

4. Glasgow and the Clyde

Forty miles west of Edinburgh, Scotland's largest city stands on the banks of the River Clyde, which was the birthplace of the *Queen Mary* and *Queen Elizabeth,* plus many other ocean-going liners. Here is housed half of Scotland's population. The Firth of Clyde is one of the loveliest waterways in the world, with its long sea lochs, islands, and hills.

GLASGOW: The commercial capital of Scotland, and Britain's third-largest city, Glasgow is very ancient, making Edinburgh, for all its wealth of history, seem comparatively young. The village that became the city grew up beside a ford 20 miles from the mouth of the River Clyde, which is famous for its shipbuilding, iron and steelworks. Glasgow was a medieval ecclesiastical center and seat of learning. The ancient city is buried beneath 19th-century Glasgow, which is now undergoing vast urban renewal. Glasgow was founded by St. Kentigern, also called St. Mungo, who selected the site 1400 years ago for his church.

In 1136 a cathedral was erected over his remains; in 1451 the university was started—the second established in Scotland. Commercial prosperity began in the 17th century when its merchants set out to dominate the trade of the western seas. The Clyde was widened and deepened, and the city's expansion engulfed the smaller towns of Ardrie, Renfrew, Rutherglen, and Paisley, whose roots are deep in the Middle Ages.

The smoking industrial city of Glasgow is blighted, in parts, by the "Gorbals," some of the worst slums in Europe, which are now giving way to urban development schemes.

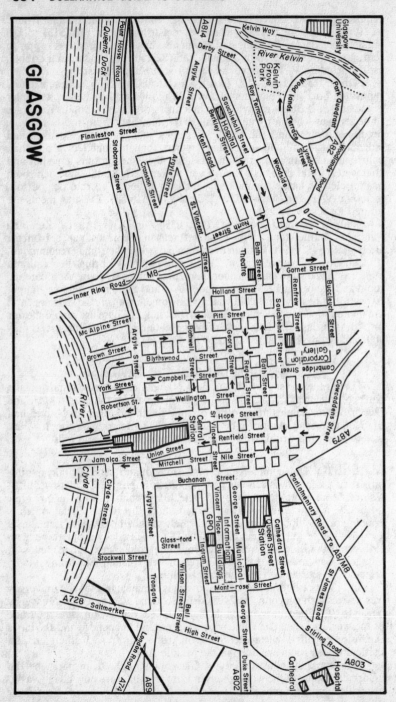

Glasgow does contain some sightseeing attractions—enough to make the city a worthy goal for many visitors. But mainly it's a good center for touring central Scotland. For example, you can sail on Loch Lomond and Lock Katrine on the same day, and the resorts along the Ayrshire coast are only an hour away by frequent train service. From Glasgow you can also explore the Burns Country, the Stirling area, Culzean Castle, and the Trossachs.

The Sights

In Glasgow, the center of the city is **George Square,** dominated by the City Chambers which Queen Victoria opened in 1888. Of the statues in the square, the most imposing is that of Sir Walter Scott on an 80-foot column. Naturally, you'll find Victoria along with her beloved Albert, plus Robert Burns. The Banqueting Hall, lavishly decorated, is open to the public on most weekdays.

The **Cathedral of St. Kentigern,** first built in 1136, was burned down in 1192 but rebuilt soon after. The Laigh Kirk, the vaulted crypt said to be the finest in Europe, remains to this day. Visit the tomb of St. Mungo in the crypt where a light always burns. The edifice is one of mainland Scotland's few complete medieval cathedrals, dating from the 12th and 13th centuries. Formerly a place of pilgrimage, 16th-century zeal purged it of all "monuments of idolatry." For the best view of the cathedral, cross the Bridge of Sighs into the necropolis, the graveyard containing almost every type of architecture in the world. The graveyard is built on a rocky hill and dominated by a statue of John Knox. It was first opened in 1832, and the first person to be buried there was a Jew—typical of the mixing of all races in this cosmopolitan city where tolerance reigns until the rival local football teams meet. The necropolis is full of monuments to Glasgow merchants, among them William Miller (1810–1872) who wrote "Wee Willie Winkie."

The **Art Gallery and Museum,** at Kelvingrove Park (tel. 334-1134), is the finest in Britain outside London. The gallery contains such a superb collection of old masters, including Dutch and French painters, that one first-time woman visitor questioned their authenticity—she could not believe her eyes. Displayed are works by Giorgione (*Adulteress Brought before Christ*), Rembrandt (*Man in Armour*), Rubens, and Bellini, incuding four galleries of British paintings from the 16th century to the present. The gallery of 19th-century French paintings includes all the famous names. Even Salvador Dali gets in on the act with his *Christ of St. John of the Cross*. Scottish painting, of course, is also well represented.

The museum has an outstanding collection of European arms and armor, displays from the ethnography collections featuring the Eskimo peoples, Africa, and Polynesia, as well as a large section devoted to natural history. There are also small, regularly changing displays from the decorative art collections of silver (especially Scottish), ceramics, glass, and jewelry. The museum and gallery are open weekdays from 10 a.m. to 5 p.m., on Sunday from 2 to 5 p.m.

Haggs Castle is a branch museum for children, with displays showing the history of the castle, temporary exhibitions, and a workshop for activities. It is open from 10 a.m. to 5 p.m. daily (from 2 to 5 p.m. on Sunday). For information, telephone 427-2725.

St. Enoch Exhibition Centre is a gallery for temporary exhibitions of contemporary film and decorative arts.

If time remains, **Provands Lordship,** 3 Castle St., is the oldest house in

Glasgow, built in 1471. Mary Queen of Scots is said to have written the notorious "Casket letters" there. The house contains 17th- and 18th-century furniture and domestic utensils. It is now in the care of Glasgow Museums and Art Galleries. The house is open daily Monday through Saturday from 10 a.m. to 5 p.m., from 2 to 5 p.m. on Sunday. Admission is free. For information, telephone 334-1134.

Glasgow also offers a number of branch museums, including the **Museum of Transport,** 25 Albert Dr. (tel. 423-8000). Once Glasgow's trams were famous. You can see seven displayed here, dating from 1894. Many Scottish-built vintage cars are also exhibited, along with railway locomotives. Recent extensions house a magnificent display of nearly 200 ship models and a reconstruction of the old Glasgow underground. Hours are weekdays from 10 a.m. to 5 p.m., on Sunday from 2 to 5 p.m. There is a self-service tea room and also a souvenir shop.

Pollok House in Pollok Park was built around 1750, with additions in 1890 to 1908 designed by Sir Robert Rowand Anderson. It houses the Stirling Maxwell Collection of Spanish and other European paintings, as well as displays of furniture, ceramics, glass, and silver, mostly 18th century. The house may be visited weekdays from 10 a.m. to 5 p.m. and on Sunday from 2 to 5 p.m. For information, telephone 632-0274.

The **Burrell Collection,** Pollok Park (tel. 649-7151), is housed in a building opened in 1983 to display the rich treasures left to Glasgow by Sir William Burrell, a wealthy Glaswegian shipowner, who amassed a vast aggregation of furniture, textiles, ceramics, stained glass, silver, art objects, and pictures, especially 19th-century French art. The collection may be visited from 10 a.m. to 5 p.m. Monday to Saturday, 2 to 5 p.m. on Sunday. It's closed on Christmas and New Year's Day. Admission is free. There's a restaurant, and you can roam through the surrounding lawns and trees of the park.

People's Palace Museum, Glasgow Green (tel. 554-1223), is a museum of Glasgow history from 1175 to the present. Collections cover early Glasgow, the rise of the tobacco trade in the 18th century, and domestic and social life in the 19th century. The museum is open weekdays from 10 a.m. to 5 p.m., on Sunday from 2 to 5 p.m.

The park in which the palace is situated, **Glasgow Green,** is the oldest public park in the city. Once a common pasture for the early town, it has witnessed much history. Seek out, in particular, Nelson's monument, the first of its kind in Britain; the Saracen Fountain, opposite the palace; and Templeton's Carpet Factory, modeled on the Doge's Palace in Venice.

The principal shopping district is **Sauchiehall Street,** Glasgow's fashion center, containing many shops and department stores where you'll often find quite good bargains, particularly in woolen goods. The major shopping area, about three blocks long, has been made into a pedestrian mall.

Although it's blighted by much industry and stark commercial areas, Glasgow contains many gardens and open spaces. Chief among these is **Bellahouston Park,** Paisley Road West (tel. 427-5454). The park is 171 acres of beauty with a sunken wall and rock gardens. Here you'll find the **Bellahouston Sports Centre** (tel. 427-5454), which is a base for a variety of indicated trails that make up runners' training courses.

Glasgow's **Botanic Gardens,** Great Western Road, covers 40 acres, an extensive collection of tropical plants and herb gardens. It too is open all year, daily, including Sunday, from 7 a.m. to dusk.

Linn Park, on Clarkston Road, is 212 acres of pine and woodland, with many lovely walks along the river. Here you'll find a nature trail, pony rides for children, an old snuff mill, and a children's zoo. The park is open all year, from 8 a.m. to dusk daily.

Greenock is an important industrial and shipbuilding town on the Clyde Estuary a few miles west of the center of Glasgow. It was the birthplace in 1736 of James Watt, inventor of the steam engine. A huge Cross of Lorraine on Lyle Hill above the town commemorates Free French sailors who died in the Battle of the Atlantic during World War II.

Upper-Bracket Hotels

Albany, Bothwell Street (tel. 248-2656), is a contemporary tower block hotel in the heart of Glasgow, rising nine stories and offering a total of 250 well-furnished rooms, all with private baths. The rate in a single is £48 ($72), rising to £62 ($93) in a twin or double, including service and VAT. Windows are double glazed against the noise, and air conditioning and color TV sets are what you'd expect in a hotel of this standing. However, in spite of its modernity, the Albany is efficiently and beautifully run in the grand tradition of Scottish hospitality. The staff extends a friendly welcome, and you don't feel part of a computer. The restaurant, Four Seasons, exudes formality, offering a well-chosen French menu, although you may prefer the Carvery, typical of such places already recommended in London. At any hour of the day, you can order drinks and sandwiches brought to your room. The public rooms are well appointed, of a first-class international standard, and there are ample bars, including a Scandinavian-style Cabin Bar if you want to sneak away to the cellar for a light snack.

The **North British Hotel,** George Square (tel. 332-6711), is an old-fashioned and handsome hotel looking out over the green trees and lawns of the square in the center of this busy, commercial city. It is close to the Queen Street Station where trains depart for the north of Scotland. There is a comfortable lounge bar for a quiet rest, or the Devil's Elbow, a bright and lively pub. The addition of a new wing means that you will almost certainly get an accommodation with private bath. Singles go for £18 ($27) to £38 ($57), and doubles or twins run from £26 ($39) to £45 ($67.50), the top price being charged midweek for rooms with bath. The dining room, open from 7 to 10:30 p.m., is enormous and discreet, and the food is standard, although quite good.

Central Hotel, Gordon Street (tel. 221-9680), still retains its Victorian aura, although it has been completely updated to meet modern demands. Owned by British Railways, the hotel stands at the Central Station where it has been welcoming train travelers for more than a century. Its rooms, some of which are cavernous, are comfortable and well appointed, and of the 211 accommodations available, at least 150 contain their own private baths. Singles range in price from £22 ($33) to £44 ($66), and doubles go from £29 ($43.50) to £50 ($75), the latter charges being levied in high season for units with bath. VAT, service, and breakfast are included.

Excelsior Hotel, Glasgow Airport (tel. 887-1212), stands at the Glasgow Airport at Abbotsinch, and is not to be confused with the international Prestwick Airport. The Excelsior is modern, and like many other concrete-and-glass buildings these days, is absolutely geared to the needs of today's traveler. All rooms, for example, contain private baths with shower, and there are radio and TV sets as well. The 24-hour room service promised by the hotel really works. I asked for sandwiches and drinks at 3 a.m. and got them promptly and cheerfully. In the rooms are coffee- and tea-making equipment for do-it-yourselfers. Singles rent for £45 ($67.50) and doubles go for £55 ($82.50), including VAT and service. There are the usual lounges and bars, plus a well-designed and pleasantly paneled dining room with quite a wide menu of international and Scottish dishes, as well as a cut-and-come-again Carvery. All meals are extra, but not expensive.

The Middle-Bracket Hotels

Tinto Firs Thistle Hotel, 470 Kilmarnock Rd. (tel. 637-2353), is a modern two-story building in a residential sector away from the city center. It's small—only 27 bedrooms, all of which have private baths. It is efficiently run, but the welcome from the staff is almost old-fashioned, it is so warm and personal. The bedrooms are well designed and compact, costing from £38 ($57) to £42 ($63) for a single, £45 ($67.50) in a double or twin, and £55 ($82.50) for a suite. The food is of a good standard and competently served.

Lorne, 923 Sauchiehall St. (tel. 334-4891), is a modern hotel, with compact, functional bedrooms that are, nevertheless, attractively decorated and most comfortable. It's best suited for a stay of only one or two nights. Of its 86 chambers, only 50 contain private baths. Singles rent for £22 ($33) to £34 ($51), going up to £32 ($48) to £42 ($63) in a double, VAT, service, and breakfast included. The hotel serves dinner till around 9:30 p.m., offering such specialties as chicken Devonshire and steak tartare, although grills are the main feature. One of the Lorne's cocktail lounges stays open until the last resident has departed, and sometimes that means all night.

Bellahouston, 517 Paisley Rd. (tel. 427-3146), a modern, three-story hotel, is especially preferred by business people, as it's convenient to the Glasgow Airport, although about a ten-minute ride from the center of the city. It is also quite near Bellahouston Park, from which it takes its name. There's plenty of parking, which makes the hotel even more alluring. Each of its 50 functional bedrooms contains a private bath and TV, renting for £32 ($48) to £44 ($66) in a single, from £40 ($60) to £50 ($75) in a double, including a full breakfast, VAT, and service. The fully licensed hotel has central heating, an elevator, TV lounge, and cocktail bar, as well as a restaurant serving a set lunch for £10 ($15). In winter there is dancing on Saturday night.

The **Crest Hotel Glasgow City,** Argyle Street, opposite the Anderson Bus Station (tel. 248-2355), is a modern block of 120 bedrooms, all with bath, standing in the heart of the city, within easy reach of the main railway stations. Somewhat stark in appearance, it offers rooms that have been equipped with many conveniences, such as auto-dial telephones, electric alarm clocks, color TVs, tea- and coffee-making facilities, and individually controlled central heating. Opened in 1974, the hotel charges £42 ($63) in a single, from £54 ($81) in a double or twin. The Crest also features a specialty restaurant, plus two bars. A set lunch costs £6.50 ($9.75), from £10 ($15) for a set dinner.

A Budget Hotel

Hazelcourt Hotel, 232 Renfrew St. (tel. 332-7737), is small and quiet, a pleasantly furnished hotel in the heart of the city, convenient to bus depots, the rail and air terminals, plus shops and theaters, even the Kelvin Hall and Art Galleries. The comfortable rooms are centrally heated, containing hot and cold running water, shaver sockets, and electric radiators. The

Hazelcourt has only eight bedrooms, none with private bath, charging from £11.50 ($17.25) in a single, from £18.50 ($27.75) in a double, these tariffs including breakfast.

Favorites for Dining

Fountain, 2 Woodside Crescent, Charing Cross (tel. 332-6396), attracts a clientele of gourmets and Glasgow's most fashionable people. It is sophisticated and formal, and a new chef is revitalizing this much respected restaurant. You can select from many popular dishes, including grills, salmon, duck, and good fresh vegetables. A set lunch costs £8.50 ($12.75), and a set dinner starts at £12 ($18), the price dependent on your main-dish choice. You can also dine à la carte, for around £21 ($31.50) to £24 ($36) per person, the price including your wine. The wine list is excellent, and the staff makes a conscious effort to find wines from different regions, as well as the traditional clarets and burgundies. For some reason, it seems out of place in Glasgow, but that's part of its charm. No lunch is served on Saturday, and the restaurant is closed all day Sunday.

Ambassador, 19 Blythswood Square (tel. 221-2034), is a cellar restaurant specializing in continental dishes, including such specialties as scampi Ambassadeur (in a white sauce served with rice), tender escalope de veau, and of course, the finest rib of roast Angus beef on the bone. The licensed restaurant features dancing to a live band, and the service by the waiters is polite and attentive. Lunch is from 12:30 to 2:30 p.m., costing £8 ($12) if you order from the set menu. A special lure of the Ambassador is its pre-theater set meal, costing the same price as the lunch. However, if you dine à la carte, anytime before 11 p.m., expect to pay about £18 ($27) per person. The restaurant closes on Sunday and bank holidays.

Poachers, Ruthven Lane (tel. 339-0932). There are those who have suggested that this is the best restaurant in Glasgow; others are more modest in their appraisals. However, Poachers is clearly a winner in both cuisine and service. Oriental umbrellas make for an inviting ambience, but the decor is restrained. The chef pays special care in the selection of his fresh produce and meat and fish. Specialties change constantly, depending on the shopping at the market. It is open daily except Sunday from noon to 2:30 p.m. and from 6:30 to (last orders) 10:30 p.m. Count on spending about £17 ($25.50) and up for a fine meal.

Ubiquitous Chip, 12 Ashton Lane, at Hillhead (tel. 334-5007), is run by Mr. Bryden and Mr. Clydesdale. It enjoys an enviable local reputation for its fine food. It doesn't dazzle you with a wide choice, but what you get is select and fresh. Often, dishes are created that show the ingenuity of the chef. In winter you can retreat to the dining room, but you'll prefer a spot in the courtyard in fair weather. The staff is most helpful and attentive, and you get some well-prepared lamb here, along with fresh fish, depending on the market that particular day. It is closed Sunday but open otherwise for lunch from noon to 2:30 p.m. and for dinner from 5:30 until the last orders go in at 10:30 p.m. Count on spending about £15.70 ($26.25) per person.

Danish Food Centre, 56 St. Vincent St. (tel. 221-0518), offers what you'd expect, the celebrated Danish cold table and those delectable open-face sandwiches known as smørrebørd. You are rarely disappointed here. The smoked fish, in particular, is fresh and most reliable—so good, in fact, I've often make an entire meal of it. Beverages and open-face sandwiches are served from 8:30 a.m. until 5 p.m., and in the evening you can order from a really filling menu between 5:30 and 10:30 p.m., when last orders are taken. Expect to pay about £10 ($15) per person for your meal. The service is friendly and efficient. Closed on bank holidays.

A Couple of Pubs

The **Horseshoe Bar and Restaurant,** 17 Drury St., is worth taking a look at even if you don't stop for a drink or a pub lunch or dinner. Drury is a narrow, short street, probably little changed for a century or so. There's lots of highly polished brass edging the door, and frosted-glass door panels. The pub has dark wood paneling and a real pub flavor. Lunches are served from noon to 2:30 p.m., and meals are available in the public bar from 5 to 7:30 p.m.

Archie's Bar, 27 Waterloo St. (tel. 221-2210), is a modern pub where you'll find some of the finest beer in Glasgow. The host, Don Tindall, offers good snacks from noon to 10 p.m., with a self-service counter displaying pies, chili, cold meats, salad, grills, moussaka, lasagne, and such desserts as Dutch apple pie with cinnamon and cheesecakes. A plate costs about £2 ($3), and beer runs from 75p ($1.13) a glass.

Living on the Outskirts

Gleddoch House Hotel, at Langbank in Renfrewshire (tel. 047-554/ 711), is the former residence of Sir James Lithgow, which was converted in 1974 to a deluxe hotel set on enormous grounds, including farmlands, riding stables, golf course, and gardens. The 20 rooms are named for birds— Golden Eagle, Mallard, Osprey—and have good bathrooms, radio, color TV, and coffee- or tea-making equipment. Fresh milk and shortbread biscuits are provided as well. A single room, including a Scottish breakfast, ranges from £38 ($57) to £60 ($90), a double going from £52 ($78) to £72 ($108). Weekend rates are cheaper.

The paneled hallway is bright with a roaring fire, and there's a cozy bar. The residents' sitting room is upstairs. Breakfast is a leisurely, help-yourself affair. Dinner is a five-course meal, costing £16.50 ($24.75), more on Saturday. Appetizers are likely to include smoked Argyll trout or pheasant consommé, followed by a small fish course, then a choice of lamb cutlets, duckling, or beef, all served with fresh vegetables and the appropriate sauces. A vast array of desserts awaits you on a central table, and you can wallow in lemon mousse, chocolate cake, and trifles.

There's also a set luncheon or à la carte grills, but the more energetic repair to the Golf Club House to mingle with sportsmen, who usually order the hot dish of the day.

Glenddoch House is a perfect place to unwind after a transatlantic flight. There are a sauna and a plunge pool, as well as horseback riding. Trout fishing is available on the 250-acre estate and, of course, golf.

To get there, drive west along the A8/M8 from Glasgow and the Erskine Bridge toward Greenock and Gourock. Turn left at the sign for Langbank on the B789, going left again under the railway bridge and then steeply up the hill to the hotel entrance on the right.

5. The Trossachs and Loch Lomond

"The Trossachs" is the collective name given that wild Highland area lying east and northeast of Loch Lomond. Both the Trossachs and Loch Lomond are said to contain Scotland's finest scenery in moor, mountain, and loch. The area has been famed in history and romance ever since Sir

Walter Scott included vivid descriptive passages in *The Lady of the Lake* and *Rob Roy*.

In Gaelic, the Trossachs means "the bristled country," an allusion to its luxuriant vegetation. The thickly wooded valley contains three lochs—Vennachar, Achray, and Katrine. The best centers for exploring are the villages of the Trossachs and the "gateways" of Callander and Aberfoyle.

Legendary Loch Lomond, the largest and most beautiful of Scottish lakes, is known for its "bonnie banks." Lying within easy reach of Glasgow, the loch is about 24 miles long. At its widest point, it stretches for five miles. At Balloch in the south the lake is a Lowland loch of gentle hills and islands. But as it moves north, the loch changes to a narrow lake of Highland character, with moody cloud formations and rugged steep hillsides.

CALLANDER: For many, this small burgh, 16 miles northwest of Stirling by road, makes the best base for exploring the Trossachs and Loch Katrine, Loch Achray, and Loch Vennachar. For years, motorists—and before them passengers traveling by bumpy coach—stopped here to rest up on the once-difficult journey between Edinburgh and Oban.

Callander stands at the entrance to the **Pass of Leny** in the shadow of the Callander Crags. The Teith and Leny Rivers meet to the west of the town. British TV viewers know of Callander as the "Tannochbrae" of the B.B.C. "Dr. Finlay's Casebook."

For miles beyond the Pass of Leny, with its beautiful falls, lies **Loch Lubnaig** ("the crooked lake"), divided into two reaches by a rock and considered fine fishing waters. Nearby is **Little Leny,** the ancestral burial ground of the Buchanans.

More falls are found at **Bracklinn, 1½** miles northeast of Callander. In a gorge above the town, Bracklinn is considered one of the most scenic of the local beauty spots. Other places of interest include the **Roman Camp,** the **Caledonian Fort,** and the **Foundations of St. Bride's Chapel.** The tourist office will give you a map pinpointing the above-recommended sights. While there, you can also get directions for one of the most interesting excursions from Callander, to **Balquhidder Church,** 13 miles to the northwest, the burial place of Rob Roy.

The leading hotel is **Roman Camp** (tel. Callander 30003), once a 17th-century hunting lodge with pink walls and small gray-roofed towers, built on the site of what was believed to have been a Roman camp. The Dukes of Perth once came to this turreted establishment, lodging here for "hunting and hawking." Entering through a gate, the modern-day traveler drives up a splendid driveway, with shaggy Highland cattle and sheep grazing on either side and well-manicured yew hedges. The setting, if you'll pardon the cliché, is like a picture postcard. Naturally, a river runs through the 20-acre estate. Inside a walled garden, vegetables and fruit—used in the hotel's kitchen—are grown. In summer flowerbeds are in full bloom.

Once inside, you are welcomed to a country house furnished in a gracious manner. The hotel contains eight bedrooms and three suites, with private baths in nine units and showers in the other two, plus hair dryers, radios, and TVs. The charge is from £35 ($52.50) for single occupancy, from £55 ($82.50) for a double. Prices include VAT and service.

The dining room, converted in the '30s from the old kitchen, has been redesigned by a local Scottish architect who lectures at the Edinburgh College of Art. The ceiling design is based on the old Scottish painted ceilings of the 16th and 17th centuries, which were a feature of Scottish houses around the time the Roman Camp hunting lodge was built. The meals—"Scottish country-house fare," as one reader described them—are served until 9 o'clock in the evening. In the afternoon, tea and homemade shortbread are available. There is a small cocktail bar, but the library, with its plasterwork and paneling, remains undisturbed. For the tradition-minded, the Roman Camp is one of the finest choices in the Trossachs. The hotel closes down in December and January.

ABERFOYLE: Looking like an Alpine village, in the heart of the Rob Roy country, this small holiday resort is the gateway to the Trossachs, near Loch Ard. A large crafts center contains a wealth of gift items related to the Highlands.

Bailie Nicol Jarvie Hotel (tel. 08772/202) is an old-fashioned hotel on the road between Loch Ard and Aberfoyle. If you're passing through the Trossachs, it makes a suitable overnight stopover. The hotel takes its name from Nicol Jarvie, the Glasgow magistrate who used to visit the outlaw, Rob Roy, at a former inn on this site. The hotel is one of character, somewhat dated in appeal.

Many of the rooms have high ceilings and are furnished in "comfy" pieces. The B&B rate is £20 ($30) per person nightly, increasing to £25 ($37.50) per person for half board. All 39 rooms contain private baths. Lovers of antiquity are drawn to Bailie Bar, a cocktail lounge hung with weaponry. The hotel serves good country meals, using farm produce when available. It's open from April to October.

THE TROSSACHS: The Duke's Road (A821) north from Aberfoyle climbs through the Achray Forest, past the **David Marshall Lodge** information center, operated by the Forestry Commission, where you can stop for snacks and a breathtaking view of the Forth Valley. The road runs to the Trossachs—the "bristly country"—between Lochs Achray and Katrine.

Loch Katrine, at the head of which Rob Roy was born, owes its fame to Sir Walter Scott who set his poem *The Lady of the Lake* there. The loch is the principal reservoir of the city of Glasgow. A small steamer, S.S. *Sir Walter Scott,* plies the waters of the loch which has submerged the Silver Strand of the romantic poet.

Sailings are from mid-May to the end of September between Trossachs Pier and Stronachlachar. Round-trip fare is about £2.50 ($3.75) for adults, £1.50 ($2.25) for children. Complete information as to the sailing schedules is available from the Strathclyde Water Department, Lower Clyde Division, 419 Balmore Rd., Glasgow, Scotland G22 6NU.

Trossachs Hotel, Trossachs (tel. 08776/232), became famous in Victoria's heyday. Built on the site of one of the old posting inns of Scotland that dated from the 18th century, it was erected by Lady Willoughby as a castle in 1826, converting to a hotel in 1852. After a long career the hotel, now mellowed with time, is still going strong, although it's rather shabby, which accounts for its low rates. Rooms come in a variety of styles with a wide range of plumbing, costing about £15 ($22.50) to £18 ($27) per person in a double for B&B. Add about £2 ($3) to those rates for single occupancy. Usually you pay another small supplement for the privilege of private bath. The Shield Hung Dining Room is draped with the plaids of the ancient clans and has a timbered ceiling, serving dinners for about £9 ($13.50). You can also take lunch in the dining room for about £7 ($10.50). The location is right in the heart of the Trossachs, two miles from Loch Katrine where you can sail on the loch steamship *Sir Walter Scott.*

On Loch Achray, lying between Lochs Vennachar and Katrine, stands the **Loch Achray Hotel,** Trossachs (tel. 08776/229), run by Mr. Penny. The hotel stands in an estate of 45 acres between Callender and Aberfoyle on the A821. From the hotel you can step directly into the Achray Forest, part of the vast Queen Elizabeth National Park, which abounds in wildlife, including roe deer. The original building of the hotel dates from Jacobean times. The Achray Burn is an overflow of Loch Katrine and runs through the hotel grounds. This hotel is a good stopping place for a two-day tour out of Edinburgh or for those on their way north. A pleasant hotel, it offers views over the loch. Rooms are basic but comfortable—only two have private baths—and the first-floor lounge is well furnished. They charge from 15 ($22.50) per person for B&B, or you can stay here on half-board terms of £20 ($30) per person nightly.

LOCH LOMOND: This largest of Scotland's lochs was the center of the ancient district of Lennox, in the possession of the branch of the Stuart family from which sprang Lord Darnley, second husband of Mary Queen of Scots and father of James VI of Scotland, who was also James I of England. The ruins of Lennox Castle are on Inchmurrin, one of the 30 islands of the loch—one having ecclesiastical ruins, one noted for its yew trees planted by King Robert the Bruce to ensure a suitable supply of wood for the bows of his archers. The loch is fed by at least ten rivers from west, east, and north. On the eastern side is Ben Lomond, rising to a height of 3192 feet.

The song "Loch Lomond" is supposed to have been composed by one of Bonnie Prince Charlie's captured followers on the eve of his execution in Carlisle Jail. The "low road" of the song is the path through the underworld that his spirit will follow to his native land after death more quickly than his friends can travel to Scotland by the ordinary high road.

The road from Dumbarton to Crianlarich runs along the western shore of the loch, but the paddle steamer *Maid of the Loch* is an interesting, if slower, way to see the "banks and braes." It sails daily during the summer from Balloch Pier which is reached by the railway. There is a large car park serving the pier.

Traveling around Loch Lomond from the east, you'll find:

ARROCHAR: At the head of the sea-arm of Loch Long, 1½ miles west of Loch Lomond, this village, easily reached by road and railway from Glasgow, is a center for climbers.

A pleasant accommodation is the **Lochside Guest House** (tel. Arrochar 467), a small place with a garden overlooking the shores of Loch Long. There, Joe and Marilyn Sullivan will welcome you to one of their singles for 10 ($15) or to a double for £18 ($27), including breakfast. For 15 ($22.50) per person they'll provide not only your room and breakfast, but also a good, hearty dinner—quite a bargain. Receiving guests year round, the Sullivans can arrange for a small-boat rental (also chartered sea fishing). Naturally, anglers flock to Lochside.

Heading west from Loch Long and Loch Lomond on the A83 toward Inveraray and Loch Fyne you'll come to:

CAIRNDOW: Barely visibly from the main highway, the A83, this little town nestles between a hill and Loch Fyne, on the loch's eastern shore. It is a peaceful haven with a view of the loch and the high mountains. **Stone Gardens,** open on Sunday from April 1 to September 30 and by arrangement otherwise, has in its pine forest the tallest tree in Great Britain.

The **Cairndow Inn** (tel. Cairndow 286) is a fully licensed, stone gem of an old stagecoach inn overlooking the loch. The building dates from before the 1745 rebellion. The stone staircase, with a low ceiling, leads to nine immaculate and cozy bedrooms on the second and third floors, one with private bath. You'll pay £11 ($16.50) per person for B&B. Bar snacks and meals are available for lunch. Dinner, for around £7.50 ($11.25), is served in the fine restaurant overlooking Loch Fyne, created from the stables left over from coaching days.

Chapter XX

NORTHEAST SCOTLAND

1. Exploring Tayside
2. Aberdeen and Royal Deeside

COVERING THE REGIONS of Tayside and Grampian, Northeast Scotland beckons the visitor with much scenic grandeur, although some come just to hit the Whisky Trail.

Three of Scotland's most important cities, Dundee, Aberdeen, and Perth, are tucked away in this corner, and the section also contains three of the country's best known salmon rivers, the Dee, the Spey, and the Tay.

The land is riddled with historic old castles, and will give you a view of Highland majesty—imposing, grand, tumultuous, including Queen Victoria's favorite view. The best known of the traditional Highland gatherings takes place at Braemar.

1. Exploring Tayside

The trouble with exploring Tayside is that you may find it so fascinating in scenery you'll never make it on to the Highlands. Carved out of the old counties of Perth and Angus, Tayside is named for its major river, the 119-mile Tay. Its tributaries and dozens of lochans and Highland streams are some of the best salmon and trout waters in Europe. One of the loveliest regions of Scotland, Tayside is filled with heatherclad Highland hills, long blue lochs under treeclad banks, and miles and miles of walking trails.

It is a region dear to the Scots, a symbol of their desire for independence, as exemplified by the Declaration of Arbroath and the ancient coronation ritual of the "Stone of Destiny" at Scone. In cities, Perth and Dundee are among the leading six centers of Scotland.

Tayside also provided the backdrop for many novels by Sir Walter Scott, including *The Fair Maid of Perth, Waverley,* and *The Abbot.*

Its golf courses are world famous, ranging from the trio of 18-hole courses at Gleneagles to the open championships links at Carnoustie.

We'll begin our trip in an offshoot southern pocket of the county at Loch Leven, then take in Perth and its environs, heading east to Dundee, and later along the fishing villages of the North Sea, cutting west again to visit Glamis Castle, finally ending our journey of exploration even farther west in the lochs and glens of the Perthshire Highlands.

LOCH LEVEN: "Those never got luck who came to Loch Leven." This proverbial saying sums up the history of the ruined **Loch Leven Castle,** on Castle Island, dating from the late 14th century. Among its more ill-fated prisoners, none was more notable than Mary Queen of Scots. Within its forbidding walls she signed her abdication on July 24, 1567. However, she effected her escape from Loch Leven on May 2, 1568. Thomas Percy, seventh Earl of Northumberland, supported her cause. For his efforts he too was imprisoned and lodged in the castle for three years until he was handed over to the English, who beheaded him at York.

Lying to the north of Dunfermline (head toward Kinross), the loch has seven islands. Loch Leven Castle, of course, is in ruins. So is the **Priory of Loch Leven,** built on the site of one of the oldest Culdee establishments in Scotland, and lying on St. Serf's, the largest of the islands in the loch.

In Kinross, 25 miles north of Edinburgh, you can make arrangements to visit Loch Leven Castle by boat, the only means of access.

For dining or lodgings, try **Nivingston House,** on the B9097, two miles south of Kinross at Cleish (tel. Cleish Hills 216), which serves some of the finest food in Tayside. The place is run by Pat and Allan Deeson, who offer seven modernized rooms for £30 ($45) in a single, £48 ($72) in a double, both with breakfast included.

However, most visitors arrive to sample the wares of the kitchen. I've never had the same meal here twice, as one must depend on the inspiration of the chef. But that's hardly a problem. Meals, costing around £10.25 ($15.38) for lunch and £14.50 ($21.75) for dinner, are concocted principally from local produce, such as fish, Scottish lamb and beef, and veal, as well as charcoal-grilled sardines. Try, if featured, his fish terrine and the king prawns, or the delectable house pâté. Desserts are luscious and velvety, your selection made from a trolley wheeled to your table. Hours are from 12:30 to 2 p.m. and from 7:30 to 9 p.m. Always reserve a table, and men should wear a jacket and tie in the evening. The hotel stands on ten acres of grounds.

Hawthorn Vale (tel. 0577/63117) has a picture-postcard look to it, a small stone house set in a garden, with a stone wall along the road, overlooking Loch Leven. It's the private home of Mrs. P. Warder, who has three double rooms, one with twin beds, that she rents reasonably at £9 ($13.50) per person for B&B. Each of her rooms is acceptably attractive and comfortable, with hot and cold running water. Along the hall is a separate toilet. In Mrs. Warder's guest lounge is a TV set and a radio at your disposal. Two of her rooms overlook her garden (and she's rightly proud of how well kept it is). Her breakfasts are filling and done as you like them. It's best to stay here on the half-board plan, sampling one of her dinners in the evening, the tariff for all this, including your room and breakfast, only £13 ($16.50) per person.

Kirklands Hotel, High Street (tel. 0577/63313), is a village hotel, all glistening white with bright shutters and a modernized interior. It has Georgian touches in its entry and the pillars in the residents' lounge. Warm colors have been used throughout; even the bedrooms carry out the autumnal theme. Each bedroom is pleasant, with hot and cold water. Patricia and Edward Wootten, the owners, charge £15 ($22.50) per person in doubles or twins and £16 ($24) for a single room for B&B. And what a breakfast—properly made porridge with Drambuie and cream, finnan haddie with an egg on top, among the other dishes. This is the place to try haggis with Drambuie for dinner. A four-course evening meal with coffee goes for around £15 ($22.50).

PERTH: From its majestic position on the Tay, the ancient city of Perth was the capital of Scotland until the middle of the 15th century. Here the Highland meets the Lowland. Sir Walter Scott immortalized the royal burgh in *The Fair Maid of Perth.* On Curfew Road you can still see the house of Catherine Glover, the fair maid herself.

The main sightseeing attraction of "the fair city" is the **Church of St. John the Baptist,** of which the original foundation, it is believed, dates from Pictish times. However, the present choir dates from 1440 and the nave from 1490. In 1559 John Knox preached his famous sermon here attacking idolatry, and it caused a wave of iconoclasm to sweep across the land. The church was restored as a World War I memorial in the late 1920s. In the church is the tombstone of James I, who was murdered by Sir Robert Graham.

Food and Lodging

Royal George, Tay Street (tel. Perth 24455), is royal because it once listed on its guest list the illustrious name of Queen Victoria. But since that monarch's day, the hotel has been considerably updated with the latest amenities. Now run by Trusthouses Forte, the Royal George opens onto views of the River Tay and the Bridge of Perth. All of its roomy, solidly furnished bedrooms contain private baths, renting for £35 ($52.50) in a single, from £50 ($75) in a double. The lounges are still large enough to evoke if not Victoria's day, then Edward's. The food is traditional Scottish fare. The Ox and Claret restaurant serves à la carte meals, costing from £10 ($15), and the Riverside Buffet features a set three-course meal for £6.50 ($9.75).

The **Station Hotel,** Leonard Street (tel. Perth 24141), also evokes Queen Victoria, although she never, to my knowledge, stayed there. However, like the Royal George, it has been considerably updated, and its bedrooms are well equipped and maintained. Some of the bathrooms, at least the one I had, would have pleased Lillie Langtry at least, as it was as large as most bedrooms in many modern hotels. The lounge is faithful to the old style, and the drinks in the bar seem generous if you order enough of them. You can even stroll in the garden, inspecting the lime trees. Singles pay from £18.50 ($27.75) to £30 ($45), doubles cost from £34 ($51) to £48 ($72). All units have color TV and bedside controls. A set lunch is offered for £6.50 ($9.75), and dinner costs the same.

For dining, I recommend **Timothy's,** 24 St. John St. (tel. Perth 26641), which has a convivial informality, and also serves the best food in this ancient city, far superior to that I've encountered in the dining rooms of the staid Victorian hotels. Ever had a Scottish smörgåsbord? If not, then try the table offered by the owners, Caroline and Athole Laing. Roast beef (served rare and tender), smoked trout, tasty sausages, crabmeat wrapped in smoked salmon, and truly homemade soups are well prepared and pleasantly served here. Perhaps you might like to try salmon caught in the River

Tay, only 50 miles away, brought here fresh each morning and served at lunch and dinner during the season. Meals are from noon to 2:30 p.m. and 7 to 10 p.m., and it's necessary to call for a reservation, as the restaurant can fill up rapidly, particularly in summer. For a complete meal, expect to pay 10 ($15) per head. Closed Sunday and Monday.

SCONE: On the River Tay, Old Scone was the ancient capital of the Picts. On a lump of granite, the "Stone of Destiny," the monarchs of the Dark Ages were enthroned. The British sovereign to this day is still crowned on the stone, but in Westminster Abbey. Edward I moved the stone there in 1296. Charles II was the last king crowned at Scone; the year: 1651.

Scone Palace (tel. 0783/52300), the seat of the Earl of Mansfield and birthplace of David Douglas of fir tree fame, was largely rebuilt in 1802, incorporating the old palace of 1580. Inside is an impressive collection of French furniture, china, ivories, and 16th-century needlework, including bed hangings executed by Mary Queen of Scots. A fine collection of rare conifers is found on the grounds in the Pinetum. Rhododendrons and azaleas grow profusely in the gardens and woodlands around the palace. To reach the palace, head north of Perth on A93. It lies two miles from the center of Perth. The site is open Easter Sunday to mid-October on weekdays from 10 a.m. to 5:30 p.m., on Sunday from 2 to 5:30 p.m. Admission is £1.80 ($2.70) for adults, £1.50 ($2.25) for children, including entrance to both the house and grounds.

GLENEAGLES: This is a famous golfing center on a moor between Strath Earn and Strath Allan, and in addition, it provides a good, although lethal in expense, base from which to explore the major attractions of Central Scotland. The center gets its name from the Gaelic Gleann-an-Eaglias, "glen of the church." The golf courses here are said to be unrivaled anywhere in the world.

CRIEFF: At the edge of the Perthshire Highlands, Crieff makes a pleasant stopover, what with its possibilities for fishing and golf. This small burgh, 18 miles from Perth, was the seat of the court of the Earls of Strathearn until 1747. In its marketplace, gallows were once used to execute Highland cattle rustlers.

You can take a "day trail" into Strathearn, the valley of the River Earn, the very center of Scotland. Highland mountains meet gentle Lowland slopes, and moorland mingles with rich green pastures. North of Crieff, the road to Aberfeldy passes through the narrow pass of the Sma' Glen, with hills rising on either side to 2000 feet. The glen is a well-known beauty spot.

In addition, you can explore a distillery, glassworks, a pottery center, and an aircraft museum.

The Sights

Glenturret Distillery Ltd. (tel. Crieff 2424) is Scotland's oldest distillery, established in 1775. On the banks of the River Turret, it is reached from Crieff by taking the A85 toward Comrie. At a point three-quarters of a mile from Crieff, turn right at the crossroads. The distillery is a quarter of a mile up the road. It is all signposted. Visitors can see the milling of malt, mashing, fermentation, distillation, and cask filling, followed by a free "wee dram" dispensed at the end of the tour. Visitors are welcome March to October, Monday to Friday from 10 a.m. to 12:30 p.m. and 1:30 to 3:45 p.m. The last morning tour is at 12:15 p.m., the last afternoon tour at 3:45 p.m. Tours leave every ten minutes. In July and August, tours are Monday to Saturday from 10 a.m. to 4 p.m. The Glenturret Heritage Centre incorporates a 100-seat audio-visual theater and an exhibition display museum. Glenturret whiskies of 8, 12, and 15 years' aging are available at the distillery shop.

Stuart Strathearn, Muthill Road (tel. Crieff 2942), is a factory welcoming visitors wanting to see how handmade crystal is produced. From June to September it is open Monday to Saturday from 9 a.m. to 5 p.m., on Sunday from noon to 5 p.m. You can see the traditional craftsman's skill in the Stuart Crystal film demonstrated by factory glassworkers. The shop on the premises has a large selection of Stuart Crystal seconds and its own engraved crystal giftware. In the grounds of the factory is a picnic area, plus a children's playground.

A. W. Buchan & Co. Ltd., also on Muthill Road (tel. Crieff 3515), is a pottery where you can see the thistle decoration applied. The thistle, national emblem of Scotland, is applied entirely by hand, as are such other blooms as heather and bluebell. The pottery shop is open from 9:30 a.m. to 5 p.m. Monday to Friday, from 10 a.m. to 5 p.m. on Saturday and Sunday. The Sunday opening is only from April to mid-December. Conducted tours of the pottery are given at 10:15 and 11 a.m. and at 1:30 and 4 p.m. Monday to Thursday. On Friday, tours are at 10:15 and 11:30 a.m. There are no conducted tours on Saturday and Sunday.

The **Strathallan Aircraft Collection** is at Strathallan Airfield, near Auchterarder (tel. Auchterarder 2545). From Auchterarder, follow the B8062 for Crieff and then the signs for the museum. From Crieff, take the A822 to Muthill and follow the signs. The collection is open daily April 1 to October 31 from 10 a.m. to 5 p.m. (later in July and August). Aircraft on display include a Lancaster bomber, a Hurricane fighter, and a Westland Lysander. There are also displays of aero engines and many other items of a nostalgic nature. Wet weather need not deter a visitor, as most exhibits are indoors. Flying weekends are held every Sunday during the summer.

Three miles south of Crieff, you can visit the gardens of **Drummond Castle,** the property of Lady Willoughby who inherited it from her late father, the Earl of Ancaster. The second Earl of Perth laid out the ten-acre gardens in 1662 along continental lines. The grounds are open daily from 2 to 6 p.m. from the last week in May until the end of August. During the first three weeks in May and in September they are open only on Wednesday and Sunday from 2 to 6 p.m. Admission is £1 ($1.50) for adults, 50p (75¢) for children.

Food and Lodging

The **Murraypark Hotel,** Connaught Terrace (tel. Crieff 3731), is small, offering ten rooms with private baths, but its standards are first rate. Each year the hotel seems to improve a bit. The bedrooms have a pleasing decor and are comfortably furnished. Singles rent for £20.50 ($30.75) for B&B, doubles going for between £35 ($52.50) and £41 ($61.50). Before dinner you can meet in one of two bars, after having strolled around the hotel, enjoying views across Strathearn. Meals are based on country-house fare, costing from £11 ($16.50) for four courses.

Gwydyr, Comrie Road (tel. Crieff 3277), now a century old, is a fine house about a five-minute walk from the center of the burgh. Ian and Christine Gillies, along with their warm and hospitable staff, welcome you to this friendly and gracious hotel. The B&B charge is about £12 ($18) per person nightly, and all of their accommodations contain hot and cold running water. The beds are comfortable, and as an added convenience you're given facilities for making tea or coffee. The dining room serves well-prepared food, using local ingredients whenever possible. They offer a selection of dishes, all reasonably priced. The dining room is open from 7 to 8 p.m. Prices range from about £7.50 ($11.25) for a set dinner. The cellar is well stocked with wines, beers, and liquors. In the residents' lounge, guests gather around a color television. Gwydyr stands on its own grounds, almost an acre of charming garden overlooking MacRosty Park. You'll have an uninterrupted view of Ben Vorlich and Glen Artney to the south.

COMRIE: An attractive little village in Strathearn, 25 miles from Perth, Comrie stands at the confluence of the Earn, Ruchill, and Lednock Rivers. The A85 runs through the village to Lochearnhead, Crianlarich, Oban, and the Hebrides in the west. It's convenient as an overnight stop for travelers crossing Scotland. Waterskiing, boating, and sailing are available on Loch Earn.

The **Royal Hotel,** Melville Square (tel. Comrie 70200), was awarded the "royal" after the visit of Her Majesty, Queen Victoria. It's not, as you might imagine, a Victorian hotel, but rather an L-shaped stone inn dating back to 1765, with white trim and six bedroom dormers. Its cocktail bar with copper-top tables, furnished and decorated in the proprietor's own Gordon tartan, is noted for its selection of malt whiskies, and on the walls are framed prints and photographs with signatures of numerous famous guests who have stayed here over the years, including that of "Monty," Lloyd George, actress Sarah Bernhardt, and Queen Victoria's faithful servant, John Brown. The dining room is equally attractive, with an open log fire and autumnal colors. The bedrooms are most comfortable, consisting of a three-room suite with one four-poster bed, plus 13 bedrooms of which 10 have private bathroom or shower, and all have telephone, TV, radio, tea- and coffee-making facilities, electric blanket, and self-selection heating control. The lounge offers color television in comfortable and well-appointed surroundings. The charge per person nightly for B&B is £18 ($27), rising to £21 ($31.50) per person with private bath. Dinner prices start at £10 ($15), although you can also choose à la carte.

DUNDEE: This royal burgh and old seaport is an industrial city, one of the largest in Scotland, lying on the north shore of the Firth of Tay. It's noted for its flax, jute, and marmalade. Spanning the Firth, the Tay Railway Bridge was opened in 1888. It's nearly two miles long, one of the longest in Europe.

In the suburbs, at **Broughty Ferry,** 3½ miles from Dundee, the **castle** dates from 1498. For a spectacular view, go to **Dundee Law,** a 572-foot hill just a mile north of the city.

Most visitors pass through Dundee en route to Glamis Castle, 12 miles north. However if you'd like to stop for the night, there is the—

Angus Thistle Hotel, 101 Market Gait (tel. 0382/26874), the best equipped hotel in the heart of town, a glass-and-concrete structure. On my most recent stopover I encountered a number of businessmen from Pakistan who export raw materials to Dundee used in making jute. Don't stay here seeking historical romance. But if you want a comfortable accommodation, you'll find all the amenities. The furnishings throughout are well maintained, and most bedrooms contain private baths. In a single the rate is £42 ($63) to £50 ($75). A double rents for £53 ($79.50) to £58 ($87), including VAT, service, and a continental breakfast, the higher prices being charged in high season. The hotel also possesses three bars and a main dining room serving a standard cuisine.

ARBROATH: Samuel Johnson wasn't that much impressed with Scotland on his jaunt there, but he did say that the view of Arbroath repaid him for some of the hardships suffered in his journey. Arbroath is a popular coastal resort with a colorful fishing harbor and rugged, red sandstone cliffs weathered into grotesque shapes. Smugglers once used the sandstone caves along the coast. Arbroath "smokies" (smoked haddock) are one of the fish delicacies along the east coast of Scotland.

The "Fairport" of Sir Walter Scott's *The Antiquary,* the royal burgh of Arbroath lies 17 miles northeast of Dundee. On its High Street are the ruins of a red sandstone abbey, once the richest in Scotland. It was founded by William the Lion in 1178, and the king was buried in its precincts in 1214. The Scottish Parliament met there in 1320 and sent the pope a famous letter asserting the independence of their country. In the abbey a historical pageant is presented every year.

Two miles to the west stands **Kellie Castle** (tel. Arbroath 72271), built in 1170 and restored in 1679. Of pink sandstone, the castle is noted for its unique courtyard and left-handed spiral stairway. Robert the Bruce once came into possession of it, during the "Black Parliament." It is open from April until October 1, daily except Tuesday, from 10:30 a.m. to 5:30 p.m., charging adults £1.75 ($2.63) for admission to both the castle and grounds; children pay half price.

Hotel Seaforth, Dundee Road (tel. Arbroath 72232), has been modernized and refurnished, a stone structure that is made inviting by the excellent food, good service, and pleasant staff. It is personally supervised by the proprietors, Jean and Alex Mann, who extend a warm welcome. The hotel, which has a southern exposure, overlooks the sea. It is some 200 yards from the beach and within minutes of the center of town. Roomy, comfortable bedrooms rent for £18 ($27) in a bathless single, £25 ($37.50) in a single with bath. A bathless double goes for £32 ($48), £35 ($52.50) for a double with a complete bath. Tariffs include VAT, service, and a full Scottish breakfast. The cuisine consists of an extensive à la carte menu specializing in a "Taste of Scotland," using mostly local fresh ingredients. A three-course set lunch goes for £5 ($7.50), and a three-course dinner for £7.50 ($11.25), coffee included.

MONTROSE: Instead of heading immediately for Glamis Castle, I suggest you continue along the coastal road from Arbroath toward Montrose. Along the way you'll pass stretches of rugged beauty. Sandstone cliffs rise sharply out of the water, and little slate-roofed cottages house the families who make their living from the often turbulent sea.

Montrose stands on a bottleneck of Montrose Basin, a broad estuary inhabited by hundreds of wild birds, notably pink-footed geese. This harbor town, with its well-known golf links, is a North Sea coastal resort for holiday makers. Its spired church and town hall date from the 18th century. David I granted Montrose its charter, and in 1352 it became one of Scotland's many royal burghs. Montrose lies 30 miles northeast of Dundee by road.

The Links Hotel (tel. 0674/72288) is modern and attractive, the successful adaptation of a grand old house with interesting stained glass. Latter-day additions have been made, and central heating has been added. The bedrooms are brightly furnished and spotlessly kept, and the service provided by the friendly, helpful staff is excellent. A single room costs £28 ($42), a twin or double going for £38 ($57), and a family room priced at £42 ($63), all tariffs including VAT, service, and a full Scottish breakfast. You can lunch on bar snacks, ranging from 75p ($1.13) to £3 ($4.50). An à la carte dinner, costing £10 ($15) on the average, is likely to include salmon from its own fisheries and Aberdeen Angus rib roast. There is entertainment every evening in the Toff's Disco and a dinner-dance every Friday in the Kingfisher Restaurant, the set meal costing £8.50 ($12.75).

Central Hotel, High Street (tel. 0674/72142), is one of the Welcome Inn chain, which gives one assurance of a well-run hostelry. It's in the heart of town, where you can get all the necessities and sleep in peace, with the prospect of a full Scottish breakfast. Rent for B&B in a single is £13.50 ($20.25); with shower, £18 ($27). Doubles without bath rent for £24 ($36); with shower, £29 ($43.50). In a twin-bedded room you'll pay £26 ($39) if it's bathless, £30 ($45) with a shower. In the Steakhouse, lunch starts at £1.50 ($2.25) for a set menu, from £3 ($4.50) if you select from the à la carte listing. You can enjoy a high tea for around £2.50 ($3.75). Dinner, à la carte, costs from £4 ($6). All prices include VAT.

KIRRIEMUIR: This town of narrow streets is the birthplace of Sir James Barrie, the "Thrums" of his novels. The Scottish dramatist and novelist, whose best loved play is *Peter Pan,* was born here in 1860, of a father who was employed as a hand-loom weaver of linen. **Barrie's Birthplace,** 9 Brechin Rd. (tel. 05752/72646), a property of the National Trust for Scotland, contains manuscripts and mementos of the writer and is open May 1 to September 30 weekdays from 10 a.m. to 12:30 p.m. and 2 to 6 p.m. (only afternoons on Sunday), charging 75p ($1.13) admission for adults, 40p (60¢) for children.

If you're in the area for lunch, the **Thrums Hotel,** Bank Street (tel. 05752/72758), suitable honors J. M. Barrie by offering some old-fashioned and traditional Scottish cookery, including Tayside salmon, Angus steaks, clootie dumpling, and of course, Peter Pan porridge. For dessert, why not try the Kirriemuir gingerbread? Lunch, served from noon to 2 p.m., is inexpensive: you'll rarely spend more than £6 ($9). Should you stay for dinner, which is served from 6:30 to 9 p.m., expect to spend around £12 ($18), especially if you order the Angus steak or Tayside salmon.

From Kirriemuir, it's a four-mile drive south to—

GLAMIS CASTLE: After Balmoral Castle, most visitors to Scotland want to see Glamis Castle at Glamis (pronounced Glaams), for its architecture, its Shakespearian link (Macbeth was Thane of Glamis at the beginning of the play), and its link with the Crown. For ten centuries it has been connected to British royalty. Her Majesty, Queen Elizabeth, the Queen Mother, was brought up here; her daughter, now Queen Elizabeth II, spent a good deal of her childhood here; and Princess Margaret, the Queen's sister, was born here, becoming the first royal princess born in Scotland in three centuries. The existing castle dates in part from the middle of the 14th century, but there are records of a castle's having been in existence in the 11th century, at which time it was one of the hunting lodges of the kings of Scotland. King Malcolm II was carried there mortally wounded in 1034 after having been attacked by his enemies while hunting in a nearby forest.

Glamis Castle has been in the possession of the Lyon family since 1372, when it formed part of the dowry of Princess Joanna, daughter of King Robert II, when she married John Lyon, secretary to the king. The castle was altered in the 16th century and restored and enlarged in the 17th, 18th, and 19th centuries. It contains some fine plaster ceilings, furniture, and paintings.

The present owner, the Queen's cousin, is the 17th Earl of Strathmore and Kinghorne. He lives at the castle with his wife and three children. He is the direct descendant of the first earl.

The castle is open to the public, who have access to the Royal Apartments and many other rooms, and also to the gardens and grounds, daily except Saturday, May 1 to October 1, from 1 to 5 p.m. (also Easter weekend). Admission to the castle and gardens is £1.70 ($2.55) for adults, 80p ($1.20) for children. If you wish to visit the grounds only, the charge is 60p (90¢) for adults. Children are admitted free.

Also in Glamis, you may want to visit the **Angus Folk Museum, Kirkwynd Cottages,** run by the National Trust for Scotland. From the former county of Angus, rich in folklore, were collected domestic utensils, agricultural implements, furniture, and clothing. The museum is open May 1 to September 30 from noon to 5 p.m., charging adults £1 ($1.50); children, 50p (75¢). Last entry is at 4:30 p.m.

DUNKELD: A cathedral town, Dunkeld lies in a thickly wooded valley of the Tay River, at the edge of the Perthshire Highlands. Once a major ecclesiastical center, it is one of the seats of ancient Scottish history. It was an important center of the Celtic church, for example.

The National Trust for Scotland has been effective in restoring many of the old houses and shops around the marketplace and cathedral that had fallen into decay.

The **Cathedral of Dunkeld** was founded in 815. David I converted the church into a cathedral in 1127. The 14th and 15th centuries witnessed subsequent additions. The cathedral was first restored in 1815, and at that time traces of the 12th-century structure clearly remained, as they do to this day.

Finally, Shakespeare fans may want to seek out the oak and sycamore in front of the destroyed **Birnam House,** a mile to the south. This was believed to be a remnant of the Birnam wood to which the Bard gave everlasting literary fame in *Macbeth*. In Shakespeare's drama, you may recall, the "woods of Birnam came to Dunsinane."

The **Dunkeld House Hotel** (tel. 03502/243) offers the quiet dignity of life in a Scottish country house. Built for the seventh Duke of Atholl in the

19th century, the house was erected on the banks of the Tay, and the surrounding grounds were planted with trees and flowering bushes, making for a park-like setting. You reach the house by going down a long drive. Guests can fish for trout and salmon on the grounds.

The house is well preserved and beautifully kept, and, as befits such a place, accommodations come in a wide range of styles, space, and furnishings. A single on the second floor, without bath, is £20 ($30) in low season, £24 ($36) in high. Doubles or twins with bath but no view cost £25 ($37.50) in low season, the price in high season for double accommodations with view being £30 ($45). All rates are per person and include VAT, service, and a full Scottish breakfast. You can have a set lunch or dinner for £9.75 ($14.63), or if you prefer, you can order à la carte. A Sunday buffet lunch for £13 ($19.50) draws locals as well as visitors to the area. The hotel is open all year.

Cardney House (tel. Butterstone 222) is an elegant 18th-century manor on a private estate outside Dunkeld, three miles from the town on the A923 Blair Gowrie road. The house is surrounded by hills, forests, and lochs, and on the grounds rare and beautiful shrubs are grown, as well as orchids, stephanotis, and lemon and orange trees. Here you are received like the guest at a private party at a country home by the charming and hospitable hosts, Lieutenant Commander (retired) and Mrs. MacGregor, who because of "crippling taxes" now receive paying guests. The gracious home is well furnished, often with antiques, and the atmosphere is one of refinement and tranquility, a style set so admirably by the proprietors.

They have available now only two singles and six doubles, charging £18 ($27) per person for B&B, £25 ($37.50) per person for half board, including VAT. Dinner, a Cordon Bleu cuisine, is served until 8 in the evening, and you definitely feel you are dining family style. The food is well prepared and beautifully served, and meals are complemented by a first-class wine cellar. Men are expected to change into lounge suits or dinner jackets; women, long or short dresses. Guests relax freely in the lounges, which are furnished with family treasures, often antiques. Surprisingly, there's an elevator. During the day, shooting and fishing expeditions can be arranged. Mistress MacGregor, as she likes to be called, is an active concert singer, and musical evenings are given regularly at Cardney.

PITLOCHRY: After leaving Edinburgh, many motorists stop here for the night before continuing on the Highland road to Inverness. However, once they discover the charms of Pitlochry, they want to linger. This popular holiday resort center is a touring headquarters for the Valley of the Tummel.

It is particularly renowned for its **Pitlochry Festival Theatre,** Scotland's "theater in the hills." Telephone 0796/2680 for information. Founded in 1951, the festival theater draws people from all over the world to its repertoire of plays, usually presented from early April until late October. Performances in the evening begin at 8 p.m., and on Wednesday and Saturday there is a matinee at 2 p.m. A new theater next to Pitlochry's dam and salmon ladder opened in 1981.

The **Pitlochry Dam** was created because a new power station was needed, but in effect the engineers created a new loch. The famous "Salmon Ladder" was built to help the struggling salmon upstream. An underwater portion of the ladder—a salmon-observation chamber—has been enclosed in glass to give fascinated sightseers a look.

Pitlochry doesn't just entertain visitors, although it would appear that way in summer. It also produces scotch whisky and tweeds.

Food and Lodging

Green Park (tel. 0796/2537) lies about half a mile from the center, at the northwest end of Pitlochry, and it's one of the best hotels in the area, the preferred choice of many. Against a backdrop of woodland, the white-painted mansion with its carved eaves enjoys a top scenic position, its lawn reaching to the shores of Loch Faskally, the only hotel so situated. Visitors who reserve well in advance get one of the half dozen or so snappy modern rooms in the garden wing, each with a private bath and all enjoying a view of the loch. Depending on where you anchor, singles range from £21.50 ($32.25) to £23.50 ($35.25), and doubles from £40 ($60) to £45 ($67.50), the higher tariffs for rooms with private baths. Guests enjoy drinks in a half-moon-shaped lounge overlooking the water. Many diners come here during festival season to enjoy not only the good food and wine, but the panoramic views. The hotel is closely supervised by Anne and Graham Brown. Dinner is served until 8 p.m., and many traditional Scottish dishes are featured. The Green Park is open from mid-March until November 1.

The **Pitlochry Hydro Hotel,** Knockard Road (tel. 0796/2666), was originally known by the English gentry who came here in summer to enjoy the fresh air of the Perthshire Highlands. Built in the Scottish baronial mansion style, the hotel has kept up with much-needed modern improvements, and now ranks with Green Park as the preferred choice of accommodations in Pitlochry. The hotel stands on large, well-manicured grounds, offering tennis and a nine-hole golf course, as well as a solarium, putting green, and croquet lawn. The merchants of Pitlochry and their wives come here on Saturday nights for dancing.

At latest count, the hotel had nearly 70 rooms, all with private baths. Ask for one of the turreted corner rooms when making a reservation. Rates in a single range from £30 ($45) to £35 ($52.50), and in a double from £45 ($67.50) to £51 ($76.50), including VAT, service, and a full Scottish breakfast. A set lunch costs £8.50 ($12.75), and a set dinner, £11 ($16.50). Cabaret is put on twice weekly in summer. The hotel is open throughout the year.

Pine Trees Hotel, Strathview Terrace (tel. 0796/2121), is a charming country house hotel built in the 1890s and situated in 14 acres of private grounds, only about a 15-minute walk to the town center and the golf course, home of the Highland Open Championships. An exceptionally well-appointed family-run hotel, Pine Trees has spacious, comfortable public rooms, an atmosphere of friendliness, warmth, and relaxation, and an enviable reputation for good food and wine. Most of the 27 bedrooms have private baths, and prices in the high season are from £22 ($33) to £25 ($37.50) per person for B&B. Bar lunches and full luncheon and dinner are offered, with fresh and smoked salmon always on the menu. Trout and salmon fishing can usually be arranged.

Moulin Inn (tel. 0796/2196) is an old Highland coaching inn converted to a comfortable hotel, lying less than a mile from the center of Pitlochry in the attractive old-world village of Moulin. It is within easy reach of the theater and all the attractions of Pitlochry. A detached annex at the Moulin contains more modern rooms. For B&B one person pays £16.50 ($25) to £18 ($27); two persons, from £34 ($51) to £39 ($58.50). The food is good.

The dining room opens onto beautiful views of the hills. In summer umbrella-shaded tables are set out for drinks, although when the wind blows, patrons prefer the modern lounge bar, where they can also order snacks and sandwiches. Tariffs include VAT. A lunch at the hotel or a packed lunch are à la carte, and dinners start at £10 ($15). The hotel is open all year.

Excursions from Pitlochry

From the town you can make excursions in almost any direction. Heading northwest for four miles, you come to the **Pass of Killiecrankie,** where "Bonnie Dundee" and his Jacobites won their victory over the armies of General Mackay fighting for King William in 1689. This is one of the scenic highlights of the area.

If time remains, try to see another attraction, **Queen's View,** where Victoria herself picnicked. The view is reached by taking the road alongside Loch Tummel. At the eastern end, Victoria looked down the length of the loch toward Schiehallion.

BLAIR ATHOLL: Eight miles to the northwest of Pitlochry stands the gleaming white **Blair Castle** (tel. 079/681355), the home of the Duke of Atholl, just off the A9. Built in Scottish baronial style and dating from 1269, it has the distinction of being the last castle in the British Isles to be besieged. Today, in more than 32 rooms open to the public, you can see impressive collections of furniture, paintings, china, lace, arms and armor, and Jacobite relics. It is open Sunday and Monday in April and during Easter week, then every day from the first of May until the second Sunday in October. Hours weekdays are from 10 a.m. to 6 p.m. and from 2 to 6 p.m. on Sunday. Last admission to the castle is 5 p.m.

For both food and lodging, you might prefer a stopover in Blair Atholl to Pitlochry. If so, I'd recommend **Atholl Arms** (tel. 0796/205). Once lords and ladies who couldn't find room at Blair Castle stayed here, and some of the grand balls of old Perthshire were held here. Now the Atholl Arms is a roadside inn, built of stone and gabled with large bays, attracting motorists en route to Inverness. A cocktail lounge has been redecorated, and there's a public bar as well, attracting the locals. The ballroom has been turned into an arched-roof restaurant, complete with a minstrels' gallery. There's also a more intimate dining room with antiques and mahogany chairs. Both rooms offer a substantial menu. The bedrooms are individually styled and well fitted, and each one I inspected had a completely different character. The B&B price is around £15 ($22.50) per person, or you can take half board for £22 ($33) per person daily.

ABERFELDY: The "Birks o' Aberfeldy" is one of the beauty spots made famous by Robert Burns. Once a Pictish center, this small town makes a fine base for touring Perthshire's glens and lochs. Loch Tay lies 6 miles to the west; Glen Lyon, 15 miles west; and Kinloch Rannoch, 18 miles northwest.

General Wade in 1733 built the bridge spanning the Tay. In the town's shops you'll find good buys in tweeds and tartans, plus other items of Highland dress.

The **Cruachan Hotel,** Kenmore Street (tel. 0887/20545), stands at the edge of town in about three acres of flowery gardens and greenery. The hotel is small and immaculately kept, renting out only three singles, six doubles, and one family room, each containing hot and cold running water. Some of the rooms contain private baths, for which the charge is an additional £3 ($4.50) per person nightly. Evening meals, and well-prepared ones at that, are served from 7 to 8 p.m. It's best to take the half-board arrangement, costing from £18.50 ($27.75) per person daily. At lunch, it's possible to order those open-face Danish sandwiches. The centrally heated, fully licensed, private hotel is closed in December, January, and February. On the grounds is a nine-hole putting green for the use of guests.

KILLIN: Just over the border from Tayside in the Central Region, Killin is a village on the Dochart at the lower end of Loch Tay. Lying 45 miles west of Perth by road, Killin is both a summer holiday resort and a winter sports center. The **Falls of Dochart** are world famous, but the town is also noted for beauty spots, and there are sights of historical interest as well.

Killin Church contains a font more than 1000 years old. Less than a quarter of a mile from the church stands an upright stone, said to mark the grave of Fingal. An island in the Dochart was the ancient burial place of the MacNab Clan.

The ruins of **Finlarig Castle** contain a beheading pit near the castle gate that was written about in Scott's *The Fair Maid of Perth*. Perched 1000 feet above the loch, the castle was the seat of "Black Duncan of the Cowl," a notoriously ruthless chieftain of the Campbell Clan.

For accommodations or meals, I recommend **Bridge of Lochay** (tel. 05672/272), which retains some of its 16th-century character, although it has seen many alterations and additions since that time. Half a mile from **Killin,** the "bridge"—an attractive, rambling, white-painted building—lies on the banks of the Lochay River, at the tip of Loch Tay. A. G. Symon, the owner, welcomes you to one of his 17 bedrooms, simply but comfortably furnished, each containing hot and cold running water. The overnight charge is £13 ($16.50) per person for a bed and a large Scottish breakfast. Guests can enjoy good drinks in the bar or sit in front of peat and log fires in the lounges. The food is plain Scottish cooking, quite good. If you stay at least three nights, you'll be quoted a half-board tariff of £25 ($37.50) per person daily. The hotel is open from April to October.

Morenish Lodge (tel. 05672/258) is now a small Highland hotel, although formerly it was the shooting lodge of an earl, lying 200 feet above Loch Tay and less than three miles from Killin (on the A827 Aberfeldy road). The hotel, run by Graeme and Maureen Naylor, offers only a dozen bedrooms, with hot and cold running water, a few with private bath, for which £2 ($3) extra is charged. Furnishings are comfortable and old-fashioned. B&B costs £12 ($18), but it's best to stay here on a half-board arrangement, costing from £20 ($30) per person nightly. Many of the public rooms face the loch, and you can enjoy a good meal with wine in the Tay View room; and in the Laird's Bar, scotch whisky, both blended and malt, is served.

Dall Lodge Hotel (tel. 05672/217) is a 19th-century stone house overlooking the River Lochay on the outskirts of Killin. The hotel specializes in serving many traditional Scottish foods, such as salmon, trout, venison, haggis, Aberdeen Angus beef, Scottish hill lamb, cloutie dumplings, and Scottish raspberry shortcake. A five-course dinner costs £7.50 ($11.25). The hotel carries a wide range of fine wines and a comprehensive choice of Scottish malt whiskies. All bedrooms have hot and cold running water and tea- and coffee-making facilities, and they offer splendid views. Some units have private baths. The price for B&B is £9.60 ($14.40) per person. All tariffs include VAT.

2. Aberdeen and Royal Deeside

Traveling north from the lochs—previewed in the section above—heading toward Royal Deeside, you can't help but go through Glen Shee and Glen Clunie, a most spectacular route which will give you your first taste of Highland scenery.

As you journey across uncrowded roads into Scotland's northeast, you'll pass heather-covered moorland and peaty lochs, wood glens and salmon-filled rivers, granite-stone villages and fishing harbors, even North Sea beach resorts.

This is the Grampian region, with such centers as Aberdeen and Braemar, and such sights as Balmoral Castle and the "Whisky Trail." Even the Queen comes here for holidays.

BRAEMAR: This little Deeside resort is the site of the **Royal Highland Gathering,** which takes place there annually, either in late August or early September. It is usually attended by Queen Elizabeth. The "royal link" dates from the 1840s when Queen Victoria first attended the games.

The capital of the Deeside Highlands, Braemar is overrun with foreign visitors, as well as the British, during the gathering. Anyone thinking of attending would be wise to make application for accommodation anywhere within 20-mile radius of Braemar not later than early April.

The gathering in Braemar is the most famous of the many Highland games. The spectacular occasion is held in the **Princess Royal and Duke of Fife Memorial Park.** Competitions include tossing the caber, throwing the hammer, sprinting, vaulting, a tug-o'-war, the long leap, Highland dancing, putting a 16-pound ball, sword dancing, relay races, and, naturally, a bagpiping contest. At a vast refreshment tent, Scottish lassies serve tea, coffee, buns, and other refreshments.

The romantic 17th-century **Braemar Castle** (tel. Braemar 213) lies half a mile northeast of Braemar on the A93. A fully furnished private residence of architectural grace, scenic charm, and historical interest, it is the seat of Capt. A. A. Farquharson of Invercauld. It can be visited from early May until the first Monday in October—daily from 10 a.m. to 6 p.m., costing adults £1 ($1.50); children under 13 pay 50p (75¢).

Food and Lodging

Invercauld Arms Hotel (tel. 03383/605) is a lovely old granite building of which the original part dates back to the 18th century. In cool weather there's a roaring log fire on the hearth, and the friendly staff offers you traditional Highland hospitality. You can go hill walking and see deer, golden eagles, and other wildlife. Fishing and, in winter, skiing are other pursuits in the nearby area. To spend a few days in this thoroughly pleasant hotel visiting fine old castles and fascinating whisky distilleries makes a perfect respite from the rush of modern city life. In the pub close by you'll meet the "ghillies" and "stalkers" and then return to the Castleview Restaurant to sample a "Taste of Scotland" with fresh Dee salmon,

Aberdeen Angus beef, venison, and grouse, together with the "dreaded haggis," on the extensive menu of local specialties. Of course, you'll find kippers and porridge with the full Scottish breakfast that is included in the room rates. A coffeeshop has been opened recently, and there is also the well-known Colonel's Bed bar, which offers entertainment on occasion. A room with private bath, single or double, goes for £25 ($37.50) per person in season. Lower rates are offered out of season, and there are half-board and "special break" terms available too.

Fife Arms Hotel, Mar Road, near the center of Braemar (tel. Braemar 644), is a pleasant stone building surrounded by gardens. It contains a comfortable lounge with two bars to slake your thirst. Many of the bedrooms have baths and cost from £20 ($30) per person nightly, based on double occupancy. That becomes quite a bargain when you realize that it also includes a full breakfast plus a good-tasting dinner that evening. The owners, Dennis and Marion Davies, run a busy, bustling place. During the day, they do bar meals and set lunches from noon to 2 p.m. There is a more ambitious menu in the evening, going for £7.50 ($11.25) and likely to include Scottish salmon or trout. However, either of these delicacies is likely to run the tab up another £3 ($4.50). Coffee is served later in the lounge.

Braemar Lodge Hotel (tel. Braemar 617) is run by the delightful Mrs. McKay, who is frightfully apologetic that on reservations in advance she must insist on a £5 ($7.50) deposit. The house is an old hunting lodge but has been converted into a friendly hotel with a small lounge for guests. The bedrooms are warm and neat, and there are adequate bathroom facilities. B&B costs £12 ($18). Dinner, served at 7 p.m. (and don't be late), costs from £8 ($12). You can sit afterward in the lounge, ordering coffee and Drambuie if you wish. Local information is willingly given, and the small staff will go out of their way to make you feel at home. Mrs. McKay spends a lot of time in the kitchen, and the food is plain and excellent, served by attractive young women. When booking, say whether you plan to be there for dinner, as that helps Mrs. McKay plan the meals. Opposite the hotel is the cottage where Robert Louis Stevenson wrote *Treasure Island*.

THE WHISKY TRAIL:
Extending north from Braemar, from Grantown and Dufftown to Elgin, are many distilleries of scotch whisky. Many are open for visits only by appointments—collect the list of telephone numbers from the local tourist office at Braemar. However, **Glenfiddich Distillery** in **Dufftown** is open Monday to Friday from 10 a.m. to 12:30 p.m. and from 2 to 4:30 p.m. Visitors are shown an audio-visual presentation about the history of scotch whisky and then shown around the distillery. The process is explained by guides dressed in tartan. At the finish of the tour, you're given a free dram of malt whisky—and the whole tour is free. For information, telephone 0340/20373).

BALLATER:
On the Dee River, with the Grampian mountains in the background, Ballater is a holiday resort center where visitors flock to attend one of Scotland's most popular sightseeing attractions, Balmoral Castle (see below).

The town still centers around its **Station Square,** where the royal family used to be photographed as they arrived to spend holidays. The railway has since been closed.

From Ballater you can drive west to view the magnificent scenery of **Glen Muick** and **Lochnagar,** where you'll see herds of deer.

Food and Lodging

Tullich Lodge, on the A93, 1½ miles east of Ballater (tel. 0338/55406), is a turreted country house built in the Scottish baronial style, standing in five acres of its own gardens and woods above Royal Deeside and Ballater. The attractive hotel is tastefully decorated and furnished, often with antiques, its brass fittings and wood paneling providing the traditional touches. Your pleasant hosts, Hector Macdonald and Neil Bannister, offer only ten bedrooms, but they're of generous size and are beautifully furnished. At least eight contain private baths, the rest showers. Half-board rates are £45 ($67.50) per person in a single or double. The lodge closes from December through March.

Its dining room, commanding panoramic views of the "royal valley," serves some of the finest food along Royal Deeside. One of the chef's specialties is casseroles, although he does all the standard dishes with above-average flair, including locally caught trout and salmon, game and especially venison in season, as well as crab and lobster. The homemade soups are particularly enjoyable. A table d'hôte dinner, served from 7:30 to 9 p.m., goes for about £17 ($25.50). A bar luncheon is at 1 p.m. with no fried foods. It's essential to make a reservation. In an amusing bar, with a model railway, you can order from a good selection of malt whiskies. For guests to get the most out of the surrounding countryside, as well as this special hotel, I'd recommend whenever possible that they stay a minimum of two nights. In this way, they won't have to live out of suitcases all the time and will have a chance to settle in.

The **Invercauld Arms** (tel. 0338/55417) is a whitewashed Victorian hotel right in the heart of Royal Deeside. Queen Victoria used to visit it when at court at Balmoral. Mr. and Mrs. James Anderson, the proprietors, will welcome you most kindly, offering good food, comfortable bedrooms, and solid service. The atmosphere is informal, and visitors quickly get to know each other. All the bedrooms contain private baths. In some of the more traditionally furnished units the antiques were made by Victoria's cabinet-maker. Singles cost from £19 ($28.50) to £26 ($39), depending on the season. Twins and doubles go for £33 ($49.50) to £45 ($67.50), all tariffs including VAT, service, and a full Scottish breakfast.

The fully licensed hotel was built as a coaching inn in the early 1800s, and offers a wide range of pursuits such as game fishing, tennis, bowling, and golf. The hotel's spacious restaurant is especially fine, not only opening onto beautiful views, but serving a country-house fare of standard dishes that are well prepared, using fresh ingredients. The roasts are especially good. Lunch is served from noon to 2:30 p.m., dinner from 7:30 to 9:30 p.m. Expect to pay about £10 ($15) for dinner. Lunch served in the bar is from a cold buffet table, with prices starting at £2.50 ($3.75). The hotel is open all year.

Balmoral Castle

"This dear paradise" is how Queen Victoria described this castle, rebuilt in the Scottish baronial style by her beloved Albert. It was completed in 1855. Today Balmoral, eight miles west of Ballater, is still a private residence of the British sovereign. Albert, the prince consort, acquired the property in 1847, and the royal family first arrived there in 1848. As the little castle left by the Farquharsons proved too small, the present castle was rebuilt. Its principal feature is a 100-foot tower. On the grounds are many memorials to the royal family. Only the grounds, incidentally, can be visited—daily, except Sunday in May, June, and July from 10 a.m. to 5 p.m. However, no visits are allowed if the royal family is in residence. Admission is £1.25 ($1.88) for adults, 60p (90¢) for children.

BANCHORY: On lower Deeside, this pleasant resort is rich in woodland and river scenery. From this base, you can take excursions to two of the most popular castles in the Grampian region.

The Sights

Crathes Castle and Gardens, (tel. 033-044/525) two miles east of Banchory, is a fine early Jacobean building which is celebrated for its gardens with sculptured yews dating from 1702. Just north of the A93 on the north bank of the Dee, this baronial castle contains remarkable painted ceilings. Gardens and grounds are open all year from 9:30 a.m. to sunset. The castle is open at Easter, then May 1 until September 30 Monday through Saturday from 11 a.m. to 6 p.m. (on Sunday from 2 to 6 p.m.). Admission to the grounds is as follows: cars, 70p ($1.05); and minibuses, £1.55 ($2.33). To visit just the castle, adults pay £1 ($1.50); children, 50p (75¢). If you desire to see only the gardens, the charge is 50p (75¢) for adults, 25p (38¢) for children. A combined ticket costs adults £1.55 ($2.33); children, 80p ($1.20). There is a licensed restaurant serving light meals during the hours the castle is open.

Structurally unchanged since its completion in 1626, Craigievar Castle (tel. 033-983/635) is an example of Scottish baronial architecture at its greatest height. Original molded plaster ceilings are to be seen in most rooms. The castle has been continually inhabited by the descendants of the builder, William Forbes, and is now preserved by the National Trust for Scotland. It is open daily except Friday from May to September, from 2 to 7 p.m., charging an admission of £1.20 ($1.80) for adults, 60p (90¢) for children. The grounds are open all year from 9:30 a.m. to dusk, and admission is by donation.

A mile from the castle is Macbeth's Cairn, where, according to legend, Macduff put an end to Macbeth.

Food and Lodging

Raemoir House (tel. 03302/2846) is an 18th-century manor standing on 3500 acres of grounds with such sporting attractions as shooting, fishing, and riding. It is a journey into nostalgia, with its ballroom, antiques, and fine tapestries, and log fires burning in the colder months. The rooms are handsomely decorated, most of them quite large, and at least 18 of the 24 bedchambers contain private baths. What is so lovely about Scotland is its curious mixtures—in this case, an 18th-century manor house with its own helipad. This place is run by one of the most charming women you could find anywhere, Mrs. Kit Sabin, who has been here since 1942. She is ably assisted by Miss Molly Grant, her manager of 30 years. Meals are served in an attractive Georgian dining room, featuring a standard repertoire of familiar dishes, rather well done. Service is informal and prompt. Depending on the plumbing, the B&B rate ranges from £29 ($43.50) per person in a bathless room to £33 ($49.50) with bath. Dinner, bed, and breakfast ranges from £42 ($63) to £45 ($67.50). All prices include VAT and morning tea or coffee.

The hotel is run just like a private house—no keys to bedroom doors, but you can bolt yourself in for privacy. The office is an old desk in the cubbyhole under the splendid staircase. The adjoining Ha' Hoose with rentable rooms was once used by Mary Queen of Scots. The place is unique, its special character not recommended for Hilton/convenience food/21st-century fans.

Tor-Na-Coille, Inchmarlo Road (tel. 03302/2242), is a country house hotel—really a Victorian mansion—standing on its own wooded grounds of about six acres. Public rooms are suitably spacious, most comfortable, and the whisky always tastes better in the modern bar. If you're on your way to see Balmoral Castle or to attend the Highland gathering at Braemar, you will be able to relax here, enjoying the gracious hospitality of Mr. Graham. The bedrooms, many quite large, are restful; 60% of them have private baths, and all of them have color TV, radio, phone, and coffee-making equipment. Singles cost from £28 ($42) with private baths and doubles begin at £24 ($36) per person with private bath, including a full breakfast and VAT. A half-board rate applies for stays of more than three nights. The hotel is interesting architecturally, and the room you may be assigned could have much character.

Lunches are light meals in the bar, including smoked venison sausage blended with rum and red wine. Sunday lunch is a grander affair, when the main dishes include roast beef, turkey, and leg of pork. Food at night is by candlelight, and here might be your chance to try real Scottish salmon (the salmon leap at the Falls of Feugh nearby). Dinner is likely to feature the chef's special pheasant. The hotel has a high reputation for its food. Bar lunches and suppers are offered, as well as a table d'hôte dinner from £11 ($16.50). If you order an à la carte dinner, expect to pay from £15 ($22.50).

Banchory Lodge Hotel (tel. 03302/2625), built in 1738, was once the home of a well-known Deeside family. But when Maggie and Dugald Jaffray took it over, it was almost derelict. With dedication and hard work they transformed it into the pleasant country house it is today, with much Georgian charm. On its own grounds, on the banks of the Dee, where it is joined by the Water of the Feugh, the lodge is open all year, accommodating guests in some 27 bedrooms, many of which overlook the river; 25 have private baths. The B&B rate is about £25 ($37.50) per person, increasing to £30 ($45) for half board. In the dining room, overlooking the river, furnishings and decor are in period style. Maggie Jaffray supervises the kitchen, where specialties include fresh Dee salmon and Aberdeen Angus roast beef. Guests can fish from the lawn or in one of the hotel's boats by arrangement.

ABERDEEN: The harbor in this seaport in the northeast of Scotland is one of the largest fishing ports in the country, literally infested with kipper and deep-sea trawlers. The **Fish Market** is well worth a visit, as it's the liveliest in Britain.

Bordered by fine sandy beaches (delightful if you're a polar bear), Scotland's third city is often called "the granite city," as its buildings are constructed largely of granite, in pink or gray, hewn from the Rubislaw quarries.

Aberdeen has become the capital of the oil workers pouring into northeast Scotland to help harvest the riches from six North Sea oilfields. The city lies on the banks of the salmon- and trout-filled Don and Dee Rivers. Spanning the Don is the world-famous **Brig o' Balgownie,** a steep Gothic arch, begun in 1285.

In Castlegate is the **Mercat Cross,** a hexagonally shaped structure, built in 1686, and considered the handsomest of the old crosses in Scotland.

The **University of Aberdeen** (tel. 0224/40241) is a fusion of two separate colleges. King's College, the older, was founded under a Papal Bull issued in 1495. It contains the oldest school of medicine in Great Britain. The college's chapel is topped by a closed (imperial) crown that was erected about 1505 but was blown down in a storm and quickly replaced in 1633 by an exact copy. Marischal College, founded in 1593, is recognized as one of the finest granite buildings in the world. The two colleges were rival institutions until a royal ordinance enacted in 1860 united them both under the title of the present university.

The university is in the Old Aberdeen, as is the **Cathedral of St. Machar,** founded in 1131, although the present structure dates from the 15th century. Its splendid heraldic ceiling contains three rows of shields representing the kings and princes of Europe along with the Scottish ecclesiastical and aristocratic hierarchy. The modern stained-glass windows are magnificent, the work of Douglas Strachan.

Provost Skene's House, 45 Guestrow, is named for a rich merchant who was lord provost of Aberdeen during 1676–1685. Off Broad Street, it is now a museum with period rooms and artifacts of domestic life. Admission is free, and it can be visited Monday to Saturday from 10 a.m. to 5 p.m. For more information, telephone 0224/641086. There's parking available.

Food and Lodging

Because of the increasing numbers of tourist and business visitors to the Granite City, now established as Europe's Offshore Oil Capital, hotels, which are expensive, are likely to be heavily booked at any time of year. If you need help, it's best to go to the **Information Centre,** St. Nicholas House, Broad Street (tel. 0224/632727), which is open seven days a week during the summer. A member of the staff there will assist with hotel or guest house reservations.

For those willing to reserve in advance, here are my favorite selections:

Holiday Inn, Oldmeldrum Road, Bucksburn (tel. 0224/713911), is especially popular with business people from the oil-related concerns flocking to Aberdeen. Even though Laird's Bar is done up in a Highland baronial flavor, you're likely to hear customers ordering Jack Daniel's and Old Grand-Dad as much as malt scotch. The 99-unit Holiday Inn is a fresh package, all accommodations containing fully tiled private baths. In decor the tone is traditional rather than modern. Singles rent for £36 ($54) to £55 ($82.50), and doubles range from £52 ($78) to £63 ($94.50). The Mariner Restaurant, serving until 10:30 p.m., evokes nostalgia for the days of the Aberdeen clipper ships.

Prince Regent Hotel, Waverly Place (tel. 0224/55071), is a small, attractive, and well-kept hotel run by Mr. and Mrs. Ashdown. Their little oasis lies only yards from the West End of Union Street. The public rooms have a Regency decor, and the bedrooms, although simply furnished, have all the necessities, and all of them come with private baths. Singles begin at £35 ($52.50), and doubles or twins rent for about £42 ($63), including VAT, service, and a full Scottish breakfast. The cookery is quite fine and is handsomely presented, the hotel offering both table d'hôte and à la carte menus. A table d'hôte lunch goes for £5 ($7.50), the set dinner price going up to £10 ($15). Guests can enjoy apéritifs in the Regency Buck or drinks in the Jug.

Malacca Hotel, 349 Great Western Rd. (tel. 0224/28901), is one of the best of the small hotels of Aberdeen. Actually, it offers only eight bedrooms, seven of which contain private baths and showers. Singles rent for £30 ($45) nightly, doubles going for £40 ($60), including VAT, service, and a full Scottish breakfast. The granite town-house hotel, with its surrounding stone wall and trees, is much better known for its restaurant, an attractively decorated dining room with bentwood caned chairs, a sophisticated setting for the international dishes served here, everything from bouillabaisse to chicken jubilee to duck in orange sauce. You can dine here à la carte for about £18 ($27) per person. Lunch is served until 2 p.m. and dinner until 10:30 p.m.

On the outskirts, if you're heading for Royal Deeside, I'd suggest a dining stopover at **Marycutler House** (tel. 0224/732124), about six miles from Aberdeen on the South Deeside road. World traveler Mrs. Martin purchased this 17th-century house beside the river, imaginatively decorating the dining rooms with treasures brought back from her trips. The baronial bar has an eclectic collection—an African mask, an Early English settle, a Victorian sofa, and Adam bar. In addition to the bar are two handsome dining rooms as well as one with a glass roof, evoking memories of Marrakesh. The menu is likely to change by the time of your visit, but it's international in scope—tagliatelle Florentine, stilton soup, quail with grapes and almonds, port venison, or Greek salad, perhaps followed by peaches in wine or, a favorite, brown bread ice cream. Expect to spend from £15 ($22.50) and up for a complete à la carte meal. Lunch is until 2 p.m., and dinner (make a reservation) is from 7:30 to 9:30 p.m. If you're stopping in for lunch, you can have a light pub meal in front of the fireplace. Closed Sunday. The house is likely to be closed for dinner from January until April. Mrs. Martin rents a few rooms, all with private baths, at £24 ($36) per person for B&B.

Excursions in "Castle Country"

Aberdeen is the center of "castle country," as 40 inhabited castles lie within a 40-mile radius. Two of the most popular castle excursions are previewed below. For others, refer above to Banchory.

Drum Castle: The handsome mansion (tel. 03308/204) was added in 1619, but the great square tower dates from the late 13th century, making it one of the three oldest tower houses in the country. Historic Drum lies ten miles west of Aberdeen, off the A93. The castle is open May to September daily from 2 to 6 p.m., charging adults £1.05 ($1.58); children, 55p (83¢). The grounds are open all year from 9:30 a.m. to dusk, and admission is by donation.

Muchalls Castle: Built by the Burnetts of Leys in 1619, this castle is now lived in by Mr. and Mrs. Maurice A. Simpson. It is noted for its elaborate plasterwork ceilings and fireplaces. The castle lies five miles north of Stonehaven, nine miles south of Aberdeen. It is open May to September on Tuesday and Sunday from 3 to 5 p.m., charging adults 40p (60¢); children, 15p (23¢).

Chapter XXI

HIGHLANDS AND ISLANDS

**1. Aviemore, Speyside, and Elgin
2. Inverness and Loch Ness
3. Fort William and Lochaber
4. Kyle of Lochalsh and Skye
5. Oban and District
6. The Inner Hebrides
7. Kintyre, Arran, and Islay**

FROM ITS ROMANTIC GLENS and its rugged mountainous landscapes, the Highlands suggest a timeless antiquity. Off the coast, mysterious islands, such as Skye with its jagged peaks, rise from the sea, inviting further exploration. These lands are sparsely inhabited even today, and much wildlife, such as the red deer, still flourishes.

As the unofficial capital of the Highlands, Inverness is the terminus of the rail journey from London, a distance of some 570 miles. As such, many visitors use it as a base for Highland adventures.

From Inverness, you can journey along Loch Ness (especially if you're a monster watcher) to Fort William, dominated by Ben Nevis, the highest mountain in Britain. Oban is the main resort on Scotland's West Highland coastline. It is also one of the major ports for journeying to the Hebridean islands.

If at all possible, try to explore some of these islands, the largest of which is Lewis, where the Standing Stones of Callanish, a prehistoric monument, evokes Stonehenge. Numerous inter-island air services allow you to go "island hopping."

Many pleasure trips are possible to the islands in the Firth of Clyde, Scotland's greatest yachting center. Dominated by the peak of Goat Fell, Arran is the largest of these Clyde islands.

1. Aviemore, Speyside, and Elgin

Aviemore is the winter sports capital of Britain, but it also enjoys mass popularity in summer. Aviemore Centre, previewed below, is Scotland's most modern holiday resort, an all-year, all-weather center, endowed with a multitude of outdoor pursuits, such as golfing, angling, skiing, or ice skating.

Those seeking a more traditional Scottish ambience will gravitate to one of the many Speyside villages, each with its own attractions and atmosphere. Ranking next to Aviemore, Grantown-on-Spey is another major center.

The Spey is the fastest flowing river in the British Isles, famed not only for its scenery but also for its salmon and ski slopes.

Finally, on your way to Inverness, you might care to stop off at the old cathedral city of Elgin.

Our first stop up the Spey follows.

NEWTONMORE: This Highland resort on Speyside is a good center for the Grampian and Monadhliath Mountains, and it offers excellent fishing, golf, pony trekking, and hill walking. Most motorists zip through it on the way to Aviemore, but sightseers may want to stop off and visit the **Clan MacPherson House & Museum** (tel. Newtonmore 332), at the south end of the village. Displayed are clan relics and memorials, including the Black Chanter and Green Banner as well as a "charmed sword," and the broken fiddle of the freebooter James MacPherson—a Scottish Robin Hood. Sentenced to death in 1700, he is said to have played the dirge "MacPherson's Rant" on his fiddle as he stood on the gallows at Banff. He then offered the instrument to anyone who would think well of him. There were no takers, so he smashed it. The museum is open from May to September on weekdays from 10 a.m. to noon and from 2 to 6 p.m.

A track from the village climbs past the Calder River to Loch Dubh and the massive Carn Ban (3087 feet), where eagles fly. Castle Cluny, ancient seat of the MacPherson chiefs, is six miles west of Newtonmore.

A good place to stay is the **Pines Hotel,** Station Road (tel. Newtonmore 271), on a hill overlooking the Spey Valley, with the Cairngorms, the Grampians, and the Monadhliath Mountains all in view. The resident proprietors, John and Fran Raw, offer seven rooms in their attractive stone house, all with heaters and hot and cold running water. They charge £10.50 ($15.75) to £14.50 ($21.75) for B&B in low season, £11.50 ($17.25) to £15.50 ($23.25) in high season. The cuisine here is excellent. Such choices as trout, salmon, venison, beef, and lamb are offered, all locally supplied. All the food is home-cooked, and a substantial wine list is offered. The hotel has a pleasant residents' lounge where guests enjoy malt whisky and fine liqueurs. As its name implies, the hotel is in the middle of a pine grove.

KINGUSSIE: Your next stop along the Spey might be at this little summer holiday resort and winter ski center (it's pronounced King-youcie), the so-called capital of Badenoch, a district known as "the drowned land" because the Spey can flood the valley when the snows of a severe winter melt in the spring. There you can visit the six-acre **Highland Folk Museum,** on Duke Street, just off High Street, with its comprehensive collection of artifacts, including weaponry, bagpipes, and fiddles, illustrating more than two centuries of Highland customs, plus the work of craftspeople. Naturally, there are tartans. A furnished cottage with a mill, a central Highlands house with cruck-frame construction and turf walls, and a farming shed that has been expanded to become a farming museum stand on the grounds. It is open all year from 10 a.m. to 3 p.m. but stays open as late as 6 p.m. from April to October. The admission is £1 ($1.50) for adults, 45p (68¢) for children.

If you'd like to stop here instead of at Aviemore, I'd recommend the following establishments:

Scott's Hotel (tel. 05402/351) is more personal than the leading hotel at Kingussie, the Duke of Gordon. Scott's is really more of a B&B house, under the personal supervision of its resident proprietors, Mr. and Mrs. Patrick John Cook, who are most hospitable. Rooms are comfortable and well appointed. One reader wrote, "Our stay here was the happiest in Scotland." The hotel has mostly double rooms, charging £8.50 ($12.75) per person for an overnight stay, this tariff including a full Scottish breakfast, service, and VAT. The hotel has a residential license, and its cuisine is home cooking, family style. Dinners cost £6 ($9) to £8.50 ($12.75). In winter this hotel is very busy housing skiers.

If you're not dining at a hotel, try the **Wood'n Spoon,** 3 High St. (tel. 05402/488), on the A9, run by Mr. and Mrs. David Russell. It is considered by some the only "real pub" in the Highlands, and it serves excellent home-cooked food. For lunch (11:30 a.m. to 2:30 p.m.) there is a cold display and numerous hot dishes made to order. In the evening from 5:30 to 9:30 p.m. (Highland dining is early), a more extensive selection is available. Dishes offered are, as much as possible, made from local produce including fish from the Spey and venison from the nearby glens. The Russells also offer a large selection of homemade jams and chutneys for sale. Try their stovie potatoes (that is, diced potatoes with onions and minced beef), or the venison casserole. Appetizers include smoked fish pâté, and there's always a soup of the day made from a real stockpot so it's always different. Desserts feature a Scottish trifle. A meal ranges in price from £5 ($7.50) to £8 ($12).

AVIEMORE CENTRE: This year-round holiday complex on the Spey was opened in 1966 in the heart of the Highlands, at the foot of the historic rock of Craigellachie. This rock was the rallying place for Clan Grant.

In winter, ski runs are available for both beginners and experts (four chair lifts and seven T-bar tows). Après-ski activities include swimming in a heated indoor pool 82 feet long, folk singing, table tennis, or just relaxing and drinking in one of the many bars in the complex.

The ice rink is the second-largest indoor ice rink in Britain, with seven curling lanes and ice skating on a separate 4000-square-foot pad. At night younger people are attracted to the discos, although others seek out one of the Scottish nights, country dancing, supper dances, or dancing in the large Osprey Ballroom with a sprung maple floor.

In summer, sailing, canoeing, pony trekking, hill walking, and mountain climbing, as well as golf and fishing, are just some of the many activities. The **Speyside Theatre,** seating 720, changes its film programs every day, and often is host to live shows and concerts. The center's shopping precincts cover a wide range of services, ranging from banking to hairdressing to car-rental offices.

Children always like to visit **Santa Claus Land,** set on a six-acre site, with a log cabin, toy factory, dollhouse, and a permanently frozen "North Pole" in peppermint colors. It also includes pony rides, a cowboy trail, veteran cars, and a gingerbread house. Since it's Scotland, there is also Santa Shortbread.

Adjacent to Santa Claus Land is the **Highland Craft Centre,** where wood-carvers, potters, jewelers, weavers, blacksmiths, and engravers maintain the ancient skills and crafts of the Highlands. Their products are offered for sale.

Later, you can visit **Alan Keegan's Craft Shop,** where you can see 135 different kinds of scotch whisky from 65 different distilleries. He doesn't sell drinks. Collecting scotch whisky is his hobby. He's good at it too, as his collection is considered the largest in Scotland. The most expensive is a Springbank whisky. Only one cask was ever produced.

Food and Lodging

The following hotels in the complex are recommended:

Strathspey Thistle Hotel (tel. 0479/810681) is an ideal family holiday hotel offering excellent facilities for a comfortable, relaxed stay in a friendly Highland setting. The 88 bedrooms all have private baths, color TVs, radios, phones, tea- and coffee-making facilities, baby-listening service, and superb views of the surrounding hills and mountains. Some rooms feature bunk beds for children, for whom special rates are quoted. The tariff, including a full Scottish breakfast, dinner, and VAT, is from £40 ($60) per person. There is live entertainment in the lounge most nights, and the hotel offers two bars, sauna baths, sunbeds, and a licensed disco for your enjoyment. Residents are also entitled to unlimited free use of Aviemore Centre indoor swimming pool and skating rink, only 200 yards from the hotel, and there is a supervised playroom for children under 8 years of age.

Post House (tel. 0479/810771) is one of the increasingly popular post houses belonging to Trusthouses Forte. (At a post house, you don't get room service, but every other amenity seems to be there.) The hotel is spread informally over a hillside, which often causes a split-level effect. The style here is most casual and informal, a holiday atmosphere. The spacious layout is balanced effectively by a warm color scheme. Picture windows and terraces open onto country views. The staff is most helpful and friendly. The bedrooms are all equipped with private baths, and some family rooms are available. Singles rent for £35 ($52.50), the tariff increasing to £44 ($66) in a double, including VAT and service.

You can drink in the Illicit Still Bar, with its shiny copper-topped tables and a copper whisky still, or else in the White Lady Bar, named after one of the Cairngorm ski runs. The Baked Potato Engine is for light meals, and the main restaurant is crowned by a tall pyramidal ceiling, from which a quartet of chandeliers hangs. The service and the food are first class. I'd highly recommend the roast ribs of Scottish beef. In the game room is a resident nanny—so, if you have children, you're free to hit the slopes without them.

Badenoch Hotel (tel. 0479/810261) overlooks the Craigellachie Nature Reserve and its much-photographed rock. The hotel gives summer and winter holidaymakers a choice of both luxury and economy rooms. In this starkly modern Highland building, 60 rooms are streamlined and functional, all large size, all with the modern amenities. For these you pay £28 ($42) in a single, from £19 ($28.50) in a twin. There are 16 bunk-bedded rooms with adjacent baths and showers going for £15 ($22.50) in a single and from £13.50 ($20.25) in a twin. The hotel's facilities include a sauna, solarium, cocktail bar, Viking Bar, and games room, plus a shop and restaurant specializing in Scottish fare.

Aviemore Chalets Motel (tel. 0479/810618) offers comfortable, moderately priced double-story chalets with four units on each floor. Each chalet is centrally heated, carpeted, and adequately furnished with double-tiered bunks, two wash basins with hot and cold running water, private showers, toilets, and heated drying cupboards. Based on four persons in a room, the rate is from £8.50 ($12.75) per person. The reception chalet offers a snackbar, large lounge, and an attractive licensed lounge bar, the Craigellachie. For meals, the Pinewood is a cafeteria (self-service) restaurant, but in Das Stübel, an Austrian-style grillroom, friendly waitresses serve your meals. There are also seven self-catering apartments, each sleeping six, with cooking facilities and color television. The latest addition is a collection of 24 deluxe twin-bedded rooms, with private shower, toilet, drying cupboard, color TV, and tea- and coffee-making facilities. These rent for £16 ($24) per person.

The Rank organization has the following offering:

Stakis Coylumbridge Hotel, Rothiemurchus (tel. 0479/810661), suggests northern Sweden rather than northern Scotland. Christened by the Duke of Edinburgh, the Coylumbridge stands on 65 acres of tree-studded grounds, facing the slopes of the Cairngorms. The bedroom decor is chalet style, with pinewood used profusely. Cheerful appointments evoke both a summer and a winter holiday atmosphere. All rooms have private bathroom, color TV, radio, telephone, and coffee maker. Singles are £43 ($64.50), and doubles or twins go for £58 ($87), including VAT, service, and a full Scottish breakfast.

The Coylumbridge is geared for the winter skier, with instruction and equipment available. In summer, pony-trekkers, fishermen, and golfers check in. One some nights there is disco dancing. It's really a self-contained unit, with a heated swimming pool, sauna, Jacuzzi, coffeeshop, a skating rink (ice in winter, roller in summer), a game room, a hairdresser, plus a pleasant modern restaurant, the Epicure, offering a continental cuisine in the evening, a set dinner costing from £10 ($15). As well as the restaurant, the hotel has a Chieftain Grill, open seven days a week.

Another leading hotel in the area is the **High Range** (tel. 0479/810636), standing above the main Perth–Inverness road. This chalet hotel enjoys a wooded setting of natural birch. From the windows of the single -story chalets, you look out onto the Rothiemurchus Forest and the snow- or heather-covered slopes of the Cairngorms.

In the main block, built of western red cedar, are housed a restaurant, a cocktail bar, and public lounges, all evoking the atmosphere of a ski lodge. The rooms are pleasantly and attractively decorated, offering single, double, twin, and family rooms, each with bath or shower and the majority with bidet. A room costs £22 ($33) in winter, £26 ($39) in summer. Rates include VAT, service, and a Scottish breakfast.

The restaurant at High Range is one of the best at Aviemore, serving dinner only, from 7:30 to 10:30 p.m. The attractive modern dining room draws a lively, youthful crowd to its capable bistro cooking. On my last visit, in summer, the vegetables were garden fresh, and the fish, salmon from the Spey, was exquisitely tender. The soups were interesting too, and the service alert and efficient but definitely not rushed. Meals prepared by the chef, John Fraser, are served in the bistro for £6 ($9) up to £18 ($27).

Fish 'n' Chips

At the **Happy Haggis Chip Shop**, Grampian Road (tel. 0479/810430), you can get fish and chips to take out. A wrapping of plaice and chips costs £1.50 ($2.25).

GRANTOWN-ON-SPEY:

This holiday resort, with its gray granite buildings, stands in a wooded valley and commands splendid views of the Cairngorm mountains. It is a key center for winter sports in Scotland. Fishermen are also attracted to its setting, because the Spey is renowned for its salmon. Lying 34 miles southeast of Inverness by road, it was one of Scotland's many 18th-century planned towns, founded on a heather-covered moor in 1765 by Sir James Grant of Grant, becoming the seat of that ancient family. Grantown became famous in the 19th century as a Highland tourist center, enticing visitors with its planned concept, the beauty of surrounding pine forests, the Spey River, and the mountains around it.

From a base here you can explore the valleys of the Don and Dee, the already-mentioned Cairngorms, and Culloden Moor, scene of the historic battle in 1746.

In hotels, the leading recommendations follow:

Grant Arms, The Square (tel. 0479/2526). When Queen Victoria stayed here in 1860, she is reported to have said, "My bed was hard, but at least it was clean." Her old room with its four-poster is still there—and still clean—although not at all hard. Into its second century of hospitality, the Grant Arms is still the best place to stay at the resort. The hotel has been considerably modernized, yet it retains traditional touches. The color-coordinated bedrooms are well maintained, and some of them are deluxe in their appointments. At least 40 of the 55 units contain private baths, and another 15 come equipped with showers. In the peak season, the overnight charge ranges from £23 ($34.50) in a single, from £36 ($54) in a double, this rate including a full Scottish breakfast.

At the Grant Arms a former ballroom has been converted into the Balmoral Restaurant, where tour groups often dine. It serves what is perhaps the best food in Grantown-on-Spey, not only the national dishes of Scotland, but fresh salmon and trout and venison in season. The service is expert even when the Balmoral seems crowded. Lunch is from noon to 2:30 p.m. and dinner from 7 to 8:45 p.m.

Craighlynne, Woodland Terrace (tel. 0479/2597), is spacious and sprawling, standing on its own grounds overlooking the wooded valley and the hills beyond. Resident ski instructors—and equipment for renting —are on hand in winter, and in summer pony-trekkers check in. Accommodations come in a variety of styles, plumbing, and space. The bedrooms are pleasant and bright, well maintained, although some are somewhat spartan in decor. Most rooms have private bath or shower (only four without). The charge is £16 ($24) to £19 ($28.50) per person, including VAT, service, and a Scottish breakfast. Dinner and B&B cost £19 ($28.50) to £23 ($34.50) per person. The tartan bar with its peat fire is the center of après-ski life. In season there is entertainment every evening. The dining room is light and airy, serving good country fare, including such Scottish dishes as haggis and malt gravy.

ROTHES: A Speyside town with five distilleries, Rothes lies just to the south of the lovely Glen of Rothes. You can stay in Rothes and explore "The Whisky Trail," detailed earlier. It is but a short ride from here to **Dufftown,** containing at least seven distilleries, including **William Grant's Glenfiddich Distillery,** operating a reception room from March to October and showing visitors how malt whisky is produced.

After your career up "The Whisky Trail," **Rothes Glen Hotel** in Rothes (tel. Rothes 254) may appear to be a mirage. The old turreted house, with many of its original pieces of furniture, stands back from the road, surrounded by about 40 acres of fields with grazing Highland cattle—how can they see to eat with all that shaggy hair? This historic castle-like building was designed by the architect who built Balmoral. Inside the house a warm fire greets you. Bedrooms are well furnished and relaxing. Owner Donald Carmichael charges from £25 ($37.50) in a single without bath to £28 ($42) in a single with bath. Doubles with bath cost £50 ($75), including VAT and a full breakfast. The dining room is paneled in wood, and good wholesome meals are served in true Scottish tradition. The bar lunches are very popular, with a wide choice offered, including fried fresh haddock, a three-course meal with coffee going for about £5.50 ($8.25). A set four-course dinner with coffee and mints costs £16 ($24). As an alternative, there is an à la carte menu from which individual dishes may be chosen. A favorite specialty is mince, tatties, and skirlie (fried oatmeal and onions). This goes very well with roast pheasant for dinner, a local delicacy. Lunch is from 12:30 to 2 p.m. and dinner from 7 to 8:30 p.m. The hotel shuts down from mid-November to March 1.

FOCHABERS: This village, on the Inverness–Aberdeen road, dates from 1776 and was created as one of the early planned towns by John Baxter, for the fourth Duke of Gordon. Most of the buildings along High Street are protected and have not been changed much in 200 years. On the Spey, Fochabers is distinguished by its **Market Cross** and **Tower of Gordon Castle.**

The **Gordon Arms** (tel. Fochabers 820508) is a well-known 18th-century coaching inn, run by Mr. and Mrs. Pern, who are justly proud of the hospitality they offer wayfarers of today. Bedrooms are both traditional and modern, either in the old wing or the new. Singles without bath cost £20 ($30), rising to £25 ($37.50) with bath, and doubles cost from £35 ($53) to £40 ($60), including a full breakfast and VAT. Only 7 of the 17 rooms contain private baths. Fishermen are fond of the place, as revealed by the "salmon house" for the storing of rods and tackle.

The Perns are noted for their catering, and their food is some of the best along Speyside, including many national dishes Mrs. Pern cooks for her visitors, such as herring rolled in oatmeal and grilled. The Moray beef and salmon are rarely equaled. Sometimes continental dishes appear on the menu. Meals, costing from £5 ($7.50) to £10 ($15), are served from 12:30 to 2 p.m. and from 7 to 8:30 p.m. It's important to make a reservation, incidentally. On the wall are paintings by local artists. If you're stopping on a summer afternoon, you might have tea in the garden.

ELGIN: The center of local government in the Moray district, an ancient royal burgh, this cathedral city lies on the Lossie River, 38 miles from Inverness by road. Once called the "lantern of the north," the **Cathedral of Moray** is now in ruins. It was founded in 1224 but extensively damaged in 1390 by the "wolf of Badenoch," the natural son of Robert II. After its destruction, the citizens of Elgin rebuilt their beloved cathedral, turning it into one of the most attractive and graceful buildings in Scotland. The architect's plan was that of a Jerusalem cross. However, when the central tower fell in 1711, the cathedral was allowed to fall into decay. But a faithful cobbler still respected its grandeur, and he became its caretaker. By the time of his death in 1841 he had removed most of the debris that had fallen. Today visitors wander among its ruins, snapping pictures. Best preserved is the 15th-century chapter house.

Samuel Johnson and Boswell came this way on their Highland tour, reporting a "vile dinner" at the Red Lion Inn in 1773.

I'm sure you'll fare better at the **Eight Acres Hotel,** Sheriffmill (tel. Elgin 3077), a modern, low-lying, motel-type unit, all 40 of its streamlined, functionally furnished rooms offering a private bath or shower. Standing on spacious grounds, the hotel lies on the western approaches to Elgin on the main A96 Inverness road. The public rooms are spacious, and the restaurant attracts a lot of motorists bound for Inverness. Rates in a single are £28 ($42), rising to £45 ($67.50) in a double, including breakfast. The hotel offers quite a bit of entertainment at various times of the year, not only a disco and dinner—dancing to a live band, but occasional Scottish folk evenings. However, entertainment is not on a regular basis.

Less expensive is the **Royal Hotel,** corner of Station Road and Moss Street (tel. Elgin 2320), a pleasant, privately owned hotel standing on its own grounds about a four-minute walk from the center of Elgin. It lies adjacent to the railway station and in close proximity to golf, bowling, swimming, and tennis courts. The owners, Mr. and Mrs. Iain Grant McAllister, ask £12.50 ($18.75) per person per night for bed and a traditional Scottish breakfast. There are ten rooms, each with hot and cold water, shaver points, gas fires, electric blankets, tea- and coffee-making facilities, and comfortable furnishings. High tea, with a variety of menus, is served between 5 and 7 p.m. at reasonable prices. Guests are invited to relax in the TV lounge, where a beautiful antique fireplace is a focal point. The double staircase with old-fashioned wrought-iron balusters and a mahogany rail is a striking feature leading from the front hall. The house was constructed in 1865 by James Grant, founder of the Glen Grant Distillery, who also built the railways in northern Scotland. This three-story structure is surrounded by a garden and car parking space.

The McAllisters also have the beautifully situated **Hotel St. Leonards** around on the next street, Duff Avenue. It is slightly more expensive, as bedrooms with private baths are available.

FINDHORN: As you travel westward from Elgin to Forres, a turn to the right and then to the left will bring you to Findhorn, a tiny village whose name has become internationally known through its connection with the University of Light in Forres and as a gathering place for persons seeking a place where communal living and creativity have burgeoned. Actually, a caravan park just before you arrive in Findhorn is the center of these activities. Findhorn is on a unique tidal bay at the mouth of the River Findhorn, which makes it ideal for yacht racing, sailing, and waterskiing.

Across the bay from Findhorn is the Culbin Sands, under which lies a buried village.

In Findhorn, a good place to stay is the **Culbin Sands Hotel** (tel. 03093/2252), which has panoramic views of the Moray Firth across to Ross and Cromarty, Caithness, Sutherland, Findhorn Bay, and the Culbin Forest. There are eight miles of sandy beach within two minutes' walk of the hotel. Owned by R. M. Sinclair, the hotel has 15 bedrooms, all with hot and cold water, renting nightly for £14 ($21) in a single, £25 ($37.50) in a double with shower for B&B, including VAT, service, and a full Scottish breakfast. Children under 12 pay half price, and cots are available. The hotel boasts three well-stocked bars, a pleasant dining room, and a color TV lounge. Bar lunches are served seven days a week, and high teas and dinners are also offered to guests. The hotel, open all year, is a mile from the Findhorn Foundation and is the home of the Royal Findhorn Yacht Club. There are ample facilities for fishing, pony trekking, waterskiing, and sailing. It's best to reserve well in advance if you plan to visit Findhorn in the high season.

The **Crown and Anchor Inn** (tel. 03093/2243), run today by Robin Graham and Gay Robertson, dates from 1739 when it was built to cater to travelers making the run between Edinburgh and Inverness. The hospitable inn is run as a "free house," renting out five comfortably furnished bedrooms, including a family room with a double bed and two bunk beds. Each accommodation has its own shower and toilet. Including a full Scottish breakfast, the charge in a single is from £15 ($22.50) per night, rising to £25 ($37.50) and up in a double. Bar snacks and meals are served all day seven days a week. Locals drop in to enjoy the real ales and malt whiskies served in the bar.

FORRES: This ancient burgh, mainly residential in character, stands on the Aberdeen–Inverness road, between Elgin and Nairn (ten miles to the east). Near the mouth of the Findhorn, it is one of Scotland's oldest towns. Once a castle associated with Duncan and Macbeth stood here. Nearby is **Sueno's Stone,** a 23-foot sandstone monolith containing 10th- and 11th-century Celtic carvings with intricate figures of men. The **Witches' Stone,** in the same vicinity, marks the site of the burnings of persons accused of witchcraft.

The best hotels include the **Ramnee,** Victoria Road (tel. 0309/72410), a charming house set back from the road and entered through well-kept gardens. Mrs. Jill Martini personally supervises the day-to-day running of the place, keeping it spotless. There is a lounge plus a pleasant dining room with wood panels and gleaming napery where meals are served. A full breakfast is included in the overnight cost, and dinner consists of simple grills, steak, and fish. There is as well a bar for the use of residents. The bedrooms are large and, where bathrooms have been added, the workmanship has been professional—you don't feel that your toilet has been carved out of a corner of your room. The charge is £18 ($27) per person, £3 ($4.50) extra for a room with bath. A set dinner costs from £10 ($15).

Built in an informal 19th-century style, the hotel is sited within a garden in the Laigh of Moray. To reach it, pull off the A96 Aberdeen–Inverness road on a clearly marked driveway leading to the hotel. The view from the front of the hotel is the richly wooded Cluny Hill of *Macbeth* witches fame. To the rear the view stretches out many miles over Findhorn Bay and the Culbin Sands Forest.

Nearby, the **Park Hotel,** Victoria Road (tel. 0309/72328), is very much the same sort of house. Set on spacious, well-kept grounds, it overlooks Findhorn Bay and the Moray Firth. The bedrooms are comfortable and well appointed, containing hot and cold running water. In season fresh fruit and vegetables come from the garden, the produce used in the hotel's kitchen. Mr. and Mrs. James Noble welcome guests, charging them £15 ($22.50) per person for B&B, including VAT, service, and a full Scottish breakfast. Bar lunches are served. The hotel also has a cocktail bar, drawing room, and television lounge.

2. Inverness and Loch Ness

After Glasgow, most motorists wanting to explore the Highlands head for Inverness, its ancient capital. From its doorstep, one can explore a romantic land of hills, lochs, and lots of myths.

Of course, the most popular excursion is to Loch Ness, where one sets up an observation point to await the appearance of "Nessie," the Loch Ness monster. But even if the monster doesn't put in an appearance, the loch itself has splendid scenery. I have a scattering of recommendations around the loch for those wanting to base there.

Finally, visitors going east may want to explore the old town of Nairn, and those adventurous readers wanting to venture into the forlorn and relatively uninhabited section of northwest Scotland may want to do so from a base at the old spa of Strathpeffer.

INVERNESS: The capital of the Highlands, Inverness is a royal burgh and seaport, at the north end of Great Glen, lying on both sides of the Ness River. It is considered the best base for touring the north. At the Highland Games, with their festive balls, the season in Inverness reaches its social peak.

The city has a new and luxurious theater complex on the bank of the Ness, the **Eden Court Theatre,** Bishops Road, which has a superb restaurant, bars, and an art gallery. Included in the repertoire are variety shows, drama, ballet, pop music, movies, opera, rock and folk concerts, and a summer-season traditional Scottish show with top stars. The theater, which opened in 1976, was constructed with an ingenious use of hexagonal shapes and has a horseshoe-shaped auditorium. Programs are advertised in most hotels and guest houses. The box office is open from 10:30 a.m. to 8 p.m., Monday through Saturday (tel. 0463/221718).

Inverness is one of the oldest inhabited localities in Scotland.

On **Craig Phadrig** are the remains of a vitrified fort, believed to date from the fourth century B.C., where the Pictish King Brude is said to have been visited by St. Columba in A.D. 565. The old castle of Inverness stood to the east of the present Castlehill, the site still retaining the name **Auld Castlehill.** Because of the somewhat shaky geography of Shakespeare in dramatizing the crime of Macbeth by murdering King Duncan, some scholars claim that the deed was done in the old castle of Inverness while others say it happened at Cawdor Castle, 4½ miles to the south where Macbeth held forth as Thane of Cawdor.

King David built the first stone castle in Inverness around 1141. The **Clock Tower** is all that remains of a fort erected by Cromwell's army between 1652 and 1657. The 16th-century **Abertarff House** is now the headquarters of An Comunn Gaidhealach, the Highland association that preserves the Gaelic language and culture.

Inverness today has a castle, but it's a "modern" one—that is, dating from 1835. Crowning a low cliff of the east bank of the Ness, the **Castle of Inverness** occupies the site of an ancient fortress blown up by the Jacobites in 1746. The castle houses county offices and law courts. Mary Queen of Scots was denied admission to the castle in 1562, and she subsequently occupied a house on Bridge Street. From the window of this house, she witnessed the execution of her cousin, Sir John Gordon. For not gaining admission to the castle, she took reprisals, taking the fortress and hanging the governor.

Opposite the town hall is the **Old Mercat Cross,** with its **Stone of the Tubs,** an Inverness landmark said to be where women rested their washtubs as they ascended from the river. Known as "Clachnacudainn," the lozenge-shaped stone was the spot where the early kings were crowned.

Inverness Museum and Art Gallery, at Castle Wynd (tel. 0463/237114), contains the display "The Hub of the Highlands," the story of the people, wildlife, environment, and culture of the Inverness district, as well as silver and changing exhibitions. It's open daily except Sunday from 9 a.m. to 5 p.m.

West of the river rises the wooded hill of **Tomnahurich,** known as "the hill of the fairies." It is now a cemetery, and from here the views are magnificent.

In the Ness are wooded islands, linked to Inverness by suspension bridges and turned into parks.

From Inverness, you can visit **Culloden Battlefield,** six miles to the east. This is the spot where Bonnie Prince Charlie and the Jacobite army were finally crushed at the battle on April 16, 1746. A cairn marks the site on Drummossie Moor where the battle raged. **Leanach Cottage,** around which the battle took place, still stands and was inhabited until 1912. A path from the cottage leads through the Field of the English, where 76 men of the Duke of Cumberland's forces who died during the battle are said to be buried. Features of interest include the **Graves of the Clans,** communal burial places with simple stones bearing individual clan names alongside the main road and through the woodland; the great memorial cairn, erected in 1881; the **Well of the Dead,** a single stone with the inscription: "The English Were Buried Here"; and the huge **Cumberland Stone** from which the victorious "Butcher" Cumberland is said to have reviewed the scene. The battle lasted only 40 minutes; the prince's army lost some 1200 men out of 5000 and the king's army 310. A visitors' center and museum are open all year.

Between Inverness and Nairn, also about six miles to the east of Inverness, are the **Stones of Clava,** one of the most important prehistoric monuments in the north. These cairns and standing stones are from the **Bronze Age.**

Back in Inverness, we'll investigate—

Food and Lodging

Culloden House, near Culloden Moor, six miles from Inverness (tel. 0463/790461), is a Georgian mansion with extensive gardens and parkland. It includes part of the Renaissance castle in which Bonnie Prince Charlie slept the night before the last great battle on British soil, the Battle of

Culloden. Superbly isolated, it is perfect for a relaxed Highland holiday. Public rooms, furnished in the grand style, are suitably spacious and comfortable. The bedrooms are cheerful, cozy, and agreeably furnished. All 21 of them contain private baths and showers. Depending on your room assignment, singles pay from £60 ($90); doubles, from £95 ($142.50) to £120 ($180)—including VAT and breakfast.

The hotel maintains pleasantly traditional ideas of personal service. The food, in my opinion, is of exceptional quality, and it's served against an impressive backdrop of refinement and elegance. Simple and complex dishes are virtually flawless, and the finest of fresh local ingredients are used. Expect to pay about £25 ($37.50) per person for dinner.

Station Hotel, Academy Street (tel. 0463/231926), adjacent to the railway station, offers a high standard of first-class service, comfortable accommodations, and well-prepared food. The occupants of those baronial Highland mansions like to stop here when they're in Inverness on shopping or social expeditions, gathering for somewhat lively chats in the conservatory lounge. Grandly Victorian, the bedrooms are tastefully decorated and welcoming, costing from £34.50 ($51.75) with bath or shower, from £48 ($72) in a double, tariffs including a full Scottish breakfast.

The dining room is one of the finest in Inverness, serving good-quality Scottish dishes, plus some excellently cooked continental favorites. Courteous waiters create a friendly atmosphere. Lunch is served from 12:30 to 2 p.m. and dinner from 7 to 9 p.m. A table d'hôte evening meal costs £9.50 ($14.25), but expect to pay £14 ($21) if you're ordering à la carte, sampling the French specialties.

Dunain Park, 2½ miles southwest of Inverness (tel. 0463/230512), stands in six acres of garden and woods, between Loch Ness and Inverness. This 18th-century house was opened as a hotel in 1974, and is furnished with fine antiques, china, and clocks, allowing it to retain its atmosphere of a private country house. Although Dunain Park has won its fame mainly as a restaurant, it does offer six bedrooms, four of which contain private baths and one of which has an antique four-poster bed. The rates range from £40 ($60) to £65 ($97.50) in a double or twin. A host of thoughtful details and pretty, soft furnishings have gone into the bedrooms. The breakfast served here is exceptional—in fact, the homemade marmalade was the best I've ever tasted, and you can buy some to take with you.

You can order a simple lunch (in the garden, if you prefer). Snack meals are served from 12:30 to 1:30 p.m. But it is at dinner that the chef really delivers, offering a set meal for about £17 ($25.50), fully inclusive. This menu changes daily, depending on the availability of high-quality produce, fish, and meat. The chicken with ginger and honey and cod's-roe pâté are particular favorites. The restaurant and hotel are closed from mid-November until mid-March.

Kingsmills Hotel, Culcabock Road (tel. 0463/237166), is an 18th-century house of much charm set in four acres of woodland garden only a mile from the center of Inverness. Once a private mansion, it stands adjacent to an 18-hole golf course, and the hotel has its own private squash courts. Angus and Lillian MacLeod have carefully maintained a country-house atmosphere, with a small, pleasantly informal, and most hospitable Highland staff. Furnishings throughout the hotel is of a high quality, and all 54 bedrooms have private bath, radio, color TV, and telephone. Single room rates range from £40 ($60) to £48 ($72), and doubles go from £54 ($81) to £65 ($97.50), according to location and season. Bed-sitting rooms and family rooms are also available. The rates include a full Highland breakfast. Dinner, offered from 7 to 10 p.m., costs £12.50 ($18.75). All prices include VAT. The fish dishes are exceptionally good. Bar lunches and snack meals offer a wide choice, including Scottish fare. A notice in the lobby tells you that Robert Burns dined here in 1787, and the "Charles" who signed the guest register in 1982 was (you guessed it) the Prince of Wales. Centrally heated, the hotel remains open all year.

Mercury Motor Inn, Nairn Road, at the junction of the A9 and the A96 (tel. 0463/239666), is without surprises, each uniform room well furnished with a high degree of comfort, an ideal center for those who want to tour the Highlands. Accommodations come with private bath, toilet, color TV, radio, and tea- or coffee-making facilities. In all, 108 rooms are offered, ranging in price from £34 ($51) to £40 ($60) in a single and from £48 ($72) to £54 ($81) in a double or twin, including VAT and service. The inn offers a conically shaped grill and two fully licensed bars.

Glen Mhor Hotel, 10 Ness Bank (tel. 0463/234308), looks out onto the River Ness. A house of gables and bay windows, it is a hospitable, family-run hotel with an endearing charm in spite of its creaky quality. The Manson family has provided many thoughtful touches, such as a log fire blazing in the entrance lounge. From many of the individually styled bedrooms, you have views of the river, castle, and cathedral. Some of these are suitable for families, and children sharing a room with two adults are accommodated free. Amenities in the rooms include private baths or shower rooms with toilets, color TVs, and baby-listening service. The B&B rate starts at about £18 ($27), rising to about £33 ($49.50) per person in a room where H.R.H. Prince Charles once dined. In a restaurant overlooking the river and specializing in Scottish dishes, you will enjoy such fine food as salmon caught in the river outside, shellfish, lamb, and beef. The wine list is considered one of the best in the country. In addition to the cozy cocktail lounge, there's a charming Parisian Bistro bar called Nico's, which is open for food and drinks at lunchtime and in the evening. It's a popular nightspot. The hotel is ideally situated for touring the north of Scotland, angling, golfing, horseback riding, and hunting, all of which can be arranged by the hotel.

Redcliffe, 1 Gordon Terrace (tel. 0463/232767), is a small hotel set on its own grounds, commanding a peaceful perch above the Ness and the castle, yet lying within a three-minute walk of the main shopping district. Your hosts, Mr. and Mrs. Acock, have completely modernized the interior, but have kept the traditional stone facade intact. The bedrooms are pleasantly decorated and have hot and cold running water. The B&B rate is £14 ($21) per person, increasing to £15.50 ($23.25) if you request a private bath. VAT is extra. In a spacious, comfortable lounge, guests gather to watch TV. At the hotel is a permanent exhibition of the work of local artists, with all art for sale. The hotel also serves excellent Highland dinners with pheasant, haggis, venison, and salmon (the latter should be requested in advance when making a reservation). All the food is home-cooked.

In the Environs

North of Inverness is a fertile peninsula known as the **Black Isle** because it is seldom whitened by snow. Here tropical plants flourish, and **Cromarty,** at the northeast tip, has fine sandy beaches. The cottage there where Hugh Miller, noted geologist, was born in 1802 is now a geological museum. **Fortrose,** an ancient town facing the Moray Fifth, has a sheltered bay for yachting.

Dingwall is a town in Easter Ross district near the mouth of the River Conon. The town arms, a starfish, are displayed on the tolbooth (originally a booth for collecting tolls), dating from 1730. In front of this is the shaft of a former Mercat Cross, and beside it is an iron gate of the old town jail.

Strathpeffer, about six miles west of Dingwall, is a good center for touring Easter Ross, where the countryside is dominated by the 3433-foot summit of Ben Wyvis.

Heading back toward Inverness, an interesting stop is at **Beauly,** 12 miles west of the city, where you can visit the ruins of a Valliscaulian priory built in 1230. On the south bank of the River Beauly southwest of the town is **Beaufort Castle,** a 19th-century baronial mansion that is the seat of the Frasers of Lovat whose ancestor was the "Lovat of the Forty-five." The original seat of the Lovats was Castle Dounie, built about 1400, but it was destroyed by "Butcher" Cumberland after his victory at Culloden.

ULLAPOOL: Northwest of Inverness, on an arm of the sea called Loch Broom, the little town of Ullapool is an embarkation point for travelers crossing The Minch, a section of the North Atlantic separating Scotland from the Outer Hebrides. The road from Inverness takes you through the wild Northwest Highlands, and a car-ferry from Ullapool will deposit you in Stornaway on Lewis, one of the Western Isles.

Altanaharrie Inn, at Ullapool, Wester Ross (tel. Dundonnell 230), is one of those places that you feel you should not tell anyone about, as it is small (only three bedrooms). But it is one of those places that calls for inclusion because of its uniqueness and total integration into the life of the region. The Altanaharrie was once a drovers' inn on the banks of Loch Broom. There is no access by road so guests are brought over the loch by private launch. Tell them what time you are arriving at Ullapool, and they'll come and meet you.

Once you've landed, Fred Brown greets you with a warm log fire in a bar for a dram before dinner, which is likely to consist of locally caught seafood. Much meat, local venison, and fish such as trout and lobster are obtained locally. They make their own bread, and they like to know beforehand if you are eating "in" so that they can cater accordingly.

Overnight will cost you £38 ($57) per person, including dinner, VAT, and breakfast.

Fred also operates Summer Isles Charters for cruising aboard a sailing yacht among the offshore islands or, for the more ambitious, to Skye or the Outer Hebrides, with or without skipper. This is a serious business, and you should write to Fred before you embark on such a venture, giving details of your experience. Otherwise he may not let you take a boat out.

NAIRN: A favorite family seaside resort on the sheltered Moray Firth, Nairn is a royal burgh, lying at the mouth of the Nairn River. Its fishing harbor was constructed in 1820, and golf has been played here since 1672, as it still is today. A large uncrowded beach, tennis, and angling draw a horde of vacationers in summer.

At **Cawdor Castle** (tel. Cawdor 615), to the south of Nairn, you encounter 600 years of Highland history. Since the early 14th century it's been the home of the Thanes of Cawdor. The castle has all the architectural ingredients you associate with the medieval: a drawbridge, an ancient tower (this one built around a tree), and fortified walls. The severity is softened by the handsome gardens, flowers, trees, and rolling lawns. As I mentioned earlier, even the Scots can't agree as to where Macbeth, who actually was made Thane of Cawdor by King Duncan, committed his foul deed of murdering the king—at Cawdor or in the castle that once stood on Auld Castlehill in Inverness, if at all. The castle is open to the public from 10 a.m. to 5:30 p.m. every day from May 1 to October 3. Admission is £2 ($3) for adults, £1 ($1.50) for children. The castle has extensive nature trails, a snackbar, and a licensed restaurant.

Food and Lodging

The **Clifton Hotel,** Viewfield Street (tel. 0667/53119), reflects the dynamic personality of J. Gordon Macintyre, the owner of this honey-colored sandstone, vine-covered Victorian mansion. The Clifton has been owned by the same family probably longer than any other hotel in the north of Scotland. Fully licensed, it stands on the seafront, three minutes from the beach and golf links.

Mr. Macintyre has spent a lot of time, trouble, and money in decorating the house, often with interesting prints, and in selecting the furnishings, as exemplified by the Clifton's old-fashioned parlor. The collection of pictures, paintings, prints, engravings, etchings, and drawings is unusual and extensive, not only in public rooms, the drawing room, the writing room, and the bar and restaurant, but also in the long corridor. The bedrooms on the first floor are better equipped, each pleasantly appointed, while those on the second floor are more spartan, yet the view from this higher perch seems to compensate. Singles rent for £25 ($37.50); doubles, from £48 ($72). All bedrooms have baths, except one which has a shower; some, however, do not have toilets. Musical and theatrical performances are often staged in the hotel.

The Clifton also serves the best food in Nairn—in fact, it's some of the best in the north of Scotland. The cooking is often in the hearty Highland tradition—that is, game pie, pigeons in wine, lamb in a mustard sauce—although French specialties also tempt. Dinner hours are from 7 to 9:30 p.m. Luncheon, from 12:30 to 2:30 p.m. daily, is served in the new Green Room, whose menu is based on what is available that day in the way of fish and shellfish, such as lobster, oysters, brill, prawns, and sole. The room is quite elegant, its china being Wedgwood Old and New. With only four tables, it is advisable to reserve your table by phoning early. Breakfast is special too. There is no menu as such. Since the hotel is stocked with all the necessary ingredients, guests are asked what they would like cooked. The ultimate aim is to try to make guests feel they are staying in a well-run private house. The emphasis is on good taste, without making things too overly refined or too "precious." The hotel and restaurant are shuttered from November until February.

Newton, Inverness Road (tel. 0667/53144), a castle-like hotel, stands just outside town in an attractive park of 35 acres, offering views across sweeping lawns and the golf course to the sea. Considered one of the finest of the "manor house" hotels of Scotland, it is spacious and sumptuous, drawing a clientele likely to include everybody from a prime minister to a Glasgow industrialist. Prices have a pedigree too: a single rents for £32

($48) to £35 ($52.50), and a double or twin goes for £50 ($75) to £55 ($82.50), including VAT and a full breakfast. It's also possible to stay here on the half-board rate, from £40 ($60) per person, including VAT. The public rooms are furnished with taste, and the Moray Firth, viewed on a day when the sun is shining brightly, forms a spectacle of beauty from many of the Newton's windows. The bedrooms have many fine appointments—sedate, comfortable, although unpretentious. All 34 of them contain private baths. There is a high standard of maintenance and personal service.

The **Windsor Hotel,** Albert Street (tel. 0667/53108), is a fine sandstone building that has been renovated and refurbished to good effect. The resident proprietors, Mr. and Mrs. Charles Woolley, see to it that the hotel provides a comfortable family atmosphere and first-class cuisine. The hotel is centrally heated, and each bedroom contains its own basin with hot and cold running water. There are numerous bathrooms, showers, and toilets throughout the hotel. The color TV lounge, residents' lounge, and fully licensed cocktail bar add to the guests' enjoyment. A single without bath costs £22 ($33), rising to £25 ($37.50) with bath. A bathless double costs £38 ($57), going up to £42 ($63) with bath, including VAT, service, and a full breakfast. Special rates are allowed for children. A four-course dinner costs £10 ($15). The hotel is close to centers of transportation and sports facilities. It is open all year.

DRUMNADROCHIT: This pleasant little hamlet lies about a mile from Loch Ness at the entrance to Glen Urquhart. The ruined **Urquhart Castle,** one of Scotland's largest castles, is a mile and a half southeast on a promonotory overlooking Loch Ness. The chief of Clan Grant owned the castle in 1509, and most of the existing building dates from that period. In 1692 the castle was blown up by the Grants to prevent its becoming a Jacobite stronghold. It is here at Urquhart Castle that sightings of the Loch Ness monster are most often reported.

In 1980 a **Loch Ness Monster Exhibition** opened in the village, and it's been packing them in ever since. You can view fuzzy pictures and movies of the so-called monster and learn about serious attempts by scientists to get to the heart of the age-old mystery. For example, submarines have been lowered into the murky water, as have cameras and diving bells. Talk to Tony Harmsworth, curator. He makes a convincing case for the existence of the creature—or creatures.

In the vicinity stands the **Lewiston Arms,** Lewiston, near Drumnadrochit (tel. Drumnadrochit 225), an old whitewashed coaching inn lying just off the principal road in the village of Lewiston. Many motorists prefer to stop off here instead of going on to Inverness. The inn offers only one single and seven doubles, none with private bath. The tariffs are £12 ($18) in a single, £22 ($33) in a double. You might ask for the dinner, bed, and breakfast rate of £19 ($28.50) per person. Bedrooms are simply but adequately furnished. Outside is an attractive garden. In all, it's a good center for exploring the Loch Ness district. The place is owned and run by Nicholas and Helen Quinn, a team with a spotless little inn off the fast A82, right beside the castle.

FORT AUGUSTUS: This Highland touring center stands at the head (the southernmost end) of Loch Ness. The town took its name from a fort named for the Duke of Cumberland. Built after the 1715 Rising, the present Benedictine abbey stands on its site.

In accommodation, it offers the **Inchnacardoch Lodge** (tel. 0320/6258), a family-run hotel in a beautiful setting overlooking Loch Ness from most of the bedrooms. You can monster-watch in comfort. The old-fashioned house of many gables, once owned by Lord Lovat, clan chief of the Clan Fraser, offers 20 comfortable and well-equipped bedrooms, six with baths, charging from £15 ($22.50) to £17 ($25.50) for a single, from £30 ($45) to £34 ($51) in a double, including VAT, service, and a full Scottish breakfast, which provides porridge, kippers, and black pudding on the menu. You can enjoy a wee dram of the malt in one of the two lounge bars and then a succulent Scottish steak (either beef or salmon) in the fully licensed restaurant. An à la carte dinner costs £6 ($9) to £10 ($15), and bar lunches are offered from £2 ($3). Open all year, the hotel is owned and run by Mr. and Mrs. Donald MacFadyen, both of whom were born and brought up in the Highlands. They enjoy meeting their guests. Music is provided on Friday and Saturday night in season.

INVERGARRY: A Highland center for fishing and deer stalking, Invergarry is noted for its fine scenery. It too is a good center for exploring Glen More and Loch Ness. At Invergarry is the beginning of the road through the West Highland glens and mountains, forming one famous "Road to the Isles" that terminates at Kyle of Lochalsh.

Near Invergarry, you can visit the **Well of the Heads,** on the west side of Loch Oich near its southern tip, erected in 1812 by MacDonnell of Glengarry to commemorate the decapitation by the family bard of seven brothers who had murdered the two sons of a 17th-century chief of Clan Keppoch, a branch of the MacDonnell Clan. The seven heads were washed in the well before being presented to the chief of the MacDonnells at Glengarry.

The **Glengarry Castle Hotel,** at Invergarry (tel. 254), stands on the River Garry, which runs into Loch Oich. The castle hotel is privately owned and run by Mr. and Mrs. MacCallum and Mrs. Paterson. Their 100-year-old house lies on extensive grounds and has recently been modernized to provide comfort to the passerby or to be a pleasant base for a week or so of country holiday with fishing, tennis, walking, and rowing. On the grounds are the ruins of **Glengarry Castle,** the historic seat of the MacDonnells.

There are two spacious lounges where drinks can be served to residents, and the dining room offers excellent meals made from local produce. They charge £15 ($22.50) per person in a bathless room, £20 ($30) per person with bath. Lunch costs from £6 ($9); dinner, from £10 ($15); and tariffs quoted include VAT and service.

SPEAN BRIDGE: This village is a busy intersection of the Fort William–Perth and Fort William–Inverness roads, as well as having daily train service to Fort William, Glasgow, and London, and bus service to Inverness and Fort William. Two miles outside the town, in Glen Spean, is the striking **Commando Memorial** by Scott Sutherland that the Queen Mother unveiled in 1952. In this area many commandos were trained during World War II. Numerous war movies have been filmed here.

On the outskirts of the village on the A86 going toward Newtonmore and Perth is **Coire Glas** (tel. 039-781/272), a motel-style guest house with 15 bedrooms. Mr. and Mrs. MacFarlane have added onto the back of their one-story home, to come up with an attractive and convenient place for visitors to stay overnight or for long periods. All the rooms are equipped with hot and cold running water, and ample bathroom facilities are provided. Three bedrooms have shower and toilet en suite. The MacFarlanes charge £10 ($15) per person per night for B&B. Dinner costs from £6.50 ($9.75), and the house is licensed to sell alcohol with meals. A lunch will be packed for you upon request. Spean Bridge is a central area for touring the loch country, and from Coire Glas, looking across a wide, grassy lawn, you can see Ben Gurry, which is a part of the Ben Nevis range.

3. Fort William and Lochaber

Fort William, the capital of Lochaber, is the major touring center for the western Highlands. Wildly beautiful Lochaber, the area around Fort William, has been called "the land of bens, glens, and heroes."

Dominating the area is **Ben Nevis,** Britain's highest mountain, rising 4418 feet. In summer when it's clear of snow, there's a safe path to the summit. Fort William stands on the site of a fort built by General Monk in 1655, which was pulled down to make way for the railroad. This district is the western end of what is known as Glen Mor—the Great Glen, geologically a fissure that divides the northwest of Scotland from the southeast and contains Loch Lochy, Loch Oich, and Loch Ness. The Caledonian Canal, opened in 1847, linked these lochs, the River Ness, and Moray Firth. It provided sailing boats a safe alternative to the stormy route around the north of Scotland. Larger steamships made the canal out of date commercially, but fishing boats and pleasure steamers still use it. Good roads run the length of the Great Glen, partly following the line of General Wade's military road. From Fort William you can take steamer trips to Staffa and Iona.

The ruins of **Old Inverlochy Castle,** scene of the famous battle in 1645, can be reached by driving on the A82 two miles north of Fort William. At a point just one mile north of Fort William is **Glen Nevis,** one of the most beautiful in Scotland.

About 15 miles west of Fort William, on the A830 toward Mallaig, at Glenfinnan at the head of Loch Shiel, is the **Glenfinnan Monument,** which marks the spot where Bonnie Prince Charlie unfurled his proud red-and-white silk banner on August 19, 1745, in the ill-fated attempt to restore the Stuarts to the British throne. The monument is topped by the figure of a kilted Highlander. At a Visitors' Centre one may learn of the prince's campaign from Glenfinnan to Derby and back to the final defeat at Culloden.

FORT WILLIAM: The name evokes redcoats billeted in rough barracks to keep the Highlanders of Lochaber under control. Fort William today is a busy tourist town on the shores of Loch Linnhe. Although it stands in the shadow of Ben Nevis, the mountain can't be seen from town. While the town is most often used as a touring center, in Fort William itself you can visit the **West Highland Museum,** on Cameron Square, containing all aspects of local history, especially the 1745 Jacobite rising, plus sections on tartans and folk life. The museum is open Monday to Saturday from 9:30 a.m. to 5:30 p.m. in June and September, to 9 p.m. in July and August, and

9:30 a.m. to 1 p.m. and 2 to 5 p.m. the remainder of the year. Admission is 50p (75¢) for adults, 25p (38¢) for children.

Where to Stay

In Fort William, I'd recommend the following accommodations, beginning first with a deluxe suggestion:

Inverlochy Castle (tel. 0397/2177) is another one of the places where Queen Victoria stayed. In her time it was newly built (1863), a Scottish baronial mansion belonging to Lord Abinger. The monarch claimed in her diary, "I never saw a lovelier or more romantic spot." I do not wish to detract from that long-ago sentiment. In fact, Inverlochy Castle today remains one of the premier places of Scotland for food and accommodations.

Against the scenic backdrop of Ben Nevis, the castle hotel has a mood inside of elegance and refinement, luxurious appointments and antiques, artwork and crystal, plus a profusion of flowers. Danish-born Mrs. Hobbs, the owner, is a delight, equally at home in welcoming a prime minister or an American couple from the Midwest.

Only 14 bedrooms, each with private bath, are offered, and all of them are beautifully furnished. The prices reflect the opulence, however—from £75 ($112.50) in the only single, from £110 ($165) in a double, including VAT, a full Scottish breakfast, and service.

The cuisine is one of the finest in all of Scotland. Every dish emerging from the kitchen of French chef François Huguet is cooked to order and served on silver platters. Sparkling crystal and fine china are placed on hand-carved polished tables where the fortunate guests enjoy such fare as salmon from the Spean or crayfish from Loch Linnhe, even produce from the hotel's own garden. Monsieur Huguet is a natural-born cook, an unusually gifted one at that, adding a creative touch to food yet instinctively preserving its natural flavor. Only dinner is served, and reservations are mandatory. It is likely you'll spend about £25 ($37.50) per person, including tax and service charge, before leaving the table a most satisfied diner. The hotel and restaurant are closed from mid-November to March.

Alexandra (tel. 0397/2241) is a familiar sight, a hotel with tall gables and formidable granite walls, so common in this part of the Highlands. But the hotel is no antiquated mansion—rather, it has been completely modernized, offering 76 double rooms and 11 singles that are pleasantly and attractively furnished. The rate in a bathless double or twin is £30 ($45), rising to £42 ($63) in a double or twin with bath. A single, depending on whether it is bathless or not, ranges in price from £18 ($27) to £27 ($40.50). These tariffs include VAT, service, and a Scottish breakfast. Service and housekeeping standards are good. The chef makes excellent use of fresh fish, and the wine cellar is amply endowed. The vegetables are simply cooked with enjoyable results. A set dinner costs from £10 ($15).

Croit Anna Hotel (tel. 0397/2268) is on the A82 highway 2½ miles south of Fort William, overlooking Loch Linnhe and having fine views of the Ardgour Hills. Many of its rooms have private bathrooms, and several also have color TVs. Singles rent for £22.50 ($33.75) nightly, with doubles or twins going for £21.50 ($32.25) per person, including VAT and service. In the hotel dining room, a set lunch is £6 ($9), with a set dinner costing £10 ($15) and a four-course à la carte meal from £15 ($22.50). Hotel facilities include a game room, TV lounge, panoramic lounge, gift shop, lounge bar, and guest launderette. It's open from April to October, and entertainment is provided on most evenings in season. The hotel is owned and managed by the same family who designed and built it on a traditional Highland croft that has been in their possession for more than 250 years.

Where to Dine

Like its counterpart in Oban, **McTavish's Kitchens** and the coffeeshop are under the same management on the High Street (tel. 0397/2406) and are dedicated to preserving the hearty Scottish cuisine. McTavish's has a self-service cafeteria on the ground floor and a large licensed restaurant upstairs. The cafeteria is open from mid-May until the end of October, with light meals served throughout the open hours. Homemade soup of the day is offered with a range of chef's specials that change from day to day. Main courses include haggis and salmon mayonnaise. The cafeteria is licensed, and you can enjoy dinner with a glass of wine for as little as £5 ($7.50) per person.

If you prefer waitress service, go to the restaurant upstairs, where you can have a predinner drink in the adjoining Laird's Bar, surrounded by photographs of the old Scottish laird. The restaurant's specialties include venison, smoked salmon, fresh local prawns from Loch Linnhe, lobster when available, and Scotland's national dish, haggis. A budget special includes homemade soup, a main course served with vegetables, and a dessert of deep-dish apple pie with cream, costing £6 ($9). If you choose a "Taste of Scotland" menu, the price is £12 ($18).

The restaurant features a Scottish evening in summer, mid-May until the end of September, from 8:30 to 10:30 p.m., with singers, a piper, a Highland dancer, a fiddler, and a small dance band. Admission for the entertainment is £1.55 ($2.33) for adults, 90p ($1.35) for children.

ONICH: On the shores of Loch Linnhe, this charming little village lies to the north of the Ballachulish Bridge. It's a good center if you're taking the western route to Inverness, or going to Skye and Fort William. My favorite hotels in the area follow.

Creag Dhu Hotel (tel. 08553/238) was once the country home of Lady McPherson and takes its name from the rallying cry of her clan. Now a family-run hotel, it lies between Ben Nevis and Glencoe, with expansive lochside and mountain views. The loch views are of prawn-filled Linnhe and Leven. Creag Dhu is an imposing country home with modern additions. All the rooms contain private baths. B&B rates range from £19 ($28.50) per person in low season to £21 ($31.50) per person in high season, including a full breakfast and VAT. Ceilidhs, evenings of Scottish music and song, as well as talks and slide shows are among events held at the hotel. Special musical weekends take place in the spring and autumn, and there are courses in painting, spinning, and other crafts. Such activities as boating, sailing, waterskiing, and aqualung diving are offered, along with good sea and freshwater fishing, pony trekking, riding, golfing, swimming, and tennis. Receiving guests from April to October, the hotel has an enthusiastic repeat clientele.

Onich Hotel (tel. 08553/214) is handsomely perched on the shores of Loch Linnhe, commanding views of the Ardgour and Glencoe Mountains and the Firth of Lorne. Its gardens slope down to the water. Under family management, the hotel definitely reflects a personal touch, both in its welcome of real Highland hospitality and in the appointments of its bedrooms and lounges. The hotel is owned by Ian and Ronald Young, brothers who have run the inn since 1964. They have a loyal band of guests who return yearly. Their cookery enjoys a good reputation for its consistency. Ronald cooks, incidentally, and Ian looks after the administration of the hotel. The bright, airy bedrooms—25 in all—have been modernized and rent for £14.50 ($21.75) per person for B&B. The bed, breakfast, and evening meal rate is £22 ($33) per person. Rooms do not contain private baths, however. The hotel attracts the athletic-minded, as it's a center for walking, climbing, loch bathing, putting, fishing, sailing, and pony trekking. The cuisine is of a good standard, backed up by a fine wine list. Guests gather either in the Clan cocktail bar or the Deerstalker lounge bar. The hotel is open all year.

BALLACHULISH: This small village enjoys a splendid scenic position on the shores of Loch Leven at the entrance to Glencoe. The Ballachulish Bridge links North and South Ballachulish. A good center for touring the western Highlands, the village has the following recommended hotel:

Ballachulish Hotel (tel. 08552/239) stands right on the shores of Loch Leven, at the point where hills split Leven from Loch Linnhe. Built in the style of a Scottish manor house, it offers hospitality, warmth, relaxation—just what you're seeking in a Highland hotel. The bedrooms have a high standard of comfort and convenience, although they vary considerably in style and plumbing. Singles go for £12 ($18) to £18 ($27); twins or doubles, from £26 ($39) to £32 ($48). These tariffs include VAT, service, and a full breakfast. Receiving guests from April to October, the hotel also serves good food, handsomely presented, with fresh ingredients. There are very good bar snacks. The fare offers everything from sandwiches to pizzas, from fish and fresh chips to hot and cold meat dishes. Residents from nearby gather in the hotel's bars, mingling with foreign visitors (and by that I mean the English). From the windows of the hotel you can look out onto views of hill and loch. The staff will arrange boat trips on the lochs or fishing expeditions.

GLENCOE: On the shores of Loch Leven, near where it joins Loch Linnhe, the Ballachulish Bridge now links the villages of North and South Ballachulish, at the entrance to Glencoe. The bridge saves a long drive to the head of the loch if you are coming from the north, but many visitors enjoy the scenic drive to Kinlochleven to come upon the wild and celebrated Glencoe from the east.

Glencoe runs from Rannoch Moor to Loch Leven between some magnificent mountains, including 3766-foot Bidean nam Bian. Known as the "Glen of Weeping," Glencoe is where, on February 11, 1692, Campbells massacred MacDonalds—men, women, and children—who had been their hosts for 12 days. Although massacres were not uncommon in those times, this one shocked even the Highlanders because of the breach of hospitality. When the killing was done, the crime of "murder under trust" was regarded by law as an aggravated form of murder, and carried the same penalties as treason.

The glen, much of which now belongs to the National Trust for Scotland, is full of history and legend. A tiny lochan is known as "the pool of blood" because by its side some men are said to have quarreled over a piece of cheese, and all were killed.

This is an area of massive splendor, with towering peaks and mysterious glens where you can well imagine the fierce battle among the kilted Highlanders to the skirl of the pipes and the beat of the drums.

In the Glen

Almost where Glen Etive joins Glencoe, under the jagged peak of Buchaille Etive Mor dominating the road (A82), lies the **King's House Hotel** (tel. 08552/259), several miles from the village of Glencoe. A building has stood here since the late 14th century. During the Jacobite Rising of 1745, it was required to accommodate troops on their way south from Fort William. It is now a center for skiing and attracts thousands from far and near. Believed to be the oldest licensed inn in Scotland, the hotel has been enlarged and completely modernized. Whichever way you drive through Glencoe, from the rolling east or the dramatic and narrow west, the hotel lying to the north of the road is a welcoming outpost. Simple yet comfortable bedrooms go for £16 ($24) per person if bathless, rising to £19 ($28.50) per person with bath, including breakfast. A set dinner is £10 ($15), and lunchtime snacks are served in the bar, decorated with antlers and paintings of the Glen and surrounding area.

A ski lift is almost opposite the hotel. The Buachaille Etive Mor guards Glencoe's eastern end. This mountain provides a challenge for climbers and was the training ground for Sir John Hunt and the party he took to the top of Everest in the coronation year. This is great climbing and walking country, and rescue techniques evolved and taught here have been widely used.

Besides access from the Glasgow–Inverness highway, guests at the King's House Hotel can be met at the Bridge of Orchy railway station by arrangement.

Glen Orchy, to the south, is well worth a visit too, with the wild river and mountain scenery being beautiful and photogenic. It was the birthplace of the Gaelic bard Duncan Ban MacIntyre, whose song, "In Praise of Ben Doran," is considered a masterpiece.

In Glencoe Village

As you turn away from Loch Leven to enter the historic glen, you will find a number of accommodations available in the village of Glencoe, including—

Glencoe Hotel (tel. 08552/245) is a spruce and stucco building with a slate mansard roof, dominating its area. In the hotel are 13 rooms, including one with a double bed and a private bathroom, one twin-bedded with a private bath, while the other doubles, twins, and singles have hot and cold running water. The hotel charges from £12 ($18) off-season rising to £16 ($24) in high season per person for B&B. Snack lunches are available in all public rooms, and dinner is offered from £7.50 ($11.25). VAT is included in all charges. The hotel is open all year.

MALLAIG: This small fishing village is a good touring center for the western Highlands and the islands. Steamers call here for the Kyle of Lochalsh, the Isle of Skye, the Outer Hebrides, and the sea lochs of the northwest coast. At the tip of a peninsula, Mallaig is a bustling little fishing village, and it is surrounded by moody lochs and hills. The distance between Morar and Mallaig is just three miles.

In the village you can find food and lodging at the **West Highland Hotel** (tel. 0687/2210), Mallaig's major hotel, situated above the port, its bedroom windows looking upon the harbor and the Isle of Skye. The hotel is antiquated, but it offers good old-fashioned comfort and pleasant Highland hospitality. Only a handful of rooms contain private baths, however. Depending on room assignment, singles rent for £15.50 ($23.25) to £20 ($30), and doubles cost £25 ($37.50) to £35 ($52.50), including breakfast. The B&B-and-dinner rate is £25 ($37.50) to £28 ($42). The hotel is open from May to September.

Less expensive is the **Marine Hotel,** near the railway station and ferry terminal (tel. 0687/2217), a family-owned operation that has passed to the third generation. The hotel has been brought up to date, offering some rooms with private baths, hot and cold running water in all rooms, heaters, shaving points, and tea- and coffee-making facilities. The cost is £13 ($19.50) in a single, from £24 ($36) in a double, although you'll pay £4 ($6) extra for a private bath. The Marine is open all year. The location is above a bank.

4. Kyle of Lochalsh and Skye

From the Kyle of Lochalsh you can take a ferry to the mystical Isle of Skye, off the northwest coast of Scotland. The island has inspired many of the best loved and best known of Scottish ballads such as "Over the Sea to Skye" and "Will Ye Not Come Back Again." On the 48-mile-long island, you can explore castle ruins, duns, and brochs, enjoying a Highland welcome. For the Scots, the island will forever evoke images of Flora Macdonald, who conducted Bonnie Prince Charlie to Skye. She disguised him as Betty Burke after the Culloden defeat.

Once on Skye, you'll find ferry service back to Kyle or to Mallaig from Armadale. The Armadale ferry transports cars, but the service is less frequent than the one to Kyle. If you're planning to take your car, reservations are recommended.

Caledonian MacBrayne, The Pier, Gourock, near Glasgow (tel. Gourock 34664), runs ferry services to Skye and to Mull. The company also offers inclusive tours for people and cars to island-hop, using their services between islands. This is an ideal opportunity to visit places well away from the beaten track. The information office at Gourock is most helpful, and someone there will assist you in planning a trip if you wish to make up your own journey.

The largest island of the Inner Hebrides, Skye is separated from the mainland by the Sound of Sleat on its southeastern side. At Kyleakin, on the eastern end, the channel is only a quarter of a mile wide and thus the ferry docks there. Dominating the land of summer seas, streams, woodland glens, mountain passes, cliffs, and waterfalls are the Cuillin Hills, a range of jagged black mountains. The Peninsula of Sleat, the island's southernmost arm, is known as "The Garden of Skye."

DORNIE: This small crofting village on the road to the Isle of Skye is the meeting place of three lochs—Duich, Long, and Alsh. On a rocky islet stands **Eilean Donan Castle,** Wester Ross at Dornie, eight miles east of Kyle of Lochalsh on the A87. This romantic castle was built in 1220 as a defense against the Danes. In 1719 it was shelled by the British frigate *Worcester.* In ruins for 200 years, it was restored by Colonel MacRae of Clan MacRae in 1932 and is now a clan war memorial and museum, containing Jacobite relics, mostly with clan connections. It is open April to September 30 daily, including Sunday, from 10 a.m. to 12:30 p.m. and 2 to 6 p.m., charging £1 ($1.50) for admission.

South of Dornie and Eilean Donan Castle is Shiel Bridge. From here, an "unclassified road" leads to **Glenelg,** after a twisting climb over Ratagan Pass with a fine view of the mountain range known as the **Five Sisters of Kintail,** which is dominated by Sgurr Fhuaran, 3505 feet high. In summer a car-ferry crosses the Sound of Sleat to Skye. It was from Glenelg that Dr. Johnson and James Boswell crossed to Skye in 1773. In Gleann Beag, two miles to the southeast, stand two of the best preserved Iron Age brochs on the Scottish mainland—**Dun Telve** and **Dun Troddan.** Brochs are stone towers with double walls, probably built more than 2000 years ago by the Picts for protection against raiders. The walls of the two brochs are more than 30 feet high.

Just outside Dornie, across Loch Long and at the end of Loch Duich, the **Loch Duich Hotel,** Ardelve, near Kyle of Lochalsh (tel. 059-985/213), is among my favorite hotels, in a dream location overlooking one of the Highland's most photogenic castles, Eilean Donan. It's now owned by Rod and Gerry Stenson, a young couple who have brought their enthusiasm and energy to the place. They lived for two years on the island of Rhum, running the castle and guest house there where they learned to be self-sufficient.

Gerry cooks—really cooks! She turns out bread, oatcakes, cakes, scones, shortbread, pâtés, broth, and even makes yogurt from their own goats' milk as well as cream cheese from the same herd. Vegetarians are welcome—just give them fair warning, as Gerry is adept in balancing a suitable diet and producing appetizing meals.

Behind the hotel is a pub, reached through the hallway or outside-and-round-the-corner. It's well patronized by locals and guests alike in the evenings. At lunch, bar snacks include a hot dish along with a substantial soup and homemade bread, plus freshly made, well-filled sandwiches.

The hotel has a small lounge and bar where you can wait for dinner, from £10 ($15). It's likely to be a magnificent meal of fresh chowder or pâté, followed by local venison (melt in your mouth) or perhaps a local fish. Rod's worry is that in winter they can't always provide fresh vegetables in this wild part of the island. But you can rest assured that everything that possibly can be is fresh.

Bedrooms are simple, and many overlook Eilean Donan and the loch. Including an enormous freshly cooked breakfast with porridge and eggs and bacon—you name it—they charge £16 ($24) per person.

They also have a boat which you can rent to go fishing (Gerry will cook your catch for supper). For those so inclined, the National Trust for Scotland Ranger Service, 5 Charlotte Square, Edinburgh EH2 4DU (tel. 031/226-5922 in Edinburgh), will arrange for you to make the six-mile guided hike through some of Scotland's wildest country along the Seven Sisters Kintail. Advance reservations are necessary, as this is no country stroll, and you must be suitably clad and fit.

From Dornie, it is a short drive to the—

KYLE OF LOCHALSH: This popular center for touring the western Highlands is also a good jumping-off point to the islands. A car-ferry leaves for Kyleakin on the Isle of Skye. There is no need to book in advance. The journey is only ten minutes. The ferry shuttles back and forth all day, and you will have plenty of time to drive the length of Skye in a day, returning to the mainland by night if you want to. If that is your intent, you might register at:

Lochalsh Hotel (tel. 0599/4202) occupies a choice situation right beside the loch where the ferry to Skye sails in front of the windows. Rooms have been modernized, a single renting from £18 ($27) to £32 ($48), and a double from £35 ($52.50) to £65 ($97.50), including a Scottish breakfast and VAT.

Lunch is served in the Ocean Bar, a choice of snacks including grilled mussels in garlic, smoked fish mousse, homemade soup, fisherman's kebab, grilled herrings in oatmeal, omelets, and a hot dish of the day. If you happen to be on the "Road to the Isles" on a nippy day, try afternoon tea here with pancakes and scones, covered with jam, along with buttered toast and pastries, served with coffee or tea. This will amply fill you and revive your spirit. A set dinner at £11.50 ($17.25) is likely to include a choice of four appetizers such as mackerel and horseradish sauce, followed by a selection of five main dishes, including grilled or roast meat, a fish dish, plus a choice from the dessert trolley. The chef does a number of interesting house specialties—scallops, collops, and venison.

BALMACARA: Those planning to stay in the Kyle of Lochalsh district, taking the car and passenger ferry to Skye, may prefer a more peaceful oasis for a day or two. In the Balmacara estate, now the property of the National Trust for Scotland, the **Balmacara Hotel** (tel. Balmacara 283) is a quiet, unassuming choice. On the road along Balmacara Bay, facing the Cuillins of Skye, it has been preferred by many readers, although I personally have not stayed there. Guests are received all year and charged from £22 ($33) with bath in a single, from £38 ($57) in a double with bath, including breakfast. An evening meal will cost from £10 ($15). A fishing party can be arranged.

A hotel courtesy bus can be arranged to meet you at Kyle Railway Station when coming from Inverness, or at the Skye ferry terminal.

ISLE OF SKYE: Skye is the largest of the Inner Hebrides, 48 miles long and between 3 and 25 miles wide. It is separated from the mainland by the Sound of Sleat (pronounced Slate). There are many stories as to the origin of the name, Skye. Some believe it is from the Norse "ski," meaning a cloud, while others say it is from the Gaelic word for winged. There are Norse names on the island, however, as the Norsemen held sway for four centuries before 1263. Overlooking the Kyle is the ruined Castle Maol, once the home of a Norwegian princess.

For those who want to overnight or spend a longer holiday on the island, I offer the following suggestions, scattered in the various hamlets. However, in summer be sure to reserve in advance, as accommodations are extremely limited.

There are coach tours three or four times a week in summer from Kyleakin where the ferry lands to Dunvegan Castle or to the north end of the island. They generally start at 10 a.m., returning to Kyleakin around 6 p.m., so you need not take your car across with you. Telephone 0599/4328, **Clan Coaches,** for further information.

If you're staying at Portree in the center of the island, **W. J. Sutherland,** Glenbrittle, Skye (tel. Carbost 267), operates a round trip from Portree to Sligachan, then Carbost where the Talisker Whisky Distillery is. Then it goes on to Portnalong and Fiskavaig on the west coast where there is a sandy beach for a day of relaxation before the return journey at 5 p.m. The round trip costs £2.50 ($3.25).

Kyleakin

The ferry from Kyle of Lochalsh docks at this tiny waterfront village. For those seeking a quiet, well-kept place to stay, I'd recommend:

Dunringell Hotel (tel. 0599/4180) sits in 4½ acres of extensive lawns in which rhododendrons, azaleas, and other flowering shrubs provide a riot of color from March to July. Dunringell is a spacious structure, built in 1912, with large bedrooms and public rooms. Mr. and Mrs. MacPherson charge £15 ($22.50) with bath, £12.50 ($18.75) without bath, per person for B&B. For half board, the tariff per person is £20 ($30) with bath, £18 ($27) without. Both a smoking and no-smoking lounge are maintained for guests. For those who wish to participate, the MacPhersons hold a short worship service in one of the lounges each evening.

Broadford

This town is the meeting point for the ports of Armadale, Kylerhea, and Kyleakin.

Broadford Hotel (tel. Broadford 204) is a venerated old inn dating from 1611, when it was established by Sir Lauchlin MacKinnon. It was here that a descendant of his first came up with the secret recipe for Drambuie liqueur, now a symbol throughout the world of Highland hospitality.

The Broadford has seen a lot of changes since those days, and it's been completely modernized and brought up to date, both in its bedrooms and public facilities. The inn lies by the waters of Broadford River, and guests are allowed to fish for salmon and trout. If you'd like this congenial center for exploring the southern part of Skye, you can request a double room for £33 ($49.50) to £41 ($61.50), the latter with bath, or a single for £17.50 ($26.25), depending on the plumbing. If you're traveling with a child, it costs £8 ($12) extra to have a bed added to the room. Rooms are comfortable and unpretentious.

The old inn offers good Scottish cooking, making fine use of the local produce. A dinner goes for £8.50 ($12.75). You can stop in for a drink in the cocktail bar. The inn lies four minutes from the Skye airfield, where there is direct daily service to Glasgow. Nearby are the ruins of the farmhouse where Samuel Johnson and his companion, Boswell, spent a night on their tour of the Highlands.

Sligachan

Sligachan Hotel (tel. Sligachan 204) stands in the middle of the islands on its own moorland at the head of a beautiful loch, affording views of water and hills. As such, the hotel is the most convenient center from which to explore the entire island. Climbers who love "to go up in the heather" book its 23 simply furnished bedrooms, only nine of which contain private baths. April to October, they cost from £19 ($28.50) to £21 ($31.50), including a big Scottish breakfast that often features kippers and porridge. The meals are excellent, comprising, for example, homemade soups, steak-and-kidney pie with a flaky crust, salmon, followed by fresh fruit and cream, ending with good coffee. A complete dinner costs from £10 ($15). At Sligachan guests in their classic tweeds (which have been well broken in) mingle freely in good companionship, and the talk is of fishing for trout and salmon and of motorboat excursions through the Outer Hebrides.

Portree

Skye's capital, Portree, is the port for steamers making trips around the island and linking Skye with the 15-mile-long island Raasay. Sligachan, nine miles south, and Glenbrittle, seven miles farther southwest, are centers for climbing the Cuillin (Coolin) Hills.

Royal Hotel (tel. 0478/2525) stands on a hill facing the water and is said to have offered hospitality to Bonnie Prince Charlie during his flight in 1746. In less dramatic and rushed circumstances, you can book one of its comfortable bedrooms, the preferred ones opening onto the sea. A double- or twin-bedded room costs £18 ($27) if bathless, £24 ($36) with bath. A bathless single costs £21 ($31.50). À la carte meals and bar snacks are offered, a dinner in the restaurant averaging £12 ($18). Bar snacks cost about £1.50 ($2.25) and up per plate. The hotel is open all year.

Rosedale Hotel, Beaumont Crescent (tel. 0478/2531), lying in one of the more secluded parts of Portree, opens directly onto the sea. Owned and run by the Andrews family since 1950, it is a warm and friendly place. The hotel offers 20 bedrooms decorated in the modern style, most of which have private baths or showers and toilets en suite. The Rosedale is open only from May to October, charging £15 ($22.50) per person in a bathless room, the rate increasing to £19 ($28.50) per person with bath. These tariffs include a big Scottish breakfast. In a lounge, you can be served a good range of Highland malt whiskies. The food is good too.

Uig

This village is on Trotternish, the largest Skye peninsula, and ferry port for Harris and Uist in the Outer Hebrides. It is 15 miles north of Portree and 49 miles from Kyle of Lochalsh. **Monkstadt House,** a mile and a half north, is where Flora MacDonald brought Prince Charles, in the guise of a girl named Betty Burke, after their escape flight from Benbecula. In **Kilmuir** churchyard, five miles north, Flora was buried, wrapped in a sheet used by the prince. Her grave is marked by a Celtic cross.

Uig Hotel (tel. Uig 205) has been furnished with warmth, imagination, and creativity. In home-like comfort, guests are welcomed and shown to the lounge with its pleasant, harmonious colors. The hotel stands on a hillside overlooking a small bay and a tiny fishing harbor. The food, excellently prepared Scottish fare, is served in a cheerful dining room with a view of the bay. The 24-room hotel comes equipped with private bath or shower in every chamber. Rates range from £16.50 ($24.75) to £26.50 ($39.75) for singles, £33 ($49.50) to £52 ($78) for doubles, including a full Scottish breakfast and VAT. Half-board rates go from £25 ($37.50) to £35 ($52.50) per person. The hotel is open from April to the end of September.

Dunvegan

The village of Dunvegan grew up around **Dunvegan Castle,** the principal man-made sight on the Isle of Skye, seat of the chiefs of Clan MacLeod who have lived there for 700 years. The castle, which stands on a rocky promontory, was once accessible only by boat, but now the moat is bridged and the castle open to the public. It holds many fascinating relics, including a "fairy flag." It is reputed to be the oldest inhabited castle in Britain. It is open March 31 to mid-May from 2 to 5 p.m., mid-May to the end of September from 10:30 a.m. to 5 p.m., and for most of October from 2 to 5 p.m. It is closed all day Sunday. Adults pay £1.50 ($2.25) for admission; children, 75p ($1.13).

The **Black House museum,** four miles from Dunvegan on the Glendale road (tel. Glendale 291), contains implements and furniture of bygone days and has a peat fire burning throughout the day. A replica of an illicit whisky still can be seen behind the museum, which is open daily from 10 a.m. to 7 p.m.

There's also a pottery and silversmith in Glendale, along with a watermill and an art gallery specializing in local views. **Skye Venture Cottage Industry,** 18 Holmisdal, Glendale-by-Dunvegan (tel. Glendale 316), specializes in hand- and machine-made sweaters, waistcoats, hats, and scarves, with a wide range of Arran, Fair Isle, and Icelandic garments. The store is open Monday to Saturday from 10 a.m. to 6 p.m.

At **Trumpan,** nine miles north of Dunvegan, are the remains of a church that was set afire in 1597 by MacDonald raiders while the congregation, all MacLeods, were inside at worship. Only one woman survived. The MacLeods of Dunvegan rushed to the defense, and only two MacDonalds escaped death.

Atholl House Hotel (tel. 047-022/219), owned by John and Mary Laing, is a small Highland hotel offering hospitality to guests seeking B&B and evening dinner. The hotel is in the village of Dunvegan close to the historic Dunvegan Castle. Enjoy traditional Scottish cooking in the dining room overlooking Loch Dunvegan and MacLeod's Tables. Then relax in the lounge with a malt whisky to the sound of the great Highland bagpipe if you wish. Overnight accommodation with dinner and breakfast costs around £20 ($30) per person.

Skeabost Bridge

Eastward from Dunvegan is Skeabost Bridge, with an island cemetery of great antiquity. The graves of four Crusaders are here.

Nearby is the **Skeabost House Hotel** (tel. 047-032/202), one of the most comfortable, refreshing, and inviting country homes of Skye, receiving paying guests from May 1 to mid-October. Thoroughly modernized, it is interesting architecturally with its dormers, chimneys, tower, and gables, everything a weather-worn beige. Inside, the taste level is high, with wood paneling and carpets. Once a private estate, it has been converted into a lochside hotel, standing on beautiful grounds that in summer are studded with flowering bushes. The location is 35 miles from Kyle of Lochalsh and 5 miles from Portree.

Sportsmen are attracted to the hotel, gathering in the firelit lounge for a mellow scotch whisky. The atmosphere is of hardy tweeds with the distinctive aroma of a good cigar. The loch outside is well stocked with salmon and trout.

Of the 27 handsomely furnished rooms, 16 contain private baths. Singles are accepted at a rate of £18.50 ($27.75) to £24 ($36), and doubles cost from £17.50 ($26.25) to £24 ($36) per person, including a big Scottish breakfast. The Scottish fare, including smoked salmon, is served on fine china and elegant silver, a dinner costing from £12 ($18).

RAASAY: For an offbeat adventure, I suggest a side trip to this 14-mile-long island, which has a fine panoramic view over the Isle of Skye. A car-ferry, leaving from Sconsar on Skye, is in service about three times a day (check at the tourist office on Skye for exact times of departure). From June 25 to around mid-August, the service is increased to four times a day. Each passenger must pay $2.50 (U.S.) for a one-way fare or about $20 per car.

On a recent visit, I didn't find the gaiety and laughter Johnson and Boswell did. The local school is rapidly dwindling in enrollment, and only about 100 people still inhabit the island, most of them apparently hovering around the age of 65. The island's young people have mostly gone on to such cities as Glasgow, returning only for the Christmas holidays, and sometimes not even then.

It is this very remoteness that attracts many to Raasay, visitors who like to wander around a depopulated countryside, enjoying the quiet of country lanes, the uncrowded feeling everywhere, and the beautiful, but out-of-the-way, scenery, with an eye out for birdlife.

You can find lodging and food on the island at the **Raasay Hotel** (tel. Raasay 222), which is run by Alistair Nicolson, a man who long ago grew accustomed to rugged winter weather. He is also the captain of the ferryboat that brought you over the sea from Skye. His is the only guest house on the island, and he has many stories— often sad—to relate about the depopulation of his island. However, he has hopes for the future, especially the growth of tourism, and he has made enlargements and improvements to his Edwardian house.

Captain Nicolson has a dozen rooms, all with private plumbing, renting for about $40 (U.S.) per person per day on a half-board arrangement. Scottish breakfasts are hearty here. You'll need one to fortify you for the day.

5. Oban and District

Oban (meaning "small bay") is the great port for the Western Isles and a center of Gaelic culture. It is the gateway to Mull, largest of the Inner Hebrides; to the island of Iona, the cradle of Scottish Christianity; and to Staffa, where Fingal's Cave inspired Mendelssohn to write his Hebrides Overture. The ferries to the offshore islands run only twice a day until summer; then there are cruises to Iona from early June to late September. For information about island ferry services to Mull, Iona, and the Outer Hebrides, get in touch with **MacBraynes Steamers** at their office in Oban (tel. 0631/62285).

Back on the mainland, I'll include a number of colorful sites, such as Fort Appin and Inveraray, for those who prefer to soak up atmosphere away from the major towns.

OBAN: One of Scotland's leading coastal resorts, the bustling port town of Oban is set in a sheltered bay that is almost landlocked by the island of Kerrera. A yachting center and small burgh, it lies about 50 miles south of Fort William.

From Pulpit Hill in Oban there is a fine view across the Firth of Lorn and the Sound of Mull. Overlooking the town is an unfinished replica of the Colosseum of Rome, built by a banker, John Stuart McCaig, in 1897–1900 as a memorial to his family and to try to curb local unemployment during a slump. Its walls are two feet thick and from 37 to 40 feet high. The courtyard within is landscaped and the tower is floodlit at night. It is known locally as **McCaig's Folly.**

In September the Oban Highland Games are held, with massed pipe bands marching through the streets. The Oban Pipe Band plays regularly throughout the summer, parading up and down main street. Paul W. Ware, New Providence, Pennsylvania, writes: "During evening, the promenade is traversed by little dogs pulling their masters who are wearing tweed jackets and smoking pipes. But the town also attracts young people."

On the island of Kerrera stands **Gylen Castle,** home of the Mac-Dougalls, dating back to 1587.

Near the little granite **Cathedral of the Isles,** one mile north of the end of the bay, is the ruin of the 13th-century **Dunollie Castle,** seat of the Lords of Lorn who once owned a third of Scotland.

You can visit **Dunstaffnage Castle,** 3½ miles to the north, which was believed to have been the royal seat of the Dalriadic monarchy in the eighth century. The present castle was probably built in 1263. "The Stone of Destiny," now in Westminster Abbey, was kept here before its removal to Scone.

In Oban, Gaelic is taught in schools as a "leaving certificate subject."

Where to Stay

As a holiday resort, Oban has a number of good hotels and guest houses within easy reach of the seafront and the piers from which cruises to the offshore islands can be booked.

Alexandra, Esplanade (tel. 0631/62381), is a stone hotel with gables and a tower, plus a Regency-style front veranda, enjoying a sunny perch on the promenade. From its public rooms, you can look out onto Oban Bay. Two sun lounges overlook the seafront. The bedrooms are substantial and pleasing, offering comfort and conveniences at a rate in a single that ranges from £32 ($48), in a double from £48 ($72), including VAT, service, and a full breakfast. Of the 60 bedrooms, nearly half contain private baths. The restaurant, serving good food, also opens onto the panorama. Bar lunches are available for around £4 ($6), a complete dinner in the evening averaging around £12 ($18). Dinner is accompanied by live music and dancing. The hotel is open from Easter to the end of October.

Lancaster, Esplanade (tel. 0631/62587), is distinguished by its attractive pseudo-Tudor facade. On the crescent of the bay, it commands views from its public rooms of the islands of Lismore and Kerrera, even the more distant peaks of Mull. Open all year, the hotel is managed by its resident owners, Mr. and Mrs. J. T. Ramage, who welcome you to one of their well-furnished bedrooms, charging from £15 ($22.50) per person, including breakfast. For bed, breakfast, and evening meal, the charge is £21 ($31.50) per person nightly. A number of rooms offer central heating, and a few have private baths or showers. The fully licensed Lancaster is the only hotel in Oban featuring a heated indoor swimming pool, a sauna, a Jacuzzi, and a solarium.

Wellpark Hotel (tel. 0631/62948) is a substantial stone house with a gabled bay window, positioned on the seafront and commanding views of the bay and the islands of Kerrera, Mull, and Lismore. It's also one of the best bargains in Oban. Mr. and Mrs. R. B. Dickison welcome you, charging £16.50 ($24.75) per person nightly for bed, dinner, and a full Scottish breakfast, based on double occupancy. Their rooms—simple, pleasantly comfortable—contain hot and cold running water and are equipped with electric blankets. Many contain private showers and toilets. The hotel receives guests from May to October, and there is full central heating.

Where to Dine

McTavish's Kitchens, George Street (tel. 0631/63064), like its cousin in Fort William, is dedicated to preserving the local cuisine. Downstairs is a self-service cafeteria providing à la carte breakfasts from 9 to 11:30 a.m. and light meals served throughout the day and evening, seven days a week. There are, in addition, Laird's Bar, opening onto a beautiful view over Oban Bay, and the Mantrap Bar with a "real mantrap." The licensed second-floor restaurant has a more ambitious Scottish and continental menu with higher prices. It's open only from mid-May to the end of September, from 6 to 10:30 p.m.

Specialties include lobster (when available), scallops in wine sauce, local mussels, "Heilan steak" (two small filets of beef, one with white wine sauce, the other with red wine sauce), venison steak (local red deer), Lochfyne kippers (kippered by a man with two generations of kipperers before him), local haddock, and salmon. If you wish a budget meal, have the special lunch, £2 ($3) for two courses, including fresh salmon mayonnaise, or the early-evening special, served from 6 to 10:30 p.m., costing £3 ($4.50). You'll have the salmon mayonnaise, haddock, bread and butter, and tea or coffee. You can also feast on a 12-ounce rump steak or choose a light à la carte meal.

A feature of the restaurant is the Scottish evenings, with songs in Gaelic and English, piping, Highland dancing, and accordion playing. Most evenings, there is also fiddle music. The entertainment is held nightly from 8:30 to 10:30 from mid-May until the end of September. Admission is £1.50 ($2.25) for adults, 75p ($1.13) for children. For younger patrons, a pop band plays every Friday from 11 p.m. to 1:30 a.m., and a disco is held every Saturday from 11 p.m. to 1 a.m.

On the Outskirts

The Isle of Eriska Hotel, Ledaig, Connel, near Oban, in Strathclyde (tel. 0631-72/371), is a glorious Victorian house that welcomes you at the end of a winding drive. From the main road it takes about five minutes to reach the house, which must remind one of a clan castle with the house flag flying strongly from the tower. A magnificent front door leads to the paneled entrance hall, with a log fire to back up the central heating.

A wide staircase leads to the spacious bedrooms which are well furnished with wax-polished furniture, comfortable beds, and warm, cheerful draperies. Modern bathrooms with showers as well as tubs have been installed, and thoughtful touches include nail brushes, large cakes of soap, and bath crystals. Fresh fruit is presented, and conveniences include phone and radio. Dinner, bed, and breakfast is around £60 ($90) to £69 ($103.50) per person, including VAT and service. The Isle of Eriska is owned and very personally run by Mr. and Mrs. Robin Buchanan-Smith.

Settled in, you're expected to wear jacket and tie for dinner, as you descend for a drink in the bar before embarking upon a six-course meal. You get no choices, except for appetizers. The main course is nearly always a roast joint. If you're worried, you have only to discuss your diet with the chef, who will arrange something else. Nonresidents are charged £15 ($22.50) per person for dinner. Afterward, you repair to the lounge or the hall for coffee.

Breakfast is an adventure, a step back into the past. Silver dishes on the sideboard contain kippers, haddock, bacon, sausages, kidneys, tomatoes, eggs, you name it. If it's not usually there, it will be by the next morning. Try porridge the proper way, that is, cooked slowly for more than 12 hours on the stove.

After breakfast, you can charter the seven-ton Bermudan rig yacht for fishing or visiting the islands on the loch. Or you can ride a Highland pony across the countryside, play tennis, or just walk in the beautiful gardens. It's also possible to visit the home farm whence much fresh produce comes to the kitchens.

Lunch is an informal buffet meal of cold meats, salads, and cheese. On Sunday a traditional lunch is served, and that evening supper is a relaxed meal set out on the sideboard for you to help yourself. Morning coffee and afternoon tea are served free to residents.

PORT APPIN: To the north of Oban lies a beautiful lochside district, including Lismore Island. On an islet nearby is a landmark, **Castle Stalker,** the ancient seat of the Stewarts of Appin, built in the 15th century by Duncan Stewart, son of the first chief of Appin. Dugald, the ninth chief, was forced to sell the estate in 1765, and the castle slowly fell into ruin. It was recently restored and is once again inhabited. According to myth, there's a subterranean undersea passage at Port Appin where a piper supposedly entered with his dog. Only the dog returned, and he was hairless. Port Appin itself is a small hamlet of stone cottages.

Airds Hotel (tel. 063-173/236) is an old ferry inn, one of the most outstanding in its classification, dating from 1700, in one of the most beautiful spots in the historic district of Appin. You're assured of serenity if you take a room at this tranquil choice on Loch Linnhe, midway between Oban and Fort William. The hotel overlooks not only Loch Linnhe, but the island of Lismore and the mountains of Morvern, an ideal center for touring this area of the country. You can take forest walks in many directions, or go pony trekking, sea angling, or trout fishing. Boats can be rented and trips arranged to see the seals and to visit the island of Lismore.

The resident proprietors, Mr. and Mrs. Allen, welcome you to one of their comfortably furnished bedrooms, 11 of which contain private baths (in the new addition). The daily rate for dinner, bed, and breakfast is £40 ($60) per person. The food is excellent, using fresh produce when possible. By all means try to return to the inn for a bountiful Scottish tea in the late afternoon, with home-baked scones and cakes. Guests are received from March to October. The hotel has a cocktail bar, a public bar, and residents' lounges.

LOCH AWE: Twenty-two miles long and in most places only about a mile wide, Loch Awe for years acted as a natural moat protecting the Campbells of Inveraray from their enemies to the north. Along its banks and on its islands are many reminders of its fortified past. There is a ruined castle at Fincharn, at the southern end of the loch, and another on the island of Fraoch Eilean. The **Isle of Inishail** has an ancient chapel and burial ground, and at the northern end of the loch are the ruins of **Kilchurn Castle,** built by Sir Colin Campbell in 1440. The bulk of Ben Cruachan, 3689 feet, dominates Loch Awe at its northern end and attracts climbers. On the ben is the world's second-largest hydroelectric power station, which pumps water from Loch Awe to a reservoir high up the mountain. Below the mountain are the **Falls of Cruachan** and the wild **Pass of Brander,** where Robert the Bruce routed the Clan MacDougall in 1308.

In this area, the Forestry Commission maintains the vast forests, and a new road now makes it possible to travel around Loch Awe, so that it is more than ever a popular angling center. Sharp-eyed James Bond fans may even recognize some scenes that appeared in one of the films.

The Pass of Brander where Loch Awe narrows was the scene of many a fierce battle in bygone times, and something of that bloody past seems to brood over the narrow defile. Through it the waters of the Awe flow on their way to Loch Etive. This winding sealoch is 19 miles long, stretching from Dun Dunstaffnage Bay at Oban to Glen Etive, reaching into the Moor of Rannoch at the foot of the 3000-foot Buachaille Etive (the Shepherd of Etive), into which Glencoe also reaches.

The **Portsonachan Hotel,** Lochaweside, by Dalmally (tel. 08663/224), is in a delightful position on the south shore of the loch, where an inn has stood since the 15th century. It's on the old drove road from Oban to the cattle markets of central Scotland, and has retained the charm of bygone years. You get good accommodation, morning tea served in your room, and excellent meals. The price per person per night depends on which floor of the hotel you are on. If you're on the first floor, you'll pay £32 ($48) for dinner, bed, and breakfast in a bathless room, £36 ($54) in a room with a complete bath. In a bathless room on the second floor, you'll be charged £28 ($42) for full board. The hotel has a public bar where you'll see mementos of the past and a recently refurbished and enlarged cocktail bar. In the main lounge, an open peat/log fire welcomes you, and there is a small lounge with TV. Reader Mrs. Ella Crabb of West Vancouver, B.C., says she found this an excellent "middle of the road" hotel so far as prices go in the area.

THE CRINAN CANAL: The nine-mile-long canal, constructed between 1793 and 1801, was designed to provide water communication between the Firth of Clyde, Argyll, the western Highlands, and the islands. It runs roughly north from Ardrishaig and curves gradually to the west before reaching Loch Crinan on the Sound of Jura. Four miles north of **Cairnbaan,** on the canal, is the ruined hill-fort of **Dunadd,** once capital of Dalriada, kingdom of the Scots. There are numerous Bronze Age stone circles in the vicinity, and **Kilmartin churchyard,** five miles north of Cairnbaan, has a carved cross dating from the 16th century. **Carnasserie Castle,** also to the north of the canal, built in the late 16th century, was the home of John Carswell, the first post-Reformation bishop of the isles, whose translation of John Knox's liturgy into Gaelic was the first book to be published in that language.

Crinan, a yachtsman's haven on the Sound of Jura, is overlooked by the early 11th-century **Duntrune Castle,** one of the oldest castles in Scotland, and still inhabited by the descendants of the original owners, the Clan Malcolm. Crinan is a charming little village.

Lochgilphead, a pleasant little town sitting just where the canal turns westward, is the address of my recommendation for a stopover in this area:

The **Cairnbaan Motor Inn** (tel. 0546/2488). Formerly an old coach inn and now a privately owned hotel, this is an excellent base for touring Argyll and the islands. Nearby are safe beaches, and for the sportsman there is loch fishing, sea angling, and salmon fishing on the River Add. The motor inn has comfortable, modern bedrooms, some with private bathrooms and verandas. All bedrooms have built-in wardrobes, wash basins, razor sockets, radios, intercoms, and baby listening service. The tariff is £16 ($24) per person.

The split-level dining room has a superb view southward down the busy canal. Emphasis for the cuisine is on Scottish dishes. There is a handsome cocktail bar and a comfortable sun lounge with a patio beyond.

Crinan Hotel (tel. Crinan 235), off the B841, seven miles northwest of Lochgilphead, is an inn with a bright, attractive decor and modern comforts and conveniences. Because of its location on a canal and yacht basin, it is naturally a favorite with yachtsmen, who book its 22 rooms with private bath in July and August, the peak sailing months. If you're reserving (and I highly recommend that you do), ask for one of the rooms with private balconies opening onto mountains and lochside sunsets.

The hotel is managed by Nicolas Ryan, who once worked as a bellboy on the old *Queen Mary,* later rising rapidly within the Cunard organization. Bedrooms rent for £28 ($42) in a single, from £45 ($67.50) to £50 ($75) in a double, including a breakfast that often features oatcakes and hot croissants.

Open all year, the hotel serves good food—dishes such as fresh salmon, Crinan clams mornay, roast duckling in black cherry sauce, and Scottish sirloin. Meals are served from noon to 2 p.m. and from 7 to 9 p.m. A table d'hôte luncheon goes for £7.50 ($11.25), a set dinner for £15 ($22.50), although you are likely to pay £20 ($30) if you order from the seafood menu. Luncheon in fair weather is served alfresco. The hotel is one of the best run in the area. As efficient as Mr. Ryan's staff is, they never overlook old-fashioned Scottish hospitality and friendliness.

INVERARAY: This small resort and royal burgh occupies a splendid Highland setting on the upper shores of Loch Fyne. The hereditary seat of the Dukes of Argyll, **Inveraray Castle** has been headquarters of the Clan Campbell since the early 15th century. In 1644 the original village was burned by the Royalist Marquess of Montrose, was rebuilt, and then the third Duke of Argyll built a new castle between 1744 and 1788. The 11th duke opened the castle to the public and it is now presided over by the present laird, the 12th Duke of Argyll and 26th MacCailein Mor, chief of the Clan Campbell. A special welcome is given anyone who is related to Clan Campbell. The castle is among the earliest examples of Gothic revival in Britain, and offers a fine collection of pictures and 18th-century French furniture, old English and continental porcelain, and a magnificent Armoury Hall, which alone contains 1300 pieces. There is a castle shop for souvenirs and a tea room where tea, coffee, and snack meals are served. The castle is open daily except Friday from 10 a.m. to 1 p.m. and 2 to 6 p.m. in April, May, June, September, and October. In July and August, hours are 10 a.m. to 6 p.m. daily. Sunday hours are 2 to 6 p.m. year round. Admission is £2 ($3) for adults, £1.25 ($1.88) for children. A family ticket is available for £5.50 ($8.25). The castle is closed on Friday from the opening date until the end of June each year and in September and October.

At one end of the main street of the town is a Celtic burial cross from Iona. The parish church is divided by a wall enabling services to be held in Gaelic and English at the same time.

The **Auchindrain Museum of Country Life** (tel. Furnace 235), six miles southwest of Inveraray, is an open-air museum of traditional Highland farming life. It is a unique survivor of the past, whose origins are so far back as to be a subject for archeology. The farming township stands more or less as it was in the 1800s, but studies are now revealing at least four centuries before that. At present, Auchindrain consists of 20-odd acres of the "infield," about which stand 21 houses and barns of the 18th and 19th centuries. Some are furnished to their appropriate period, and others contain displays. There is also an exhibit center and a museum shop. The land is being brought back into use, and it is already growing traditional crops and supporting livestock. Open daily during the summer, it charges £1.50 ($2.25) for adults, 75p ($1.13) for children over 7 years old. The museum is closed Saturday during April, May, and September. Auchindrain and mid-Argyll are in an area crammed with things and places of interest for historians, antiquarians, and archeologists.

A fine woodland garden may be visited at **Crarae Lodge,** four miles southwest of the village.

Vacationing fishing enthusiasts may want to visit the **Castle Fisheries** (tel. 0499/2233), two miles north past the castle on the Oban road. Primarily a farm providing trout for the table, facilities are set up so that visitors can try their luck in one of the trout ponds, while the children play in the playground area or enjoy snacks from the refreshment stand. Other facilities include a baby deer park and even a hospital for sick fish. Admission is 75p ($1.13) for adults, 40p (60¢) for children, with an additional charge to those who go fishing. It's open 10 a.m. to 6 p.m., from April to October (fishing all year). If you want to fish, you must pay £4.75 ($7.13) for a day's license, plus 80p ($1.20) for a rod. There's a small charge for each fish you catch over the minimum size (those you throw back, of course).

For food and accommodations in Inveraray, I'd suggest the **George,** Main Street (tel. 0499/2111), which is a small inn, open all year. The overnight rate is £12 ($18) to £14 ($21) per person, including a full Scottish breakfast, service, and VAT. The rooms are simply furnished, with a minimum of plumbing, decidedly old-fashioned. The dining room, however-er, is attractively modern with bright furnishings. A four-course dinner costs from £7.50 ($11.25), and bar snacks for lunch range from bacon rolls to fresh salmon salad. Downstairs there's a public bar with stone walls and a flagstone floor, a part of which was connected with the stables when the George was a stagecoach inn. Here you can order snacks at lunch along with your lager.

6. The Inner Hebrides

Geologists wandering through bog and bracken used to happen on painters and birdwatchers and stumble across an occasional sea angler or mountain climber. That era of solitude was some time ago, however. These special-interest individuals still frequent the islands of the Hebrides, but now you'll find more and more general tourists.

Nearly everybody has heard of Mull and Iona, but what about Rhum, Eigg, and Muck? (Sounds like a goblin Christmas recipe.) On these little islands of the Inner Hebrides, visitors can meet crofters (small farmers) and fisher folk, even join in a real island *ceilidh* (singing party).

Arran, Islay—that most southerly of the Hebridean islands—and the Isle of Jura, along with romantic Skye, are covered in other sections.

Mull, featured in Robert Louis Stevenson's *Kidnapped,* has wild scenery, golf courses, and a treasure trove of tradition. Iona played a major part in the spread of Christianity in Britain, and a trip there usually includes a visit to Staffa, a tiny, uninhabited volcanic island where Fingal's Cave inspired Mendelssohn.

These places are on the regular tourist circuit. However, more adventurous readers will seek out Coll and Tyree, along with Rhum, Eigg, Muck, and Canna.

This chain of islands lies just off the west coast of the Scottish mainland. To visit them, you'll be following a worthy tradition—in the footsteps of Dr. Samuel Johnson and his faithful Boswell.

Caledonian MacBrayne (tel. 0475/33755) provides the main link for boat transportation around the Inner Hebrides. Call them for information about departures.

MULL: The largest island in the Inner Hebrides, Mull is rich in legend and folklore, a land of ghosts, monsters, and the wee folk. Over log fires that burn on cold winter evenings, the talk is of myths and ancient times. The island is wild and mountainous, characterized by sea lochs and sandy bars.

The capital is **Tobermory,** lying on a bay guarded by **Duart Castle,** restored in 1912 and still the seat of the once-fiery MacLeans, who shed much blood in and around the castle during their battles with the Lords of the Isles. In the bay—somewhere—lies the *Florencia,* the Spanish galleon that went down laden with treasure. Many attempts have been made to bring it up, but so far all of them have failed.

To the southeast, near Salen, are the ruins of **Aros Castle,** once the stronghold of the Lords of the Isles.

On the far south coast at Lochbuie, **Moy Castle** has a water-filled dungeon. The wild countryside of Mull was the scene of many of David Balfour's adventures in *Kidnapped* by Robert Louis Stevenson.

Roads on Mull are few and can be quite rough. If you're taking a bus tour, the driver often has to stop to let sheep and cattle cross.

From Oban you can take one of the car-ferry services to Mull, operated by **Caledonian MacBrayne.** For information in Oban, telephone 0631/62285. In Tobermory, on Mull, you can reach the steamer office by telephoning 0688/2017. The cost of taking a car to Mull from Oban for a round-trip excursion is £26.80 ($40.20). Passengers are charged £3 ($4.50) for a round-trip excursion. A special weekend rate is offered charging £18.60 ($27.90) per car and £2.75 ($4.13) per person Friday to Tuesday. In high season, the car rate rises to £30.80 ($46.20) for a round trip, while passengers are charged £3.15 ($4.73). The high-season weekend bargain rate is £21.60 ($32.40) for a car, passengers still being charged £3.15 ($4.73) each. There are reductions in the off-season and also an "Island Hopscotch" for those who wish to visit several islands.

Always make a reservation if you're planning to spend the night on Mull.

I'll follow with a selection of hotels scattered across the island, beginning first at—

Tobermory

Western Isles (tel. 0688/2012) has a beautiful location above the harbor, looking out upon the bay. It's a large, gray stone country inn on a bluff above Tobermory. Derek and Kathy McAdam are the proprietors of this comfortable establishment. They have researched the history of the building and believe it was constructed by the Sandeman sherry company in the 1880s as a hunting and fishing lodge for their top-level staff and customers. It was owned for a number of years by the MacBrayne shipping company. The McAdams welcome visitors to rooms decorated in a mixture of styles, but they're homey, spotless, and have electric heaters. A single goes from £18 ($27), and doubles cost from £35 ($52.50) to £39 ($58.50), including a full Scottish breakfast. You also get good meals here, especially fish dishes. The chef is adept at both Scottish and French cuisine. I heartily recommend the lamb. Lunches in the bar range from £3.50 ($5.25), and a four-course dinner goes for £10 ($15). The hotel is closed from October to mid-March.

Carnaberg Hotel, 55 Main St. (tel. 0688/2479), lies right on the quay, overlooking the harbor and the Sound of Mull. The house has been pleasantly redecorated, and the rooms are comfortable. Ian MacLean charges £9 ($13.50) per person, this tariff including a Scottish breakfast and VAT. If you're there on a cold night, you might be given a hot-water bottle to take to bed with you, but only after you've been offered a snack before retiring. And what a snack! On one recent occasion, it consisted of four different kinds of cake, including chocolate, and three types of cookies (the oatmeal ones are especially good).

Mishnish Hotel (tel. 0688/2009) is a personal favorite. It's small, only 15 rooms, but its owners, the "MacCleod clan," have run it for four generations, giving island hospitality and creating a congenial atmosphere for guests. They never seem too busy that they can't stop and give advice and directions for exploring both Mull and Iona. Open all year, the Mishnish charges from £12 ($18) to £18 ($27) in singles without bath, £24 ($36) to £39 ($58.50) in bathless twins or doubles. For a room with private bath, you will pay from £28 ($42) to £42 ($63). All tariffs include a full Scottish breakfast, service, and VAT. The food is simple but the portions are ample, the ingredients fresh. An à la carte lunch starts at £6 ($9), a dinner at £10 ($15). There's live pipe music every evening in summer. The hotel contains lots of low ceilings and narrow passageways, and many of its furnishings have been polished for years with loving care. Residents can ask about boats for rent. In all, the Mishnish is a plain, simple, and friendly choice.

Suidhe Hotel, 59 Main St. (tel. 0688/2209), was originally recommended by readers Joseph and Elizabeth Mooney, and I agree fully with their point of view. Suidhe is Gaelic for "sit, rest, or a break in a journey," and that's exactly what this place is. Jim and Christine Scott, delightful people, run this clean, friendly little hotel, charging £17 ($25.50) per person nightly, including bed, breakfast, and evening dinner. The meals are well prepared and good tasting. All rooms have hot and cold water. Trout fishing, sea angling, and pony trekking are available locally. Suidhe is in a village off the western coast, right on the harbor, facing mountains covered with all shades of rhododendron in spring. In the village is a very good craft shop in a former church.

Craignure

Isle of Mull (tel. Craignure 351) is a first-class hotel that opened in 1971. It stands near the ferry and the meeting point of the Sound of Mull and Loch Linnhe. From the picture windows of its public rooms you'll have panoramic vistas of mountains and the island of Lismore. Each of its 60 bedrooms, all handsomely furnished, comes equipped with private bath and good views. The single rate is £30 ($45), increasing to £48 ($72) in a double, plus VAT. The food is good and pleasantly served in the attractive dining room, which faces both sea and hills. The chef does both British and continental dishes. The sea trout is superb. Hopefully, you'll be there on a night when the specialty is roast haunch of venison with gooseberry sauce. A set lunch costs about £4.50 ($9.75), a dinner going for around £7.50 ($11.25). Bar lunches begin at £2 ($3). Other facilities include a cocktail bar and a residents's television lounge. The hotel is open from the first of May until the end of September.

Dervaig

Bellachroy (tel. 06884/225) is a small hotel consisting of only eight rooms, but it remains open all year, welcoming visitors and charging them £12.50 ($18.75) per person nightly for a comfortable bed in a room with a heater and an electric blanket, plus a hearty Scottish breakfast next morning. You can also stay here on half-board terms of £19 ($28.50) per person nightly. On the premises are two bars, one of which serves meals, and there is musical entertainment every Thursday night in summer. The Bellachroy is run by resident proprietors Andrew and Anne Arnold. The hotel was once mentioned in *Gourmet* magazine for its good food. Loch and river trout and salmon fishing are available, plus sea angling nearby.

READERS' INN SELECTIONS: "Tiroran House, on the Isle of Mull (tel. 06815/232), is a tiny inn with six double rooms (five with private baths) and two singles, each individually decorated with utter charm and exquisite taste. Many of the furnishings and accessories are quite obviously family heirlooms. Sitting in 12 acres of lovely grounds with flowering shrubs and golden pheasants, Tiroran House is serenely remote but also easily accessible to many of the area's most interesting sights. The inn is owned by Robin and Sue Blockey, who make a point of letting you know that Tiroran House is their home, and indeed when you stay here you feel more like a welcome house guest than a paying customer. When we descended to the drawing room for drinks before dinner, our host, a careful and considerate man with a quiet sense of humor, introduced us to all the other guests—de rigueur in your own home but something we've never before experienced in a hotel. Mrs. Blockey, a handsome Englishwoman with appealing warmth, does the cooking, using home-grown vegetables and homemade cheeses with local game and seafood. We doubt that there is a finer example of haute cuisine anywhere in Scotland. Dinner and B&B cost £40 ($60) per person. There's a fine wine list, and prices of drinks are reasonable" (Leah and Ralph Toporoff, New York, N.Y.).

"I came upon a most charming inn on the Isle of Mull, Druimnacroish (tel. 06884/274). It is, in my opinion, absolutely charming, with about 11 rooms. The proprietor acts as the maître d', and his wife does chef duty. The food is excellent, the accommodations the best we found on our trip throughout Scotland, and the rates most reasonable. Singles rent for £32 ($48) for B&B and dinner, with doubles priced at £60 ($90)" (Paul Marcus, Hastings-on-Hudson, N.Y.). . . . **"Druimnacroish Country House Hotel,** also at Dervaig (tel. 06884/274), is a hotel of character and charm. The hotel is on an Ordnance Survey Map as a 'ruin.' It was, but it's been carefully and thoughtfully rebuilt into a country house hotel that offers good, comfortable amenities, including two lounges and an attractive dining room. All seven bedrooms have private bath, TV, and tea- or coffee-making facilities. Towels are changed daily, and this is the only hotel where I could walk barefoot on clean carpets. I could cover a page about the gourmet-quality food, cooked by Wendy McLean and served graciously by her husband Donald. Dishes include Scottish salmon and venison in season. Most of the produce is from their own garden. In the bedroom is a welcoming miniature bottle of Tobermory whisky. Dinner and breakfast service is impeccable, leisurely but not slow. Donald and Wendy go out of their way to be helpful" (Mrs. J. McG. Alexander, Blairgowrie, Scotland).

IONA: Someone once said, "When Edinburgh was but a barren rock and Oxford but a swamp, Iona was famous." It has been known as a place of spiritual power and pilgrimage for centuries. It was the site of the first Christian settlement in Scotland. A remote, low-lying, and treeless island, Iona lies off the southwestern coast of Mull and is only 1 mile by 3½ miles in size. It is accessible only by passenger ferry from the Isle of Mull (cars must remain on Mull). The ferry to Iona is run by local fishermen, and it's quite informal in service, depending in large part on the weather.

Since 1695 the island was owned by the Dukes of Argyll, but the 12th duke was forced to sell to pay $1 million in real estate taxes owed since 1949. The island was purchased by Sir Hugh Fraser, the former owner of Harrods and other stores. He secured Iona's future and made it possible for money raised by the National Trust for Scotland to be turned over to the trustees of the restored abbey.

Iona is known for its **"Graves of the Kings."** A total of 48 Scottish kings, including Macbeth and his victim Duncan, were buried on Iona, as were four Irish kings and eight Norwegian kings.

Today the island attracts nearly 1000 visitors a week in high season. Most of them come here mainly to see the **Abbey of Iona,** part of which dates back to the 13th century. But they also visit relics of the settlement founded there by St. Columbia in 563, from which Celtic Christianity spread through Scotland. The abbey has been restored by an ecumenical group called the Iona Community, which conducts workshops on Christianity, sponsors a youth camp, offers tours of the abbey, and leads a seven-mile hike to the various holy and historic spots on the island each Wednesday. It's possible to stay at the abbey.

Although there are many visitors to the abbey, the atmosphere on the island remains very rare, peaceful, and spiritual. It's possible to walk off among the sheep that wander freely everywhere to the top of Dun-I, a small mountain, and contemplate the ocean and the landscape as if you were the only person on earth.

There is much to do on Iona, but perhaps best of all, you can simply do nothing and absorb the kind of atmosphere that has drawn people on pilgrimages here for centuries.

One reader, Capt. Robert Haggart, Laguna, California, described his experience this way: "I was enchanted by the place. It really has a mystic atmosphere—one *feels* something ancient here, something spiritual, sacred, long struggles and wonderment about the strength of religion.''

Most of the islanders live by crofting and fishing. In addition, they supplement their income by taking in paying guests in season, charging usually very low or at least fair prices. You can, of course, check into the hotel recommended below, but a stay here in a private home may be an altogether rewarding travel adventure. If you don't stay on Iona, you must catch one of the ferries back to Mull, and they rarely leave after 5 p.m.

The **St. Columba Hotel** (tel. 06817/304) stands right outside the village, in the vicinity of the cathedral. Offering a total of 29 simply furnished rooms (only two of which have private baths), the hotel accepts guests from March to October. Singles range in price from £22 ($33) to £24 ($36), and doubles run from £22 ($33) to £25 ($37.50) per person, including dinner, bed, a full Scottish breakfast, plus VAT and service. There are reduced rates for guests staying four nights or longer. The food is good, especially the fish dishes, but, remember, the last order for dinner is taken at 7 p.m. People turn in early on Iona. Try to get a room overlooking the sea, but know that it's virtually impossible to secure an accommodation here in season without a reservation made well in advance.

STAFFA: Fingal's Cave,

on Staffa, a 75-acre island in the Hebrides off Scotland's west coast, has been attracting visitors for more than 200 years. It has been the inspiration for music, poetry, paintings, and prose. No less a personage than Queen Victoria visited the cave in the 19th century and wrote: "The effect is splendid, like a great entrance into a vaulted hall. The sea is immensely deep in the cave. The rocks under water were all colors—pink, blue and green." The sound of the crashing waves and swirling waters caused Mendelssohn to write the "Fingal's Cave Overture." Turner painted the cave on canvas, and Keats, Wordsworth, and Tennyson all praised it in their poetry.

The cave is unique in that it is the only known cave in the world formed of basalt columns. Over the centuries, the sea has carved a huge cavern in the basalt, leaving massive hexagonal columns to create the "vaulted hall" effect that enchanted Queen Victoria.

The Gaelic name of the cave is An Uamh Ehinn or the musical cave.

Although the island of Staffa has not been inhabited for more than 160 years, visitors can still explore the cave, thanks to the Laird of Staffa, Alastair de Watteville. In his hydrojet-equipped boat, *Fulmar,* the laird makes three trips a day from the quay at Ulva Ferry on the Isle of Mull to the rocky shores of Staffa. After docking, visitors are led along the basalt path and into Fingal's Cave. Inside, the noise of the pounding sea is deafening.

Another cave, **Clamshell Cave,** can also be visited, but only at low tide. Appropriately named, **Boat Cave** is accessible only by water.

Kenway Travel operates a range of excursions, cruises, and tours from Oban and Argyll. There are daily sailings in summer (May to September) to Staffa, Iona, Mull, and a variety of beauty spots on the Argyll coast. Visits to Staffa include opportunities to land on this unique island, explore Fingal's Cave, and study the remarkable sea caves formed in the hexagonal slabs of basalt. All trips present views of dramatic, beautiful scenery and sights of varied marine and seabird life. Puffins, cormorants, gannets, kittiwakes, fulmars, and many kinds of gull are frequently seen, as are seals and porpoises.

Kenway Travel Centre is at 113 George St., Oban (tel. 0631/64747).

RHUM: This enticingly named island lies about nine miles southwest of the previously explored Isle of Skye. There are those who will tell you not to go. "If you like a barren desert where it rains all the time, you'll love Rhum," a skipper in Mallaig recently told me.

It's stark, all right. And wet. In fact, with more than 90 inches of rainfall recorded annually, this is said to be the wettest island of the Inner Hebrides.

Since the mid-1950s Rhum has been owned by the Nature Conservation Board, which has wisely selected a considerate, conscientious warden, Laughton Johnston, to preside over the little "kingdom," about eight miles wide by eight miles long. Obviously, conservation is of paramount importance on the island, and attempts are being made to bring back the sea eagle, which used to live here in Queen Victoria's day.

On this storm-tossed outpost, mountain climbers arrive in summer to challenge the rugged peaks, and anglers are attracted to the oceanic island by reports (accurate, I must say) of its good trout fishing. Bird-lovers seek out the Manx shearwaters, which live on Rhum in great numbers. Red deer and ponies add color, along with the wildflowers of summer, to an otherwise bleak landscape.

Astonishingly, in such a forbidding place, you come upon a hotel, **Kinloch Castle** (tel. Mallaig 2037), which is a mansion of imposing stature and grandeur, built by a wealthy British industrialist, Sir George Bullogh, at the turn of the century. He wanted a retreat from the world, and in this monument to the opulence of the Edwardian era, he found it on Rhum. The location is at the top of a loch on the eastern coast of the island.

From around March until September, guests are accommodated at the castle, paying around $55 (U.S.) a day for a room and all meals, served on a dining table rescued from a yacht. The food is good, and in season you are likely to be served Scottish salmon and venison. Only one bedroom has a private bath, as no one has seen fit to alter the original house plans—but who would want to? Anyway, the shared baths are quite grand. The decor is exactly what you'd expect in a castle: monumental paintings and lots of stuffed animals. Here you can experience what the lifestyle of a wealthy laird was all about.

To reach Rhum, you can take a passenger ferry from Mallaig, on the western coast of Scotland. It leaves about four times a week, and no cars are carried. A one-way passenger fare from Mallaig to Rhum is about $8 (U.S.).

EIGG: "Egg island," as it is called, is reached by passenger ferry from Maillaig at a cost of $5 (U.S.) per person. Boats sail infrequently, so it's best to check with **Caledonian MacBrayne** (tel. 0475/33755).

The tiny island, about 4½ miles by 3 miles, lies some 4 miles southeast of the just-explored Rhum. The laird of the island, Keith Schellenberg, an Englishman, purchased Eigg in 1975 at a reported cost of half a million dollars. He welcomes visitors who come here to see the **Sgurr of Eigg,** a tall column of lava, said to be the biggest such pitchstone mass in the United Kingdom. Climbers on its north side try to reach its impressive height of 1300 feet.

After your arrival at Galmisdale, the principal hamlet and pier, you can take an antique omnibus to Cleadale. Once there, you walk across moors to Camas Sgiotaig, with its well-known beach of the Singing Sands (its black and white quartz grains are decidedly off key). The cost of a ride across the green glen to the Singing Sands is only $3 (U.S.) for a one-way ticket.

If you want lunch or dinner, call **Mrs. Margaret Alderson** (tel. 0687/82428), who will provide something suitable for about £8 ($12). She'll also put you up overnight in a B&B establishment, charging from £12 ($18) per person, including a Scottish breakfast.

MUCK:
Directly to the southwest of Eigg, Muck, unlike Rhum, has such an unappetizing name that visitors may turn away and not want to explore it. This little 2½-square-mile isle is misnamed. Muck is not used in the sense we know it. It is based on a Gaelic word "muic," meaning the "island of the sow." Admittedly that doesn't conjure up a much more appealing picture, but the island is more attractive than its name, and many seabirds find it a suitable place for nesting.

Often storm tossed, Muck is actually a farm run by its resident laird, Lawrence MacEwen. There are hardly more than two dozen people on this island, all of them concerned in some way with the running of the farm.

Laird MacEwen runs the one hotel, **Port Mhor House** (tel. Mallaig 2362), which is actually a cottage that was skillfully converted to receive guests. The food often uses produce from the farm's garden, and the fare here is hearty. You can call ahead and reserve space in the dining room, even if you aren't a resident. Expect to spend from £10 ($15) for a meal. Later, you can enjoy a malt whisky around an open log fire. A double bedroom rents for about £22 ($33) per night. For reservations, write to the laird at Gallanach, Isle of Muck, Inverness.

Naturalists come here looking for everything from rare butterflies to otters. Visitors are allowed to tour the farm.

A one-way ferry ride from Mallaig (passengers only) costs $6 (U.S.).

CANNA:
Some three miles northwest of Rhum, Canna is another of the so-called Small Isles and is really one of the hardest to reach. A one-way ferry from Mallaig is infrequent and unreliable, costing about $10 (U.S.) per passenger. Canna, like Muck, is really not in the tourist business, and only the most persistent may want to seek it out.

The laird of the island, John Lorne Campbell, is concerned with farming, including the raising of Cheviot sheep and Highland cattle. He married a native of Pennsylvania, Margaret Shaw, and they have owned the island since before World War II. They are traditionalists, believing mightily in the preservation of the Gaelic language and culture. In 1981 the laird willed the island to the National Trust for Scotland.

A wooden bridge connects Canna to Sanday, a tidal island, which makes a good day's exploring. You can seek out a Celtic cross and the outline of a Viking burial ship.

Canna is not really geared to receive tourists, yet the National Trust for Scotland (tel. 031/226-5922) in Edinburgh might arrange accommodations if you write them far enough in advance.

COLL AND TYREE: If you like your scenery stark and tranquil, try Coll and Tyree, tiny islands that attract visitors seeking remoteness. On Tyree (also spelled Tiree), the shell-sand machair increases the cultivable area, differentiating it from the inner isles. A lot of British pensioners live on Coll and Tyree, and they seem to like to keep the place pretty much to themselves.

The outside world intrudes, however, when the ferry arrives—which sometimes it doesn't do, as gales often cause cancellations. The ferry stops at Mull and then, if conditions are right, goes on to Coll and Tyree. If you go at the wrong time of year (and nobody knows exactly when the right time is!), you can easily be stranded for a while waiting for the next departure.

By car-ferry from Oban, via Mull, passengers are charged about $20 (U.S.) for the trip, with cars, depending on the size, being assessed at a rate ranging from $85 to $110. These are round-trip tariffs. Loganair also flies directly to Tyree from Glasgow, with about six scheduled flights weekly, an excursion fare costing $75.

Don't despair if you can't get back anytime soon, as the islands do have some limited accommodations.

On Tyree, try **Tyree Lodge Hotel** (tel. Scarinish 368), which has about eight rooms and is comfortable and immaculate, charging around $32 (U.S.) per person per night, which includes a good Inner Hebrides breakfast and a hearty dinner.

Also on Tyree, **Balephetrish House** (tel. Scarinish 549) welcomes visitors to one of its small rooms, only five in all. Again, everything is kept spic and span, and your fellow guest that night is likely to be a geologist or a pensioner. Rates are cheaper than at the previously recommended lodge: about $25 per day per person for a good breakfast and a filling dinner, along with your room, of course.

Coll offers the appropriately named **Isle of Coll Hotel** (tel. Coll 334), which looks to some people a little run-down, but in this part of the world you welcome whatever comfort you find. Rates are from $38 to $42 (U.S.) per person per night for half board.

If you're economizing more seriously, try **Tighna-Mara Guest House** (tel. Coll 329), a B&B establishment with half a dozen rooms. Rates of $26 to $28 per person per night are charged for a filling breakfast, adequate supper, and a bed. Comfort might be minimal, but the welcome is maximum.

7. Kintyre, Arran, and Islay

For many foreign visitors, the Atlantic seaboard of the old county of Argyll will represent a journey into the unknown. For those who want to sample a bygone age, this is one of the most rewarding trips off the coastline of western Scotland. My recommendations lie on islands, easily reached by ferries—except the Kintyre Peninsula which is a virtual island in itself. You'll soon discover that the Gaelic traditions of the islands endure. Peace and tranquility prevail.

ISLE OF ARRAN: At the mouth of the Firth of Clyde, this island is often described as Scotland in miniature, because of its wild and varied scenery, containing an assortment of glens, moors, lochs, sandy bays, and rocky coasts for which the country is known. Ferry services, making the 50-minute crossing, operate from Ardrossan to Brodick, the major village of

Arran, lying on the eastern shore. There are also ferry connections linking the northern part of Arran with the Kintyre Peninsula and the Highlands. Once on Arran, you'll find buses to take you to the various villages, each with its own character. A coast road, 60 miles long, runs the length of the island.

Arran contains some splendid mountain scenery, notably the conical peak of **Goatfell** in the north, reaching a height of 2866 feet. It's called "the mountain of the winds."

Students of geology flock to Arran to study igneous rocks of the Tertiary Age. Cairns and standing stones at **Tormore** intrigue archeologists as well.

Arran is also filled with beautiful glens, especially **Glen Sannox** in the northeast and **Glen Rosa,** directly north of Brodick. In one day you can see a lot, as the island is only 25 miles long, 10 miles wide.

After the ferry docks at Brodick, you may want to head for Arran's major sight—**Brodick Castle,** 1½ miles north of the Brodick pierhead. The historic home of the Dukes of Hamilton, the castle dates from the 13th century and contains superb silver, antiques, portraits, and objets d'art. It is open in April after Easter on Monday, Wednesday, and Saturday from 1 to 5 p.m. From May 1 to September 30, hours are daily from 1 to 5 p.m. The award-winning gardens and the new Country Park are open all year, daily from 10 a.m. to 5 p.m. Admission to both the castle and gardens is £1.50 ($2.25) for adults, 75p ($1.13) for children. For information, telephone 0770/2202.

South from Brodick lies the village and holiday resort of **Lamlash,** opening onto Lamlash Bay. From here a ferry takes visitors over to **Holy Island,** with its 1000-foot peak. A disciple of St. Columba founded a church on this island.

One of the best known centers on the western coast is **Blackwater Foot,** which offers pony trekking and golfing.

Finally, in the north, **Lochranza** is a village with unique appeal. It opens onto a bay of pebbles and sand, and in the backdrop lie the ruins of a castle that reputedly was the hunting seat of Robert the Bruce.

Brodick

Glenartney (tel. 0770/2220) is a two-story, 17-bedroom hotel on a convenient hillside location overlooking the bay, with the castle and mountains beyond. The hotel offers comfortable rooms, good food, and a cozy atmosphere, and is licensed for residents. Singles peak at £13 ($19.50) and doubles at £23 ($34.50), including breakfast. Lunch, costing from £4 ($6), is by arrangement, and dinner can be ordered for from £6 ($9). There is full central heating, and tea- and coffee-making equipment and electric blankets are in all rooms, some of which have private baths and TV. The hotel is open year round, with off-season discounts as well as reductions for children sharing a room with their parents. A wide variety of sporting activities can be arranged by the proprietors, Graham and Vi McKelvie, on request.

Whiting Bay

The **Whiting Bay Hotel** (tel. 07707/247) has excellent sea views of the Firth of Clyde. The restaurant offers cuisine of a high standard, specializing in local seafood and other local produce. Most bedrooms have private baths, B&B costing from £15 ($22.50). The hotel is fully licensed, with a choice of three bars with varied entertainment put on in the function suite. There's ample parking for cars. You can arrange to go golfing, fishing, diving, and participate in other sports.

Lamlash

Although I missed this on my latest rounds, the **Carraig Mhor,** Lamlash, Arran (tel. 07706/453), continues to get accolades from food writers and has been awarded rosettes. This highly-spoken-of restaurant is open nightly except Sunday and Monday, and you can expect to pay from £8.50 ($12.75) to £10.50 ($15.75) for a meal. Always telephone ahead for a reservation, however.

KINTYRE PENINSULA: The longest peninsula in Scotland, Kintyre is more than 60 miles in length, containing much beautiful scenery, pleasant villages, and magnificent gardens on the Isle of Gigha, which lies off its western shores. The largest center on Kintyre is Campbeltown, although Tarbert in the north is also popular. In the evening you just might hear the music of the *ceilidhs* in hotels and village halls.

The major sight is an excursion to Gigha's famous gardens. They're called **Achamore** and are located a quarter of a mile from Ardminish on the Isle of Gigha. The island is reached by ferry boat that picks up passengers at the Tayinloan jetty on Kintyre. Weather permitting, sailings are four times daily. It is advisable to check times with Cal/Mac Ltd. (tel. 088-073/253).

These extensive gardens contain roses, hydrangeas, rhododendrons, camellias, and azaleas. They are open March to October from 10 a.m. to dusk, charging adults 50p (75¢); children, 25p (38¢).

At Carradale, near the ruins of Aird Castle on the eastern coast, you can visit the **Carradale Forest Centre** and the gardens of Carradale House.

TARBERT: A sheltered harbor protects this fishing port and yachting center that lies on a narrow neck of the northern tip of the Kintyre Peninsula, between West Loch Tarbert and the head of herring-filled Loch Fyne. Nearby is the finest accommodation on the Kintyre Peninsula.

Stonefield Castle Hotel (tel. 08802/207), occupying a commanding position, is a luxuriously appointed and magnificent hotel on 100 acres of wooded grounds and park-like gardens on Loch Fyne, two miles outside Tarbert. The grounds are studded with rare shrubs, and from the gardens come the flowers for the exquisite arrangements inside the house. Extended from the central square tower are tall step-gabled wings, with highly pitched windows and rows of dormers. From this impressively handsome building are seemingly unlimited views. Older readers especially find it a tranquil oasis. The castle was formerly owned by a member of the Campbell clan. Nowadays the proprietor is James H. Scot, whose son, Graeme, is the manager. Both are still in constant attendance. Its public rooms are lofty, decorated, in part, with antiques.

Try to get one of the well-furnished bedrooms in the main building, although you may be assigned an accommodation in the more modern wing. In all, there are 34 rooms, 29 with private bath. Singles range from £32 ($48) to £35 ($52.50), and doubles run from £54 ($81) to £58 ($87), including a full Scottish breakfast, service, and VAT. Meals utilize produce from the hotel's own garden. In the kitchen the staff does its own baking.

The paneled dining room is decorated in a formal style, and the service is superb.

Lunch in the bar costs about £5 ($7.50), and dinner ranges from £15 ($22.50). The hotel has many excellent facilities, including a spacious drawing room overlooking the loch, a cocktail bar, tennis court, putting green, a large library, an outdoor swimming pool, a sauna, even yacht anchorage. Sea fishing can be arranged. It's imperative to book well in advance, as Stonefield has a large repeat clientele. It is closed from November to March.

Considerably less expensive, the **Tarbert Hotel** (tel. 08802/264) stands on the quayside where the Kintyre fishermen anchor with their herring-filled boats. The hotel is really like a pub, painted in white, and the frugal Scots book the comfortable and simply furnished rooms which cost from £14 ($21) to £25 ($37.50) per person, including VAT, service, and a full breakfast. Dinner is £11 ($16.50) per person. If you don't lunch in the main room, you'll find a goodly assortment of snacks. The lounge bar is usually well stuffed with the local people, enjoying their Scottish & Newcastle.

The **West Loch Hotel** (tel. 08802/283), a small, family-managed hotel, is also good, although it contains only six bedrooms, renting for £20 ($30) in a single, from £32 ($48) in a double, including a full breakfast. The rooms are immaculately maintained, furnished in an old style. The main building dates back to old coaching days. You really should take the half-board rate of £28 ($42) per person, or else drop in for a meal, because the cookery is first rate. Fresh ingredients are used whenever available, and the fish dishes are superb. In season game is featured. Hot and cold snacks as well as full meals are served both in the bar and dining room at noon, costing from 75p ($1.13) to £8 ($12). Nonresidents can dine here for £15 ($22.50). The black-and-white inn overlooks West Loch—hence its name. It lies one mile south of the village on the Campbeltown road. It's popular with yachtsmen from the east harbor. The hotel is conveniently situated for ferries sailing to Arran, Islay, and Jura. A nine-hole golf course, pony trekking, forestry walks, and the sandy West Coast beaches are all within easy reach.

ISLE OF ISLAY: The southernmost island of the Inner Hebrides, Islay lies 16 miles west of the Kintyre peninsula and less than a mile southwest of Jura, from which it is separated only by a narrow sound. At its maximum breadth, Islay is only 15 miles wide (25 miles long).

Called "the Queen of the Hebrides," it is a peaceful unspoiled island of moors, salmon-filled lochs, sandy bays, and wild rocky cliffs. Islay was the ancient seat of the Lords of the Isles, and today you'll see the ruins of two castles and several Celtic crosses.

Near Port Charlotte are the graves of the U.S. seamen and army troops who lost their lives in 1918 when their carriers, the *Tuscania* and *Otranto*, were torpedoed off the shores of Islay. There's a memorial tower on the Mull of Oa, eight miles from Port Ellen.

The island is noted for its distilleries, producing single-malt Highland whiskies by the antiquated pot-still method.

MacBrayne Steamers operate a daily service to Islay—you leave West Tarbert on the Kintyre peninsula, arriving at Port Askaig on Islay.

The island's capital is Bowmore, on the coast across from Port Askaig. There you can see a fascinating round church—no corners for the devil. But the most important town is Port Ellen, on the south coast, a holiday and golfing resort as well as Islay's principal port.

As accommodations are limited on Islay, always arrive with a reservation in your pocket.

Port Askaig

Port Askaig Hotel (tel. Port Askaig 245) is a genuine old island inn, dating from the 18th century, built on the site of an even older inn. It stands on the Sound of Islay overlooking the pier where a MacBrayne steamer berths daily. The hotel is quite charming, offering island hospitality and Scottish fare, including broiled trout, cock-a-leekie soup, roast pheasant, smoked Scottish salmon, and of course, haggis. The hotel is a major destination for anglers on Islay, and the bar at the inn is popular with local fishermen. All year the friendly staff welcomes you to one of its modestly furnished bedrooms, costing from £20 ($30) in a single and from £30 ($45) in a double, including a continental breakfast. Dinner costs from £10 ($15). The hotel, incidentally, offers only nine rooms, half of which contain private baths.

Port Ellen

White Hart (tel. 049-683/2311) is modest, but pleasantly situated, standing on a tiny promenade on the skirttails of Port Ellen. The furnishings are in good taste, offering unassuming comfort. The hotel rents out 19 rooms, of which only 5 contain private baths. All year singles cost from £18 ($27); doubles, from £30 ($45)—including a full breakfast. The half-board rate is £26 ($39) per person. A room with a private bath costs a £2 ($3) supplement. Meals are good, although simple, and are served in a dining room opening onto a view of the water. Log fires burn in the attractive lounge. If given proper notice, the staff will arrange fishing expeditions for guests.

Bridgend

Bridgend Hotel (tel. 049-681/212) is a good base if you're crossing Islay, making your headquarters around the capital at Bowmore. All year the resident owners of this hotel will welcome you to their quiet retreat, opening onto Loch Indaal. The hotel is plainly furnished, although a nice touch is added by the pictures of wild bird life on Islay and the seascape paintings of local artists. The Bridgend offers only nine doubles and two singles, none of which contains a private bath. Singles cost £18 ($27), and doubles are priced at £34 ($51), including VAT, service, and a full Scottish breakfast. For B&B and dinner, the charge is £26 ($39). Meals—good, simple, unassuming cookery—are served between 7 and 7:30 p.m. The hotel also has a fully licensed cocktail bar.

ISLE OF JURA: This is the fourth-largest island in the Inner Hebrides. It perhaps takes its name from the Norse *Jura,* meaning "deer island." The red deer on Jura outnumber the people by about 20 to 1. At four feet high, the deer are the largest wild animals roaming Scotland. The hardy islanders number only about 250 brave souls, and most of them live along the east coast. The west coast is virtually uninhabited.

The capital, **Craighouse,** is hardly more than a hamlet. It is connected by steamer to West Loch Tarbert on the Kintyre peninsula. If you're already on Islay, you can journey to Jura by taking a five-minute ferry ride from Port Askaig, docking at the Feolin Ferry berth.

The breadth of Jura varies from two to eight miles, and at its maximum length it is 27 miles long. The island's landscape is dominated by the **Paps of Jura,** reaching a peak of 2571 feet at Beinn-an-Oir. An arm of the sea, **Loch Tarbert** nearly divides the island, cutting into it for nearly six miles.

As islands go, Jura is relatively little known or explored, although its mountains, soaring cliffs, snug coves, and moors make it an inviting paradise—nowhere is there overcrowding. The island has actually lost population drastically.

The square tower of **Claig Castle** is now in ruins, but once it was the stronghold of the MacDonalds until they were subdued by the Campbells in the 17th century.

Literary historians may be interested to know that George Orwell in the bitter postwar winters of 1946 and 1947 lived at Jura. Even then a sick and dying man, he wrote his masterpiece, *1984,* a satire on modern politics. He almost lost his life on Jura when he and his adopted son ventured too close to the whirlpool in the Gulf of Corryvreckan. They were saved by local fishermen, and he went on to finish *1984,* only to die in London of tuberculosis in 1950. His life span hardly matched that of Gillouir MacCrain, said to have been 180 when he died on Jura in the days of Charles I.

In accommodations, the **Jura Hotel** (tel. Craighouse 243) at Craighouse is the only licensed premises on the island. Overlooking the sea, it actually has palms growing on its grounds, thanks to the benevolence of the Gulf Stream. All year it rents 18 bedrooms, four of which contain private baths. The single tariff is £18 ($27); the double rate, £36 ($54)—including breakfast. The half-board terms are from £26 ($39) per person daily. Rooms are simply although agreeably furnished. However, bring along some mosquito repellent to deal with the pest of the islands.

NOW, SAVE MONEY ON ALL YOUR TRAVELS!
Join Arthur Frommer's $25-A-Day Travel Club

Saving money while traveling is never a simple matter, which is why, over 22 years ago, the **$25-A-Day Travel Club** was formed. Actually, the idea came from readers of the Arthur Frommer Publications who felt that such an organization could bring financial benefits, continuing travel information, and a sense of community to economy-minded travelers all over the world.

In keeping with the money-saving concept, the annual membership fee is low—$15 (U.S. residents) or $18 (Canadian, Mexican, and foreign residents)—and is immediately exceeded by the value of your benefits which include:

(1) The latest edition of any TWO of the books listed on the following page.

(2) An annual subscription to an 8-page quarterly newspaper *The Wonderful World of Budget Travel* which keeps you up-to-date on fastbreaking developments in low-cost travel in all parts of the world—bringing you the kind of information you'd have to pay over $25 a year to obtain elsewhere. This consumer-conscious publication also includes the following columns:

Travelers' Directory—members all over the world who are willing to provide hospitality to other members as they pass through their home cities.

Share-a-Trip—requests from members for travel companions who can share costs and help avoid the burdensome single supplement.

Readers Ask ... Readers Reply—travel questions from members to which other members reply with authentic firsthand information.

(3) A copy of *Arthur Frommer's Guide to New York.*

(4) Your personal membership card which entitles you to purchase through the Club all Arthur Frommer Publications for a third to a half off their regular retail prices during the term of your membership.

So why not join this hardy band of international budgeteers NOW and participate in its exchange of information and hospitality? Simply send $15 (U.S. residents) or $18 U.S. (Canadian, Mexican, and other foreign residents) along with your name and address to: $25-A-Day Travel Club, Inc., 1230 Avenue of the Americas, New York, NY 10020. Remember to specify which *two* of the books in section (1) above you wish to receive in your initial package of members' benefits. Or tear out this page, check off any two books on the opposite side and send it to us with your membership fee.